Taylor's Master Guide *to* Gardening

Editor-in-Chief: Frances Tenenbaum
Editors: Rita Buchanan, Roger Holmes
Designer: Deborah Fillion
Illustrator: Steve Buchanan
Copy Editor: Nancy J. Stabile

Taylor's Master Guide to Gardening

HOUGHTON MIFFLIN COMPANY

Boston • New York • 1994

Library of Congress Cataloging-in-Publication Data

Taylor's master guide to gardening / editor-in-chief, Frances Tenenbaum ; editors, Rita Buchanan and Roger Holmes ; illustrator, Steve Buchanan.
     p.   cm.
  Includes bibliographical references and index.
  ISBN 0-396-64995-1
  1. Landscape gardening. 2. Gardening. 3. Landscape plants.
I. Tenenbaum, Frances. II. Buchanan, Rita. III. Holmes, Roger.
IV. Title: Master guide to gardening. V. Title: Gardening.
SB473.T425 1994   93-48865
635.9 — dc20   CIP

Color separations by Sfera, Milan
Printed and bound by Sfera/Garzanti, Milan

Printed in Italy

SFE   10 9 8 7 6 5 4 3 2 1

In memory of Norman Taylor (1883–1967)
Author of *Taylor's Encyclopedia of Gardening*

Contents

Contributors

Of the many people who have contributed to this book, none are more important than those who agreed to share the knowledge they've accumulated in a lifetime of involvement with gardening and horticulture. The editors wish to thank these authors and consultants for their efforts and for their patience with the sometimes frustrating process of melding numerous voices into a single work.

CREATING A GARDEN

Kevin Connelly wrote the essays "Hedges and screens" and "Meadow gardens" and the sidebar "Annuals in winter." He is a professional landscape gardener and specialist in California native plants and drought-tolerant gardens. A frequent contributor to newspapers and magazines, Connelly is the author of *Gardener's Guide to California Wildflowers.* He lives in Arcadia, California.

John R. (Dick) Dunmire wrote the essays "Shrubs," "Trees," and "Covering ground." He was a senior editor in the gardening department of *Sunset Magazine* at his retirement in 1990. During his 27 years with *Sunset,* he edited three editions of the *Western Garden Book.* A resident of Los Altos and Inverness, California, Dunmire has long been active in horticultural organizations on the West Coast.

Diane Ipsen, who wrote "The front garden" essay, is a landscape architect in Denver, Colorado, specializing in residential design. She writes about horticulture, design, and landscape history for local publications as well as lecturing and teaching at the Denver Botanic Gardens.

Glenn Morris wrote the essays "Designing your garden," "Putting it on paper," "Establishing structure," "Composing a picture with plants," "Seasons in the garden," and "Water in the garden." Trained in landscape architecture, Morris has worked as landscape design editor for *Southern Living* magazine. Now a landscape designer and consultant in Greensboro, North Carolina, he writes frequently about gardening in the South.

Judith Phillips wrote the two essays on planning as well as "Underfoot in the garden" and "Making shade." She is a landscape designer and co-owner of a nursery specializing in drought-tolerant native and locally adapted plants in the Albuquerque, New Mexico, area. A frequent contributor to gardening books, Phillips is the author of *Southwestern Landscaping with Native Plants.*

Rob Proctor wrote the essays "Gardening across America," "Annuals and biennials," "Patios, terraces, and restful nooks," and "Making the most of a small space." Author of several gardening books, including *Annuals* and *The Outdoor Potted Bulb,* Proctor is also an accomplished botanical illustrator and photographer. He lives in Denver, Colorado, and teaches at the Denver Botanic Gardens.

Lauren Springer wrote the essays "Perennials," "Color in the picture," "Gardening in the shade," "Beds and borders," and "Rock gardens." She is the author of *Water-wise Gardening* and *The Undaunted Garden.* Springer also designs gardens in her hometown of Windsor, Colorado.

Alice Yarborough, who wrote the essay "Gardening for wildlife," lives in Carnation, Washington. Her garden writing, photography, and humorous essays have appeared in newspapers, magazines, and books.

ENCYCLOPEDIA OF PLANTS

The following people provided information for the descriptions of individual species and cultivars as well as the "How to grow" sections in the plant encyclopedia.

Kevin Connelly (see above).

John R. (Dick) Dunmire (see above).

Galen Gates is a horticulturist at the Chicago Botanic Garden in Chicago, Illinois. His special interest is ornamental grasses and plants with winter interest.

Betty Graubaum is an estate gardener in Sharon, Connecticut, where she grows a wide variety of hardy shrubs and perennials and unusual annuals.

Tim Hohn is curator of collections at the Washington Park Arboretum in Seattle, Washington. He previously worked as horticulturist for the New York Zoological Garden.

Peter Loos, head of forestry for the city of Houston, Texas, has a special interest in native shrubs and trees of Texas and the South.

Rob Nicolson, horticulturist at Smith College Botanic Garden in Northampton, Massachusetts, is a specialist in woody plants.

Gregory Piotrowski, a horticulturist at the New York Botanical Garden, Bronx, New York, is a specialist in daylilies.

Rob Proctor (see above).

Alan Rollinger, a landscape architect in Denver, Colorado, teaches courses on hardy trees and shrubs at the Denver Botanic Gardens.

Elisabeth Sheldon formerly ran a nursery specializing in unusual perennials and herbs. Now retired, she gardens and writes in Lansing, New York.

Mary Ellen Tonsing gardens in Littleton, Colorado, and has a special interest in hardy ferns and other perennials for shade.

The editors would like to thank **Allan Armitage, Steve Frowine, Harold Greer, Gary Keim, Gary Koller,** and **Guy Sternberg** for supplying additional information on specific plants.

GROWING HEALTHY PLANTS

Nancy Beaubaire, consultant on controlling pests and diseases, lives in Waterbury, Connecticut, and is executive editor of *Fine Gardening* magazine.

Steve Bender, senior writer for *Southern Living* magazine, contributed material on lawns. He lives in Birmingham, Alabama.

Jim Borland, owner of Native Concepts, a landscape consulting firm in Denver, Colorado, and frequent contributor to trade and scientific journals, provided material on propagation.

Nancy Carney, who contributed material on planting, lives in Newtown, Connecticut, where she writes and lectures on gardening.

John R. (Dick) Dunmire (see above) contributed material on lawns.

Kim Hawks is the owner of Niche Gardens in Chapel Hill, North Carolina, where she sells nursery-propagated plants. She contributed material on meadow gardening.

Dr. John W. Mastalerz, professor emeritus of horticulture at Pennsylvania State University, contributed material on fertilizing.

Robert Parnes, consultant on compost, is a former director of a soil-testing service and author of *Fertile Soil: A Grower's Guide to Organic and Inorganic Fertilizers.*

Dr. H. Brent Pemberton, associate professor at the Texas A&M University Agricultural Research and Extension Center in Overton, Texas, contributed material on how plants grow.

Warren Schultz, former editor-in-chief of *National Gardening* magazine and author of *The Chemical-Free Lawn,* contributed material on lawns.

Lauren Springer (see above) contributed material on preparing a new garden bed.

Guy Sternberg, a landscape architect with the Illinois Department of Conservation and owner of Starhill Forest in Petersburg, Illinois, provided material on pruning.

Gayle Weinstein, owner of Eletes Consultants in Denver, Colorado, and consulting director of education at Bernheim Arboretum and Research Forest in Louisville, Kentucky, consulted on watering.

EDITORIAL

Rita Buchanan was a co-editor of this book with primary responsibility for the Gallery and Encyclopedia sections, for which she wrote the plant descriptions. She has worked as a botanist and horticulturist in Texas, Colorado, Virginia, Connecticut, England, and Costa Rica. A former editor of *Fine Gardening* magazine, she now edits and writes gardening books from her home in Winsted, Connecticut.

Roger Holmes, co-editor of this book, was responsible for two sections, Creating a Garden and Growing Healthy Plants. He was the founding editor of *Fine Gardening* magazine and is now a freelance editor and writer based in Lincoln, Nebraska.

About this book

Of the many pleasures of gardens and gardening—flowers and foliage, fragrance, turning the earth, and caring for plants—one in particular stands at the heart of this book. Many gardeners derive as much enjoyment from cultivating gardening friends as they do from cultivating plants. Many a garden bed has been dug with the aid of such friends, planted with seeds and divisions of their favorite plants, and tended with an ear cocked to the friendly voices of experience.

Like gardeners everywhere, those who have contributed to this book enjoy sharing. They can't help dig your garden or donate a favorite plant, but they can pass on knowledge gained from gardening friends and mentors as well as that acquired through trial and (especially) error in their own gardens.

What is this "master guide"? It is a one-volume reference book for gardeners, a compendium of authoritative information and advice to consult as you plan, plant, and build in your home landscape. Between these covers, you'll find all the information you need for years of happy gardening.

In planning the book, we were guided by a few basic considerations. First, for many, many gardeners, the pleasures of gardening are to be found as much in the work—planning, designing, digging, planting, pruning—as in the results. Consequently, this guide is a book for hands-on, dirt-under-the-fingernails gardeners.

Second, as inspiring as large, beautifully designed and planted estates can be, most of us are likely to possess less grand surroundings, gardening ambitions, and finances. The *Master Guide* is about making the most of the resources we have, rather than those we might covet.

Finally, North America possesses diverse climates and topography—deserts, rain forests, vast prairies, towering mountains. Where you live makes a big difference to how you garden. To ensure that the *Master Guide* serves American gardeners in all their diverse needs, we drew our authors and experts from every region of the country and asked them to keep regional considerations firmly in mind.

To help you make best use of the book, let's take a brief tour of its contents, which are divided into four major sections.

Creating a Garden

Some 30 chapters in this section examine the elements basic to creating a pleasing and functional home landscape. The chapters will help you assess your landscaping needs and desires (planning) and learn how to satisfy those needs (design). Other chapters introduce the major categories of plants—annuals, perennials, shrubs, and trees—and examine how you can use them to cast shade, define space, create privacy, provide color, and so on. You'll also learn about a variety of gardening situations and possibilities, from annual beds, perennial borders, and mixed plantings to woodland gardens, meadow and wildflower gardens, and water gardens. In each chapter, carefully selected color photographs help bring relevant ideas and concepts to life.

The Gallery and the Encyclopedia

Just as plants are at the heart of a garden, the Gallery of Plants and the Encyclopedia of Plants are at the heart of this book. The Gallery section includes about 1,000 color photos of outstanding garden plants. The Encyclopedia contains descriptions of more than 3,000 plants, including all of the plants shown in the photo gallery plus many related species and cultivars.

We invited a panel of expert gardeners from around the country to recommend plants for this book and imposed certain criteria in compiling the final list. We chose plants that are readily available from local nurseries or established mail-order suppliers, not rare plants that are difficult to find. We looked for plants that have more than one noteworthy characteristic and contribute to the garden over a long season—for example, plants with fragrant flowers in spring and colorful foliage in fall. We included many plants just for their beauty, but we added others that are less dramatic but very useful for practical landscaping purposes such as providing shade, screening views, covering steep slopes, filling the space under trees, or defining property lines.

Some of the plants in this book do well throughout the United States; others are regional favorites that require certain climate or growing conditions. We used the USDA zone ratings to indicate hardiness to winter cold, and we note in the descriptions plants that are especially tolerant of or sensitive to summer heat, humid or dry air, drought, poor drainage, lean or rich soil, or other conditions. Consider all of this information when selecting plants for your garden. If carefully chosen and properly sited, most of the plants in this book require only routine maintenance and are relatively free of pests and diseases.

The photos in the Gallery are organized into 12 categories: deciduous trees, deciduous shrubs, evergreen trees, palms, evergreen shrubs, conifers, vines, grasses and bamboos, ferns, perennials, herbs, and annuals. You can use the photos to compare different candidates for a particular role in your garden, such as a small flowering tree for the front yard, an evergreen shrub for hedging, or a colorful annual for patio containers. Or you can browse through the photos to make a shopping list of new plants you'd like to try. The photos can also help you identify plants that came with your house or plants that you notice around your town or neighborhood.

Along with the photos in the Gallery are brief descriptions of each plant. For more information, turn to the Encyclopedia section. There the plants are organized alphabetically by genus. A brief description of the genus is followed by entries for selected species and cultivars. These entries point out the plant's desirable characteristics, such as foliage, flowers, or growth habit, and provide suggestions for using it in the garden. They also tell how to grow the plant, giving its requirements for sun, soil, water, and maintenance.

We describe many more plants in the Encyclopedia than we could show in the Gallery. Usually these additional plants resemble the illustrated entries but differ in minor ways such as flower or foliage color, hardiness, or size. Most of the Encyclopedia entries feature one particular species or cultivar, but some describe major groups of related plants. For example, the entries for lilies, daffodils, rhododendrons, and roses give you an overview of these indispensable plants and recommend some of the many outstanding cultivars.

The entries in the Gallery and Encyclopedia are organized by the Latinate names assigned to them by botanists, but common names are given when possible. If you know only the common name for a plant, look it up in the index, and you will find where to turn. We use Latin names instead of common names for three reasons: Some plants don't have common names; sometimes the same plant goes by different common names in different parts of the country; and sometimes one common name is used for two or more different plants. By contrast, each plant has its own unique Latin name that's used around the world. (Actually, the Latin names for some plants have been changed over the years. If you can't find an Encyclopedia listing under the name you know, look for that name in the index in case the plant is listed under a synonym.)

Most plant names have two parts that name the genus and the species. The name of a genus (called the generic name) is often used as a common name. For example, magnolias are trees in the genus *Magnolia.* The name for a species (called the specific epithet) always follows the generic name, to indicate a particular kind of plant within that genus. For example, *Magnolia macrophylla* is the magnolia with large leaves. Many garden plants are hybrids between two species; in this case, the species name is preceded by the symbol ×, such as *Magnolia × loebneri.*

Cultivars are plants selected for their outstanding qualities and usually propagated by cuttings, division, or grafting to maintain those traits. (A few cultivars come true from seed.) Cultivar names are capitalized and appear within single quotation marks. Most cultivars are selections within a species, and their botanical names have three parts, such as *Magnolia stellata* 'Royal Star'. Other cultivars are hybrids between species, and their names have just two parts, such as *Magnolia* 'Elizabeth'. All of this may seem confusing at first, but you'll find that you gradually become more familiar with plant names as you learn more about the plants themselves.

Growing Healthy Plants

Regardless of size or design, all successful gardens have one thing in common—healthy plants. Few of us are blessed with good soil, a benign climate, and a green thumb. To grow healthy plants, you will probably need to augment what nature has provided, by improving the soil or by supplementing rainfall and nutrients. Sometimes you'll need to temper nature, shading plants from the heat, insulating them from the cold, or protecting them from insects and disease.

The chapters in this section of the book cover these subjects and many others—how to grow plants from seed and increase their numbers by division or cuttings; how to prune to maintain health, control size, or enhance form; how to start and maintain a lawn. Informative black-and-white drawings illustrate many of the techniques.

Creating a Garden

The pleasures of gardening

Since the dawn of civilization, people have been growing plants—digging, sowing, cultivating in order to survive. But for as long as gardening has been a labor of necessity, it has also been a labor of love, a source of great delight. Today, when few in our affluent society have to grow plants, many choose to do so. Some take more pleasure in the labor than in its fruits; others are fulfilled by the bounty or the beauty of their efforts. Many find equal satisfaction in the work and in its results.

As generation after generation has tilled the soil, a vast store of knowledge, literature, and lore about gardening has accumulated. Today universities devote whole departments to the study of horticulture; scholars and scientists as well as practicing gardeners fill libraries with their findings, observations, and advice. Each year thousands of businesses, great and small, earn millions of dollars serving the public's desire for this information and for the plants, tools, and accessories that, we're promised, will make our garden dreams reality.

Yet of all our many pastimes, gardening is perhaps the simplest and most accessible. It doesn't require a workshop full of tools, a wallet full of money, or hours of practice. Plant a few seeds in a bit of earth and you're on your way. For the beginner, overwhelmed by gardening books, catalogs, experts,

workshops, and products, there is great comfort—and encouragement—in the knowledge that every garden, no matter how grand, shares these humble origins.

Like its essential practices, gardening's pleasures are also, at heart, simple. Some are fleeting—the first scent of lilac in the spring; a hummingbird glimpsed drawing nectar from a trumpet vine; a dew-laden rose backlit by the rising sun. Others endure for days or weeks—a perennial border in full early summer bloom; the brilliant berries of hollies and pyracanthas in the autumn and winter. The most profound of gardening's attractions—the mystery that transfixes and delights us as children watching a bean emerge from a soil-filled paper cup—lasts a lifetime.

Gardens, of course, enrich our daily lives in numerous ways. We may fortify ourselves for the day's work by sipping a cup of coffee on a sunny patio surrounded by fragrant plants; in the evening we unwind in the same spot with a glass of wine. Children play ball on the lawn, climb the big shade tree, or chase butterflies that hover over the phlox. We welcome our guests in the courtyard garden and entertain them on the patio, perhaps serving a meal harvested from the vegetable garden tucked behind the garage.

Gardening is, above all, an active pursuit. A gardener's work is never done—soil to till, seeds to sow, shrubs to prune—and gardeners wouldn't have it any other way. A garden that appears to the casual viewer to be perfect in all its parts is a work in progress to its creator. A clump of perennials is crowding its neighbors and needs to be divided. The color combination in that corner isn't quite right. A place must be found for our latest plant enthusiasm—perhaps the time has come to enlarge the bed.

Change is one of gardening's most powerful appeals. A garden is never the same two days in a row, much less two months or two years in a row. While some change is due to the ever-active gardener, much is grounded in the rhythms of nature. Annuals follow their yearly cycle from seed to flower to seed; perennials pass from dormancy to growth and back again. Year after year, trees and shrubs branch out, bloom, and set fruit.

We mark the changing seasons as much by their manifestations in the garden as by changes in the temperature or length of day. Pushing aside a dusting of snow, the first crocus heralds the end of winter; daffodils, tulips, and cherry blossoms speckle the greening landscape with color. Peonies, irises, and daylilies attend the first days of summer. When other flowers have faded, sturdy coneflowers and black-eyed Susans brave the heat of high summer while the shade of an old oak shelters the gardener. Fall has its own blossoms—asters, chrysanthemums—but this season belongs to brilliant leaves and golden grasses. In winter we ponder the garden's bones—the evergreens, the gnarled branches of the old oak, the rattle of the wind through dry seed heads—and plan for the spring.

Our gardening interests and energies change, too. When we're young, juggling the demands of jobs and children, perhaps moving every few years, we do our gardening on the fly, grateful for a respite, however brief, from the bustle of daily life. As we settle in one place and the children grow up and leave home, gardening expands to fill the newly available time and

Gardening reaches across all sorts of boundaries. It occasions lifelong friendships and brings old and young, rich and poor together. It is, above all, an active pursuit, offering invigorating exercise, fresh air, and the satisfaction of working in partnership with nature to help things grow.

space. The garden, along with our dreams for it, begins to grow. We may develop a passion for roses or rock gardens, water plants or natural landscapes. The lawn that we struggled to keep healthy despite its punishment by youthful soccer players gives way to flower beds, shrub borders, perhaps an orchard.

Then, as retirement approaches, with its tantalizing prospects of more time for gardening, the body lodges a protest. No matter how much we enjoy digging, planting, and weeding, these activities are hard work. The big perennial border now seems a bit too big; the woodland garden is in danger of becoming a thicket. Reluctantly, we cut back, maybe even move to a smaller property.

Fortunately, the pleasures of gardening are not dependent on the size of the garden. Gathering some of our favorite plants in a smaller, more intimate setting, we savor them no less than when they billowed across the entire backyard. Gardeners, like everyone, grow old; our gardens keep us from feeling old.

Planning: What do you have?

Gardeners are an active breed, happiest with shovel or pruning shears in hand. Of course, we love to relax on the patio and admire our plantings. But many of us enjoy the labor of gardening as much as its fruits, whether we're casually snipping spent blossoms off a favorite rose or digging up half the yard for a new flower bed.

Unfortunately, our enthusiasm for action sometimes leads us astray, particularly if we're new to gardening and impatient to bring our dreams to life. We need to remember that the best home landscapes—those that manage to be beautiful, inviting, and functional without making slaves of their owners—are landscapes that fit their sites and situations. The more familiar you are with your property, in both its natural and man-made aspects, the more successful you'll be in creating a landscape that is pleasing and practical.

You may be surprised by how much there is to know about your small domain. In addition to noting nature's contributions—temperature, rain, snow, wind, soil, and existing plants—you'll need to observe the ways you and your family and friends make use of and interact with the site. Some things are quick and easy to ascertain—the number of existing trees or the condition of the front fence. Others take time. Seasonal differences, for example, require a full year to experience. And certain things keep changing: shadows lengthen as trees and shrubs mature; traffic patterns alter as children grow.

While there's always something for an observant gardener to discover, no matter how long you've been at it, some sort of systematic examination is particularly important for beginning gardeners (and for experienced gardeners starting out on a new site). Even the placement of a simple flower bed requires that you know where and for how long the sun shines on various spots on the property. As you progress to more complicated planning—organizing trees, shrubs, beds, borders, paths, fences, patios, and so on into an attractive and functional whole—the information that you gather about your property and the insight that you acquire about your own gardening needs and desires (see the next chapter) will be indispensable.

Recording your observations

It can be helpful to draw a site plan (an accurately scaled, bird's-eye view of your property and what's on it), but many people are intimidated by the idea and never get past that very large blank sheet of paper. When you're starting out, a small notebook makes more sense. Jot your observations in it while they're fresh; record all sorts of things—how patterns of sun and shade change during the course of a day and over the seasons, as well as your thoughts about what to plant in the soggy spot at the bottom of the slope. If you keep it up, your notebook will be far more valuable than any site plan.

Photographs can be an effective aid to note taking, helping you recall the quality of light in a particular season or a view that you might find hard to conjure up from memory. In the dead of winter, surrounded by seed catalogs, you can use photos to help chart the course for spring—maybe a touch more blue in that spot or some silver foliage to blend with the pinks over there. As the years pass, it can also be rewarding to look back over a photo chronicle of your garden's evolution.

Old landscape or new?

The process of analyzing a site is like using a mental zoom lens. First, you focus on the broad view: the character, geography, and condition of the property as a whole as well as its relation to the neighborhood and even to the region. Then you gradually narrow the perspective until you're at your back door.

If you're new to gardening but not to your property, you have a head start. You already know a lot about your site, particularly how you feel about it—you're tired of staring at the neighbor's garage; you know you'd like to plant something in that spot just outside the bedroom window. You may not know, however, specific information important to successful gardening—where the frost pockets are, how the shade changes from season to season, the qualities of your soil.

When you move to a previously lived-in home, you're inheriting someone else's landscape—the house, garage, driveways and walkways, walls and fences, and established plantings. If you share the previous residents' tastes and have similar needs, you can pick up where they left off. If not, you'll have to decide which parts of the existing landscape to keep or restore and which to change.

Sites that have been newly built on present fewer givens. The contractor may have graded the land and installed a lawn and a few shrubs and trees. But such sites are still more open and exposed, more unformed, than an older property. Where the new house is surrounded by bare soil, the mud, blowing dust, and weeds that soon flourish may lend a greater urgency to landscape projects. While you may be able to renovate an existing landscape at a more leisurely pace, the prospect of beginning with a "clean slate" can be invigorating.

Finally, if you're building your own house or buying a yet-to-be-completed new house, you can affect features that are givens in other circumstances—the contours and grading of the entire property, the position and character of driveways and sidewalks, sometimes even the orientation of the house itself.

Whether you've lived on your site for years or you're building a new house, familiarize yourself with the larger surroundings. Look at your neighborhood with a gardener's eye. All properties have a natural history, and knowing that your plot was once meadow, pasture, or woodland will give you a good idea of the kinds of plants that should do well there. If this history was scraped away during construction, take your notebook with you on walks through the

neighborhood or the surrounding countryside and note the plants that grow well—particularly those that thrive unaided. Visit local nature centers; add field guides of local flora and fauna to your library.

Climate

Rain, snow, heat, frost, and wind—these constituents of climate are critical to the well-being of plants. North America contains a wide range of climates, which influence an equally wide range of habitats, from rain forest to desert, prairie to woodland. A garden in the Pacific Northwest, where temperatures are moderate and rainfall abundant, will be completely different from one in hot, dry Albuquerque. It's not difficult to find statistics about your climate—annual rainfall and snowfall, frost dates, yearly high and low temperatures. The USDA Hardiness Zone map in this book, for example, will give you a general idea of the lowest temperatures common to where you live. Your local library, newspaper, or Cooperative Extension Service can provide more of this sort of information.

But these general facts are only part of the picture. Temperature, wind, and humidity can combine to produce conditions in small areas that differ considerably from those that generally characterize a large region. These local climatic variations, often called microclimates, can be as big as a valley or as small as a nook between a house wall and a fence. Microclimates can be very important to your garden. For instance, if your property is on a north-facing hillside, you may find that your last frost occurs a week or two later than the date for your region.

You can establish a profile of your property's climate by observation and some rudimentary measurement. Get a rain gauge and a thermometer (some of the latter automatically record the day's high and low), and enter their readings in your notebook. Although you may not take daily readings, it's useful to note unusual weather conditions. Plants that are otherwise heat and cold tolerant, for example, may be sensitive to sudden swings in temperature from day to night.

As you walk around the site, note how heat varies from place to place. South-facing exposures are generally warmer than other exposures. In northern and high-elevation gardens, a south-facing site often offers the best gardening possibilities. But in warmer climates, a southern exposure can be too hot for most plants (and most gardeners). An east-facing site is versatile, one of gentle morning light and afternoon shade. West is warmer than east, and afternoon sun there is harsher and hotter than morning light, and therefore harder on some plants. A northern exposure is slowest to warm in spring and quickest to cool in fall. Where the sunlight is strong, plentiful, and unobstructed by trees or structures, exposure can affect microclimates to such an extent that the south side of the house can resemble Arizona while the north is like Quebec.

In addition to exposure, structures and materials in or near the garden bed can affect the heat and light that reach it. A stone or brick wall, a concrete path, a dark mulch can all intensify heat. A white wall reflecting light and heat into a shady site can make it suitable for more plants, but a mulch of white river rock in full sun can fry plants growing nearby. A dark mulch will warm the soil beneath it and make plants start growth earlier. A wall of somber gray stone will appear to steal what little light is available in a shady corner.

Winds, whether they originate off the vast expanse of ocean or sweep the desert or prairie, can stage limb-wrenching assaults on weak trees and shrubs. Exposure to prevailing winds can lower temperatures and dry out plants. The effects of wind can be tempered by fences and rows of sturdy, good-size plants. But remember that wind also helps keep insects and diseases at bay and promotes strong, bushy growth in plants.

Plants vary remarkably in their reactions to humidity. Entire regions, of course, are known for their humid or arid conditions. Microclimates may offer some relief (a shady, sheltered area with trees will be moister than a windy, sunny spot) or may intensify the condition. But it's difficult to affect humidity enough to satisfy certain plants. Some woodland plants that are comfortable in humid eastern gardens, for example, struggle in the arid West, no matter how much you might change the soil, add water, and otherwise pamper them.

Getting started: Plant while you plan

FEW PEOPLE would dream of starting to build a house without first completing detailed plans. A home landscape can be complex, too, but fortunately you needn't postpone the pleasure of digging until you have a detailed blueprint in hand.

At the very least, start a little flower bed at the same time you embark on the process of evaluating your site and your gardening needs and desires. Firsthand knowledge of plants is every bit as important as the other insights you'll gather. And gaining it is a lot of fun.

Soil and the lay of the land

Of all the elements of the site, none is more important than the one you find beneath your feet—the soil. Although some plants will grow in a wide range of soils, most garden plants prefer a loose, well-drained soil full of organic matter. Unfortunately, very few of us find this in our yards. You can learn a lot about your soil by digging a few holes around the property and by noting where existing plants seem to grow well or where water stands after rain. Later, when you're considering where to put flower beds, trees, and shrubs, you may decide to send soil samples to a laboratory for tests. (See "Evaluating your soil" for more on this subject.)

The lay of the land—flat, rolling, sloping, or rock strewn—will have a big influence on your landscaping plans. While a steep slope without natural rock outcroppings or vegetation to hold the soil can pose erosion problems, you might see it as the chance to build a magnificent terraced garden. Gentle rolling contours make a flat site more interesting to the eye. Contours also provide a diversity of growing conditions—slopes being drier, swales and basins damper—with opportunities to harvest runoff in drier climates or to facilitate drainage in wetter ones. It's usually difficult and expensive to make major changes in the contours of your property, but with structures and plantings you can introduce a little "roll" to a flat site or "level out" a hilly one.

Existing vegetation

Trees and shrubs already on the site can be valuable assets or formidable obstacles. They may be quality, long-lived specimens in good condition, providing spring flowers, summer shade, or autumn color while forming the bones of a well-thought-out structure for the entire landscape planting. Or they may be fast-growing, weak-wooded species that drop branches in the slightest breeze and obstruct warming sunlight or cooling breezes. Below ground, they may undermine foundations or sewage lines, or their shallow root systems may hog the nutrients, water, and space that other plants need to grow.

With the exception of invasive species, the more perennials and annuals you find on the site the better. At worst you'll eventually dig them up and replace them with plants you like; at best they'll give you a good head start on making your own garden. A lawn, like trees and shrubs, can be a mixed blessing— an asset if it's healthy, a time-consuming pain if it's not. And even a healthy lawn can be a liability if its vigor is dependent on large infusions of water and fertilizer. In areas where water is in short supply, many people are substituting drought-tolerant ground covers for turfgrass.

If you're unfamiliar with the plants you find on a new property, particularly the trees and shrubs, ask a knowledgeable friend or a landscape professional to help you identify them and to explain their advantages and disadvantages.

People in the landscape

No amount of knowledge about climate, soil, and plants can save a flower bed that is placed across the kids' favorite shortcut to the ball park. People, no less

than nature, affect the home landscape, by the ways they use and interact with it and by the structures and services they build on it. Here are some human factors to consider.

Note the routes most commonly taken to typical destinations, such as the garage, parking area, trash bins, clothesline, or sandbox. Do these coincide with "formal" paths, or are they well-worn ruts in the lawn? Are your entryways inviting, convenient, and safe—well lit, no loose steps or low branches? Is the driveway large enough, and is there enough off-street parking? Be sure to examine the condition of existing garden structures, walls, and fences.

Identify the legal boundaries of the site as well as the fences, hedges, and buildings that visually define them. Locate aboveground and buried utilities: electricity, gas, cable TV, telephone, septic and sewage, and water (including permanent irrigation systems). Most municipalities will locate buried public utilities for free, to reduce the hazards and cost of landscapers cutting into the lines. (These and other tangible elements—boundaries, walls, and driveways as well as major existing trees and shrubs—might be usefully marked on a site plan. See "Putting it on paper" for more on making plans.)

As you investigate your property, don't forget the subtle ways it influences you and your family. Are the views from the windows pleasing, or do overgrown shrubs nearby cast a dismal pall on the room? What about the views of the house from the garden, and views from one part of the garden to another? How do people amuse themselves when they're outside? If the children enjoy burrowing around in that thicket of shrubs along the lot line, you may decide to renovate it rather than remove it. Are there secluded spots where you can steal a moment of relaxation during a busy day?

Every site has a character of its own. Whether you find your site charming or problematic, the more intimately you know it, the better you'll be able to shape it to serve your needs and desires.

The house is the dominant element on most residential properties. With plants and other landscape features you can enhance a house's good points and mask its bad ones. A large grass garden and planting of perennials and shrubs makes the house above much more inviting than did its previous, formal setting of sheared evergreens, right.
A little meadow planting complements the informality of the adobe house below.

Planning:
What do you want?

You may want a patio for entertaining, outdoor eating, and relaxation with friends and family, or a simple, secluded spot to enjoy your garden on your own. Perhaps you want both.

A garden grows as much from the personality of the gardener as it does from seeds and compost, stone and timber. Understanding what you and your family bring to your property—likes and dislikes, needs and desires—is just as important as discovering what your property offers to you.

Households often include people with very different tastes and interests. Moreover, one person frequently harbors two conflicting ideas or desires at the same time. When you plan a landscape, you must serve, among other things, as a mediator between different agendas. Defining your preferences and those of other family members as clearly as possible makes it much easier to arrive at good choices or to find mutually acceptable compromises.

Gardener, know thyself

Some people are fully aware of their preferences and tastes and can list them like items on a menu. But if you're not so sure, take a look around you. Chances are your surroundings will reflect your personality. If your house has open, generously lit rooms, you may be most comfortable with a rambling, open landscape. A house of small, intimate rooms may suggest a desire for privacy and enclosure. (If you didn't choose your home for its looks, noting what you don't like about it can be just as revealing.)

How you furnish your home—rooms crammed with knickknacks and collectibles, or simple and spare as a Shaker's kitchen—will give you an idea of the planting density and diversity you might prefer in your garden. Likewise, if your sock drawer is always in need of organizing and you haven't seen the surface of your desk in months, your ideal garden may be an overwhelming profusion of plants. If your checkbook always balances to the penny and your files are actually in alphabetical order, a highly structured, organized landscape may please you most.

Other hobbies and interests may provide clues to possible gardening enthusiasms or landscape needs. It's safe to assume that an avid collector of antiques or stamps, comic books or rocks will sooner or later find herself amassing salvias or veronicas, penstemon or primulas. An ardent cook might want a kitchen garden, herb garden, or orchard; a weaver may want a place for sheep, a hunter for dogs.

Gardens inspired by nature's habitats and their characteristic plants and creatures are becoming increasingly popular. If your idea of fun on a weekend is to hike a challenging trail to a secluded wilderness spot, consider creating a "natural" garden—a meadow, woodland, or water garden—on part or all of your property. In these areas, young children can monitor the changes from cocoon to butterfly and from egg-filled nest to extended feathered family, or watch a spider capture her prey or bees collect pollen. Adults can enjoy the same natural wonders as well as cultivate some of the interesting plants that inhabit these areas.

Memories of favorite places, often from childhood, shape our preferences. Does the scent of lilacs or roses carry you back to grandma's garden? Does a cool, leafy hideaway remind you of playing hooky from chores on hot summer days? Even if you can't re-create fond memories in your garden, you may be able to include elements—a scented plant, a picket fence, a small pond—that bring them to mind.

The best way to discover or to develop your tastes in plants and garden design is, of course, to visit gardens, the more the better. Botanic gardens and noted public gardens offer a wealth of garden styles and plants, but a friend's modest home landscape can be just as informative. When you visit these places, subject them and your reactions to them to a little scrutiny. Note the color combinations that you most enjoy. Are they dramatic collections of bold, contrasting colors, or subtle blends of pastels? Try to ascertain the underlying structure in a handsome perennial border or to figure out why a friend's deck seems to relate so well to the house and the surrounding plantings. Such analysis can help you understand more clearly what you like and why you like it, and ultimately help you achieve similar effects in your landscape.

Living in the landscape

Balancing the often abstract considerations of personal taste are the very concrete demands we make of our home landscapes. We live in our landscapes much as we do in our homes. We cook and entertain on the patio or deck, we relax with a good book under a favorite shade tree. We exercise, play games, or fix the car in the open spaces. We store firewood or keep animals along the boundaries. Each of these demands, along with many others, has consequences for your landscape.

If outdoor entertaining is important to you, you may want an intimate space for two, room to accommodate a crowd, or both. You might decide to develop outdoor areas adjacent to your kitchen or family room, making the movement of food and guests between the house and the garden convenient and inviting. You might extend the flagstone, wood, or tile flooring inside the house out onto the patio to emphasize the flow between the two spaces. In the Southwest, a patio or courtyard with an overhead lath sunscreen or a vine-covered arbor creates a transitional area between indoors and outdoors. In colder or wetter climates, a patio with a solid roof would fulfill the same function while offering more protection.

Farther from the house, lawns can serve as both patio extensions for entertaining and open play areas for children, adults, and pets. If yours is a sports-minded family, you'll want open space for ball games, badminton, or just horsing around. A swimming pool provides exercise and entertainment. Embellished with plantings, dramatic lighting, or a fountain, a pool can also be a beautiful focal point in the landscape. If a swimming pool is too big or too expensive for you, consider making a smaller, "natural" pool with a plastic liner. Planted with water-loving plants and inhabited by a few frogs and fish, a small pool can fascinate children for hours while enhancing the look of your garden.

Although all of us enjoy activities with family and friends, we also need time to ourselves. If your bedroom or study opens to the outside, you may want to develop the adjacent space as a quiet retreat. Smaller in scale and more subdued in tone than the rest of the landscape, such an area might be physically screened by plants or walls, an ideal place for a spa or a hammock, a trickling fountain, muted lighting. On larger lots, there may be a niche isolated from the social areas, where you can read or relax in private. You need only a meandering path to get you to it and a bench to keep you comfortably there. Not everyone unwinds sitting down, however. If your escape from care is slamming a ball against a wall or overhauling an engine, you'll want to make sure that your landscape provides for these, too.

The home landscape is also the stage for numerous mundane things. Kennels and dog runs, clotheslines, firewood storage, trash and recycling bins, pool gear, garden tools, bicycles, outdoor toy storage, potting shed and cold frames, the compost pile, and even the vegetable garden might be included among necessities that need to be readily accessible but screened from public view. Depending on your site, a single large area might accommodate most of these needs, or you may have to disperse them around the property.

Maintaining your landscape

From time to time, as your landscaping wish list grows, remember the story of the little red hen. Who will care for all this wonderful stuff? Trees and shrubs need pruning; perennials need dividing, staking, and deadheading. Everything needs watering. Patios and paths will need to be mended, as will decks, trellises, lath houses, and gazebos. Water features, whether a swimming pool or a lined pond, are always demanding attention.

You may love to roll up your sleeves and get to work, but does anyone else in your family? And how much time, realistically, does your work schedule allow for the garden—an hour every evening from spring through fall, or two hours a week? Which chores do you relish, which are drudgery? If you have tidy tastes and less time than you'd like for gardening, you should consider a landscape of trees and shrubs. If you have lots of time and are happiest with dirt under your fingernails, you may wish to tackle a large perennial border.

There is little joy in a home landscape that nags at you to weed and water, sweep and paint when all you have the energy to do is sit on the patio and watch the sunset. Be realistic about how much time you can invest in maintenance, and plan accordingly. If you're new to gardening and uncertain of its demands, start small.

If your tastes run to riotous colors, you may prefer an informal garden filled with cheerful flowers like the bed of gloriosa daisies, yarrow, and peony poppies, above right. A shrub border like the one at right may appeal to those with more subdued, formal tastes.

Organizing your landscape to serve the needs of children and adults can be a challenge. This New England garden satisfies vegetable-gardening adults and pleasure-seeking youngsters by locating a miniature lighthouse/playhouse among the raised beds.

Money matters

One of the most important boundaries of your home landscape is your budget. Although most of us think of plants when we plan our landscape, it's the hardscape—paths, walls, fences, decks, patios, and so on—that constitutes its biggest cost. Installing these elements over a period of years, and doing as much of the work as you can yourself, will help keep these costs in bounds. The choice of materials also makes a huge difference. Brick, tile, or stone paving is beautiful, but it's more expensive than concrete. Crushed gravel is even more economical. Use expensive materials where they'll make the greatest impact, or where their durability will pay off in reduced maintenance.

Compared with the hardscape, plants are one of the least expensive elements of the landscape. Still, when you consider plants there are several ways to stretch your gardening dollar. Many perennials can be grown from seed, although they may take a year or two longer than container-grown plants to reach mature size. When you buy plants, select those that are well adapted to your region. (See "Buying plants" for more advice.)

Your garden will cost less in the long run if you identify and plan for expensive or permanent items (large trees and shrubs as well as hardscape) as early as possible. You may not install parts of your plan for months or even years, but having a plan for major landscape elements will help ensure that what you put in place first won't conflict with what is to come. If your pockets aren't very deep, take heart. The most beautiful gardens are often those that cost comparatively little in cash but that are richly endowed with the spirit of their creators.

As your garden grows

A garden, resonating life itself, is always changing. Its colors and moods shift with the seasons. Over the years, trees grow, expanding their shade, inching sun-loving plants out of their space. As windbreaks fill in, they provide protected niches for tenderer plants. Our lives also change, our energies and interests wax and wane, our needs evolve. Children grow up and the swingset and basketball court become places for an herb garden or a climbing rose. The large perennial border you eagerly cared for as a young adult may begin to overwhelm you in later life.

A new interest in orchids or lilies, cacti or koi may not be predictable, but if you or other family members have a history of grand passions, allow for such diversions by leaving room for growth. If you anticipate expanding the family room but want a patio in that spot now, pave it with bricks laid on sand instead of with poured concrete. Such foresight will reduce the cost of reworking spaces as the garden evolves.

Despite your best efforts, there are many changes that you won't be able to anticipate. Perhaps that's just as well. The potential for change engages us in gardening from the start and fuels our continuing fascination. Why not embrace it?

Gardeners frequently develop passions for particular plants (roses, for example) and devote considerable energy and space to them. Sometimes these plants can be integrated in existing beds; at other times they take over the garden.

There is often a delicate balance to be struck between the need for privacy and the desire to present a friendly face to neighbors and to offer a warm welcome to visitors. This adobe wall, gateway, and planting addresses all these needs quite effectively.

Do you need help?

IF THE WHOLE BUSINESS of analyzing your landscaping needs and desires, not to mention figuring out what your site has to offer, is making your head ache, consider seeking out a knowledgeable, experienced gardening friend or a landscape professional. These consultants can often open your eyes to possibilities and perils you might never take into account on your own, or dispel confusion by helping you sort out your options and establish priorities.

You can ask a consultant to guide you through the whole process of evaluation and planning, or you can request help on specific problems. If your strong suit is plants, you may want someone to advise you on hardscape (all the parts of the landscape that aren't plants—paving, walls, garden structures, irrigation systems, and so on). If you're already a regular at the local building supply but a novice when it comes to perennials, trees, or shrubs, a horticultural consultant can identify the existing plants on your site and suggest what new plants will best accomplish your goals. Sometimes you'll find people who have a mix of these skills. If no one among your gardening friends fills the bill, a local garden group can sometimes recommend landscape designers or contractors who have proven themselves in your area.

One of the most rewarding aspects of gardening is seeing your dreams and hard work transform your property. In just five years, a love both of plants and of Japanese garden design created a richly varied little world on this small suburban front yard.

Gardening across America

Ours is a vast country. Mountains, deserts, rain forests, and grasslands; arctic tundra and tropical beaches—you can find all these, and more. Our climates are equally diverse. At the same moment that a blizzard howls through Maine, a light spring rain may be cooling a 70° F afternoon in San Diego.

It's small wonder that gardeners who move from one part of the country to another often have to

Midwestern gardeners have begun to take greater advantage of the grasses and wildflowers of their native prairies. In the photo at right, coneflowers, gayfeather, and black-eyed Susans brighten a Wisconsin garden.

Urban gardeners must make the most of limited space and difficult conditions. High above Manhattan, the rooftop garden shown below offers an oasis of plant life amid acres of concrete.

hone their skills from the ground up. They must not only adjust to the limitations and possibilities of new conditions—rainfall, length of growing season, heat and cold, soil, and so many other variables—but they must also become familiar with the style of life and traditions prevalent in their new region.

In this nation of immigrants, domestic traditions from many cultures have been transplanted, and old ways have been adapted to new conditions. Homes, for example, historically have varied by region. Abundant fieldstone and timber were fashioned into dwellings in New England; in the treeless Southwest and Great Plains, homes were formed of earth (adobe) or sod; structures of artfully stacked logs rose in the evergreen forests of the Rockies and Pacific Northwest.

The diversity of nature and of human society has given rise to myriad expressions in American gardens. These differences may have been more pronounced in earlier times, when new arrivals from England, Spain, China, or Scandinavia were more isolated physically and culturally from each other. Today mass communication has brought gardeners much closer together. We learn from each other and share many of the same problems and concerns. After all, deer are deer—and they eat gardens—whether you live in Georgia or Montana. Many of the same approaches to gardening are applicable no matter where you live. Sound horticultural practices—soil management, irrigation, pest control, and recycling—are essentially the same across the land.

A sense of place

What differs is the attitude toward gardening, which reflects the ways in which people live. And the diversity of lifestyles is in significant ways a reflection of the natural environment. A practical approach to gardening relies on an understanding of the natural features and weather in your region and an appreciation of your region's history and culture.

One question a gardener should ask is, "What grows here naturally?" What plants have evolved to cope with the region's weather—rain, drought, wind, cold, heat, hail, humidity—and its natural features—soil type, altitude, and topography? It is certainly possible to grow plants that are not naturally adapted to a particular region—an iris in the desert or a cactus in the woods—but you must ask yourself if the effort is worth the trouble. Have you spent too much of your time and resources for the reward?

Growing a majority of plants adaptable to your region is a sensible approach. Fortunately, the range of plants for each region is large when you consider not only the plants native to your area but also the many that have evolved in similar climates throughout the world.

In each region of the country, native plants have adapted to the prevailing conditions of soil and climate. Much of a region's character comes from the kinds of plants that grow wild there and their annual cycle of growth. For example, conditions in the eastern United States support a forest of deciduous trees whose appearance changes dramatically through the seasons. The eastern landscape is bright and open in winter, gauzy with pastel buds in spring, dim and occluded in summer, and dazzling with color in fall. By contrast, the coniferous forests of the western

Venerable moss-draped live oaks and colorful azaleas, like these in Charleston, South Carolina, evoke a strong sense of place for many southerners.

Towering maples shelter this rambling house on the edge of a small New England town. Blessed with abundant rainfall and moderate temperatures, gardeners in this region grow a wide variety of native and exotic plants, often in beds and borders that reflect the area's British roots.

Employing desert plants, adobe construction, and a stretch of cool water, this Phoenix home combines the traditions of the Southwest with the contemporary interest in natural landscaping. An interior courtyard in the same home, at right, harks back to landscape practices of early Spanish settlers in the region.

mountains and Pacific Northwest are a towering dark presence year-round. In the vast midwestern prairies, the waving grasses cycle from green to golden brown to green again, ever present but never screening your view of the horizon. Increasingly, gardeners are taking a new look at the landscapes that surround their communities and designing gardens that reflect the natural patterns.

Garden styles

Many American gardens are as distinctive as the land itself. There is no one right way to garden across the land or, indeed, within each zone. What has evolved, however, is similarities within each region. In some cases, these derive from architectural preferences and cultural influences as well as climatic factors.

There is no denying, for example, the influences of English settlers in the Northeast. But these take many forms, from the saltbox houses of the coast to the elegant brownstones of the cities. With a backdrop of deciduous trees and colonial stone walls, the gardens of the eastern woodlands often reflect a British legacy of perennial borders and lush lawns. Other European cultures have also played a part in shaping the landscape, however, including the French, Dutch, Irish, German, and Italian. Native plants play an important role where gardeners seek to integrate their gardens into existing or reestablished woodlands.

The English influence is also felt throughout the South, but so is that of the French and Spanish gardening traditions. Symmetry and formality characterize many of the region's gardens. Climate accounts for some of the decidedly different turn taken by southern gardens from their northern counterparts. Native pines provide the backdrop for magnolias and azaleas as well as many subtropical plants from around the world.

As the country pushed its boundaries west, the Great Plains offered new horticultural challenges. New cities reflected the Victorian influence of the day, and stately, ornate "Queen Anne" homes are still features in established neighborhoods throughout the Midwest. Sweeping lawns, trees planted for shade (now venerable specimens), picket fences, and colorful "carpet" beds of flowers were distinguishing features. These traditions still linger, although a new appreciation of native prairie ecology has resulted in a recent trend toward a more natural, relaxed look in gardens.

The Spanish and Native Americans influenced the style of the western deserts. Adobe and stucco construction is still a notable feature, as is the ranch-style home. Lacking the shade trees of many other parts of the country, gardens of the Southwest often create their own enclosures for an oasis, just as many Spanish and Mediterranean gardens do. Walled gardens, pergolas, and shaded patios provide protection for people and plants. Lawns may be replaced by drought-tolerant ground covers, desert wildflowers, and some of the unique shrubs and cacti of the region.

The Rockies and Pacific Northwest, being relatively "new" areas of the country, borrow heavily from existing styles in the rest of the United States, adapting them for local conditions. Denver, Boise, Salt Lake City, and San Francisco all have Victorian architectural roots, and this influences many gardens. A dramatic landscape and a variety of native plants have also led to a more naturalistic style where the beauty of rocks and streams are re-created.

Although Spanish mission settlements in California predate English colonization in the East, much of California is only recently developed. While the Spanish influence is deeply felt in the western deserts, California has almost invented itself. Notable is the impact of immigrants from the Pacific Rim; Japanese garden sensibilities, in particular, are widespread. Whatever the stylistic preferences, everyone tries to take advantage of the marvelous climate, and homes are often built for equal indoor and outdoor living. In these outdoor rooms, native plants vie for attention with tropical and subtropical plants from both the Old and New World.

An overview of natural ecology and cultural influences is useful, but it does not take into account a prime factor—American ingenuity. As the space and time for gardening have decreased, many gardeners have managed to create new approaches to gardening. Cities blossom with innovative gardens that salute the past but embody modern living. These thrive on rooftops, balconies, and fire escapes. They provide green havens amid concrete and steel. Where space is abundant but time is not, imaginative low-maintenance landscapes have appeared. American gardens continue to grow, influenced by the past but with an eye to the future.

In this rural Rocky Mountain setting, an informal perennial garden seems right at home against spectacular scenery.

The greening of suburbia

IN THE BUILDING BOOM following World War II, developers stamped out carbon-copy houses in vast numbers across the country. From coast to coast, regardless of natural surroundings and conditions, they created a banal domestic landscape—houses corseted by narrow bands of evergreen shrubs afloat on seas of closely cropped bluegrass. Recent suburbs are more varied, but many share the same unimaginative landscaping.

Just as suburban homeowners have customized their houses to suit individual needs and tastes, it is possible to transform dull suburban landscapes. The first step may be to hitch up the Jeep and pull out the overgrown shrubs that obscure many otherwise lovely homes. Take a fresh look at your house, play up its strong points, reconsider how you use the property.

Most important, become familiar with your region—the land and its plants, its history of building and design. Introducing native plants, indigenous stone, or traditional building materials into the landscape will help give it—and you—a sense of place. Put your personal stamp on your property, salute your regional heritage, and express your own interests.

To a remarkable extent, suburbs exist outside the physical and traditional expressions of place. At street level, this suburban development in San Francisco would be hard to distinguish from numerous contemporaries across the country.

Annuals and biennials

Grown in pots, annuals can create a miniature garden on patios, porches, or anywhere space or soil is limited.

A hanging basket of nasturtiums, marigolds, and petunias hovering over a carpet of geraniums brings life and color to this hard-edged brick corner.

Annuals make showy additions to any garden; in fact, some people make gardens entirely of annuals. Beginning gardeners often find great success and build their confidence and skills by growing annuals, but this diverse group of plants has much to offer gardeners of all abilities.

Annuals are easy to grow and are relatively inexpensive (especially if you grow them from seed). Because there are so many annuals, you can find one for every condition in the garden, from sun to shade and from dry to moist, and in many sizes, shapes, and colors. There are towering giants such as cleome, hollyhocks, and Mexican sunflowers, and diminutive creepers such as sweet alyssum and lobelia.

A short, happy life

True annuals grow, bloom, set seed, and die in a single gardening season. They invest no resources in surviving for another year, concentrating instead on producing seed to continue their species. This results in a great profusion of flowers and often a very long season of bloom.

Biennials have a different, two-year life cycle. The first year, they produce only foliage, which provides the energy for the following year's flowers. After flowering the second year, biennials set seed and die, and the cycle begins again. It's true that there are far fewer biennials from which to choose, but many, such as foxgloves, hollyhocks, silver-dollar plant, and mulleins, are especially interesting and beautiful and worth the extra patience required to grow them. (For convenience, we'll include biennials under the term *annuals* in the remainder of this chapter.)

In addition to true annuals and biennials, a number of tender perennials are grown as annuals in much of North America. Often of tropical or subtropical origin, these perennials have much to offer despite the fact that they are not winter-hardy. Long-blooming, adaptable, and easy to care for, tender perennials such as geraniums and wax begonias are routinely grown as annuals where conditions preclude their survival over the winter.

In the garden and landscape

Annuals and biennials serve a variety of needs in many different kinds of gardens. In the mid-19th century, when annuals first came into vogue in England, and later, in America, vast numbers of these new and exotic plants were started from seed or cuttings in large greenhouses and then transplanted to outdoor beds, where their brilliant flowers formed geometric patterns.

These extravagant plantings came to be known as "carpet beds," after the colorfully patterned Orien-

tal carpets that were also the rage at the time. The bedding craze relied heavily on compact, uniform annuals with bright flowers or foliage that could be planted in blocks or lines; beds might be replanted in new patterns several times during the course of a growing season. These plantings were most spectacular in the large public and private gardens that could afford legions of gardeners to maintain them.

Today you can see examples of these grand plantings in public parks and gardens. Few home gardeners have the time or energy to concoct elaborate patterns and grow all the plants needed to execute them, but bedding plants appear in home gardens on a smaller scale, usually as one of several elements in a formal design, or in container gardens.

Short, free-blooming bedding plants are, however, just the beginning of annual choices. Many annuals possess other useful qualities. Those with outstanding flowers and lovely foliage—often with a more "natural" look than the traditional bedding plants—are especially valuable in a perennial or mixed border. Here, where plants are evaluated and included for their height, spread, bloom time, color, texture, and ability to complement and contrast with others, many annuals play a role.

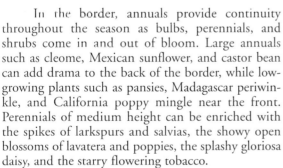

Given enough space, energy, and imagination, you can make a whole border of annuals. At left, a colorful collection of annual zinnias mingles with salvias and Madagascar periwinkle, both perennials grown as annuals. Above, a dooryard garden of vegetables and flowers delights the eye as well as the palate at this New Jersey home.

Annuals in winter

GARDENERS IN THE LOWER CORNERS of the continental United States and the state of Hawaii live in climates very different from one another—subtropical, tropical, mild temperate, desert, and Mediterranean. Yet they share the special gardening privilege of being able to grow annuals outdoors in the winter.

Because so many of the plants we grow as annuals are really tender perennials used as annuals, having winter color can be as casual as just leaving your summer annuals where they are. Madagascar periwinkle, impatiens, and petunias will keep on going in mild-winter areas until they are cut down by frost.

With a good understanding of the local climate, you can take a more planned approach to the winter garden. In areas of the Pacific Coast, Southwest, and Southeast that experience only light to moderate frosts, hardy annuals are planted in the fall for bloom in late winter and spring. Pansies, violas, snapdragons, calendulas, Iceland poppies, and cinerarias can be set out in late August in cool, coastal areas. Planting is better put off in hotter inland locations until October or even November for flowers such as Iceland poppies that really dislike heat.

In California, fall is also the season to sow native wildflowers such as California poppies and lupines. A number of introduced plants, especially those from the Mediterranean basin, naturalize so easily that they behave like wildflowers in the garden. Johnny-jump-up, rocket larkspur, sweet alyssum, borage, and corn poppy are easy to grow, whether from small plants set out in the fall or from seed sown in the fall where the plants are to bloom.

Tender annuals can be grown in winter in the frost-free zones of Hawaii and southern Florida, as well as in small enclaves of the Pacific Coast and desert Southwest that are subject to only very light frosts, mostly in December and January. In southern Florida, petunias, marigolds, and impatiens are popular fall-planted flowers. Petunias, which are summer flowers in coastal southern California, are a winter flower just two hours' drive away in Palm Springs, at the western edge of the Sonoran Desert.

In the border, annuals provide continuity throughout the season as bulbs, perennials, and shrubs come in and out of bloom. Large annuals such as cleome, Mexican sunflower, and castor bean can add drama to the back of the border, while low-growing plants such as pansies, Madagascar periwinkle, and California poppy mingle near the front. Perennials of medium height can be enriched with the spikes of larkspurs and salvias, the showy open blossoms of lavatera and poppies, the splashy gloriosa daisy, and the starry flowering tobacco.

Annuals serve practical purposes, too. They disguise the yellowing foliage of bulbs and hide the unattractive stems and foliage of many taller perennials or the underpinning hoops and stakes. They can be used as quick-growing, dense screens to cover unsightly objects or views. Climbing annuals such as morning glory and sweet pea can dress up a screening wall or fence; grown on a trellis or an arbor, they can provide shade or privacy on a porch or a patio.

Many annuals become permanent fixtures by sowing themselves each year. This faithful bunch (which varies by region) is especially valuable in naturalistic gardens such as cottage gardens or meadows. Few of these annuals make pests of themselves; once

Towering above their perennial neighbors, annual tobacco and cleome contribute rich rose-colored flowers to this misty Northwest border. In the evening, the tobacco sweetens the air with fragrance.

Some annuals, such as these coleus, are grown for their foliage rather than for their flowers.

Other aromatic annuals contribute to the scented garden. Some, such as marigolds, have a pungent aroma that many gardeners associate with high summer. Many annual herbs, such as dill, basil, and sweet marjoram, have aromatic foliage; rubbing a leaf between your fingers releases the fragrance.

Fetching foliage. Annuals grown primarily for their attractive leaves complement flowering plants and add dramatic touches of color and texture over a long season. Dusty-miller's finely cut, silver-gray leaves highlight blossoms of almost every color as well as provide a foil for green leaves of many shapes and sizes. The multicolored leaves of coleus do much the same thing in shady areas, but they have a large color range that invites combination with many other plants. Coleus are also standouts on their own, glowing in shades ranging from chartreuse to beet red and near-black maroon, while many are splattered with contrasting pigments.

Outstanding foliage is provided by tropical perennials grown as annuals, including cannas, caladiums, gingers, and bananas, all valued for their large, bold leaves. Annual grasses, such as fountain grass and squirreltail, with thin, linear foliage and spiky seed heads, add motion and textural interest to a planting.

In pots, boxes, and barrels. Container gardening brings fresh flowers and foliage to the most-used areas outdoors. Hard-working and dependable, annuals lend a lush, romantic feeling to container gardens. They brighten shady patios and gazebos, while a wide array of annuals enlivens a sun-drenched terrace, deck, or rooftop. Pots of annuals are especially welcome near doorways; on steps, landings, and window ledges; or around seating areas. Identical pots of flowering annuals may be lined on railings and balconies for a dramatic statement.

Almost every annual can be successfully grown in a container, provided the plants have adequate light, moisture, and drainage. Planted in exciting combinations or as bold, solitary displays of a single kind, container-grown annuals provide a very long period of beauty for only a few minutes of care every day or so. Many of the foliage annuals are especially recommended for container growing, their leaves lending contrast and balance to the mass of blossoms of petunia, marigold, lobelia, and ageratum. You can choose the classic terra-cotta pot for annuals or opt for containers made of wood, plastic, or metal. From large barrels and tubs to groups of varying, small pots, a number of looks can be achieved.

Whether you grow annuals in pots or in the ground, take care to match the plant to its site. Most annuals thrive in ordinary garden soil with about an inch of water each week. Some, such as California poppy, gazania, and globe amaranth, take to sunny, dry spots. At the other end of the sun and moisture scale the choices are more limited, but they still include a number of annuals such as impatiens, asparagus fern, caladium, and begonias. Many annuals are adaptable and may still thrive out of their favored habitats with some extra care. Coleus and wax begonias, for example, will grow just as well in sun as in shade if they have a steady supply of moisture. Annuals have many uses, and creativity is the key to enjoying them most of the year.

you learn to recognize the leaves of the individual species, unwanted seedlings can be pulled or be transplanted to other areas. Where the seedlings are too crowded, a little thinning will provide room to grow and flower well.

Cutting gardens. Gardeners often make special garden beds for specific purposes. One of the most popular is the cutting garden, where many plants, especially annuals, are grown for a continuous supply of fresh flowers for indoor bouquets as well as for drying. A cutting garden can be a small, out-of-the-way patch; a section of a vegetable or herb garden; or a grand production occupying the whole backyard.

Cutting gardens typically include long-stemmed, easy-care annuals noted for their profusion of bloom. Sunflower, larkspur, zinnia, bells-of-Ireland, China aster, gloriosa daisy, snapdragon, and mealy-cup sage are especially favored by flower arrangers. Everlasting annuals, such as strawflower and statice, are equally valuable.

Fragrant annuals. Besides their attractive flowers, many annuals offer an added bonus: scent. These annuals are especially rewarding when planted near outdoor living areas, such as patios and decks, or close to the house itself, where their fragrances will waft indoors. Among the most richly scented annuals are stock, with a spicy, clove scent, and flowering tobacco, a tall, old-fashioned favorite whose pure, sweet scent is most prominent after dark. Old-fashioned petunias carry a heady, sweet perfume, and sweet alyssum is much treasured for the honeylike scent of its white flowers.

Annuals and biennials, such as the lovely hollyhocks flanking a Santa Fe doorway shown in the photo above, can grow to considerable size and can serve some of the same purposes as shrubs.

Annuals are important players in meadow plantings, photo left. California poppies (yellow flowers) and scorpion weed (Phacelia spp.; blue flowers) light up this desert meadow in Phoenix from late February to mid-May.

Engulfing a rough fence in the photo below, annual sweet peas form a delightful boundary or screen planting.

Annuals for cut flowers

Gladiolus
(*Gladiolus* cultivars)

Cut stalks when the first few flowers have opened. The rest will open in the vase.

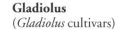

Stock
(*Matthiola incana*)

Flowers are very fragrant. Grows best in cool weather. Plant in fall or early spring.

Strawflower
(*Helichrysum bracteatum*)

Pick flowers just as the buds open. They dry easily and make colorful everlasting arrangements.

Snapdragon
(*Antirrhinum majus*)

Grow tall kinds for cutting. Each plant makes several stalks. Grows best in cool weather.

Cosmos
(*Cosmos bipinnatus*)

Condition fresh-cut flowers in a tall pail of cool water overnight to extend vase life.

Sweet William
(*Dianthus barbatus*)

Flowers have a warm spicy fragrance. Transplant in early fall for bloom the next spring.

Dahlia
(*Dahlia* hybrids)

Remove lower leaves and dip stem ends briefly in very hot water to extend vase life.

Shirley poppy
(*Papaver rhoeas*)

Cut flowers as soon as they open. Sear stem ends briefly with a flame to prolong vase life.

Larkspur
(*Consolida ambigua*)

Good for both fresh and dried arrangements. Grows best in cool weather.

Zinnia
(*Zinnia elegans*)

Grow tall kinds for cutting. Remove lower leaves before placing stems in water.

Sunflower
(*Helianthus annuus*)

Pinch the seedling to make a bushy plant with several small flowers instead of one big one.

Feverfew
(*Chrysanthemum parthenium*)

Flowers and foliage last for weeks in water. Keeps blooming until late fall.

Perennials

From tiny crocuses braving a late winter snow to robust asters blazing away in autumn, there are perennials for every season.

Tulips, daffodils, and other familiar bulbs are among the most well-loved perennials. (The tulip cultivar 'Palestrina' is shown here.)

I n many ways, perennials are ideal garden plants. There are perennials for every season, climate, soil, and site. And there is a perennial for every taste, from the lush sensuality of the swamp mallow's huge crimson blossoms to the dainty chartreuse froth of lady's-mantle flowers, from the bold exclamation point that is a clump of stiff reed grass to the gently drooping native bleeding-heart, encased in a doily of lacy leaves.

Trees and shrubs can test a gardener's patience: they grow slowly and often don't bloom or set fruit for several years. Perennials, on the other hand, are faster growing and easier to plant, move, or remove. They give the impatient gardener a full, lush look in only a year or two. What's more, you can cram a wide assortment of them into a limited space.

Perennials offer much more than quick results and convenience—otherwise we'd just plant annuals and be done with it. A garden of perennials has character, which unfolds with the passage of the seasons. Flowers, foliage, and seed heads all interweave to create a complex canvas of everchanging color, form, and texture, transforming the garden many times over the course of a year.

What is a perennial?

In simplest terms, any plant that lives for more than one growing season is a perennial. Technically, then, woody plants are perennials, but horticulturists and gardeners commonly use the term only for non-woody, or herbaceous, plants. (We include those perennials commonly known as bulbs in this chapter, too.) Herbaceous perennials have adapted to various climatic rigors—extreme cold, heat, or drought—by going dormant for a period of time during the year. In this dormant phase, the majority

die back to the ground, although some retain their foliage but stop all aboveground growth. Eventually, triggered by longer days, warming temperatures, or moisture, the living plant beneath the ground sends up new shoots, and the cycle of growth and dormancy repeats.

While all perennials are expected to live longer than one growing season, some, such as columbines and feverfew, die after a few years. Others, such as the peony, can outlive the gardener. Perennials also vary considerably in their tolerance of growing conditions. Oriental poppies, for example, can be found in gardens in the most far-flung corners of the globe. Other perennials, many of the penstemons for instance, are suited only to a highly specific climate and soil and will sulk and die elsewhere. These demanding plants are nevertheless a great boon to gardeners with difficult conditions—select the right site-specific perennials, and you can have a thriving garden almost anywhere.

Perennials are good plants for beginning a garden—many grow quickly and can be divided in a few years, providing free plants for your expanding garden. Most can be moved easily. Perhaps that red Maltese-cross clashes with the pink mallow; it takes only a minute or two to move it next to the orange geum, while popping a blue cranesbill next to the mallow. You can also pull out a languishing, sickly perennial with few regrets. A small tree may decide after a slow decline of five years or so that your garden isn't the best site for it and die. A perennial may prove equally unsuccessful, but you're usually out only one year and a few dollars at most.

There are a vast and constantly increasing number of perennials available to gardeners. Every year new species are discovered and tamed for garden use, and new forms of old favorites are bred and developed. Even the greediest, most insatiable plant collector will long be satisfied by a diet of perennials.

Perennials in the landscape

Perennials have been valued garden plants for a very long time. Although influences from around the world are found in North American gardens, those from Europe, particularly Great Britain, have dominated. The herb garden, often a formal arrangement of mostly perennial plants grown for medicinal or culinary use, dates from the European monastery or cloister gardens of the Middle Ages. The cottage garden, a casual profusion of floriferous plants stuffed in a small area, evolved later, when the common folk began to have a bit of land of their own. Comfrey for stomach aches, thyme for seasoning meats, and lavender for masking a lack of hygiene joined primroses, violets, and pinks, grown just for their beauty. The humble cottage garden ushered in the era of gardening for pleasure.

Several centuries later, flush with the wealth of the industrial revolution, Victorian Britain produced the herbaceous border. Featuring large, blowsy perennials tightly planted in a formal, linear framework, an herbaceous border is a sumptuous, breathtaking sight. Such beds were arrayed against a clipped hedge or a high wall; typically huge, they were frequently paired, one each side of a central path. Much admired on this side of the Atlantic, expansive herbaceous borders were installed by those with the gener-

This magnificent New England border showcases just some of the rich diversity to be found among perennials, from the simple white daisies of feverfew to the red spires of astilbe, from the low, deeply cut gray foliage of artemisia to the stately swordlike leaves of iris seen at the back of the picture.

Not all perennials are big, sun-loving plants. Many grace woodland and shade gardens. Here, the tiny flowers of rue anemone shelter beneath the large leaves of bloodroot and the smaller, three-lobed leaves of hepatica.

ous supplies of money, time, and space required to plant and maintain them.

Gardeners with smaller pocketbooks, full-time jobs, and more modest, more casual homes quickly began modifying the style and continue to do so today. The island bed is one such development: Smaller and more manageable, an island bed requires no backdrop—you can place one wherever a mass of perennials might be appealing. The plants are accessible from all sides, and the bed can take any shape, whether rectilinear or free-form.

Perhaps the most versatile and enjoyable way to use perennials is to mix them with trees, shrubs, vines, and annuals. These mixed plantings can encompass the entire yard or set off a small corner nook; they can be a formal border, complete with hedge backdrop, or an informal meadow. You might plant perennials among existing shrubs and trees near your house, perhaps flowing the perennials in soft curves out into the lawn. Or you might create a more elaborate garden, perhaps in a woodland, planting shade-loving perennials beneath large trees and an

understory of shrubs—a sea of daffodils under dogwoods and redbud trees; columbines spangling the ground beneath a grove of aspens; waves of the pastel-plumed astilbes under tall oaks and hickories.

Like woodlands, meadows and prairies have inspired an interest in "natural" garden designs. Those that emphasize ornamental grasses and native perennial meadow plants work especially well with rustic homes, modern architecture, and wide-open terrain. These plants have considerable fall and winter interest, giving the perennial garden more year-round appeal. Because of the smaller number of species and the relaxed, naturalistic feel of the plantings, deadheading, staking, edging, and other time-consuming chores of the traditional herbaceous border are reduced.

Even more specific in their relation to natural habitat are rock and desert gardens. In the rock garden, dwarf conifers, fragrant daphnes, and other small woody plants add shape among the rocks, while colorful textured cushions and buns of various low- and slow-growing perennials, many from the moun-

Many perennials offer handsome foliage in a range of colors, shapes, and textures. Flowers come and go, but foliage plantings such as this one of hostas, goatsbeard, lady's-mantle, and various grasses look good throughout the growing season.

Perennials usually take a year or more to reach mature size. Patience is rewarded, however, as these two photos show. Both pictures were taken in October, one of the newly planted bed, the other of the same bed two years later.

tainous regions of the world, are tucked in between. In the desert garden, a backdrop of drought-tolerant shrubs, cacti, and agaves acts as elegant living architecture above a fine-textured jamboree of water-conserving perennials and annuals, ephemeral but brilliant in bloom.

Perennials need not be grown exclusively in beds or borders. A well-placed clump of arching, feathery fountain grass, for example, can provide a focal point in the landscape as effectively as a specimen tree or shrub. Accents of large individual plants or groups of perennials in a landscape dominated by woody plants and lawn can be a welcome touch without increasing maintenance too much or altering the serene, green mood of such a landscape. Many perennials make excellent ground covers, adding texture and color to a landscape while reducing erosion and weeds. These include low-growing carpet-forming plants, such as evergreen vinca and snow-in-summer, and larger perennials, such as daylilies and hostas, which make effective ground covers when planted in sufficient numbers.

Flowers and foliage

Central to the successful use of perennials is the knowledge that most of these plants, unlike many annuals, bloom for weeks rather than months. The challenge of perennial gardening is to select and combine plants that will make your garden attractive in each season. Following early-spring-blooming bulbs, there are a large number of perennials that bloom in late spring and early summer. A mid- to late summer lull precedes autumn's blaze of asters, chrysanthemums, and sedums. Then it is winter. In a garden carpeted by snow, dried seed heads of grasses shimmer in the pale sunlight, while in a warm desert garden, evergreen succulents create colorful texture. Mixed plantings make the task of seasonal interest easier, particularly in winter, when evergreen shrubs and trees and the handsome scaffolding and bark of deciduous species provide interest in a dormant landscape.

Because a perennial may bloom for only a few weeks, you need to pay more attention to its foliage than when planning a garden with annuals. It is the leaves in their varied colors, shapes, and textures that create the backdrop against which the ephemeral flowers come and go. In fact, you can create a stunning perennial garden with only foliage—imagine a woodland garden, softly dappled by sun and shadow, where waves of green, cream, gold, and blue-gray hosta leaves lap up against the fine, feathery texture of various ferns.

Growing perennials

The practical aspects of selecting, planting, and maintaining perennials are discussed in detail in the last section of this book, Growing Healthy Plants, but there are a few points worth reiterating here. All plants require effort on the gardener's part, and perennials are no exception. As with other plants, you'll have the most success when you select perennials that thrive in the conditions found on your property—soil, sun, shade, heat, cold, wind, and moisture.

The temptation to plant new perennials close together is great. The little plant in the 4-inch pot may look as though it desperately needs company, but it won't in a year or so when it's a 4-foot by 4-foot behemoth. If you're discouraged by the meager looks of a new perennial bed, plant some annuals to fill it out. By the second year, most perennial gardens begin to fill in nicely. By the third and fourth years, a perennial garden has hit its stride. The fifth year is often the best—by that time you'll have pulled out ill-chosen plants and moved those that were poorly placed.

Maintaining perennials can be some of the most pleasurable work in a garden—the essence of the word "puttering." After the first year, weeds will be shaded out by large perennials or smothered by mulch; those that remain can be tugged out as you take your daily garden stroll. Staking can be a nuisance; you'll either decide to grow plants that don't need it, or suffer the chore as the price of those gorgeous delphiniums or double peony blossoms. With the exception of digging the bed initially, dividing perennials is probably the most strenuous work you'll encounter. But as that's the only cost of the resulting plants, it's more easily borne.

The pleasures and possibilities perennials offer are as varied as the plants themselves. Ask your site what it offers; ask yourself what you like. Size, color, form, texture—the palette is huge. Whether combined with other types of plants or with each other, there are no limits to the ways perennials can enhance a garden.

There are perennials to suit every climate and condition. The plants in the hillside border shown above—lavender, santolina, euphorbia, and feather reed grass, among others—were chosen to thrive in a hot, dry climate on rainfall alone.

Although they may cost a few dollars to purchase, many perennials repay your initial investment in a few years when you divide them. The dozen daylily divisions shown at left came from a single clump.

Shrubs

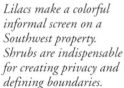

Lilacs make a colorful informal screen on a Southwest property. Shrubs are indispensable for creating privacy and defining boundaries.

Above right, evergreen shrubs, such as the creeping juniper, mugo pine, and dwarf Norway spruce in this planting, add color and form to winter landscapes. The shapes and textures of these shrubs take the hard edge off the angular house and paving.

Shrubs are to the garden what furniture is to the house—and more. They can also be the pictures, the floral arrangements, the carpets or rugs, the windows and interior walls, and even, as they change through the seasons, the entertainment center. Selected to match conditions in your garden, many shrubs will thrive for years without much attention. Shrubs are ideal where water conservation is a concern; their deep roots make them less dependent on frequent irrigation than are herbaceous plants. They are increasingly used as bank and hillside cover for erosion control, or as lawn substitutes.

Just what are these versatile plants? While it's easy enough to say that shrubs are perennial plants with woody stems, further definition can be confusing. Most shrubs are smaller than trees; you seldom walk or sit under them. But some shrubs can be trained into trees, just as some trees can be pruned into shrubs. Most shrubs are freestanding; unlike woody vines, they need no additional support. Again, however, it must be admitted that some shrubs can be cajoled into vining, and that some woody vines can be restrained into behaving like shrubs, or even trees. (Wisteria is a notable example of the latter.)

Further complications are presented by a group of plants called subshrubs, shrubby perennials, or half-hardy shrubs. The woody stems of these plants die back to the ground or to well-hardened wood each winter. Butterfly bush and crape myrtle, for example, freeze to the ground in cold winters but regenerate and bloom on new wood in summer. Fuchsias, which can reach to the eaves in California, often die back to hard wood after a killing frost; where winters are cold, they are grown in pots and stored in cold frames or coddled indoors. Herbs such as rosemary and lemon verbena are woody enough to

qualify as shrubs in mild climates but are often grown as perennials where the occasional severe winter limits their life span.

In the end, it's best to accept a simple existential definition: If it is sold as a shrub and people think of it as a shrub, then it is a shrub.

Evergreen shrubs

Shrubs that retain their foliage year-round are amazing in their variety. For many people, evergreen shrubs are cone-bearing plants with narrow, needlelike or scalelike leaves. But gardeners in mild-winter climates will also be familiar with a selection of broad-leaved evergreen shrubs; fortunately for northerners, a number of these handsome plants have hardy cousins.

Conifers. These evergreens include many true shrubs, varying from prostrate to near tree-size (the junipers range from one end of the spectrum to the other), along with shrubby varieties of true trees (arborvitae, false cypresses, and yews). These are especially useful for creating permanent garden structures with all-year good looks—space dividers, boundary or interior "walls," and edgings. Because they are amenable to shaping or shearing, many conifers make excellent hedges, screens, and borders of formal appearance.

Low-growing varieties of juniper are used by the millions as ground covers, while their somewhat taller, spreading relatives are classic foundation shrubs. Globular arborvitae and spirelike junipers enhance entryways and other architectural features. Dwarf, shrubby forms of cedar, fir, pine, and spruce are attractive in rock gardens. Although we expect conifers to have green foliage, they exhibit a surpris-

ing range of color, from blackish green through brighter shades to golden green, bright yellow, blue-gray, and purplish bronze. Some change color with the seasons, becoming purple or brown in winter.

Broad-leaved evergreens. These shrubs are the special darlings of mild-winter and subtropical areas. Because few tolerate sub-zero temperatures, those that do are especially treasured where winters are severe. (Selection and hybridizing are increasing the supply of hardy broad-leaved evergreens, particularly among euonymus, holly, pyracantha, rhododendron, and viburnum.)

Although some broad-leaved evergreens, notably privet and boxwood, can be trained as hedges or screens, many are grown primarily for their flowers. Gardeners in the South and on the Pacific Coast rejoice in the spectacular flowers of azaleas and camellias. Those in the Northwest and northern California grow an incredible number of rhododendron species and hybrids, while easterners keep adding new, superior varieties of hardy rhododendrons and mountain laurels. Florida and southern California gardeners grow, among scores of lesser-known species, tropical hibiscus and bottlebrush. In southern California and the Southwest, where water is scarce, gardeners are turning to drought-tolerant ceanothus, rock rose, and an increasing number of shrubs from dry-summer countries such as Australia and South Africa.

Many of these flowering shrubs offer equally handsome foliage. The rich green leaves of rhododendrons are an asset long after their showy flowers have faded. The rigidly erect stems and finely divided, almost fernlike foliage of heavenly bamboo are its chief glory. Emerging leaves of photinia and pieris are a brilliant reddish bronze. In cold weather the leaves of heavenly bamboo and Oregon grape turn red or purple, forming a striking contrast with a backdrop of snow or the dark green foliage of other evergreens. Many evergreen shrubs have variegated foliage—stripes, spots, or marbling of yellow or white.

Broad-leaved evergreens also offer pleasing fragrance and showy fruit. The flowers of gardenia are legendary for their scent, and many species of daphne have a delicious fragrance. Pyracantha, holly, and some cotoneasters have showy red to orange fruit that brightens dull fall and winter days, affords branches for holiday arrangements, and may even help sustain the birds in cold weather. Bright orange seeds in pinkish capsules are a bonus of evergreen species of euonymus grown principally for foliage.

Deciduous shrubs

Deciduous shrubs are widely grown in the colder parts of the country and should find a place in warmer climates. They have much to offer: sudden, amazing bursts of bloom; a procession of flowering that begins in late winter and continues through summer and into autumn; seasonal changes in foliage color and the beauty of winter form, bark, and buds; and, in many cases, showy fruit. Most also have the virtue of modest cost.

The spring flower show begins with forsythia, shrubby magnolias (varieties of *Magnolia stellata*), and flowering quince. Mid- to late spring brings the high season, with lilac, mock orange, the deciduous azaleas, beautybush, spirea, and the shrub and species roses. Summer brings butterfly bush, hydrangea, crape myrtle, and rose-of-Sharon, all of which often

Swathed in blossoms, azaleas (shown above) and rhododendrons paint the spring landscape in a wide range of colors. Handsome evergreen or deciduous leaves extend the appeal of many popular flowering shrubs through much of the year.

Shrubs adapted to conditions in your region and on your site are likely to cause few problems and require little maintenance. At right, drought-tolerant native shrubs, including rock rose, California lilac, and agave, fit perfectly in a suburban southern California natural landscape.

Although we usually think of them in a class of their own, roses are shrubs or serve shrublike purposes such as edging (shown above) and screening and, of course, as focal points on their own or in mixed borders.

continue into autumn. During mild spells in winter, witch hazel and wintersweet open delicate flowers.

Many of these have the added gift of fragrance. The scent of lilacs and mock oranges evokes nostalgia, and many of the native American deciduous azaleas have a delicious perfume. Less well known are the spring-blooming fothergilla, with its small brushes of white flowers, and the summer-blooming sweet pepperbush, with white or pink flowering spikes. The deep brownish red, many-petaled flowers of Carolina allspice have a spicy-sweet fragrance. Other shrubs such as spicebush, bayberry, and sagebrush have pleasantly aromatic foliage.

Some shrubs delight us by their form or their leaf shape and color. The smooth and staghorn sumacs (and their cut-leaf varieties) have long, much-divided leaves reminiscent of the tropics. Many of the smaller varieties of Japanese maple have trailing branches and a weeping, mounded shape; some of these have leaves cut to the delicacy of lace, while others display leaves of bronze-red or sport pink and white variegation. Harry Lauder's walking stick has fantastically twisted branches. A single species of shrub may offer a range of color. Japanese barberry has, in addition to basic green, varieties with dark red, yellow, or rosy purple foliage. A number of shrubs have leaves with striking white or yellow edging or marbling; notable are *Hydrangea macrophylla* 'Tricolor' and *Weigela florida* 'Variegata'.

Colorful fall foliage is another glory of deciduous shrubs. No late autumn color is so striking as the hot rose-red foliage of burning bush or of the smooth and staghorn sumacs. The dark green or purple leaves of smokebush turn to shades of yellow, orange, or red. These same shades reach a stage of near-incandescence in the leaves of fothergilla. The shrubby Japanese maples have a variety of autumn colors, from clear yellow to flaming red; in spring, their unfolding leaves bring an added dividend in tender coppery and rosy tones.

Deciduous shrubs display a wide variety of fruits in summer, autumn, and winter. Cotoneasters (evergreen species also) have red, pink, or black fruits. Many species of viburnum produce heavy clusters of rich red fruits; those of *Viburnum trilobum* make a passable sauce. Blueberry has beautiful and eminently edible blue fruits, and bright fall foliage color as well. Beautyberry strings garlands of violet-colored berries along its branches; those of snowberry are white.

In winter, deciduous shrubs enliven the garden

Shrubs vary greatly in size, as these two cotoneasters demonstrate. A small plant by nature, Cotoneaster microphyllus *has been sheared to form edgings for a set of garden steps; its outsized cousin is* C. multiflorus.

Many deciduous shrubs light up the fall landscape with an explosion of color. Tucked behind plumes of fountain grass, euonymus adds a blazing band of red to this colorful curbside scene.

with the tracery of their limbs, colorful bark, and attractive buds. Sumacs present coarse, stark trunks. Kerria displays brilliant green stems; those of various shrubby dogwoods are golden or red. Winter buds of the hazels, winter hazels, shrubby magnolias, and willows and the winter flowers of wintersweet and witch hazel are added delights.

Using shrubs in the landscape

Having seen what shrubs have to offer, how can you best make use of these gifts? Although traditional foundation plantings are less popular today, shrubs still provide the best way to soften the uncompromising line between house and earth. Rather than deploying rigidly pruned, geometric shrubs around the house, you might try shrubs chosen for their natural soft, spreading forms. Spreading yews and junipers look good year-round; evergreen azaleas are the first choice for flower color; spireas, spreading flowering quince, and a host of others thrive under more difficult conditions.

Many shrubs serve well as hedges, screens, or edgings, both trimmed and untrimmed. Hedges delineate garden areas, frame or direct views, and edge walks and drives to control foot traffic. The ideal hedge plant sprouts freely below shearing or pruning cuts and keeps its foliage to the ground. Boxwood, for example, can be pruned to grow indefinitely at a few inches in height or taller than an adult's head.

Screens can block out an undesirable vista, mark a property line, or hide a vegetable garden or work area. They can consist of a single species, such as lilac or pyracantha, or a mixture of shrubs. Like hedges, screens can be formal, as with trimmed yew or arborvitae, or informal, the shrubs allowed to take their natural form. (You can assist nature in maintaining this form at a reasonable size by occasionally cutting out the oldest wood.)

Mixed with perennials in beds and borders, shrubs lend height and substance, separate warring colors, or supplement the color scheme with their own flowers, foliage, or fruits. Many shrubs contribute notably to the cutting garden. Flowering quince and forsythia are often the earliest bouquets of the year, and lilacs are among the most loved of flowers for arrangements. Such cutting, if done properly, also benefits the plants by shaping them and inducing new growth.

Shrubs need not always be considered either as social plants to be massed for utilitarian purposes or as flower factories. They can be objects of beauty in themselves, planted singly or in small groups. On large lawns or meadows, groupings of cotoneasters, barberries, or viburnums can take the place of flower beds, relieving the expanse of grass with a change in elevation, a different green, and a seasonal show of flowers or fruits, all at far less trouble than beds of seasonal flowers. Residential landscapes consisting almost entirely of shrubs and lawn can be highly attractive and functional.

A single large shrub can be the focus of a planting or of the entire landscape. Possibilities abound: the large filigreed leaves of Japanese aralia can create a tropical atmosphere; a substantial dark evergreen such as viburnum imparts a solemn tone; the twisted branches of Harry Lauder's walking stick set a more bizarre scene. With age many shrubs assume a majestic air. A single red buckeye can create a mound 12 feet tall and half again as wide; an old, multistemmed lilac can be a powerful piece of natural sculpture. Many shrubs can be shaped into informal, multistemmed trees or single-stemmed standards, or sculpted into topiary of geometric or more fanciful shapes. Whether you admire them for their attractive flowers or fruit, their handsome foliage or striking forms, whether you plant them for utilitarian or aesthetic purposes, shrubs can provide years of gardening pleasure.

Shrub hedges don't serve just practical purposes. Curving around the fountain in this charming little scene is a low hedge of Japanese barberry, backed by a taller hedge of sheared yew and a magnolia.

Trees

One of life's little pleasures is sitting beneath a shade tree on a sunny summer's day. Trees need not be huge to provide shade; small but carefully placed flowering plums do the job nicely in this backyard garden.

There's a tree shape to suit every purpose or taste. Tall and thin, these Italian cypresses are ideal for a roadside screen, blocking the view without intruding on the road or the property behind.

Combined with other plants, trees are important players in compositions meant to please the eye. A stately weeping willow provides a visual climax of contrasting texture, color, and size in this attractive scene.

North Americans seem to have a deep, ancestral connection to trees. The eastern woodlands and great forests of the West have long sheltered robust communities. But even the loneliest prairie homestead or desert outpost is not without its cottonwood or Siberian elm, its mesquite or palo verde. And it is a poverty-stricken city indeed that cannot offer its citizens shade on sidewalks or in parks. In addition to shoring up our sense of security and well-being, trees perform many practical services, and they beautify our public and private landscapes.

In the previous chapter, we discussed the differences between shrubs and trees. Like shrubs, trees may be evergreen or deciduous, and within these classifications they exhibit many of the same qualities discussed for shrubs. Here, we'll look at some of the uses to which we put trees in our home landscapes: to provide shelter and shade, to create privacy, to screen an unattractive view or enhance a pleasant one. Trees also contribute seasonal flowers or foliage color, edible or ornamental fruit, or a background for the creation of your dream garden.

Protection from wind and sun

Hot, dry summer winds and cold, dry winter winds are hard on people and on garden plants. Trees offer defense against wind not by stopping it but rather by modifying it, breaking the full force into eddies and countercurrents. Reducing the wind's speed reduces the water loss from plants and soil, and it prevents wilting and windburn. Strategically placed in relation to the house, patio, walks, or driveway, trees can also shelter people from the unpleasant effects of wind.

Large properties may require extensive windbreaks, while a few well-placed trees, perhaps with an understory of shrubs, will cut windspeed on a smaller plot. Tough, cold-tolerant trees such as hackberry, green ash, Osage orange, and ponderosa pine serve this purpose in the Midwest and on the high plains. In California miles of evergreen eucalyptus protect citrus groves and vegetable fields from constant wind. Near the seaside, salt-tolerant trees can intercept salt spray and lessen windspeed, making it possible to grow a wider range of plants in the shielded area.

Protection against sun is equally important. A tree on the south or southwest side of a house can mitigate heat buildup inside the house from afternoon sun, resulting in lower air-conditioning bills. Deciduous trees are very accommodating in this capacity; in winter, when the house can use the radiant heat and light, they obligingly lose their leaves and let the sun shine in.

For city gardeners, trees help reduce heat and glare from streets, sidewalks, and buildings, and they provide a welcome relief from the otherwise overwhelming presence of brick, steel, stone, and concrete. Although it's unlikely that trees actually lower noise levels, they give the perception of doing so, which is just about as good. Only the toughest trees—hackberry, hawthorn, ash, gingko, sycamore, linden, and certain oaks—can withstand the dust, soot, and atmospheric pollution of cities.

Service in the landscape

Trees are to gardens as walls are to houses: they impose barriers against the great outside, providing a psychological sense of shelter and security. On large properties, great oaks, elms, ashes, or maples define our horizons, creating a comforting sense of place in wide-open surroundings or blocking out nearby bustle in built-up areas. Trees can also serve to mitigate the confinement of a smaller property by allowing us to imagine that our domain extends behind and beyond their leafy border.

Where fence height is limited by law but the height of neighboring houses is not, you can increase privacy with small to medium-size trees, pruned of side branches to the height of the fence and then permitted to spread. Some trees, such as beech, holly, yew, and hemlock, can even be pruned into formal hedges, making genuine living walls.

Trees serve admirably to edit the view, visually deleting undesirable elements or framing desirable ones. Screens can be broad, covering an entire neighboring house, or narrow enough to obscure only the utility pole that offends your eye. Nothing calls attention to a garden focal point or a distant element of the scenery so well as a frame of trees. A single tree or even a branch situated in the foreground can also lead the eye to a desired feature. (Photographers frequently include a single tree branch in the near foreground of a picture to frame the scene or to suggest distance.)

In addition to acting as walls and windows, trees can provide a number of other architectural effects. Planted in rows, they can produce corridors; a row of narrow trees, widely spaced, becomes a colonnade. And, of course, trees perform especially well as roofs or ceilings, increasing our comfort by shading our sitting or recreational areas. One broadly spreading tree may suffice to shade a terrace or outdoor dining area. If your terrace is large, you may want to shade several areas with a number of small, spreading trees, such as hawthorns, flowering cherries, crab apples, or Japanese persimmons.

Select shade trees with care. Shade is a matter of degree, and dense shade, although it may sound desirable in hot regions, can discourage (or destroy) lawn grass growing beneath it—it's not easy to grow grass under a horse chestnut, a Norway maple, or a southern magnolia, for example. Duration of shade is likewise important. If your summers are short, look for a tree such as honey locust that leafs out late and sheds leaves early, providing shade in summer while letting the sun through on chilly spring and fall days.

Plants, like people, also need shade. Shrubs such as rhododendrons and azaleas as well as quite a few perennials need shelter from strong, constant sunlight. Deep-rooted trees that provide a dappled shade, such as oaks, serve this purpose well.

In the service of beauty

Trees serve numerous purposes in the landscape, but often it's their intrinsic beauty that captures our affection—some trees you plant just because they're so pleasing to the eye. Many offer showy or fragrant flowers; others feature foliage of intriguing form, texture, or color. Many have brilliant or subtly colored fall foliage. Some have attractive or edible fruit, while others make a winter show of handsome bark or striking branch structure. And there's no end to their forms—obelisks, fountains, globes, umbrellas, pyramids, and more.

Some of the attractions of trees reward an up-close look. The frothy flowers and broad, deciduous leaves in the top photo belong to horse chestnut; the evergreen, needlelike leaves and spiky cones in the middle photo to a pine. The striking bark at bottom is that of a river birch.

There are flowering trees to brighten the spring landscape in all regions. Many, such as this dogwood, are small, suitable for properties of any size. (Wisteria, grown as a rambling vine on the roof behind, can also be trained as a small tree.)

Flowering fruit trees burst into bloom in earliest spring, when our senses most need a lift. Enveloped in clouds of white to deep pink, plums, peaches, and cherries are most often rounded trees of small to moderate size. But there are narrow spires, broad umbrellas, and weeping forms as well.

Blooming along with the flowering fruit trees are the Asiatic magnolias. The most familiar is the hybrid *Magnolia × soulangiana,* whose bare branches display huge (6 inches or more in width) cup-shaped flowers, in shades of white to purplish pink. The flowering dogwood is also a herald of spring, spreading its tiers of white or pink before the leaves appear.

Then come the flowering crab apples, heavy with more white to pink flowers. Hawthorns follow, and the flower pageant continues through summer with Japanese pagoda tree, locusts, and golden-rain trees and into fall with *Franklinia alatamaha,* whose white camellia-like flowers stand out against foliage that is beginning to turn scarlet. In late fall, on mild days in winter, and in earliest spring, the branches of witch hazels (which can be grown as trees or as shrubs) froth with wispy yellow, orange, or red fragrant flowers.

Spectacular as they are, flowers are short lived, while foliage lasts at least from midspring to midfall. Many trees have beautiful foliage. The graceful, informally layered branches of the Japanese maples *Acer palmatum* and *A. japonicum* carry lacy leaves in purplish red, golden, or variegated colors. Opening in spring in delicate salmon-pink tones, they exit in a blaze of brilliant scarlet, orange, or yellow in autumn.

The broad leaves of catalpa suggest the tropics, as do the large compound leaves of staghorn sumac. In overwhelmingly green landscapes, trees with colored foliage can provide welcome relief. European beech has purple, golden, and variegated forms, and there are purple-leaved forms of plum, birch, crab apple, and maple.

Many trees come into their full glory in autumn, when their leaves turn to shades of gold, orange, pink, purple, or red. In addition to the familiar maples, oaks, sweet gum, and ginkgo, a host of lesser-known trees, such as *Parrotia persica* and Chinese pistache, are equally striking.

Autumn is also the season of fruits, edible and ornamental. Apple, pear, and plum can be useful and ornamental dooryard trees, if you're willing to undertake the necessary training, pruning, spraying, and harvesting. Where hardy, the Japanese persimmon (especially the cultivar 'Hachiya') provides good form, fall color, and spectacular and delicious orange fruit in exchange for very little maintenance and pest trouble. Crab apples return to center stage in autumn and winter with profuse displays of red or yellow fruit, some of which (the cultivars 'Hopa' and 'Red Jade', for example) make good jelly or preserves.

Winter strips away the summer clothing of deciduous trees and shows their essential form—the broad fans of elm and zelkova, the columns of fastigiate oaks and poplars, the tiered structure of dogwoods, the frozen fountains of weeping willow or birches. The tracery of their branches against the sky, intricate or massively simple, has a somber beauty.

Bark, too, has its interest. The chalk white of birches; the bronzy polish of flowering cherry or Japanese tree lilac; the red or yellow twigs of certain willows; the checkered and flaking bark of sycamores, stewartias, and the lace-bark pine are only a few of the winter attractions that can enliven the landscape.

Winter is not without its greenery. Mild-winter gardeners can choose from a variety of broad-leaved evergreen trees, among them evergreen oaks and magnolias, holly, camphor, citrus, and the hosts of eucalyptus species. Colder areas must rely on conifers. These needled evergreens are generally too large and too uncompromisingly geometrical for small properties, but the slow-growing blue spruce is a splendid ornament to a lawn, and a rugged Japanese black pine, lovingly pruned, can be the making of a garden in the Japanese style. On large grounds the big conifers come into their own. Full-size firs, pines, spruces, hemlocks, and true cedars can be magnificent with the sky as background and an ample lawn as foreground. In the majority of gardens, however, the most useful conifers will be compact or dwarf selections often sold as shrubs.

In many communities the selection of trees to be planted near the street is in the hands of official agencies such as park or engineering departments. In some areas homeowners are given a choice of trees or a list of trees forbidden because of their greedy root systems, brittle branches, offensive fruit or flowers, or susceptibility to locally serious pests and diseases. But once you cross the sidewalk your tree choices broaden. Your possibilities are now limited only by your climate, your lot size, and your imagination.

Certain trees appeal to us because of their evocative forms. Some pines develop a distinctive character as they age. In Japanese-style gardens (top photo) this craggy, layered form is often encouraged and hastened by selective pruning and pinching.

Trees are one of the chief glories of the autumn landscape (middle photo). This multitrunked birch combines attractive fall color with eye-catching bark.

Though fewer and farther between in arid regions, trees add a distinctive character to gardens there. This drought-resistant palo verde blooms in the spring (bottom); its leaves drop early, but the tracery of fine branches provides light shade and a striking profile.

Designing your garden

Of all the many aspects of gardening, few are as misunderstood or as intimidating as design. Experienced gardeners, who may be on intimate terms with hundreds of plants, often feel inadequate when the subject is raised. And beginners, already nervous about all the things they don't know, too frequently throw up their hands in frustration at its mention.

Part of the problem is the common belief that design is an arcane practice, the province of professionals initiated into the discipline's secrets or of amateurs blessed with some innate artistic skill. But ordinary people design things every day. Your

Whether you're combining two plants or dozens, you're doing design. If you're a beginner, start out small and apply the lessons you learn about design—color, form, texture, repetition, symmetry, and so on—as you enlarge your garden.

arrangement of the table setting for a holiday feast is design; the placement of accessories, artifacts, and books on a shelf or of furniture in a room is also design. When you mark the outline of a proposed patio with a garden hose, combine three or four annuals or perennials in a bed, or choose and place a shade tree in the backyard, you are committing landscape design. In each of these activities, you arrange objects into a composition to serve a predetermined purpose. That's design.

There's nothing mysterious about the process. Let's look at a simple example. Suppose your neighbor's bright blue speedboat dominates the view from your kitchen window. Since he has no other place to park it and you can't paint the boat gray, you quietly resolve to screen it from your line of sight with plantings.

Your first thought is to plant half a dozen or so shrubs at regular intervals to create a screen. You might even trim the shrubs to make a shaped hedge. With the help of a few reference books, you identify six suitable plants of differing size and shape: evergreens with varying foliage texture, and several deciduous flowering shrubs. Each of these appealing plants would bring something different to the garden setting and still accomplish the intended purpose.

In a fit of imagination, you choose three different types of shrub. Two are evergreen—one tall and spirelike, one an upright but rounded rapid grower. The third is a rangy deciduous shrub, with flowers in spring and colorful foliage in autumn. Buying several of each kind, you plant them in an irregular arrangement that blocks out the blue blight next door while creating nooks and corners on your property—ideal settings, you quickly realize, for more plants. What you've done, from start to finish, is garden design.

Design often involves making multiple decisions to accomplish a simple end. You could have erected an 8-foot-high plywood fence (zoning permitting), but by making a little more effort, you increased the reward. The plant collage is attractive on its own and adds interest to a previously ordinary corner of the property. A visitor (now unable, of course, to see the boat) would think that the planting was purely decorative. Design is problem solving; good design is imaginative problem solving.

Start small; grow with confidence

Like cooking, sewing, or woodworking, garden design is a skill, and like those other skills, it takes time and practice to become good at it. Attempting too much too soon leads to frustration. Your property will present many exciting possibilities, some small or simple, others large or complicated. Don't feel that you need to tackle them all at once. While it is very helpful to start with firm ideas about all the things you'll need and want from your landscape, you need not come up with design solutions to all of them right away. A garden that evolves along with your knowledge, skills, and interests, one that takes shape over a period of years, is likely to suit you and your family best in the long run—and the process will provide as much pleasure as the results.

So start small. If you're a beginner feeling overwhelmed by a neglected, overgrown property, pick a corner and change it. If you're confronting a barren construction site, pick a sunny spot and make a simple flower bed. Its cheerful flowers will give you courage as you ponder the placement of trees, screens, paths, and patios. If you later determine that you need a path or a shade tree in that spot, it's an easy matter to move the bed. Or you may like it there and decide to expand it. The following year, it may become obvious that the larger bed needs some sort of backdrop—just the job for some favorite evergreen shrubs you've always wanted. And so, as one thing leads to another, your garden will grow.

Along the way, you'll gain valuable hands-on experience with many of the design principles discussed in subsequent chapters—color, contrast, rhythm, symmetry and asymmetry, balance, unity. As you undertake more projects, you'll get better at defining the problems you hope to solve or the desires you wish to realize. A clear and specific purpose is essential to the design process. If all you can say is that you'd like some shade on the house, you may not have given yourself enough information. If you can say that you want light shade on your bedroom window in the morning during summer only and you don't want to obscure the view from that window, you've narrowed the possible solutions considerably and greatly increased your chances of coming up with a successful one.

Good design doesn't happen in a vacuum. Seek inspiration from other gardens, keep a file of design ideas clipped from magazines. Don't hesitate to ask for help if you're stumped. A friend or paid consultant will bring a fresh perspective. The consultant also brings wide experience to bear; an hour or two of

his or her time may be a very wise investment before tackling a major project.

It's worth stressing the importance of imagination. While design as a skill and method is a fairly logical process, logic has its limits. Often you'll get the urge to do something for reasons that may be murky—it "feels right" or "looks right." Trust your instincts and intuition. Knowing how to solve problems using design as a tool is very useful; acting on your "irrational" impulses can be fun and can lead to some inspired gardening.

The big picture

Eventually, many gardeners come to think of large parts of their landscape (sometimes the entire property) as a single composition. You'll realize, perhaps, that adding a planting of mixed evergreen and deciduous shrubs across the lawn from the now-extensive border will visually balance the scene as viewed from the deck. You may have to add a path or a flowering tree, remove or reposition a shrub or a bench, or extend the patio or front porch to knit part of the picture together, and the process may take years.

Some people have an image of a complete, mature landscape in mind from the very beginning of their efforts. Others are able to decide on a basic structure early on, and they fill in the details over the years. Many gardeners clearly see the whole picture only after they've painted it. Whatever your path, if you stay with it your landscape will develop character and personality, perhaps as many-faceted as that of its creator.

The designer of this small patio garden addressed many of the considerations faced by every home gardener, no matter how large or small the property. He allocated available space among a variety of needs and desires—a place to sit or to entertain, a vegetable garden, flower beds. He provided shade and paths, and he selected plants to make pleasing combinations.

Putting it on paper

The simplest method of design is the most direct—moving whatever you're working with around until you arrive at an arrangement that pleases you and satisfies your purposes. Whereas this hands-on approach is easy to do with dried flowers or a selection of container-grown plants for a small garden bed, it's much more difficult when the elements are trees and shrubs, paths and patios. At this scale, working ideas out on paper is easier on your back and on your wallet. On paper you can give your imagination full rein, conjuring up far more possibilities than you could by shifting real, full-size materials around.

As a design tool, drawings range from purposeful doodles to precisely scaled blueprints rendered on a drafting board. Doodles work just fine for much of what we need to figure out in our landscapes. Rough sketches can give you a good idea of relationships between sizes, shapes, and spacings. If you're good with a pencil, you can get an even better notion by doing perspective sketches.

Unfortunately, many of us don't draw very well. While we may be able to sketch the outlines of individual trees, shrubs, and perennials, we can't render the site in which we want to put them realistically enough to be useful to us. If you have this problem, you might try drawing on photographs. Take photos of the area on which you're working (slide or print film will do); a variety of views is often helpful. Then have inexpensive 8x10 black-and-white enlargements made. Cover the prints with a sheet of clear acetate and draw in the features you want. China marker easily wipes off the acetate (or the glossy surface of the photo itself), so you can try out numerous ideas.

A similar technique is to project a color slide onto a sheet of paper taped to a wall and trace the important features onto the paper. You can produce as many worksheets as you'd like with a photocopier.

Site plans

A site plan is a bird's-eye view drawn to scale and indicating the location of some or all of what is on your property. As a design tool, a site plan is useful for working out spatial relationships between certain large elements in the garden. It is generally true that if the shapes of beds, lawns, and paths relate harmoniously on the plan, they are likely to be harmonious in the garden. Within an individual bed or border, a plan view can be a good way to work out color schemes, perhaps making one for each season.

A site plan is also a useful record. It can help you keep track of the location of buried services such as gas lines and water mains, and electrical or irrigation lines you may install. If you note changes as you make them, it can be fun to look at your site plan to see how far you've come.

Unless you have drafting equipment, the easiest way to make a plan is on graph paper; depending on the paper, it's usually most convenient to have one square on the grid equal one square foot. Measuring from the boundaries of the property, draw the house, garage, driveway, and sidewalks. (You might start

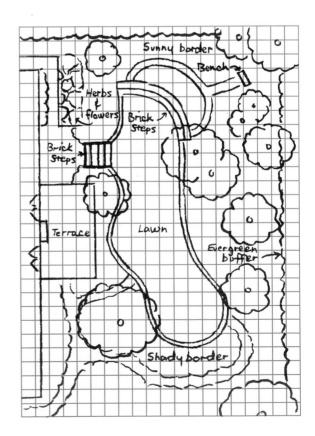

A site plan, a bird's-eye view of your property drawn to scale, is a valuable tool for designing the large, structural features in a landscape—patios, paths, trees and shrubs, lawn, borders and beds. It's easy to see proportion, spacing, and overall composition on this site plan of a small suburban backyard in Atlanta, a view of which is shown above. Smaller details, such as the individual plants in the sunny border, are best worked out at a larger scale—often this is done by trial and error, adding and moving plants over a period of years.

deciduous shade tree

evergreen foundation planting

climbing roses

evergreen screen

brick path

parking area

flowerbed

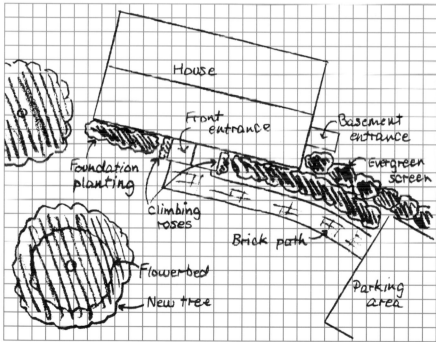

House

Front entrance

Basement entrance

Evergreen screen

Foundation planting

Climbing roses

Brick path

Flowerbed

New tree

Parking area

A site plan can show you the big picture, but it doesn't give you much of an idea of what that picture will look like in reality—as you stand, feet on the ground, in this or that spot. A quick, easy way to get this "people's-eye view" is shown here. Take photos of the area on which you're working and have inexpensive black-and-white enlargements made. Cover the photos with sheets of acetate and sketch your ideas with a china marker. (Acetate and markers are available at art-supply stores.) Marks erase quickly with window cleaner or rubbing alcohol and a tissue.

with the survey of your property done when you purchased it, a scale drawing showing property lines and utility easements; if the drawing is too small, have it enlarged to a usable scale.)

You can locate major features such as trees, walks, big rocks, and garden beds by triangulation. Measure from two points whose location you've already plotted to determine the position of a third, unplotted element. For example, you might locate a tree by measuring to it from two corners of the house. On the plan, set a compass to the first measurement and draw an arc with its center at the first house corner. Reset the compass to the second measurement and draw an arc from the second corner. The intersection of the arcs precisely locates the tree.

Or not...

Although gardeners are frequently encouraged to make site plans, such detailed drawings often turn out to be a waste of time. After doing some rough sketches, it often makes more sense to go outside and lay out your idea full-size than to do more-detailed drawings. Outlining a flower bed or a flagstone patio with a garden hose or powdered limestone, you can examine its actual relationships with its surroundings rather than having to imagine them while hovering (figuratively) above a two-dimensional graph-paper world. If you find yourself struggling with pencil and paper, remember that many beautiful, even complex landscapes have been created by people who never once set anything down on paper.

Establishing structure

Structure can dominate a landscape, as in the photo at top, where the hedges, paths, shrubs, outbuildings, and the house itself are tied firmly together by unwavering geometry. Conversely, in the landscape above, structure is minimal, but no less effective. In a wide-open space, the low stucco fence and stylized gate symbolize enclosure rather more than they provide it, while the table and chairs introduce a simple but strong sense of place.

Creating structure in a home landscape is almost easier to do than it is to explain. When you mark the boundaries of your property with trees and shrubs, plot a meandering path through a woodland garden, or screen the children's play area from the compost pile with a patch of giant sunflowers, you are creating structure. Like the bones of a skeleton, structural elements furnish a framework that brings order and coherence to a portion or the whole of your landscape.

Walls and walkways, hedges and trees, individual shrubs or entire flower beds can provide structure in a large area. The distinctive form of a single plant can do the same for a small group of annuals or perennials. A structural element may be unobtrusive—a simple path alongside a gorgeous perennial border. Or it may be the first thing you notice—a garden pool, flowering tree, or vine-covered arbor.

Structural elements frequently perform several tasks at once. A hedge or fence along the wall of a carport, for example, may screen the carport clutter from view, form a handsome backdrop for a perennial border (while protecting the flowers from errant basketballs), and provide privacy by blocking the view of your patio from an adjoining property. Like most structural elements, the hedge or fence defines two different landscape "spaces" (the carport and driveway/basketball court on one side, the border and patio area on the other), each with its own purpose, character, and mood.

As the example shows, structural elements may combine utilitarian and aesthetic purposes. They organize the landscape for use, delineating areas for parking, play, entertaining, storage, gardening, or work. They also shape what we see and experience, directing our gaze in this way or that, creating a sense of enclosure or privacy, giving an overall sense of unity, or marking a graceful transition from one area or composition to another.

Structure and function

Whether you're starting with a mature landscape or with an undeveloped lot, considerations of structure should begin with function. Above all, you want your landscape to suit your needs. In an earlier chapter ("Planning: What do you want?") we identified some of these: a place to park the car; a welcoming entrance; a play area for children; a place to gather or to entertain; secluded private spots; shade from the summer sun and shelter from winter winds; and, of course, flower beds, borders, and other plantings.

Because of their size, prominence, and permanence, landscape features that satisfy our daily needs—driveways and storage sheds, patios and entryways—unavoidably structure a property. But how they do so is often up to you; even inherited features can be altered in character or style without expensive rebuilding.

To accomplish their purposes, utilitarian fea-

Built structures—fences, stairs, retaining walls, deck, and gateway—not only help organize steep hillsides such as this for use and enjoyment, but they also are often what makes it possible to garden there at all.

A path is an ideal way to divide space in the garden without introducing a barrier to vision or to movement.

This lovely garden uses unaltered the standard structures found in many residential neighborhoods: concrete sidewalk running in a straight line from the street to the front door through a small front yard enclosed by a low fence. The fence and tall shrubs on the perimeter provide privacy without shutting out the neighborhood.

A single element can play a major role in organizing a garden. A birdbath serves as a focal point in a small setting (top), a place for the eye to start, to return to, or to rest as it surveys the diverse planting. On a larger scale (above), a pond lies at the center, both physically and psychologically, of a woodland garden.

tures must fulfill certain requirements. A driveway, for example, has to be a firm, well-drained surface long enough and wide enough to accommodate the car. Beyond these essentials, you have considerable latitude. The drive may rigidly parallel a property line, angle across the property, or curve gracefully in front of the house. The surface may be gravel, concrete, or brick. All these shapes and materials are functional, but each imparts a very different character to the landscape.

Structural elements are most successful when the purpose they serve is clear and unambiguous. For instance, hardscape or plantings intended to direct a visitor to the proper house entrance very often fail to do the job because their message—a series of visual clues that tell a guest where to go—is murky. Given no clear sign as to which of two possible routes leads from the parking area to the main entrance, the visitor usually chooses the closest one, which often as not results in a tour of the laundry room and kitchen. Visual clues should be immediately evident and their message unmistakable. A widened parking pullover adjacent to a paved landing that is flanked by shrubs and is well lit at night resonates with the message, "Approach this way, please."

Structure and the senses

Although structural elements shape the garden in all sorts of practical ways, we lavish attention on them in order to enhance the pleasure they give our senses. A straight path will get you from one end of the yard to the other, but one that meanders through lovely flowers and handsome shrubs will make the journey enjoyable.

Structural elements can alter our perception of space and scale. By framing a distant view, several well-placed trees can make a small property seem larger; by cutting up an expanse of lawn, a tall hedge or screen can make a large space into several smaller ones. Lots, whether large or small, can be divided by paths, plantings, fences, or the placement of furniture into garden "rooms," each with its own mood or theme.

Trees, shrubs, hedges, screens, and various built structures can help create a small world of your own making on a wide-open, featureless suburban lot. Gardeners who prefer open vistas might favor a prairie or meadow planting, where clumps of ornamental grasses, small trees and shrubs, paths, and rustic fences provide focal points or set off areas within the garden. In a woodland setting, you may have to remove, rather than plant, in order to create structure, pruning and thinning selected trees and shrubs to produce the skeleton of your landscape.

A flowering cherry, a sculpture, a distinctive grouping of shrubs, or some other focal point can organize part of the landscape. These elements can provide a start or a finish for the eye's exploration as well as a visual cue that locates an area with a specific purpose, such as an entrance or an area for sitting and chatting. (Focal points are also discussed in "Composing a picture with plants.")

On many lots, geography (or geology) is destiny. The lay of the land—flat, hilly, undulating—will determine where paths run and the placement of planting beds and built structures. Sometimes natural features such as large rock outcroppings or ponds will provide both structure and theme for the landscape. But geography can be mitigated, too. Clustered in a

Like the walls of a house, hedges, arbors, fences, and borders can all serve to divide a garden into "rooms." The arbor at left allows just enough of a glimpse of the room beyond to pique our interest.

A few simple touches create a garden room equally suited to a large gathering or an intimate picnic, photo top right. A perennial border forms the room's far wall, a rectilinear patchwork of grass and bluestone pavers constitutes its floor. The small evergreen tree at right seems to hover like a solicitous waiter.

Tall sheared yews and high backdrop hedges bring order to what could be an overwhelming riot of colors and shapes in the large border at bottom right.

swale, trees or shrubs can "raise" such a low spot, at least so far as the eye is concerned. Planting larger trees in the foreground than on higher ground behind can likewise "lower" an elevation by playing tricks with our sense of perspective.

On most properties, the house is the dominant structure, its architectural style weighing heavily on the possibilities for landscaping. A formal house, symmetrical, perhaps austere, may seem to command its surroundings—balanced masses of trees and shrubs; a broad, meticulously clipped lawn; and, maybe, a large, formal perennial border. A woodland bungalow, on the other hand, may appear to have grown from the forest floor; although the bungalow's landscape may be as carefully structured as the previous example, the hand of the gardener is evident only in subtle ways.

In residential neighborhoods, the house usually divides the landscape into public and private domains, the public being visible from the street, the private more hidden from view. Often these areas serve very different purposes. Most front gardens are intended to present an attractive "face" to passersby and to provide a welcoming entrance for visitors. The private areas frequently accommodate a wide range of family activities. (See "The front garden" for a discussion of how the role of that part of the landscape is changing.)

It's easy to overlook the importance of the lawn, even though it typically occupies far more area than any other landscape feature. (To prove the point, look out your window and imagine that your lawn is bright red, and see how dominant it becomes.) The character of a home landscape can be drastically altered merely by changing the lawn's out-

line. The shape of the lawn can reinforce the crisp rectilinear lines of a house on a rectangular lot, or it can curve and arc within the frame. Like a tablecloth under a table setting, a lawn ties together all other landscape features. So take time to consider its shape and area as you're laying out beds, borders, planting areas, paths, and patios.

Installing structure

As we discussed in the chapter on design, many gardeners develop their landscape slowly; if they have an overall concept, it is often vague and subject to repeated change. While this poses few problems for some projects, it presents a dilemma when dealing with some of the large elements that provide the garden's underlying structure and character.

Trees are the best example. Trees take years to reach maturity. If you wait to plant them until you've determined the overall plan of your landscape—which may also take years—you'll spend too much time in a landscape of skimpy saplings. So screw up your courage and plant the trees as soon as you've identified solid needs—to shade a specific spot, to provide a windbreak, to frame a view of the house from the street, to screen an eyesore, to "lift" a low spot on the property, and so on. Then allow the landscape to evolve around them.

This strategy can also be employed for decks, patios, terraces, driveways, and walkways. But remember that major constructions and plantings are not easily or inexpensively altered. Although it's a good idea to install these elements as soon as possible, if you're unsure about them, advice from a landscape architect or designer can be invaluable.

Composing a picture with plants

Grouping plants together to create an effect that none of them alone could provide is one of gardening's most stimulating challenges. Composing a single striking view or delicate vignette is highly satisfying. Creating an entire garden whose every aspect seems to capture or caress the eye is, for some, the happy work of a lifetime.

For a few gifted individuals, crafting a garden composition is a breeze. Like a television watercolor artist painting before the camera, they make it look easy. Most of us, however, find first efforts difficult; we load our brushes with too much water and too little paint, and the results are murky, at best. But unlike paint on paper, you can always move a plant. A composition requires at least a season, if not several, to prove its worth, but patience and dirt-under-the-fingernails experience will pay off.

It can be helpful to think of garden compositions according to how we view them. Some are meant to be seen from one or more specific spots—from the kitchen window, the patio, or a strategically placed bench, for instance. Others are meant to be viewed on the move, as a sequence of vignettes or shifting relationships that reveal themselves as the viewer strolls along.

There is much overlap between these types, and, indeed, the same broad principles of composition apply to both. Once you are comfortable composing a simple garden picture from a single vantage point, tackling larger compositions, whether with single, multiple, or moving vantage points, won't be so daunting.

Frame and focal point

Garden vignettes share several characteristics with works of fine art. Like a painting, a garden vignette is usually "framed" for the viewer, either by structures in the garden or by plants placed specifically for this purpose. Within the frame, vignettes frequently have a focal point, an element or area that attracts and holds the viewer's eye.

A composition that doesn't "look good" probably lacks one of these two elements. Where the frame is missing or is ill defined, you may have trouble separating the composition from its surroundings or be uncertain where it begins or ends. Lacking a focal point, a composition is without a prime organizing

A garden scene can be framed like a picture, as shown at top. Or the effect can be subtle—in the photo at left, gentle masses of foliage unobtrusively bracket the bench as viewed from the path.

element; the eye has no place to start, finish, or rest as it explores the scene.

Generally speaking, framing directs the eye of the viewer by limiting the scope or size of the composition. For example, the trees flanking Washington's Capitol Mall frame the view of the Capitol in one direction and of the Washington Monument in the other. In your landscape, you might use evergreen trees to frame a view of a distant mountain, large shrubs to frame a gazebo, or several peonies to set off a birdbath or statuary. The arching branch of a small ornamental tree may be all that's needed to frame a favorite view of the perennial border from a bench on your patio.

A focal point may be an architectural object, such as a sculpture or garden pool; it may be a specimen plant or group of plants; or it may be a distant vista. Architecture is almost always more visually compelling than horticulture (flowering and fall color are short lived by comparison). Because sculpture or structure can easily become a focal point, whether intended or not, use it with care.

A focal point may catch the eye by virtue of its position in the composition or its contrast in form, color, or texture with the composition's other elements or background. Frequently, a focal point is centered; some formal compositions, such as knot gardens, reinforce strong central focal points by symmetry, flanking them with identical elements. Off-center focal points can be equally effective; other elements in the composition often help direct the eye to them.

Simple garden compositions

A simplified garden setting serves well to introduce some basic principles of composition. Imagine a relatively small area backed by a tall fence and viewed from the kitchen window, which frames the scene.

Place one plant centered in front of the fence and you have the simplest (and most boring) composition—a single focal point dividing the space symmetrically down the middle. Alternatively, you could place two identical plants an equal distance from the center of the fence. This composition is also symmetrical, but, interestingly, the space between the two plants draws the eye and becomes the focal point. Inserting a third identical plant in the middle makes the focal point tangible, but the composition is still dull. By selecting a middle plant of a different species with an entirely different form than the other two—a tree and two identical low shrubs, for instance—you introduce the element of contrast, strengthening the focal point and making the composition more interesting.

Now start over. Divide the space in front of the fence in half; place the tree in the half on the left and the two shrubs in the half on the right. The composition is no longer symmetrical, but it is balanced. The two shrubs have the same visual presence or weight as the single tree, although the tree, by virtue of its height, remains the focal point. If all of the plants differ—say, a small upright evergreen tree, a chest-high deciduous shrub, and a clump of daylilies—the center of the composition may shift to the space between them, but the arrangement still pleases the eye because of the balance of forms, colors, and textures.

Whereas the symmetrical compositions described earlier rely on the similarity of the plants for success, asymmetrical compositions depend on how well the differing forms, textures, and colors of the plants relate. As the number of these variables increases, the careful selection of the plants becomes more important.

Form, texture, and color

A plant's basic form—upright, spreading, vase-shaped, and so on—is its most constant characteristic. This is obviously true for evergreen plants, but even when dormant and leafless, deciduous plants maintain a "skeletal" representation of their foliated form. Some plants change form as they age. Red maple, for example, develops a somewhat "weeping" habit as it matures; in red cedar, a great shaggy dig-

These two gardens could hardly be more different—one strictly symmetrical, the other strongly asymmetrical— yet both are pleasantly balanced and unified compositions. Note that each uses statuary as a focal point—the urn helps organize the scene at top, while the statue in the bottom photo provides the eye a resting place amidst the relentless duplication of every other element in the garden.

Texture, color, and form play an important role in garden compositions, both small and large. Employing stark contrasts in form, color, and materials, the striking combination of cream-colored Douglas irises and rounded black pebbles at right is one of those little details that make a garden memorable. Gathered around a variegated hosta (below), a variety of leaf shapes make a pleasing composition despite the limited palette of colors. The mounded forms of the cut-leaf maples in the Japanese garden at bottom are suggestive of weather-worn mountains.

nity replaces adolescent fuzziness. Generally speaking, however, a plant's form does not change—if it is upright today, it will be upright 15 years from now.

Certain forms lend themselves to certain uses. Spreading or cascading plants are useful for making a transition between vertical and horizontal elements, from the wall of a two-story house to the lawn, for instance. Upright plants are horticultural exclamation points. Weeping trees are among the most visually powerful plants, almost automatic focal points in a garden—because of this, they should be used sparingly. The conical shape of some evergreens, such as American holly or the larger arborvitae, is almost as commanding. More widespread in nature than the weeping form, conical forms can be employed in the garden with less danger of unintentionally stealing the show.

Texture, determined primarily by leaf size and shape and to a certain extent by branching habit, is the second most constant characteristic. Small leaves give a fine texture; large leaves, a coarse texture. American plane tree and many magnolias are coarse-textured trees; oakleaf hydrangea is an example among shrubs. White birch, honey locust, and spirea are examples of fine-textured trees and shrubs. Compared with most deciduous trees, needle-leaved evergreens are fine textured. But such categories are relative. Planted alongside creeping juniper, Japanese black pine, with its long needles and large cones, appears coarse. Such contrast is the key to composing with textures.

Compared with form and texture, color can be a fleeting attribute. Evergreens, of course, retain their color more or less year-round, though the color can change considerably with the seasons. Deciduous trees and shrubs may offer light greens in the spring, dark greens in the summer, and a rainbow of color in the fall, followed by a winter of gray tracery. With the exception of annuals, flowers usually occupy a brief span on a plant's calendar and are best considered as an accent for a particular season. (See the following chapter for more on color in the garden.)

Distance and movement affect the selection of form, texture, and color in compositions. Generally speaking, the closer you are to the composition and the slower you move by it, the more delicate the textures, the subtler the colors, and the smaller the forms can be and still be effective.

Expanding your horizons

Complex garden compositions are often assemblages of simple groupings. A rock and a tree in a ground-cover bed may be a freestanding garden composition, or they may together form the focal point of a larger composition that also includes groups of shrubs or perennials with a lawn foreground and a woodland backdrop. In addition to frame and focal point, symmetry and balance, you'll encounter other principles as you begin to create more complex compositions; here are some of the most common.

Repetition and rhythm. One of the easiest principles to employ is repetition. Placing clumps of white flowers or sword-shaped foliage, for example, at several carefully considered locations in the garden creates the subtle effect of an echo. You can repeat forms, colors, or textures; single species, single plants, or groups of plants. Repeated elements may be identical, or they may be just similar enough to make the necessary association in the viewer's mind.

Rhythm is patterned repetition; for example, fence panel, post, fence panel, post. Rhythmic patterns in the garden can mark progress or motion, like telephone poles along a highway. Rhythm often is employed along pathways or in long borders.

Sequence and perspective. Typically, sequence involves several similar elements, each of which differs from its predecessor so as to draw the viewer's attention from one to the next. For instance, a sequence of rocks of increasing size might lead the eye to a small waterfall; a sequence of shrubs, from creeping to spreading to upright, might draw a visitor

It may seem odd to talk of composing a naturalistic landscape. But a great deal of planning and selection goes into creating a scene as "natural" as the one above.

Big borders are often enhanced by repetition (recurring colors, forms, or textures) and rhythm (patterned repetition), as shown at left.

to the main entrance of the house. Spaces, as well as plants or objects, by changing in some recognizable manner, can also encourage movement in one direction or another.

Certain sequences can create illusions of distance. Imagine you're standing at the end of a double row of trees flanking a path to a house. If the trees increase in size as they near the house, the house will appear closer to you. If the trees decrease in size, the house will seem farther away.

Unity. This is a composition's most desired, and most elusive, quality. The elements may be harmonious, soothing and pleasing to the senses; or they may be dissonant, purposely jarring to the eye. Whether the effect is calm, clash, or a combination of the two, if the elements combine in a coherent form, a composition has unity.

Saying that a composition has unity is perhaps just a fancy way of saying that it "looks right." If something in the garden doesn't "look right," it probably isn't. The challenge and the fun of making garden compositions is to find out why. Is something too large, the wrong color, in the wrong spot? The only way to solve the problem is to change it, and change it again, until it "looks right" to you.

Color in the picture

A cool, informal combination of purple-blue lavender, light pink geraniums, and striped ornamental grass soothes the eye (above). At the other end of the design spectrum, the regimented bands of hot-colored tulips at right shout for attention.

Of all the visual enticements gardening has to offer, none has the punch, immediacy, or emotional appeal of color. Placed in a grassy field dotted with wildflowers, most of us, like the birds and the bees, pass by the leaves and the delicate grasses, so strongly are we drawn to the colorful blossoms. In a garden, flowers are often the dominant players, but they do not act in a vacuum. Behind them, harmonizing or contrasting, surrounding and supporting, is a backdrop of color—foliage, earth, and sky or the wood, stone, concrete, and steel we use to fashion our homes and shape our landscape.

When visiting other gardens, most of us know right away whether we like or dislike this or that combination of colors. Orchestrating pleasing combinations—being creator rather than audience—is more difficult. This chapter offers some basic observations about the nature and workings of color and some seat-of-the-pants guidelines about combining colors. Remember that the enjoyment of color is highly personal. As with so much about gardening, discovering your own preferences requires experience and experimentation. Don't be afraid to break the rules, or to try something outlandish.

Ways of seeing

Many of our color preferences originate in personal taste. It's difficult, perhaps impossible, to explain why one person loves bright, brassy colors, while another enjoys calmer pastels. Some differences, however, may be physical—people perceive color differently. Where one person identifies only a few shades of a single color, another may discern a whole range of shades differentiated by the finest nuances.

Color varies not only from eye to eye but also

from one region to another, from one season to another, and even during the course of a day. These variations are all a result of differences in the light that illuminates our gardens. When light hits an object, certain wavelengths are reflected back, and the rest are absorbed by the object; we perceive different reflected wavelengths as different colors. Change the light, and you change the color—hence the marked difference between the colors in your garden on a bright sunny day and on a cloudy one.

Traditional English flower borders, with their enticing pastel flowers, have seduced many North American gardeners. The diffuse, soft light common in overcast, humid, northerly England enhances soft colors—muted pink, pale yellow, white, cream, lavender, powder blue, and silver—and emphasizes fine distinctions between hues. Sadly, these colors often lose much of their beauty and grace in the bold light of a sun-kissed American garden. The strong sunlight that dominates most of this continent (including summers in the cloudier regions of the Northwest and Northeast) is ideal for displaying the brilliant colors beloved in our native wildflowers—orange California poppies, purple asters, brassy goldenrods, blue lupines, red paintbrush, shocking pink penstemons. If your garden is situated in light shade, by all means indulge in the ethereal, shimmering effects of pastel flowers. But if you have sun, make the most of it with rich, brilliant colors.

Colors vary by season as the angle of the sun's rays changes. The difference between summer, when the sun is high in the sky, and winter, when it arcs nearer the horizon, is well known to gardeners in the South and Southwest, who can compare foliage and flower colors of the two seasons. Where winters are cold, gardeners may be more likely to notice differ-

You can work out color combinations with crayons and paper or, better yet, experiment by shifting potted plants (below), which provide texture and form as well as color.

ences between spring or fall, when the sun is lower, and high summer.

Changes in light over the course of a day can also affect colors dramatically. Morning light is generally whiter and more neutral, giving it a cooler effect, whereas late afternoon light tends to take on golden hues, mellowing all it touches. Some plants are transformed when backlit by morning or late afternoon sun. Hibiscus, Japanese anemones, poppies, and other plants with translucent petals or leaves are lovely in such situations.

Midday is a photographer's least favorite time of day and for good reason, for the light is at its harshest and least subtle. Drowned in this intense light, flowers can appear flat, without depth or dimension. Surfaces that at other hours add rich color to a garden scene—an emerald lawn, an aquamarine pool, a charcoal slate patio, or a wall of warm apricot adobe—lose much of their impact to reflected light and glare. Deep, bright colors are better able to hold their own than are pale or subtle hues at this time of day.

Painting with the gardener's palette

There are many approaches to using color in the garden. They reflect plant and color preferences as well as aesthetic sensibilities. Some depend on theories or rules; others rely on "what looks good." Regional character plays a part in an increasing number of gardens and, of course, affects the choice and combination of colors. Here is a sampling of possibilities and rules of thumb.

Because of the importance of color to gardeners and to painters, the two sometimes influence each other. Among gardeners, the Impressionist painter

In the casual setting of this woodland garden, the red azaleas, blue forget-me-nots, and green grass path make a striking contrasting combination.

Claude Monet is as admired for the lovely garden he created as for the paintings he made of it. Many have been inspired by Monet, seeking to achieve in their own gardens the same shimmering haze of color, where plants of little individual importance are mixed almost randomly and hundreds of points of color create a scene both scintillating and soothing.

If you prefer a bolder approach, you might concentrate color in uninhibited splashes against a diffuse background. Consider a dry hillside planted with the fine-textured gray foliage and shimmering white flowers of snow-in-summer. Across this, paint a sweeping brush stroke of brilliant orange California poppies. This river of bright color gives the planting drama and focus. For a similar effect on a smaller scale, snake a ribbon of blue salvia through a bed of silver lamb's-ears. A more formal effect with blocks of color might be a rectangular bed of hot pink roses edged in the cooling green of a sheared boxwood hedge.

Color can create or reinforce structure in the landscape. Concentrated in a spot and contrasted with surrounding hues, color becomes a bold accent, a beacon for the eye. By placing color accents at strategic places, you can lead a viewer's eye through a landscape. Likewise, in a traditional herbaceous border, colors are repeated throughout the length of the planting to give it cohesion and to move you along. Often silver and white are used. These colors are universal unifiers, going well with all other colors, separating hues that would do battle next to one another, giving deep shades and pale tints more richness, and lightening the more domineering bright colors.

Beyond blossom. In some carefully orchestrated gardens, the rich hues of foliage are as important as flowers (or more so) in the color composition. Consider a shady garden where blue-leaved hostas mingle with golden-leaved oregano and the green-and-cream foliage of variegated red-twig dogwood. Even in a garden that emphasizes flowers, foliage dominates the scene when blooming is at an ebb.

The colors of nonliving components play such an important role in some garden styles and settings that they must be considered before you go about choosing the color palette of the plants. Take, for example, a rock garden; if the stone is a cool gray granite, you will probably choose a completely different group of colors to work with than if you were

Sunlight differs in quality and intensity across the country. Bright colors suit the strong sunlight and deep blue skies of the Southwest.

The color wheel

WHEN DETERMINING COLOR combinations, many gardeners make do with trial and error, but a simple tool, the color wheel (shown here) can be helpful. Colors directly opposite each other on the wheel—red and green, blue and orange, yellow and purple—are most likely to give the greatest contrast. These pairs are called complementary colors; placed together, the two colors produce a lively, vibrant effect. Contrast diminishes as colors draw nearer on the wheel. Adjacent

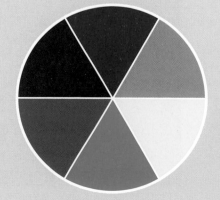

colors, such as yellow and orange, harmonize in combination.

The subtlest color combinations of all go beyond the simple wheel, into the realm of tints (a color mixed with white), tones (mixed with gray), and shades (mixed with black). Using these, a lovely, complex garden picture can be composed using only variations of one color—say, pink or white. Foliage and background colors ensure that such a garden is never truly monochromatic.

When you think of color, think of foliage as well as flowers. The silvery leaves of artemisia and the green ribbons of daylily foliage are as much a part of the composition above as are the bright flowers. And after flowers are long gone, the foliage, stems, and seed heads of many plants are still enlivening the garden, as shown at left.

Gardens restricted to just a few colors—white, silver, and green in this example—require considerable knowledge of plants, but the results can be lovely.

dealing with a warm reddish or peach sandstone. Some soils and gravels of the Southwest have a rich pink, orange, or mauve cast that may provide a desert garden's strongest note of color when nothing is in bloom—a vibrant canvas against which the plants' shades of green, sage, and gray and the blue of the sky are set.

Where the house or other structures feature prominently, they must be integrated into the color scheme. The color of walls, the patio floor, containers, statuary, and even the color of water in a pool or fountain all help determine the colors you choose for the plants.

Colors warm and cool. Most of us associate certain colors with certain emotions. Red, yellow, and orange are said to be warm—they give a sense of vibrancy and intensity, calling to mind the heat of the sun or a burning flame. These colors jump out at you, full of energy and immediacy. When placed at a distance, they make you feel that they're closer than they actually are. Purple, blue, and green—the cool colors—have the opposite effect, a soothing, cooling, gentle mood, tranquil and aloof. The blue of the ocean or the horizon, the green of a woodland, the purple of distant mountains all give a sense of serenity. These colors recede, giving the impression of distance.

Some of the most effective plant combinations join a warm color and a cool color. An edging of fragrant lavender, chartreuse lady's-mantle, or misty blue catmint cools down a bed of smoldering crimson roses. Along the roadsides of Texas, indigo spikes of wild lupine are nature's wonderful foil for scarlet Indian paintbrush. Even a homeowner's nightmare—a deep green lawn dotted with bright yellow dandelions—is a lovely sight if you can put aside your thoughts of weeding for a minute.

Warm and cool are not completely clear-cut, however. Yellow and pink can be either. Take the pale yellow of 'Moonbeam' coreopsis and combine it with soft pink Mexican evening primrose for a cool combination. The bright, cheery golden yellow of 'King Alfred' daffodils and the vivid pink flowers of a redbud tree raise the temperature considerably.

Color, whether warm or cool, flower or foliage, creates a mood in the garden. Strong contrast adds energy and interest and can give a garden a delightful sense of surprise if done in unexpected places and ways. Subtle combinations lend a feeling of harmony and repose. Whether you believe in restraining your palette or in diving headlong into the rainbow, follow your instincts. Don't shy from breaking rules—shocking pink and scarlet verbenas can look stunning tangling together on a fiery embankment, even if the two colors are said to "clash." Remember, changing what you don't like is as easy as moving a plant.

Seasons in the garden

North America's temperate climate affords its gardeners a wonderful opportunity. In the same space, we can have two, three, or even four different gardens—one for each season of the year. Too often, however, we think primarily of spring and summer flowers. With some diligent observation and creativity, you can offer some feature or collage of elements that brings intrigue and interest even in the least likely season.

In an area as large as North America, the timing and the length of the seasons vary considerably depending on where you live. Take the month of April, for example. While azaleas and dogwoods are exploding with blossom in South Carolina, folks in Wisconsin may still be shoveling snow. Winter in New Orleans comes and goes in January; it lasts a good five months in New England and longer up in the Rockies. Spring unfolds for nearly four to six weeks in the mid-South, while it's a fortnight's hiatus in some more northerly spots.

In many respects our most remarkable season is fall, that joyous, frisky farewell to the productive summer, gorgeously flagged by deciduous plants. It's a horticultural display virtually unparalleled elsewhere in the world. At its most spectacular in New England's wooded hills, autumn offers something special in most regions.

Inevitably, you must work with the seasonal character of your area; remember that in certain regions, local climates vary substantially within short distances. Every area has possibilities for seasonal displays; in some, the task is just a little more challenging. Here's a quick tour of the seasons and some tips for capitalizing on their qualities.

Winter: the season of contemplation

In much of North America, this is the bare-bones (bare-limbs, actually) landscape. Shorn of its deciduous foliage, your property will be more open, and its underlying structure (trees, shrubs, fences, garden beds, paths, and so on) will be clearly evident. Evergreen shrubs and trees add welcome color and texture to the landscape in both cold- and warm-winter areas. These structural elements should maintain at least some of the sense of enclosure or shelter that they provide in lusher seasons—unpleasant views should continue to be obscured, and you should feel secure and private in outdoor areas that you use during the winter.

In California and the lower South, winter is camellia time; in coastal southern California and Florida, winter can be nearly as colorful as summer (and more comfortable). Where the climate keeps you indoors more of the time, winter features will need to be visible from a distance and from vantage points inside the house. Introduce plants with unusual form, attractive branch structure, or colorful, textured bark. If the garden will be covered with snow, use plants and structures to create interesting patterns of silhouette and shadow against the snowy backdrop. Take full advantage of natural features, such as rock outcroppings, or create your own constructions of rock or other materials to provide focal points. Where lawn grasses turn brown, increase the contrast between the shapes of lawns and the seasonally barren planting beds. And feed the birds—they're garden color on the wing. Remember that fruiting plants (nuts, berries, seed heads) are attractive to birds as well as to people.

Spring: the season of renewal

There are actually several springs, or can be. One is the flamboyant awakening heralded by quince or forsythia and climaxed by a charge of daffodils, tulips, azaleas, rhododendrons, flowering cherries, crab apples, and other trees. There is also a more subdued spring, when the muted hues of buds and new leaves paint a gentler salute to new beginnings.

Where winter relinquishes its grip slowly, press the season to begin by planting early-blooming shrubs, perennials, or bulbs. Take advantage of different sun exposures of your property to lengthen the blooming season—a plant will bloom sooner on a south- or west-facing site than it will on the north. Planting a variety of spring-blooming plants throughout the garden instead of in one location makes the garden seem larger and certainly more interesting. Using the same plants in different locations will impart a pleasing rhythm to a springtime stroll around your property.

Summer: the season of flowers and foliage

Summer is the blue-collar season for plants, when they do the important work of growing and reproducing. With most of the showy spring and early-summer trees and shrubs clad in workmanlike green, a dynamic swirl of colorful annuals and perennials come into their own. Now is when your experiments with form, foliage, and flower prove themselves.

Concentrate colorful displays in time and place. Try not to have the entire garden blooming at once; pick plants to keep something, somewhere continually in show. Use annuals to bridge sequences and places. Remember that foliage has its attractions, too—not the least of which is providing the eye with restful pauses between more glittering sights. Consider shadow and shade as well for the part they can play in setting the mood of a garden.

Fall: the season of farewell

Although this is the season when the largest plants in the garden are at their showiest, gardeners all too often don't plan for it, they just let it happen. A little planning would go a long way—the majority of fall color is provided by a relatively small number of tree and shrub species. After shape and size, fall color is perhaps the most important consideration in the selection of woody plants.

Silhouetted against a contrasting backdrop, less colorful trees and shrubs can create a calligraphic effect in the garden—a feature that carries on into the winter. Fruit and seeds also add interest in the fall, as do ornamental grasses in lovely shades of gold, straw, and russet. And if that isn't enough for you, it's easy to replace faded annuals with bright, container-grown chrysanthemums.

Selecting plants with an eye to seasonal change can be challenging and rewarding. As these photos show, even a small spot in the garden can be very different, but equally engaging, from season to season. Blazing sumac leaves, the pale leaves of mock orange, and graceful fountain grass make autumn the most colorful season. The garden's skeleton draped with a gentle mantle of snow, winter's scene is etched like a woodcut. In spring, the spot is open to the sky, flecked with color from tulips, spirea, and a ground cover of barren strawberry; a stream gurgles over the rocks. Lush growth closes in on the path in summer; the spindly stems of sumac have filled with leaves, while daylilies and cardinal flowers stand out against the green.

Hedges and screens

A hedge makes an ideal backdrop for colorful flowers. The meticulously sheared hedge above mimics the walls of a room, complete with door at the far end. By creating distinct areas in your landscape, screens and hedges can help expand the number of things you can do there. At right, a high, dense screen of passionflower vines shelters an intimate garden retreat, well protected from activities just feet away.

Hedges and screens are the unsung heroes of the garden. So much of what is pleasing about a garden—its sense of mystery, the comforting feeling of being enclosed in a world of one's own—is the result of their leafy work. Hedges and screens hide unwanted views, ensure privacy, divide the garden into pleasant roomlike spaces, and make backdrops or borders for other plants. They may not pull at our heartstrings the way flowers do, but they enhance the beauty of flowering plants in many ways.

The terms *hedge* and *screen* can be confusing. Both elements are more or less continuous, uniform plantings of shrubs or trees. We usually use *hedge* to refer to such a planting whose growth is controlled by shearing—all branches, twigs, and leaves are cut along a straight or curved plane to produce a tightly geometrical form. When individual branches or twigs are selectively pruned to a more natural appearance, the hedge is called "informal" or "natural."

The term *screen* commonly refers less to the way a planting is maintained than to its purpose—to block unwanted views of objects outside or within the garden, to prevent others from looking in, or to block troublesome winds. A screen may be a formal hedge; it may be informally pruned or, in some circumstances, not pruned at all. Finally, a third descriptive term that's sometimes used is *barrier,* a planting so dense or thorny that it precludes physical intrusion. These terms frequently overlap. A row of tall, closely spaced, and neatly clipped yews along a boundary is at once a hedge (it is sheared), a screen (it obscures a view), and a barrier (it blocks entry).

Hedges and screens at work

Each of the many uses of hedges and screens has its own requirements. The main job of hedges and screens is space definition. On the perimeter they establish boundaries, hide the house next door or the tall building on the horizon, or frame a beautiful vista. Only a visual presence is needed to establish a boundary—the plants may be large or small, evergreen or deciduous; the foliage may be dense or

impenetrable as a lath and plaster wall. Or you may want a more open garden room, bounded by loose deciduous shrubs that allow you to see out into the rest of the garden. It doesn't take much to define a space—a few well-placed shrubs, several paving stones, a table and a couple of chairs will do the trick.

Hedges and screens may not be year-round necessities. If the little setting described above is used only during the summer, clumps of ornamental grass would serve as well as the shrubs. A compost heap that is an eyesore in the summer, when the nearby play area is in constant use, but not in the winter might be screened with a deciduous flowering vine on a lightweight trellis.

Hedges add a formal touch as edging along a walkway or a flower bed, enhancing the natural forms of the plants by strong contrast. A bed of perennials or roses surrounded by a low hedge is like a jewel in its setting. A garden in which beds are edged with hedges has a strong, unified appearance, and when the flowering plants have gone dormant, the framework of hedges remains and becomes a focal point in itself. As edging, hedges can be more informal, perhaps a small shrub such as lavender allowed to assume its natural shape. Hedges are also the traditional backdrop to large perennial borders, a green canvas that is flecked with floral color in ever-changing patterns.

Choosing the right plant

Many trees and shrubs are suitable for hedges and screens. The trick is to get a good match between plants and purpose. There are a great many things to consider, and we'll discuss some important ones here. Because a hedge or screen requires a major commitment of space, time, and money, it makes sense to seek out a knowledgeable consultant, a friend or a professional, if you're the least bit uncertain about the purpose of the planting, its design, or the selection of plants for it.

Shrubs and trees whose growth is to be controlled by regular shearing need good powers of rejuvenation, for it is the growth engendered by repeated shearing that gives a formal hedge its dense, uniform surface. Plants that don't sprout from old wood, such as cypress, are formed into hedges, but they can't be rejuvenated if they get out of hand. (For more on this, see the chapters on pruning in the final section of this book, Growing Healthy Plants.)

Where your purpose is to create a more or less uniform, leafy wall, the branching pattern and type of leaf are important. These plants should retain leafy lower branches down to the ground even when they grow to treelike height. Conifers such as yews, hemlocks, and arborvitae are favorites in cold-winter areas; broad-leaved evergreens, including viburnums, myrtle, and hollies, serve well in milder climates. There are also a number of excellent candidates among deciduous shrubs, including burning bush, flowering quince, and rugosa roses, all of which are grown widely throughout the country.

Plants with small leaves closely spaced along the stem make the best hedges because they look good when sheared. Many conifers and such broad-leaved species as boxwood, myrtle, and abelia are classic hedge plants for this reason. Large leaves are unattractive when cut by shears, their scarred and

Annuals produce edgings for paths or flower beds quickly (top). This low annual hedge contains impatiens, cupflower, browallia, and dusty miller. Above, a low, clipped shrub hedge provides a formal touch to a bed of marigolds.

A whole range of plants can be pressed into service to screen trash cans, compost heaps, and other small eyesores around the property. Here, a clump of hollyhocks hides a rough lean-to that houses garbage cans.

loose; the form may be compact or sprawling.

More often than not, however, boundary plantings also serve additional purposes. In areas buffeted by strong winds, they can be windbreaks, preventing damage to plants (shredded leaves and flower blossoms, even stunted growth) and people. As a bonus, in winter a windbreak can create microclimates at least one climate zone warmer than in unprotected surrounding areas.

Plantings that screen views must be tall enough to intercept the line of sight and dense enough to obscure what is behind. For year-round effectiveness, the plants must be evergreen or must have a sufficiently dense thicket of branches to obstruct the view when they are leafless. Remember that you don't necessarily need giant trees to block the view from your patio of the four-story apartment building next door. The closer the screen is to the patio, the lower it can be and still cut the line of sight.

Requirements for dividing spaces within your landscape are equally varied. You may wish to enclose a private patio with a sheared evergreen hedge as

Where space is tight, a fence, perhaps laced with vines (above left), may be the best solution for a screen or a boundary. At right, an inspired combination of weathered snow fence and bright poppies is as effective as any formal, sheared hedge in marking the boundary of this property—and far more in keeping with the surroundings.

Good hedges make good neighbors

NOTHING SEEMS TO stimulate the planting of hedges as much as an open expanse of lawn stretching across several parcels in a new suburban neighborhood. In no time, long rows of forsythia march up and down property lines previously visible only on the surveyor's map.

A successful boundary planting depends on many factors, but none is more important than good planning and cooperation between neighbors. Both sides of a formal hedge or informal screen boundary require maintenance; timely consultation will prevent your neighbor from feeling that he or she has been saddled with an unwanted and recurring chore.

Choose plants whose ultimate size will do the intended job and no more. In California thousands of Italian cypresses have been planted for screening on the margins of small suburban lots. While their 60-foot spires look great lining the approach to a grand Mediterranean villa, they have proved to be a landscape-maintenance disaster in reduced spaces. Similarly, many conflicts have arisen in coastal areas when one person's tall windbreak has spelled doom for a neighbor's ocean view.

Each region of the country has its tried-and-true favorites for boundary plantings; widely planted, these local favorites can give neighborhoods a visual sense of unity as well as a spectacular show of color when they all bloom together. On the other hand, they can be planted in such numbers that they threaten to become landscape clichés. If your neighborhood is well stocked with the local favorite, ask at your nursery for a few alternatives.

In the West oleanders are a top choice for boundary plantings, prized for their tolerance of heat and drought as much as for their long season of bloom. For a change of pace, consider the native California holly, which also blooms in summer but has the bonus of red berries for the holiday season, or the pineapple guava, which combines drought tolerance and evergreen habit with edible flowers and fruit.

In cold-winter areas where forsythia is abundant on boundaries, a short list of attractive alternatives includes flowering quince, Japanese barberry, and some of the beautiful new hybrid hollies (cultivars of *Ilex × meserveae*).

In the arid Southwest a variety of cactus species have been favored as easy and convincing barrier plants. If your relationship with your neighbors warrants a more friendly interface than a thorny wall of cacti, some colorful alternatives include such heat lovers as mountain mahogany and Texas ranger.

Informal hedges of sumac and spirea impart a casual feel to this brick path. Planted as hedges, many shrubs look much better when pruned to enhance their natural growth forms than when sheared in geometric shapes.

Screens of trees and shrubs are indispensable for creating privacy in residential neighborhoods. These medium-size evergreens block a neighboring house almost completely from view.

torn edges turning brown, but they are a great asset in screen plantings that are informally pruned. (Oleander is a prime example of a shrub that looks poorly when sheared but makes a superb screen when lightly pruned.)

Size, spread, growth rate, and longevity are prime considerations. Size and spread need little explanation; because local conditions affect size, it's prudent to find out how large and fast a plant will grow in your area rather than relying entirely on figures in a book. Growth rate is important but sometimes overemphasized. When there is a pressing need to hide an objectionable view or a strong urge for greater privacy, there is a tendency to opt for the fastest-growing alternative. Fast growers, however, may also spread fast. Golden bamboo forms a quick screen, but when it shoots up in your lawn (or worse, in your neighbor's lawn) many feet from the original planting, you may lose your enthusiasm for it.

Remember, too, that what grows fast sometimes doesn't live long. Purple hopseed bush, a widely adapted, fast-growing shrub, makes a handsome screen, but it may last less than 10 years in the garden. You may want to look for a more long-lived plant even if it has a distinctly more moderate growth rate. Interspersing fast and slow growers is easier said than done. Shaded and subjected to root competition from the faster growers, the slow growers usually fail. A better tactic might be to install a temporary fence that would give a degree of instant privacy while the moderate-growing hedge that you planted next to it comes into its own.

Growth rate is also a consideration if you're planning a formal hedge—keeping a rapid grower looking neat can be a major chore. In the end, the wisest choice for hedges and screens may be the classic long-lived species of slow to moderate growth rate; yews, boxwood, and sweet bay, all in use for centuries, fit this description.

Hedges can provide colorful foliage; screens, whose buds aren't regularly sheared off, can add both foliage and flowers. Try to select plants with leaf colors that will enhance the adjacent plantings either by harmonizing with their colors or by making a carefully planned contrast. A dark green screen planting of osmanthus, for example, is a great background for a purple-leaf plum.

Hedges and screens aren't always uniform plantings. A mixed border of evergreen shrubs, perhaps containing spring- and fall-blooming species, may be a better solution than a uniform planting of Japanese privet. What distinguishes a shrub border from a screen planting is mainly the motivation of the gardener. One person planting with privacy in mind and another choosing shrubs for their flowers could end up with quite similar plantings.

There are times when the screening job you want to accomplish does not require the mass of a shrubby hedge, or perhaps there is simply too little room. Bear in mind that vines and even annuals can be of value for screening. To partially mask the bare side of a garage, a row of hollyhocks or sweet peas trained up wires might be all you need. Something you want completely out of view, such as an unattractive ensemble of trash containers, can be hidden behind a small trellis covered with vines such as Carolina jessamine, gold-flame honeysuckle, or variegated English ivy.

Large annuals make excellent temporary screens; they are ideal for testing to see if you want a permanent screen in a particular spot. Above, cleome separates two areas in a large garden physically and visually.

For year-round privacy, impenetrability, and traditional decorum, it's hard to beat a sheared hedge, such as the barberry one at left. In other circumstances, however, adventurous gardeners are experimenting with different types of hedge, such as the one above of feather reed grass.

Shrubs for hedges and screens

Wax myrtle
(*Myrica cerifera*)

Evergreen foliage is glossy and fragrant. Can be pruned if you choose. Tolerates poor soil and salt spray.

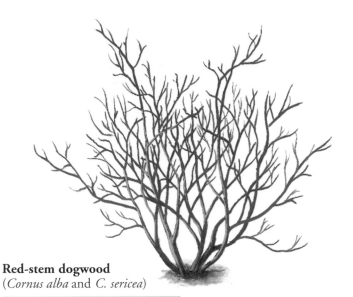

Red-stem dogwood
(*Cornus alba* and *C. sericea*)

Colorful stems make a see-through screen in winter. Foliage is dense and bushy in summer. Prune to the ground every few years.

Red-tip photinia
(*Photinia* × *fraseri*)

A tough and easy evergreen, especially popular for clipped hedges. New shoots are bright red in spring.

Hemlock
(*Tsuga canadensis* and *T. caroliniana*)

A fine-textured conifer with feathery branches and soft needles. Makes a lovely clipped hedge where summers aren't too hot or dry.

Shrub rose
(*Rosa rugosa* and others)

Both old-fashioned and modern types of shrub roses make excellent hedges with lovely flowers and colorful fruits. They require little pruning or other care.

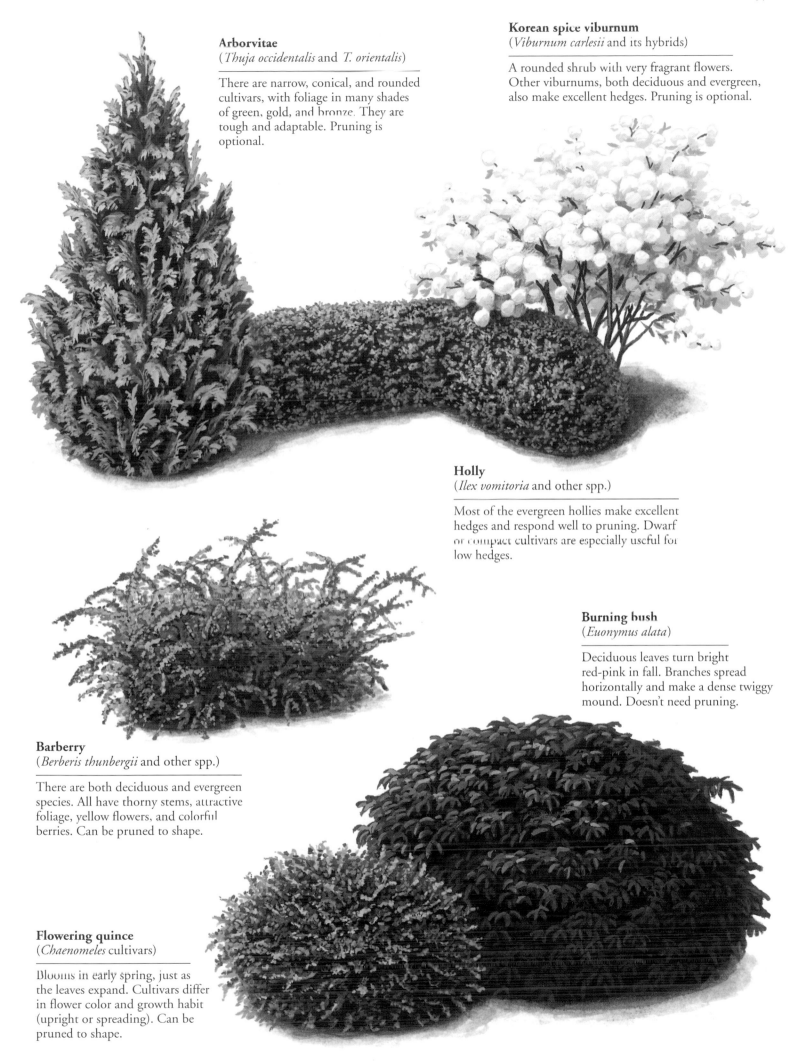

Arborvitae
(*Thuja occidentalis* and *T. orientalis*)

There are narrow, conical, and rounded cultivars, with foliage in many shades of green, gold, and bronze. They are tough and adaptable. Pruning is optional.

Korean spice viburnum
(*Viburnum carlesii* and its hybrids)

A rounded shrub with very fragrant flowers. Other viburnums, both deciduous and evergreen, also make excellent hedges. Pruning is optional.

Holly
(*Ilex vomitoria* and other spp.)

Most of the evergreen hollies make excellent hedges and respond well to pruning. Dwarf or compact cultivars are especially useful for low hedges.

Burning bush
(*Euonymus alata*)

Deciduous leaves turn bright red-pink in fall. Branches spread horizontally and make a dense twiggy mound. Doesn't need pruning.

Barberry
(*Berberis thunbergii* and other spp.)

There are both deciduous and evergreen species. All have thorny stems, attractive foliage, yellow flowers, and colorful berries. Can be pruned to shape.

Flowering quince
(*Chaenomeles* cultivars)

Blooms in early spring, just as the leaves expand. Cultivars differ in flower color and growth habit (upright or spreading). Can be pruned to shape.

Underfoot in the garden

Like a pair of comfortable shoes, a good garden path needn't be showy to be effective. This wide woodland path is ideal for strolling two abreast, and the wood-chip surface fits perfectly with the surroundings.

Whether your aim is to stroll among the flowers in style or to trundle a wheelbarrow efficiently to the compost heap, you need to be able to move around your property comfortably and safely. In addition to getting people from place to place, paths and walkways help organize a landscape, defining and separating its various parts. They also contribute to the landscape's character. Their layout, proportions, and materials should entice as well as serve.

If you're new to your property, it's wise to observe your family's traffic patterns for a time before making decisions about paths. Some paths—from sidewalk or parking area to front door, for example—may already exist. But don't be surprised to see that people choose to cut across the lawn rather than following existing walkways. Adopting and enhancing the most convenient traffic patterns is much easier than trying to train family members to use alternative routes. While you consider your options, you can build temporary paths of gravel, wood chips, or stepping-stones.

Usually paths take the shortest route from one place to another. This may make sense for getting from the back door to the garage, storage shed, or clothesline, but such a path might be out of place in a garden of curving lines and soft contours. A clear understanding of the purposes a path is meant to serve is essential. The walkway to your home's main entrance should be welcoming and easily identifiable to visitors. Formal stairs ascending through a hillside planting may be the focal point of the design, while unobtrusiveness may be the chief virtue for a wood-chip path meandering through a woodland or a meadow.

The practical requirements of paths are straightforward. The surface should be safe, durable, and well drained. Of course, these qualities vary by situation. The uneven surfaces of a stepping-stone path may be charming winding through a rock garden but dangerous as a walkway to the front door. A grassy path may hold up well where traffic is light but wear to bare ground under constant use. If you live in an area of regular rainfall or cold winters, avoid materials that are slippery when wet or that make snow removal difficult.

Consider the amount and type of traffic. Where several people are apt to stroll side by side, proportion your path generously. If the path is a highway for wheelbarrows, tillers, or lawn mowers, make sure that the surface is smooth, the grade and turns as gentle as possible.

Take the time to provide an adequate foundation and drainage for each path. It's no fun to try to raise sunken bricks or flagstones back up to level, or to dodge puddles after every rain. The discussion of materials below provides general guidelines for construction, but requirements vary according to the site and soil, climate, and amount of use. If you're not certain of how to proceed, seek advice from an experienced friend or a landscape professional—a little money spent on consultation can save additional expense and headaches later.

Addressing practical considerations is necessary; determining the layout, look, and feel of your paths is fun. You can choose materials to blend in with and complement the plantings or nearby structures, or you can choose them to contrast with their surroundings. You can manipulate the way in which a viewer will see your garden—changes of direction, material, width, grade, and so on can influence a walker's speed, where her attention is focused, even her mood. The best way to learn how to create these effects, some of which can be very subtle, is to visit as many gardens as you can and note how the paths contribute to the way you experience each one.

Materials for paths

People make paths out of a great many materials. We'll introduce some of the most common here, but remember that there are many varieties of brick, gravel, stone, and so on throughout the country, each with its own qualities.

Ground-cover paths. A cool green swath of grass, creeping thyme, or Irish moss makes a very inviting path for light-traffic areas. Of the three, a grass well adapted to the site will be the most tolerant of wear. A crowned surface (higher in the center than at the edges) and well-prepared soil will help ensure good drainage. Setting flagstones or stepping-stones along the most traveled sections will keep the plants from wearing thin and the soil from becoming compacted with more frequent use. (Plastic reinforcement cells—set at soil level, the grass growing up through them—are available, too.) A strong, permanent edging may be needed to keep the path from gradually inching its way into surrounding plantings.

Needles and chips. Paths made of pine needles or wood chips (or similar local materials, such as cacao hulls and pecan shells) have a soft, rustic appeal and are inexpensive and easy to build. Construction is simple—spread a 4-inch layer of needles or chips on a surface that has been cleared of vegetation and crowned to aid drainage. (Tamping the surface increases durability, and an underlayment of weed-barrier fabric will check unwanted plants.) The path might have a brick, steel, or timber edge, or it may blend into the adjoining mulch or planting beds. Steel edging lasts indefinitely and creates strong lines without drawing attention to itself. Depending on climate and traffic, you may need to add new material every year or two.

Gravel. There are many types of gravel suitable for garden paths; the size, color, and texture can have considerable effect on the "feel" of a garden. A path of white crushed marble, for instance, might brighten a shady garden, but it may create an unpleasant glare in the unrelenting sunshine of a desert setting.

A common method for making a gravel path is to lay down 4 inches of $1/2$-inch to $3/4$-inch

When planning paths, keep in mind the purposes they'll serve. This path provides the only flat workspace in a terraced garden and must be wide enough to accommodate various tasks and tools as well as appreciative garden visitors.

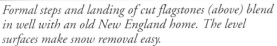

Formal steps and landing of cut flagstones (above) blend in well with an old New England home. The level surfaces make snow removal easy.

Ascending a gradual slope, the path above right combines steps and platforms (long, flat sections requiring several paces to cross). Large timbers frame and hold the gravel surface in place.

Where traffic isn't excessive, grass makes a comfortable path (right). Flagstone edgings and divisions hold the soil in place and give the path more presence. Note also that the stones are placed across the path where the grade changes and wear on grass would be heaviest.

A path of rounded river rock laid in sand suggests a dry streambed, an effect enhanced by varying the height of the stones and allowing them occasionally to cascade off the path—note that there is always a relatively flat surface to follow when walking.

A path can reinforce the character of its surroundings. The geometry of the square-cut flagstones at top, carefully trimmed hedge, and cleanly edged lawn are all of a piece. The rough-cut stones (above) seem equally at home among a profusion of shade-loving plants. The formal path might encourage a brisk passage, from car to entrance, for example, while the other path invites a lingering stroll.

crushed stone on a cleared, crowned, and tamped bed, bordered with a hard edge of steel or wood. Spread a 2-inch layer, rake it level, and compact it by rolling or tamping, then repeat the process with the remaining gravel. Gravel fines (a by-product of screening gravel that is the consistency of coarse sand mixed with small rock chips or slivers) and decomposed granite (a natural material of similar texture) can be laid the same way and make pleasantly smooth surfaces.

Gravel paths may double as drainage channels to help drain a property during heavy rains. In the arid Southwest, dry streambed paths lend a regional flavor to the garden and help capture and channel runoff into planted areas. Such gravel paths have a 4- to 6-inch base of 3/4-inch crushed stone to make a comfortable walking surface that will also withstand a flow of water. Spreading larger gravel at the path edges creates a natural-looking meander. At grade changes, boulders serve as stairsteps and help prevent washouts.

Stone. Few materials are at home in as many different situations as stone is. Pieces of rough slate seem just right hopscotching through a cottage garden; a mortared path of meticulously cut and fitted granite couldn't be more appropriate between a pair of flawless boxwood hedges.

There are many regional variations, from slate or schist, bluestone, and limestone to cut granite and sandstone. All have two more or less parallel flat faces, but they vary in size and thickness. Pieces whose edges are cut straight tend to look more formal and are easier to fit together than pieces broken from the mother rock. Look for good-quality hard stone that resists splintering.

Stones may be set individually in grass or ground cover, laid in gravel or sand, or mortared in place. In each instance a well-prepared, compacted base is essential. Because thicknesses vary and faces are often not truly flat, setting and leveling stones requires time and skill, regardless of whether the base is earth, gravel, or mortar.

A mosaic of russet flagstones adds color to the scene above, set off by an edging of snow-in-summer.

Brick. Like stone, bricks set on sand drain well, are beautiful, and, if constructed properly of high-quality materials, are long lived. Weathered brick salvaged from old buildings is seductively attractive, but it's not as durable as brick, patio pavers, or interlocking blocks made specifically to resist the weather and wear suffered by a path. Brick laid on tamped earth and leveled sand needs some sort of solid edging (steel strips, boards, or mortar) to keep it from unraveling.

Wood. Slippery when wet and relatively quick to rot, wood isn't the best material for most paths, but it does have its place. Sections of wooden decking can serve as a transition between a large deck area and other paths, particularly where there are changes of level. Boardwalks are often the best solution for bridging boggy areas or streambeds (dry or wet). Where the wood will contact soil, use pressure-treated or rot-resistant wood. A rustic path can be made by laying thick transverse sections of logs in a ground cover or on a sand bed. The wood will rot eventually, but the effect is charming while it lasts.

Concrete. For durability and low maintenance, it's hard to beat a concrete path. With an array of surface treatments—broom finished, salt pitted, pattern stamped, and color tinted—concrete is no longer the plain-Jane option it once was. When poured in place, concrete requires precise grading, accurate forms, allowance for expansion, and enough skill to make professional help the best option for most homeowners. Committed do-it-yourselfers might try making simple forms to produce individual concrete pavers that can be laid like flagstones.

A wooden path, while material- and labor-intensive to build, is ideal for raising the path above damp or marshy ground; or where, as in the photo above, it just looks good.

Steps

On properties with any sort of grade change, steps can be a handsome feature; where slopes are steep, they are a necessity. Gradual slopes are ideal for ramps or platform steps, which require several paces or more to cross. Steeper slopes will need stairs, unless you have the space to lay out a path with switchbacks. These can be formal, attention-grabbing stairways or a few deftly placed stones that "just happen" to be in the right spots. Formal or naturalistic, each step should be 5 to 7 inches high, at least 12 inches deep, and as wide as the path.

All the materials discussed above are suitable for ramps or steps. It is particularly important that steps not be slippery, and those frequently used at night will be far safer if they are well lit. As with all paved surfaces, steps should be built on compacted soil and an appropriate base to avoid settling.

Made of materials similar or complementary to those of the house, a path can help give a landscape unity and coherence. This wide, carefully laid brick path complements in color, form, texture, and dignified character the house to which it leads.

Set in gravel, thick transverse sections from a tree trunk make a distinctive path. Cut this way, wood wears extremely well, but it's even more susceptible to rot than usual.

Patios, terraces, and restful nooks

Whether it's a simple plank bench or an elaborate terrace, every garden needs somewhere to entertain friends or to relax in solitude—many gardens provide both.

What is the point of making a beautiful garden if you never take time to relax and enjoy it? Although there is considerable pleasure in digging and planting, even the most hardworking soul needs moments of repose. Some people may prefer a good book and a comfortable bench secluded by shrubs. Others want to relax with family or entertain friends on a large patio or deck overlooking their garden kingdom.

Meeting your needs

Whether large or small, an extension of your home or an integral part of the garden, any outdoor living space must be convenient and comfortable. Let's look at some things you should consider to make it so.

Study the traffic patterns in and around your home. A logical and popular choice for a terrace, deck, or patio is off the most used room, such as the family room, living room, or kitchen. If your retreat is to be more private, consider creating a small patio or balcony off your master bedroom, study, or home office. You may prefer something out in the garden. Away from the daily bustle around the home, a vine-covered gazebo, bower, or pergola offers old-fashioned charm and a quiet rest in a hammock or good conversation with a small group of friends.

When you're locating an outdoor living area, remember to consider the seasons and time of day you're likely to make the most use of it. The warmth of direct sunshine can be welcome on a crisp autumn morning but oppressively hot on an August afternoon. Note the position of the sun throughout the year and during the course of a day. (Here's where a diligently kept garden notebook proves invaluable.) Observe the extent and type of shade (deep, dappled, and so on) cast by the house, neighboring buildings, and trees.

If you wish to use the area during cool seasons, try to find a space that traps the sun during those months. In the summer you might mitigate sunlight and heat with an awning or overhead lattice, then remove it during the winter. Deciduous trees, shrubs, and vines shade an area during hot summers and allow sun to penetrate after the leaves drop.

Evenings are often the best time to entertain—the day's work is done and temperatures have cooled. Outdoor lighting can increase the usefulness and appearance of an outdoor area after dusk. Indirect lighting works best, either shining up—into the trees, for example—or shining down—illuminating steps or changes of level. Carefully placed spotlights shining out onto the garden can provide pleasant views. Please the nose as well as the eyes by growing some night-scented plants, such as nicotiana, close to the patio or deck.

Privacy is important to most outdoor living areas. You can create a green sanctuary blocked off from the rest of the world, or screen off only enough to feel comfortable without obscuring a good view or alienating your neighbors. Urban dwellers often find that a row of evergreens or a carefully placed potted tree will do the trick. Trellises and latticework also work, and the degree of privacy can be increased by training vines over them.

It may be impractical to remove or radically change an existing outdoor area. Renters face this dilemma, as do people with existing concrete slab patios, which are expensive to demolish and may be perfectly serviceable. The challenge is to make them work for you. Options include laying stone or brick on top of the concrete, or building a wooden deck above it. You can extend the area outward with planters, beds, or staged potted plants, or upward with trellises for climbing roses, grapes, or bougainvillea. As in an indoor room, durable, comfortable furniture adds immensely to the livability of an outdoor area.

Plants and patios

The plantings on and around a deck or patio are almost as important as the structure itself. A family-oriented area may open onto a lawn, but that doesn't mean the patio still can't be partially enclosed by a low wall, raised beds, trellised vines, or evergreen hedges so that the parents might have a bit of space to themselves while still being able to keep an eye on the kids.

Plants should be tough and durable, especially for areas where children play. (Remember that thorny plants and small children don't mix.) Pay special attention to the mature size of trees and shrubs so that you won't end up spending hours pruning to keep the steps or view clear. Some people use their patio as a garden center, equipping it with a potting area or bench, tools, supplies, pots, soil, and water. Prized potted plants hang from beams or rest on shelves, railings, and stands. Rooftop gardeners create their whole gardens with cleverly arranged planters and pots.

Integrating patio and home

Architectural and regional influences play an important role in designing an outdoor living area. Take into consideration the style and materials of your home, and extend them into your deck or patio. For example, the simple addition of brick edging to a concrete patio will tie it into a brick home. Pathways and steps from the area may repeat existing materials or introduce new, complementary ones. Be sure to use durable materials. Brick, stone, or concrete patios and terraces, if installed correctly, require little maintenance and last for many years, as do wooden decks and balconies, when properly sealed from the elements.

A formal two-story home may look best with a rectilinear patio, but geometric or free-form shapes may work well with other styles of architecture. Consider a half circle that projects into the garden, or a part that sweeps around your house. Enliven flat properties by changing the level of the patio or deck, adding railings or walls to break up monotony as well as to delineate areas for specific uses—dining, sunbathing, or exercise.

A patio may be closely integrated by design and materials with the house, as shown above. The terrace at top, on the other hand, is skillfully constructed to resemble a natural formation of stone; plants tucked between slabs enhance this effect.

Making the most of a small space

It's hard to imagine a spot less conducive to gardening (or anything else) than this corridor between house and garage. Yet a little imagination, along with some hard work, has created this delightful garden; the statue of Saint Francis at the far end unifies the whole scheme.

Bigger isn't always better, especially in gardening. A small space may present a challenge, but many gardeners turn what might be a liability into an asset. The key is to understand how to make every inch of space work for you.

Some gardeners, particularly in urban areas, live on small lots with limited room for gardening. Condominium or townhouse dwellers may be allowed to plant a small area not included in the communally maintained property. Gardeners with relatively large properties may find small areas within their gardens that require special consideration. These may be narrow side yards or strips between the drive or sidewalk and your house or the street.

Small front gardens may not offer the scope for much active use, but they can provide a decorative welcome to the house. If so, year-round interest and low maintenance may be most important to you. Where there isn't enough space to grow plants in the ground, the front garden (and other small areas) can rely on containers, including pots, tubs, hanging baskets, and window boxes.

Too many small backyard areas serve mainly as storage depots, full of rusting barbecues and stacks of firewood. If you can provide adequate storage elsewhere, a tiny back garden can become a truly functional outdoor room, more private than a similar space in front of the house. A verdant oasis is a lovely place to spend time in activities you might normally do inside. Bring out your reading, knitting, or painting. Cook, dine, and entertain guests surrounded by inviting greenery and fragrant flowers.

Small spaces at the sides of our houses may be the most abused or ignored of all potential garden sites. Inevitably, they become dumping grounds for hoses, tools, and other items lacking a permanent

home. Or they may serve only for hanging laundry or as a dog run. With imagination and organization, you can transform a narrow side yard into a lovely place. If sunny, it might support vegetables and herbs; dappled with light shade, a side yard may become a relaxing retreat.

Designing for a small space

There are no secrets to making effective and attractive use of limited space. The planning and design suggestions outlined elsewhere in this book apply to large and small spaces alike. Regardless of lot size, you need to evaluate your site and conditions and determine your needs and desires. Plants, play, entertaining, storage, privacy—all are concerns for large and small areas alike.

There are, of course, differences that derive from size. Assigning priorities to your needs and wants is essential when space is limited—there just won't be enough room to do everything. On the other hand, less space can mean less maintenance and more time to pursue the outdoor activities you deem most important, whether that's entertaining guests or fussing over a collection of bonsai or roses.

Certain design principles or "tricks" also prove especially useful for small spaces. Rounded or curved lines (a meandering path or a free-form seating area) provide interest in a small space and can give a sense of distance or additional room where very little actually exists. You can "borrow" space by framing views from the garden. A bower of roses or a vine-covered brick archway captures and high-

Instead of the usual strip of lawn between hedge and drive, this gardener has created a lovely spring display. Note how well the small flowering tree fits the space.

Selected carefully for appropriate size and maintained regularly, shrubs and trees have a place in small spaces. The urban garden at left puts on a colorful show in the spring when the azaleas are in bloom.

This diminutive meadow is ideal for a small sunny yard. The brick path curves away from a raised terrace, providing a counterpoint to the informal planting while adding interest and utility.

lights the view beyond as well as providing a handsome feature on its own.

Even where no view exists, you can create the illusion that one beckons just beyond a door, gate, or corner by playing up that feature. In a narrow garden with a meandering path, partitions, screens, or taller plants can obscure the view of what's ahead, furthering the illusion of depth. When the entire garden is not apparent at first glance, it seems larger. A small-space garden, by its nature, is intimate. By accenting that quality, you can achieve a "secret garden" effect.

Changes in level add dimension and delineate areas. Raised beds or a raised deck for seating works especially well in small, enclosed rectangular areas. A sunken area may accommodate a patch of lawn, a reflecting pool, or a sandbox. Changes of level also make more space for planting. Plants tumble out of raised beds or cascade over retaining walls. Low walls or railings hold potted specimens.

Practical matters

Some practical concerns may be easier to address on a small scale than on a large one. Soil improvement, for example: Compacted or worn-out soil can be amended or dug up and replaced in a small area, or you can import rich topsoil to fill raised beds, planters, and containers.

Other practical matters may be more intractable. Unlike large properties, which offer a variety of exposures, a small property will likely provide less choice. A garden that enjoys lots of sun may over-

heat, particularly if there are walls and paving nearby to collect and radiate heat. You may be able to modify conditions by shading the area or planting vines on the walls, but be sure to select plants able to stand the fluctuations in temperature. Shady conditions may be more difficult. You can trim your own trees and, possibly, prevail upon neighbors to trim theirs, but if you're hemmed in by tall buildings, there's not much you can do about shady conditions other than seek out shade-tolerant plants.

Plants for small spaces

In a small space, each individual plant becomes more important, so take care in choosing them. Don't restrict the possibilities—like larger gardens, a small-space garden can contain a mixture of small trees or shrubs, perennials, annuals, and bulbs, and container plants can complement those in the ground.

Each plant should offer several attractions. Flowering plants should have not only pretty blossoms but also interesting foliage of varied shapes and textures. Seek out candidates with a long season of bloom, fall foliage color, or an arresting "skeleton" for the winter. Pay attention to scale. What was a

A row of handsome older houses in this Pennsylvania town are very close to the sidewalk. A profusion of low, colorful annuals and perennials and several small shrubs make this difficult space a delight.

Strict condominium rules allowing the use of only a minuscule space didn't deter this avid gardener from growing and enjoying favorite flowers and vegetables.

A few stones, a little water, and several plants make a charming garden in a tiny space. A vignette like this might stand on its own or be integrated into a larger garden.

medium-size plant in another garden may appear as a towering plant in a small space. Don't rely overmuch on pruning—try to find plants whose natural mature sizes fit your garden.

In a shady area, you may wish to focus on foliage, displaying the bold leaves of hostas and the contrasting delicate fronds of ferns. If the shade is cast by deciduous trees, the garden can include snow-drops, squills, crocuses, daffodils, and other bulbs that bloom before the trees have completely leafed out. It is also a place for woodland perennials, such as ferns, primroses, lilies-of-the-valley, foamflowers, and bleeding-hearts.

You might opt for a subtropical touch to a shaded garden, showcasing the brilliant flowers and leaves of impatiens, coleus, browallia, begonias, and caladiums. For a formal look, consider training ivy and yew into blocks of greenery, clipped specimens, and topiary, perhaps joined by statues and urns.

In a small sunny area, a formal herb garden with brick paths and potted tender bay trees, citrus, and scented geraniums may suit your tastes. Or try a knot garden. Comprising clipped plants in an intricate, geometric pattern, a knot garden is especially appealing viewed from a balcony or deck. Those with less formal taste might prefer a sunny patch of wildflowers or cacti and succulents.

Several types of specialty gardens work well in small spaces. A water garden, built around a fountain or pool, can be home to water plants and fish and complement a backdrop of tropical exotics. The splash and babble of the water is a soothing antidote to noises of the city. Rock gardens are ideal for those with an urge to collect plants but not much space to accommodate them—you can fit many tiny alpine jewels attractively into a small area. Oriental gardens, with their minimalist aesthetic, are good candidates, as are small kitchen gardens with vegetables in raised beds, large containers, and even window boxes.

Small trees, big benefits

Offering spring flowers, summer shade, fall color, interesting form and bark in the winter, and even edible fruit, small trees can pack a big punch in a limited space. In urban areas, a single tree can help establish a welcome link with a natural world that may be otherwise little in evidence. Outstanding small trees include several maples (amur maple, hedge maple, and some forms of Japanese maple), flowering cherries, fringe tree, redbud, a number of hawthorns, crab apples, magnolias, and dogwoods.

Espaliers—plants trained to grow flat against a wall, fence, or trellis—are excellent in a small-space garden. With light pruning and the removal of unwanted growth tips, you can direct a plant to grow into a formal pattern or in a more naturalistic way. Pears, apricots, and apples are frequently espaliered and offer blossoms in spring and fruit later. Hollies, pyracanthas, flowering quince, and saucer magnolia also lend themselves to training.

Space, or the lack of it, need not limit your gardening pleasure. You can choose tailored precision or a rustic, informal effect; grow as many different plants as possible or concentrate on a few favorites; construct a quiet getaway or a neighborhood gathering place. Small spaces pose few limits that can't be overcome by imagination and ingenuity.

Container gardening

WHILE WE OFTEN THINK of a display of potted annuals as a feature for the deck or patio, potted plants can cascade from balconies and window boxes, brighten dark corners, make a cheerful invitation on porches and around entrances, or line steps and walls. Potted gardens offer tremendous flexibility. You can grow a wide variety of plants in a small space, and change displays from season to season or even week to week. Containers also allow you to grow some plants that aren't suitable for your garden's soil or climate.

From hollow tree stumps to old boots, almost any container (provided it has a drainage hole) can be employed for growing plants. The classic is the terra-cotta pot, which affords good drainage and aeration but heats up quickly in the sun. Wood is a better insulator, and wooden window boxes, planters, and half-barrels are widely used. Stone, plastic, ceramic, and concrete containers are also common.

Annuals, with their long bloom time, make excellent container plants. But don't stop there. Perennials, vines, small shrubs, and dwarf trees all find a place in containers. Large-leaved cannas, colorful coleus, delicate ferns, and other plants with distinctive or dramatic foliage enhance container gardens or stand on their own. Trailing plants such as lobelia, vinca, lamiastrum, and ivy hide the edges of containers and cascade from hanging baskets and window boxes. Many catalogs and nurseries offer small-space vegetables that lend themselves to the sunny patio.

Staging containers is an art in itself. The same principles of color combination, rhythm, repetition, contrast, and so on described for larger gardens can be applied to container gardens. No matter how small the site, you need never be without a garden—there's bound to be room for at least one container.

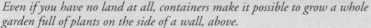

Even if you have no land at all, containers make it possible to grow a whole garden full of plants on the side of a wall, above.

Part of the fun of container gardening is making imaginative use of pots. Above right, a brood of the sempervivum known as hen-and-chickens snuggles up in their terra-cotta namesakes.

The compact tomato 'Patio Prize' cascades over the edge of the potted edible landscape at right. Other plants include parsley, basil, marigold, and Madagascar periwinkle.

Deciduous trees for small spaces

Kousa dogwood
(*Cornus kousa*)

White floral bracts last up to 6 weeks in early summer. Also has showy fruits, bright fall foliage, and colorful flaking bark.

Eastern redbud
(*Cercis canadensis*)

Pink or white flowers are an early sign of spring. Heart-shaped leaves turn gold in fall.

Mountain ash
(*Sorbus aucuparia*)

Clusters of bright-colored fruits are very showy in fall. White flowers open in spring.

Hybrid crab apple
(*Malus* hybrids)

Clouds of blossoms in spring are followed by colorful small fruits that last through fall and winter.

Hybrid witch hazel
(*Hamamelis* × *intermedia*)

Clusters of fragrant flowers open in late winter, while most trees are still dormant.

Weeping cherry
(*Prunus subhirtella* var. *pendula*)

Single flowers open in early spring.
Drooping branches sway
gracefully in the breeze.

Sourwood
(*Oxydendrum arboreum*)

Drooping flower clusters last all
summer. Makes a slender tree with
brilliant fall color.

Paperbark maple
(*Acer griseum*)

Even young trees have decorative
peeling bark. Compound leaves turn
red in late fall.

Crape myrtle
(*Lagerstroemia indica*)

Large flower clusters open from
summer until frost. Smooth trunks
are handsome in winter.

Magnolia
(*Magnolia* × *loebneri*)

White or pink flowers open
late enough to avoid frost injury.
A fast-growing, adaptable tree.

Red buckeye
(*Aesculus pavia*)

Red flowers are showy in early
summer. Compound leaves have
a bold, coarse texture.

Smoke tree
(*Cotinus coggygria*)

Fluffy flower stalks last all
summer. Small rounded
leaves are green or purple.

Making shade

Planted 40 years ago, the mature trees on this suburban midwestern property provide cooling shade and protection from wind, as well as a sense of enclosure for people and a habitat for shade-loving plants.

From Maine to San Diego, rare is the homeowner who doesn't desire some sort of shade. What better way to pass a hot summer's day than sitting in the shade with a glass of lemonade. The lofty canopy of oak or maple, ash or sycamore can cool the temperature 15 degrees beneath it. Aptly placed shade trees can cut energy consumption for air conditioning and filter dust and pollutants from the air we breathe. And, of course, as gardeners, we require shade to grow many favorite plants—prize begonias, sweet-scented lilies-of-the-valley, and diminutive Dutchman's-breeches.

The degree to which we value shade and how we make it depend on where we are. In the forested Northwest, for example, where the climate is cool and cloudy days are abundant, clearing spaces to garden in the sun can be more of a concern. In snowy northern climes, gardeners must choose species whose branches are sturdy enough to bear a hefty snow load but open enough to allow the winter sun to warm the house.

On the plains, shade trees mediate between the vast sky and fragile humanity, providing a sense of enclosure that comforts the spirit while sheltering us from the winds that once swept tall grass prairies. In the deserts of the Southwest, where shade offers relief from unrelenting heat, water-conscious gardeners are replacing fast-growing but thirsty trees planted years ago with clusters of small, drought-tolerant trees.

Building shade

Choosing and growing quality trees and shrubs for shade takes time. Building shade can provide immediate comfort during the process, and it can sometimes be a long-term solution as well. Shade structures are usually lightweight frameworks, freestanding or attached to the house and covered with wood lath, woven shade cloth, canvas, reed, bamboo, or fiberglass panels. They can complement the architecture of the house or the style of the garden or suggest regional character—a latilla ramada in the Southwest, a post-and-beam lean-to in Montana, or a Victorian gazebo in New Orleans.

A shade structure is an ideal support for vines, which, with their leafy canopy, provide an extra measure of cooling. Trumpet vine or coral honeysuckle will also lure hummingbirds; roses and wisteria perfume the air; and grapes provide an edible harvest. What could be more efficient than having your shade and eating it too? Vines such as wisteria may take a few years to yield much shade, but they will endure for decades. Fast-growing vines such as silver-lace vine are often short lived, but they're useful while you're figuring out which trees are best suited to your needs and local conditions and while you're waiting for slower-growing shade plants to mature.

Shade trees

Aside from the obvious prerequisite that it be leafy in summer, a shade tree (or a shrub or vine, for that matter) should be well adapted to conditions on its site and pest-resistant. Be sure it won't outgrow its intended space or invade its surroundings with a greedy, competitive root system. A pleasing form and seasonal interest are nice, too.

The density of shade is important for trees that will shelter shade-loving plants. You may need to provide a range of filtered light, from dappled to dark, to grow the lilies and columbines, camellias and scillas, trilliums and hellebores you desire. The tree's root system, deep and noninvasive or shallow and highly competitive for water and nutrients, will greatly affect what will grow well beneath it. Learning the assets and liabilities of the trees you're considering is especially important because the drawbacks usually don't become apparent until you have time and care invested in them. It's difficult to cut down a tree after you've nurtured it for a few years, even when its greedy and messy personality begins to starve and smother the plants it's supposed to be sheltering.

Besides an aggressive root system, some trees, by virtue of their size or their flower or seed production, can be garden thugs. Sycamores not only shed prodigious amounts of leaves, they drop seed clusters and slough off bark as well. Some crab-apple varieties are gorgeous in flower, filter the sun wonderfully all summer, provide a foliage color show in autumn, and then rain a dubious bounty of golf-ball-sized fruit all winter. Any tree that flowers prolifically will produce some litter, though it's harder to think of a pink mulch of cherry blossoms as messy than it is to grumble when pelted with horse chestnuts.

Plants vary in their compatibility with each other. Although aggressive competition for shared resources is common, some trees and shrubs, notably black walnut, salt cedar, tree-of-heaven, and creosote bush, may go so far as to alter the chemistry of the soil they grow in to suppress the growth of other plants nearby.

Shade placement

A number of considerations affect the placement of shade trees. Where the sun tracks relatively low in the sky, trees throw shadows well beyond their drip line. The farther south you live, the more directly overhead the sun is throughout the summer, and the less effective a tree is at shading a garden or roof that isn't directly beneath its branches. By shading the east side of the house early in the day and reducing the heat reflected off the soil and walls, you can mitigate the heat buildup in a house exposed to midday overhead sun.

Most large shade trees, including ash, elm, oak, sycamore, linden, and poplar, should be sited 20 feet from the foundations of walls and hard paving. Smaller trees, especially deeply rooted ones such as redbud and desert willow, may be planted as close as 8 feet. Small gardens require careful planting, since one large tree can easily overwhelm a space. Small, deeply rooted trees are particularly practical in these niches, especially those that provide seasonal flower color as well as shade.

For quick shade, you can cover a patio with a lath roof, a popular garden structure in southern California, where the photo at top was taken. In a Texas garden (above), a rustic pergola supporting climbing roses makes a cool, fragrant, and lovely oasis.

Two smallish maples and a vine-covered bower make this small patio garden in Connecticut a cozy, shady spot. Picking similar trees with different-colored leaves is a nice touch.

Gardening in the shade

Shade plants are often less eye-catching than their sun-loving cousins, but their subdued flowers and foliage are no less beautiful. Mottled foliage and pale yellow flowers of trilliums and spotted leaves and pale lavender flowers of pulmonaria repay close inspection.

Many popular garden plants—roses, lilacs, irises, peonies, and most annuals—are sun lovers, so it isn't surprising when a novice gardener's heart sinks at the prospect of a shady site. But what appears to be a bane may be a blessing. In most regions of North America there are several months of the year when spending time out-of-doors in full sunshine is not only unhealthy but downright uncomfortable. A shade garden offers an oasis, an intimate, restful outdoor living space. You can meander down an inviting path through a woodland garden softly dappled by light and shade, sip a cool drink on a north-facing patio or porch surrounded by lushly planted beds, or sink with a good book in hand onto a comfortable bench under a large tree. The pleasures derived from shade gardens are both physical and spiritual.

Shade also allows you to broaden the variety of interesting and handsome plants you can grow. Throughout the world, wooded regions—be they the deciduous forests of eastern North America; the conifer-dominated woods of the Rocky Mountains, Sierra Nevada, Cascades, and Alps; or the tropical jungles of Asia and Central and South America— play host to innumerable garden-worthy plants adapted to less than a full day's sun. Enough of these plants are available at garden centers or from specialty nurseries to keep the most devoted plant lover happy for years.

The nature of shade

Shade is a lot more variable and complex than you might suspect. Consider just a few of the terms used to describe it: filtered, dappled, heavy, light, thin, full, high, half, open, medium, intermittent, dense, constant, deep, and partial. What really matters is that shade varies with the object causing it, the time of day, and the time of year. Each of these factors greatly affects what will grow and how well.

Most shade-loving plants prefer a high canopy of deciduous trees or strong, indirect reflected light. The light is friendly and soft, the shade cool but not dark and somber. Both plants and people take well to these situations. Full morning sun and afternoon shade suits many. A few will thrive in constant shade, as long as it is not truly deep and dark. Areas where sun never reaches and even reflected light is dim, as under dense evergreens, in a narrow alley between walls or fences, or close to the north side of a tall structure, are best left to the mosses or mulch.

Two other "shady" situations won't generally support shade plants. The first is where the mornings are shady and afternoons sunny, as on the west side of a structure. Because the afternoon sun is so much hotter and more intense, only sun-loving plants can take the shock of the transition. The same effect occurs in the second situation, where an area is in full sun during the heat of summer when the sun is at its highest arc in the sky, and in shade during the cooler months.

Woodland gardens

You may be fortunate enough to have one of the most versatile types of shade already in place on your property—a deciduous woodland. Most shade plants love such a site. The majority of North American woodland natives bloom in the spring, when the

One of the pleasures of shade gardens is watching the dramatic changes that take place in just a few weeks in the spring. Before the trees leaf out (left), primroses sparkle against the mulch. Just a few weeks later (above), ferns dominate the scene.

Warmed by sunlight only partially filtered by young leaves overhead, spring is the season of bloom in the shade garden. The path shown above is flanked by low-growing, white-flowered sweet woodruff.

canopy of tree foliage is still thin enough to let in some soft spring sunlight, so the main challenge of this type of garden consists of finding shade-loving plants that provide interest in other seasons. By combining some later-blooming plants with plants that have attractive leaves, you can create a gentle, pleasing harmony through the rest of the year.

Let the many natural models found across the continent inspire you. You might want to leave the woodland as is, not planting anything at all, just cleaning up from time to time. Or you may take a more active role, removing crowded trees, judiciously pruning low-hanging limbs, thinning underbrush, and removing "weedy" species. Paths of chopped leaves or bark mulch impart a "natural" feel; stone, brick, wood, or gravel might suit a more formal approach. You may want to add some small understory trees or shrubs for flower, fruit, or fall foliage effects. Perennials and bulbs—native, exotic, or both—add diversity to the woody framework.

Maintenance of a woodland garden is straightforward. Remove dead wood regularly, and if leaf fall is heavy, rake off the heaviest layers, shred them, and return them as fine mulch. Otherwise they may smother the more delicate plants and hinder the germination of self-sown seedlings that can add so much to the display.

Under a shade tree

The most common type of shade on residential lots is created by one or a few large trees. Trees with dense canopies, such as Norway maple or horse chestnut, let little light or rain penetrate, limiting the choice of plants that will grow in their shade. High-crowned trees such as elm or small-leaved trees such as honey locust let in more light and broaden the spectrum of understory plant possibilities.

There is more to a tree than meets the eye. As much is at stake for the future of the shade garden below ground as above. Some trees have mercifully deep or diffuse root systems, leaving plenty of soil, food, and water for plants growing in their shadows. Others dominate the root zone, where only the very toughest plants can compete. As mentioned in the previous chapter ("Making shade"), black walnut and a few other trees actually do chemical warfare with other plants, emitting poisons from their roots. Some plants are less susceptible to these substances than are others, but your best bet may be to build a patio or just spread mulch under these trees, adding a few well-placed, richly planted large containers for interest.

Even the most benevolent trees rob the soil beneath them of moisture and nutrients over time, and it will greatly help any new planting to add some organic matter. Don't go overboard and smother the tree roots with a foot or more of compost, or bring in

Rhododendrons are excellent large understory plants for a woodland garden. They reward the protection from wind, frost, and excessive sun that can damage their flowers and leaves with a breathtaking display of blossom.

Shade gardens can be dense and tropical, like the one shown at right, where large understory plants fill in the space beneath the canopy. In the garden shown above, on the other hand, substantial trunks rise branchless for many feet, creating a high umbrella-like canopy above a relatively open area; phlox blooms in the foreground.

the tiller, damaging most of the trees' feeder roots. A few inches of rich organic mulch or compost applied annually will go a long way toward establishing and maintaining a healthy tree-shaded garden.

In the shadow of a wall

When shade is provided by a solid structure such as a wall, fence, or building, the exposure defines the shade. Western exposures, as previously mentioned, should be treated as sunny sites even if the first half of the day is shaded. East-facing gardens of this sort are much more hospitable to shade-loving plants; in hotter regions, they are ideal for growing sun-loving plants from cooler areas that are not adapted to the local heat or intensity of light. A garden on the north side of a building may receive no direct sunlight but may still be bright enough to support plants if it is open to the sky or if the structures nearby reflect light onto the planting. The partial or dappled shade cast by a picket fence or a thin hedge, for example, will usually support a wider variety of plants than will solid shade.

Shade-loving plants

For all but the very darkest shaded situation, you'll find a good selection of desirable plants. Most shade plants share a few general characteristics. Some, such as hostas and ligularias, have large, pliable leaves. Others, including many ferns and meadow rue, possess very thin, fragile foliage. Shade lovers tend toward lushness—loose and leafy rather than tight, dense mounds. Few have spines, prickles, or hairy, silver or gray leaves. Because sunlight easily burns pale areas on a leaf, gold- or variegated-leaved plants usually require some shade, even if their green-leaved cousins prefer full sun, as do the relatives of golden oregano and variegated garden phlox.

Colors change dramatically in the shade. The paler colors—whites, yellows, and pastels—which are a blurry, indistinguishable haze in bright sunshine, come into their own in softer light, where they seem more vivid, even glowing. On the other hand, deeper colors—dark reds, purples, and blues—fade into obscurity as the light diminishes.

Most plants bloom less profusely in the shade, so foliage becomes all the more important. Leaves are as varied as blossoms, with shape, size, color, and surface texture all coming into play. You can contrast fine, ferny leaves with large, sumptuous, tropical-looking ones, or experiment with variegation and unusual foliage colors. Variegated leaves make lovely patterns of light and dark that show to great effect in the shade. And don't forget to consider fall color and, for winter, interesting bark or branching patterns.

Like their sun-loving counterparts, shade plants

have preferences for specific soil and moisture conditions. Humidity, temperature, wind, and angles of the sun all affect shade, so a plant that prefers morning sun and afternoon shade in the Northeast may want a more complete shade in the South or in the drier parts of the West. Dry shade supports a far smaller number of plants than does the exact same type of shade given more moisture.

When choosing plants for a shaded garden, research their origins. All plants, sun lovers and shade lovers alike, prefer conditions in cultivation similar to those they experienced in the wild. Many plants are quite adaptable to new conditions, so don't be afraid

to experiment—and to fail. One reason shaded lawn grass is so often half-dead is that lawn grasses, in general, need sunshine; beneath a tree they are the wrong plant in the wrong place.

Shade-garden maintenance differs in many ways from its sunny counterpart. If the soil has a good supply of organic matter (perhaps augmented by a water-holding mulch), heat stress and watering will be much less of a problem. When dense foliage or a structure shelters the site from rainfall, you'll have to water, as you will in dry climates. Drip irrigation or soaker hoses work best in a shade garden. Overhead sprinklers can flatten the lax, floppy foliage of many shade plants, and the wet foliage contributes to the spread of fungal diseases. As further protection against fungal diseases, space plants to provide good air circulation.

The play of light and shadow, flower and foliage in a shade garden works a soothing magic. Whether it's an extensive woodland or a small strip in the shadowy lee of your home, the calm, cool oasis that is the essence of a shade garden will be a welcome addition to your landscape.

At top, in the shade of this wall, hostas thrive where sun-loving plants would struggle. Though the flowers last only briefly, the handsome foliage remains for months. Above, hemmed in by two high walls and shaded by trees at each end, this charming courtyard garden nevertheless offers a lush and colorful display. Potted annuals bloom on the side that receives more sun, while shade-tolerant shrubs line the other side.

Plants that grow in shade

Cardinal flower
(*Lobelia cardinalis*)

Red flowers last for weeks in late summer. New hybrids have blue and purple flowers. Prefers moist soil.

Bleeding-heart
(*Dicentra* spp.)

Sprays of dangling pink or white flowers spread like a fountain over a lush mound of delicate foliage.

Caladium
(*Caladium* × *hortulanum*)

Large leaves come in many colors and patterns. Not hardy to frost; usually treated as an annual.

Variegated Solomon's-seal
(*Polygonatum odoratum* 'Variegatum')

White-edged leaves look fresh and bright all summer. Spreads gradually. Tolerates fairly dry soil.

Astilbe
(*Astilbe* × *arendsii* hybrids)

Fluffy plumes of red, pink, or white flowers bloom in summer. Compound leaves are dark and glossy.

Lady's-mantle
(*Alchemilla mollis*)

Makes a broad mound of neatly pleated leaves, with billows of tiny chartreuse flowers in summer.

Hosta
(*Hosta* spp., hybrids, and cultivars)

A diverse group of excellent shade plants. They form generous clumps of foliage in shades of green, blue, gold, and variegated. Flowers are purplish or white.

Alumroot
(*Heuchera micrantha* 'Palace Purple')

Clumps of dark purple or bronzy foliage make a colorful accent that lasts all season. Blooms in summer.

Ferns
(*Osmunda cinnamomea* is shown here)

All ferns grow well in shade. Some prefer moist soil, but others tolerate dry sites. Most hold their fronds in vaselike clumps, but some spread to form a patch.

Bugbane
(*Cimicifuga simplex* 'White Pearl')

Spreads to form a low patch of foliage, topped in late fall by arching clusters of small white flowers.

Hellebore
(*Helleborus foetidus* and other spp.)

Dark green leaves are evergreen in mild climates. Pale green, pink, or white flowers open in early spring.

Covering ground

Low-growing junipers make excellent ground covers, and they're frequently used on slopes. During the several years they'll take to fill in, a heavy mulch will keep down weeds and keep up appearances.

If trees are the walls and roof of a garden and shrubs the furniture, lawns and ground covers are the flooring and carpets. The grass lawn has been the carpet of choice since the days of the great English estates. While our home landscapes are decidedly more modest, they follow the same formula of a large lawn, dotted with trees and edged by borders of shrubs or flowers.

A well-manicured lawn is undeniably attractive, and it's unsurpassed as a surface for all sorts of activities. But lawns have their drawbacks. They're not practical on steep slopes, in moderate to heavy shade, or in the increasing number of places where water is scarce. Even where water is plentiful, a lawn requires a heavy expenditure in labor (mowing, weeding, aerating, edging) and materials (fertilizer, pest and disease controls, herbicides).

Fortunately, there are alternatives, plants that need little upkeep and thrive where traditional turfgrass struggles. Loosely gathered under the umbrella term *ground covers,* these include low-growing, creeping, or spreading shrubs, vines, perennials, and some annuals. Long a staple of parks, highway verges, and other public landscapes, ground covers are finding a place in the home landscape. In addition to handling problem spots and cutting down on lawn maintenance, ground covers provide an exciting design element: their wide range of foliage and flowers can add large splashes of color or texture to the garden.

It's worth examining for a moment why we "cover" the ground in the first place. In arid regions, where tracking mud into the house is seldom a worry and the natural vegetative cover is sparse, trying to carpet the ground with plants makes little sense. The Spanish courtyard garden, with its cover of dust or pebbles, and the desert, where a few succulents are scattered across a gravelly surface, are models worth considering.

Where conditions favor lusher vegetation, however, if you don't plant ground covers of some sort, nature is only too happy to provide them—usually in the form of weeds. A leafy cover of your own choosing will inhibit weeds, keep the soil cool, and break the force of drenching rain. Beneath the surface, its roots will hold the soil against erosion and improve water penetration.

The installation, care, and maintenance of traditional turfgrass lawns is covered in the final section of this book, Growing Healthy Plants. Here we'll take a look at other ground covers and what they can do for your landscape.

Ground covers for special sites

Trees pose two problems for lawn grass: shade and competition from roots. One or the other can make growing grass difficult; the two together permit a threadbare lawn at best. There are a number of tough

ground covers that do better. Where winters are cold, English ivy and its hardier Baltic variety are the most reliable and fastest growing among evergreen ground covers. In mild-winter areas, large-leaved Algerian ivy is even faster. Other woody-stemmed evergreen competitors are St.-John's-wort and winter creeper. Barely woody candidates include periwinkle and pachysandra.

Delicately scented, with fragile-looking flowers, lily-of-the-valley is one of the toughest competitors with tree roots. It disappears in winter, but its matted rhizomes suppress weeds effectively. Supremely attractive in leaf and flower, bishop's-hats (*Epimedium* spp.) are slow to spread and can be hard to find at local nurseries, but they're worth a browse through the mail-order catalogs. Easier to find are the ajugas, with blue, white, or pink flowers and green, bronze, or variegated leaves. Violets lend fragrance, while hostas and bergenias are larger plants with magnificent foliage and quite adequate flowers. For a grassy look where grass won't grow, you should consider mondo grass and lilyturf.

It's important to note that wherever oak root rot or honey fungus (*Armillaria*) is a serious threat, ground covers that need frequent irrigation should

Low, flowering ground covers, including sedums, thyme, and saxifrage, offer a colorful, meadowlike alternative to a lawn for this Santa Fe home (left).

Dense colonies of pachysandra solve several classic landscaping problems on this property (above)—heavy shade, sloping terrain, and, between the walk and the house, an area too narrow to conveniently mow. The result is also quite pleasing to the eye.

not be planted up to the bases of trees. Constantly damp soil can cause rotting of the tree's cambium layer at the soil line, which can kill the tree.

Steep slopes. Lawns are difficult to establish and maintain on steep slopes. The steeper the slope, the greater the danger of erosion and earth slippage, and hence the greater the need for ground cover. Although coarse grasses such as annual rye can stabilize bare slopes quickly, you can find better solutions among shrubs and vines.

Various ivies root freely as they run, knitting the soil in place. Hall's honeysuckle is even quicker to cover (much too quick, in the view of many who have suffered it as an invasive nuisance). Junipers are attractive throughout the year and require little maintenance. Cotoneasters, evergreen or deciduous, put on a winter display of red or rosy fruits. Where soil is acidic and quick-draining, heathers are effective, with colorful flowers or foliage. The West and Southwest have an impressive array of drought-tolerant native bank covers, including species of arctostaphylos, baccharis, and ceanothus. In semitropical climates, bougainvillea and natal plum are sturdy and showy.

Certain perennials can hold slopes, too. In the West, the smaller ice plants carpet slopes with incandescent sheets of yellow, orange, pink, red, or purple flowers. Less obvious but equally effective as a ground cover are daylilies, which eventually expand into a weed-smothering mass.

Cramped quarters. Most home landscapes have some area that isn't big enough for a lawn. Where entry or patio gardens are too small for a lawn mower, think of a patch of ground cover as a throw rug. In such situations, prostrate plants such as creeping thyme, Irish moss, and some of the sedums are easy to maintain. These plants can also flow around boulders and between stepping-stones.

Irish moss and creeping thyme withstand some foot traffic, too, as do chamomile and *Mazus reptans*. Korean grass (*Zoysia tenuifolia*) may well be considered here because, although a true grass, it never needs mowing.

The narrow strips of ground between a curb and a fence or a wall or between driveway and sidewalk are well suited to restrained ground covers. Irises, daylilies, and compact, spreading perennials such as creeping phlox and hardy geraniums will sup-

press weeds and give a fine show of flowers. In mild-winter climates, gazania, Peruvian verbena, and ivy geranium give months of bloom.

Expansive covers. In large areas not subject to traffic, consider massed shrubs instead of turfgrass. Deciduous candidates include barberry, forsythia, privet, and spirea; abelia, juniper, Oregon grape, pyracantha, and yew are evergreen. Spaced so that the mature plants just touch, these moderately tall shrubs produce a pleasant, undulating surface. To make the same waves on a smaller scale, try lower-growing shrubs such as heather, dwarf nandina, and potentilla.

The meadow, nearly wiped out by the plow and the builder, is making a comeback in the home landscape. Comprising pasture grasses and wildflowers (annual and perennial), meadows usually cover large open spaces, but smaller areas spangled with larkspur, poppies, and blue or scarlet flax are seen more often every year. In a variation on the meadow theme, you might plant certain turfgrasses but not mow them. Red fescue is widely used as bank or slope cover in the West. The rich green blades ripple in the wind just like a natural meadow, and like a meadow red fescue is mowed once a year.

Painting the landscape with ground covers

The wide range of color and texture found in the foliage and flowers of ground covers can be deployed in the landscape much as a painter uses color on a canvas, to create bands, drifts, or large pools of color.

Foliage color, because it persists through much or all of the year, creates permanent effects. In regions where dark evergreen forests prevail, the lively gold or blue-gray of massed junipers brings a welcome contrast. Conversely, masses of dark evergreen foliage stand out in the gray or white winter landscape of cold climates. During the growing season, the gray foliage of lamb's-ears makes any nearby greenery seem more verdant. Some ajugas have purple or bronze leaves, and variegated archangel, a similar plant, has leaves with strong white variegation, pale enough to be luminous against lawn or dark shrubbery. If you live in the intermountain region of the West, try the variegated form of bishop's weed (*Aegopodium podagraria*); gardeners in the East, however, may find it too aggressive.

Contrasting foliage forms and textures are also a joy to the eye. The smooth, broad leaves of berge-

Arrayed in wide swaths, large plants can be effective ground covers. The perennials in the top photo at left include sedums, black-eyed Susans, yucca, and ornamental grasses.

Turning bronze in the autumn, a thicket of deciduous azaleas runs along a low ridge on a New England property, center photo.

A wide variety of grasses can substitute for traditional turfgrass, bottom photo. They require little if any mowing and minimal maintenance, and they come in a range of heights, colors, and textures, often with colorful seed heads. The bluish grass here is sheep fescue, which grows only 8 to 12 inches high. Behind it is feather reed grass.

nia or hosta are especially effective when contrasted with bordering grasses or grasslike daylily, lilyturf, and mondo grass. The velvety softness of lady's-mantle shows to good advantage against the succulent crispness of London-pride (*Saxifraga umbrosa*).

Flowering ground covers provide painterly effects. Ajuga in flower make pools of blue in shade or sun; snow-in-summer sheet the ground with white. Many of the sedums supplement their evergreen foliage with drifts of white or yellow flowers; creeping phlox makes carpets of white, pink, red, or lavender. The flowers of ice plants dazzle in orange, red, and purple. Large-flowered clematis, usually seen on trellises or fences, makes a spectacular ground cover.

Practical matters

Attractive as ground cover can be, it is economic considerations—the saving in resources and labor—that guarantee its increasing use. Nowhere is this saving more visible than in the use of water. The lawn is by far the thirstiest customer in the home landscape, the greediest in its use of fertilizers, and the most demanding of attention. The dry West, which has for decades faced the problem of a rapidly growing population and a scanty water supply, has begun to legislate the use of water-conserving ground-cover plants and restrict the planting of turfgrasses. Consequently, a vast number of drought-tolerant shrubs and perennials have been introduced there. Many are native to the region, while others have come from low-rainfall areas around the world. Other regions will very likely follow suit as population pressure and industrial demand grow while the water supply remains static.

Ground covers also require less labor than turf lawns. Once established they can usually take care of themselves, with only an annual grooming and occasional damage repair. A good start is the key to minimal cost down the line. Select plants adapted to your site and conditions, and prepare the ground carefully.

The hard part is suppressing weeds while plants are getting established. Once the plants shade the ground, they'll provide their own weed control. To accomplish this effectively, plant mounding shrubs of limited spread close together. Trailers can be more widely spaced, as can plants that spread by surface or underground runners or by layering (rooting where branches touch the ground). This last group is especially useful in holding soil on cut or filled banks and in preventing erosion.

Ground covers that present a close-cropped, lawnlike appearance for low-traffic areas include Irish moss (shown at top) and thyme. The mondo grass on the left of this photo is ideal where a taller, dense ground cover is suitable.

In woodland or shady areas where a casual, natural look is wanted, a variety of low-growing flowering plants, such as the sweet woodruff and false miterwort shown in the middle photo, spread quickly to fill large spaces.

A ground cover of spring cinquefoil provides much more texture and character to the small planting shown in the bottom photo than turfgrass could—and the ground would have to be much smoother and more uniform to allow grass to be mowed.

Ground covers

Yellow archangel
(*Lamiastrum galeobdolon*)

Silvery foliage contrasts well with dark evergreens. Easy to grow and fills in fast. Can be invasive.

Japanese honeysuckle
(*Lonicera japonica*)

A tough and aggressive vine, useful in dry climates but weedy in damp areas. Periodically needs severe pruning. Flowers are very fragrant.

Pachysandra
(*Pachysandra terminalis*)

Ideal for filling large areas under and around trees. Makes a dense mat of evergreen foliage and needs virtually no care.

English ivy
(*Hedera helix*)

A carefree cover for small or large areas. There are dozens of cultivars, differing in hardiness and in leaf size, shape, and color.

Ribbon grass
(*Phalaris arundinacea* 'Picta')

Very easy to grow. Needs some sun but tolerates almost any soil, wet or dry. Mow in late summer to promote fresh new growth. Dies down in winter.

Periwinkle
(*Vinca minor*)

Easy and adaptable. Tolerates sun or shade, heat or cold. Glossy leaves are evergreen. Has lavender or white flowers in spring.

Bishop's-hat
(*Epimedium grandiflorum*)

Compound leaves are neat and attractive from spring to fall. Prefers rich, moist soil and shade. Spreads slowly. Related species are all desirable.

European ginger
(*Asarum europaeum*)

Spreads slowly to make a low mat of evergreen, heart-shaped leaves. Needs rich, moist soil and part shade.

Lilyturf
(*Liriope muscari*)

Makes thick clumps of glossy green or variegated foliage, topped with lavender or white flowers in summer.

Bugleweed
(*Ajuga reptans*)

Cultivars differ in leaf color and size and in flower color. All stay low and spread fast. Good for sun or shade. Easy to grow.

Creeping juniper
(*Juniperus horizontalis*)

A favorite for well-drained, sunny sites. Cultivars differ in foliage color and texture. Most hug the ground and spread fast.

Rockspray cotoneaster
(*Cotoneaster horizontalis*)

Trails gracefully down a bank or over a wall. Has fine-textured deciduous foliage and bright red berries in fall. There are many cultivars of this and related species. Some are evergreen.

Beds and borders

This small border, with its towering delphiniums and lupines and cheerful poppies, plays very effectively against the white stucco and bright blue trim of the house.

For many North Americans, *flower bed* and *garden* are interchangeable terms. Although there can be a great deal more to a garden than a clearly bounded plot of plants in effusive bloom, there is no denying that beds, and their cousins, borders, are at the heart of countless gardens.

Their widespread appeal reflects an enormous range of possibilities. At one extreme is the small patch of colorful annuals lovingly tended by a child. At the other is a horticultural symphony of color, texture, and form a dozen feet wide and 10 times as long, containing hundreds of plants from every corner of the globe and requiring the ministrations of a small army of gardeners.

Most of our beds and borders are more ambitious than the child's but far more modest than the symphony—lack of time, space, money, and energy, if nothing else, limits our efforts to a fugue or a sonata. But "ordinary" beds and borders can be quite spectacular to the eye and enormously satisfying to the gardening spirit.

Bed and border basics

A bed can be any shape, from rigidly geometric to casually curved and free-form. Accessible from one or more sides, it is densely planted and designed to pack as much visual punch as possible. An island bed allows access from every point on its perimeter, making it an exceptionally interactive planting offering a variety of views.

A border is a special sort of bed, one that is linear and viewed principally from one long edge

(which can be straight or curved). A backdrop of some sort—a hedge, a line of trees, a wall, or a fence—forms the other long edge. The classic border, made famous by the English at the beginning of the 20th century, is long and deep and filled with herbaceous plants arranged in complex combinations of color, form, and texture that change through the seasons. Such borders can range from formal to casual, but in essence they are stylized artistic expressions, far removed from any natural model.

They are also highly time-consuming. The work is simple to learn and, aside from initial soil preparation, not particularly backbreaking. But if you get lazy about the ongoing weeding, deadheading, staking, dividing, and replanting required, the planting shows your negligence immediately. Unlike more relaxed, loosely naturalistic plantings, the classic herbaceous border can easily deteriorate into a sloppy mess.

Seeking the same exuberant effect in less space and for less effort, many gardeners have turned to beds or borders that combine a potpourri of plants. By incorporating easy-care woody plants and ground covers with more labor-intensive perennials and annuals, you cut down considerably on your work. Mixed beds and borders allow for more informal

This grand perennial border is the result of 25 years of enthusiastic gardening effort. Situated on a slight slope, backed by evergreen rhododendrons, it presents itself handsomely to the viewer strolling on the lawn. Planning for show in each season is one of the most stimulating challenges in designing a border; in this border the spring display of tulips and daffodils (above) is followed by peonies and early daylilies before the garden reaches its peak (left).

Shrub borders are generally less work than their perennial counterparts. Although flowers can play an important part in such borders, much of their attraction derives from the foliage and form of the plants.

design than does the classic border and are more easily adapted to existing terrain or "natural" schemes. Mixed plantings also offer four-season attractions—when the herbaceous perennials have died to the ground, the lovely structure, bark, or evergreen foliage of the woody plants and the graceful rustling fountains of the ornamental grasses remain.

You will, of course, want to put your bed or border in the best possible location. Perhaps you want a showy backdrop to an outdoor entertainment area or a focal point for the front yard. Is it to be viewed mainly from a special spot inside the house, or to be enjoyed by walking along or through it? Consider also prevailing winds and shade; most herbaceous plants do best with some protection from strong wind and at least half a day of sun. Pay close attention to the "borrowed scenery" supplied by the surrounding landscape. The colors, shapes, textures, and mood of nearby trees and buildings or distant fields, hills, or mountains will affect your design.

Whether your dream is a classic border or a mixed planting, your chances of success will greatly improve if you start small and choose your plants carefully. Even if you have a border-perfect 90-foot stretch down one side of your property, resist the temptation to dig it up all at once. Preparing, plant-

ing, and caring for a border a third as long could keep you busy for several years.

Choosing plants

In the grand borders of British estates, many of the plants (lupines, for example) offer only a brief moment of glory before fading. Whereas the visual holes such plants leave after blooming are less noticeable in a large bed or border, they can leap at the eye from a smaller planting. By choosing plants with an extended flowering period and/or handsome foliage, you can avoid much of the problem. During the first year or two, annuals fill in gaps between the small perennials and add color while the youngsters are still shy to bloom. In a border dominated by trees and shrubs, carpet the bare soil between immature woody plants with perennials, ground covers, and bulbs. As the shrubs and trees grow larger and closer together, the herbaceous plants recede, weakened by lack of light and root competition, their role fulfilled.

If you don't want to devote every spare hour to your border, avoid plants that need tedious staking and primping, frequent division and replanting, or regular pest and disease control. If delphiniums blow over in the wind, break in early summer showers, or

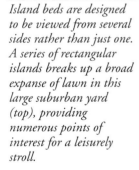

Island beds are designed to be viewed from several sides rather than just one. A series of rectangular islands breaks up a broad expanse of lawn in this large suburban yard (top), providing numerous points of interest for a leisurely stroll.

Beds and borders are most often parts of a home landscape that includes lawn, patios, shrubs, and trees. Here, however, the gardening urge has taken over and filled almost the entire yard with flower beds (bottom).

suffer an assortment of maladies in your region, try annual larkspur for the blue spike effect, or drought-tolerant, tough foxtail lilies if it's the spike more than the color you're after. Choose the least labor-intensive plants that still give a similar effect. And always avoid invasive plants; their aggressive, bossy ways are ill suited for a bed or border of well-behaved perennials.

The right plants for your region. Perhaps the best advice for a gardener about to embark on designing a bed or border is to start with plants that do well in your area. If these are the same plants that inhabit the magnificent English borders you see in books, so much the better. But you can still have a beautiful planting if they're not. In the West, a border may overflow with water-thrifty penstemons; in the heat and humidity of the South, tropical salvias bloom for months on end; in the hot summers and frigid winters of the Midwest, indigos and other prairie wildflowers add as much color and texture as any tenderer prima donna.

In some regions, the range of herbaceous plants that do well is more limited than in others; there, shrubs with beautiful flowers and leaves are important players in beds and borders. The hot, humid South offers a vast choice of shrubs, both native and exotic—abelia, wintersweet, gardenia, and camellia, with their season-stretching flowers;

rhododendrons, hollies, Indian hawthorn, and pittosporum, with their evergreen foliage and handsome flowers and fruit.

California's mildest climates, where perennials are limited by the absence of a dependably cool dormant season, are home to thriving plantings of shrubs and subshrubs. Innovative, water-wise borders and beds spill over with colorful bottlebrush, oleander, rock rose, Jerusalem sage, lavender and native Cleveland sage, ceanothus, and shrubby buckwheat, giving any perennial border a run for its money.

In colder or extremely dry climates that are more hospitable to annuals and perennials than to woody plants, adapted shrubs and small trees add a dimension to an herbaceous planting. In the arid Southwest, floriferous Texas sage and fairy-duster contribute form and color, while dainty palo verde and acacia trees give much-needed shade.

A sight for each season. One of the greatest challenges in making a bed or border is providing interest throughout as much of the year as possible. In temperate climates, many perennials bloom for four to six weeks beginning in June (in hotter climates, it's April); too great a reliance on these plants results in a short, almost surreal flush of color followed by little else. To overcome this pitfall, make an effort to include plants that bloom at other times of the year

pleasing harmonies and symmetry or surprising contrasts. Classic borders often repeat blocks of color in a formal composition; for a more fluid, informal look, weave ribbons of plants through the bed. Remember the all-important role of foliage as a lasting backdrop and frame; greens, grays, and silver serve as go-betweens.

Monochromatic designs are much in fashion, but the subtle color gradations and the balance of form and texture so vital to their success require knowledge of a large number of plants and an artistic eye. Instead of just one color, select two or three; this is a much easier approach with predictably good results. Try using a touch of a harmonious color in a border dominated by one hue. For example, a predominantly blue-flowered planting is enhanced by the addition of a few soft yellow blossoms or leaves; a pale pink scheme is enlivened by strategically placed rich purple or burgundy plants.

Beyond color, consider the shape and texture of the flowers and leaves and how they play off one another. Too much busy fine texture, too many spiked flowers, or an overabundance of bold, dramatic plants makes a design less effective. The same can be said for plant shapes. A common mistake in designing perennial borders is selecting plants with similar rounded forms; the result is a planting with a boring, lumpy look. Vary the shapes by including a smattering of dramatic vertical spikes, weeping grasses, and stiffly linear leaves.

Place taller, more substantial plants toward the middle of an island bed; by hiding other parts of the design from certain vantage points, they introduce the element of surprise. In a more formal border, you can introduce spontaneity and surprise by breaking the typical gradation of plant heights—low in front, tall at the back—with an occasional large, bold plant in the foreground or smaller, creeping ones weaving from front to back.

A bed or border takes time to develop; be patient with the planting and with yourself. Mistakes are inevitable; fortunately, beds and borders are among the easiest garden styles to alter when things don't work out as planned. Regular maintenance and a sense of adventure will assure you of a wonderfully gratifying result in due time. What may surprise you more than anything is that the process turns out to be as satisfying as the eagerly awaited result.

Stuffed with colorful annuals and presided over by a little tree, the timber-enclosed raised beds at left make the most of a difficult strip of land between the house and the street.

Although most perennial beds and borders are at their peak in early summer, when plants are blooming profusely, the maturing seed heads and lanky foliage of autumn have a certain ripe charm.

or for extended periods and plants whose foliage maintains interest long after the bloom is gone. When you plan plant combinations and sequences, consider creating seasonal pockets of interest. It's more effective, for instance, to group asters, goldenrods, and maiden grass together for a concentrated lovely fall picture than to spread them individually throughout the planting.

Herbaceous plants die down to the ground each dormant season, so they are at their worst in winter and early spring. In early spring, when the perennials are just beginning to show signs of life, let a redbud, crab apple, magnolia, or other early-blooming tree enliven the area. An underplanting of bulbs adds to the display; as the bulbs finish, the perennials fill in and cover the yellowing bulb foliage. After the fall color fades, woody plants, evergreen and deciduous, and plants with interesting seed heads can reward a casual stroll by the border.

Some design tips

The discussions of design, structure, and color elsewhere in this book should prove helpful when planning your bed or border. Here are some reminders.

Color is what many beds and borders are about; use it for exciting accents, restful repetition and unity, optical effects of depth and distance, and

Fragrant plants for beds and borders

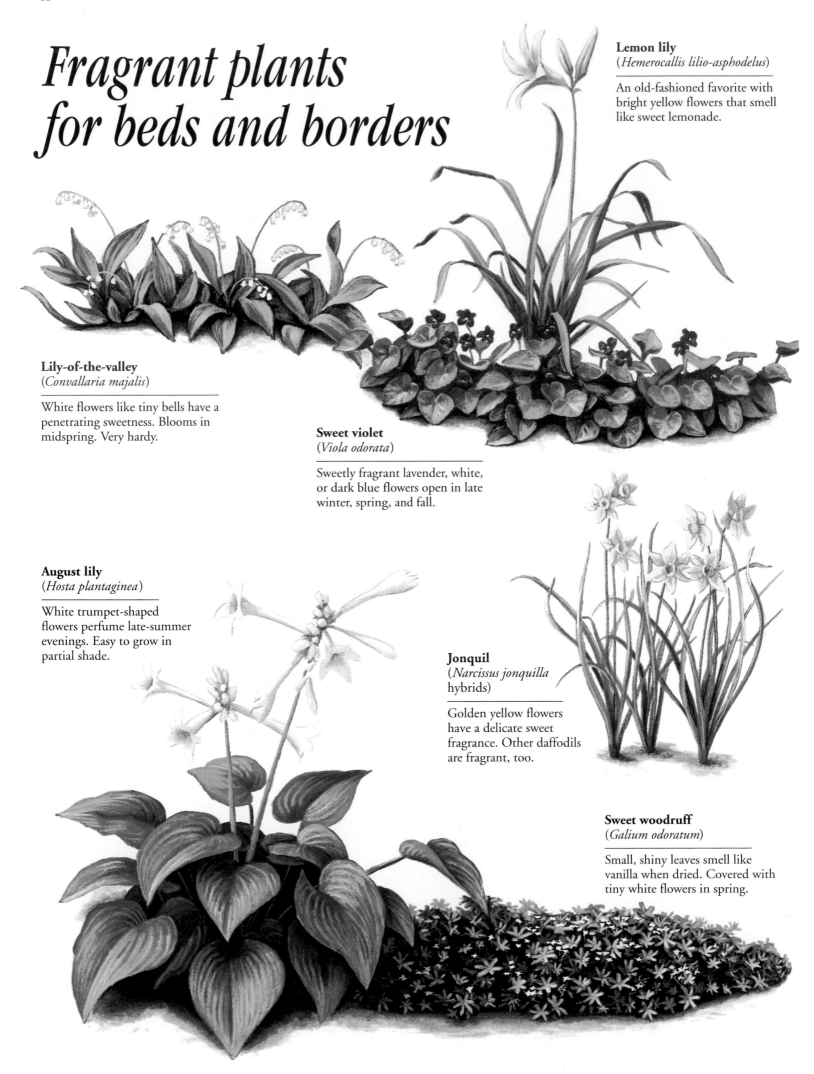

Lemon lily
(*Hemerocallis lilio-asphodelus*)

An old-fashioned favorite with bright yellow flowers that smell like sweet lemonade.

Lily-of-the-valley
(*Convallaria majalis*)

White flowers like tiny bells have a penetrating sweetness. Blooms in midspring. Very hardy.

Sweet violet
(*Viola odorata*)

Sweetly fragrant lavender, white, or dark blue flowers open in late winter, spring, and fall.

August lily
(*Hosta plantaginea*)

White trumpet-shaped flowers perfume late-summer evenings. Easy to grow in partial shade.

Jonquil
(*Narcissus jonquilla* hybrids)

Golden yellow flowers have a delicate sweet fragrance. Other daffodils are fragrant, too.

Sweet woodruff
(*Galium odoratum*)

Small, shiny leaves smell like vanilla when dried. Covered with tiny white flowers in spring.

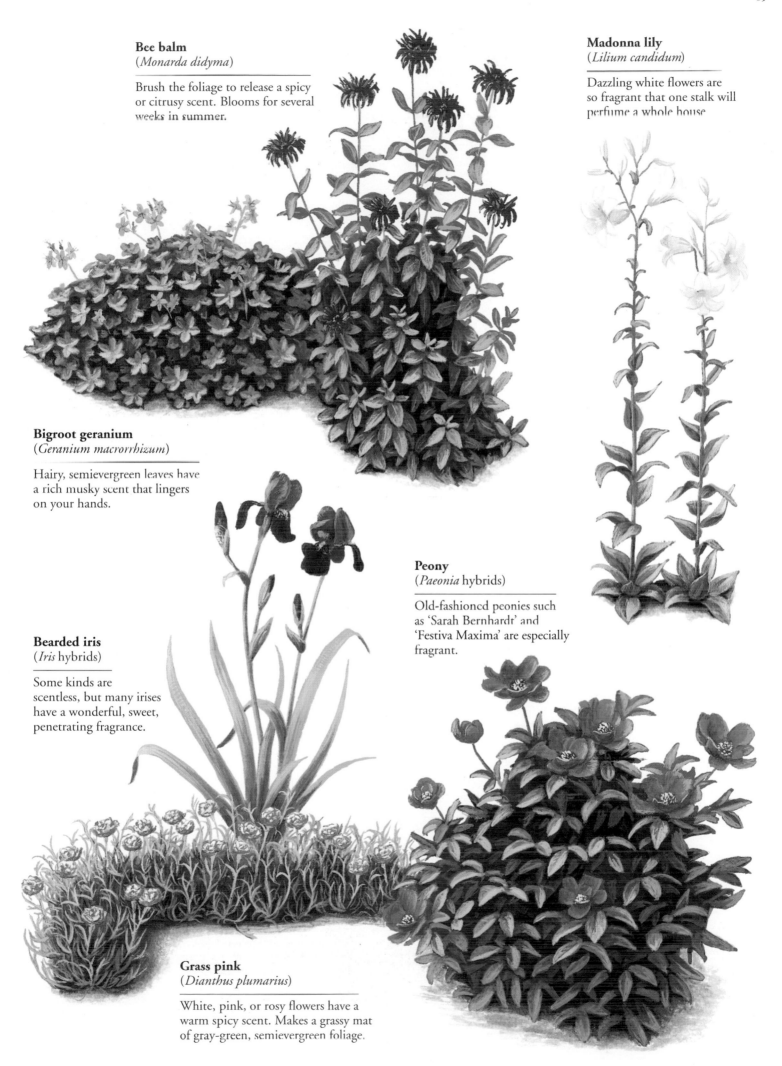

Bee balm
(*Monarda didyma*)

Brush the foliage to release a spicy
or citrusy scent. Blooms for several
weeks in summer.

Madonna lily
(*Lilium candidum*)

Dazzling white flowers are
so fragrant that one stalk will
perfume a whole house.

Bigroot geranium
(*Geranium macrorrhizum*)

Hairy, semievergreen leaves have
a rich musky scent that lingers
on your hands.

Peony
(*Paeonia* hybrids)

Old-fashioned peonies such
as 'Sarah Bernhardt' and
'Festiva Maxima' are especially
fragrant.

Bearded iris
(*Iris* hybrids)

Some kinds are
scentless, but many irises
have a wonderful, sweet,
penetrating fragrance.

Grass pink
(*Dianthus plumarius*)

White, pink, or rosy flowers have a
warm spicy scent. Makes a grassy mat
of gray-green, semievergreen foliage.

The front garden

Where there isn't much room in the front yard (above), you can usher visitors on their short journey to the front door through a blaze of color. Where there's no front yard at all (below), colorful container plantings do the job.

For years Americans have thought of the "front yard" as a semipublic domain. Like many a formal living room, it is prim, proper, and unsuited for any real day-to-day living. A sward of well-manicured lawn, tidy shrubs up next to the house, and perhaps an edging of colorful annuals along the walkway are meant to elicit approval from passersby rather than to provide pleasure or utility to the occupants.

Old notions stick like sandburs, but more and more people are transforming front yards into front gardens. Some continue to play to the passing audience, but they do so with imaginative and varied plantings that stimulate the gardener as well as welcome the visitor. Others, perhaps lacking space elsewhere on the property, create private areas for gardening, entertaining, and play, screened from the sidewalk and street by fences, walls, or plantings. Land is a precious commodity these days—why not reclaim the parcel in front of the house for your own use and expression?

Reconsidering your front yard

A good way to start is to think in terms of usable spaces rather than of a calendar picture that would look good to the folks across the street. In different regions of this country, front gardens have been used for all kinds of purposes and have taken various forms in response to those purposes. Colonial New England, for example, featured dooryard gardens, areas fenced off from marauding livestock, where householders cultivated the herbs, berries, and flowers indispensable in the operation of the home.

Similarly, immigrants in the mining regions of the Upper Great Lakes, bringing with them European traditions, wasted no part of their modest yards. Front gardens were devoted to the growing of food, a task that also offered an antidote to industrial stress. In rural areas of the Deep South, domestic chores such as cooking or tinkering with machinery often spilled out-of-doors into a "swept yard," an outdoor room so named because the bare compacted earth beneath tall pines was swept clear of debris with dogwood brooms. In warm areas of the country such as the Southwest and southern California, courtyard gardens at the entrances to homes reflected the outdoor living possible there year-round. Variations on these gardens exist today, successful now as then because they suit human purposes.

Your purpose may be as simple as creating a bit of privacy and providing shade. You may want to create an enchanting entryway, a small wooded Eden for a visitor arriving from the busy street. If your front lawn requires too much water, fertilizer, or attention, you might replace much of it with ornamental ground covers, perennials, or even edible plants, artfully arranged on trellises, arbors, or walls, perhaps tended and viewed from a meandering path. In the Southwest, a dryland garden might complement the architecture and the environment.

Except for walking to and from the car or mailbox and mowing the lawn, you may not have spent much time in the front yard, so it is particularly important to take stock of the area as described in the chapters on planning. Spend some time noting conditions at different times of the day, in different seasons. In the morning when the back garden is in shade, is there a choice sunny spot out front where it would be nice to sip coffee? Would the front door be cooler and more inviting on a summer afternoon if shaded by a carefully placed tree; would a windscreen of shrubs protect winter visitors?

Consider the relationship of the front yard to the inside of the house as well. Are there potentially attractive views from the living room, dining room, or second-floor bedrooms? Would removing that overgrown yew or juniper jammed up against the windows bathe the dining room in welcome sunlight? If so, would a carefully placed curbside bed of perennials and shrubs enhance the view for the diners?

Comings and goings

Whatever other purposes you have in mind for your front garden, one is almost certain to be a given—getting people to the main entrance of the house. The driveways, walks, steps, porches, and entry courts required to orchestrate a person's progress to the front door will likely play a large role in the organization of the front garden.

Of these, the path to the front door is often the most important—and often terribly boring. Instead of making a beeline from the street or driveway to the door, you can "choreograph" the journey through a succession of pleasant, surprising, or intriguing views. The path should be clear and logical, but it can offer more rewards than just arrival at the front door.

For example, a front garden above street level could feature entry steps at an angle to the public sidewalk. Mounting the steps, your gaze is directed toward a clematis in flower, supported by a handsome railing. Curving under an archway, the path leads to a small grove of river birch that slightly conceals the entry. In the Great Plains or Southwest, stepping-stones nestled in a silver-gray ground cover might wind through clumps of ornamental grasses, interplanted with a collection of dryland native plants featuring masses of intensely colored flowers.

Don't forget practical concerns. The path should be easily perceived at night, but avoid lighting it like an airport landing strip. Lights should draw attention to the walkway and, perhaps, nearby plantings, not to themselves. The materials and design should complement the architecture and suit the climate and the level of traffic. Where winters are snowy, the path should be easy to shovel. Steer clear of materials such as wood chips that are easily tracked inside. (See "Underfoot in the garden" for more on paths.)

Driveways and garages

Whereas the front walkway may be the most important element in the front garden, the driveway is often the dominant one, and the biggest design headache. It's fairly easy to relocate a path or a walkway, but few of us have the space or resources to move the drive.

Visitors to this suburban home are treated to an interesting stroll by several plantings along a wide brick path. The occupants of the house can sip coffee and read the paper on the bench in the morning or enjoy the evening there with a few friends.

92

Making this large driveway-side planting away from the house creates an element of surprise for a visitor, who can readily discern the path to be taken, yet can't see everything to be encountered on the journey. The tall plants in the bed also screen the driveway from people relaxing on the lawn on the other side.

Lawn dominates most front yards, but here the gardener has eliminated the lawn, turning the entire area into a garden of fascinating profusion.

This small front courtyard in Connecticut, paved with brick and planted with herbs and perennials, is a contemporary version of the dooryard gardens traditional to New England.

You can weaken the attention-grabbing power of the driveway and garage with plantings, carefully placed so that they don't encroach on space needed to open and close car doors. Additional structures (retaining walls, steps, a dry streambed) in combination with plantings can dramatize the route intended for foot traffic, wresting the viewer's attention from the mundane drive and garage.

For too many homes, the driveway serves as walkway for most of the journey to the door, giving the impression that it is more important to accommodate the automobile than the people in it. If visitors are likely to park on the street, provide a welcoming path from the street to the front door. If your property includes off-street parking, make sure that an obvious walkway connects it to the entrance. If the driveway is the only practical route, consider laying a brick walkway adjacent to it. Or try to emphasize the point in the journey at which the path takes over from the drive; a change of surface, a change of level, or attractive plantings will mark the spot.

The front porch

Closer to the front door, a porch, a terrace, or at the very least a stoop creates a transition zone from the public front garden to the interior of the home. Such features are more effective if they are preceded by a series of interesting spaces that move the visitor from the public to the private domain. The series need not be elaborate or extensive—moving from the sidewalk through a small garden can make a very pleasant welcome.

Perhaps the most charming of all transition spaces is the courtyard or dooryard garden. Some are simply a widening in the walkway defined by shrubs or a wall. Others are extensive, patio-like, almost another room of the house. They may be accessible, through French doors perhaps, from a living or dining room and serve to extend those areas outdoors for parties or daily living. Fences, walls, or tall plantings provide privacy from the street, affording the visitor a sheltered, intimate approach to the entrance, and the occupant another private outdoor space.

Special plants can be shown to great advantage

Foundation plantings

FROM MAINE TO ARIZONA, in small town, inner city, and suburb, perhaps no other element is as common to home landscapes as foundation plantings—trees and shrubs, usually small and evergreen, that hug the base of the house. Although there are tasteful, attractive examples, too often the overall effect resembles clumps of parsley garnishing a turkey.

Part of the problem is that foundation plantings have come adrift from their historical mooring. Victorian houses sat high off the ground on stone or brick foundations and virtually begged for a skirt of shrubs to reduce their imposing scale and to conceal their awkward-looking underpinnings. When smaller bungalows arrived, generous foundation plantings created the impression that the house had "grown" from its surroundings. Through subsequent changes in house and garden styles, foundation plantings have hung on doggedly, sometimes to hide architectural flaws, more often out of force of habit.

Of course, planting around a house is both needed and desirable—few lawns can gracefully continue right up to the building wall. But we can design these plantings far more effectively. Here are some guidelines.

Choose plants that won't outgrow their space and purpose—we've all seen houses entombed by evergreens that weren't right for the spot. Expand your plant horizons; consider perennials and deciduous trees and shrubs with evergreens to take advantage of the delightful march of the seasons. Finally, think of the plantings near the house as a part of the total design of the front garden, coordinated with its pathways, structures, and other plantings, as discussed elsewhere on these pages. So reconsider the traditional foundation planting—extend the walls of your house rather than smother them.

Instead of a tight symmetrical skirt of closely cropped evergreens, like the one at above left, try something new. The hosta garden and flagstone path at bottom accomplish the same task (dressing up an unappealing facade), are more inviting to the eye, and require less maintenance.

in this architectural setting. Fragrant flowers and plants requiring more care or water may be more fully enjoyed and more easily tended in a dooryard garden. Plant a linden tree, gardenia, or fragrant viburnum within range, or allow a sweet-scented honeysuckle vine to scamper over the fence. In arid parts of the country, a dooryard garden or entry court may appeal to those seeking a more imaginative lawn substitute than gravel or ground covers.

For entertaining, family dinners, or sunbathing, people want the privacy usually afforded by a backyard garden. But often we want to feel more connected—to the street activity, to our neighbors walking by on a summer evening, to a larger, more open space—and the back garden is just too isolated. A front garden or half-hidden entry court fulfills those needs. And, whether you choose to create an intimate private space or plan a garden that's open and shared, whether your plant palette includes flowers to fuss over or elegant sweeps of low-maintenance plantings, or whether you combine all the options through a staging of successive spaces, a front garden provides yet another realm for growing and enjoying plants.

Rock gardens

Rock-garden plants are fascinating, adapted as they are to extreme sites and climates. Inhabiting a miniature world, the plants shown here (including common aubrieta, basket-of-gold, a tiny-leaved sedum, and dwarf wallflower) cling to pockets of soil among the rocks.

The rock garden, a marriage of plant and stone, evokes the natural world in ways that other garden styles do not. Inspired by fascinating plants in glorious mountain settings, early rock gardeners went to great lengths to summon beautiful montane scenes. Today the concept of rock gardening has expanded. Some gardeners create miniature scenes in small, rough-hewn stone troughs. Others adorn a rocky hillside or a weathered stone wall with rock-loving plants. Still other gardeners undertake serious construction, grading and hauling in tons of gravel and stone to fabricate the right setting.

Alpine plants are the traditional stars of rock gardens, but you don't have to be a plant nut or avid alpinist to have a rock garden. Among well-placed rocks, you can compose a beautiful, low-maintenance garden with a few showy, easy-to-grow plants (some of which have little connection to mountains). Because many rock-garden plants are small, gardeners cramped for space can create an immensely satisfying, complex garden in only a few square yards. Covered with a cooling rocky mulch, rock gardens also conserve water, a considerable advantage in arid regions.

The construction of an appropriate setting and the selection and care of rock-garden plants are more complicated, even for a simple rock garden, than for many other types of gardening. The following is merely a brief overview of the essential ingredients— rocks and plants. If you're intrigued, consult the bibliography for further reading, or, better yet, seek out rock gardeners in your community and learn more firsthand.

The rocks

Rocks are as important to the plants as they are to the garden's looks. They can shade plants or warm them by reflecting heat; they can cool roots and improve drainage. Rocks often protect plants from frost and wind, and, depending on the type, they may affect the alkalinity or acidity of the soil.

If you have stone formations on your site, you can use them to set off plants and add natural structure and architecture to the garden picture. Lacking natural stone or rock, you need to select your site with care. Where will the rocks look best? Where is the optimum light? Large rocks have more impact, but they cost more and are harder to install—particularly as they look best when buried to two-thirds their depth. Rocks have different qualities—shape, texture, color, hardness, heat reflection, effect on soil pH. Using only one kind of rock from a local source is a good way to simplify things.

In nature, alpine plants grow in a variety of habitats, from soilless ledges, to gravellike fields of scree, to depressions filled with soil. A serious rock gardener may concoct several types of soil, each appropriate for certain plants. For beginners, a mix that accommodates a range of rock-garden plants consists of one part sand (a mix of fine to rough), one part pea-sized gravel, and one part good garden loam.

The plants

A large number of rock-garden plants are tough and drought-tolerant. Many come from places with extreme climates: rocky shores, windswept cliffs, hot steppes, harsh mountainsides. They thrive in intense sunlight, thin soil, cold winters, and strong wind. In fact, the adaptations that make survival possible account for some of their appealing qualities. The attractive small, dense shapes—known as buns and cushions—of many rock-garden plants protect them from wind and drought. The plant acts like a mulch over its own roots, keeping the soil beneath from drying out, from becoming too hot or too cold, or from simply eroding away. The intricate, small forms and textures invite closer scrutiny, fostering a more intimate relationship between the plants and the gardener.

Profuse, tightly packed flowers nestled close to the leaves are also less likely to be windblown and shattered. The abundance of showy flowers helps lure pollinating insects that may be few and far between or active only for a short time during the favorable season. These mats of flowers offer a more agreeable landing site to the pollinator than would a more exposed flower wobbling in the wind on a taller stem.

Beautiful silver, blue, or gray foliage, common among rock-garden plants, results from hair or wax on the leaf surface. The hairs trap rain or dew and also shade and cool the leaf. Wax keeps moisture within the leaf, slowing the wilting process. Leathery, small, often evergreen leaves catch as much sun as possible while minimizing desiccation by heat and wind. Add to the rocky setting and beautiful foliage a careful selection of plants that bloom at many different times of the year, not only the majority of showy spring bloomers, and you can create a most fulfilling year-round garden.

A rock garden needs to be approached with a good deal of patience. Many rock-garden plants are slow-growing—a perennial border matures much more quickly—so consider planting a few of the quicker and less finicky ones to give color and size early on to satisfy you. Then as the garden matures and your taste for the unusual and challenging broadens, you can replace the starter plants with rarer specimens. Like fine wine, a rock garden mellows with the years, the rocks and the plants settling into a comfortable, harmonious relationship.

The rocky hillside planting shown at top is a far cry from the enthusiast's rock garden, filled with rare alpine plants. But it is a lovely solution using common plants (such as the white snow-in-summer) for a difficult site.

Sometimes the rocks can be as compelling as the plants in a rock garden. It takes considerable skill to select and place rocks in a convincing arrangement—the striking example shown above looks perfectly "natural" but is entirely man-made.

With a selection of drought-tolerant plants available, rock gardens are ideal for arid climates. Planted in pockets of amended soil, the plants in this southern California garden (left) include New Zealand flax and several bunchgrasses.

Water in the garden

Flowing water has a special fascination and soothing effect, whether it's a large-scale stream and waterfall, or a gentle trickle into a small rock basin, as shown above.

If space is scarce, consider a vertical water garden. This resourceful example fits a trickling waterfall and pond into a space not much bigger than a generous garden bench.

Water, that fundamental element of all life, has a magical effect in the garden. Lapping serenely at the side of a pond or pool, it soothes, calms, and comforts. Dancing from a fountain or frolicking down a rocky streambed, it supplies music and mirth. Trickling slowly from a length of bamboo onto a weathered stone, it presents an opportunity for contemplation.

Water also provides the means to introduce some fascinating and often unusual plants into the home landscape. Some plants, such as water lilies, with their distinctive pads and beautiful flowers, grow up through the water from submerged rootstocks. Others, such as water hyacinths, float on the surface. A larger group of plants, including marsh marigolds and several irises, prefer "wet feet," growing partially submerged on the banks of a stream or in boggy ground. Essential to many pool, pond, or barrel gardens are plants such as anacharis that oxygenate the water, enabling other plants and fish to survive. Whether your water garden consists of a half-barrel on an urban patio or a half-acre pond in the country, you won't lack for interesting plants.

Fit the feature to the garden

Our natural affinity for water is so powerful that a water feature can easily dominate a garden or a corner of a garden. Integrated thoroughly in the overall garden design, a water feature can be an enormous asset. Ill conceived or poorly executed, such a domineering element can knock the garden scheme out of whack. In an enclosed courtyard garden planted as a miniature mountain meadow or lush rain forest, a lava-rock waterfall can be the perfect touch. Plopped in the middle of a flat suburban lawn, it is more likely to evoke thoughts of miniature golf.

Because a water feature can so easily steal the show (or ruin it), and because some can require extensive construction, consider it very early on when designing your landscape. If you're thinking of putting a water feature into an established landscape, make every effort to match its scale, materials, and style with what is already in place, or be prepared to make substantial alterations to accommodate aspects of the feature that don't "fit" the surroundings.

Construction

If your heart is set on a courtyard fountain or a bubbling backyard stream, it pays to consult an experienced landscape architect or contractor. Any combination of water and electricity, from pumps to pond-side lighting, requires such assistance for your own safety.

Modest pools are well within the boundaries of

most people's skills, budget, and energy. This is largely due to the improvements in vinyl liners, which have replaced concrete construction in many water features. Available from most swimming-pool supply companies, larger garden centers, and specialty mail-order and retail outlets, vinyl liners come in almost any size.

Construction of a linered pool is straightforward, albeit labor-intensive. Because garden pools need only be a few feet deep, many can be dug with pick and shovel. More ambitious projects (or wearier gardeners) may call for an hour or two of a backhoe operator's time. Contoured and padded with an inch or two of sand and a layer of newspaper, the hole is ready for the liner, which must be carefully tucked and smoothed into place. Large flat rocks laid dry or with mortar around the perimeter conceal and pro-

Vinyl liners have made pond building accessible to energetic do-it-yourselfers. The small linered pond above is particularly effective because care has been taken to make it an integral part of the surrounding garden.

A very satisfying water garden can be had in a very small space. The potted patio pond at left contains a half dozen different plants, including cattail, dwarf papyrus, water hyacinth, and two water-lily cultivars.

If water gardening captures your fancy, it might take over your property, as has the lovely backyard creation shown below.

tect the edges of the liner and form a transition to the surrounding landscape.

Lacking a swampy spot on your property, you can construct a bog garden in a similar manner—fill the liner with soil rather than with water. Buy your liner from an experienced, reputable firm, and you'll likely get good advice on installing pools or bogs.

If you haven't the space or energy for a pool or bog, you can make a small water garden in a half-barrel. Set it on the patio, or bury it in the ground to make a miniature pond. You can plant a water-lily tuber in a submerged tub, float a water fern on the surface, maybe even add a colorful fish (along with an oxygenating plant to keep it alive). Beware the fascination of water, however—soon you'll be digging up the backyard, pursuing visions of that placid pond or rippling brook.

Meadow gardens

Depending on where you live, a meadow can be an expanse of colorful wildflowers against a treeless horizon (above); a swath of grasses, daylilies, and black-eyed Susans behind the house (center); or a grassy clearing in the woods (top, facing page).

When an open, sunny area is planted with grasses and flowers so artfully that we are reminded of nature itself at work, the result is what gardeners refer to as a meadow garden. Like its close relative, the woodland garden, the meadow garden derives its appeal equally from our desire to capture some of the unkempt beauty of the "natural" landscape and the desire to commune with the forces shaping those landscapes. Whether you grow a small plot of wildflowers or transform your entire property, meadow gardening can provide many pleasures.

The word *meadow* means different things to different people. To farmers it might signify a grassy swale that is sometimes mown for hay. To mountaineers the word probably evokes a sunny opening in the forest where an ancient sediment-filled lakebed provides a marshy haven for alpine sedges and wildflowers. Both of these sunny, moist, grassy, mostly level areas can serve as models for gardens.

But what if your garden is hilly and your climate so hot and dry that even a small lawn is a luxury? Don't give up on meadow gardening. On a California hillside that bakes under rainless skies seven months a year or on a stretch of desert scrub in

New Mexico, you'll probably call your creation a wildflower garden rather than meadow. Still, by using native plants and others well suited to your local conditions you can develop a garden that has the "natural" feel of a meadow, offering a welcoming habitat for a variety of plants and animals as well as for your family and friends.

Plants for meadow gardens

Meadows (and their cousins, prairies) are by definition grasslands, and the graceful presence of grasses is an indispensable ingredient of the meadow garden. Whether tiny tufts of blue grama huddled against boulders or stately stands of tall bluestem, perennial grasses give the meadow its feeling of place and permanence. Rustling in the wind, they animate the garden, imparting a palpable unity to the scene.

Colorful flowers are the other essential ingredient. Local native wildflowers, plants that evolved together to cope with the climate and soil of your area, make especially satisfying subjects. The huge sunflower family alone provides scores of appropriate plants for the meadow no matter where you garden in North America, from the New England aster to

If you don't have a lot of space, you can still have a meadow planting. The strip of raucous wildflowers and grasses above (including blanket flower, bachelor's-button, and crested wheatgrass) would be just as appealing on an even smaller scale.

the sea dahlia of southern California. But with the entire flora of your area to discover, there is no need to stop with daisies. The meadow garden can host wildflowers as tall and regal as lilies or as down-to-earth as the tiny bird's-foot violets.

Using local native plants helps ensure the compatibility of grasses and flowers. In a prairie garden, strong perennial wildflowers such as purple coneflower won't be smothered by sod-forming prairie grasses. In California and the desert Southwest, desert marigold and other annuals adapted to brief rainy seasons will fill in the spaces between clump-forming grasses. Wildflowers from other regions and even such familiar garden flowers as sweet William, foxglove, and cornflower are candidates, provided they're compatible with the local natives.

Practical matters

Like other gardens, a meadow can be established from seed, from nursery stock, from divisions of existing plants, or from collected specimens. Seed is economical, but cast a critical eye on commercial "wildflower garden" mixtures, which may contain cheap, even weedy, species. Nurseries specializing in native plants of your region can be a prime source of high-quality seeds and plants as well as of reliable information on planting and maintenance.

Creating a meadow garden requires more than just scattering seeds and standing back to watch. Unless you're truly letting nature take its course, some plants will need nurturing, others eradication—weed control is a necessity in the first year or two. Your biggest obstacle may prove to be the disapproval of neighbors who are used to mowed turf and sheared shrubbery. Gentle education and tidy habits—don't let the more rampant self-seeders colonize the neighborhood—help win over skeptics. (For more on starting and maintaining a meadow, see "Making a meadow garden.")

A meadow garden can be enormously satisfying. In addition to its beauty, the workings of its self-perpetuating ecosystem of plants, insects, and animals are an endless source of fascination. When the monarch butterflies return from their fantastic journey to Mexico they will reward you by visiting your meadow, rather than the meticulous expanse of lawn across the street, to sip nectar and lay their eggs. A well-maintained meadow is likely to win you not only admirers but also imitators.

Gardening for wildlife

Even the lowly dandelion can have a place in wildlife gardens. These shelter a toad, a belching basso of prehistoric visage beloved by small children (and not a few adults).

Every gardener is the habitat manager for a diverse population of critters that fly, hop, burrow, scuttle, creep, or crawl. Because of the voracious appetites of a few, we often view creatures in the garden as nuisances or worse and spend considerable energy trying to get rid of them. But for many of us, nesting birds, nectar-seeking butterflies, philosophical toads, and chirping crickets are as great a source of pleasure as flowers. Though these creatures can be found in any garden, it is not difficult to increase their numbers and diversity.

Most wildlife gardeners start small, making gradual changes in their plantings and design as they observe wild visitors and come to know their needs. Virtually any style of garden, with some imaginative planning, can serve as a wildlife garden. Whether you just want to attract some hummingbirds and butterflies to your perennial border or intend designing a full-scale, intensively focused wildlife garden, the same principles apply.

All the world loves butterflies, but only some love raccoons. Animals don't respect property lines; the raccoon you entice to visit won't be so welcome in your neighbor's corn patch. Weigh the possible results of encouraging any particular form of wildlife. And remember that gardening for wild creatures is full of surprises. Nature is complex, and the expected often doesn't happen. The caterpillars nibbling on your big patch of borage may become a feast for wasps rather than the beautiful painted lady butterflies you hoped for.

Gardening for butterflies

Butterflies love sunshine and nectar, and they will avoid shady or windy gardens. Tall lilacs, butterfly bush, and various viburnums can screen breezes while their flowers are rich sources of nectar. Many well-loved flowers are sought by nectaring butterflies. Phlox, lavender, honeysuckle, pinks, bougainvillea, centranthus, candytuft, and sedums are especially favored. Just about all daisy-shaped blossoms, from black-eyed Susans to mammoth sunflowers, are rich in nectar.

Native wildflowers have a special attraction for butterflies. Skippers and sulphurs may mob a native aster while ignoring a less tasty hybrid growing alongside. Joe-Pye weed rates highest marks as a striking accent plant and a superb butterfly flower. If you get serious about butterfly gardening, you'll want to include plants preferred by hungry butterfly caterpillars. Most state wildlife departments and many county extension services furnish listings of nectar plants, emphasizing local native species, and can provide advice on caterpillar delicacies.

Attracting birds

Offer birds suitable foods, clean water, and adequate shelter, and they'll move in. Shelter means nesting sites and refuge areas that provide protection from predators and severe weather. Most birds (like other wild creatures) nest and feed at particular heights. Juncos nest on the ground; chickadees stick to trees, bushes, and stumps. Evaluate your existing plantings; if you have only tall trees and tall shrubs, you're missing part of the show.

The best habitat plants furnish both shelter and food. A small thicket of elderberries feeds a variety of fruit-eating birds and affords good cover, too. Hollies and junipers provide both food and refuge in the cold months. Position feeders adjacent to sheltering evergreens or dense thickets, so songbirds can dash to safety when a hungry shrike or merlin swoops in. Brush piles and wood piles also make fine cover as well as winter insect-hunting grounds. Hollow trees (and man-made snags with drilled cavities) offer nesting sites and winter shelter for woodpeckers, owls, and nuthatches.

Ideally, the garden should afford a year-round source of varied foods: nuts, small seeds, fruits, and insects. Native plants are particularly useful for attracting birds as well as butterflies. Wild cherries, willows, hazels, and alders support and tolerate sizable insect populations. Hummingbirds frequent many of the same nectar flowers as do butterflies. They favor tubular red flowers, but blue pulmonarias, Siberian irises, red-hot-pokers, columbines, monardas, and fuchsias are all popular.

Fresh water is the most important ingredient in a wildlife garden. Animals will travel considerable distances to obtain it. Install a birdbath, a small pool or pond, or a simple drip faucet in your garden, and watch your wild visitors increase in numbers and variety. Remember that small mammals and amphibians need cover, and site your water habitat beside vegetation.

Above all, don't blitz the garden with chemical pesticides. Most birds, especially young birds in the nest, require insects as a first food. The majority of garden insects are not detrimental, but insecticides kill all indiscriminately. The larvae of ladybugs, syrphid flies, and green lacewings are all voracious aphid-eaters. Many leaf-chewing caterpillars become glamorous butterflies. Spare your six-legged visitors—hungry baby robins will thank you.

Depending on your interests, there are many other creatures you may wish to attract to your garden—frogs, toads, salamanders, lizards, garter snakes, chipmunks, bats, and myriad insects. Once you begin to pay attention, you can discover an astonishing variety of wildlife in even the smallest garden. And when you create a haven for this or that creature, the habitat you will end up enriching the most will be your very own.

Providing sites for nesting as well as food and water makes your garden more attractive to birds. Here, a mourning dove and offspring nest in a cholla in a Tucson garden. The birds' coloring is a perfect match for that of the cactus, affording them protection and us a lovely sight.

Viewed up close, monarch caterpillars feasting on butterfly weed (left) are scarcely less beautiful than the lovely creatures they'll ultimately become, like those above seeking nectar from Joe-Pye weed. Wildlife gardeners are willing to trade some chewed leaves for such rewards.

A wildlife garden provides a front-row seat to the wonders of nature, such as this white-lined sphinx moth, which sucks nectar from a zinnia through its long, flexible proboscis.

Acer, Maples

Maples are outstanding specimen and shade trees, popular wherever they grow. All are deciduous, and their leaves often turn brilliant gold, orange, or scarlet in fall. Some are valued for their uniquely shaped leaves; others offer conspicuous flower clusters in spring, colored twigs, or textured bark.

Most maples grow best in rich, moist soil and prefer cool climates, but a few tolerate poor soil and hot, dry weather. Choose one that's adapted to your climate and soil to minimize the risk of insect and disease problems.

Acer ginnala

Acer buergerianum

Acer buergerianum. Trident maple. Height: 25–30 ft. Glossy 3-lobed leaves are dark green in summer, yellow to red in late fall. Tolerates poor soil. Compact enough for patio or courtyard sites. Full or part sun. Zone 4.

Acer campestre. Hedge maple. Height: 40 ft. Long-lasting, dark green, 5-lobed leaves; yellow in fall. Dense crown. Not suitable for mixed plantings. Drought-tolerant. Can be pruned as a hedge. Full sun. Zone 4.

Acer ginnala. Amur maple. Height: 20–25 ft. Leaves are shiny bright green in summer, scarlet in fall. Fragrant flowers form 2-in. star clusters. Tolerates poor soil and dryness. Full or part sun. Zone 3.

Acer campestre

Acer (continued)

Acer japonicum 'Aconitifolium'.
Full-moon maple.
Height: 25 ft. A spreading tree with a rounded crown and many trunks. Lacy or feathery leaves turn crimson to violet in fall. Best in dappled sun or part shade. Zone 5.

Acer japonicum 'Aureum'.
Full-moon maple.
Height: 25 ft. A small spreading tree with a rounded crown and many trunks. Leaves, edged with 7–11 triangular points, are soft gold in summer, bright red in fall. Zone 5.

Acer palmatum 'Bloodgood'.
Japanese maple.
Height: 8–20 ft. Often multitrunked, with a round tiered crown. Deeply lobed, dark reddish purple leaves. Red fruits in fall. Slow-growing. Part sun. Zone 6 or 5.

Acer palmatum 'Dissectum'.
Japanese maple.
Height: 8–25 ft. Often wider than tall, with a round tiered crown. Deeply cut leaves in shades of green, red, bronze, purple, and variegated. Moist, fertile soil. Zone 6 or 5.

Acer rubrum 'October Glory'.
Red maple.
Height: 40–80 ft. Fast-growing, with showy clustered red flowers in early spring, brilliant red foliage in late fall. Ordinary soil and watering. Full sun. Zone 4 or 3.

Acer saccharum.
Sugar maple.
Height: 70–90 ft. A beautiful shade tree for large sites, with spectacular fall color. Full or part sun. Definitely needs fertile, well-drained, moist soil. Zone 3.

Acer japonicum 'Aconitifolium'

Acer saccharum

Acer palmatum 'Bloodgood'

Acer rubrum 'October Glory'

Acer palmatum 'Dissectum'

Acer japonicum 'Aureum'

Betula pendula

Betula platyphylla var. *japonica* 'Whitespire'

Carpinus betulus 'Fastigiata'

Broussonetia papyrifera

Catalpa speciosa

Carpinus caroliniana

Betula pendula.
European white birch.
Height: 40 ft. An erect trunk and drooping branchlets of shiny diamond-shaped leaves that turn gold in fall. Graceful silhouette. Ordinary watering. Full or part sun. Zone 2.

Betula platyphylla var. *japonica* 'Whitespire'.
Height: 45 ft. Narrow upright habit. Chalky white bark is marked with black triangles. Dark green leaves in summer, yellow in fall. Resistant to borers. Zone 4.

Broussonetia papyrifera. Paper mulberry.
Height: 30–50 ft. Fast-growing, with a dense spreading crown. Large heart-shaped or deeply lobed gray-green leaves with rough texture. Tough enough for city streets but can be weedy. Zone 5.

Carpinus betulus 'Fastigiata'.
European hornbeam.
Height: 50 ft. Upright with a narrow symmetrical crown. Can be pruned into formal hedges. Neat foliage is dark green in summer, gold in fall. A healthy tree. Zone 5.

Carpinus caroliniana. American hornbeam.
Height: 15–25 ft. Has a distinctly fluted trunk with taut bluish gray bark. Dark green leaves turn yellow or orange in fall. Small, slow, and neat; good for patios or city gardens. Zone 3.

Celtis occidentalis, above and at right

Carya ovata

Carya illinoinensis

Carya illinoinensis. Pecan.
Height: 125 ft. or more. A stately shade tree with an upright trunk and round crown. Gold fall foliage. Choose grafted cultivars for their large, sweet, thin-shelled nuts. Full sun. Zone 5.

Carya ovata. Shagbark hickory.
Height: 100 ft. An upright crown and drooping branches. Gray bark breaks into long, vertical, curved plates. Leaves turn bright gold in fall. Tasty nuts with woody shells. Full or part sun. Zone 4.

Catalpa speciosa. Southern catalpa.
Height: 40–60 ft. Giant clusters of showy white flowers in early summer. Coarse heart-shaped leaves. Skinny dry pods hang from bare winter limbs. Moderate- to fast-growing. Full sun. Zone 6.

Celtis occidentalis. Hackberry.
Height: 40–90 ft. Upright with a rounded oval crown and drooping branches. Tough gray fins of bark stud the trunk. Small dark berries. Useful for shade in poor soil or on windy sites. Zone 3.

Cercidium floridum. Blue palo verde.
Height: 20–30 ft. Smooth green bark on the trunk and twigs. Covered with yellow flowers in spring. Tiny leaves drop early. Makes light filtered shade for patios and walks. Full sun. Zone 9 or 8.

Cercidium floridum

Cercis canadensis

Chionanthus retusus

Chionanthus virginicus

Cladrastis lutea

Cornus florida

Cornus florida var. *rubra*

Cercis canadensis. Eastern redbud.
Height: 20–35 ft. Stalkless clusters of small pink (sometimes white) flowers dot the bare branches in early spring. Heart-shaped leaves turn gold in fall. Full or part sun. Zone 5.

Chionanthus retusus.
Chinese fringe tree.
Height: to 30 ft. Small, shiny, leathery leaves. Dangling clusters of fragrant white flowers in early summer. Female trees produce blue fruits. Full or part sun. Zone 5.

Chionanthus virginicus. Fringe tree.
Height: to 30 ft. Multitrunked dome. Clusters of white flowers with spicy fragrance in late spring. Females produce dark blue fruits. Native to the Southeast. Full or part sun. Zone 5.

Cladrastis lutea. Yellowwood.
Height: 30–50 ft. Foot-long drooping clusters of sweet, white, pealike flowers in early summer. Compound leaves are bright green in summer, yellow in fall. A perfect shade tree. Full sun. Zone 3.

Cornus florida. Flowering dogwood.
Height: 25 ft. Clouds of white blossoms cover the branches in early spring. (Var. *rubra* has pink flowers.) Leaves turn maroon in fall as red berries ripen. Zone 5.

Cornus florida 'Cherokee Sunset'.
Flowering dogwood.
Height: 25 ft. Variegated foliage is green and gold all summer, turning bright red and orange in fall. Rosy pink blossoms in spring. Red berries. Takes part sun or shade. Zone 5.

Cornus florida 'Cherokee Sunset'

Cornus mas

Cornus kousa

Crataegus crus-galli

Crataegus phaenopyrum

Crataegus viridis 'Winter King'

Cornus kousa.
Kousa dogwood.
Height: to 25 ft. Blossoms in early summer, after flowering dogwood. Bracts are pointed, not rounded. Strawberry-like fruits ripen in late summer. Older trees have attractive flaking bark. Resistant to anthracnose disease. Zone 5.

Cornus mas.
Cornelian cherry dogwood.
Height: 20 ft. Pale yellow clusters of flowers bloom in very early spring. Bright red cherrylike fruits can be made into preserves. Foliage turns yellow, orange, or red in fall. Grows as a large shrub or small tree. Zone 4.

Crataegus crus-galli. Cockspur hawthorn.
Height: 25–30 ft. A strong-thorned tree with a spreading crown. White flowers in late spring. Small red fruits last well into winter. Leaves turn gold, orange, or red in fall. Zone 4.

Crataegus phaenopyrum.
Washington hawthorn.
Height: 25 ft. A tough and adaptable tree with year-round interest. Small white flowers bloom in June. Glossy foliage turns red in fall. Bright red fruits attract birds in winter. Zone 3.

Crataegus viridis 'Winter King'.
Height: 25 ft. A vase-shaped tree with spreading limbs. Clusters of white flowers bloom in late spring. Bright red-orange fruits last through winter. Tough and trouble-free. Zone 4.

Elaeagnus angustifolia

Fagus sylvatica 'Atropurpurea'

Diospyros kaki

Ficus carica

Fagus sylvatica 'Tricolor'

Franklinia alatamaha

Diospyros kaki.
Japanese persimmon.
Height: to 30 ft. A very ornamental tree with large sweet fruits that hang on the branches from fall to winter. Fall foliage is gold to red. Easy to grow. Full sun. Zone 8.

Elaeagnus angustifolia. Russian olive.
Height: 20 ft. or more. Very tough and fast, good for screens or windbreaks on difficult sites. Foliage is shimmering and silvery. Flowers in May are small but very fragrant. Zone 2.

Fagus sylvatica 'Atropurpurea'.
Copper beech.
Height: 60 ft. or more. A majestic specimen tree for large lawns. Leaves are dark blackish purple or purple-green in summer, bronze in fall. Gray bark is very smooth and tight. Zone 5.

Fagus sylvatica 'Tricolor'. Tricolor beech.
Height: 25 ft. or more. Small and slow-growing, this is the best beech for smaller properties. Purple leaves are edged with pink and white. Needs good soil and constant moisture. Zone 5.

Ficus carica. Common fig.
Height: 20–30 ft. Several cultivars are grown for their sweet fruits. Large lobed leaves make a bold contrast with other foliage. Grow in portable tubs where winters are cold. Zone 8 or 7.

Franklinia alatamaha. Franklin tree.
Height: 10–20 ft. Fragrant, frilly, pure white flowers with golden stamens bloom on the

Fraxinus americana

Fraxinus ornus

Fraxinus oxycarpa 'Raywood'

Fraxinus velutina 'Modesto'

tips of branches in late summer and fall. Dark green leaves turn crimson in fall. Full or part sun. Zone 6 or 5.

Fraxinus americana. American ash. Height: 50 ft. or more. A large shade tree with an upright oval crown. Dark green compound leaves turn yellow and purple in fall. Needs deep rich soil to do well. Disease-prone if stressed. Zone 3.

Fraxinus ornus. Flowering ash. Height: 40 ft. Good shade tree with a domed crown. Large clusters of fragrant white flowers in May; winged fruits in summer or fall. Dark green leaves turn yellow in fall. Full or part sun. Zone 6 or 5.

***Fraxinus oxycarpa* 'Raywood'.** Narrow-leaved ash. Height: 25–35 ft. Dark green leaves with long narrow leaflets have purplish red fall color. This cultivar is seedless and makes a tidy street or lawn specimen. Zone 6.

***Fraxinus pennsylvanica* 'Summit'.** Green ash. Height: 50–60 ft. A good shade tree for the plains. Grows fast in any soil. Can be underplanted with perennials. This cultivar is seedless. Compound leaves turn yellow in fall. Zone 2.

***Fraxinus velutina* 'Modesto'.** Arizona ash. Height: to 50 ft. Compound leaves are fuzzy gray at first, turn bright green as they expand, then turn golden in fall. Fast-growing. Good shade tree for the Southwest. Full sun. Zone 6.

Fraxinus pennsylvanica 'Summit'

Ginkgo biloba

Gleditsia triacanthos var. inermis

Gymnocladus dioica

Halesia carolina

Jacaranda mimosifolia

Ginkgo biloba. Ginkgo.
Height: 50–80 ft. Clusters of delicate
fan-shaped leaves turn clear yellow in fall.
Irregular branching makes an angular
specimen. Very tough and adaptable. Zone 4.

Gleditsia triacanthos var. inermis.
Thornless honey locust.
Height: 40–60 ft. Spreading crown of lacy
compound leaves casts a light filtered shade.
Foliage turns yellow in fall. May bear a few
long curved pods. Fast-growing. Zone 4.

Gymnocladus dioica. Kentucky coffee tree.
Height: 60–70 ft. Large leaves have small
leaflets. Bark curls into scaly ridges. Fragrant
greenish white flowers in late May or June.
Females bear woody pods. Zone 4.

Halesia carolina. Carolina silver-bell.
Height: 30–50 ft. Dangling white blossoms
are lovely in spring; woody pods are
interesting later. Native to eastern woodlands;
needs rich, moist, acidic soil and can take
light shade. Zone 4.

Jacaranda mimosifolia. Jacaranda.
Height: to 40 ft. Large, showy, long-lasting
clusters of wide blue-violet flowers bloom in
spring or summer. Delicate, fernlike,
compound leaves drop only when the flowers
appear. Full sun. Zone 9.

Koelreuteria paniculata. Golden-rain tree.
Height: 30–35 ft. Yellow flowers in
midsummer are followed by puffy pinkish
beige pods that last into winter. Has deep
roots, so it's good for underplanting. Zone 5.

Lagerstroemia fauriei. Crape myrtle.
Height: to 25 ft. Flowers are not as showy as
those of *L. indica,* but the bark is prettier and
the tree is hardier. Zone 6.

Lagerstroemia indica. Crape myrtle.
Height: to 25 ft. Very popular in the South
and Southwest. Bright flowers are showy all
summer; fall color is vivid; flaking bark is
striking in winter. Zone 7.

Lagerstroemia 'Natchez'. Crape myrtle.
Height: to 25 ft. This is one of several new
cultivars released by the National Arboretum,
with mildew-resistant foliage and particularly
handsome bark. Dies back but recovers in
Zone 6.

Liquidambar styraciflua 'Palo Alto'.
Sweet gum.
Height: 60 ft. or more. An easy-to-grow tree
with outstanding fall color even if
temperatures aren't very cold. Winged twigs
and prickly seed balls look interesting in
winter. Zone 6.

Liriodendron tulipifera. Tulip tree.
Height: 70 ft. or more. An eastern native that
grows fast in rich, moist soil. Flowers in early
summer. Unusual-shaped leaves turn warm
yellow in fall. Gets too big for small gardens.
Zone 5.

Koelreuteria paniculata

Lagerstroemia fauriei

Lagerstroemia indica

Lagerstroemia 'Natchez'

Liriodendron tulipifera

Liquidambar styraciflua 'Palo Alto'

Magnolia, Magnolias

Magnolias are fine specimens for year-round interest. They are best loved for their large showy flowers, which are often quite fragrant. Most kinds bloom in spring, before or as the leaves open. The foliage is healthy and attractive all summer. The conelike fruits release bright-colored seeds in fall, and the furry flower buds and gray twigs are handsome in winter.

Some of these deciduous magnolias stay quite small and might be called shrubs, not trees. Others get taller and develop a wide, spreading crown. Most grow best in deep, well-drained soil topped with a thick layer of mulch. They need little pruning and have few pests or diseases.

Magnolia 'Galaxy'

Magnolia 'Betty'

***Magnolia* 'Betty'.**
Height: to 10 ft. Usually makes an upright shrub, not a tree. Fragrant flowers open late enough to avoid spring frosts. One of the Kosar-DeVos hybrids. Zone 5.

***Magnolia* 'Elizabeth'.**
Height: 35 ft. or more. A vigorous, healthy tree. Clear yellow flowers are lightly scented. Blooms late enough to avoid frost damage. Zone 5.

***Magnolia* 'Galaxy'.**
Height: 20–30 ft. A new hybrid with a narrow upright habit, ideal for small spaces or as a street tree. Vigorous and fast-growing. Flowers in spring. Zone 6 or 5.

***Magnolia* × *loebneri* 'Merrill'.**
Height: 20–30 ft. A vigorous large shrub or small tree. Fragrant flowers open late enough to avoid frost damage. An adaptable tree; grows well across the United States. Zone 4.

Magnolia sieboldii. Oyama magnolia.
Height: 12–15 ft. Round flowers are very fragrant. Blooms mostly in May and June but continues throughout summer. A small, neat tree. Can take part shade.
Zone 7.

Magnolia* × *soulangiana.
Saucer magnolia, tulip tree.
Height: to 30 ft. One of the most popular magnolias. Flowers open just before the leaves and are damaged by late frosts some years. Adapts to many soils and climates. Zone 5.

Magnolia sieboldii

Magnolia 'Elizabeth'

Magnolia × *soulangiana*

Magnolia × *loebneri* 'Merrill'

Magnolia (continued)

Magnolia stellata

Malus 'Donald Wyman'

Magnolia tripetala

Magnolia stellata. Star magnolia.
Height: 10–15 ft. The first magnolia to
open in early spring (February to April,
depending on where you live). Plant on
the north or east side of a building or
fence to protect it from frost damage.
Grows slowly; stays small for years.
Zone 5 or 4.

Magnolia tripetala.
Umbrella magnolia.
Height: to 40 ft. Large fleshy fruits are
showy in fall. Has very large leaves, like
M. macrophylla, that give a tropical effect.
An eastern native, hardy to Zone 5.

Magnolia virginiana.
Sweet-bay magnolia.
Height: 20–60 ft. A variable plant—can
be deciduous or evergreen, shrubby or
tree-sized. In any form, it has spicy-
scented leaves and fragrant white flowers
in summer. Tolerates wet soil and shade.
Zone 5.

Malus 'Red Jewel'

Magnolia virginiana

Malus 'Selkirk'

Malus floribunda

Malus 'Donald Wyman'.
Crab apple.
Height: 20 ft. Bright red fruits last for months, sometimes until the new flowers open in spring. Forms a rounded crown. Disease-resistant. Zone 4.

Malus floribunda.
Japanese crab apple.
Height: 20–25 ft. Buds are red; flowers are pink fading to white. Small fruits ripen from yellow to reddish brown in fall. Grows well in most of the United States. Needs well-drained soil. Zone 4.

Malus 'Hopa'. Crab apple.
Height: to 30 ft. An old standby that looks pretty in bloom but is very vulnerable to scab, rust, and mildew, especially in humid climates. Can look quite ragged by midsummer. Zone 4.

Malus 'Red Jewel'.
Crab apple.
Height: 15 ft. Forms an upright oval crown. Flowers are pure white. Fruits turn golden brown by midwinter. Disease-resistant. Zone 4.

Malus 'Selkirk'. Crab apple.
Height: 25 ft. Forms an open vase-shaped crown. Fruits are glossy reddish purple. Disease-resistant. Zone 4.

Nyssa sylvatica.
Sour gum.
Height: 30–60 ft. An eastern native with outstanding fall color, even where autumn weather is warm. Color begins early and lasts long. Not fussy about soil. Adaptable and pest-free. Zone 3.

Oxydendrum arboreum. Sourwood.
Height: 30 ft. or more. White flowers open in summer. Fall color starts early and develops into blazing scarlet, orange, and burgundy. Prefers well-drained, acidic, organic soil. Zone 4.

Malus 'Hopa'

Nyssa sylvatica

Oxydendrum arboreum

Parrotia persica, above and at right

Phellodendron amurense

Pistacia chinensis

Parkinsonia aculeata

Parkinsonia aculeata. Jerusalem thorn. Height: 25–30 ft. A tough small tree that tolerates heat and drought. Blooms mostly in spring and again after summer rains. Branches are spiny. Tiny leaflets cast a filtered shade. Zone 8.

Parrotia persica. Persian parrotia. Height: 15–20 ft. or more. A small tree with yearlong interest: flaking bark, small reddish flowers, and healthy leaves that turn brilliant shades of gold, pink, and red in fall. Zone 3.

Phellodendron amurense. Amur cork tree. Height: 30–45 ft. Attractive bark matures into corky ridges. Compound leaves cast a light shade. Black fruits in fall are ornamental but messy, and seedlings can be weedy. Zone 4.

Pistacia chinensis. Chinese pistache. Height: 40 ft. or more. One of the best trees for fall color in warm climates. Tough, adaptable, and neat. Tolerates alkaline soil and drought. No serious pests. Zone 7 or 6.

Platanus occidentalis. American sycamore. Height: 100 ft. A native tree with very distinctive bark. Grows wild in rich, moist soil throughout the eastern United States. Old trees are massive. Susceptible to insects and diseases. Zone 5.

Populus deltoides. Eastern cottonwood. Height: 60–100 ft. Useful as a fast-growing shade tree, especially in the Great Plains. Gold fall color. Choose male cultivars to avoid the mess of cottony seeds. Roots are invasive. Zone 3.

Prosopis glandulosa. Honey mesquite. Height: to 30 ft. Grows wild across much of Texas and the Southwest. Has fragrant yellow flowers in spring, tan pods in fall.

Populus deltoides

Prunus cerasifera 'Thundercloud'

Platanus occidentalis

Prunus subhirtella var. *autumnalis*

Tolerates poor, dry soil; can't take wet soil. Zone 6.

Prunus cerasifera 'Thundercloud'.
Purple-leaf plum.
Height: 15 25 ft. Has single pink flowers in early spring. Plums are edible but not tasty. Needs full sun for good foliage color. Fast-growing but often short lived. Zone 5.

Prunus sargentii. Sargent cherry.
Height: 40–50 ft. The largest flowering cherry, and the best to use as a street tree. Blooms for weeks in midspring. Leaves turn bright orange-red in fall. Zone 4.

Prunus subhirtella var. autumnalis.
Autumn cherry.
Height: 20–30 ft. Has double white or pale pink flowers in late fall, during mild spells in winter, and most abundantly in early spring. Zone 6.

Prosopis glandulosa

Prunus sargentii

Prunus × yedoensis

Robinia pseudoacacia

Pterostyrax hispidus, above and at right

Sapium sebiferum

Pyrus calleryana 'Bradford'

Prunus × yedoensis. Yoshino cherry.
Height: 25–45 ft. Blooms in early spring.
Most of Washington, D.C.'s celebrated
cherry trees belong to this species. There are
various rounded or weeping forms with
single or double, pink or white flowers.
Zone 6.

Pterostyrax hispidus.
Fragrant epaulette tree.
Height: 40 ft. Has fragrant white flowers in
May or June, after the leaves have expanded.
Develops a round open crown. Hard to find
at nurseries but easy to grow and pest-free.
Zone 5.

***Pyrus calleryana* 'Bradford'.** Bradford pear.
Height: 30–60 ft. Flowers in early spring.
Glossy leaves are dark green in summer and
often turn bright red, orange, yellow, or
purple in fall. Tolerates poor growing
conditions. Zone 5.

Quercus. (See pp. 126–127.)

Robinia pseudoacacia. Black locust.
Height: 50 ft. or more. Large clusters of
white flowers are very fragrant in spring.
A fast-growing native tree that tolerates poor
soil. Lacy compound leaves cast a filtered
shade. Seedlings are weedy. Zone 4.

***Salix alba* 'Tristis'.**
Golden weeping willow.
Height: 50 ft. or more. A graceful tree that
thrives in damp soil. Slender leaves turn
yellow in late fall. Twigs are yellow in winter.
Flowers and leafs out in early spring. Zone 2.

***Salix matsudana* 'Tortuosa'.**
Twisted Hankow willow.
Height: 30 ft. Twigs and stems twist and
spiral like a corkscrew. Slender leaves are
dark green in summer, yellow in fall. Grows
fast, especially in moist soil. Zone 5.

Salix alba 'Tristis'

Salix matsudana 'Tortuosa'

Sassafras albidum, above and at right

Sapindus drumondii.
Soapberry.
Height: 40–50 ft. A good shade tree for difficult sites with very poor, dry soil. Compound leaves turn yellow in fall, and grape-sized yellow fruits hang on into winter. Zone 6.

Sapium sebiferum.
Chinese tallow tree.
Height: 25–50 ft. A fast-growing tree that tolerates poor, dry soil. Has spread like a weed in the South but not (yet) in other regions. Leaves are dark green in summer, red in fall. Zone 7.

Sassafras albidum. Sassafras.
Height: 40–60 ft. A native tree, hard to transplant but easy to grow. All parts have a rich spicy fragrance. Lobed leaves resemble mittens and develop wonderful fall color. Zone 5.

Sapindus drumondii

Quercus, Oaks

Oaks are majestic trees that make ideal specimens for large lawns. Their leaves provide shade all summer and color in the fall, their acorns feed birds and wildlife, and their spreading limbs and rugged bark offer an interesting winter silhouette. Nearly all of the deciduous oaks grown in this country are native species. The key to success is choosing the right oak for any particular site. Given suitable soil, moisture, and climate, oaks grow steadily, require little pruning, and live for hundreds of years.

Quercus coccinea

Quercus acutissima

Quercus falcata

Quercus gambelii

Quercus alba

Quercus acutissima. Sawtooth oak. Height: 35–50 ft. Leaves turn tan or gold in fall. Does best in well-drained, acidic soil. Tolerates dry soil. Fast-growing. Zone 5.

Quercus alba.
Eastern white oak.
Height: 50–100 ft. Forms a broad open canopy. Leaves turn red or purple in fall. Prefers rich, deep, well-drained soil. Zone 4.

Quercus coccinea. Scarlet oak.
Height: 50–100 ft. Resembles pin oak, *Q. palustris,* but is more tolerant of dry or alkaline soil. Good fall color. Zone 5.

Quercus falcata. Southern red oak.
Height: 50–70 ft. Resembles northern red oak, *Q. rubra,* but has leaves with fewer lobes and tolerates poor, dry soil. Zone 7.

Quercus gambelii.
Gambel oak.
Height: 15–30 ft. More shrubby than treelike. Often spreads slowly to make a low colony. Tolerates dry, rocky soil. Zone 5.

Quercus macrocarpa. Bur oak.
Height: 70–80 ft. The best oak for the plains states. Bark, twigs, and acorns have lots of character. Very hardy. Zone 3.

Quercus phellos. Willow oak.
Height: 50–90 ft. Has slender willowlike leaves. A fine shade tree. Prefers damp soil. Does well in the South. Zone 6 or 5.

Aronia melanocarpa

Berberis thunbergii 'Atropurpurea Nana'

Berberis koreana

Berberis × mentorensis

Buddleia alternifolia 'Argentea'

Buddleia davidii 'Fascination'

Berberis × mentorensis. Mentor barberry.
Height: 6 ft. Forms a spiny, upright,
multistemmed dome. Teardrop-shaped leaves
turn fiery red-orange in fall. Dense and
durable. Useful as a hedge or barrier. Zone 5.

Berberis thunbergii 'Atropurpurea Nana'.
Japanese barberry.
Height: 2 ft. Very compact and naturally
round. Deep crimson foliage turns gold in
fall. Thorny stems and bright red berries.
Good as an entryway planting. Full sun.
Zone 4.

Buddleia alternifolia 'Argentea'.
Fountain butterfly bush.
Height: 15 ft. Arching branches with dense
clusters of fragrant lilac flowers in early
summer. Silky silvery leaves. Cascades down
a hillside or embankment. Full sun. Zone 5.

Buddleia davidii 'Fascination'.
Butterfly bush.
Height: to 10 ft. Long clusters of fragrant
pink flowers at the tips of arching branches
attract butterflies from midsummer to fall.
Other cultivars have purple, blue, or white
flowers. Zone 5.

Caesalpinia gilliesii

Callicarpa dichotoma

Calycanthus floridus

Caryopteris × clandonensis

Chaenomeles japonica

Caesalpinia gilliesii. Bird-of-paradise. Height: 10 ft. Feathery twice-compound leaves. Clusters of yellow flowers with bright red stamens bloom all summer. Quick-growing but needs hot weather. Showy accent or screen. Zone 8.

Callicarpa dichotoma. Korean beautyberry. Height: 4 ft. Arching stems have paired clusters of small flowers in spring, bright violet-lilac berries in fall. Good for mass plantings. Full or part sun. Zone 6 or 5.

Calycanthus floridus. Sweet shrub. Height: 6–9 ft. Large, fragrant, maroon flowers in midspring. Glossy oblong leaves turn bright yellow or gold in fall. Sun or shade. Zone 4.

Caryopteris × clandonensis. Bluebeard. Height: 2–3 ft. Fluffy clusters of lavender-blue flowers attract butterflies in August and September. Leaves and stems are soft and gray. Cut to the ground each spring. Full sun. Zone 6 or 5.

Chaenomeles speciosa 'Toyo Nishiki'

Clerodendrum trichotomum

Chimonanthus praecox

Clethra alnifolia 'Rosea'

Clethra barbinervis

Chaenomeles japonica. Flowering quince. Height: 4–6 ft. Small and spreading, with crooked thorny branches. Bright scarlet, crimson, orange, pink, or white scentless flowers in early spring. Fragrant fruits make a tasty jelly. Zone 4.

Chaenomeles speciosa 'Toyo Nishiki'. Height: 8 ft. White, pink, red, and two-tone flowers bloom all on the same plant. Upright growth habit. Yellow-green fruits smell spicy-sweet in fall. Zone 4.

Chimonanthus praecox. Wintersweet. Height: 9 ft. Irregular and multistemmed, with clusters of very fragrant, pale yellow flowers in late winter. Plant nearby, where it will perfume entryways or patios. Full or part sun. Zone 7.

Clerodendrum trichotomum. Harlequin glory-bower. Height: 10–15 ft. A large spreading shrub with upright stems. Makes showy clusters of white flowers with long-lasting, purple-red calyxes and bright blue, pea-sized berries. Zone 6.

Clethra alnifolia 'Rosea'. Sweet pepperbush. Height: 9 ft. A slow-spreading shrub with upright stems topped with spires of very fragrant, pale pink flowers in midsummer. Leafs out in late spring. Full or partial sun. Zone 5.

Clethra barbinervis. Japanese clethra. Height: 12–15 ft. Slender clusters of sweet flowers at the branch tips in midsummer. Older stems have shedding gray-brown bark. Good in a border shaded by tall trees. Part sun. Zone 6.

Comptonia peregrina. Sweet fern. Height: to 4 ft. Fragrant dark green leaves have a leathery texture. Spreads slowly to make small patches. Tolerates disturbed soil, sandy or acidic sites. Full or part sun. Zone 3.

Comptonia peregrina

Cornus alba 'Elegantissima'

Cornus sericea 'Cardinal'

Cornus sericea 'Flaviramea'

Cornus sericea

Corylopsis pauciflora

***Cornus alba* 'Elegantissima'.**
Variegated Siberian dogwood.
Height: 6–8 ft. Pretty all year. White flowers in spring; variegated leaves in summer and fall; bright red twigs in winter. Easy to grow in sun or shade. Zone 2.

Cornus sericea. Red-osier dogwood.
Height: to 10 ft. An adaptable native for hedges or mass plantings. Stems are bright red in winter. White flowers in spring. Leaves turn purple in fall. Easy to grow. Zone 2.

***Cornus sericea* 'Cardinal'.**
Height: to 10 ft. Outstanding in winter, as bark color changes from cherry red to watermelon pink to chartreuse. White flowers in spring; lush green foliage all summer. Easy to grow. Zone 2.

***Cornus sericea* 'Flaviramea'.**
Height: to 10 ft. Stems turn golden yellow in winter. Good for mixed hedges or borders. Can be used to stabilize soil along a pond edge or creek bank. Full sun, part sun, or shade. Zone 2.

Corylopsis pauciflora.
Buttercup winter hazel.
Height: 4–6 ft. Fragrant primrose yellow flowers in early spring. Needs a site protected from late frosts. Small, bluish green, heart-shaped leaves turn yellow in fall. Zone 5.

***Corylus avellana* 'Contorta'.**
Harry Lauder's walking stick.
Height: 7 ft. A distinctive plant for the winter garden. Shiny brown branches twist into irregular spirals. Long dangling catkins in late winter and early spring. Zone 4.

Corylus avellana 'Contorta'

Cotoneaster apiculatus

Cotinus coggygria 'Notcutt's Variety'

Cotoneaster divaricatus

Cotoneaster horizontalis

Cotinus coggygria 'Notcutt's Variety'.
Smoke tree.
Height: 12–18 ft. Rich purple foliage
contrasts dramatically with other plants.
Fluffy flower stalks last all summer. Tolerates
poor soil. Prune hard each year for best
appearance. Zone 3.

Cotoneaster apiculatus.
Cranberry cotoneaster.
Height: 3 ft. A good ground cover for cold
climates. Layers of arching stems trail down
slopes or over walls. Small glossy leaves turn
burgundy in fall. Red fruits. Zone 3.

Cotoneaster divaricatus.
Spreading cotoneaster.
Height: 5–6 ft. Makes an open airy mound
with small leaves that turn red in fall. Most

graceful if unpruned. Pink flowers in May.
Bright red berries from late summer into
winter. Zone 5.

Cotoneaster horizontalis.
Rockspray cotoneaster.
Height: 3 ft. Branches form a distinctive
herringbone pattern and make a layered
mound. Fine-textured foliage reddens in fall.
Red berries in fall and winter. Good over a
wall or bank. Zone 4.

Cotoneaster multiflorus.
Many-flowered cotoneaster.
Height: 10 ft. Very showy, with abundant
white flowers and large clusters of red fruits.
Graceful fountainlike habit. Give it plenty
of room. Full or part sun. Zone 3.

Cotoneaster multiflorus

Cytisus × praecox 'Warminster'

Cytisus × praecox 'Hollandia'

Daphne × burkwoodii 'Carol Mackie'

Daphne caucasica

***Cytisus × praecox* 'Hollandia'.** Broom. Height: 3–5 ft. A twiggy shrub with many gray-green stems, leafless most of the year. Covered with two-tone pinkish red and white flowers in spring. Needs good drainage. Zone 5.

***Cytisus × praecox* 'Warminster'.** Warminster broom. Height: 3–5 ft. Showy creamy white or pale yellow flowers last for weeks in spring. Twiggy habit combines well with conifers or other evergreens. Needs full sun and well-drained soil. Zone 5.

***Daphne × burkwoodii* 'Carol Mackie'.** Height: 3–4 ft. A dense, compact, mounded shrub. Oval green leaves are edged with gold. Blooms profusely in late spring. Small, starry, pale pink flowers are very fragrant. Adaptable but slow-growing. Zone 4.

Daphne caucasica. Height: 6 ft. Fragrant white flowers begin in late spring. Makes an upright open shrub that needs little pruning. Small leaves are evergreen in mild climates. Zone 6 or 5.

Daphne mezereum. Height: 2–3 ft. White, pink, purplish, or dark purple flowers are notably fragrant in early spring. Bright red berries in summer and fall. Slow-growing and tricky, but deserves a try. Zone 4.

Deutzia gracilis. Slender deutzia. Height: 3–4 ft. Clusters of snow-white blossoms weigh down the branches in late spring, after most shrubs have finished. Prune after flowering. Easy to grow. Full sun. Zone 4.

Enkianthus campanulatus. Height: 10–15 ft. Profuse clusters of red-veined, light yellow, bell-shaped flowers in spring. Leaves turn orange-red in fall. Grows narrowly erect; can fit beside a building. Part shade. Zone 5.

***Euonymus alata* 'Compacta'.** Dwarf burning bush. Height: to 6 ft. Remarkable for its brilliant red-pink fall color. Often used as a hedge. Looks best unpruned. Branches form soft overlapping layers. Very adaptable and tough. Zone 3.

***Exochorda × macrantha* 'The Bride'.** Pearlbush. Height: 3–5 ft. An old-fashioned favorite. Pearllike buds on arching stems open into snow-white blossoms. Blooms in April or May. Foliage is blue-green in summer, yellow in fall. Zone 5 or 4.

Exochorda racemosa. Common pearlbush. Height: to 15 ft. Arching branches carry bright white buds and blossoms in spring. Inconspicuous when not in bloom. Grows quite large and can be trained into a small multitrunked tree. Zone 4.

Daphne mezereum

Enkianthus campanulatus

Exochorda racemosa

Deutzia gracilis

Euonymus alata 'Compacta', at left and above

Exochorda × macrantha 'The Bride'

Forsythia × intermedia

Fothergilla major

Hamamelis × intermedia 'Jelena'

Hamamelis mollis

Hamamelis virginiana

Forsythia × intermedia. Forsythia.
Height: 8 ft. or more. Showy, cheerful yellow flowers are among the first to appear in early spring. Spreads into a broad arching mound. Foliage is purplish in fall. Tough and adaptable. Full sun. Zone 4.

Fothergilla major.
Large fothergilla.
Height: 6–10 ft. Dense bottlebrush-like clusters of honey-scented flowers form at the ends of twigs in spring. Leathery dark green leaves turn red, orange, and yellow in fall. Zone 5.

Hamamelis × intermedia 'Jelena'.
Witch hazel.
Height: 15–20 ft. or more. Coppery orange flowers open in very early spring. Sometimes reblooms in late summer. Fall foliage is red, orange, and yellow. A lovely small tree. Zone 6 or 5.

Hamamelis mollis.
Chinese witch hazel.
Height: 15–20 ft. or more. Flowers are small but intensely fragrant when they open in late winter. Blooms for up to 4 weeks. Fall foliage is clear yellow. Easy to grow. Zone 6 or 5.

Hamamelis virginiana.
Common witch hazel.
Height: 10 ft. or more. Native to moist sites throughout the eastern United States. Fragrant yellow flowers open in fall, as the leaves drop off. Spreads to make a thicket. Zone 4.

Hibiscus syriacus 'Diana'.
Rose-of-Sharon.
Height: about 8 ft. This is one of several new cultivars that have large single flowers and don't set seed. Blooms from midsummer to fall. Adaptable and carefree. Zone 5.

Hydrangea macrophylla.
Hydrangea.
Height: 4–8 ft. A popular shrub for mild climates. Rounded clusters of flowers are pink, blue, or white. Leaves are thick and glossy. Hardy to Zone 6 but flowers only where winters are mild.

Hibiscus syriacus 'Diana'

Hydrangea macrophylla 'Mariesii Variegata'

Hydrangea macrophylla

Hydrangea paniculata 'Grandiflora'

Hydrangea macrophylla 'Mariesii Variegata'.

Height: 2–3 ft. Worth growing for its foliage, which brightens a shady corner, but this variegated form grows slower than all-green types. Hardy to Zone 6 but flowers only in Zone 9 or 8.

Hydrangea paniculata 'Grandiflora'.

Peegee hydrangea.

Height: 10–25 ft. Flowers open white in summer and darken to pink or tan, lasting all fall and winter. Leaves turn bronzy in fall. Easy, adaptable, and fast-growing. Zone 3.

Hydrangea quercifolia 'Snowflake'.

Oakleaf hydrangea.

Height: 4–8 ft. Has 12-in. clusters of double flowers, larger and showier than the wild species. Large oaklike leaves turn red, orange, or purplish in fall. Slow but trouble-free. Zone 5.

Hydrangea quercifolia 'Snowflake'

Hypericum calycinum

Hypericum 'Hidcote'

Ilex decidua 'Warren Red'

Ilex 'Sparkleberry'

Ilex verticillata 'Winter Red'

Itea virginica

Kerria japonica 'Pleniflora'

Hypericum calycinum.
Height: 12–18 in. Flowers off and on from
June to September. Often dies back to the
ground in winter but recovers quickly and
blooms on new wood. Makes a good ground
cover. Zone 5.

Hypericum 'Hidcote'.
Height: 3–4 ft. Clusters of 3-in. flowers keep
opening all summer. Makes a neat leafy
mound. Recovers quickly from frost damage
or heavy pruning. Trouble-free. Zone 5.

Ilex decidua 'Warren Red'.
Possum haw.
Height: 15 ft. or more. Pea-sized red berries
hang on well into winter, until birds eat
them all. Needs full sun for best fruiting.
Grows in almost any soil. Pest-free. Zone 5.

Ilex 'Sparkleberry'.
Height: to 12 ft. A vigorous hybrid that
bears tremendous crops of berries, even as a
young plant. Showy throughout fall and
winter months. Tolerates poorly drained soil.
Zone 3.

Ilex verticillata 'Winter Red'.
Winterberry holly.
Height: to 9 ft. An upright shrub with many
branching stems. Red berries ripen in fall and
last into winter. Native to wetlands; tolerates
poorly drained soil. Pest-free. Zone 3.

Itea virginica.
Virginia sweetspire.
Height: 3–5 ft. or more. A hardy native with
fragrant white flowers and bright green leaves
in midsummer. Turns scarlet in fall. Grows
well near ponds and streams. Needs moist,
fertile soil. Zone 5.

Jasminum nudiflorum.
Winter jasmine.
Height: to 4 ft. A trailing vinelike shrub,
good for spilling down a bank or climbing a
wall. Blooms off and on for several weeks,
starting in late winter. Needs pruning to
control size. Zone 6.

Kerria japonica 'Pleniflora'.
Height: to 6 ft. Blooms mostly in spring,
sporadically in summer. Does best in part
shade. Stems are bright green in winter. This
cultivar has double flowers. Easy to grow.
Zone 4.

Kolkwitzia amabilis.
Beautybush.
Height: 10 ft. or more. Blooms for about
3 weeks in spring or early summer. Bristly
pink fruits are pretty in summer. Prune after
flowering to stimulate new shoots. Zone 5.

Lespedeza thunbergii 'Alba'.
Bush clover.
Height: 6–8 ft. Brightens the garden in late
summer with white flowers that attract
butterflies. Prune to the ground each spring;
blooms on new wood. Tolerates poor, dry
soil. Zone 5.

Jasminum nudiflorum

Kolkwitzia amabilis

Lespedeza thunbergii 'Alba'

Ligustrum obtusifolium **var.** *regelianum.*
Regel's border privet.
Height: 5–6 ft. The most interesting and attractive privet for northern gardens, and so tough that it's planted along highways. Good for hedges or as a specimen. Flowers in June. Zone 3.

Ligustrum sinense **'Variegatum'.**
Chinese privet.
Height: 6 ft. or more. White-variegated leaves are bright all season, and white flowers open in summer. Very tough and adaptable; grows in any soil with no care. Zone 7.

Lonicera fragrantissima. Winter honeysuckle.
Height: 8 ft. Small white flowers are very sweet in early spring. Birds eat the red berries in summer. Spreads quite wide unless you keep it pruned. Hardy to Zone 5, but flower buds may freeze.

Lonicera **'Freedom'.**
Height: 8–12 ft. A new hybrid with resistance to the aphids that disfigure (and can kill) common Tartarian honeysuckle. Good for windbreaks or screens on difficult sites. Zone 4 or 3.

Malus sargentii.
Sargent crab apple.
Height: 6–10 ft. Spreads $1^1/_2$–2 times as wide as it is tall, with dense, horizontal, zigzag branches that look interesting in winter. Blooms later than other crab apples, and blooms more heavily in alternate years. Red fruits attract birds. Zone 5.

Myrica pensylvanica.
Bayberry.
Height: 8–10 ft. Leaves look particularly fresh and glossy all summer; are semievergreen in the South. Silver-gray berries are coated with a fragrant wax, used to make bayberry candles. Tolerates poor, sandy soil and salt spray. Spreads slowly. Zone 4 or 3.

Philadelphus coronarius.
Common mock orange.
Height: 10 ft. An old-fashioned shrub, common around old farmhouses. Blooms for 1–2 weeks in late spring. Flowers have a penetrating sweet fragrance. Easy to grow. Zone 4.

Philadelphus × *virginalis* **'Miniature Snowflake'.**
Height: 3 ft. A low, spreading shrub with very fragrant double flowers in late spring. Smells just as sweet as common mock orange but takes much less space; better for small gardens. Zone 4.

Potentilla fruticosa **'Abbotswood'.**
Bush cinquefoil.
Height: 2–3 ft. Blooms all summer. Other cultivars have pale or deep yellow flowers. Makes a low, spreading, rounded shrub. Good for mass plantings in dry, sandy soil. Zone 2.

Punica granatum **'Flore Pleno'.**
Pomegranate.
Height: 15–20 ft. Blooms for months where summers are hot. Flowers are double or single, usually bright orange-red. Can be espaliered or shaped as a shrub or small tree. Zone 8.

Ligustrum obtusifolium var. *regelianum*

Ligustrum sinense 'Variegatum'

Lonicera fragrantissima

Lonicera 'Freedom'

Malus sargentii

Myrica pensylvanica

Philadelphus coronarius

Philadelphus × virginalis 'Miniature Snowflake'

Potentilla fruticosa 'Abbotswood'

Punica granatum 'Flore Pleno'

Rhododendron, Azaleas

Deciduous azaleas are hardy shrubs with upright or spreading forms. There are many species (including several natives) and hundreds of hybrid cultivars to choose from. The flowers come in a wide range of colors, and many kinds have a penetrating sweet fragrance. The bloom season starts in very early spring and continues through July or August. Many deciduous azaleas have very handsome foliage that turns bright colors for several weeks in fall.

Most grow best in rich, moist, well-drained, acidic soil with sun or part shade. Choosing the right site and preparing the soil are the keys to success. Once planted, these shrubs require little care and offer years of satisfaction.

Rhododendron arborescens

Rhododendron mucronulatum 'Cornell Pink'

Rhododendron periclymenoides

Rhododendron arborescens.
Tree azalea.
Height: 6–8 ft. or more. White or pale pink flowers have a very sweet, penetrating fragrance. Blooms for 2 weeks or more in late June and July. Native to the Appalachians. Zone 5 or 4.

Rhododendron mucronulatum 'Cornell Pink'.
Height: 6 ft. A deciduous rhododendron, native to China and Korea. Blooms in very early spring, before the leaves expand. Very easy and trouble-free. Zone 5.

Rhododendron periclymenoides.
Pinxterbloom azalea.
Height: 4–6 ft. White or pink flowers are very fragrant in April or May. Spreads by underground runners to make a colony. A native shrub. Tolerates drier soil than most azaleas. Zone 4.

Rhododendron prunifolium.
Plum-leaved azalea.
Height: 8 ft. or more. Blooms much later than other azaleas. Scentless orange-red flowers last for up to a month in July and August. Native to the Southeast. Zone 6 or 5.

Rhododendron schlippenbachii.
Royal azalea.
Height: 6 ft. Large flowers are fragrant and bloom in early spring. Foliage is attractive and develops good fall color. Grows upright, with open branching. Native to Asia. Zone 5.

Rhododendron vaseyi.
Pink-shell azalea.
Height: 6–8 ft. Masses of scentless pink flowers open just before the leaves in April or May. Spreads wider than tall. Native to the Southeast. Zone 6 or 5.

Rhododendron viscosum.
Swamp azalea.
Height: to 8 ft. Blooms in late June or July.
White or pink flowers have an intensely
sweet fragrance. Grows wild in swamps and
tolerates poor drainage, unlike other azaleas.
Zone 4.

**Rhododendron yedoense
var. poukhanense.**
Height: to 6 ft. Slightly fragrant rose or lilac
flowers open in March or April. Technically
considered an evergreen azalea, but it usually
drops most or all of its leaves. Zone 6 or 5.

Rhododendron prunifolium

Rhododendron vaseyi

Rhododendron schlippenbachii

Rhododendron viscosum

Rhododendron yedoense var. *poukhanense*

Rhododendron (continued)

Rhododendron Ghent hybrids

Rhododendron Exbury hybrids

Rhododendron Mollis hybrids

Rhododendron Northern Lights hybrids

Rhododendron Exbury hybrids.
Height: 4 ft. or more. This diverse group
includes hundreds of cultivars with flowers in
shades of white, cream, yellow, orange, red,
rose, or pink. Most kinds bloom in May.
'Gibraltar' is shown above. Zone 5.

Rhododendron Ghent hybrids.
Height: 5–8 ft. These are upright shrubs
with fragrant flowers in shades of yellow,
orange, pink, or red. They flower later than
the Mollis hybrids. 'Wilhelm III' is shown
above. Zone 5.

Rhododendron Mollis hybrids.
Height: 4–6 ft. These are rounded shrubs
with scentless flowers in shades of white,
yellow, pink, or red. Flowers open just before
the leaves, usually in May. Zone 6 or 5.

Rhododendron Northern Lights hybrids.
Height: to 6 ft. These are the hardiest azaleas
and bloom reliably even after very cold
winters. Fragrant flowers come in several
colors. 'Rosy Lights' is shown above. Zone 3.

Rhus aromatica 'Gro-Low'

Rhus copallina

Ribes speciosum

Rhus typhina 'Dissecta'

Ribes alpinum

Rhus aromatica 'Gro-Low'. Fragrant sumac.
Height: 2 ft. A good ground cover for sunny sites
with poor, dry soil. Can spread up to 8 ft. wide.
Compound leaves are glossy green all summer,
turn red or purple in fall. Zone 3.

Rhus copallina.
Shining sumac, winged sumac.
Height: 12 ft. or more. A tough, trouble-free
native shrub that spreads to make a dome-shaped
colony. Compound leaves are shiny bright green
in summer, crimson in fall. Thick stems are
topped with greenish flowers in summer, red
fruits in fall. Zone 4.

Rhus typhina 'Dissecta'. Staghorn sumac.
Height: 15–25 ft. or more. This cultivar has
compound leaves divided into many fine
segments. Cut back hard in spring to produce
vigorous suckers with especially large leaves. A
tough, adaptable, pest-free shrub that tolerates
heat and cold. Zone 4.

Ribes alpinum. Alpine currant.
Height: 3–6 ft. Can be pruned as desired or left
to grow naturally into a compact mound.
Twiggy branches carry small shiny leaves. Grows
in any well-drained soil and takes sun or shade.
Zone 3.

Ribes speciosum. Fuchsia-flowered gooseberry.
Height: to 10 ft. A California native that thrives
in dry shade. Blooms prolifically in winter and
early spring. Hummingbirds visit the dangling
crimson blossoms. Zone 7.

Rosa, Roses

Roses are beloved for their beautiful fragrant flowers, but when choosing a rose for your garden, think past the blossoms and look at the whole plant. How big does it grow? What shape is it? Is it hardy and disease-resistant? Is the foliage attractive? How long does it bloom? Are there colorful hips for winter interest?

Rose growers today offer a remarkable selection of plants, old and new. Most start blooming the year you plant them and just get better over time. For best results, choose a site in full sun with fertile, well-drained soil, and use plenty of mulch. The roses here are carefree plants that require little pruning or spraying.

Rosa 'Don Juan'

Rosa 'Bonica'

Rosa 'Carefree Beauty'

Rosa 'Bonica'.
Height: 4–5 ft. A shrub rose that's covered with small double flowers all season. Makes a good low hedge. Hardy.

Rosa 'Carefree Beauty'.
Height: 4 ft. A shrub rose with fragrant flowers all summer. Orange hips are showy in fall and winter. Healthy and hardy.

Rosa 'Don Juan'.
Height: 8–10 ft. A pillar rose. Flowers are very fragrant. Blooms midseason and repeats in fall. Not reliably hardy.

Rosa 'The Fairy'.
Height: 2 ft. A polyantha rose that blooms from summer until frost. Spreads 3 ft. wide; good for mass planting. Hardy.

Rosa 'Harison's Yellow'.
Height: 5–7 ft. A shrub rose. Blooms once, in early season. Canes are very thorny. Leaves are small and delicate. Not hardy.

Rosa 'Iceberg'.
Height: 4 ft. A floribunda rose with fragrant flowers 3 in. wide. Reblooms throughout the season. Grows upright. Hardy.

Rosa 'Mary Rose'.
Height: 5 ft. An English rose with fragrant flowers all season. A compact, healthy shrub. Hardy.

Rosa 'Penelope'.
Height: 6 ft. A hybrid musk rose. Makes a large shrub with an open habit, good for hedges. Flowers are fragrant. Hardy.

Rosa 'The Fairy'

Rosa 'Harison's Yellow'

Rosa 'Iceberg'

Rosa 'Mary Rose'

Rosa 'Penelope'

Rosa (continued)

Rosa hugonis

Rosa palustris

Rosa rubrifolia

Rosa 'Frau Dagmar Hartopp'

Rosa moyesii

Rosa 'Hansa'

Rosa hugonis. Father Hugo's rose. Height: 6–8 ft. One of the best single yellow roses, with slightly fragrant 2-in. flowers early in the season. Hardy.

Rosa moyesii. Height: to 10 ft. Red hips are very showy in fall. Has single red flowers in early to midseason. Grows upright. Hardy.

Rosa palustris. Swamp rose. Height: 6 ft. or more. A native wild rose that tolerates poorly drained soil. Flowers are very sweet. Grows upright. Hardy.

Rosa rubrifolia. Height: 4–8 ft. Valued for its dark reddish purple foliage and shiny red hips. Red canes are almost thornless. Hardy.

Rosa 'Frau Dagmar Hartopp'. Height: to 4 ft. A rugosa hybrid. Fragrant flowers are followed by large red hips. A low grower. Disease-resistant. Very hardy.

Rosa 'Hansa'. Height: to 6 ft. A rugosa hybrid. Large flowers are very fragrant. Hips are orange-red. Grows upright. Very hardy.

Salix caprea 'Pendula'

Salix elaeagnos

Spiraea × bumalda 'Lime Mound'

Salix purpurea 'Nana'

Spiraea × cinerea 'Grefsheim'

Salix caprea 'Pendula'.
Weeping pussy willow.
Height: 5–10 ft. This cultivar is usually sold as a standard with a weeping crown grafted on a short trunk. Regular pussy willows grow upright, with many slender stems. Flowers in early spring. Zone 4.

Salix elaeagnos. Rosemary willow.
Height: 8–12 ft. or more. Slender leaves are dark green above and white below and sparkle when rippled by the breeze. A fine-textured dense shrub for damp or average soil. Zone 5.

Salix purpurea 'Nana'. Purple osier willow.
Height: to 5 ft. A compact shrub with very slender twigs and thin blue-gray leaves 1–2 in. long. A good specimen or low hedge that responds well to annual pruning. Zone 4.

Spiraea × bumalda 'Lime Mound'.
Height: to 3 ft. Leaves change from yellow to lime green to orange-red as the season progresses. Has pink flowers in early summer. Easy and adaptable. Needs little pruning or care. Zone 3.

Spiraea × cinerea 'Grefsheim'.
Height: 5–6 ft. An excellent choice for informal hedges. Foliage is pale green in summer, gold in fall. It's covered with fragrant white flowers in spring, before the leaves unfold. Zone 4.

Spiraea japonica 'Little Princess'

Spiraea nipponica 'Snowmound'

Symphoricarpos albus

Spiraea × vanhouttei

Syringa laciniata

Syringa meyeri 'Palibin'

Syringa patula 'Miss Kim'

Syringa vulgaris

Vitex agnus-castus

Vaccinium corymbosum

Weigela florida 'Variegata'

Spiraea japonica 'Little Princess'.
Height: 1¹/₂ ft. A compact shrub that
blooms in summer, after the other spireas.
Good for foundation planting, edging beds
or borders, or containers. Pest-free and easy
to grow. Zone 3.

Spiraea nipponica 'Snowmound'.
Height: 4 ft. Arching branches make a
spreading rounded profile. Flowers in May or
June. Fine-textured foliage is blue-green and
combines well with other plants. Easy to
grow. Zone 4.

Spiraea × vanhouttei.
Height: 6–8 ft. The most commonly planted
spirea, very tough and easy to grow. Allow
plenty of space for the branches to spread
into a graceful fountain. Flowers in May or
June. Zone 4.

Symphoricarpos albus. Snowberry.
Height: 3–6 ft. Juicy white berries ripen in
fall and last a few months. A tough plant that
thrives where little else will grow. Tolerates
poor, gravelly soil. Sun or shade. Zone 3.

Syringa laciniata. Cut-leaf lilac.
Height: 4–6 ft. Has clusters of fragrant
flowers all along the branches in spring.
Leaves are deeply lobed and have a lacy
appearance. A good lilac for small gardens.
Zone 4.

Syringa meyeri 'Palibin'. Dwarf Meyer lilac.
Height: 6–8 ft. Stays compact and doesn't
get leggy. Even young plants flower
generously. Flowers are very fragrant. Leaves
resist mildew and sometimes develop fall
color. Zone 4.

Syringa patula 'Miss Kim'. Miss Kim lilac.
Height: 4–8 ft. A compact lilac, covered with
fragrant flowers in early summer. Mildew-
resistant leaves turn purple in fall. Needs full
or part sun, average soil and watering. Zone 4.

Syringa vulgaris. Common lilac.
Height: to 20 ft. There are hundreds of
cultivars with single or double flowers in
shades of lilac, violet, blue, purple, magenta,
pink, or white. Most kinds require a cold
winter or they won't bloom. Old plants get
very tall and large. Zone 4.

Vaccinium corymbosum.
Highbush blueberry.
Height: 6–15 ft. An excellent native shrub.
Has small pale flowers in spring, loads of
tasty berries in summer, and rich fall color.
Needs acidic soil. Fruits best in full sun.
Zone 4.

Viburnum. (See pp. 154–155.)

Vitex agnus-castus. Chaste tree, pepperbush.
Height: 10–20 ft. Blooms over a long season
from midsummer through fall. Crushed
leaves have a spicy or peppery fragrance.
Thrives in hot weather and tolerates poor,
dry soil. Zone 7.

Weigela florida 'Variegata'.
Variegated weigela.
Height: 4–6 ft. Blooms for about 2 weeks in
late spring. Green leaves have creamy white
margins. Smaller and more interesting than
common weigela but just as easy to grow.
Zone 5.

Viburnum, Viburnums

The deciduous viburnums offer fragrant flowers in spring, rich fall color, and bright berries that last for months and feed the birds. They make excellent specimens or hedges for both formal and casual gardens. There are dozens to choose from, including several native species. All are hardy, adaptable, and carefree.

Viburnum dilatatum 'Erie'

Viburnum carlesii 'Compactum'

Viburnum dentatum

***Viburnum carlesii* 'Compactum'.**
Korean spice viburnum.
Height: 3 ft. Pink buds open into white flowers with a rich spicy fragrance. Blooms as the leaves expand, usually in April. Zone 4.

Viburnum dentatum. Arrowwood.
Height: to 15 ft. Toothed leaves are glossy dark green in summer and develop good fall color. An adaptable native shrub. Zone 3.

***Viburnum dilatatum* 'Erie'.**
Height: 6 ft. or more. Berries last well into winter. Has white flowers in spring and good fall foliage colors. Zone 5.

Viburnum × juddii.
Height: 6–8 ft. A hybrid of *V. carlesii* with very fragrant flowers in April or May. Leaves turn purple in fall. Zone 4.

***Viburnum lantana* 'Mohican'.** Wayfaring tree.
Height: 10 ft. Berries change color as they ripen, darkening from orange to red to black. Tolerates drier soil than most viburnums and makes a good hedge or screen. Zone 4.

***Viburnum plicatum* var. *tomentosum* 'Shasta'.**
Double file viburnum.
Height: 6 ft. A lovely shrub. Tiers of horizontal branches spread about twice as wide as it is tall. Spring flowers are followed by summer berries and red-purple fall foliage. Zone 6.

Viburnum trilobum. American cranberry bush.
Height: 8–10 ft. Bright scarlet fruits hang on through winter. Has white flowers like lacecap hydrangeas in spring. Similar to *V. opulus* but even hardier. Zone 2.

***Viburnum trilobum* 'Compactum'.**
Compact American cranberry bush.
Height: 6 ft. A native shrub selected for compact habit. Makes a good informal hedge with minimal pruning. This cultivar often fails to flower or set fruit. Zone 2.

Viburnum × *juddii*

Viburnum plicatum var. *tomentosum* 'Shasta'

Viburnum trilobum

Viburnum lantana 'Mohican'

Viburnum trilobum 'Compactum'

Evergreen trees

Acacia baileyana

Arbutus unedo

Arbutus menziesii

Brachychiton acerifolius

Callistemon viminalis

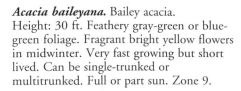

Acacia baileyana. Bailey acacia.
Height: 30 ft. Feathery gray-green or blue-green foliage. Fragrant bright yellow flowers in midwinter. Very fast growing but short lived. Can be single-trunked or multitrunked. Full or part sun. Zone 9.

Arbutus menziesii. Madrone.
Height: 50 ft. or more. An irregular oval crown. Broad leathery leaves and colorful mottled bark. Clusters of creamy flowers in May are followed by orange-red berries. Hard to transplant. Zone 8.

Arbutus unedo.
Strawberry tree.
Height: 20 ft. Upright with a rounded crown. Reddish twigs and shiny leathery leaves. Clusters of small white to pink flowers and bright red fruits in October. Likes hot, dry sites. Zone 8.

Brachychiton acerifolius. Flame tree.
Height: 50 ft. Drops its leaves temporarily in May to cover itself with showy clusters of red bell-shaped flowers. Heavy trunk and woody fruit. Good street tree. Full sun. Zone 9.

Callistemon viminalis.
Weeping bottlebrush.
Height: to 30 ft. An upright trunk with slender hanging branches. Leathery, light bluish green leaves and bottlebrush-like spikes of bright red flowers are followed by long-lasting pods. Zone 9.

Cassia leptophylla. Gold medallion tree.
Height: 25 ft. Spreading, often multitrunked, with an open habit. Notable for the giant clusters of yellow flowers produced all summer, followed by long pods. Zone 9.

Cassia leptophylla

Citrus × paradisi 'Marsh'

Ceratonia siliqua

Citrus limon 'Eureka'

Cinnamomum camphora

Ceratonia siliqua. Carob.
Height: 30–40 ft. Dense and mounded, with shiny leathery leaves. Beanlike pods are the source of a chocolate substitute. Makes a durable hedge. Tolerates heat, drought, and poor soil. Zone 9.

Cinnamomum camphora. Camphor tree.
Height: 50 ft. or more. Has a thick trunk and heavy limbs; aromatic leaves and bark. Clusters of tiny yellow flowers in spring; small black fruits in fall. Good shade tree. Full sun. Zone 9.

Citrus limon 'Eureka'.
'Eureka' lemon.
Height: 20–25 ft. Shiny green leaves, fragrant blossoms, and edible fruits. All citrus are excellent trees for year-round beauty. Full sun. Zone 9.

Citrus × paradisi 'Marsh'.
'Marsh' grapefruit.
Height: 25–30 ft. Another excellent citrus for home gardens. Seedless fruits ripen from December to May. Very ornamental and highly productive. Full sun. Zone 9.

Cupaniopsis anacardiodes

Eriobotrya japonica

Cupaniopsis anacardiodes. Carrotwood. Height: 25–40 ft. A neat and handsome tree with an erect trunk and a spreading crown. Smooth, leathery, dark green compound leaves. Flowers are inconspicuous. Very tough and adaptable. Zone 9.

Eriobotrya japonica. Loquat. Height: 20–30 ft. A tropical-looking tree with a dense crown of large, thick, leathery leaves. Cherry-sized fruits ripen in spring and have a pleasant flavor. Likes hot, dry weather. Zone 7.

Eucalyptus camaldulensis. Red gum. Height: 80 ft. or more. A huge tough tree for large open spaces. Makes a spreading crown with weeping branches. Foliage is leathery and gray-green. Inconspicuous white flowers. Zone 8.

Eucalyptus citriodora.
Lemon-scented gum.
Height: 60–100 ft. A slender tree that fits next to buildings. Thin leathery leaves have a strong lemon scent when crushed. Inconspicuous flowers. Makes a lovely grove. Zone 9.

Eucalyptus ficifolia. Red-flowering gum. Height: to 40 ft. A large spreading tree. Leaves are thick and rubbery. Forms spectacular huge clusters of red, pink, or white flowers. Blooms mostly in summer. Zone 9.

Eucalyptus polyanthemos.
Silver-dollar gum.
Height: 30–75 ft. Young shoots have round silvery leaves, popular for fresh or dried arrangements. Old trees have mottled bark. Grows fast and tolerates repeated pruning. Zone 8.

Eucalyptus sideroxylon.
Red ironbark.
Height: 30–90 ft. A good screen or street tree with a weeping habit, blue-green foliage, and dark bark. Powderpuff flowers are white, pink, or red. Trouble-free. Zone 8.

Ficus microcarpa var. ***nitida.***
Indian laurel fig.
Height: 25–30 ft. Has a neat dense crown of bright green, glossy, thick, oval leaves. Pale gray bark. Tiny inedible fruits. Tolerates heat and urban conditions. Full sun. Zone 9.

Geijera parviflora.
Australian willow.
Height: 25–30 ft. Looks like an evergreen weeping willow with long leathery leaves. Tiny star-shaped flowers in spring. Neat and trouble-free. Good as a patio or street tree. Zone 9.

Gordonia lasianthus. Loblolly bay. Height: to 40 ft. Wide fragrant flowers with snow-white petals and golden stamens bloom from June to frost. Smooth, glossy, dark green leaves. Native to the Southeast. Full sun. Zone 7.

Eucalyptus camaldulensis

Eucalyptus citriodora

Eucalyptus ficifolia

Eucalyptus polyanthemos

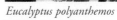

Eucalyptus sideroxylon

Ficus microcarpa var. *nitida*

Geijera parviflora

Gordonia lasianthus

Ilex aquifolium 'Argentea Marginata'

Ilex × attenuata 'East Palatka'

Ilex × attenuata 'Foster #2'

Ilex 'Nellie R. Stevens'

Ilex latifolia

Ilex aquifolium 'Argentea Marginata'. English holly.
Height: about 30 ft. Spiny leaves have white edges. This form is female and makes red berries. Can't take hot summers. Zone 6.

Ilex × attenuata 'East Palatka'. Topal holly.
Height: 25 ft. or more. Grows upright with a neat conical shape. Leaves are almost spineless. Has red berries. Zone 7.

Ilex × attenuata 'Foster #2'. Topal holly.
Height: 25 ft. or more. A slender tree, good for small gardens. Has spiny leaves and red berries. Doesn't mind heat. Zone 7.

Ilex latifolia. Lusterleaf holly.
Height: 20 ft. or more. An outstanding specimen tree. Shiny leaves can be 8 in. long. Flowers are fragrant. Red berries are quite large. Slow-growing but trouble-free. Zone 7.

Ilex 'Nellie R. Stevens'.
Height: 15–25 ft. Makes a pyramidal tree or can be pruned into a dense hedge. Adaptable, fast-growing, and very popular. Leaves have few spines. Berries are bright red. Zone 7.

Ilex opaca. American holly.
Height: to 50 ft. More cold-hardy than English holly. Leaves are leathery with spiny edges; berries are dull red. Needs moist, well-drained, acidic soil. Zone 5.

Leptospermum laevigatum. Australian tea tree.
Height: to 30 ft. Blooms in spring. Makes a dense hedge if pruned or a picturesque, twisted tree if allowed to spread naturally. Tolerates hot, dry weather. Zone 9.

Ligustrum lucidum. Glossy privet.
Height: to 30 ft. A small tree with a loose open habit. Glossy leaves are 4–6 in. long. Strong-scented white flowers bloom in early summer. Easy to grow. Zone 8 or 7.

Lithocarpus densiflorus. Tanbark oak.
Height: 30 ft. New leaves are covered with buff-colored fuzz; older leaves are smooth and leathery. Does best in dry West Coast gardens. Zone 8.

Magnolia grandiflora. Southern magnolia.
Height: to 80 ft. Large glossy leaves are dark green above, covered with rust-colored hairs below. Creamy white flowers have a rich lemony or fruity fragrance. Zone 7.

Maytenus boaria. Mayten.
Height: 25–50 ft. Resembles an evergreen weeping willow. Leaves are thin and glossy. Flowers are inconspicuous. Surface roots can be a problem in lawns. Zone 8.

Olea europaea. Olive.
Height: 25–30 ft. A fine lawn or street tree with silvery foliage and attractive branching. Let it spread naturally, or shear it into a formal shape. Fruitless cultivars are best unless you specifically want to harvest the olives. Zone 8.

Ilex opaca

Leptospermum laevigatum

Ligustrum lucidum

Lithocarpus densiflorus

Maytenus boaria

Magnolia grandiflora

Olea europaea

Pyrus kawakamii

Prunus caroliniana 'Bright 'N Tight'

Quercus agrifolia

Quercus ilex

Quercus laurifolia

Quercus suber

Quercus virginiana

***Prunus caroliniana* 'Bright 'N Tight'.**
Carolina cherry laurel.
Height: under 30 ft. More compact than
ordinary cherry laurels. Good for formal
hedges or specimens because it tolerates
repeated pruning. Small white flowers are
very sweet in spring. Zone 7.

Pyrus kawakamii. Evergreen pear.
Height: 15–30 ft. Blooms for weeks in late
winter. Leaves are glossy dark green. Can be
trained as a standard tree with a spreading
crown or espaliered against a wall. Zone 8.

Quercus agrifolia. Coast live oak.
Height: 50 ft. or more. A California native.
Old trees can reach 100 ft. wide. Young trees
grow quickly, up to 2 ft. a year. Needs dry
soil; subject to root rot if overwatered. Zone 9.

Quercus ilex. Holly oak.
Height: 60 ft. A rugged, fairly fast growing
oak for West Coast gardens. Native to the
Mediterranean region, it tolerates dry soil,
sea salt, and wind. Can be pruned as desired.
Zone 8 or 7.

Quercus laurifolia. Laurel oak.
Height: 70 ft. or more. A southeastern
native, good as a street tree or lawn shade
tree. Leaves stay green well into winter but
drop by spring. Tolerates poorly drained soil.
Zone 8 or 7.

Quercus suber. Cork oak.
Height: 70–90 ft. Glossy dark green leaves
are small and leathery. Soft bark forms thick
ridges and furrows on the trunk and limbs;
it is harvested and used as cork. Zone 7.

Quercus virginiana. Southern live oak.
Height: 60 ft. or more. A southeastern
native. Old trees spread much wider than
tall, with open crowns. Young trees have
dense rounded crowns. Zone 7.

Rhus lancea. African sumac.
Height: 25 ft. A tough tree for hot, dry
climates. Dark green leaves have a smooth
leathery texture. Trunk has deeply checkered
blackish red bark. Zone 9.

Schinus molle. California pepper tree,
Peruvian pepper tree.
Height: to 40 ft. A tough tree with lots of
character. Trunk is heavy and gnarled, and
branches and foliage are quite graceful. Roots
are shallow and invasive, however, and it
hosts several insect pests. Zone 9.

Schinus terebinthifolius.
Brazilian pepper tree, Florida holly.
Height: 30 ft. Big clusters of berries are very
showy in fall and winter, but seedling trees
have become a major weed in Florida. Not a
problem (yet) in California. Zone 9.

Tristania conferta. Brisbane box.
Height: 40–60 ft. A neat tree with leathery
leaves and attractive, flaking, two-tone bark.
Small white flowers look like snowflakes in
summer. Easy and trouble-free. Zone 9.

Schinus molle

Schinus terebinthifolius

Rhus lancea

Tristania conferta

Palms

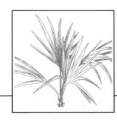

Arecastrum romanzoffianum

Butia capitata

Brahea armata

Chamaerops humilis

Livistona chinensis

Arecastrum romanzoffianum. Queen palm. Height: 40–50 ft. Very straight trunk. Clusters of long, glossy, pinnate leaves. Fast-growing. Good street tree. Full sun. Zone 9 or 8.

Brahea armata. Fan palm. Height: to 40 ft. Erect and often multitrunked, with ring-striped bark. Sometimes thorny. Long, narrow, pale silvery blue leaves. Clusters of creamy white flowers in spring. Edible yellow fruits. Zone 9.

Butia capitata. Pindo palm. Height: 10–20 ft. Long, arching, gray- or blue-green pinnate fronds atop a stubby trunk. White or yellow flowers in late spring. Edible yellow to red fruits. Can be grown in tubs, urns, or concrete-edged beds. Zone 9 or 8.

Chamaerops humilis. European fan palm. Height: 6–20 ft. Forms low clumps. Bright leaves spiral around the trunk and fan out into long slender leaflets. Inconspicuous

flowers and fruits. Slow-growing. Use by patio or pool or in a container. Sun or shade. Zone 8.

Livistona chinensis. Chinese fan palm. Height: usually under 15 ft. Leaf blades are 3–6 ft. wide. Grows slowly and can live for years in a large tub. Zone 9 or 8.

Phoenix canariensis. Canary palm. Height: 50 ft. Has a thick erect trunk topped with an umbrella of arching fronds 15–20 ft.

Phoenix canariensis

Rhapis excelsa

Sabal palmetto

Trachycarpus fortunei

Washingtonia filifera

long. Starts out slow but eventually gets too large for most gardens. Zone 9 or 8.

Rhapis excelsa.
Lady palm.
Height: 5 ft. or more. An elegant palm for special sites. Does very well in containers. Grows slowly, so it's expensive to buy, but it lives for decades and gets better every year. Zone 8.

Sabal palmetto.
Cabbage palm.
Height: 20–40 ft. The state tree of South Carolina and Florida. Slowly grows a tall trunk with a crown of coarse dark green fronds. Adapts to sun or shade and tolerates poor soil. Zone 8.

Trachycarpus fortunei.
Windmill palm.
Height: 20 ft. A showy little palm, quite hardy and easy to grow. Forms a thick

shaggy trunk and a round or umbrella-shaped crown. Grows well in the ground or in containers. Zone 8.

Washingtonia filifera.
Washington palm.
Height: 30–50 ft. A large palm with a sturdy trunk and a wide round crown. Fronds are divided into slender segments edged with loose fibers. Tolerates heat and drought. Zone 8.

Evergreen shrubs

Abelia × grandiflora

Arctostaphylos densiflora 'Howard McMinn'

Arctostaphylos 'Emerald Carpet'

Arctostaphylos uva-ursi

Abelia × grandiflora.
Glossy abelia.
Height: 6–10 ft. An oval mound of arching branches with shiny leaves. Small bell-shaped flowers from early summer to fall. Excellent hedge or screen. Zone 6.

Arctostaphylos densiflora 'Howard McMinn'. Manzanita.
Height: 4–6 ft. Crooked reddish stems, small round leaves, waxy pink flowers, and tiny applelike fruits. Good as a specimen, hedge, or ground cover. Long lived. Zone 8.

Arctostaphylos 'Emerald Carpet'.
Height: 9–12 in. Shiny bright green leaves, glossy reddish brown bark, and inconspicuous pink flowers. Low and spreading. Good ground cover for hillsides or banks. Full or part sun. Zone 8.

Arctostaphylos uva-ursi.
Bearberry.
Height: under 12 in. Foliage is glossy green in summer, bronzy reddish purple in winter. Makes a good ground cover for well-drained soil or rocky slopes. Full or part sun. Zone 3.

Aucuba japonica 'Crotonifolia'.
Height: 6–10 ft. Leathery toothed-edge leaves, heavily spotted with light yellow. Other aucubas have green or variegated leaves. Only females make red berries. Part to full shade. Zone 7.

Baccharis pilularis 'Twin Peaks'.
Coyote brush.
Height: to 3 ft. Low and compact. Small, thick, resinous, dark gray or gray-green leaves. Makes a good ground cover for West Coast gardens. Full sun. Zone 9.

Aucuba japonica 'Crotonifolia'

Berberis julianae

Berberis verruculosa

Baccharis pilularis 'Twin Peaks'

Buxus microphylla var. *koreana* 'Green Beauty'

Buxus sempervirens

Buxus sempervirens 'Suffruticosa'

Berberis julianae.
Wintergreen barberry.
Height: 8 ft. Dense twiggy habit, abundant foliage, and clusters of needlelike thorns make this an excellent hedge or barrier plant. Yellow flowers in spring; blue-black berries in fall. Zone 5.

Berberis verruculosa. Warty barberry.
Height: to 6 ft. Upright habit with dense thorny stems. Smooth, glossy, hollylike leaves turn purplish or bronzy in winter. Yellow flowers and blue-black berries. Zone 6 or 5.

Buxus microphylla var. **koreana** **'Green Beauty'.**
Littleleaf box.
Height: to 4 ft. Dense glossy foliage. Ideal for low hedges, foundation plantings, containers, or topiaries. Slow-growing. Quite hardy but may turn yellowish brown in winter. Zone 5.

Buxus sempervirens.
English box.
Height: 3–20 ft. A classic hedge plant, holding its dense foliage all the way to the ground. Naturally forms a round or oval shape, eventually growing quite large. Zone 5.

Buxus sempervirens 'Suffruticosa'.
Dwarf boxwood.
Height: 4–5 ft. Grows slowly into a dense mound. Foliage is neat and fine-textured. Can be sheared into a low hedge or left unpruned. Full or part sun. Zone 5.

Callistemon citrinus

Calluna vulgaris 'Robert Chapman'

Camellia hiemalis 'Showanosakae'

Camellia sasanqua 'Yuletide'

Camellia japonica 'Glen 40'

Callistemon citrinus. Lemon bottlebrush.
Height: 10–15 ft. Red flowers at the ends of
arching branches bloom year-round. Lemon-
scented leaves unfold pink, turn green as they
mature. Fast hedge or specimen for mild
climates. Zone 9.

Calluna vulgaris 'Robert Chapman'.
Heather.
Height: 10 in. A low, spreading mound of
wiry branches with minute gold to reddish
overlapping leaves. Thousands of small
mauve flowers in late summer and fall.
Zone 4.

Camellia hiemalis 'Showanosakae'.
Height: to 3 ft. Small and spreading, with
open, willowy, tiered branches. Profuse light
pink flowers from autumn to winter. Good
for containers, even hanging baskets. Part
sun. Zone 8.

Camellia japonica 'Glen 40'.
Height: 6–15 ft. Formal double blooms of
showy waxy blooms. Other cultivars have
red, pink, or white flowers, single or double,
borne from fall to early spring. Part sun.
Zone 8 or 7.

Camellia sasanqua 'Yuletide'.
Height: to 10 ft. Single deep red flowers in
midwinter. Other cultivars are red, pink, or
white. All are tidy plants with neat glossy
foliage and make lovely specimens. Part sun.
Zone 8.

Cassia artemisioides.
Feathery cassia.
Height: 3–5 ft. Narrow, compound,
needlelike leaflets of gray or silver. Showy
clusters of coin-sized yellow flowers from
winter through spring. Makes a good hedge.
Full sun. Zone 9.

Ceanothus 'Dark Star'.
Height: 6 ft. Fast-growing. Dense, with
leathery leaves, reddish buds, and profuse
clusters of fragrant dark blue flowers in
spring. Good as an informal hedge or screen.
Full sun. Zone 8.

Ceanothus griseus var. *horizontalis* 'Yankee
Point'. Carmel creeper.
Height: 2–3 ft. Beautiful clusters of fragrant,
tiny, deep blue flowers from March to April.
Fast-growing ground cover. Zone 8.

Ceanothus thyrsiflorus 'Skylark'.
California lilac.
Height: to 15 ft. Compact and fast-growing.
Glossy bright leaves. Clusters of deep blue
flowers in March and April. Can be trained
as a single-trunked or multitrunked tree.
Zone 8.

Cercocarpus ledifolius.
Curl-leaf mountain mahogany.
Height: 10–20 ft. Stiff leaves are dark green
on top, silver underneath. Decorative spiraled
seed heads have fine silver hairs. Whole plant
is fragrant. Long lived. Zone 4.

Cassia artemisioides

Ceanothus griseus var. *horizontalis* 'Yankee Point'

Ceanothus 'Dark Star'

Cercocarpus ledifolius

Ceanothus thyrsiflorus 'Skylark'

Choisya ternata

Cistus × corbariensis

Cotoneaster dammeri

Cotoneaster lacteus

Cotoneaster salicifolius 'Emerald Carpet'

Choisya ternata. Mexican orange.
Height: 10 ft. Erect mounded habit. Shiny compound leaves. Clusters of very fragrant, star-shaped white flowers at the branch tips early spring through summer. Zone 8.

Cistus × corbariensis. White rock rose.
Height: 3–5 ft. Spreading, with crinkled gray-green leaves that release fragrance on warm days. Showy white flowers in late spring. Good bank or hillside cover. Zone 8.

Cotoneaster dammeri. Bearberry cotoneaster.
Height: 1 ft. A fast-growing ground cover. Bright, firm, oval leaves turn dull green or purple in cold weather. White flowers in spring; bright red berries in late summer. Zone 5.

Cotoneaster lacteus. Red clusterberry.
Height: 5–9 ft. Flowers in spring. Red berry clusters last nearly all winter. Thick, oval, dark green leaves are silvery below. Arching shape makes a graceful screen or hedge. Looks best unpruned. Zone 7 or 6.

Cyrilla racemiflora

Daphne cneorum 'Eximia'

Dodonaea viscosa 'Purpurea'

Daphne odora 'Aureo-Marginata'

Elaeagnus pungens 'Maculata'

Erica carnea 'Myretoun Ruby'

Cotoneaster salicifolius 'Emerald Carpet'.
Willowleaf cotoneaster.
Height: to 2 ft. A good ground cover that can spread several feet. Slender dark green leaves turn purple (and may drop) in cold weather. Berries are bright red. Full or part sun. Zone 6.

Cyrilla racemiflora. Titi.
Height: 15 ft. or more. Evergreen in the South but deciduous (with good fall color) farther north. Showiest when covered with long sprays of fragrant white flowers in summer. Tolerates very wet soil. Zone 6 or 5.

Daphne cneorum 'Eximia'.
Garland flower.
Height: 1 ft. Clusters of fragrant deep pink flowers cover the foliage in spring. Sometimes reblooms in fall. Forms a low mat that spreads and drapes over a wall or slope. Zone 4.

Daphne odora 'Aureo-Marginata'.
Winter daphne.
Height: 4 ft. Glossy leaves have cream-white variegation. Clusters of white flowers are very fragrant in early spring. Plant it near the house where you'll pass it often. Zone 7.

Dodonaea viscosa 'Purpurea'. Hopbush.
Height: 12–15 ft. Makes a good hedge or screen, with thin, leathery, purplish leaves. Clusters of pink fruits are showy in late summer. Tolerates desert heat and drought. Zone 8.

Elaeagnus pungens 'Maculata'.
Thorny elaeagnus.
Height: 10 ft. or more. Very tough and easy to grow, used for hedges and barriers. Has an irregular angular profile and thorny twigs. Tiny flowers are fragrant in fall. Zone 7 or 6.

Erica carnea 'Myretoun Ruby'.
Winter heath.
Height: 6–9 in. Long clusters of ruby red, bell-shaped flowers last from winter to spring. Forms a mat of needlelike foliage. A good ground cover or edging for sandy, acidic soil. Zone 5 or 4.

Euonymus fortunei 'Emerald 'n' Gold'

Euonymus kiautschovica 'Manhattan'

Euonymus fortunei 'Variegatus'

Euonymus fortunei var. radicans

Euonymus japonicus

Euonymus fortunei 'Emerald 'n' Gold'.
Winter creeper.
Height: to 2 ft. Compact and dense. Dark green leaves are edged with gold in summer, turn purplish-green and pink in winter. Good for foundation plantings or mixed borders. Zone 5.

Euonymus fortunei var. radicans.
Winter creeper.
Height: varies. Thick, glossy, dark green leaves. Grows as a shrub or vine and can climb up to 40 ft. Pinkish red fruits have bright orange seeds inside. Not fussy about soil. Sun or shade. Zone 5.

Euonymus fortunei 'Variegatus'.
Winter creeper.
Height: varies. Small leathery leaves can be either all-green, green and white, or all-white. Grows as a shrubby bush, sprawling ground cover, or climbing vine. Sun or shade. Zone 5.

Euonymus japonicus. Japanese euonymus.
Height: 10 ft. Very tough and adaptable. Makes a dense upright oval with many leafy stems. Variegated forms are the most popular. Leaves are green with white or gold spots or edges. Zone 8 or 7.

Euonymus kiautschovica 'Manhattan'.
Spreading euonymus.
Height: 6 ft. or more. A rounded shrub, good for hedges or foundation plantings. Leaves are glossy dark green in summer, sometimes yellowing or browning in severe winters. Zone 6.

Euryops pectinatus.
Height: 4–6 ft. A thick rounded shrub that blooms almost nonstop. Deeply cut foliage can be gray or bright green. Easy to grow in borders or containers. Tolerates dry soil. Zone 9.

Fatsia japonica.
Height: 5–7 ft. Tropical-looking, with large, glossy, palmately lobed leaves. Round clusters of tiny white flowers are followed by small dark fruits. Grows well in containers. Part sun or shade. Zone 8.

Feijoa sellowiana 'Coolidge'.
Pineapple guava.
Height: 10 ft. or more. White flowers have bright red stamens. Dark green leaves are

Euryops pectinatus

Fatsia japonica

Feijoa sellowiana 'Coolidge'

Fremontodendron 'California Glory'

Gardenia jasminoides

Heteromeles arbutifolia

gray below. Fragrant yellow fruits are sweet and tasty. This cultivar is self-pollinating. Zone 8.

Fremontodendron 'California Glory'. Flannel bush.
Height: 15–20 ft. Gold-yellow flowers bloom from March through June. Branches and leaves are covered with hairs. A California native, perfect for dry landscapes or slopes. Zone 9.

Gardenia jasminoides. Gardenia.
Height: 5–8 ft. or more. Grown for its very fragrant, waxy flowers, white aging to creamy yellow. Leaves are glossy, smooth, and dark green. Fussy about soil and subject to many pests. Zone 8.

Heteromeles arbutifolia. Toyon.
Height: 30 ft. This is the "holly" of Hollywood. Has fragrant white flowers and bright red berries. Tolerates poor, dry soil and heat. Zone 8.

Ilex, Hollies

Evergreen hollies are among the most useful plants for home landscaping, popular for foundation planting, hedges, or screens or as pruned or unpruned specimens. The leaves can be smooth or spiny, tiny or large. The plants range from compact to large. Some are slow, but others grow quite fast. Several cultivars can be treated as shrubs and kept small by regular pruning, or they can be allowed to mature into full-size trees. Many produce colorful berries on the female plants (a male is needed for pollination). Note that hollies differ considerably in their tolerance of cold and heat, wet or dry soil, acidic or alkaline conditions, and salt. Ask local nurseries to identify which cultivars do best in your region.

Ilex × altaclerensis 'Wilsonii'

Ilex cornuta 'Rotunda'

Ilex glabra

Ilex × altaclerensis **'Wilsonii'.** Wilson holly. Height: to 20 ft. Can grow as a mounded shrub or a small tree. Makes a good hedge. Tough and vigorous. Tolerates heat, dry soil, wind, sea salt, and city conditions. Zone 7 or 6.

Illex cornuta **'Rotunda'.** Chinese holly. Height: to 4 ft. Formidably spiny, with stiff glossy leaves. Doesn't make berries. Tolerates heat, drought, and alkaline soil. Good for foundation plantings or barrier hedges. Zone 7.

Ilex crenata **'Helleri'.** Japanese holly. Height: usually under 4 ft. Grows naturally into a low dense mound, even without pruning. Makes a trouble-free substitute for boxwood. Needs acidic or neutral soil and full or part sun. Zone 6.

Ilex glabra. Inkberry. Height: to 8 ft. Native to eastern wetlands but tolerates ordinary garden conditions. One of the hardiest evergreen hollies. Needs pruning to make it compact and dense. Zone 5 or 4.

Ilex crenata 'Helleri'

Ilex × *meserveae* 'Blue Girl'

Ilex vomitoria 'Nana'

Ilex pedunculosa

Ilex × meserveae 'Blue Girl'.
Height: 10–15 ft. Even young plants have showy red berries. Blue-green foliage is very glossy. Excellent for foundation planting on the east or north side of a building. Zone 5 or 4.

Ilex pedunculosa. Long-stalked holly.
Height: 20–25 ft. An unusual holly with graceful limbs, toothless leaves, and berries on long stalks. Lustrous foliage turns yellow-green in winter. Hardier than many evergreen hollies. Zone 5.

Ilex vomitoria 'Nana'. Yaupon holly.
Height: 3–5 ft. Naturally makes a compact mound or can be sheared into any shape desired. Grows quickly and isn't fussy about soil. Tough and easy but hardy only to Zone 7.

Lantana camara

Lantana montevidensis

Illicium floridanum

Kalmia latifolia

Illicium floridanum.
Florida anise.
Height: 10–15 ft. Crushed leaves have a strong licorice fragrance. Starry blooms are hidden in the foliage. Can be pruned into a formal hedge. Part to full shade. Zone 8.

Kalmia latifolia. Mountain laurel.
Height: usually under 10 ft. A hardy evergreen native to the eastern United States. Grows slowly. New cultivars offer a range of white, pink, or red flowers. Needs moist, acidic soil. Zone 4.

Lantana camara.
Common lantana.
Height: 2–4 ft. Blooms from spring until frost, with clusters of white, yellow, gold, pink, orange, red, or two-tone flowers. Spreads into a low mound. Leaves have a pungent aroma. Zone 8 or 7.

Lantana montevidensis.
Trailing lantana.
Height: 2 ft. A good ground cover for rough banks. Grows well in containers, too. Blooms for months. Tolerates poor soil, drought, and heat. Spreads quickly. Zone 7.

Leptospermum scoparium 'Ruby Glow'.
New Zealand tea tree.
Height: 6–8 ft. Blooms abundantly in spring and summer. Foliage is fine-textured. Other cultivars have white or pink flowers. Needs full sun and well-drained soil. Zone 9.

Leucophyllum frutescens. Texas sage.
Height: 6–8 ft. Leaves are covered with soft hairs. Violet-purple flowers open in flushes. Needs pruning to develop a dense bushy shape. Tolerates heat, drought, and alkaline soil. Zone 8.

Leucothoe axillaris. Coast leucothoe.
Height: 2–4 ft. Good for foundation plantings because it stays compact. Resistant to leafspot diseases. Fragrant flowers open in April or May. Foliage turns purplish bronze in winter. Zone 5.

Leucothoe fontanesiana.
Drooping leucothoe.
Height: 3–6 ft. Flowers in spring. Good along the north or east wall of a building or under deciduous trees. Hardy to cold but can't take heat. Leaves are subject to fungal diseases. Zone 4.

Ligustrum japonicum. Wax-leaf ligustrum.
Height: 10–15 ft. White flowers release a heavy fragrance in early summer. Has dark berries in fall and winter. Tolerates frequent heavy pruning. Makes a fast screen. Zone 8 or 7.

Loropetalum chinense.
Height: to 5 ft. Blooms mostly in early spring but sometimes repeats in summer and fall. Spreading, arching branches need little pruning. Prefers acidic, organic soil and shade. Zone 7.

Leptospermum scoparium 'Ruby Glow'

Leucophyllum frutescens

Leucothoe fontanesiana

Leucothoe axillaris

Loropetalum chinense

Ligustrum japonicum

Mahonia bealei

Mahonia aquifolium 'Compacta'

Mahonia repens

Mahonia 'Golden Abundance'

Mahonia lomariifolia

Mahonia aquifolium 'Compacta'.
Oregon grape.
Height: 2–3 ft. A dwarf form of this shrub, good for ground cover or foundation plantings. Blooms in spring. Hardy to Zone 6 or 5, but the foliage turns brown or dies back in severe winters.

Mahonia bealei.
Leatherleaf mahonia.
Height: 8–10 ft. A distinctive, architectural plant. Very fragrant yellow flowers last for a few weeks in early spring. Silvery blue fruits are showy in fall and winter. Zone 7 or 6.

Mahonia 'Golden Abundance'.
Height: 8 ft. A hybrid derived from *M. aquifolium* with vigorous growth, dense foliage, abundant flowers, and large fruit clusters. Makes a showy informal hedge or screen. Zone 7 or 6.

Michelia figo

Myrica cerifera

Nandina domestica

Myoporum parvifolium

Myrtus communis

Nandina domestica 'Harbour Dwarf'

Mahonia lomariifolia.
Height: 10 ft. Makes a narrow clump of unbranched stems topped with many long drooping leaves. Leaflets are stiff and glossy. Has large showy clusters of yellow flowers in spring and blue berries in fall. Zone 8.

Mahonia repens.
Creeping holly grape.
Height: 2–3 ft. A tough ground cover, native to the western mountains. Has yellow flowers in late spring, dark blue fruits in fall. Foliage turns purple-bronze in cold weather. Hardy to Zone 5 or 4 but needs protection from winter sun.

Michelia figo.
Banana shrub.
Height: 10–15 ft. Flowers smell rich and fruity like bananas—only better! Blooms in spring and summer. Makes a dense compact shrub. Plant one near a window to enjoy the fragrance indoors. Leaves are thick and glossy. Zone 8.

Myoporum parvifolium.
Height: 2–3 in. A quick, flat, bright green ground cover, good for controlling erosion and weeds on hillsides or steep streambanks. Blossoms in summer. Needs good drainage and requires little water once established. Zone 9.

Myrica cerifera.
Wax myrtle.
Height: to 30 ft. A good low-maintenance shrub for much of the South. Slender light green leaves are smooth and leathery and smell wonderful when crushed. Makes a good screen and tolerates (but doesn't need) repeated pruning. Zone 7.

Myrtus communis. Myrtle.
Height: usually 5–6 ft. A tough, drought-resistant shrub with a rounded habit and dense foliage, very useful for sheared hedges and edgings. Grows slowly. Small white flowers have a sweet scent and bloom all summer. Zone 8.

Nandina domestica. Nandina.
Height: to 6–8 ft. Heavy sprays of shiny red berries last from fall to spring. Creamy white flowers bloom in early summer. Foliage makes a changing display of subtle colors. Needs little care. Zone 7 or 6.

Nandina domestica 'Harbour Dwarf'.
Nandina.
Height: under 2 ft. Makes a good ground cover; stays low and spreads by suckers. Foliage turns bronzy orange or red in winter. There are several other dwarf forms of nandina. Zone 7 or 6.

Nerium oleander 'Algiers'

Osmanthus × fortunei

Opuntia humifusa

Osmanthus heterophyllus 'Gulftide'

Opuntia polycantha

Nerium oleander 'Algiers'. Oleander. Height: 6–8 ft. An intermediate-size oleander. Other cultivars grow up to 12 ft. or more or stay under 4 ft. Flower colors include red, pink, salmon, and white. All are tough plants that grow in almost any soil and tolerate heat and drought. Zone 8.

Opuntia humifusa. Hardy prickly pear. Height: 1 ft. A low-growing cactus with spiny stems flattened into round or oval "joints" or sections about 6 in. long. Waxy yellow flowers, 3 in. wide, bloom in early summer. Tolerates poor, dry soil but thrives in ordinary soil. Full sun. Zone 4.

Opuntia polycantha. Hardy prickly pear. Height: 1 ft. Small, juicy, reddish purple fruits ripen in fall. Blooms in late spring, with waxy 4-in. flowers in shades of yellow, pink, or red. Native to dry hillsides in the Great Plains. Makes a tough ground cover where all else fails. Zone 3.

Osmanthus × fortunei. Sweet olive. Height: 6 ft. or more. Thick glossy leaves are spiny-edged, like holly. Grows slowly into a dense mound; can eventually reach 20 ft. Tiny flowers release an intensely sweet fragrance in fall. Zone 7.

Osmanthus heterophyllus 'Gulftide'. Holly-leaf osmanthus. Height: usually 8–10 ft. Leathery, thick, dark green leaves resemble English holly. Tiny white flowers are sweetly fragrant. Blooms in fall. Grows fairly slowly. Sun or shade. Zone 7 or 6.

Photinia × fraseri. Red-tip photinia. Height: 10–12 ft. New leaves and stems are shiny bright red in spring, later turning dark green. Often sheared into formal hedges or foundation specimens. Unpruned specimens bloom in spring, with white flowers on second-year wood. Zone 7.

Photinia × fraseri

Photinia serrulata

Pieris floribunda

Pieris 'Brouwer's Beauty'

Pieris japonica

Photinia serrulata. Chinese photinia. Height: to 30 ft. Usually grows as a multitrunked shrub or tree. New leaves are coppery red, changing to dark green. Has white flowers in spring, clusters of red berries in fall. Zone 8 or 7.

Pieris 'Brouwer's Beauty'. Height: 3–6 ft. A hybrid between *P. floribunda* and *P. japonica*. Horizontal clusters of deep purplish-red flower buds are showy all winter, then open into small white flowers in spring. Hardy, healthy, and very desirable. Zone 4.

Pieris floribunda. Mountain andromeda. Height: 4–6 ft. More compact than Japanese andromeda and more tolerant of cold, heat, and alkaline soil. Fragrant white flowers open in March or April. Leaves are red or bronzy when new, darkening to green. Zone 4.

Pieris japonica. Japanese pieris, Japanese andromeda. Height: 9–12 ft. Very popular for its glossy foliage and early spring bloom but subject to various fungal diseases and insect pests. Cultivars feature white or pink flowers and new leaves colored red, pink, or bronze. Needs acidic soil. Zone 5.

Pittosporum crassifolium

Pittosporum eugenioides

Pittosporum tobira 'Wheeler's Dwarf'

Pittosporum tobira 'Variegata'

Plumbago auriculata

Pittosporum crassifolium.
Height: 10 ft. or more. Purplish fruits are conspicuous in summer and fall. Gray-green leaves are thick and leathery, 1–2 in. long. Makes a good hedge or can be shaped into a small tree. Grows well along the seacoast. Tolerates dry spells. Zone 8.

Pittosporum eugenioides.
Height: to 40 ft. Responds well to pruning and makes a fine clipped hedge, a tall screen, or a specimen tree. Light green leaves are shiny and crisp. Tiny star-shaped yellow flowers are strongly honey-scented and bloom for weeks in spring. Zone 9.

Pittosporum tobira 'Variegata'.
Height: about 6 ft. Gray-green leaves are mottled with white and brighten a shaded patio or entryway. Makes an irregular mounded dome. Small creamy white flowers are very fragrant in early summer. Tough and adaptable. Zone 8.

Prunus lusitanica

Pyracantha koidzumii 'Santa Cruz'

Pyracantha coccinea 'Lalandei'

Prunus laurocerasus 'Otto Luyken'

Pyracantha koidzumii 'Victory'

Pyracantha 'Gnome'

Rhaphiolepis indica 'Springtime'

Pittosporum tobira 'Wheeler's Dwarf'.
Height: 3–4 ft. Small enough for townhouse gardens, foundation plantings, or containers. Grows dense and compact without pruning. Leaves stay glossy dark green all year. White flowers are very fragrant in early summer. Zone 8.

Plumbago auriculata. Cape plumbago.
Height: 6 ft. Good as a ground cover along driveways or banks or can be trained to cover a fence or trellis. Blooms all summer. Colors include white and many shades of clear blue. Tolerates heat and dry soil once established. Zone 9.

Prunus laurocerasus 'Otto Luyken'.
Cherry laurel.
Height: 4 ft. A compact cultivar that spreads 6–8 ft. wide. Blooms profusely, even if growing in shade. Small white flowers have a very sweet fragrance. A tough plant that tolerates poor, dry soil. Good for massing under trees. Zone 7.

Prunus lusitanica.
Portugal laurel.
Height: 10–20 ft. Forms a dense crown of thick glossy leaves, excellent as an unsheared screen or background planting. Has slender clusters, up to 8 in. long, of sweet-scented white flowers in midspring. Grows in sun or shade. Zone 7.

Pyracantha coccinea 'Lalandei'.
Scarlet firethorn.
Height: 8–10 ft. A vigorous shrub with stiff thorny branches. Can be trained into a hedge, specimen, or espalier. Has fragrant white flowers in spring. Orange-red berries last all winter. Other cultivars have redder berries. Zone 6.

Pyracantha 'Gnome'.
Height: under 6 ft. A compact, spreading hybrid with dense evergreen foliage, white flowers in spring, and orange berries in fall and winter. One of the hardiest pyracanthas. Zone 5.

Pyracantha koidzumii 'Santa Cruz'.
Firethorn.
Height: 3 ft. A low prostrate form, small enough to fit in a foundation planting. Develops an interesting mounded shape. Berries are bright red and last all winter. Zone 7.

Pyracantha koidzumii 'Victory'.
Firethorn.
Height: 10 ft. A vigorous upright grower that can get quite large. Makes a good specimen along property lines or corners. Dark red berries color in late fall and last all winter. Zone 7.

Rhaphiolepis indica 'Springtime'.
Indian hawthorn.
Height: 2–5 ft. Small flowers last for weeks in spring, followed by blue berries in late summer. Good for hedges or foundation plantings. Easy to grow. Flowers best in full sun. Zone 7.

Rhododendron catawbiense

Rhododendron cultivars

Rhododendron 'Boule de Neige'

Rhododendron kiusianum

Rhododendron yakusimanum

Rhododendron cultivars.
Height: 2–10 ft. or more. These colorful flowering shrubs do especially well in the Northwest and Northeast. There are hundreds of cultivars. Most bloom in April, May, or June. Zone 6 or 5.

Rhododendron catawbiense.
Height: 6–10 ft. An Appalachian native, parent of many hardy hybrid cultivars with lilac, purple, rose, pink, or white flowers. Has large dark leaves. Zone 5.

Rhododendron kiusianum.
Height: 2 ft. An evergreen azalea that spreads wider than tall. There are white, pink, orchid, and purple forms. Native to Japan. Semievergreen but hardy in Zone 6.

Rhododendron yakusimanum.
Height: 3 ft. An especially desirable species, parent of several cultivars and hybrids. New leaves are thickly covered with soft white hairs. Pink flower buds open into snowy flowers. Zone 5.

Rhododendron 'Boule de Neige'.
Height: 5 ft. One of the best white-flowering hybrid rhododendrons, with glossy dark foliage and a broad round habit. Tolerates sun and heat better than most. Zone 5.

Rhododendron 'George Lindley Taber'.
Height: 8–10 ft. A Southern Indica evergreen azalea. These are upright shrubs with medium-size leaves and flowers up to 3 in. wide. Zone 9 or 8.

Rhododendron 'Gumpo Pink'.
Height: to 3 ft. The Gumpo azaleas are dense, spreading, slow-growing plants with small leaves and large flowers. There are also rose-pink and white forms. Zone 7.

Rhododendron 'George Lindley Taber'

Rhododendron 'Hino Crimson'

Rhododendron 'Scintillation'

Rhododendron 'Gumpo Pink'

Rhododendron 'Roseum Elegans'

Rhododendron 'Hino Crimson'.
Height: 3–4 ft. A Kurume evergreen azalea.
These are compact bushy plants with small
glossy leaves. In April or May they are
covered with red, rose, pink, or white
flowers. Zone 7.

Rhododendron 'Roseum Elegans'.
Height: 6 ft. A large vigorous shrub. Related
cultivars have clear pink flowers without the
trace of purple. Zone 5.

Rhododendron 'Scintillation'.
Height: 5 ft. One of the best pink
rhododendrons, with abundant flowers and
excellent foliage. A vigorous grower. Zone 5.

Rhododendron 'Unique'.
Height: 4 ft. Creamy yellow flowers open
from pink buds. A compact rounded shrub
with good foliage. Zone 6.

Rhododendron 'Unique'

Skimmia japonica

Sophora secundiflora

Tecoma stans

Sarcococca hookerana var. *humilis*

Sarcococca hookerana var. humilis.
Sweet box.
Height: 18 in. A splendid evergreen ground cover for deep shade. Foliage looks fresh all year. Tiny white flowers are very fragrant in late winter. Wants rich soil. Zone 6.

Skimmia japonica.
Height: 3–5 ft. A neat, low-growing, naturally rounded shrub. White flowers are conspicuously fragrant in spring. Female plants have shiny red berries in winter. Part or full shade. Zone 7.

Sophora secundiflora.
Texas mountain laurel, mescal bean.
Height: 10–30 ft. Large purple flowers have a sweet fruity fragrance. Compound leaves are glossy dark green. Grows slowly into an upright rounded specimen. Needs good drainage. Zone 7.

Tecoma stans. Yellowbells.
Height: to 20 ft. A fast-growing shrub. Big bell-shaped flowers open from spring to late fall. Bright green foliage always looks crisp and fresh. Freezes back but soon recovers. Zone 8 or 7.

Ternstroemia gymnanthera.
Height: 4 ft. or more. A low rounded shrub with glossy foliage, small fragrant flowers in summer, and red-orange berries in fall. Needs acidic, fertile, well-drained soil. Sun or shade. Zone 7.

Viburnum davidii.
Height: 3 ft. A low, spreading shrub with pleasant but scentless flowers in spring, followed by lovely bright blue berries. Large dark green leaves have deep parallel veins. Zone 7.

Viburnum 'Pragense'.
Height: 10 ft. Small shiny leaves are semievergreen. Flowers in spring. Berries ripen from red to black. Vigorous and fast-growing. A hybrid of *V. rhytidophyllum.* Zone 5.

Viburnum suspensum.
Sandankwa viburnum.
Height: 10 ft. A large round shrub with dense evergreen foliage, white flowers in spring, and red berries in fall. Makes a good screen or hedge for large properties. Part shade. Zone 8.

Viburnum tinus. Laurustinus.
Height: 6–12 ft. An erect narrow shrub that makes a good hedge for smaller gardens. Has smooth shiny leaves, slightly fragrant white flowers, and pretty blue berries. Zone 7.

Xylosma congestum. Xylosma.
Height: 8–10 ft. A versatile shrub that can make a clipped 3–5-ft. hedge or a graceful, spreading, 6–10-ft. screen. Flowers are inconspicuous, but leaves are glossy and bright. Zone 8.

Ternstroemia gymnanthera

Viburnum davidii

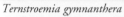

Viburnum suspensum

Viburnum 'Pragense'

Viburnum tinus

Xylosma congestum

Conifers

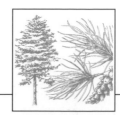

Abies concolor

Abies koreana 'Prostrate Beauty'

Cedrus deodara

Chamaecyparis lawsoniana 'Lutea'

Chamaecyparis nootkatensis

Chamaecyparis pisifera 'Boulevard'

Abies concolor. White fir.
Height: 50–150 ft. A massive tree with spreading branches, best for large properties. Blue needles curve upward. Young trees are shaped like and often used for Christmas trees. Zone 4.

Abies koreana 'Prostrate Beauty'. Korean fir.
Height: to 3 ft. Short stiff needles are dark green on top, silver below. Makes purple cones. Spreads horizontally along a bed or over a stone wall. Slow-growing. Zone 5.

Cedrus deodara. Deodar cedar.
Height: 60 ft. Long, soft, silvery blue-green needles create a feathery appearance. Young trees are conical; older trees are flat-topped. Needs plenty of space to expand when mature. Zone 6.

Chamaecyparis lawsoniana 'Lutea'. Lawson cypress.
Height: to 60 ft. A slender, dense cone shape. Foliage arrayed in flat fanlike sprays. 'Lutea' has gold foliage; other cultivars are green, blue-green, or blue-gray. Zone 6.

Chamaecyparis nootkatensis. Nootka cypress.
Height: to 60 ft. A slender cone shape. The shiny green foliage is arranged in flat sprays. Not fussy about soil and tolerates cold but can't take much heat. Zone 6.

Chamaecyparis obtusa 'Nana Gracilis'. Hinoki cypress.
Height: 6–12 ft. A slow-growing dwarf form. Shiny dark emerald foliage in dense, curving, feathery sprays. Excellent foundation, rockery, or patio plant. Zone 5.

Cryptomeria japonica 'Elegans'

Cunninghamia lanceolata 'Glauca'

Cupressus glabra

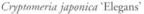

Chamaecyparis obtusa 'Nana Gracilis'

× *Cupressocyparis leylandii*

Cupressus sempervirens 'Stricta'

Chamaecyparis pisifera 'Boulevard'.
Sawara cypress.
Height: 10 ft. or more. An irregular conical shape. Soft fluffy foliage is silver-blue in summer, tinged purple in winter. Slow-growing; good for small gardens. Zone 5.

Cryptomeria japonica 'Elegans'.
Plume cedar.
Height: 20–25 ft. Forms a dense pyramid of fluffy feathery foliage, gray-green in summer and purplish bronze in winter. Needs little care. Full or part sun. Zone 6.

Cunninghamia lanceolata 'Glauca'.
China fir.
Height: 50–60 ft. A tall formal tree with stiff, sharp, blue-gray foliage. Can substitute for Colorado blue spruce in southern gardens. Older trees lose lower branches. Zone 6 or 5.

× Cupressocyparis leylandii. Leyland cypress.
Height: 20–40 ft. Fast-growing and good for screens or hedges, with flat sprays of feathery foliage. Young trees have a neat conical shape. Older trees often get straggly. Zone 6.

Cupressus glabra. Smooth Arizona cypress.
Height: 30–40 ft. A fast-growing conifer for screens or specimens in hot desert climates. Fine-textured foliage, handsome bark, and small round cones. Zone 7.

Cupressus sempervirens 'Stricta'.
Italian cypress.
Height: 30–40 ft. An unusually narrow and columnar tree with dense dark green foliage. Very formal profile. Plants with multiple leaders make interesting irregular specimens. Zone 8.

Juniperus, Junipers

Tough, adaptable, and vigorous, junipers are indispensable for home and commercial landscaping. The cultivars used as ground covers and foundation plants are most common, but other kinds make large shrubs or even trees with conical or rounded crowns. The foliage can be needlelike or scaly—sometimes both variations occur on the same plant—in shades of pale to dark green, silvery blue, or purple-bronze. The leaves and berries of most species release a pleasant fragrance if crushed.

Almost all junipers grow best in full sun and need good air circulation and well-drained soil. Most tolerate both cold and heat. Young junipers at the nursery are as cute as puppies. Old specimens often outgrow their space and may get straggly; if that happens, replace them with compact new plants.

Juniperus conferta 'Blue Pacific'

Juniperus chinensis 'Hetzii'

Juniperus chinensis 'Torulosa'

***Juniperus chinensis* 'Hetzii'.**
Height: to 10 ft. Multiple trunks radiate like a broad inverted pyramid. Can spread 12 ft. wide. Grows fast. Foliage has a pleasant fragrance. Zone 5 or 4.

***Juniperus chinensis* 'Torulosa'.**
Hollywood juniper.
Height: to 20 ft. or more. Irregular branching makes an interesting asymmetric profile. Scalelike foliage stays bright green all year. Tolerates heat and drought. Zone 5.

***Juniperus conferta* 'Blue Pacific'.**
Shore juniper.
Height: to 1 ft. A good ground cover for dry soil. Stays low and spreads up to 8 ft. wide. Tolerates sea salt. Fine short needles have a soft texture. Zone 6.

***Juniperus horizontalis* 'Bar Harbor'.**
Height: under 1 ft. Flat branches hug the ground, spreading 4–6 ft. wide. Foliage is blue-gray in summer, blue-purple in winter. Very hardy. Zone 2.

***Juniperus horizontalis* 'Blue Chip'.**
Height: under 2 ft. Makes a low mound up to 4 ft. wide. Foliage stays silver-blue all year. Zone 2.

***Juniperus sabina* 'Buffalo'.** Savin juniper.
Height: to 1 ft. A tough ground cover that spreads up to 8 ft. wide, good for covering rough banks. Foliage stays bright green all year. Needs sun and good air circulation. Zone 3.

***Juniperus scopulorum*.**
Rocky Mountain juniper.
Height: 30 ft. or more. Hardy enough to thrive in the Rocky Mountains and Great Plains, where it makes a good specimen or screen. Foliage has a pleasant aroma. Tolerates drought. Zone 4.

Juniperus sabina 'Buffalo'

Juniperus horizontalis 'Blue Chip'

Juniperus horizontalis 'Bar Harbor'

Juniperus scopulorum

Juniperus (continued)

Juniperus squamata 'Blue Star'.
Height: 2–3 ft. One of the best junipers for foundation plantings, because it doesn't grow too fast or get too big. Forms an irregular mound of sparkly foliage. Zone 4.

Juniperus virginiana. Eastern red cedar.
Height: to 30 ft. Very common throughout the eastern United States. Grows fast and makes a dense screen in any soil. Tolerates pruning. Zone 2.

Juniperus virginiana 'Skyrocket'.
Eastern red cedar.
Height: to 30 ft. A narrow, erect form that stays very skinny and never rounds out. Foliage is silvery blue all year. Zone 2.

Juniperus virginiana 'Skyrocket'

Juniperus virginiana

Juniperus squamata 'Blue Star'

Larix kaempferi. Japanese larch.
Height: 75 ft. Needles are soft green in spring, bright green in summer, clear gold in fall. Deciduous in winter. Grows fast and gets big. Needs moist, acidic, well-drained soil. Zone 4.

Metasequoia glyptostroboides.
Dawn redwood.
Height: 80 ft. or more. A deciduous conifer. Needlelike leaves turn bronze before they drop in fall. Can grow 2 ft. or more a year. Makes a lovely lawn specimen or grove. Zone 5.

Picea abies. Norway spruce.
Height: 100 ft. or more. Widely planted in the past; less so now that people see how big these trees can get. Easy to grow and makes a symmetrical cone with no pruning. Roots are shallow. Zone 3.

Picea glauca 'Conica'. Dwarf white spruce.
Height: 10 ft. Grows very slowly, with dense compact branches. Short pale needles are crowded on the twigs. Makes a formal specimen for foundation plantings or rock gardens. Zone 3.

Picea omorika. Serbian spruce.
Height: to 100 ft. A narrow and graceful tree, usually only one quarter as wide as it is tall. Short flat needles are dark green all year. Does especially well in the Northeast. Zone 4.

Picea orientalis. Oriental spruce.
Height: 60 ft. or more. Grows slower than other spruces. Glossy green needles are densely crowded on the twigs. An excellent specimen tree. Needs well-drained soil. Zone 5.

Picea pungens 'Blue Spreader'. Blue spruce.
Height: 1–2 ft. One of several dwarf cultivars, ideal for foundation plantings or rock gardens. Grows quite slowly. Zone 3.

Larix kaempferi

Picea orientalis, above and at right

Metasequoia glyptostroboides

Picea abies

Picea glauca 'Conica'

Picea omorika

Picea pungens 'Blue Spreader'

Pinus, Pines

Gardeners from coast to coast appreciate the versatility, fragrance, and character of pine trees. There are dozens of native and exotic species to choose from. They differ in foliage, habit, ultimate size, rate of growth, hardiness, adaptability to different soils, and susceptibility to insects and diseases. Ask a local nursery to recommend the best pines for your region.

Some pines, especially when young, achieve Christmas-tree symmetry without any pruning. Others, especially as they mature, develop irregular profiles and have lots of "character." Some pines grow too fast and get too big for small gardens, but if space is limited, you can choose from a wonderful variety of slow-growing species or dwarf cultivars.

Pinus mugo and *Pinus nigra*

Pinus bungeana. Lace-bark pine.
Height: 50 ft. Valued for its handsome flaking bark. Dark green needles are stiff and sharp. Grows very slowly. Zone 5.

Pinus cembra. Swiss stone pine.
Height: 35 ft. or more. Uncommon but desirable. Young trees fit easily into small gardens. Foliage is dense and rich. Zone 4.

Pinus densiflora 'Umbraculifera'.
Tanyosho pine.
Height: 10–25 ft. Grows slowly but makes a handsome specimen at all ages. Trunks have attractive flaking bark. Zone 5.

Pinus flexilis 'Glauca'. Limber pine.
Height: 25–50 ft. Tolerates dry, rocky soil and wind; a fine substitute for eastern white pine on difficult sites. Zone 4.

Pinus halepensis. Aleppo pine.
Height: to 60 ft. Grows fast and has interesting irregular branching. Tolerates desert heat and drought. Zone 8.

Pinus mugo. Dwarf mugo pine.
Height: can reach 15 ft. Some forms are more compact than others, but all have dense dark green foliage. Tolerates salt. Zone 3.

Pinus nigra. Austrian black pine.
Height: 40–60 ft. Very adaptable and widely planted. Foliage is especially dark green, even in winter. Tolerates salt. Zone 4.

Pinus ponderosa. Ponderosa pine.
Height: 60 ft. or more. Older trees have an open crown and furrowed bark. Coarse needles are 4–8 in. long. A western native. Zone 4.

Pinus strobus. Eastern white pine.
Height: 80 ft. or more. Fine needles have a very soft texture. Grows fast. Prefers rich, moist, organic soil. Zone 3.

Pinus sylvestris 'Watereri'.
Dwarf Scotch pine.
Height: 10 ft. or more. A slow-growing cultivar with blue needles. Tolerates poor, dry, sandy, acidic soil. Zone 3.

Pinus thunbergiana.
Japanese black pine.
Height: 20–80 ft. Especially useful for seaside plantings, because it tolerates salt spray and winds. Grows fast. Zone 6.

Pinus bungeana

Pinus cembra

Pinus densiflora 'Umbraculifera'

Pinus strobus

Pinus halepensis

Pinus thunbergiana

Pinus flexilis 'Glauca'

Pinus sylvestris 'Watereri'

Pinus ponderosa

Podocarpus macrophyllus

Taxus cuspidata

Sequoiadendron giganteum

Thuja occidentalis 'Rheingold'

Thuja orientalis 'Aurea Nana'

Taxodium distichum

Podocarpus macrophyllus. Yew pine. Height: to 30 ft. Grows narrowly upright. Responds well to pruning—can be kept small, used as a hedge, or trained for espalier or topiary. Leathery needles are 3–4 in. long. Zone 8.

Sequoiadendron giganteum. Big tree, giant sequoia. Height: 80 ft. Gets huge in old age, but a young tree forms a dense narrow pyramid. Gray-green needles are short and sharp. Needs very little care. Average soil and watering. Zone 7.

Taxodium distichum. Bald cypress. Height: to 100 ft. Drops its needles in winter; grows new ones in spring. They turn dark green in summer and rusty red in fall. A fast-growing and adaptable tree. Zone 5.

Taxus cuspidata. Japanese yew. Height: varies. Cultivars can be spreading or upright, and they differ in rate of growth and ultimate size. All can be sheared into neat formal shapes or allowed to spread naturally. Foliage may turn bronze in winter or stay green all year. Zone 4.

Taxus × media

Thuja occidentalis 'Woodwardii'

Thuja plicata

Tsuga canadensis 'Sargent's Weeping'

Taxus × media. Hybrid yew.
Height: varies. There are several cultivars. A popular choice for hedges, foundation plantings, and specimens. Can be sheared into formal shapes. Foliage may turn bronze in winter or stay green all year. Zone 5 or 4, depending on cultivar.

***Thuja occidentalis* 'Rheingold'.**
Rheingold arborvitae.
Height: 3–4 ft. Makes a small cone of dense foliage in rich metallic shades of gold, copper, and bronze. Looks pretty all year in a rock garden or mixed border. Zone 3.

***Thuja occidentalis* 'Woodwardii'.**
Globe arborvitae.
Height: 8 ft. Grows naturally into a rounded shape. Stays small for years but eventually gets quite large. Commonly offered and popular, but foliage is subject to winterburn. Zone 3.

***Thuja orientalis* 'Aurea Nana' ('Golden Ball').**
Height: 3 ft. A compact dwarf. Flat sprays of foliage are arranged in vertical alignment. Color is bright gold from spring to fall but darkens to bronze in cold weather. Zone 6.

Thuja plicata.
Western arborvitae, giant arborvitae.
Height: 50–70 ft. Young trees grow fast and make a narrow cone or pyramid, spreading wider with age. Fragrant foliage is bright green in summer, golden brown in cold weather. Zone 5.

***Tsuga canadensis* 'Sargent's Weeping'.**
Weeping Canada hemlock.
Height: to 15 ft. One of the best weeping conifers. Feathery foliage stays rich green all year. Upright forms make good specimens or hedges. Needs cool, moist, acidic soil. Zone 4.

Vines

Actinidia deliciosa

Actinidia kolomikta

Akebia quinata

Ampelopsis brevipedunculata

Antigonon leptopus

Actinidia deliciosa. Kiwi.
Height: 30 ft. Vigorous and sprawling. Round wide leaves; creamy flowers on old growth in spring. Edible egg-sized fruits with green flesh and fuzzy brown skin. Quickly covers a trellis, fence, arbor, or patio. Zone 8.

Actinidia kolomikta.
Height: 20 ft. Heart-shaped green leaves splashed with pink and white. Males have showier leaves. Females have edible yellow fruits. Vigorous and hardy but doesn't take heat well. Full or part sun. Zone 5.

Akebia quinata. Five-leaf akebia.
Height: 20 ft. Fast-growing. Wide, glossy, palmate leaves have 5 rounded leaflets. Inconspicuous fragrant flowers; edible purple fruits. Evergreen in mild climates. Good as shade for an entry or arbor. Zone 5.

Ampelopsis brevipedunculata.
Porcelain berry.
Height: 20 ft. Fast-growing. Climbs by tendrils. Toothed 3-lobed leaves are dark green in summer, red in fall. Small berries ripen to metallic turquoise-blue. Zone 5.

Antigonon leptopus. Coral vine.
Height: 10–40 ft. A fast-growing climber with papery heart-shaped leaves. Clusters of rosy pink flowers in late summer or fall. Makes a lacy edging for a porch or arbor. Full sun. Zone 8.

Aristolochia durior. Dutchman's-pipe.
Height: to 30 ft. Fast-growing, with a shinglelike array of wide heart-shaped leaves. Pipe-shaped green and burgundy flowers open briefly in spring or summer. Dark gray fruits in fall. Zone 4.

Aristolochia durior

Bignonia capreolata

Bougainvillea 'Barbara Karst'

Campsis radicans, above and below

Celastrus orbiculatus

Bignonia capreolata. Cross vine.
Height: 60 ft. Orange to red trumpet-shaped flowers in late spring. Needs full sun to bloom abundantly. Evergreen leaves turn purplish in winter. Climbs by tendrils. Zone 6.

Bougainvillea 'Barbara Karst'.
Height: to 20 ft. Sturdy, with tough thorny stems and evergreen leaves. Papery floral bracts last for months. Colors include bright shades of red, pink, magenta, orange, and white. Good in a container or in the ground, or as a shrub if pruned hard. Zone 10 or 9.

Campsis radicans. Trumpet vine.
Height: 30 ft. or more. Clusters of reddish orange flowers attract hummingbirds from June to fall. Dry woody pods last all winter. Tendrils can damage roofs, masonry, or screens. Zone 5.

Celastrus orbiculatus. Oriental bittersweet.
Height: 30 ft. or more. Clusters of orange berries are very showy after the leaves drop in fall and winter. Climbs by twining and can strangle other plants; keep it away from small trees and shrubs. Zone 5.

Clematis, Clematis

The most popular of all garden vines, clematis are easy to grow and versatile. Use one to decorate a mailbox or lamppost, shade a porch or pergola, scramble over a shrub or into a tree, screen an undesirable view, trace an "eyebrow" along the top of a fence or wall, or weave among perennials as a ground cover.

Clematis thrive in ordinary garden soil with regular watering. For best results, choose a site where the foliage and flowers can grow in the sun but the roots are shaded by a rock, wall, or generous mulch. Clematis require little care beyond annual pruning.

Clematis 'Nellie Moser'

Clematis 'Comptesse de Bouchard'

Clematis armandii

Clematis armandii. Evergreen clematis. Height: 20 ft. or more. Abundant fragrant white flowers in early spring. Feathery-tailed seeds in fall. Excellent for a porch, arbor, fence, or wall. Sun or shade. Zone 8.

Clematis 'Betty Corning'. Height: to 15 ft. Pale lavender bells bloom on new growth. Slender stems of leathery dark green foliage. Let it climb over a shrub or hedge. Zone 5.

Clematis 'Comptesse de Bouchard'. Height: to 15 ft. Spectacular, soft rosy pink flowers with large rounded sepals. Climbs vigorously up a lightpost, trellis, or tree. Also good as a ground cover. Zone 5.

Clematis macropetala. Downy clematis. Height: 6–10 ft. Wide, flaring, scentless double flowers from white to deep blue in spring to summer. Feathery seed clusters in fall. Good over shrubs, on a trellis, or as a ground cover. Zone 5.

Clematis maximowicziana. Sweet autumn clematis. Height: 20 ft. or more. Covered with small, starry, fragrant white flowers in late summer. Silvery plumelike fruits through fall. Aggressive. Part sun. Zone 4.

Clematis montana. Anemone clematis. Height: 25 ft. or more. Makes a spectacular display of white or pinkish almond-scented flowers in spring. Develops a strong trunk and will cover a large wall or fence. Sun or shade. Zone 6.

Clematis 'Nellie Moser'. Height: to 15 ft. Outstanding flat pink blossoms with a reddish center stripe. Dark foliage. Old shoots bloom in spring, new shoots in summer. Vigorous climber. Zone 5.

Clematis 'Betty Corning'

Clematis montana

Clematis macropetala

Clematis maximowicziana

Clematis (continued)

Clematis tangutica. Golden clematis.
Height: 9–10 ft. Bright yellow, bell-shaped,
scentless flowers on slender stalks in summer and
fall. Masses of feathery seed clusters from fall
into winter. Bright green foliage. Zone 5.

Clematis texensis **'Étoile Rosé'.**
Scarlet clematis.
Height: 6–15 ft. Small bell-shaped flowers with
silver-edged rosy purple sepals in spring and
summer. Tolerates heat and dryness. Not
aggressive. Zone 7.

Hedera canariensis 'Variegata'

Clematis tangutica

Hedera helix 'Baltica'

Clematis texensis 'Étoile Rosé'

Hedera helix 'Needlepoint'

Clytostoma callistegioides.
Violet trumpet vine.
Height: 30–40 ft. Clusters of lavender or light purple tubular flowers from late spring to fall. Bright green leaves. Quick cover for a fence, wall, balcony, or eave. Zone 9 or 8.

Distictis buccinatoria.
Blood-red trumpet vine.
Height: to 30 ft. Clusters of trumpet-shaped flowers, orangish red to purplish red with yellow throats. Blooms repeatedly throughout warm weather. Shiny dark foliage. Zone 9.

Euonymus fortunei.
Winter creeper.
Height: varies. One of the hardiest evergreen vines, good as a ground cover or climber. Spreads fairly quickly and needs little maintenance. Adapts to most soils. Grows in sun or shade. Zone 5.

Euonymus fortunei 'Gracilis'.
Winter creeper.
Height: varies. Small green leaves are variegated with white or cream in summer; pale area turns pinkish in winter. Good as a ground cover or climber. Tolerates sun or shade. Zone 5.

Ficus pumila.
Creeping fig.
Height: to 25 ft. or more. An evergreen vine that clings tenaciously to wood, stone, or brick. Young plants are delicate. Older plants have coarser stems and larger leaves. Zone 8.

Gelsemium sempervirens.
Carolina jasmine.
Height: to 20 ft. Covers itself with fragrant yellow flowers in early spring. Slender dark green leaves may turn purplish in winter. Often planted on mailbox posts or fences. Zone 8.

Hedera canariensis 'Variegata'.
Algerian ivy.
Height: 50 ft. or more. Both this and a solid green form are very fast, tough ground covers for sun or shade in mild climates. Leaves are thick and leathery, up to 8 in. wide. Zone 9.

Hedera helix 'Baltica'.
English ivy.
Height: to 50 ft. A vigorous ground cover or climber with medium-size leaves that stay dark green all winter. Very hardy. Zone 5.

Hedera helix 'Needlepoint'.
English ivy.
Height: to 10 ft. Relatively slow growing and compact, good for small corners. Leaves are small but set close together. May freeze back but recovers from the roots. Zone 6.

Clytostoma callistegioides

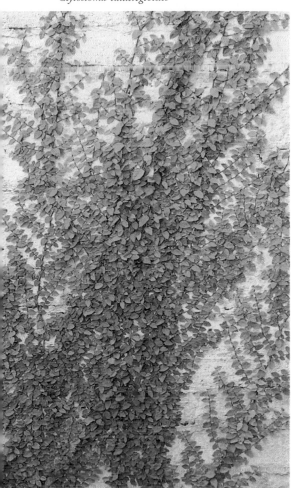

Ficus pumila

Distictis buccinatoria

Euonymus fortunei

Euonymus fortunei 'Gracilis'

Gelsemium sempervirens

Hydrangea anomala subsp. petiolaris

Lonicera × heckrottii

Lonicera sempervirens

Lonicera japonica 'Halliana'

Mandevilla × amabilis 'Alice du Pont'

Hydrangea anomala subsp. petiolaris.
Climbing hydrangea.
Height: 60–80 ft. Climbs slowly up a tree, wall, or chimney. Flowers for weeks in midsummer on shoots that project about 3 ft. from the anchored stems. Takes sun or shade. Zone 5.

Lonicera × heckrottii.
Gold-flame honeysuckle.
Height: 10–20 ft. Blooms most heavily in spring but continues until frost. Smooth blue-green foliage is evergreen where winters are mild. Grows fast but isn't invasive. Full or part sun. Zone 5 or 4.

Lonicera japonica 'Halliana'.
Hall's honeysuckle.
Height: 15–20 ft. An invasive weed in parts of the East and South; vigorous but safe to plant in dry climates. Flowers are intensely sweet. Blooms spring to fall. Zone 5 or 4.

Lonicera sempervirens.
Trumpet honeysuckle.
Height: 10–15 ft. Flowers are scentless but attract hummingbirds. Climbs by twining or can be quite shrubby. Easy to grow but not weedy or invasive. Native but uncommon. Zone 4.

Mandevilla × amabilis 'Alice du Pont'.
Height: 10 ft. or more. Tender but widely available and commonly grown as a summer patio plant. Grows well in containers and climbs quickly to cover a trellis. Evergreen. Zone 10.

Parthenocissus quinquefolia.
Virginia creeper.
Height: 40–50 ft. A versatile vine that can climb up a tree, cover a fence or wall, or scramble as a ground cover. Grows fast. Large compound leaves turn bright red in early fall. Zone 2.

Parthenocissus tricuspidata

Parthenocissus quinquefolia

Passiflora × alatocaerulea

Parthenocissus tricuspidata.
Boston ivy.
Height: 40–50 ft. This is the "ivy" at Ivy League colleges. Does best on north or east walls. Stems cling tight. Small leaves overlap like shingles. Turns bright scarlet in fall. Zone 2.

Passiflora × alatocaerulea.
Passionvine.
Height: 20 ft. A vigorous vine that climbs or scrambles over anything it touches. Intricate flowers are very fragrant. Blooms all summer. Freezes to the ground in severe winters. Zone 8 or 7.

Polygonum aubertii. Silver fleece vine.
Height: 25–35 ft. Grows very fast and climbs on fences or into trees. Covers itself with fragrant white flowers in midsummer. May freeze to the ground but blooms on new growth. Zone 5.

Polygonum aubertii

Rosa banksiae 'Lutea'

Rosa 'Blaze'

Rosa 'Golden Showers'

Solanum jasminoides

Rosa 'New Dawn'

Rosa banksiae 'Lutea'. Lady Banks rose. Height: 20–30 ft. Slender, nearly thornless canes can be trained on a trellis, fence, or other support. Scentless 1-in. flowers open in early spring. There's also a white form. Not hardy.

Rosa 'Blaze'.
Height: to 12 ft. Blooms over a long season and requires little care. Semidouble flowers are 2½–3 in. wide. Can be trained to a vertical or horizontal support. Tolerates both heat and cold.

Rosa 'Golden Showers'.
Height: 8–10 ft. Semidouble flowers are fragrant, 3½–4 in. wide. Can be trained against a wall or up a post or grown as an upright shrub. Blooms over a long season. Fairly hardy.

Rosa 'New Dawn'.
Height: 12–15 ft. Semidouble flowers are fragrant, 3–3½ in. wide. Blooms midseason and repeats in fall. Vigorous, disease-free, and hardy.

Solanum jasminoides.
Potato vine.
Height: 15 ft. or more. Blooms most in spring but continues all year in very mild areas. Quickly covers a trellis or wall. Foliage is semievergreen. Zone 10 or 9.

Trachelospermum asiaticum.
Asian jasmine.
Height: 12 in. A tough evergreen ground cover. Grows dense enough to keep out weeds or to stabilize a slope. Interplant with daffodils for spring color. Usually doesn't flower. Zone 8.

Trachelospermum asiaticum

Trachelospermum jasminoides

Vitis rotundifolia

Wisteria sinensis

Vitis vinifera

Wisteria floribunda

Trachelospermum jasminoides.
Confederate jasmine, star jasmine.
Height: to 20 ft. Blooms mostly in late spring and early summer. Flowers are very fragrant, especially in the evening. Can be used as a ground cover or trained up a tree trunk or trellis. Zone 8.

Vitis rotundifolia.
Muscadine grape.
Height: 20 ft. or more. Large leaves are green all summer, gold in fall. Self-pollinating cultivars such as 'Carlos' and 'Noble' make large tasty grapes. Grows best in the South. Zone 8 or 7.

Vitis vinifera. Grapes.
Height: 20 ft. or more. Beautiful as well as productive, grapes thrive in warm sunny weather. Ask locally to determine which kinds grow best in your area. 'Purpurea', shown above, is grown more for its red-purple foliage than its fruits. All grapes need annual pruning. Zone 8 or 7.

Wisteria floribunda.
Japanese wisteria.
Height: 30 ft. or more. Blooms in spring. Violet, blue, or white flowers hang in slender clusters up to 3 ft. long. A tough vigorous vine. Provide a strong trellis or support. Zone 5.

Wisteria sinensis.
Chinese wisteria.
Height: 30 ft. or more. Can climb any support but is often trained into a small weeping standard with a thick trunk. White, blue, or violet flowers are very fragrant in spring. Zone 5.

Grasses, bamboos, and grasslike plants

Acorus gramineus 'Ogon'

Bambusa oldhamii

Buchloe dactyloides

Calamagrostis × *acutiflora* 'Karl Foerster'

Acorus gramineus 'Ogon'.
Japanese sweet flag.
Height: 12 in. Upright fans of slender
yellow-striped leaves. Thrives in moist soil.
Slow-spreading. Part sun or shade. Zone 6.

Arundinaria viridistriata.
Running bamboo.
Height: 30 in. Spreading rhizomes and leafy
upright stems. New leaves are vibrant gold
with bright green stripes. Controls erosion on
steep banks. Tolerates shade. Zone 4.

Bambusa oldhamii.
Giant timber bamboo.
Height: 50–55 ft. A clump-forming bamboo
with thick woody stems. Evergreen leaves up
to 12 in. long make a dense mass of foliage.
Plant singly or in pairs to line an entryway.
Full sun. Zone 8.

Buchloe dactyloides. Buffalograss.
Height: 3–5 in. A perennial creeping grass.
Fine, curly, sage green blades turn straw-tan
and stiff in cold weather. Makes a good lawn
or ground cover for hot, dry climates.
Zone 5.

Calamagrostis × acutiflora 'Karl Foerster'.
Feather reed grass.
Height: 5–6 ft. Forms strongly vertical
clumps of slender leaves with tall flower
stalks that develop in June, hold through
winter. Seed heads ripen from gold to silver.
Cut back in spring. Zone 5.

Carex buchananii.
Leatherleaf sedge.
Height: 2 ft. Airy tufts of shiny cinnamon-
colored foliage that goes well with blues,
whites, and greens. Delicate arching leaves
curl gracefully at the tips. Part sun or shade.
Zone 6.

Carex morrowii 'Aureo-variegata'.
Variegated Japanese sedge.
Height: 12 in. Neat, low, evergreen tufts
of bright yellow-and-green striped leaves.
Brightens dark shady areas or the edges of
borders, ponds, or rock gardens. Easy to
grow. Zone 6 or 5.

Chasmanthium latifolium.
Northern sea oats.
Height: 3–5 ft. Broad close-set leaves are
green in summer and fall, tan in winter. Flat
oatlike seed heads. Self-sows and spreads as a
ground cover on slopes or in a woodland.
Shade-tolerant. Zone 4.

Cortaderia selloana. Pampas grass.
Height: 8 ft. or more. Makes large clumps
of slender, arching, sharp-edged leaves.
Flowering plumes on long stems last from
late summer through midwinter. Easy to
grow. Zone 7.

Dasylirion texanum. Sotol.
Height: 2–3 ft. Slender spiny edged leaves
are evergreen. Makes flower stalks up to 15
ft. tall in late spring. Full or part sun.
Tolerates poor soil. Easy to grow. Zone 8.

Chasmanthium latifolium

Carex buchananii

Carex morrowii 'Aureo-variegata'

Cortaderia selloana

Dasylirion texanum

Festuca ovina var. *glauca*

Festuca ovina 'Sea Urchin'

Erianthus ravennae

Deschampsia caespitosa

Hakonechloa macra 'Aureola'

Helictotrichon sempervirens

Hordeum jubatum

Imperata cylindrica 'Red Baron'

Miscanthus sinensis 'Gracillimus'

Miscanthus sinensis var. *purpurascens*

Deschampsia caespitosa. Tufted hair grass. Height: 2–3 ft. Forms clouds of tiny delicate flowers in summer. Foliage is semievergreen, even in the North. Excellent for mass plantings. Part shade. Zone 4.

Erianthus ravennae. Ravenna grass. Height: 9–12 ft. A huge dramatic grass for specimens or screening. Forms a mound of coarse wide leaves and stiff reedlike stalks. Flower plumes last into winter. Zone 4.

Festuca ovina var. glauca. Blue fescue. Height: 6–12 in. Forms pincushions of blue foliage, evergreen in mild climates. Most plants sold are seedlings, and "blueness" varies. Needs full sun and good drainage. Zone 4.

Festuca ovina 'Sea Urchin'. Height: 6–12 in. Makes a small clump of bright blue foliage that holds its color all winter. Flower stalks reach 12 in. tall in summer. Easy and long lived. Rarely needs dividing. Zone 4.

Hakonechloa macra 'Aureola'. Height: 1–1¹/₂ ft. Makes a soft mound of variegated foliage. Flowers are inconspicuous. Perennial, spreading slowly from year to year. Takes part sun. Zone 5.

Helictotrichon sempervirens. Blue oat grass. Height: 18–30 in. Comparable to blue fescue grass, but it makes a larger clump. Foliage stays pretty into winter. Needs well-drained soil. Perennial. Full or part sun. Zone 4.

Hordeum jubatum. Foxtail barley. Height: 18–30 in. Awned flower heads are showy in the garden and last well in fresh or dried arrangements. Self-seeds and can be weedy. Usually grown as an annual.

Imperata cylindrica 'Red Baron'. Japanese blood grass. Height: 12–18 in. Grown for its bright red foliage, which is especially striking if backlit by the sun. Grows best in moist, fertile soil with full or part sun. Zone 6.

Miscanthus sinensis 'Gracillimus'. Height: 5–6 ft. Has slender gray-green leaves with distinct white midribs. Flowers in late September or October; may not bloom in northern gardens. Zone 5.

Miscanthus sinensis var. purpurascens. Height: 3–4 ft. Foliage is green in summer, turning red, orange, and/or gold in fall and buff in winter. Flowers open early and last all winter. Prefers moist sites. Spreads by rhizomes. Zone 6.

Miscanthus sinensis 'Silverfeather'

Miscanthus sinensis 'Variegatus'

Miscanthus sinensis 'Zebrinus'

Panicum virgatum

Molinia caerulea 'Variegata'

Miscanthus sinensis 'Silverfeather'.
Height: 6–9 ft. Forms a wide clump. Leaves are fairly broad. Flowers open in August, earlier than most cultivars, and last well into the winter. Zone 5.

Miscanthus sinensis 'Variegatus'.
Height: 5–6 ft. Has a creamy white stripe down the center of each leaf. Doesn't bloom until late September or October; may not bloom in northern gardens. Zone 5.

Miscanthus sinensis 'Zebrinus'.
Height: 6–8 ft. Makes a soft open clump of unusual foliage. Leaves have crosswise stripes of green and gold. Flowers open in September. Zone 5.

Molinia caerulea 'Variegata'.
Variegated purple moor grass.
Height: 18 in. (foliage). Arching leaves are yellow with green stripes. Brown-purple flowers and seeds wave 8–12 in. above the leaves in late summer. Makes an undulating ground cover. Zone 5.

Panicum virgatum.
Switch grass.
Height: 3–6 ft. A native grass, easy and adaptable. Upright clumps of foliage hold up all winter. Airy masses of flowers last from July to fall. Named cultivars have colored foliage. Zone 4.

Pennisetum orientale. Fountain grass.
Height: 1–2 ft. (foliage). Graceful spikes of flowers spread 1 ft. above the clump of foliage in summer. Grown as an annual north of Zone 7. *P. alopecuroides* is similar but grows bigger and is hardy to Zone 5.

Pennisetum setaceum 'Rubrum'.
Crimson fountain grass.
Height: 2–3 ft. Flower spikes wave above the foliage from June to fall. This form doesn't set seed and isn't weedy. Perennial in Zone 8; grown as an annual in colder regions.

Pennisetum villosum. Feathertop.
Height: 2–2 1/2 ft. Fluffy white flower plumes look good from July through September but don't last into winter. Perennial in Zone 8; grown as an annual in colder regions.

Phalaris arundinacea 'Picta'. Ribbon grass.
Height: 2–4 ft. Pretty but very invasive. Useful as a ground cover for difficult spots or in confined areas. Grows in any soil. Cut back in midsummer to renew the foliage. Zone 4.

Phormium tenax. New Zealand flax.
Height: 8–9 ft. Not a grass but used like one. Makes crowded clumps of bright-colored, sword-shaped, evergreen leaves. Flowers in summer. Compact cultivars fit smaller gardens. Zone 8.

Pennisetum orientale

Pennisetum villosum

Phormium tenax

Pennisetum setaceum 'Rubrum'

Phalaris arundinacea 'Picta'

Phyllostachys aureosulcata

Phyllostachys nigra

Sasa palmata

Sasa veitchii

Schizachyrium scoparium 'Blaze'

Semiarundinaria murielae

Sorghastrum nutans

Yucca filamentosa

Sporobolus heterolopis

Yucca flaccida 'Golden Sword'

Phyllostachys aureosulcata.
Yellow-groove bamboo.
Height: 15–20 ft. Spreads to make a grove of woody culms up to 1¹/₂ in. thick. Must be confined with deep edging or it will take over the neighborhood. Overgrown patches are common throughout the South. Leaves and culms are hardy to Zone 6.

Phyllostachys nigra.
Black bamboo.
Height: 15–25 ft. Culms are shiny black, up to 1 in. thick. Must be confined or it will spread many feet in all directions. Makes a lovely grove for a Japanese-style garden. Zone 7.

Sasa palmata.
Height: 6 ft. or more. A vigorous bamboo that spreads fast by underground runners. Install deep barriers at planting time if you want to keep it in place. Grows in sun or shade. Zone 7.

Sasa veitchii.
Height: 2–3 ft. Evergreen leaves are green in summer but turn creamy around the edge in fall. Makes a good ground cover for shady spots. Spreads, but not as fast as some bamboos. Zone 7.

Schizachyrium scoparium.
Little bluestem.
Height: 2–3 ft. A small native grass that forms erect clumps. Summer flowers mature into fluffy seed heads that sparkle when backlit. 'Blaze', shown on p. 214, has excellent fall color. Zone 3.

Semiarundinaria murielae.
Height: to 15 ft., usually less. Slender culms arch gracefully. Makes a clump that spreads slowly and isn't too invasive. Dense foliage makes an effective screen. Takes sun or shade. Zone 7.

Sorghastrum nutans. Indian grass.
Height: 3–5 ft. A native prairie grass that makes a good informal screen or background.

Slender leaves turn bronze or burnt orange in fall. Adaptable and easy to grow. Zone 4.

Sporobolus heterolopis.
Prairie dropseed, northern dropseed.
Height: 18–24 in. Delicate leaves are emerald in summer, gold in fall and winter. Flowers have a unique, pleasant fragrance. Native to moist prairies but tolerates poor, dry soil. Zone 3.

Yucca filamentosa.
Bear grass, Adam's needle.
Height: 2–3 ft. (foliage); 5–6 ft. (flowers). A tough, adaptable, long-lived perennial for sunny dry sites. Leaves are evergreen. Flowers in June. Has interesting woody pods. Zone 5.

Yucca flaccida 'Golden Sword'.
Variegated bear grass.
Height: 2–3 ft. Variegated foliage is evergreen, but leaves may droop in very cold weather. Spreads slowly to form a patch of many clumps or rosettes. Needs well-drained soil and full sun. Zone 5.

Ferns

Adiantum capillus-veneris

Adiantum pedatum

Athyrium filix-femina

Athyrium goeringianum 'Pictum'

Adiantum capillus-veneris.
Southern maidenhair fern.
Height: 6–12 in. Fans of lacy, soft green fronds on wiry black stipes. Needs shade and constant moisture. Grows well in cracks and crevices of stone walls and fences. Zone 8.

Adiantum pedatum.
American maidenhair fern.
Height: 1–2 ft. Dainty fan-shaped fronds on wiry stems. Delicate in appearance but quite hardy. Good in crevices of a rock garden or shaded pockets. Shade or part sun. Zone 3.

Athyrium filix-femina. Lady fern.
Height: 2–3 ft. Divided arching fronds are wide at the base and narrow at their tips. Easy to grow. Plant on the north side of a building or fence or in a shady border. Zone 3.

Athyrium goeringianum 'Pictum'.
Japanese painted fern.
Height: 12–18 in. Triangular tricolor fronds of burgundy, silver-gray, and green. Good clustered in a shady border or woodland garden. Part or full shade. Zone 3.

Cyrtomium falcatum.
Holly fern.
Height: 2–3 ft. Forms an arching clump of leathery, glossy, dark green fronds with long toothed leaflets. Good for containers or sheltered sites. Part sun or shade. Zone 9.

Dryopteris affinis.
Height: 2–3 ft. Forms neat clumps of leathery glossy fronds that are broad at the base and taper to the tip. Stems have golden scales. Stays green well into winter. Part sun or shade. Zone 4.

Cyrtomium falcatum

Dryopteris affinis

Dryopteris filix-mas

Dryopteris marginalis

Dryopteris erythrosora.
Japanese autumn fern.
Height: 24–30 in. Mature fronds are shiny
dark green; new growth is coppery pink.
Good in mass plantings with evergreen
shrubs. Part sun or shade. Zone 4.

Dryopteris filix-mas. Male fern.
Height: 2–4 ft. Forms large clumps of long,
wide, leathery fronds, dissected into many
fine segments. Stems are scaly brown. Good
as a specimen or in mass plantings. Part sun
or shade. Zone 3.

Dryopteris marginalis.
Marginal shield fern.
Height: 18–24 in. Arching lance-shaped
fronds are yellow-green when new and
mature to dark blue-green. Before fronds
unfurl, coarse brown scales cover the crown.
Zone 3.

Lygodium japonicum.
Japanese climbing fern.
Height: 10–15 ft. Climbs on trees or shrubs
(doesn't hurt them) or makes a soft curtain
of green on a fence or arbor. Semievergreen.
Naturalized in the South. Zone 8.

Dryopteris erythrosora

Lygodium japonicum

Matteuccia struthiopteris

Nephrolepis exaltata

Osmunda cinnamomea

Matteuccia struthiopteris. Ostrich fern. Height: to 5 ft. Giant clumps of feathery fronds look wonderful in spring but usually turn brown by late summer. Spreads to make a large colony. Needs rich soil and must never dry out. Zone 2.

Nephrolepis exaltata. Sword fern. Height: to 5 ft. Very common as a ground cover for part sun or shade where winters are mild. Spreads by runners. Erect fronds are evergreen. Also grows well in containers. Zone 9.

Osmunda cinnamomea. Cinnamon fern. Height: 2–3 ft. Fertile fronds emerge in early spring and look like cinnamon sticks. Large sterile fronds are bright green all summer. Forms a big clump. Prefers damp soil. Zone 3.

Osmunda claytoniana. Interrupted fern. Height: 2–4 ft. Fronds are white with wool when they first unroll in early spring, bright green all summer, gold in fall. A rugged, long-lived fern. Can grow in rocky, dry soil. Zone 3.

Osmunda regalis. Royal fern. Height: 5–6 ft. or more. Grows taller than many shrubs but dies to the ground each winter. Frond segments resemble honey-locust tree leaves. Needs moist, fertile, acidic, organic soil. Zone 3.

Polystichum acrostichoides. Christmas fern. Height: 2–3 ft. Leathery evergreen fronds are glossy green, up to 5 in. wide and 2–3 ft.

long. Grows wild in eastern woodlands. Needs rich, moist soil. Part sun or shade. Zone 3.

Polystichum munitum. Sword fern. Height: 2–4 ft. Large fronds are leathery and evergreen. Forms clumps that spread slowly. A West Coast native. Tolerates some heat or dryness but not both at the same time. Zone 4.

Polystichum polyblepharum. Tassel fern. Height: 2 ft. Stiff glossy fronds are evergreen. Good for shady corners or the north side of a house. Needs rich, acidic soil and constant moisture. Protect from sun and wind. Zone 4.

Polystichum setiferum. Soft shield fern. Height: 3 ft. Narrow fronds have a soft texture and lie close to the ground. Looks delicate but tolerates poor, dry soil. There are many cultivars with unique foliage. Semievergreen. Zone 5.

Rumohra adiantiformis. Leatherleaf fern. Height: to 3 ft. The toughest and most tolerant fern for warm-winter climates. Cut fronds make excellent greenery for bouquets. Needs shade from hot sun. Prefers moist, fertile soil. Zone 9.

Thelypteris kunthii. Wood fern. Height: to 3 ft. One of the best ferns for southern gardens. Spreads steadily by rhizomes but isn't invasive. Use it to fill shady corners or to replace the grass under trees. Zone 8 or 7.

Osmunda claytoniana

Osmunda regalis

Polystichum acrostichoides

Polystichum munitum

Polystichum polyblepharum

Polystichum setiferum

Rumohra adiantiformis

Thelypteris kunthii

Perennials

Acanthus mollis

Achillea 'Coronation Gold'

Achillea millefolium 'Summer Pastels'

Achillea 'Moonshine'

Aconitum napellus

Acanthus mollis.
Bear's-breeches.
Height: 3 ft. Tall spikes of whitish, lilac, or rose flowers with green or purplish bracts. Glossy, lobed, toothed leaves with small soft spines. Needs light shade. Zone 8.

Achillea 'Coronation Gold'.
Yarrow.
Height: 3 ft. Sturdy, with pungent, gray-green, fernlike leaves. Dense flat clusters of small bright yellow flowers in summer. Good in borders. Full or part sun. Zone 3.

Achillea millefolium 'Summer Pastels'.
Height: 2–3 ft. Rose, reddish, pale pink, salmon, yellow, and creamy white flowers. Pungent, gray-green, fernlike leaves. Ideal in meadow gardens and as a ground cover. Zone 3.

Achillea 'Moonshine'. Yarrow.
Height: 2 ft. Clusters of lemon yellow flowers bloom on long stalks from June to August. Forms a basal mound of pungent, soft gray, finely dissected leaves. Good in borders. Full sun. Zone 3.

Aconitum napellus. Monkshood.
Height: 3–5 ft. Spikes of hoodlike blue or purple flowers bloom on tall stalks for 3–4 weeks in late summer and fall. Forms a low mound of glossy, deeply lobed leaves. Good as an accent in a shaded border. Zone 2.

Agapanthus orientalis. Lily-of-the-Nile.
Height: to 5 ft. Spheres of blue flowers on tall stems. Basal mound of firm arching leaves. Other forms have pale blue or white flowers. Does well in containers. Part to full sun. Zone 8.

Agapanthus orientalis

Ajuga reptans 'Burgundy Glow'

Alchemilla mollis

Agave attenuata

Agave vilmoriniana

Agave attenuata. Century plant.
Height: 5 ft. Forms a squat rosette of fleshy pale jade leaves. Eventually produces a tall spike of greenish yellow flowers. Good for dry landscapes. Full sun; part shade in the desert. Zone 9.

Agave vilmoriniana. Octopus agave.
Height: 4 ft. Pale green, curling and twisting leaves with spiny tips and smooth edges. Occasionally bears a tall spike of yellow flowers in spring or summer. Full sun; part shade in the desert. Zone 9.

Ajuga reptans 'Burgundy Glow'.
Bugleweed.
Height: 4–8 in. Has shiny multicolored leaves and blue flowers. Other ajugas have plain green or variegated foliage. All make good ground covers, spreading fast in damp soil. Sun or shade. Zone 3.

Alchemilla mollis. Lady's-mantle.
Height: 1–2 ft. Clouds of small chartreuse flowers on tall stalks in spring. Wide, pleated, and scalloped leaves unfold to form a soft gray-green mound. Sun or shade. Zone 3.

Allium cernuum

Allium christophii

Allium moly

Allium neapolitanum

Aloe arborescens

Aloe saponaria

Allium cernuum,
Nodding wild onion,
Height: 8–12 in. Clusters of pink to purple
starlike flowers bloom in early summer.
Slender and delicate, with pungent leaves.
Makes a good cut flower. Plant in small
groups. Full sun. Zone 4.

Allium christophii.
Star of Persia.
Height: to 30 in. Large globes of amethyst or
purplish flowers bloom in late spring and
early summer. Wide, blue-green, straplike
leaves. Flower heads dry well. Full sun.
Zone 4.

Allium moly. Lily leek.
Height: 12 in. Forms a low compact clump
with bright yellow starlike flowers in late
spring. Flat leaves turn yellow after the
flowers fade. Easy and fast-spreading. Full or
part sun. Zone 2.

Allium neapolitanum. Naples onion.
Height: 12 in. Umbel of sweet-scented,
starlike white flowers blooms for a month in
early spring. Can be forced in pots like
daffodils. Needs well-drained soil. Full sun.
Zone 7.

Aloe arborescens.
Candelabra plant.
Height: usually 8–12 ft. Rosettes of thick
tooth-edged leaves on branching woody
trunks. Red-orange winter flowers attract
hummingbirds. Tolerates poor soil. Full sun.
Zone 9.

Aloe saponaria. Soap aloe.
Height: 9–12 in. Clumps of white-spotted,
reddish green leaves. Scarlet, yellow, shrimp
pink, or orange-red flowers 2–3 times a year.
Good for hot, dry landscapes. Fast-growing.
Zone 9.

Aloe vera.
Height: 2 ft. Plump gray-green leaves, tinged
with red, are edged with soft spines. Long
racemes of tubular yellow flowers open in
spring. Medicinal uses. Good in containers
or on dry slopes. Zone 8.

Alstroemeria **Ligtu hybrids.**
Peruvian lilies.
Height: 3–5 ft. Leafy stalks of lilylike white,
yellow, pink, salmon, or red flowers bloom
from spring to summer. Make excellent cut
flowers. Full or part sun. Zone 8.

Amsonia tabernaemontana.
Bluestar.
Height: 2–3 ft. Clusters of starlike pale blue
flowers in spring. Slender, shiny, pale green
leaves turn yellow in fall. Tolerates constant
moisture. Full or part sun. Zone 3.

Anemone blanda '**White Splendor**'.
Grecian windflower.
Height: 6–8 in. Wide, daisylike white flowers
in early spring. Deeply dissected, hairy leaves.
Lovely when naturalized in mass plantings.
Part shade. Zone 4.

Aloe vera

Alstroemeria Ligtu hybrids

Amsonia tabernaemontana

Anemone blanda 'White Splendor'

Aquilegia caerulea

Anemone × hybrida 'Honorine Jobert'

Aquilegia canadensis

Aquilegia chrysantha

Anemone vitifolia 'Robustissima'

Aquilegia hybrids

Artemisia absinthium 'Lambrook Silver'

Artemisia lactiflora

Artemisia ludoviciana 'Silver King'

Artemisia 'Powis Castle'

Anemone × hybrida 'Honorine Jobert'.
Japanese anemone.
Height: 3–5 ft. Dozens of clear white, single flowers on branching stalks in late summer and early fall. Dark foliage is handsome, too. Good for mass plantings or partly shaded borders. Other cultivars have light or rosy pink flowers. Zone 4.

Anemone vitifolia 'Robustissima'.
Grapeleaf anemone.
Height: 3–4 ft. Wide pink flowers bloom on upright stalks for several weeks in late summer. Makes a vigorous ground cover of healthy attractive foliage. Full or part sun. Zone 4.

Aquilegia caerulea.
Rocky Mountain columbine.
Height: 1–2 ft. Blue-and-white flowers with spurs on tall branched stalks. Basal mound of delicate lacy foliage. Good for a semiwoodland border and for cutting. Zone 3.

Aquilegia canadensis. Columbine.
Height: 2–3 ft. Spurred red-and-yellow flowers bloom for about 6 weeks in spring and attract hummingbirds. Long branched stalks. Lacy foliage is evergreen in mild winters. Part sun. Zone 3.

Aquilegia chrysantha. Golden columbine.
Height: about 3 ft. Showy and fragrant yellow flowers with long straight spurs bloom from late spring through midsummer. Vigorous. Tolerates some heat and dryness. Zone 3.

Aquilegia hybrids. Columbine.
Height: 2–3 ft. Soft mounds of fine-textured foliage. Flowers in pastel, bright, or bicolored shades of blue, red, white, pink, violet, and yellow. Full or part sun. Zone 4.

Artemisia absinthium 'Lambrook Silver'.
Wormwood.
Height: 30 in. Forms a mass of silvery, silky, finely divided leaves with a strong aroma.

Stems are topped with panicles of tiny yellow flowers in summer. Full or part sun. Zone 5.

Artemisia lactiflora.
White mugwort.
Height: 4–5 ft. Plumes of fragrant creamy flowers last for weeks in late summer, dry well for winter wreaths. Dark green, pinnately divided leaves. Full or part sun. Zone 4.

Artemisia ludoviciana 'Silver King'.
Height: 2–3 ft. Aromatic, silvery gray stems and foliage make excellent fresh or dried bouquets. May be floppy; spreads underground unless confined. Full sun. Zone 3.

Artemisia 'Powis Castle'.
Height: 3 ft. Forms an exuberant but noninvasive mound of aromatic stems and silvery filigree foliage. Flowers are inconspicuous. Tolerates dryness. Full or part sun. Zone 6.

Arum italicum

Asarum canadense

Aruncus aethusifolius

Asarum europaeum

Asclepias tuberosa

Arum italicum. Italian arum.
Height: 18 in. Large, dark green, arrow-shaped leaves develop in fall and remain through winter. Clusters of bright orange-red berries ripen in late spring. Good for shady borders. Zone 4.

Aruncus aethusifolius. Goatsbeard.
Height: to 12 in. Showy spikes of tiny creamy white flowers appear in early summer. Leaves are sharply divided. Perfect for a shady spot next to a stream. Part sun or shade. Zone 5.

Asarum canadense. Eastern wild ginger.
Height: 6 in. Wide heart-shaped leaves rise from ginger-scented rhizomes. Deciduous. Spreads slowly to form a mat. Good ground cover or edging for a shady border or woodland path. Zone 2.

Asarum europaeum.
European wild ginger.
Height: 6 in. Wide, dark green, heart-shaped leaves with a glossy leathery texture. Evergreen. Makes an excellent ground cover

near an entry or walkway. Filtered sun to dense shade. Zone 4.

Asclepias tuberosa. Butterfly weed.
Height: 1–1½ ft. Makes a clump of upright stems with milky sap and narrow green leaves. Clusters of waxy, bright orange flowers attract butterflies in summer. Full sun. Zone 3.

Asparagus densiflorus 'Myers'.
Ornamental asparagus.
Height: 2 ft. or more. Looks like a bouquet of foxtails. Evergreen but tender to frost. Does very well in containers. Trouble-free. Full or part sun. Zone 9.

Aspidistra elatior. Cast-iron plant.
Height: 30 in. Long lasting and tough. Tolerates low light, dry air, dust, and erratic watering. Excellent as a container plant and in heavily shaded areas. Creeping rhizome spreads slowly. Zone 7.

Aster × frikartii 'Monch'.
Height: 2–3 ft. Makes a clump of upright

branching stems. Lightly fragrant blossoms of pale lavender-blue in summer and fall, and into winter in mild climates. Full or part sun. Zone 6.

Aster lateriflorus var. horizontalis.
Calico aster.
Height: 2–4 ft. Forms a mound of branched stems with small reddish leaves. White or lavender blossoms with purplish disks. Tolerates sun and dry soil. A tough native. Zone 3.

Aster novae-angliae 'Purple Dome'.
New England aster.
Height: 18 in. Deep purple flowers with yellow disks bloom for up to 6 weeks. Naturally compact form doesn't need staking. Full or part sun. Zone 3.

Aster tataricus.
Tartarian daisy.
Height: to 7 ft. Tall erect stems are topped with violet-blue blossoms late into fall. Lower leaves are up to 2 ft. long. Striking in large gardens. Full sun. Zone 3.

Asparagus densiflorus 'Myers'

Aspidistra elatior

Aster × frikartii 'Monch'

Aster lateriflorus var. *horizontalis*

Aster novae-angliae 'Purple Dome'

Aster tataricus

Astilbe × arendsii 'Fanal'

Astilbe × arendsii hybrids

Astilbe chinensis 'Pumila'

Astilbe simplicifolia 'Sprite'

Astilbe chinensis var. *taquetii* 'Superba'

Astilbe × arendsii 'Fanal'.
Height: 30 in. Fluffy plumes of tiny deep red flowers appear in early midsummer over mounds of dark bronze, fernlike leaves. A mainstay of shady borders; easy and durable. Zone 2.

Astilbe × arendsii hybrids.
Height: 2–3 ft. Tiny flowers in shades of white, pink, deep purplish, or carmine red, opening between June and September. Foliage is deep green to bronze. Part sun or shade. Zone 2.

Astilbe chinensis 'Pumila'. Plume flower. Height: under 1 ft. Dark green, deeply divided leaves. Bottlebrush-like spikes of tiny pinkish lavender flowers in late summer. A low-spreading ground cover or edging. Zone 4.

Astilbe chinensis var. taquetii 'Superba'.
Height: to 3½ ft. Tall thin panicles of pink flowers in late summer turn beige and last into fall. Neat clumps of long fernlike leaves. Part sun or shade. Zone 4.

Astilbe simplicifolia 'Sprite'.
Height: 10 in. Dwarf form with plumes of pink flowers that bloom in midseason. Finely cut foliage starts out bronze, turns dark green. Needs very little care. Part sun or shade. Zone 4.

Aurinia saxatilis. Basket-of-gold.
Height: 1–2 ft. Dense masses of small, fragrant gold flowers in spring. Low rosettes of soft gray leaves on trailing stems. Plant at the front of a raised bed or where it can cascade. Full sun. Zone 3.

Baptisia australis. False indigo.
Height: 3–4 ft. Racemes of pealike, indigo blue flowers appear in midspring above shrubby mounds of light blue-green foliage. Large, woody, charcoal pods from midsummer into winter. Good for borders or meadows. Zone 3.

Belamcanda chinensis. Blackberry lily.
Height: 2–3 ft. Flat sheaves of irislike leaves on zigzag stalks topped with dark-spotted orange flowers in summer. Pods of shiny black seeds resemble blackberries. Full sun. Zone 6 or 5.

Bergenia cordifolia. Heartleaf bergenia.
Height: 18 in. Clumps of thick, cabbagelike green leaves that turn glossy red in fall. Clusters of pink flowers on short upright stalks. Good edging or ground cover. Zone 3.

Boltonia asteroides 'Pink Beauty'.
Height: 3–5 ft. Large upright clumps hold clusters of asterlike blossoms with light pink rays and yellow disks in late summer and fall. Full or part sun. Zone 4.

Aurinia saxatilis

Baptisia australis

Belamcanda chinensis

Bergenia cordifolia

Boltonia asteroides 'Pink Beauty'

Brunnera macrophylla

Calamintha nepeta

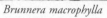

Callirhoe involucrata

Campanula persicifolia 'Alba'

Camassia leichtlinii

Campanula carpatica

Campanula glomerata 'Joan Elliott'

Campanula portenschlagiana

Canna hybrids

Campanula poscharskyana

Canna hybrid

Brunnera macrophylla.
Siberian bugloss.
Height: 18 in. Sprays of blue forget-me-not flowers in spring and often again in summer. Heart-shaped, coarse, hairy leaves. Good ground cover. Full or part sun. Zone 3.

Calamintha nepeta.
Height: 12–24 in. A graceful mound of shiny, mint-scented, gray-green foliage with clusters of tiny white or lilac flowers in summer and fall. Attracts bees. Full sun or afternoon shade. Zone 6 or 5.

Callirhoe involucrata.
Purple poppy mallow.
Height: 6–12 in. or more. Large, wine-colored, cupped flowers and deeply lobed green foliage from spring to early summer. Plant individually or massed. Tolerates dry soil and heat. Zone 4.

Camassia leichtlinii. Camas.
Height: to 3 ft. Spikelike clusters of white or blue flowers in spring. Slender grasslike leaves. Good for damp meadows or low garden spots. Full or part sun. Zone 4.

Campanula carpatica.
Carpathian bellflower.
Height: 8–18 in. Cup-shaped flowers in shades of lavender, purple, or white, borne abundantly in midsummer. Spreads slowly to form low mounds. Full or part sun. Zone 3.

Campanula glomerata 'Joan Elliott'.
Clustered bellflower.
Height: 18 in. Tight clusters of funnel-shaped, violet-purple flowers on tall single or branched stems in late spring. Soft hairy leaves form a basal mound. Zone 3.

Campanula persicifolia 'Alba'.
Peach-leaved bellflower.
Height: 2–3 ft. Bell-shaped white flowers on slender stems. Blooms in early summer. Basal rosette of leathery evergreen leaves. Good cut flower. Full or part sun. Zone 3.

Campanula portenschlagiana.
Dalmatian bellflower.
Height: 6–9 in. Tight mound of ivylike leaves with long, trailing, winding stems. Violet-blue or white cupped flowers. Excellent rock-garden or wall plant. Zone 4.

Campanula poscharskyana.
Serbian bellflower.
Height: 6–9 in. Clusters of starry lavender-blue or white spring flowers on long trailing stems. Fast-spreading and can be invasive. Makes a good ground cover. Zone 3.

Canna hybrid. Variegated canna.
Height: 3–4 ft. Decorative broad leaves have creamy stripes radiating out from the midrib. Other variegated forms have yellow flowers. Prefers steady moisture. Full or part sun. Zone 8.

Canna hybrids.
Height: 2–6 ft. Erect stems with broad tropical-looking leaves in shades of green, reddish green, or bronze. Big bright red, orange, salmon, pink, yellow, or white flowers, summer to frost. Zone 8.

Centaurea montana

Centranthus ruber

Ceratostigma plumbaginoides

Cheiranthus 'Bowles Mauve'

Chelone lyonii

Centaurea montana. Perennial cornflower.
Height: 18–24 in. Wide blossoms with
fringed rays in shades of blue-purple, rose, or
white on clumps of leafy stems. Blooms in
early summer. Fast-spreading. Doesn't like
hot summers. Zone 3.

Centranthus ruber. Red valerian.
Height: 3 ft. Dense clusters of fragrant
crimson, pink, or white flowers in late spring
and early summer. Long stems of blue-green
foliage. Tolerates difficult conditions. Good
cut flower. Zone 5.

Ceratostigma plumbaginoides.
Dwarf plumbago.
Height: 12 in. Spreading, with dense heads
of blue flowers from summer through fall.
Dark green leaves turn reddish purple in fall.
Makes a good ground cover. Full or part sun.
Zone 5.

Cheiranthus 'Bowles Mauve'. Wallflower.
Height: 2 ft. Small, sweet-scented mauve
flowers on a low mound of soft gray-green
foliage. Easy, but needs annual division and
replanting. Best in well-drained, fertile soil.
Full sun. Zone 6.

Chelone lyonii. Turtlehead.
Height: 3 ft. Clear pink flowers in dense
clusters on upright spikes bloom from late
August until frost. Large lance-shaped leaves.
Plant beside a pond or stream. Full or part
sun. Zone 3.

Chrysanthemum coccineum.
Painted daisy.
Height: 18–30 in. Single unbranched stalks
of yellow-disked white, pink, or rosy red
flowers. Fernlike foliage. Colorful for mass
plantings. Makes a long-lasting cut flower.
Zone 4.

Chrysanthemum frutescens.
Marguerite.
Height: 3 ft. Smooth, bright green, coarsely
toothed leaves. Abundant white, pink,
or yellow daisies. Blooms in summer and
fall, intermittently in winter and spring.
Fast-growing. Tender to cold. Full sun.
Zone 9.

**Chrysanthemum leucanthemum 'May
Queen'.**
Height: 1–3 ft. Large, white, single blossoms
on unbranched stems in early summer, off
and on until fall. Basal rosettes of thick
leaves. Good for wildflower gardens. Full
sun. Zone 4.

Chrysanthemum × morifolium.
Hardy garden chrysanthemum.
Height: to 3 ft. There are thousands of
cultivars in a wide range of flower colors,

Chrysanthemum coccineum

Chrysanthemum frutescens

Chrysanthemum × morifolium

Chrysanthemum leucanthemum 'May Queen'

sizes, and forms, blooming from late summer through winter. All need full sun and well-drained soil. Some are hardy to Zone 6 or 5; others only in Zone 7 or warmer.

Chrysanthemum nipponicum.
Nippon daisy.
Height: to 30 in. Thick, smooth, lustrous green leaves all along the stems throughout summer. Wide white daisies bloom in fall, too late for many northern gardens. Full sun. Zone 5.

Chrysanthemum rubellum 'Clara Curtis'.
Height: 12–18 in. Mounds of slender branched stems with clear pink daisies that bloom for many weeks in mid- to late summer. Fast-spreading. Good cut flower. Zone 4.

Chrysanthemum rubellum 'Clara Curtis'

Chrysanthemum nipponicum

Cimicifuga simplex 'White Pearl'

Cimicifuga racemosa

Colchicum 'Lilac Wonder'

Coreopsis verticillata 'Moonbeam'

Coreopsis auriculata 'Nana'

Coreopsis grandiflora 'Early Sunrise'

Cimicifuga racemosa.
Black cohosh.
Height: 2 ft. (foliage) to 8 ft. (flowers).
Branching wiry stems with long wands of
starry white flowers. Long lived, dramatic,
and easy to grow. Needs moisture. Part sun
or shade. Zone 3.

Cimicifuga simplex 'White Pearl'.
Height: 2 ft. (foliage) to 3–4 ft. (flowers).
Long sprays of flowers on arching stems in
late fall. Makes a compact mound of foliage.
Spreads slowly. Part sun or shade. Zone 3.

Colchicum 'Lilac Wonder'.
Meadow saffron.
Height: under 1 ft. Lavender-pink, crocuslike
fall flowers open wide on sunny days, close at
night. Smooth grassy leaves in spring. Full or
part sun. Zone 4.

Convallaria majalis.
Lily-of-the-valley.
Height: 8 in. Very fragrant, small, white,
bell-like flowers bloom in midspring on
slender curved stalks. Smooth oval leaves
turn gold in fall. A tenacious ground cover.
Zone 2.

Coreopsis auriculata 'Nana'.
Height: to 1 ft. Abundant golden yellow
daisies bloom in spring. Dark green, lobed
foliage. Low and compact; makes a good
ground cover for woodland gardens. Part
sun or shade. Zone 4.

Coreopsis grandiflora 'Early Sunrise'.
Height: 1–2 ft. Compact and strong
stemmed, with bright golden yellow daisies
from late spring to summer. Easy from seed.
Good for meadow gardens. Full or part sun.
Zone 5.

Coreopsis verticillata 'Moonbeam'.
Height: 2–3 ft. A dense clump with pale
yellow flowers and fine feathery foliage.
Forms dense textured patches. Good in a
border or meadow. Full sun. Zone 3.

Crambe cordifolia.
Height: 6 ft. Forms a loose mound of wide,
coarse, heart-shaped leaves. Clouds of dainty
white flowers float on tall much-branched
stems in early summer. Give it plenty of
space. Zone 6.

Crinum hybrids.
Milk-and-wine lilies.
Height: 2 ft. or more. Fragrant, lilylike white
flowers with pink or wine stripes. Floppy
straplike leaves. Giant bulbs. An old southern
favorite. Sun or shade. Zone 7.

Crocosmia 'Lucifer'.
Crocosmia, montbretia.
Height: 3 ft. Bright red flowers on long
stalks in summer are excellent for cutting.
Fans of slender ribbed leaves. Underground
corms multiply rapidly. Needs good
drainage. Full sun. Zone 5.

Convallaria majalis

Crinum hybrids

Crambe cordifolia

Crocosmia 'Lucifer'

Crocus ancyrensis 'Golden Bunch'

Crocus speciosus

Crocus chrysanthus

Crocus vernus

Crocus ancyrensis 'Golden Bunch'.
Golden bunch crocus.
Height: 6 in. Narrow grassy leaves mix with clusters of small, bright golden spring blossoms. Good as part of a natural lawn or in drifts under early-blooming shrubs. Full sun. Zone 3.

Crocus chrysanthus.
Golden crocus.
Height: 4–6 in. More delicate than common crocuses. Masses of honey-scented flowers bloom in early spring. Available with yellow, white, blue, purple, striped, or bicolor petals. Zone 4.

Crocus speciosus. Autumn crocus.
Height: 4–6 in. Small flowers with blue, lavender, purple, or white petals bloom in fall. Grassy foliage emerges with the flowers, then dies back in winter. Full sun. Zone 5.

Crocus vernus. Dutch crocus.
Height: 4–8 in. The most commonly grown crocus, popular for early spring bloom. Flowers are fairly large, in white, purple, yellow, or lilac. Plant where the soil warms early. Zone 5.

Cyclamen hederifolium. Baby cyclamen.
Height: 3–4 in. Pink or white flowers with crimson eyes bloom in fall. Large, waxy, heart-shaped leaves are pale green with silvery spots and last all winter. Spreads in the shade. Zone 6.

Delosperma cooperi. Purple ice plant.
Height: 2–4 in. A good ground cover for dry sites. Spreads quickly but isn't invasive. Makes a dense mat. Showy, bright magenta, daisylike flowers bloom from June until frost. Zone 6 or 5.

Delosperma nubigena. Hardy ice plant.
Height: 2–4 in. Bright green summer foliage turns red in winter. Yellow daisylike blossoms appear in late spring and summer. A vigorous ground cover for dry soil. Full sun. Zone 6 or 5.

Delphinium × elatum hybrids.
Hybrid delphiniums.
Height: to 6 ft. Tall branching stalks are crowded with flowers in shades of blue, purple, lavender, pink, or white. Cultivar heights vary. Plants grow best where summers are cool. Full sun. Zone 3.

Dianthus × allwoodii hybrids.
Height: 12–20 in. Clove-scented single or double flowers are red, rose, pink, or white. Bloom late spring through summer. Form dense mats of slender blue-green leaves. Zone 4.

Dianthus deltoides. Maiden pink.
Height: 1 ft. Forms low mats of grassy leaves. Scentless red, rose, or white flowers bloom abundantly in early summer and sometimes later. Good as a ground cover. Full or part sun. Zone 3.

Dianthus gratianopolitanus 'Tiny Rubies'.
Cheddar pink.
Height: 4 in. A compact mat of slender blue-green leaves and hundreds of small, double, deep pink flowers in late spring and early summer. Very fragrant. Zone 4.

Dianthus plumarius.
Cottage pink.
Height: 12–18 in. Wide, fringed, pink flowers—single, semidouble, or double—with a spicy fragrance bloom on floppy stems. Forms a loose mound of slender gray-blue foliage. Full sun. Zone 4.

Delosperma cooperi

Delosperma nubigena

Cyclamen hederifolium

Dianthus deltoides

Dianthus gratianopolitanus 'Tiny Rubies'

Delphinium × *elatum* hybrids

Dianthus × *allwoodii* hybrids

Dianthus plumarius

Dicentra 'Luxuriant'

Dicentra spectabilis

Dictamnus albus

Echinacea purpurea 'Bright Star'

Echinops 'Taplow Blue'

Dicentra 'Luxuriant'. Bleeding-heart.
Height: 2–3 ft. Unusual flowers are cherry
red. Blooms over a very long season from late
spring through summer. Flowers hang from
arching stalks over ferny foliage. Part shade.
Zone 2.

Dicentra spectabilis.
Common bleeding-heart.
Height: 2–3 ft. Arching sprays of rosy pink
and white flowers in late spring. Delicate lacy
foliage forms a basal mound. Dies back in
hot weather. Needs fertile soil. Part shade.
Zone 2.

Dictamnus albus. Gas plant.
Height: 2–4 ft. Glossy dark green leaves are
strongly aromatic. Pure white flowers in
summer; ornamental pods in fall. Lives for
decades and needs no care. Also available
with pinkish flowers. Zone 3.

Doronicum caucasicum.
Leopard's-bane.
Height: 1–2 ft. Bright green basal leaves are
topped with wide, daisylike yellow blossoms
in early spring. Good for cutting. Usually
goes dormant in hot weather. Part sun or
shade. Zone 4.

Echinacea purpurea 'Bright Star'.
Purple coneflower.
Height: 1½–3 ft. A prairie wildflower with
blossoms like large rosy pink daisies. Blooms
all summer and attracts butterflies. Leaves
and stalks have a rough texture. Full sun.
Zone 4.

Echinops 'Taplow Blue'. Globe thistle.
Height: 2–4 ft. Upright stalks with round,
steel blue flower heads; stiff bristly bracts;
and spiny-toothed leaves. Makes a big clump.
Good for dried arrangements. Full sun.
Zone 3.

Doronicum caucasicum

Epimedium × rubrum 'Pink Queen'

Epimedium × youngianum 'Niveum'

Endymion hispanica

Ensete ventricosum 'Maurellii'

Endymion hispanica.
Spanish bluebell.
Height: 18 in. Clusters of lovely blue flowers open for about 3 weeks in spring. Ideal for naturalizing under deciduous trees. Bulbs are inexpensive and multiply quickly. Zone 5.

***Ensete ventricosum* 'Maurellii'.**
Height: 12–15 ft. Dark red trunk with an umbrella of wide, long, red-edged leaf blades. Can be grown in a container and overwintered indoors. Looks exotic and tropical. Zone 10 or 9.

***Epimedium × rubrum* 'Pink Queen'.**
Height: 1 ft. An excellent ground cover to plant under trees and shrubs. Spreads slowly into a weed-proof mat. Rosy pink flowers are showy in spring. Foliage is evergreen. Zone 5.

***Epimedium × youngianum* 'Niveum'.**
Height: to 8 in. An excellent ground cover to plant under trees and shrubs. Spreads slowly into a weed-proof mat. Shorter than other epimediums. Has white flowers in spring. Zone 5.

Eriogonum umbellatum

Eryngium varifolium

Eupatorium coelestinum

Eupatorium purpureum

Eremurus × isabellinus

Erigeron speciosus 'Forster's Darling'

Eremurus × isabellinus.
Shelford hybrid foxtail lilies.
Height: 4–6 ft. Tall dense stalks of bright-colored flowers in late spring and early summer. Available in yellow, orange, white, pink, or red. Need good drainage. Die back after bloom. Zone 5.

Erigeron speciosus 'Forster's Darling'.
Fleabane.
Height: 1–2 1/2 ft. Bright pink blossoms start in spring and continue sporadically through summer. Blooms are 2–3 in. wide. Makes neat clumps of basal foliage. Full or part sun. Zone 5.

Eriogonum umbellatum.
Sulphur buckwheat.
Height: 1 ft. Umbels of bright gold, pale yellow, or creamy flowers in midsummer turn reddish as they mature. Puffy seedpods are good for dried arrangements. Thrives in dry soil. Zone 7.

Eryngium varifolium. Sea holly.
Height: to 2 ft. Tight blue flowers with spiny blue bracts on stems that are also blue near the top. Rounded leaves with conspicuous white veins are semievergreen. Zone 5.

Eupatorium coelestinum. Hardy ageratum.
Height: 2 ft. Fluffy powder blue flowers continue for weeks in late summer and fall. Lush light green foliage. Good in sunny meadows or on creek banks. Full or part sun. Zone 5.

Eupatorium purpureum.
Joe-Pye weed.
Height: 5–9 ft. Makes impressive clumps of tall stalks topped with broad clusters of flowers that are pinkish purple in late summer, fading to pinkish beige in fall. Needs room. Zone 4.

Euphorbia griffithii 'Fireglow'.
Height: 3 ft. Bright orange-red floral bracts are showy for weeks in midsummer. Foliage turns bronze in fall. Milky sap may irritate skin. Full sun. Zone 6 or 5.

Euphorbia myrsinites.
Height: 8–12 in. Stiff, fleshy, blue-gray leaves spiral around trailing stems. Flowers open in early spring. Good in a raised bed or planter. Full or part sun. Zone 6.

Filipendula rubra 'Venusta'.
Queen-of-the-prairie.
Height: 6–8 ft. Fluffy pink plumes open in mid- to late summer. Dark green compound leaves have toothed leaflets. Makes a giant clump. Prefers moist soil. Easy and carefree. Zone 3.

Fragaria chiloensis.
Wild strawberry.
Height: 4–8 in. Makes a good ground cover that roots as it spreads. Glossy green leaves turn maroon in winter. Small white flowers in spring. Sometimes makes red berries. Full or part sun. Zone 5.

Euphorbia griffithii 'Fireglow'

Euphorbia myrsinites

Filipendula rubra 'Venusta'

Fragaria chiloensis

Gaillardia × *grandiflora* 'Goblin'

Gaura lindheimeri

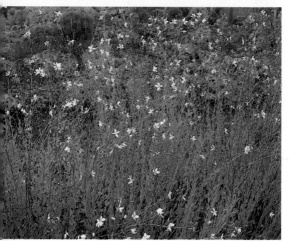

Gazania rigens var. *leucolaena*

Geranium × *cantabrigiense* 'Biokovo'

Galanthus nivalis

Geranium 'Johnson's Blue'

Geranium sanguineum var. *striatum*

Gerbera jamesonii

Geranium endressii 'Wargrave Pink'

Gaillardia × grandiflora 'Goblin'.
Blanket flower.
Height: 1 ft. Daisylike flowers are good for cutting. Blooms all summer. Forms a mound of rough-textured foliage. Tolerates poor, dry soil. Full sun. Zone 3.

Galanthus nivalis.
Snowdrop.
Height: 6–9 in. Flowers in late winter and isn't hurt by snow. Good for naturalizing under trees. Bulbs multiply to form clumps; also spreads by seed. Full sun or summer shade. Zone 4.

Gaura lindheimeri.
Height: 3–5 ft. Airy masses of delicate starlike flowers float on slender stems from midspring to frost. Blossoms open white and age to pink. Forms a clump. Not fussy about soil. Zone 6.

Gazania rigens var. leucolaena.
Trailing gazania.
Height: to 1 ft. Soft-textured white leaves accented by wide yellow-orange daisies. Good as a ground cover or in containers or hanging baskets. Easy to grow. Prefers dry soil. Zone 9.

Geranium × cantabrigiense 'Biokovo'.
Height: 1 ft. Blooms in late spring. Bright green leaves release a fragrance when rubbed. Can spread as a ground cover or trail over a wall. Easy and trouble-free. Zone 5 or 4.

Geranium endressii 'Wargrave Pink'.
Height: 1–1½ ft. Blooms for many weeks. Makes a big floppy mound. Trailing stems can hang over a wall or climb on shrubs. Showy but easy. Needs well-drained soil. Zone 4.

Geranium 'Johnson's Blue'.
Height: 1½–2 ft. Flowers are pretty for a few weeks in late spring. Makes a neat mound of foliage if you keep it trimmed, or can sprawl casually in a natural garden. Easy to grow. Zone 4.

Geranium macrorrhizum.
Bigroot geranium.
Height: 12–15 in. Fuzzy leaves have a distinct lingering aroma. Semievergreen foliage turns colorful in winter. Small flowers in late spring. Good ground cover for dry, shady spots. Zone 3.

Geranium sanguineum var. striatum.
Height: 6–12 in. Pale pink flowers with red veins cover lacy leaves in late spring and early summer and continue sporadically through summer. Spreads fast. Tolerates hot, dry weather. Zone 4.

Gerbera jamesonii. Gerbera daisy.
Height: to 18 in. The ultimate daisy. Large blossoms on long stalks are very long lasting and excellent for cutting. Also does well in containers, outdoors or as a houseplant. Zone 9.

Geranium macrorrhizum

Gypsophila paniculata

Hamelia patens

Hedychium coronarium

Hedychium gardneranum

Helenium 'Moerheim Beauty'

Gypsophila paniculata. Baby's-breath. Height: 3 ft. Delicate clouds of bloom make a perfect filler in the garden or in arrangements. Needs well-drained, limy soil. May need staking. Cut back in summer to encourage rebloom. Zone 3.

Hamelia patens. Firebush. Height: 4–5 ft. Bright flowers, 2 in. long, attract hummingbirds. Blooms nonstop in hot weather, continuing until frost. Needs well-drained soil and does well in containers. Zone 8.

Hedychium coronarium. Butterfly ginger. Height: 5–6 ft. Very fragrant white flowers are 2–3 in. wide. Needs a long, warm summer to bloom well. Spreads slowly to make a dense patch of sturdy stalks. Prefers moist soil. Zone 8 or 7.

Hedychium gardneranum. Kahili ginger. Height: 6 ft. or more. Forms a large clump of strong stalks with broad leaves and giant clusters of exotic flowers. Does best in moist, fertile soil. Zone 9.

Helenium 'Moerheim Beauty'. Sneezeweed. Height: 4–5 ft. Blooms for many weeks from midsummer to fall. Other cultivars are orange, bronze, gold, or yellow. Easy to grow but can be floppy and often needs staking. Zone 3.

Helianthemum nummularium. Rock rose. Height: 1½–2 ft. Flowers are 1 in. wide in bright shades of red, copper, peach, apricot, pink, yellow, or white. Makes loose mounds. Good for walls, dry slopes, or rock gardens. Zone 5.

Helianthus angustifolius. Narrow-leaved sunflower. Height: 5–10 ft. Robust and showy. Makes a big clump of tall stalks with attractive slender leaves. May need staking. Flowers open in late summer and fall. Zone 6.

Heliopsis helianthoides 'Summer Sun'. False sunflower. Height: 2–3 ft. Bright blossoms are good for cutting. Blooms from summer into fall if deadheaded regularly. Usually doesn't need staking. Zone 4.

Helleborus foetidus. Stinking hellebore. Height: 18 in. Leathery foliage is evergreen. Slowly forms a dense patch in good soil. Pale green flowers appear in late winter or early spring, before the new leaves. Zone 3.

Helleborus orientalis. Lenten rose. Height: 18–24 in. The easiest hellebore to grow. Blooms last for weeks in early spring. Flowers can be pink, plum, white, or chartreuse. Glossy foliage is evergreen. Zone 4.

Helianthemum nummularium

Helianthus angustifolius

Heliopsis helianthoides 'Summer Sun'

Helleborus foetidus

Helleborus orientalis

Hemerocallis 'Mary Todd'

Hemerocallis lilio-asphodelus

Hemerocallis 'Becky Lynn'

Hemerocallis 'Ed Murray'

Hemerocallis 'Stella d'Oro'

***Hemerocallis* 'Becky Lynn'.** Daylily.
Height: 2 ft. Rosy pink flowers are almost
7 in. wide on 20-in. scapes. Blooms early to
midseason; sometimes reblooms. Zone 4.

***Hemerocallis* 'Ed Murray'.** Daylily.
Height: 2$^1/_2$ ft. Dark red flowers have yellow
throats and are 4$^1/_2$ in. wide on 30-in.
scapes. Blooms in midseason. Zone 4.

Hemerocallis lilio-asphodelus.
Lemon lily.
Height: 2 ft. Blooms in May or June, earlier
than hybrid daylilies. Yellow flowers are very
sweet-scented. Zone 4.

***Hemerocallis* 'Mary Todd'.** Daylily.
Height: 2–2$^1/_2$ ft. Yellow flowers are 6 in.
wide on 26-in. scapes. One of the first
tetraploid daylilies. Zone 4.

***Hemerocallis* 'Stella d'Oro'.** Daylily.
Height: 1 ft. Gold flowers are 3 in. wide on
12-in. scapes. Blooms continually from early
summer through fall. Vigorous. Zone 4.

Hesperaloe parviflora. Red yucca.
Height: 2 ft. Evergreen leaves are stiff and
tough. Flowers for many weeks in spring and
summer, on stalks up to 5 ft. tall. Tolerates
poor, dry soil and hot weather. Zone 6.

Hesperis matronalis. Dame's rocket.
Height: 2–3 ft. Blooms in late spring. White
or lavender flowers are very fragrant,
especially in the evening. Renews itself and
spreads by self-seeding. Very easy. Zone 3.

Hesperaloe parviflora

Hesperis matronalis

Heuchera micrantha 'Palace Purple'

Heuchera × *brizoides* 'Coral Cloud'

Hibiscus coccineus

Hibiscus moscheutos

Heuchera × brizoides 'Coral Cloud'.
Coralbells.
Height: 12–18 in. Remarkable in bloom, and the foliage is lovely, too. Different cultivars have red, pink, salmon, or white flowers. Needs well-drained soil and frequent watering. Zone 4.

Heuchera micrantha 'Palace Purple'.
Height: 12 in. Foliage color varies from deep purplish red to bronze or brownish. Looks best if grown in part to full shade. Needs well-drained soil and regular watering. Zone 4.

Hibiscus coccineus.
Wild red mallow.
Height: to 6 ft. Grows as big as a shrub every summer but doesn't spread much from year to year. Red flowers open daily for many weeks. Prefers moist, fertile soil. Zone 6.

Hibiscus moscheutos.
Rose mallow.
Height: to 6 ft. Native to wetlands but does well in ordinary garden soil. New cultivars have flowers up to 12 in. wide in shades of white, pink, rose, or red. Fast and easy. Zone 6 or 5.

Hosta, Hostas

Hostas are among the most popular perennials and are particularly valuable in shady gardens. They are very easy to grow and thrive with almost no maintenance, forming larger, more beautiful clumps every year. There are short, medium, and tall plants, useful for edgings, ground covers, or specimens. Hostas are valued chiefly for their leaves, but their flowers can add color—and, in some cases, fragrance—to the garden in late summer.

Most hostas do best in full or part shade and prefer well-drained soil with regular watering. For best results, prepare the soil by mixing in plenty of organic matter, and apply a generous layer of mulch each spring. Clumps can live in the same spot for decades and don't need to be divided. The hostas shown here are all hardy to Zone 4.

Hosta fortunei 'Hyacinthina'

Hosta 'Ginko Craig'

Hosta 'Krossa Regal'

Hosta fortunei **'Hyacinthina'.**
Height: under 18 in. Spreads vigorously.

Hosta **'Ginko Craig'.**
Height: under 12 in. Brightens a shady corner.

Hosta **'Gold Standard'.**
Height: under 18 in. Tolerates part sun.

Hosta **'Hadspen Blue'.**
Height: under 12 in. Leaves have rich texture and substance.

Hosta **'Krossa Regal'.**
Height: under 18 in. Flower stalks reach up to 6 ft. tall.

Hosta plantaginea **'Grandiflora'.**
Height: 2 ft. or more. Flowers are very fragrant in August.

Hosta sieboldiana **'Frances Williams'.**
Height: 2 ft. or more. One of the most popular hostas.

Hosta sieboldii **'Kabitan'.**
Height: under 12 in. Good for edging beds or walks.

Hosta venusta.
Height: about 4 in. A miniature hosta for rock gardens or pots.

Hosta **'Wide Brim'.**
Height: under 18 in. Leaf edges mature from creamy to gold.

Hosta venusta

Hosta sieboldiana 'Frances Williams'

Hosta 'Hadspen Blue'

Hosta sieboldii 'Kabitan'

Hosta 'Gold Standard'

Hosta 'Wide Brim'

Hosta plantaginea 'Grandiflora'

250

Iris, Irises

Although it's easy to recognize an iris as an iris, there's wonderful diversity within the genus. The flowers can be small or large, with broad or narrow segments. Some kinds bloom at ground level; others are 3 ft. tall. The flowering season begins in late winter and continues through early summer. Many irises are quite fragrant, and any with long stalks make good cut flowers. The dried seedpods are also attractive in arrangements.

Iris plants can have spreading rhizomes or rounded bulbs, with sword-shaped or grassy leaves. Some thrive in dry soil; others grow in shallow water. A few are tender to cold, but most are quite hardy.

Iris bearded hybrids

Iris foetidissima

Iris cristata

Iris 'Beverly Sills'

Iris ensata

Iris pseudacorus

Iris pallida 'Variegata'

Iris Pacific Coast hybrids

Iris bearded hybrids.
Height: to 3 ft. There are dwarf, intermediate, and tall forms; they bloom in that sequence, over a period of weeks. Need fertile, well-drained soil. May go dormant in summer. Zone 3.

Iris 'Beverly Sills'.
Height: about 3 ft. One of the most popular tall bearded irises. There are hundreds of other cultivars, in a wide range of colors. Some kinds are fragrant. All make good cut flowers. Zone 3.

Iris cristata.
Dwarf crested iris.
Height: to 8 in. (foliage); 4–6 in. (flowers). A southeastern wildflower that flowers in early spring. Spreads to make a low carpet of bloom. Tolerates dry soil and summer heat. Zone 3.

Iris ensata. Japanese iris.
Height: 2–3 ft. Blooms in early summer. Flowers are exquisite but fragile. There are hundreds of cultivars in many color combinations. Prefers heavy, rich, damp, acidic soil. Zone 4.

Iris foetidissima.
Stinking iris.
Height: 2 ft. Pods full of shiny bright red seeds are colorful in the autumn garden and last well in arrangements. Flowers in spring. Makes an erect clump that spreads quite slowly. Zone 7.

Iris Pacific Coast hybrids.
Height: to 2 ft. A new group of irises, developed by crossing native species. Do best where summers are dry and not too hot. Available in a wide range of colors. Hardiness not established.

Iris pallida 'Variegata'. Orris root.
Height: 3 ft. An old-fashioned favorite. Lavender-blue flowers are very fragrant in spring. Foliage is lovely all summer. Needs good drainage. Tolerates hot, dry weather. Zone 4.

Iris pseudacorus. Yellow flag.
Height: 2½–3½ ft. The original fleur-de-lis. Grows best in shallow water but tolerates ordinary soil and watering. Zone 3.

Iris (continued)

Iris reticulata. Reticulated iris.
Height: 3 in. (flowers); 12 in. (foliage). Plant bulbs in fall. Blooms in early spring, along with crocuses. Zone 3.

Iris sibirica. Siberian iris.
Height: 2–3 ft. Blooms in late spring, in shades of purple, blue, or white. Spreads slowly to make large clumps of grassy foliage. Prefers moist soil and tolerates part shade. Zone 4.

Iris sibirica 'White Swirl'. Siberian iris.
Height: 2–3 ft. Blooms in late spring. Other cultivars have blue or purple flowers. Spreads slowly to make large clumps of grassy foliage. Prefers moist soil and tolerates part shade. Zone 4.

Iris Xiphium hybrids. Dutch irises.
Height: 18–24 in. Plant bulbs in fall for flowers in late spring. Excellent cut flowers. Need moisture from fall to spring but tolerate hot, dry summers. Plants multiply slowly. Zone 6.

Iris sibirica 'White Swirl'

Iris sibirica

Iris reticulata

Iris Xiphium hybrids

Hyacinthus orientalis

Hyacinthus orientalis. Hyacinth.
Height: 6–10 in. Flowers are intensely sweet and bloom for about 2 weeks in early spring. Plant bulbs close together, almost touching. They usually don't multiply or spread. Zone 5.

Iberis sempervirens. Candytuft.
Height: 9–12 in. Blooms for weeks in spring if the weather stays cool and sometimes reblooms in fall. Good for well-drained spots, in rock gardens or raised beds. Zone 3.

Kniphofia hybrids. Torch lilies.
Height: 3 ft. Make a coarse tangle of grassy leaves. Bright red, orange, gold, or yellow flowers attract hummingbirds. Flower stalks grow up to 6 ft. tall. Like hot, dry spots. Zone 5.

Lamiastrum galeobdolon 'Herman's Pride'.
Yellow archangel.
Height: 1–2 ft. A popular ground cover that spreads by runners; too invasive to include in a mixed planting. Has yellow flowers in early summer. Takes part or full shade. Zone 6.

Lamium maculatum 'White Nancy'.
Spotted dead nettle.
Height: 12 in. An easy and adaptable ground cover, fast but not too aggressive. Other kinds have pink flowers. Grows best in moist, fertile soil with full or part sun. Zone 4.

Leucojum aestivum. Summer snowflake.
Height: 12–18 in. White flowers are about 1 in. wide, in small clusters. Needs no care for years on end, gradually forming big clumps. Good for naturalizing in rich, moist soil. Zone 4.

Liatris spicata. Blazing-star.
Height: 3–4 ft. Flowers for weeks in midsummer and attracts many butterflies. 'Kobold' (at right in photo) is a compact cultivar only 30 in. tall. Long lived and easy to grow. Full sun. Zone 4.

Kniphofia hybrids

Iberis sempervirens

Lamiastrum galeobdolon 'Herman's Pride'

Lamium maculatum 'White Nancy'

Leucojum aestivum

Liatris spicata

Lilium, Lilies

Gardeners have grown and cherished lilies since biblical times, and the selection today is better than ever. In addition to the traditional favorites such as Madonna, regal, and tiger lilies, there are hundreds of new hybrid cultivars with excellent color, fragrance, form, and vigor. Three groups—the Asiatic, Aurelian, and Oriental hybrids—are especially popular and reliable. Lily flowers come in all colors but blue. Many have a very sweet fragrance, and all make excellent cut flowers. Most bloom between June and August. The leafy stalks range from 1 to 8 ft. tall.

Lilies combine well with other perennials in mixed beds or borders or with a low ground cover such as ajuga, lamium, or sweet woodruff. They also do well in containers. In any case, they need well-drained soil enriched with plenty of organic matter and topped with a thick mulch. Under favorable conditions, a clump can live in one spot and flower abundantly year after year with very little care.

Lilium 'Enchantment'

Lilium longiflorum

Lilium canadense

Lilium lancifolium

Lilium 'Stargazer'

Lilium 'Black Dragon'

Lilium candidum

Lilium martagon var. *album*

Lilium regale

Lilium 'Black Dragon'.
Height: to 8 ft. One of the Aurelian, or trumpet, hybrids. These lilies are very fragrant and bloom in July or August. Forms a clump of tall stems topped with very large flowers. Zone 4.

Lilium canadense. Meadow lily.
Height: 2–5 ft. An eastern wildflower that prefers moist soil and part shade. Colors include yellow, orange, and red. Zone 4.

Lilium candidum. Madonna lily.
Height: 3 ft. Cherished since biblical times. Flowers are very fragrant. Blooms in June or July. Tolerates alkaline soil and summer heat better than most lilies do. Zone 4.

Lilium 'Enchantment'.
Height: 3 ft. One of the Asiatic hybrids. This group blooms from late May through June. They are easy to grow and multiply quickly. There are hundreds of cultivars in white, yellow, orange, pink, lavender, or red. Most are not fragrant. Zone 4.

Lilium lancifolium. Tiger lily.
Height: 4–6 ft. A vigorous plant; very easy to grow. Hybrid tiger lilies have red, orange, yellow, or white flowers, all with dark dots. Carries a virus that infects other lilies. Zone 4.

Lilium longiflorum. Easter lily.
Height: 2–3 ft. Flowers are very fragrant. Planted in the garden, it blooms in June, not at Easter. Zone 7.

Lilium martagon var. album.
Height: 3–6 ft. Slow to get going but lives for decades once established. Tolerates more shade than other lilies do. Flowers in June. Martagon hybrids look similar, with colored blooms. Zone 3.

Lilium regale. Regal lily.
Height: 5–6 ft. Flowers are very fragrant, especially in the evening. Blooms in July. Zone 4.

Lilium 'Stargazer'.
Height: 2–3 ft. One of the Oriental hybrids. These flower in late summer. Almost all have a very sweet fragrance. Colors include white, many shades of pink, and red. Zone 5.

Limonium latifolium

Liriope muscari 'Majestic'

Linum perenne

Liriope spicata

Limonium latifolium. Sea lavender.
Height: 2–3 ft. Sprays of tiny flowers are excellent fillers for cut or dried arrangements. Evergreen leaves are thick and leathery. Needs good drainage and shouldn't be crowded. Zone 3.

Linum perenne. Flax.
Height: to 18 in. Flowers open in the morning and close by midafternoon. Blooms for several weeks in summer. Dry stalks and round seedpods look good in fall and winter. Zone 4.

Liriope muscari 'Majestic'. Lilyturf.
Height: 2 ft. A good ground cover or edging for part shade. Forms clumps of broad, grassy, evergreen leaves. Other cultivars have blue or white flowers. Some kinds have variegated leaves. Zone 6.

Liriope spicata. Creeping lilyturf.
Height: under 12 in. Spreads quickly and makes a solid mass of evergreen foliage under trees or in shady spots. Needs curbing or it will invade adjacent beds. Zone 6 or 5.

Lobelia cardinalis. Cardinal flower.
Height: 4 ft. Clear red flowers attract hummingbirds. Blooms for weeks in late summer. Plants are short lived but usually self-sow. Prefers rich, moist soil and takes part shade. Zone 2.

Lycoris radiata. Spider lily.
Height: 12–18 in. Flowers suddenly in early fall, usually soon after a good rain. Leaves develop after bloom and last until spring. Slow to establish but long lived. Zone 8 or 7.

Lysimachia clethroides.
Gooseneck loosestrife.
Height: 2–3 ft. Blooms for several weeks in midsummer. Arching flower clusters grow up to 12 in. long. Spreads fast, especially in damp soil. Can be used as a ground cover. Zone 3.

Lysimachia nummularia.
Moneywort.
Height: 2–3 in. A good ground cover for moist, shady spots. Stems cling to the ground and root as they go. Flowers in summer. Fast, easy, and pest-free. Zone 3.

Macleaya cordata. Plume poppy.
Height: 6–8 ft. or more. A showy plant for the back of the border. Grows tall but doesn't need staking. Spreads to form large clumps. Blooms in midsummer. Zone 3.

Malva moschata. Musk mallow.
Height: 2–3 ft. Makes a soft bushy mound, good for meadows or natural gardens. *M. alcea* 'Fastigiata' has larger flowers and grows more erect. Both are easy and spread by seed. Zone 4.

Malvaviscus arboreus.
Turk's-cap.
Height: 3–5 ft. An old favorite for southern gardens. Blooms throughout summer and fall. Hummingbirds like the flowers. Other birds eat the small cherrylike fruits. Zone 8.

Lobelia cardinalis

Malva moschata

Lycoris radiata

Macleaya cordata

Lysimachia clethroides

Lysimachia nummularia

Malvaviscus arboreus

Mazus reptans

Mertensia virginica

Monarda didyma 'Gardenview Scarlet'

Nepeta × *faassenii* 'Six Hills Giant'

Monarda fistulosa

Nelumbo nucifera

Muscari armeniacum

Nymphaea odorata

Oenothera missourensis

Oenothera speciosa 'Rosea'

Oenothera tetragona

Mazus reptans.
Height: 2 in. A low ground cover for sun or part shade. Stems root as they run. Flowers in spring. May invade lawns but looks pretty there and tolerates light foot traffic. Zone 3.

Mertensia virginica.
Virginia bluebells.
Height: 1–2 ft. A native woodland wildflower. Emerges and soon flowers in early spring; goes dormant by summer. Nodding bell-shaped flowers are pale blue, fading to pink. Zone 3.

Monarda didyma 'Gardenview Scarlet'.
Bee balm.
Height: 2–4 ft. Blooms for several weeks in summer. Leaves release a pleasant fragrance. Unlike older cultivars, this has resistance to powdery mildew. Easy to grow and spreads quickly. Zone 4.

Monarda fistulosa. Bergamot.
Height: 2–4 ft. Flowers for several weeks in summer. Fuzzy leaves have a sweet fragrance. A prairie wildflower. Tolerates poor soil, hot sun, and dry weather. Zone 3.

Muscari armeniacum. Grape hyacinth.
Height: 6–8 in. Flowers have a rich fruity fragrance. Blooms in early spring, goes dormant in summer, makes new leaves in fall. Good for naturalizing; spreads slowly and needs no care. Zone 4.

Narcissus. (See pp. 260–261.)

Nelumbo nùcifera. Lotus.
Height: to 5 ft. above water. Flowers open during the day and have an intensely sweet fragrance. Blooms in midsummer. A vigorous plant that spreads quickly and can fill a shallow pond. Hardy to Zone 4 if the tubers are protected from freezing.

Nepeta × faassenii 'Six Hills Giant'.
Catmint.
Height: 3 ft. Flowers heavily in June; shear after flowering to encourage rebloom in late summer. Needs plenty of space and prefers well-drained soil. Combines well with roses. Zone 4.

Nymphaea odorata. Water lily.
Height: floats on water. Specialists offer both hardy and tropical water lilies with small to large flowers in a wide range of colors. Plants can be miniature or giant. Hardy water lilies can survive in Zone 4; tropical kinds are usually grown as annuals.

Oenothera missourensis. Ozark sundrops.
Height: 1 ft. Good for dry sites. Clear yellow 4-petaled flowers open 4–6 in. wide in late afternoon. Blooms for several weeks in summer. Large winged fruits are interesting, too. Zone 5.

Oenothera speciosa 'Rosea'.
Showy primrose.
Height: 1–2 ft. Few plants give as much color for so long with so little care. It is tough and adaptable and spreads quickly. Flowers open daytimes from spring through summer. Zone 5.

Oenothera tetragona. Sundrops.
Height: to 2 ft. Blooms daytimes for up to a month in summer. New foliage develops in fall. Spreads by underground runners to make a wide patch. Good ground cover for sunny banks. Zone 4.

Narcissus, Daffodils

The genus *Narcissus* includes all the various plants called daffodils, jonquils, and narcissus. They grow well throughout the United States and bring joy wherever they are planted. Different kinds bloom in sequence over a long season from late winter to late spring. The flowers can be small or large, borne singly or in clusters. Colors range from bright yellow or gold to creamy white, orange, or pink. Many kinds are fragrant. All make good cut flowers.

Naturalizing them in the grass is just one way to grow daffodils. Plant them along the edge of a woodland. Mix them with hostas, daylilies, ornamental grasses, or chrysanthemums in mixed borders. Use a special clump to accent a rock, tree, or bench. Pot them in containers for forcing indoors or to brighten the patio or entryway in spring. The bulbs are inexpensive to start with and multiply fast, so you can plant them generously. All those listed below are hardy to Zone 4, except as noted.

Narcissus 'Dutch Master'

Narcissus 'Hawera'

Narcissus 'Actaea'

Narcissus 'Suzy'

***Narcissus* 'Actaea'.** Pheasant's-eye narcissus. Height: 18 in. A poeticus hybrid. Flowers are very sweet-scented. Late spring.

Narcissus bulbocodium.
Hoop-petticoat daffodil.
Height: 6 in. A species narcissus. Plants are small, good for containers, rock gardens, or naturalizing. Midspring.

***Narcissus* 'Dutch Master'.**
Height: 14–18 in. A trumpet daffodil. Very popular for naturalizing. Early to midspring.

***Narcissus* 'Geranium'.**
Height: 14 in. A tazetta hybrid. Flowers are very fragrant, excellent for cutting. Late spring. Zone 5.

***Narcissus* 'Hawera'.**
Height: 8 in. A triandrus hybrid. This miniature daffodil is good for rock gardens or very special niches. Mid- to late spring.

***Narcissus* 'Ice Follies'.**
Height: 14–18 in. A long-cup daffodil. Naturalizes well. Flowers open yellow and fade to white. Early to midspring.

***Narcissus* 'Peeping Tom'.**
Height: under 8 in. A cyclamineus hybrid. One of the first daffodils to bloom in very early spring.

***Narcissus* 'Suzy'.**
Height: to 16 in. A jonquilla hybrid. Has a very sweet fragrance. Mid- to late spring.

***Narcissus* 'Tahiti'.**
Height: 12–16 in. A double daffodil. Flowers in this group range from 1 to 4 in. wide. Mid- to late spring.

Narcissus 'Tahiti'

Narcissus 'Geranium'

Narcissus 'Ice Follies'

Narcissus 'Peeping Tom'

Narcissus bulbocodium

Ophiopogon japonicus

Ophiopogon planiscapus 'Nigrescens'

Pachysandra terminalis

Paeonia 'Edulis Superba'

Papaver orientale

Ophiopogon japonicus. Monkey grass. Height: 6–12 in. A good substitute for turfgrass in shady places. Tolerates only light foot traffic but makes a dense ground cover. Flowers and fruits are small and hide in the foliage. Zone 7.

Ophiopogon planiscapus 'Nigrescens'. Black mondo grass. Height: 6–12 in. A striking accent for small spaces. Contrasts well with gold, silver, or light green plants. Needs part sun to develop rich foliage color. Spreads slowly. Zone 7.

Pachysandra terminalis. Pachysandra. Height: 8 in. A hardy evergreen ground cover for part or full shade, under and around trees and shrubs. Glossy leaves are arranged in rosettes on short stalks. Blooms briefly in spring. Zone 5.

Paeonia 'Edulis Superba'. Hybrid peony. Height: $2^{1}/_{2}$–$3^{1}/_{2}$ ft. An old favorite with very fragrant, double, rosy pink flowers. Excellent for cutting. Blooms early in the season. Does well in both the North and South. Zone 3.

Paeonia tenuifolia. Fernleaf peony. Height: 12–18 in. Unusual lacy foliage is lovely in spring and makes a bushy mound under the round waxy flowers. Dies back and leaves a gap in late summer. Needs rich soil. Zone 3.

Paeonia 'Toro-no-maki'. Hybrid peony. Height: 3 ft. A Japanese-style peony with single flowers that have a mounded tuft of gold stamens. Foliage is attractive from spring to fall. Blooms midseason. Zone 3.

Paeonia 'Toro-no-maki'

Penstemon digitalis 'Husker's Red'

Paeonia tenuifolia

Penstemon barbatus

Penstemon smallii

Papaver orientale. Oriental poppy.
Height: to 3 ft. Vivid glossy flowers, 4–6 in.
wide, have crinkled petals in shades of scarlet,
orange, red, pink, or white. Blooms in late
spring or early summer; dies back by
midsummer. Zone 2.

Penstemon barbatus.
Height: to 3 ft. A bushy plant with loose
spikes of tubular flowers, 1 in. long, in
shades of red, pink, purple, orange, or white.
Thrives in dry sandy or gravelly soil.
Zone 3.

Penstemon digitalis 'Husker's Red'.
Height: 2–4 ft. Worth growing for the dark
reddish purple foliage, which combines well
with many perennials. Large flowers like
white foxgloves open for a month in early
summer. Zone 3.

Penstemon smallii.
Height: 1–2$^{1}/_{2}$ ft. Flowers in early summer.
Foliage is usually evergreen. Can grow in the
dry soil under trees. Zone 6.

Perovskia atriplicifolia

Phlox maculata 'Miss Lingard'

Phlox stolonifera

Phlomis fruticosa

Phlox divaricata

Physostegia virginiana

Phlox paniculata 'Bright Eyes'

Platycodon grandiflorus

Phlox pilosa

Phlox subulata

Perovskia atriplicifolia. Russian sage.
Height: 3–5 ft. Coarse-toothed leaves have a pleasant fragrance. Makes a loose open clump of silvery foliage topped with thousands of small lavender flowers. Needs good drainage. Zone 5.

Phlomis fruticosa. Jerusalem sage.
Height: 4 ft. A shrubby perennial, good for dry, sunny spots. Thick wrinkly leaves and tough stems are covered with fuzzy hairs. Blooms repeatedly if you cut it back each time. Zone 7.

Phlox divaricata. Wild sweet William.
Height: 8–12 in. An ideal ground cover or filler for shady spots. Blooms for many weeks in spring. Usually has light blue flowers, but there are white and dark blue-purple forms. Zone 3.

***Phlox maculata* 'Miss Lingard'.**
Spotted phlox.
Height: 2–4 ft. Thick glossy leaves resist mildew and look good all season. White flowers last 2–3 weeks in early summer. Other cultivars are pink or purple. Prefers rich, moist soil. Zone 3.

***Phlox paniculata* 'Bright Eyes'.**
Garden phlox.
Height: 2 ft. Erect leafy stems are topped with domed clusters of fragrant flowers in late summer. Dozens of other cultivars differ in height and flower color. Spreads to make big clumps. Zone 4.

Phlox pilosa. Prairie phlox.
Height: 1–1¹/₂ ft. Spreads generously but doesn't get in the way. Similar to *P. divaricata* but tolerates sun, heat, and dry soil. Flowers for several weeks in early summer. Zone 3.

Phlox stolonifera. Creeping phlox.
Height: 6–12 in. Forms loose mats that trail along a path or wander among spring bulbs. Spreads but isn't invasive. Flowers can be blue, violet, pink, or white. Blooms in midspring. Zone 2.

Phlox subulata. Moss phlox.
Height: 6–9 in. Makes a solid sheet of color in spring. It's ideal for carpeting dry, sunny slopes. Colors include bright and soft shades of pink, magenta, lavender, blue, white, and red. Needlelike foliage is evergreen in mild climates. Zone 2.

Physostegia virginiana.
Obedient plant.
Height: 3 ft. An eastern wildflower, good for damp spots where it can spread freely. Pretty but invasive in borders. Has pink, lavender, or white flowers in late summer. Zone 2.

Platycodon grandiflorus.
Balloon flower.
Height: 1¹/₂–3 ft. Puffy buds open into lovely 5-pointed flowers, 2 in. wide, in shades of blue, violet, pink, or white. Slow to establish but long lived. Blooms all summer. Zone 3.

Polemonium caeruleum

Polygonatum odoratum 'Variegatum'

Polygonum bistorta 'Superbum'

Polemonium caeruleum.
Jacob's-ladder.
Height: 2–3 ft. Blooms for several weeks in late spring. Nodding flowers are 1 in. wide. Can't take hot summers. Needs cool, moist, well-drained, organic soil. Zone 2.

***Polygonatum odoratum* 'Variegatum'.**
Variegated Solomon's-seal.
Height: 1½–3 ft. Fragrant white flowers, 1 in. long, bloom in spring. Grows well under trees or shrubs; tolerates dry shade better than most perennials do. Spreads slowly to make a patch. Zone 3.

***Polygonum bistorta* 'Superbum'.** Knotweed.
Height: 2–3 ft. Large smooth leaves, 4–6 in. long, have wavy edges and distinct white midribs. Brushy spikes of tiny pink flowers make good cut flowers. Spreads fast in damp soil. Zone 3.

Primula denticulata. Drumstick primrose.
Height: 10–15 in. Flowers in early spring, in shades of lavender, pink, or white. Can survive short dry spells but does better with constant moisture. Needs rich, organic soil. Zone 3.

Primula japonica. Japanese primrose, candelabra primrose.
Height: 1–2 ft. Tiers of rosy red, pink, magenta, or white flowers are stacked one above another. Blooms in May or June. Needs moist soil and can't survive dry spells. Zone 5.

Primula × polyantha. Polyanthus primrose.
Height: 8–12 in. The easiest primrose to obtain and to grow. Among the earliest plants to bloom in spring—and often the latest in fall. Available in many colors. Zone 3.

Primula sieboldii. Japanese star primrose.
Height: 9–15 in. Blooms in spring. Flowers can be pink, white, lilac, or magenta. Unlike most primroses, it can survive summer heat and dry soil by going completely dormant. Zone 4.

Primula vulgaris. Common primrose.
Height: 6–9 in. Beloved by generations of gardeners for its simple charm. Fragrant yellow flowers open in early spring. Excellent for woodland gardens or along streams. Zone 5.

***Prunella webbiana* 'Pink Loveliness'.**
Self-heal.
Height: 12–18 in. Forms a compact mat or clump of smooth dark green leaves, attractive at the front of a border. Doesn't spread like its weedy relatives. Blooms for several weeks in summer. Zone 5.

Pulmonaria angustifolia. Blue lungwort.
Height: 6–9 in. Blooms for several weeks in early spring. Spreads slowly and makes a good ground cover among bulbs. May go dormant in the heat of summer, then reappear in fall. Zone 3.

Primula denticulata

Primula japonica

Primula sieboldii

Primula × polyantha

Primula vulgaris

Pulmonaria angustifolia

Prunella webbiana 'Pink Loveliness'

Ratibida columnifera

Romneya coulteri

Rudbeckia fulgida 'Goldsturm'

Rudbeckia laciniata 'Golden Glow'

Rudbeckia nitida 'Herbsonne'

Ratibida columnifera.
Coneflower, Mexican hat.
Height: 12–18 in. A prairie wildflower that combines well with grasses. Blooms from May to September. Needs full sun and well-drained soil. May be short lived but usually self-sows. Zone 4.

Romneya coulteri. Matilija poppy.
Height: 8 ft. One of California's most famous wildflowers. Blooms from May to July. Spreads fast and needs plenty of space. Full sun. Tolerates poor soil, heat, and drought. Zone 8.

Rudbeckia fulgida 'Goldsturm'.
Black-eyed Susan.
Height: 18–30 in. Makes a big splash of color from summer into fall. Flowers are good for fresh or dried arrangements. Gather them often; the more you pick, the more it blooms. Zone 3.

Rudbeckia laciniata 'Golden Glow'.
Height: 6–8 ft. Blooms from summer to fall. Flowers are good for cutting. Spreads underground and makes a big clump. Can be invasive. Best used in informal or country gardens. Zone 3.

Rudbeckia nitida 'Herbsonne'.
Height: 4–6 ft. Lemon yellow flowers combine easily with other colors. Blooms for weeks in late summer and autumn. Easy to grow in average soil and full sun. May need staking. Zone 4.

Salvia azurea var. grandiflora. Azure sage.
Height: 3–5 ft. Blooms from summer to frost. Bees and butterflies love it. Good for

Salvia azurea var. *grandiflora*

Salvia clevelandii

Salvia coccinea

Salvia greggii

meadows, as it competes well with grasses and tolerates moist soil and periodic mowing. Zone 5.

Salvia clevelandii. Cleveland sage.
Height: 4 ft. A shrubby plant, woody at the base. Evergreen foliage is very aromatic. Blooms from spring to summer. Needs well-drained soil. Tolerates heat and drought. Zone 9 or 8.

Salvia coccinea. Scarlet sage.
Height: 2–3 ft. A graceful alternative to the familiar bedding salvia, *S. splendens*. Perennial in the South, it grows fast from seed and makes a good annual in the North. Zone 8 or 7.

Salvia farinacea. Mealy blue sage.
Height: to 2–3 ft. Blooms nonstop from late spring to hard frost. Long-stalked flower spikes are good for fresh or dried arrangements. Flowers can be dark blue, light blue, or white. Perennial in Zone 8 or 7; makes a good annual in colder climates.

Salvia greggii.
Cherry sage, autumn sage.
Height: 3 ft. A low bushy plant with colorful flowers from spring to fall. Available with flowers in shades of rosy pink, red, salmon, purple, or white. Needs well-drained soil. Zone 9 or 8.

Salvia guaranitica. Blue sage.
Height: 3–5 ft. A bushy plant with fragrant dark green leaves and dark violet-blue flowers. Blooms from midsummer to frost. A Texas wildflower, like *S. farinacea*. Zone 8.

Salvia farinacea

Salvia guaranitica

Salvia leucantha

Salvia pratensis

Salvia × superba 'May Night'

Sanguinaria canadensis

Salvia leucantha. Mexican bush sage.
Height: 3–4 ft. A big bushy plant that thrives
in hot, dry weather and blooms from
midsummer to late fall. Give it plenty of
space. Cut back older stems to promote new
growth. Zone 8 or 7.

Salvia pratensis.
Meadow sage, meadow clary.
Height: to 3 ft. Forms a rosette of large,
hairy, fragrant, dark green leaves. Upright
stalks carry lavender-blue, violet, rosy, or
white flowers for a month or so in summer.
Zone 3.

Salvia × superba 'May Night'.
Height: 1½ ft. Blooms from May to frost if
you remove spent flower spikes. Makes a
mass of color in the garden and a good cut
flower, too. Full or part sun. Tolerates dry
soil. Zone 4.

Sanguinaria canadensis. Bloodroot.
Height: to 8 in. A spring wildflower that
blooms before the trees leaf out. Large,
lobed, blue-green leaves die down by
midsummer. Spreads underground to form a
patch and also self-sows. Zone 4.

Sanguisorba canadensis. Canadian burnet.
Height: 3–6 ft. Blooms in late August or
September, after most perennials are finished.
Foliage looks good all season; leaflets have
very neat scalloped edges. Moist soil. Zone 3.

Santolina chamaecyparissus.
Lavender cotton, gray santolina.
Height: 2 ft. Grows naturally into an
irregular mound or can be trimmed into
neater shapes. Rough-textured evergreen
foliage is strong-scented. Has yellow flower
heads in summer. Zone 7 or 6.

Santolina virens. Green santolina.
Height: 2 ft. Yellow flowers last for weeks in
summer. Dark foliage is evergreen, with
slender leaves like twisted pine needles. Can
be clipped into neat formal shapes. Zone 6.

Saponaria ocymoides. Rock soapwort.
Height: 4–8 in. Makes a carpet of bright
pink flowers, ½ in. wide, in early summer.
Dark green foliage is semievergreen. Grows
easily from seed. Likes a sunny, well-drained
site. Zone 4.

Saxifraga stolonifera.
Strawberry geranium, strawberry begonia.
Height: 6 in. An easy ground cover for mild,
shady spots. Blooms in early summer.
Spreads like a strawberry, making baby plants
at the ends of slender runners. Prefers moist
soil. Zone 7.

Scabiosa caucasica. Pincushion flower.
Height: 18–24 in. A desirable and long-
lasting cut flower, also showy in a summer
border. Available in pale and deep blue, lilac,
lavender pinkish purple, and white. Zone 3.

Sanguisorba canadensis

Saponaria ocymoides

Saxifraga stolonifera

Santolina chamaecyparissus

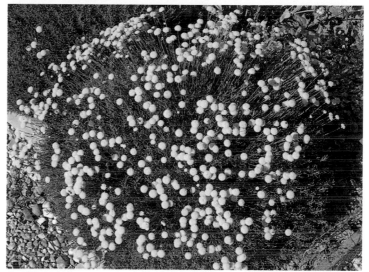

Santolina virens

Scabiosa caucasica

Scilla sibirica 'Spring Beauty'

Sedum 'Autumn Joy'

Sedum 'Ruby Glow'

Sedum kamtschaticum 'Weihenstephaner Gold'

Sedum spurium 'Dragon's Blood'

Scilla sibirica 'Spring Beauty'.
Squill.
Height: 4–8 in. Blooms in early spring.
Small starry flowers are a gorgeous shade of blue. Bulbs are inexpensive; plant dozens where they can naturalize under trees or shrubs. Zone 3.

Sedum 'Autumn Joy'.
Height: 2–3 ft. Flowers for weeks in late summer and fall. Flowers open pink, gradually darken to rusty red, and fade to tan in winter. Foliage is plump and succulent. Adaptable and easy. Zone 3.

Sedum kamtschaticum 'Weihenstephaner Gold'.
Height: 4–8 in. An excellent noninvasive ground cover for almost any soil. Yellow flowers are followed by red seed heads. Succulent foliage stays fresh and healthy all season. Zone 3.

Sedum 'Ruby Glow'.
Height: 12 in. Fleshy leaves are blue-gray tinged with maroon. Brilliant ruby red flowers last for several weeks in fall. Butterflies love it. Needs good drainage. Zone 3.

Sedum spurium 'Dragon's Blood'.
Height: to 6 in. An easy ground cover or edging for sunny spots. Creeping stems root at the nodes. Leaves are purple-bronze. Blooms for several weeks in summer. Spreads fast. Zone 3.

Sempervivum tectorum.
Hen-and-chickens.
Height: 4 in. Forms a "hen," closely surrounded by many smaller "chicks." Flat clusters of starry reddish flowers top thick stems in midsummer. Good for rock walls, crevices, or pots. Zone 4.

Sempervivum tectorum

Smilacina racemosa

Sidalcea malviflora

Sisyrinchium bellum

Sisyrinchium striatum 'Variegatum'

Sidalcea malviflora.
Prairie mallow, checkerbloom.
Height: 2¹/₂–4 ft. A graceful wildflower with flowers like small hollyhocks. Blooms for about 2 weeks in June or July. Cultivars differ in height and flower color. Zone 5.

Sisyrinchium bellum.
Blue-eyed grass.
Height: 6–18 in. Starry blue-violet flowers on flat winged stalks bloom in late spring and early summer. Individual plants are small; mass several together to make a show. Zone 8.

Sisyrinchium striatum 'Variegatum'.
Height: 1¹/₂–2¹/₂ ft. A unique and striking plant. Irislike leaves are gray-green striped with cream. Creamy yellow flowers bloom in spring. Prefers moist, well-drained soil. Zone 7.

Smilacina racemosa.
False Solomon's-seal.
Height: 2–3 ft. A woodland wildflower that spreads slowly to form thick patches. Blooms in spring; has red berries in fall. Needs shade and deep, loose, moist, acidic soil. Zone 3.

Solidago rugosa

Solidago vigaurea 'Peter Pan'

Stachys byzantina

Strelitzia reginae

Stokesia laevis

Tagetes lemmonii

Thalictrum aquilegifolium

Thermopsis caroliniana

Tiarella cordifolia

Tulbaghia violacea

Solidago rugosa.
Rough-leaved goldenrod.
Height: 4–5 ft. Sturdy stems branch near the top into many flowering side shoots. Makes a large vase-shaped clump. Doesn't spread as fast as most goldenrods. Zone 4.

Solidago vigaurea 'Peter Pan'.
Height: 2–3 ft. Makes a compact mound of bright yellow flowers in fall. More refined than most goldenrods. Zone 4.

Stachys byzantina. Lamb's-ears.
Height: 8 in. Ear-shaped leaves are soft, thick, and woolly. Spreads to make a low mat of semievergreen foliage, excellent for edging flower beds. Flower stalks reach 18 in. Zone 5.

Stokesia laevis. Stoke's aster.
Height: to 2 ft. Flowers in summer, in shades of blue, lavender-blue, pink, white, or pale yellow. An adaptable plant that tolerates part shade, poor or dry soil, and hot weather. Zone 5.

Strelitzia reginae.
Bird-of-paradise.
Height: to 5 ft. A dramatic plant with exotic flowers that are excellent for cutting. Needs a frost-free climate, plenty of sun, and rich, moist soil. Grows well in a large container. Zone 9.

Tagetes lemmonii. Mexican bush marigold.
Height: 3–6 ft. A bushy plant with bright 1-in. blossoms, especially in winter and spring but continuing all year. Evergreen foliage has a strong marigold odor. Zone 9.

Thalictrum aquilegifolium.
Columbine meadow rue.
Height: 2–3 ft. Flowers are showy for about 2 weeks, but lacy blue-green foliage lasts all season and makes a nice background for other flowers. Prefers rich, moist soil. Zone 4.

Thermopsis caroliniana. Carolina lupine.
Height: 3–6 ft. Bright yellow flowers last for 1–2 weeks in late spring, then form fuzzy flat pods. Combines well with other wildflowers and grasses. Trouble-free. Lives for years. Zone 4.

Tiarella cordifolia. Foamflower.
Height: 6–12 in. Plump flower spikes are showy for several weeks in late spring. Foliage is semievergreen. Makes a good ground cover or edging for shady gardens. Zone 3.

Tulbaghia violacea. Society garlic.
Height: 1–2 ft. Blooms mostly in summer but repeats throughout the year. Makes a good cut flower, but stems and leaves smell like garlic. Grow in containers where winters are cold. Zone 9.

Tulipa Darwin tulips

Tulipa 'Monte Carlo'

Tulipa 'White Emperor'

Tulipa tarda

Tulipa 'Red Riding Hood'

***Tulipa* Darwin tulips.**
Height: 18–30 in. The most popular garden tulips. Flowers are shaped like deep cups and held on tall stalks. They come in a very wide range of colors and bloom in late spring. Zone 4.

***Tulipa* 'Monte Carlo'.**
Height: 12 in. A double early tulip. This class has many-petaled flowers on short stems. They bloom in early spring. Double late tulips reach 24 in., in late spring. Zone 4.

***Tulipa* 'Red Riding Hood'.**
Height: 8–12 in. A Greigii tulip. This class has dark green leaves mottled with red or purple. Flowers are usually red, orange, or yellow, in midspring. Zone 4.

***Tulipa* 'White Emperor'.**
Height: 18 in. A Fosteriana or emperor tulip. These are single early tulips with large flowers on rather short stalks. Colors include red, orange, pink, yellow, and white. Zone 4.

Tulipa tarda.
Height: 5 in. A species tulip. Flowers open 2 in. wide and last for about 2 weeks in early spring. They are borne in groups of 3–6 on short stalks. Needs well-drained soil. Zone 4.

Verbascum chaixii.
Height: 3 ft. A showy plant for dry, sunny sites. It's short lived but usually self-sows. Flowers for several weeks in summer. Basal rosette is semievergreen. Zone 5.

Verbascum olympicum.
Height: 5 ft. or more. A short-lived perennial or biennial. Makes a bold rosette of large silvery leaves the first year, then flowers the second summer. Often self-sows. Zone 5.

Verbena bonariensis.
Height: 3–4 ft. Violet flowers bloom from early summer to frost. Doesn't need staking or deadheading. Good for covering the gap over spring bulbs. Grows as an annual in cold zones. Zone 7.

Verbena canadensis. Rose verbena.
Height: 1 ft. A showy wildflower that thrives in dry, sandy soil and full sun. Blooms for a month or longer. Easy to grow. Usually short lived, but it self-sows. Zone 6.

Verbena rigida.
Height: 1–2 ft. A carefree plant with masses of violet, lavender, or white flowers all summer. Fills in fast and can be grown as an annual, like *V. bonariensis.* Zone 8.

Verbascum chaixii

Verbena bonariensis

Verbascum olympicum

Verbena canadensis

Verbena rigida

Veronica 'Crater Lake Blue'

Veronica 'Sunny Border Blue'

Veronica incana

Vinca major

Vinca minor

Viola labradorica var. *purpurea*

Viola pedata

Viola odorata

Waldsteinia ternata

Zauschneria californica

Zephyranthes candida

Zinnia grandiflora

Veronica 'Crater Lake Blue'.
Height: 1 ft. Beautiful blue flowers last for about 2 weeks in late spring. Forms a loose mat of medium green foliage for the rest of the season. Zone 3.

Veronica incana.
Woolly speedwell.
Height: 1–2 ft. Silvery foliage makes a good edging along the front of a well-drained bed. Slender spikes of blue flowers last for several weeks in summer, but flower stalks usually need support. Zone 3.

Veronica 'Sunny Border Blue'.
Height: 2 ft. A bushy upright plant that flowers all summer and requires very little care. Butterflies love the flowers. Leaves are shiny dark green, with a crinkled texture. Zone 4.

Vinca major. Large periwinkle.
Height: 1 ft. An evergreen ground cover with trailing stems that root where they touch the ground. Blooms in early spring. A variegated form is often used in window boxes or planters. Zone 7.

Vinca minor.
Common periwinkle.
Height: 6–12 in. A versatile evergreen ground cover that grows well in sun or shade. Very long lived and carefree. Blooms in spring. Flowers can be lavender-blue, purple, or white. Zone 4.

Viola labradorica var. purpurea.
Labrador violet.
Height: 4 in. A low violet that spreads quickly and makes a pretty ground cover. Shiny dark leaves can be green or purple. Has small violet-blue flowers, mostly in spring. Zone 3.

Viola odorata. Sweet violet.
Height: 4–6 in. Very fragrant lavender, white, or dark blue flowers bloom for many weeks in late winter and early spring. Spreads fast and makes a good semievergreen ground cover. Zone 4.

Viola pedata. Bird's-foot violet.
Height: 6 in. A popular wildflower with lobed leaves that are shaped like a bird's foot. Flowers are larger than those of many violets. Needs well-drained sandy or gravelly soil. Zone 4.

Waldsteinia ternata. Barren strawberry.
Height: 4–6 in. A good ground cover for sunny, well-drained sites. Shiny leaves are semievergreen, turning reddish purple in cold weather. Flowers in late spring and early summer. Zone 4.

Zauschneria californica.
California fuchsia.
Height: 1–2 ft. Hummingbirds love it. Trumpet-shaped flowers open from July to October. There are also pink and white forms. A California wildflower, good for informal gardens. Zone 8.

Zephyranthes candida.
Height: 1 ft. Clear white flowers open 2 in. wide. One of several similar species; the others have white, pink, or red flowers. All bloom in spring or summer. Many do well in pots. Zone 9.

Zinnia grandiflora.
Desert zinnia, Rocky Mountain zinnia.
Height: 6–8 in. Spreads slowly but gradually fills in to make a dense, tough, long-lived ground cover for hot, dry sites in the West. Keeps blooming for months and months. Zone 5.

Herbs

Agastache foeniculum

Allium schoenoprasum

Allium tuberosum

Aloysia triphylla

Agastache foeniculum.
Anise hyssop.
Height: 4 ft. Perennial, with dense spikes of blue-purple flowers from July to September. Fragrant leaves can be used to make a licorice-flavored tea. Full or part sun. Zone 6.

Allium schoenoprasum. Chives.
Height: 12 in. A bulb-forming perennial with pungent onion-flavored leaves. Balls of lavender flowers on stiff stalks bloom in late spring. Long lived. Full or part sun. Zone 3.

Allium tuberosum. Garlic chives.
Height: 24 in. Slender clumps of garlic-flavored flat leaves in spring and summer. Round clusters of white flowers on tall stalks in late summer or early fall. Perennial. Full sun. Zone 3.

Aloysia triphylla. Lemon verbena.
Height: to 10 ft. A slender-twigged shrub with a loose open habit. Whorls of thin papery leaves with intense lemon fragrance. Grow as an annual or in containers where winters are cold. Full sun. Zone 8.

Angelica archangelica

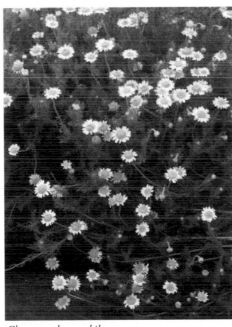

Anethum graveolens

Artemisia abrotanum

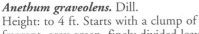
Artemisia dracunculus var. sativa

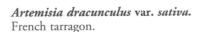
Chamaemelum nobile

Borago officinalis

Anethum graveolens. Dill.
Height: to 4 ft. Starts with a clump of fragrant, gray-green, finely divided leaves, then makes yellow flowers on tall stalks in midsummer. Used in cooking. Fast-growing annual.

Angelica archangelica. Angelica.
Height: to 6 ft. Makes big clumps of stout stems with glossy compound leaves and large umbels of greenish white flowers. Seeds are fragrant. Part sun or shade. Perennial or biennial. Zone 4.

Artemisia abrotanum. Southernwood.
Height: 3–5 ft. Fragrant, finely divided, gray-green leaves. Easily shaped into a compact ball. Dried lemon-, tangerine-, or camphor-scented foliage makes sachets or potpourri. Zone 5.

Artemisia dracunculus var. sativa.
French tarragon.
Height: 2 ft. or more. A slow-spreading perennial with slender flavorful leaves that have many culinary uses. Rarely bears small greenish flowers. Full or part sun. Zone 3.

Borago officinalis. Borage.
Height: 24 in. Star-shaped, sky blue flowers. Large oblong leaves are rough and hairy. Flowers and new leaves add flavor to salads; flowers are also used as a garnish. Full sun. Annual.

Chamaemelum nobile. Roman chamomile.
Height: 4–12 in. Flat and spreading, with finely dissected, aromatic leaves. Daisylike flowers make an apple-flavored tea. Good ground cover or lawn substitute. Perennial. Full sun. Zone 4.

Chrysanthemum parthenium

Conradina verticillata

Coriandrum sativum

Cymbopogon citratus

Foeniculum vulgare 'Purpureum'

Chrysanthemum parthenium. Feverfew.
Height: 1–3 ft. Aromatic ferny foliage.
Cheerful daisylike blossoms open throughout
summer and fall, last well as cut flowers.
Foliage has medicinal properties. Perennial.
Zone 5.

Conradina verticillata.
Cumberland rosemary.
Height: 15 in. Forms a low-growing,
spreading mound. Fine dark green leaves
with a strong minty aroma. Small pale pink-
purple flowers in midspring. Can make a low
hedge or ground cover in sandy soil. Zone 5.

Coriandrum sativum. Cilantro, coriander.
Height: 1–3 ft. Fast-growing rosettes of
strong-scented compound leaves. Umbels of
white or pale pinkish flowers. Fresh leaves
and aromatic seeds are used in cooking. Full
sun. Annual.

Cymbopogon citratus. Lemongrass.
Height: to 6 ft. Dense clumps of long,
slender, sharp-edged, pale green leaves have a
strong lemony flavor and aroma. Flowers
infrequently. Grows well in a large pot. Full
sun. Zone 10.

Foeniculum vulgare 'Purpureum'.
Bronze fennel.
Height: 3–6 ft. Fragrant purple-bronze
foliage makes a fluffy mound in spring,
topped with clusters of tiny yellow flowers on
tall hollow stalks in late summer. Full sun.
Zone 4.

Galium odoratum. Sweet woodruff.
Height: 4–9 in. A useful ground cover that
spreads quickly, even in poor soil and shade.
Whorled leaves are dark green in summer,
tan after hard frost, vanilla-scented when dry.
Zone 4.

Hyssopus officinalis. Hyssop.
Height: 18–24 in. Blooms in midsummer.
Can be sheared to make a dense low hedge.
Aromatic leaves are sometimes used for
fragrance and flavoring. Semievergreen in
mild climates. Zone 3.

Galium odoratum

Hyssopus officinalis

Lavandula angustifolia

Lavandula stoechas

Laurus nobilis. Sweet bay.
Height: 10–40 ft. Stiff leathery leaves have a pleasant fragrance and flavor. Easily pruned and shaped into formal shapes for standards or topiary. Makes a dense evergreen hedge. Zone 8.

Lavandula angustifolia. English lavender.
Height: 1–2 ft. Flowers are wonderfully fragrant in early summer. Different cultivars have pink, lavender, or purple blossoms. A shrubby perennial. Needs well-drained soil. Zone 5.

Lavandula stoechas. Spanish lavender.
Height: 18–24 in. Slender gray leaves have a pleasant fragrance. Flower spikes are topped with dark purple bracts. A shrubby perennial. Needs well-drained soil. Zone 8 or 7.

Levisticum officinale. Lovage.
Height: 4–6 ft. A robust perennial with bold leaves, stiff stalks, and large flower heads. Leaves and seeds are used for flavoring. Does best in rich, moist soil. Zone 3.

Laurus nobilis

Levisticum officinale

Marrubium vulgare

Matricaria recutita

Mentha hybrids

Melissa officinalis

Marrubium vulgare. Horehound.
Height: 2–3 ft. Gray-green leaves produce a bitter compound that relieves sore throats and suppresses coughs. Grows well in sandy or gravelly soil; gets floppy in rich or moist soil. Full sun. Zone 4.

Matricaria recutita. German chamomile.
Height: 24–30 in. Ferny foliage has a sweet fragrance. Dried flower heads make a soothing tea. An annual, easily grown from seed sown direct in early spring. Ordinary soil and full sun.

Melissa officinalis. Lemon balm.
Height: 2 ft. Shiny crinkled leaves have a wonderful lemony aroma and flavor. Makes a bushy mound if pruned repeatedly or a sprawling patch if left alone. An easy-to-grow perennial. Zone 5.

Mentha hybrids. Mints.
There are hundreds of mints, differing in flavor, foliage, plant height, and vigor and sold under a babel of names. Many, but not all, spread invasively. Most are hardy to Zone 5.

Mentha pulegium. Pennyroyal.
Height: to 12 in. Makes a good ground cover for damp spots or between stepping-stones and is not invasive. Flowers in midsummer. Not reliably winter-hardy but may self-sow. Zone 6.

Mentha spicata. Spearmint.
Height: 2–3 ft. Notorious both for its sweet minty aroma and for its vigorous invasive growth. Spreads quickly to make a dense patch. Prefers but doesn't require damp soil. Zone 5.

Mentha pulegium

Mentha spicata

Mentha suaveolens

Myrrhis odorata

Nepeta cataria

Mentha suaveolens. Pineapple mint.
Height: 1 ft. or more. The most ornamental
of all mints. Less invasive than spearmint or
peppermint, it's safer to include in herb
gardens or flower borders. Has a mild flavor.
Zone 5.

Myrrhis odorata. Sweet cicely.
Height: 3 ft. Makes a bushy clump of
fragrant ferny foliage that turns gold in fall.
White flowers in spring are followed by
clusters of conspicuous ribbed fruits.
Perennial. Zone 4.

Nepeta cataria. Catnip.
Height: 3 ft. Cats get excited by the bitter
fragrance of the leaves, which are also used
for tea. Leaves and stems are covered with
soft hairs. Easy to grow but invasive.
Perennial. Zone 3.

Ocimum basilicum

Ocimum basilicum 'Purpurascens'

Origanum vulgare subsp. *hirtum*

Origanum majorana

Origanum vulgare subsp. *vulgare* 'Aureum'

Ocimum basilicum. Sweet basil.
Height: to 2 ft. Shiny leaves have a
wonderful fragrance and flavor. Makes a
bushy erect plant with stiff stems. Several
strains are available from seed. A tender
annual, quite sensitive to cold.

Ocimum basilicum **'Purpurascens'.**
Purple basil.
Height: to 2 ft. More ornamental but not
as tasty as common sweet basil. The dark
foliage is a welcome contrast to greens and
grays. Annual.

Origanum majorana. Sweet marjoram.
Height: 1–2 ft. Leaves have a delicious
fragrance and are used in cooking and
perfumery. Tiny flowers are nestled in
knotlike bracts. Usually grown as an annual;
perennial in Zone 9.

Origanum vulgare **subsp.** ***hirtum.***
Oregano.
Height: 2 ft. This is the oregano to use in
Italian food. Leaves have a distinct
penetrating fragrance. Flowers are dull white.
Spreads to make a patch. Hardy to Zone 5 if
mulched.

Origanum vulgare **subsp.** ***vulgare***
'Aureum'. Golden oregano.
Height: under 6 in. Makes a creeping mat of
gold-green foliage. Leaves are ornamental but
virtually scentless. Spreads as a ground cover
and tolerates dry soil. Hardy to Zone 5 if
mulched.

Pelargonium graveolens.
Rose geranium.
Height: 2–3 ft. Different cultivars have
different fragrances—sweet, pungent, fruity,
or flowery. Most grow bushy and upright.
Some are variegated. Overwinter in a pot on
a sunny windowsill.

Pelargonium tomentosum.
Peppermint geranium.
Height: under 2 ft. Spreads wider than tall
and can cover several square feet by late
summer. Soft furry leaves have a rich minty
aroma. A tender perennial often grown as an
annual.

Petroselinum crispum. Parsley.
Height: 1 ft. A biennial grown as an annual.
Makes a rosette of tasty, fragrant, dark green
foliage. Both curly- and flat-leaved types are
commonly available. Prefers deep, rich,
moist soil.

Rosmarinus officinalis. Rosemary.
Height: 4 ft. A favorite culinary herb.
Evergreen foliage is very aromatic. Flowers in
winter and spring. Does well in pots and can
be overwintered indoors. Zone 8.

Rosmarinus officinalis **'Prostratus'.**
Prostrate rosemary.
Height: 1 ft. An evergreen ground cover that
will trail down a bank or over a wall. Needs
good drainage and tolerates heat and
drought. Zone 8.

Pelargonium graveolens

Pelargonium tomentosum

Petroselinum crispum

Rosmarinus officinalis

Rosmarinus officinalis 'Prostratus'

Ruta graveolens 'Jackman's Blue'

Salvia elegans

Salvia officinalis

Salvia sclarea

Ruta graveolens 'Jackman's Blue'.
Jackman's Blue rue.
Height: 1½–2 ft. This cultivar forms a compact sphere and doesn't flower. Rue foliage is strong-scented and has historic uses, but handling the plant causes a skin rash in some people. Zone 5.

Salvia elegans. Pineapple sage.
Height: 4–5 ft. Grows fast and makes a shrub-sized plant in a single season. Leaves have a strong pineapple fragrance and flavor. Blooms from late summer until frost. Zone 9.

Salvia officinalis. Garden sage.
Height: 2 ft. Fragrant leaves are used for seasoning or tea. Spikes of blue flowers are showy in early summer. Variegated forms are hardy only to Zone 8 or 7. Common gray-green variety is hardy to Zone 5. Needs well-drained soil and full sun.

Salvia sclarea. Clary sage.
Height: 3–4 ft. A biennial that makes a broad rosette of large, crinkly-textured, gray-green leaves the first year and flowers in the second year. Foliage has a rich aroma. Zone 4.

Satureja montana. Winter savory.
Height: to 1 ft. Small, glossy, evergreen leaves have a strong flavor and are used for seasoning. Has white, lavender, or pink flowers in late summer. Needs well-drained soil and sun. Zone 6.

Tagetes lucida.
Mexican mint marigold.
Height: to 3 ft. A good substitute for French tarragon in hot climates, with a rich anise fragrance and flavor. Grows well as an annual in the North but usually doesn't flower there. Zone 8 or 7.

Tanacetum vulgare. Tansy.
Height: to 3 ft. Finely dissected leaves have a pungent fragrance and are used to repel insects. Plant it in a remote corner or put a barrier around the roots, because it spreads fast. Zone 4.

Teucrium chamaedrys. Germander.
Height: 1 ft. Flowers are showy and attract bees in midsummer. Let it sprawl, or shear it into a neat mound. Pungent foliage is shiny and semievergreen. Needs good drainage. Zone 5.

Thymus × citriodorus 'Aureus'.
Golden lemon thyme.
Height: 6 in. Has a distinct lemony aroma. Glossy dark green leaves are edged with yellow. Cut off any shoots that revert to solid green. Forms a low mat that doesn't spread fast. Zone 4.

Thymus herba-barona. Caraway thyme.
Height: 6 in. Has a distinct caraway aroma. Makes a good ground cover for sunny, well-drained sites. Can take light foot traffic and mowing. Flowers in midsummer. Zone 4.

Thymus pulegioides. Mother-of-thyme.
Height: to 12 in. A variable plant, often raised from seed and sold under several names, including *T. serpyllum*. Makes flat or bushy mats of green or gray-green foliage, sometimes quite fragrant. Very showy when it blooms in summer. Zone 4.

Satureja montana

Tanacetum vulgare

Teucrium chamaedrys

Tagetes lucida

Thymus × citriodorus 'Aureus'

Thymus herba-barona

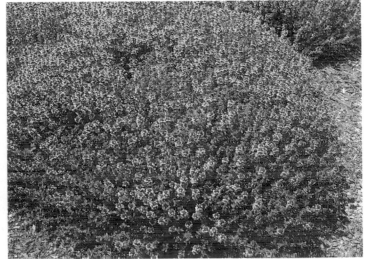

Thymus pulegioides

Annuals

Ageratum houstonianum

Alcea rosea

Amaranthus tricolor

Antirrhinum majus, at left and above

Ageratum houstonianum. Flossflower.
Height: 6–30 in. Fuzzy rounded leaves and
dense heads of tiny lavender-blue, pink, or
white flowers. Blooms all summer. Dwarf
forms are great for edging or containers. Full
or part sun.

Alcea rosea. Hollyhock.
Height: 3–9 ft. Dramatic tall stalks with
rough gray-green leaves and double or single
flowers in white, yellow, apricot, red, rose,
pink, or purple. Grows best as a biennial.
Full sun.

Arctotis hybrids

Baileya multiradiata

Begonia Tuberhybrida hybrids

Begonia × *semperflorens-cultorum*

Amaranthus tricolor.
Joseph's-coat.
Height: 1–4 ft. A tough plant with large thin leaves of brilliant red, orange, and yellow scattered along the stems and clustered on top. Flowers are tiny. Grows best in hot weather.

Antirrhinum majus.
Snapdragon.
Height: 6–36 in. Bears spikes of velvety, colorful, two-lipped flowers, sometimes fragrant. Tall forms are best for borders and cutting, dwarf varieties for edging and containers. Full sun.

Arctotis hybrids.
African daisies.
Height: 12–18 in. Plants form low clumps of gray-green foliage with dark-eyed, long-stemmed daisies of white, pink, coral, red, yellow, or orange. Good edging along a bed or patio. Full sun.

Baileya multiradiata.
Desert marigold.
Height: 12–18 in. Bright yellow daisylike flowers bloom on leafless stems for several months. Woolly white foliage. Good for desert gardens, borders, or mass plantings. Takes dry heat.

Begonia × semperflorens-cultorum.
Wax begonia.
Height: 6–12 in. Makes compact bushy mounds of shiny foliage and red, pink, or white blossoms. Blooms for months. Excellent for edging, beds, or containers. Needs shade from hot afternoon sun.

Begonia Tuberhybrida hybrids.
Tuberous begonias.
Height: to 2 ft. Huge single or double flowers with plain or frilled petals in many colors. Good in beds, window boxes, or hanging planters. Delicate; need protection from hot sun and dry winds.

Bellis perennis

Brassica oleracea

Caladium × *hortulanum*

Calendula officinalis

Catharanthus roseus

Celosia argentea
var. *plumosa*

Bellis perennis. English daisy.
Height: 6 in. Wide blossoms with a daisylike yellow center and fine rays of pink, rose, red, or white on short stalks. Low, dark green leaf rosettes. Good for edging. Full or part sun.

Brassica oleracea. Flowering kale.
Height: 12 in. Crinkly rosettes of bright pink, lavender, purple, white, and/or green leaves. Grows and looks best in fall; tolerates considerable frost. Easy in containers or beds. Full sun.

Caladium × **hortulanum.**
Height: 1–3 ft. Large, papery, arrowhead-shaped leaves in solid, mottled, or spotted patterns of crimson, rose, pink, pale green, and white. Plant tubers in spring; dig in fall. Best in shade.

Calendula officinalis.
Height: to 2 ft. Cheerful daisylike blossoms of cream, yellow, gold, or orange on long stalks with slightly hairy leaves. Compact strains are best for bedding. Does best in cool weather.

Catharanthus roseus.
Madagascar periwinkle.
Height: 1–2 ft. A bushy mound of glossy green foliage with 5-petaled flowers in white, pink, or rose. Good for mass plantings and in containers. Thrives in hot weather and blooms all summer.

Celosia argentea var. **plumosa.**
Cockscomb.
Height: to 2 ft. Tiny red, orange, gold, salmon, or pink flowers in dense fluffy

plumes. Dwarf forms are available. Good as cut flowers, fresh or dried. Prefers hot weather.

Centaurea cyanus.
Bachelor's-button.
Height: to 30 in. Inch-wide blossoms in shades of bright blue, pink, rose, or white. Slender gray leaves on branched stems. Good cut flower, fresh or dried. Fast-growing. Full sun.

Cleome hassleriana.
Spider flower.
Height: 4–5 ft. A fast-growing airy mass of tough stems and rounded clusters of pink or white flowers that bloom nonstop from midsummer to frost. Give it plenty of space to spread. Full sun.

Centaurea cyanus

Cleome hassleriana

Coleus blumei

Consolida ambigua

Coleus blumei. Coleus.
Height: 1–2 ft. Grown mostly for the showy fringed or ruffled leaves in shades of red, pink, purple, cream, and green. Spikes of blue flowers. Excellent for partly shaded beds or containers.

Consolida ambigua. Larkspur.
Height: 1–4 ft. Upright stalks of showy blue, lilac, pink, or white flowers. Good in mass plantings or as cut flowers, fresh or dried. Prefers cool weather. Best sown direct. Full sun.

Coreopsis tinctoria. Dyer's corcopsis.
Height: 1–3 ft. Abundant yellow, maroon, and/or bicolor daisylike blossoms on upright branching stalks. Scant foliage. A prairie wildflower, good for meadow gardens.

Coreopsis tinctoria

Cosmos bipinnatus

Cosmos sulphureus

Dahlia 'Double Pompon'

Dahlia 'Rigoletto'

Cosmos bipinnatus. Cosmos.
Height: to 6 ft. Abundant daisylike blossoms with yellow disks and rays of pink, rose, lavender, purple, or white on branching stems. Open, airy habit. Easy to grow. Full sun.

Cosmos sulphureus.
Yellow cosmos.
Height: to 3 ft. A small, bushy, branching plant with rough stems and bright yellow, orange, or reddish orange daisylike flowers. Blooms for months if deadheaded. Full sun.

***Dahlia* 'Double Pompon'.** Dahlia.
Height: to 6 ft. Bright glossy blossoms are round and full. Blooms from midsummer to frost. Dig tubers in fall to save from year to year. Needs rich soil and regular watering.

***Dahlia* 'Rigoletto'.**
Height: 1–1½ ft. This strain is raised from seed and sold as bedding plants. Blooms from midsummer to fall, with semidouble blossoms in several colors. Bushy plants are killed by frost. Needs fertile soil and full sun.

Dianthus barbatus. Sweet William.
Height: 1–2 ft. Usually grows as a biennial. Stiff leafy stalks are topped with flat clusters of round flowers. Colors are white, rose, pink, dark red, or bicolored. Some kinds have a spicy fragrance. A very long-lasting cut flower. Zone 3.

***Dianthus chinensis* hybrids.**
China pinks.
Height: to 18 in. Easy from seed and quick to bloom. Flat clusters of scentless single or double flowers are red, pink, white, or bicolored. Stiff upright stems branch repeatedly.

Digitalis purpurea. Common foxglove.
Height: 4–5 ft. Usually grows as a biennial. Makes a basal rosette of large furry leaves. Bell-shaped flowers on tall stalks are purple, lavender, rose, pink, apricot, or white. All parts are poisonous. Zone 4.

Dolichos lablab. Hyacinth bean.
Height: 20 ft. A fast-growing vine that thrives in hot weather. Foliage is dense and dark. Pealike flowers are white or purple. Needs a long summer to produce magenta-purple pods.

Eschscholzia californica.
California poppy.
Height: 9–24 in. Cuplike, vivid orange flowers bloom from March to May or longer. Delicate, pale gray-green foliage. Easy to grow in well-drained soil and full sun. Often self-seeds.

Euphorbia marginata.
Snow-on-the-mountain.
Height: 18–24 in. Grown for its foliage; flowers are inconspicuous. White-edged leaves on erect stems are showy from midsummer until frost. Milky sap may irritate skin.

Dianthus barbatus

Dianthus chinensis hybrids

Digitalis purpurea

Dolichos lablab

Euphorbia marginata

Eschscholzia californica

Felicia amelloides

Fuchsia hybrids

Helianthus annuus

Gaillardia pulchella

Gladiolus callianthus

Gladiolus cultivars

Felicia amelloides. Blue marguerite. Height: 12–18 in. Bright blue daisylike blossoms with yellow centers on long stalks. Thick dark green leaves on sprawling branches. Needs regular trimming. Perennial in Zone 9.

Fuchsia hybrids.
Height: 3 ft. or more. Popular for hanging baskets or containers and sometimes used for bedding. Showy dangling flowers in many shades of pink, purple, red, or white bloom all summer and attract hummingbirds. Need moist, fertile soil and part shade.

Gaillardia pulchella. Indian blanket. Height: 1–2 ft. Daisylike blossoms of brownish or purplish red and yellow open from summer to fall. Basal foliage is hairy and gray-green. A fast-growing wildflower. Needs full sun.

Gladiolus callianthus. Peacock orchid. Height: 2–3 ft. Delicate flowers have a sweet fragrance and are good for cutting. Leaves are tall and slender. Hardy to Zone 7; farther north, dig corms in fall and store indoors.

Gladiolus cultivars. Hybrid gladioli. Height: 3–6 ft. Excellent cut flowers, with tall spikes of showy flowers with flaring, ruffled, or frilled petals. Long sword-shaped leaves. Need fertile soil, moisture, and full sun. Dig corms in fall to store indoors.

Gloriosa superba

Gomphrena globosa

Gloriosa superba. Gloriosa lily.
Height: 6 ft. A tender vine that climbs by tendrils at the leaf tips. Greenish yellow buds open into showy crimson flowers that attract hummingbirds. Dig tubers each fall. Full or part sun.

Gomphrena globosa. Globe amaranth.
Height: 18–24 in. Clusters of small round flower heads in bright purple, pink, red, orange, or white. Good for dried arrangements. Thrives in hot weather and doesn't mind poor, dry soil.

Helianthus annuus.
Common sunflower.
Height: 4–10 ft. Fast, vigorous, and fun. New cultivars have small multicolored blossoms on bushy plants. Use several to make a temporary screen or hedge. Birds love the seeds. Full sun.

Helichrysum bracteatum. Strawflower.
Height: to 30 in. An excellent flower for dried arrangements, available in many bright colors. Plants look coarse, so grow them in a cutting garden or vegetable garden. Full sun.

Iberis umbellata. Globe candytuft.
Height: 6–12 in. Grows fast and blooms abundantly, then goes to seed. Flowers and seedpods are good for small arrangements. Direct-sow in fall or early spring. Full or part sun.

Helichrysum bracteatum

Iberis umbellata

Impatiens wallerana

Ipomoea purpurea

Ipomopsis rubra

Lathyrus odoratus

Lavatera trimestris

Limonium sinuatum

Lobelia erinus

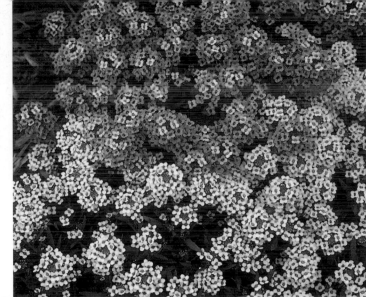

Lobularia maritima

Lunaria annua

Lupinus texensis

Impatiens wallerana. Impatiens.
Height: to 2 ft. One of the best annuals for shade. Blooms all summer and makes a bushy mound without needing to be pruned or pinched. Excellent under trees or in containers. Tender to frost.

Ipomoea purpurea. Morning glory.
Height: to 15 ft. Climbs quickly to cover a trellis or fence with a screen of large heart-shaped leaves. New flowers open daily. Doesn't need rich soil and tolerates some dryness. Full sun.

Ipomopsis rubra. Standing cypress.
Height: 3 ft. or more. Easy to grow. Bright flowers attract hummingbirds all summer. Useful as a filler in mixed plantings. Self-sows readily. Tolerates heat and dry soil. Full or part sun.

Lathyrus odoratus. Sweet pea.
Height: to 6 ft. Plant seeds in fall or very early spring. Flowers best in cool weather and dies back in the heat of summer. Excellent for cutting, but not all kinds are fragrant.

Lavatera trimestris.
Tree mallow.
Height: 2–4 ft. Makes a bushy mound with no pinching or pruning and flowers from midsummer until frost. Flowers are 3–4 in. wide. Gather whole stalks to use as cut flowers. Full sun.

Limonium sinuatum. Annual statice.
Height: 18 in. Bright-colored papery flowers are popular everlastings; cut stalks before the flowers open completely and hang upside down in a dark place to dry. Easy to grow. Full sun.

Lobelia erinus. Edging lobelia.
Height: 4–8 in. Trailing types are good for containers; upright forms are useful for edging beds. Blooms all summer. Tiny flowers are usually blue, sometimes white or reddish. Sun or part shade.

Lobularia maritima. Sweet alyssum.
Height: to 6 in. Popular everywhere for easy care and nonstop bloom. Forms a low mat, good for edging beds. Shear in midsummer to promote fresh new growth. Some kinds are very fragrant.

Lunaria annua. Honesty.
Height: 30–36 in. A biennial that blooms in spring, with small purple or white flowers. Gather the flat round pods when they turn tan to use for dried arrangements. Often self-sows. Zone 4.

Lupinus texensis. Texas bluebonnet.
Height: 6–16 in. Usually grown in mass as a wildflower for a carpet of blue flowers in mid- to late spring. Let plants mature if you want them to self-seed. Tolerates poor, dry soil. Full sun.

Matthiola incana

Mimulus × hybridus

Mirabilis jalapa

Myosotis sylvatica

Nicotiana alata

Nicotiana sylvestris

Oenothera biennis

Matthiola incana. Stock.
Height: 1–2¹/₂ ft. Classic cut flowers with a pervading, unforgettable, spicy fragrance. Needs a long, cool spring to do well. Plant in fall or very early spring in rich, moist soil.

Mimulus × hybridus. Monkey flower.
Height: 6–12 in. Unusual 2-lipped flowers come in bright shades of yellow, rose, or red. Needs moist, fertile soil. Thrives in cool weather and can't take heat. Will bloom in the shade.

Mirabilis jalapa. Four-o'clock.
Height: to 3 ft. Easy to grow in any well-drained soil. Blooms throughout the hottest weather. Flowers open in late afternoon and close by dawn. Overwinters in mild climates.

Myosotis sylvatica. Forget-me-not.
Height: 9–12 in. Self-seeds and forms wide patches in rich, moist soil. Good for interplanting with spring bulbs. New strains have larger flowers in brighter shades of blue, pale pink, or white.

Onopordum acanthium

Papaver nudicaule 'Champagne Bubbles'

Papaver rhoeas

Nicotiana alata. Flowering tobacco.
Height: 1–3 ft. Blooms all summer. New strains stay open during the day. Some kinds are sweetly fragrant. Leaves are covered with sticky hairs. Does well in beds or containers.

Nicotiana sylvestris. Woodland tobacco.
Height: 4–6 ft. A dramatic plant with loose drooping clusters of white flowers that are intensely fragrant at night. They're pollinated by hawkmoths that resemble tiny hummingbirds.

Oenothera biennis. Evening primrose.
Height: to 6 ft. Fragrant, clear yellow flowers open at dusk, so fast you can see them move. Long stalks of seedpods are good for dried arrangements. Good for natural landscapes.

Onopordum acanthium. Scotch thistle.
Height: to 8 ft. Biennial. Makes a broad rosette of woolly white leaves with spiny-tipped lobes the first year. Shoots up fast and blooms in early summer the second year. Don't let it self-sow.

Papaver nudicaule 'Champagne Bubbles'. Iceland poppy.
Height: 1–2 ft. Mildly fragrant, cup-shaped flowers have 4 or 8 crinkled silky petals. Prefers cool weather. Usually raised from seed in mixed colors.

Papaver rhoeas. Shirley poppy.
Height: 1–3 ft. Has single or double flowers in shades of white, pink, or red. Blooms in summer. Direct-sow the tiny seeds in fall or early spring. Often reseeds.

Pelargonium × domesticum

Petunia × hybrida

Pelargonium × hortorum

Pelargonium peltatum

Portulaca grandiflora

Phlox drummondii

Rudbeckia hirta

Ricinus communis

Salvia splendens

Salvia viridis

Senecio cineraria

Pelargonium × domesticum.
Martha Washington geranium.
Height: to 3 ft. Showy flowers resemble
azaleas, in shades of red, pinkish purple, or
white. Grows well in containers. Root
cuttings to overwinter indoors, or buy new
plants each year.

Pelargonium × hortorum.
Common geranium.
Height: 1–3 ft. Excellent for bedding or
containers. New strains are very compact and
flower nonstop. Available in red, pink,
salmon, magenta, or white. Some kinds have
variegated leaves.

Pelargonium peltatum. Ivy geranium.
Height: 1 ft. The best geranium for hanging
baskets, raised planters, and window boxes.
Also a good ground cover for Zone 9. Stems
trail like vines. Leaves are thick and glossy.

Petunia × hybrida.
Common garden petunia.
Height: 1–3 ft. Round flowers can be single
or double, in shades of red, rose, pink,
purple, violet-blue, pale yellow, white, or
striped combinations. Some kinds have a
very sweet fragrance.

Phlox drummondii.
Height: 6–18 in. A Texas wildflower that
tolerates poor, dry soil and hot weather. New
cultivars bloom all summer if deadheaded, in
many shades of red, pink, purple, or white.
Good for edging beds or walks.

Portulaca grandiflora. Moss rose.
Height: under 1 ft. Succulent leaves and
stems help it survive on hot, dry sites.
Blooms from early summer until frost. Good
for edging paved walks or driveways or in
containers. Self-seeds.

Ricinus communis. Castor bean.
Height: 8 ft. or more. Grows fast from seed
to make a shrub-sized plant in one season.
Large leaves can be green, bronze, or red.
Warn children that the seeds, though
attractive, are poisonous.

Rudbeckia hirta.
Gloriosa daisy.
Height: 1–3 ft. These were developed from
wild black-eyed Susans. The big colorful
daisies have long stalks and are excellent
for cutting. Easy and self-seeds readily.

Salvia splendens. Salvia.
Height: 1–3 ft. Blooms all summer, even
if you never deadhead it. There are dwarf,
medium, and tall strains, with red, pink,
salmon, lavender, purple, or white flowers.
Easy to grow.

Salvia viridis. Tricolor sage.
Height: 18 in. Slender flower spikes are
topped with leaflike bracts in bright blue-
purple, rose, and white. Will self-sow in a
mixed bed and surprise you by sticking up
through other plants.

Senecio cineraria. Dusty-miller.
Height: to 12 in. Valued for its beautiful
silvery gray or white leaves, which combine
well with any color of flowers. Excellent for
bedding or edging. Usually overwinters in
mild zones.

Tagetes erecta

Tagetes patula

Tagetes tenuifolia 'Lemon Gem'

Tropaeolum majus

Viola × wittrockiana

Viola tricolor

Tithonia rotundifolia

Tagetes erecta. African marigold.
Height: to 3 ft. Big bushy plants have glossy green foliage and full flower heads in shades of yellow, orange, or creamy white. Easy to grow. Blooms nonstop from early summer to frost.

Tagetes patula.
French marigold.
Height: 6–18 in. The many dwarf forms are especially good for edging, bedding, or pots. Flowers can be yellow, orange, red, mahogany, or bicolor. Blooms from early summer to frost.

Tagetes tenuifolia 'Lemon Gem'.
Lemon gem marigold.
Height: to 8 in. Delicate lacy foliage has a mild, lemony fragrance. Single blossoms have the charm of wildflowers. Uncommon at garden centers but easy to grow from seed.

Tithonia rotundifolia. Mexican sunflower.
Height: 6 ft. Use this for a quick specimen or a temporary hedge or screen. Quickly makes a big bushy plant. Flowers are about 3 in. wide. Thrives in hot weather and blooms all summer.

Tropaeolum majus. Nasturtium.
Height: 1 ft. Easy, adaptable, and colorful. Climbs or sprawls 2 ft. or more. Spicy-scented flowers come in bright shades of yellow, orange, red, mahogany, cream, or bicolor. Self-sows.

Verbena × hybrida.
Garden verbena.
Height: 6–12 in. Thrives in hot, sunny weather and blooms nonstop all summer. Sprawling stems make a tangled mat. Can be used as an annual ground cover for full sun or part shade.

Verbena × hybrida

Zantedeschia albomaculata

Zinnia angustifolia

Zinnia elegans cultivars

Viola tricolor. Johnny-jump-up.
Height: to 12 in. Charming, cheerful, and easy to grow. Blooms in spring and early summer, continuing until the weather gets hot. Plants often overwinter and self-sow readily.

Viola × wittrockiana. Pansy.
Height: to 12 in. Excellent bedding plants that bloom from fall to spring where winters are mild and from spring to fall where summers are cool. Facelike flowers come in a wide range of colors and have a pleasant fragrance.

Zantedeschia albomaculata.
Calla lily.
Height: 2 ft. Looks exotic and tropical, but it's as easy to grow as a gladiolus. Plant tubers in rich, moist soil in spring; dig when the tops turn yellow in fall and store in a warm, dry place for the winter. Flowers are excellent for cutting.

Zinnia angustifolia.
Height: 12 in. An uncommon zinnia that looks more like a wildflower than a bedding plant. Small flowers open throughout the hottest weather. Available with white or orange flowers.

Zinnia elegans cultivars.
Common zinnias.
Height: 1–3 ft. Easy to grow and excellent for bedding or bouquets. Most strains have double flowers, ranging from 1 to 6 in. wide, available in all colors but blue. Plants range from compact dwarfs to tall cut-flower types.

Encyclopedia of Plants

About the encyclopedia

The entries in this section are organized alphabetically by genus. A short description of the genus is followed by individual entries for featured species and cultivars. Many entries include short references to related or similar plants. Sometimes recommended species or cultivars are highlighted in a box. Page numbers following the entries are keyed to photos in the Gallery section.

Names: Plant taxonomists are continually reclassifying plants or changing their names, so many of the plants in this book are known by two or more names. We have alphabetized plants under their most widely accepted and used names and have listed synonyms where appropriate. Common names are given when possible, but some plants don't have common names.

Cold-hardiness: The USDA Hardiness Zone rating indicates a plant's ability to tolerate the cold temperatures of an average winter. See the map on pages 576–577 to identify which zone you live in. Zone ratings are averages, based on the performance of many plants in gardens across the country. The survival of any particular plant in your garden depends on many factors in addition to temperature, and the plant may prove more or less hardy than predicted.

In many parts of the country, plants are stressed more by summer heat than by winter cold, but there is no zone map for average summer high temperatures. The individual entries note plants with either poor or outstanding ability to tolerate heat, drought, pollution, and other stresses.

Height and spread: The figures given are for mature (but not record-setting) specimens that are well established in average conditions. Individual plants vary and may grow larger or smaller, depending on their genetic potential, where they are sited, and how you care for them. Perennials, grasses, and ferns often reach their mature size in just a few years; shrubs and vines may take a decade or more; most garden trees take at least 25 years to approach their mature height, and longer to reach their full mature spread.

How to grow: Full sun means a plant requires or tolerates at least 6 hours of full midday sun during the growing season. Shade means a plant does not need or tolerate full direct sun. The entries note any special requirements.

Once established, many plants grow well in average soil with regular watering; exceptions are noted. Young plants often require extra care—more frequent watering and shelter from extreme heat, cold, and wind—for the first year or two after planting.

These entries describe any special requirements for seasonal and long-term maintenance, such as pruning, mulching, and dividing. Pests and diseases are noted if they are commonly encountered and potentially severe.

Abelia

A-beel´ee-a.

Caprifoliaceae. Honeysuckle family.

Evergreen or deciduous shrubs with fine-textured foliage and many small flowers from summer to fall. About 30 spp., native to Asia and Mexico.

× *grandiflora* (p. 166)

Glossy abelia.

Semievergreen shrub. Zone 6.

H: 6–10 ft. S: 4–6 ft.

A tough, adaptable shrub for most landscape situations. It forms an oval mound of graceful arching branches covered with slender shiny leaves. Leaves turn purplish and remain through winter in mild climates but are deciduous where winters are cold. Small, bell-shaped, white or pale pink flowers are borne continuously from early summer through early fall. Excellent as a hedge or screen. 'Prostrata' and 'Sherwood' are dwarf forms, suitable for foundation planting or as ground covers. *A.* 'Edward Goucher' stays under 5 ft. tall and has showier, rosy lavender flowers.

How to grow: Full or part sun. Ordinary soil and watering. Can be pruned anytime and will continue to bloom. Renew old plants by cutting some stems to the ground.

Abies

Ay´bees. Fir.

Pinaceae. Pine family.

Tall evergreen conifers, shaped like and often used as Christmas trees, with short flat needles and erect cones. Several dwarf forms have been collected and named. About 40 spp., most native to moist or mountainous habitats in the north temperate zone. Firs generally don't do well in urban areas.

concolor (p. 188)

White fir, Colorado white fir.

Conifer. Zone 4.

H: 50–150 ft. S: 30–40 ft.

A massive, stately tree with striking blue needles, best used as a specimen on large properties. Forms a broad cone with spreading branches. The needles are about 2 in. long and curve upward from the twigs. 'Candicans' and 'Violacea' have particularly handsome needles. 'Compacta' is a dwarf that stays under 7 ft. tall.

How to grow: Full or part sun. Tolerates infertile soil and dryness better than other firs do but appreciates a layer of mulch. Fails in heavy or alkaline soil. Plant in fall, allowing plenty of space for the tree to spread up and out. Consider white fir as a substitute for Colorado blue spruce; it has a softer appearance and fewer insect problems.

koreana (p. 188)

Korean fir.

Conifer. Zone 5.

H: 30–45 ft. S: 15–20 ft.

A slow-growing conifer with ideal Christmas-tree shape. The needles are short and stiff, dark green on top and silver below. Attractive purple cones, about 3 in. long, are produced even on young trees. Use this as the centerpiece for a planting of dwarf conifers such as weeping blue spruce or golden false cypress. 'Prostrate Beauty' stays low and spreads horizontally along the front of a bed or over a stone wall.

How to grow: Full sun. Ordinary soil and watering. Remove extra leaders; no other pruning or maintenance required. Trouble-free in cool climates but can't tolerate extreme heat, drought, or air pollution.

Acacia

A-kay´sha.

Leguminosae. Pea family.

Evergreen trees or shrubs, often bearing exceptional displays of yellow flowers. Many have feathery compound leaves; some are thorny. About 1,200 spp., most native to hot, dry regions, particularly Australia.

baileyana (p. 156)

Bailey acacia, often called mimosa.

Evergreen tree. Zone 9.

H: 30 ft. S: 30 ft.

An attractive tree with feathery gray-green or blue-green foliage and an abundance of fragrant, brilliant yellow blossoms in midwinter. Extremely fast growing but not long lived. Endures drought, heat, and wind. Use for minimum-maintenance landscaping with native or other Mediterranean-climate plants.

How to grow: Full or part sun. Tolerates poor and dry soil. For sturdiest growth, set out small plants and do not stake. Train as a single-trunked or multitrunked tree. Prune after bloom to reduce pod set. Often self-sows, and seedlings bloom in 3–4 years.

other acacias

A. dealbata and *A. decurrens* are larger (to 50 ft.) and bloom later than *A. baileyana*. *A. melanoxylon*, to 40 ft., is an incredibly tough tree with dark green leaves and creamy blossoms and is tolerant of salt, wind, and poor soil. *A. redolens*, only 2 ft. tall but up to 15 ft. wide, is a useful ground cover for large rough areas. Check local nurseries to find other species that do well in desert areas of the Southwest.

Acanthopanax

A-kan-tho-pan´ax.

Araliaceae. Aralia family.

Deciduous shrubs or trees, usually prickly, with palmately compound leaves and round clusters of dark berries. A few spp., native to Asia.

sieboldianus 'Variegatus' (p. 130)
(now *Eleutherococcus sieboldianus* 'Variegatus')
Deciduous shrub. Zone 4.
H: 8 ft. S: 8 ft.

The creamy white borders on this shrub's fan-shaped leaves will brighten up a shady spot and hold your attention all summer long. Excellent as a single specimen or focal point, it can also be used as a hedge; its dense habit and small thorns form an effective barrier and can help keep the neighbors' pets out of your garden.

How to grow: Very tolerant of a wide range of conditions, including sun or shade, poor soil, heat, and drought. One of the best variegated shrubs for dry shade. Pest-free and requires no pruning. Dig and transplant suckers if they appear. For a hedge, plant 5 ft. apart and allow suckers to fill in.

Acanthus

A-kan'thus. Bear's-breeches.
Acanthaceae. Acanthus family.

Perennial herbs or shrubs with large toothed leaves and erect spikes of showy flowers. About 30 spp., most native to dry climates around the Mediterranean.

mollis (p. 220)
Bear's-breeches, artist's acanthus.
Perennial. Zone 8.
H: 3 ft. S: 3 ft.

Forms a clump of handsome glossy leaves, 2–3 ft. long, deeply lobed, and toothed with small soft spines. Admired by artists, these leaves inspired the design of Corinthian columns. Dozens of whitish, lilac, or rose flowers with green or purplish bracts crowd robust spikes, up to 6 ft. tall, from late spring to early summer. Dramatic as an accent in light shade under trees or useful as a pest-free, easy-to-grow ground cover. 'Latifolius' has especially large leaves and is more frost-hardy. 'Oakleaf' has deep green, oak-leaf-shaped leaves. *A. spinosus* grows only 1¹/₂ ft. tall, has leaves with narrow lobes, and produces spiny-toothed bracts. It's more tolerant of cold, heat, and humidity.

How to grow: Part sun or shade. Does best in deep, well-drained soil with constant moisture but tolerates poor soil and dryness. Plant 2 ft. apart; divide clumps in fall (or in winter in mild areas). Spreads by roots. Not aggressive, but it's difficult to eradicate old plants because a new plant sprouts from each piece of root left in the soil. Goes dormant after blooming (in mild areas) or in winter (in colder zones).

Acer ginnala

Acer

Ay'sir. Maple.
Aceraceae. Maple family.

Most are deciduous trees or shrubs with palmately lobed or compound leaves, often turning brilliant colors in fall. Valued as specimen and shade trees, particularly where the soil is rich and moist. More than 110 spp., native to the north temperate zone.

buergerianum (p. 107)
(*A. trifidum*)
Trident maple.
Deciduous tree. Zone 4.
H: 25–30 ft. S: 20 ft.

A tidy, compact, oval-crowned tree for urban landscapes, with glossy 3-lobed leaves that are dark green in summer, coloring from yellow to red (depending on climate) in late fall. On mature trees the flaking bark shows layers of gray, brown, and orange. Useful for street, patio, or courtyard sites; unlike most maples, can be combined with perennials, since its shade and root competition are not prohibitive. Selected varieties and cultivars offer distinctive leaf shapes.

How to grow: Full or part sun. Tolerates poor soil. Once established, is drought-tolerant and trouble-free.

campestre (p. 107)
Hedge maple, field maple.
Deciduous tree. Zone 4.
H: 40 ft. S: 30–35 ft.

A very neat, well-shaped, medium-size shade tree. With its full dense crown nearly sweeping the ground, it is the very picture of arbor royalty and makes an ideal specimen for the lawn. The 5-lobed leaves are rather small, dark green, and unblemished all summer, long-lasting and yellow in fall. Often used for hedging in Britain and Europe because it tolerates (but doesn't require) heavy pruning. The crown is too dense and the roots too greedy for this tree to be used in mixed plantings. There are white-variegated, red-leaved, pendulous, fastigiate, and compact varieties and cultivars.

How to grow: Full sun. Easily transplanted in spring or fall. Tolerates unamended and alkaline soils. Drought-tolerant and trouble-free.

ginnala (p. 107)
(now *A. tataricum* subsp. *ginnala*)
Amur maple.
Deciduous tree. Zone 3.
H: 20–25 ft. S: 25 ft.

A very tough and superhardy small tree or shrub that forms an irregular dome with many stems arching from the ground. The shiny 3-lobed leaves, 4 in. long, are bright green in summer, scarlet in fall. The creamy flowers are fragrant (unusual for a maple) and form starry 2-in. clusters as the leaves unfurl. The winged fruits turn red in summer. Plant as a specimen in the lawn, or use several for a colorful but undemanding mass planting, screen, or hedge. Dwarf forms are sometimes offered.

How to grow: Full or part sun. Tolerates poor soil and dryness. Plant singly or 15–25 ft. apart. Remove dying stems from older plants to encourage new growth. Verticillium wilt and other diseases are occasional problems.

japonicum (pp. 108, 109)
Full-moon maple.
Deciduous tree. Zone 5.
H: 25 ft. S: 25 ft.

A small spreading tree with many trunks and a rounded crown. Its rounded leaves are edged with 7–11 triangular points, soft green in summer and bright red in fall. More cold-hardy than *A. palmatum*. There are several cultivars with distinct leaf shapes and colors. 'Aconitifolium' has deeply divided, lacy or feathery leaves that make a vivid display of crimson to violet in fall.

How to grow: Dappled sun or part shade is best; can't take intense sun or dry wind. Ordinary soil okay, but cover the root zone with mulch, and water during dry spells.

palmatum (pp. 108, 109)
Japanese maple.
Deciduous tree. Zone 6 or 5.
H: 8–25 ft. S: often wider than tall.

These mounding shrubs or small trees are popular nationwide as specimens for small-scale plantings. Most have overlapping tiers of arching branches that form a wide, rounded crown. The foliage is outstanding in summer and fall, and the bark and branching are attractive in winter. Hundreds of cultivars vary in leaf shape and color, overall habit and size, and hardiness. 'Bloodgood' has deeply lobed leaves that are dark reddish purple all season, produces red fruits in fall, and slowly grows up to 20 ft. tall and wide. 'Oshi Beni' has a spreading habit, and the leaves are brightly colored in both spring and fall. 'Sango Kaku' has bright coral-red bark on the younger twigs and brilliant fall color. The Dissectum group ('Dissectum' or var. *dissectum*) includes many forms with very deeply cut leaves in shades of green, red, bronze, or purple as well as variegated. Don't disdain unnamed seedlings; they're usually faster, easier to grow, and tougher than the cultivars.

How to grow: Sun/shade requirements vary with foliage color and type. Green-leaved types can take full sun. Red- and purple-leaved forms need part sun to develop their color but tend to "bronze" in full sun. Variegated or extra-lacy types need afternoon shade to prevent leaf scorch. All kinds prefer moist, fertile soil with a layer of mulch over the root zone.

rubrum (p. 109)
Red maple, swamp maple.
Deciduous tree. Zone 4 or 3.
H: 40–80 ft. S: 30–40 ft.

A fast-growing shade tree that provides showy color in two seasons: the clustered red flowers are among the first to open in early spring, and the foliage glows bright red, orange, or pink in fall. Leaves are about 3 in. wide, with 3 lobes. Color varies among seedlings, but the cultivars are reliable. 'October Glory' has phenomenal red color in late fall; 'Red Sunset' turns orange to red earlier. Superb as a specimen in the lawn. A row of these as street trees would guarantee house sales in fall.

How to grow: Full sun. Native to wet sites throughout the eastern United States but adaptable to ordinary soil and watering. Prone to fungal leafspot in late summer. The shallow roots limit the potential for underplanting.

saccharum (p. 108)
Sugar maple.
Deciduous tree. Zone 3.
H: 70–90 ft. S: 50–60 ft.

The stunning fall color of this maple has come to symbolize the grace and beauty of New England. A beautiful shade tree for large sites. Grows upright with a rounded crown, 5-lobed leaves up to 5 in. wide, and greenish yellow flowers in spring. The gray bark on old trees forms deep ridges and furrows. Selected cultivars have distinctive forms, increased vigor, and stress tolerance. *A. barbatum*, the southern sugar maple, is similar but smaller (to 25 ft.) and better adapted to hot summers.

How to grow: Full or part sun. Best in fertile, well-drained, moist soil; harmed by road salt, compacted soil, and acid rain. Stressed by heat and drought and attacked by several insects and diseases.

other maples

A. griseum, the paperbark maple, is grown for its outstanding bark: thin papery strips peel off sideways to reveal a glossy, reddish brown inner layer. Plant it near a path or window where you'll enjoy looking at it all year long. The compound leaves have 3 toothed leaflets and turn dull or bright red in late fall. It's a small tree, slowly growing to 30 ft.

A. platanoides, the Norway maple, is planted everywhere and has naturalized in the eastern United States. It grows fast, provides quick shade, and tolerates air pollution and neglect. The clusters of bright yellow-green flowers catch your eye in spring, and the leaves turn a pretty yellow quite late in fall. There are dozens of cultivars with unique leaf shapes and colors; 'Crimson King', with garnet leaves all summer, is the most popular. Despite its advantages, Norway maple is not highly recommended. It is subject to verticillium wilt and other fungal diseases, has aggressive shallow roots, and casts shade too dense for underplanting.

A. pseudoplatanus, the sycamore maple, is a large (to 60 ft.) shade tree that tolerates difficult conditions such as alkaline soil and salty sea winds. Native to Europe, it prefers cool climates and does especially well in the Pacific Northwest. The dark green leaves have 5 coarsely toothed lobes; the gray bark peels off in large plates. Some cultivars have dark or multicolored foliage.

A. saccharinum, the silver maple, is a big, fast-growing tree with deeply lobed leaves. It transplants easily, tolerates poor soil, and survives through floods and droughts. Although it provides quick shade where little else will grow, it's not recommended. The wood is weak and brittle, and whole trees split apart in heavy storms.

The shallow, aggressive roots wreck sidewalks and sewers, and scores of pests and diseases attack the foliage.

Achillea

A-kil-lee′a. Yarrow.
Compositae. Daisy family.

Perennials with pungent gray or green leaves, often finely divided, and flat clusters of small flowers. About 80 spp., native to the north temperate zone. Hybridization has produced many excellent garden varieties.

'Coronation Gold' (p. 220)
Perennial. Zone 3.
H: 3 ft. S: 3 ft.

This is a sturdy, self-sufficient candidate for a border of warm-colored perennials. Forms a mat of ferny, gray-green leaves, up to 10 in. long, topped in summer with bright yellow flowers in dense flat clusters, 3 in. wide, on long stalks. The flowers last several weeks in the garden; gather them just before they fully open to dry for winter bouquets. *A. filipendulina,* a parent of this hybrid, is taller and has greener foliage. *A. f.* 'Gold Plate' has 6-in.-wide clusters of deep yellow flowers. All look wonderful with rudbeckias, grasses, and daylilies.

How to grow: Full or part sun. Tolerates poor soil and dryness; may flop over in rich or moist soil. Divide in spring or early fall if a clump gets too big or has been infiltrated by grass or weeds. Plant at least 18 in. apart. Trouble-free.

Achillea millefolium

millefolium (p. 220)
Common yarrow.
Perennial. Zone 3.
H: 2–3 ft. S: 2–3 ft. or more.

Old-fashioned common yarrow is a traditional European herb that grows as a wildflower throughout the United States, with flat clusters of small white flowers held above pungent, gray-green, fernlike leaves. A natural for meadow gardens, it also tolerates mowing and light traffic and spreads to make a surprisingly versatile ground cover. Modern cultivars and the new Galaxy hybrids from Germany have a range of flower colors—dark rose, reddish, pale pink, salmon, and creamy white. They make good cut flowers and bloom for a long season, although the colors fade rapidly from bright to dusty shades.

How to grow: Full or part sun. Grows tall and floppy in rich, damp soil; is much sturdier and more compact in lean, dry conditions. No pests attack it, but it may need staking. New cultivars are not invasive. Propagate by division.

'Moonshine' (p. 220)
Perennial. Zone 3.
H: 2 ft. S: 18 in.

Even without flowers, the basal mound of soft gray, finely dissected leaves would deserve a prominent place in the border, but the pure lemon yellow flowers, borne in 2-in. clusters on 2-ft. stalks, harmonize with most other perennials and continue from June to August if deadheaded. Try combining it with veronicas, artemisias, and salvias. *A. taygetea,* a parent of this hybrid, has greener foliage and pale sulphur flowers and can bloom from late May to October.

How to grow: Full sun. Prefers light soil with good drainage. Doesn't need staking. Tolerates dry heat but gets foliar diseases in hot, humid, rainy areas. Propagate by division in spring or fall.

Aconitum

Ak-o-ny′tum. Monkshood.
Ranunculaceae. Buttercup family.

Perennials with distinctive hoodlike or helmet-shaped flowers, usually blue or purple, on tall stalks. Basal leaves are lobed or cleft. Roots are thick and sometimes tuberous. All parts are dangerously poisonous to eat but not to touch. About 100 spp., native to the north temperate zone.

Aconitum napellus

napellus (p. 220)
Monkshood.
Perennial. Zone 2.
H: 3–5 ft. S: 2 ft.

Forms a low mound of deeply cut, glossy green leaves topped with spikes of rich blue or purple flowers for 3–4 weeks in late summer and fall. Makes a tall accent in a shaded border with late-flowering *Astilbe chinensis* or ferns and hostas. 'Album' has white flowers on 3–4-ft. stalks. Other species and hybrids vary in height and flower color.

How to grow: Part sun. Prefers cool, moist soil with added leaf mold or compost. Plant crowns just below the surface, 1 ft. apart. Do not divide or move. Doesn't need staking, but deadhead to renew bloom.

Acorus

Ak′o-rus. Sweet flag.
Araceae. Arum family.

Rhizomatous perennials with upright fans of slender leaves and tiny flowers in a thumblike cluster. Only 2 spp., native to wetlands in Eurasia and North America.

Acorus gramineus

gramineus '**Variegatus**' (see below for photo)
Variegated Japanese sweet flag.
Grasslike perennial. Zone 6.
H: 12 in. S: 12 in.

Forms a low tuft of slender white-striped leaves that brightens any moist, shady spot. Thrives beside a stream or pond or in a shallow tray of water. Spreads rather slowly. 'Ogon' (p. 208) is similar, with yellow instead of white stripes. *A. calamus* 'Variegatus' is a larger plant, up to 3 ft. tall; its leaves have similar variegation and a spicy fragrance.

How to grow: Part sun or shade. Needs good or fertile soil and constant moisture. No maintenance required. North of Zone 6, grow in a container and bring it indoors to enjoy over winter.

Actinidia
Ak-ti-nid´ee-a.
Dilleniaceae. Dillenia family.

Deciduous woody vines with vigorous growth and handsome foliage. Some, such as the kiwi vine, have edible fruits. About 30 spp., native to Asia.

deliciosa (p. 198)
(*A. chinensis*)
Kiwi, Chinese gooseberry.
Woody vine. Zone 8.
H: 30 ft. or more.

A vigorous, sprawling, twining vine that quickly covers a trellis, fence, arbor, or patio with a luxuriant mass of deciduous foliage. Leaves are rounded, up to 8 in. wide; new shoots are covered with red fuzz. Creamy flowers are produced on old growth in spring. The delicious egg-sized fruits have green flesh under a fuzzy brown skin. For fruit set, you need both male and female plants. 'Hayward' ('Chico') is the best-known cultivar; 'Vincent' requires the least winter chill; 'Blake', though rare, is self-fertile. *A. arguta*, the hardy kiwi, is hardy to Zone 5, with small leaves and flowers and fuzzless grape-sized fruits that are edible, skin and all. 'Issai' is self-fertile.

How to grow: Full or part sun. Ordinary soil and watering. Plant 10–15 ft. apart and provide a sturdy support. Prune to establish 1 or 2 main trunks and 4 principal arms; shorten long canes and remove old wood in winter. Can be damaged by late or early frosts. Pest-free.

kolomikta (p. 198)
Woody vine. Zone 5.
H: 20 ft.

Grow this hardy vine for its showy foliage—the heart-shaped green leaves, 4–6 in. long, are splashed with pink and white. One plant is enough to make a show on a big trellis or climbing into a tree. The males have prettier leaves, but plant a female too for edible yellow fruits.

How to grow: Full or part sun. Ordinary soil and watering. Provide support, and prune to control size and to remove dead or tangled wood. Hardy and tough but doesn't take heat well.

Adiantum
Ad-ee-an´tum. Maidenhair fern.
Polypodiaceae. Fern family.

Ferns with dark, stiff, wiry stems and thin delicate leaflets. About 200 spp., most native to tropical America.

capillus-veneris (p. 216)
Southern maidenhair fern.
Fern. Zone 8.
H: 6–12 in. S: 12 in. or more.

A dainty fern that thrives in warm sheltered areas with high humidity. Lacy, soft green fronds fan out from shiny black stipes. Grows well in the cracks and crevices of stone walls and fences.

How to grow: Needs shade, constant moisture, and moist, fertile, well-limed soil. If your plant isn't thriving, top-dress with crushed eggshells. Spreads slowly by rhizomes and is easily divided—simply cut off a section of the rhizome and replant $1/2$ in. deep. Makes a lovely houseplant in cold climates.

pedatum (p. 216)
American maidenhair fern.
Fern. Zone 3.
H: 1–2 ft. S: 1–2 ft. or more.

Fan-shaped fronds on thin wiry stems give this popular fern a delicate appearance, though it's actually quite hardy and tough. To accentuate its daintiness, combine it with broad-leaved plants such as *Asarum europaeum,* pulmonaria, or hellebores. Thrives in shaded pockets or crevices of a rock garden, where the rocks provide a cool root run.

How to grow: Shade or part sun. Moist, fertile soil. Divide like *A. capillus-veneris.*

Aesculus
Es´kew-lus. Horse chestnut, buckeye.
Hippocastanaceae. Horse chestnut family.

Deciduous trees or shrubs with large palmately compound leaves, dense clusters of large flowers, and glossy nutlike seeds in leathery capsules. 13 spp., native to Europe, Asia, and North America.

Adiantum pedatum

californica (p. 130)
California buckeye.
Deciduous shrub. Zone 9.
H: 10–20 ft. S: 10–20 ft.

Interesting all year. In spring, fans of smooth, 3–6-in.-long, dark green leaflets appear, followed from April to June by dense clusters of 1-in.-wide white or pale pink flowers with orange anthers. Leaves fall in midsummer if unirrigated, late summer or early fall otherwise. Attractive gray branches, good structure, and large handsome seedpods provide interest through the dormant period.

How to grow: Full sun. Tolerates poor or dry soil and heat. No pruning needed, but produces some litter.

× *carnea* 'Briotii' (p. 106)
Red horse chestnut, red-flowered buckeye.
Deciduous tree. Zone 5.
H: 35 ft. S: 20 ft.

An erect, round-crowned tree with robust leaves with 5–7 leaflets up to 10 in. long, thick twigs, and showy panicles of bright scarlet flowers. Prettier and less susceptible to drought injury and brown leaf scorch than is its parent, *A. hippocastanum*. Most attractive in bloom; use as a specimen or shade tree.

How to grow: Full sun. Ordinary soil.

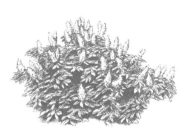

Aesculus parviflora

parviflora (p. 130)
Bottlebrush buckeye.
Deciduous shrub. Zone 5.
H: 10–20 ft. S: 15 ft. or more.

A wide-spreading shrub with tropical-sized leaves; bristly spikes of white flowers in midsummer, after most shrubs have finished; and big seeds in leathery husks atop long upright stems in fall and winter. Makes a screen or mass planting at the end of a property or the edge of a woods. Tolerates shade and can be planted under large trees. Slow-growing but eventually gets quite large.

How to grow: Full sun, part sun, or shade. Ordinary soil. If you plant a single specimen in the lawn, allow plenty of room for it to spread.

pavia (p. 130)
Red buckeye.
Deciduous shrub. Zone 6.
H: 5–25 ft. S: 10 ft.

Masses of this large, open shrub or small tree are attractive along woodland edges or in shrub borders. Also can be trained into a small single-trunked lawn or patio tree. Its leaves are among the first to appear in spring, followed by dense, eye-catching plumes of red flowers. *A. sylvatica,* the painted or Georgia buckeye, is similar but with yellow flowers.

How to grow: Like *A. parviflora.*

Agapanthus orientalis

Agapanthus
Ag-a-pan´thus.
Amaryllidaceae. Amaryllis family.

Evergreen or deciduous perennials with firm straplike leaves, thick roots and rhizomes, and large round umbels of blue, violet, or white flowers. 9 spp., native to South Africa, and many named hybrid cultivars.

orientalis (p. 221)
Lily-of-the-Nile.
Tender perennial. Zone 8.
H: to 5 ft. S: 2 ft.

Beautiful spheres of blue flowers on tall slender stems rise above substantial clumps of broad, arching, evergreen leaves. Stalks bear as many as 100 individual flowers and last well in the garden or as cut flowers. Useful in borders, for ground cover (set 1 to 1 1/2 ft. apart), and as entryway or patio plants in pots or tubs. 'Alba' has white flowers. *A.* 'Peter Pan' is an evergreen dwarf cultivar with foliage clumps to 12 in. tall and blue flowers on 12–18-in. stalks. The 'Headbourne' hybrids are more cold-hardy and reach 2 1/2 ft.

How to grow: Part to full sun. Best in moist, fertile soil but tolerates ordinary soil if regularly fed and watered. Slugs and snails harbor in the foliage but do little damage. Divide every 5 years or when crowded. In cold climates, grow in pots and bring indoors for the winter.

Agastache
A-guh-sta´key.
Labiatae. Mint family.

Perennials with strong upright stems topped with dense spikes of small flowers. Leaves are plain but often very fragrant. About 30 spp., native to North and Central America and to Asia.

foeniculum (p. 280)
Anise hyssop.
Perennial herb. Zone 6.
H: 4 ft. S:·2 ft.

Forms a clump of stiffly upright, 4-sided stalks topped with spikes of blue-purple flowers that attract bees, butterflies, and hummingbirds from July to September. Fresh or dried, the leaves make a tasty anise-flavored hot or iced tea. The lower leaves drop early, so plant this behind a shorter herb such as echinacea or wormwood.

Other agastaches, available from herb specialists, have bright red, orange, or pink flowers.

How to grow: Full or part sun. Tolerates moist soil but not drought. Pest-free and easy to grow. Self-sows readily.

Agave
Uh-gav´ee. Century plant.
Agavaceae. Agave family.

Large succulents with thick, often spiny leaves. Many form a squat rosette, but some have short woody trunks. Tall flower stalks like candelabras develop quickly; after flowering, the old leaves die but new shoots grow from the base. About 300 spp., native from the southern United States through South America.

attenuata (p. 221)
Large succulent. Zone 9.
H: 5 ft. S: 5 ft.

Makes a statuesque rosette of fleshy, pale jade leaves, a natural sculpture for dry landscapes, seaside gardens, or containers. One plant is enough for most gardens. Safe near patios and pools because it has no spines. After many years, suddenly produces a long-lasting spike of greenish yellow flowers that shoots up 12–14 ft., then bends over almost to the ground. After bloom, the parent rosette dies but the "pups" carry on.

How to grow: Full sun, but part shade in the desert. Ordinary soil; tolerates dryness. Protect from severe frost.

vilmoriniana (p. 221)
(*A. mayonensis*)
Octopus agave.
Large succulent. Zone 9.
H: 4 ft. S: 6 ft.

Curling, twisting leaves give the plant the look of a giant octopus. Makes a magnificent and unusual specimen in a garden of succulents and cacti or in a pot or tub. The pale green leaves have spiny tips but smooth edges. Yellow flowers are produced on 15-ft. spikes in spring or summer.

How to grow: Like *A. attenuata.*

other agaves
A. americana, the century plant, is much larger, with ferociously spiny leaves up to 6 ft. long and a flower stalk 20–40 ft. tall. Removing a dead (or live) rosette is a terrible chore, so don't plant one of these unless you're sure you want it. *A. parryi* is smaller, to 3 ft. wide, and looks like a giant blue-gray artichoke with dark spines along the leaf edges and tips. *A. deserti* rosettes are just 2 ft. wide, but one plant will spread fast to form large colonies. It has narrower, gray-green, spiny leaves.

How to grow: Like *A. attenuata.*

Ageratum
A-jur-ay´tum.
Compositae. Daisy family.

Most are annuals with abundant fuzzy-looking clusters of blue, purple, pink, or white flowers. More than 40 spp., native to tropical America.

houstonianum (p. 290)
Flossflower.
Annual. All zones.
H: 6–30 in. S: 6–18 in.

An indispensable edging plant for summer flower beds, with fuzzy, soft, rounded leaves and dense heads of tiny lavender-blue, pink, or white flowers. Blooms all summer until frost and makes a good foreground for zinnias, marigolds, catharanthus, or phlox. Also excellent in containers. There are many dwarf forms, some only 4–6 in. and some 9–12 in. tall. Taller forms, up to 30 in., are good for cutting.

How to grow: Full or part sun. Ordinary or fertile soil. Needs steady moisture, especially in hot areas. Plant 6–10 in. apart after frost. Deadhead for neatness. Pest-free.

Ajuga
A-joo´ga. Bugleweed.
Labiatae. Mint family.

Perennial ground covers with semievergreen foliage and spikes of blue or violet flowers in spring. Most stay close to the ground and spread by runners. About 50 spp., native to the Old World.

reptans (p. 221)
Bugleweed, carpet bugle.
Perennial. Zone 3.
H: 4–8 in. S: 8 in. and beyond.

One of the best ground covers for sun or shade. Excellent as an edging, in the border, or for planting under shrubs and trees. The foliage is attractive and colorful for a long season. Short spikes of blue, purple, or white flowers top the foliage for a few weeks in early summer. 'Burgundy Glow' has wonderful variegations of cream, pink, and green. 'Royalty' has dark purple leaves that are crimped and puckered. 'Silver Beauty' or 'Variegata' is gray-green and creamy white. 'Bronze Beauty' has large bronze-purple leaves, and 'Catlin's Giant' has especially large bronze-green leaves.

How to grow: Sun or shade. Ordinary soil and watering. Plant small-leaved cultivars 8 in. apart; give larger ones 1 ft. or more. The species is invasive and spreads into lawns, but cultivars are more restrained. If the ajuga planting is invaded by grass or weeds, the best solution is to fork up the whole mat, remove the grass or weeds, and replant the ajuga. It's also easy to lift and relocate new plants from rooted stolons. No pests or diseases. Can't take extreme heat or humidity.

Ajuga reptans

Akebia
A-kee´bi-a.

Lardizabalaceae. Lardizabala family.

Twining woody vines with glossy compound leaves, evergreen in mild climates. Female plants occasionally bear purple sausagelike fruits. Only 2 spp., native to eastern Asia.

quinata (p. 198)
Five-leaf akebia.

Woody vine. Zone 5.

H: 20 ft.

A fast-growing, twining vine with delicate lacy foliage (evergreen where winters are mild) and inconspicuous but vanilla-scented flowers. The palmate leaves are 6 in. wide with 5 rounded leaflets. Use it to shade an entry or arbor or to scramble over a derelict stump or dead tree. Be careful in cool, moist, mild climates, where it can smother small or young shrubs. The purple, 3-in.-long fruits are edible but insipid.

How to grow: Sun or shade. Prefers rich, fertile soil with ordinary watering. Pinch when young to encourage many stems; later, thin occasionally to prevent tangling. Provide support.

Albizia
Al-bizz´ee-a.

Leguminosae. Pea family.

Deciduous trees or shrubs with pinnately compound leaves and flower clusters like tassels or pincushions. All but the silk tree are tender. About 150 spp., native to South America, Asia, Africa, and Australia.

julibrissin (p. 106)
Silk tree, mimosa.

Deciduous tree. Zone 6.

H: 30–35 ft. S: 30–35 ft.

A fast-growing tree with a low, spreading, umbrella-shaped crown. The twice-compound leaves have very fine leaflets and fold shut at night. Fragrant pink flowers in powderpuff-like clusters open daily from June to August. Makes a handsome specimen and casts a light, airy shade, but the fallen flowers and pods are messy and the numerous seedlings grow like weeds. 'Rosea' has deeper pink flowers.

How to grow: Full sun. Tolerates poor and alkaline soil, heat, and dryness. Train to a single trunk, but avoid severe pruning, which hastens the death of the tree. Mimosa wilt, a soilborne fungal disease, has killed many trees in the South; 'Charlotte' is a resistant cultivar.

Alcea
Al-see´a. Hollyhock.

Malvaceae. Mallow family.

Biennials or perennials with rough or felty leaves and tall unbranched stems bearing large stalkless flowers. About 60 spp., native to Eurasia.

rosea (p. 290)
Hollyhock.

Usually biennial. Zone 5.

H: 3–9 ft. S: 3 ft.

A quintessential plant of English cottage gardens; its dramatic tall spikes make a splendid accent against a wall or fence. The rough gray-green leaves are rounded or shallowly lobed. Flowers can be single or double in colors ranging from white, yellow, apricot, and red to pink, rose, and purple. Even the "smaller" modern forms are back-of-the-border biggies. Old-fashioned kinds are real garden giants, sometimes reaching 9 ft.

How to grow: Full sun. Ordinary soil and watering. Sow seeds in place for bloom the following year. (Some kinds bloom the first year and others continue as perennials, but most grow best as biennials.) Stake tall stalks, and cut down after blooming. Very prone to rust (destroy infected leaves) and other fungal diseases and attacked by slugs, snails, Japanese beetles, and other pests.

Alchemilla
Al-ke-mill´a.

Rosaceae. Rose family.

Perennials with lobed or compound leaves and sprays of tiny greenish yellow flowers. About 200 spp., most native to the north temperate zone.

Alchemilla mollis

mollis (p. 221)
Lady's-mantle.

Perennial. Zone 3.

H: 1–2 ft. S: 2 ft.

Lovely as an edging plant around fountains or in mass plantings on slopes. The pleated and scalloped 6-in.-wide leaves unfold to make a soft gray-green clump in early spring, then frothy clouds of small chartreuse flowers on 2-ft. stalks spill over the top. The flowers last a long time in the garden, and they also dry well for winter bouquets. *A. alpina* and *A. erythropoda* are dainty relatives with particularly lovely leaves.

How to grow: Sun or shade. Tolerates poor conditions but does better with good soil and regular watering. An almost perfect plant—decorative, easy to grow, and well behaved. Needs no maintenance and has no pests. To increase your stock, divide in spring or summer.

Allium

Al'li-um.

Amaryllidaceae. Amaryllis family.

Bulb-forming perennials with flat or hollow leaves and round clusters of small flowers. Many, including onion and garlic, have pungent leaves and bulbs, but the flowers may smell quite sweet. About 700 spp., all native to the Northern Hemisphere.

cernuum (p. 222)

Nodding wild onion.
Perennial. Zone 4.
H: 8–12 in. S: 12 in. or more.

Plant in small groups and enjoy the nodding clusters of pink to purple starlike flowers in early summer. Native throughout much of the United States. Makes a good cut flower and combines well with other small perennials. The leaves are slender and delicate.

How to grow: Full sun. Well-drained soil. Easy to grow; spreads by division and seed to form natural clumps or drifts.

christophii (p. 222)

(*A. albopilosum*)
Star of Persia.
Perennial. Zone 4.
H: to 30 in. (flowers). S: 12 in.

Both leaves and flowers are beautiful in late spring and early summer. The leaves are wide, strap-shaped, and glaucous blue-green. The spiderlike amethyst or purplish flowers form a globe up to 10 in. wide on a stalk up to 30 in. tall. The flower head dries well and lasts for years as an indoor decoration. In the garden, plant near purplish red roses or purple-leaved shrubs and combine with perennials that will fill in when the allium leaves die down. *A.* 'Globemaster', a new hybrid, produces giant heads with more than 1,000 violet flowers on a stalk more than 3 ft. tall.

How to grow: Full sun. Needs well-drained soil; tolerates dry soil and heat. Plant bulbs in fall, 6 in. deep and 8 in. apart, and mark the site so that you won't pierce dormant bulbs when digging nearby.

moly (p. 222)

Lily leek, golden garlic.
Perennial. Zone 2.
H: 12 in. S: 12 in. or more.

Rapidly spreads into a low, compact clump that explodes with starry, cheerful yellow flowers in late spring. Each bulb grows 2 flat lance-shaped leaves, 2 in. wide, that turn yellow after the flowers fade (it doesn't hurt to cut them off before they wither). Combine it with something like *Veronica* 'Crater Lake' or 'Royal Blue', which will fill in to cover the space.

How to grow: Full or part sun. Tolerates poor soil and dryness. Plant bulbs in fall about 2 in. deep. Blooms in 1 year from seed. Requires no effort and has no problems.

neapolitanum (p. 222)

Naples onion, daffodil onion.
Perennial. Zone 7.
H: 12 in. S: 12 in.

Bears a lovely umbel of sweet-scented, starry white flowers that last a month in early spring. Combine with scillas, daffodils, and grape hyacinths for a garden display in mild climates, or pot up a few and force like daffodils in the North. Var. *grandiflorum* is larger, more vigorous, and showier.

How to grow: Full sun. Well-drained soil. Plant bulbs in fall, 5 in. deep, and mulch well. Self-sows where suited.

schoenoprasum (p. 280)

Chives.
Perennial herb. Zone 3.
H: 12 in. S: 18 in.

Plant a few clumps of chives along the front of a flower bed where you can snip the fresh onion-flavored leaves from spring to fall. (Chop and freeze for winter use, or pot up a plant to keep on the windowsill.) The lavender flowers in 1-in.-wide heads on stiff stalks last a month in late spring; they also make good cut flowers, can be dried for winter bouquets, and look pretty (but taste chaffy) in salads.

How to grow: Full or part sun. Ordinary soil and watering. Easy from seed started indoors or out in spring, or divide an old clump into dozens of new starts. Shear after flowering to tidy up the plant and to promote new growth. Long lived and trouble-free.

tuberosum (p. 280)

Garlic chives.
Perennial herb. Zone 3.
H: 24 in. S: 12 in.

Just a slender inconspicuous clump of leaves in spring and summer but bears lovely round clusters of white flowers on 2–3-ft. stalks in late summer or early fall. The leaves have a mild garlic flavor. Regular chive leaves are thin hollow tubes; garlic chive leaves are solid flat ribbons.

How to grow: Full sun. Ordinary soil and watering. Easy to grow; just remove faded flowers to prevent rampant self-sowing.

Aloe

Al'oh, al'o-ee.

Liliaceae. Lily family.

Succulents with thick fleshy leaves that are sometimes spiny and clusters of brightly colored, long-lasting flowers on tall stalks. Most form clumps of dense rosettes at ground level, but some have branching woody trunks and grow several feet tall. More than 360 spp., native to arid regions in the Old World, particularly Africa.

Allium cernuum

Aloe arborescens

arborescens (p. 222)
Candelabra plant, octopus plant, torch plant.
Shrub-sized succulent. Zone 9.
H: usually 8–12 ft. S: 8–12 ft.

An exotic yet virtually carefree winter-blooming succulent for mild climates. Branching trunks support rosettes of plump, tooth-edged leaves 2 ft. long. Tubular red-orange flowers, attractive to hummingbirds, are borne in dense racemes held above the leaves. It looks tropical but needs little water; makes a dramatic center-piece for a Mediterranean-style garden.

How to grow: Full sun. Tolerates heat and poor, dry soil. Remove flower stalks after blooming and old dry leaves. Usually planted singly, but plants could be spaced 3–5 ft. apart to make a barrier.

saponaria (p. 222)
(*A. latifolia*)
Soap aloe.
Succulent. Zone 9.
H: 9–12 in. S: to several ft.

Fast and easy to grow; excellent in containers or hot, dry landscapes. Spreads by suckers, forming clumps of sharply toothed, reddish green leaves with dull white spots. Two or three times a year it bears tubular scarlet, yellow, shrimp pink, or orange-red flowers on stout 18–36-in. stalks. Attracts hummingbirds.

How to grow: Full or part sun. Ordinary or poor soil. Tolerates heat and dryness. Groom after bloom. Divide old clumps and replant in spring or fall. Destroy plants with leaves deformed by thrips.

vera (p. 223)
(*A. barbadensis*)
Succulent herb. Zone 8.
H: 2 ft. S: to several ft.

This famous medicinal aloe used for burns, skin problems, and shampoo is also an easy-to-grow, drought-tolerant ornamental that blooms freely and attracts hummingbirds. Grow in containers, near swimming pools, or on dry slopes. The plump gray-green leaves, 1–2 ft. long, are tinged red, spotted when young, and edged with soft spines. Tubular yellow flowers in 3-ft. racemes usually open in spring but may bloom again later.

How to grow: Like *A. saponaria.*

Aloysia
A-loyz´ee-a.
Verbenaceae. Verbena family.

Deciduous or evergreen shrubs with fragrant leaves. About 30 spp., native to Central and South America.

triphylla (p. 280)
(*Lippia citriodora*)
Lemon verbena.
Tender woody herb. Zone 8.
H: to 10 ft. S: to 6 ft.

The whorls of 3 or 4 thin, papery leaves have a wonderfully intense lemon fragrance; use them in iced drinks, apple jelly, and potpourri. Usually deciduous outdoors but semievergreen in mild winters or if wintered indoors. Bears open clusters of tiny lilac or white flowers in summer. A slender-twigged shrub with a loose, open habit—tuck it behind low mounding shrubs or perennials, or pinch repeatedly to make it denser.

How to grow: Full sun. Ordinary or better soil and regular watering. In cold climates buy a new plant each spring to treat as an annual, or grow one in a pot and bring it into a bright, cool, dry place for the winter.

Alstroemeria
Al-stro-meer´ee-a. Peruvian lily.
Amaryllidaceae. Amaryllis family.

Perennials with upright leafy stems topped by broad clusters of brightly colored lilylike or azalea-like flowers. About 50 spp., native to South America, and many new garden hybrids.

Ligtu hybrids (p. 223)
Perennials. Zone 8.
H: 3–5 ft. S: 2–3 ft. or more.

This group makes a splendid mass of color for 4–6 weeks from spring to summer, when the leafy stalks are topped with 20 or more flowers in shades of white, yellow, pink, salmon, or red, often marked with darker spots. Brilliant in the garden with Shasta daisies or delphiniums and excellent as cut flowers. Spreads by seed and can be a pest, but a magnificent one.

The new Cordu hybrids and other "evergreen" hybrids come in many colors and bloom over a long season. *A. aurea* (formerly *A. aurantiaca*), to 3 ft. and a rampant spreader, is nearly evergreen and bears umbels of heavily spotted orange, yellow, or red flowers. *A. pelegrina* has spotted lavender and white flowers.

How to grow: Full or part sun. Ordinary or better soil. Can't tolerate heat; they go dormant and need no water in late summer and fall. Sow seeds in place, or set out container-grown plants in fall or winter. Transplanting is difficult because the tuberous roots are deep and brittle. Pull—don't cut—the dead stalks after the flowers fade.

Alstroemeria pulchella

pulchella
(similar or identical to *A. psittacina*)
Perennial. Zone 8.
H: 12–18 in. S: to several ft.

Spreads to make a scattered colony of erect stems with smooth, thin, evergreen leaves 3 in. long, topped in spring and summer with clusters of tubular, flared, lilylike flowers. The flowers aren't showy, but they have fascinating colors and markings at close range—dark red tipped with green, and spotted with purple. Grows well in the shade of conifers and makes a good ground cover with ferns, ajugas, and sweet woodruff.

How to grow: Part sun or shade. Ordinary soil and watering. Plant one and wait; it will spread by underground runners and by seed. Dig individual plants with a clump of tubers to share with friends at any time. Needs no care; can be invasive in loose, leafy woodland soil.

Amaranthus
Am-a-ran'thus.
Amaranthaceae. Amaranth family.

Annuals, often coarse and weedy, sometimes grown for their brightly colored foliage or their edible seeds. About 60 spp., native or naturalized around the world.

tricolor (p. 290)
Joseph's-coat.
Annual. All zones.
H: 1–4 ft. S: 1–2 ft.

A sturdy, bushy annual with large thin leaves scattered up the stems and clustered on top. The flowers are inconspicuous, but the leaves glow in brilliant shades of red, orange, and yellow. Fast and easy for a show of bright color in hot weather.

How to grow: Full sun. Tolerates poor soil and dryness. Sow in place or set out seedlings only when the soil is thoroughly warm.

Amelanchier
Am-e-lang'ki-er. Serviceberry, shadbush, Juneberry.
Rosaceae. Rose family.

Deciduous shrubs or trees with white flowers in early spring, small edible fruits, and brilliant fall color. Only 6 spp., native to North America.

laevis (see below for photo)
Serviceberry, shadbush, sarvisbush.
Deciduous shrub or small tree. Zone 4.
H: 15–25 ft. or more. S: 15 ft. or more.

An easy-to-grow native that provides 3-season interest. Dangling clusters of white or pinkish flowers are one of the first signs of new life in early spring. Clusters of berrylike dark purple fruit make a tasty treat (for you or the birds) in June or July. The small leaves turn superb yellows, oranges, or reds in fall. A perfect size for most gardens, filling the often-overlooked gap between shrubs and tall trees. *A. arborea* (p. 106) is similar; *A.* × *grandiflora* is a hybrid between the two. (Even professionals have trouble telling which is which.) Selected cultivars offer upright habit, abundant bloom and fruit, and/or outstanding fall color. Other species of *Amelanchier*, native to different regions of the country, also make fine ornamental shrubs or trees.

How to grow: Full or part sun. Well-drained acidic soil; tolerates dry soil and heat. Prune to a single trunk if desired; rarely needs other pruning. Susceptible to various insects and diseases but not badly damaged by them.

Amelanchier laevis

Ampelopsis
Am-pel-op'sis.
Vitaceae. Grape family.

Deciduous vines with compound leaves and small blue berries. Tendrils are branched but don't have suction-cup disks. Only 2 spp., native to North America and Asia.

brevipedunculata (p. 198)
Porcelain berry.
Deciduous woody vine. Zone 5.
H: 20 ft.

A vigorous vine that climbs by tendrils and quickly covers a trellis, pergola, arch, or wall. The coarsely toothed, 3-lobed leaves are dark green in summer, turn red in fall. The small berries, which ripen from greenish white to metallic turquoise-blue, are exquisite and attract birds. 'Elegans' is less vigorous and has smaller leaves marked with pink and white. 'Citrulloides' has more attractive, deeply 5-lobed leaves.

How to grow: Full sun or shade (the more sun, the more berries). Ordinary soil and watering. Tolerates heat. Provide support and allow plenty of room; prune as needed to keep it in bounds. Japanese beetles will strip it bare, but it has few other problems.

**Amsonia
tabernaemontana**

Amsonia

Am-sown´ee-a.
Apocynaceae. Dogbane family.

Perennials forming clumps of upright stems containing milky sap, with slender shiny leaves and star-shaped flowers in spring. About 20 spp., native to North America and Japan.

tabernaemontana (p. 223)

Bluestar, willow herb.
Perennial. Zone 3.
H: 2–3 ft. S: 3 ft.

One of the toughest and most attractive plants for the perennial bed or moist meadow. Makes a bushy clump. Clusters of starry pale blue flowers top the stems for 3–4 weeks in spring, combining well with peonies and irises. The slender, smooth, pale green leaves turn a pleasing yellow in fall. Related species are similarly desirable and carefree.

How to grow: Full or part sun. Tolerates constant moisture. Increase by division in fall or early spring. Cut off the tops of the stems after bloom to encourage a flush of compact fresh growth.

Anemone

Uh-nem´o-nee.
Ranunculaceae. Buttercup family.

A diverse group of perennials. Roots are tuberous or fibrous; leaves divided or compound; stems 6 in. to 4 ft. tall; and flowers white or brightly colored, appearing from spring to fall. About 120 spp., from throughout the north temperate zone, and many hybrid cultivars.

blanda (p. 223)

Grecian windflower.
Perennial. Zone 4.
H: 6–8 in. S: 6 in.

A drift of these rich blue, daisylike flowers is a welcome sight in early spring, and they make good cut flowers, too. Naturalize them with other spring-flowering bulbs in a woodland garden or in grass. The hairy leaves are 3 in. wide and deeply dissected. Flowers are up to 2 in. wide. Available in various shades of blue, purplish, pink, or white.

How to grow: Part shade. Needs cool, moist, well-drained, fertile soil; doesn't do well in hot climates. Soak the rounded tubers overnight and plant 2 in. deep. Spreads itself by seed.

× hybrida (p. 224)

Japanese anemone.
Perennial. Zone 4.
H: 3–5 ft. S: 2 ft.

Lovely in mass plantings or a shady border, with a large mound of handsome, dark green, deeply lobed leaves and dozens of blossoms on erect branching stalks for several weeks in late summer and early fall. Flowers are 2–3 in. wide, single to double, in shades of white, rose, or deep pink. 'Honorine Jobert' is a popular old cultivar with clear white, single flowers. Some new cultivars have larger flowers, 4–5 in. wide.

How to grow: Part shade; protect from hot sun. Likes deep, fertile, well-drained but moisture-retentive soil topped with mulch. Plant 12–18 in. apart and divide every 3–4 years. Tall forms may need staking.

vitifolia (p. 224)

(*A. tomentosa*)
Grapeleaf anemone.
Perennial. Zone 4.
H: 3–4 ft. S: 2 ft. or more.

The deeply lobed, grapelike leaves make a handsome ground cover that spreads quickly. The upright branching stalks bear dozens of single white flowers, 2–3 in. wide, for several weeks in late summer. Looks pretty beside *Artemisia* 'Silver King', or plant several in one area around and between shrubs and underplant with spring-flowering bulbs. 'Robustissima' is especially vigorous and hardier and has pink flowers. Similar but smaller, *A. sylvestris,* the snowdrop anemone, has fragrant white flowers on 18-in. stalks in spring and sometimes again in fall.

How to grow: Sun or part sun. Likes well-mulched, fertile soil. Will tolerate sun if kept moist. Spreads quickly. Separate new plants from the runners in spring and replant or give them away.

Anemone × hybrida

Anethum

A-nee´thum. Dill.
Umbelliferae. Carrot family.

Annual herbs with fragrant threadlike leaves and tasty seeds. Only 2 spp., native to the Old World.

graveolens (p. 281)

Dill.
Annual herb. All zones.
H: to 4 ft. S: 1 ft.

Seedlings grow quickly to make a low rosette of grayish green, finely divided leaves with wonderful flavor and fragrance. The stalks shoot up in midsummer, each branch topped with an umbel of tiny yellow flowers, which are also edible. Grow more than you want to eat, and cut extra flowers as fillers for fresh flower arrangements, or let them go to seed and gather the seeds for flavoring or the dry seed heads for winter arrangements. New varieties have denser foliage and don't rush into bloom.

How to grow: Full sun. Ordinary soil. Sow seeds where they are to grow in early spring and again in midsummer for a fall crop. After the first year, watch for volunteer seedlings.

Angelica

An-jel´i-ka.
Umbelliferae. Carrot family.

Perennial or biennial herbs forming large clumps of strong stems with bold compound leaves and large umbels of pale flowers. Many species are used medicinally in Asia. About 50 spp., native to the Northern Hemisphere and New Zealand.

archangelica (p. 281)

Angelica.
Herb. Zone 4.
H: to 6 ft. S: 2–3 ft.

Use this dramatic sculptural plant as a background for smaller herbs or flowers. It has stout ribbed stems; triply divided leaves with dark, glossy, toothed leaflets; and giant umbels of small greenish white flowers. The stems can be candied to flavor desserts, and the fragrant seeds are used in perfumery. *A. gigas* is even more attractive, with unusual puffed-out leaf bases and purple flowers.

How to grow: Part sun or shade. Prefers rich soil with plenty of moisture; doesn't grow as big in ordinary or dry soil. Sow seeds immediately after ripening in late summer, and transplant seedlings when they are still small the following spring. The plant will die if allowed to set seed but will self-sow if happy in its position.

Antigonon

An-tig´o-non.
Polygonaceae. Rhubarb family.

Deciduous or evergreen, fast-growing vines with generous clusters of bright flowers through-out summer and fall. Only 2 or 3 spp., native to Mexico and Central America.

leptopus (p. 198)

Coral vine, queen's-wreath.
Deciduous vine. Zone 8.
H: 10–40 ft.

An easy, healthy vine that grows quickly and climbs by tendrils to cover its support with a mass of heart-shaped leaves up to 4 in. long. After the first good rain in late summer or fall, it's covered with a froth of rosy pink flowers. Can frame a porch or arbor like an edging of fine lace. 'Album' has white flowers.

How to grow: Full sun. Well-drained soil. Tolerates heat well but dies back with the first frost. Plant in spring so that it has all season to develop the tubers, which overwinter. Easy from seed. Provide support and assist climbing when necessary.

Antirrhinum

An-ti-ry´num.
Scrophulariaceae. Foxglove family.

Perennials or annuals with upright leafy stems and colorful two-lipped flowers. About 40 spp., native to the New and Old World.

majus (p. 290)

Snapdragon.
Perennial grown as an annual. All zones.
H: 6–36 in. S: 8–18 in.

A popular annual with velvety flowers in a wide range of colors and forms, from the traditional "snapping" shape loved by children to broader, more open shapes like penstemons or azaleas. There are dwarf varieties, which are good for edging and containers, and tall ones, which fit into mixed borders and make excellent long-lasting cut flowers. For the best selection, order seeds and grow your own plants.

How to grow: Full sun. Ordinary soil and watering. Sow seeds in shallow flats to germinate and grow at 60° F. Pinch seedlings to promote branching. In mild-winter areas, set out plants in early fall for winter or spring bloom. In colder regions, plant in spring for summer bloom. Cut back after blooming, and the plants will often bloom again. Often overwinters in protected and well-drained sites. Watch for brown spots on the leaves, the symptom of rust infection. Destroy infected plants. The following year, choose resistant varieties, and plant them in a different spot.

Aquilegia

Ak-wi-leej´ee-a. Columbine.
Ranunculaceae. Buttercup family.

Perennials with delicate lacy foliage and unique flowers on long branched stalks. The flowers have long or short spurs in back and come in every color, pastel or bright. About 70 spp., native to the north temperate zone.

caerulea (p. 224)
Rocky Mountain columbine.
Perennial. Zone 3.
H: 1–2 ft. S: 12–18 in.

A lovely plant that lifts its large blue-and-white flowers on tall stalks that branch above a basal mound of dainty, deeply divided leaves. Flowers are 2 in. wide and have 2-in.-long spurs; they make excellent cut flowers. Lovely in a semiwoodland border with ferns, hostas, and brunnera or pulmonaria. Individual plants live just a few years, but they self-sow freely. *A. vulgaris,* a European species, has similar flowers with shorter curved spurs. There are many hybrids derived from these species, with different flower forms and colors.

How to grow: Best in part sun and moist, well-drained soil. Doesn't tolerate heat and is susceptible to aphids, leafminers, and powdery mildew. Remove old flower stalks if tidiness matters, or let the seedpods develop. Birds will come to eat the seeds, and you'll get a crop of seedlings, too.

canadensis (p. 224)
Columbine, Canadian columbine.
Perennial. Zone 3.
H: 2–3 ft. S: 1 ft.

Attractive to humans and hummingbirds alike, the nodding red-and-yellow flowers bloom for about 6 weeks in spring. The delicate lacy foliage is evergreen in mild winters. At home in a wide range of habitats. *A. formosa,* the western columbine, has similar flowers on taller stalks.

How to grow: Like *A. caerulea* but is easier to grow. Tolerates sun if the soil is moist, tolerates heat if given shade, and stands up well to leafminer infestations.

chrysantha (p. 224)
Golden columbine.
Perennial. Zone 3.
H: about 3 ft. S: 1 ft.

One of the showiest columbines, bearing fragrant yellow flowers from late spring through midsummer. The flowers are 2–3 in. wide, with straight spurs more than 2 in. long. The plant itself is vigorous, with many branching, upright stalks. Of the many cultivars, 'Yellow Queen' has large, lemon yellow flowers; 'Alba Plena' has pale yellow flowers; and 'Nana' is a dwarf form (1¹/₂ ft. tall).

How to grow: Like *A. caerulea* but can take sun, drier soil, and some heat.

hybrid cultivars (p. 224)
Columbine.
Perennials. Zone 4.
H: 2–3 ft. S: 1 ft.

These are graceful yet tough and hardy perennials for beds and borders, with soft mounds of fine-textured foliage topped with dozens of flowers in pastel, bright, or bicolored shades of blue, red, white, pink, violet, and yellow. 'McKana Giants' and 'Spring Song' grow 30–36 in. tall and have large flowers on strong stems, good for cutting. 'Music' and 'Dwarf Fairyland' are shorter, better for open, windy sites. All come in a range of colors.

How to grow: Full or part sun. Ordinary or better soil. Prefer constant moisture. Easy from seed; start in pots or flats. Plant seedlings or nursery stock from spring to fall; they will bloom the next year. Discard plants after a few years, when they get woody at the base or flowering diminishes. Subject to aphids, leafminers, and spider mites.

Arbutus
Ar-bew´tus.
Ericaceae. Heath family.

Evergreen trees or shrubs with leathery leaves, conspicuous red bark, small pink or white flowers, and orange berries. About 14 spp., native to western North America and Europe.

menziesii (p. 156)
Madrone.
Evergreen tree. Zone 8.
H: 50 ft. or more. S: 30 ft.

One of the most beautiful broad-leaved evergreen trees, it makes a picturesque specimen with an irregular oval crown. The bark is outstanding—tan twigs, maroon branches, and peeling patches of buff and cinnamon on the trunk. Drooping clusters of small creamy flowers cover the tree for 3 weeks in May; fleshy orange-red fruits follow.

How to grow: Full or part sun. Tolerates poor, dry soil and heat and should *not* be irrigated in summer—irrigation leads to root rot and can kill the tree. Does best in maritime and Mediterranean climates along the Pacific Coast. Should be grown from seed sown in place, which germinates readily if fresh. Seedlings grow fast, often reaching 10 ft. in 2–3 years. Naturally abundant in areas where it grows well.

unedo (p. 156)
Strawberry tree.
Evergreen tree. Zone 8.
H: 20 ft. S: 20 ft.

An upright shrub or small tree with a rounded crown, reddish twigs, and shiny, leathery, evergreen leaves. Drooping clusters of small white to pinkish flowers appear in October, blooming alongside the pebbly-textured, bright red, spherical fruits. Ideal for small or urban gardens along the West Coast; nice in combination with lavenders, rock roses, and other Mediterranean shrubs and perennials. Very effective as a specimen or screen on hot, dry sites. 'Compacta' is a shrubby form, to 5 ft. tall, that flowers and fruits almost continuously.

How to grow: Full sun. Tolerates heat and poor, dry soil. Plant container-grown specimens in fall or spring. Once established, it is extremely drought-tolerant, needs no maintenance, and has no pests or diseases.

Aquilegia canadensis

Aquilegia hybrids

Arctostaphylos

Ark-toe-staff'i-los.

Ericaceae. Heath family.

Evergreen shrubs with crooked stems, small leathery leaves, waxy bell-shaped flowers, and fruit like tiny apples. About 50 spp., most native to western North America, and several hybrids and cultivars.

densiflora 'Howard McMinn' (p. 166)

Manzanita.

Evergreen shrub. Zone 8.

H: 4–6 ft. S: 7 ft.

The most dependable, healthiest, and longest lived of the cultivated manzanitas. Unpruned, it makes an informal mounded specimen or hedge. Pinch off the branch tips after the flowers fade to shape a formal planting. Can be used as a large-scale ground cover. The rounded leaves are small and glossy; twigs are smooth and reddish. Small, pale pink flowers in February and March are followed by tiny, glossy red berries. 'Harmony' grows somewhat taller and broader; 'Sentinel' is more upright, not as mounded.

How to grow: Full or part sun but can't take desert heat. Needs well-drained soil. Plant 4 ft. apart, preferably in fall, setting the top of the root ball slightly above grade. Needs rain or irrigation until it's established; can tolerate drought later. Branches root where they touch the ground.

'Emerald Carpet' (p. 166)

Evergreen shrub. Zone 8.

H: 9–12 in. S: 4–5 ft.

A splendid low evergreen ground cover for dry-summer climates, with shiny bright green leaves about 1/2 in. long. The bark is glossy reddish brown; the pink flowers are inconspicuous, hidden among the leaves. Use it on hillsides and banks, in rock gardens, or to cover plantings of bulbs. *A. hookeri* 'Monterey Carpet', to 1 ft. tall and 10–12 ft. wide, is similar but has more-open growth and slightly larger leaves.

How to grow: Like 'Howard McMinn' but grows low and spreads by itself; no pruning required.

uva-ursi (p. 166)

Bearberry, kinnikinick.

Evergreen shrub. Zone 3.

H: under 12 in. S: 15 ft. or more.

A maintenance-free ground cover ideal for rock gardens and hillsides. Makes a good substitute for lawns on steep slopes; combines well with pines or other conifers. The leathery coin-sized leaves are glossy green in summer, bronzy reddish purple in winter. The spring flowers are white, tipped with pink; lustrous red fruits (like tiny apples) are produced in fall. Selected varieties have a more prostrate habit, larger fruits, and/or resistance to leafspot diseases. Cultivar names such as 'Point Reyes', 'Vancouver Jade', and 'Massachusetts' indicate bearberry's wide adaptability.

How to grow: Full or part sun. Needs well-drained soil. Hardy enough to be useful in New England and the Rocky Mountains but also popular in the Pacific Northwest. Plant 2 ft. apart for ground cover, and use mulch to control weeds until it fills in. Can take infrequent foot traffic, which actually helps push the stems into the ground, where they root.

Arctotis

Ark-toe'tis.

Compositae. Daisy family.

Perennials or annuals with a basal rosette of rough or hairy lobed leaves and daisylike flowers on long stalks. About 50 spp., native to southern Africa.

hybrids (p. 291)

African daisies.

Annuals. All zones.

H: 12–18 in. S: 12 in.

Easy annuals for warm, sunny spots, with 3-in.-wide, long-stemmed daisies in shades of bright white, pink, coral, red, yellow, or orange, usually with dark "eyes." Plants form a low clump of rough gray-green leaves, 6 in. long, with toothed or lobed edges. They look cheerful along the edge of a bed or patio, and they make good cut flowers, too. *A. stoechadifolia* var. *grandis* grows taller and has silvery white daisies with deep blue eyes.

How to grow: Full sun. Ordinary soil and watering. Sow seeds in place. Plant in fall for spring bloom only where winters are very mild; otherwise, sow in spring for summer bloom. Deadhead regularly to prolong flowering.

Arecastrum

A ree-ka'strum.

Palmae. Palm family.

An erect palm with pinnate leaves. Only 1 sp., native to South America.

romanzoffianum (p. 164)

(now *Syagrus romanzoffianus*)

Queen palm.

Palm. Zone 9 or 8.

H: 40–50 ft. S: 20 ft.

A fast-growing palm with an exceptionally straight trunk, topped with a cluster of glossy feather-type leaves up to 15 ft. long. Used as a street tree in the mild regions of Florida, Texas, and California. *Archontophoenix cunninghamiana*, the king palm, is similar but more tender to frost.

How to grow: Full sun. Tolerates unamended soil but needs regular watering. Transplant when small. Remove old dead leaves to expose the handsome trunk.

Arecastrum romanzoffianum

Aristolochia

A-ris-toe-low´kee-a.
Aristolochiaceae. Birthwort family.

A diverse group of evergreen or deciduous vines, shrubs, or herbs. All have peculiar, dull-colored flowers designed to trap pollinating insects. Perhaps as many as 300 spp., mostly tropical.

durior (p. 199)

(*A. macrophylla*)
Dutchman's-pipe.
Deciduous vine. Zone 4.
H: to 30 ft.

A hardy vine native to eastern woodlands. It grows quickly to cover any support with a shinglelike array of large (to 12 in. wide) heart-shaped leaves. Intriguing 3-in.-long, pipe-shaped flowers of mottled green and burgundy open for a few weeks in spring or summer, followed by dark gray, pickle-shaped fruits in fall. Use it to hide an eyesore, to shade a porch, or to clothe a fence with a curtain of green. *A. californica*, a hardy native of western mountains, has smaller flowers and 5-in. leaves and doesn't climb as high.

How to grow: Sun or shade. Prefers organic, well-drained soil. Tolerates heat in summer but needs cold winters. Easy from seed and can be grown as an annual in mild climates. To make a screen, plant 1–2 ft. apart along a support. Tie the stems at first. Pinch the growing tips to encourage branching. Prune as needed when dormant.

Aronia

A-rone´ee-a. Chokeberry.
Rosaceae. Rose family.

Deciduous shrubs that form a thicket of stems with blossoms like pears, bright red fall foliage, and red or black berries. Only 2 spp., native to North America.

arbutifolia (p. 130)

Chokeberry.
Deciduous shrub. Zone 4.
H: 6–10 ft. S: 4–6 ft.

A useful shrub for mass plantings, for casual borders, or in the transition zone between managed landscapes and natural areas. Forms spreading clumps with many upright stems and narrow oval leaves that turn bright red in fall. Covered with clusters of small white flowers in spring and bright red berrylike fruits. Combine it with beautyberries, deciduous hollies, and quince for a fruit display to admire on winter days. 'Brilliantissima' has especially vivid fall foliage and fruits. *A. melanocarpa* is similar but doesn't grow as tall and has purple-black fruits.

How to grow: Full or part sun. Native to wetlands; tolerates low, wet areas but grows fine in ordinary garden conditions. An easy, vigorous, and adaptable plant. Plant in spring, 4–6 ft. apart. Trim suckers if you want to control its spread. Subject to fire blight, rust, and leafspot.

Aronia arbutifolia

Artemisia

Ar-te-miss´ee-a.
Compositae. Daisy family.

Evergreen or deciduous shrubs or perennials. Most have aromatic foliage, often silver or gray. Flowers are small, rarely conspicuous. About 300 spp., native to dry regions in the Old and New World.

abrotanum (p. 281)

Southernwood, old-man, lad's-love.
Deciduous shrubby herb. Zone 5.
H: 3–5 ft. S: 3 ft.

An old-fashioned favorite valued for its fine aromatic foliage. The finely divided, almost feathery leaves are a light gray-green; a dusting of tiny yellowish flowers may appear in fall. Open and straggly if unpruned but easily shaped into a compact ball. Makes a good companion for shrub roses, or plant it near a path where you'll brush against its foliage and appreciate the scent. Lemon-, tangerine-, and camphor-scented forms are available. Cut and dry some foliage for sachets or potpourri.

How to grow: Full or part sun. Tolerates poor soil and dryness. Cut back drastically in spring to control size and shape; no other attention necessary.

absinthium 'Lambrook Silver' (p. 225)

Wormwood.
Shrubby perennial. Zone 5.
H: 30 in. S: 24–36 in.

Makes a foaming mass of silvery, silky, shimmering leaves and gives no trouble, aside from flopping over onto small neighboring plants. Leaves are finely divided, 2–5 in. long, and strongly aromatic. Stems are topped with panicles of tiny yellow flowers in summer. Looks good in front of purple-leaved shrubs. Common wormwood, *A. absinthium*, grows taller and the leaves aren't quite as delicate. Historically, it was used as a medicinal herb and to flavor the alcoholic beverage absinthe.

How to grow: Like *A. abrotanum*, but trim back by at least a third in spring and again in midsummer to prevent floppiness. Hardy to cold but can be lost in winter if the soil stays too wet.

dracunculus var. *sativa* (p. 281)

French tarragon.
Perennial herb. Zone 3.
H: 2 ft. or more. S: 2 ft. or more.

It's a plain, even drab-looking plant, but the slender leaves have a wonderful anise flavor, popular in vinegar or salad dressings and tasty with chicken or fish. Forms a slowly spreading colony of leafy upright stems. Rarely bears small greenish flowers. Sniff a leaf before you buy the plant; true French tarragon is a sterile variety that must be propagated from cuttings or by division. Russian tarragon, *A. dracunculus*, is cheaply raised from seed and often sold, but it has no flavor and is useless for culinary (or any other) purposes.

How to grow: Like *A. abrotanum* but must be watered during periods of drought.

lactiflora (p. 225)
White mugwort.
Perennial. Zone 4.
H: 4–5 ft. S: 2–3 ft.

Creamy plumes of sweetly fragrant flowers top the stems for up to a month in late summer and dry well for winter wreaths or bouquets. Dark green, pinnately divided leaves grow all the way up the stems. Makes an impressive background for blue or purple flowers such as asters.

How to grow: Full or part sun. Prefers rich, moist soil but tolerates ordinary soil and watering. May need staking if stems seem floppy. Spreads slowly; divide every few years.

ludoviciana 'Silver King' (p. 225)
(*A. albula*)
Perennial. Zone 3.
H: 2–3 ft. S: rapidly forms patch.

One patch provides a generous supply of pleasantly aromatic, silvery gray stems and foliage for fresh or dried bouquets. Cut stems when the flower buds look like tiny gray knobs. Lovely with blue, lavender, pink, and red border flowers, but it should be confined in a pot or bottomless bucket or it will run all over the bed. 'Silver Queen' has prettier (more deeply cut) leaves but weaker stems than 'Silver King' and usually needs support.

How to grow: Full sun. Does best in poor or dry soils and tolerates heat. Spreads by underground roots; to keep it under control, dig and divide every spring and plant new starts 1 ft. apart.

'Powis Castle' (p. 225)
Perennial. Zone 6.
H: 3 ft. S: 4 ft.

Forms a generous mound of silvery filigree foliage that couldn't be prettier. It is exuberant but not invasive and doesn't need staking. Try combining it with dark reds and purples.

How to grow: Full or part sun. Ordinary soil. Tolerates heat and dryness. Leave 2 ft. of space on all sides or the branches will cover its neighbors. Trim back old shoots to force new growth in spring. In cold climates, take cuttings in midsummer and pot them up to keep indoors over winter; these new plants will shape up faster than old plants that have frozen down.

other artemisias
California sagebrush, *A. californica,* is an evergreen shrub native to coastal California and hardy to Zone 9. Two prostrate forms, 'Canyon Gray' and 'Montana', make dense, fragrant, mounding and spreading ground covers with fine-textured, gray-green leaves.

Threadleaf sage, *A. filifolia,* is a semievergreen shrub hardy to Zone 4, growing 3–4 ft. tall and wide. The very fine, threadlike, semievergreen leaves are silver-blue in summer, silver-gray in winter, and the whole plant is sweetly pungent.

A. schmidtiana 'Silver Mound' is widely sold but not highly recommended. Only in cool, dry summers does it mound into a silky, silvery dome; exposed to heat and humidity, it flops apart into a soggy gray doughnut.

Beach wormwood, *A. stellerana,* is a low-growing perennial hardy to Zone 3 that looks like dusty-miller.

Sagebrush, *A. tridentata* (now *Seriphidium tridentatum*), is a hardy (Zone 4) evergreen shrub whose velvety soft leaves have a sweet pungent aroma, especially noticeable after a rain. The fine-textured foliage stays silvery gray all year. Old plants have a gnarled shape and shredding bark.

Artemisia tridentata

Arum
Air´um.
Araceae. Arum family.

Perennials with tuberous roots, large leaves, and callalike blossoms on short stalks. About 15 spp., native to Europe and the Mediterranean region.

italicum (p. 226)
Italian arum.
Perennial. Zone 4.
H: 18 in. S: 12 in.

An unusual perennial for the shady border, it reverses the usual growing seasons. The arrow-shaped leaves, dark green with paler midrib and veins, appear in fall and remain all winter, disappearing in late spring when the stout clusters of bright orange-red berries ripen. The berries last for weeks, held just above the ground on short stalks. Interplant it among creeping phlox or other ground covers. 'Pictum' has narrow, spear-shaped leaves with cream-colored veins.

How to grow: Part sun. Ordinary soil and watering. Plant tubers at least 3 in. deep (6 in. in colder zones). Mature plants form tubers as deep as 15 in. Spreads by seed, or divide big clumps in spring or fall.

Aruncus
A-run´kus.
Rosaceae. Rose family.

Perennial herbs with large, pinnately divided leaves and showy plumes of small white flowers. Only 2 or 3 spp., native to North America and Asia.

Artemisia californica

Aruncus dioicus

dioicus (see below for photo)
Goatsbeard.
Perennial. Zone 5.
H: 4–6 ft. S: 3 ft.

This impressive streamside perennial produces long spikes of tiny white flowers in early summer. Its height and large (2–3 ft. long) compound leaves make it useful as a background plant for moist shady spots. Needs plenty of space but makes a dramatic cloud of bloom. 'Kneiffii' stays under 3 ft. tall, and its leaves are more finely divided. *A. aethusifolius* (p. 226) is smaller yet (under 12 in.), with creamy flowers and sharply cut leaves.

How to grow: Part sun or shade. Ordinary or better soil. Prefers constant moisture and can't tolerate much heat. Divide in spring or fall.

Arundinaria

A-run-di-nayr′ee-a.
Gramineae. Grass family.

Hardy bamboos with spreading rhizomes and leafy upright stems. Flowering is rare; when it occurs, all members of a species flower simultaneously over a large area. About 30 spp., native to the Old and New World.

viridistriata (p. 208)
(now *Pleioblastus viridistriatus;* has been given many other names)
Running bamboo. Zone 4.
H: 30 in. S: indefinite.

Use this spreading bamboo as a ground cover to control erosion on steep banks or as a tough, low-maintenance cover for areas surrounded by concrete sidewalks or drives. It is invasive but less so than other dwarf running bamboos. The new leaves are vibrant gold with bright green stripes. Use it to brighten a shady corner or woodland edge, and try interplanting it with gold or purple crocuses, yellow narcissus, and red or purple tulips. Can be grown in a container on a deck or patio. *A. variegata,* 1–3 ft. in height, is similar but has white-striped leaves; it runs aggressively and must be confined.

How to grow: Tolerates shade, but sun makes the leaves a brighter yellow. Ordinary soil and watering. Hardier than formerly acknowledged; tops freeze back, but runners survive. Buy one to start with; you can soon divide it if you want more. Use hand pruners or a string trimmer to mow off old stems in spring.

Asarum

Ass′a-rum. Wild ginger.
Aristolochiaceae. Birthwort family.

Evergreen or deciduous perennials that spread to form a low carpet of heart-shaped leaves. Many have ginger-scented rhizomes, used as medicine but not for seasoning. The unusual dark flowers hide under the leaves in early spring. About 70 spp., native to the north temperate zone.

canadense (p. 226)
Eastern wild ginger.
Perennial. Zone 2.
H: 6 in. S: 12 in.

Plant this deciduous ground cover at the edge of a shady border or along a woodland path where its thick-textured, heart-shaped, 6-in.-wide leaves can contrast with lacy ferns, astilbes, or aruncus. An easy-to-grow wildflower, it spreads slowly to make a thick carpet. *A. caudatum,* a western native, has glossier leaves.

How to grow: Filtered sun to dense shade. Needs well-drained, organic soil and prefers constant moisture. Plant 12 in. apart for ground cover. Propagate by division at any time during the period of active growth. Seeds take 2 years to germinate and another 2 years to mature. Carefree but subject to slugs and snails.

Asarum europaeum

europaeum (p. 226)
European wild ginger.
Perennial. Zone 4.
H: 6 in. S: 12 in.

Plant this evergreen ground cover close to your entry or walkway so you can enjoy its glossy, leathery, dark green leaves every day of the year. The heart- or kidney-shaped leaves are 3 in. wide. *A. hartwegii,* native to the Sierras, has especially pretty evergreen leaves with silver veins. *A. shuttleworthii* (also called *Hexastylis shuttleworthii*), native to the southern Appalachians, has mottled evergreen leaves and tolerates heat better than other wild gingers do.

How to grow: Like *A. canadense.*

Asclepias

As-klee′pee-us. Milkweed.
Asclepiadaceae. Milkweed family.

Perennials with upright stems, milky sap, simple leaves, clusters of waxy flowers, decorative pods, and silky-plumed seeds. About 120 spp., most native to North America.

tuberosa (p. 226)
Butterfly weed.
Perennial. Zone 3.
H: 1–1¹/₂ ft. S: 1–2 ft.

Forms a clump of upright stems surrounded with narrow green leaves and topped with spectacular flat clusters, 2–5 in. wide, of bright orange flowers in summer. Makes a long-lasting fresh cut flower, and cutting often induces a second round of bloom. Gather the slender tan pods in fall for dried bouquets. The 'Gay Butterflies' strain includes flowers in shades of

Asclepias tuberosa

orange, yellow, and red. *A. curassavica* is a tropical species with similar flowers in smaller clusters; it blooms in 4 months from seed and can be grown as an annual. All attract butterflies.

How to grow: Full sun. Tolerates poor or dry soil and heat. Sow fresh seeds in fall for bloom in 2–3 years. Choose a site and leave it there; old plants have large brittle roots, which makes transplanting difficult. Occasionally defoliated by monarch butterfly larvae, but that doesn't permanently damage the plants. Susceptible to aphids and powdery mildew.

Asparagus

As-pair´a-gus.
Liliaceae. Lily family.

Perennials, sometimes woody or thorny, with thick or tuberous roots. Stems branch repeatedly to make a fluffy mass of green, but the true leaves are inconspicuous dry scales. The starry flowers, which often are fragrant, are followed by plump colored berries. About 100 spp., native to the Old World, including the vegetable asparagus.

densiflorus (p. 227)

Ornamental asparagus, asparagus fern.
Tender perennial. Zone 9.
H: 2 ft. or more. S: 3 ft. or more.

Forms a clump of slender, sometimes prickly stems clothed with thousands of thin flat branchlets that look like evergreen needles or leaves. Dotted with fragrant, starry white flowers in late spring. 'Sprengeri' has arching or drooping stems (up to 6 ft. long) with bright green or yellow-green needles in bunches of 3. 'Myers' has stiffly erect stems (to 2 ft. or more) with dark green needles and looks like a bouquet of fluffy green foxtails. Both are excellent for containers, outdoors or in. 'Sprengeri' drapes gracefully from a hanging basket, window box, or raised bed. 'Myers' is an unusual and effective companion for bedding plants such as impatiens.

How to grow: Full or part sun. Ordinary soil and watering. Stores water in fleshy tubercles on roots and can withstand dry periods but looks better with generous moisture. Fertilize potted specimens frequently from spring to fall. The tops may freeze, but plants resprout from the base. Divide old clumps in spring. Trouble-free.

Aspidistra

As-pi-dis´tra.
Liliaceae. Lily family.

Tender evergreen perennials with creeping rhizomes and long-lasting, broad, leathery leaves held straight up. Dull flowers at ground level. Only 3 spp., native to eastern Asia.

elatior (p. 227)

Cast-iron plant.
Perennial. Zone 7.
H: 30 in. S: forms patch.

Tough, glossy, evergreen leaves, up to 30 in.

tall and 3–4 in. wide, arise singly from a creeping rhizome. Called cast-iron plant for its unique tolerance of low light, dry air, dust, erratic watering, and other vagaries of indoor life, but with good care it makes a handsome specimen to be proud of. A top container plant and also extremely useful in heavily shaded areas—under stairs, for example. In better light it makes an attractive companion/understory for azaleas or camellias. Variegated forms have leaves striped, streaked, or speckled with white; too much fertilizer can make them revert to all green.

How to grow: Part sun or shade. Ordinary soil and watering. Divide and/or repot in spring or fall every few years. Tolerates heat. Subject to spider mites where the air is very dry; hosing dust off the leaves helps keep these pests at bay.

Aster

As´ter.
Compositae. Daisy family.

Perennials of variable habit, from 6 in. to 7 ft. tall. Most have leafy branching stems topped with blossoms in summer or fall. The round daisylike blooms have threadlike purple, blue, pink, or white rays around a yellow or orange disk. About 250 spp., native to the Old and New World. The native species are increasingly popular in the East, and several hybrids and cultivars are grown across the country.

×frikartii (p. 227)

Perennial. Zone 6.
H: 2–3 ft. S: 2 ft.

Forms loose mounds of healthy, fairly mildew-resistant foliage, and each branch is tipped with a fragrant, 2½-in. daisy. Blooms for months in summer and fall, continuing into winter in mild climates. Lovely combined with the rosy pea-blossoms of *Lespedeza thunbergii*. 'Monch' is a strong upright plant with blossoms in a particularly lovely shade of pale lavender-blue. 'Wonder of Staffa' has weaker stems (may need staking) and darker flowers.

How to grow: Full or part sun. Ordinary or better soil. Cut back after flowering, and divide at least every other year in spring. Often listed as hardy in Zone 5 but doesn't survive there, even if protected with boughs.

novae-angliae (p. 227)

New England aster, Michaelmas daisy.
Perennial. Zone 3.
H: to 6 ft. S: 3 ft.

A symbol of the fall landscape in New England, these asters give lots of color at the end of the season when not much else is blooming. The rough-surfaced stems are stiff—almost woody—and clothed from the base with gray-green leaves 4–5 in. long, branching at the top to bear dozens of 1–2-in. daisies that open for several weeks between August and October. All forms have yellow disks, but the rays can be purple, violet, or shades of pink. Stake them early, before the stems fall over, and hide the lower

Aspidistra elatior

Aster novae-angliae

leaves (which often discolor early) behind a bushy clump of Japanese anemones or artemisias. Popular cultivars include 'Alma Potschke' (hot pink blooms for up to 6 weeks), 'Harrington's Pink' (salmon-pink flowers late in the season), 'Treasurer' (violet flowers on very tall stems), 'Hella' (deep violet-purple flowers), and 'Purple Dome' (deep purple flowers on a compact plant only 18 in. tall).

A. *novi-belgii,* New York asters, are also called Michaelmas daisies. They tend to grow shorter than New England asters but are more vulnerable to foliar diseases. These have been hybridized to yield a wonderful range of flower colors—everything from snowy white and palest lavender through darker purple, deep red, and pink—on dwarf, medium, and tall plants. Unless the weather is terribly hot and dry, you can have mounds of bloom for many weeks.

How to grow: Full or part sun. Ordinary soil. Divide every year or two in spring, replanting the outer new growth and discarding the old center. Spacing them generously and keeping the soil moist helps reduce the severity of foliar mildew. Cut stems back halfway in early summer to make shorter, stronger, and bushier clumps. Even so, you'll probably need to stake tall cultivars.

tataricus (p. 227)
Tartarian daisy.
Perennial. Zone 3.
H: to 7 ft. S: 3 ft.

A stately giant for large gardens, with lower leaves up to 2 ft. long. The tall erect stems are topped with violet-blue daisies late into the fall. Combine it with the cheery sunflowers of *Helianthus angustifolius* and the silvery plumes of *Miscanthus sinensis* 'Silver Feather' to close the season in triumph.

How to grow: Full sun. Ordinary soil. Tolerates both cold and heat. Divide every year or two. May hold up without staking.

Selected cultivars of hybrid astilbes

'Bressingham Beauty': pure pink, late midseason, 36 in.

'Bridal Veil': pure white, midseason, 36 in.

'Cattleya': orchid pink, late, 42 in.

'Deutchland': white, early, 18 in.

'Fanal': deep red, early midseason, 30 in.

'Glow' ('Glut'): dark red, late, 36 in.

'Peach Blossom': salmon-pink, early midseason, 24 in.

'Red Sentinel': deep purplish red, midseason, 20 in.

'Rheinland': carmine-pink, early, 24 in.

'White Gloria': creamy white, midseason, 24 in.

other native asters (p. 227)

A. *alpinus,* the alpine aster, is a compact (under 12 in.) plant that blooms in late spring, unlike most asters. The 1–2-in.-wide daisies are borne singly and have yellow disks and lavender, blue, white, or dark pink rays.

A. *divaricatus,* the white wood aster, prefers shady spots, where it spreads to make a clump 2–3 ft. high and wide, filling gaps in the summer garden and hiding the foliage of early bloomers. It has handsome green leaves, burgundy stems, and dense clusters of small white flowers in September.

A. *ericoides,* the heath aster, is a bushy plant 1–3 ft. tall, with dainty leaves and starry 1/2-in. daisies on wiry, twiggy stems. Easy to grow and charming in a casual border or natural planting. 'Ring Dove' reaches 3 ft. tall and has pale blue flowers. Can grow for years without being divided.

A. *lateriflorus* var. *horizontalis,* the calico aster, forms a 2–4-ft. mound of much-branched stems with small reddish leaves. In fall the whole plant is speckled with 1/2-in.-wide blossoms with white or lavender rays and purplish disks. Tolerates sun and dry soil.

A. *linarifolius,* the stiff-leaved or bristly aster, looks like a small evergreen, forming distinct rounded clumps (to 18 in. tall) of stiff, deep green, glossy foliage. Blooms for 3–4 weeks in early fall, with blue to violet rays and yellow or reddish disks.

Astilbe
As-till´bee.
Saxifragaceae. Saxifrage family.

Perennials with a mound of simple or compound leaves and upright plumes of tiny pink, red, or white flowers. About 14 spp., two from the Appalachians, the rest from eastern Asia. Most of the cultivars are hybrids.

× *arendsii* hybrids (p. 228)
Perennials. Zone 2.
H: 2–3 ft. S: 2–3 ft.

Astilbes are the backbone of the shady border wherever summers aren't too hot. They lift plumes of tiny flowers over mounded clumps of fernlike divided leaves. Foliage is deep green to bronze. Flowers come in shades of white, pale to dark pink, and deep purplish and carmine reds, opening between June and September; spent flowers turn reddish brown and remain attractive for months. Plant them in large drifts with hostas, bergenias, and ferns, or include them as accents in a border.

How to grow: Part sun or shade. Astilbes need fertile soil amended with organic matter and constant moisture. The site must be well drained during winter dormancy. Plant 15–18 in. apart. Divide clumps and amend the soil with peat moss or leaf mold every 2–3 years in early spring (or fall in mild climates). Astilbes are heavy feeders but otherwise are trouble-free.

Astilbe chinensis 'Pumila'

chinensis 'Pumila' (p. 228)
Plume flower.
Perennial. Zone 4.
H: under 1 ft. S: 1 ft. or more.

Use this low spreader as a ground cover or edging plant. It tolerates drier soil and more heat than other astilbes do, and it flowers later than most. Makes a crowded mat of dark green, deeply divided leaves, topped with bottlebrush-like spikes of tiny pinkish lavender flowers in late summer. Combine it with hostas or leathery polystichum ferns, or plant it in front of shrubs.

How to grow: Like *A. × arendsii,* but plant 12 in. apart.

chinensis var. taquetii 'Superba' (p. 228)
(*A. taquetii* 'Superba')
Perennial. Zone 4.
H: to 3¹/₂ ft. S: 2–3 ft.

Forms neat clumps of fernlike leaves up to 18 in. long. The latest astilbe to bloom, with tall thin panicles of pink flowers in late summer, fading to an attractive beige and lasting into fall. 'Purpurkerze' is similar, but flowers, stems, and leaves are all tinged with purple.

How to grow: Like *A. × arendsii.* Prefers fertile soil and constant moisture but endures poor soil and weeks of drought—it grows slower and stays shorter, but it blooms anyway.

simplicifolia 'Sprite' (p. 228)
Perennial. Zone 4.
H: 10 in. S: 8 in.

A dwarf astilbe with pink flowers in midseason. Leaves are finely cut and airy, bronzy at first and dark green later. Lovely as a single specimen nestled against a rock, or use it as a ground cover beneath deciduous shrubs. 'William Buchanan' is even smaller and has creamy flowers and reddish new leaves.

How to grow: Like *A. × arendsii.* Needs dividing less often; gets just slightly larger year by year.

Athyrium
A-theer´ee-um.
Polypodiaceae. Fern family.

Deciduous ferns with finely divided fronds. Perhaps as many as 180 spp. worldwide.

filix-femina (p. 216)
Lady fern.
Deciduous fern. Zone 3.
H: 2–3 ft. S: 2–3 ft.

One of the easiest ferns to grow, with delicate, finely divided, arching fronds, wider at the base and pointed at the tip. It contrasts nicely with large-leaved perennials and shrubs. Plant on the north side of a building or fence, under deciduous trees, or in a shady border. Interplant with spring-flowering bulbs. Dwarf and crested forms are sometimes available.

How to grow: Part or full shade. Plant 2 ft. apart in well-drained but constantly moist, fertile loam, in a protected area out of the wind. Place the crown on top of the soil, and mulch well with aged compost, leaf mold, or pine needles. Do not remove old fronds; they make an excellent mulch. Divide mature plants in early spring or late fall.

goeringianum 'Pictum' (p. 216)
(*A. nipponicum* 'Pictum')
Japanese painted fern.
Deciduous fern. Zone 3.
H: 12–18 in. S: 18 in.

This is America's most beautiful and most popular garden fern. The triangular fronds are tricolored in burgundy, silver-gray, and green. Plant several in a shady border or woodland garden, combined with black mondo grass, *Heuchera* 'Purple Palace', blue-leaved hostas, or deep pink primulas. *A. otophorum,* 18–24 in. tall, is another colorful fern, maturing from pale silver and greenish gold to dark green and red.

How to grow: Like *A. felix-femina,* but plant 18 in. apart.

Athyrium goeringianum

Aucuba
Aw-kew´ba.
Cornaceae. Dogwood family.

Evergreen shrubs with thick shiny leaves and red berries. Only 3 or 4 spp., native to eastern Asia and Japan.

japonica (p. 167)
Evergreen shrub. Zone 7.
H: 6–10 ft. S: 5–8 ft.

A stalwart evergreen for dark entryways that face north or for massing under trees. Also a fine container plant. Tough and undemanding, but the leathery leaves (4–8 in. long, with toothed edges) are attractive, and the females hold sealing-wax red fruits for months. (You'll need one male plant to get berries.) The variegated forms brighten shady corners. 'Variegata' (male or female), the gold-dust plant, has leaves speckled with bright yellow. 'Crotonifolia' (male) is heavily spotted with light yellow. 'Picturata' (female) leaves have a yellow center and a green edge. 'Sulphur' (female) has green leaves with a yellow edge.

How to grow: Needs some shade; tolerates heavy shade. Ordinary soil and watering. Plant from containers any time of year. Prune only to control size and form; in late winter or spring, cut back unwanted growth to just above a leaf.

Aucuba japonica

Aurinia

Aw-ri′nee-a.
Cruciferae. Mustard family.

Perennials with low rosettes of foliage and dense clusters of tiny yellow or white flowers in spring. About 7 spp., native to Eurasia.

saxatilis (p. 229)

(*Alyssum saxatile*)
Basket-of-gold, gold-dust alyssum.
Perennial. Zone 3.
H: 1–2 ft. S: to 2 ft.

One of the most cheerful sights in spring, with its fragrant masses of little gold flowers. Forms loose mounds of soft gray leaves, 2–5 in. long, on curved stems that rise from a woody base. Best planted at the front of a raised bed or where it can cascade over rocks or walls or down steps. Plant near spring bulbs; combine it with blue, gold, or white, but not pink. 'Citrinum' ('Luteum') has pale lemon yellow flowers, easier to combine with other colors in the garden. There are also dwarf, double, and variegated cultivars.

How to grow: Full sun. Does best in lean, gritty soil and must have good drainage; will not remain healthy and compact in rich soil. Takes cold but not heat. Plant in spring or fall for bloom the following year. Cut back after flowering. Easy from seed, or divide old plants in fall.

Baccharis

Bak′kar-is.
Compositae. Daisy family.

Evergreen or deciduous shrubs, some with leafless green stems. Separate male and female plants; females sometimes have showy white seed heads. About 350 spp., native to North America.

pilularis (p. 167)

Coyote brush.
Evergreen shrub. Zone 9.
H: 3 ft. S: 10 ft.

Selected male forms of this coastal California native make excellent evergreen ground covers for West Coast gardeners. Leaves are small, thick, and resinous, dark green or gray-green. 'Twin Peaks' is a low, compact form; 'Pigeon Point', with light green leaves, is fast-growing.

Gardeners in the East can plant *B. halimifolia,* a hardy (Zone 6) coastal shrub that tolerates salt spray and constantly wet soil but also does well in ordinary garden conditions. Its light gray-green leaves persist into winter, and the large clusters of white fruiting heads on female plants are very showy in late fall.

How to grow: Full sun. Tolerates poor or dry soil and heat but isn't hurt by irrigation. Plant in fall, 3–4 ft. apart. Prune or shear as often as once a year to shape or to control height. Overgrown plants can be cut back by half to rejuvenate.

Baccharis halimifolia

Baileya

Bay′lee-a.
Compositae. Daisy family.

Perennials with woolly leaves and stems and yellow daisy blossoms. Only 4 spp., native to the southwestern United States and Mexico.

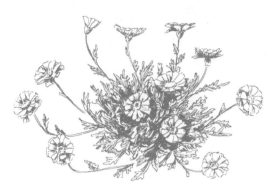

Baileya multiradiata

multiradiata (p. 291)

Desert marigold.
Biennial or short-lived perennial. Zone 6.
H: 12–18 in. S: 12–18 in.

An excellent addition to very hot, dry desert gardens, suitable for borders, in mass plantings, or naturalized. Clear, bright yellow, daisylike flowers, about 1 1/2 in. in diameter, rise on nearly leafless stems above mounds of woolly white foliage. Depending on when seeds germinate, plants may flower from April to October; individual plants flower for several months.

How to grow: Full sun. Tolerates poor or dry soil and heat. Sow fresh seeds in fall. A stand will self-seed, but the surface of the soil must be repeatedly disturbed to ensure adequate germination. (Dogs running regularly through a patch will do the trick.) Rosettes require a period of cold-weather dormancy to set buds.

Bambusa

Bam-boo′sa. Bamboo.
Gramineae. Grass family.

Clump-forming bamboos, some with large woody culms. About 100 spp., native to tropical and warm climates.

multiplex 'Alphonse Karr'

Clumping bamboo. Zone 8.
H: 10–20 ft. S: 10–12 ft.

Makes a tall graceful fountain of arching stems topped by clouds of feathery green foliage. Stems are vertically striped bright yellow and green. Thin papery leaves, 4 in. long by 1/2 in. wide, are bright green with an occasional faint yellow stripe. Doesn't spread, so it's safe to plant several for a tall screen.

How to grow: Sun or shade. Ordinary soil and watering. For screens, plant 5–6 ft. apart. Divide in spring if you want more plants. Occasionally remove old stems that are tattered or leafless.

oldhamii (p. 208)
Giant timber bamboo.
Clumping bamboo. Zone 8.
H: 50–55 ft. S: 20 ft.

Truly a giant, it makes a huge green fountain for tropical or Oriental effects. The stems are green, turning yellow, up to 4 in. thick, and make good poles for fencing or other garden structures. The thin, bright green leaves are up to 12 in. long. Use single plants or pairs to mark an impressive entry. Plant with bananas, elephant's-ear, or gingers for a tropical effect. This bamboo is a clumper. Another giant timber bamboo, *Phyllostachys bambusoides,* is a runner and will in time form open groves to 45 ft. tall, with 6-in. stems. It is hardier (Zone 7) than *B. oldhamii.*

How to grow: Full sun. Ordinary soil and watering okay, but grows larger with fertile soil and ample water. One plant is usually enough. For a really big screen to block undesirable views, plant 10–15 ft. apart. To divide old plants, use pick, ax, and saw in spring. The fallen leaves of all bamboos may be considered litter, or you could think of them as an attractive, weed-suppressive mulch.

Baptisia

Bap-tiz´ee-a. False indigo, wild indigo.
Leguminosae. Pea family.

Perennials forming bushy clumps of upright stems with trifoliate leaves, pealike flowers, and inflated pods. About 17 spp., native to eastern North America.

Baptisia australis

australis (p. 229)
False indigo.
Perennial. Zone 3.
H: 3–4 ft. S: 4–6 ft. or more.

One of the best perennials for borders, meadow gardens, or naturalized landscapes. Attractive throughout the season. Foot-long racemes of small (1 in.), indigo blue flowers appear in midspring and last for 3–5 weeks. The shrubby mound of light blue-green foliage is a perfect backdrop all summer. From midsummer into winter the plant displays large, woody, charcoal-colored pods. *B. alba* grows slightly taller and has tall spikes of white flowers. *B. leucantha* has large white flowers and blooms later than the other species. All are native to the eastern or central states.

How to grow: Full or part sun. Prefers fertile, organic soil. Tolerates poor or dry soil and

heat. Can be raised from seed but won't flower for a few years. Set purchased plants in their permanent location; they develop big root systems and don't transplant well. Established plants are trouble-free and long lived.

Begonia

Bee-go´nee-a.
Begoniaceae. Begonia family.

Tender perennials or shrubs, often divided as having tuberous, rhizomatous, or fibrous roots. Leaves exhibit a tremendous variety of sizes, shapes, colors, and textures. Many kinds of begonias have abundant, brilliant, waxy flowers. About 900 to 1,000 spp., native to tropical climates, with more than 10,000 recorded hybrids and cultivars.

× ***semperflorens-cultorum*** (p. 291)
Wax begonia.
Tender perennial grown as an annual. All zones.
H: 6–12 in. S: 6–12 in.

A favorite for bedding and containers, these compact, leafy plants are covered with flowers for months on end. The fleshy stems branch repeatedly, making bushy mounds. The green, green-and-white, reddish purple, or bronze leaves always look fresh and shiny. Look closely and you'll see that the red, pink, or white blossoms occur in separate clusters of male flowers (slightly larger, with a tuft of yellow stamens) and female flowers (smaller, with a winged ovary behind the petals).

Use begonias with impatiens and ferns to fill partly shaded beds under tall trees or along the east or north side of buildings or fences. The bronze- or purple-leaved forms are darkest if grown in the sun; use them with ageratum or dusty-miller to edge beds and borders. All begonias are excellent for window boxes and patio planters. Dozens of strains are listed in every seed catalog and available at local nurseries every spring.

How to grow: Full or part sun. Prefers fertile soil and regular moisture. Tolerates occasional dryness but can't take soggy conditions. Cuttings root easily, and seeds, though tiny, germinate and grow quickly. Plant outdoors after frost, then sit back and enjoy them all summer.

Tuberhybrida hybrids (p. 291)
Tuberous begonias.
Tender perennials grown for summer display. All zones.
H: to 2 ft. S: to 2 ft.

A triumph in the art and science of plant breeding, tuberous begonias produce huge flowers in every color except blue. The hanging types are perhaps the most spectacular of all plants for baskets and raised planters. The upright types need staking but reward you with blossoms of incredible lushness. Flowers are single, semidouble, or double, with plain or frilled petals, 2–8 in. wide, in white, cream, yellow, orange, pink, apricot, salmon, red, or crimson. For the widest

***Begonia* hybrid**

selection, order tubers from specialty nursery catalogs.

How to grow: Filtered shade. Tuberous begonias need fertile soil and regular watering. They do best where summers are cool and moist—along the Pacific Coast or in the Northeast. Start tubers in flats indoors, several weeks before the last frost, and pot or plant them out when the shoots are 3 in. tall. In fall, let the tops dry out and die down, then lift the tubers and store them in a cool, dry place.

Belamcanda
Bel-am-kan´da.
Iridaceae. Iris family.

Perennials with stout rhizomes, irislike leaves, colorful flowers, and seed clusters that resemble blackberries. Only 2 spp., native to eastern Asia.

chinensis (p. 229)
Blackberry lily, leopard lily.
Perennial. Zone 6 or 5.
H: 2–3 ft. S: 1 ft.

An interesting plant with flat sheaves of leaves on zigzag stalks, topped in summer with dark-spotted orange flowers. Best of all are the pods stuffed with shiny black seeds. This display lasts for weeks in the garden, or you can gather them for winter arrangements. A hybrid originated by Park Seed, × *Pardancanda norrisii,* has larger flowers in a wide range of colors.

How to grow: Needs full sun; is floppy in shade. Needs well-drained soil. Tolerates heat and dryness but doesn't get as tall. Easy from seed, and blooms the first or second year. Remove all debris in fall to reduce problems with iris borers and foliar leafspot.

Bellis
Bel´lis.
Compositae. Daisy family.

Perennials with low leafy rosettes and aster-like blossoms on short stalks. About 7 spp., native to Europe.

perennis (p. 292)
English daisy.
Grown as an annual. Zone 4.
H: 6 in. S: 6 in.

This was once a humble lawn weed, but plant breeders have developed new strains with flowers large enough to be quite showy. The daisylike blossoms, 1^1/$_2$–3 in. wide, have a yellow disk surrounded by hundreds of needle-fine rays in pink, rose, red, or white. Blossoms are borne singly on short stalks, above a rosette of simple dark green leaves. A favorite edging plant, charming when planted among stepping-stones or in rockeries, or a pretty low companion for spring bulbs.

How to grow: Full or part sun. Ordinary soil and watering okay, but prefers moist, fertile soil. Plant seedlings 4 in. apart in autumn for bloom the following spring. Deadhead to prolong flowering, but plants will die in the heat of summer.

Berberis
Ber´ber-iss. Barberry.
Berberidaceae. Barberry family.

Evergreen or deciduous shrubs, usually spiny, with bright yellow wood. Some have abundant yellow flowers and persistent red, yellow, or black berries. About 450 spp., native to Eurasia and Africa.

julianae (p. 167)
Wintergreen barberry.
Evergreen shrub. Zone 5.
H: 8 ft. S: 8 ft. or more.

A hardy evergreen shrub with a dense twiggy habit, abundant foliage, and clusters of needlelike thorns. Makes an excellent barrier planting—a barberry hedge would stop the neighborhood horde from invading. Leaves are long, thin, and willowlike, with spiny edges and a thick leathery texture. Bright yellow flowers in spring and dark blue-black berries in fall add contrast. 'Nana' is a dwarf cultivar, about 4 ft. tall and wide.

How to grow: Full sun. Ordinary or unimproved soil. Tolerates heat and dryness. Plant 6 ft. apart to make a hedge. Remove dead stems and prune to shape after flowering. This may be the hardiest evergreen barberry, but its leaves will turn brown or drop if exposed to cold, dry, winter winds. A sheltered site or a covering of snow will protect the leaves from damage.

koreana (p. 131)
Korean barberry.
Deciduous shrub. Zone 3.
H: 6 ft. S: 4–6 ft.

Noteworthy among barberries for its drooping clusters of yellow flowers in late spring, followed by bright red berries that dangle like beaded earrings in fall and winter. Foliage is dark green in summer, maroon to magenta until late fall. Very hardy and tough, ideal for barriers but handsome enough to include in mixed borders. Makes a dense mound of spiny stems.

How to grow: Like *B. julianae,* but plant 4 ft. apart for a hedge.

× *mentorensis* (p. 131)
(*B. julianae* × *B. thunbergii*)
Mentor barberry.
Deciduous shrub. Zone 5.
H: 6 ft. S: 6 ft. or more.

A tough, durable shrub with teardrop-shaped leaves that turn a fiery red-orange in fall. Semievergreen in mild climates. It forms a multistemmed, upright, densely branched dome that's loaded with spines. Most useful as a hedge or barrier planting, but it does tend to catch blowing papers or litter.

How to grow: Like *B. julianae.* Makes a dense hedge naturally and doesn't need pruning.

Berberis thunbergii

thunbergii (p. 131)
Japanese barberry.
Deciduous shrub. Zone 4.
H: to 6 ft. S: to 6 ft.

Long a staple for hedges, the newer cultivars of this tough, reliable shrub offer compact habit and richly colored foliage. All have dense thorny stems, small teardrop-shaped leaves, and bright red berries in fall. For best color, plant in full sun. The compact cultivars grow naturally round without pruning and are easy but handsome additions to a foundation or entryway planting. The purple-leaved forms are useful in mixed borders because they combine well with most pink- or blue-flowered perennials.

The following cultivars are especially popular and do well in most parts of the country. The Atropurpurea group (full-size plants) includes those with purplish red foliage that turns gold in fall. 'Rosy Glow' (full-size) has new leaves mottled rosy pink and silver, maturing to reddish purple. 'Aurea' (to 4 ft.) has leaves that emerge golden yellow and turn green later in the season. 'Sparkle' (to 4 ft.) has foliage that turns red, orange, and yellow in fall. 'Atropurpurea Nana', also called 'Crimson Pygmy', has deep crimson coloring and a very compact, rounded shape (2 ft. high by 5 ft. wide). 'Kobold' is equally compact, with bright green leaves.

How to grow: Like *B. julianae*. Very hardy to cold but weakened by extremely hot summers.

verruculosa (p. 167)
Warty barberry.
Evergreen shrub. Zone 6 or 5.
H: to 6 ft. S: to 6 ft.

"Warty" refers to the rough little bumps on the stems; this shrub's foliage is smooth and glossy. It's a handsome evergreen for cold climates, with hollylike leaves that turn purplish or bronzy in winter, bright yellow flowers, and dark blue-black berries. Grows upright with branches sticking out at random but can be pruned to a rounded contour. *B.* × *gladwynensis* 'William Penn', another hardy evergreen barberry, has a more compact, mounded habit and stays under 4 ft. tall.

How to grow: Like *B. julianae*.

Bergenia
Ber-jean'ee-a.
Saxifragaceae. Saxifrage family.
Perennials, often evergreen, forming large clumps of substantial leaves with clusters of small flowers on upright stalks. Fewer than 10 spp., native to eastern Asia, and many hybrids.

cordifolia (p. 229)
Heartleaf bergenia.
Perennial. Zone 3.
H: 18 in. S: 12–24 in.

This hardy and vigorous perennial forms a clump of large, thick, cabbagelike leaves, waxy and green in summer, turning rich glossy red in fall as the temperature starts to drop. In mild climates the foliage stays pretty all winter. Nodding clusters of pink flowers rise barely above the leaves in spring. Use it as an edging in the front of a border or along walkways or as a ground cover under deciduous trees. Makes a nice contrast with the divided foliage of ferns or astilbes. Many nurseries now carry hybrid cultivars selected for outstanding winter foliage or prettier flowers on taller stalks. These include 'Bressingham White', 'Rotblum', 'Silver Light' ('Silberlicht'), and 'Sunningdale'.

How to grow: Sun or part shade. Ordinary soil. Water during hot, dry periods. In cold areas, mulch lightly to protect the leaves from winter sun. Plant the thick rhizomes 12–15 in. apart. Divide crowded plantings in spring or fall. The leaves must be as tender and tasty as cabbage—they attract just as many pests, including aphids, slugs, snails, caterpillars, rabbits, chipmunks, and squirrels.

Betula
Bet'you-la. Birch.
Betulaceae. Birch family.
Deciduous trees or shrubs, most fast-growing but short lived. Many have white or colored peeling bark, a graceful weeping habit, and/or golden fall color. About 60 spp., most native to cool northern climates in the Old and New World.

jacquemontii (p. 106)
(*B. utilis* var. *jacquemontii*)
Himalayan birch.
Deciduous tree. Zone 5.
H: 40 ft. S: 20 ft.

The bark of this tree is simply outstanding—it's so white as to appear painted or artificial. It makes a stunning specimen, especially when backed by evergreens. Combine it with colored-twig dogwoods and bright-berried deciduous hollies for a striking winter scene. Grows upright with a single trunk and a narrow oval crown. The coarsely toothed leaves are dark green in summer, golden in fall.

How to grow: Full or part sun. Ordinary soil and watering, with supplemental irrigation during dry periods. Newly planted trees may need staking for the first year or two. This tree is somewhat resistant to leafminers and bronze birch borers, but close monitoring is advised.

Betula nigra

nigra (p. 106)
River birch, red birch, black birch.
Deciduous tree. Zone 4.
H: 40–70 ft. S: 40–60 ft.

Its shimmering leaves and light, shredding bark on single or multiple trunks make river birch handsome year-round. Especially useful for troublesome wet sites and in hot, humid climates where other birches may not survive. 'Heritage' has lighter bark that peels in large curly sheets and makes a good substitute for paper birch in warmer regions.

How to grow: Full or part sun. Transplant when dormant. Prefers fertile, organic, acidic soil. Tolerates constant moisture and heat. Roots are shallow, so don't plant it near walks, driveways, or fences. Crotches of multiple trunks can weaken with age.

pendula (p. 110)
(*B. alba, B. verrucosa*)
European white birch.
Deciduous tree. Zone 2.
H: 40 ft. S: 20 ft.

A graceful tree with an erect trunk, drooping branchlets, white bark, and shiny, bright, diamond-shaped leaves that turn gold in fall. Plant a clump or grove against a background of conifers for a northern forest look. Attractive beside a pool or stream, and the winter silhouette softens the walls of a tall house. Two unique forms are 'Dalecarlica' ('Laciniata'), a graceful weeping tree with deeply lobed leaves, and 'Trost's Dwarf', a bonsai-sized mound of arching branches with skeletal leaves. Gardeners in New England and the Great Lakes states often plant the native white or paper birch, *B. papyrifera*. It is less graceful but more resistant to bronze birch borers than the European white birch is.

How to grow: Full or part sun. Ordinary soil and watering. Can't take desert heat or the damp heat of the Deep South. Plant dormant trees in early spring. Prune in winter to correct the form or to thin for better light penetration to the interior. Aphids on the foliage drip honeydew on everything below. Birch borers and leafminers are serious problems in some areas; ask locally. Surface roots can impede lawn maintenance, so use a ground cover instead of turf.

platyphylla **var.** ***japonica*** **'Whitespire'**
(p. 110)
Whitespire birch.
Deciduous tree. Zone 4.
H: 45 ft. S: 20 ft.

This is the best white-barked birch. It is resistant to bronze birch borers, has a narrow upright habit that fits today's shrinking landscapes, and has a strong central leader that holds up to snow and ice. The bark is chalky white with black triangles at the base of branches. Leaves are glossy dark green in summer, warm yellow in fall. Plant it outside a window or patio door where you can appreciate the bark in winter months, and hang a bird feeder nearby.

How to grow: Full or part sun. Ordinary soil and watering. Plant 10–15 ft. apart to make a grove.

Bignonia
Big-known´ee-a. Trumpet vine.
Bignoniaceae. Trumpet creeper family.

Woody vines with showy flowers. Formerly a large genus, but most trumpet vines have been reclassified. Now only 1 sp., native to the southeastern United States.

Bignonia capreolata

capreolata (p. 199)
Cross vine.
Evergreen vine. Zone 6.
H: 60 ft.

This easy-to-grow vine will climb and cover masonry walls, fences, trees, arbors, and trellises. It's an interesting and unusual plant. Trumpet-shaped flowers, yellow outside and red within, smother the foliage for a few weeks in late spring just as the ruby-throated hummingbirds return. Beanlike seedpods ripen from green to brown and hang on through winter. The compound leaves have 2 long, narrow leaflets on either side and a branching, disk-tipped tendril in the center. Cut through the stem to see the "cross" pattern inside. Some nurseries carry a special form with purplish red flowers.

How to grow: Needs full sun for the best flowering and foliage display but can grow in part shade. Tolerates poorly drained soil. Provide support and prune to shape.

Boltonia
Bole-ton´ee-a.
Compositae. Daisy family.

Perennials forming clumps of upright leafy stems with small but profuse asterlike blossoms in late summer and fall. Fewer than 10 spp., native to the eastern United States and eastern Asia.

asteroides (p. 229)
Perennial. Zone 4.
H: 3–5 ft. S: 4–5 ft.

This large, open plant with fine, blue-green leaves is covered for 3–5 weeks in late summer with clusters of 1-in. blossoms that have white rays and yellow disks. Best for moist, open, natural plantings where it can freely spread among and blend with brighter fall colors. 'Snowbank', an erect cultivar that doesn't need staking, is best for borders. 'Pink Beauty' has light pink rays.

How to grow: Full or part sun. Prefers fertile, organic soil. Tolerates heat. Plant 3 ft. or more apart. Divide every 2–3 years in fall or early spring. Cut the stems back by a third in late spring to keep them from flopping over later.

Borago
Bo-ray´go. Borage.
Boraginaceae. Borage family.
Annuals or perennials with hairy leaves and stems and star-shaped blue flowers. Only 3 spp., native to the Mediterranean region.

officinalis (p. 281)
Borage.
Annual herb. All zones.
H: 24 in. S: 12 in.
Grow borage for its starry, sky blue flowers, 3/4 in. wide, which make a beautiful garnish for drinks or dinner plates, and use the flowers or the most tender new leaves to add a cucumber flavor to salads. The large oblong leaves are rough and hairy.

How to grow: Full sun. Tolerates heat and dryness. Start seeds in peat pots or direct-sow in the garden, but do not cover, as they need light to germinate. Once started, borage usually self-sows in subsequent years. It grows fast but is attractive only when young, so plant successive crops where summers are long.

Bougainvillea
Boo-gan-vil´ee-a.
Nyctaginaceae. Four-o'clock family.
Evergreen woody vines, often spiny, sometimes shrublike. The actual flowers are small, but the bright-colored papery bracts make a show that lasts for months. About 14 spp., from Central and South America, and many hybrid cultivars.

hybrids (p. 199)
Woody vines. Zone 10 or 9.
H: to 20 ft.
Although hardy in only the mildest regions of the United States, bougainvilleas are increasingly popular as container plants to grow outdoors in summer and bring indoors for winter protection. Stems are tough and thorny, and if pruned hard they're sturdy enough to stand upright like a shrub. Where hardy, they can climb a building or wall or sprawl over a hillside. The plain green leaves are evergreen without cold but drop at the slightest frost. The masses of papery floral bracts keep their bright colors for months. Blooms form on new growth, so the plants recover quickly from frost damage or pruning. There are dozens of cultivars in colors ranging from red, orange, pink, and purple to yellow and white, including double-flowered and variegated-leaf forms. Some are dwarfs that can live in the same pot for years.

***Bougainvillea* hybrid**

'Barbara Karst' has red flowers and does well in the ground or in containers.

How to grow: Full sun in most areas; light shade in the hottest desert regions. Ordinary soil. Can tolerate occasional drying out, which seems to promote more abundant flowering. Be very careful not to disrupt the brittle roots when transplanting. Young plants are very tender, but older plants can survive a light frost. Prune away the damaged wood in spring and new growth will soon replace it. In cold climates, bring pots into a cool, bright room for the winter, and water just enough to keep the leaves from wilting.

Brachychiton
Brack-ee-ky´ton. Bottle tree.
Sterculiaceae. Chocolate family.
Evergreen or deciduous trees with swollen trunks, showy clusters of red or yellow flowers, and woody fruits. About 30 spp., native to Australia.

populneus (see below for photo)
(*Sterculia diversifolia*)
Bottle tree.
Evergreen tree. Zone 9.
H: 50 ft. S: 30 ft.
A tough tree that tolerates desert heat and dryness but has shiny, bright green leaves that shimmer like those of an aspen or poplar. The trunk is very heavy at the base, tapering quickly like a bottleneck. Useful as a street tree or a tall screen against sun, wind, or unwanted views. The flowers are not showy, but the woody 2–3-in. seedpods are conspicuous (and a minor source of litter). *B. acerifolius* (p. 156), the flame tree, drops its 10-in.-wide lobed leaves briefly in May and June, when it's covered with clouds of bell-shaped red flowers.

How to grow: Full sun. In desert areas, amend the soil with sulfur and organic matter to lessen the danger of Texas root rot. Prune only to shape or to groom.

Brahea
Bra-he´a.
Palmae. Palm family.
Fan palms, sometimes thorny, usually with a single upright trunk. Only 12 spp., native to limestone regions in Central America.

Brahea armata

armata (p. 164)
Fan palm. Zone 9.
H: to 40 ft. S: to 10 ft.

An erect, often multitrunked palm topped with palmate leaves divided into narrow 4–5-ft. strips. The leaves are pale silvery blue, and big woolly clusters of creamy white flowers appear in spring. The yellow fruits are edible. Removing the old leaves exposes the ring-striped bark on the trunk. A single plant makes a fine specimen.

How to grow: Full sun. Takes drought, heat, and wind. Grows fairly slowly but requires little care. Holds dead leaves for years until you remove them.

Brassica
Brass´i-ka.
Cruciferae. Mustard family.

A diverse group of annuals, biennials, and perennials, including cabbage, Chinese cabbage, kale, broccoli, cauliflower, mustard, turnips, canola, and some ornamentals. About 30 spp., native to the Old World, and thousands of varieties and cultivars.

oleracea (p. 292)
Flowering kale, flowering cabbage.
Annual. All zones.
H: 12 in. S: 18 in.

Looks like a giant crepe-paper flower, but the crinkly-textured rosette is actually made of brightly colored leaves. The bright pink, rose, lavender, purple, white, and/or green leaves stay crisp and colorful for months. Grows and looks best in fall and isn't damaged by frost until temperatures go below 20° F. Cheerful and easy as the centerpiece of a container planting or when surrounded with white or pink alyssum in a bed.

How to grow: Full sun. Ordinary soil and watering. Sow seeds in summer or buy plants to set out in early fall. Spring-started plants are liable to bolt in hot weather. Subject to all the pests that attack cabbage, but these usually don't do much damage late in the season.

Broussonetia
Broo-so-net´ee-a. Paper mulberry.
Moraceae. Mulberry family.

Deciduous trees or shrubs with milky sap and mulberry-like fruits. Only 7 spp., native to eastern Asia.

papyrifera (p. 110)
Paper mulberry.
Deciduous tree. Zone 5.
H: 30–50 ft. S: 30–40 ft.

A very tough and rugged tree that survives where others can't. Useful as a street or shade tree in urban environments because it tolerates compacted soil, heat, drought, and pollution. Grows fast, with a dense spreading crown. The large (up to 9 in. long and 5 in. wide) leaves may be heart-shaped or deeply lobed and have a rough sand-papery texture and gray color. In Polynesia the bark of this tree is made into a papery fabric called tapa cloth.

How to grow: Sun or shade. Grows in any soil. Needs pruning to remove suckers and to eliminate narrow branch forks. No serious pests, but the wood is brittle and easily broken by storms.

Brunnera
Brun´er-a.
Boraginaceae. Borage family.

Perennials with hairy stems, large rounded leaves, and blue forget-me-not flowers. Only 3 spp., native to Asia.

macrophylla (p. 230)
Siberian bugloss.
Perennial. Zone 3.
H: 18 in. S: 24 in.

Holds airy sprays of bright blue forget-me-not flowers on 18-in. stalks above the foliage in spring, sometimes repeating in late summer. The heart-shaped leaves, 6–8 in. wide, are dark green, hairy, and coarse. Use it as a ground cover under deciduous shrubs or naturalized in a woodland area, interplanted with spring-flowering bulbs.

How to grow: Full or part sun. Ordinary soil and watering. Plant 2 ft. apart to start. Self-sows freely and will spread by itself. Divide large clumps every few years. Slugs can be a problem.

Buchloe
Bu-klo´ee.
Gramineae. Grass family.

Perennial creeping grass with short curly blades. Only 1 sp., native to the Great Plains.

dactyloides (p. 208)
Buffalograss.
Perennial grass. Zone 5.
H: 3–5 in. S: 2 ft.

This is an excellent lawn grass for hot, dry climates, requiring deep infrequent watering, one annual fertilizing, and monthly (or less) mowing from May to September. Sage green, fine, and soft bladed when growing, straw tan and stiffer when dormant, it's an attractive ground cover when unmowed.

How to grow: Full or part sun. Tolerates poor or dry soil and heat. Sow seeds from May to August, 3–6 lb. per 1,000 sq. ft. Plant plugs 1 ft. apart. Fertilize mowed, trafficked areas in spring; no-mow areas may not need fertilizing once established. Excess water or fertilizer can lead to pest and disease problems.

Buddleia
Bud´lee-a. Butterfly bush.
Loganiaceae. Buddleia family.

Deciduous or evergreen shrubs or small trees with clusters or spikes of small flowers, often fragrant and quite popular with butterflies. About 100 spp., native to tropical and subtropical regions in the Old and New World.

alternifolia (p. 131)
Fountain butterfly bush.
Deciduous shrub. Zone 5.
H: 15 ft. S: 15 ft.

The hardiest butterfly bush, this is a large shrub or small tree with arching willowlike branches. Dense clusters of mildly fragrant lilac-purple flowers cover the previous year's stems in early summer. 'Argentea' is the prettiest form, with silky silvery leaves that sparkle in the sun. Can be trained as a single-trunked or multi-trunked tree for a graceful lawn specimen, or let it fountain down a hillside or bank.

How to grow: Full sun. Tolerates poor, dry soil. Prune after bloom by cutting some of the older stems a few inches above the ground.

Buddleia davidii

davidii (p. 131)
Butterfly bush, summer lilac.
Deciduous or semievergreen shrub. Zone 5.
H: to 10 ft. but usually less. S: to 10 ft.

A trouble-free shrub with long clusters of fragrant flowers at the tip of every arching branch. Blooms on new wood from midsummer to fall. Combine it with other shrubs and perennials in a bed or border, or plant one close to a window or patio where you can watch all the butterflies (and bees, too) come hover around the blossoms.

There are many cultivars, differing mostly in flower color. Whatever the petal color, most forms have a bright orange eye in the center of the flower. 'Charming' and 'Fascination' are pink; 'Peace' and 'White Profusion' are white; 'Empire Blue' is bluish violet; 'Fortune' is lilac; 'Black Knight' and 'Dubonnet' are rich purple. The 'Nanho' series are compact or dwarf plants, with white, blue, or purple flowers. 'Lochinch' is a hybrid between *B. davidii* and *B. fallowiana* with silvery gray leaves on especially vigorous stems and lovely lavender-blue flowers.

How to grow: Full sun. Ordinary or poor soil. Needs good drainage; tolerates considerable dryness. Looks best if you prune it to the ground each spring to force a fountain of fresh shoots each year. They'll grow at least 5 ft. tall in a season. Generally pest-free, but spider mites may attack plants in hot, dry areas.

other butterfly bushes
Buddleias are increasingly popular because their flowers are fragrant and attract butterflies. Their hardiness is uncertain above Zone 7 or 8; they may survive on well-drained sites as dieback shrubs. Try them in a sheltered spot, against a south wall perhaps, and mulch heavily in fall. The following are now available from specialty mail-order suppliers as seeds or plants.

B. asiatica is evergreen with drooping spikes of white flowers. *B. crispa* has woolly white, deciduous leaves and shorter clusters of lilac flowers. *B. fallowiana* has slender deciduous leaves and panicles of lavender flowers at the ends of the new growth. *B. globosa* is semievergreen with ball-shaped clusters of orange flowers. *B. × weyeriana* 'Sungold' is similar but has even brighter golden flowers. *B. salvifolia* has semievergreen sagelike leaves and creamy white flowers.

Butia
Bew´tee-a.
Palmae. Palm family.

Feather palms with long arching fronds atop relatively short trunks. About 8 spp., native to South America.

capitata (p. 164)
Pindo palm, jelly palm.
Feather palm. Zone 9 or 8.
H: 10–20 ft. S: to 20 ft.

One of the toughest and most durable palms, especially tolerant of growing in tubs, urns, or concrete edged beds. Has a stubby trunk topped with a lollipop-like crown of arching pinnate fronds, 6–10 ft. long by 2 ft. wide. The fronds are gray- or blue-green. Creamy white or yellow flowers fill a showy stalk in late spring, followed by edible but pulpy yellow to red fruits (sometimes gathered to make jelly).

How to grow: Full sun. Grows in any soil. Tolerates heat and dryness. Trim off the old leaves to neaten the trunk. Don't plant near a sidewalk or patio where the dropping fruits would make a messy litter.

Buxus
Bucks´us. Boxwood.
Buxaceae. Box family.

Evergreen shrubs or trees with a dense, branching, rounded habit and smooth leathery leaves. Flowers are inconspicuous. About 30 spp., native to the Old and New World.

'Green Velvet'
(*B. microphylla* var. *koreana* × *B. sempervirens*)
Evergreen shrub. Zone 4.
H: 3 ft. S: 3 ft.

An excellent evergreen for northern gardens. It keeps its deep green color even in severely cold winters and grows naturally round without any pruning. The small rounded leaves are thick and glossy, and there are inconspicuous but fragrant flowers in early spring. Ideal for foundation planting and provides structure and color to mixed borders throughout the barren winter months. Resistant to deer. This is one of a series of new hybrids that combine the hardiness of Korean box with the green winter color of common box. 'Green Mound' and 'Green Gem' are similar to 'Green Velvet'. 'Chicagoland Green' is faster growing and finer textured. 'Green Mountain' forms an upright oval, 5 ft. by 3 ft., instead of a ball and is excellent for hedging.

How to grow: Full or part sun. Plant in spring to summer in good soil, mulch to cover the shallow roots, and water regularly for the first year. You'll never have to touch it again, but you'll enjoy it for years to come.

microphylla (p. 167)
Littleleaf box.
Evergreen shrub. Zone 5.
H: to 4 ft. S: to 4 ft.

The dense branching and closely set, glossy, fine-textured foliage make this ideal for low hedges, foundation plantings, or containers, and it can be sheared into formal shapes or topiary.

There are two main varieties and many cultivars, which differ in habit and mature size, winter foliage color, and hardiness. Var. *japonica* is the most robust, with an open, spreading habit. It tolerates dryness, heat, and alkaline soil. Var. *koreana* grows slower and shorter. It's quite hardy, but it can turn an ugly yellowish brown in winter. 'Compacta', 'Green Beauty', 'Winter Beauty', 'Winter Gem', and 'Wintergreen' are selected cultivars with a compact habit and good green color even in cold winters.

How to grow: Full or part sun. Needs well-drained soil and regular watering. Boxwoods have shallow roots that need special attention. Apply mulch to keep them from drying out, but leave an open space around the trunk to prevent stem rot. Be careful when weeding, and never cultivate in the root zone. Subject to several pests, including leafminers, spider mites, and nematodes.

sempervirens (p. 167)
English box, common box.
Evergreen shrub. Zone 5.
H: 3–20 ft., depending on cultivar.
S: equal to height.

A fine-textured evergreen shrub for specimens, screens, or accents. It grows naturally into a round or oval mound, or you can shear it into formal shapes. Old plants reach considerable size but hold their leaves all the way to the ground. The leaves have a distinct fragrance, appreciated by some but not by all. The flowers in spring are also fragrant.

Boxwood is especially popular along the East Coast, where it's associated with stately old homes. The specimens at Colonial Williamsburg and other historic sites in Virginia are truly impressive. There are many cultivars, erect and spreading, solid green and variegated.

'Suffruticosa' is a compact, slow-growing form often used to edge formal beds. Unpruned, it makes a low billowing mound.

How to grow: Full or part sun. Needs well-drained soil and regular watering. Can't tolerate extreme heat or alkaline soil. Subject to root rot, leafminers, spider mites, and nematodes. Where it grows well, it's easy. Where it doesn't, don't bother planting it.

Caesalpinia
See-zal-pin´ee-a.
Leguminosae. Pea family.

Evergreen or deciduous shrubs or small trees with pinnately compound leaves and bright red or yellow flowers. About 100 spp., from tropical and subtropical regions in the Old and New World.

gilliesii (p. 132)
Bird-of-paradise.
Deciduous shrub. Zone 8.
H: 10 ft. S: 10 ft.

An easy, quick-growing shrub that thrives in hot weather, with feathery twice-compound leaves on long shoots tipped with clusters of exotic flowers. Blooms all summer. Flowers have yellow petals and bright red stamens, 4–5 in. long, and attract hummingbirds. It drops leaves and then freezes to the ground in cold weather, but it sprouts back from the base the following year. Makes a showy accent or a quick screen. *C. pulcherrima,* the red bird-of-paradise, has wonderful bright orange-red flowers but is hardy only to Zone 10.

How to grow: Full sun. Needs well-drained soil. Tolerates dry spells with occasional deep watering. Cut to the ground if frozen back or to renew dense growth from the base.

Caladium
Ka-lay´dee-um.
Araceae. Arum family.

Tender perennials with basal tubers sprouting clumps of large, often colorful leaves. About 7 spp., native to tropical South America.

× *hortulanum* (p. 292)
(*C. bicolor*)
Tender perennial grown as an annual. All zones.
H: 1–3 ft. S: 2 ft.

Plant tubers in spring and enjoy the brightly colored foliage until frost. The large (to 12 in. long) arrowhead-shaped leaves have a delicate papery texture and come in solid, mottled, or spotted patterns of crimson, rose, pink, pale green, and translucent white. Lovely mixed with ferns and often planted in partly shady beds underneath trees or on the north side of a house. Also does well in containers.

Two related plants, *Alocasia macrorrhiza* and *Colocasia esculenta,* both called elephant's-ear, are like giant green caladiums with huge heart-shaped or arrowhead-shaped leaves up to

Caladium × hortulanum

6 ft. long. Grow one for a tropical effect, or just for fun.

How to grow: Part sun or shade. Ordinary or better soil and regular watering. Plant tubers bumpy side up in pots indoors and put them in a warm place for a few weeks to develop roots, then plant them outdoors when frost danger is past and the soil is warm. Stop watering and let the leaves die down (or freeze down) in fall, then dig the tubers and let them dry for a week in a warm place before burying them in a box of vermiculite or sawdust. Store at 50°–60° F for the winter.

Calamagrostis
Kal-a-ma-gross´tis.
Gramineae. Grass family.

Annual or perennial grasses that form large erect clumps. About 250 spp., native to the temperate zones.

× *acutiflora* 'Karl Foerster' (p. 208)
Feather reed grass.
Perennial grass. Zone 5.
H: 5–6 ft. S: 2 ft.

A strongly vertical plant that makes an exclamation point in the garden, a good contrast to low mounded perennials or shrubs. Makes a clump of very slender, wiry leaves 3 ft. long, with much taller flower stalks spiking up through the center of the clump. The flowers appear in June; the seed heads, slim as pipe cleaners, look pretty all summer and fall as they ripen from gold to silver. Leave it untouched at the end of the season; this grass is strong enough to weather the vagaries of winter. 'Stricta' is more strongly upright, grows 6–7 ft. tall, and starts blooming about 2 weeks later than 'Karl Foerster'.

How to grow: Full or part sun. Grows well in ordinary or poor soil. Tolerates either wet or dry conditions. Divide and plant in spring, 18 in. apart for mass plantings. The only maintenance required is an annual shearing in spring.

Calamintha
Kal-a-minth´a.
Labiatae. Mint family.

Perennials, sometimes woody at the base, with scented leaves and small clusters of pale flowers. Only 7 spp., native to Eurasia.

nepeta (p. 230)
(sometimes listed as *C. nepetoides*)
Perennial. Zone 6 or 5.
H: 12–24 in. S: 18 in.

One of the most charming plants introduced to gardeners in recent years. Makes a mound of gracefully arranged gray-green foliage topped with a hazy cloud of tiny white or lilac flowers for weeks in summer and fall. Bees love it. The leaves are shiny and mint-scented. The long, leafy sprays make a great filler in fresh flower arrangements. Plant it along the front of a bed, with *Heuchera* 'Palace Purple', *Berberis* 'Crimson Pygmy', or *Ajuga* 'Tricolor'. Shop at herb nurseries to find other calamints, including the lovely white-splotched *C. grandiflora* 'Variegata'. All are pretty and fragrant.

How to grow: Full sun or afternoon shade. Needs well-drained soil. Cut back long stems in fall and mulch with pine boughs where winters are cold. Self-sows readily; if the parent plant dies in winter, new seedlings will almost surely replace it. Has no pests or diseases.

Calendula
Ka-len´dew-la.
Compositae. Daisy family.

Annuals or perennials with slightly hairy leaves and long-stemmed daisylike blossoms. About 20 spp., most native to the Mediterranean region.

officinalis (p. 292)
Annual. All zones.
H: to 2 ft. S: 1 ft.

Bright and cheerful blossoms on long stalks top this easy-to-grow annual. Use it to fill gaps in a border or to add quick color to a new planting. Traditionally called pot marigold in England, the flowers are edible and can be used fresh or dried to add color and a mild flavor to salads, soups, or rice. Flower colors range from pale cream to yellow, gold, and bright orange. The compact strains are best for bedding; the taller ones make good cut flowers.

How to grow: Full sun. Ordinary soil and watering. The seeds are big enough to handle easily. Direct-sow or set out transplants; space 12 in. apart. Often attacked by aphids or slugs. Does best in cool weather. Grow for summer bloom in the North, for fall to spring bloom where winters are mild. Deadhead to prolong blooming.

Callicarpa
Kal´li-kar-pa. Beautyberry.
Verbenaceae. Verbena family.

Deciduous or evergreen shrubs or trees with opposite leaves. Stems are lined with paired clusters of small flowers followed by pink, violet, or purple berries. About 140 spp., most native to tropical and subtropical regions.

dichotoma (p. 132)
Korean beautyberry.
Deciduous shrub. Zone 6 or 5.
H: 4 ft. S: 4 ft.

You won't notice this shrub in summer, but it's stunning in fall when clusters of bright violet-lilac berries make every branch glow like a string of Christmas lights. Forms a mound of arching stems that droop under the weight of the berries. Fruits more heavily and makes the most impressive display if several are planted in a group. The berries are held tight and last well in cut-flower arrangements. *C. bodinieri* var.

giraldii 'Profusion' grows more upright and has rosy purple foliage in fall as well as abundant violet berries. Other beautyberries, including some white-fruited forms, are offered by specialty nurseries.

How to grow: Full or part sun. Prefers moist, loamy soil with good drainage. Set 2–3 ft. apart for mass plantings. Best grown like an herbaceous perennial; prune severely in early spring, as berries are borne on new wood. Pest-free.

Callirhoe
Kal-lir´oh-ee.
Malvaceae. Mallow family.

Annuals or perennials with thick taproots, tough stems, and large showy flowers. About 8 spp., native to North America.

involucrata (p. 230)
Purple poppy mallow, wine cup.
Perennial. Zone 4.
H: 6–12 in. or more. S: 6–12 in. or more.

Large (to 2 1/2 in. wide), wine-colored, cup-shaped flowers rise above deeply lobed green foliage from spring to early summer (through fall with moisture). Spectacular as individuals or massed, in borders or naturalized. Self-sows without becoming weedy.

How to grow: Full sun. Tolerates poor or dry soil and heat. Sow seeds in fall or increase by division.

Callistemon
Kal-i-stee´mon. Bottlebrush.
Myrtaceae. Myrtle family.

Evergreen shrubs or trees with leafy stems and distinctive bottlebrush-like spikes of red or yellow flowers. About 20 spp., native to Australia.

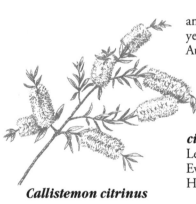

Callistemon citrinus

citrinus (p. 168)
Lemon bottlebrush.
Evergreen shrub. Zone 9.
H: 10–15 ft. S: 10–15 ft.

A mounded shrub with arching branches that makes a fast and easy hedge or specimen or can be trained into a small tree. The bright red flowers make 6-in. "bottlebrushes" near the ends of the branches; flushes of bloom appear sporadically in all seasons and attract hummingbirds. Interesting woody seed capsules persist on the stems for years. The slender lemon-scented leaves are silky and pink at first, turning dark green and firm as they mature.

How to grow: Full sun. Ordinary soil. Tolerates heat and dryness. Set 4–5 ft. apart for a hedge or screen. To train a tree, provide a stake and remove lower branches until a head is formed. Can be trained as an espalier.

viminalis (p. 156)
Weeping bottlebrush.
Evergreen tree. Zone 9.
H: to 30 ft. S: 15 ft.

An attractive weeping tree with an upright trunk and slender branches that hang straight down. Bright red 8-in. bottlebrushes dangle in the breeze. The narrow leathery leaves are light bluish green. 'Captain Cook' is a dwarf (to 6 ft.) variety. Colorful and showy as a specimen or lawn tree or in a shrub border.

How to grow: Like *C. citrinus*. Prune long branches in fall to prevent winter wind damage.

Calluna
Ka-loo´na. Heather.
Ericaceae. Heath family.

Evergreen shrubs that form a low mound of flexible stems with tiny scalelike leaves, tipped with spikes of small flowers in late summer and fall. Only 1 sp., native to Europe and Asia Minor, but hundreds of cultivars.

vulgaris (p. 168)
Heather.
Evergreen shrub. Zone 4.
H: to 24 in. S: to 24 in.

Heathers form low mounds of wiry branches clothed with minute overlapping leaves. Many change color from summer to winter, ranging from shades of pale to dark green, gold, and gray to bronze and reddish purple. Thousands of tiny flowers cover the plants with a cloud of white, pink, lavender, or rosy purple. Choose cultivars that bloom in sequence for continuous color from midsummer to late fall. Heathers are often combined with heaths (*Erica* spp.) and dwarf or low-growing conifers for a year-round display of color and texture.

The following cultivars are especially popular: 'County Wicklow' has green foliage, a mounding habit (12 in. by 20 in.), and pink flowers. 'H. E. Beale' is gray-green and upright (30 in. by 24 in.), with deep pink flowers. 'J. H. Hamilton' is dark green and spreading (6 in. by 12 in.), with deep pink flowers. 'Robert Chapman' is gold to reddish and spreading (10 in. by 30 in.), with mauve flowers.

How to grow: Best in full sun. Needs acidic soil with excellent drainage; add peat and sand or gravel to make raised beds. Easy in cool climates but can't tolerate hot summers, wet or dry. Set 1 ft. apart for mass plantings. Grows slowly for the first few years, then thrives for decades with no care. Lightly prune to shape after flowering, if desired.

Calycanthus
Kal-ee-kan´thus.
Calycanthaceae. Sweet shrub family.

Deciduous shrubs with large, fragrant, reddish brown flowers in spring. Only 2 spp., native to North America.

Calycanthus floridus

floridus (p. 132)
Sweet shrub, Carolina allspice.
Deciduous shrub or small tree. Zone 4.
H: 6–9 ft. S: 6–10 ft. or more.

One of the easiest and most versatile native shrubs, sweet shrub serves as an understory shrub for shade, a transition plant along a woodland edge or building, or a specimen clump along a path. The large, oblong, glossy leaves turn bright yellow or gold in fall. Unusual maroon flowers with numerous ribbonlike petals appear in midspring for 3–4 weeks and sporadically through early summer. Spreads slowly to form dense clumps, ideal for an informal fence. The floral fragrance varies from plant to plant; other parts of the plant have a spicy scent when crushed. *C. occidentalis,* a California native, grows 4–12 ft. tall and is hardy to Zone 8.

How to grow: Full or part sun or shade. Best in fertile, organic soil with even moisture but adapts to most soils. Tolerates heat. Prune off sprouts to maintain as a small multitrunked tree.

Camassia
Ka-mas'see-a.
Liliaceae. Lily family.

Perennials with bulbs, slender grasslike leaves, and showy clusters of white, blue, or violet flowers on long bare stalks. Only 5 spp., native to North and South America.

quamash (see below for photo)
(*C. esculenta*)
Camas.
Perennial. Zone 4.
H: to 24 in. S: 12–18 in.

Mass plantings make pools of blue in damp meadows or low spots in the garden. The flowers are 6-petaled stars, 1–1½ in. wide, in erect spikelike clusters that last for 2–3 weeks in spring. The slender grassy leaves make a clump 18 in. tall. Lovely naturalized with azaleas, lilies, and hostas at the edge of a woodland. 'Orion' and 'San Juan' have deeper blue flowers. *C. cusickii,* 18–30 in. tall, has light blue flowers. *C. leichtlinii* (p. 230) grows to 3 ft. and has white or blue flowers.

How to grow: Full or part sun; needs some shade where summers are hot and dry. Ordinary or damp soil. Plant 4 in. deep, 4 in. apart in fall. May be dug and divided if too crowded after many years.

Camellia
Ka-mee'lee-a. Camellia.
Theaceae. Tea family.

Evergreen shrubs or trees with leathery leaves. Many have showy waxlike flowers in fall, winter, or spring. About 80 spp., native to eastern Asia, and thousands of cultivars.

japonica (p. 168)
Evergreen shrub. Zone 8 or 7.
H: 6–15 ft. S: 6–15 ft.

These camellias are handsome evergreen shrubs to combine with azaleas, dwarf hollies, ferns, and hostas for beds or foundation plantings. They grow well in containers for a patio or entryway, and they can be trained into standards or espaliers. The oval, dark green leaves are glossy and leathery. Plump round flower buds at the ends of the branches open into showy single or double flowers in white, shades of pink, or red. Flowers are usually scentless, but they have exquisite petals and make lovely corsages.

There are hundreds of cultivars, each blooming for a long season, starting in fall, winter, or early spring. Most gardeners choose formal double blooms such as the white 'Alba Plena' and 'Purity' or the red 'Glen 40' and 'Pope Pius IX'. Fanciers prefer the newer, larger, less formal types such as the rose-red 'Guilio Nuccio' or the pink 'Mrs. D.W. Davis'. 'Elegans' has large, pink, anemone-type flowers on an arching, mounded, tiered shrub; 'C.M. Wilson' (pale pink) and 'Shiro Chan' (white) are similar.

C. reticulata is grown chiefly for its spectacular flowers, which can reach 9 in. across in some varieties—an astonishing sight in a winter garden. The flowers are round with fluted petals, pink to deep purplish red, often marked with white. The plant itself tends to be open and lanky, reaching 10 ft. tall and 6 ft. wide, and is not particularly handsome out of bloom. Put one in a container that you can move to a featured spot from midwinter to early spring, or plant in a woodland garden. Cultivars have different flower colors, shapes, and sizes. New hybrids of *C. reticulata* and *C. japonica* are handsome shrubs with exquisite flowers but are very tender to cold.

How to grow: Part sun. Needs well-drained soil amended with plenty of peat or organic matter. Apply a 2-in. layer of organic mulch such as ground bark or pine needles. Use an acid-type fertilizer. Water weekly, if needed, to keep the soil moist. Camellias are most dormant when in bloom, so that's the best time to plant them. Position the top of the root ball slightly higher than the surrounding soil. Prune only to shape, after blooming.

In marginal areas, protect plants from hard freezes by growing them in containers that can be moved to shelter. Plants hit by hard frost may sprout back, or they may die. Even if the plants aren't hurt, freezing temperatures make the flowers turn brown. Camellia petal blight occurs in some areas; the removal and destruction of damaged flowers is the best control. Fungal leafspot and scale insects also cause problems.

Camellia japonica

sasanqua (p. 168)
Evergreen shrub. Zone 8 or protected sites in Zone 7.
H: to 10 ft. S: to 6 ft.

Compared with the camellias described above, these tend to be smaller, neater, more easily shaped shrubs, with smaller leaves and flowers. They tolerate more sun, and they can be used as informal hedges or mass plantings or featured as specimens. The leathery leaves are shiny dark green all year. Flowers are single or double, 2–3 in. wide, in shades of white, pink, or red, and they're borne profusely over a long period from autumn into winter. Some have light fragrance. 'Jean May' is compact and upright, with double pink flowers. 'Mine-No-Yuki' ('White Doves') has double white flowers on limber shoots that are easily trained to climb or to trail. 'Yuletide' has single deep red flowers in midwinter on a compact upright shrub.

Cultivars of *C. hiemalis,* often grouped with *C. sasanqua,* are small (2–3 ft. tall by 5–6 ft. wide) spreading shrubs with tiered or layered branches. They're especially lovely arching over a wall or trailing from a planter and can even be grown in hanging baskets. 'Shishi Gashira' is low and compact, with semidouble, bright rose flowers. 'Showanosakae' grows faster and is more open and willowy, with light pink flowers.

How to grow: Like *C. japonica,* but these plants are more versatile and easier to use in the landscape. Select and transplant when plants are blooming. Pinch branch tips to fatten the shrubs. When established, these camellias tolerate full sun or considerable shade. Hardiness varies among cultivars. Most finish blooming before the coldest part of winter, so flower buds are usually not damaged.

Hardier camellias for colder climates

Gardeners in Zones 7 and 6 can grow camellias, too. You won't find these at local nurseries, but mail-order specialists are starting to offer a selection of hardy camellias. As more people learn about these, they'll become more widely available.

C. oleifera, the oil-seed camellia, is perhaps the hardiest. The plants resemble *C. sasanqua,* with fragrant, 2-in., single white flowers, shaded pink at the edges, starting in October. Plants have survived 15° F below zero, completely unharmed. The Ackerman hybrids were developed by crossing *C. oleifera* with other species. These new plants have a dense habit, small evergreen leaves, and lovely single or double flowers up to 4 in. wide. Sheltered from dry winter winds, they're hardy in Zone 6 and worth a try in Zone 5.

C. sinensis, hardy to Zone 6, is the plant from which tea is made. It's a dense shrub that tolerates repeated pruning—on tea plantations, the new leaves are plucked several times a year. It makes a dense hedge or screen, dotted with hundreds of fragrant, small white flowers from late summer to cold weather. A pink-flowered form is also available.

Campanula
Kam-pan´you-la. Bellflower.
Campanulaceae. Bellflower family.

A popular and diverse group of perennials, biennials, and annuals, varying in size and form but most with showy blue, violet, pink, or white flowers. About 300 spp., most native to the north temperate zone.

carpatica (p. 230)
Carpathian bellflower.
Perennial. Zone 3.
H: 8–18 in. S: 12 in.

Makes slowly spreading tussocks of small dark green leaves; blooms for many weeks starting in midsummer. The cup-shaped flowers, in shades of lavender, purple, or white and up to 2 in. wide, are borne singly or several to a stalk. An easy, cooperative plant, always attractive whether blooming or not. Use it in the front of the border, with dianthus and creeping thyme. Cultivars such as 'Blue Clips', 'White Clips', and 'China Doll' are compact and low-growing, under 10 in. tall.

How to grow: Full or part sun. Needs good drainage and tolerates gravelly or dry soil. Easily raised from seed. Every other year, lift the clumps and divide into two or three pieces, then replant. Hardy to cold but doesn't like hot summers.

glomerata (p. 230)
Clustered bellflower.
Perennial. Zone 3.
H: 12–30 in. S: 18–24 in.

Tall single or branched stems rise above a mound of softly hairy leaves to display tightly packed clusters of upward-facing, funnel-shaped flowers in gorgeous shades of blue, violet, purple, or white. Enjoy masses of color throughout the cool, damp weather of late spring. Var. *acaulis* (8 in.) has medium purple flowers on short stems. 'Crown of Snow' (12–18 in.) has snowy white flowers for weeks in early summer. 'Joan Elliott' (18 in.) has violet-purple flowers. 'Superba' (3 ft.) has tight clusters of violet-blue flowers on stems that don't flop, and it tolerates heat better than other forms do.

How to grow: Full sun in the North, part shade in the South or West. Needs ordinary or better soil and regular watering. Plant 12–18 in. apart, depending on cultivar height. Divide after flowering. It spreads fast from running roots and can be invasive, but it's easy to lift and remove extra plants.

persicifolia (p. 230)
Peach-leaved bellflower.
Perennial. Zone 3.
H: 24–36 in. S: 12–18 in.

Bell-shaped flowers, 1 in. or wider, face in all directions from the top of slender nodding stems. The white forms are pure white; "blue" forms are usually lavender-blue. All are lovely in the garden with antique roses or hardy geraniums and do well as fresh cut flowers. Blooms appear in early summer and once again later if deadheaded. The basal rosette of narrow leathery leaves is evergreen, but rabbits may devour the foliage in winter unless it's protected with pine boughs, chicken wire, or snow.

How to grow: Full or part sun. Ordinary soil and watering. Can't take much heat. May self seed where you don't want it; lift and relocate stray plants when they aren't blooming. Divide in fall. Use brushy twigs or stakes to support the stems so that they won't flop over during rainstorms.

portenschlagiana (p. 231)
(*C. muralis*)
Dalmatian bellflower.
Perennial. Zone 4.
H: 6–9 in. S: 12 in. or more.

An excellent rock-garden or wall plant. The tight mound of shiny green, ivylike leaves is attractive even without flowers. Long trailing stems emerge from this mound and wind gracefully around rocks, carrying clusters of marvelous violet-blue (or white) flowers like little bells or cups. Try using it as a ground cover or an edging plant, or plant some in a container and let it spill over the edge.

How to grow: Full or part sun. Needs well-drained soil. Plant 18 in. apart. No attention required unless it begins to crowd other plants; in that case, cut back or divide. Can be invasive, but it's lovely.

poscharskyana (p. 231)
Serbian bellflower.
Perennial. Zone 3.
H: 6–9 in. S: 12 in. or more.

Long trailing stems spread rapidly from a central mound to fill a sunny area. Plants are covered with loose clusters of starry lavender-blue or white flowers in spring. Tolerates dryness and makes a showy ground cover for rocky areas but grows fast and can be invasive.

How to grow: Like *C. portenschlagiana.*

Campanula medium

other campanulas

C. lactiflora, the milky bellflower, grows 4 ft. tall (and may need staking) in moist, fertile soil. The branching stems are topped with loose clusters of mildly fragrant white, pale pink, or pale blue flowers. Blooms over a long season through summer and fall. Hard to transplant but self-sows readily in favorable sites.

C. medium, Canterbury-bells or cup-and-saucer, is a biennial with single or double cup-shaped flowers up to 2 in. wide, in shades of pink, lavender, blue, or white. The flowers are slightly fragrant and make good cut flowers. The stems are upright (to 3 ft.) and branching. Set out plants in early fall for bloom the next spring.

C. rapunculoides has pretty blue flowers on 3-ft. spikes, but be warned: Once you've planted it, you'll never get rid of it. Any bit of unpulled root can sprout a new shoot.

C. rotundifolia, bluebell or harebell, has bright blue or white flowers on slender stalks up to 1 ft. tall. It's pretty in mountain gardens or northern climates, but it can't take heat. Self-seeds and can be weedy where it grows well.

Campsis
Kamp´sis.
Bignoniaceae. Trumpet creeper family.

Deciduous woody vines with pinnately compound leaves and large, showy, red or orange flowers. Only 2 spp., one from the eastern United States and the other from eastern Asia, and their hybrid.

radicans (p. 199)
Trumpet vine, trumpet creeper.
Woody vine. Zone 5.
H: 30 ft. or more.

A vigorous, tough, easy vine for covering fences, stumps, old buildings, or anyplace you want summer color without having to water. Red, orange, or yellow trumpets, 3–4 in. long, are borne continuously from June to fall in clusters at the tips of shoots. Hummingbirds love them. Dry woody pods hang on all winter. The compound leaves have a bold, coarse texture. The strong stems climb via aerial rootlets. *C.* × *tagliabuana* 'Madame Galen' is a hybrid with larger, showier, salmon-red flowers.

How to grow: Sun or shade. Grows in any soil and needs no special care. Choosing an appropriate site is the only concern; the tendrils cling tight and can damage roofs, masonry, or window screens. Also spreads by root suckers. These can be controlled by mowing or by planting in beds confined by adjacent pavement.

Canna
Kan´na.
Cannaceae. Canna family.

Tender perennials with thick starchy rhizomes, leafy upright stems topped with large showy flowers, and seeds like shiny beads. About 25 spp., native to the New World tropics.

hybrids (p. 231)
(*C.* × *generalis*)
Tender perennials. Zone 8.
H: 2–6 ft. S: 2–3 ft.

Old-fashioned but still popular, cannas are among the easiest perennials to grow. They have big flowers in bright red, orange, salmon, pink, yellow, or white and bloom from early summer to fall. Plants make a clump of erect stems, each

Canna hybrid

with several broad leaves in shades of green, reddish green, bronze, or variegated. Can be mixed with other perennials in a border, but a mass planting will soften the straight lines of a wooden fence or fill a difficult corner. A single large clump adds color beside a pool or pond.

There are many cultivars, differing in flower color, leaf color, and stature. The 'Pfitzer Dwarfs' (2–4 ft.) come in crimson, pink, coral, and yellow. 'The President' (3 ft.) has bright red flowers and deep green leaves. 'Wyoming' (4 ft.) has orange flowers and bronze leaves. 'Striped Beauty' (3–4 ft.) has yellow flowers and cream-striped green leaves.

How to grow: Full or part sun. Cannas prefer good soil and steady moisture but tolerate some dryness. Remove faded flowers for prolonged bloom. Leaf caterpillars are the only pest.

In Zone 8 or warmer, plant rhizomes in spring and divide every few years. To grow as an annual in Zone 7 or colder, start rhizomes in pots indoors, a month before the last frost, and put them in a warm place to start growing roots. Wait until the soil is warm before planting them out. When frost kills the tops in fall, dig up the rhizomes and dry them for a few days before storing them in a box of damp peat moss for the winter.

Carex
Kay′rex. Sedge.
Cyperaceae. Sedge family.

A huge genus of grasslike perennials, most forming tufts or clumps of slender leaves. All sedges bear clusters of separate male and female flowers on solid, 3-sided stalks. More than 1,000 spp., found worldwide in cool, wet climates.

buchananii (p. 209)
Leatherleaf sedge.
Grasslike perennial. Zone 6.
H: 2 ft. S: 1 ft.

Making an airy tuft of shiny cinnamon-colored foliage, the fine delicate leaves arch gracefully and curl at the tips. It offers relief from the green that dominates all gardens, but it also complements blue, white, or reddish brown plants. Combine it with silver-leaved thyme and yellow primroses for winter and spring. It rarely flowers.

How to grow: Part sun or shade. Ordinary or better soil. Space 1 ft. apart for mass plantings. Divide in spring. Cut foliage back in late fall or early spring. In cold climates, grow one in a container and bring it indoors to a sunny window for the winter.

morrowii 'Aureo-variegata' (p. 209)
Variegated Japanese sedge.
Grasslike perennial. Zone 6 or 5.
H: 12 in. S: 18 in.

This is a must for gardeners who shy away from the unkempt appearance of some grasses. It forms a neat, low, evergreen tuft of leaves striped bright yellow and green. Use it to brighten a dark shady area or to edge a border, pond, or rock garden. Flowers are inconspicuous.

How to grow: Part sun or shade. Prefers moist, fertile soil but tolerates ordinary soil and watering. Plant 12–15 in. apart so that the mounded clumps will remain distinct. Needs minimal maintenance; simply prune away any damaged foliage in spring.

Carpinus
Kar-py′nus. Hornbeam.
Betulaceae. Birch family.

Deciduous trees of small to medium size, with notably hard wood, alternate toothed leaves, and dangling catkins of tiny flowers. About 35 spp., native to the north temperate zone.

betulus (p. 110)
European hornbeam.
Deciduous tree. Zone 5.
H: 50 ft. S: 80 ft.

A medium-size tree of very neat habit. The crown is often very symmetrical and almost has a manufactured look. Leaves are dark green (yellow in fall) with conspicuous veins and are notably healthy and unblemished. Yellow-green catkins dangle in spring. The fluted trunk has smooth gray bark. 'Fastigiata', an upright form, makes a good lawn specimen and can also be used for hedging. In Europe, hornbeams are often pleached or espaliered, as they respond well to pruning and training. There are several cultivars with distinct leaf shapes.

How to grow: Full or part sun. Ordinary soil and watering. Pest-free and easy to grow.

caroliniana (p. 110)
American hornbeam, musclewood.
Deciduous tree. Zone 3.
H: 15–25 ft. S: 10–15 ft.

An attractive, slow-growing, small tree, good for patios or city gardens. The trunk is often crooked and has a distinctly lean and muscular appearance, with taut bluish gray bark. The dark green leaves turn yellow or orange in fall and color well even in shade. Interesting papery bracts surround the fruits. It's a good tree for children to climb, because of the strong wood and wide-spreading branches.

How to grow: Sun or shade. Grows naturally as an understory tree in moist soil along rivers and streams. Tolerates most soil types but can't take prolonged dryness. Pest-free and needs no maintenance.

Carya
Kare′ee-a.
Juglandaceae. Walnut family.

Deciduous trees, sometimes quite large, with pinnately compound leaves and strong hard timber. Pecans and some hickories bear tasty nuts in woody shells. About 20 spp., many native to eastern North America.

illinoinensis (p. 111)
Pecan.
Deciduous tree. Zone 5.
H: 125 ft. or more. S: 100 ft.

A stately shade tree, too large for many lots but handsome and graceful where it has room to spread. Has an upright trunk and rounded crown. The large pinnate leaves turn yellow in fall. Grows well but doesn't bear many nuts in cold climates of the Northeast and Midwest. Bears generously in warm climates; one tree can yield gallons of nuts each year. "Native" pecans have small nuts with thick, hard shells. Selected cultivars (grafted or budded onto seedlings) have much larger nuts with thin shells that are easy to crack.

How to grow: Full sun. Native to fertile bottomlands, it prefers good soil and plenty of moisture. Pecans are big trees; don't plant one if space is limited. Tent caterpillars infest the foliage, and many insects (and also bluejays and squirrels) relish the nuts. Check with local Cooperative Extension agents for varieties and care recommendations.

ovata (p. 111)
Shagbark hickory.
Deciduous tree. Zone 4.
H: 100 ft. S: 40 ft.

A tall tree with an upright crown and drooping branches, best known for its remarkable gray bark, which breaks into long vertical plates that curve out at the top and bottom ends. Older trees have a distinctive shaggy appearance. The large pinnate leaves are smooth and green all summer, turn bright gold in fall, and have a pleasant pungent odor when bruised. The nuts are tasty but have a hard woody shell. Squirrels love them.

Many other native hickories are also common throughout the eastern United States. Most are strong, slow-growing, handsome trees. Try not to disturb them (in particular, don't dig around or drive over their roots) if you're clearing land to build a new house in a wooded area.

How to grow: Full or part sun. Ordinary soil and watering. Tent caterpillars may attack the leaves. Big mushrooms under a tree manifest a fungus that infects damaged roots.

Caryopteris
Kare-ee-yop´ter-is. Bluebeard.
Verbenaceae. Verbena family.

Deciduous shrubs or perennials with simple leaves and abundant clusters of tiny blue, violet, or white flowers. About 6 spp., native to eastern Asia, and a few hybrids.

× clandonensis (p. 132)
Bluebeard, blue spirea.
Deciduous shrub. Zone 6 or 5.
H: 2–3 ft. S: 2–3 ft.

A small shrub that combines very well with perennials. Cut to the ground each spring, it quickly sends up new shoots with neatly spaced pairs of downy gray leaves. Fluffy clusters of lavender-blue flowers tip each shoot in August and September and attract butterflies. Combines well with lespedeza, *Sedum* 'Autumn Joy', late-blooming roses, and lavender. 'Blue Mist' has an informal rounded shape and pale flowers. 'Dark Knight' is upright, with dark violet blossoms. 'Longwood Blue' has abundant sky blue flowers.

How to grow: Full sun. Prefers sandy loam with excellent drainage. Tolerates heat and dry soil. Plant 30 in. apart. Cut back drastically in spring to promote shapely new growth. May freeze in severe Zone 5 winters but will come back from the roots. Often self-seeds. Pest-free.

Cassia
Kas´ee-a. Senna.
Leguminosae. Pea family.

A diverse group of woody and herbaceous plants with pinnately compound leaves and showy clusters of yellow flowers. Some species are used medicinally, others for tanning leather. More than 500 spp., most from warm or tropical climates.

artemisioides (p. 169)
Feathery cassia, silver cassia.
Evergreen shrub. Zone 9.
H: 3–5 ft. S: 3 ft.

A choice desert plant with handsome gray or silver foliage and showy yellow flowers. The compound leaves are divided into narrow needlelike leaflets. Coin-sized flowers are borne in clusters from winter through spring. Can make an informal hedge, or combine it with cacti, yuccas, and other desert plants. *C. phyllodenia*, with needlelike gray leaves, and *C. sturtii*, with narrow woolly gray leaves, both grow about 6 ft. tall as hedges or specimens and have bright yellow flowers.

How to grow: Full sun. Needs well-drained soil; very tolerant of heat and dryness. Water until established, then only infrequently. Easy from seed soaked in hot water before sowing. Cut off old flowers to prolong bloom and to avoid seedpods.

leptophylla (p. 156)
Gold medallion tree.
Evergreen tree. Zone 9.
H: 25 ft. S: 20 ft.

An open, spreading, often multitrunked tree with evergreen compound leaves. Stunning 1-ft.-wide clusters of golden yellow flowers decorate the branch ends over a long summer season. Each flower is 2–3 in. wide, and there are 30–50 flowers per cluster. The long pods that follow are interesting or messy, depending on your point of view. Excellent combined with buddleia or vitex or displayed against a dark background of pines or other conifers.

How to grow: Like *C. artemisioides*. Train to one or many trunks. Freezes back but recovers from 15° F cold snaps.

Catalpa
Ka-tal′pa.
Bignoniaceae. Trumpet creeper family.

Deciduous trees with saucer-sized leaves and traffic-stopping clusters of very showy flowers in early summer, followed by long, slender, woody pods. About 11 spp., native to North America and eastern Asia.

speciosa (p. 110)
Southern catalpa.
Deciduous tree. Zone 6.
H: 40–60 ft. S: 30–40 ft.

A moderate- to fast-growing tree with an upright trunk and a rounded crown. The heart-shaped leaves are coarse and large, up to 10 in. long. For up to 2 weeks in early summer, the tree is covered with giant clusters of big white (dotted with yellow and brownish purple) flowers that look like spilled popcorn when they drop on the lawn. Skinny dry pods, 1/2 in. thick and 12–16 in. long, hang from the bare limbs all winter. Handsome as a lawn specimen, but you'll have to rake up a mess of pods in early spring. *C. bignonioides,* the northern catalpa, is hardy to Zone 4. It has fewer flowers per cluster, but each flower is larger. Otherwise, the two trees are similar.

How to grow: Full sun. Does best in moist, fertile soil but tolerates ordinary conditions. No serious pests or problems.

Catharanthus
Kath-a-ran′thus.
Apocynaceae. Dogbane family.

Perennials or annuals with simple opposite leaves and white or rosy flowers with 5 broad petals. About 8 spp., most native to Madagascar.

roseus (p. 292)
(*Vinca rosea*)
Madagascar periwinkle.
Perennial grown as an annual. All zones.
H: 1–2 ft. S: 1 ft. or more.

Grows quickly from seed to make a mounding bushy plant of glossy green foliage covered with cheerful 5-petaled flowers in shades of white, pink, or rose, often with a contrasting eye. Thrives in hot weather, dry or humid, and keeps blooming after other annuals have given up. Use it in mass displays, containers, or difficult sites where heat is reflected from nearby buildings or pavement. Many cultivars are available from seed catalogs or local garden centers. Beyond its beauty, this is a powerful plant with a long history of medicinal applications, including the ability to inhibit cancerous tumors.

How to grow: Full or part sun. Ordinary soil and regular watering. Transplant seedlings 12–16 in. apart after danger of frost is past. Self-seeds in warm climates. Pest-free and needs no maintenance.

Ceanothus
See-a-no′thus.
Rhamnaceae. Buckthorn family.

Deciduous or evergreen shrubs or small trees, usually with dense branching. Clusters of tiny blue, violet, or white flowers can hide the foliage for weeks on end. About 55 spp., all native to North America.

griseus var. *horizontalis* (p. 169)
Carmel creeper.
Evergreen shrub. Zone 8.
H: 2–3 ft. S: 6–15 ft.

Prized for its tremendous display of fragrant, tiny, pale blue flowers, borne in dense 1-in.-long clusters from March to April. The small evergreen leaves are glossy and leathery. A fast-growing ground cover for dry-summer, mild-winter areas. 'Yankee Point' (to 10 ft. wide) has deeper blue flowers. 'Santa Ana' (to 15 ft. wide) has tiny dark green leaves and rich deep blue flowers.

How to grow: Full sun. Native to the California coast, it tolerates dry soil but needs afternoon shade in hot inland areas. Avoid overwatering. Plant in fall, 6 ft. apart for ground cover. Pinch the tips to fatten the plant; prune to remove dead or damaged wood.

Ceanothus griseus var. ***horizontalis***

thyrsiflorus (p. 169)
California lilac, blueblossom.
Evergreen shrub. Zone 8.
H: to 25 ft. S: to 25 ft.

Evergreen shrubs with blue flowers are rare, and this is one of the best and easiest for the West. Exceptionally fast-growing and drought-tolerant, it's useful at the edge of a garden or woods, as a large-scale bank or ground cover, or along rural roads. Leaves are glossy bright green, and large clusters of fragrant, light to deep blue flowers appear in March and April. Can be trained as a single-trunked or multitrunked tree or allowed to grow as a big bush. 'Skylark' is smaller and more compact, with deeper blue flowers; it is fairly tolerant of summer water. 'Snow Flurry' reaches 10 ft. tall and has white flowers.

How to grow: Sun or shade. Needs good drainage. Tolerates dryness but can't take heavy summer irrigation or damp heat. Plant 6–8 ft. apart for screening.

hybrids (p. 169)
Evergreen shrubs. Zone 8.
H: varies. S: varies.

There are many ceanothus hybrids, all fast-growing with leathery evergreen leaves and profuse clusters of fragrant, tiny blue flowers in spring. Choose erect or spreading cultivars to use for informal hedges or screens and for bank or ground covers. 'Julia Phelps' (6 ft. by 6 ft.) is dense, with tiny dark green leaves and darkest blue flowers that open from reddish buds. 'Dark Star' and 'Concha' are similar to 'Julia Phelps' but somewhat more tolerant of summer water. 'Ray Hartman' has large mid-green leaves and medium blue flowers and grows as a tree to 20 ft.

How to grow: Full sun. All need good drainage and die if overwatered in summer. Prune only to remove dead or broken branches.

hardy ceanothus
The most commonly grown *Ceanothus* species and hybrids are all tender, but at least two species are hardy to Zone 4. *C. americanus,* New Jersey tea or red root, is a small (3–4 ft. tall and wide) deciduous shrub, native to the eastern states and used during colonial days as a tea substitute. It has small fluffy clusters of creamy white flowers in early summer. Needs good drainage and tolerates dry gravelly soil where other shrubs would fail. Prune back by a third in spring to force denser growth.

C. velutinus, snowbrush, is one of the few broad-leaved evergreens native to the western mountains. In early summer, clusters of fragrant, creamy white flowers contrast nicely with the dark, balsam-scented foliage. Grows 3–5 ft. tall and wide. Protect new plants from dry winds the first winter.

Cedrus
See'drus. Cedar.
Pinaceae. Pine family.

Evergreen conifers with tufts of stiff needles and upright cones with many layers of scales. These are the true cedars. Only 4 or fewer spp., native to the mountains of North Africa and the Middle East.

atlantica 'Glauca' (see below for photo)
Blue atlas cedar.
Conifer. Zone 6.
H: 60 ft. S: 30–40 ft.

Native to the mountains of Morocco and Algeria, this conifer can tolerate heat and dry alkaline soil. It offers rich blue color and strongly architectural branch structure and silhouette. The bluish silver needles are stiff and bristly, held in tufts on short spurs. The barrel-shaped cones are 3 in. long. Young trees are conical, with branches pointing up at a 45° angle. Older trees are broader and flat-topped. Use one as a specimen in large dry courtyards or planted at the end of an expanse of lawn. Makes a good background for red- or maroon-leaved shrubs. 'Glauca Pendula' is a weeping cultivar with pliable

branches that are easily espaliered or trained against a wall. *C. deodara* (p. 188), the deodar cedar, has silvery blue-green needles that are longer (to 1 1/4 in.) and softer, giving the tree a fine feathery texture. 'Kashmir' and 'Shalimar' are considered the hardiest cultivars. Compact, prostrate, and gold-needled forms are also available.

How to grow: Full sun. Tolerates poor, dry soil and heat. Plant in fall in its permanent site and don't try to move it later. It gets big, so don't put it too close to buildings. Avoid exposed or windy locations, as cold winter winds make the needles turn brown. Prune out any double leaders. Subject to borers, weevils, and root rot.

Celastrus
Sel-las'trus. Bittersweet.
Celastraceae. Staff-tree family.

Deciduous woody vines or shrubs that climb by twining. Most have simple leaves and inconspicuous flowers, but in winter the bare vines are covered with clusters of bright gold or orange berries in an orange or crimson hull. About 30 spp., native to the Old and New World.

orbiculatus (p. 199)
Oriental bittersweet.
Woody vine. Zone 5.
H: 30 ft. or more.

A vigorous vine that can squeeze and smother to death small trees and shrubs, but it makes an unforgettable display of orange berries, revealed in fall when the leaves turn gold and drop and persisting through winter until eaten by birds. Separate male and female plants are needed to set fruit. Let it climb on a trellis or arbor or run along the top of a fence, but keep it away from your trees. Once planted on highway medians in New England, it now ensnarls the region's forests. *C. scandens,* the native American bittersweet, is less vigorous but hardier (Zone 3) and has red berries wrapped in yellow hulls.

How to grow: Full or part sun. Not fussy about soil or water. May wait a few years before flowering and fruiting. Prune heavily to keep it under control.

Celosia
Sel-lo'see-a.
Amaranthaceae. Amaranth family.

Annuals or perennials with strong upright stems, thin leaves, and dense heads or plumes of tiny, chaffy, brightly colored flowers. About 50 spp., native to tropical climates.

argentea (p. 292)
Cockscomb.
Annual. All zones.
H: to 2 ft. S: 1 ft.

A heat-loving annual that's colorful in all parts, with particularly brilliant red, orange, gold, salmon, or pink flower heads. The individual

Cedrus atlantica 'Glauca'

flowers are tiny, but they're crowded into dense fluffy plumes in var. *plumosa* or into odd wavy crests in var. *cristata*. All make good cut flowers, fresh or dried. Both dwarf and taller forms are commonly available. Gardeners who disdain big masses of bright colors should check the specialty seed catalogs; there are other celosias with graceful slender spikes of pale flowers.

How to grow: Full sun. Ordinary soil. Thrives on heat and tolerates dryness. Wait until nights are warm before transplanting seedlings into the garden. Space close together if you want single-stemmed flower heads; allow more space and pinch out the tips for branched plants with many smaller heads.

Celtis
Sel´tis. Hackberry.
Ulmaceae. Elm family.

Most are deciduous trees similar to elms, with strong wood, toothed leaves, inconspicuous flowers and small round fruits. About 60 spp., some native to the United States.

occidentalis (p. 111)
Hackberry.
Deciduous tree. Zone 3.
H: 40–90 ft. S: 30–40 ft.

Not a showy tree, but a tough one. It has an upright trunk and a round or oval crown with arching or drooping branches. The oval leaves are green in summer, pale yellow in fall. The small dark berries are very sweet and tasty but have big seeds inside. Most interesting are the tough gray fins of bark that stud the trunk. Useful as a shade tree in poor soil on city lots or on windy sites or alkaline soil throughout the Midwest and West.

C. laevigata, the sugar hackberry or sugarberry, is similar but usually has smooth bark. *C. reticulata,* the western hackberry, native from eastern Washington to Arizona, is a smaller tree with reddish brown berries.

How to grow: Full sun. Tolerates the poorest conditions. It has no serious problems, but sometimes a virus makes the twigs branch out like a witch's broom, and it may get harmless but warty-looking leaf galls. Often hosts mistletoe in the South.

Centranthus ruber

Centaurea
Sen-tor´ee-a.
Compositae. Daisy family.

A large group of mostly herbaceous plants with diverse leaves and blossoms that resemble thistles but aren't as prickly. About 450 spp., most native to the Mediterranean region.

cyanus (p. 293)
Bachelor's-button, cornflower.
Annual. All zones.
H: to 30 in. S: 12 in.

A fast and easy annual with slender gray leaves on branching stems topped with 1-in.-wide flower heads in bright blue, pink, rose, or white. Often included in mixtures of "meadow" seeds and lovely combined with Shirley poppies in a mass planting. Self-sows for a few years but doesn't compete with invasive grasses or perennials. Makes a good cut flower, fresh or dried. Seed catalogs list many varieties, including some shorter, compact ones. *C. moschata,* sweet-sultan, is a heat-loving annual with 2-in.-wide thistlelike heads of sweetly scented yellow, lilac, or white flowers.

How to grow: Full sun. Stands up and flowers best in lean, dry soil; grows soft and floppy if the soil is too rich and moist. Direct-sow in early spring in colder climates, late fall where winters are mild.

montana (p. 232)
Perennial cornflower, mountain bluet.
Perennial. Zone 3.
H: 18–24 in. S: 24 in.

Forms loose clumps of leafy stems topped with solitary 2–3-in.-wide blossoms with fringed rays in shades of blue-purple, rose, or white. Blooms for a few weeks in early summer. Spreads fast to fill in vacant areas.

How to grow: Full or part sun. Ordinary or poor, dry soil. Does best in cool northern or mountain climates and can't take much heat and humidity. Plant 2 ft. apart. Lift and divide regularly to keep it from taking over the garden.

Centranthus
Sen-tran´thus.
Valerianaceae. Valerian family.

Most are tough perennials that form clumps of leafy stems topped with dense clusters of red or white flowers. About 10 spp., native to Europe.

ruber (p. 232)
Red valerian, Jupiter's-beard, fox's-brush.
Perennial. Zone 5.
H: 3 ft. S: 4 ft.

Dense clusters of fragrant crimson, pink, or white flowers top the long stems of smooth blue-green foliage, mostly in late spring and early summer (continuing intermittently through the year in mild climates). Extremely tolerant of difficult conditions and will survive many months of total drought and continue blooming anyway. In England it grows from crevices in brick or rock walls. In California it thrives on dry slopes or in raised beds. Makes a good cut flower. 'Albus' has white flowers.

How to grow: Full or part sun. Needs good drainage and prefers limy soil. Divide in spring or fall and plant 3 ft. apart for mass plantings. Deadheading prolongs bloom, removes untidy seed heads, and prevents an overabundance of volunteer seedlings. Cut straggly plants back to 6 in. to renew them and to force a second show of bloom.

Ceratonia

Ser-ra-tone′ee-a. Carob.
Leguminosae. Pea family.

Evergreen trees with pinnate leaves and pods filled with sweet edible pulp. Only 2 spp., native to Arabia and Somalia.

siliqua (p. 157)

Carob, St.-John's-bread.
Evergreen tree. Zone 9.
H: 30–40 ft. S: 30–40 ft.

A dense mounded shrub or tree with shiny, leathery, evergreen compound leaves. It is very tolerant of heat and drought and makes a durable hedge that needs little maintenance. If pollinated, female trees produce 1-ft.-long pods with sugary pulp and hard seeds inside. The pulp is soft, sticky, and tasty. Carob powder, ground from the dried pods, is often used as a substitute for chocolate.

How to grow: Full sun. Tolerates poor soil and dryness when established. Plant 6–8 ft. apart for a screen. To grow as a tree, shorten the lower branches and then remove them only after a head is formed at the proper height. The roots will lift pavement if planted too close; these trees need more space than is usually allowed between sidewalk and street.

Ceratostigma

Ser-rat-o-stig′ma.
Plumbaginaceae. Plumbago family.

Shrubs or woody perennials with simple leaves and dense heads of blue flowers. About 8 spp., native to Africa and Asia.

plumbaginoides (p. 232)

Dwarf plumbago.
Perennial. Zone 5.
H: 12 in. S: 12 in. or more.

A spreading perennial with dense heads of small clear blue flowers. Bloom continues from the heat of summer through fall. Leaves are smooth and plain, dark green in summer and turning reddish purple in fall. Makes a good companion for spring bulbs, as it leafs out in late spring and then fills in the gaps when the bulb foliage dies down. Also lovely when its fall colors complement autumn foliage and ripe red berries.

How to grow: Full or part sun. Ordinary or dry soil. Tolerates heat if partly shaded. Goes dormant in winter even in the mildest climates. Cut old stems to the ground in spring, and remove old woody crowns in favor of vigorous young shoots. Rooted stolons can be transplanted in spring or fall. Space 8–12 in. apart for a mass planting or ground cover.

Cercidium

Ser-sid′ee-um.
Leguminosae. Pea family.

Deciduous small trees or shrubs with bright green bark. They are leafless most of the year but have attractive silhouettes and wonderful masses of yellow flowers. About 10 spp., native to the southwestern United States and Mexico.

floridum (p. 111)

(now *Parkinsonia florida*)
Blue palo verde.
Deciduous tree. Zone 9 or 8.
H: 20–30 ft. S: 20–30 ft.

An unusual native tree with smooth green bark on the trunk, branches, and twigs. It bears tiny leaves for only a short time in spring. Billows of small yellow flowers in clusters 2–4 in. long add color in spring, sometimes repeating through summer, depending on rainfall. Flat thin pods, 2–3 in. long, ripen yellow-brown in summer. *C. microphyllum,* the yellow foothills palo verde, is more drought-tolerant; *C. praecox,* the Sonoran palo verde, is more open and "clean"-looking but less cold-hardy.

How to grow: Full sun. Dry soil; tolerates poor soil and heat. Deep but infrequent watering is best. Its noninvasive roots make it ideal for shading patios and walks and make underplanting easy. Leave twiggy growth on major limbs to protect from sunscald. Treat the trunks of newly transplanted trees with insecticide for a few years. Trees that have been weakened by sunscald or by too much water and fertilizer are prone to borers.

Cercidium floridum

Cercis

Sir′sis. Redbud.
Leguminosae. Pea family.

Deciduous small trees or shrubs with stalkless clusters of pink or white pealike flowers sprouting directly from the branches or trunk in early spring, before the leaves open. Only 6 or 7 spp., native to North America, southern Europe, and China.

canadensis (p. 112)

Eastern redbud.
Deciduous tree. Zone 5.
H: 20–35 ft. S: 25–35 ft.

Redbuds welcome spring with a showy display of small pealike rose, pink, or lavender flowers that open 2–3 weeks before the leaves develop. In nature redbuds often grow in combination with and flower at the same time as dogwoods. After bloom the heart-shaped leaves start with a maroon cast, darken to green, and then turn gold in fall. The flat dry pods are interesting but can be messy. Selected cultivars have clear white or true pink flowers; the new leaves of 'Forest Pansy' are especially bright reddish purple.

Other native redbuds are stocked by nurseries around the country. *C. occidentalis,* the western redbud, has similar flowers and leaves but is shrubbier and usually has multiple trunks; it is very drought-tolerant and is hardy to Zone 8. *C. reniformis* 'Oklahoma' has rich reddish purple flowers and thick glossy leaves that are particularly handsome.

Cercis canadensis

How to grow: Full or part sun. Prefers fertile, organic soil. Tolerates poor or dry soil and heat. Avoid poorly drained sites. Redbuds are fairly fast-growing but sometimes short lived, as the leaves, wood, and roots are all subject to fungal diseases. Remove dead branches and prune to shape after blooming. Often self-seeds but isn't weedy.

Cercocarpus
Ser-ko-kar´pus.
Rosaceae. Rose family.
   Evergreen or deciduous shrubs or small trees with leathery leaves and feathery fruits that catch the light in fall. About 6 spp., native to the mountains and foothills in western North America.

ledifolius (p. 169)
Curl-leaf mountain mahogany.
Evergreen shrub. Zone 4.
H: 10–20 ft. S: 10–30 ft.
   A long-lived, hardy, and trouble-free evergreen equally useful as a bushy screen or windbreak or pruned as a specimen tree. The small leathery leaves, stiff and slightly hairy, are dark green on top, silver underneath. Flowers are inconspicuous. The seed heads—short spiraled plumes with fine silver hairs—are eye-catching, particularly when backlit, in late summer and fall. The whole plant has a spicy aroma. *C. montanus* is smaller and deciduous, perhaps hardier.
   How to grow: Full or part sun. Tolerates poor or dry soil and heat. Periodic deep watering maintains the density of the foliage.

Chaenomeles
Kee-nom´e-lees. Flowering quince.
Rosaceae. Rose family.
   Deciduous shrubs with picturesque crooked branches, bright flowers in late winter or early spring, and fragrant applelike fruits. Only 3 spp., native to China and Japan, but many hybrid cultivars.

cultivars (see below for photos)
Flowering quince.
Deciduous shrubs. Zone 4.
H: 4–8 ft. S: 4–6 ft.
   Among the first shrubs to bloom in spring, with flowers like apple blossoms, 1–2 in. wide, in shades of bright scarlet, crimson, orange, pink, or white. The flowers are scentless but last for weeks in cool weather. Cut a few branches in late winter and force them indoors. The shrubs themselves are tough and thorny, with Oriental-looking crooked twigs. They make carefree shrubs for hedges or barrier plantings or can be trained against a wall or pruned as specimens. The round yellow-green fruits smell spicy-sweet when they mature in fall and can be used for preserves.
   C. speciosa is a medium to tall, round or upright shrub. *C. japonica* (p. 132) is smaller

and more spreading. *C.* × *superba* is a hybrid between them. There are dozens, perhaps hundreds, of cultivars belonging to one species or another, differing mostly in flower color and form but also in growth habit (upright or spreading). Shop locally and buy plants while they're in bloom to be sure that you get the color you want, particularly if you're buying several for a hedge. 'Cameo' (apricot-pink), 'Jet Trail' (white), and 'Texas Scarlet' (tomato red) are low spreaders. 'Apple Blossom' (light pink), 'Snow' (white), and 'Crimson Beauty' (red) grow more upright. 'Toyo Nishiki' (p. 133) is a tall shrub with white, pink, red, and two-tone flowers all at the same time.
   How to grow: Full or part sun. Can tolerate infertile neutral or acidic soil, but alkaline conditions make the leaves turn yellow. Tolerate heat and cold. Need ordinary watering. Remove older stems every few years. Shear right after flowering if you choose; new growth will flower the following year.

Chamaecyparis
Kam-ee-sip´ar-is. False cypress.
Cupressaceae. Cypress family.
   Evergreen conifers with needlelike juvenile foliage and scaly adult foliage. Wild trees grow huge and yield important timber, but hundreds of dwarf forms are better suited for gardens. About 7 spp., native to North America and eastern Asia.

lawsoniana (p. 188)
Lawson cypress.
Conifer. Zone 6.
H: to 60 ft. S: 20 ft.
   Makes a slender dense cone that's pleasing on its own or when used as a foil or backdrop to contrasting conifers or deciduous trees with white, red, or yellow bark. The shiny green foliage has a fine texture and is arrayed in flattened fanlike sprays. The cones are marble-sized, and the reddish brown bark forms long vertical strips or plates. There are hundreds of cultivars, many less hardy than others, in varying size and hues. 'Ellwoodii' is especially hardy. 'Allumii' has soft blue-gray foliage and a compact upright form; planted 3 ft. apart, it makes a tidy narrow hedge. 'Minima Aurea' is a gold-foliaged upright dwarf, reaching only 2 ft. in a dozen years. 'Silver Queen' is large, fast-growing, and conspicuously variegated.
   C. nootkatensis, the Nootka cypress, is not as fussy about soil and tolerates more cold but less heat than the Lawson cypress does. *C. n.* 'Pendula' has drooping side branches; 'Aurea' and 'Lutea' have gold or yellow new growth.
   How to grow: Full or part sun. Prefers fertile soil with constant moisture. Does best in mild western climates; can't tolerate southern or desert heat. Shearing for hedges is best done in summer. Cut only into green wood.

***obtusa* and its cultivars** (p. 189)
Hinoki cypress.
Conifers. Zone 5.
H: 40–60 ft. S: 15–30 ft.

The Hinoki cypress's rich emerald green color is a joy when the feathery branches are dusted with snow. The flattened sprays of tiny rounded scales have a texture that invites touching. The species makes a gorgeous tall hedge or screen, and the dwarf forms make excellent foundation, rockery, or patio plants. There are hundreds of cultivars, differing in foliage color and texture, rate of growth, mature size, and habit. 'Nana Gracilis' (slowly growing to 6 ft. and eventually reaching 10–12 ft.) has shiny dark green foliage arranged in dense curving sprays; it's one of the most popular of all dwarf conifers. 'Nana' and 'Kosteri' are even more dwarf, reaching only 3 ft. after decades. 'Crippsii' (to 30 ft.) has broad sprays of golden foliage. 'Coralliformis' or 'Torulosa' (to 10 ft.) has bright green foliage compressed into slender cordlike strands.

How to grow: Full or part sun. They prefer moist, fertile soil but tolerate ordinary conditions. Plant in fall and mulch well. Protect from winter sun and wind, which can discolor or scorch the foliage.

***pisifera* cultivars** (p. 188)
Sawara cypress.
Conifers. Zone 5.
H: varies. S: varies.

The species, infrequently grown, makes a broad cone and loses its lower limbs with age. The many cultivars are much more popular and make prime specimens for foundation planting or mixed beds. 'Squarrosa' has silvery gray-green foliage and makes a compact cone when young but grows loose and open when it matures at 30 ft. or more. 'Boulevard' or 'Cyano-Viridis' makes an irregular cone, slowly reaching 10 ft. or more, and has especially soft and fluffy foliage, silver-blue in summer, tinged purple in winter. Both 'Squarrosa' and 'Boulevard' have the flaw of retaining dead brown foliage, and they need pruning for tidiness and to reveal the branch structure as they age. 'Filifera Aurea Nana' or 'Golden Mop' has long, threadlike, golden foliage on a small dense plant. 'Nana' makes a very small (2 ft.), flat-topped, dark green bun.

How to grow: Like *C. obtusa.*

Chamaecyparis pisifera

Chamaemelum
Kam-e-mel´um.
Compositae. Daisy family.

Perennial herbs with aromatic feathery leaves and small daisylike blossoms. Only 3 or 4 spp., native to Europe and the Mediterranean region.

nobile (p. 281)
Roman chamomile.
Perennial herb. Zone 4.
H: 4–12 in. S: 12–18 in.

Makes a flat, spreading, branching mat with finely dissected leaves. Can be planted between flagstones or used as a ground cover that tolerates light foot traffic. The leaves release a pungent fragrance when stepped on or mowed. The solitary flower heads, like tiny daisies with white rays and yellow disks, open from summer into fall. The dried flowers make a soothing tea with an applelike fragrance; in Spanish the plant is called *manzanilla,* or "little apple." 'Grandiflora' has larger flowers, and 'Flore-Pleno' has double flowers.

How to grow: Full sun. Tolerates heat. Prefers dry soil. Plant seedlings or divisions 1 ft. apart for quick cover. Trim back in spring. If used as a lawn substitute, mow 3–4 in. high.

Chamaerops
Ka-mee´rops.
Palmae. Palm family.

A fan palm that usually forms low clumps. Only 1 sp., native to the Mediterranean region.

humilis (p. 164)
European fan palm.
Fan palm. Zone 8.
H: 6–20 ft. S: 6–8 ft.

Carefree and tough, this is one of the most attractive of the slow-growing, clump-forming palms. The bright green leaves spiral around the trunk and fan out into long slender leaflets. Flowers and fruits are inconspicuous. Use one clump by a pool or patio for a tropical effect. Can also be grown in containers.

How to grow: Sun or shade. Tolerates heat and is hardy to 10° F for brief periods. Grow in ordinary or poor soil with regular rainfall or watering. Separate suckers from older plants if the clump gets too dense.

Chamaerops humilis

Chasmanthium
Kaz-man´thee-um.
Gramineae. Grass family.

Perennial grasses that form clumps or small patches, with uniquely flat seed heads that dangle over the broad leaf blades. Only 5 spp., native to eastern North America.

Chasmanthium latifolium

latifolium (p. 209)
Northern sea oats, spangle grass.
Perennial grass. Zone 4.
H: 3–5 ft. S: 2 ft. or more.

Easy to grow and shade-tolerant, this clump-forming grass makes an excellent ground cover on slopes or open woodland; smaller clumps can accent a pathway or add contrast to a perennial border. The close-set leaves are broad for a grass, green in summer and fall and warm tan in winter. The flat drooping clusters of oat-like seed heads sway above the leaves in the slightest breeze and look wonderful in winter when displayed against a fence or snow. As cut flowers, they last in dried arrangements for more than a year. Spreads fast (by seed) in wet sites, less invasive in dry conditions.

How to grow: Full or part sun or shade. Looks best in full sun and moist, fertile soil. Tolerates poor or dry soil and heat. Sow seeds or increase by division in spring; space 2 ft. apart for mass plantings. Cut back to the ground in early spring.

Cheiranthus
Ky-ran´thus. Wallflower.
Cruciferae. Mustard family.

Low-growing perennials with very sweetly scented flowers in early spring. About 10 spp., native to Europe and Asia.

'Bowles Mauve' (p. 232)
(*Erysimum* 'Bowles Mauve')
Wallflower.
Perennial. Zone 6.
H: 2 ft. S: 3 ft.

Makes a handsome mound of soft gray-green foliage, covered for weeks in early spring with small mauve flowers that draw raves from garden visitors. A single clump makes a fine specimen in a border of purple, pink, and white flowers. Easy to grow and especially popular in southern gardens. Wallflowers, *C. cheiri*, are bushy biennials or perennials topped with clusters of sweet, bright flowers in many shades of yellow, orange, red, pink, and rose. They look lovely with tulips but require cool summers and mild winters for best growth.

How to grow: Full sun. Grows best in well-drained, fertile soil with regular watering. Plants form a neat mound the first year but tend to sprawl and flop apart in later years. It's best to start new plants from seeds or tip cuttings every summer. For best bloom, all wallflowers should be planted by late summer so that their leaves and roots can grow steadily through autumn.

Chelone
Ke-low´nee. Turtlehead.
Scrophulariaceae. Foxglove family.

Perennials with leafy stems bearing dense spikes of white, pink, or purplish flowers. Only 5 or 6 spp., native to wetlands in eastern North America.

Chelone lyonii

lyonii (p. 232)
Turtlehead.
Perennial. Zone 3.
H: 36 in. S: 30 in.

The clear pink flowers (which really do look like little turtles' heads) are tightly clustered in upright spikes that draw attention from late August until frost. The large, lance-shaped, green leaves are lush and full all season. Lovely beside a pond or stream, combined with sweet pepperbush. *C. glabra* has white or very pale pink flowers; *C. obliqua* has deep rosy purple flowers over a very long period.

How to grow: Full or part sun. Prefers moist, fertile, organic soil. Tolerates ordinary soil and heat if regularly watered. Plant in spring, 3 ft. apart. Doesn't need staking. Pest-free.

Chimonanthus
Ki-mo-nan´thus.
Calycanthaceae. Sweet shrub family.

Deciduous shrubs with fragrant yellow flowers in late winter, before the leaves open. Only 4–6 spp., native to China.

praecox (p. 133)
Wintersweet.
Deciduous shrub. Zone 7.
H: 9 ft. S: 12 ft.

You wouldn't notice this irregular, multi-stemmed shrub in summer or fall, but the sweet spicy fragrance of its pale yellow (blotched with purplish brown) flowers is a distinct treat in winter. Blooms between December and March, with clusters of 1-in. flowers on the previous year's wood. Plant it where you'll pass it often, near a door or sidewalk. Can be trained against a wall to perfume entryways or patios. 'Luteus' has brighter yellow flowers; var. *grandiflorus* has larger leaves and flowers. *C. nitens* is an ever-green species for warmer climates, with white flowers.

How to grow: Full or part sun. Tolerates summer heat if shaded. Ordinary soil and watering. Prune or train immediately after flowering. Pest-free.

Chionanthus
Ki-o-nan´thus.
Oleaceae. Olive family.

Deciduous trees or shrubs with dangling clusters of white flowers in late spring and blue berries in late summer. Only a few spp., native to eastern North America and China.

virginicus (p. 112)
Fringe tree, old-man's-beard, snow tree.
Deciduous tree. Zone 5.
H: to 30 ft. S: to 30 ft.

Usually growing as an open, multitrunked dome, fringe tree is spectacular in bloom. Clusters of fleecy white flowers with a spicy fragrance blanket the tree for about 2 weeks in late spring or early summer. It blooms profusely even

Chionanthus virginicus

when young. Male trees have larger flowers; females (if pollinated) produce small dark blue fruits that attract birds in late summer. The large oval leaves are dark green in summer, often turning bright yellow in fall. Awkward as a specimen because it leafs out late, but it fits well along the edge of a property or into a mixed shrub border (prune to keep it in scale). A small grove of fringe trees would be outstanding. *C. retusus*, the Chinese fringe tree, is similar but has smaller, shiny, leathery leaves and flowers a little later.

How to grow: Full or part sun; flowers best in sunny sites. Prefers fertile, organic, acidic soil but tolerates poor or dry soil and heat. Grows disappointingly slowly but needs no special care once established.

Choisya

Choy'si-a.
Rutaceae. Citrus family.

Evergreen shrubs with glossy compound leaves and fragrant white flowers. About 7 spp., native to the southwestern United States and Mexico.

ternata (p. 170)

Mexican orange, mock orange.
Evergreen shrub. Zone 8.
H: 10 ft. S: 10 ft.

An easy-to-grow shrub with an erect mounded habit, useful as an informal hedge or low screen, as a clipped hedge, or in foundation plantings. The shiny, thin, bright green compound leaves have 3 oval leaflets. Star-shaped white flowers, 1 in. wide, form dense clusters at the branch tips in early spring and intermittently through summer. Blossoms are very fragrant and last well as fresh cut flowers.

How to grow: Full or part sun. Needs ordinary or better soil and infrequent but deep watering. Plant 4–5 ft. apart for a hedge. Grows quickly. Thin from time to time to encourage new growth from within.

Chrysanthemum

Kri-san'thee-mum.
Compositae. Daisy family.

Gardeners and taxonomists have different visions of the genus *Chrysanthemum*. To gardeners, it's a group of easy-to-grow annuals, perennials, and subshrubs with daisylike blossoms that are cheerful in the garden and long lasting as cut flowers. Their foliage often has a pungent fragrance. The plants gardeners grow belong to just a few species, but there are thousands of cultivars.

Taxonomists used to lump between 100 and 200 species, including many of no interest to gardeners, into the genus *Chrysanthemum*, but it was a motley grouping that invited revision. There have been various attempts to regroup the species into several smaller genera, which explains why the Latin names listed below have so many synonyms. Fortunately, the common names are much less confusing and generally reliable for distinguishing one plant from another.

coccineum (p. 233)

(*Pyrethrum roseum, Tanacetum coccineum*)
Painted daisy, pyrethrum.
Perennial. Zone 4.
H: 18–30 in. S: 12 in.

Makes a feathery mound of finely cut, fernlike foliage. Single, upright, unbranched stalks carry solitary 2–3-in.-wide daisies in shades of white, pink, or rosy red, all with yellow disks. The yellow disk flowers from a related species, *C. cinerariifolium*, are the main source of the insecticide pyrethrum. Painted daisies make long-lasting cut flowers, and several shades massed together make a wonderful display in the garden, especially when combined with bearded irises, lupines, or catmint. Several strains, including doubles and dwarfs, are easily raised from seed.

How to grow: Full sun, or part shade where summers are hot. Needs well-drained soil and regular watering. Sow seeds in spring. Mixes will produce some excellent and some inferior plants—save and divide the best ones and discard the others. Set 12–18 in. apart. May need staking. Cut flower stalks to the ground after bloom fades.

frutescens (p. 233)

(*Anthemis frutescens, Argyranthemum frutescens*)
Marguerite.
Tender perennial. Zone 9.
H: 3 ft. S: 4–5 ft.

Valuable for their quick growth and abundant bloom, marguerites can fill a large container in one season or add mass and color to a new garden. One plant can make a 3–4-ft.-wide mound in a single growing season. The smooth, bright green, coarsely toothed leaves are smothered with white, pink, or yellow daisies, $1^{1}/_{2}$–$2^{1}/_{2}$ in. wide, throughout summer and fall and intermittently in winter and spring. Cultivars differ in flower color, size, and form. 'White Lady' and 'Pink Lady' have buttonlike flower heads. 'Snow White' has double anemone-type flowers and a more restrained habit.

How to grow: Full sun. Ordinary or poor soil and regular watering. Tolerates heat. Tender to cold but makes a good patio plant where it isn't hardy in the ground. Plants are fast-growing but short lived. Root tip cuttings or buy replacements every 2–3 years. Space 3–4 ft. apart for a quick mass planting. Subject to leafminers, thrips, root gall, nematodes, and fasciation (cresting), which deforms flowering branches.

× *morifolium* (p. 233)
(*Dendranthema × grandiflorum*)
Hardy garden chrysanthemum, florist's chrysanthemum.
Perennial. Hardiness depends on cultivar.
H: usually under 3 ft. S: 3 ft. or more.

Popular for their brightly colored, long-lasting flowers in fall, chrysanthemums are easy to grow in containers, raised planters, beds, or borders. There's an endless array of cultivars, colored white, yellow, bronze, orange, pink, red, or purple, sometimes with two or more colors in the same flower. Some have tall erect flower stalks, good for cutting. Others form low spreading mounds. Blossoms may be single (like daisies), double (flat in back but rounded and fluffy in front), pompom (ball-shaped), button (less than 1 in. wide and rounded), or fancy forms with "petals" shaped like spoons or quills. Don't bother transplanting the fancy types grown in florists' greenhouses; they usually don't do well outdoors. There are plenty of good garden varieties hardy even in Zone 6 or 5.

Chrysanthemums need "short days"—actually long nights—to flower. They begin to form flower buds as the nights get longer in late summer and fall. Early bloomers need fewer hours of darkness to begin budding; some start blooming as early as late August, so they avoid hard frosts in northern gardens. Late bloomers need more hours of darkness to initiate buds. They get frozen in cold northern gardens, but they start late and continue past Christmas in California and the South. In mild climates, mums may keep blooming or bloom again in spring, since nights are long all winter.

How to grow: Full sun or light shade part of the day. Needs well-drained, fertile soil and regular watering. Fertilize twice, in spring and summer. Local nurseries sell potted plants in late summer and fall that will continue to bloom for weeks after you plant them in the garden. After flowering, cut the stalks back to 6-in. stubs and use a loose mulch to protect the crown over winter. In spring, divide the clump into separate rooted shoots or root tip cuttings. You can also buy a wide variety of rooted cuttings from mail-order suppliers in spring. Several strains of hardy chrysanthemums can be raised easily from seed and will blossom the first year from an early spring sowing. Pinch the tips back hard two or three times to shape low growers into dense bushy mounds. Stake tall forms if you want straight stems, and remove side buds if you want just one big flower per stalk. Watch for and control aphids and spider mites.

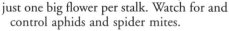

nipponicum (p. 233)
(*Nipponanthemum nipponicum*)
Nippon daisy.
Perennial. Zone 5.
H: to 30 in. S: 24 in.

Doesn't bloom until fall, with typical white daisies about 2 in. wide, but earns its place all summer with a show of particularly handsome foliage. The rich green leaves, borne all the way up and down the stems, are thick, smooth, and lustrous. Looks nice with slender elements such as grasses or iris leaves and seedpods. *C. pacificum* (best in Zone 7 and warmer climates) is grown primarily for its foliage—the small scalloped leaves are gray-green edged with white. It forms a low spreading mound, 1 ft. high by 3 ft. wide. Blooms too late for northern gardens but bears clusters of little gold buttons in the South.

How to grow: Full sun. Needs well-drained ordinary or better soil and regular watering. Easy to grow and pest-free. Pinch several times to encourage branching, but stop pinching a few months before frost so that the buds will have time to develop. Old plants get woody at the base and are hard to divide. Start new plants by rooting tip cuttings in spring.

parthenium (p. 282)
(*Matricaria capensis, Tanacetum parthenium*)
Feverfew.
Perennial herb. Zone 5.
H: 1–3 ft. S: 1–2 ft.

Carefree and easy to grow, with pungently aromatic ferny foliage and masses of $1/2$-in. daisies off and on all summer and fall. Start it once, and you'll have it forever. Sprinkled or massed here and there, the flowers add light and harmony to a mixed planting and are lovely combined with lavender and roses. The leaves are used medicinally (to cure migraines) and as an insect repellent. Cut flowers are very long lasting in water. There are double forms, both white and yellow. 'Aureum' has golden yellow foliage.

How to grow: Full sun. Well-drained soil with regular watering. Not reliably winter-hardy in the North, nor summer-hardy in the South, but it self-sows, and double-flowered or gold-leaved forms usually come true from seed. Cut back after flowering to encourage repeat bloom. Attacked by aphids but has few other pests.

rubellum 'Clara Curtis' (p. 233)
(*Dendranthema zawadskii* var. *latilobum*)
Perennial. Zone 4.
H: 12–18 in. S: 24 in.

Spreads fairly rapidly, making mounds of slender branched stems topped with 2–3-in. clear pink daisies. Starts blooming in mid- to late summer and continues for many weeks. Nice massed in the garden and makes good cut flowers. Attractive paired with silvery artemisias. 'Duchess of Edinburgh' has coppery red flowers.

How to grow: Full sun. Prefers light sandy soil and ordinary watering. Divide and replant

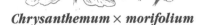

Chrysanthemum × morifolium

every year or two in spring. Monitor and treat for insect pests to avoid distorted leaves and flowers.

× *superbum* (see below for photo)
(*Leucanthemum* × *superbum*)
Shasta daisy.
Perennial. Zone 4.
H: 12–36 in. S: 18 in.

Large, white, wide-awake daisies are good companions for nearly all border perennials and make fine cut flowers. Several cultivars have been developed since Luther Burbank first produced this hybrid in 1890. Most form a low mat of shiny, smooth, coarsely toothed, dark green leaves that are nearly evergreen. The daisies are borne singly on erect stalks. 'Alaska' (2–3 ft.) and 'Miss Muffet' (to 1 ft.) have single flowers. 'Marconi', 'Mount Shasta', and 'Wirral Pride' have double flowers.

C. leucanthemum 'May Queen' (*Leucanthemum vulgare* 'May Queen'; p. 233) is an improvement on the common oxeye daisy or field daisy, with single blossoms 1–2 in. wide on unbranched stems. Blooms in early summer, then off and on until fall. The dark green leaves, in basal rosettes, are thick and leathery. Stalks are strong and don't need staking. Lovely in cottage gardens or wildflower meadows.

How to grow: Full sun. Ordinary or better soil and regular watering. Needs good drainage, particularly in winter. Buy plants or start seeds indoors in early spring (plants from the latter may not bloom the first year). Divide every spring and replant rooted stems 1–1¹/₂ ft. apart. (Don't divide in fall; late transplants rarely survive the winter.) Deadhead regularly, and cut all flower stems to the ground after blooming. Tall cultivars will probably need staking. Watch for aphids.

Cimicifuga
Sim-i-cif'u-ga.
Ranunculaceae. Buttercup family.

Perennials with upright stems, large compound leaves, and tall wands of white flowers. Some are used medicinally. About 15 spp., native to rich woodlands in the north temperate zone.

racemosa (p. 234)
Black cohosh, bugbane, black snakeroot.
Perennial. Zone 3.
H: 2 ft. (foliage) to 8 ft. (flowers). S: 3–4 ft.

A long-lived, easy-to-grow perennial that covers acres of woodland understory in the East. Tall wiry stems emerge from the foliage, branching and carrying long tapered wands of starry white flowers for 3–4 weeks in mid- to late summer. Unsurpassed for producing a dramatic effect against a dark background of trees. Combine it with Japanese anemones and garden phlox. *C. simplex* 'White Pearl' is more compact, with long sprays of flowers on arching stems, 3–4 ft. tall, in late fall.

How to grow: Part sun or shade. Needs fertile, acidic soil and constant moisture. Top-dress with aged manure or compost every year. Plant in spring or fall, spaced 2 ft. apart. Divide only when the clump gets too big. In spite of its height, it does not need staking.

Cinnamomum
Sin-na-mo'mum.
Lauraceae. Laurel family.

Evergreen tropical trees or shrubs with aromatic leaves and bark, providing camphor, cinnamon, and fragrant timber. About 250 spp., native to eastern and southeastern Asia and Australia.

camphora (p. 157)
Camphor tree.
Evergreen tree. Zone 9.
H: 50 ft. or more. S: 50 ft.

A broad, bulky shade tree with a thick trunk and heavy limbs, good for large lawn areas or broad parking strips. Leaves are shiny pale green. New growth is flushed with red. Clusters of tiny yellow flowers in spring are followed by small shiny black fruits in fall. All parts are fragrant; camphor is distilled from the wood and bark.

How to grow: Full sun. Ordinary soil and watering. Avoid planting near a sidewalk, as the roots will lift paving. Thin the limbs occasionally to lessen wind resistance, and remove broken or dead wood. Self-sows freely and can be a pest around flower beds.

Cistus
Sis'tus. Rock rose.
Cistaceae. Rock rose family.

Mostly evergreen shrubs of low spreading habit with simple opposite leaves and wide, open flowers. Some yield fragrant resins. About 17 spp., native to the Mediterranean region, and a few cultivated hybrids.

× *corbariensis* (p. 170)
(*C. hybridus*)
White rock rose.
Evergreen shrub. Zone 8.
H: 3–5 ft. S: 3–4 ft.

An easy, showy shrub for hot, dry climates. Makes a spreading mound of crinkled, gray-green, 2-in.-long leaves that release an incenselike fragrance on warm, still days. Round white flowers, 1¹/₂ in. wide, open over a long period in late spring. Makes a good cover for banks or hillsides; blends well with California natives and other Mediterranean-climate plants.

How to grow: Full sun. Ordinary or poor, unamended soil. Loves heat; tolerates drought when established. Plant in fall where winters are mild and wet. Space 3 ft. apart for mass plantings. Pinch tips to fatten young plants. Thin old branches from established plants. Pest-free and easy to grow.

Chrysanthemum leucanthemum

Cistus ladanifer

other rock roses

C. ladanifer, the crimson-spot rock rose, has larger flowers with a crimson dot at the base of each white petal; thick, dark green, 4-in.-long leaves with a gummy surface; and delightful fragrance. Var. *immaculatus* has unspotted white flowers. 'Blanche' and 'Paladin' are lower-growing (to 3 ft.) and have 4-in.-wide white flowers. *C. × purpureus* has 3-in.-wide reddish purple flowers with dark red eyes, and rough, leathery, dark green leaves 1–2 in. long. *C. salviifolius* (often sold as *C. villosus prostratus*), the sageleaf rock rose, is low and spreading (2 ft. high by 6 ft. wide). It has thick fuzzy gray leaves and white flowers and makes a good ground cover for poor soil and hot exposures.

How to grow: Like *C. × corbariensis.*

Citrus

Sit′rus.

Rutaceae. Citrus family.

Evergreen trees or shrubs, usually spiny, with glossy simple leaves, richly fragrant white or pale pink flowers, and aromatic juicy fruit. This genus includes oranges, lemons, grapefruits, limes, and other citrus fruits; all are notably handsome plants. About 16 spp., native to southern and southeastern Asia.

limon 'Eureka' (p. 157)

'Eureka' lemon.

Evergreen tree. Zone 9.

H: 20–25 ft. S: 20–25 ft.

Where the climate allows, all citrus fruits give 4-season beauty with shiny, leathery, bright green leaves; powerfully fragrant blossoms; and showy, tasty fruit. Most citrus are available on dwarfing rootstock; such plants are best for small gardens. They bear full-size fruit on half-size plants and make excellent shrubs in the ground or in containers. Full-size trees can furnish shade and screening as well as ornament.

The 'Eureka' lemon is selected here only because of its culinary utility and ability to ripen in coolish summers. Where hardy, it is seldom out of fruit. Many other citrus are excellent landscape plants. The 'Lisbon' lemon is somewhat more heat-tolerant. 'Improved Meyer' is hardier to cold and tends to be a smaller plant, with rounded, orange-yellow, less-acid fruit. Other good choices include the 'Bears' seedless lime, 'Minneola' tangelo, 'Dancy' tangerine, 'Marsh' seedless and 'Ruby' grapefruits, 'Valencia' and 'Washington' navel oranges, and 'Owari Satsuma' mandarin.

A few nurseries in the South and the Pacific Northwest are experimenting with citrus supposed to be hardy in Zone 8, but these are not yet widely available. Gardeners in cold climates can maintain a dwarf citrus tree for years in a 12-in. pot, taking it outdoors for the summer and overwintering it in a cool sunroom or greenhouse, or even a bright window.

How to grow: Full sun. Needs ordinary or better soil and deep, infrequent watering.

Citrus 'Marsh' grapefruit

Fertilize for good appearance and good crop. Little pruning is needed. Subject to many pests and diseases, but few concern home gardeners. Watch for spider mites, scale, snails, and fruitworms.

Cladrastis

Kla-dras′tis.

Leguminosae. Pea family.

Deciduous trees with pinnate leaves, drooping clusters of white pealike flowers, and thin flat pods. About 5 spp., one from the eastern United States and the rest from eastern Asia.

lutea (p. 112)

(*C. kentuckea*)

Yellowwood.

Cladrastis lutea

Deciduous tree. Zone 3.

H: 30–50 ft. S: 40–50 ft.

Its medium size, broad rounded crown, and spreading branches make yellowwood a perfect shade tree, especially where space is limited. The compound leaves are glossy bright green in summer, yellow in fall. The 1-ft.-long drooping clusters of sweet white flowers last for 3–4 weeks in early summer. 'Rosea' has pink flowers.

How to grow: Full sun. Prefers well-drained, fertile, organic soil. Tolerates some heat. Prune to shape when dormant. Spread or eliminate narrow crotches, which are prone to split during storms. Pest-free. Its deep roots allow underplanting.

Clematis

Klem′a-tis.

Ranunculaceae. Buttercup family.

Most clematis are deciduous vines, but some are evergreen vines and a few are deciduous perennials or semishrubs. In climbing types, the leaf petiole wraps like a bent elbow around a wire or other support. Most have wide flat flowers with 4 to many sepals (in clematis, what look like petals are actually sepals); some have smaller, nodding, urn-shaped flowers. In fall, watch for fluffy clusters of feathery-tailed seeds. About 250 spp., nearly all native to the north temperate zone, and hundreds of hybrid cultivars. The large-flowered hybrids are perhaps the most popular of all garden vines.

armandii (p. 200)

Evergreen clematis.

Evergreen vine. Zone 8.

H: 20 ft. or more.

A magnificent vine for covering a porch or pergola, running an "eyebrow" along a fence or wall, or covering a derelict tree or outbuilding. The leathery, firm, dark green leaves are divided into 3 slender leaflets and have a bold effect. Bears an abundance of fragrant, big (to 3 in.) white flowers for a long season in early spring.

How to grow: Sun or shade. Ordinary or improved soil and average watering. One plant is enough for most gardens. Train it up the support to get it started. Prune hard after bloom to prevent tangling and to keep new growth coming from below. Its only problems are rampant growth and a tendency to go bare at the base.

macropetala (p. 201)

Downy clematis.
Deciduous vine. Zone 5.
H: 6–10 ft.

This clematis has flaring double flowers (to 4 in. wide) reminiscent of a ballerina's tutu. Flowers on seed-grown plants range from white to deep blue; most are lavender-blue, and 'Markham Pink' is pink. The flowers open from spring to summer and are scentless. The showy, feathery seed clusters last into fall. The compound leaves are dark green. More restrained than some clematis, this looks good scrambling over shrubs, as a ground cover, at the edge of a woodland, or on a trellis.

How to grow: Full or part sun. Ordinary or fertile soil and regular watering. Prune immediately after bloom.

maximowicziana (p. 201)

(*C. terniflora, C. dioscoreifolia, C. paniculata*)
Sweet autumn clematis.
Deciduous vine. Zone 4.
H: 20 ft. or more.

A tough carefree vine that sprawls over fences or clambers on trees and shrubs. Covered in late summer with a cloud of small, starry, fragrant (some say vanilla-scented) white flowers. The silvery plumelike fruits are decorative through fall. An old-fashioned favorite and still very popular. Indispensable for softening and disguising chain-link fences. It's aggressive, but you can let it run through a hedge or climb a conifer if you cut it back hard every few years. Don't worry about all its Latin names; just ask for sweet autumn clematis and most nurseries will know exactly what you want.

How to grow: Part sun. Ordinary soil and watering. Its only problem is its extreme vigor in mild climates; it's more restrained where winters are cold. Cut back frozen shoots to healthy wood in spring. Blossoms on new growth.

montana (p. 201)

Anemone clematis.
Deciduous vine. Zone 6.
H: 25 ft. or more.

Gives an overwhelming show of white or pinkish almond-scented flowers in spring, each 2–3 in. wide, with 4 large sepals—like dogwood blossoms on a vine. Not invasive, but it is massive and can cover a large wall or pergola. Let it grow into a pine or yew tree and it will spray festoons of flowers against a dark background. Can decorate yards of fence top or chain-link fence.

Var. *rubens* has bronzy new growth and pink flowers and is somewhat hardier. 'Tetrarose' has larger (4 in.) deep pink flowers.

How to grow: Sun or shade. Ordinary or better soil and regular watering. Provide a sturdy support; one plant can become quite large, eventually with a heavy trunk. Prune immediately after flowering to thin and control growth.

tangutica (p. 202)

Golden clematis.
Deciduous vine. Zone 5.
H: 9–10 ft.

Unusual for its bright yellow, bell- or lantern-shaped, 2–4-in.-wide flowers that nod from slender stalks. They are scentless but showy over a long season in summer and fall, followed by masses of feathery seed clusters that shine bright and silvery into winter. Foliage is bright green and smooth. Not too aggressive for train-

Clematis jackmanii

Favorite hybrid clematis and their flower color

florida-type hybrids

'Belle of Woking': smaller double mauve flowers.
'Duchess of Edinburgh': larger double white flowers.

jackmanii-type hybrids

jackmanii: velvety purple-blue with wide sepals.
'Comptesse de Bouchard': soft rosy pink with rounded sepals.
'Hagley Hybrid': pale pink with brown stamens.
'Madame Edouard André': crimson with yellow stamens.
'Mrs. Cholmondeley': pale lavender-blue with long pointed sepals.
'Niobe': deep ruby red with gold stamens.

lanuginosa-type hybrids

'Candida': white with pale yellow stamens; large.
'General Sikorski': medium blue with puckered edges.
'Nellie Moser': pink with reddish center stripe.
'Ramona': lavender-blue with dark stamens.

patens-type hybrids

'Dr. Ruppell': pink with red center stripe.
'Lasurstern': blue with wavy edges and white stamens.
'Miss Bateman': white with brown stamens.
'The President': deep violet-purple with pointed sepals.

viticella-type hybrids

'Betty Corning': pale lavender bells.
'Ernest Markham': glowing velvety red.
'Lady Betty Balfour': deep violet-blue with cream centers.
'Madame Julia Correvon': wine red with yellow stamens.
'Ville de Lyon': bright red with darker edges.

ing through a shrub or tree, or let it sprawl among perennials. *C. orientalis,* the orange-peel clematis, is similar, with gray-green foliage. It has smaller but very thick-textured golden yellow flowers.

How to grow: Full or part sun. Ordinary or better soil and regular watering. Prune in early spring to encourage new flowering shoots, to limit height, and to keep from heaviness.

texensis (p. 202)
Scarlet clematis.
Deciduous vine. Zone 7.
H: 6–15 ft.

An unaggressive vine with dense leathery foliage and small (1 in.), nodding, bell-shaped flowers in spring and summer, sometimes continuing until fall. The 4 thick-textured sepals are red, rusty, maroon, or rosy pink. Tolerates heat and dryness better than most clematis do. 'Étoile Rosé' is a hybrid with silver-edged rosy purple sepals. Other Texas species have various shades of lavender flowers; look for them at native-plant nurseries.

How to grow: Full or part sun. Ordinary or dry soil. Dies back to the ground in winter, so it never gets very big. Prune in early spring; blooms on new growth. Can be grown in containers.

large-flowered hybrids (pp. 200, 201)
Deciduous vines. Zone 5.
H: to 15 ft.

Outstanding in bloom, hybrid clematis have flat blossoms 3–8 in. wide, with 4–8 or more large sepals in shades from white and pink to rich red, purple, and blue. There are hundreds of cultivars, grouped according to their parent species and differing in flower color and season of bloom (see box on p. 357). Most have similar foliage (dark green and leathery) and habit (slender stems that look weak but climb vigorously). A single plant trained up a lightpost or trellis by your entryway will make a brilliant mass of color for weeks. Plant one by the mailbox, along a fence, or against an evergreen hedge. Let another climb through a viburnum or dogwood tree. Plant several (4 ft. apart) for a ground-covering carpet of bloom. No more gorgeous hardy vine exists.

How to grow: These clematis are a bit fussy, but it's worth creating just the right conditions to have one of these beauties in your garden. Transplant from containers in early spring. They grow best with foliage and flowers in the sun but roots shaded by a rock, wall, or generous mulch. They prefer well-drained but moist, rich, neutral or limy soil. Insect pests do attack clematis but are rarely severe.

Pruning is important, but the timing depends on whether plants bloom on new or old shoots. The *jackmanii-* and *viticella-*type hybrids bloom on new growth. Prune them hard, cutting back to within 1 ft. of the ground in earliest spring when the buds begin to expand. Provide support immediately for the new shoots, which are brittle and break easily in the wind.

The *florida-, lanuginosa-,* and *patens-*type hybrids bloom on old shoots in spring and on new shoots in summer. Remove only dead or damaged shoots in very early spring; do the main pruning-back immediately after bloom in spring.

Cleome
Klee-oh´me.
Capparaceae. Caper family.

Most are perennials or shrubs with sticky foul-scented leaves and tough stems but lots of showy pink or white flowers. Some are edible or medicinal. About 150 spp., from warm and hot climates worldwide.

hassleriana (p. 293)
Spider flower.
Annual. All zones.
H: 4–5 ft. S: 3 ft.

A fast-growing, heat-loving annual that reaches bushlike proportions by late summer. Makes a big but airy mass. Blooms nonstop from midsummer to frost, with rounded clusters of rosy pink or white flowers at the tips of the branches. Use it to fill space in new gardens, as a temporary hedge, or at the back of a perennial border. Don't plant it close to a path; the strong, almost woody stems and small palmate leaves have a prickly texture and a fetid odor.

How to grow: Full sun. Ordinary soil and watering. Start seeds indoors and transplant about the time of last frost. Self-sows abundantly. After the first year, watch for volunteer seedlings after the soil warms and move them around when they're still small.

Clerodendrum
Klee-ro-den´drum.
Verbenaceae. Verbena family.

Evergreen or deciduous trees, shrubs, or vines with opposite oval leaves and big clusters of bright flowers with colorful lingering calyxes. About 400 spp., most from the Old World tropics.

trichotomum (p. 133)
Harlequin glory-bower.
Deciduous shrub. Zone 6.
H: 10–15 ft. S: 10 ft. or more.

Showy in late summer and fall, when it's covered with flower clusters 6–9 in. wide. The fleshy purplish red calyxes make a striking contrast with both the fragrant white 1-in.-long flowers and the sapphire blue pea-sized berries that follow. It "moves" by underground stems and forms a spreading clump of many upright stems with plain green leaves. Plan to control it with regular pruning, or tuck it in a far corner, out of harm's way.

How to grow: Full sun. Ordinary soil and watering. Dies back to the ground in severe winters but comes back and blooms on the current season's growth. Prune back early in the season to encourage branching and increased flower

Cleome hassleriana

production. Can be pruned to a single-leader tree in mild climates.

Clethra
Kleth´ra.
Clethraceae. Summer-sweet family.

Deciduous or evergreen shrubs or trees with terminal clusters of fragrant white or pink flowers. About 60 spp., most native to tropical climates.

alnifolia (p. 133)
Sweet pepperbush, summer-sweet.
Deciduous shrub. Zone 5.
H: 9 ft. S: 12 ft.

One bush will fill the whole garden with a sweet spicy fragrance when it blooms in midsummer. Spreads slowly to form a clump of upright stems, each topped with a 4–6-in. spire of small white flowers. Leafs out in late spring. 'Rosea' has pale pink flowers; 'Pinkspirc' is rosy pink.

How to grow: Full or part sun. Prefers moist, fertile soil. Tolerates seasonal flooding and poor drainage but also grows in ordinary borders if well watered and shaded from hot afternoon sun. Plant 5–6 ft. apart for a hedge. Needs little pruning.

barbinervis (p. 133)
Japanese clethra.
Deciduous shrub. Zone 6.
H: 12–15 ft. S: 12 ft.

A large shrub or small tree with sweetly fragrant flowers in slender 6–8-in. clusters at the branch tips in midsummer, when most shrubs are finished. The older stems have shedding gray-brown bark, handsome all winter. Makes a good companion for azaleas, rhododendrons, and pieris, in a border shaded by tall trees. Use ferns, hostas, or other perennials to fill around the base.

How to grow: Part sun. Prefers well-drained, organic soil and ordinary watering. Needs little pruning. Pest-free.

Clytostoma
Kly-tos´to-ma.
Bignoniaceae. Trumpet creeper family.

Evergreen vines or climbing shrubs with showy tubular flowers. About 9 spp., native to South America.

callistegioides (p. 203)
Violet trumpet vine.
Evergreen vine. Zone 9 or 8.
H: 30–40 ft.

Furnishes a quick evergreen cover for a fence or wall or an "eyebrow" for a balcony or eave. The compound leaves each have 2 shiny, substantial, oblong, bright green leaflets. Lavender or light purple trumpet flowers, 3 in. wide, are clustered at the shoot tips from late spring to fall. Makes a good background for hibiscus, geraniums, or showy annuals.

How to grow: Full or part sun. Ordinary soil and watering. An aggressive grower that needs hard pruning in late winter to prevent tangles; it can build up into an untidy jungle if not controlled. Freezes to the ground but recovers in Zone 8.

Colchicum
Kol´chi-kum.
Liliaceae. Lily family.

Perennials with white, purple, or yellow crocuslike flowers in fall or spring; grassy or bladelike leaves; and bulblike corms. The bulbs produce colchicine, a poisonous compound used in plant breeding and to treat gout. About 65 spp., native to Europe, Asia, and northern Africa.

hybrids (p. 234)
Meadow saffron.
Perennials. Zone 4.
H: under 1 ft. S: under 1 ft.

Plants make a clump of smooth straplike leaves (3–4 in. wide by 12 in. long) in spring, go dormant in summer, then suddenly produce showy rosy purple, pink, or white flowers in autumn, just when you thought the growing season was over. Flowers open 6 in. wide on sunny days and close at night. Use a low-growing ground cover such as periwinkle or ajuga to provide a background and to help support the floppy blossoms, which often collapse after a rain. 'Autumn Queen' (deep violet), 'Lilac Wonder' (lavender-pink), 'The Giant' (mauve and white), and 'Waterlily' (double lavender) are some of the best cultivars. The parent species, *C. autumnale* and *C. speciosum,* are less showy.

How to grow: Full or part sun. Ordinary soil. Can tolerate heat and dry soil. Plant corms 3–4 in. deep and apart in late summer, when they're dormant, where you can leave them undisturbed for years. Plants spread slowly by seed and offsets.

Coleus
Ko´lee-us.
Labiatae. Mint family.

Perennials or annuals, usually succulent, with square stems, opposite leaves, and small white or pale lavender flowers. About 150 spp., native to the Old World tropics.

blumei (p. 293)
(*Solenostemon scutellarioides*)
Coleus.
Tender perennial grown as an annual. All zones.
H: 1–2 ft. S: 1–2 ft.

Their glowing colors make coleus good leafy companions for wax begonias and impatiens in lightly shaded summer beds. Useful in containers and raised beds and especially beautiful when seen backlit. There are hundreds of cultivars and seed strains. Some are more compact, some are

Clethra alnifolia

multicolored, some have fringed or ruffled leaves. Leaf colors include green, chartreuse, yellow, cream, pink, salmon, orange, and red. The spikes of tiny blue flowers aren't unattractive, but they detract from the leaves.

How to grow: Part sun, filtered shade. Prefers fertile soil and constant moisture. Start seeds indoors 8 weeks before last frost or buy plants at local nurseries; plant 8–16 in. apart when the soil is warm. Choose just a few of the many color variations to avoid a jumbled look in mass plantings. To encourage compact, bushy plants, pinch tips and remove flower buds as they form. Feed often with a high-nitrogen liquid fertilizer. Cuttings root easily in a glass of water if you want to grow favorite plants on a windowsill in winter and save them from year to year.

Comptonia

Komp-to´ni-a. Sweet fern.
Myricaceae. Wax myrtle family.

A deciduous shrub with fragrant leaves reminiscent of fern fronds. Only 1 sp., native to eastern North America.

peregrina (p. 133)
Sweet fern.
Deciduous shrub. Zone 3.
H: to 4 ft. S: 4 ft. or more.

A very tough, adaptable plant for acidic soils. The dark green leaves, 2–4 in. long by 1/4 in. wide, have rounded lobes along both edges, a leathery texture, and a spicy fragrance. Flowers are inconspicuous. Spreads slowly to make a flat-topped colony. Combine it with grasses as a ground cover for exposed, infertile, difficult sites.

How to grow: Full or part sun. Tolerates sandy, acidic sites with scant topsoil. Transplant from containers in spring or fall. No maintenance needed.

Comptonia peregrina

Conradina

Kon-ra-dee´na.
Labiatae. Mint family.

Low shrubs with aromatic needlelike leaves and pale mintlike flowers. Only 4 spp., native to restricted sites in the southeastern United States.

verticillata (p. 282)
Cumberland rosemary.
Evergreen woody herb. Zone 5.
H: 15 in. S: 12 in. or more.

This small shrub is rare and endangered in its native habitat—sandy riverbanks in eastern Tennessee and Kentucky—but nursery-propagated plants are increasingly popular in gardens from New England to Texas. It forms a spreading mound of thin stems with fine, dark green leaves that resemble rosemary foliage but have a strong minty aroma. Small pale pink-purple flowers appear in midspring. Makes a fine low hedge or ground cover in sandy soil.

Convallaria majalis

How to grow: Full or part sun. Requires well-drained soil and tolerates dry sites. Plant 1–2 ft. apart. Prune to shape as desired. No maintenance required. Easily propagated by layering, from cuttings, or from seed.

Consolida

Kon-sol´i-da.
Ranunculaceae. Buttercup family.

Annuals with leaves like birds' feet and unusual spurred flowers in shades of blue, pink, purple, or white. About 40 spp., native to Europe and Asia.

ambigua (p. 293)
Larkspur, annual delphinium.
Annual. All zones.
H: 1–4 ft. S: 1 ft.

A cool-loving annual with showy spikes of blue, lilac, pink, or white flowers. Cut flowers last well in water and hold their color when dried. Leaves are divided into narrow segments. The branching flower stalks are strongly upright. Different strains vary in height; tall varieties may need staking or support. Combines well with foxgloves, Canterbury-bells, sweet Williams, and Shirley poppies. A mass planting is very showy in late spring and early summer.

How to grow: Best in full sun. Ordinary soil and watering. Sow seeds directly where they are to grow, in late fall or very early spring. Seedlings are hardy to frost and prefer cool, damp weather. Plants self-sow readily, and they sometimes continue for years where conditions are favorable.

Convallaria

Kon-va-lair´ee-a. Lily-of-the-valley.
Liliaceae. Lily family.

Deciduous perennials that spread as a low dense ground cover. Sweet white flowers that dangle like tiny bells are followed by pea-sized red berries. Only 3 spp., native to the north temperate zone.

majalis (p. 235)
Lily-of-the-valley.
Perennial. Zone 2.
H: 8 in. S: forms patch.

The marvelously fragrant flowers hang like little white bells from a slender curved stalk. Blooms for 2 weeks in midspring. Smooth oval leaves with pointed tips arise from creeping rootstocks and make a solid patch of green, turning gold in fall. It's vigorous and invasive in cold climates, where regular mowing won't keep it from spreading into a lawn. There it's best used as a ground cover to carpet a woodland or to fill space under shrubs on the north or east side of a house. Where summers are hot or dry, it's much less aggressive, even puny, but worth coddling for its unequaled perfume.

How to grow: Part sun or shade. Tolerates unamended and dry soil; competes well with shallow-rooted trees. Divide and replant anytime during the growing season. Specially prechilled "pips" are sold each winter for forcing early bloom indoors; keep them growing in the pot until you can plant them into the garden.

Coreopsis

Ko-ree-op´sis.
Compositae. Daisy family.

Perennials or annuals, most with abundant displays of yellow daisylike blossoms. More than 100 spp., native to the New World and Africa.

auriculata (p. 234)
Perennial. Zone 4.
H: 1–2 ft. S: 1 ft. or more.

Unusual among coreopsis, this native of the woodland and forest edge grows best in light shade and blooms in spring. The 1–2-in. golden yellow daisies rise above lobed, dark green foliage. 'Nana', a dwarf form, is the most popular. Plant it along the front of a shady border, or use it for an evergreen ground cover in a woodland garden.

How to grow: Part sun or shade. Prefers well-drained, fertile, organic soil. Raise the crown slightly above the soil surface when transplanting. Divide every few years for increased vigor.

grandiflora (p. 234)
Perennial. Zone 5.
H: 1–2 ft. S: 2 ft.

Easy to grow, with bright golden yellow daisies from late spring to early summer, continuing later if you deadhead conscientiously. The dark green leaves are deeply divided into slender leaflets. This species and the similar *C. lanceolata* are common wildflowers, suitable for meadow gardens and natural areas but too floppy for most borders. New cultivars such as 'Early Sunrise', 'Sunburst', and 'Sunray' are much more compact, stronger stemmed, and longer blooming than the parent species. Combine them with rudbeckias, Shasta daisies, or daylilies.

How to grow: Full or part sun. Tolerates poor or dry soil and heat. Deadheading increases the flowering period. Plants are short lived; divide regularly or cultivate the plentiful self-sown seedlings.

tinctoria (p. 293)
(*Calliopsis tinctoria*)
Dyer's coreopsis.
Annual. All zones.
H: 12–36 in. S: 6 in.

Popular in meadow gardens and prairie plantings; its tall slender form blends well with grasses. Foliage is scant, but the upright branching stalks carry dozens and dozens of bright yellow, maroon, and/or bicolor blossoms. Blooms from June to September if deadheaded.

How to grow: Full sun. Tolerates poor or dry soil and heat. Easy to grow from seed sown in fall or spring. Self-sows readily.

Coreopsis grandiflora

verticillata (p. 234)
Thread-leaved coreopsis.
Perennial. Zone 3.
H: 2–3 ft. S: 2–3 ft.

Valued for its deeply divided, fine, feathery foliage and pale golden yellow blossoms, 1–2 in. wide, borne for 4–6 weeks in midsummer. Spreads by thin stolons to form dense patches that add a distinctive texture to the mid-border or meadow. 'Moonbeam' forms a dense clump with pale yellow flowers. 'Zagreb' is compact (about 1 ft. tall), with darker yellow flowers. *C. rosea* has similar delicate foliage and 1-in. pale pink flowers. Unlike most coreopsis, it does well in damp, heavy soil.

How to grow: Full sun. Needs good drainage; tolerates dry or poor soil and heat. Increase by division in spring. There are too many flowers to deadhead individually, but you can trim off the top of the plant to encourage a second bloom.

Coriandrum

Ko-ree-an´drum.
Umbelliferae. Carrot family.

Annual herbs with strong-scented compound leaves, umbels of pale flowers, and fragrant edible fruits. Only 2 spp., native to Eurasia.

sativum (p. 282)
Cilantro, Chinese parsley, coriander.
Annual herb. All zones.
H: 1–3 ft. S: 1 ft.

Matures too fast to keep its place in an ornamental planting, but it's a must for herb gardens. The fresh leaves are a staple in Mexican and Oriental cookery, and the aromatic seeds are used in curries and ground as a spice. Quickly forms a rosette of lobed or pinnately compound leaves, then bolts up to bear umbels of white or pale rosy lavender flowers. 'Long Standing' coriander is leafier and waits longer before bolting.

How to grow: Full sun. Not fussy about soil. Sow small patches at 2–4-week intervals, starting in early spring where the plants are to grow, and thin seedlings to 6 in. apart.

Cornus
Kor´nus.
Cornaceae. Dogwood family.

An attractive group of trees and shrubs. Most are deciduous, with simple opposite leaves. Some have round clusters of small white or yellow flowers, while others have large, showy, white or pink bracts, all of which are followed by shiny berries that birds love. About 45 spp., native to the north temperate zone.

alba (p. 134)
Siberian dogwood.
Deciduous shrub. Zone 2.
H: 6–8 ft. S: 10–12 ft.

Makes a splendid addition to the shrub border, with interest in every season: the 2-in. clusters of small creamy flowers last for about 3 weeks in spring, the pale bluish white berries attract birds in summer, the oval leaves turn reddish purple in fall, and the young twigs are a glowing bright red in winter. 'Elegantissima', with white-variegated leaves, is particularly effective in shade. 'Spaethii' has leaves edged with yellow. 'Sibirica' has bright coral-red stems. Siberian dogwood is similar to *C. sericea* (listed on p. 363) but makes a more compact clump of stems and doesn't spread as fast.

How to grow: Full sun, part sun, or shade. Not fussy about soil and watering. Space 5–6 ft. apart for mass plantings. Cut older stems to the ground to force new growth, which has the best color. Very cold-hardy but doesn't grow well in the South or Southwest where summers are hot. Pest-free.

Cornus florida

florida (pp. 112, 113)
Flowering dogwood.
Deciduous tree. Zone 5.
H: 25 ft. S: often wider than height.

Beloved throughout the eastern United States, flowering dogwood is a small native tree that flowers in early spring, just before it and the other forest trees leaf out. The actual flowers are quite small, but each flower cluster is framed by 4 large white or pink bracts, and the overall effect is a cloud of bloom floating among the slender spreading branches. The smooth green leaves are dark green all summer and consistently turn red or maroon in fall, about the same time as the clusters of bright red berries ripen. Dogwoods are ideal for small gardens and are small and neat enough to plant near a building or patio. They're especially lovely along the edge of a woods or planted in the shade of tall, high-pruned oaks or pines.

Don't try to transplant a wild tree. It's much better to buy a nursery-propagated cultivar. Favorites include 'Cherokee Chief', with reddish pink bracts; 'Cherokee Daybreak', with white bracts and green-and-white variegated leaves; 'Cherokee Sunset', with red bracts and yellow-edged leaves; and 'Cloud 9', which is thickly covered with bracts even as a young tree.

C. nuttallii, the Pacific flowering dogwood,

Cornus kousa

looks similar, with 4–8 large white or pale pink bracts, but its buds freeze in cold winters and the tree is fussy about soil. 'Eddie's White Wonder', a hybrid of *C. florida* and *C. nuttallii,* is hardier and more vigorous, with blooms that completely cover the foliage in spring.

How to grow: Part sun or shade, especially where summers are hot or dry. Prefers well-drained, acidic soil with a layer of mulch. Prune lightly to develop shape. Susceptible to borers and various leafspots, and a fungal disease called anthracnose has killed many dogwoods in the Northeast and the southeastern mountains. Plants in shaded or sheltered locations where the foliage stays wet after dew or rain are most vulnerable to the fungus; pruning surrounding trees to increase air circulation is a worthwhile precaution.

kousa (p. 113)
Kousa dogwood.
Deciduous tree. Zone 5.
H: to 25 ft. S: to 25 ft.

This Asian dogwood flowers in early summer, about 3 weeks after the native flowering dogwood and well after the glossy green foliage has developed. The large creamy white bracts last up to 6 weeks. Worth planting for its flowers alone, it also offers plump red raspberry-like fruits from August to October and yellow-orange to scarlet fall color. If you have room, plant one where you can view it backlit against the sun in fall. Leave the lower branches for a broad, spreading specimen, or remove them to reveal the flaking gray, tan, and rich brown bark on the trunks and limbs of older trees. This tree's colors and horizontal branching make a handsome complement to a brick ranch-style house. There are several cultivars of Kousa dogwood, not commonly available, with pink bracts, weeping or upright habits, or variegated foliage.

The Stellar dogwoods (*C.* × *rutgersensis*) are newly released hybrids between flowering dogwood and Kousa dogwood. They bloom in the interval between the parent species and are particularly vigorous, healthy, and free-flowering.

How to grow: Full or part sun. Tolerates ordinary soil and watering but prefers well-drained, organic soil and constant moisture. Kousa dogwood is more cold-hardy than flowering dogwood but can't take as much summer heat. Tolerates but does not require any pruning. Unlike flowering dogwood, Kousa dogwood is highly resistant to both borers and anthracnose fungus.

mas (p. 113)
Cornelian cherry dogwood.
Deciduous tree. Zone 4.
H: 20 ft. S: 15 ft.

An excellent plant for northern gardeners because it blooms very early, well before forsythia and other familiar symbols of spring. The clustered small flowers are pale yellow and show up best against a dark building or evergreen tree; they last for up to 3 weeks. Bright red fruits like small cherries ripen in summer; you can use them for preserves if the birds don't get them first. The smooth healthy foliage turns yellow, orange, or red in fall, varying from tree to tree and year to year. Usually grown as a densely branched shrub, this dogwood can screen views, traffic, or wind. It can also be trained as a multitrunked small tree. 'Golden Glory' has an upright habit, especially dark green leaves, and more profuse flowers and fruits. 'Flava' has yellow fruits. There are also variegated forms.

How to grow: Full or part sun. Prefers ordinary conditions but tolerates unamended soil and dryness better than other dogwoods do. It's one of the toughest, most drought-tolerant trees for cities in the Northeast and Midwest. Pruning is optional. Very pest-free.

sericea (p. 134)
(*C. stolonifera*)
Red-osier dogwood.
Deciduous shrub. Zone 2.
H: to 10 ft. S: to 10 ft.

A wonderful shrub for cold climates, where the bright red or yellow stems are a cheerful sight against a background of snow or dark conifers. The clusters of white flowers are showy in spring and are followed by white berries in early fall. The oval leaves are dark green in summer, purplish in fall. 'Cardinal' is an excellent selection with stems that change from cherry red to watermelon pink to chartreuse over the course of the winter. 'Kelseyi' is a dwarf (to 2 ft.) with large leaves and red stems; it doesn't flower or fruit much. 'Flaviramea' has golden yellow stems in winter. 'Silver and Gold' has cream-variegated leaves and yellow stems.

How to grow: Full sun, part sun, or shade. Native to swampy sites and prefers moist or seasonally wet soil but tolerates ordinary conditions. The fibrous roots will stabilize soil along a pond edge or creek bank. Space 5–6 ft. apart for a hedge or mass planting. Fast-growing. Prune old stems to the ground every 2–3 years to encourage new growth from the base. Specimens can be trimmed to the ground every spring for maximum color.

other tree dogwoods
Two other dogwoods are increasingly popular as specimen trees with attractive silhouettes.

C. alternifolia, the pagoda dogwood, is a large shrub or small tree (15–25 ft.) with branches that spread horizontally and bend up at the tips, like the roof of a pagoda. Handsome all year, it has clusters of small flowers in spring and reddish berries in summer. It is native throughout the East and hardy to Zone 3. *C. controversa*, the giant dogwood, is an Asian species that grows quickly into a large spreading tree, clothed with creamy white flowers in spring. Both species have white-variegated forms that are especially striking.

Cortaderia
Kor-ta-dee'ree-a. Pampas grass.
Gramineae. Grass family.

Perennial grasses that form huge clumps of slender, arching, sharp-edged leaves. Feathery plumes on woody stalks rise in the center of the clumps. About 24 spp., native to South America and New Zealand.

selloana (p. 209)
Pampas grass.
Clumping grass. Zone 7.
H: 8 ft. or more. S: 8 ft. or more.

Tough as nails but very showy. Makes a huge billowing clump of slender leaves that rise up through the center and arch over to the ground; foliage is nearly evergreen in Zone 9, turns tan in colder zones. Cotton-candylike flowering plumes on stiff stalks lift 2 ft. or more above the foliage in late summer and remain showy through midwinter. Female plants are showier than the males. It is most often used as a single specimen in mid-lawn but is perhaps better as a barrier hedge or wind screen, because it gets quite big and the leaf edges are dangerously sharp. 'Rosea' and 'Rubra' have pink plumes. 'Pumila' is a dwarf with flower stalks only 6 ft. tall.

How to grow: Full or part sun. Grows anywhere; not fussy about soil or watering. Space 10 ft. apart for mass plantings. Remove old plumes in spring. Cutting back old foliage is a major chore every few years; burning it off is an easier solution if allowed in your area.

Corylopsis
Kor-ril-lop'sis. Winter hazel.
Hamamelidaceae. Witch hazel family.

Deciduous shrubs or small trees with fragrant yellow flowers that appear before the leaves in spring. Only 7 spp., native to eastern Asia.

glabrescens (see below for photo)
Fragrant winter hazel.
Deciduous shrub. Zone 5.
H: 8–15 ft. S: 8–15 ft.

Fragrant pale yellow flowers dangling from the bare branches are a welcome sign of winter's end, and they can be forced into earlier bloom indoors. Makes a multistemmed dome, open at the base and rounded on top with arching branches. The heart-shaped leaves are soft bluish green in summer, yellow in fall. Best used along a woodland walkway, in a shrub border, or at the edge of a property, underplanted with blue-leaved and a few contrasting gold and green hostas. *C. pauciflora* (p. 134), or buttercup winter hazel, is daintier and more compact (4–6 ft. tall), with smaller leaves and primrose yellow flowers.

How to grow: Full or part sun. Needs ordinary or improved soil and regular watering. Best in a protected site; flowers can be damaged by late frosts. Needs little pruning and has no pests.

Corylus

Kor´i-lus. Hazelnut, filbert.
Betulaceae. Birch family.

Deciduous shrubs or trees with drooping catkins in spring, toothed leaves that make a dense crown in summer, and edible nuts in fall. About 10 spp., native to the north temperate zone.

avellana 'Contorta' (p. 135)

Harry Lauder's walking stick.
Deciduous shrub. Zone 4.
H: 7 ft. S: 6 ft.

Most interesting in winter, this is a curiosity with contorted branches that twist into irregular spirals. The bark is shiny brown. Male catkins up to 3 in. long dangle conspicuously in late winter and early spring. Leaves are coarse and dull. Most effective as a specimen on a rocky site or combined with dwarf conifers and winter-hardy cacti and succulents. *C. avellana* and *C. americana* are both vigorous multistemmed shrubs that make dense hedges and bear edible hazelnuts.

How to grow: Full sun. Ordinary soil and watering. These plants are almost always propagated by grafting, but the understock inevitably suckers vigorously, making corrective pruning an annual ritual. Cut all straight shoots back to the base. Subject to various blights and diseases.

Cosmos

Kos´mos.
Compositae. Daisy family.

Perennials or annuals with slender branching stems, finely divided opposite leaves, and bright daisylike blossoms on long stalks. About 26 spp., native to the southwestern United States and Mexico.

bipinnatus (p. 294)

Cosmos.
Annual. All zones.
H: to 6 ft. S: to 4 ft.

Robust and easy to grow, and blooms abundantly for several weeks. The daisylike blossoms, up to 4 in. wide, have yellow disks and pink, rose, lavender, purple, or white rays. Cut them for bouquets, or let them go to seed and feed the goldfinches. Old-fashioned varieties get quite large but still look graceful and delicate, because the leaves are divided into slender segments and the stems branch repeatedly with an open, airy habit. Useful as a quick filler or temporary screen in new gardens, or allow it to naturalize among perennials or shrubs. 'Sensation' has large single blooms; 'Sonata' has 3-in. flowers on compact 2-ft. plants. Other forms have striped, curled, or double flowers.

How to grow: Full sun. Ordinary or unimproved soil. Almost carefree but needs an occasional soaking during long dry spells. Sow seeds indoors 6 weeks before last frost, or sow directly in the garden after frost. Volunteers readily.

sulphureus (p. 294)

Yellow cosmos.
Annual. All zones.
H: to 3 ft. S: to 2 ft.

Smaller and brighter than common cosmos and even more tolerant of poor soil, heat, and dryness. The rough stems branch repeatedly and make a bushy plant with no pinching. The daisylike flowers are bright yellow, orange, or reddish orange. Blooms nonstop for months if deadheaded regularly. Combine with other bright colors—sunflowers, heleniums, and daylilies—or contrast with soft-colored foliage such as gray artemisias or blue fescue. 'Diablo', 'Bright Lights', and 'Sunny Red' are popular strains, listed in most seed catalogs.

How to grow: Like *C. bipinnatus.*

Cotinus

Kot´i-nus, ko-ty´nus. Smoke tree.
Anacardiaceae. Sumac family.

Deciduous shrubs or small trees with a bushy upright habit and rounded leaves that turn bright colors in fall. The flowers are small and drop soon, but the much-branched flower stalks expand into hairy puffs that last all season. Only 3 spp., one each from the southeastern United States, Asia, and China.

coggygria (p. 135)

Smoke tree.
Deciduous shrub. Zone 3.
H: 12–18 ft. S: 10 ft.

This is a tough, trouble-free, tolerant shrub or tree that grows well even in abused urban soils, but it's attractive enough to earn a space in the finest mixed borders. The pingpong-paddle-shaped leaves are smooth and healthy, bright green or purple in summer and turning orange, scarlet, or maroon in fall. The fluffy clouds of pink or purple "smoke" that cover the foliage all summer are wiry, much-branched flower stalks; the actual flowers are small and drop quickly. 'Notcutt's Variety', 'Royal Purple', and several other cultivars all have rich purple foliage that makes an excellent companion for pink, blue, or white perennials or contrasts with pale yellow. *C. obovatus,* the American smoke tree, grows wild on rocky limestone ledges from the Appalachians down into Texas. Easily trained as a single-trunked tree, it has larger leaves that turn vivid shades of red, orange, and gold in fall.

How to grow: Full or part sun. Tolerates poor soil, acidic or alkaline, and summer dryness. Blooms on new growth, so prune in early spring. Cutting the stems back to the ground each year forces tall straight shoots with larger, brighter-colored leaves. No serious pests or diseases.

Cotoneaster

Ko-to´nee-as-ter.
Rosaceae. Rose family.

Evergreen or deciduous shrubs with white or pink flowers and red or dark fruits that last from fall to spring. Most branch repeatedly; some grow upright, while others spread sideways. About 50 spp., native to Europe and Asia.

apiculatus (p. 135)

Cranberry cotoneaster.
Deciduous shrub. Zone 3.
H: 3 ft. S: 5 ft.

An excellent woody ground cover for cold climates, with arching stems that stack up in layers, gradually forming low mounds. The roundish 1/2-in. leaves have wavy margins and are glossy dark green in summer, burgundy in fall. Small pale pink flowers appear in late spring, cranberry-sized bright red fruits in fall. Looks wonderful trailing over a limestone retaining wall, where the light-colored background accentuates the herringbone branching pattern. *C. adpressus* var. *praecox,* or early cotoneaster, is very similar in all ways.

How to grow: Full or part sun. Prefers fertile, amended soil but tolerates both acidic and alkaline conditions. Space 2 ft. apart for mass plantings. Established plants tolerate some dryness but are subject to spider mites and fire blight when stressed by heat or drought. Doesn't do well in the South or Southwest.

dammeri (p. 170)

Bearberry cotoneaster.
Evergreen shrub. Zone 5.
H: 1 ft. S: 6 ft. or more.

A fast-growing woody ground cover for sun or shade. Forms a low, densely branched mat, and the stems root where they touch the ground. The narrowly oval leaves, under 1 in. long, are firm and leathery, bright green in summer, turning dull green or purplish in cold weather. The white flowers are fleeting in spring, but the bright red 1/2-in. berries are showy in late summer. Covers a bank quickly, or can spill over walls. Combine it with conifers or evergreen ferns, or contrast its daintiness with bold-leaved hostas. 'Coral Beauty' (or 'Royal Beauty') has coral-red fruits and grows up to 2 ft. tall. 'Lowfast' stays under 1 ft. and quickly spreads 12–15 ft. wide.

How to grow: Like *C. apiculatus.* Plant 3–4 ft. apart for ground cover. Fire blight can be a problem. Prune out stricken branches well behind the afflicted area, and sterilize clippers with diluted household bleach between cuts.

divaricatus (p. 135)

Spreading cotoneaster.
Deciduous shrub. Zone 5.
H: 5–6 ft. S: 10–12 ft.

An open, airy shrub that does well in shade and makes a mounded understory under large trees. The small shiny leaves turn red in fall. Pink flowers in May are followed by bright red

berries that last into early winter. Handsomest if unpruned and given enough room to develop its natural spreading shape.

How to grow: Like *C. apiculatus.* Plant 4–5 ft. apart when massing; allow 10 ft. or more for a specimen.

horizontalis (p. 135)

Rockspray cotoneaster.
Deciduous shrub. Zone 4.
H: 3 ft. S: 5–6 ft.

A low, spreading shrub with a distinctive herringbone branching pattern. Branches overlap into layered mounds that spill gracefully over a wall or bank. Also can be espaliered against a north or east wall. The fine-textured foliage is dark green in summer, red in fall. Small red berries add interest in fall and winter. A few cultivars are particularly low-growing and follow the contours of the ground. 'Variegatus' has tiny leaves edged in white and is dainty but very slow-growing.

How to grow: Like *C. apiculatus.*

lacteus (p. 170)

(*C. parneyi*)
Red clusterberry.
Evergreen shrub. Zone 7 or 6.
H: 5–9 ft. S: 5–9 ft.

Has red berries in 2–3-in. clusters that last nearly all winter, displayed against the evergreen foliage. The oval 2-in. leaves are thick and leathery with distinct veins, dark green above and silvery beneath. Makes an arching, fountain-shaped shrub with a dense but graceful form, useful as an informal screen or hedge or in a shrub border. *C.* × *watereri* grows twice the size, with larger leaves and fruits.

How to grow: Like *C. apiculatus.* Looks best with minimal pruning, just thinning and heading back where necessary. Don't shear. Tolerates heat and dryness when established.

multiflorus (p. 135)

Many-flowered cotoneaster.
Deciduous shrub. Zone 3.
H: 10 ft. S: 15 ft.

One of the most ornamental large deciduous shrubs, with the showiest flowers of any cotoneaster, refreshing gray-green foliage, abundant red fruits in fall, and a spreading fountain-like habit that's attractive in the winter months. Leaves are 2 in. long. The white flowers are 1/2 in. wide, borne in clusters of 3–12. Give it plenty of room to develop, and use it as a focal point or specimen. The gray stems in winter stand out best when planted against conifers or a dark stone or brick wall or building.

How to grow: Like *C. apiculatus.* Prune only as needed to develop character and help shape its natural form. Relatively immune to fire blight.

Cotoneaster dammeri

salicifolius (p. 170)
Willowleaf cotoneaster.
Evergreen shrub. Zone 6.
H: 10 ft. or more. S: to 10 ft.

The species is an upright shrub with arching branches, but low-growing cultivars are more popular. The simple slender leaves, up to 3 in. long, are shiny dark green in summer, usually turn purple in winter, and may be damaged or drop in cold climates. The bright red berries last into winter. 'Autumn Fire' ('Herbstfeuer'), 'Emerald Carpet', 'Repens', and 'Scarlet Leader' are ground-cover types that stay under 2 ft. tall and spread several feet wide.

How to grow: Like *C. apiculatus*. Relatively free of fire blight.

Crambe

Kram´be.
Cruciferae. Mustard family.

Perennials or annuals with coarse leaves and dainty flowers. Some have edible shoots or seeds. About 20 spp., all from the Old World.

cordifolia (p. 235)
Perennial. Zone 6.
H: 6 ft. S: 4 ft.

A dramatic, magnificent plant for a large garden. Forms a loose mound of coarse, scratchy, heart-shaped leaves, 2 ft. wide. Strong branched stems shoot up and produce clouds of small 4-petaled white flowers in early summer. Finches like the seeds that follow. Needs plenty of space. Site it at the back of a border, behind peonies or other mid-height perennials, or against a fence or wall.

How to grow: Full sun. Ordinary or limy soil. Needs good drainage. Easy from seed and blooms the second or third year, or divide the thick woody rootstock in early spring. Bloom stalks need staking. Foliage is prey to slugs and caterpillars.

Crataegus

Kra-tee´gus. Hawthorn.
Rosaceae. Rose family.

Deciduous small trees or shrubs, usually thorny, with branches that zigzag horizontally. They have white flowers in spring and attractive summer foliage but are most conspicuous in fall and winter when laden with gold, red, or dark fruits that look like tiny apples. At least 300 spp., native to the north temperate zone, and many hybrids and varieties.

crus-galli (p. 113)
Cockspur hawthorn.
Deciduous tree. Zone 4.
H: 25–30 ft. S: 20–25 ft.

A small tree with a wide-spreading crown. The clusters of 1-in.-wide white flowers look pretty but smell foul in spring. The simple glossy leaves turn gold, orange, or red in fall. The red fruits are pea-sized. The fierce branched thorns, up to 3 in. long, make a dramatic silhouette in winter but are so threatening that some cities have ordinances banning this tree. Var. *inermis* is thornless and makes a fine, harmless specimen.

How to grow: Full sun. Ordinary soil and watering. Prune to shape, training one or multiple trunks, and remove lower limbs to allow underplanting. Very hardy and tough, but pests and diseases may disfigure the foliage.

phaenopyrum (p. 113)
Washington hawthorn.
Deciduous tree. Zone 3.
H: 25 ft. S: 20 ft.

An excellent small tree with multiple trunks and spreading branches. Clusters of many small white flowers open in June, after most other trees have blossomed, followed by bright red fruits that color in late summer and hang on through winter. The glossy triangular or oval leaves turn bright red in fall. Best used as a specimen set in the open or against a dark background; also effective for mass plantings or tall screens. The sharp thorns, 1–3 in. long, limit use near sidewalks or play areas.

How to grow: Full or part sun. Very tolerant of poor soil conditions—alkalinity, compaction, low organic matter, seasonal wetness or dryness. Needs minimal pruning. Relatively problem-free; one of the best hawthorns for gardens.

viridis 'Winter King' (p. 113)
Deciduous tree. Zone 4.
H: 25 ft. S: 25 ft.

A top-notch tree with year-round interest. It has a vase-shaped habit with spreading limbs and very few thorns. It bears 2-in. clusters of small white flowers all along the branches in late spring, followed by a profusion of fruits that ripen red in fall, then turn orange in winter, attracting cedar waxwings and other birds in spring. The glossy leaves are thick and healthy. Older specimens have flaking silver, gray, and brown bark. Makes a very handsome specimen, underplanted with woodland wildflowers or shade perennials.

How to grow: Like *C. phaenopyrum*.

other hawthorns

The three species above are native to the eastern United States. Many other native species do well in cultivation and are increasingly available. *C. brachyarantha*, or blueberry haw (Zone 7), has blue fruits. *C. marshallii*, or parsley haw (Zone 7), has unique foliage—the leaves look like parsley—and musclelike trunks with mottled bark. *C. mollis*, or downy hawthorn (Zone 3), looks like an apple tree, with soft gray-green leaves and large red fruits that drop in September. *C. opaca*, or mayhaw (Zone 6), has red fruits that ripen in May, rather than in fall, and grows in poorly drained soil where water collects in spring.

Species native to Europe and the British Isles are popular in gardens there and are often grown here. 'Paul's Scarlet', 'Crimson Cloud' (or 'Superba'), and other cultivars of *C. laevigata*, or

English hawthorn (Zone 5), grow about 15 ft. tall and are beautiful in bloom. *C. monogyna,* or singleseed hawthorn (Zone 4), has particularly sweetly scented flowers (most hawthorns have a foul, musty odor); the cultivar 'Biflora', or Glastonbury thorn, is legendary for its habit of flowering at Christmastime.

Crinum

Kry'num.
Amaryllidaceae. Amaryllis family.

Tender perennials with giant bulbs and floppy straplike leaves, but valued for their lilylike white, pink, or red flowers. About 130 spp., native to tropical climates, and some hybrids.

hybrids (p. 235)
Milk-and-wine lilies.
Perennials. Zone 7.
H: 2 ft. or more. S: 1–2 ft.

Most crinums are large, tender perennials with giant bulbs, cornlike foliage, and fragrant lilylike flowers. Several species and hundreds of hybrids and cultivars are cultivated in mild climates. Many forms, commonly called milk-and-wine lilies, have white petals with pink or wine stripes. Some kinds have such slender petals that the flowers look spidery. Hybrids between *Amaryllis* and *Crinum* have lovely fragrant flowers and more-refined foliage. All crinums are extremely tough and long lived and do best if left alone for years.

How to grow: Sun or shade. Most crinums aren't fussy about soil; many tolerate seasonal wetness or dryness. Propagate by removing offsets from old clumps. Pest-free and require no maintenance.

Crocosmia

Kro-kos'mee-a.
Iridaceae. Iris family.

Perennials with small corms, slender irislike leaves, and long stalks of very bright flowers. About 10 spp., native to South Africa, with a few hybrids and cultivars.

'Lucifer' (p. 235)
Crocosmia, montbretia.
Perennial. Zone 5.
H: 3 ft. S: 1 ft.

Makes wonderful long sprays of clear bright red flowers in summer, long lasting in the garden and excellent as cut flowers. The color absolutely gleams on a sunny day. Also makes a handsome fan of slender ribbed leaves. Underground corms multiply rapidly to form showy clumps. Other crocosmias are old-fashioned favorites with yellow, orange, red, or bicolor flowers.

How to grow: Full sun. Grows fine in ordinary soil in the summer but needs good drainage to survive the winter outdoors. Plant on slopes or in raised beds, or lift bulbs in the fall and store indoors like gladioli. Divide every few years. Trouble-free.

Crocus

Kro'kus.
Iridaceae. Iris family.

Perennials with small corms, grassy leaves, and bright white, yellow, blue, or purple flowers on short stems in spring or fall. About 80 spp., native from the Mediterranean region to China.

ancyrensis 'Golden Bunch' (p. 236)
Golden bunch crocus.
Perennial. Zone 3.
H: 6 in. S: 6 in.

Welcomes spring with cheery clusters of small bright golden flowers. Each corm produces as many as 10 blossoms. Narrow grassy leaves emerge with the flowers and grow for 2–3 months before withering. Can be naturalized in a part of the lawn that doesn't need early mowing, or plant it in drifts under early-blooming shrubs such as daphnes, winter hazel, witch hazel, or fragrant honeysuckle.

How to grow: Full sun. Grows best in well-drained, gritty soil amended with leaf mold or fine compost. Plant in early fall, about 4 in. deep. Grouped bulbs look better than uniformly spaced individuals. Set bulbs in groups about 2 in. apart. Allow the leaves to ripen naturally after flowering. Every few years, when flowering is reduced by crowding, fork up the clumps after the leaves have withered, then divide and replant the bulbs. Squirrels, chipmunks, and gophers are the worst enemies of crocuses. If you can control these pests by means of an industrious cat or traps, the crocuses will spread by division and by self-sowing.

chrysanthus (p. 236)
Golden crocus.
Perennial. Zone 4.
H: 4–6 in. S: 6 in.

Smaller and more delicate than the common Dutch crocuses, with masses of honey-scented flowers in early spring. Easy to grow and ideal for naturalizing in "wild" gardens. There are many cultivars with flowers in shades of yellow, white, blue, or purple, including some with striped or bicolor petals. 'Blue Pearl', 'Cream Beauty', 'E. A. Bowles', 'Ladykiller', and 'White Triumphator' belong to this species.

How to grow: Like *C. ancyrensis.*

speciosus (p. 236)
Autumn crocus, showy crocus.
Perennial. Zone 5.
H: 4–6 in. S: 6 in.

This flowers during fall foliage season, and the delicate little blossoms make a poignant contrast to colored leaves, ripe berries, and gone-to-seed perennials. Petals are blue, lavender, purple, or white, sometimes with dark veins. Grassy foliage emerges with the blossoms and continues to develop through fall, then dies back in winter. *C. sativus,* or saffron, is another fall-blooming crocus with lilac flowers. Its bright orange stigmas are used to color and flavor food.

How to grow: Like *C. ancyrensis.*

Crinum hybrid

vernus (p. 236)
Dutch crocus, common crocus.
Perennial. Zone 5.
H: 4–8 in. S: 6 in.

These are the most commonly grown crocuses, popular for early spring bloom. Plant clumps of them along the south side of the house or on a south-facing slope where the soil warms early. Flowers open in the sun and close at night or on cloudy days. The large-flowered (2–4 in. long by 1–3 in. wide) cultivars are hybrids of this species. 'Peter Pan' is white, 'Pickwick' is lilac with darker stripes, 'Remembrance' is purple, and 'Yellow Mammoth' is just like its name.

How to grow: Like *C. ancyrensis.*

Cryptomeria

Krip-to-meer´ri-a. Japanese cedar.
Taxodiaceae. Bald cypress family.

An evergreen conifer with a strong upright trunk, drooping branches, and short, slightly curving needles. Only 1 sp., native to eastern Asia.

japonica (p. 189)
Plume cedar.
Conifer. Zone 6.
H: 40–60 ft. S: 15–20 ft.

A tall, fast-growing tree resembling a coast redwood in size and form, with a narrowly erect habit, often leaning to one side. Sometimes planted in groves to counterfeit Japanese castle gardens or forest effects. 'Elegans' is one of many dwarf cultivars, better suited for small gardens. It makes a dense pyramid, 20–25 ft. tall, of fluffy, feathery foliage, gray-green in summer and turning purplish bronze in winter. Plant a single specimen or a pair at an entryway, or a row along a substantial driveway.

How to grow: Full or part sun. Ordinary soil and watering. Dislikes alkaline soil. Shear lightly to restrict size, if desired.

Cunninghamia

Kun-ning-ham´ee-a.
Taxodiaceae. Bald cypress family.

Evergreen conifers with a thick trunk, drooping branches, and stiff pointed needles. Only 2 spp., native to eastern Asia.

lanceolata (p. 189)
China fir.
Conifer. Zone 7 or 6.
H: 50–60 ft. S: 20–30 ft.

A tall, rather formal pyramidal tree. Young trees retain lower whorls of branches that sweep the ground like a long skirt; older specimens lose lower limbs to reveal bark that peels in long vertical strips. Needles are stiff and fairly sharp, to 2 in. long by 1/4 in. wide, dark green in summer and purplish bronze in winter. Best used as a residential lawn specimen; sometimes planted in parks, on campuses, or near large buildings.

'Glauca' has blue-gray foliage year-round and is widely adapted; it is hardier (Zone 6 or 5) than the species but also makes a good substitute for Colorado blue spruce in southern gardens.

How to grow: Full or part sun. Ordinary soil and watering. Does best in sheltered locations; both hot summer wind and cold winter wind can scorch the foliage. Prune away suckers at the base of the trunk.

Cupaniopsis

Kew-pan-i-op´sis.
Sapindaceae. Soapberry family.

Evergreen trees or shrubs with handsome pinnately compound leaves and inconspicuous flowers. About 60 spp., native to Australia and the South Pacific islands.

anacardiodes (p. 158)
(*C. anacardiopsis*)
Carrotwood, tuckeroo.
Evergreen tree. Zone 9.
H: 25–40 ft. S: 25–40 ft.

A neat and handsome evergreen tree with an erect trunk and a spreading crown. The compound leaves have 4–12 oblong leaflets and are smooth, leathery, and dull dark green. The tiny clustered flowers are inconspicuous but lightly fragrant in spring and are sometimes followed by yellow-orange fruits.

How to grow: Full sun. Very tough and tolerant. Used mostly as a street tree in mild climates, where it endures heat, wind, ocean spray, and poor soil, wet or dry. Grows easily from seed; fruit and self-sown seedlings can be a nuisance. Prune to thin mature trees as desired. Pest-free.

× *Cupressocyparis*

Kew-press-o-sip´a-ris. Leyland cypress.
Cupressaceae. Cypress family.

An evergreen conifer with flat sprays of feathery foliage. Quickly grows into a nice conical shape. Only 1 sp., a unique hybrid between *Cupressus macrocarpa* and *Chamaecyparis nootkatensis,* found in an English garden in 1888.

leylandii (p. 189)
Leyland cypress.
Conifer. Zone 6.
H: 20–40 ft. S: 20 ft.

Because this graceful conifer is fast-growing and tolerates many soils and exposures, it is often planted for a hedge or screen or used for a quick specimen in subdivisions or newly developed sites that lack mature trees. It is also grown commercially on Christmas-tree plantations. Young plants can grow 2 ft. or more each year, and they grow naturally in a neat conical shape. Older trees have a more open, spreading, informal habit. Limbs branch into flattened sprays clothed with tiny, flat, scalelike leaves that have a rich green color year-round and a pleasing

× *Cupressocyparis leylandii*

aroma when crushed. There are several cultivars. 'Green Spire' forms a dense column of bright green foliage. 'Naylor's Blue' is pyramidal, with blue-gray foliage. 'Silver Dust' has new growth blotched with white.

How to grow: Full or part sun. Ordinary or unimproved soil. Tolerates occasional drying out. Roots rot on poorly drained or wet sites. Plant 5–10 ft. apart for a quick hedge or screen. Needs no pruning. Bagworms are a major pest in some regions, and a severe infestation can defoliate and kill a tree.

Cupressus
Kew-pres'sus. Cypress.
Cupressaceae. Cypress family.

Evergreen conifers with round woody cones and fragrant scalelike leaves that hug the twigs. 13 spp., native to warm regions in the Northern Hemisphere.

arizonica (see below for photo)
Arizona cypress.
Conifer. Zone 7.
H: 30–40 ft. S: 15–25 ft.

A fast-growing conifer native to northern Mexico and the Southwest, popular for windbreaks, screens, or specimens in hot desert climates. The silhouette can be rounded, conical or pyramidal, or columnar, always with a strong central trunk. Foliage is fine-textured; leaves are small and flat, like scales. Cones are 1-in. balls. Older plants have handsome peeling bark. 'Gareei' has a pyramidal shape and silvery blue foliage, attractive summer and winter; it is hardy throughout Zone 7 and southern Zone 6. *C. glabra* (p. 189), the smooth Arizona cypress, is so similar that some botanists include it with *C. arizonica*. It's unusually drought-tolerant. The trunk sheds its outer bark to reveal smooth, shiny, dark red inner bark.

How to grow: Full sun. Thrives in hot, dry conditions and tolerates poor soil but responds well to amended soil, fertilizing, and watering. Grows quickly but sometimes dies young. Subject to bark beetles, bagworms, spider mites, and juniper blight or cankers.

sempervirens 'Stricta' (p. 189)
Italian cypress.
Conifer. Zone 8.
H: 30–40 ft. S: 6–10 ft.

The skinniest of trees, this makes a narrow column of dense, dark, dull green, scalelike foliage. It's very conspicuous in a garden because of its distinct shape; use one or two at a gate or doorway, or plant a row at measured spacing to emphasize a formal drive or property line. Plants often have multiple leaders. Let them spread apart for an irregular, interestingly shaped specimen, or tie them together to make a neatly columnar tree. Various narrow, dense clones are sold under the name 'Stricta'. 'Glauca' has blue-green foliage.

How to grow: Full sun. Tolerates heat.

Grows very quickly if fertilized and watered regularly. Bagworms and juniper blight are problems in hot, humid climates. Spider mites attack plants in hot, dry sites.

Cyclamen
Sick'la-men, sy'kla-men.
Primulaceae. Primrose family.

Perennials with a tuft of waxy-textured rounded leaves that sprout from flattish corms. Long-lasting white, pink, or magenta flowers have thrown-back petals and nod above the foliage on long stalks. 17 spp., native from central Europe to the Middle East.

hederifolium (p. 237)
(*C. neapolitanum*)
Baby cyclamen.
Perennial. Zone 6.
H: 3–4 in. S: 8–12 in.

It's worth bending down for a closer look at this plant. It blooms in fall, with pink or white flowers on single stalks about 4 in. tall. The crimson "eye" in the center of the flower looks down at the ground, but the twisted petals sweep upward. The large (to 5 in. long) heart-shaped leaves, pale green marked with silvery spots and veins, have a thick texture and a waxy surface. They appear in fall, last all winter, then disappear in late spring. Forms stout corms, up to 6 in. wide, right beneath the soil surface. Wonderful for naturalizing under deciduous or evergreen trees on well-drained sites. Specialists offer other species of cyclamen, but this is the easiest to grow. There are white, pink, and sweetly scented strains.

How to grow: Shade. Needs well-drained soil, preferably amended with organic matter and coarse sand or grit. Needs ordinary watering from fall to spring, infrequent water during summer. Plant dormant corms in summer, 12 in. apart, and cover with 1/2 in. of soil. Do not cultivate around the corms. Roots emerge from the upper surface, and leaf petioles and flower stalks creep several inches under the soil before ascending. Leave plants undisturbed for years, and they will gradually multiply. Easy from seed, but takes 3–4 years to reach blooming size. Relatively pest-free.

Cupressus glabra

Cymbopogon
Sim-bo-po'gon.
Gramineae. Grass family.

Tropical grasses forming dense clumps of slender arching leaves. Many are very aromatic, used for fragrance and flavoring. More than 50 spp., native to tropical climates in the Old World.

citratus (p. 282)
Lemongrass.
Tender perennial grassy herb. Zone 10.
H: to 6 ft. S: 6 ft.

A clumping grass whose pale green leaves, 1/2 in. wide and up to 6 ft. long, have a strong lemon aroma. The leaves are used fresh or dried for tea and in Thai cooking. Harvest leaves from the outside of the clump whenever you want them; be careful of their sharp edges. Native to tropical Asia, lemongrass flowers infrequently in temperate gardens. A related species, *C. nardus,* is the source of the citronella insect repellent.

How to grow: Full sun. Prefers moist soil. Can't withstand frost and is hardy outdoors only in the mildest regions. In most of the United States, a plant set in the ground after frost will make a nice clump by midsummer. Dig and divide it in fall to pot up a start for overwintering indoors, or buy new plants every spring.

Cyrilla
Sigh-ril′la.
Cyrillaceae. Cyrilla family.

A semievergreen shrub with shiny leaves that turn bright colors in fall and showy clusters of small white flowers in summer. Only 1 sp., native to the southeastern United States.

racemiflora (p. 171)
Titi, leatherwood.
Semievergreen shrub. Zone 6 or 5.
H: 15 ft. or more. S: 10 ft. or more.

A native shrub or small tree with shiny, dark green, oblong leaves, 2–4 in. long, that are mostly evergreen in mild climates but turn bright fall colors before dropping in cold climates. Showiest in early summer when the fragrant tiny white flowers open. They are borne on slender racemes up to 9 in. long that sprout from all sides of the previous year's stems, looking like giant floppy bottlebrushes. After the flowers fade, small tan fruits develop and persist on the stalks until the following spring. Can be trained as a single-trunked or multitrunked specimen tree, or mixed with other shrubs in a border or screen. *Cliftonia monophylla,* or buckwheat tree, belongs to the same plant family and grows in similar conditions. It has smaller clusters of fragrant white or pale pink flowers in late spring.

How to grow: Best in full sun; tolerates shade but doesn't bloom as much. Prefers moist, acidic soil. Native to swampy sites and tolerates standing water, but grows in ordinary garden settings if watered during dry spells. Grows fairly quickly when established. Wild plants can reach 30 ft. tall and spread by suckering to form broad thickets. No serious pests or diseases.

Cyrtomium
Sir-toe′mee-um.
Polypodiaceae. Fern family.

Evergreen ferns with leathery pinnate fronds. About 10 spp., native to the Old World. Sometimes combined with the New World genus *Phanerophlebia.*

falcatum (p. 217)
Holly fern.
Evergreen fern. Zone 9.
H: 2–3 ft. S: 2–3 ft.

Hardy only in mild climates but attractive as a container plant to winter indoors in cold regions. Forms an arching clump of leathery, glossy, dark green fronds. The toothed leaflets, up to 4 in. long, look somewhat like English holly leaves. Best used in sheltered sites along with other ferns, begonias, and gingers.

How to grow: Part sun or shade. Tolerates hot, dry air better than other ferns do. Needs ordinary or amended soil and regular watering. Be careful not to plant it too deep. Don't bury the crown (the growing point at the center of the rosette). Needs no maintenance beyond occasional grooming. Pest-free.

Cytisus
Sigh′ti-sus. Broom.
Leguminosae. Pea family.

Bushy shrubs with prolific displays of pealike flowers. Some are deciduous, some evergreen, some nearly leafless with bright green twigs. More than 30 spp., native to the Mediterranean region, and several hybrids.

× *praecox* 'Warminster' (p. 136)
Warminster broom.
Deciduous shrub. Zone 5.
H: 3–5 ft. S: 4–6 ft.

Very showy in spring when the branches are covered with masses of creamy white or pale yellow flowers, 1/2 in. wide, that resemble pea blossoms. The flowers last a long time but have a faintly unpleasant smell. Short narrow leaves appear in spring but drop quickly. Most of the year the bush is a compact mound of wiry gray-green twigs. Although deciduous, it has year-round interest and makes an interesting contrast to broad-leaved evergreens. Use a single specimen in a mixed border, or mass several to cover a bank or slope. Other cultivars differ mostly in flower color. 'Allgold' has bright yellow flowers. 'Hollandia' has two-tone flowers, pinkish red and white.

'Moonlight', a low, mounding form of the related species *C. scoparius,* has very pale yellow or cream flowers. *C. scoparius* itself is a fast-growing weedy shrub that has spread by seed throughout northern California, the Pacific Northwest, and scattered locations in the East. It's a big coarse shrub with too many stiff upright branches, and it's almost impossible to eradicate, but it does have lovely bright yellow flowers in spring.

How to grow: Full sun. Needs good drainage and prefers neutral or acidic soil. Tolerates heat and dryness. Plant 4 ft. apart for ground cover. Prune after flowering to prevent leggy growth and to reduce seed production. Start pruning while plants are young; cutting back into old wood is not successful. Pest-free.

Dahlia

Dahl'ya.
Compositae. Daisy family.

Tender perennials with tuberous roots, pinnate leaves, and composite flowers on long stalks. Once grown for the edible tubers; now hundreds of hybrid cultivars are prized for their colorful flowers. About 28 spp., native from Mexico to Colombia.

hybrids (p. 294)
(*D. hortensis*)
Dahlias.
Perennials grown as annuals. All zones.
H: 1–6 ft. S: 1–3 ft.

Remarkable for their bright blossoms that come in all colors but blue, dahlias are a classic plant for summer bedding and a choice cut flower. The innumerable cultivars are grouped according to the size and shape of their blossoms, which can be as small and round as golf balls, as big and flat as dinner plates, or any combination in between. Many have twisted, curled, or quill-like florets. Bloom starts in midsummer and continues until frost.

Dahlias have opposite, pinnately compound leaves on sturdy upright stalks ranging from 1 ft. to 6 ft. tall. Dwarf varieties are useful for edging and fit even the smallest gardens. Give larger forms a bed of their own, edged with blue ageratum for color contrast and even more beautiful cutting material.

For bedding purposes, it's easy to grow dahlias from seed. They bloom the first summer and form tubers that you can save if you choose. For fancier flowers, buy tubers of named cultivars. Local nurseries sell a small assortment of dormant tubers in spring. Mail-order specialty nurseries offer a much wider selection.

How to grow: Full sun. Dahlias need well-drained, fertile soil and an average of 1 in. of water weekly. Plant tubers about 4 in. deep and 3 ft. apart when the soil has warmed in spring, after danger of frost is past. Install a stake at planting time for tall varieties, and use a soft string to secure the stalk as it grows. Pinch tips for bushy bedding plants with many smaller blossoms; remove side shoots and buds to produce fewer, larger blossoms on tall varieties. Save plants you like by digging clumps of tubers in fall, shaking off the soil, and storing them in a cool, dark place. Separate the tubers carefully in spring, and replant the ones with the most vigorous buds and shoots. ·

Daphne

Daf'nee.
Thymelaeaceae. Daphne family.

Deciduous or evergreen shrubs with simple alternate leaves and small 4-lobed flowers that are usually very fragrant. All parts, particularly the bright-colored fruits, are poisonous. About 50 spp., native to Europe and Asia.

× *burkwoodii* (p. 136)
(*D. caucasica* × *D. cneorum*)
Semievergreen shrub. Zone 4.
H: 3–4 ft. S: 3–4 ft.

Forms a dense, compact, mounded shrub with neat, small, oval leaves. A profusion of small, starry, pale pink flowers covers the plant for several weeks in late spring. They are deliciously fragrant, and one plant perfumes the entire garden. 'Carol Mackie' has striking foliage; the leaves are green edged with gold. 'Somerset' has green leaves and a more upright growth habit. Plant one where you'll pass it often.

How to grow: Full sun in cool climates, part shade where summers are hot. Prefers well-drained soil amended with plenty of organic matter. Tolerates hot weather and occasional dry spells. Needs no pruning beyond the removal of damaged shoots. Slow-growing but free of pests or diseases.

caucasica (p. 136)
Semievergreen shrub. Zone 6 or 5.
H: to 6 ft. S: 3–4 ft.

An erect airy shrub with small narrow leaves. Clusters of sweetly fragrant white flowers appear from late spring through early summer and occasionally throughout the year in mild climates. Lovely at the sunny edge of a woodland garden, framed with a carpet of dwarf crested irises, miniature dianthus, or other low ground covers.

How to grow: Like *D.* × *burkwoodii*. Easily propagated from fresh seed.

cneorum (p. 171)
Garland flower.
Evergreen shrub. Zone 4.
H: 1 ft. S: 3–4 ft.

Spreads to form a low mat that combines well with dwarf conifers or rock-garden plants and flows nicely over the edge of a wall or terrace. Clusters of small, starry, pink flowers completely cover the evergreen foliage in spring; sometimes a few appear in fall. The fragrance is lovely. 'Ruby Glow' has deeper pink flowers opening from reddish buds. 'Eximia' has larger, deep pink flowers. 'Alba' has white flowers on a smaller plant.

How to grow: Like *D.* × *burkwoodii*.

mezereum (p. 137)
Deciduous shrub. Zone 4.
H: 2–3 ft. S: 3 ft. or more.

Delightful in very early spring, when the bare twigs are covered with clusters of fragrant pink or purplish (sometimes white or dark purple) flowers. Simple leaves, 1–3 in. long, expand after the flowers and spiral around the erect branching stems. Bright red berries are showy from summer to fall. Attractive in front of evergreens and compatible with hostas, epimediums, and other shade lovers.

How to grow: Part sun. Needs good drainage. Slow-growing. Prone to die with no warning, succumbing to mysterious causes. While alive, it needs no pruning or special care.

Daphne odora

odora (p. 171)
Winter daphne.
Evergreen shrub. Zone 7.
H: 4 ft. S: 4 ft.

A lovely shrub for mild climates, with perhaps the sweetest fragrance of all daphnes. Forms a perfect symmetrical mound covered with glossy leaves up to 3 in. long. Decorative clusters of buds tip each branch in fall and winter, opening from reddish purple to white in very early spring. Lovely near the front door or along a path, where you can appreciate the fragrance daily. Combines well with hollies, junipers, and other evergreens in foundation plantings. 'Aureo-Marginata' has cream-edged leaves.

How to grow: Full sun. Must have good drainage; tolerates sandy or gravelly soil and summer dry spells. Plant the top of the root ball slightly above ground level to reduce risk of root rot. Needs no pruning or maintenance. Grows slightly bigger and better each year but may succumb for no apparent reason.

Dasylirion

Daz-i-leer´ee-on. Bear grass.
Agavaceae. Agave family.

Woody-based perennials with very short or sometimes medium-height trunks topped with dense clusters of long, slender, often spiny-edged leaves. The rounded leaf base is called a "desert spoon." About 18 spp., native to the Southwest and Mexico.

texanum (p. 209)
Sotol, bear grass.
Shrubby perennial. Zone 8.
H: 2–3 ft. (leaves). S: 3 ft. or more.

Makes a rounded mound of swordlike leaves, 2–3 ft. long and 1/2–1 in. wide, that radiate from a stubby trunk like a giant pincushion. Older plants spread underground to form a clump of rosettes. Leaves are medium to dark green with yellowish spines along the margin. Slender flower stalks up to 15 ft. tall arise in late spring, topped with wormlike clusters of small greenish, yellow, or white flowers that last for several weeks. Useful for desert gardens, combined with succulents and shrubs. Several other species are offered by native-plant nurseries.

How to grow: Full to part sun. Needs good drainage. Tolerates hot, dry sites; unamended soil; and caliche. Remove old bloom stalks. Needs no other maintenance.

Delosperma

De-lo-sper´ma.
Aizoaceae. Carpetweed family.

Mostly tender succulent herbs or shrubs with densely branched, spreading habits and small but numerous bright-colored flowers over a long season. About 130 spp., native to South Africa and Madagascar.

cooperi (p. 237)
Purple ice plant.
Succulent perennial. Zone 6 or 5.
H: 2–4 in. S: 12 in. or more.

A showy ground cover for hot, dry sites or xeriscape plantings, with narrow succulent leaves and bright magenta daisylike flowers from June until frost. Spreads quickly but isn't invasive. Hardy to cold on well-drained sites but dies out in wet winters.

How to grow: Full sun. Needs good drainage. Tolerates heat and dry soil. Space about 12 in. apart for ground cover. Requires no maintenance. Trouble-free.

nubigena (p. 237)
Hardy ice plant.
Succulent perennial. Zone 6 or 5.
H: 2–4 in. S: 12 in. or more.

More aggressive than purple ice plant, this is a showy and hardy ground cover. The succulent foliage is bright green in summer, turning red in winter. Yellow daisylike blooms are produced in late spring and summer.

How to grow: Like *D. cooperi.*

Delphinium

Del-fin´ee-um.
Ranunculaceae. Buttercup family.

Annuals, biennials, or perennials with palmately lobed or divided leaves and upright stalks of bright blue, pink, white, scarlet, or yellow flowers with distinct spurs. About 250 spp., native to the north temperate zone.

× ***elatum*** **hybrids** (p. 237)
Hybrid delphiniums.
Perennials. Zone 3.
H: to 6 ft. S: 2 ft.

Delphiniums are dramatic plants for the perennial border. Their tall branching stalks are densely crowded with flat flowers, 2–3 in. wide, in many shades of blue, purple, lavender, pink, or white. Flowers are scentless (and poisonous) but good for cutting. They combine well with foxgloves, mulleins, tall bearded irises, and other large-scale perennials. There are many types, differing in overall height and flower size and form. The Giant Pacific hybrids reach 5 ft. or more, usually with double flowers. The Connecticut Yankee hybrids are short (under 3 ft.) and bushy, with single blossoms.

How to grow: Full sun. Require well-prepared organic soil, frequent light fertilization, and constant moisture. Tall forms need staking. Cut back after first bloom and fertilize to encourage reblooming in fall. Delphiniums prefer cool, moist summers and last just a year or two in hot climates, but new plants are easily raised from seed. Space seedlings 2 ft. apart, planting in fall for bloom the following year.

Deschampsia

Des-champs'ee-a. Hair grass.
Gramineae. Grass family.

Clumping perennial grasses with rough leaves and masses of delicate-looking flower stalks. About 50 spp., most native to cool regions in the Northern Hemisphere.

caespitosa (p. 210)

Tufted hair grass.
Clumping grass. Zone 4.
H: 2–3 ft. S: 2 ft.

Excellent for mass plantings, where it creates an ethereal cloud of bloom throughout the summer. Flowers are pale greenish yellow tinged with purple, held in panicles above mounds of spiky or arching foliage. Cut the flower stalks for fresh or dried bouquets. The foliage is semievergreen even in northern climates; include this species in a border of plants for winter interest. 'Tardiflora' blooms 2–3 weeks later than the species.

How to grow: Best in part shade. Tolerates acidic or alkaline conditions if the soil is fertile and moist. Plant 2 ft. apart in masses for best effect. Cut flower stalks back in late summer and cut foliage to the crown in early spring (or late summer where summers are hot). Cold-hardy but doesn't take heat well.

Deutzia

Doot'si-a.
Saxifragaceae. Saxifrage family.

Deciduous shrubs with opposite leaves and showy clusters of scentless, usually white flowers in spring. About 40 spp., native to Asia and Central America.

gracilis (p. 137)

Slender deutzia.
Deciduous shrub. Zone 4.
H: 3–4 ft. S: 4 ft.

Extends the bloom season for deciduous shrubs. Clusters of snow-white blossoms cover the graceful arching branches for about 2 weeks in late spring. Then it remains a neutral green mound for the rest of the growing season. Can be used alone or combined with other shrubs in hedges, or included in a large mixed border. 'Nikko' is a dwarf form (2–3 ft.) and has maroon foliage in fall. *D. × lemoinei* (to 6 ft.) has larger leaves and broad clusters of white flowers tinged with pink. *D. scabra* is much larger (to 10 ft.) and makes a showy waterfall of white flowers.

How to grow: Best in full sun. Ordinary soil and watering. Space 3 ft. apart for a hedge. Blossoms form on the previous year's growth. Prune just after flowering, removing about one-third of the oldest stems every year. Cutting unsightly old plants to the ground rejuvenates them by forcing new growth.

Dianthus

Dy-an'thus. Pink.
Caryophyllaceae. Pink family.

Low-growing annuals, biennials, or perennials. The opposite leaves are often as slender as blades of grass, thickening at the base where they join the stem. Flowers are borne singly or on branched stalks. They have 5 to many petals, sometimes with fringed edges, in shades of pink, rose, or white, sometimes red, purplish, or yellow. Many have a very sweet or spicy fragrance. About 300 spp., most from Europe and Asia.

× *allwoodii* hybrids (p. 237)

Cottage pinks, border carnations, Allwood pinks.
Perennials. Zone 4.
H: 12–20 in. S: 12 in.

A large and popular group of hybrids, worth growing for both their flowers and their foliage. Slender blue-green-gray leaves form closely packed tufts or mats, evergreen in mild climates, handsome until deep winter in colder zones. The very fragrant clove-scented flowers are single or double, 1½–2 in. wide, in shades of dark red, rose, pink, or white. Bloom continues from late spring through summer, sometimes lasting 2 full months. Excellent for cottage gardens, combined with larkspurs, lavender, and campanulas.

'Aqua' (pure white), 'Doris' (salmon with a dark eye), 'Ian' (scarlet), and other named cultivars have lovely flowers but are not as hardy and rarely survive Zone 5 winters. The 'Alpinus' strain, easily raised from seed, is very hardy (Zone 3). It forms tight mounds of blue-gray foliage, topped with very fragrant single flowers in many shades. The *D. × allwoodii* hybrids result from crossing *D. caryophyllus* and *D. plumarius*.

How to grow: Full sun. Must have excellent drainage to survive the winter. Plant in light soil amended with plenty of organic matter and lime. Space 1 ft. apart in spring or late summer. Divide and replant after 2–3 years. Use twiggy sticks to support the flower stalks of tall forms. Shear off faded flowers to prolong blooming or to encourage repeat blooming.

Dianthus barbatus

barbatus (p. 295)

Sweet William.
Biennial. Zone 3.
H: 1–2 ft. S: 1 ft.

Pretty in the garden and long lasting in bouquets. Forms a loose mat of deep green leaves, ½ in. wide by 2–4 in. long. Individual flowers, ½–1 in. wide, are grouped in flat round clusters up to 4 in. wide atop stiff erect stalks. Colors include white, rose, pink, dark red, and bicolors. Some kinds are very spicily fragrant, but others are scentless. Most bloom in late spring, lasting up to a month. Cut flowers last 2 weeks in water. Seed catalogs list several strains, including dwarfs (under 8 in.) and long-stemmed cut-flower types (to 30 in.). Most are sold as mixed colors. Nurseries sell individual plants of a few named cultivars.

How to grow: Full sun. Does best in fertile, well-limed soil with regular watering. Although classified as biennials, sweet Williams may flower the first year if seeds are started early indoors. Other times, plants will hang on like perennials, blooming every summer for 2 or 3 years. The normal practice is to sow seeds in early summer and transplant to their final location by late summer. The bigger the rosette of foliage in fall, the more flowers in spring. Cut flowering stems to the ground after bloom unless you want to encourage self-sowing. Make divisions or cuttings to propagate the plants you like best.

caryophyllus
Carnation.
Tender perennial grown as an annual.
Zone 8.
H: 1–3 ft. S: under 1 ft.

This species includes the classic florist's carnations, which are grown mostly in greenhouses. Those long-stemmed cutting types are fussy to grow; they need staking and disbudding, and suffer from many pests and diseases. Contrary to the enticing photos in seed catalogs, it's very difficult to produce florist-quality carnations outdoors. The types known as hardy or border carnations, such as 'Dwarf Fragrance', with spicy 2-in. flowers on 12-in. plants, make a better choice for containers or gardens.

How to grow: Full sun. Needs fertile, well-limed, well-drained soil and regular watering. Start seeds early indoors for bloom 4–6 months later. All forms, even the dwarfs, need staking. Subject to aphids, spider mites, and thrips; also to fungal and viral infections, particularly in humid climates.

chinensis hybrids (p. 295)
China pinks.
Annuals. All zones.
H: to 18 in. S: 12 in.

These are easy from seed and quick to flower, continuing throughout the summer, even in hot weather. Most have stiff upright stems that branch repeatedly, topped with flat clusters of several small single or double flowers in shades of red, pink, white, or bicolors. They are usually scentless, but they provide months of color as edging or bedding plants.

How to grow: Full sun. Ordinary soil and watering. Start seeds indoors and set plants out about the time of last frost, or direct-sow where they are to grow. They start flowering in as little as 10 weeks from seed. Plants need no maintenance, not even deadheading.

deltoides (p. 237)
Maiden pink.
Perennial. Zone 3.
H: 1 ft. S: 2 ft. or more.

Forms a low mat of grassy green leaves, suitable as a ground cover for sandy slopes. Flowers are scentless, single, 3/4 in. wide, and red, rose, or white, often with dark marks in the center. Blooms abundantly for several weeks in early summer, often repeating later if the first flower stalks are sheared off when the petals fade. Named cultivars, some available from seed, are selected for flower size and color. All self-sow prolifically. Start maiden pinks once, and you'll never be without them.

How to grow: Takes partial shade. Needs good drainage and prefers gritty soil with added lime. Tolerates dry soil. Space seedlings or divisions 1 ft. apart. May die in cold wet winters (North) or hot humid summers (South) but will return from self-sown seedlings.

gratianopolitanus (p. 237)
Cheddar pink.
Perennial. Zone 4.
H: 9–12 in. S: 12 in. or more.

An indispensable perennial with marvelous foliage and lovely flowers with a heavenly fragrance. Forms a tightly packed mat of slender blue-green leaves. The wiry stems bear one or two 1/2–3/4-in. flowers for several weeks in late spring/early summer. Excellent for walls, rock gardens, or the front of the border. Try it with low silvery artemisias, balloon flower, and catmint. 'Bath's Pink' is a new cultivar with single soft pink flowers. 'Tiny Rubies' is an old favorite. It makes a very compact mat of foliage, covered with hundreds of small, double, deep pink flowers on 4-in. stems.

How to grow: Full sun. Needs good drainage and prefers gritty soil with added lime. Tolerates dry spells. Space at least 12 in. apart. Shear twice yearly. Cut off all flower stalks when blooms fade; and cut back all straggly growth in spring, reducing the plant to one-third its former size. If the center dies out, sift gritty soil into the bare spot, and new growth will come up through it. Named cultivars must be propagated by division. If all you want is pretty pinks, gather seeds and sow them.

Rabbits like to eat dianthus leaves in winter. Discourage them by covering the plants with pine boughs or chicken wire. Mice like to nest underneath, chopping up leaves and stems for bedding. Set traps or get a cat.

plumarius (p. 237)
Cottage pink, grass pink.
Perennial. Zone 4.
H: 12–18 in. S: 12–18 in.

Ideal for cottage gardens, these pinks are easy to grow and have lovely fringed flowers with a delicious spicy fragrance. The slender gray-blue leaves form loose mounded hummocks. Flowers are 1–1 1/2 in. wide and are single, semidouble, or double, usually held in groups of 2 or 3 on

Dianthus plumarius

floppy 12-in. stems. They combine well with lavender, catmint, Shirley poppies, feverfew, and roses. There are many seed strains and named cultivars, with flowers in shades of red, pink, or white. These old-fashioned pinks form looser mounds of foliage and grow more slowly than the Allwood hybrids do.

How to grow: Full sun. Tolerates, even prefers, richer soil and more moisture than other pinks do. Space 12 in. apart in spring or late summer. Use twiggy sticks to support the floppy flower stalks. Deadhead to prolong the blooming period. After 3–4 years, divide plants in late summer. Also easily grown from seed. No pests other than rabbits and mice, which eat the foliage.

Dicentra
Dy-sen´tra.
Fumariaceae. Bleeding-heart family.

Hardy perennials, most forming a clump of basal leaves with a lacy or ferny texture. Flowers with unusual spurs or pouches droop from upright or arching stalks. About 19 spp., native to North America and Asia.

spectabilis (p. 238)
Common bleeding-heart.
Perennial. Zone 2.
H: 2–3 ft. S: 2 ft.

An old-fashioned favorite with arching sprays of rosy pink and white flowers (pure white in the cultivar 'Alba') that dangle above the delicate fluffy foliage in late spring. Unfortunately, it stops blooming and usually dies back when hot weather arrives. The common bleeding-heart

Dicentra eximia

comes from Japan. Two native species, though smaller (usually under 18 in.), have branching stalks with more flowers and keep blooming all summer. *D. eximia*, the fringed bleeding-heart, is native to eastern forests; *D. formosa,* the Pacific bleeding-heart, grows wild from British Columbia to California. Hybrids between these species, including 'Bountiful' (dark reddish pink flowers) and 'Luxuriant' (cherry red flowers), are particularly attractive and long blooming. Combine any bleeding-heart with other shade lovers such as wild gingers, ferns, and hostas.

How to grow: Part shade. Needs fertile, well-drained soil and steady moisture. Divide older plants in spring or fall, breaking the rhizome into chunks with 3 or more buds. Plant 2 ft. apart. Pest-free.

Dictamnus
Dik-tam´nus.
Rutaceae. Citrus family.

A hardy perennial with pinnately compound leaves and white or pink flowers. The foliage releases an aromatic oil; legend says that you can touch a match to a leaf and burn this oil without harming the plant. Only 1 sp., native from southern Europe to northern China.

albus (p. 238)
Gas plant, fraxinella.
Perennial. Zone 3.
H: 2–4 ft. S: 3 ft.

Looks good all season, with elegant foliage and flowers. Leaves are glossy dark green and have a strong citrusy or medicinal fragrance. In summer the sturdy erect stems are topped with loose clusters of striking pure white flowers with conspicuous outstretched stamens, followed by ornamental seedpods. Mature clumps are very elegant, especially when posed against a dark background of trees or combined with irises, hardy geraniums, or *Campanula persicifolia.* Selected forms have reddish purple or rosy flowers with darker veins.

How to grow: Full sun. Best in fertile, well-drained soil. Starts slowly from seed and resents transplanting, so buy a container-grown plant and put it in its permanent location. Lives for decades, very gradually developing into a large clump, and never needs division. Needs no staking or care. Does best where summer nights are cool.

Digitalis
Di-ji-tal´is. Foxglove.
Scrophulariaceae. Foxglove family.

Perennials or biennials with a basal rosette of large simple leaves and upright stalks crowded with bell-shaped flowers. The leaves of the common foxglove provide the heart medicine digitalis, but gardeners should treat the plant as poisonous. About 19 spp., native to Europe, the Mediterranean region, and central Asia.

Digitalis purpurea

purpurea (p. 295)
Common foxglove.
Biennial. Zone 4.
H: 4–5 ft. S: 2–3 ft.

An old-fashioned plant with lots of charm, always pictured in storybook gardens. Tall stalks with thimble-sized flowers dangling from one side rise above broad rosettes of large, furry, wrinkled, oblong leaves. Flowers are usually purple-pink spotted with purple, but lavender, rose, white, and apricot forms are available from seed. The 'Excelsior' strain has flowers all the way around the stem, not just on one side, and reaches 5–7 ft. tall. 'Foxy' is only 2–3 ft. tall, with several shoots, and blooms the first year from seed. *D.* × *mertonensis,* the strawberry foxglove, is a hybrid of the common foxglove. It has larger flowers in a luscious shade of pink and handsome, dark green, velvety leaves. Although sold as a perennial, it must be renewed every 2–3 years by division or from seed. All foxgloves are beautiful in partly shaded gardens or woodland plantings.

How to grow: Part shade; avoid hot afternoon sun. Needs fertile, well-drained soil and regular watering. Space 2 ft. or more apart, establishing plants by fall for bloom the following year. Cut spent flower stalks to the ground to prolong the bloom season. Gather seed or let some stalks mature to self-sow, and watch for volunteer seedlings in spring.

Diospyros
Dy-os´pi-rus.
Ebenaceae. Ebony family.

Most are large tropical trees harvested for their hard, dark wood, called ebony. Some, called persimmons, are valued for their sweet, rich, pulpy fruits. About 475 spp., almost all native to the tropics.

kaki (p. 114)
Japanese persimmon.
Deciduous tree. Zone 8.
H: to 30 ft. S: to 30 ft.

An attractive tree with a broad rounded crown; leathery oval leaves; splendid gold to orange-red fall color; and large, plump, edible fruits. Handsome as a garden or lawn tree and requires less maintenance than other fruit trees do. Used in southern Europe as umbrellas over outdoor dining terraces (the fruit ripens after the outdoor dining season has ended). 'Hachiya' is a shapely tree with large fruits, astringent until mushy-ripe, then sweet and delicious. 'Fuju' has firm crisp fruits that are edible before they soften.

How to grow: Full sun. Ordinary soil and watering. Needs little care beyond the removal of dead or awkwardly placed branches. Don't plant near sidewalks or patios unless you plan to gather the fruit; unwanted fruit makes a mess where it drops.

Distictis
Dis-tick´tis.
Bignoniaceae. Trumpet creeper family.

Tender woody vines with showy clusters of trumpet-shaped flowers. About 9 spp., native to Mexico and the West Indies.

Distictis buccinatoria

buccinatoria (p. 203)
Blood-red trumpet vine.
Woody vine. Zone 9.
H: to 30 ft.

One of the showiest evergreen vines, with shiny dark green foliage and big clusters of trumpet-shaped 4-in. flowers, orangish red to purplish red with yellow throats. Bursts of bloom repeat throughout warm weather. Use it to cover a wall or fence, to hide a dead tree, or to shade an arbor. *D.* 'Rivers' (sometimes sold as *D. riversii*), the royal trumpet vine, is similar but more restrained, with 5-in. purple trumpets.

How to grow: Full sun. Tolerates desert heat. Needs well-amended, fertile soil and constant moisture. Provide a sturdy support and tie the young plant to it; it will soon climb on its own by tendrils and adhesive pads. Thin from time to time to restrict growth, to prevent tangling, and to remove dead twigs beneath the canopy.

Dodonaea
Do-don´ee-a.
Sapindaceae. Soapberry family.

Tropical evergreen shrubs or trees, often with sticky resinous secretions that have some medicinal properties. About 50 spp., most native to Australia.

viscosa (p. 171)
Hopbush.
Evergreen shrub. Zone 8.
H: 12–15 ft. S: 12–15 ft.

Native to the Arizona desert and incredibly tough, this is an easy and tolerant shrub for informal hedges or screens. It usually grows as an erect multitrunked shrub but can be trained into a single-trunked tree. Leaves are thin and leathery. Flowers are inconspicuous, but clusters of winged pinkish beige fruits show up in late summer. 'Purpurea' has purplish leaves and is more commonly grown than the native green-leaved form.

How to grow: Full sun. Tolerates poor, dry soil. Space 6–8 ft. apart for a hedge. Tip-pinch to fatten young plants, or stake the trunk and remove lower branches to form a tree. Problem-free.

Dolichos
Dol'li-kos.
Leguminosae. Pea family.

Mostly twining vines, not woody, with trifoliate leaves and long-stalked clusters of pealike flowers. About 60 spp., native to the Old World tropics.

lablab (p. 295)
(*Lablab purpureus*)
Hyacinth bean.
Annual vine. Zone 6.
H: 20 ft.

Grows quickly, with many side branches that spread and drape to cover a fence, trellis, or arbor. Foliage is dense and dark green; the compound leaves have 3 oval leaflets. Makes an impressive display of pealike, sweetly fragrant, white or purple blossoms in late summer or fall, followed by flat magenta-purple pods, 1 in. wide by 3 in. long. Combines well with any of the blue, lavender, or white salvias. Very easy and showy but needs hot weather and a long growing season to produce flowers and pods.

How to grow: Full or part sun. Ordinary soil and watering. Sow after danger of frost is past, thinning seedlings to one per foot. Self-sows in mild climates.

Doronicum
Do-ron'i-kum. Leopard's-bane.
Compositae. Daisy family.

Hardy perennials with a basal clump of large, long-petioled leaves and blossoms like yellow daisies on upright stalks. About 35 spp., native to Europe and Asia.

caucasicum (p. 239)
Leopard's-bane.
Perennial. Zone 4.
H: 1–2 ft. S: 1 ft.

A trouble-free plant topped with cheery yellow 2-in. daisies in early spring. They make good cut flowers. Combine it with purple money plant (*Lunaria*) or blue scillas in a woodland or semishaded garden. The basal leaves form a bright green clump in spring, but the whole plant dies back and goes dormant in hot weather; be prepared to fill the gap with annuals. 'Spring Beauty' is very early, 18 in. tall, with double flowers. 'Finesse' blooms later than the species, with 3-in. blossoms on stalks 18–24 in. tall. 'Miss Mason', a hybrid, flowers over a longer season and doesn't always go dormant.

How to grow: Part sun or shade. Does best where summers aren't too hot. Ordinary soil and watering. Space 1 ft. apart. Divide every 3–4 years. Problem-free.

Dryopteris
Dry-op'ter-is.
Polypodiaceae. Fern family.

A large genus of hardy or tropical, deciduous or evergreen ferns. Most form a clump of more or less finely divided fronds. About 150 spp., from around the world.

affinis (p. 217)
Semievergreen fern. Zone 4.
H: 2–3 ft. S: 2 ft.

A neat fern that looks fresh all summer and stays green well into winter, too. Forms large clumps of leathery, glossy fronds, broadest at the base and tapering to the tip, with golden scales on the stipe (stem). Combine it with early spring-flowering bulbs, primroses, trilliums, or hostas, tucked among shrubs in a mixed border.

How to grow: Part sun or shade. Can tolerate full sun if the soil is constantly moist. Needs fertile, organic, well-drained soil. Position the crown on top of the ground when planting, and apply a generous layer of composted leaves or other organic mulch. Established plants need no maintenance. Don't remove old fronds, as they break down into excellent mulch. To propagate by division, lift the whole plant out of the ground in early spring, wash the soil away from the roots, and use a strong knife to cut the crown into sections. Replant immediately.

erythrosora (p. 217)
Japanese autumn fern, red shield fern.
Semievergreen fern. Zone 4.
H: 24–30 in. S: 12–18 in.

New fronds of this fern have a coppery pink color like autumn leaves. They mature to a shiny dark green. The fronds are triangular in outline but divided into fine segments. Looks best when several clumps are massed together in front of dark evergreen shrubs, to show off the color of the new fronds. Combines well with epimediums or wild gingers. Evergreen in mild climates, deciduous where winters are cold.

How to grow: Like *D. affinis*.

filix-mas (p. 217)
Male fern.
Semievergreen fern. Zone 3.
H: 2–4 ft. S: 2 ft.

A large, dominant fern that forms erect clumps of long leathery fronds, up to 8 in. wide but dissected into many fine segments. Stipes (stems) are scaly brown. Use a single clump as a specimen, or plant masses among shrubs and trees to hide bare trunks and create a lush, woodsy look. 'Barnesii' has narrower fronds with serrated edges and is much prettier than the common male fern.

How to grow: Like *D. affinis*.

marginalis (p. 217)
Marginal shield fern.
Evergreen fern. Zone 3.
H: 18–24 in. S: 24 in.

A tough but graceful fern native to rocky woodlands. Easy to grow with spring wildflow-

Dryopteris marginalis

ers under deciduous trees. The arching, lance-shaped fronds are leathery and shiny, yellow-green when new, maturing to dark blue-green. The crown is covered with coarse brown scales before the new fronds uncurl. Forms clumps but doesn't spread.

How to grow: Like *D. affinis.*

other species

D. goldiana resembles the male fern but has a lovely gold-green color. *D. spinulosa* has deep green fronds, 3 ft. long, divided into hundreds of lacy segments. *D. wallichiana* has long narrow fronds with ruffled edges. New fronds, appearing through the season, are golden green, maturing to leathery dark green. Evergreen but hardy only to Zone 7. Many other species are also cultivated; most require similar conditions and care.

Echinacea

Ek-i-nay′see-a. Purple coneflower.
Compositae. Daisy family.

Hardy perennials with rough or hairy leaves at the base and up the stalks and daisylike blossoms with prominent cone-shaped disks and drooping rays. About 10 spp., native to the eastern United States.

purpurea (p. 238)

Purple coneflower.
Perennial. Zone 4.
H: 1½–3 ft. S: 2 ft.

A strong plant with coarse-textured dark green leaves on rough, almost woody stalks and 3–4-in.-wide daisylike blossoms. Rays are rose to pink; disk florets are bright orange, ripening to brown. Attracts many butterflies. Combines well with monarda, phlox, daisies, daylilies, and other sun-loving perennials. 'Bright Star' has deep pink rays and a maroon cone. 'White Swan' has white rays and a bronze cone.

How to grow: Full sun. Tolerates poor or dry soil and heat. Easy from seed and may bloom the first year. Divide older plants in spring or fall. Deadheading prolongs bloom in summer, but let the seed heads ripen in fall to feed the birds and to provide winter interest.

Echinops

Ek′i-nops.
Compositae. Daisy family.

Perennials or biennials with prickly, lobed or dissected, thistlelike foliage and round flower heads with stiff bristly bracts. About 120 spp., native to the Old and New World.

ritro (see below for photo)

Globe thistle.
Perennial. Zone 3.
H: 2–4 ft. S: 3 ft.

Easy to grow and very handsome, with a bold architectural shape and texture. Makes big, slowly spreading clumps. Leaves are pinnately

Echinacea purpurea

dissected into spiny-toothed segments. The upright branched stalks end in tightly packed globes of tiny metallic blue flowers. Pick flower heads just before they open to dry for winter arrangements. Handsome in the garden with yellow daylilies and pink boltonia. 'Taplow Blue' (p. 238) is floriferous, with steel blue 2-in. globes. 'Veitch's Blue' has smaller but darker blue flower heads. Taxonomists disagree over the proper identity of these plants, but gardeners enjoy them under any name.

How to grow: Full sun. Ordinary soil. Tolerates heat and dry soil. Space 2 ft. apart. Rarely needs staking or dividing—a good thing, since the leaves are quite prickly and unapproachable. Insects may damage the foliage, but they rarely hurt the flower heads.

Elaeagnus

Eel-ee-ag′nus.
Elaeagnaceae. Oleaster family.

Deciduous or evergreen shrubs or small trees. Most have thorny stems, silvery foliage, and clusters of small but fragrant flowers followed by heavy crops of berries. About 40 spp., most native to Europe and Asia.

angustifolia (p. 114)

Russian olive.
Deciduous tree or shrub. Zone 2.
H: 20 ft. or more. S: 15–20 ft.

An extremely tough plant that tolerates cold, heat, wind, drought, and infertile or compacted soil. Often multitrunked, with shreddy bark on crooked stems that have "character." Young shoots and the slender willowlike leaves are covered with dense silvery scales. The creamy flowers that appear in May are small and are not showy, but they have a sweet fragrance that carries on the breeze. The silvery fall fruits are edible, but most people prefer real olives and leave these for the birds.

E. commutata, or silverberry, is a smaller shrub with especially bright silvery leaves. *E. umbellata,* the autumn olive, has green and silver leaves and spreads to form a thicket. Quite similar but native to North America are *Shepherdia canadensis* and *S. argentea,* the buffaloberries, with silvery foliage and reddish fruits. All are fast-growing and most useful for difficult situations, often planted for quick screening along

Elaeagnus pungens

roadsides or as a windbreak or shelter on open sites. The silvery foliage contrasts well with pines, junipers, and other evergreens.

How to grow: Full sun. Tolerates poor, dry soil and heat. Does best in dry areas. Subject to fatal root rot where soil is heavy or wet. Prune as desired to increase branching or to shape into a tree.

pungens (p. 171)
Thorny elaeagnus.
Evergreen shrub. Zone 7 or 6.
H: 10 ft. or more. S: 10 ft.

A large spreading shrub with an irregular angular profile. Twigs are tough, often thorny. The oval leaves have wavy margins and are drab green above, silvery gray below. Tiny flowers in fall release a wonderful fragrance. Birds eat the fruits in spring. 'Maculata' has leaves with a gold blotch in the middle. Other silver- and yellow-variegated forms are also attractive and are used widely throughout the South and Southwest. Variegated forms of the hybrid *E.* × *ebbingei* have even prettier leaves and a more compact habit. All can be used as hedges, screens, or barriers.

How to grow: Full or part sun. Tolerates poor, dry soil and coastal salt and winds. Space 10 ft. apart. Fast-growing and very tough but requires major pruning at least once a year to look good.

Endymion
En-dim'ee-on.
Liliaceae. Lily family.

Hardy bulb-forming perennials that produce a clump of strap-shaped leaves and upright clusters of clear blue, violet, or white flowers in spring. Only 3–4 spp., native to western Europe and northwest Africa.

hispanica (p. 239)
(formerly *Scilla hispanica*; now *Hyacinthoides hispanica*)
Spanish bluebell, wood hyacinth.
Perennial. Zone 5.
H: 18 in. S: 12 in.

Charming in spring, when every clump produces several flower stalks, each with 10 or more nodding blue bells. Looser and less formal than true hyacinths and suitable for naturalizing among deciduous shrubs and trees. Flowers last about 3 weeks. The strap-shaped leaves, 1 in. wide, are handsome before bloom but ratty soon after; unlike with most bulbs, it's okay to remove them as soon as they turn yellow. Interplant with a ground cover such as dwarf plumbago (*Ceratostigma plumbaginoides*) for foliage and color later in the season. 'Excelsior' has deep blue flowers. There are also pink and white forms. *E. non-scriptus,* or English bluebell, has shorter stalks with fewer, smaller flowers.

How to grow: Sun or part shade; grows well under deciduous trees. Ordinary soil and watering. Tolerates, actually prefers, dry soil when dormant in summer. Bulbs are inexpensive and

clumps multiply quickly. Divide and replant in fall, 3–6 in. deep and 6 in. apart.

Enkianthus
En-ki-an'thus.
Ericaceae. Heath family.

Deciduous shrubs with simple leaves crowded at the ends of the branches and drooping clusters of tiny bell-shaped flowers. About 10 spp., native from the Himalayas to Japan.

campanulatus (p. 137)
Deciduous shrub. Zone 5.
H: 10–15 ft. S: 8 ft.

Usually a narrowly erect shrub but sometimes trained as a small tree, with azalea-like foliage turning a lovely orange-red in fall. It blooms profusely in spring, with clusters of dainty bell-shaped flowers, light yellow with red veins. Flowers are scentless but very attractive, especially when viewed up close. Selected forms have white, pink, rosy, or red flowers. Combines well with azaleas, rhododendrons, pieris, and other acid-loving shrubs.

How to grow: Part shade. Needs well-drained, acidic soil amended with plenty of organic matter. Position the top of the root ball slightly higher than the surrounding soil. Established plants need no pruning or maintenance.

Ensete
En-see'tee.
Musaceae. Banana family.

Large palmlike plants with huge leaves. The swollen leaf bases make a thick fleshy trunk, topped with an umbrella of broad leaf blades. Just 7 spp., native to the Old World.

ventricosum (p. 239)
(*Musa ensete*)
Abyssinian banana.
Tender palmlike perennial. Zone 10 or 9.
H: 20 ft. S: 10 ft.

A large dramatic plant with a lush tropical look. The leaf blades can grow 2–3 ft. wide and 10–20 ft. long. On windy sites they shred into fluttering ribbonlike strips. After a few years outdoors in a mild climate, a clump will flower, bear small inedible bananas, and die, usually sending up a few replacement shoots from the base. 'Maurellii' is smaller (12–15 ft.), with a dark red trunk and red-edged leaf blades. Banana plants look out of place in most gardens, but try one anyway—they're easy, fast, and so much fun to grow. Children love them, and your neighbors will be impressed.

How to grow: Full or part sun. Ordinary soil and frequent watering. Hardy only where winters are mild. In colder zones, wait until frost kills the leaf blades, then dig up the trunk (it's very heavy), wrap it in burlap, store in a frost-free garage or basement over winter, and replant in spring. Can be grown in a pot but may need daily watering. Several catalogs offer the pea-sized seeds, which sprout easily in warm soil and make big plants the first year.

Epimedium

Ep-i-mee´dee-um.
Berberidaceae. Barberry family.

Low, spreading perennials with semiever-green foliage. Leaves have 3 or more leaflets. Four-parted flowers, often with spurred petals, appear in spring. About 21 spp., native to the Mediterranean region and Asia. Many of the cultivated forms are hybrids.

grandiflorum (see below for photos)
Bishop's-hat.
Perennial. Zone 5.
H: 1 ft. S: forms colony.

A fine ground cover with graceful elegant foliage and pretty, curiously shaped flowers. Grows very well under and around deciduous trees and shrubs. The compound leaves with heart-shaped leaflets up to 3 in. long are thin but tough and are evergreen in mild climates. New leaves are bronze, turning light green, then dark-ening to reddish brown in winter. Trimming off old leaves exposes the clusters of white, pink, red, or violet blossoms in spring; each square, spurred flower is about 1 in. wide.

There are many epimediums, with confus-ingly similar names, and the plants are much alike. All are trouble-free and desirable. *E. g.* 'Rose Queen' has red flowers with white spurs. *E. × rubrum* 'Pink Queen' (rosy pink; p. 239) and 'Snow Queen' (white) are robust plants with showy flowers. *E. × versicolor,* with smaller flowers and new leaves mottled with reddish brown, is a tough plant that tolerates dry shade. *E. × youngianum* 'Niveum' (white; p. 239) and 'Roseum' (pink) are shorter plants (under 8 in.) with reddish leaves in spring and fall.

How to grow: Part or full shade. Best if soil is amended with plenty of peat moss or organic matter. Prefers constant moisture, but estab-lished plants tolerate short dry spells. Space 12 in. apart and be patient. Although slow to get started, plants will eventually make a dense ground cover impenetrable to weeds. The rhi-zomes are quite tough and woody. Divide in fall or late winter.

Epimedium × youngianum

Eremurus

Air-re-mure´us. Foxtail lily.
Liliaceae. Lily family.

Perennials with tall tough stalks densely packed with bright-colored, bell-shaped flowers. The narrow leaves form a stiff basal tuft. The spreading roots are thick and tough. About 35 spp., most native to western and central Asia.

× *isabellinus* (p. 240)
Shelford hybrid foxtail lilies.
Perennials. Zone 5.
H: 4–6 ft. S: 3 ft.

These magnificent plants throw tall candles of bloom above yard-wide clumps of foliage in late spring and early summer, then leave a big space when they die back later. Flowers up to 1 in. wide come in many shades of yellow, orange, white, pink, or red. They make excellent, if over-whelming, cut flowers. Dried stalks of the seed-pods are decorative, too. Plant as accents in well-drained borders, among shrubs, on banks or hillsides, or in wild or meadow gardens. Use clumping grasses or spreading perennials such as gypsophila or yarrow to fill the after-bloom gap. Other foxtail lilies include *E. stenophyllus,* under 3 ft., with yellow flowers aging to brown; and *E. robustus,* to 8 ft., with pink flowers.

How to grow: Full sun. Good drainage is critical; plant the huge octopus-shaped roots on a bed of sand and cover with 2–3 in. more sand. Insert a stick near the crown so that stakes can be set later as the flower stalk begins to lengthen. Leave the stick as a reminder not to dig into the roots by mistake after the leaves die down. Don't divide unless the clump gets very crowded, and be very careful not to bruise or break the roots.

Erianthus

Air-ee-an´thus.
Gramineae. Grass family.

Perennial grasses with tall reedy stems, flat spreading leaf blades, and silky flowering plumes. About 20 spp., native to temperate and tropical climates. Some botanists now combine *Erianthus* with *Saccharum,* the genus that includes sugar cane.

ravennae (p. 210)
Ravenna grass, plume grass.
Clumping grass. Zone 4.
H: 9–12 ft. S: 5–6 ft.

A dramatic grass for large landscapes, with fluffy flower plumes that lighten from purplish to beige to silver, lasting from September through winter. Cut them to use for fresh or dried arrangements. The stiff reedy stalks hold the plumes well above the coarse 1-in.-wide leaves. Keep the mature size in mind when plac-ing this plant; it would be overwhelming beside a patio or next to a narrow walkway but makes a good screen or backdrop for a border. You'll enjoy its constant movement and rustling sound on breezy days. Although big, this plant is not invasive—it forms a clump and doesn't spread.

How to grow: Full sun. Best in relatively infertile, dry soil, where it stays upright and strong; requires staking in fertile or moist condi-tions. Cut old stalks to the ground in early spring.

Erica

Air´i-ka. Heath.
Ericaceae. Heath family.

Evergreen shrubs or small trees whose branching twiggy stems are crowded with needlelike leaves. Plants produce small bell-shaped flowers in nodding clusters, usually rosy red, pink, purplish, or white. About 665 spp., the majority native to South Africa, with some from the Mediterranean region and Europe.

carnea (p. 171)
Winter heath.
Evergreen shrub. Zone 5 or 4.
H: 6–9 in. S: 18 in.

The easiest and hardiest of the heaths, with attractive fine-textured foliage and pretty flowers. Spreads to form a dense mat and makes an excellent ground cover for sandy or acidic soils. Use it to edge a grouping of rhododendrons and azaleas, or mass it with other heaths and heathers for a Persian-carpet effect. The whorled leaves are short and pointy, bright to dark green. Tiny bell-shaped flowers in long slender clusters at the branch tips last for weeks from winter to spring, in shades of white, pink, or red. 'Springwood White' has light green foliage and white flowers, 'Springwood Pink' has bright green foliage and pink bloom, and 'Myretoun Ruby' has dark green foliage and ruby red flowers. *E. cinerea* has a more upright habit and flowers in spring. *E.* × *darleyensis,* a hybrid between *E. carnea* and *E. cinerea,* flowers over a long season from winter to spring and tolerates heat or cold weather and acidic or alkaline soil. Specialty nurseries offer many other species, both hardy and tender.

How to grow: Full or part sun. Good drainage is most important. Likes slightly acidic soil; if the soil is mildly alkaline, add lots of peat moss or compost. Doesn't tolerate hot summers, dry or humid. Space 18 in. apart for ground cover. Cut back hard after bloom for dense growth and a tidy appearance.

Erigeron

Air-ij´er-on. Fleabane.
Compositae. Daisy family.

Perennials, biennials, or annuals with hairy leaves in a basal clump and clasping the upright flower stalks. The composite blooms have yellow disks and two or more dense layers of needlelike rays. About 200 spp. worldwide, most native to North America.

speciosus (p. 240)
(*E.* × *hybridus*)
Fleabane.
Perennial. Zone 6.
H: 1–2½ ft. S: 1–2 ft.

Provides masses of asterlike blossoms early in the season, sometimes continuing sporadically through the summer. Blooms are 2–3 in. wide, with pink, lavender, or purple rays and yellow disks, borne on strong leafy stalks above a neat clump of basal foliage. The low-growing types are good for edging. The tall forms mix well with bearded irises and columbines. Several cultivars have been selected for their flower color. 'Forster's Darling' is hardier than most (Zone 5), with bright pink semidouble blooms.

How to grow: Full or part sun. Does best in well-drained soil with ordinary watering. Space 1–2 ft. apart; divide in spring. Tall flower stalks will need support. Cut back after flowering to encourage rebloom.

Eriobotrya

Air-ee-o-bot´ri-a.
Rosaceae. Rose family.

Evergreen shrubs or small trees with thick, large, short-stalked leaves, usually with toothed edges, sometimes with rusty hairs. Flowers are not showy. About 27 spp., native to eastern Asia.

japonica (p. 158)
Loquat.
Evergreen tree. Zone 7.
H: 20–30 ft. S: 20–30 ft.

An erect, dense-crowned tree that's usually planted for its bold, tropical appearance. The thick leathery leaves are 2–4 in. wide and 6–12 in. long. Tight woolly clusters of fragrant but tiny flowers in fall or winter yield yellow-orange 1–2-in. fruits in spring. Fruits are seedy but have a pleasant flavor; if you like them, look for grafted varieties such as 'Champagne', 'Gold Nugget', or 'MacBeth'. If you just want to grow the tree for its foliage, any seedling will do. Makes a good lawn tree, can be espaliered on a fence or wall, and does well in containers.

How to grow: Full or part sun. Ordinary soil and watering. Tolerates hot, dry weather when established. The tree survives cold spells, but the fruit may be damaged. If fire blight strikes, prune out damaged wood well behind the blackened wilted parts, sterilizing clippers with diluted household bleach after each cut.

Eriobotrya japonica

Eriogonum

Air-ee-og´o-num.
Polygonaceae. Buckwheat family.

Perennials or shrubs, some forming low mounds, often with woody crowns and roots. The simple leaves often are covered with silvery wool. Showy yellow, white, pink, or red flowers are borne in clusters. About 150 spp., native to the southern and western United States.

umbellatum (p. 240)
Sulphur buckwheat.
Perennial. Zone 7.
H: 1 ft. S: 2 ft.

A choice rock-garden plant with cheery umbels of bright gold, pale yellow, or creamy flowers in midsummer, turning reddish as they mature. Both the flowers and the puffy seedpods dry well for arrangements. Forms a low mat of leaves, green above and woolly beneath. A widespread species, native across the Southwest, and

Eriogonum umbellatum

varying in height, habit, and flower color.

How to grow: Full or part sun. Tolerates poor or dry soil and heat. Needs good drainage. No special care.

Eryngium

Air-rin´ji-um.
Umbelliferae. Carrot family.

Dramatic perennials with spiny leaves, usually lobed or divided, and dense white or purple flower heads collared with spiny bracts. The foliage or bracts often have a metallic silvery or purple color. About 230 spp., occurring worldwide.

amethystinum (see below for photo)
Sea holly.
Perennial. Zone 5.
H: to 3 ft. S: 2 ft.

Uncannily beautiful, with spiny blue bracts and tight thimbles of blue flowers. Attractive in arrangements, fresh or dried, and in borders. The basal leaves, 6 in. long, are spiny and finely cut. Stems are stiffly erect, tinted blue near the top. Flower heads are poised on a saucer of 2-in. bracts. Combine with grasses, black-eyed Susans, baby's-breath, and sneezeweed in colder zones; with succulents and desert shrubs in mild climates. Some plants sold under this name are actually *E. planum* or hybrids between the two species. Other species are worth seeking out. *E. alpinum* has especially vivid blue flower heads and bracts. *E. varifolium* (p. 240) is unusual because it has rounded leaves with conspicuous white veins, and the foliage looks good well into winter. Both are smaller than *E. amethystinum*, staying under 2 ft. tall.

How to grow: Full sun. Needs well-drained, ordinary or unamended soil. Best planted in groups of 3 or more, 2 ft. apart. The only care needed is the cutting back of old stalks.

Eschscholzia

Esh-sholt´zi-a.
Papaveraceae. Poppy family.

Perennials or annuals with shiny bright poppylike flowers on single stalks. Leaves are smooth and finely dissected. Only 8–10 spp., native to western North America.

californica (p. 295)
California poppy.
Perennial grown as an annual. All zones.
H: 9–24 in. S: 9–24 in.

California's state flower, these easy-to-grow plants are perfect for naturalizing with other wildflowers in a drought-tolerant garden. The cuplike flowers are vivid orange with a satiny sheen. They bloom most heavily from March to May in nature but continue much longer in the garden. The delicate-looking foliage is pale gray-green. Selected forms have gold or creamy flowers. *E. mexicana* is similar but smaller, with golden orange flowers.

Eschscholzia californica

How to grow: Full sun. Needs good drainage and tolerates poor or dry soil. Water during dry spells to prolong bloom. The best plants come from sowing the tiny seeds directly in fall or winter in mild-winter areas, spring in colder zones. Self-sows readily.

Eucalyptus

You-ka-lip´tus. Gum tree.
Myrtaceae. Myrtle family.

Evergreen trees, some small and shrubby and others very tall. Most have leathery foliage, which is sometimes very aromatic. Individual plants usually produce leaves of at least two different sizes and shapes as they develop from seedlings to mature trees. The brushy flowers are often very brightly colored, followed by curious woody pods. In Australia the different species are grouped according to their bark, which can be smooth, flaky, more or less stringy or fibrous, or hard and fissured. Eucalyptus trees have been planted throughout the tropics and mild temperate zones for timber and firewood and as ornamentals. About 450 spp., almost all from Australia.

camaldulensis (p. 158)
Red gum, river red gum.
Evergreen tree. Zone 8.
H: 80 ft. or more. S: 80 ft. or more.

A huge tough tree for ranches, rural roads, and large open spaces. Grows fast and makes a spreading crown with weeping branches. The lance-shaped leaves, up to 10 in. long, are thin, leathery, and green or gray-green. The clusters of scentless white puffy flowers are inconspicuous but produce a big crop of woody pods. Makes a windbreak if pruned hard to increase density. Can be cut back to the ground and it will resprout. Too big for most city lots, and roots are too greedy for underplanting.

How to grow: Full sun. Tolerates poor, dry soil and is exceptionally heat-tolerant. Plant from containers, buying the smallest plants available to avoid tangled roots. Straighten out any curled roots at planting time. Thin branches to avoid top-heaviness. Young plants have slender, pliable trunks. Stake well, but tie loosely enough that the trunk can sway a little—such movement actually helps thicken and strengthen it.

citriodora (p. 158)
Lemon-scented gum.
Evergreen tree. Zone 9.
H: 60–100 ft. S: 30–40 ft.

Grown principally for its magnificent straight white trunk, which looks good with contemporary architecture. The thin leathery leaves, 3–7 in. long by 1 in. wide, have a strong lemon scent when crushed. Flowers in winter often go unnoticed. Fast enough from seed to grow as an annual if you love lemon-scented plants, and northern gardeners can keep one in a pot for a few years. Used as a lawn tree in California, and it makes lovely groves if planted close together. Grows quickly into a narrow column; later develops a broad crown.

How to grow: Like *E. camaldulensis*.

ficifolia (p. 159)
Red-flowering gum.
Evergreen tree. Zone 9.
H: to 40 ft. S: to 40 ft.

A spreading tree with dense foliage. The rubbery, thick, dark green leaves are 3–7 in. long, up to 2 in. wide. Flowers form spectacular 1-ft.-long clusters of red (sometimes pink or white) powderpuffs. Bloom is sporadic, heaviest in summer. Useful at a property edge or by the street; seldom thrives in lawns. *E. calophylla* is similar but has showy white or creamy flowers.

How to grow: Like *E. camaldulensis*. Fine for seaside plantings. Prune heavy seedpods from young trees to keep branches from drooping.

polyanthemos (p. 159)
Silver-dollar gum (U.S.), red box (Australia)
Evergreen tree. Zone 8.
H: 30–75 ft. S: 15–45 ft.

A shapely, informal, fast-growing tree with a mottled brown, gray, and pink trunk. Cut back as needed to encourage young shoots, which have round silver-dollar leaves that dance in the breeze. Unpruned trees will gradually shift to mature foliage, with narrow, oval, bright green leaves. Flowers are inconspicuous white puffs. Use it for a tall screen or windbreak or as a street or specimen tree. *E. cinerea* also has decorative silver-dollar juvenile foliage that is used by florists and interior designers. It's a scrawny, irregular tree, but it grows fast and tolerates repeated pruning.

How to grow: Like *E. camaldulensis*.

Eucalyptus sideroxylon

sideroxylon (p. 159)
(*E. sideroxylon* 'Rosea')
Red ironbark.
Evergreen tree. Zone 8.
H: 30–90 ft. S: 30 ft. or more.

The rather open, weeping growth habit creates open shade. The blue-green foliage makes a strong contrast to the dark reddish to blackish brown bark. Clusters of powderpuff flowers, 1 in. wide, are white to pink or red. Good for tall screens or as a street tree. Trouble-free.

How to grow: Like *E. camaldulensis*.

Other eucalyptus

E. gunnii, or cider gum, is a tall, dense, quick-growing, deep green tree hardy to 5° F, possibly colder. 40–75 ft. tall.

E. leucoxylon, or white ironbark, is slender and upright, with drooping branches. Shredding bark exposes the white trunk. Showy white to pink powderpuff blossoms in spring. 20–80 ft. tall.

E. mannifera, or spotted gum, is a broad, open-crowned, heavy-limbed tree with showy white bark blotched with brown. 20–50 ft. tall.

E. melliodora is a shapely well-mannered tree with slightly weeping branches, honey-scented flowers, and very little litter. 30–100 ft. tall.

E. microtheca is dense and bushy and has blue-green foliage. Its tolerance to wind and drought makes it a good desert tree. 35–40 ft. tall.

E. robusta takes heat, wind, drought, and wet soil. Shiny dark green leaves and pinkish white flowers in winter. To 90 ft. tall.

Euonymus
You-on´i-mus.
Celastraceae. Spindletree family.

Deciduous or evergreen shrubs, creeping vines, or small trees. Most have simple opposite leaves and inconspicuous flowers. Bright-colored red, orange, or pink fruits open in fall to reveal even brighter seeds, attractive to birds but poisonous to humans. More than 170 spp., native mostly to Asia.

alata (p. 137)
Burning bush.
Deciduous shrub. Zone 3.
H: 8–10 ft. S: 10 ft.

A workhorse of a shrub: tough, hardy, tolerant of most soils, and easy to grow. The simple opposite leaves slowly turn from dark green in summer to pale greenish pink and finally brilliant scarlet in fall. It's one of the most vivid and reliable plants for fall color. Also interesting in winter, when the corky winged twigs are revealed. Looks best when unpruned, as the branches spread horizontally into graceful overlapping tiers. Makes a good single specimen or a showy mass planting or hedge. 'Compacta' is smaller (to 6 ft.), with even more intense red-pink fall color and slender wingless twigs.

How to grow: Full sun, part sun, or shade. Ordinary soil and watering. Needs no special care or pruning.

fortunei selections (pp. 172, 203)
Winter creeper.
Evergreen vines or shrubs. Zone 5.
H: varies. S: varies.

This species has contributed many attractive hardy evergreen vines and shrubs. Several of the most popular forms are described in the box

Euonymus fortunei

below. The vining forms make good ground covers for small or large spaces, or can climb a wall, fence, chimney, or tree. The shrubby upright forms combine well with conifers or evergreens in foundation plantings or mixed borders, or can be used as low hedges. Sprawling "juvenile" plants rarely flower; upright "adult" forms do. The actual flowers are inconspicuous, but the pea-sized fruits are startlingly colorful: the pinkish red hulls open to reveal bright orange seeds and hang on through winter.

How to grow: Full sun, part sun, or shade. Not fussy about soil but need good drainage. Tolerate dry spells. Easy to establish; plant from containers in spring or early fall. Require no special care or pruning. Subject to leafspot and powdery mildew, especially in humid conditions or where air circulation is poor. Euonymus is unusually susceptible to scale insects, and severe infestations can be fatal. Check often, and spray with horticultural oil if needed. Stem or tip cuttings root easily in summer if planted in a shady spot and covered with a glass jar.

Euonymus fortunei *selections*

E. f. 'Coloratus' spreads to make a good ground cover, 1 ft. tall and several feet wide. Leaves are 1–2 in. long, dark green in summer and purple-maroon in winter. Set the lawn mower high and mow in early spring for a more uniform and formal appearance, or let it spread naturally to cover a rough slope or rock wall.

E. f. 'Emerald 'n' Gold' is a compact shrub, usually under 2 ft. tall and wide. Its 1–1^1/$_2$-in. leaves are dark green edged with gold in summer, purplish-green and pink in winter.

E. f. 'Gracilis', also sold as 'Silver Edge', is a trailing ground cover, usually just a few inches tall and spreading up to 2 ft. wide. The relatively thin green leaves are edged with white or cream in summer, turning pink in winter.

E. f. 'Kewensis' is a dainty plant with tiny leaves only ^{1}/$_4$ in. long. It hugs the ground like a rug and makes a charming ground cover for small spaces. It also climbs nicely, but the leaves get larger as it goes higher. Climbing specimens occasionally flower and fruit.

E. f. var. *radicans* is tough and versatile, with thick, glossy, dark green leaves 1 in. long. It can grow as a shrubby bush, sprawl over the ground, or climb 40 ft. up a wall or tree. *E. f.* 'Variegatus' is equally versatile, with variably green-and-white, all-green, or all-white leaves.

E. f. 'Sarcoxie' is a shrubby form, growing about 4–6 ft. tall, and makes a good hedge. It has thick, glossy, dark green leaves and often flowers and fruits.

E. f. var. *vegetus* is usually a shrub about 4–5 ft. tall and wide, but it sometimes takes off as a vine and climbs up to 40 ft. The broadly elliptical leaves, 1–2 in. long, are thick and glossy. This is the hardiest of evergreen vines and is very useful as an evergreen shrub. It regularly flowers, so plant it where you can enjoy the colorful fruits all winter, displayed against the rich green foliage.

japonicus selections (p. 172)
Japanese euonymus.
Evergreen shrubs. Zone 8 or 7.
H: 10 ft. S: 6 ft.

Tough as nails and ubiquitous in mild-winter climates, these are dense, many-stemmed shrubs thickly clothed with glossy leathery leaves 1–3 in. long. They grow naturally into an upright oval but are often pruned into geometric shapes. The species has plain green leaves, but variegated forms are more popular. There are many cultivars, some apparently with two or more names, but basically the options are green leaves edged with gold, cream, or silvery white; or green leaves with a center spot of gold, cream, or silvery white. These are all striking plants, and if they were rare they would be collector's items. In fact, they are very common, especially in commercial landscaping. Less familiar is 'Microphyllus', a dwarf (2 ft.) form with small narrow leaves. It makes an inexpensive substitute for boxwood, with fewer insect and disease problems, and makes a fine low hedge around a bed of roses or herbs.

How to grow: Full sun, part sun, or shade. Ordinary or unimproved soil. Tolerate coastal wind and salt, acidic or alkaline soil conditions, heat, and drought (when established). Tolerate pruning or shearing, but the natural shape is fine for informal gardens. Watch for scale, thrips, and spider mites, and spray as needed.

kiautschovica 'Manhattan' (p. 172)
Spreading euonymus.
Evergreen shrub. Zone 6.
H: 6 ft. or more. S: 4–5 ft.

Almost problem-free (subject to scale) and ideal for hedges or foundation plantings. Grows naturally in an erect, dense, rounded shape, or can be pruned or sheared, trained into a standard, or espaliered against a wall or fence. The glossy leaves, 2–3 in. long, are dark green in summer; they hold fine through mild winters but look discolored and ratty after severe winters. Fruits regularly, with pinkish hulls and orange seeds. Other cultivars are sometimes listed and look quite similar.

How to grow: Full sun, part sun, or shade. Ordinary or unimproved soil and regular watering or rainfall. Tolerates even desert heat if watered. Supposedly originated in Manhattan, Kansas, but isn't reliably hardy in the upper Midwest. Prune as desired, and watch for scale infestations.

Eupatorium
You-pa-toe´ree-um.
Compositae. Daisy family.

Perennials with opposite or whorled leaves on upright stalks topped with showy clusters of many small flower heads. Many species have been divided out of this formerly large genus. Remaining are about 40 spp., native to the eastern United States and Eurasia.

coelestinum (p. 240)
(now *Conoclinium coelestinum*)
Hardy ageratum.
Perennial. Zone 5.
H: 2 ft. S: 2 ft. or more.

Branched clusters of fluffy, powder blue flowers enliven the garden for 4–6 weeks in late summer and fall. The lush, light green foliage is attractive throughout the growing season. Ideal for moist sunny meadows or creek banks. 'Alba' has white flowers.

How to grow: Sun or part shade. Tolerates constant moisture and heat. Can be invasive in rich, moist soils. Space plants 1½–3 ft. apart. Divide in spring. Remove spent flowers to limit self-seeding.

Eupatorium purpureum

purpureum (p. 240)
Joe-Pye weed.
Perennial. Zone 4.
H: 5–9 ft. S: 2–4 ft.

Growing bigger than many shrubs, this is no plant for small gardens, but it makes a wonderful focal point in the fall border. Established clumps produce 20 or more strong stalks punctuated with whorls of 3–5 large, toothed, vanilla-scented leaves. Broad (12–18 in.) clusters of tiny pinkish purple flowers top the stalks in late summer, gradually fading to pinkish beige and lasting through fall. Combine it with maiden grass, New England asters, and perennial sunflowers. *E. fistulosa* and *E. maculatum,* also called Joe-Pye weed, are similar. Compact (under 5 ft.) and darker purple-colored forms are sometimes offered.

How to grow: Full sun. Does best in fertile, organic, moist soil. Cut stems back by one-third in late spring to encourage branching and to reduce overall height. Doesn't need staking. Cut to the ground in late winter. Increase by division in fall or early spring.

Euphorbia
You-for'bee-a.
Euphorbiaceae. Spurge family.

A giant and diverse group of herbaceous annuals and perennials, succulents, shrubs, and trees. All have a milky sap that causes a skin rash in some people. The actual flowers are usually small but may be surrounded with large, colorful, showy bracts. About 1,600 spp., native worldwide.

***griffithii* 'Fireglow'** (p. 241)
Perennial. Zone 6 or 5.
H: 3 ft. S: 2 ft.

Brilliant in midsummer, with glowing orange-red bracts spread over a rounded clump. The leafy stalks of foliage hold up well and turn bronzy in fall. Combine it with grasses or bright yellow achilleas or coreopsis. Not common yet in the United States but available from mail-order perennial nurseries.

How to grow: Full sun. Best in sandy, well-drained soil with regular watering. Cut to the ground in fall and mulch crowns where winters are cold.

marginata (p. 295)
Snow-on-the-mountain.
Annual. All zones.
H: 18–24 in. S: 8–12 in.

Easy but showy from midsummer until frost, with clusters of white-edged leaves atop erect stems. The actual flowers are inconspicuous. Use it to fill spaces between perennials in a new garden, or combine it with white and yellow four-o'clocks and purple perilla for a long-lasting annual display. Can be used in flower arrangements, but don't let the milky sap get on your skin—it can be irritating.

How to grow: Full or part sun. Tolerates poor soil, dryness, and heat. Sow indoors 6 weeks before last frost, or sow in place when the soil is warm. Self-sows but isn't invasive.

myrsinites (p. 241)
Perennial. Zone 6.
H: 8–12 in. S: 24 in.

Admired for the handsome blue-gray color of its stiff fleshy leaves, which whorl around the stem in close spirals and are evergreen in mild climates. Flat clusters of chartreuse or yellow flowers develop at the ends of the shoots in early spring. Nice in a raised bed or planter where the color and form can be appreciated up close, or trailing over a rock wall or down a bank. *E. rigida* has the same color foliage but is more tender (Zone 8) and more erect (to 2 ft.).

How to grow: Full or part sun. Tolerates unamended soil, dryness, and heat. Cut out old stems as they turn yellow.

Euryops
Yur'yops.
Compositae. Daisy family.

Evergreen shrubs with yellow daisylike blossoms on single stalks, borne over a long season. About 97 spp., many from South Africa.

pectinatus (p. 173)
Evergreen shrubby perennial. Zone 9.
H: 4–6 ft. S: 4–6 ft.

A chubby plant that blooms almost continuously, with bright 1–2-in. yellow daisies held above furry, deeply cut, silvery gray-green foliage. (The cultivar 'Viridis' is identical but has smooth, bright green leaves.) Combines well

Euryops pectinatus

with shrubs or perennials in mixed borders, or makes a low-maintenance cover on banks. Does well in containers and can be trained as a lollipop standard on a short trunk.

How to grow: Full sun. Ordinary soil and watering. Needs good drainage and tolerates dry soil when well established. Cut off old flowers to prolong bloom. Prune after heaviest bloom in early summer to control size. Pest-free.

Exochorda

Ecks-o-kor'da. Pearlbush.
Rosaceae. Rose family.

Hardy deciduous shrubs or trees with bright white flowers in spring. Only 4 spp., native to Asia.

× *macrantha* 'The Bride' (p. 137)

Pearlbush.
Deciduous shrub. Zone 5 or 4.
H: 3–5 ft. S: 4–5 ft.

Lovely in April or May, when the pearllike buds open into flowers like apple blossoms. Flowers cover the arching stems of this compact mounded shrub. Foliage is smooth, blue-green in summer and yellow in fall. An old-fashioned favorite, ornamental and easy but unfortunately not common in nurseries. Small enough to fit easily in a mixed border.

How to grow: Full or part sun. Ordinary soil and watering. Does poorly on limy soil. Prune after flowering, cutting out the oldest wood every year. Problem-free.

racemosa (p. 137)

Common pearlbush.
Deciduous shrub or small tree. Zone 4.
H: to 15 ft. S: 10–15 ft.

Grown for its spring show of clean white buds and blossoms; lovely displayed against a background of dark evergreens. It usually makes a tall shrub with arching, sometimes flopping branches but looks better if trained as a multi-trunked small tree. It leafs out early, then recedes into the background after flowering. Useful in a mixed shrub border, perhaps along property lines.

How to grow: Full or part sun. Ordinary soil and watering. Tolerates hot, dry summers. Prune after flowering. Choose a few trunks and remove lower limbs to train as a tree; continue by removing the oldest flowering shoots each year.

Fagus

Fay'gus. Beech.
Fagaceae. Beech family.

Large deciduous trees with smooth gray bark, spreading limbs, slender twigs, toothed leaves, and small angular seeds (beechnuts) in prickly shells. 10 spp., native to the north temperate zone.

Fagus grandifolia

sylvatica (p. 114)

European beech.
Deciduous tree. Zone 5.
H: 60 ft. or more. S: 40 ft.

Beeches are stately, graceful trees, handsome in all seasons. Unfortunately, they grow too big for most city or suburban lots, but they're wonderful for larger sites. The bark is appealingly smooth and tight, light to dark gray, often compared to elephant hide. Foliage is glossy and dense in summer, in shades of green, copper, or purple, turning bronze in fall. The main trunk is strongly upright, but the branches spread wide, often drooping to the ground like a long skirt. Twigs are slender, with delicate pointed buds.

Many forms have been selected and propagated by nurseries in Europe and the United States; sometimes similar forms have different names. 'Atropurpurea', 'Purpurea', and 'Riversii' have dark blackish purple or purple-green foliage; 'Cuprea' has lighter purple leaves. 'Tricolor', or 'Roseo-marginata', has purple leaves edged with pink and white, a lovely effect but vulnerable to scorching in hot, dry weather. It grows slowly enough to include in a smaller garden, eventually reaching 25 ft. or more. 'Pendula' has weeping branches that form a waterfall of foliage; children can play house under the tentlike canopy. *F. grandifolia,* the American beech, which is native on rich, moist sites throughout the eastern United States, is equally lovely, with green leaves in summer turning a warm golden bronze in fall, and persisting through winter on young trees or lower limbs of older trees.

How to grow: Best in full sun. Prefers moist but well-drained soil with acidic pH. Doesn't tolerate compacted or waterlogged soil. Needs good soil, plenty of moisture, and part shade where summers are hot. Beech roots are shallow, often lifting above the soil. Don't try to maintain turfgrass under a beech tree. Use mulch or tough ground covers such as epimediums, or let the tree's lower limbs sweep to the ground. When established on a suitable site, beech trees are hardy and pest-free and need no maintenance.

Fatsia

Fat'si-a.
Araliaceae. Aralia family.

An evergreen shrub with large, glossy, palmately lobed leaves. Only 1 sp., native to Japan.

japonica (p. 173)

Evergreen shrub. Zone 8.
H: 5–7 ft. S: 4–6 ft.

An upright shrub with big, coarse, glossy, palmately lobed leaves, often 12 in. wide and long. Sometimes makes rounded clusters of tiny white flowers on branched stalks, followed by small dark fruits. Valued for its boldness, which goes well with modern architecture, or can be combined with gingers, bananas, palms, and

Fatsia japonica

other large-leaved plants for a tropical effect. Crossed with *Hedera hibernica,* it produced the hybrid × *Fatshedera lizei,* which has big ivylike leaves on mostly unbranched stems that don't quite stand alone but look good trained against a wall. Both *Fatsia* and × *Fatshedera* grow well in containers and are often used as houseplants.

How to grow: Part sun or shade; protect from hot afternoon sun. Not fussy about soil or watering. Does well under eaves, in entryways, or in other dry, shady spots. Hard to shape by pruning; tends to grow as it chooses. Subject to spider mites and other pests, especially if grown as a houseplant.

Feijoa

Fee-jo′a.
Myrtaceae. Myrtle family.

Evergreen shrubs with opposite oblong leaves, ornamental flowers, and edible fruits. Only 2 spp., native to South America.

sellowiana (p. 173)

Pineapple guava.
Evergreen shrub. Zone 8.
H: 10 ft. or more. S: 10 ft.

Attractive and useful, this densely branched shrub has healthy oval leaves, dark green above and gray below, and showy flowers, 1¹/₂ in. wide, with waxy white petals and lots of bright red stamens. The round fruits, like small yellow eggs, are very fragrant and tasty. It flowers in early summer; fruit ripens in fall. Grows well in containers, and a single specimen makes a good patio plant. (Can be wintered indoors in colder climates.) Suitable for hedges, left unpruned for a casual mounded profile or sheared into formal shapes. If you want to eat the fruit, look for 'Coolidge', 'Nazemeta', or 'Pineapple Gem'—all are self-pollinating and have good flavor.

How to grow: Full or part sun. Ordinary well-drained soil; tolerates dry soil but not wet sites. Space 10 ft. apart for a hedge. Branch tips may freeze back in severe winters, but it recovers with bushy new growth. Pest-free.

Felicia

Fe-liss′ee-a.
Compositae. Daisy family.

Annuals, perennials, or small shrubs with composite flowers on long stalks, usually with yellow disks and blue, lavender, pink, or white rays. About 83 spp., most from South Africa.

amelloides (p. 296)

Blue marguerite.
Grown as an annual. All zones.
H: 12–18 in. S: 3–4 ft.

Fast enough to grow as an annual where winters are cold, this is actually a shrubby perennial, evergreen outdoors in Zone 9. The long-stalked daisylike blossoms, pure bright blue with yellow centers, open almost continuously through mild weather. The egg-shaped dark green leaves are somewhat rough and thick. Branches sprawl and look untidy if not trimmed regularly but look good spilling from window boxes or over walls, or spreading along the front of a bed or border. 'San Gabriel', 'San Luis', and 'Santa Anita' are vigorous forms with extra-large 2–3-in. blooms.

How to grow: Full sun. Ordinary or better soil and regular watering. Cut flowers often; prune to control shape. Where grown as a perennial, prune hard in late summer to encourage renewed bloom.

Festuca

Fes-too′ka. Fescue.
Gramineae. Grass family.

Annual or perennial grasses, most forming clumps of flat narrow blades or slender, curling, almost threadlike leaves. Flowers are borne in narrow panicles. Some species are used as forage, others in lawns, and a few are ornamental. About 300 spp., most from temperate regions.

ovina var. glauca (p. 210)

Blue fescue.
Clumping grass. Zone 4.
H: 6–12 in. S: 8–10 in.

A small clumping grass, ideal for small courtyard gardens, rock gardens, or raised beds, where its diminutive habit can be appreciated. Blue combines well with many other colors, and while blue flowers come and go, this plant's blue foliage remains through the growing season and into winter (it's "everblue" in mild years). Use it as a specimen or edging along the front of a border. Massed as a ground cover, it makes a sea of billowing mounds. Combines well with hardy geraniums. Narrow spikes of flowers appear sporadically in summer; leave them if you like, but removing them focuses the plant's energy on foliage production.

Seedling plants are commonly sold but vary considerably in blueness. The best bright blue forms, such as 'Elijah's Blue' and 'Sea Urchin', must be propagated by division. *F. amethystina,* the large blue fescue (18–24 in. or more), makes bigger, showier clumps, but the foliage is equally delicate and blue. It tolerates heat better than regular blue fescue does.

How to grow: Full sun. Needs well-drained soil and tolerates dryness better than wetness. Space 8–10 in. apart for ground cover. Cut back once a year, in fall or spring. Clumps can (and should) go years without division.

Feijoa sellowiana

Ficus
Fy′kus. Fig.
Moraceae. Mulberry family.

Trees, shrubs, or clinging vines, nearly all with thick evergreen leaves. All figs have sticky milky sap and bear flowers and seeds inside a fleshy receptacle—the fig. About 800 spp., from tropical and warm climates worldwide.

carica (p. 114)
Common fig.
Deciduous tree. Zone 8 or 7.
H: 20–30 ft. S: 20 ft.

A distinctive shrub or tree, often multi-trunked, with large, coarse, lobed leaves on thick stems. Makes a bold, interesting specimen. The tiny flowers develop into sweet, tasty figs. One crop is borne in early summer, on the previous year's wood; the main crop forms on new wood and ripens in fall. Cultivars differ in fruit size, flavor, color, and tolerance of heat and cold. 'Kadota' and 'Mission' have large sweet fruits and are popular in California. 'Brown Turkey', an old favorite with dark purple-brown fruits, is hardier (Zone 7 or 6) than most figs. Figs can be grown as lawn trees but do especially well if planted against the south wall of a building, where reflected heat helps ripen the fruit. Gardeners in cold zones can grow a fig tree in a large tub or planter, rolling it out on the patio for summer and wintering it in a garage or basement that stays near freezing temperatures.

How to grow: Full or part sun. Needs good drainage and tolerates dry soil better than wet. Prune to control size and shape, removing weak or crossed limbs. Watch out for the milky sap— it stains hands and clothing.

Ficus carica

microcarpa var. *nitida* (p. 159)
(often sold as *F. retusa*)
Indian laurel fig.
Evergreen tree. Zone 9.
H: 25–30 ft. S: 15–20 ft.

One of the cleanest-looking, shapeliest evergreen trees and highly tolerant of urban conditions. It has an erect trunk with smooth, pale gray bark and a dense crown of glossy, thick, bright green, oval leaves, 2–4 in. long. This tree gets huge in tropical climates, but it can be pruned anytime to maintain its form and shape—even sheared into topiary. The tiny fig fruits are dry and inedible, small enough not to be messy. The species, *F. microcarpa,* has similar foliage but is weeping in form, with branches trailing nearly to the ground unless trimmed.

How to grow: Full sun. Tolerates heat. Ordinary well-drained soil with regular rainfall or watering. Cuban laurel thrips are a serious disfiguring pest; control by systemic sprays. The cultivar 'Green Gem' is less subject to thrips damage. Severe freezes can disfigure or kill trees.

pumila (p. 203)
(*F. repens*)
Creeping fig.
Evergreen vine. Zone 8.
H: to 25 ft. or more.

An evergreen vine that clings tenaciously to stone, brick, wood, or metal walls, spreading and branching to make a vertical carpet of foliage. Often seen covering the brick walls of courtyard gardens in Charleston, New Orleans, and other old southern cities, where it makes a soft green background for flowering perennials and shrubs. Young plants have slender stems and "juvenile" foliage: thin, papery, heart-shaped leaves 1/2–1 in. long. Older plants that have climbed partway up a wall develop stout branches of "adult" foliage: thick, leathery, oval leaves 2–4 in. long. 'Minima' has small leaves and grows slowly. 'Variegata' has small leaves blotched with white.

How to grow: Part sun; scorches brown or yellow in hot afternoon sun or winter sun. Ordinary or constantly moist but well-drained soil; doesn't recover well from drying out. Don't hesitate to prune if the vine gets too big or if you don't like the coarseness of the adult foliage. Usually recovers from frost injury that kills the tops of the shoots. Subject to spider mites.

Filipendula
Fill-i-pen′dew-la. Meadowsweet.
Rosaceae. Rose family.

Hardy perennials with pinnately compound leaves and upright stems topped with fluffy clusters of tiny flowers. Formerly used as medicinal plants. About 10 spp., native to the north temperate zone.

Filipendula rubra

rubra (p. 241)
Queen-of-the-prairie.
Perennial. Zone 3.
H: 6–8 ft. S: 4 ft. or more.

Truly a grand and statuesque plant, with fluffy pink plumes, 6–9 in. wide, waving above all the other plants in the border. Blooms in mid- to late summer. The foliage—dark green pinnately compound leaves with jagged leaflets—is almost as beautiful as the blossoms. Does especially well in a damp meadow or beside a pond or stream, combined with Japanese irises or other moisture-loving plants. 'Venusta' has darker pink flowers.

How to grow: Full or part sun. Prefers fertile, organic soil and steady moisture. Won't grow very tall in dry soil. Give it plenty of room—2–3 ft. on all sides—to begin with. It will spread quickly to fill the space but isn't difficult to control. The sturdy stalks stand up well to wind and rain and don't need staking. Pest-free.

Foeniculum

Fee-nick´you-lum. Fennel.
Umbelliferae. Carrot family.

A perennial or annual herb with compound leaves divided into fine needlelike segments, umbels of yellow flowers, and aromatic seeds. Only 1 sp., native to Europe and the Mediterranean region, with 3 varieties.

vulgare (p. 282)
Fennel.
Perennial herb. Zone 4.
H: 3–6 ft. S: 2 ft.

Three varieties of fennel are commonly grown: one with tasty seeds, another with leaf bases swollen into an anise-flavored bulb, and a third with ornamental purple-bronze foliage. The last, *F. v.* 'Purpureum', or bronze fennel, makes a fluffy mound of fragrant, finely dissected foliage early in the season, then sends up tall hollow stalks topped with doilylike clusters of tiny yellow flowers. Easy to grow and combines well with most flower colors.

How to grow: Full sun. Ordinary soil and watering. Cut off seed heads before they mature to prevent self-sowing; can be weedy in some areas. Sometimes damaged by black-and-yellow caterpillars, the larvae of swallowtail butterflies.

Forsythia

For-sith´ee-a.
Oleaceae. Olive family.

Deciduous shrubs with showy, yellow, 4-petaled flowers in early spring before the leaves appear. Just 7 spp., native to Europe and Asia.

× intermedia (p. 138)
Forsythia.
Deciduous shrub. Zone 4.
H: 8 ft. or more. S: 12–15 ft.

One of the first shrubs to bloom in spring, with cheerful bright yellow flowers covering the stems before the leaves expand. (Don't be surprised to find scattered blooms again in late fall.) Forsythia is vigorous, tough, and adaptable to various soils and climates, but it's often misused. Uninteresting for 50 weeks of the year, it does not make a good specimen for small lots. Repeated pruning makes it even worse, forming a twiggy knot that looks awful in winter. Instead, give it plenty of room to spread naturally into a broad, gracefully arching mound, or let it scramble, vinelike, into big pines or other trees. Selected cultivars have more compact growth and bigger or brighter-yellow flowers. Extreme cold can damage buds and prevent bloom, even though the plant itself is un-

harmed. 'Northern Sun' and 'Meadowlark' have buds hardy to -25° F. The closely related white forsythia, *Abeliophyllum distichum,* is not as rampant and has fragrant white flowers.

How to grow: Full sun. Ordinary soil and watering; wilts badly in dry weather. Allow plenty of space when planting. Dig up suckering shoots and replant in early spring. After flowering, remove the oldest shoots by cutting to the ground.

Forsythia × intermedia

Fothergilla

Foth-er-gil´la.
Hamamelidaceae. Witch hazel family.

Deciduous shrubs with brushy clusters of fragrant white flowers in spring, before the leaves expand, and bright fall foliage. Only 2 spp., native to the eastern United States.

major (p. 138)
Large fothergilla.
Deciduous shrub. Zone 5.
H: 6–10 ft. S: 8–10 ft.

A spreading shrub with honey-scented flowers in dense little bottlebrushes at the end of each twig in spring. The leathery rounded leaves expand later, are healthy dark green all summer, and turn beautiful shades of red, orange, and yellow in fall. Combines well with deciduous azaleas and witch hazels, with an underplanting of spring bulbs or wildflowers. *F. gardenii* is smaller, 2–3 ft. tall by 3–4 ft. wide; its cultivar 'Blue Mist' has blue-green leaves.

How to grow: Full or part sun. Prefers well-drained, acidic soil with plenty of organic matter. Needs no maintenance if planted in a suitable site. Fairly slow-growing.

Fothergilla major

Fragaria

Fra-gay´ree-a. Strawberry.
Rosaceae. Rose family.

Low-growing perennials that spread by runners. The glossy leaves have 3 toothed leaflets; some are evergreen, turning purple in cold weather. The small, white, 5-petaled flowers are followed in some species by sweet fleshy fruits. About 12 spp., native to the north temperate zone and Chile.

chiloensis (p. 241)
Wild strawberry.
Perennial. Zone 5.
H: 4–8 in. S: 8–12 in.

An ideal ground cover, spreading by rooting runners, and particularly suitable for naturalizing among trees and shrubs. The compound leaves, with 3 toothed leaflets, are glossy green above, pale below. The small white flowers are borne on upright stalks and are sometimes followed by firm red fruits. This species is native along the Pacific coast. *F. virginiana,* the eastern wild strawberry, is similar, with smaller, sweeter fruits. Both hold foliage well into or through the winter, turning maroon in cold weather.

Fragaria chiloensis

How to grow: Full or part sun. Ordinary soil and watering. Space 8–12 in. apart for ground cover. Place the crown level with or slightly above, never below, the soil surface. Easily increased by division. Mow or cut off old foliage in early spring, before new shoots develop.

Franklinia

Frank-lin´ee-a.
Theaceae. Tea family.

A deciduous shrub or small tree with white flowers like single camellias in summer and fall. Only 1 sp., extinct from its native habitat in Georgia but propagated by nurseries and popular in gardens far beyond its native range.

alatamaha (p. 114)

Franklin tree.
Deciduous tree or large shrub. Zone 6 or 5.
H: 10–20 ft. S: 6–12 ft.

Lovely in late summer and fall, when the fragrant flowers spread 3 in. wide at the branch tips. Five snow-white, frilly petals surround a mass of golden stamens. The oblong leaves are shiny dark green in summer, crimson in fall. Usually has multiple trunks and forms an upright open crown. Uncommon but special. Combine it with azaleas or rhododendrons to add interest after their flowers have passed.

How to grow: Full or part sun. Needs acidic, fertile soil amended with plenty of organic matter. Choose a site protected from cold winter winds. Best planted from containers as a small tree; grows at a medium rate. Surprisingly fast and easy from seeds (if you can get them), blooming in 6–10 years.

Fraxinus velutina

Fraxinus

Frax´in-us. Ash.
Oleaceae. Olive family.

Deciduous or evergreen trees with opposite leaves, usually pinnately compound. Trees produce small flowers in early spring, winged fruits in summer or fall. Many species are harvested for their strong resilient timber. About 65 spp., most native to the north temperate zone.

americana (p. 115)

American ash.
Deciduous tree. Zone 3.
H: 50 ft. or more. S: 50 ft. or more.

A big shade tree when mature and fast-growing when young. Makes a strongly upright trunk with an oval crown. Thick twigs with precise opposite branching look distinctive in winter. The pinnately compound leaves are dark green in summer, yellow and purple in fall. Handsome and vigorous where well sited but prone to insects and diseases, especially if stressed by dry or compacted soil. Several cultivars have been selected for vigor, neat habit, and good foliage color.

How to grow: Full sun. Best in deep, well-drained, organic soil. Not fussy about pH. Too big for small lots but fine in the country. Volunteer seedlings pose little problem in a lawn (regular mowing kills them) but are irritating in flower beds.

ornus (p. 115)

Flowering ash, manna ash.
Deciduous tree. Zone 6 or 5.
H: 40 ft. S: 30 ft.

Unique among ashes for its conspicuous 5–7-in. clusters of fragrant white flowers in May. The dark green compound leaves (turning yellow in fall) and smooth gray bark are also handsome. Grows medium-fast; develops a domed oval crown. Makes a good specimen for medium or large properties.

How to grow: Full or part sun. Tolerates unamended soil and dry conditions but is subject to several pests and diseases. Prune to eliminate narrow crotches.

oxycarpa (p. 115)

(*F. angustifolia*)
Narrow-leaved ash.
Deciduous tree. Zone 6.
H: 25–35 ft. S: 25–35 ft.

A neat, tidy, small to medium street or lawn tree with a delicate lacy look. Casts moderate shade. The firm, dark glossy green leaves have long narrow leaflets. Young trees are narrow, rounding out as they mature. Seedless cultivars are best. 'Raywood' has purplish red fall color; 'Flame' is similar but turns brighter red.

How to grow: Full sun. Ordinary soil and watering. Tolerates heat. Needs only routine pruning. Pest-free.

pennsylvanica (p. 115)

(*F. pennsylvanica* var. *lanceolata*)
Green ash.
Deciduous tree. Zone 2.
H: 50–60 ft. S: 40–60 ft.

A good shade tree for the plains: very upright and fast-growing (2 ft. or more a year) and not at all fussy about soil. The compound leaves cast medium shade, turn yellow in fall. Plant only nursery-propagated cultivars, which have neat symmetrical branching and don't produce seeds; seedlings are a nuisance and grow into irregular, weedy trees. Look for 'Bergeson', 'Marshall's Seedless', 'Newport', 'Patmore', or 'Summit'. Easy to transplant, and roots aren't bothered by cultivation, so you can underplant with shrubs and perennials.

How to grow: Full or part sun. Tolerates almost any soil conditions, including dry soil, and heat. Needs only routine pruning. Subject to borers and scale insects.

velutina (p. 115)

Arizona ash.
Deciduous tree. Zone 6.
H: to 50 ft. S: 30–40 ft.

A tough, fast tree for quick shade and golden fall color. The compound leaves, with 3–5 leaflets, are covered with gray fuzz at first, turning greener as they expand. Flowers are inconspicuous, and cultivars are seedless. Planted widely throughout the Southwest as a street tree. 'Modesto' has brighter green foliage. 'Rio Grande' has larger, thicker, dark green leaflets and isn't hurt by heat or wind.

How to grow: Full sun. Ordinary soil and watering. Prune to eliminate narrow branch crotches. Anthracnose can disfigure the foliage in wet springs. Aphids and psyllids feeding on the foliage drip messy honeydew on cars parked below. Resistant to oak root fungus.

Fremontodendron 'California Glory'

Fremontodendron

Free-mont-o-den´dron. Flannel bush.
Sterculiaceae. Chocolate family.

Semievergreen shrubs or small trees with woolly foliage and showy gold flowers for many weeks in spring. Only 2 spp., native to California and Baja California.

'California Glory' (p. 173)
(*F. californicum* × *F. mexicanum*)
Flannel bush.
Semievergreen shrub. Zone 9.
H: 15–20 ft. S: 20–30 ft.

Perfect for dry landscapes, especially spacious slopes, this is the showiest of California's spring-blooming shrubs. From March through June its branches are thickly covered with waxy lemon-yellow flowers, 3 in. wide. The thick, leathery, dark green leaves are handsome but have irritating hairs, as do the branches. Ideal companion for blue-flowered ceanothus and orange California poppies.

How to grow: Full sun. Needs dry soil. Tolerates poor soil and heat. Plant in fall. Give it plenty of room, and stake against wind. Grows quickly. Once it's established, do not water in summer.

Fuchsia

Few´sha.
Onagraceae. Evening primrose family.

Most are tender evergreen shrubs or small trees, with simple leaves and showy flowers that dangle like earrings from the stems. About 100 spp., most native to Central and South America.

hybrids (p. 296)
Hybrid fuchsias.
Tender shrubs grown as annuals. All zones.
H: 3 ft. or more. S: 3 ft. or more.

Where summers are cool and foggy along the Pacific coast, fuchsias make splendid flowering shrubs. In most parts of the United States, they are grown as annuals in hanging baskets, planters, or sometimes garden beds. The growth habit can be upright, spreading, or trailing. Plump round buds open into dangling flowers with 4 flared-back sepals (usually white, red, or pink), 4 to many rounded petals (white, pink, red, or purple), and prominent protruding stamens and pistil. There are hundreds of cultivars, with flowers 1/2–4 in. wide, single or double, solid-color or two-tone. The blossoms are scentless but attract hummingbirds, and they open continuously from early summer to fall. Most fuchsias are killed by a hard frost, but there is a hardy fuchsia sold as *F. magellanica* or fuchsia 'Riccartonii'. It dies to the ground but recovers in Zone 7, bearing red-purple flowers on upright stems that reach 3 ft. or more in a season.

How to grow: Part sun or shade. Don't tolerate hot sun or dry air. Need fertile soil amended with plenty of organic matter and constant moisture. Pinch tips often to promote branching. Fertilize lightly every 2 weeks. Watch for spider mites, whiteflies, and aphids. Hosing the foliage frequently helps discourage pests.

Gaillardia

Gay-lar´dee-a.
Compositae. Daisy family.

Annuals, biennials, or perennials with hairy leaves and showy daisylike blossoms, usually in various combinations of purple, dark red, and yellow. About 28 spp., most native to North America.

× *grandiflora* (p. 242)
Blanket flower.
Perennial. Zone 3.
H: 2–3 ft. S: 3 ft.

Rewarding and easy to grow, blooming all year in mild areas and throughout the summer and fall months in colder regions. The daisylike blossoms are 3–4 in. wide; red to yellow with orange, red, or maroon banding; and good for cutting. The basal foliage is rough-textured and gray-green. Forms a mounding clump in beds or borders. 'Goblin' is a popular dwarf cultivar.

How to grow: Full sun. Tolerates poor soil and hot, dry weather. Plant 'Goblin' 12 in. apart, larger types 2–3 ft. apart. Deadheading improves appearance and prolongs bloom. Easy from seed and may bloom the first year. Volunteers readily and sometimes naturalizes in wild areas.

pulchella (p. 296)
Indian blanket, blanket flower.
Annual. All zones.
H: 1–2 ft. S: 1–2 ft.

Fast and easy, providing color from summer to fall, even in hot, dry conditions. The daisylike blossoms are brownish or purplish red and yellow. Looks nice with grasses in "meadow" plantings.

How to grow: Like *G.* × *grandiflora.*

Gaillardia pulchella

Galanthus

Ga-lan´thus. Snowdrop.
Amaryllidaceae. Amaryllis family.

Bulb-forming perennials with 2 or 3 strap-like basal leaves and small flowers. Only 12 spp., native from Europe to central Asia.

nivalis (p. 242)

Snowdrop.
Bulbous perennial. Zone 4.
H: 6–9 in. S: 4–6 in.

A small plant with nodding, white, 1-in.-long flowers and slender straplike leaves. It appears, cheerfully, at the bleakest time of year and doesn't mind being snowed under, emerging afterward just as good as new. Plant masses of them under and around shrubs or trees; the more the better. Each bulb eventually multiplies to form a clump. Also spreads by seed. 'Flore-Pleno' is slightly taller, with double flowers. *G. elwesii*, or giant snowdrop, is 9–12 in. tall, with 2-in. flowers a bit later in spring.

How to grow: Full sun or summer shade from deciduous trees. Prefers well-drained soil; tolerates summer dryness. Plant 3 in. deep and 3 in. apart in fall. To divide, lift bulbs immediately after flowering, while the leaves are still healthy and green.

Galium

Gay´lee-um. Bedstraw.
Rubiaceae. Madder family.

Perennials with spreading rhizomes and floppy, often prickly-textured stems. Slender straight leaves are whorled around the stems. The small 4-petaled flowers, usually white or yellow, are sometimes numerous and showy. About 400 spp., native worldwide. Some European species are naturalized and weedy in the United States.

Galium odoratum

odoratum (p. 283)

(*Asperula odorata*)
Sweet woodruff.
Perennial herb. Zone 4.
H: 4–9 in. S: indefinite.

A perfect plant for problem areas in shade, even deep shade. Once it gets going it will form a solid thick mat of pretty whorled leaves, dotted in spring with starry white flowers. Foliage is deep green all summer, dies and dries to a warm tan in winter. When dry, it smells like vanilla. Runners creep underground and spread relentlessly, competing well with tree roots. Can be interplanted with lilies but will overwhelm daintier perennials.

How to grow: Part sun or shade; tolerates sun in the North. Ordinary soil and watering. Tolerates summer dryness but may go dormant. Space 1 ft. apart. Pull up runners that go out of bounds. Lift and divide clumps anytime.

Gardenia

Gar-deen´ee-a.
Rubiaceae. Madder family.

Evergreen shrubs or trees with glossy smooth leaves and large, waxy-textured, extremely fragrant white or creamy yellow flowers. About 200 spp., native to the Old World tropics and subtropics.

Gardenia jasminoides

jasminoides (p. 173)

(*G. augusta*)
Gardenia.
Evergreen shrub. Zone 8.
H: 5–8 ft. or more. S: 3–5 ft. or more.

Unequaled for fragrance, gardenias have lovely flowers with thick tender petals, white aging to creamy yellow. Blossoms may be single or double, up to 4 in. wide, depending on cultivar. The oval leaves are glossy dark green. 'August Beauty', 'Mystery', and 'Veitchii' are upright shrubs, useful for hedges, borders, specimens, or foundation plantings. 'Radicans' (or 'Prostrata') is a miniature form with small leaves and flowers. It trails gracefully from planter boxes.

How to grow: Full or part sun. Gardenias are fussy and need fertile, acidic soil amended with plenty of organic matter, and special acid fertilizer containing iron and other micronutrients. If conditions aren't right, the leaves turn sickly yellow. Use mulch to protect the roots, and water regularly. Watch for aphids, spider mites, whiteflies, and scale; horticultural oil spray will control them all without damaging the foliage.

Gaura

Gaw´ra.
Onagraceae. Evening primrose family.

Perennials or annuals with plain leaves and small white or pink flowers during hot weather. About 20 spp., native to North America.

lindheimeri (p. 242)

Perennial. Zone 6.
H: 3–5 ft. S: 2–4 ft.

A Texas native, tough and tolerant, that makes a delicate airy mass of bloom in any perennial border. Forms a spreading, sprawling clump with a carrotlike taproot. New flowers open continually at the tips of the long slender stems from midspring to hard frost. Individual blossoms are starlike, about 1 in. wide, opening white and aging to pink.

How to grow: Sun or shade. Not fussy about

soil. Needs occasional watering or goes dormant during prolonged droughts. Prune old shoots to the ground in spring. Self-sows but isn't weedy.

Gazania

Ga-zay´nee-a.
Compositae. Daisy family.

Most are perennial herbs with a basal rosette of variably lobed leaves and composite flowers borne singly on long stalks. About 16 spp., most native to South Africa.

Gazania rigens var. leucolaena

rigens var. leucolaena (p. 242)
Trailing gazania, treasure flower.
Tender perennial. Zone 9.
H: to 1 ft. S: 2 ft.

A trailing plant with brilliant yellow-orange daisies, 1½ in. wide, and felty-white leaves. Makes a quick filler among new shrubs or a ground cover on banks. Good in containers or hanging baskets, too. There are many hybrid gazanias, some with dark-eyed blossoms and green rather than gray foliage. All are handsome, tough, and easy. Blossoms open wide in sun, then close at night or on cloudy days.

How to grow: Full sun. Tolerates heat and needs little water. Ordinary or unimproved soil okay. May die out in patches and need to be replaced; new cultivars show some resistance to dieback. Space 12–18 in. apart. Divide in spring or fall.

Geijera

Guy-jay´ra.
Rutaceae. Citrus family.

Evergreen shrubs or trees with simple glossy leaves and small yellowish flowers. About 7 spp., native to Australia and the South Pacific.

parviflora (p. 159)
Australian willow.
Evergreen tree. Zone 9.
H: 25–30 ft. S: 15–30 ft.

An extremely well behaved tree with habit and foliage like an evergreen weeping willow. It has a short thick trunk, a broad mounded head, and drooping leathery leaves ½ in. wide and 8 in. long. Clusters of tiny starry flowers appear briefly in early spring and have a curious aroma. Casts light shade; makes a good patio or street tree.

How to grow: Full or part sun. Ordinary soil. Tolerates dry soil when established. Needs only routine pruning. Trouble-free.

Gelsemium

Jel-see´mee-um.
Loganiaceae. Buddleia family.

Woody evergreen vines with fragrant yellow funnel-shaped flowers, most abundant in late winter. All parts of the plant are poisonous. Only 2 or 3 spp., one or two from eastern North America, the other from eastern Asia.

Gelsemium sempervirens

sempervirens (p. 203)
Carolina jasmine, yellow jasmine.
Evergreen vine. Zone 8.
H: to 20 ft.

A versatile vine, it climbs well on fences, trellises, lampposts, and mailboxes or can serve as a ground cover. Clusters of fragrant yellow blossoms, about 1 in. long, open first in very early spring, sometimes continuing off and on for several weeks. The slender leaves are dark green in summer, often purplish in winter. 'Pride of Augusta' has double flowers.

How to grow: Full or part sun. Ordinary soil and watering. Tolerates hot sun. Prune after flowering to encourage branching and to keep it tidy.

Geranium

Ger-ray´nee-um.
Geraniaceae. Geranium family.

Annuals, perennials, or a few shrubs with palmately divided or lobed leaves, 5-petaled white or pink flowers, and fruits with long beaks, like a crane's bill. About 300 spp., from around the world. Many hybrids and cultivars are becoming available as these easy, showy plants gain popularity in U.S. gardens.

× cantabrigiense 'Biokovo' (p. 242)
(*G. dalmaticum* × *G. macrorrhizum*)
Perennial. Zone 5 or 4.
H: 1 ft. S: 1–2 ft.

Both flowers and foliage are decorative, and it all but takes care of itself. The bright green leaves, 1–3 in. wide, are lobed and divided and release a pleasant fragrance when rubbed. The 1-in. white flowers, flushed pink in the center, are held just above the foliage in late spring. Looks nice with mat-forming dianthus, along the front of a well-drained border or trailing over a wall. Spreads to make a ground cover.

How to grow: Full sun, part sun, or shade. Avoid afternoon sun in hot climates. Needs well-drained, fertile soil. Space 18 in. apart for ground cover. Cut back trailing stems before winter. Divide every few years.

endressii 'Wargrave Pink' (p. 243)
Perennial. Zone 4.
H: 1–1½ ft. S: 1½–2½ ft.

Worth growing for its handsome foliage and long season of bloom, with 1–1½-in.-wide bluish pink flowers all summer in cool climates, spring and fall where summers are hot. The jagged leaves, 2–4 in. wide, are divided into 5 segments. Not invasive underground but greedy for space above ground—unchecked, it will flop over and smother its neighbors. Cut back severely after the first flush of bloom to keep it within bounds. Some gardeners let it clamber on shrubs or prop it up with peasticks. Easier yet, plant it on top of a retaining wall and let it cascade down.

How to grow: Like *G.* × *cantabrigiense.* Space at least 2 ft. apart.

'Johnson's Blue' (p. 242)

(*G. himalayense* × *G. pratense*)
Perennial. Zone 4.
H: 1¹/₂–2 ft. S: 2–3 ft.

Makes a pretty hemisphere of foliage in early spring, with long-stalked leaves 2–8 in. wide, divided into 7 narrow lobed segments. The flat 2-in.-wide flowers, violet-blue, last 2 weeks or more in late spring. After it blooms, the leafy stems start to flop and sprawl. Cut the foliage almost to the ground when flowering is finished, and a neat dome of new leaves will appear. Or combine it with grasses and wildflowers in a "wild" garden, where floppiness wouldn't matter. For even richer blue flowers, look for *G.* × *magnificum.* It has deep violet-blue flowers with dark veins and lovely leaves with overlapping segments.

How to grow: Like *G.* × *cantabrigiense.* Space 1¹/₂–2 ft. apart.

macrorrhizum (p. 243)

Bigroot geranium.
Perennial. Zone 3.
H: 12–15 in. S: 15 in. or more.

A fine ground cover for dry shady spots. Forms mounded clumps with an underground network of thick rhizomes and deep roots. The deeply lobed leaves have a sticky, fuzzy surface and release a pungent, musky aroma that lingers on your hands for hours. Magenta, pink, or white flowers, 1 in. wide, are held above the foliage for weeks in late spring. 'Album' has white flowers; 'Ingwersen's Variety' has pale pink flowers and smoother leaves than the species.

How to grow: Full sun, part sun, or shade. Ordinary soil and watering. The thick rhizomes allow it to endure summer dry spells without wilting. Easy to grow. Space at least 1 ft. apart.

sanguineum var. *striatum* (p. 243)

(often sold under the name 'Lancastriense')
Perennial. Zone 4.
H: 6–12 in. S: 12 in. or more.

Can be prostrate or mound-forming, with deeply divided, lacy-looking leaves. Spreads fast, and looks neat and attractive all summer long. Covers itself in late spring and early summer with flat 1–1¹/₂-in. flowers, pale pink with red veins. Occasional blossoms continue off and on all summer. The flowers look good with any other color in the garden. The species *G. san-*

guineum, called bloody cranesbill, is a tough plant with magenta flowers. The cultivar 'Album' is vigorous and aggressive but worth the extra trouble for its large pure white flowers. 'Shepherd's Warning' is quite small (under 6 in.), with deep rosy pink flowers.

How to grow: Full or part sun. Ordinary soil and watering. Tolerates hot, dry summers. Lift and divide every few years.

Gerbera

Jer´ber-ra, ger´ber-ra.
Compositae. Daisy family.

Perennials with a basal rosette of oblong lobed leaves and large daisylike blossoms on solitary stalks. About 35 spp., most native to Africa or Asia.

jamesonii (p. 243)

Gerbera daisy, Transvaal daisy.
Perennial. Zone 9.
H: to 18 in. S: to 18 in.

The most aristocratic and shapely daisy, and an excellent cut flower with nice long stalks. The yellow-eyed daisies, to 5–6 in. wide, have cream, yellow, orange, pink, or red rays. It blooms most in summer and fall, off and on in winter and spring. Individual blossoms last a week or more. Makes a basal rosette of narrow lobed leaves, to 10 in. long, smooth green above and woolly gray below. Hardy outdoors only in mild climates but grows well in containers and makes a fine houseplant if you can give it bright light and cool (60° F) nights.

How to grow: Full sun or afternoon shade. Needs well-drained, fertile, organic soil with regular watering and frequent fertilizing. When planting, be careful not to bury the crown, and don't let soil wash in and cover the crown later. Divide old plants in early spring, leaving 2 or 3 eyes on each division. Seeds are expensive, but seedlings bloom the first year. Snails and slugs eat the leaves outdoors; aphids, whiteflies, and spider mites attack them indoors.

Ginkgo

Gink´o. Maidenhair tree.
Ginkgoaceae. Ginkgo family.

A deciduous tree with delicate fan-shaped leaves borne in clusters on stubby branchlets. Introduced from China in the 1700s and widely cultivated, but now rare or extinct in the wild. Judging from the fossil record, ginkgo trees existed 200 million years ago, looking just as they do today. Only 1 sp.

biloba (p. 116)

Ginkgo, maidenhair tree.
Deciduous tree. Zone 4.
H: 50–80 ft. S: 30–40 ft.

An excellent tree for difficult conditions—infertile or alkaline soil, air pollution, or hot city streets. Forms an upright pyramid when young, spreading irregularly with age. The fan-shaped

Ginkgo biloba

leaves, divided into 2 lobes at the broad end, move in the slightest breeze. Bright green all summer, they turn clear yellow in fall (fertile soil can inhibit fall color), dropping all at once when the temperature dips below about 25° F. Female trees produce edible but very smelly and messy fruits; males don't. 'Autumn Gold' is a male with good fall color and a uniform, broadly conical outline. 'Princeton Sentry' or 'Sentry' is a male with a slender tapered crown.

How to grow: Full or part sun. Not fussy about soil. Needs no special care. Trouble-free. A good candidate for underplanting with perennials—it doesn't cast too much shade, and the roots aren't too greedy.

Gladiolus

Glad-ee-o′lus.
Iridaceae. Iris family.

Tender perennials with underground corms, sword-shaped leaves, and large showy flowers in a wide range of colors. About 180 spp., many from South Africa, and thousands of named cultivars.

callianthus (p. 296)

(*Acidanthera bicolor*)
Peacock orchid.
Tender perennial often grown as an annual.
Zone 7.
H: 2–3 ft. S: 1 ft.

Grown for its delicate, sweetly scented flowers. Flowers are 2–3 in. wide, with white petals and dark marks in the throat, and are borne in groups of 2–10 on slender arching stems that reach above the spiky basal leaves. Plant a few in a bed or border—they don't take much room, and the flowers are very good for cutting.

How to grow: Full or part sun. Ordinary soil and watering. Plant corms 6 in. apart and 3–4 in. deep. In Zone 7 and warmer, dig every few years in spring to divide and replant the new cormels. In Zone 6 and colder, dig corms after fall frost and store for the winter in dry peat or vermiculite.

cultivars (p. 296)

Hybrid gladioli.
Tender perennials usually grown as annuals.
Zone 9.
H: 3–6 ft. S: 1 ft.

Grown for their tall spikes of showy colorful flowers, 2–5 in. wide, with flaring petals, sometimes ruffled or frilled. Available in all colors but blue, in both pastel and very deep shades. Leaves are sword-shaped, about 12 in. long. Plants form underground corms that can carry them through 8 months of dormancy. Gladioli can be included in beds or borders of annual and perennial flowers, but for the best flowers, give them plenty of space and well-prepared, fertile soil in a separate cutting garden. Cut spikes when the first flower opens.

How to grow: Full sun. Buy top-sized corms, at least 2–3 in. wide, and plant them 6–8 in.

deep and 1–2 ft. apart in rich, well-drained, deeply dug soil. Water regularly and apply a layer of mulch. Dig up the corms 4–6 weeks after blooming; it isn't necessary to wait for the leaves to die. Remove the foliage, discard the old corms, and spread the new corms and cormels to dry. Store in a cool, dry place over winter. Watch for and destroy plants with diseased spots on the foliage or corms.

Gleditsia

Gle-dit′see-a. Honey locust.
Leguminosae. Legume family.

Deciduous trees with pinnately compound leaves, stout branched thorns, small greenish flowers, and large flattened woody pods. About 14 spp., native to the Old and New World.

triacanthos var. inermis (p. 116)

Thornless honey locust.
Deciduous tree. Zone 4.
H: 40–60 ft. S: 50 ft.

A large tree with a spreading crown. The bipinnately compound leaves cast a lacy filtered shade that allows underplanting with turfgrass, ground covers, perennials, or shrubs. Grows fast and is quite tough and tolerant. Foliage is green in summer, yellow in fall. Most cultivars bear some, but not many, long curved pods. 'Imperial', 'Moraine', 'Shademaster', and 'Skyline' are recommended for their vigor and shape.

How to grow: Full or part sun. Native to rich bottomlands in the eastern United States but isn't fussy in cultivation. Tolerates alkaline soil, road-salt runoff, and summer droughts. Subject to several pests and diseases, particularly a canker disease that can be fatal. Prune in winter to remove dead or damaged limbs.

Gloriosa

Glo-ree-oh′sa.
Liliaceae. Lily family.

Tuberous-rooted climbing vines with showy flowers. Various forms are now grouped into 1 spp., native to tropical Asia and Africa.

superba (p. 297)

Gloriosa lily.
Tender perennial grown as an annual.
All zones.
H: 6 ft. S: 2 ft.

Aptly named, this is a glorious, superb plant. Greenish yellow buds open into brilliant crimson flowers with dramatic, flared-back tepals, aging to a rich dark red. Hummingbirds fight over these flowers, visiting many times a day. Each tuber produces one or more brittle, branching stalks with shiny leaves tapering into tendrils that reach for support, curling around any nearby wire, string, or twig. Scarlet sage (*Salvia coccinea*) makes a good filler around the base of the stalks.

How to grow: Full or part sun. Ordinary soil and watering. Plant tubers 3 in. deep after danger of frost is past. Provide support—a trellis, strings, or brushy sticks. Vines will turn yellow about 2 months after flowering, or when frost strikes. Carefully dig the tubers, remove soil and old stalks and roots, and pack them in dry peat moss or crumpled paper. Store in a cool room for the winter.

Gomphrena

Gom-free′na.
Amaranthaceae. Amaranth family.

Annuals or perennials with simple leaves and small flowers clustered in dense chaffy heads. About 100 spp., native to southeastern Asia, Australia, and Central America.

globosa (p. 297)

Globe amaranth.
Annual. All zones.
H: 18–24 in. S: 12 in.

Provides bright color all summer in the garden, thriving in hot dry weather, and very popular for dried arrangements. The marble-sized flower heads look like clover blossoms but have a stiff papery texture. Comes in many shades of purple, pink, red, orange, or white. Some seed strains are mixed; others are available in separate colors. 'Buddy' is compact (6–8 in. high), with brilliant magenta-purple blossoms.

How to grow: Full sun. Ordinary soil and watering. Tolerates heat but is very tender to cold. Sow seeds indoors 6 weeks before last frost; space transplants 8 in. apart. Cut flowers for drying before they fade.

Gordonia

Gor-doan′ee-a.
Theaceae. Tea family.

Evergreen shrubs or trees with simple leathery leaves and large camellia-like flowers. About 70 spp., native to southeastern Asia and the southeastern United States.

lasianthus (p. 159)

Loblolly bay.
Evergreen tree or shrub. Zone 7.
H: to 40 ft. S: 10–15 ft.

A lovely tree, tall and slender with smooth, glossy, dark green leaves. Fragrant flowers, 3 in. wide, with 5 snow-white petals and numerous golden stamens, unfold continually from June to frost. Because it is slender, try planting it in groups of 3–5. Native to wetlands along the Atlantic coastal plain.

How to grow: Full sun. Prefers moist, fertile soil. Look for container-grown plants at native-plant nurseries. Slow to establish, and subject to root rot when young. Carefree once it settles in.

Gymnocladus

Jim-nock′lay-dus.
Leguminosae. Pea family.

Deciduous trees with large leaves on stout twigs. Male and female flowers are produced on separate trees. The large hard seeds were once used as a coffee substitute. Only 5 spp., native to North America and Asia.

dioica (p. 116)

Kentucky coffee tree.
Deciduous tree. Zone 4.
H: 60–70 ft. S: 40–50 ft.

A rugged native tree, excellent for difficult sites. The bipinnately compound leaves, 2 ft. wide by 3 ft. long, have small blue-green leaflets. As with many trees having compound leaves, the branching pattern is relatively open and makes a bold silhouette that doesn't obstruct welcome rays of sun in winter. Even on young trees, the dark gray bark forms interesting scaly ridges that curl outward. The big clusters of greenish white flowers are fragrant in late May or June. Females develop stout pods, fuzzy and green in summer, woody and brown all winter, and briefly messy when they drop in spring. Some gardeners might prefer males, because they don't make pods, but these trees are rarely identified as male or female at the time of sale.

How to grow: Full sun. Ordinary soil and watering. Tolerates alkaline soil, city conditions, and drought. Needs no special care.

Gypsophila

Jip-sof′fil-la. Baby's-breath.
Caryophyllaceae. Pink family.

Annuals or perennials with opposite small leaves that disappear under a cloud of bloom. Flowers are small but very numerous, borne in profusely branched panicles. About 125 spp., native to the Old World.

paniculata (p. 244)

Baby's-breath.
Perennial. Zone 3.
H: 3 ft. S: 3 ft.

No other plant furnishes such clouds of tiny blossoms. Lovely planted near roses, hardy geraniums, and lavender. Wonderful, too, for fresh and dried bouquets. The rounded, sometimes sprawling clumps are a tangle of branching stems with narrow gray-green leaves and hundreds of single or double white or pink flowers. 'Bristol Fairy' has double white flowers; 'Compacta Plena' and 'Pink Fairy' are smaller (1½–2 ft.), more dependable plants with smaller double white or pale pink flowers.

How to grow: Full sun. Needs well-drained, light, limy soil. Plant in spring. The double cultivars are often grafted; if so, plant with the graft below the soil surface. Space 2–3 ft. apart. Shearing back after the first flush of bloom often produces second flowers. Large plants may need staking. Needs winter mulch in cold regions.

Hakonechloa

Hack-oh-nee-clo´a.
Gramineae. Grass family.

Only 1 sp. of perennial grass, native to Japan.

macra 'Aureola' (p. 210)

Clumping grass. Zone 5.
H: 1–1¹/₂ ft. S: 3 ft.

Layers of ribbonlike leaves form a soft graceful mound of green tinted with gold, buff, and bronze—an effect that livens up a dull shady corner and contrasts well with hostas or ferns. Greenish yellow flowers appear in August and last into winter but are inconspicuous against the foliage.

How to grow: Part sun. Needs well-drained soil with good moisture retention. Work in plenty of organic matter before planting. Spreads slowly by rhizomes but isn't a problem. Cut back hard once a year.

Halesia

Ha-lee´zee-a. Silver-bell.
Styracaceae. Storax family.

Deciduous trees with white flowers in spring and dry fruits with 2 or 4 wings. Only 5 spp., native to eastern China and the eastern United States.

carolina (p. 116)

(*H. tetraptera*)
Carolina silver-bell.
Deciduous tree or large shrub. Zone 4.
H: 30–50 ft. S: 30 ft.

Small clusters of snowy white bell-shaped flowers dangle from the branches in early spring. The simple leaves turn yellow-green and drop early, but woody pods add interest in winter. Young trees have striped bark; with age, the bark flakes into a pattern of grays and browns. Pretty along the edge of a woodland or natural area. Other species, sometimes offered, are similar.

How to grow: Full or part sun. Needs acidic, well-drained, organic soil, as for rhododendrons and azaleas. Prune out extra shoots to make a multitrunked tree, if desired, or let it grow full and bushy. Trouble-free.

Hamamelis

Ha-ma-mell´is. Witch hazel.
Hamamelidaceae. Witch hazel family.

Deciduous shrubs or small trees with sweet-scented flowers in fall, winter, or early spring. The rounded leaves have coarse teeth and turn red or gold in fall. Only 5 or 6 spp., native to eastern Asia and eastern North America.

× *intermedia* (p. 138)

Hybrid witch hazel.
Deciduous tree or shrub. Zone 6 or 5.
H: 15–20 ft. or more. S: 15 ft.

Witch hazels brighten the dreariest of winter days. They are handsome vase-shaped small trees, ideal for small or shaded yards. Flowers with 4 straplike petals line the limbs for 3–4 weeks in late winter. Cultivars differ in flower color, time of bloom, and fragrance. Choose two or more to extend the season. Position light-colored forms against dark backgrounds; use backlighting to highlight darker flowers.

'Arnold Promise' has fragrant clear yellow flowers and is one of the last to bloom. 'Diane' has coppery red to maroon flowers and scarlet and maroon fall color. 'Jelena' has large coppery orange flowers and marbled red, orange, and yellow fall color; it sometimes reblooms in late summer. 'Primavera' has abundant primrose yellow flowers and marbled fall color. 'Sunburst' has clear yellow flowers and blooms early. 'Winter Beauty' has small but abundant tangerine flowers, which are very fragrant, and blooms early.

How to grow: Part sun or shade. Prefers fertile soil amended with organic matter and regular watering. The cultivars are sold as grafted plants, and rootstock suckers will appear; remove them in summer. Needs only routine pruning. Trouble-free.

mollis (p. 138)

Chinese witch hazel.
Deciduous shrub or tree. Zone 6 or 5.
H: 15–20 ft. or more. S: 15 ft.

The intensely fragrant yellow-and-red flowers are an absolute delight to unsuspecting winter eyes and noses. The flower-lined branches make a gauzy yellow haze when backlit with the soft winter sun and look wonderful against a rich green background of conifers and broad-leaved evergreens. Blooms for up to 4 weeks in late winter. The rounded, slightly fuzzy leaves are dull green in summer, clear yellow in fall. 'Pallida' has soft yellow flowers, more abundant than those of the species.

How to grow: Like *H.* × *intermedia*.

vernalis (see below for photo)

Vernal (spring) witch hazel, Ozark witch hazel.
Deciduous shrub or small tree. Zone 4.
H: 10 ft. or more. S: 10 ft.

A reliable performer even where winters are cold. The red to yellow blooms are small (under 1 in.) and spidery, but they release an indescribable aroma. The petals start to unfurl during mild spells in February, curling back if the temperature drops. This witch hazel's small stature and vase-shaped habit fit well into gardens. Consider grouping 3 or more as a petticoat for a big spruce or fir, with winter and spring bulbs sprinkled underneath. *H. virginiana* (p. 138), or common witch hazel, is a larger plant with fragrant yellow flowers in fall and winter. Its bark is distilled to make the medicinal and astringent witch-hazel extract. Both species have gold foliage in fall.

How to grow: Like *H.* × *intermedia*. Both *H. vernalis* and *H. virginiana* spread by suckers, especially in moist soil. If you don't have room for a thicket, remove them.

Halesia carolina

Hamamelis virginiana

Hamelia
Ha-mee'lee-a.
Rubiaceae. Madder family.
>Deciduous shrubs with showy red or yellow flowers. About 16 spp., native to Central America.

patens (p. 244)
Firebush, hummingbird bush.
Woody-based perennial. Zone 8.
H: 4–5 ft. S: 4–5 ft.
>Thrives in hot weather, blooming nonstop from early summer to frost. The red to red-orange flowers are tubular, about 2 in. long, dropping quickly but constantly replaced by new buds. The simple opposite leaves are dark green with a red midrib. Plant it near the patio (does well in containers, if ground space is limited) where you can watch the hummingbirds come and go.

>**How to grow:** Full sun. Needs well-drained soil, but give it water when it wilts. Shear to control shape and height and to promote perpetual bloom. Cut back to the ground after fall frost. No pests or problems.

Hedera
Hed'er-a. Ivy.
Araliaceae. Aralia family.
>Woody evergreens with different juvenile and adult appearance. Juvenile shoots are clinging vines with lobed leaves. Adult growth is upright and bushy with elliptical leaves and bears umbels of greenish flowers followed by dark blue-black berries. Only 4 or 5 spp., most native to the Mediterranean region, but hundreds of distinct forms have been propagated and named.

Hedera helix

canariensis (p. 202)
(now *H. algeriensis*)
Algerian ivy.
Evergreen woody vine. Zone 9.
H: 50 ft. or more.
>There is no faster or tougher ground cover for shade or sun in mild-winter climates. Also climbs and covers fences (especially chain-link), posts, porch columns, dead tree stumps, or eyesores. The broadly triangular, lobed leaves are thick and leathery, deep green or variegated, up to 8 in. wide. Mature shoots reach stiffly upright and have simple leaves, flowers, and berries. 'Variegata' or 'Gloire de Marengo' has strong white or ivory mottling on gray-green leaves. *H. colchica*, or Persian ivy, has similar large leaves but is hardy on protected sites in Zone 7 and perhaps Zone 6.

>**How to grow:** Full sun, part sun, or shade. Very tough but needs protection from full sun in desert areas. Ordinary soil and watering. Space 1–1¹/₂ ft. apart for ground cover, 3 ft. apart for fence cover. Water and feed regularly until established. Trim 2–3 times a year to keep it from invading lawn or flower beds. If stems build up into a mat, cut back hard in early spring with a sturdy power mower. Chewed by slugs and snails and may harbor rats and mice. Control bacterial leafspot with copper sprays.

helix (p. 202)
English ivy.
Evergreen woody vine. Zone 6 or 5.
H: to 50 ft.
>Versatile and widely grown throughout the United States. There are hundreds of cultivars, varying in leaf shape and size, coloring and variegation, vigor, and hardiness. Some make robust, weed-choking ground covers; others trace a delicate pattern on walls or tree trunks; some are compact, almost bushy. Most cultivars are juvenile forms with lobed leaves and rooting stems. 'Baltica' and 'Thorndale' are vigorous ground covers with medium-size leaves that stay dark green through winter. 'Needlepoint' grows more slowly and has close-set small leaves with pointed lobes. 'Glacier' has pale foliage splotched with white and gray, usually turning pinkish in winter. 'Goldheart' has dark green leaves with big yellow spots in the center.

>**How to grow:** Sun or shade. Ordinary soil and watering. Space 8–12 in. apart for ground cover. Set plants deeply, removing a few lower leaves and covering that part of the stem, to encourage deep rooting. Water regularly the first year after planting. Be patient if the top dies in winter; the plant may come back from the roots. Once established, prune or mow as needed to control spread. Despite rumors, ivy doesn't kill trees, no matter how high it climbs.

Hedychium
Hed-dick'ee-um. Ginger lily.
Zingiberaceae. Ginger family.
>Robust perennials with thick spreading rhizomes and tall leafy stalks topped with showy clusters of fragrant flowers. About 50 spp., native to eastern Asia.

coronarium (p. 244)
Butterfly ginger.
Perennial. Zone 8 or 7.
H: 5–6 ft. S: forms patch.
>One of the easiest gingers to grow, with very fragrant, butterfly-shaped white flowers, 2–3 in. wide, in loose clusters at the tops of the stalks. Needs a warm summer to bloom well. Stalks have alternate leaves, 12 in. or longer by 2–4 in. wide. The leaves are arranged so that a clump of foliage looks like a bouquet of giant feathers. Spreads slowly by thick rhizomes. Will freeze to the ground but recovers.

>**How to grow:** Full or part sun. Tolerates unamended soil, clay or sand. Prefers constant moisture during the growing season and thrives near ponds or pools. Will survive and bloom in dry soil, but the leaves turn brown along the edges. Divide every few years in early spring and replant the divisions 3 ft. apart. Can be grown in large containers.

gardneranum (p. 244)
Kahili ginger.
Tender perennial. Zone 9.
H: 6 ft. or more. S: forms patch.

Grows taller than butterfly ginger and has long spikes of fragrant yellow flowers with projecting red stamens. The erect stalks have smooth green leaves, up to 18 in. long by 6 in. wide. Makes an exotic and long-lasting cut flower.

How to grow: Like *H. coronarium.*

Helenium

Hell-lee´nee-um. Sneezeweed.
Compositae. Daisy family.

Annuals or perennials with rather coarse leaves and abundant clusters of composite flowers, usually in shades of yellow, maroon, reddish brown, or purple. About 40 spp., native to North America.

Helenium autumnale

autumnale (see below for photo)
Sneezeweed, Helen's-flower.
Perennial. Zone 3.
H: 4–5 ft. S: 1¹/₂–3 ft.

Highly adaptable to various climates and conditions and easy to grow. Large (2–3 in.) composite blossoms with yellow rays and raised dark or yellow disks bloom for up to 10 weeks from midsummer to fall. Spreads to make a patch and sends up lots of shoots. The midribs of the lance-shaped leaves continue down the stems, forming vertical wings or ridges. Blends well with grasses, daylilies, goldenrods, rudbeckias, and perennial sunflowers. 'Moerheim Beauty' (p. 244) has brick red rays and dark disks; other hybrid cultivars come in a variety of reddish, orange, and bronze shades. All make good cut flowers and don't cause sneezing, despite the common name.

How to grow: Full sun. Prefers fertile, organic soil and regular watering. Prune stems back by one-third in early summer to force branching and to reduce height; even so, tall forms may be floppy and need staking. If it spreads too far, pull out extra shoots or divide and replant in spring or fall.

Helianthemum

He-lee-an´thee-mum. Rock rose.
Cistaceae. Rock rose family.

Low, spreading shrubs or perennials with hairy foliage and small 5-petaled roselike flowers in bright colors. More than 100 spp., native to the Old and New World.

nummularium (p. 245)
Rock rose.
Shrubby perennial. Zone 5.
H: 1¹/₂–2 ft. S: 2–3 ft.

Makes loose mounds of sprawling stems, ideal for tumbling over the edge of a wall or cascading down dry sun-baked slopes. Blooms for weeks in summer, repeating in fall. Flowers are like single 5-petaled roses, 1 in. wide, displayed above the gray-green foliage, and are usually bright shades of red, copper, peach, apricot, pink, yellow, or white. The small, narrow, evergreen leaves are often slightly hairy, green or gray-green. Many forms are offered.

How to grow: Full sun. Needs very good drainage. Tolerates dry soil and heat. Usually planted singly in rock gardens. Space 2 ft. apart for ground cover on banks. Shear after summer bloom and again to tidy up in spring. Apply protective mulch where winters are cold. Often short lived.

Helianthus

He-lee-an´thus. Sunflower.
Compositae. Daisy family.

Robust annuals or perennials with stiff, almost woody stems; hairy foliage; and cheerful composite blooms, usually with yellow rays and yellow to dark brown or purple disks. Almost 70 spp., native to North America.

angustifolius (p. 245)
Narrow-leaved sunflower.
Perennial. Zone 6.
H: 5–10 ft. S: 3 ft.

Excellent plants for large borders or for naturalizing in damp meadows. The long slender leaves are attractive all summer. Hundreds of golden yellow blossoms, 2–3 in. wide, open in late summer and fall. Wonderful in the South but sometimes hit by frost in northern gardens. Birds flock to eat the seeds. *H. salicifolius,* the willow-leaved sunflower, has slenderer leaves. Both go well with tall grasses, New England asters, and Joe-Pye weed.

How to grow: Full sun. Prefers fertile soil and regular watering. Prune back by one-third in early summer to promote branching and to reduce height. May need staking anyway. Pest-free.

annuus (p. 296)
Common sunflower.
Annual. All zones.
H: 4–10 ft. S: 2–3 ft.

Strong, fast, vigorous plants with woody stalks, rough leaves, and big cheerful blooms.

Giant forms with 1-ft.-wide blooms on 10-ft. stalks are fun to grow and win prizes at the county fair, but new cultivars with smaller, multicolored gold, orange, red, rust, and cream blossoms are more useful for borders and cutting. Children love them all, and so do the birds.

How to grow: Full sun. Ordinary or improved soil and regular watering. Sow groups of 3 or 4 seeds in hills 3 ft. apart, then thin to a single seedling per hill. Hoeing soil around the roots helps hold the plant upright. Unless you want just one tall stalk, pinch out the growing tips to force branching. This makes bushy plants with many smaller flowers. Can be used as a temporary hedge.

Heliopsis helianthoides

Helichrysum

Hell-i-kry′zum. Everlasting.
Compositae. Daisy family.

A big genus of annuals, perennials, and shrubs, most with rounded flower heads composed of many rows of stiff, papery, bright-colored bracts around a yellow disk of tiny tubular flowers. About 500 spp., most native to South Africa and Australia.

bracteatum (p. 297)

Strawflower.
Annual. All zones.
H: to 30 in. S: 12 in.

Grown for the bright-colored papery bracts that form 1–3-in. flower heads. Available in shades of red, rose, pink, orange, yellow, or creamy white, usually mixed in the seed packet. The plants are ugly ducklings with thick stalks of wilty foliage; tuck them in a cutting garden, out of sight.

How to grow: Full sun. Ordinary soil and watering. Start 6 weeks early indoors, or sow in place after danger of frost is past. Space 12 in. apart. Gather flowers every 2–3 days, cutting them in the bud stage, as the bracts continue to unfold after cutting. Cut the stalk short and press a florist's wire up into the base of the flower head before it dries.

Helictotrichon

Hel-ick-toe-try′kon.
Gramineae. Grass family.

Clump-forming perennial grasses with arching leaf blades and rather sparse flowers. About 30 spp., native to Eurasia and North America.

sempervirens (p. 211)

(*Avena sempervirens*)
Blue oat grass.
Clumping perennial grass. Zone 4.
H: 18–30 in. S: 18–24 in.

Makes a tufted mound of slender blue leaves, lovely from spring to fall and sometimes on through winter. Comparable to the blue fescues (*Festuca* spp.) but bigger, with leaves up to 18 in. long by 1/8 in. wide. It doesn't flower much, especially in cool climates, but its foliage

lasts longer than any flowers. Combine it in a foundation planting with a dwarf blue spruce and one of the dwarf blue-colored junipers, or contrast it with perennials of different habits and leaf shapes.

How to grow: Full or part sun. Needs well-drained soil to perform well, especially where winters are wet. Develops the best blue color in dry soil. Cut back once a year. Divide older clumps in spring.

Heliopsis

He-lee-op′sis.
Compositae. Daisy family.

Upright perennials with simple opposite leaves and sunflower-like blossoms, usually with yellow or gold rays and darker disks. About 13 spp., native to Central and North America.

helianthoides (p. 245)

False sunflower.
Perennial. Zone 4.
H: 3–6 ft. S: 2–2 1/2 ft.

A big bushy plant with erect branching stems, coarse-toothed leaves 5 in. long, and lots of 3–4-in. blossoms over a long season from summer into fall. Blooms are single to double, in shades of yellow or gold, too brassy to put with pastel flowers but sunny and bright with black-eyed Susans or asters. Good for cutting. 'Summer Sun' has 4-in. yellow-orange blossoms on 2–3-ft. stalks, comes fairly true from seed, and tolerates heat well.

How to grow: Full sun. Ordinary soil and watering. Tolerates worse conditions but looks ratty. Deadhead regularly to prolong blooming. Usually doesn't need staking. Divide every few years in spring or fall.

Helleborus

Hell-e-bore′us. Hellebore.
Ranunculaceae. Buttercup family.

Low, spreading perennials with thick rhizomes and roots that are quite poisonous. Leaves are mostly basal, palmately lobed. Flowers are showy in winter or spring. About 20 spp., native to Europe and Asia.

foetidus (p. 245)

Stinking hellebore.
Perennial. Zone 3.
H: 18 in. S: 18 in.

One of the first plants to bloom in late winter or early spring, with foliage that is pretty all year long. It has strong stalks topped with leafy clusters of nodding, cup-shaped, pale green flowers, sometimes purple-rimmed, about 1 in. wide. Flowers smell unpleasant, but only if you stick your nose in. Leaves are divided into a fan of 4–9 long, narrow, dark green leaflets. Plant under deep-rooted trees or shrubs, where it will spread slowly into a dense patch. Lovely with daffodils.

How to grow: Part sun or shade. Needs well-drained soil amended with plenty of organic matter and plenty of lime. Ordinary watering okay. Plant 18 in. apart, and leave in place—hellebores resent disturbance and reestablish slowly if moved or divided. It's better to look for volunteer seedlings and transplant them when young. Remove winter-damaged old leaves in spring, when shiny new ones will soon take their place.

Helleborus orientalis

orientalis (p. 245)
Lenten rose.
Perennial. Zone 4.
H: 18–24 in. S: 24 in. or more.

The easiest and most widely adapted of all hellebores, excellent for naturalizing under deciduous trees. Clusters of several nodding cup-shaped flowers, 2–3 in. wide, open in early spring. Flowers come in many shades of pink, plum, white, or chartreuse speckled with maroon; float some flowers in a shallow bowl where you can observe their markings. Forms a glossy mound of long-stalked evergreen leaves, sometimes 1 ft. wide, divided into 5–11 coarse-toothed leaflets. Don't confuse Lenten rose with the so-called Christmas rose, *H. niger*, which has fine-toothed dark evergreen leaves and saucer-shaped clear white flowers up to 4 in. wide. It's more temperamental than other hellebores and blooms in early spring, if at all.

How to grow: Like *H. foetidus*.

Hemerocallis
Hem-mer-o-kal´lis. Daylily.
Liliaceae. Lily family.

Perennials with funnel- or bell-shaped flowers held on a branched stalk above a clump of narrow arching leaves. About 15 spp., most native to China or Japan, and many hybrids. There are thousands of named cultivars.

hybrids (p. 246)
Hybrid daylilies.
Perennials. Zone 4.
H: 1–6 ft. S: 2 ft. or more.

The most popular perennials for sunny spots, easy to grow throughout the United States. Each flower lasts only a day, but new buds open over a period of weeks. Flowers range from 2 in. to 7 in. wide, in shades of cream, yellow, orange, salmon, pink, rose, brick red, purplish red, lavender, or green. Some are bicolors, and many have contrasting midribs or throats.

All (except the doubles) have 3 petals and 3 sepals, which may be similar or different in shape and color. Modern hybrids offer a variety of flower forms, ranging from the traditional lilylike shape to round flat flowers with wide ruffled petals, spiderlike flowers with long slender petals, and double flowers with a puff of extra petals. A few kinds have a slight sweet fragrance. Many of the newer cultivars are tetraploid plants with unusual vigor; their flowers have more substance and are borne abundantly on thick sturdy stalks.

Most cultivars have one major burst of flowering and are classified as early-, mid-, or late-season bloomers. Some rebloom later in the year, and a few bloom almost continuously. By planting several kinds, you can have nonstop bloom from May or June through late September.

Daylily plants are long lived and form dense clumps or spreading patches of long slender leaves. Kinds with evergreen foliage do best in mild-winter regions. The deciduous types are more reliable where winters are cold. Usually the mound of foliage is about 1–2 ft. tall. The flower stalks, called scapes, range from 1 ft. to 6 ft. tall, depending on variety.

Hemerocallis 'Stella d'Oro'

Popular daylily cultivars

'Becky Lynn': Rosy pink flowers, 7 in. wide, on 20-in. scapes. Early to midseason; sometimes reblooms.

'Betty Woods': Chinese yellow flowers, 5$\frac{1}{2}$ in. wide, on 26-in. scapes. Early.

'Condilla': Deep gold double blossoms, nicely rounded, 4$\frac{1}{2}$ in. wide, on 20-in. scapes. Early to midseason.

'Ed Murray': Dark red flowers with a yellow throat and rim, 4$\frac{1}{2}$ in. wide, on 30-in. scapes. Midseason.

'Fairy Tale Pink': Ruffled pink 5$\frac{1}{2}$-in. flowers on 24-in. scapes. Midseason.

'Hyperion': Light yellow flowers, 6 in. wide, on 42-in. scapes; lovely fragrance. One of the oldest and most widely planted cultivars. Midseason.

'Joan Senior': Nearly white 6-in. flowers on 25-in. scapes. Early to midseason; sometimes reblooms.

'Mary Todd': Yellow flowers, 6 in. wide, on 26-in. scapes. One of the first tetraploids, and still a winner. Early.

'Ruffled Apricot': Apricot flowers, 7 in. wide, on 28-in. scapes. Early to midseason.

'Statuesque': Unusually tall, with golden yellow flowers, 3$\frac{1}{2}$ in. wide, on 56-in. scapes. Flowers abundantly. Midseason.

'Stella d'Oro': Gold flowers, 3 in. wide, on 12-in. scapes. Blooms continuously from early summer through fall. 'Happy Returns' is similar, with yellow flowers.

Most nurseries sell potted daylily plants, but for the widest selection and best prices, buy from mail-order specialists. Their catalogs list hundreds of varieties, labeled according to flower color and form, scape height, and season of bloom.

How to grow: Full sun, or light afternoon shade where summers are hot. For best results, prepare the soil well by digging about 12 in. deep and working in plenty of organic matter. Space plants 18–24 in. apart and mulch well. Water regularly from spring to fall. Rarely touched by insects or diseases, daylilies require very little maintenance. Some multiply fast enough to be divided every few years; others can grow undisturbed for decades. Divide crowded plants in spring or fall and replant in freshly prepared soil.

lilio-asphodelus (p. 246)
(*H. flava*)
Lemon lily.
Perennial. Zone 4.
H: 2 ft. S: 2 ft.

An old-fashioned favorite from grandmother's garden. Lemon lilies bloom in May or June, earlier than hybrid daylilies, and have very sweetly scented clear yellow flowers. Leaves are slender, almost grassy.

How to grow: Like hybrid daylilies. Spreads by rhizomes and quickly fills a bed. Divide anytime.

Hesperaloe
Hes-per-al´ow.
Agavaceae. Agave family.

Woody-based perennials that make a clump of slender evergreen leaves and bear tall stalks of many small flowers. Only 3 spp., native to the Southwest and Mexico.

parviflora (p. 247)
Red yucca.
Evergreen perennial. Zone 6.
H: 2 ft. (flowers to 5 ft.). S: 4 ft.

Arching wandlike stems of small, tubular, coral to salmon-pink (never true red) flowers attract hummingbirds from spring to late summer. Makes a clump of tough slender leaves, blue-green in summer, purplish in winter. Old plants gradually spread sideways. Use it singly or grouped, with ornamental grasses or evergreen shrubs.

How to grow: Full or part sun. Needs good drainage. Tolerates poor, dry soil and heat. Remove old flower stalks as they dry.

Hesperis
Hes´per-iss.
Cruciferae. Mustard family.

Erect branching biennials or perennials with 4-parted flowers, usually white to purple, often fragrant. About 30 spp., native to Europe and Asia.

Hesperaloe parviflora

matronalis (p. 247)
Dame's rocket, sweet rocket.
Perennial or biennial. Zone 3.
H: 2–3 ft. S: 2 ft.

Pretty, fragrant, and easy to please. Forms an erect clump of leafy stems topped with big clusters of dime-sized white or lavender flowers that are very fragrant, especially in the evening. Blooms in late spring. Best used in meadow gardens or semiwild areas where it can naturalize.

How to grow: Best in part shade. Ordinary or unamended soil. Gets by on natural rainfall and tolerates dryness. Plant anytime, 2 ft. apart. In gardens, cut back the flower stalks after bloom to prevent self-sowing. May die after flowering, so plant annuals nearby to fill in gaps. Individual plants are short lived, but it is a prolific self-seeder and once introduced will go on forever.

Heteromeles
Het-er-om´e-leez. Toyon.
Rosaceae. Rose family.

An evergreen shrub or small tree with red berries in winter. Only 1 sp., native to southern California.

arbutifolia (p. 173)
Toyon, California holly.
Evergreen shrub or small tree. Zone 8.
H: 30 ft. S: 15 ft.

This is the "holly" of Hollywood. It's a long-lived, drought-tolerant shrub or small tree with leathery dark green leaves, clusters of fragrant small white flowers in June and July, and abundant crops of small bright red berries from November until February. Use it for hedging or as a specimen.

How to grow: Full or part sun. Tolerates poor, dry soil and heat. Plant 6 ft. apart for a hedge. Subject to fire blight; sterilize pruners with diluted bleach as you cut out infected wood.

Heuchera
Hew´ker-a. Alumroot.
Saxifragaceae. Saxifrage family.

Perennials with thick rhizomes, a tuft of rounded or lobed basal leaves, and many tiny cup-shaped flowers on slender stalks. About 55 spp., native to North America.

× *brizoides* (p. 247)
Coralbells, alumroot.
Perennial. Zone 4.
H: 12–18 in. S: 12–18 in.

A good old-fashioned perennial, worth growing for both its foliage and its flowers. Makes a compact mound of thick, leathery, almost evergreen leaves, which may be round or kidney-shaped, toothed or lobed, crimped or ruffled. The wiry leafless stalks hold tiny pink, red, or creamy white flowers well above the foliage, forming an airy cloud of bloom. Use it as an edging plant, among shrubs, or massed as a ground cover.

The following hybrids may be listed under *H.* × *brizoides* or *H. sanguinea*, a red-flowered species native to the Southwest. Their parentage is uncertain, but they're all excellent plants for gardens in most parts of the United States. 'Coral Cloud' has salmon-pink flowers. 'Chatterbox' and 'Tattletale' are pink. 'June Bride' and 'White Cloud' are white. 'Pluie de Feu' ('Rain of Fire') is bright red, and 'Mount St. Helens' is dark red.

How to grow: Full sun where summers aren't too hot; part shade otherwise. Needs well-drained soil and frequent watering. Space about 18 in. apart, positioning the crown level with the soil surface. Divide every few years in early spring. Remove entire stalks of faded flowers to prolong bloom. Mulch in fall to prevent heaving—plants tend to shove up out of the soil and must be reset. New cultivars sometimes develop brown leaves and die a mysterious, untimely death. Older varieties are long lived.

micrantha 'Palace Purple' (p. 247)
Perennial. Zone 4.
H: 12 in. S: 12–15 in.

A recent introduction, welcomed by gardeners who love purple-leaved plants. Forms a semievergreen mound of shiny lobed and toothed leaves, up to 4 in. wide, on tall stalks. Foliage color ranges from deep purplish red to bronze or brownish, varying among plants and generally prettier if shaded from midsummer sun. Some people like and others trim off the wiry stalks of tiny white flowers. Combines well with any silver-gray perennial and also with blues or whites.

How to grow: Best in part to full shade; discolors in hot sun. Needs well-drained, fertile soil and regular watering. Space 12–18 in. apart. Nurseries often sell seedlings, which vary in color. Plant several, and divide the ones you like best.

Hibiscus
Hy-bis´kus. Mallow.
Malvaceae. Mallow family.

A diverse group of annuals, perennials, shrubs, and trees, most with showy bell-shaped flowers. Many are grown as ornamentals; others provide food, tea, medicine, or fibers. About 200 spp., native to the Old and New World.

coccineus (p. 247)
Wild red mallow.
Perennial. Zone 6.
H: to 6 ft. S: 4 ft.

A handsome shrublike perennial to use in large borders or as a specimen. Makes a nice clump that doesn't spread much; fills the same space year after year. It has reddish stems and reddish green leaves palmately divided into 5 slender, toothed segments. Vivid red 5-petaled flowers, 5–6 in. wide, open daily from midsummer through September. Native to the south-

eastern United States. 'Lord Baltimore', a hybrid cultivar, is more readily available than the species.

How to grow: Full sun. Native to damp sites and prefers moist, fertile soil; can take ordinary soil and watering. Cut down old stalks, which are woody enough to use for staking other perennials, in fall or early spring. Be patient; new shoots don't emerge until quite late in spring.

moscheutos (p. 247)
Rose mallow.
Perennial. Zone 6 or 5.
H: to 6 ft. S: 4 ft.

Rose mallow is a native eastern wildflower, abundant in sunny marshes; its various cultivars and hybrids are more common in gardens. They have flowers up to 12 in. wide, in shades of white, pink, rose, or red, often with darker-colored centers. All make big clumps of tough stalks with large papery-textured leaves. Too big and bold for most perennial borders but good for summer color in a hedge of spring-blooming shrubs. Try massing several over a bed of daffodils, tulips, or other spring bulbs; the mallows emerge late, then fill in quickly and cover the yellowing bulb leaves. 'Southern Belle' has red, pink, or white 10-in. flowers on a 3–4-ft. plant.

How to grow: Like *H. coccineus*. Several strains, including 'Southern Belle', are easily raised from seed and bloom the first year if started early indoors. Japanese beetles can ravage both foliage and flowers.

syriacus (p. 139)
Rose-of-Sharon.
Deciduous shrub. Zone 5.
H: to 15 ft. S: 5 ft. or more.

An old-fashioned favorite that blooms from midsummer to fall, after most other shrubs, with single or double flowers 3–4 in. wide in shades of white, pink, red, or lavender-blue. Young plants are narrowly upright, gradually spreading when mature. Makes a good specimen for small gardens and can be trained into tree form. Four new cultivars from the National Arboretum all have large (to 6 in.) single flowers that drop off neatly and don't set seeds. They grow about 8 ft. tall. 'Aphrodite' is deep rose-pink with a red eye; 'Diana' is pure white; 'Helene' is white with a reddish purple eye; and 'Minerva' is lavender-pink with a darker eye.

How to grow: Full sun. Ordinary soil and watering. Tolerates dry soil and heat but is subject to spider mites under those conditions. Prune to shape when dormant. A tough and carefree shrub.

Hordeum
Hor´dee-um. Barley.
Gramineae. Grass family.

Annual or perennial grasses with dense, bristly flower heads. Includes the cereal grain barley. About 20 spp., native to the north temperate zone.

Heuchera sanguinea

Recommended hostas

'Blue Cadet': Medium. Makes a sturdy clump of blue-gray foliage with small heart-shaped leaves.

fortunei **'Francee':** Medium-large. A fast-growing variegated ground cover. Leaves are forest green edged in bright white. Tolerates almost full sun.

fortunei **'Hyacinthina':** Medium-large. Makes rounded mounds of gray-green leaves edged with a white hairline. Spreads vigorously.

'Ginko Craig': Medium. The lance-shaped leaves are green with white edges. *H. tardiflora*, a similar edging hosta with dark green lance-shaped leaves, blooms very late in fall.

'Gold Standard': Medium-large. Grows fast, making broad mounds of big heart-shaped leaves, gold edged with green. Tolerates part sun.

'Hadspen Blue': Medium. The extremely blue leaves have rich texture and substance.

'Krossa Regal': Medium-large. Shaped like a vase, with leaves flowing outward at the top. The large heart-shaped leaves are powdery blue-gray. The light orchid flowers are borne on 6-ft. stalks. Makes a distinctive specimen.

plantaginea: Large. Called August lily for its deliciously fragrant, trumpet-shaped white flowers in August. The smooth leaves are light green. The cultivar 'Grandiflora' has slightly larger flowers. 'Aphrodite', recently introduced from China, has fragrant double white flowers. 'Honeybells' has light green leaves and fragrant pale violet or lavender flowers. 'Royal Standard' is a vigorous hybrid with rich green leaves and fragrant white flowers; it adapts well to shade or sun. All of these fragrant hostas are lovely in the garden and make long-lasting cut flowers that will perfume a room.

sieboldiana **'Elegans':** Large. The rounded leaves have rich substance and a seersucker texture, with a lovely blue-gray color in shade, blue-green in sun. *H. sieboldiana* itself has rich green leaves.

sieboldiana **'Frances Williams':** Large. The rounded, cupped leaves have heavy substance and a seersucker texture, with a blue-green center and irregular green-gold margins. One of the most popular hostas nationwide, it makes quite a specimen. Tolerates sun and dry soil better than many hostas do.

sieboldii **'Kabitan':** Medium. An edger that almost hugs the ground. The narrow leaves are gold with ruffled dark green edges. Spreads by rhizomes.

'Sum and Substance': Large. A spectacular plant that makes huge mounds of glossy, heavy-textured foliage. Leaves can be 2 ft. wide. Color is chartreuse in shade, bright gold in half-day sun. Very reliable. Pest-resistant.

ventricosa **'Aureo-Marginata':** Medium-large. The rich green leaves with irregular creamy or white margins have wavy edges and twisted tips.

venusta: Small. The leaves are only 1–2 in. wide, and mature clumps are 4 in. high by 8 in. wide. *H. v.* 'Variegata' is similar, but its leaves have cream centers and two-tone green edges. Both are tiny and look precious in pots.

'Wide Brim': Medium-large. The blue-green leaves have irregular creamy margins that darken to gold. Vigorous.

jubatum (p. 211)
Foxtail barley, squirreltail grass.
Grass. Zone 4.
H: 18–30 in. S: 18 in.

A short-lived grass, often grown as an annual for cut-flower arrangements or massed in informal gardens. It's very showy for several weeks in early summer, when the flower heads sparkle in the sun and dance in the wind. The spikes are 4 in. long, and each floret is topped with a hairlike 3-in. awn. Colors change from green and reddish purple to beige as the flowers mature and seeds ripen. Pick early for dried arrangements.

How to grow: Full or part sun. Not fussy about soil or watering. Plant seeds in spring. If you don't harvest or cut back the seed heads by late August, it will probably self-sow and may become weedy.

Hosta

Hoss´ta. Plantain lily.
Liliaceae. Lily family.

Perennials that make neat clumps of broad-bladed leaves. The small lilylike flowers are usually violet, blue, or white, sometimes very fragrant. Plants spread slowly by underground rhizomes. About 40 spp., native to China, Korea, and Japan, and many hybrids and thousands of cultivars.

species and cultivars (pp. 248–249)
Hostas, plantain lilies, funkias.
Perennials. Zone 4.
H: 6 in. to 3 ft. (foliage). S: most wider than tall.

Hostas are the preeminent perennials for shady gardens coast to coast. They are very easy to grow and thrive with almost no maintenance, forming larger, more beautiful clumps every year. Tufts of long-stalked, wide-bladed leaves rise directly from short underground stems. Older plants have dozens of these tufts crowded closely together. Single plants mature into mounded specimens. Mass plantings form into a ground cover that banishes weeds.

Hostas are valued chiefly for their leaves, which can be slender, lance-shaped, heart-shaped, or rounded. Texture can be smooth, crinkled, or ruffled. Colors include light to dark green, blue-green, blue-gray, and gold. There are

Hosta plantaginea

Hosta 'Krossa Regal'

many white-variegated or gold-variegated forms. Generally, the blue-leaved forms grow and look best in full shade, but the gold-leaved forms need part sun to brighten their color.

Most hostas have lavender or purplish flowers borne on erect stems about twice the height of the foliage. The tubular 6-lobed flowers can be horizontal or drooping. Some gardeners think that hosta flowers detract from the impact of the foliage and remove them. Others let them develop. *H. plantaginea* and its cultivars are exceptional for having large white flowers that are showy and wonderfully fragrant.

Plant sizes range from doll-sized to jumbo, and their landscape uses vary accordingly. Small hostas are under 8 in. tall and are good for rock gardens or small gardens. Medium hostas grow up to 12 in. high and 18 in. wide and are good for edging paths or beds. Medium-large hostas grow up to 18 in. tall and 2–3 ft. wide; often massed as ground covers, they also make fine specimens. Large hostas grow over 2 ft. tall and make clumps several feet wide, excellent as a background for other perennials.

How to grow: Full shade to part sun. Best in well-drained soil amended with plenty of organic matter. Hostas are most luxuriant if the soil is constantly moist. They survive short dry spells without permanent damage but don't do well in arid climates. Spreading a generous layer of mulch around the plants every spring helps retain soil moisture. Where slugs and snails are common pests, hostas are their favorite food, and black vine weevils are a problem in the South.

Hostas rarely need division; they can live for years in one place. If you want to multiply your stock, dig clumps in spring when the leaves first emerge. Cut or pull the clump into smaller clusters, each with several shoots and plenty of roots. Or, use a sharp spade to slice a wedge out of an established clump (like cutting a piece of pie) in early spring. If necessary, hostas can be transplanted or divided later in the growing season. Just be sure to keep them well watered afterward.

Hyacinthus

Hy-a-sin´thus. Hyacinth.
Liliaceae. Lily family.

Bulb-forming perennials with a few strap-shaped leaves and a stubby stalk of sweet-scented flowers in spring. Only 3 or 4 spp., native to the Mediterranean region.

orientalis (p. 252)

Hyacinth.
Bulbous perennial. Zone 5.
H: 6–10 in. S: 6 in.

Popular for its intense fragrance and sturdy cheerful appearance. Blooms last for about 2 weeks in early spring. Each bulb makes one spike with dozens of single or double flowers in pink, blue, lavender, rose, yellow, or white. Leaves appear with the flowers and remain for 2–3 months. Combine with Spanish bluebells, grape hyacinths, and other spring bulbs under deciduous shrubs or trees.

How to grow: Needs full sun in spring, takes part shade after bloom. Ordinary soil and watering. Bulbs may rot if the soil is wet. Tolerates heat and dry soil in summer, while it is dormant. Plant 6 in. deep and close together (almost touching) in fall. Reblooms for years, gradually bearing fewer flowers, but doesn't multiply. Replace every 2–3 years for best display.

Hydrangea

Hy-dran´jee-a.
Saxifragaceae. Saxifrage family.

Deciduous or evergreen shrubs with opposite rounded leaves and bushy clusters of white, pink, or blue flowers. More than 20 spp., native to North and South America and eastern Asia.

anomala subsp. petiolaris (p. 204)

(*H. petiolaris*)
Climbing hydrangea.
Deciduous woody vine. Zone 5.
H: 60–80 ft.

An excellent vine, slow to establish but worth the wait. It has slightly fragrant white flowers in flat 6–8-in. clusters for several weeks in summer, and its beautiful cinnamon-colored bark is handsome in winter. The rounded leaves are glossy dark green all summer and fall. Clings by rootlets to a trellis, arbor, chimney, wall, or tree. Leafy flowering branches reach out about 3 ft. from the anchored stems. Eventually grows quite large, with a strong trunk. Tolerates shade, and looks most attractive clambering up a large tree, with its white flowers brightening an otherwise dark area. *Schizophragma hydrangeoides,* the Japanese hydrangea-vine, is similar but stays flat against its support and doesn't project its branches.

How to grow: Full sun, part sun, or shade. Prefers rich, fertile soil amended with plenty of organic matter and acidic to neutral pH; gets chlorotic in alkaline soil. Carefree and grows steadily once established.

Hydrangea quercifolia

macrophylla (p. 139)
Hydrangea.
Deciduous shrub. Zone 6.
H: 4–8 ft. S: 6–10 ft.

A popular shrub for foundation plantings or mixed borders, with showy rounded clusters of white, pink, red, or blue flowers in summer and fall. Has lots of thick, erect, unbranched stems that reach their full height in a single season. The big opposite leaves have a thick texture and shiny green color; fresh healthy foliage is handsome by itself.

Hundreds of cultivars compose two groups. 'Pia', 'Nikko Blue', and other hortensia types have domed clusters of flowers that are all sterile, with conspicuous papery petallike sepals. 'Mariesii' and other lacecap types have flatter clusters with small fertile flowers in the middle and a lacy ring of sterile flowers around the edge. 'Mariesii Variegata' has lovely green-and-white leaves and blue flowers; it grows slowly and stays 2–3 ft. tall.

Flower color varies with soil pH. Acidic conditions (pH below 5.5) improve blue coloring. Neutral to alkaline conditions (pH of 6.5 or higher) favor the pink and red colors.

Hardiness varies among cultivars. Most produce flowers on the previous year's shoots, and they fail to bloom if a cold winter kills the shoots to the ground, even though the roots will survive and produce a vigorous crop of new shoots. Flowering is reliable only where winters are mild in the Deep South or Pacific coastal regions. In colder climates plants must be grown in containers and overwintered in a cool garage or basement.

For reliable bloom where winters are cold, plant *H. arborescens* 'Annabelle' or 'Grandiflora'. Both have big clusters of sterile flowers, borne on new shoots that grow 3–5 ft. tall in a season. Treat them like herbaceous perennials, cutting all stems to the ground each winter. Their flowers start out as green buds, lighten to creamy white as they expand, and darken to tan as they age.

How to grow: Full or part sun. Needs fertile soil amended with plenty of organic matter and constant moisture. Use aluminum sulfate to acidify soil for blue flowers and lime to produce red flowers. Remove stems that have flowered while plants are dormant. Further thinning will promote larger flower clusters. Dig up suckering shoots to make new plants. Hydrangeas are long lived and trouble-free.

paniculata 'Grandiflora' (p. 139)
Peegee hydrangea.
Deciduous shrub or small tree. Zone 3.
H: 10–25 ft. S: 10–20 ft.

A fast-growing shrub with 6–12-in. clusters of papery flowers that open white in summer and gradually darken to pinkish tan in fall, hanging on through winter. The clusters are borne at the ends of thick arching limbs. The large opposite leaves turn bronzy in fall. Very showy in late summer when other shrubs are finished. Cut flowers last for years in dried arrangements.

How to grow: Full or part sun. Prefers fertile soil and constant moisture but isn't fussy and survives even in difficult urban conditions. Prune hard when dormant, removing old flowering stems. Blooms on new wood. A tough plant, easy to grow.

quercifolia (p. 139)
Oakleaf hydrangea.
Deciduous shrub. Zone 5.
H: 4–8 ft. S: 6–8 ft.

This southeastern native has large, lobed, oaklike leaves, dark green in summer, turning red, orange, or purplish in late fall. It makes a thicket of stout, usually unbranched stems with attractive reddish brown bark. Long clusters of white flowers top the branches in early summer. 'Snowflake' has 12-in. clusters of double flowers. 'Snow Queen' has dense clusters of larger than normal flowers. Good in partly shaded mixed borders or massed at the edge of a woods.

How to grow: Part sun or shade. Prefers fertile soil with plenty of organic matter. Tolerates dry soil but looks better with regular watering. Grows slowly. Spreads by suckers; propagate by division. Stem tips and flower buds are likely to freeze in cold winters; prune off damaged parts in spring. Trouble-free.

Hypericum

Hy-per'i-kum. St.-John's-wort.
Hypericaceae. St.-John's-wort family.

A big group of perennials and shrubs, most with 5-parted yellow flowers having a prominent tuft of stamens and simple opposite leaves with clear or dark dots. About 370 spp., native to the Old and New World.

calycinum (p. 140)
Semievergreen shrub. Zone 5.
H: 12–18 in. S: 18–24 in.

A versatile small shrub with 3-in. shiny bright yellow flowers off and on from June to September. Fills in quickly as a colorful ground cover, or combines well with daylilies, yarrows, daisies, and other perennials in a mixed border. The new shoots are soft and tend to sprawl. The simple opposite leaves are oval, 2–4 in. long, dark green in summer and fall, turning purplish in cold weather. Often dies back over winter but recovers quickly if cut to the ground in early spring.

How to grow: Full or part sun. Grows best with ordinary soil and watering but tolerates poor, dry, sandy soil. Space 12–18 in. apart for ground cover. Spreads by suckers; propagate by division. Trouble-free.

'**Hidcote**' (p. 140)
Semievergreen shrub. Zone 5.
H: 3–4 ft. S: 3 ft.

This hybrid St.-John's-wort makes a leafy mound of neat foliage and blooms throughout the summer months. The simple opposite leaves, 2 in. long, are neatly spaced along slender arching twigs and hang on into winter. The golden yellow flowers, to 3 in. wide, are borne in clusters of 1–5. Very showy in mass plantings.

How to grow: Full or part sun. Grows best with ordinary soil and watering. Shoots freeze in cold winters; prune back to live wood in early spring. In cold regions, this means cutting it to the ground and treating it like an herbaceous perennial. It will flower on new growth. Trouble-free.

Hyssopus
Hi-so´pus.
Labiatae. Mint family.

Perennials or small shrubs with square stems, opposite leaves, and 2-lipped flowers. Only 5 spp., native to Eurasia.

officinalis (p. 283)
Hyssop.
Shrubby perennial herb. Zone 3.
H: 18–24 in. S: 12–18 in.

A bushy plant with lots of upright leafy stems topped with whorled spikes of blue-purple flowers in summer. Bees love them. The dark green leaves are slender, 1 in. long, and are semi-evergreen in mild climates. The leaves are very aromatic, formerly used to flavor food, now used commercially in liqueurs and perfumes. Single plants are colorful in flower or herb gardens. Can be trimmed into a low hedge or edging. Herb nurseries offer hyssop with white or pink flowers as well as a dwarf blue-flowered form.

How to grow: Full sun. Does best in well-drained, sandy, neutral or limy soil. Tolerates dry heat but not high humidity. Propagate by division or seed. Flowers the first year from seed. Space 12–15 in. apart for a hedge. Prune to the ground in spring and shear after flowering to keep it compact. Pest-free.

Iberis
Eye-beer´is. Candytuft.
Cruciferae. Mustard family.

Annuals or evergreen perennials, mostly small and low, with clusters of white, pink, or purplish flowers. About 30 spp., native to Europe and the Mediterranean region.

sempervirens (p. 253)
Candytuft.
Shrubby perennial. Zone 3.
H: 9–12 in. S: 18–30 in.

Makes tufts or spreading mats of trailing stems densely packed with blunt, oblong, evergreen leaves. Small, 4-petaled, bright white flowers form clusters up and down the stems in spring, continuing for weeks if the weather stays cool. Sometimes reblooms in fall. Makes a good companion for early spring bulbs. Cascades over a stone wall or down a rocky bank. 'Snowflake' grows 12 in. tall, with larger than normal leaves and flowers. 'Little Gem' is only 4–6 in. tall, good for rock gardens.

How to grow: Full or part sun. Needs well-drained, neutral or limy soil. Ordinary watering. Propagate by seed or division. Shear hard after blooming to keep plants neat and compact. Trouble-free.

umbellata (p. 297)
Globe candytuft, annual candytuft.
Annual. All zones.
H: 6–12 in. S: 6–12 in.

Easy, fast-growing, and cheerful. Forms a mat of slender stems with thin leaves, then quickly covers itself with flat 2-in. clusters of pink, rose, purple, carmine, or white flowers. The flowers last well in fresh arrangements, and the beige seed heads are pretty in dried arrangements. Blooms once and goes to seed; doesn't continue all summer. Sow seeds in fall for early spring bloom, to fill the spaces around late starters such as balloon flower or hardy hibiscus.

How to grow: Full or part sun. Ordinary soil and watering. Sow seeds where they are to bloom, in fall or early spring. Thin seedlings to 6 in. apart.

Ilex
Eye´lecks. Holly.
Aquifoliaceae. Holly family.

Mostly evergreen (some deciduous) trees or shrubs, usually with thick leathery leaves, sometimes spiny, and round red, gold, or black fruits. About 400 spp., native worldwide, and many hybrids and cultivars.

Hollies produce male and female flowers on separate plants; you need both sexes for good berry production. Hybrids can be pollinated by either parent; what's most important is that the flowers must be open at the same time. Usually one male will suffice to pollinate 10–20 females. They don't need to be planted side by side, as bees will carry the pollen several hundred yards. If there's already a suitable male holly in your neighborhood, you don't need to plant another.

× *altaclerensis* 'Wilsonii' (p. 174)
(*I. aquifolium* × *I. perado*)
Wilson holly.
Evergreen shrub or tree. Zone 7 or 6.
H: to 20 ft. S: to 10 ft.

A tough and vigorous holly that usually grows as a mounded shrub 6–8 ft. tall but can be trained into a single-trunked or multitrunked tree 15–20 ft. tall. The large (3 in. by 5 in.), thick, leathery leaves have a few tiny spines along the edges. Bears heavy crops of bright red berries. (Can be pollinated by a male English holly, *I. aquifolium*.) Grown commercially in the Pacific Northwest and Mid-Atlantic states for holiday wreaths. Makes a good specimen tree or clipped hedge.

How to grow: Full sun, part sun, or shade. Ordinary soil and watering. Not a fussy plant—tolerates heat, dryness, wind, and seacoast and city conditions.

aquifolium (p. 160)
English holly.
Evergreen tree. Zone 6.
H: to 30 ft. or more. S: 15 ft. or more.

This is the quintessential holly, with a tidy—almost artificial—pyramidal growth habit; glossy, rigid foliage; and showy crops of bright red berries. The small white flowers are fragrant for about 2 weeks in May or June. Although best adapted to the Pacific Northwest, it can also be grown in parts of the Mid-Atlantic states and Southeast where summers are not too hot and humid. Where it thrives, it makes wonderful specimens, screens, or hedges. There are hundreds of cultivars, differing in leaf color (many are variegated with white or yellow), leaf size (usually 1–3 in. long), spininess, berry production, and hardiness. Females need a nearby male for pollination. 'Argentea Marginata' is a female with white-edged leaves. 'Balkans' (both male and female) is the hardiest English holly. 'Scotica' has spineless leaves. 'Sparkler' bears heavy crops of shiny berries, even as a young plant.

How to grow: Full sun, part sun, or shade. Grows best in well-drained soil with ordinary watering. Dormant oil sprays control various insect pests, particularly scale. Needs minimal pruning.

× ***attenuata*** (p. 160)
(*I. cassine* × *I. opaca*)
Topal holly.
Evergreen tree. Zone 7.
H: 25 ft. or more. S: 15 ft. or more.

This is a group of hybrid American hollies, selected and grown mostly in the southeastern states. Most are upright, slender, pyramidal trees with narrow evergreen leaves and red berries. Many selections were made by E. E. Foster in Alabama. 'Foster #2', one of the most popular, is a female with spiny leaves. 'Foster #4' is a male pollinator. 'East Palatka' has broad spineless leaves and abundant red berries. All make handsome, healthy specimen trees that fit into small gardens.

How to grow: Full sun, part sun, or shade. Ordinary soil and watering. Tolerates heat and humidity. Requires no special care.

cornuta (p. 174)
Chinese holly.
Evergreen shrub. Zone 7.
H: usually under 10 ft. S: to 10 ft.

Chinese hollies are popular landscape plants in the South and Southwest. They thrive in hot weather. Most make irregular mounded shrubs, useful in foundation plantings and for hedges and specimens. The evergreen leaves feel like plastic and have a shiny rich green color. Berries are very big, bright red, and long lasting, but plants need a long hot summer for berries to develop.

The typical Chinese holly has nearly rectangular leaves, 2–3 in. long, with sharp spines at the corners and tip. It makes a large upright

***Ilex cornuta* 'Burfordii'**

shrub. 'Burfordii' is a vigorous grower that gets 15–20 ft. tall, has almost spineless leaves that cup downward, and bears a heavy crop of berries. It makes a good hedge or can be pruned into tree form, but it grows too fast and too big for foundation plantings. 'Dwarf Burford' has small (1½ in.) leaves, bears smaller and less abundant berries, and grows more slowly, reaching about 10 ft. 'Carissa' has spineless leaves, does not produce berries, and stays under 4 ft. tall. 'Rotunda' has stout spines on the leaves and no berries; it grows to 4 ft. tall and makes a formidable burglar-proof barrier planting under windows. 'Willowleaf' is a large broad shrub with spreading limbs; long, narrow, twisted leaves; and dark red berries.

How to grow: Full or part sun. Not fussy about soil and watering. It's a tough plant that tolerates alkaline conditions, heat, and drought. Quite susceptible to scale; treat with dormant oil spray.

crenata (p. 175)
Japanese holly.
Evergreen shrub. Zone 6 or 5.
H: usually under 4 ft.; can reach 20 ft. S: varies.

Most forms grow slowly into low dense mounds. The thick, leathery, dark green leaves are small ovals (¼ to ¾ in. long) with tiny marginal teeth. The small inconspicuous berries are black. Japanese hollies are often used as a trouble-free substitute for boxwood in foundation plantings or small gardens. Cultivars vary in size, habit, and hardiness. 'Helleri' is compact and bushy, usually under 4 ft. 'Compacta', 'Convexa', 'Glory', and 'Hetzii' reach about 6 ft. 'Golden Gem' has gold foliage if grown in the sun. 'Convexa', 'Glory', and 'Northern Beauty' are undamaged by winter lows in Zone 5.

How to grow: Full or part sun. Needs acidic or neutral soil; don't plant near concrete, which leaches an alkaline residue. (Use *I. vomitoria* 'Nana' in alkaline soil.) Ordinary watering. Needs minimal care or pruning. Grows naturally into a compact dense shrub. Subject to spider mites in hot, dry conditions but otherwise trouble-free.

decidua (p. 140)
Possum haw, swamp holly.
Deciduous shrub or small tree. Zone 5.
H: 15 ft. or more. S: 10–15 ft.

A tough southeastern native that offers a showy display of red (sometimes orange or yellow) pea-sized berries that attract birds throughout fall and winter. Branches densely with many small gray twigs. Leaves are smooth, oval, and toothless, green in summer and gold in fall. Adds winter interest to an informal border of deciduous and evergreen shrubs. Can be pruned into a small specimen tree. There are several cultivars with abundant red or red-orange berries, including 'Warren Red', 'Council Fire', and 'Pocahontas'. 'Byers Golden', with bright yellow fruits, is choice but scarce because it's hard to propagate. Plant one male for every 3–5 females.

Can also be pollinated by a male *I. opaca*. Possum haw is similar to winterberry holly (*I. verticillata*) but grows faster and gets bigger.

How to grow: Needs full sun for best fruiting but tolerates part or full shade. Not fussy about soil; tolerates heavy clay, sand, or alkaline conditions. Grows wild in wetlands but tolerates dry soil. Grows fairly quickly. Prune to shape as desired. No serious pests.

glabra (p. 174)
Inkberry.
Evergreen shrub. Zone 5 or 4.
H: to 8 ft. S: to 10 ft.

A tough and hardy evergreen holly with small, thin, spineless, oval leaves (to 2 in. long) and dark blue-black berries. Native to wetlands throughout the eastern United States, where it spreads to make dense thickets. The foliage is similar to that of the Japanese hollies (*I. crenata*), but the plant tends to grow more upright and get leggy at the base. 'Compacta' is a dense-growing female, 4–6 ft. tall, good for hedging. 'Nordic' and 'Shamrock' are even more compact and should be hardy in Zone 4. 'Ivory Queen' has white berries.

How to grow: Full sun, part sun, or shade. A good holly for damp sites but also tolerates dry soil. Can be sheared into formal hedges. Older plants may need heavy pruning to force new growth from the base. Spreads by suckers.

latifolia (p. 160)
Lusterleaf holly.
Evergreen tree. Zone 7.
H: 20 ft. or more. S: 10 ft.

A wonderful broad-leaved evergreen that surprises many gardeners, who don't recognize it as a holly. Leaves are large and luxuriant, up to 8 in. long. The small yellowish flowers are notably fragrant in early spring. The red berries are quite large, borne in generous clusters that nearly encircle the branches. Grows strongly upright, nearly columnar, with a dense crown. Makes a sentry by an entryway or gate, or a wonderful contrast to fine-textured companions such as nandina or bamboo.

How to grow: Part sun or shade. Ordinary soil and watering. Tolerates some heat and dryness. Fairly slow growing. Trouble-free.

× *meserveae* cultivars (p. 175)
(*I. aquifolium* × *I. rugosa*)
Meserve hybrid hollies.
Evergreen shrubs. Zone 5 or 4.
H: 8–15 ft. S: to 10 ft.

This group of hybrids, developed by Mrs. Kathleen Meserve on Long Island, New York, combines outstanding evergreen foliage with good cold-hardiness. Most have spiny-margined blue-green leaves, purple stems, and showy red berries, even on very young plants. Excellent for foundation planting in cold climates, where the shiny foliage and berries look bright and cheerful throughout the winter months. 'Blue Girl', 'Blue Boy', and the other "Blue" cultivars all have dark blue-green foliage. Most grow into shrubby upright pyramids.

Mrs. Meserve also introduced the hybrid 'China Boy' and 'China Girl' hollies (*I. cornuta* × *I. rugosa*). They are handsome mounded plants with rich dark green leaves, and they tolerate hot weather better than the "Blue" hollies do.

How to grow: Part sun. All do best if shaded from direct sun in winter; avoid planting on the south side of a building. Ordinary soil and watering. Prune to shape anytime. Pest-free.

'Nellie R. Stevens' (p. 160)
(*I. aquifolium* × *I. cornuta*)
Evergreen tree or shrub. Zone 7.
H: 15–25 ft. S: 10–15 ft.

A tough, durable hybrid holly that makes a handsome pyramidal tree or can be pruned into a dense hedge. Very popular in the South and California. Fast-growing and trouble-free. The dark green evergreen leaves are waxy-textured, 1–2 in. long, with just a few spines. Can be pollinated by a male Chinese holly (*I. cornuta*) and bears a heavy crop of bright red berries. Good as a specimen or hedge. Named for its originator, who lived in Maryland.

How to grow: Full or part sun. Not fussy about soil and watering. Tolerates heat, humidity, and dryness. Space 5–10 ft. apart for a hedge.

opaca (p. 161)
American holly.
Evergreen tree. Zone 5.
H: to 50 ft. S: 30 ft.

A stately evergreen native to the eastern United States, where its cultivars are common and popular. Grows upright with a rounded or pyramidal crown. The leathery leaves have spiny edges and may be dark green or a yellowish olive green. Berries are dull red. Selected cultivars such as 'Christmas Carol', 'Merry Christmas', and 'Greenleaf' have much prettier leaves and berries than most wild plants do. 'Canary' has yellow berries that look bright even on dark winter days.

How to grow: Full or part sun. Foliage is damaged by winter sun or cold, dry winds. Prefers slightly acidic, well-drained, moist soil; gets chlorotic in alkaline soil. Subject to several pests, including leafminers and scale.

Ilex opaca

pedunculosa (p. 175)
Long-stalked holly.
Evergreen shrub or tree. Zone 5.
H: 20–25 ft. S: 10–15 ft.

Unusual for a holly, with red berries borne on long stalks, like cherries; quite showy in fall, until the birds eat them all. The pointed toothless leaves are 1–3 in. long, lustrous dark green in summer, yellow-green in winter. Makes a large upright shrub or small pyramidal tree; branches are more graceful and not as stiff as those of many hollies. Uncommon but very attractive; also hardier and more adaptable than English or American hollies. Male trees are more cold-hardy than the females.

How to grow: Full or part sun. Best in slightly acidic, moist, well-drained soil but tolerates adversity. Prune anytime. No serious pests or diseases.

verticillata (p. 140)
Winterberry holly.
Deciduous shrub. Zone 3.
H: to 10 ft. S: to 10 ft.

A wonderful native shrub for northern gardens, covered with bright red berries for several months in fall and winter. It's easy, showy, and colorful and attracts cedar waxwings, robins, and other birds. Usually makes several upright stems that branch repeatedly. The thin-textured spineless leaves, 1–2 in. long, are bright green in summer, sometimes turning yellow before they drop in fall. Excellent planted in mass for a winter display, against a background of conifers, a light-colored brick or painted building, or a snow-covered lawn or field. 'Winter Red', 'Sunset', 'Fairfax', 'Cacapon', and 'Afterglow' are female cultivars chosen for heavy berry production. Include one male plant for pollination.

Hybrids of *I. verticillata* and the Japanese winterberry, *I. serrata,* are vigorous plants that bear tremendous crops of berries. Outstanding in this group is 'Sparkleberry', a female with an upright habit, reaching 12 ft. tall, that bears brilliant red fruits. Use 'Apollo' (similar in size and habit) as its male pollinator.

How to grow: Full or part sun. Best in fertile, slightly acidic soil with ordinary watering. Tolerates constant moisture; a good choice for difficult, poorly drained sites. Doesn't grow too fast but tends to get leggy. Prune hard if needed to force more shoots from the base.

vomitoria (p. 175)
Yaupon holly.
Evergreen shrub or tree. Zone 7.
H: 15–20 ft. S: to 10 ft.

A southeastern native with small, narrow, dark green leaves and huge crops of small, juicy-looking, red berries. Easily trained as a small multitrunked tree with picturesque crooked trunks and limbs. Dwarf cultivars make compact mounds of foliage and can be sheared into any desired shape. Grows quickly and makes a good hedge or screen; also popular for foundation plantings. 'Nana' makes a dense twiggy hemisphere, 3–5 ft. high and wide, covered with tiny leaves but few berries; 'Stokes Dwarf' is even smaller. 'Pendula' has an upright trunk and weeping branches.

How to grow: Full or part sun. Not fussy about soil; tolerates alkaline conditions, clay, sand, and wet or dry sites. Responds well to pruning. No serious pests. Tougher and easier than *I. crenata* but not as hardy.

Ilex verticillata

Illicium
Il-lis'i-um. Anise tree.
Illiciaceae. Anise family.

Evergreen trees or shrubs with glossy foliage, many-petaled flowers, and many-pointed woody pods. Seeds of some species are used in flavoring or medicine. About 42 spp., native to eastern Asia and eastern North America.

floridanum (p. 176)
Florida anise.
Evergreen shrub. Zone 8.
H: 10–15 ft. S: 6–10 ft.

A native southeastern shrub with evergreen leaves, 4–6 in. long. Crushed leaves have an anise or licorice fragrance that some people appreciate; others call this stinkbush or stinking laurel. The starry blooms have reddish brown or purplish petals and smell odd, but they're hidden in the foliage and easily overlooked. Forms an irregular mound, or can be sheared into a dense formal hedge. *I. parviflorum,* the small anise, is similar but more tolerant of dry soil. *I. anisatum,* or Japanese anise, has leaves that smell like root beer. Its fruits are the "star anise" sold as a spice. It makes an attractive 15–25-ft. tree but is susceptible to freeze damage.

How to grow: Part to full shade. Prefers well-drained but constantly moist, fertile soil. Space 5–10 ft. apart and prune regularly to make a dense hedge. Trouble-free.

Impatiens
Im-pay'shens. Balsam, jewelweed, touch-me-not.
Balsaminaceae. Balsam family.

Annuals or perennials, most with succulent stems, 5-parted flowers, and fruit capsules that burst open to eject the seeds. About 850 spp., many native to Africa and Asia.

Impatiens wallerana

wallerana (p. 298)
Impatiens.
Tender perennial grown as an annual.
All zones.
H: to 2 ft. S: to 2 ft.

One of the best annuals for shade, popular in all parts of the United States. The succulent light green stems branch repeatedly, making a bushy mound without needing to be pruned or pinched. The thin leaves look good in shade but wilt quickly in hot sun. Flowers are 1–2 in. wide in shades of red, orange, pink, purple, or white, sometimes striped or two-tone. Some forms have double flowers like little roses. Excellent for massing under deciduous trees, for edging shady borders, or in containers. Combines well with begonias, ferns, hostas, and hydrangeas.

How to grow: Part shade. Fertile, well-drained soil and regular watering. Plants bloom better if the soil is slightly dry, but not dry enough to wilt the foliage. Easy from seed sown indoors 10 weeks before last frost; don't cover the seeds (they need light to germinate), and put in a warm place (70°–75° F). Outdoors, space 8–12 in. apart after danger of frost is past. Before first frost, root a few cuttings in water and pot them up for winter houseplants.

Imperata
Im-per-ay´ta.
Gramineae. Grass family.
A small group of perennial grasses, mostly from tropical climates. Only 8 spp.

cylindrica 'Red Baron' (p. 211)
Japanese blood grass.
Perennial grass. Zone 6.
H: 12–18 in. S: to 12 in.
Grown for its bright red foliage. The slender upright leaves are red on top, and the color intensifies in fall. Use it for an accent plant, especially on a west-facing lawn or ridge where it will be backlit by the setting sun. Also makes a colorful ribbon running along a lawn or edging a perennial border. The species itself has plain green leaves and is a vigorous spreader. A major weed problem in Old World tropics, it is on the federal noxious weed list and cannot be sold in this country.
How to grow: Full or part sun. Best in fertile, moist but well-drained soil. Propagate by division. Cut back once a year. If all-green shoots appear, remove and destroy them immediately.

Ipomoea
Ip-po-mee´a. Morning glory.
Convolvulaceae. Morning glory family.
A diverse group of annuals, perennials, vines, and shrubs, all with 5-lobed funnel-shaped flowers. Includes the sweet potato (*I. batatas*) and other food and medicinal plants, several ornamentals, and some weeds. About 500 spp., most native to warm or tropical climates worldwide.

purpurea (p. 298)
(*I. tricolor*)
Morning glory.
Annual vine. All zones.
H: to 15 ft.
A twining vine that climbs quickly to cover a trellis or fence with a screen of large heart-shaped leaves. The funnel-shaped flowers, up to 5 in. wide, open in the morning and last just one day. Flowers can be blue, lavender, pink, red, or white, often with contrasting markings like 5-pointed stars. The moonflower, sold either as *I. alba* or as *Calonyction aculeatum,* is a vigorous vine that needs a sturdy support. Its large white flowers open at dusk and are sweetly fragrant. *I. batatas* 'Blackie' is grown for its striking dark foliage.
How to grow: Full sun. Ordinary soil; don't fertilize, as it causes rank growth. Ordinary watering; can tolerate some dryness. Soak seeds overnight before planting in the garden after danger of frost is past. Thin seedlings to 6 in. apart. Provide support immediately. Often self-seeds, but doesn't spread by deep perennial roots like the weedy wild morning glory or bindweed (*Convolvulus arvensis*).

Ipomopsis
Ip-po-mop´sis.
Polemoniaceae. Phlox family.
Mostly perennials, with leafy stems and clusters of small tubular flowers. About 24 spp., native to North and South America.

rubra (p. 298)
Standing cypress.
Biennial or annual. All zones.
H: 3 ft. or more. S: 1–2 ft.
A bushy erect plant with fine-textured feathery foliage. Stems are topped with clusters of small, trumpet-shaped, red-orange (occasionally yellow) flowers that attract hummingbirds from June to August. Seeds are often included in wildflower mixes. Showy as a filler in mixed plantings.
How to grow: Full or part sun. Needs good drainage; tolerates dry soil. Sow seeds in spring. Self-sows readily. Thin to 6–12-in. spacing. Cut stalks back in late spring to make shorter, denser plants. Unpruned plants get top-heavy with bloom and may flop over. Trouble-free.

Ipomopsis rubra

Iris
Eye´ris.
Iridaceae. Iris family.
Perennials that form either rhizomes or bulbs, with flat sword-shaped or linear leaves. The characteristic flowers have 3 inner segments (the standards) and 3 outer segments (the falls). Although it's easy to recognize an iris as an iris, there's wonderful diversity within the genus. About 300 spp., most native to the north temperate zone, and some hybrids and many cultivars.

bearded hybrids (p. 250)
Bearded irises.
Perennials. Zone 3.
H: to 3 ft. S: 1 ft. or more.
Most gardeners are familiar with the taller members of this group, but not many realize that there are intermediate and dwarf forms as well. All have large showy flowers with upright standards and fuzzy beards on the down-curved falls, borne on sturdy, erect, branching stalks. Flower

Bearded iris

colors include all shades of white, yellow, gold, orange, pink, blue, lavender, and purple; many types are bicolored, and some are sweetly fragrant as well as beautiful. All make good cut flowers.

Dwarf bearded irises include miniature plants (4–10 in. tall) and standard dwarfs (under 15 in.). Although the plants are small, the flowers can be 3–4 in. wide. This group is the first to flower. Next to bloom are the intermediate bearded irises, with large flowers on stalks 15–28 in. tall. Last to flower are the tall bearded irises, with stalks at least 28 in. tall. Planting some of each type will prolong the bloom season for several weeks. Breeders have now developed some repeat bloomers—bearded irises that bloom again in late summer or fall.

Bearded irises all have thick spreading rhizomes and stiffly vertical leaves arranged in flat fans. For best results, they need well-drained soil and must be divided every few years, during the summer. Collectors grow them in special beds where it's easy to accommodate these requirements. Most gardeners prefer to include irises in a mixed border, where they join the festival of peonies, pinks, azaleas, lilacs, and other spring flowers.

How to grow: Full sun or afternoon shade. Prefer fertile soil amended with organic matter. Need good drainage and may rot on wet sites. Tolerate hot, dry weather during the summer, sometimes by going dormant. When planting, spread and bury the roots, but position the rhizome right at the soil surface. Point the leafy end in the direction you want it to grow. Space 6–18 in. apart, depending on plant height. May not bloom well until the second year after planting.

Divide every 3–4 years in summer. Lift the entire clump and cut or snap off the leafy leading ends of the rhizomes to save. Discard the older parts from the center of the clump; they won't bloom again. Trim leaves and roots to about 6 in. long, and let the divisions sit for a few hours to heal the cuts before replanting.

Borers are a major pest of bearded irises. They tunnel into the rhizome, opening the way for bacterial and fungal infections that disfigure and weaken the plant. Fungal infections also cause problems if the soil is too heavy and wet. Give bearded irises plenty of space for good air circulation, don't put mulch over the rhizomes, watch for and destroy any infested or infected plant parts, and do a thorough cleanup in fall.

Iris cristata

cristata (p. 250)
Dwarf crested iris.
Perennial. Zone 3.
H: to 8 in. (foliage); 4–6 in. (flowers). S: 2 ft.

This southeastern native makes lovely carpets for edging woodland gardens or informal perennial beds. The lavender, blue, purple, or white flowers open just above ground level in early spring. Despite their short stature, they're surprisingly large and wonderfully delicate, with yellow "crests" or ridges at the base of the falls. Fans of smooth light green leaves elongate after

flowering. Several nurseries offer forms selected for their flower color. 'Alba', with white flowers, is especially vigorous and covers the ground rapidly. *I. tectorum,* or Japanese roof iris, is another crested iris with lovely flowers and broad, ribbed, evergreen leaves. It grows 12–18 in. tall.

How to grow: Part sun or shade. Ordinary soil and watering. Tolerates dry soil and summer heat. Spreads by slender rhizomes. Can be divided in early spring, when it first peeks out of the ground, or in fall. Needs no special care. Problem-free.

Iris ensata

ensata (p. 251)
(*I. kaempferi*)
Japanese iris.
Perennial. Zone 4.
H: 2–3 ft. S: 1–2 ft.

Blooms later than the bearded iris hybrids, with huge (8–10 in. wide) flat blossoms, often mottled or delicately patterned, in shades of white, violet, blue, or purple. The flowers are exquisite but fragile, easily damaged by hot sun, dry wind, or heavy rain. Plants make an erect clump of sturdy smooth leaves with obvious midribs. Ideal for the damp banks of a pond or stream, combined with masses of Japanese primroses, but also grows fine in a bed of rich, moist, fertile soil. There are hundreds of cultivars in many color combinations. Most have very small standards and wide flat falls; some are double, with a soft mass of petals. *I. laevigata* also has spectacular large flowers in shades of white or purple. It needs constant moisture around the roots and does best in shallow water.

How to grow: Full sun. Prefers heavy, rich, damp, acidic soil. Plant in early fall, setting the rhizomes about 2 in. deep and 12–18 in. apart. Divide every 3–4 years in fall. Remove faded flowers daily. Problem-free.

foetidissima (p. 250)
Stinking iris.
Perennial. Zone 7.
H: 2 ft. S: 2 ft.

Grown not for its modest flowers but for the seedpods that split open in fall to reveal shiny bright red seeds. Those red berries look pretty for many weeks in the garden and also last well in cut arrangements. Each stalk has up to a dozen flowers and seedpods. The plant makes an erect clump of slender grassy leaves (which smell bad if you cut or crush them). Surround it with mounds of yellow chrysanthemums or daisies. There are varieties with yellow or white berries.

How to grow: Part sun or shade. Ordinary or improved soil and regular watering. Survives in Zone 6 with a winter mulch to protect the crown. The rhizomes spread slowly, and the plant can go years without division. Easily raised from seed but doesn't flower for several years.

Louisiana hybrids (see below for photo)
Perennials. Hardiness varies.
H: 1–4 ft. S: 1 ft. or more.

This diverse group includes both natural and deliberate hybrids between several species of iris that grow wild in the Deep South. All tolerate heat and humidity better than the bearded hybrids do and are ideal plants for southern gardens. The flowers are quite large and showy, without crests or beards, and come in a wide range of colors, including the best reds of any iris. There are hundreds of cultivars, varying in flower color, form, and height. Some are tender, but many are hardy up into the Midwest and New England. Breeders are striving to increase hardiness and adaptability.

In California, breeders are working with native species to develop the Pacific Coast hybrid irises (p. 251), which also come in a wide range of colors but are less adaptable to poor soil and extreme temperatures.

How to grow: Full sun. Prefer fertile soil amended with plenty of organic matter. Tolerate alkaline soil. Need constant moisture before and during bloom but can take dryness during the summer. (Some kinds go dormant in summer.) Plant rhizomes 2 in. deep in fall. They spread fairly rapidly and need division every few years. No serious pests or diseases.

pallida (p. 251)
Orris root.
Perennial. Zone 4.
H: 3 ft. S: 2 ft.

An old-fashioned perennial, tough and reliable, with very fragrant flowers in a lovely shade of lavender-blue. This plant traditionally was grown for its rhizomes, which are used in perfumery. Now it is valued as a parent of many modern tall bearded iris hybrids. The sturdy erect leaves are a silvery blue-green; a variegated form has creamy white markings that retain interest all summer. Combine it with bleeding-hearts, columbines, pinks, and other cottage-garden favorites.

How to grow: Full sun. Needs well-drained soil. Tolerates hot, dry weather. Has thick rhizomes. Divide every few years in spring or fall. Trouble-free.

pseudacorus (p. 251)
Yellow flag.
Perennial. Zone 3.
H: 2^1/$_2$–3^1/$_2$ ft. S: 2 ft. or more.

Cultivated for centuries in Europe, this iris inspired the traditional fleur-de-lis motif. Its clear yellow flowers open for 2–3 weeks in late spring; the leaves grow quite tall and look like cattails in summer. The plant grows best in shallow water and has naturalized in wetlands throughout the eastern United States, where it forms extensive patches, often mingling with the native blue flag, *I. versicolor*, which is shorter but looks similar and blooms at the same time. Both are wonderful beside garden ponds or streams but also grow well in ordinary beds. Gather the seedpods for dried arrangements.

How to grow: Full sun. Prefers rich, moist conditions but tolerates ordinary soil and watering, blooming well but not growing as tall. Easy from seed, or divide in fall. Trouble-free.

Iris versicolor

reticulata (p. 252)
Reticulated iris, violet-scented iris.
Perennial. Zone 3.
H: 3 in. (flowers); 12 in. (foliage). S: 2–3 in.

These irises grow from little bulbs that have a netlike (reticulated) covering. They are inexpensive, so plant lots of them close together. The short-stalked flowers open in early spring, along with crocuses, snowdrops, and hellebores. They smell delicious. Individual blossoms are fleeting, but a mass planting lasts a few weeks. The smooth 4-sided leaves elongate after the flowers fade, disappear by summer. 'Harmony' is dark sky blue with yellow spots on the falls; 'Cantab' is pale blue with orange spots; 'J. S. Dijt' is reddish purple. *I. danfordiae* is similar, with yellow flowers.

How to grow: Full sun. Ordinary soil and watering. Tolerates hot, dry summers. Plant bulbs 2–3 in. deep and 2–3 in. apart in fall. May be short lived, but they're easy to replace. Trouble-free.

sibirica (p. 252)
Siberian iris.
Perennial. Zone 4.
H: 2–3 ft. S: 2–3 ft.

Graceful but tough and easy to grow, these lovely irises can go untended and undivided for years. Their delicate flowers, in shades of purple, blue, or white, open after the tall bearded irises and before the Japanese irises. Selected cultivars have large flowers in outstanding colors, such as the snowy 'White Swirl' and the dark indigo 'Caesar's Brother'. The dark green leaves are narrow and grassy, with distinct midribs, and form an arching fountainlike clump. Old plants produce scores of flower stalks, each with several blooms, and the seedpods that follow are decorative in the garden or in dried arrangements. Siberian irises thrive in damp sites near water, but they tolerate ordinary soil and combine well with other perennials in a mixed border.

How to grow: Sun or part shade. Moist, fertile soil is best; tolerates ordinary soil and watering. Unnamed seedlings are usually more drought-tolerant than named cultivars are. The narrow rhizomes spread slowly in all directions, making a large clump that eventually gets a hole in the middle, like a doughnut. When this happens, dig in early fall, divide the clump into several chunks, and replant 2–3 ft. apart. May not bloom the first year after division. No pests or problems.

unguicularis
Winter iris.
Perennial. Zone 7.
H: 1–2 ft. S: 1–2 ft.

Flowers off and on for weeks on end, starting in December where winters are very mild and continuing through February. Plant it near a path where you'll pass it daily and enjoy the violet-blue (sometimes white) blossoms. Individual flowers poise on long stemlike tubes and make good cut flowers with a pleasant fragrance. The leaves are flat and grassy and tend to be floppy.

How to grow: Winter sun, summer shade. Not fussy about soil and watering. Spreads by rhizomes. Divide big clumps in fall; new plants may not bloom the first year. Subject to slugs and snails.

Xiphium hybrids (p. 252)
Dutch, Spanish, or English irises.
Perennials. Zone 6.
H: 18–24 in. S: to 12 in.

These hybrids have big bright flowers on tall erect stalks. There are many cultivars in a wide range of colors, including clear blues and yellows, orange, mauve, wine, and white. Excellent for cutting, they make showy mass plantings. Dutch irises bloom first, in late spring, with 3–4-in. flowers on stalks to 24 in. tall. Spanish irises bloom a little later, with smaller flowers. Both have leaves in winter that can be damaged by hard frosts, but neither minds hot, dry summers, when they go dormant. English irises start growing in spring, have 5-in. flowers in summer, and need rich, moist soil.

How to grow: Full sun. Best with fertile soil and regular watering during active growth. Plant bulbs 4–6 in. deep and 4 in. apart in fall. They multiply slowly. Use annuals such as sweet alyssum to fill the bare spots around the base of the stems in spring and summer. Plants may not be long lived but are inexpensive to replace.

Itea
It´ee-a.
Saxifragaceae. Saxifrage family.

Deciduous or evergreen shrubs with alternate simple leaves and small flowers. About 10 spp., native to eastern North America and eastern Asia.

virginica (p. 140)
Virginia sweetspire.
Deciduous shrub. Zone 5.
H: 3–5 ft. or more. S: 2–4 ft. or more.

A tough adaptable shrub, native to the eastern United States. Grows erect, branching near the top, with shiny leaves that are bright green in summer, rich scarlet in fall. Fragrant white flowers in upright clusters 2–6 in. long open in midsummer, after many shrubs are done. Grows well near ponds or streams with ornamental grasses and winterberry hollies. 'Henry's Garnet' grows 6–10 ft. tall and 8–12 ft. wide, has longer flowers, is slightly hardier, and holds its red-purple foliage well into winter.

How to grow: Full or part sun. Needs fertile soil amended with plenty of organic matter and constant moisture. Needs no special pruning or care.

Jacaranda
Jack-a-ran´da.
Bignoniaceae. Trumpet creeper family.

Deciduous or evergreen shrubs or trees, most with showy clusters of blue-violet flowers. About 30 spp., native to the American tropics.

mimosifolia (p. 116)
Jacaranda.
Deciduous or semievergreen tree. Zone 9.
H: to 40 ft. S: to 30 ft.

One of the very few blue-flowering trees, and the most spectacular. It bears large long-lasting clusters of tubular, flaring, 2-in. flowers in spring or summer. Fallen blossoms are attractive on the ground but can be slippery on paving. The fernlike compound leaves are delicate and cast a pleasant light shade. They drop briefly in spring, before flowering starts.

How to grow: Full sun. Ordinary soil and watering. Stake the main trunk and shorten side branches to produce a single-trunked tree.

Jasminum
Jas´mi-num. Jasmine.
Oleaceae. Olive family.

Deciduous or evergreen shrubs or vines with white, yellow, or pink flowers, often sweetly fragrant. About 450 spp., almost all native to the Old World tropics.

nudiflorum (p. 141)
Winter jasmine.
Deciduous shrub. Zone 6.
H: to 4 ft. S: to 8 ft.

Spreads and trails into a big mass of slender green branches that root where they touch the ground. Blooms off and on for several weeks, starting in late winter, with scentless bright yellow flowers about 1 in. wide. Later produces shiny green leaves with 3 small leaflets. Good for trailing down a bank but can also be trained to climb up a wall or fence. *J. mesnyi,* the primrose jasmine, is similar but less hardy (Zone 8), with larger, mildly fragrant flowers and leaves. The most fragrant jasmines are tender evergreen shrubs or vines. The shrubs are fairly compact, but the vines are quite rampant.

How to grow: Full or part sun. Not fussy about soil. Tolerates some drought but does better with ordinary watering. Roots and stems are cold-hardy, but flower buds can freeze. Prune after flowering to control size. Renew old plants by cutting to the ground.

Juniperus

Jew-nip′er-us. Juniper.
Cupressaceae. Cypress family.

Evergreen conifers, including low, spreading shrubs and upright trees. Leaves are needlelike or scalelike. Female cones are berrylike. Wood, foliage, and fruits are often very fragrant. About 50 spp., native to the Old and New World.

chinensis cultivars (p. 190)

(now *J.* × *media*)
Conifers. Zone 5 or 4.
H: varies. S: varies.

These cultivars are some of the toughest and most durable ground covers, shrubs, and specimens. Used extensively throughout the United States, they seem to thrive on neglect. The problem is that most grow faster than expected and soon outgrow their space, blocking sidewalks and entryways, shading windows, and overpowering adjacent plants. Most have needlelike juvenile foliage and scalelike adult foliage, often mixed on the same plant; the foliage has a pleasant sweet fragrance when crushed. Fruits are pea-sized blue balls. The following cultivars are especially common.

'Hetzii' is a fast grower that gets 10 ft. tall and 12 ft. or wider, with many trunks that reach out in all directions at a 45° angle. Its foliage is blue-green, often discoloring in winter. 'Mint Julep' is similar but has pretty dark green foliage year-round. 'Pfitzerana' branches at a lower angle. It usually gets about 6 ft. tall and 12 ft. wide. There are compact, gold, and blue forms of Pfitzer juniper. 'San Jose' juniper grows slowly and stays low, under 2 ft. tall and 6–8 ft. wide, with needlelike green foliage. 'Torulosa' or 'Kaizuka', commonly called Hollywood juniper, grows upright to 20 ft. or more, with irregular branching that makes an interesting asymmetric profile. It has dense, scalelike, bright green foliage.

How to grow: Full or part sun. Not fussy about soil fertility or pH. Tolerate drought but not poor drainage. Easy to transplant and need little care. Subject to bagworms and spider mites.

conferta (p. 190)

Shore juniper.
Conifer. Zone 6.
H: to 2 ft. S: to 8 ft.

Stays low and spreads wide, making a good evergreen ground cover for large areas. The leaves are fine, like needles, about 1/2 in. long, with a fairly soft texture. Color ranges from grayish to green to blue-green, depending on cultivar. 'Blue Pacific' has bright blue-gray foliage and usually stays under 1 ft. 'Emerald Sea' has pretty green foliage, spreads to 8 ft., and is hardier (Zone 5). These junipers can be used to cover rocky hillsides, trail over walls, or stabilize sandy coastal dunes.

How to grow: Like *J. chinensis*. Not damaged by salt.

davurica 'Expansa'

(*J. squamata* 'Parsoni')
Parson's juniper.
Conifer. Zone 4.
H: under 2 ft. S: to 8 ft.

Distinctly horizontal, with strong branches that spread above, not on, the ground. Makes a good ground cover and does especially well in the South. The profile is irregular, with tufts of gray-green foliage sticking out in all directions. 'Expansa Variegata' has creamy white variegation on the new growth.

How to grow: Like *J. chinensis*.

horizontalis cultivars (p. 191)

Creeping junipers.
Conifers. Zone 2.
H: under 2 ft. S: 4–6 ft. or more.

Widely used as evergreen ground covers, on rough banks, in foundation plantings, in front of shrubs or trees, or trailing over walls. There are hundreds of cultivars, varying in foliage texture (dense or loose, needlelike or scalelike), foliage color (bright green to blue in summer, turning purple or bronze in winter), and habit (ground-hugging or mounded). Some of the most common are 'Bar Harbor', with flat matted foliage, blue-gray in summer and blue-purple in winter; 'Blue Chip', mounding higher, with a good silver-blue color most of the year; 'Plumosa', with fluffy shoots that arch like a low fountain, greenish blue in summer and pinkish purple in winter; and 'Wiltonii' or 'Blue Rug', flat and trailing with silvery blue foliage.

How to grow: Full or part sun. Not fussy about soil but do best with good drainage. Native to Canada and the northern United States; quite hardy to cold but less tolerant of heat and humidity. Older plants sometimes get bald in the middle, and the only solution is to replace them. Subject to spider mites and juniper blight.

sabina cultivars (p. 191)

Savin junipers.
Conifers. Zone 3.
H: varies. S: varies.

These are spreading, not creeping, shrubs with branches that arch into soft mounds. Foliage is fine-textured, usually light to medium green in summer and yellowish green, not purplish, in winter. The crushed leaves smell unpleasant, unlike those of most junipers. Most cultivars grow too wide and too fast for foundation plantings, but they make good large-scale ground covers for banks or hillsides. 'Tamariscifolia' makes wide low mounds of blue-green foliage but is very susceptible to juniper blight. 'Arcadia', 'Broadmoor', 'Buffalo', and 'Scandia' are all bright green spreaders with good blight resistance.

How to grow: Full sun. Need well-drained soil and good air circulation; do well on open

Juniper chinensis 'Torulosa'

Juniperis horizontalis

hillsides. Tolerate drought but not humidity. Very cold-hardy.

scopulorum cultivars (p. 191)
Rocky Mountain junipers.
Conifers. Zone 4.
H: varies. S: varies.

Common and abundant throughout the Rocky Mountain region, where they grow as irregularly rounded trees, often in combination with ponderosa or pinyon pines. Selected cultivars vary in habit; most have dense foliage and make good specimens or screens. All do well throughout the Rockies and Great Plains. The blue or blue-green foliage holds its color in winter and has a very pleasing aroma when crushed. The blue raisinlike fruits take 2 years to develop. 'Blue Heaven', 'Gray Gleam', 'Pathfinder', and 'Wichita Blue' make upright pyramids of blue-green or blue-gray foliage. 'Table Top Blue' is rich silvery blue and spreads into a broad flat-topped mound. 'Blue Creeper' is a spreader that grows 2 ft. tall and 6–8 ft. wide, with bright blue color all year.

Other southwestern native junipers are tough trees for dry sunny climates. *J. flaccida,* or weeping juniper, has an erect trunk with elegant weeping branches and fine-textured blue-green foliage. It grows 20–30 ft. tall. *J. deppeana,* or alligator juniper, has rich blue foliage and checkered bark that resembles alligator hide. It grows 15–20 ft. tall.

How to grow: Full sun. Need well-drained soil. Tolerate alkaline soil and drought. Very tough plants for sunny, exposed sites. Can't take wet soils or high humidity.

squamata 'Blue Star' (p. 192)
Conifer. Zone 4.
H: 2–3 ft. S: 3–5 ft.

Unusual for its densely needled texture, irregular mounded shape, and bright blue color, this small shrub makes a colorful specimen in a foundation planting or mixed border. It has a distinctly sparkly appearance. 'Blue Carpet' has similar foliage but stays low and spreads as a ground cover.

How to grow: Like *J. chinensis.* Isn't vigorous or fast; stays in its place.

virginiana cultivars (p. 192)
Eastern red cedars.
Conifers. Zone 2.
H: to 30 ft. S: 10–20 ft.

Eastern red cedar grows wild on abandoned pastures and vacant land everywhere east of the Mississippi. It's common enough to be disdained by many gardeners, and wild trees often turn a drab brown color in winter. Nonetheless, it's a tough, adaptable tree that makes a fast screen and provides shelter and berries for birds. The fragrant reddish purple heartwood is used to make cedar chests. The rough-barked trunks are rot-resistant and can be shaped into rustic arbors or trellises or used as fence posts.

Young shoots are prickly; older branches have flat fans of scalelike foliage. The small silvery fruits develop in one year (that's the main difference between this species and *J. scopulorum*); they are sometimes abundant enough to give the tree a sparkly, frosted appearance. Selected cultivars have distinct shapes and better foliage color, summer and winter. 'Skyrocket' makes a skinny column of silvery blue. 'Canaert' is upright with spreading branches and stays rich green all year. 'Manhattan Blue' makes a dense pyramid of dark blue-green. 'Silver Spreader' makes a low fountain of silver-gray.

How to grow: Full or part sun. Not fussy about soil; tolerate acidic or alkaline, wet or dry sites. Respond to pruning better than most junipers do and can be sheared into formal shapes for hedges or specimens. Eastern red cedar is subject to bagworms, spider mites, and juniper blight and is the alternate host to a fungus called cedar apple rust. Rust outbreaks look like big blobs of orange jelly that last for a week or so in spring; later in summer the same fungus causes leafspots and defoliation on susceptible varieties of apples, crab apples, and quinces.

Kalmia
Kal′mee-a. Mountain laurel.
Ericaceae. Heath family.

Evergreen shrubs, hardy and ornamental, with leathery foliage and white, pink, or rosy flowers. All parts are poisonous. Only 7 spp., native to North America and Cuba.

Kalmia latifolia

latifolia (p. 176)
Mountain laurel.
Evergreen shrub. Zone 4.
H: usually under 10 ft. S: to 10 ft.

A hardy evergreen native to the eastern United States. Grows slowly. Young plants are compact mounds, older ones get tall (to 15 ft.) and open. The leathery leaves, 2–4 in. long, are dark green in summer, green-gold in winter. Rounded clusters of many cuplike flowers, 1 in. wide, cover the tips of the branches in June. Many new cultivars offer a range of flower colors from white and pale pink to dark pink and rosy red. Lovely as an understory to deciduous trees or combined with rhododendrons.

How to grow: Best in part shade. Needs acidic soil with plenty of organic matter and a layer of mulch. Ordinary watering. Remove flowers immediately after they fade. (Letting them go to seed reduces and sometimes prevents flowering the following year.) Subject to leafspots, scale, borers, and lace bugs.

Kerria

Ker'ree-a.
Rosaceae. Rose family.
A deciduous shrub with yellow flowers. Only 1 sp., native to eastern Asia.

Kerria japonica

japonica (p. 140)
Deciduous shrub. Zone 4.
H: to 6 ft. S: 6 ft. or more.

Easy to grow, with an upright arching habit. The slender stems are bright green in winter, a cheerful sight against the snow. Bright yellow flowers, 1¹/₂ in. wide, appear with the leaves in spring and continue sporadically throughout summer. Nice in combination with zebra grass (*Miscanthus sinensis* 'Zebrinus') and orange lilies. 'Pleniflora' has double flowers that are showier. 'Picta' has leaves edged with white and looks silvery from a distance.

How to grow: Best in part sun (flowers fade fast in full sun). Ordinary soil and watering. Prune after flowering to control shape and size. Remove old flowering shoots and any dead wood. Spreads by suckers; can be propagated by division. Slow to establish, then tough and carefree.

Kniphofia

Nip-ho'fee-a. Red-hot-poker, torch lily.
Liliaceae. Lily family.
Perennials with thick roots, tough grassy leaves, and showy spikes of bright red or yellow flowers. About 65 spp., native to Africa.

hybrids (p. 253)
Torch lilies.
Perennials. Zone 5.
H: 3 ft. (foliage); 6 ft. (blooms). S: 4 ft.

Grown for the dramatic spikes of glowing scarlet, orange-red, golden, or yellow flowers. Plants bloom in spring or summer. The 2-in.-long tubular flowers are very attractive to hummingbirds, and the spikes are spectacular and long lasting in cut arrangements. The basal foliage is a tangled mound of coarse, strongly keeled, gray-green leaves, 1 in. wide and up to 3 ft. long. Cultivars differ in flower color, bloom period, and height.

How to grow: Full or part sun. Ordinary soil and watering. Tolerate heat and dry soil. Remove old flower stalks after bloom, and trim foliage to the ground in late fall. Increase by division, taking care not to break too many of the thonglike roots. Trouble-free.

Koelreuteria

Kel-roo-teer'ee-a. Golden-rain tree.
Sapindaceae. Soapberry family.
Deciduous trees with pinnate leaves and big clusters of yellow flowers, followed by papery inflated pods. Only 3 spp., native to China and Taiwan.

paniculata (p. 117)
Golden-rain tree.
Deciduous tree. Zone 5.
H: 30–35 ft. S: 20–40 ft.

A tough tree with big (8–14 in.) clusters of small bright yellow flowers in midsummer, followed by pinkish beige inflated pods that resemble Japanese paper lanterns. The pods are interesting in dried arrangements and hang on into winter. Habit is spreading and open, with thick twigs and compound leaves. Useful as a shade tree for lawns and patios. The deep roots allow underplanting with perennials. *K. bipinnata*, the Chinese flame tree, is a larger, more formal-looking tree with larger leaves, larger flower clusters, and showy salmon-pink to red pods. It is less hardy (Zone 9).

How to grow: Full sun. Ordinary or unimproved soil; tolerates alkaline conditions. Needs watering when young but tolerates drought when established. Must be pruned to shape; branching tends to be haphazard. Sometimes self-seeds. No serious pests.

Kolkwitzia

Kolk-wit'zee-a. Beautybush.
Caprifoliaceae. Honeysuckle family.
A deciduous shrub with showy pink flowers in spring. Only 1 sp., native to China.

amabilis (p. 141)
Beautybush.
Deciduous shrub. Zone 5.
H: 10 ft. or more. S: 5–8 ft.

A large, upright, vase-shaped shrub that makes a magnificent show of bloom for about 3 weeks in spring or early summer. Borne in clusters at the branch ends, the flowers are bell-shaped, ¹/₂ in. long, with pink petals and yellow throats. Bristly pink fruits add interest for several more weeks. The simple opposite leaves are dull green with no fall color.

How to grow: Full sun. Ordinary soil and watering. Can be massed for a screen or barrier but tends to be leggy at the bottom. Prune older stems to the ground to force new growth. Removing lower limbs from a single specimen will make an umbrella shape. Thin after flowering. No serious pests.

Lagerstroemia indica

Lamium maculatum

Lagerstroemia
Lay-ger-stree′mee-a. Crape myrtle.
Lythraceae. Loosestrife family.

Deciduous or evergreen shrubs or trees with showy clusters of red, purple, or white flowers. About 55 spp., native to tropical Asia and Australia.

indica (p. 117)
Crape myrtle.
Deciduous tree or shrub. Zone 7.
H: to 25 ft. S: to 10 ft.

Popular and widely planted wherever it's hardy, crape myrtle has spectacular blooms from summer until frost. The small flowers in large clusters have a texture like crepe paper and come in many shades of pink, rosy red, purple, or white. Leaves are smooth ovals, 2–4 in. long, sometimes turning red, orange, or purplish in fall. Gray-tan outer bark flakes off the handsome muscular-looking trunks to reveal smooth mahogany inner bark. Cultivars vary in flower color and ultimate size; some are dwarfs only 3–5 ft. tall. Trees can be trained as single-trunked or multitrunked specimens. Dwarf shrubs add summer color to mixed hedges or borders. *L. fauriei,* with pretty bark but less-showy flowers, is hardier and quite resistant to powdery mildew. It has been crossed with *L. indica* to produce a series of new hybrid cultivars, recently released by the National Arboretum, that are notably healthy and hardy. Most have Native American names, such as 'Acoma', 'Hopi', and 'Sioux'; 'Natchez' has especially showy bark, pure white flowers, and good fall color.

How to grow: Full or part sun. Ordinary soil and watering. Thrives in hot weather and tolerates dry soil. Blooms on new growth; if shoots freeze back in a severe winter, it will recover the same year. Pruning and thinning can produce larger flower clusters but aren't necessary. It's better to plant a dwarf cultivar than to chop back a big tree each year. Remove suckers to expose and feature the trunks. Older cultivars were subject to powdery mildew and other foliar fungal diseases, but new ones are resistant. Aphids may infest new growth but don't cause serious or lasting damage.

Lamiastrum
Lay-me-ass′trum.
Labiatae. Mint family.

A creeping perennial with opposite leaves and yellow flowers. Only 1 sp., native from Europe to Iran.

galeobdolon 'Herman's Pride' (p. 253)
(*Lamium galeobdolon*)
Yellow archangel.
Perennial. Zone 6.
H: 1–2 ft. S: invasive.

A popular ground cover with silvery foliage that brightens a shady corner. Stems are erect but slender enough to flop over. Spreads by runners and quickly fills an area; too invasive to include in a mixed planting. Spikes of short tubular flowers, bright yellow with brown marks, appear in early summer. Looks good under dark green conifers or broad-leaved evergreens and can hold its own in competition with their roots. 'Variegata' is similar but has more green on the leaves.

How to grow: Part or full shade. Prefers fertile soil amended with plenty of organic matter and constant moisture but grows fine (and doesn't spread as fast) under ordinary garden conditions. Space 12–18 in. apart. Can't take extreme summer heat. Cut back whenever it gets shabby or spreads out of bounds. Problem-free.

Lamium
Lay′mee-um. Dead nettle.
Labiatae. Mint family.

Low-growing, creeping, and spreading annuals or perennials with 4-sided stems, opposite leaves, and small 2-lipped flowers. Many species are weedy. About 40 spp., native to northern Africa and Eurasia.

maculatum (p. 253)
Spotted dead nettle.
Perennial. Zone 4.
H: 12 in. S: 18 in.

Tolerant, adaptable, and fast-growing, this is an inexpensive but worthwhile ground cover. It doesn't spread as aggressively as *Lamiastrum.* The silver-leaved forms are prettiest. The toothed leaves are heart-shaped or oval, to 2 in. long, on upright or trailing stems. Foliage is evergreen where winters are mild. Short spikes of 1-in. tubular flowers appear from spring through summer. 'Beacon Silver' has green-edged silvery leaves and pink flowers; 'White Nancy' has similar leaves and white flowers.

How to grow: Full or part sun. Best in fertile soil with constant moisture; can't take dry soil or extreme heat. Space 8–12 in. apart. Divide in spring or fall. Shear if it gets shabby in midsummer; new growth will soon develop. Problem-free.

Lantana
Lan-ta′na.
Verbenaceae. Verbena family.

Perennials or shrubs, often with prickly stems and rough leaves, that bear rounded clusters of small bright flowers and black berries. About 150 spp., most native to tropical America.

camara (p. 176)
Common lantana.
Semievergreen shrub. Zone 8 or 7.
H: 2–4 ft. S: 2–6 ft.

A low shrub that spreads into a wide mound, hardy in mild climates and sometimes used as a bedding plant where winters are cold. It also grows well in containers—anything from patio half-barrels to hanging baskets. It blooms from late spring to frost, with 1–2-in. round clusters of papery-textured 4-lobed flowers in shades of creamy white, yellow, gold, pink, orange, or red. Individual flowers are often two-tone, and the flowers within a cluster frequently shade from one color to another, such as yellow to pink. The effect is bright and cheerful. The dark green leaves feel scratchy and smell pungent; they drop off when temperatures fall below freezing.

L. montevidensis, or trailing lantana, has sprawling stems and lavender blossoms. It trails from planter boxes or makes a good ground cover, and it's somewhat more cold-hardy than common lantana. Most lantana cultivars are hybrids between the two species.

How to grow: Full sun. Not fussy about soil. Tolerates dryness and heat (has naturalized and grows wild in Texas). Tolerates salt along the coasts. Freezes back in cold winters but recovers from the base; prune off damaged wood in spring. Prune to shape as desired. Subject to aphids, spider mites, and whiteflies.

Larix

Lar´icks. Larch.
Pinaceae. Pine family.
Tall trees with spreading limbs. Unlike most conifers, larches are deciduous and drop their needles in fall. Only 9 spp., native to cool climates in the Northern Hemisphere.

kaempferi (p. 192)
Japanese larch.
Deciduous conifer. Zone 4.
H: 75 ft. S: 40 ft.

Grows fairly quickly into a large conical tree with spreading limbs and droopy branchlets. The pincushion-like clusters of 1-in. needles are particularly appealing in spring, when they are fresh and tender. Bright green all summer, they turn clear gold before dropping in late fall. Small woody cones are conspicuous on the bare twigs in winter. Makes a distinctive specimen but needs plenty of space. *L. decidua* is a similar species from northern Europe.

How to grow: Full sun. Needs well-drained but moist soil; tolerates acidic but not alkaline conditions. Can't take heat or drought, and is subject to various pests and diseases, especially if stressed.

Lathyrus

La´thi-russ.
Leguminosae. Pea family.
Annuals or perennials with winged stems, pinnately compound leaves, and showy flowers. Many are vines that climb by tendrils. About 150 spp., most native to temperate climates in the Old and New World.

odoratus (p. 298)
Sweet pea.
Annual. All zones.
H: to 6 ft. S: 6–12 in.

An old-fashioned favorite, beloved for the penetrating sweetness of its lovely flowers, which have wavy or frilled petals in clear shades of red, pink, purple, or white. They make excellent cut flowers. The vines grow quickly, climbing up sticks, strings, trellises, or fences or clambering over shrubs. Dwarf varieties stand alone without support. Not all kinds are fragrant; be sure the catalog description or seed packet indicates sweetness. Annual sweet peas do best in cool weather and wither in hot summers. *L. latifolius,* the perennial sweet pea, blooms all summer (year after year) in shades of purplish pink or white but is scentless. Warn children that sweet peas are not like garden peas, and their seeds are not edible.

How to grow: Full sun or afternoon shade. Needs fertile soil amended with plenty of organic matter and constant moisture. Plant seeds in fall where winters are very mild, or in early spring as soon as the soil can be worked. Thin seedlings 6–8 in. apart. Pick flowers regularly to prolong bloom.

Laurus

Law´rus. Laurel.
Lauraceae. Laurel family.
Evergreen trees with aromatic leaves, long used as a flavoring. Garlands or crowns of laurel leaves symbolized honorable achievement in ancient Greece; now we speak of "resting on one's laurels." Only 2 spp., native to the Mediterranean region and adjacent Atlantic islands.

nobilis (p. 283)
Sweet bay.
Evergreen tree or shrub used as an herb. Zone 8.
H: 10–40 ft. S: 10–30 ft.

A dense evergreen that can be an impenetrable screen or a carefully shaped specimen. The pointed oval leaves are stiff, leathery, dark green, and pleasantly fragrant when crushed. They are used in soups, stews, and sauces. Tight clusters of small greenish yellow flowers are inconspicuous in early spring, but shiny black fruits are sometimes noticed in fall. 'Saratoga', which may be a hybrid between *L. nobilis* and *L. azorica,* has rounder leaves with a milder aroma and is immune to psyllids. *Umbellularia californica,* or California laurel, is a huge, slow-growing, evergreen tree. Its leaves look like those of sweet bay but have a sharper, stronger aroma.

How to grow: Full sun or afternoon shade. Ordinary soil and watering; tolerates dry spells when established. Space 3–4 ft. apart for a hedge. Shape with pruning shears, not hedge shears, to avoid mutilating the foliage. Can be trained into lollipop standards or formal cones, balls, or pyramids. Use horticultural oil spray to control scale and psyllids.

Lantana montevidensis

Lavandula angustifolia

Leptospermum laevigatum

Lavandula
La-van′dew-la. Lavender.
Labiatae. Mint family.

Perennials or shrubs, mostly evergreen in mild climates, with very fragrant foliage and flowers. About 20 spp., native to the Mediterranean region and surrounding areas.

angustifolia (p. 283)
(*L. officinalis, L. vera*)
English lavender, common lavender.
Evergreen subshrub, considered an herb. Zone 5.
H: 1–2 ft. S: 2–3 ft.

Prized for the legendary fragrance of its small lavender-purple flowers, which form crowded spikes on slender stalks in early summer. The habit is bushy, with many erect stems. The closely spaced leaves are stiff and slender, 1–2 in. long, with a fuzzy gray surface. Makes a soft low hedge or can be massed with other drought-tolerant shrubs to fill a dry sunny slope. Evergreen only in mild climates; it discolors and freezes back where winters are cold. Herb nurseries offer many cultivars. 'Hidcote' has dark purple flowers, 'Jean Davis' has pale pink, and 'Munstead' has lavender-blue. *L. × intermedia,* often called lavandin, is a hardy, vigorous, hybrid lavender. It flowers later than English lavender and has the sweetest, most intense fragrance.

Several other lavenders delight gardeners in mild climates. *L. stoechas,* or Spanish lavender, has a jaunty topknot of dark purple bracts atop broad compact flower spikes. It makes a compact mound of slender gray leaves with a pleasant fragrance and is hardy in Zone 8 and worth trying in Zone 7. *L. dentata,* or French lavender, has soft, gray-green, saw-toothed leaves that feel sticky and smell resinous. It's hardy only to Zone 9, where it blooms almost year-round.

How to grow: Best in full sun. Ordinary, sandy, or alkaline soil. Needs good drainage and tolerates drought when established. Where the soil is heavy, plant "high" by positioning the crown above the surrounding grade so that water will run away from the plant. In cold areas, prune back frozen shoots in late spring and remove old stalks as flowers fade. Don't prune after midsummer, or soft new shoots will be killed in winter. In mild regions, prune as desired. Can be cut back hard to renew leggy, untidy plants. Pest-free.

Lavatera
La-va-tee′ra.
Malvaceae. Mallow family.

Annuals, perennials, or soft-stemmed shrubs with showy flowers, very similar to the closely related genus *Malva*. About 25 spp., most native to the Mediterranean region.

trimestris (p. 298)
Tree mallow.
Annual. All zones.
H: 2–4 ft. S: 2 ft.

Grows fast and branches by itself into a shrubby mound of maplelike leaves and hollyhock-like flowers. Adds height to a planting of annuals and blooms from midsummer to frost. Flowers are 3–4 in. wide and white, pale to bright pink, or rosy pink; cut whole stalks to use as cut flowers.

How to grow: Full sun. Ordinary or improved soil and regular watering. Takes heat but not high humidity. Sow indoors 6 weeks before last frost, or sow directly where they are to bloom; space 2 ft. apart. Doesn't require constant pinching or deadheading. May self-sow. Japanese beetles are attracted to the flowers.

Leptospermum
Lep-to-sper′mum. Tea tree.
Myrtaceae. Myrtle family.

Evergreen shrubs or small trees, most with small or slender leaves. The foliage of some species is used medicinally or in herbal teas. About 30 spp., most native to Australia.

laevigatum (p. 161)
Australian tea tree.
Evergreen shrub or tree. Zone 9.
H: to 30 ft. S: to 30 ft.

If planted close together and sheared, this makes a dense gray-green hedge with stiff, leathery, oval leaves and round white flowers scattered along the branches in spring. Given more space and allowed to grow, it makes a picturesque sprawling tree with a massive twisted trunk, contorted limbs, and drooping branches. 'Compactum' is smaller, to 8 ft. 'Reevesii' is smaller yet, 4–5 ft., with broader leaves.

How to grow: Full or part sun. Tolerates sandy or rocky soil but not clay. Thrives in ocean wind. Tolerates dry spells when established, but don't let it go bone-dry. Plant 18 in. to 6 ft. apart and shear to make a dense hedge, but don't cut back into old wood. Pest-free.

scoparium (p. 177)
New Zealand tea tree.
Evergreen shrub. Zone 9.
H: 6–10 ft. or more. S: 4–6 ft.

A fine-textured evergreen shrub with small, tough, needlelike leaves. Single or double white, pink, or red flowers 1/2 in. wide are crowded along the branches over a long season in spring and summer. Makes an exuberant display of bloom. Good as a single specimen and in a mixed border, or can be trained as a single-stemmed standard in the ground or in a container. 'Pink Cascade' has a trailing habit, 1 ft. tall and 4–6 ft. wide, and pink flowers. 'Pink Pearl' is upright, 6–10 ft., with pink buds opening to double pink-and-white flowers. 'Ruby Glow' is compact and upright, 6–8 ft., with dark foliage and double dark red flowers. 'Snow White' is compact and spreading, 2–4 ft., with double white flowers.

How to grow: Full sun. Takes ordinary soil and watering, but good drainage is essential; succumbs to root rot in soggy soil. Pinch tips of young plants to encourage dense growth. Shear mature plants to shape. Don't prune back to bare wood. Pest-free.

Lespedeza
Les-pe-dee´za. Bush clover.
Leguminosae. Pea family.

Perennials or small shrubs with 3-part leaves and clusters of small pealike blossoms. About 40 spp., native to the Old and New World.

thunbergii (p. 141)
Bush clover.
Woody-based perennial. Zone 5.
H: 6–8 ft. S: 4–6 ft.

Attractive in late summer, when it bears long drooping clusters of pealike rosy purple blossoms that attract butterflies. Usually dies to the ground each winter but flowers on new wood. Stems shoot upright, then arch over in all directions like a fountain, pulled down by the weight of the flowers. The trifoliate leaves have slender 2-in. leaflets covered with silvery hairs. In addition to its ornamental appeal, this is a good plant for stabilizing and improving poor soil (as a legume, it fixes nitrogen) and is often planted along road cuts or on disturbed sites, where it thrives with no care. Combines well with pink and purple asters in fall. 'Alba' has clear white flowers that brighten any garden.

How to grow: Full sun. Tolerates poor and dry soil. Even if shoots survive the winter, it looks best if you prune it to the ground in spring. Easily raised from seed. Pest-free.

Leucojum
Loo-ko´jum. Snowflake.
Amaryllidaccae. Amaryllis family.

Small perennials with little bulbs, grassy leaves, and nodding flowers in early spring. Only 9 spp., native from Europe to the Middle East.

aestivum (p. 253)
Summer snowflake.
Bulbous perennial. Zone 4.
H: 12–18 in. S: 8 in.

Easy to grow and cheerful. Each bulb makes several shiny straplike leaves and a stalk topped with 2–8 white bell-shaped flowers, 1 in. wide. Blooms in midspring, with the daffodils. 'Gravetye Giant' has larger flowers on 18-in. stalks. *L. vernum,* or spring snowflake, blooms earlier, with 1–2 flowers on 12-in. stalks. The plants are tall but the flowers are small, so don't skimp when planting. Mass them on the edge of a woods or under deciduous trees or shrubs.

How to grow: Full or part sun. Prefers rich, moist soil. Plant bulbs in fall in large drifts, setting them 3–5 in. deep and 4 in. apart. Wait several years before dividing.

Leucophyllum
Loo-ko-fill´um.
Scrophulariaccac. Foxglovc family.

Small shrubs with silvery foliage and rosy to purplish 5-petaled flowers. Native to dry, sunny sites in Texas and Mexico.

frutescens (p. 177)
Texas sage, purple sage, ceniza.
Evergreen shrub. Zone 8.
H: 6–8 ft. S: 4–6 ft.

Makes a bushy mound that branches readily if pruned, with silver-gray, densely hairy, oval leaves clustered at the tips of the branches. Bell-shaped flowers, to 1 in. wide, appear in flushes, usually just after a rain. Easy and attractive. There are several cultivars and hybrids, offering white flowers, green foliage, or a compact habit. *L. candidum* is shorter and bushy (2–3 ft. tall), with lots of rich violet-purple flowers.

How to grow: Full sun. Needs well-drained soil; subject to root rot on wet sites. Tolerates alkaline conditions. Native to the hot, dry regions of west Texas, this shrub thrives in the summer sun and needs little care. Doesn't do well in cool or humid conditions.

Leucothoe
Loo-ko´tho-ee. Fetterbush.
Ericaceae. Heath family.

Evergreen (and a few deciduous) shrubs with simple alternate leaves and clusters of small pink or white bell-shaped flowers. More than 40 spp., native to North and South America and eastern Asia.

axillaris (p. 177)
Coast leucothoe.
Evergreen shrub. Zone 5.
H: 2–4 ft. S: 3–5 ft.

A very hardy and graceful evergreen shrub, with glossy leathery leaves, 1–3 in. long, dark green in summer and purplish bronze in winter. Branches arch into a spreading mound and tend to zigzag at the tip ends. Fragrant small white flowers form racemes 1–2¹/₂ in. long in the leaf axils in April or May. More compact than drooping leucothoe, so it fits better in small gardens. Good for foundation plantings.

How to grow: Part sun or shade. Needs fertile organic soil and constant moisture. Prefers acidic conditions; combines well with azaleas or rhododendrons. Prune after flowering. Not plagued by leafspot diseases.

fontanesiana (p. 177)
Drooping leucothoe.
Evergreen shrub. Zone 4.
H: 3–6 ft. S: 3–6 ft.

A hardy evergreen with lustrous leaves, 2–5 in. long, dark green in summer and purplish in winter. Arching stems bend gracefully under the weight of the fragrant white flowers, borne in dangling 3-in. clusters in spring. Good along the north or east wall of a building or planted under

Leucophyllum frutescens

Leucothoe axillaris

Leucothoe fontanesiana

tall deciduous trees. 'Rainbow' has leaves variegated with cream, yellow, pink, and copper but is often disfigured by fungal infections.

Though native to the Southeast, drooping leucothoe can't take much heat and fails in drought. *Agarista populifolia,* formerly identified as *L. populifolia,* is a superior plant for southern gardens. It's larger (16 ft. tall and 10 ft. wide), with small, narrow, bright green leaves and small white flowers with a honeylike fragrance. Tolerates sun and heat.

How to grow: Like *L. axillaris,* but it's more susceptible to leafspot diseases. Renew old plants by cutting some of the stems to the ground after they flower.

Levisticum

Le-vis´ti-kum. Lovage.
Umbelliferae. Carrot family.

A robust perennial herb with fragrant seeds, foliage, and roots. Only 1 sp., native to southern Europe.

officinale (p. 283)
Lovage.
Perennial herb. Zone 3.
H: 4–6 ft. S: 3–4 ft.

A handsome plant for the back of the border, with glossy thrice-compound leaves on long hollow stalks. Big umbels of greenish yellow flowers top the stalks in June, followed by decorative seed heads. The fresh or dried leaves taste like strong celery or parsley and are used in soups, stuffings, and salads. The ground seeds are tasty in cakes or breads.

How to grow: Full or part sun. Does best in rich, moist soil. Sow freshly gathered seeds in fall. Goes on for years with no special care. Can be moved or divided in spring. You'll be surprised at how big the roots are, and how good they smell.

Liatris

Lie-ay´tris.
Compositae. Daisy family.

Perennials with a basal tuft of slender leaves and tall stalks topped with spikes of small fluffy flowers, usually rosy purple. About 34 spp., native to North America.

spicata (p. 253)
Blazing-star, spike gay-feather.
Perennial. Zone 4.
H: 3–4 ft. S: 2 ft.

Popular as a long-lasting cut flower, blazing-star also provides midsummer color in a sunny border and attracts many butterflies. It looks like a tuft of shiny grass in spring, then sends up several tall leafy stalks topped with hot-dog-sized spikes of little mauve flowers. The flowers open over a period of weeks, starting at the top of the spike and working down. The species gets tall and floppy in fertile, moist soil; the cultivar 'Kobold' ('Gnome') stays under 30 in. tall and

holds itself up. 'Floristan White' has creamy white flowers, and 'Floristan Violet' is purple; both grow about 3 ft. tall. *L. spicata* is native to the eastern states.

L. pycnostachya grows wild on moist sites in the Great Plains. It's very showy in midsummer, with lilac to purple flowers in spikes up to 2 ft. long on stalks up to 4 1/2 ft. tall, but it's too big and usually too floppy for most gardens. *L. punctata* grows in the dry western states and is more compact (1 1/2–2 ft. tall). A single 5-year-old plant may produce 25 spikes of reddish purple flowers for 2–3 weeks in September.

How to grow: Full sun. Ordinary, well-drained soil. Tolerates heat and dryness. Continues for years with no special care. Divide in spring by breaking or cutting apart the crown of corms; replant divisions with at least 1 eye.

Ligustrum

Li-gus´trum. Privet.
Oleaceae. Olive family.

Deciduous or evergreen shrubs or trees with opposite leaves, clusters of small white 4-parted flowers, and black berries. The flowers have a definite strong fragrance that some people enjoy and others find offensive. Most privets have roots too dense and shallow to permit underplanting. About 50 spp., native to the Old World.

japonicum (p. 177)
Wax-leaf ligustrum, Japanese ligustrum.
Evergreen shrub or small tree. Zone 8 or 7.
H: 10–15 ft. S: 6–12 ft.

Fast-growing and tough, wax-leaf ligustrum is commonly used for hedges and foundation plantings, where it tolerates—and often needs—frequent pruning. Its smooth-edged leaves are very glossy or waxy, dark green, 2–4 in. long. Clusters of small white flowers form at the tips of new shoots in May or June, followed by blue-black berries that weigh down the branches. Excellent for fast, dense screening. Good for formal specimens at the corners of a building. Don't plant it under windows, or you'll never get a rest from pruning. 'Coriaceum' or 'Rotundifolium' grows more slowly, to 4–6 ft., and has stiffly upright stems crowded with thick rounded leaves. 'Silver Star' has leaves with creamy white edges. 'Texanum' is sometimes listed as a separate species but in fact is just wax-leaf ligustrum propagated from plants that have naturalized in Texas (birds spread the seeds around).

How to grow: Full or part sun. Grows in poor soil but does need good drainage. Tolerates heat, dry spells, and sea salt. Easily transplanted and established. Space 5–10 ft. apart for a screen. No serious pests.

lucidum (p. 161)
Glossy privet.
Evergreen shrub or small tree. Zone 8 or 7.
H: to 30 ft. or more. S: 15–20 ft.

Similar to wax-leaf ligustrum but grows larger, often reaching tree size, and has a looser,

Liatris spicata

more open habit and glossy dark green leaves 4–6 in. long; the flower clusters are also larger and looser. Responds well to pruning and can be used for medium-height hedges; also makes a fine single-trunked or multitrunked tree or a tall screen or windbreak.

How to grow: Like *L. japonicum*.

obtusifolium var. regelianum (p. 142)
Regel's border privet.
Deciduous shrub. Zone 3.
H: 5–6 ft. S: 6–8 ft.

Perhaps the most interesting and attractive privet for northern gardens, with leafy shoots that branch at right angles and look as though they've been pressed flat between the pages of a book. Limbs spread wide and stack in horizontal layers. Small clusters of starry white flowers tip each side shoot in early June. Black berries ripen in fall and hang on into winter. Use for hedges or as a specimen. So tough that it's planted along highways.

How to grow: Full or part sun. Tolerates poor, dry soil. Easy to establish. Prune anytime. Generally problem-free.

sinense 'Variegatum' (p. 142)
Chinese privet.
Deciduous shrub. Zone 7.
H: 6 ft. or more. S: 6 ft. or more.

A medium to large shrub with oval green leaves bordered in white and sprays of white flowers in early summer. Foliage hangs on late into fall. Tough and adaptable, it adds summer interest to a mixed hedge of spring-blooming shrubs and is good for brightening dark corners.

How to grow: Sun or shade. Not fussy about soil. Prune anytime. Remove suckers and seedlings that revert to the all-green form. Bird-sown plants are a common weed in the South.

vulgare
Common privet.
Deciduous shrub. Zone 4.
H: to 15 ft. S: to 20 ft.

Common indeed but tough and versatile, privet makes a fast hedge, screen, or windbreak. The smooth leaves, 1–3 in. long, are dark green in summer, turning purplish green and holding late into fall. Small dense clusters of white flowers top the branches in June. Dark blue berries last from fall to spring. 'Cheyenne' stops at about 6 ft. and is easier to maintain as a hedge. 'Lodense' is a compact dwarf, 3–4 ft. tall and wide, good for low hedges or massing in sun or shade. *L.* × *vicaryi*, the hybrid golden vicary privet, is like common privet but develops bright golden foliage if grown in full sun.

How to grow: Full sun, part sun, or shade. Not fussy about soil but tolerates moist conditions better than drought. Space 1–2 ft. apart for a dense hedge, 3–4 ft. apart for an informal screen. Prune hedges wider at the bottom than on top. Subject to powdery mildew and other foliar fungal diseases, especially in shaded or sheltered sites.

Lilium
Lil′ee-um. Lily.
Liliaceae. Lily family.

Lilies are perennial plants with scaly bulbs and leafy, upright, unbranched stalks. The showy flowers have 6 petals and sepals that all look similar; technically these should be called tepals, but gardeners call them all petals. There are about 100 spp., nearly all native to the north temperate zone. Many of the species can be grown in gardens; however, in recent decades breeders have produced a wonderful assortment of hybrid lilies with excellent color, fragrance, form, and vigor. The hybrids are generally more adaptable and easier to grow, and often more rewarding, than the species.

Lily flowers are big—up to several inches wide. They come in bright and pastel shades of red, orange, pink, salmon, peach, gold, yellow, or white; some are decorated with darker spots or freckles or raised bumps called papillae. Some are scentless, but others are intensely fragrant, with a penetrating sweetness that fills the entire garden. All lilies make excellent cut flowers. Most bloom in summer. The hybrids are described as early, midseason, or late, which roughly corresponds to June, July, and August.

Lily plants range in height from 1 ft. to 8 ft. The stems look silly when they first emerge in spring, with tufts of leaves crowded together like a topknot. As the stems elongate, the glossy bladelike leaves get spaced out into scattered or whorled arrangements. Lilies don't have much foliage in proportion to the flowers. When cutting them for arrangements, leave behind as much of the leafy stem as possible, to renew the bulb and sustain the plant.

With so many options in stem height, flower color, and season of bloom, you can choose lilies to combine with any of your other favorite perennials in mixed beds or borders. Or you can devote a special bed to lilies and underplant with a low ground cover such as ajuga, dwarf plumbago, or sweet woodruff. Lilies grow particularly well in containers, where it's easy to provide ideal soil and watering. If you plant different pots or tubs with early, midseason, and late varieties, you can have flowers on the patio all summer.

How to grow: Most lilies are fully hardy in Zone 4 or 5; in fact, they need at least 4–6 weeks of cold weather to rest and form new flower buds. Lilies also tolerate summer heat if given thick mulch, regular deep watering, and afternoon shade.

Lilies grow best in full sun or afternoon shade. Too much shade makes lily stems stretch for the light, and they get too weak to hold up their flowers. (Tall varieties often need staking anyway.) The soil must be well drained, never waterlogged. Sloping sites or raised beds are ideal. Dig deep and amend the soil with a generous dose of compost or peat moss. In containers, use top-quality peat-based potting soil. Top-dress established plantings with more compost or rotted manure each fall. To keep the soil

Lilium canadense

Lilium candidum

Species lilies (pp. 254, 255)

In addition to the hybrids, several species lilies are excellent plants for the perennial border. The following are most widely available and easiest to grow.

L. auratum, the gold-band lily, has fragrant white flowers 6–10 in. wide with crimson spots and a gold stripe down the center of each petal. Blooms July or August. Var. *platyphyllum* gets taller, with larger flowers. Zone 5.

L. canadense, the meadow lily, has whorled leaves on 2–5-ft. stems and drooping bell-shaped flowers in yellow, orange, or red. Var. *flavum* has soft yellow flowers with brown spots. Prefers part shade and moist soil. Zone 4.

L. candidum, the Madonna lily, has been cherished since biblical times for its fragrant pure white flowers. Blooms in June or early July. Unlike most lilies, it should be planted just below the soil surface. It makes an evergreen rosette of broad basal leaves in fall and has small pointed leaves on the flowering stems that develop quickly in early summer. Tolerates alkaline soil and summer heat better than most lilies do. Zone 4.

L. lancifolium (formerly *L. tigrinum*), the tiger lily, has been cultivated for centuries in China and is an old favorite in American gardens. It's a vigorous plant that grows 4–6 ft. tall and has drooping orange flowers with purple dots in midsummer. (There are also hybrid tiger lilies with red, orange, yellow, or white flowers, all with dark dots.) It is sterile and doesn't set seed, but it produces shiny black bulbils in the leaf axils; these grow quickly into new plants. Although they don't show the symptoms, tiger lilies often carry the mosaic virus and can infect other plants, so lily enthusiasts prefer to keep tiger lilies out of their gardens. Zone 4.

L. longiflorum, the Easter lily, has fragrant white flowers shaped like trumpets and held horizontally on 2–3-ft. stems. Greenhouse-forced plants can be planted outdoors after danger of frost is past; once established, they usually flower in June. Zone 7.

L. regale, the regal lily, has highly fragrant trumpet-shaped flowers that are pink-purple outside and white inside with yellow throats. (There's also a pure white form.) Holds its flowers like a crown on 5–6-ft. stalks. Zone 4.

L. speciosum is a parent of the Oriental hybrids and has flat, nodding, fragrant flowers in late season. Most common are the 'Rubrum' types with white or pale to bright pink flowers dotted with red bumps. Grows 3–5 ft. tall. Zone 5.

L. superbum, the Turk's-cap lily, is native to damp sites in the eastern United States and sometimes grows as a roadside wildflower, blooming in July or August. It has whorled leaves on 5–8-ft. stems topped with nodding red-orange flowers. The petals are strongly recurved and are dotted with many dark spots. Tolerates part shade and prefers moist soil. *L. pardalinum,* the leopard lily, is similar but grows along the Pacific coast and doesn't need extra moisture. Both Zone 5.

cool in summer, use a thick layer of organic mulch or underplant with low ground covers or spreading annuals such as sweet alyssum or lobelias.

Lily bulbs are made of many plump curved scales, with no outer covering. They never go completely dormant, and they must not be allowed to dry out. Mail-order specialists usually ship the bulbs in late fall (sometimes in spring), packed in damp peat moss and wrapped in plastic. Plant them as soon as possible after they arrive. If you must delay planting, store the bulbs in the refrigerator or a cool but not freezing garage or basement. The bagged bulbs sold at garden centers are often weakened by storage in warm, dry conditions and don't grow as well as freshly dug or refrigerated bulbs. If you want to shop locally, look for healthy container-grown lilies, which can be planted anytime from spring to fall.

The stem grows right up through the middle of the bulb, and many lilies, including most of the hybrids, produce roots along the base of the stem as well as underneath the bulb. For this reason—and also to help stabilize the often top-heavy stalk—lily bulbs should be planted two to three times as deep as their diameter. (*L. candidum* is an exception to this rule—it should be covered with just an inch of soil.) Space the bulbs about 12 in. apart, and plant groups of 3 or 5 for the best show. Lilies multiply slowly. After 3–5 years, if a clump becomes crowded, the bulbs can be dug, divided, and replanted. This is best done in fall, after the leaves have turned yellow or brown.

Lilies have few insect pests, although aphids sometimes attack the buds. Much more serious is a mosaic virus that the aphids spread. It causes yellow streaks or mottling on the leaves, disfigures the buds and flowers, and weakens the plants. (The same virus also infects tulips, causing streaked or mottled blooms.) There is no cure for this virus. Remove and destroy any plants that show symptoms. Various fungal diseases attack lily leaves and bulbs under conditions of wet soil or high temperatures and humidity; these diseases are more easily prevented (by planting in raised beds and spacing the plants far enough apart to allow good air circulation) than cured. Mice, voles, chipmunks, and gophers eat lily bulbs. Planting in wire mesh cages or buried pots offers some protection. Rabbits, deer, and slugs eat the leaves, buds, and flowers. Use fencing, barriers, or deterrents.

Asiatic hybrids (p. 254)
Perennials. Zone 4.
H: usually 3–4 ft. but can be 2–6 ft. S: 1 ft.

This is the biggest group of hybrids and includes genes from about 20 Asian species that have been crossed repeatedly. The flowers are typically 4–6 in. wide and face up, out, or down. Colors include white, yellow, orange, pink, lavender, and red. Most are not fragrant. These hybrids begin the lily season, blooming from late May through June. They are easy to grow and multiply quickly. Specialists offer hundreds of cultivars, and more are introduced each year. 'Connecticut King' has upward-facing flowers on 3-ft. stems, in a glowing shade of golden yellow with no spots. 'Enchantment' has upward-facing flowers on 3-ft. stems, orange-red with many small black spots. 'Tiger Babies' is especially vigorous and makes dozens of downward-facing flowers on 3-ft. stems, chocolate-pink outside and salmon-peach with dark spots inside.

How to grow: See main entry.

Aurelian hybrids (p. 255)
Perennials. Zone 4.
H: usually 4–6 ft.; some to 8 ft. S: 18 in.

These midseason lilies are usually very fragrant, with flowers 6–8 in. long in shades of white, yellow, gold, orange, or pink, sometimes with contrasting throats or stripes. The flowers are often trumpet-shaped, and this group is sometimes called the trumpet hybrids, but some have "sunburst" flowers that open wider with recurved petals. 'Black Dragon' is an old but prizewinning cultivar, reaching 8 ft. tall, with huge flowers that are white shading to yellow inside and maroon or chocolate-brown outside. An established clump makes a dramatic specimen—each towering stem holds a candelabra of pendant flowers. 'Pink Perfection' has fragrant deep pink flowers on 6-ft. stems. 'Golden Splendor' (gold inside with maroon on the back), 'Thunderbolt' (melon-orange), and 'White Henryi' (white with golden orange throat) are more favorites.

How to grow: See main entry.

martagon hybrids (p. 255)
Perennials. Zone 3.
H: 3–6 ft. S: 1 ft.

This is a smaller group of hybrids, developed from the Eurasian species *L. martagon*. The plants have whorled leaves and nodding flowers with curled-back petals. Most bloom in June. *L. martagon* itself has purple-pink flowers with a few dark spots. Var. *album* has waxy white spotless flowers. 'Mrs. R. O. Backhouse', a hybrid, has orange-yellow flowers flushed with rosy pink. The Paisley hybrids have martagon-type flowers in shades of yellow-orange with small maroon spots.

How to grow: Part shade; this group tolerates more shade than other lilies do. Well-drained soil with added lime and regular watering. Will continue for decades in the same spot once established. Plants are slow to get going, however, and may not even send up a stem the first year after planting.

Oriental hybrids (p. 255)
Perennials. Zone 5.
H: usually 3–6 ft.; some shorter. S: 12–18 in.

The last lilies to flower in late summer, these generally have flat flowers, 6–8 in. or more wide, with recurved petals. Most face out or down, but some new Oriental hybrids have upward-facing flowers. Almost all are fragrant, some extremely so. Colors include white, many shades of pink, and red; often with yellow stripes or throats. There are scores of cultivars; after you've grown one, you'll want to try several more. 'Casablanca' has pure white unspotted flowers up to 10 in. wide on 4-ft. stems. The 'Imperial' strain has 8-in. flowers on 5–6-ft. stems in shades of crimson, gold, pink, or white. 'Sans Souci' has pink-and-white flowers heavily marked with rosy speckles and bumps on sturdy 2-ft. stems. 'Stargazer' has upward-facing flowers on 2–3-ft. stalks, crimson edged with white and marked with dark spots.

How to grow: See main entry.

Lilium **Asiatic hybrids**

Limonium
Lee-mo′nee-um.
Plumbaginaceae. Plumbago family.

Perennials or subshrubs with sprays of small flowers that have colorful, papery, persistent calyxes. About 150 spp., native worldwide.

latifolium (p. 256)
Sea lavender, perennial statice.
Perennial. Zone 3.
H: 2–3 ft. S: 2–3 ft.

Makes a pleasant lavender haze in the garden and an excellent fresh or dry cut flower. Easier to grow than baby's-breath, which is used for the same purposes. Forms a basal rosette of thick, leathery, evergreen leaves, 6–10 in. long. Leafless flower stalks branch into wide-topped sprays of tiny flowers that last for weeks in summer. Harvest for drying when bees are most attentive to the flowers. *L. tataricum*, or German statice, is a smaller plant with leaves under 6 in. long, stiff flower stalks 12–15 in. tall, and dense heads of starry white or pinkish flowers that dry beautifully. *L. perezii* is perennial in Zone 9 or 8 but blooms as an annual if started early indoors. It makes giant (to 3 ft. wide!) bushy sprays of rich blue-purple flowers with white centers.

How to grow: Full sun or afternoon shade. Needs well-drained soil and good air circulation; gets fungal diseases in soggy soil or overcrowded beds. Tolerates heat and dryness. Plants are hard to divide but grow readily from seed.

sinuatum (p. 298)
Annual statice.
Annual. All zones.
H: 18 in. S: 12 in.

Forms a very flat, dinner-plate-sized rosette of dandelion-like leaves, then shoots up several branching stalks lined with clusters of small papery flowers in bright and pastel shades of blue, lavender, rose, peach, orange, yellow, or white, all with white centers. Blooms from midsummer to frost. Excellent for fresh and dried arrangements. Cut flowers before they open completely and hang them upside down to dry in a dark place; they stay bright and lifelike. *L. suworowii*, called rat-tail or Russian statice, is another annual species with slender curving spikes of pink to purplish flowers.

How to grow: Full sun. Ordinary soil and watering. Tolerates heat and dry soil. Start seeds indoors 8 weeks before last frost, or sow directly outside when the ground can be worked. Space 9–12 in. apart. Can be planted in the vegetable garden and used just for cutting.

Linum

Lie´num. Flax.
Linaceae. Flax family.

Annuals or perennials with slender alternate leaves and 5-petaled flowers in shades of red, yellow, blue, or white. *L. usitatissimum* is the source of linen fibers and linseed oil. About 200 spp., native worldwide.

perenne (p. 256)
Flax.
Perennial. Zone 4.
H: to 18 in. S: to 18 in.

Breathtaking on a summer morning when scores of clear blue flowers open 3/4 in. wide. Individual flowers last just one day, but more keep opening over a period of many weeks. The plant itself is open and airy, like a giant pincushion of slender stems with sparse, thin, grayish leaves. Combines easily with many other perennials. White-flowered and compact forms are available. *L. narbonense* has taller stalks with blue-green leaves and bigger flowers (to 2 in.), blue with white centers. *L. flavum* makes a compact bushy mound, 12–15 in. tall, with tough evergreen leaves and bright yellow flowers. *L. grandiflorum* is a fast-growing annual with small red flowers, good for filling gaps or covering bulbs.

How to grow: Full sun or afternoon shade. Not fussy about soil but needs good drainage. Easily raised from seed and may flower the first year. Develops a deep woody root system that can't readily be divided. Cut back after flowering, or let the stems ripen to a warm tan and hold the pea-sized pods through fall and winter. Pest-free.

Liriodendron tulipifera

Liquidambar

Li-quid-am´bar. Sweet gum.
Hamamelidaceae. Witch hazel family.

Deciduous trees that produce a sticky fragrant resin used in medicines and perfumes. The lobed leaves turn bright colors in fall. Only 4 spp., native to North America and Asia.

styraciflua (p. 117)
Sweet gum.
Deciduous tree. Zone 6.
H: 60 ft. or more. S: 40 ft. or more.

An easy-to-grow tree with outstanding fall color. The star-shaped leaves, 6 in. wide, turn bright orange, red, or purplish. Forms a narrow pyramid when young, spreading wide with age. The twigs have interesting corky wings, and the trunk has ridged bark. The prickly seed balls, 1 in. wide, look interesting on the bare limbs but

Liquidambar styraciflua

make rough litter on a lawn or sidewalk. 'Palo Alto' has bright orange or red fall foliage; 'Burgundy' turns purplish red and holds its leaves into winter. 'Rotundiloba' has leaves with rounded rather than pointed lobes and doesn't set fruit.

How to grow: Full sun. Ordinary soil and watering. Tolerates heat and dryness. Native to the Southeast but grown from New York to California. Surface roots can heave sidewalks or interfere with lawns; occasional deep soaking helps promote deeper roots. Prune only to remove lower limbs as needed. Pest-free.

Liriodendron

Lir-i-oh-den´dron. Tulip tree.
Magnoliaceae. Magnolia family.

Large deciduous trees with lobed leaves and pretty, tulip-shaped flowers. Only 2 spp., one native to eastern North America and the other to China.

tulipifera (p. 117)
Tulip tree, tulip poplar, yellow poplar.
Deciduous tree. Zone 5.
H: 70 ft. or more. S: 40 ft. or more.

A large handsome tree native throughout the eastern United States. Grows quickly, especially in rich, moist soil, with a pyramidal or rounded shape when young and a stout trunk and wide spreading crown in old age. The large lobed leaves are squared off at the ends, turn warm yellow in fall. Tuliplike flowers with orange-and-green petals develop after the leaves, in late spring or early summer. Conelike clusters of dry winged seeds mature by fall and hang on in winter. Provides shade fast but gets too big for small gardens. 'Arnold', a slender upright form, fits into narrow spaces and blooms as a young tree.

How to grow: Full sun. Needs fertile, acidic or neutral, well-drained soil and regular watering; is badly stressed by drought, which makes the leaves turn yellow and drop prematurely. Subject to aphids, and their sticky secretions invite the sooty mold fungus, which blackens the leaves. Needs only routine pruning.

Liriope

Li-rie´oh-pee. Lilyturf.
Liliaceae. Lily family.

Evergreen perennials forming tufts or spreading mats of grassy foliage. Only 5 spp., native to southeastern Asia.

muscari (p. 256)
Lilyturf.
Perennial. Zone 6.
H: 1–2 ft. S: to 1 ft.

Forms grasslike clumps or mats of leathery evergreen leaves, up to 1/2 in. wide and 12–24 in. long. (Unlike grass, though, it can't be mowed short or walked on.) Very useful as a ground cover in entryways or courtyards, under trees in the ground or in planter boxes, or as an edging along sidewalks, driveways, or borders. Makes numerous slender spikes, 12–18 in. tall, of small lavender or white flowers in summer, followed by shiny, round, blue-black berries. 'Majestic' (violet flowers) and 'Big Blue' (blue flowers) are large (2 ft. tall) plants with dark green leaves. 'Silvery Sunproof' (15–18 in.) has leaves edged with stripes that lighten from gold to creamy white, and violet flowers. 'Monroe's White' has pure white flowers held well above the dark green leaves.

How to grow: Part sun; tolerates full shade, but most cultivars don't bloom as well, and variegated forms may turn green in shade. Grows best in well-drained soil with regular watering but tolerates short dry spells. Space sprigs 4–6 in. apart; plants from quart or gallon pots can go 12–18 in. apart. Clumps fill in fairly quickly. After several years, divide crowded clumps in spring; you may need a butcher knife to cut the tough woody crowns. Cut shabby old foliage in late winter with shears or a lawn mower. No serious pests or problems.

spicata (p. 256)
Creeping lilyturf.
Perennial. Zone 6 or 5.
H: under 12 in. S: 18 in. or more.

Spreads quickly by underground runners, making a grassy mat of soft dark green leaves less than 1/4 in. wide and 18 in. long. Short spikes of pale violet flowers form in midsummer but aren't very prominent. Makes a good ground cover under trees or shrubs or in shady areas where grass won't grow. Not good for edging, as it invades adjacent beds. 'Silver Dragon' is compact (6–8 in. tall), with white-striped leaves.

How to grow: Like *L. muscari,* but it does fine in full shade.

Lithocarpus
Lith-o-kar´pus.
Fagaceae. Beech family.

Evergreen trees or shrubs with an oaklike habit, leathery foliage, and woody nuts. About 300 spp., native to Asia.

densiflorus (p. 161)
Tanbark oak.
Evergreen tree. Zone 8.
H: 30 ft. S: 15 ft.

Makes a dense formal specimen for small gardens, with outstanding foliage that contrasts well with conifers. The oblong leaves, 2–4 in. long, have distinct veins leading to sharp teeth along the edges. New leaves are covered with a soft, furry, buff-colored down; older leaves are smooth and leathery, dark green above and gray-green below. Flowers on slender erect spikes produce acorns 1–2 in. long with scaly caps. Mass plantings make an impenetrable screen—the ideal background for camellias. Also combines well with rock roses, lavender, and other Mediterranean plants.

How to grow: Full or part sun. Needs well-drained soil. Established plants are drought-tolerant and tough but can't take fertilizing or regular irrigation. Native to the Pacific coastal mountains and does best along the West Coast. Leave the lower limbs for screening, or remove them to shape a tree.

Livistona
Li-vi-sto´na. Fan palm.
Palmae. Palm family.

Tall palms with fanlike leaves. About 30 spp., native to the Old World tropics.

chinensis (p. 164)
Chinese fan palm.
Fan palm. Zone 9 or 8.
H: usually under 15 ft. S: to 10 ft.

A slow-growing palm with an erect trunk crowned with several shiny dark green leaves. The leaf blades are rounded, 3–6 ft. wide, split partway to the center into many narrow drooping segments. Old leaves drop off cleanly, exposing the ringed trunk. Does well in containers or tubs, and container-grown plants can be moved to a sheltered site for the winter.

How to grow: Full sun. Ordinary soil and watering. Needs no special care.

Lobelia
Lo-bee´lee-a.
Campanulaceae. Bellflower family.

A diverse genus of annuals, perennials, shrubs, and even some trees. All have simple alternate leaves, and their flowers, usually 2-lipped, are held upside down on pedicels that twist 180°. Flowers are often small but brilliant, in shades of red, purple, blue, yellow, or white. About 365 spp., most native to tropical and warm climates.

cardinalis (p. 257)
Cardinal flower.
Perennial. Zone 2.
H: 4 ft. S: 2 ft.

Like cardinals, these flowers are a bright clear red that gleams against a background of rich green foliage. Each upright stem is topped with dozens of unusual lobed flowers, 1 1/2 in. long, blooming for up to a month in late summer. Stems usually don't branch, so the plants make vertical accents in the garden. Cardinal flower grows wild in moist sites across much of North America. *L. splendens,* or Mexican lobelia, is similar but has bronzy leaves and stems. *L. siphilitica,* the great blue lobelia, has 1-in. blue flowers that are less showy. Nurseries are starting to offer several new hybrids bred from these species, with large flowers in a range of reds, blues, and purples, on sturdy vigorous plants that adapt well to garden conditions. All attract hummingbirds.

How to grow: Sun or part shade. Prefers damp, fertile soil but grows okay in ordinary soil

Liriope muscari

Lobelia cardinalis

with regular watering. Plants are generally short lived but self-sow freely. Plants that survive should be divided every 2–3 years.

erinus (p. 299)
Edging lobelia.
Annual. All zones.
H: 4–8 in. S: to 12 in.

Blooms throughout summer and fall, with tiny irregular flowers in all shades from light to dark blue, and also white and wine red. The trailing types are excellent for window boxes, patio containers, and hanging baskets. The upright types are bushy and compact, good for edging beds and borders. Traditionally combined with red geraniums and white petunias for patriotic displays. Several strains are available from seed catalogs or sold as small transplants in spring.

How to grow: Sun or part shade. Ordinary soil and watering. Doesn't like hot summers but can succeed if it is established before hot weather begins, shaded from the afternoon sun, and regularly watered. Start seeds indoors 10–12 weeks before last frost. Sow on the soil surface; seeds are tiny and need light to germinate. Set plants in the garden after danger of frost is past, spacing them 4–8 in. apart. Shear back partway in midsummer to rejuvenate plants if flowering slows. Pest-free.

Lobularia
Lob-you-lay′ree-a.
Cruciferae. Mustard family.

Annuals or perennials with slender sprawling stems, narrow leaves, and many small flowers over a long season. Very similar to and often merged with *Alyssum*. Only 5 spp., native to the Mediterranean region.

maritima (p. 299)
Sweet alyssum.
Annual. All zones.
H: to 6 in. S: 12 in.

Indispensable for edgings and containers, this easy, adaptable annual blooms from late spring until hard frost. Forms a spreading mound or mat of branching stems with tiny leaves and masses of 4-petaled flowers in shades of white, pink, rose, or purple. Some strains (but not all) have a sweet honeylike fragrance. Use it like a ground cover to fill the gaps between newly planted perennials or shrubs. Several strains are available from seed, and all nurseries sell the seedlings in spring.

How to grow: Full or part sun. Ordinary soil and watering. Start seeds indoors 6 weeks before last frost or sow direct. Self-sows but isn't weedy. Shear back halfway when plants get tatty in midsummer, and they will be renewed. Pest-free.

Lobularia maritima

Lonicera
Lon-iss′er-a. Honeysuckle.
Caprifoliaceae. Honeysuckle family.

Shrubs or woody vines, usually deciduous or semievergreen, with simple opposite leaves. Small or large flowers, often sweetly fragrant, are borne in pairs or whorls, followed by soft berries. About 180 spp., native to the Northern Hemisphere.

fragrantissima (p. 142)
Winter honeysuckle.
Deciduous or semievergreen shrub. Zone 6 or 5.
H: 8 ft. S: 8 ft.

Welcome in early spring, when the small creamy white flowers make a pleasant sweet aroma that fills the garden. Cut branches can be forced into earlier bloom indoors. The red berries feed the birds in summer. The opposite oval leaves, 1–3 in. long, hang on late where winters are mild. Unpruned, it makes a large wide shrub with many arching branches and some suckers. Prune after flowering to keep it compact or shapely. Tuck one into a mixed shrub border or boundary hedge where you can enjoy it in spring and ignore it the rest of the year.

How to grow: Full or part sun; tolerates shade but doesn't bloom much. Ordinary soil okay, but needs good drainage. Tolerates hot weather and dry spells. Give it water if it wilts. Easy to transplant and establishes quickly. Overgrown plants can be cut to the ground for renewal. Subject to aphids and various other pests and diseases, which can disfigure the foliage and flowers, but usually recovers with little permanent damage. Flower buds may freeze in severe Zone 5 winters.

Lonicera × heckrottii

× *heckrottii* (p. 204)
Gold-flame honeysuckle,
everblooming honeysuckle.
Semievergreen vine. Zone 5 or 4.
H: 10–20 ft.

A lovely vine with smooth, firm, blue-green leaves, opposite on lower parts of the stem but joined together into rounded disks near the top. Foliage is evergreen where winters are mild, hangs on late even in cold climates. Slender 1-in. flowers are borne in clusters, blooming most heavily in spring and continuing sporadically until frost. The flowers are carmine outside and yellow inside, fading to pink as they age. Their sweet fragrance is most pronounced on warm evenings, when it carries through the garden. Plant it on a trellis or arbor upwind of a patio or open window, let it spill over a retaining wall, or use it as a ground cover. Doesn't set berries, so it doesn't spread.

How to grow: Like *L. fragrantissima*.

japonica (p. 204)
Japanese honeysuckle.
Semievergreen vine. Zone 4.
H: 15–20 ft.

This vigorous vine is famous for its sweetly fragrant flowers and invasive growth. White flowers, 1¹/₂ in. long, are borne in pairs at the leaf axils, followed by black berries in early fall. Blooms most heavily in late spring and early summer but continues off and on for months. Useful as a ground cover or as a quick disguise for fences and posts in dry climates, where it may smother its neighbors but hasn't spread far by seed (bird-sown seedlings have entangled thousands of acres of woods and forests in the Southeast and Mid-Atlantic states). 'Halliana', or Hall's honeysuckle, is the most vigorous and most commonly grown form, with white flowers that turn yellow as they age. 'Purpurea' is a vigorous form with dark purple-green leaves and flowers that are white inside, purple outside. 'Aureo-reticulata', the gold-net honeysuckle, has leaves veined with yellow and is less vigorous.

How to grow: Like *L. fragrantissima*. For ground cover, set 3 ft. apart and cut back hard from time to time to remove the thatch of dead stems that have been shaded out. If used as a vine, provide support. Pest-free, but it can become a pest.

sempervirens (p. 204)
Trumpet honeysuckle.
Semievergreen vine. Zone 4.
H: 10–15 ft.

One of the easiest and most rewarding vines, effective on a mailbox, fence, or trellis or scrambling into a tree. Climbs by twining, or can be quite shrubby. The glossy, oval, blue-green leaves are paired below, joined together at the tops of the stems. The clusters of 2-in. tubular flowers, usually coral-red but available in yellow, are scentless but attract hummingbirds. Blooms heavily for a month or so in early summer, then intermittently through fall. Makes red berries sometimes, but not always. Growth is restrained, not aggressive like that of Japanese honeysuckle. Native throughout the eastern states but not often seen in the wild.

How to grow: Like *L. fragrantissima*.

tatarica (see below for photo)
Tartarian honeysuckle.
Deciduous shrub. Zone 4 or 3.
H: 8–12 ft. S: 8–12 ft.

Widely planted in the past as a fast-growing hedge or windbreak, this can be a handsome shrub with many arching stems and smooth blue-green foliage. It's covered with small flowers in late spring, just as the leaves unfold, and has a big crop of red berries from summer through fall. There are many cultivars with white, pale pink, rosy pink, or red flowers. Unfortunately, the Russian aphid, now a widespread pest, disfigures the shoots, reduces the vigor, and can eventually kill the plant. 'Freedom' (p. 142) is a hybrid with resistance to the Russian aphid. It has pinkish white flowers and stands up to the cold, dry, windy conditions of the Great Plains.

How to grow: Like *L. fragrantissima*.

Loropetalum
Lor-o-pet´a-lum.
Hamamelidaceae. Witch hazel family.

An evergreen shrub or small tree with white flowers in spring. Only 1 sp., native to eastern Asia.

chinense (p. 177)
Evergreen shrub. Zone 7.
H: to 5 ft. S: 6–8 ft.

Subtle and elegant, with layers of spreading, arching branches. Feathery white flowers with 4 strap-shaped 1-in. petals are clustered at the ends of the twigs in early spring and sporadically throughout summer and fall. The rounded leaves, 1–2 in. long, are light green and faintly hairy. Although evergreen, it shows an occasional red or yellow leaf. Will spill over a wall or from a container, or combines with hostas, ferns, and begonias in a shaded entryway or woodland border.

How to grow: Part sun or shade. Prefers acidic soil amended with organic matter; can't take alkaline soil. Ordinary watering. Needs little pruning and looks best if left alone. No pests.

Lunaria
Lew-nay´ree-a.
Cruciferae. Mustard family.

Biennials or perennials with erect branching stems, 4-parted flowers, and decorative pods. Only 3 spp., native to Europe.

annua (p. 299)
(formerly *L. biennis*)
Honesty, money plant.
Biennial. Zone 4.
H: 30–36 in. S: 12 in.

Grown for its round flat pods, 1–2 in. wide, which are used in dried arrangements. The papery outer covers peel off to reveal a silvery inner membrane. Seedlings make a rosette of rough heart-shaped leaves the first year, then send up tough, erect, branching stalks covered with small cross-shaped purple or white flowers the next spring. Nice in an herb garden, with lady's-mantle and chives. *L. a.* var. *variegata* 'Stella' has white flowers and foliage splotched with creamy white.

How to grow: Part sun. Ordinary soil and watering. To get started, sow seeds where they are to grow. Gather stems as the pods ripen from green to tan and dry indoors. Leave a few stalks in the garden to self-sow, and you won't have to plant it again. Look for seedlings and move them where you want in late summer or early fall.

Lunaria annua

Lupinus

Lew-pine´us. Lupine.
Leguminosae. Legume family.

Annuals, perennials, or small shrubs with palmately compound leaves and showy spikes or racemes of pealike flowers. About 200 spp., many native to the western United States.

texensis (p. 299)

Texas bluebonnet.
Annual. All zones.
H: 6–16 in. S: 18 in.

Very showy for 2–4 weeks in mid- to late spring, when it's covered with dense clusters of dark blue and white flowers. Popular in wildflower meadows or as a seasonal bedding plant. *L. subcarnosis* is similar but less showy, with lighter blue flowers. Both have 5-parted leaves with silky leaflets and branch near the base into many sprawling stems. Many other native lupines are available from wildflower specialists. Perennial gardeners often try the Russell hybrid lupines, which have impressive (to 5 ft.) spikes of bright-colored flowers in many shades, but these tend to be fussy and short-lived plants.

How to grow: Full sun. Tolerates poor, dry soil. Sow seeds outdoors in fall for spring germination. For better germination, use sandpaper to abrade the hard seed coats before sowing. To encourage self-sowing, wait until the plants mature and turn brown before mowing or trimming. Nurseries sometimes sell transplants in fall, along with pansies and other winter annuals.

Lupinus subcarnosis

Lycoris

Lie-ko´ris.
Amaryllidaceae. Amaryllis family.

Bulbous perennials with straplike basal leaves that wither away before the flower stalks arise, suddenly bearing umbels of bright spidery blossoms. Only 11 spp., native to eastern Asia.

radiata (p. 257)

Spider lily.
Bulbous perennial. Zone 8 or 7.
H: 12–18 in. S: 6–12 in.

Blooms develop suddenly in early fall, usually soon after a good rain, and last for a few weeks. The leafless stalks, 18 in. tall, are topped with spidery clusters of red (or sometimes white) flowers with slender petals and long up-curved stamens. Grassy leaves develop after bloom and last until spring. Bulbs are dormant in summer. An old favorite that has naturalized in parts of the South, where it is locally called Guernsey lily. True Guernsey lily, *Nerine sarniensis,* is similar but not as hardy. A slightly larger plant, its flowers are rosy pink to scarlet and have less prominent stamens.

How to grow: Part or full sun. Not fussy about soil but needs good drainage. Prefers winter moisture and summer dryness. Plant dormant bulbs in late summer, 3–4 in. deep and 4–6 in. apart. Wait several years before dividing; resents disturbance and will not bloom for a year or more. Pest-free.

Lycoris radiata

squamigera

Magic lily.
Bulbous perennial. Zone 5.
H: 2 ft. S: 6–12 in.

Surprising and delightful in August or September, when it suddenly shoots up 2-ft. stalks topped with several lavender-pink, trumpet-shaped flowers. Flowers are scentless, about 3 in. long. The straplike leaves make a big glossy clump in spring but look shabby for a few weeks as they die back in early summer. Can be interplanted with daylilies; it extends the bloom season, and the daylilies mask the declining foliage. This plant is sometimes called naked-lady, but that name is more commonly applied to *Amaryllis belladonna*, a similar but tenderer plant (Zone 8) with sweetly fragrant pink flowers on dark-colored stems 2–3 ft. tall.

How to grow: Like *L. radiata.*

Lygodium

Lie-go´dee-um. Climbing fern.
Schizaeaceae. Curly-grass family.

Tender ferns with unusual fronds that elongate indefinitely and twine like stems. About 35 spp., native to tropical climates.

japonicum (p. 217)

Japanese climbing fern.
Vinelike fern. Zone 8.
H: 10–15 ft. S: 4 ft.

This fern climbs on trees or shrubs but doesn't damage them. The semievergreen fronds, up to 3 in. long, are finely divided into lacy lobes. Makes a soft curtain of green on a fence, an arbor, or tree trunks. Native to Japan but naturalized in moist locations throughout the lower South.

How to grow: Sun or shade. Ordinary or unimproved soil. Prefers regular watering but tolerates periods of dry weather without damage. Prune back winter-damaged foliage just before new growth starts in spring. Can be propagated by division.

Lysimachia

Li-si-mack´ee-a. Loosestrife.
Primulaceae. Primrose family.

Annuals, perennials, or a few shrubs with simple leaves. Flowers are usually yellow or white, often with 5 petals. About 150 spp., native worldwide.

clethroides (p. 257)

Gooseneck loosestrife.
Perennial. Zone 3.
H: 2–3 ft. S: 3 ft. or more.

"Gooseneck" refers to the slender arching flower clusters that top each erect leafy stalk; a patch in bloom does resemble a flock of geese, all facing in the same direction. Small starry white flowers crowd racemes up to 12 in. long, blooming for several weeks in summer. Very desirable for cut-flower arrangements. It's easy and handsome but invasive, spreading by underground runners. Planting in a bottomless container offers some control, but watch for runners that get out. If you have space to let it go, it makes a good ground cover, especially in damp soil. There are other loosestrifes with handsome foliage and flowers; some are less invasive, but few nurseries carry them.

How to grow: Full or part sun. Ordinary or better soil. Prefers constant moisture but gets by on regular watering. Space 2 ft. apart. Divide in spring. Pest-free.

nummularia (p. 257)
Moneywort, creeping Jennie.
Perennial. Zone 3.
H: 2–3 in. S: 1 ft. or more.

An attractive ground cover for moist areas in part or full shade. The shiny, round, coin-sized (3/4–1 in. wide) leaves fit side by side on stems that lie flat on the ground. Bright yellow flowers match the leaves in size and shape. Blooms in summer. Stems root as they run, making a good cover for small bulbs or around pools and along streams. 'Aurea' is the same plant with citron yellow foliage; it brings light into dark places.

How to grow: Part sun or shade. Ordinary soil. Prefers constant moisture. Space 8 in. apart for ground cover. Divide in spring or fall. Pest-free.

Macleaya
Mak-lay´a.
Papaveraceae. Poppy family.

Large perennials with lobed leaves, small flowers, and yellow sap. Only 2 spp., native to eastern Asia.

cordata (p. 257)
(*Bocconia cordata*)
Plume poppy.
Perennial. Zone 3.
H: 6–8 ft. or more. S: 4 ft. or more.

A statuesque plant with attractive foliage and great creamy plumes that wave high in the summer wind. It makes a wonderful specimen if you have room at the back of the border. The ruffled, lobed, heart-shaped leaves are light green above, hairy and white below. Individual flowers are small but are borne in 10–12-in. panicles. Forms erect, spreading clumps. Seldom needs staking but usually needs curbing.

How to grow: Full or part sun. Ordinary or improved soil and regular watering. Can't take hot, dry summers. Give it plenty of room; it will spread. Divide in spring. Pest-free.

Magnolia
Mag-no´lce-a.
Magnoliaceae. Magnolia family.

Deciduous or evergreen shrubs or trees with many ornamental traits. Many kinds are grown for their large showy flowers, which open from prominent furry buds at the tips of the branches. The flowers are usually creamy white or purplish pink. Some have a rich fruity fragrance. Most bloom in spring, a few in summer. The conelike fruits release bright red or orange seeds in fall. Magnolia foliage is usually healthy and attractive. The leaves are oval to elliptical with smooth edges and are sometimes noteworthy for their glossy surface or extremely large size. About 125 spp., most native to eastern Asia and eastern North America, and many hybrids and scores of cultivars.

How to grow: Full or part sun. Magnolias need deep, well-drained, acidic or neutral soil amended with plenty of organic matter. Most don't do well in alkaline soil. Think twice before planting and choose the permanent location; it's difficult to transplant magnolias. Plant container-grown or balled-and-burlapped plants in spring, after new growth starts. Be careful not to break or bruise the thick fleshy roots. Apply a thick layer of organic mulch to shade the soil and to retain moisture. Water deeply and regularly during droughts.

Magnolias do well in lawns, but replace the grass immediately under the tree with mulch. Don't disturb the tree's roots by planting bulbs or annuals. It's fine if perennial ground covers planted around the edge creep toward the trunk.

Many of the hybrids and cultivars tend to have multiple trunks and grow upright when young but spread wider with age. Most develop a pleasing shape with no pruning. Simply remove dead or damaged shoots. Magnolias have few pests or diseases.

'Elizabeth' (p. 119)
(*M. acuminata* × *M. denudata*)
Deciduous tree. Zone 5.
H: 35 ft. or more. S: 25 ft. or more.

A vigorous tree with large upright buds that open into lightly scented, clear yellow flowers. Blooms late enough to avoid spring frost damage. Makes a handsome, healthy specimen. It is a hybrid, developed at the Brooklyn Botanic Garden. One parent is *M. acuminata*, the cucumber tree, the largest and hardiest (Zone 4) native American species. The showy fruits look like pink gherkins, but its flowers don't compare well with those of other magnolias, so it isn't often grown. The other parent is *M. denudata*, the Yulan magnolia from China. It's a beautiful tree with masses of ivory flowers in good years, but often the buds open too early and are browned by frost.

How to grow: See main entry.

'Galaxy' (p. 118)
(*M. liliiflora* 'Nigra' × *M. sprengeri* 'Diva')
Deciduous tree. Zone 6 or 5.
H: 20–30 ft. S: 10 ft.

A new hybrid that's becoming quite popular as a street tree. It starts flowering when only 3–4 years old, with many reddish purple blossoms up to 10 in. wide, and it blooms late enough to avoid most spring frosts. A quick grower with a

Lysimachia nummularia

Magnolia grandiflora

strong central leader and narrow upright habit. Excellent for small spaces. Both parents are also lovely trees.

How to grow: See main entry.

grandiflora (p. 161)
Southern magnolia.
Evergreen tree. Zone 7.
H: to 80 ft. S: to 40 ft.

One of our most beautiful native trees, beloved throughout the South and Texas. The main trunk is erect, with horizontal limbs. If not removed, the lower limbs sweep to the ground as gracefully as a long skirt. The large oblong leaves are thick and glossy, dark green above, covered below with a coating of dense woolly hairs, called tomentum or indumentum. The dense foliage is handsome all year but especially sparkly and cheerful in winter. The creamy white flowers have a rich lemony or fruity fragrance and form a bowl 6–10 in. wide. Bloom peaks in early summer and continues sporadically. The decorative brown fruits release shiny red seeds in fall. Leaves, flowers, and fruits are all valued by flower arrangers.

There are many cultivars, differing in the size of the flowers, the size and shape of the leaves, and the overall tree size and habit. Most are more compact than the species. All make excellent specimens.

'Edith Bogue' is the hardiest cultivar, safe in Zone 6 and worth trying on protected sites in Zone 5. It grows bushy and full to 35 ft. 'Victoria' is almost as hardy. It has large broad leaves and makes a dense 20-ft. tree.

'Little Gem' is compact enough for small gardens, slowly reaching to 20 ft., with 4-in. leaves and 3–4-in. flowers. It blooms from May until frost.

'St. Mary' (also called 'Glen St. Mary') has big flowers on a small tree, usually under 20 ft. tall. Narrow and flexible, it can be espaliered against a chimney, wall, or fence.

'Samuel Sommer' grows quickly and makes a pyramid 30–40 ft. tall. It has flowers 10–14 in. wide and leaves with thick rusty brown tomentum.

How to grow: See main entry. Plant in a site well protected from winter sun and wind to protect the foliage from browning—this is especially important at the limits of hardiness. Litter is the only drawback. Leaves keep dropping all year, and pods drop from fall to spring.

Kosar-DeVos hybrids (p. 118)
(*M. liliiflora* × *M. stellata* 'Rosea')
Deciduous shrubs. Zone 5.
H: to 10 ft. S: to 10 ft.

A group of 8 cultivars, originally called the "Girls." These are compact shrubby plants with many upright stems. They flower abundantly before the leaves open, but late enough to avoid most spring frosts, and continue blooming sporadically in summer. The erect buds open into 4–5-in. flowers. Most are rosy purple outside, the same or white inside. 'Ann' has cinnamon-scented

reddish purple flowers. 'Betty' has large fragrant flowers that are dark pink outside, white inside.

How to grow: See main entry.

× loebneri cultivars (p. 119)
(*M. kobus* × *M. stellata*)
Deciduous trees. Zone 4.
H: 20 ft. or more. S: 20 ft.

These vigorous plants grow quickly into large multitrunked shrubs or small trees. Flowers are like those of *M. stellata,* the star magnolia, but open later and usually avoid frost damage. Blooms are very abundant, even on young plants, and fragrant. 'Leonard Messel' has flowers with 12 strap-shaped petals, dark pink outside, light pink inside, and grows 15–20 ft. tall. 'Merrill' has flowers with 15 white petals and grows 20–30 ft. tall.

How to grow: See main entry. More adaptable than most magnolias, these grow well from coast to coast. They're not as fussy about soil, and they tolerate cold, heat, and wind.

macrophylla (see below for photo)
Bigleaf magnolia.
Deciduous tree. Zone 5.
H: to 50 ft. S: to 30 ft.

This southeastern native takes the prize for the largest leaves and flowers of any magnolia. The tropical-looking leaves can grow 30 in. long but are vulnerable to tearing in the wind. White flowers up to 15 in. wide open after the leaves, in June. Think twice before planting—it's a big, dramatic tree that calls a lot of attention to itself. Used right, it's a wonderful sight.

M. tripetala (p. 120), the umbrella magnolia, is another native with big leaves that expand before the white flowers open. Unlike those of most magnolias, its flowers smell unpleasant. The 12–24-in. leaves are clustered at the ends of long bare shoots (limbs may grow 2 ft. a year), an unusual but interesting effect. The tree grows to 40 ft. *M. hypoleuca,* from Japan, is similar to umbrella magnolia but has very fragrant flowers and leaves up to 18 in. long. Both are hardy to Zone 5.

How to grow: See main entry. Allow plenty of space, but choose a site protected from strong winds.

sieboldii (p. 119)
Oyama magnolia.
Deciduous shrub or small tree. Zone 7.
H: 12–15 ft. S: 12–15 ft.

A refined tree for small gardens, with round cup-shaped flowers, 3 in. wide, that face down. Flowers are very fragrant, with glossy white petals and bright red stamens, opening mostly in May to June but continuing throughout the summer. Plant it on a slope or raised bed above a path or patio, where you can walk underneath it and look up to admire the flowers. The foliage is neat and the habit is rounded. Usually multitrunked.

How to grow: See main entry. Takes part shade.

× *soulangiana* (p. 119)
(*M. denudata* × *M. liliiflora*)
Saucer magnolia, tulip tree.
Deciduous large shrub or small tree. Zone 5.
H: to 30 ft. S: to 30 ft.

Among the most popular magnolias, grown from north to south and coast to coast. White, pink, or reddish purple flowers open just before the leaves and repeat a few at a time all summer. They are shaped like cups or tulips and have no fragrance. Leaves are 6 in. long and soft-textured. Makes a single-trunked or multitrunked tree that spreads wide with age. The many cultivars are much better plants than unnamed seedlings are. 'Lennei', an old favorite, makes a broad shrub and blooms late, with flowers that are purple outside, white inside.

How to grow: See main entry. The tree itself is very hardy, but flowers that open too early are damaged by hard frost. Adapts to many climates and soils.

stellata (p. 120)
Star magnolia.
Deciduous shrub or small tree. Zone 5 or 4.
H: 10–15 ft. S: 10–15 ft.

Very popular throughout the United States, this is the first magnolia to open in early spring (February to April, depending on where you live). The slightly fragrant white (sometimes tinged with pink) flowers have many soft strap-shaped petals that flop into loose starry clusters. Dark green leaves open later and look fresh all summer. The plant grows slowly and stays small and compact for many years. 'Centennial' has flowers 5 in. wide with 28–32 petals. 'Royal Star' has 3–4-in. white flowers with 25–30 petals.

Star magnolia is a good plant, especially for small gardens, but its flowers are often damaged by spring frosts. Many gardeners prefer the later-blooming hybrid *M.* × *loebneri* (see entry).

How to grow: See main entry. Plant it on the north or east side of a wall, fence, or woods, where the ground will stay cool in spring and it won't be forced into premature bloom. Plants on the south side of a building are liable to develop early, then freeze.

virginiana (p. 120)
Sweet-bay magnolia.
Deciduous or evergreen shrub or tree. Zone 5.
H: 20–60 ft. S: 10–20 ft.

This is a variable plant, native to wet sites along the eastern seaboard from Massachusetts to Mississippi. Southern specimens are evergreen trees up to 60 ft. tall. Northern forms are deciduous shrubs, often no more than 20 ft. tall. Nurseries offer selected evergreen or deciduous forms; the deciduous ones are hardier. In either case, the leaves are leathery-textured, 3–5 in. long, dark green above with silver hairs below, and have a spicy fragrance when crushed. The cup-shaped creamy white flowers, 2–3 in. wide, have a lemony fragrance and open in June and July, sometimes repeating through summer. Grows slowly and makes a graceful specimen.

How to grow: Does best in full sun but can take more shade than other magnolias and bloom anyway. Prefers constantly moist soil and tolerates poor drainage, even boggy conditions. Thrives in humid heat but can't take dry heat. Pest-free.

Mahonia
Ma-ho´ni-a.
Berberidaceae. Barberry family.

Evergreen shrubs with thick, leathery, spiny-toothed leaves; clusters of small, cup-shaped, bright yellow flowers in early spring; and blue-black berries, often with a white coating. Mahonias are closely related to and sometimes combined with barberries (*Berberis* spp.). About 70 spp., native to eastern Asia and North and Central America.

aquifolium (p. 178)
Oregon grape.
Evergreen shrub. Zone 6 or 5.
H: 6–8 ft. S: 3–4 ft.

The state flower of Oregon, where it grows wild, this is a spreading shrub with many erect stems. The compound leaves have 5–9 spiny leaflets, 1–3 in. long, and are glossy green in summer, purplish in winter, with a few scattered red leaflets at any time. New leaves are coppery or bronzy when they open. Bright yellow flowers make 2–3-in. clusters in spring. Grapelike clusters of small silvery-frosted blue berries attract birds in fall. Large clumps or mass plantings make a good screen or background. 'Compacta' is a dwarf form that stays 2–3 ft. tall and spreads readily; it makes a good ground cover or adds year-round interest to foundation plantings. 'Golden Abundance' is a hybrid derived from *M. aquifolium* with vigorous growth, dense foliage, abundant flowers, and large fruit clusters. *M. pinnata*, the California holly grape, is similar to Oregon grape but has taller stems, spinier leaves, and more drought tolerance.

How to grow: Can take full sun but looks better if shaded from summer sun in extremely hot areas. Needs shelter from winter sun and dry winds in cold regions, or the leaves will turn brown and die. (The plant survives but recovers slowly.) Well-drained soil and ordinary watering. Spreads, but not too fast, by underground runners. You can dig and transplant well-rooted suckers. Cut off old, tattered, or too-tall stems at ground level in early spring. New growth will replace them. In the West a tiny looper caterpillar sometimes chews the leaves; control it with *Bacillus thuringiensis*.

bealei (p. 178)
(*M. japonica* 'Bealei')
Leatherleaf mahonia.
Evergreen shrub. Zone 7 or 6.
H: 8–10 ft. S: 3–4 ft.

A distinctive, architectural plant. Large leaves radiate horizontally from the stout, erect, usually unbranched stems. The leaves are com-

Magnolia stellata

Mahonia bealei

pound, with 7–15 spiny leaflets up to 5 in. long. Arching sprays of very fragrant yellow flowers last for a few weeks in early spring. Drooping clusters of blue fruits are very showy until the birds eat them. This shrub has a sculptural quality and looks striking when silhouetted against a building, fence, or dark hedge. It's a splendid choice for entryways and grows well in raised planters or containers.

How to grow: Like *M. aquifolium.*

lomariifolia (p. 178)
Evergreen shrub. Zone 8.
H: 10 ft. S: 2–3 ft.

An unusual shrub that makes a narrow clump of stems with remarkable, lustrous foliage. The fernlike leaves, up to 2 ft. long, have dozens of stiff, spiny, 3-in. leaflets; the leaves radiate from the stems, sometimes drooping gracefully. Unscented yellow flowers in erect clusters of 6-in. spikes last for weeks in late winter or early spring; blue berries follow in fall. Combines the elegance of a fern or palm with the rugged look of a holly. Use with cannas, gingers, palms, and aspidistras for a tropical effect, or contrast it with rhododendrons, azaleas, and camellias. 'Arthur Menzies' is a hybrid of *M. lomariifolia* and *M. japonica,* found as a seedling in a Seattle arboretum. It has very large clusters of yellow flowers in December and January. Other hybrids from this cross are grouped as *M. × media;* most have large leaves and are remarkably showy in bloom. All are hardy in Zone 8.

How to grow: Part sun or shade; can't take desert heat or sun. Best in fertile, organic soil with regular watering. Cut old stalks off at the base. Pest-free.

Mahonia repens

repens (p. 178)
Creeping holly grape.
Evergreen shrub. Zone 5 or 4.
H: 2–3 ft. S: 2–3 ft.

A tough ground cover, native to the western mountains, that spreads slowly by underground stems. The thick leathery leaves have 3–7 spiny leaflets. Plants have small clusters of yellow flowers in late spring or early summer, dark blue fruits in fall. Foliage is dark blue-green in summer, purple-bronze in cold weather. *M. nervosa,* the longleaf mahonia, is another good ground cover, best on shady sites and hardy to Zone 6 or 5. It usually stays under 2 ft. tall but has leaves up to 18 in. long with many leaflets.

How to grow: Part sun or shade. Needs a site sheltered from winter sun and dry winds, which kill the leaves. Snow offers ideal protection. Grows in any well-drained soil. Drought-tolerant when established. Space plants from 1-gal. cans 2 ft. apart for ground cover.

Malus floribunda

Malus
Mal´lus. Apple, crab apple.
Rosaceae. Rose family.

Deciduous trees with white or pink 5-petaled blossoms in spring, blooming as the leaves unfold, and plump fleshy fruits. The difference between apples and crab apples is the size of their fruits; apples are more than 2 in. wide, crab apples are less than 2 in. wide. There are about 25 spp. in the genus, all native to the north temperate zone. Nearly all the apples grown for fruit and the crab apples grown as ornamentals are hybrids of uncertain parentage, so they're referred to simply by the cultivar name.

floribunda (p. 121)
Japanese crab apple.
Deciduous tree. Zone 4.
H: 20–25 ft. S: 25 ft.

A graceful tree with spreading horizontal branches. Buds are red; flowers open pale pink and fade to white, and are 1–1¹/₂ in. wide. Fruits are ³/₈ in. wide, ripening from green to yellow, then darkening to a brownish red before the birds finish eating them in fall. Bears annually and abundantly. Makes a fine specimen for lawns or property borders. Has good disease resistance.

How to grow: Full sun. Needs well-drained soil. Tolerates acidic, neutral, or mildly alkaline conditions. Water during prolonged dry spells. Grows well in most of the United States, except the coastal Southeast or desert Southwest. Prune young trees to establish the shape, to encourage wide branch angles, and to remove crossed or weak branches. Mature trees need pruning only to remove damaged limbs, water sprouts (vigorous limbs that grow straight up), and suckers that arise from the rootstock. May be attacked by aphids, borers, Japanese beetles, scale, spider mites, and tent caterpillars.

sargentii (p. 142)
Sargent crab apple.
Deciduous shrub or small tree. Zone 5.
H: 6–10 ft. S: 10–15 ft. or more.

Usually a mounding shrub that spreads 1¹/₂–2 times as wide as it is tall, with dense, horizontal, zigzag branches that look interesting in winter. Can also be trained into a short tree with a broad crown. Pink buds open into fragrant pure white flowers ¹/₂ in. wide. This species blooms later than other crab apples and tends to bloom heavily in alternate years, sparsely in between. It bears abundant crops of small (¹/₄–³/₈ in.) red fruits that attract birds. A fine specimen plant, attractive in all 4 seasons.

How to grow: Like *M. floribunda.*

hybrid crab apples (pp. 120, 121)
Deciduous trees. Zone 4.
H: usually 20–30 ft. S: usually 15–25 ft.

Crab apple trees make a puffy cloud of bloom in spring, with 1–2-in. flowers in shades of white, pale to rosy pink, or purplish red. The display lasts for 1–3 weeks, depending on the weather. The leaves start expanding as the flowers open. New leaves are often reddish, turning dark green or reddish purple all summer and sometimes yellowing in fall. Unfortunately, many of the old-fashioned crab apple cultivars such as 'Hopa' and 'Almey' are highly susceptible to scab, rust, and powdery mildew; infected leaves are disfigured and drop early. Modern selections, including those listed at right, show much more disease resistance.

Fruit size varies among cultivars. Crab apples can be as big as 2 in. wide, but the big kinds usually drop off and make a terrible mess on a lawn or sidewalk in late summer. Smaller fruits tend to stay firm longer and hang on the tree until winter, when they gradually soften and are eaten by birds. Fruit color vary also, ranging from golden yellow, orange, or crimson to dark red or purple. Most fruits are apple-shaped; a few are shaped like tiny pears.

The trees grow at a moderate or fast rate. Mature size and shape vary among cultivars. Some trees are rounded; others spread wider than tall; some make upright ovals; and a few have erect trunks and weeping limbs.

How to grow: Like *M. floribunda.*

Malva

Mal′va. Mallow.
Malvaceae. Mallow family.

Annuals, biennials, or perennials with palmately lobed or divided leaves; flowers with 5 white, pink, or purplish petals; and dry fruits with seeds arranged like the spokes of a wheel. About 30 spp., native to Europe, North Africa, and Asia.

Malva alcea

alcea 'Fastigiata' (see below for photo)
Hollyhock mallow.
Perennial. Zone 4.
H: 3–4 ft. S: 1½ ft.

A favorite for cottage gardens or large borders. Makes a big clump of erect stems with downy, palmately lobed leaves at the base and plenty of flowers on top. Saucer-shaped flowers with 5 notched petals are 2 in. wide and come in shades of rose, pink, or white. Blooms for many weeks in July and August and still looks fresh and sprightly when other plants have given up. *M. moschata* (p. 257) has similar flowers in pink or white, but its stems divide into smaller branches that spread (or flop) into a bushy mound 2–3 ft. tall and wide. A European native, it has naturalized in the Northeast.

How to grow: Full or part sun. Ordinary soil and watering. Does better across the northern United States than in the South or Southwest. Space 1½ ft. apart. Easy from seed; after you buy one plant, you'll have seedlings all over the garden. Relocate seedlings while they're small, because they soon grow a long taproot. May need support.

Recommended crab apple cultivars

'**Adams**' grows 20 ft. tall with a round crown. Flowers are red-pink. Fruits are red, ⅝ in. wide.

'**Callaway**' grows 25 ft. tall with a round crown. Flowers are white and open later than most. Red-purple fruits are about 1 in. wide. The best crab apple for the South.

'**Donald Wyman**' grows 20 ft. tall with a round crown. Buds are red, flowers white. The bright red ⅜-in. fruits last until spring.

'**Indian Summer**' grows to 20 ft. with a vase-shaped crown. Flowers are rosy red. Fruits are bright red, to ¾ in. wide.

'**Molten Lava**' has spreading, slightly weeping limbs and grows 15 ft. tall. Buds are red, flowers white. The red-orange fruits are ⅜ in. wide.

'**Prairiefire**' has a spreading vase shape and grows 20 ft. tall. Flowers are reddish purple. The ½-in. fruits are dark red. Has good orange-red fall color and red-barked twigs in winter.

'**Red Jewel**' grows 15 ft. tall with an upright oval crown. It has pure white flowers and ½-in. fruits that turn from bright red to golden brown by midwinter.

'**Selkirk**' grows 25 ft. tall with an open vase-shaped crown. Flowers are rosy red. Fruits are glossy reddish purple, ¾ in. wide.

'**Sugar Tyme**' grows 20 ft. tall with a round crown. Pale pink buds open into fragrant white flowers. The red fruits are ½ in. wide.

'**Weeping Candied Apple**' grows only 10–15 ft. tall with irregular weeping branches. Flowers are pink; foliage has a reddish cast. The dark red fruits, ⅝ in. wide, last until spring.

'**Zumi Calocarpa**' grows 20 ft. tall with horizontal spreading limbs. Buds are red, flowers white and fragrant. The shiny bright red ½-in. fruits last until spring.

Malvaviscus

Mal-va-vis′kus.
Malvaceae. Mallow family.

Tender shrubs with red flowers about the size and shape of a lipstick. Only 3 spp., native to tropical America.

arboreus (p. 257)
Turk's-cap.
Grown as a perennial. Zone 8.
H: 3–5 ft. S: 5 ft.

An old favorite for gardens in Texas and the South, blooming throughout summer and fall, sometimes into November. The tubular flowers are bright red and attract hummingbirds; other birds eat the small cherrylike fruits. Makes a shrubby mound of tough stems with soft, hairy, rounded or lobed leaves up to 4 in. wide. An extremely tough and adaptable plant. 'Alba' has pure white flowers on a more compact plant. Var. *drummondii* is hardy to Zone 7.

How to grow: Full sun, part sun, or shade. Grows in any soil, acidic or alkaline, sand or clay. Drought-tolerant. Remove frozen shoots in early spring, and prune as needed in spring or summer to keep it bushy. Pest-free.

Mandevilla
Man-de-vil′la.
Apocynaceae. Dogbane family.

Tender evergreen vines or shrubs with milky sap, showy funnel-shaped flowers, and pairs of long slender pods. More than 110 spp., native to tropical America.

× *amabilis* 'Alice du Pont' (p. 204)
Evergreen vine. Zone 10.
H: 10 ft. or more.

Despite its tenderness, this vine is widely available and commonly grown as a summer patio plant. It thrives in pots or hanging baskets and blooms from the day you bring it home until killed by frost. It climbs by twining and will cover a trellis in a few months. Pinch tips to encourage branching. Pairs of large oval leaves make a dark green background for the lovely trumpet-shaped, clear pink flowers, 2–4 in. wide, with deep throats and 5 rounded petals. Individual flowers last for days. *M. sanderi* 'Red Riding Hood' has smaller, shiny, leathery leaves and 2-in. dark pink flowers with gold throats. *M. laxa*, or Chilean jasmine, is a deciduous vine that dies to the ground but grows back in Zone 8. It has heart-shaped leaves and 2-in. pure white flowers that smell like gardenias.

How to grow: Full sun or afternoon shade. Fertile soil and regular watering. Can grow all summer in a 12-in. pot but needs biweekly feeding. Stop feeding, reduce watering, and cut the stems back partway to overwinter indoors in a sunny window, or buy new plants each year. Where grown outdoors, trim back old, frozen, or tangled shoots in late winter.

Marrubium
Ma-roo′bee-um. Horehound.
Labiatae. Mint family.

Perennials with square stems and opposite leaves with a furry surface and a bitter aroma. About 30 spp., native to Europe and Asia.

incanum (see below for photo)
Silver horehound.
Perennial herb. Zone 4.
H: 2–3 ft. S: 2 ft.

One of the most beautiful herbs, with irresistibly soft, velvety foliage. The branching stems and wrinkled leaves are covered with silvery wool that combines well with anything else in an herb garden or flower border. Flowers are inconspicuous. *M. vulgare* (p. 284), or regular horehound, looks similar but isn't quite as pretty—instead of silvery, it's gray-green. The pungent leaves produce a bitter compound that relieves sore throats and suppresses coughs.

How to grow: Full sun. Needs good drainage and does well in unamended sandy or gravelly soil. Tolerates heat and drought. Makes a bushy clump in dry soil but gets floppy in rich or moist soil. Trim back in summer to correct any straggliness. May self-sow. Clumps can be divided in spring.

Matricaria
Mat-ri-kay′ree-a.
Compositae. Daisy family.

Annuals, biennials, or perennials with finely dissected leaves, a sweet or pungent fragrance, and small white and/or yellow flower heads. Only 5 spp., native to Eurasia.

recutita (p. 284)
German chamomile, sweet false chamomile.
Annual herb. All zones.
H: 24–30 in. S: 6–12 in.

A modest plant with sweet-scented (but bitter-tasting), very finely divided leaves on slender upright stems. Blossoms are white 1-in. daisies with yellow disks that become more prominent and cone-shaped as the blossoms age and go to seed. The dried flower heads make a soothing tea. A small patch provides many blossoms if harvested repeatedly.

How to grow: Full sun. Ordinary soil with good drainage. Easily grown from seed sown direct in early spring. Thin seedlings to 6 in. apart. Problem-free.

Matteuccia
Ma-too′chee-a.
Polypodiaceae. Fern family.

Large ferns that grow in damp sites. Only 3 spp., native to the north temperate zone.

struthiopteris (p. 218)
(*M. pensylvanica*)
Ostrich fern, shuttlecock fern.
Deciduous fern. Zone 2.
H: to 5 ft. S: 2–3 ft. or more.

A majestic fern for cool, moist spots in northern gardens. Its tall fronds form an upright clump shaped like a vase or shuttlecock. Individual fronds are like ostrich plumes. Spreads by underground runners to make a large colony, excellent by ponds or streams or along the edge of damp woods. Looks great in May and June but often turns brown and shabby by late summer. (For beauty that lasts into winter, plant one of the evergreen *Dryopteris* ferns.)

How to grow: Part or full shade; tolerates sun if planted where the soil never dries out. Needs moist soil amended with plenty of organic matter. Place the crown on top of the ground when planting. Divide in spring by removing well-rooted young plants that sprout from the rhizomes.

Matthiola

Math-ee´oh-la. Stock.
Cruciferae. Mustard family.

Annuals or perennials, sometimes shrubby, with fuzzy gray leaves and cross-shaped flowers, sometimes intensely sweet-scented. About 55 spp., native to the Old World.

incana (p. 300)
Stock.
Annual. All zones.
H: 1–2¹/₂ ft. S: 1 ft.

Stocks are classic cut flowers with a pervading, unforgettable, spicy fragrance. Single or double 1-in.-wide flowers fill crowded spikes on stiff leafless stalks. Colors include pink, lilac, purple, reddish, and white. Hybrid strains differ in hardiness and rate of growth. Annual or 10-week stocks develop quickly from seed sown in early spring; hardy or biennial stocks bloom in spring from plants set out the previous fall. Where they grow well, stocks are popular good bedding plants that make a colorful display in cool weather. *M. longipetala* (formerly *M. bicornis*), or night-scented stock, is not showy, but it is easy to grow and has a ravishing fragrance that fills the garden on warm summer evenings. The plant itself is an inconspicuous tangle of gray stems, with small, cross-shaped, lilac flowers that close during the day.

How to grow: Full sun. Rich, well-drained soil and regular watering. Stocks are temperature-sensitive and need a long cool spring. They don't flower well (or at all) if subjected to extreme cold or heat. Direct-sow seeds in fall or early spring or buy small plants to set out.

Maytenus

May-ten´us.
Celastraceae. Spindletree family.

Evergreen trees or shrubs with leathery leaves and clusters of small flowers. Many have medicinal properties. About 225 spp., native to tropical regions in the Old and New World.

boaria (p. 161)
Mayten.
Evergreen tree. Zone 8.
H: 25–50 ft. S: 20–40 ft.

Has the beauty of a weeping willow but is much neater and has evergreen leaves. Forms a spreading mounded crown with slender graceful branches and thin glossy leaves. Flowers are inconspicuous. 'Green Showers' has dense, unusually bright green foliage and a strongly weeping habit.

How to grow: Full sun. Ordinary soil and watering. Train and stake if you want a single-trunked tree. Prune to desired shape. In windy areas, thin branches to reduce wind resistance. Surface roots are a problem in lawns, and spading or cultivating around them causes suckers to sprout. Use mulch or a perennial ground cover under the canopy.

Mazus

May´zus.
Scrophulariaceae. Figwort family.

Low, spreading perennials with toothed leaves and small blue or white flowers. About 30 spp., native to Asia and Australia.

reptans (p. 258)
Perennial. Zone 3.
H: 2 in. S: 12 in. or more.

A mat-forming creeper with stems that root as they run. The narrow 1-in. leaves are bright green. Small 2-lipped flowers in spring are lavender spotted with white and yellow. One of the best ground covers for sun or light shade, good between paving stones or in areas planted with small bulbs. Can invade lawns; some might object, but it looks very pretty there and tolerates light foot traffic. *M. japonicus* 'Albiflorus' grows slightly larger and has paler green leaves and lovely pure white flowers.

How to grow: Full sun or part shade; needs afternoon shade where summers are hot. Ordinary soil and watering. Space 1 ft. apart. Divide every 3–4 years. Problem-free.

Melissa

Me-lis´sa. Balm.
Labiatae. Mint family.

Perennials with square stems, opposite leaves, and small flowers borne in long clusters. Only 3 spp., native to Europe and Asia.

officinalis (p. 284)
Lemon balm.
Perennial herb. Zone 5.
H: 2 ft. S: 2 ft.

Very easy to grow, with a wonderful lemony aroma and flavor. Makes a bushy mound if pruned repeatedly, or a sprawling patch if left alone. The upright stems have opposite leaves with distinct veins and toothed edges. Ordinary plants are bright green; there's also a yellow-variegated form. The crushed leaves are good in hot or iced tea.

How to grow: Full or part sun. Ordinary soil and watering. Propagate by dividing clumps in spring. Looks best if you shear it 2–3 times during the season to renew the foliage and to prevent flowering. The skinny, greenish yellow flower stalks look weedy, and the volunteer seedlings *are* weedy.

Mentha

Men´tha. Mint.
Labiatae. Mint family.

Perennials with square stems, opposite leaves that have a penetrating fragrance, and small flowers in dense heads or spikes. About 25 spp., native to the Old World, and a great many hybrids.

Matthiola longipetala

pulegium (p. 285)
Pennyroyal.
Perennial herb. Zone 6.
H: to 12 in. S: 12 in.

A low-growing mint with a strong penetrating fragrance, used to repel fleas and mosquitoes. Not recommended for culinary or medicinal use. The leafy stems branch repeatedly and spread into a dense flat mat of dark green leaves, but it isn't invasive. It's a good ground cover for damp places or for filling the gaps between stepping-stones. Small lilac flowers open in midsummer on weak upright stems 6–12 in. tall. Shear off the flower stalks for neatness, or leave them to encourage self-seeding. *M. requienii*, or Corsican mint, is much daintier, with tiny bright green leaves and a cool, lingering, crème-de-menthe fragrance. It makes a mosslike ground cover for small spaces.

How to grow: Full or part sun. Fertile soil and regular watering. Needs good drainage, especially in winter. Not reliably hardy in Zone 6 but sometimes self-seeds. Propagate by seed or by division.

Mertensia virginica

spicata (p. 285)
Spearmint.
Perennial herb. Zone 5.
H: 2–3 ft. S: 3 ft. or more.

Notorious for both its sweet minty aroma and its vigorous invasive growth. Spreads quickly to make a dense patch. The toothed leaves are usually dark green and can be smooth or hairy, veined or wrinkled. Stems are topped with long slender spikes of tiny pale lilac flowers. *M.* × *piperita,* or peppermint, is a hybrid of spearmint and water mint, *M. aquatica,* with a sharp penetrating fragrance. Its leaves are usually not hairy, but can be wrinkled, and may be green, purplish, or variegated with white. Nurseries sell many forms of spearmint and peppermint under a variety of names, and a variety of other mints also. Smelling the leaves is the best way to distinguish between them. Don't even think about growing mints from seed—what you get won't be worth the effort. Selected plants, propagated by cuttings, have much better fragrance.

How to grow: Full or part sun. Ordinary soil and watering. These mints tolerate damp soil but don't require it. Plant in an out-of-the-way spot where it won't matter if the patch spreads several feet, or limit its spread by planting in half-barrels or other large containers. Shear to the ground in winter. Divide and replant every 1–2 years in early spring.

suaveolens (p. 285)
Pineapple mint.
Perennial herb. Zone 5.
H: 1 ft. or more. S: to 3 ft.

The white-variegated form of pineapple mint is more common and much prettier than the plain green kind. It's the most ornamental of all mints and has bright green-and-white leaves about 1 in. long. Less vigorous and invasive than spearmint or peppermint, it's safer to include in herb gardens or flower borders. Use a bottomless 12-in. pot to confine it. Shear during the season to renew the foliage and to discourage flowering (the flowers aren't very decorative). The flavor is mild, but the leaves make a pretty, edible garnish for beverages or salads.

How to grow: Full or part sun. Ordinary soil and watering. Trim to the ground in winter. Divide and replant every few years in early spring.

Mertensia
Mer-ten´see-a. Bluebells.
Boraginaceae. Borage family.

Perennials with thick creeping rootstocks and many upright stems topped with clusters of blue, pink-purple, or white flowers with 5 petals. About 50 spp., native to the north temperate zone.

virginica (p. 258)
Virginia bluebells.
Perennial. Zone 3.
H: 1–2 ft. S: 1–2 ft.

An old favorite for spring gardens. The lush foliage seems to appear overnight. Delicate, nodding, bell-shaped flowers, pastel blue fading to pink, follow quickly and last a few weeks. The plant goes dormant by late spring, allowing over-planting. Combines well with foamflowers, bleeding-hearts, phlox, bloodroot, and other woodland wildflowers. 'Alba' has white flowers; 'Rubra' has pink flowers.

How to grow: Part sun or shade. Prefers moist, fertile soil amended with plenty of organic matter. Needs good drainage. Buy container-grown plants, as bare-root plants are likely to have been collected from the wild. Space 1½–3 ft. apart. Increase by dividing the crown into sections with at least one bud.

Metasequoia
Met-a-see-quoy´a. Dawn redwood.
Taxodiaceae. Bald cypress family.

A deciduous conifer related to redwoods and sequoias, first described from fossils in 1941, then discovered growing in China in 1948. Only 1 sp.

glyptostroboides (p. 193)
Dawn redwood.
Deciduous conifer. Zone 5.
H: 80 ft. or more. S: 25 ft. or more.

Grows very fast (2 ft. or more a year) and makes a narrow upright pyramid or cone. The foliage feels soft and looks feathery; the needle-thin leaves, 1/2–1 in. long, are pale green in spring, medium green in summer, and apricot or bronze in fall. The fluted trunk with shaggy reddish brown bark is revealed in winter. A single tree makes a fine lawn specimen. Plant several to make a quiet, secluded grove. Along the Pacific coast, this might be confused with the coast redwood (*Sequoia sempervirens*), but that tree is evergreen.

Easterners may confuse it with bald cypress (*Taxodium distichum*). Look closely at the leaves and branches; their arrangement is opposite in dawn redwood and alternate in bald cypress.

How to grow: Full or part sun. Does best in rich, deep, well-drained soil with regular watering. Tolerates poorer soil but doesn't grow as fast. Can be damaged by severe winters or by hard frosts in early fall. Doesn't need pruning. No serious pests.

Michelia
Mi-kee′lee-a.
Magnoliaceae. Magnolia family.

Evergreen shrubs or trees with small magnolia-like flowers in the axils of the smooth leathery leaves. About 45 spp., native to China and tropical Asia.

figo (p. 179)
(*M. fuscata*)
Banana shrub.
Evergreen shrub. Zone 8.
H: 10–15 ft. S: 6–10 ft.

A dense compact shrub with flowers that smell rich and fruity like bananas—only better! The flowers look like small (1¹/₂ in.) magnolias, creamy yellow shaded with purple. Blooms in spring and summer. The oval dark green leaves, 4 in. long, are thick and glossy. Plant it near a window to enjoy the fragrance indoors. Good for foundation planting and can be espaliered against a wall. *M. doltsopa* is a narrow evergreen tree for Zone 9. It slowly reaches 30 ft. and has very fragrant, long-lasting white flowers, 5–7 in. wide, in early spring.

How to grow: Full sun or afternoon shade. Can't take desert heat. Ordinary or improved soil and regular watering. Prune only to restrict size. Problem-free.

Mimulus
Mim′you-lus. Monkey flower.
Scrophulariaceae. Figwort family.

A diverse and widespread genus of annuals, perennials, and shrubs. Flowers come in many colors, but most have 2 lobed lips. About 150 spp., native to the Old and New World.

× hybridus (p. 300)
Monkey flower.
Annual. All zones.
H: 6–12 in. S: 12–15 in.

Covers itself with unusual flowers, 1¹/₂–2 in. wide with 2 lips, in bright shades of yellow, rose, or red, with brown or purple spots or marks. Children love them. The plants form spreading mounds, good for bedding or in containers. Combines well with primroses, forget-me-nots, and pansies. Various strains are offered as seeds. Look for 'Calypso', 'Malibu', or 'Queen's Prize'.

How to grow: Takes sun in cool climates but can bloom in the shade. Needs fertile soil amended with organic matter and constant moisture. Thrives in cool weather and can't take heat. Start seeds early indoors and set out after danger of frost is past, or sow outdoors in spring where summers are cool. Space 12 in. apart. Pinch out faded flowers to prolong bloom.

Mirabilis
Mee-rab′i-lis.
Nyctaginaceae. Four-o'clock family.

Annuals or perennials, often with tuberous roots, branching stems, and colorful round flowers. About 45 spp., native from the Southwest down through Central America.

jalapa (p. 300)
Four-o'clock.
Perennial often grown as an annual. All zones.
H: to 3 ft. S: to 3 ft.

Not as showy as many annuals but tough and easy. The erect branching stems form a leafy mound. The round flowers, 1 in. wide, open in late afternoon and close by dawn. Blooms throughout the hottest weather. The scentless flowers are usually purplish red or yellow, sometimes pink or white. A good filler for hot, dry sites. Tolerates heat reflected from pavement or buildings.

How to grow: Full sun. Not fussy about soil but needs good drainage. Seeds started indoors or direct-sown in early spring will bloom by midsummer. Often overwinters, especially in the South or Southwest, and self-sows in colder regions. Japanese beetles chew the leaves and buds.

Miscanthus
Mis-kan′thus.
Gramineae. Grass family.

Large perennial grasses with feathery flower heads and long slender leaves with distinct midribs and rough margins. Most form erect clumps. More than 15 spp., native to the Old World.

sinensis (pp. 211, 212)
Japanese silver grass.
Perennial grass. Zone 5 or 4.
H: 5–8 ft. S: 3–6 ft.

The best group of ornamental grasses, offering a wide selection of foliage types and flowering times. All make upright arching clumps of long slender leaves that sway and rustle in the wind. Large fanlike inflorescences wave above the foliage in late summer or fall. They open white, pink, or reddish purple, then ripen into feathery buff or silver seed heads that remain attractive throughout the winter.

These grasses make fine specimens for mixed borders and contrast dramatically with large-leaved perennials. Combine them with evergreens and berrying shrubs for winter interest. Space clumps side by side as a substitute for shrubs to make a screen, hedge, or background.

Miscanthus sinensis

Recommended cultivars of Miscanthus sinensis

'Gracillimus' has slender gray-green leaves with distinct white midribs and grows 5–6 ft. tall. Doesn't flower until late September or October, or not at all in northern gardens. 'Sarabande' has similar foliage but blooms a month earlier.

'Graziella' makes an upright clump 5–6 ft. tall. Leaves have a silvery midrib and turn deep burgundy in fall. Flowers in August.

'Malepartus' is a robust grower, 8–10 ft. tall, with narrow leaves that turn reddish purple in fall. Flowers in August.

'Nippon' is only 4 ft. tall, with slender leaves. Flowers open in August and are displayed well above the foliage.

Var. *purpurascens* is only 3–4 ft. tall. Foliage is green in summer, turning red, orange, and/or gold in fall. The first to flower, starting in July or August. Prefers moist sites and spreads by rhizomes.

'Silverfeather', or **'Silberfeder'**, grows 6–9 ft. tall and forms a wide clump with broader leaves. Flowers in August, earlier than most.

'Strictus' makes a stiff upright clump, 6–8 ft. tall. Leaves have crosswise stripes of green and gold—an unusual and very striking effect. Flowers open in September. 'Zebrinus' has similar leaves but makes a softer, more open clump.

'Variegatus' makes a vase-shaped clump 5–6 ft. tall. There's a creamy white stripe down the center of each leaf. The wonderful foliage adds months of interest to a perennial border. Doesn't bloom until late September or October, and often fails to bloom in northern gardens, but is worth growing anyway.

There are several cultivars to choose from, and they are widely available and inexpensive.

A related plant, *M. sacchariflorus,* forms giant clumps 7–8 ft. tall with leaves 1–2 in. wide, but it has several drawbacks: it's invasive and spreading, the lower leaves drop early, and it doesn't flower until October. If you want a big grass, *Erianthus ravennae* is a better choice.

How to grow: Full or part sun. Ordinary or unamended soil and regular watering. Adapts to acidic or alkaline conditions. Established plants are reasonably drought-tolerant. Cut to the ground in early spring, before new growth begins to show. Older plants can be divided at that time. Dig the entire clump and use a butcher knife, machete, or ax to chop it into smaller sections for replanting. No serious pests or diseases.

Molinia

Mo-lin´ee-a.
Gramineae. Grass family.

Clumping perennial grasses with soft narrow leaves and loose flower heads. Only 2 or 3 spp., native to Eurasia.

***caerulea* 'Variegata'** (p. 212)
Variegated purple moor grass.
Perennial grass. Zone 5.
H: 18 in. (foliage). S: 18–24 in.

Makes upright clumps of arching leaves, 1/2 in. wide and pointed at the ends, that are yellow with green stripes. The yellow foliage combines well with coreopsis 'Moonbeam' at the front of a sunny border, or can brighten a shady corner. Used as a ground cover, it makes an undulating sea of hummocks rather than a boring flat-topped mass. Brown-purple flowers and seeds wave 8–12 in. above the leaves in late summer. This variegated form is prettier than the species, which has plain dark green leaves.

How to grow: Full or part sun. Ordinary or improved soil and regular watering. Needs acidic to neutral soil. Cut foliage down to the ground in late fall where snow is expected, or leave it until spring where winters are mild. Crowded clumps can be divided in spring. Subject to rust and leafspot diseases under humid conditions.

Monarda

Mo-nar´da. Wild bergamot, horsemint.
Labiatae. Mint family.

Annuals or perennials with square stems, aromatic leaves, and dense clusters of tubular 2-lipped flowers. Some have culinary or medicinal uses. Only 12 spp., most native to North America.

didyma (p. 258)
Bee balm, Oswego tea.
Perennial. Zone 4.
H: 2–4 ft. S: 3–5 ft.

Monarda didyma

Flamboyant and cheerful, with moplike heads of tubular flowers that hummingbirds love. Spreads (quickly!) to make a patch with dozens of slender stems. Starts growing in early spring and begins to bloom in June, continuing for at least 3 weeks and sometimes much longer. The flower heads top the stalks. Cut back after flowering, or let the round seed heads ripen and enjoy them in fall and winter. Forms a basal mat of new foliage in fall that's evergreen (or greenish purple) where winters are mild. Powdery mildew regularly disfigures or defoliates the older cultivars such as 'Croftway Pink', but new releases such as 'Gardenview Scarlet' (red) and 'Marshall's Delight' (pink) have excellent mildew resistance and bear larger flowers over a longer season. All have mintlike leaves with a pleasant pungent fragrance.

How to grow: Full sun or afternoon shade. Native to damp sites through the East and grows best in moist, fertile soil. Doesn't tolerate extreme heat. Give it plenty of space, and expect it to spread. Divide and replant every few years in early spring.

fistulosa (p. 258)
Bergamot.
Perennial. Zone 3.
H: 2–4 ft. S: 2–4 ft.

A native of prairies and open woodlands, bergamot tolerates drier conditions and poorer soil than *M. didyma* does. It has slightly fuzzier leaves with a sweeter fragrance, and lavender flowers. New flower heads form above the old ones, as the stem keeps growing. Good for prairie plantings or dry borders. *M. citriodora,* or lemon bergamot, looks similar but has lemon-scented leaves and pink-lavender flowers and grows as an annual.

How to grow: Full sun or afternoon shade. Not fussy about soil but does best with good drainage. Subject to mildew in still, humid weather, especially if crowded by other plants. Divide and replant every few years.

Muscari

Mus-kay′ree. Grape hyacinth.
Liliaceae. Lily family.

Perennials with small bulbs, grassy leaves, and little round flowers in slender clusters at the top of leafless stalks. About 60 spp., native from Europe to Asia.

armeniacum (p. 259)
Grape hyacinth.
Perennial. Zone 4.
H: 6–8 in. S: 6 in.

These are charming little plants with fragrant violet or blue blossoms in early spring. Each bulb produces 1–3 stalks topped with 20–40 closely packed, drooping, urn-shaped flowers. Plants go dormant in summer, then send up grassy dark evergreen foliage in fall. Plant in drifts with early daffodils and tulips, or naturalize under flowering deciduous trees and shrubs. They continue for years with no care, spreading just enough and not too much. Bulb specialists offer several related species and cultivars, some with clear blue or white flowers. All are easy and long lived.

How to grow: Full or part sun. Needs well-drained, ordinary soil. Tolerates summer dryness. Plant 4 in. deep and 3–4 in. apart. Top-dress every 1–2 years with compost or organic fertilizer. Divide when clumps get crowded.

Myoporum

My-o-por′um.
Myoporaceae. Myoporum family.

Evergreen trees or shrubs with small bell-shaped flowers, bright-colored juicy berries, and dark leaves with small clear dots. More than 30 spp., most native to Australia.

parvifolium (p. 179)
Evergreen shrub. Zone 9.
H: 2–3 in. S: 6 ft. or more.

A quick, flat, bright green ground cover, good for controlling erosion and weeds on hill-sides or steep streambanks. Stems root where they touch moist soil. The thin leaves are 2 in. long and less than 1/2 in. wide and make a dense mass of foliage. Cup-shaped 1/2-in. flowers, white or pink, line the stems in summer. *M. laetum* is a fast-growing shrub or tree that makes a dense screen of dark evergreen foliage.

How to grow: Full sun. Ordinary or unimproved soil. Needs good drainage; requires little water when established. Plant 3 ft. apart for a ground cover that will fill in the first year. Prune to remove dead or damaged stems.

Myosotis

My-o-so′tis. Forget-me-not.
Boraginaceae. Borage family.

Annuals, biennials, or perennials with hairy stems and leaves and 5-petaled blue, pink, or white flowers. About 50 spp., native to temperate climates worldwide.

sylvatica (p. 300)
Forget-me-not.
Annual or biennial. All zones.
H: 9–12 in. S: to 12 in.

An easy-to-grow annual, ideal for interplanting with daffodils, tulips, or other spring bulbs. Stems are soft and hairy, topped with curving clusters of sky blue flowers 1/3 in. wide. Look closely to see the yellow eye inside each flower. Blooms for a month or so in spring, then goes to seed and dies. Self-seeds in most gardens, returning year after year. Improved strains have larger flowers in brighter shades of blue, pale pink, or white.

How to grow: Full sun or part shade. Grows fine with ordinary soil and watering. Thrives and spreads fast in rich, moist soil, forming wide patches that look like reflections of the sky. Sow seeds where they are to grow, in fall (mild regions) or early spring (cold-winter areas).

Myrica

Mir′i-ka, mir-i′ka.
Myricaceae. Bayberry family.

Deciduous or evergreen shrubs or trees, most with fragrant leaves and small, round, waxy, fragrant fruits. Some are nitrogen-fixing. About 50 spp., distributed worldwide.

cerifera (p. 179)
Wax myrtle, southern wax myrtle.
Evergreen shrub. Zone 7.
H: to 30 ft. S: to 20 ft.

A good low-maintenance shrub for much of the South, especially along the Atlantic coast, where it grows wild. Has a graceful, not stiff, appearance and sways in the wind. The slender light green leaves are smooth and leathery and smell wonderful when crushed. Clusters of small gray berries dot the stems of female plants in fall and winter. Birds like them. Makes attractive hedges and screens that tolerate (but don't require) repeated pruning. Can also be trained

Myrica cerifera

Myrtus communis

into a small tree. *M. californica* is a similar plant, native to the Pacific coast.

How to grow: Full sun or part shade. Tolerates infertile, sandy, acidic soil and salt spray; thrives in ordinary garden conditions. Space 8–10 ft. apart for a hedge. Needs no special care.

pensylvanica (p. 143)
Bayberry.
Deciduous or semievergreen shrub.
Zone 4 or 3.
H: 8–10 ft. S: 8–10 ft.

Hardier than wax myrtle but just as tough and versatile. Very pretty in summer, when the bright green leaves look particularly fresh and glossy. Stems are stiffer than those of wax myrtle and the habit is denser, less willowy. Clusters of waxy silver-gray berries on female plants are conspicuous after the leaves drop in fall. That wax is used to make bayberry candles (or, more commonly, to perfume candles made of paraffin). A good shrub for foundation planting or for massing on dry banks. Spreads by suckers, but not very fast. Tolerates sea spray and road salt.

How to grow: Full sun. Tolerates unimproved sandy soil but grows faster in ordinary garden conditions. Rarely needs pruning. Pest-free.

Myrrhis
Mir'ris.
Umbelliferae. Carrot family.

A perennial herb with fragrant ferny foliage. Only 1 sp., native to Europe.

odorata (p. 285)
Sweet cicely.
Perennial herb. Zone 4.
H: 3 ft. S: 2 ft.

Makes a bushy clump of ferny, finely cut foliage that smells like anise or licorice. Leaves are dark green all summer, gold in fall. Flat-topped umbels of tiny white flowers in early spring are soon followed by ribbed fruits, 1 in. long, that point up like rockets. Fruits slowly ripen from green to glossy dark brown and are decorative all summer and fall. Leaves and seeds are used as a sweet flavoring. Long-lived and trouble-free, it makes a good tall ground cover for shady areas such as the north side of a building or the edge of a woods.

How to grow: Part sun or shade. Likes rich organic soil and constant moisture. Space purchased plants 2 ft. apart in spring; mature clumps can be cut apart and reset in fall. May self-sow but isn't weedy. No common pests or problems.

Myrtus
Mir'tus. Myrtle.
Myrtaceae. Myrtle family.

Evergreen shrubs or small trees with opposite leaves and fragrant flowers. Only 2 spp., native to the Mediterranean region.

communis (p. 179)
Myrtle.
Evergreen shrub. Zone 8.
H: usually 5–6 ft. S: 4–5 ft.

A tough, drought-resistant shrub with a rounded habit and dense foliage, very useful for sheared hedges and edgings. The species can grow (slowly) to a 20-ft. tree, but 'Compacta' and 'Compacta Variegata' stay under 3 ft. The leathery, stiff, bright green leaves are oval with pointed tips, 2 in. long. They release a strong but pleasant fragrance when crushed. Sweet-scented white flowers like small powderpuffs open over a long season in summer, followed by dark blue berries.

How to grow: Full sun. Ordinary or unamended soil. Needs good drainage; tolerates dry soil when established. Grows slowly. Shear to shape as desired. Problem-free.

Nandina
Nan-dee'na. Heavenly bamboo.
Berberidaceae. Barberry family.

An evergreen shrub with big clusters of small white flowers and bright red berries. Only 1 sp., native to eastern Asia.

domestica (p. 179)
Nandina, heavenly bamboo.
Evergreen shrub. Zone 7 or 6.
H: to 6–8 ft. S: 2–3 ft.

Easy, versatile, and attractive. Forms a clump of erect, unbranched, bamboolike stems with horizontal tiers of lacy foliage in subtle colors. The compound leaves are divided into many smooth oval leaflets, 1–2 in. long. At first they are pastel pink or coppery, then turn light to dark green in summer and rich crimson or purple in fall and winter. Loose clusters of creamy white flowers open in early summer. Heavy sprays of shiny red berries last from fall to spring.

There are many cultivars. Various low-growing forms are called 'Nana' or 'Compacta'; some are nicer than others. 'Harbour Dwarf' is highly recommended; it stays under 2 ft. tall, spreads by suckers and makes a good ground cover, and turns bronzy orange or red in winter. 'San Gabriel' forms a 1–2-ft. mound of extremely narrow, almost needlelike leaves. 'Umpqua Chief' and 'Moyers Red' are vigorous growers that stay about 5–6 ft. tall, with bright red winter color. 'Alba' has white berries.

Nandinas fit into narrow spaces near buildings, fences, or paths and are good for foundation or entryway plantings. Taller forms make graceful hedges or screens. Dwarf forms add year-round interest at the front of a border. All grow well in containers.

How to grow: Full sun, part sun, or shade; needs some sun to develop bright foliage color. Prefers rich soil and regular watering but tolerates unamended soil and drought. Prune older stems to the ground to encourage low, dense, new growth. Tops may freeze in Zone 7 or 6; cut back to live wood in spring. No common pests or diseases.

Nandina domestica

Narcissus

Nar-sis´sus.

Amaryllidaceae. Amaryllis family.

Long-lived bulbous perennials with flat or rushlike leaves and showy yellow or white flowers. There are about 27 spp., nearly all native to Europe, and thousands of hybrids and cultivars.

Daffodils, jonquils, and narcissus

(pp. 260–261)

Perennials. Zone 4, except where noted.

H: 6–20 in. S: 4–8 in.

The genus *Narcissus* includes all the various plants called daffodils, jonquils, and narcissus. Enthusiasts group them into 12 divisions, based on flower form. The flowers have 2 parts: a round central cup, or corona; and a flat ring of 6 petallike segments, collectively called the perianth. Flowers are borne on leafless stalks, singly or in small clusters. Many kinds are fragrant. All make excellent cut flowers.

Different kinds bloom in sequence. Daffodil season starts very early and lasts up to 3 months where winters are mild. Bloom starts later and lasts 4–6 weeks where winters are cold. In any location, you can extend the season by planting some bulbs in protected south-facing sites where the soil warms early and others on the cool north-facing side of a building or slope.

Daffodils grow well throughout the United States and bring joy wherever they're planted. Interplant them with ground covers. Include clumps of fancy types as focal points in a perennial border. Plant drifts in a meadow or along woodland paths. Spread them under a hedge. The bulbs are inexpensive to start with and multiply fast, so you can plant them generously.

How to grow: Full sun or summer shade from deciduous trees. Daffodils grow in almost any soil—sand or clay, acidic or alkaline—but should have good drainage. Dampness is okay only during active growth in spring; dry soil is better when bulbs are dormant in summer. Plant bulbs in fall, after the soil has cooled below 70° F. Put large bulbs 6–8 in. deep, smaller bulbs 3–5 in. deep. Space 6–8 in. apart. Top-dress annually with compost, or scatter fertilizer on the ground in fall and again in spring when new leaves poke through the ground.

Resist the urge to trim off leaves after the flowers have faded. Let them mature and die back naturally; they feed the bulb and provide for the following year's flowers. Use hostas, daylilies, or other perennials or annuals to hide the yellowing foliage.

Naturalized plantings found in the fields or woods around old homesites thrive for decades with no care. In the garden, however, you can multiply your planting and increase flowering by dividing large clumps every few years. The easiest way to do this is to dig clumps when the leaves start to yellow, shake the soil off the roots, separate the bulbs, and replant them promptly. You can wait until the leaves die down completely, but then it's hard to find the bulbs and you risk cutting them with the spade or fork. If you do wait, separate the bulbs and spread them

Recommended daffodils and narcissus

Heights are approximate and will vary under different growing conditions. All Zone 4, except where noted. (Plants from divisions 3, 11, and 12 are usually not available.)

Trumpet daffodils, division 1: The trumpet-shaped corona is as long as the perianth segments. Flowers are 3–4 in. wide, borne singly. 'Dutch Master', 'Golden Harvest', and 'Unsurpassable' are yellow. 'Mount Hood' opens pale yellow and fades to white. 14–18 in. tall. Early to midspring.

Long-cup daffodils, division 2: This is the most popular group, with by far the most cultivars to choose from. The cup is more than one-third as long as, but less than equal to, the perianth segments. Flowers are up to 4 1/2 in. wide, borne singly. 'Carlton' is all-yellow, with a long corona. 'Ice Follies' has a broad cup that opens yellow and fades to white and a white perianth. 'Binkie' is reversed, with white cup and yellow perianth. 'Salome' has a long salmon-pink corona and a white perianth. 14–18 in. tall. Early to midspring.

Double daffodils, division 4: These have a tuft or mound of extra petals, in addition to or instead of a cup. Flowers are 1–4 in. wide, borne singly or clustered. 'Cheerfulness', sweetly fragrant, has small white flowers with pale yellow centers. 'Golden Ducat' is all-yellow. 'Tahiti' is yellow marked with red-orange. 12–16 in. tall. Mid- to late spring.

Triandrus hybrids, division 5: Flowers have a flared-back perianth and droop from the top of the stalk in groups of 2 or more. 'Hawera' is a miniature, 8 in. tall, with 1-in. flowers. 'Thalia' has white flowers 2 in. wide on 16-in. stalks. Mid- to late spring.

Cyclamineus hybrids, division 6: These have long tubular coronas and distinctly turned-back perianth segments. Flowers are about 2 in. wide, borne singly. 'February Gold' and 'Peeping Tom' are yellow. 'February Silver' is white with a yellow corona. All are short (under 8 in.). Very early spring.

Jonquilla hybrids, division 7: The sweetly fragrant flowers are 1/2–1 in. wide, with small cups, borne in clusters of 1–3. The narrow leaves are dark green. Stems are round or rushlike, not flat. 'Suzy' has a yellow perianth and an orange cup. 'Trevithian' is golden yellow. The species *N. jonquilla* has clear yellow flowers. Up to 16 in. tall. Mid- to late spring.

Tazetta hybrids, division 8: Flowers are almost flat, 1/2–1 1/4 in. wide, in clusters of 3–20. Stems are stout; leaves are broad. 'Geranium' is white with a red-orange cup, grows 14 in. tall, blooms in late spring, is hardy to Zone 5, and is very fragrant. 'Paperwhite' types, with especially fragrant white flowers, and 'Soleil d'Or', with golden yellow flowers, are hardy only in Zone 8 or warmer. They are the best daffodils for naturalizing in warm-winter climates, where they start blooming as early as Christmas. Because they don't require any cold treatment, they are especially easy to force on a sunny windowsill indoors. Just plant, water, and watch them grow.

Poeticus hybrids, division 9: 'Actaea' is the most common member of this group. Called pheasant's-eye narcissus, it has a pure white perianth and a small yellow cup with a thin red line around the edge. Very sweet-scented. 18 in. tall. Blooms at the end of the season.

Species daffodils, division 10: This group includes wild species, most with tiny bulbs and small flowers. *N. bulbocodium*, the hoop-petticoat daffodil, is one of the most popular. Its small golden flowers have wide skirtlike trumpets and very slender perianth segments. 6 in. tall. Midspring.

to dry in a shady place, then remove the withered leaves and roots. Store the bulbs in mesh bags in a cool, dry shed or cellar with good air circulation until it's time to replant them in fall.

Daffodils are trouble-free plants. Few pests or diseases attack them. Mice, voles, gophers, rabbits, and deer avoid them. Take note and warn children that daffodil bulbs, leaves, and flowers are poisonous if eaten.

Nelumbo

Nee-lum´bo. Lotus.
Nymphaceae. Water lily family.

Aquatic perennials with thick rhizomes, large round leaves, showy flowers, and interesting seedpods. Only 2 spp., one from Asia and Australia, the other from North America.

nucifera (p. 258)

Lotus, Egyptian lotus.
Perennial. Zone 4, if tubers are protected from freezing.
H: to 5 ft. above water.
S: 6 ft. or more; can spread to 20 ft.

Magnificent plants for pools or tubs. Round leaves like inverted parasols lift 2–5 ft. above the water. Many-petaled flowers, usually rosy pink or white, grow on stalks even taller than the leaves. The flowers open in the morning and close at night and are intensely fragrant. Bloom continues for several weeks through the heat of summer. The woody pods, 3–6 in. wide, have large seeds that rattle in individual cavities. They are attractive in the winter garden or in dried arrangements. 'Roseum Plenum' is a popular cultivar with double rosy pink flowers 10–12 in. wide. New dwarf cultivars have been developed for tub culture. *N. lutea,* the American lotus, is native throughout the eastern United States and has 10-in. creamy yellow flowers.

How to grow: Full sun. Needs fertile soil under 4–8 in. of still water. Plant in the bottom of a pond or in a big plastic pot or tub. Position the tuber horizontally on the soil and cover it with 3–4 in. of sand. Lotus roots spread quickly, and one plant can grow to fill a shallow pond. Confine it to a container if you don't want that to happen. Planting in containers is also a good idea in situations where a pond might freeze to the bottom. Lift the container in fall and store in a cool place for the winter. Don't let the tuber get dry. Put the container back out after the pond water warms in spring. Where it's not likely to freeze, a lotus can stay in a pond all year. No common pests or diseases.

Nelumbo lutea

Nepeta

Nep´e-ta, ne-pee´ta. Catmint.
Labiatae. Mint family.

Perennials or annuals with opposite leaves, sometimes scented, and tubular 2-lipped flowers in shades of blue, purple, pink, or white. About 250 spp., most native to dry sites in the Old World.

cataria (p. 285)

Catnip.
Perennial herb. Zone 3.
H: 3 ft. S: 2 ft. or more.

Plant this for your cats; they get excited by the bitter camphorlike fragrance of the leaves. It makes a lax clump of square-sided stems with downy, gray-green, triangular leaves 1–3 in. long. It bears spikes of small flowers in late summer if you let it, but it looks better if you shear the tops off before that happens and encourage a fresh crop of foliage. Dried leaves make good kitty toys and also make a tea that relieves cold symptoms. There's also a lemon-scented variety.

How to grow: Full or part sun. Ordinary soil and watering. Tolerates heat, dry soil, and neglect. Spreads quickly by rhizomes and can be invasive, but not like mints are. Also self-sows if you let it go to seed. A Eurasian native, it has naturalized in the northern United States.

× *faassenii* (p. 258)

(often, but erroneously, sold as *N. mussinii*)
Catmint.
Perennial. Zone 4.
H: 18–24 in. S: 18 in.

Pretty, aromatic, and trouble-free, this gives a soft effect to a flower border with its graceful loose garlands of lavender flowers and grayish foliage. Forms a lax mound of branching stems. The gray-green leaves are softly toothed and crinkled, 1¹/₂ in. long. Flowers heavily in June and again in late summer if sheared. Traditionally combined with roses, or spilling onto a brick or flagstone path. 'Dropmore' is a good cultivar with small, very gray leaves and lavender-blue flowers. 'Six Hills Giant' (sometimes identified as *N. gigantea*) grows 3 ft. tall and wide with purple flowers and tolerates damp soil better than other nepetas do.

How to grow: Full or part sun. Needs well-drained soil. Tolerates heat but not humidity. Give it plenty of space; it's apt to flop over and cover nearby plants. Shear after flowering to encourage rebloom. A sterile hybrid, it doesn't set seed. Propagate by division in early spring or after the first flush of bloom.

Nephrolepis

Nef-ro-lee´pis. Sword fern.
Polypodiaceae. Fern family.

Tender ferns with creeping rhizomes that bear tufts of slender featherlike fronds. About 30 spp., native to warm and tropical climates.

exaltata (p. 218)

Sword fern.
Evergreen fern. Zone 9.
H: to 5 ft. S: forms patch.

In mild-winter areas this fern is common and easy to the point of being invasive. It spreads by slender runners, forming tufts of erect bright green fronds. Looks fresh as a ground cover in shady corners. Grows well in containers.

N. cordifolia, often sold as *N. exaltata*, is similar but grows only 2–3 ft. tall.

How to grow: Part sun or shade. Ordinary soil and watering. Space 2 ft. apart for instant fill or 5 ft. apart for normal ground cover. Cut back to the ground if damaged by frost. Divide when crowded.

Nerium

Neer′i-um. Oleander.
Apocynaceae. Dogbane family.

Evergreen shrubs with leafy stems and big clusters of showy 5-lobed flowers. All parts are extremely poisonous. Only 2 spp., native from the Mediterranean region to Japan.

oleander (p. 180)
Oleander.
Evergreen shrub. Zone 8.
H: 6–12 ft. S: 6–12 ft.

Very tough but also very showy. Blooms throughout the heat of summer, with clusters of 2–3-in. single or double flowers in white, creamy yellow, pink, salmon, rose, or red. A few kinds are fragrant. Forms a big mound of slender leafy stems, erect or sometimes arching under the weight of the flowers. The long narrow leaves are smooth and leathery, dark green above and pale below. Excellent for screening near the beach or along highways. 'Petite Pink' and 'Petite Salmon' are compact, 3–4 ft. tall. 'Algiers' (red), 'Casablanca' (white), and 'Tangier' (pink) are intermediate size, 6–8 ft. tall. There are many other cultivars, differing in size, flower color, and hardiness (some are Zone 9).

How to grow: Full sun. Grows in almost any soil and tolerates poor drainage, drought, alkaline conditions, salt, heat, and wind. Used extensively along beaches and highways in California and Florida. Damaged by hard frost but usually recovers. Prune in winter, cutting some of the stems to the ground. Flowers on new growth. Fast-growing. Subject to scale infestation.

Nicotiana

Ni-ko-she-ay′na. Tobacco.
Solanaceae. Nightshade family.

Annuals, perennials, or a few shrubs, usually with sticky, smelly leaves. All have tubular 5-lobed flowers and make small, round, dry pods loaded with thousands of tiny seeds. *N. tabacum* leaves are dried for smoking tobacco. *N. rustica*, much higher in nicotine, is used as an insecticide. About 70 spp., native to the Old and New World.

alata (p. 300)
(*N. affinis*)
Flowering tobacco.
Annual. All zones.
H: 1–3 ft. S: 1 ft.

Blooms reliably all summer long in shades of white, pink, rose, red, crimson, or green. Flowers are like 1-in. stars with long tubular

throats, borne on erect branching stalks. Older cultivars open in the late afternoon or evening; new strains stay open all day. Some kinds are sweetly fragrant, especially in the evening. The basal leaves are large and have sticky hairs. Combines well with other annuals or perennials and also makes a good container plant. 'Lime Green' (2¹/₂ ft. tall) has green flowers. The 'Nikki' series (1 ft.) is very floriferous but has little fragrance. 'Sensation Mixed' (2–3 ft.) has fragrant blooms that stay open all day. 'Fragrant Cloud' (3 ft.) has large white flowers that are very fragrant in the evening.

How to grow: Part or full sun. Ordinary soil and watering. Seeds are small, like those of petunias. Sow indoors at 70° F 6–8 weeks before last frost. May self-sow in the garden. Cut off spent flower stalks in midsummer to reduce seeding and to renew bloom. Attacked by tomato hornworms and whiteflies.

sylvestris (p. 300)
Woodland tobacco.
Annual. All zones.
H: 4–6 ft. S: 3 ft.

A dramatic plant with tall branching stalks topped with loose drooping clusters of white flowers that are intensely fragrant at night. The flowers have long skinny tubes and flare 1¹/₂ in. wide at the end. They're pollinated by hawkmoths that resemble tiny hummingbirds. Blooms from July until frost. Forms a basal rosette of very large (to 20 in. long), sticky leaves. It's big enough to combine with shrubs, or put a few at the back of a substantial flower border.

How to grow: Like *N. alata*. Give it plenty of space. Gets top-heavy by late summer and may flop over during a storm.

Nymphaea

Nim-fay′a. Water lily.
Nymphaceae. Water lily family.

Aquatic perennials with big round leaves and showy many-petaled flowers. About 35 spp., native worldwide. Most of the cultivars are hybrids.

hybrids (p. 259)
Water lilies.
Perennials. Zone 4, if roots are protected from freezing.
H: float on water. S: 1–8 ft. or more.

Specialty nurseries offer two main categories of water lilies: hardy and tropical. Hardy ones bloom from early summer to frost, with white, yellow, pink, or red flowers that open in the daytime. Some but not all are fragrant. The flowers and plants vary considerably in size. There are miniatures that you can grow in a half-barrel lined with plastic, and robust types that need a large pool or pond.

Tropical water lilies are usually larger plants with larger, often very fragrant flowers that bloom in the day or at night. The color range is expanded to include blue and purple. Some

Nicotiana alata

Nerium oleander

Nymphaea odorata

kinds have fancy mottled foliage. Tropicals can't go in the water until its temperature reaches 65°–70° F, but they continue blooming late in fall, even after frost.

How to grow: Full sun. Need a pool of still water deep enough to cover the roots by 8–16 in. There are cultivars suitable for any size pool; when in doubt, choose a smaller plant and give it extra room, rather than crowding a big plant. Position the rhizome, buds up, horizontally on the surface of the soil at the bottom of a pond or in a broad tub filled with 6–8 in. of loamy garden soil—*not* potting soil. Cover with 1 in. of sand or gravel. Water lilies are vigorous plants and require 1 lb. of a complete fertilizer each year. Spread it on the soil around the roots.

Hardy water lilies can stay outdoors all winter if the soil doesn't freeze around their roots. In cold climates, plant one in a tub that you can lift and store in a frost-free cellar for the winter. Don't let it dry out. Put it back in the pool after the ice thaws, as early as 6 weeks before the average last frost date. Unless you live in Zone 9 or 10, it's hard to keep tropical water lilies over winter, so most gardeners grow them as annuals.

Nyssa

Nis´sa. Tupelo, sour gum.
Nyssaceae. Tupelo family.

Deciduous trees with outstanding fall color. Only 5 spp., native to North America and eastern Asia.

sylvatica (p. 121)

Sour gum, black gum.
Deciduous tree. Zone 3.
H: 30–60 ft. S: 20–30 ft.

A native eastern tree with outstanding fall color, effective even in the South and West where autumn weather is warm. Makes a handsome pyramidal tree, fine for a lawn specimen. The glossy oval leaves, 2–5 in. long, turn from dark green to bright red. Color begins early and lasts long. Flowers are insignificant, but birds like the dark blue fruits.

How to grow: Full or part sun. Not fussy about soil. Tolerates poor drainage or occasional droughts. Slow-growing but adaptable and pest-free. Prune to shape as desired.

Nyssa sylvatica

Ocimum

Oh´si-mum. Basil.
Labiatae. Mint family.

Annuals, perennials, or shrubs, most with very fragrant foliage, used for flavoring, fragrance, and medicine. About 150 spp., native to warm and tropical regions, especially Africa.

basilicum (p. 286)

Sweet basil, common basil.
Annual herb. All zones.
H: to 2 ft. S: 1 ft.

As indispensable as tomatoes in the summer garden, basil is a bushy herb with shiny, wonderfully fragrant leaves. The erect stems are woody at the base and branch repeatedly. The opposite leaves are 1/2–4 in. long, depending on the cultivar. Narrow spikes of small white or purplish flowers form at the top of the stems in summer, but most gardeners pinch them off. Regular sweet basil has excellent flavor. Many special cultivars are available from seed. 'Cinnamon' has a sweet spicy fragrance. 'Purple Ruffles' and 'Opal' are rather bland, but they have pretty dark purple foliage that combines well with flowering annuals or perennials. 'Spicy Globe' makes a 6-in. ball of tiny tasty leaves. It's good for edgings or in containers.

How to grow: Full sun. Ordinary soil and regular watering. Prefers hot weather. Easy from seed, started indoors 8 weeks before last frost or sown direct. Don't sow or transplant into the garden until the soil is warm. Attacked by Japanese beetles in the Northeast.

Oenothera

Ee-noth´er-a. Evening primrose.
Onagraceae. Evening primrose family.

Annuals or perennials with large 4-petaled flowers in bright yellow, white, or pink. Some open in the evening and last all night, but others are day bloomers. About 80 spp., native to the New World.

biennis (p. 300)

Evening primrose.
Biennial or annual. All zones.
H: to 6 ft. S: 1 ft.

Not a connoisseur's plant, but children love it. It's one of the few plants known for rapid movement. At dusk the pointed buds open in less than a minute, spreading into clear yellow, 4-petaled flowers 1–2 in. wide. The flowers are fragrant all night, then close in the morning or stay open on cloudy days. Forms a basal rosette of rough, hairy, pointed leaves, then sends up one or more flower stalks. Keeps growing taller, blooming at the top, all summer. Flower arrangers like the long stalks of dry seedpods. Goldfinches like the tiny seeds. Oil from the seeds has medicinal properties.

How to grow: Full or part sun. Ordinary or unimproved soil. Tolerates dryness and neglect. Good for meadows or semiwild landscapes. Self-seeds and has naturalized along roadsides. Pest-free.

missourensis (p. 259)

(*O. macrocarpa*)
Ozark sundrops.
Perennial. Zone 5.
H: 1 ft. S: 1 ft.

A very showy plant for dry sites. It's oddly proportioned, with giant flowers close to the ground on short weak stems. The clear yellow, 4-petaled flowers open 4–6 in. wide in late afternoon. Blooms for several weeks in early to midsummer. Plant it on the front edge of a raised bed where you can easily admire the blossoms.

In fall, gather the pinkish tan seed capsules for dried arrangements. They're egg-sized but light and papery, with 4 thin wings. *O. caespitosa* is similar, with large, fragrant white flowers.

How to grow: Full sun. This Great Plains native has a big deep taproot and needs well-drained soil, even gravel or sand. Tolerates limestone. In moist climates, plant in raised beds.

speciosa (p. 259)
Showy primrose, white evening primrose.
Perennial. Zone 5.
H: 1–2 ft. S: 3 ft. or more.

Few plants give as much color for so long with so little care. This native wildflower is tough, undemanding, pest-free, drought-tolerant, and quick-spreading. The erect stems are topped with clusters of rounded flowers 2–3 in. wide. The flowers are white or pink, slightly scented, and open daytimes from spring through summer. Spreads by rhizomes. Great for filling the strip between curb and sidewalk or covering banks. Var. *childsii* (*O. berlandieri*) is shorter, with rosy pink flowers.

How to grow: Full sun. Tolerates poor or dry soil and heat. Space 1–2 ft. apart for ground cover. Increase by division anytime. Use edging at least 8 in. deep to curb its spread when combined with other perennials or planted in rich, moist soil.

tetragona (p. 259)
Sundrops.
Perennial. Zone 4.
H: to 2 ft. S: forms patch.

Glowing lemon yellow flowers, 1–2 in. wide, bloom daytimes for up to a month in early summer. The hairy stems and leaves are dark green with a reddish purple cast or dots. Sometimes goes dormant after blooming. Forms a low mat of evergreen foliage in fall. Spreads by underground runners to make a wide patch. Useful for controlling erosion on banks. This species is very similar to and sometimes combined with *O. fruticosa*. Both are native throughout the East.

How to grow: Like *O. speciosa*.

Olea
O′lee-a. Olive.
Oleaceae. Olive family.

Evergreen trees or shrubs with leathery leaves, small flowers, and fruits with one large seed. Some species provide good timber. About 20 spp., native to warm and tropical climates in the Old World.

europaea (p. 161)
Olive.
Evergreen tree. Zone 8.
H: 25–30 ft. S: 25–30 ft.

Attractive in youth and magnificent with age, olives make fine lawn or street trees. The silvery foliage looks even more silvery when it ripples in the wind. The leathery leaves are narrow,

3 in. long. The rugged trunk and limbs are spreading and picturesque. Can be trained and pruned into a single-trunked or multitrunked tree, sheared into formal shapes, or used as a hedge. The tiny flowers are inconspicuous, but many people are allergic to the pollen. Fruits are not easy to cure and can be a nuisance. Fruiting can be prevented by a hormone spray. 'Swan Hill' produces no fruit and little pollen.

How to grow: Full sun. Ordinary or unamended soil. Thrives in heat and tolerates dry soil when established. Even large trees can be transplanted easily with a high chance of success. Grows quickly. Subject to scale infestation and verticillium wilt.

Onopordum
On-oh-por′dum.
Compositae. Daisy family.

Large biennials with spiny leaves and flower heads. About 40 spp., native to Europe and Asia.

acanthium (p. 301)
Scotch thistle, cotton thistle.
Biennial. Zone 4.
H: to 8 ft. S: to 4 ft.

Not for the timid, nor for small gardens. Makes a broad rosette of woolly white leaves with spiny-tipped lobes the first year. In rich soil, the rosette can grow 3 ft. wide. Leafy, spiny, woolly, winged stalks shoot up fast the second year, branching like a candelabra. Your neighbors will be amazed. Purple flowers like thistles bloom for up to a month in early to midsummer. Looks good and combines easily with clary sage, foxgloves, and *Crambe cordifolia*.

How to grow: Full sun. Ordinary soil and watering. Start seeds in spring or summer for bloom the following year. The only difficulty is cutting it down after it blooms, to limit the number of volunteer seedlings. The stems are tough, and you'll need long-handled loppers to get at them.

Ophiopogon
Oh-fee-oh-po′gon. Lilyturf, mondo grass.
Liliaceae. Lily family.

Evergreen perennials with grassy foliage. May form clumps or spread like sod. About 50 spp., native to eastern Asia.

japonicus (p. 262)
Monkey grass, mondo grass.
Perennial. Zone 7.
H: 6–12 in. S: 6 in.

Dark green and fine-textured, this can substitute for turfgrass in shady places. Tolerates only light foot traffic, but makes a dense ground cover in courtyards, a low edging for paths and beds, or a carefree ring under live oaks or southern magnolias. The thin leathery leaves are 6–12 in. long—shorter and narrower than liriope leaves. Flowers and fruits are small and hide in the foliage. 'Nana', or 'Nippon', is a neat com-

Oenothera berlandieri

Ophiopogon japonicus

pact form, only 3 in. tall, perfect for finely detailed small gardens or as a ground cover for container specimens. *O. jaburan* is a coarser plant, with wider leaves up to 18 in. long. There are some variegated cultivars. *O. planiscapus* 'Nigrescens' (sometimes listed as *O. arabicus*), or black mondo grass, has very dark purple-black foliage. It's too expensive to use as a ground cover, but it makes a striking accent in contrast to silver, gold, or lime green plants.

How to grow: Part sun or shade; foliage is damaged by full sun. Ordinary soil and watering; tolerates dry soil when established. For mass plantings, divide large clumps or plants from 1-gal. containers into individual sprigs, and trim the roots and tops by one-third. Be sure each division is about the same size. Space 6 in. apart. This works much better than spacing big plants farther apart—the planting fills in faster and looks more uniform.

Shear the foliage back by one-third to one-half in late winter or early spring for uniformity and neatness. Use the high setting of the lawn mower for large areas or hand clippers for small plantings. Can grow for years without division. No serious pests or diseases.

Opuntia
Oh-pun´shee-a.
Cactaceae. Cactus family.

Shrubby or treelike succulents with plump, green, flat or round stems divided into a series of joints or pads. Flowers are often large and bright with many waxy petals. The seedy fruits may be juicy or dry. About 300 spp., all native to the New World.

Opuntia humifusa

humifusa (p. 180)
Hardy prickly pear.
Evergreen shrubby succulent. Zone 4.
H: 1 ft. S: to 5 ft.

A low-growing cactus with spiny stems flattened into round or oval "joints" or sections about 6 in. long. The waxy yellow flowers, 3-in. wide, are as pretty as roses in early summer. Small, soft purplish fruits ripen in late summer. The stems turn reddish purple and wrinkle up like raisins in the winter; they get plump and green again come spring. Useful on rough rocky hillsides, on sandy beaches, or in planter beds surrounded by hot pavement where little else will grow. Combines well with spreading conifers and clumping grasses for low-maintenance mass plantings. *O. polycantha* is similar but spinier and has waxy 4-in. flowers that are yellow, pink, or carmine. Native to dry hillsides in the Great Plains, this makes a tough ground cover where all else fails and is hardy to Zone 3. *O. imbricata*, the cholla or walking-stick cactus, has cylindrical stems that branch repeatedly and make a dense spiny clump 6–8 ft. tall. Hot pink or purple cup-shaped flowers, 2–3 in. wide, cover the stems in summer. Small bright yellow fruits ripen in fall. It's hardy to Zone 6.

How to grow: Full sun. Needs good drainage. Tolerates poor or dry soil but thrives with ordinary soil and watering. Sold in containers. Increase by cuttings: sever a joint, let it callus in dry air for a few days, then insert it in warm, well-drained soil. Avoid sites with blowing litter, as cleanup is difficult. Use a thick layer of gravel mulch to discourage weeds. No common pests or diseases.

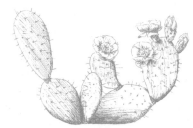

Opuntia microdasys

prickly pears for desert gardens
Gardeners in the hot, arid Southwest can choose from many other species of prickly pears. Contact cactus specialists or native-plant nurseries to find the following favorites.

O. bigelovii, the teddy-bear cactus, has woody trunks and armlike branches densely covered with golden spines. *O. ficus-indica* has plump, round, usually spineless pads. Both the pads and the juicy red or yellow fruits are edible. It grows fast and is used for hedging. *O. microdasys,* or bunny-ears, is a bushy little plant with many thin round pads closely dotted with tufts of short bristles. *O. violacea* has flat pear-shaped pads in an unusual shade of lavender-blue and showy yellow-orange flowers.

All require full sun and good drainage. They tolerate freezing nights but are damaged by extreme winters.

Origanum
Oh-rig´a-num.
Labiatae. Mint family.

Annual or perennial herbs, sometimes woody at the base. The simple opposite leaves may be very fragrant or odorless; several kinds are valued as seasonings. Some species have showy flowers. About 36 spp., native to Eurasia.

majorana (p. 286)
(formerly *Majorana hortensis*)
Sweet marjoram, knotted marjoram.
Tender perennial herb grown as an annual.
Zone 9.
H: 1–2 ft. S: 1–2 ft.

Forms a bushy branching mound of slender stems with pairs of small, oval, gray-green leaves. The leaves have a delicious fragrance and are used in cooking and perfumery. Stems are topped with rounded knotlike clusters of gray bracts that surround inconspicuous white flowers. Lives over where winters are mild but may get straggly. Grows easily from seed, and first-year plants are fresh and compact. *O.* × *majoricum* is a hybrid with the fragrance of sweet marjoram but is hardier.

How to grow: Full sun. Prefers well-drained soil with added lime. Start seeds indoors 8 weeks before last frost or buy started plants to set out. Pinch or harvest frequently to promote bushiness.

vulgare (p. 286)
Perennial herb. Zone 5.
H: to 2 ft. S: 2 ft.

There are several distinct forms within this species. Subsp. *vulgare,* or wild marjoram, makes a patch of erect stems 2 ft. tall with pretty rosy-red flowers in late summer. It is commonly sold as oregano, but unfortunately its leaves have little flavor. To season Italian food, choose subsp. *hirtum,* often sold as *O. heracleoticum.* The plant looks like wild marjoram with dull white flowers, but the aroma is distinctly pungent. Subsp. *vulgare* 'Aureum' or 'Golden Creeping' oregano is unscented, but it makes a cheery mat of creeping stems with yellow-green leaves.

How to grow: Full sun. Needs good drainage. Tolerates dry soil. The best way to get a fragrant plant is to choose it in person at the nursery, sniffing the leaves before you buy. Renew established plants by dividing and replanting every few years. Plant in a raised bed and mulch with pine boughs to maximize winter hardiness. Basal foliage is evergreen in mild climates.

Osmanthus
Oz-man´thus.
Oleaceae. Olive family.

Evergreen shrubs or trees with tough leathery leaves, sometimes spiny-toothed, and small but very fragrant flowers. About 15 spp., most native to eastern Asia.

fragrans (see below for photo)
Sweet olive.
Evergreen shrub. Zone 9.
H: to 30 ft. S: 20–25 ft.

A bulky shrub—dense, erect, and eventually treelike—with an unforgettable sweet, fruity fragrance. The clusters of tiny white flowers are powerful enough to perfume the entire garden in spring and summer and sporadically through the year. The pointed oval leaves, to 4 in. long, are thick and leathery. Use as a single specimen or for a tall screen. Can be kept small in a container. 'Aurantiacus' is similar but has pale orange flowers that are even more fragrant; it blooms heavily from September to November. *O.* × *fortunei* (p. 180) is a hybrid between *O. fragrans* and *O. heterophyllus.* It is hardy to Zone 7 and has fragrant flowers in autumn and spiny-edged hollylike leaves. It grows slowly to about 6 ft. tall; can reach 20 ft.

How to grow: Full or part sun. Ordinary soil and watering. Allow plenty of room for this large shrub. Prune only to shape, if desired. Pest-free.

heterophyllus (p. 180)
(*O. aquifolium*)
Holly-leaf osmanthus.
Evergreen shrub. Zone 7 or 6.
H: usually 8–10 ft. S: usually 4 ft.

This is a slow-growing shrub, excellent for screens, hedges, or containers. The leathery, thick, dark green leaves resemble English holly (*Ilex aquifolium*) but are opposite rather than alternate. The tiny white flowers are sweetly fragrant, blooming mostly in autumn. 'Gulftide' is especially compact and dense. 'Variegatus' has leaves bordered with creamy white.

How to grow: Full sun, part sun, or shade. Ordinary soil and watering. Plant from containers. Space tall kinds 3–4 ft. apart for screening, dwarf ones 2 ft. apart for hedges. Prune only to maintain size and form. Easy and problem-free.

Osmunda
Oz-mun´da. Flowering fern.
Osmundaceae. Osmunda family.

Large tough ferns that make upright clumps of big fronds and mats of coarse fibrous roots. About 10 spp., native to the Old and New World.

cinnamomea (p. 218)
Cinnamon fern.
Deciduous fern. Zone 3.
H: 2–3 ft. S: 1 ft.

This striking fern makes a good specimen for damp sites. The fertile fronds emerge first in spring and look like cinnamon sticks—stiff, erect, narrow, club-shaped, about 1 ft. long. Then the coarse, twice-cut, sterile fronds unroll. They are large and strong, colored yellow-green or dark waxy green. Grows as a clump, only gradually enlarging. Thrives in waterlogged soil along streams or ponds, combined with candelabra primroses or Japanese irises.

How to grow: Part sun or shade; will tolerate some sun if kept moist. Buy container-grown plants propagated from spores. Plant in constantly damp, acidic soil. Once established, needs no special care. Difficult to propagate by division.

claytoniana (p. 219)
Interrupted fern.
Deciduous fern. Zone 3.
H: 2–4 ft. S: 1 ft.

One of the first ferns to appear in spring. The fronds are white with wool when they first uncurl from a central crown. Sterile fronds reach 4 ft. tall, 1 ft. wide at the midpoint. Fertile fronds are erect and taller; spore-bearing segments soon drop off, leaving a long bare spot at the center of the stalk. Rugged and persistent, it makes a long-lived specimen for shady borders or woodland gardens. Contrasts well with the large leaves of bergenias.

Osmunda cinnamomea

Osmanthus fragrans

How to grow: Full or part sun. Ordinary soil and watering. Prefers stony, dry, mildly acidic soil. Established plants tolerate some drought but do better with summer watering. Top-dress annually with compost. Shouldn't be disturbed or divided.

regalis (p. 219)
Royal fern.
Deciduous fern. Zone 3.
H: 5–6 ft. or more. S: 2–3 ft.

The largest of our native ferns, this makes massive majestic specimens if grown in rich, moist soil. The large coarse fronds are divided into segments that resemble honey-locust tree leaves. The color is a translucent pale green in sun, deeper green in shade. Fertile fronds have curly, light brown tops that look like faded astilbe flowers. Grows naturally in wetlands and tolerates standing water along streams or ponds. 'Cristata' has crested fronds. 'Purpurascens' has coppery pink new growth and purplish stalks.

How to grow: Part sun or shade. Needs fertile, acidic soil amended with plenty of organic matter. Best in very wet soil and light shade; must not be allowed to dry out. Continues in one spot for years; shouldn't be moved or divided.

Oxydendrum
Ok-si-den´drum. Sourwood.
Ericaceae. Heath family.

A deciduous tree with drooping clusters of small white flowers in summer and red fall foliage. Only 1 sp., native to the eastern United States.

Oxydendrum arboreum

arboreum (p. 121)
Sourwood.
Deciduous tree. Zone 4.
H: 30 ft. or more. S: 15–20 ft.

Grows slowly into a handsome specimen tree with a slender profile. Lacy clusters of bead-like white flowers drape gracefully over the glossy dark green leaves in summer, after most other trees have finished blooming. Fruits ripen into a dry tawny lace. Fall color starts early and develops into blazing scarlet, orange, and burgundy. Grows well at the sunny edge of a woods or in the open.

How to grow: Full or part sun. Native to eastern woodlands and prefers well-drained, acidic, organic soil. Best if mulched—roots don't compete well with lawns or underplantings.

Pachysandra
Pak-i-san´dra.
Buxaceae. Box family.

Low-growing perennials, woody at the base, with evergreen foliage. Only 5 spp., one from the southeastern United States, the rest from eastern Asia.

Pachysandra terminalis

terminalis (p. 262)
Pachysandra, Japanese spurge.
Evergreen perennial. Zone 5.
H: 8 in. S: 8 in.

Very popular as a ground cover for part or full shade, under and around trees and shrubs. Underground runners form a dense intertwined mat that defies weeds and erosion. The short upright stalks are topped with rosettelike clusters of glossy dark green leaves. Small white flowers are briefly conspicuous in spring. A silver-edged form is pretty but less vigorous. *P. procumbens,* the native Allegheny spurge, has wider leaves mottled with purplish gray and spreads slowly.

How to grow: Part sun or shade; foliage yellows in full sun. Ordinary soil and watering. Doesn't tolerate extreme heat or dryness. Use 4 plants per square foot for ground cover. Older plantings can be divided. Pest-free but subject to various fungal diseases.

Paeonia
Pee-oh´nee-a. Peony.
Paeoniaceae. Peony family.

Perennials or low shrubs with compound leaves and rounded flowers, often large and showy. More than 30 spp., most native to Europe or Asia. Most common garden peonies are hybrids.

hybrids (pp. 262, 263)
Herbaceous peonies.
Perennials. Zone 3.
H: $2^1/_2$ –$3^1/_2$ ft. S: 3 ft.

Old-fashioned favorites—easy, long lived, and attractive from spring to fall. The long-stemmed flowers, 4–8 in. wide, are excellent for cutting. They can be single or double, in shades of white, pink, rose, or red. Some of the double kinds are very fragrant. After flowering, the bushy clump of jagged foliage stays handsome and glossy green, then turns purplish or gold in fall. Peonies combine well with irises and roses in mixed borders. A row of peonies makes a lovely low hedge.

There are hundreds of cultivars, varying in flower color, doubleness, fragrance, plant height, and season of bloom (late spring to early summer; spanning about 6 weeks). 'Edulis Superba' has very fragrant, double, rosy pink flowers; very early. 'Festiva Maxima' has fragrant, double, pure white flowers, sometimes flecked with red; early. 'Kansas' has double, watermelon red flowers; early. 'Krinkled White' has single, snow-white flowers with gold stamens; early. 'Sarah Bernhardt' has fragrant, double, pink flowers, speckled with red; late.

Peonies thrive where winters are cold and don't do well where temperatures rarely dip below freezing. Bud formation requires winter chilling. Also, the flowers don't last long in hot weather, so choose only the early cultivars for gardens in the South or Southwest.

Tree peonies, hybrids of *P. suffruticosa,* are deciduous shrubs, 3–6 ft. tall, with picturesque branching, distinctive foliage, and exquisite flowers in late spring. Though expensive and slow-growing, they are hardy, long lived, and trouble-free. The flowers are ephemeral in hot, dry, or windy weather.

P. tenuifolia, the fernleaf peony, has unusual foliage; the leaves are divided into slender lacy segments. It makes a low bushy mound in spring but goes dormant and leaves a gap by late summer. Ball-shaped flowers, 2–3 in. wide, open in early summer. 'Rubra Plena', with double deep red flowers, is most commonly offered.

How to grow: Full sun; tolerate light shade in the South, but too much shade prevents blooming. Need well-drained, fertile, acidic or neutral soil amended with plenty of organic matter. Carefully choose and prepare the site before planting; peonies can continue in one place for decades. Allow at least 3 ft. per plant, and keep away from competing tree or shrub roots. Plant in fall. Position the roots with the pink buds or eyes exactly 1–2 in. below soil level. (Peonies won't bloom if planted too deep.) Use hoop-type supports to keep the stems from flopping. After bloom, remove developing seedpods and fertilize lightly.

Don't worry about ants crawling on the flower buds; they do no harm. More troublesome is botrytis—a fungal infection that can disfigure the foliage and flowers, especially in warm, rainy weather. Plant where air circulation is good, and use copper fungicide if needed. After hard frost in fall, cut stems to the ground and burn or discard them—do not compost—to eliminate fungal spores.

Panicum

Pan´i-kum. Panic grass.
Gramineae. Grass family.

A diverse genus of annual or perennial grasses. About 600 spp., native worldwide.

virgatum (p. 212)
Switch grass.
Perennial grass. Zone 4.
H: 3–6 ft. S: 2–3 ft.

This North American native is well adapted to the vagaries of our climate and tolerates both wet and dry sites. Its sturdy, narrow, upright clumps can screen undesirable views or define intimate spaces. Adds fall color and winter interest to perennial borders. The slender leaves, 1–2 ft. long, are medium green in summer, turning bright yellow, gold, or orange in fall. Flower panicles form an airy mass 12–16 in. above the foliage and look good from July into fall. They open dark reddish purple and fade to beige. 'Heavy Metal' grows 4–5 ft. tall and has stiff metallic blue leaves. 'Rostrahlbusch' grows 3–4 ft. tall and has red fall color.

How to grow: Full or part sun. Ordinary or unimproved soil and ordinary watering. Cut down to the ground in early spring. May spread but isn't invasive. Older clumps can be divided.

Papaver

Pa-pay´ver. Poppy.
Papaveraceae. Poppy family.

Annuals or perennials with showy flowers borne singly on long stalks, lobed or dissected basal leaves, and milky sap. About 50 spp., native to the Old and New World.

nudicaule (p. 301)
Iceland poppy.
Perennial grown as an annual. Zone 2.
H: 1–2 ft. S: 1–2 ft.

A beautiful series of garden flowers developed from an Arctic wildflower. The mildly fragrant, cup-shaped flowers have a mass of golden stamens nested in 4 or 8 crinkled silky petals. Colors include shades of yellow, orange, pink, red, and white. The light gray-green basal leaves are lobed or jagged along the edges. Both leaves and flower stalks are covered with whiskery hairs. Usually raised from seed in mixed colors. 'Champagne Bubbles' and 'Sparkling Bubbles' are popular strains. Makes a good cut flower if you cauterize the base of the stem by searing it with a candle or match flame or by dipping it in hot water. Be careful when gathering the flowers, as the sap will stain your clothes.

How to grow: Full sun. Ordinary soil and watering. Iceland poppies can't take summer heat and are grown as winter annuals in the South and California. Set out small plants in fall for bloom the following spring, and discard after bloom. Northern gardeners can sow the tiny seeds indoors 8–10 weeks before last frost or buy small plants in spring for bloom in early summer; the same plants will rebloom for another year or two. In all areas, deadheading helps prolong bloom.

orientale (p. 262)
Oriental poppy.
Perennial. Zone 2.
H: to 3 ft. S: to 3 ft.

Popular in northern gardens for its vivid glossy flowers, 4–6 in. wide, with crinkled ruffled petals in brilliant shades of scarlet, orange, red, pink, or white. Look inside to see the jet black patch at the base of each petal. There are several cultivars with flowers of different colors and sizes. All bloom in late spring or early summer. The pinnately lobed foliage, pale green with bristly hairs, develops early but dies down in midsummer when the plants go dormant. Use 1 or a group of 3 in a perennial border, combined with gypsophila, boltonia, or asters to fill the gap for late summer and fall.

How to grow: Full sun. Ordinary soil and watering. Plant when dormant in late summer or early fall. Place roots 3 in. below the soil surface. Divide every 5 years or so, when dormant. Poppies are long lived and trouble-free in cold climates but don't live long where winters are mild.

rhoeas (p. 301)
Corn poppy, Flanders poppy.
Annual. All zones.
H: 1–3 ft. S: 6–12 in.

Native to European fields, bright red corn poppies are often included in seed mixes for wildflower or meadow gardens. They regularly self-sow from year to year. The cup-shaped, 4-petaled flowers open 2–3 in. wide on tall wiry stalks. Blooms for a few weeks in June or July. Forms a lacy clump of light green basal leaves; leaves and flower stalks have scattered hairs. The dry seedpods remain interesting, but the foliage dies soon after bloom. Shirley poppies were developed from this species and have single or double flowers in shades of white, pink, or red.

Many gardeners think that *P. somniferum*, the opium poppy, is the best annual poppy. It grows 3–4 ft. tall and bears many 3–5-in. flowers in rich shades of pink, purple, red, or white. Some forms have double flowers that resemble peonies. It tolerates hot weather and blooms well into summer. Technically, it's illegal to grow opium poppies in the United States, but they self-seed readily and are very common in old-fashioned cottage gardens, especially in the South and Midwest.

How to grow: Full sun. Ordinary soil and watering. Direct-sow the tiny seeds where they are to grow, in late fall or very early spring. Thin seedlings to 6 in. apart. Deadhead to prolong flowering. Let a few plants go to seed each year to renew the planting.

Parkinsonia
Par-kin-so'nee-a.
Leguminosae. Legume family.

Spiny shrubs or trees with showy yellow flowers. They are usually leafless, but photosynthesis takes place in the green-barked limbs and twigs. The genus *Cercidium* is now combined with *Parkinsonia*. About 20 spp., most native to arid regions in the Southwest and Central America.

aculeata (p. 122)
Jerusalem thorn, retama.
Deciduous tree. Zone 8.
H: 25–30 ft. S: 20–25 ft.

A tough and durable small tree that tolerates heat and drought. Forms a single trunk with an umbrella-like crown. The compound leaves have 20–30 pairs of tiny oval leaflets; the foliage has an airy delicate effect and casts a filtered shade. Loose 4–6-in. clusters of fragrant bright yellow flowers open mostly in spring, with flushes of bloom after summer rains. The green branches are quite spiny. Grows fast, but the wood is strong.

How to grow: Full sun. Tolerates poor unamended soil, alkaline conditions, and drought. Stake and train young trees; established trees need little pruning. Remove frozen shoots after severe winters. Self-seeds and can be weedy.

Parrotia
Par-ro'tee-a.
Hamamelidaceae. Witch hazel family.

A deciduous tree with ornamental foliage and bark. Only 1 sp., native to Iran.

persica (p. 122)
Persian parrotia.
Deciduous small tree. Zone 3.
H: 15–20 ft. or more. S: 10–15 ft.

Slow-growing but worth the wait, this is a handsome small tree with 4-season interest. Usually has multiple trunks and wide-spreading limbs. The outer bark flakes off in irregular patches, revealing smooth white inner bark. Small clusters of reddish flowers line the twigs in spring. The oval leaves are dark green in summer, turning brilliant shades of gold, pink, or red in fall. An excellent specimen for lawns or borders.

How to grow: Full or part sun. Ordinary soil and watering. Can be trained to a single trunk if desired. Tolerates heat, but in sunny climates wrap the trunk to prevent sunscald on young trees. No serious pests or diseases.

Parthenocissus
Par-then-o-cis'sus. Woodbine.
Vitaceae. Grape family.

Deciduous woody vines with compound or lobed leaves. They climb by branching tendrils, often with sticky disks at the tips. About 10 spp., native to North America and Asia.

Parthenocissus quinquefolia

quinquefolia (p. 205)
Virginia creeper.
Deciduous vine. Zone 2.
H: 40–50 ft.

A versatile vine that can climb up a tree, cover a fence or building wall, or scramble as a ground cover. Adhesive disks at the ends of the tendrils cling to any surface (including wood siding, shingles, and masonry, where they can be problematic). The palmately compound leaves, with 5 leaflets 3–6 in. long, are glossy dark green in summer, turning bright red in early fall, before most trees start to color. Flowers are small and inconspicuous; the dark purple berries get eaten soon after they ripen. Native throughout the eastern United States. *P. inserta,* a western form, has similar leaves but no sticky disks, so it sprawls rather than climbs.

How to grow: Full sun, part sun, or shade.

Grows in almost any soil with normal rainfall or ordinary watering. Hardy to cold and heat. Space container-grown plants 1–2 ft. apart for ground cover, and mow every few years to thicken the growth. Think twice before planting it next to a house—you can pull off the vines when they grow too far, but the sticky disks leave marks that are hard to erase. Subject to several leafspot diseases and ravaged by Japanese beetles.

tricuspidata (p. 205)
Boston ivy.
Deciduous vine. Zone 2.
H: 40–50 ft.

Not as coarse as Virginia creeper but just as hardy and versatile. This is the "ivy" that covers brick and stone buildings at Ivy League colleges. The stems cling tight and trace a delicate pattern that's very attractive against masonry walls. Leaves, with 3 lobes or 3 leaflets, are 2–5 in. long; on a wall, they overlap like shingles to make a dense cover. Glossy bright green in summer, they turn scarlet in fall. Can also be used as a low, creeping ground cover. 'Veitchii' has smaller leaves that open reddish purple, changing to green.

How to grow: Part sun or shade. Does best on the north or east side of a building or fence. Ordinary soil and watering. Space 1 ft. apart for ground cover. Climbs on any surface. Attacked by Japanese beetles and spider mites.

Passiflora
Pas-si-flo´ra. Passionflower.
Passifloraceae. Passionflower family.

Mostly evergreen vines that climb by tendrils. The large round flowers are fascinating and complex and sometimes very fragrant. Some kinds are valued for their sweet fruits. About 350 spp., most native to tropical America.

× *alatocaerulea* (p. 205)
Passionvine, passionflower.
Semievergreen vine. Zone 8 or 7.
H: 20 ft.

A rambunctious vine with unbelievably intricate flowers, 3–4 in. wide, in shades of purple or white. Very fragrant and blooms all summer. The vine climbs or scrambles over fences, trellises, or shrubs, clinging by tendrils. Good for quick shade on an arbor or for hiding an ugly view. Leaves are 3-lobed, 3–4 in. long. Evergreen and aggressive where winters are mild. Dies back to the ground after hard freezes but blooms on new growth the next year.

The hybrid *P.* 'Incense' is hardy to Zone 5 in a protected site against a building foundation or wall. It has violet flowers, 5 in. wide, with a lacy corolla and an intensely sweet fragrance. *P. incarnata,* the hardy native maypop, is a deciduous vine that spreads both underground and aboveground, with sweet lavender-colored flowers 3 in. wide and egg-sized fruits with yellow rind and sweet pulp.

How to grow: Full or part sun. Ordinary soil and watering. Allow plenty of space—this vine gets big fast. Needs annual pruning to thin the tangle of stems. Various caterpillars eat the leaves but do no serious harm. Volunteer seedlings can be a nuisance.

Pelargonium
Pel-ar-go´nee-um. Geranium.
Geraniaceae. Geranium family.

Perennials, shrubs, and some annuals. Some are succulent. True geraniums (*Geranium* spp.) have "regular" flowers—radially symmetrical, with all petals the same. These have "irregular" flowers—with a top and bottom, like a face. Many species have leaves with a distinctive shape, marking, or fragrance. About 280 spp., most native to South Africa, and hundreds of hybrid cultivars.

× *domesticum* (p. 302)
Martha Washington geranium, regal geranium.
Tender perennial grown as an annual. All zones.
H: to 3 ft. S: 2–4 ft.

Has the showiest flowers of any geranium, often likened to azaleas, but borne in loose round clusters on long stalks. Individual flowers can be 2–3 in. wide, in shades of red, pinkish purple, or white, usually with darker blotches and veins. Leaves are rounded or lobed, with coarse teeth and wavy edges. There are many cultivars.

How to grow: Full or part sun. Well-drained, fertile soil and regular watering. In containers, use peat- or bark-based potting soil that drains quickly. Feed biweekly with a dilute fertilizer solution. Plants are compact when you buy them but may get straggly later unless you keep pruning and pinching the tips. Root tip cuttings in late summer to overwinter indoors on a sunny windowsill, or buy new plants each year. (In Zone 9, geraniums are hardy outdoors.) Whiteflies, aphids, and tobacco budworm are common pests.

× *hortorum* (p. 302)
Common geranium, zonal geranium.
Tender perennial grown as an annual. All zones.
H: 1–3 ft. S: 2 ft.

One of the best and easiest flowering plants for containers, and a fine bedding plant, too. Makes big spherical clusters of 1-in.-wide flowers in many shades of red, pink, salmon, magenta, or white. Each cluster is long-lasting, and the plants bloom almost continuously. The circular to kidney-shaped leaves have scalloped or toothed edges and a soft hairy surface. Most have a band or zone of a darker color; some kinds have distinct variegation. Stems are fleshy and erect. Old-fashioned geraniums used to get tall and straggly by late summer. These have been superseded by new compact strains that stay just 1–1½ ft. tall.

How to grow: Like *P.* × *domesticum.* New compact strains are grown from seed, sown indoors in winter for bloom 15–20 weeks later.

Pelargonium × *hortorum*

peltatum (p. 302)
Ivy geranium.
Tender perennial grown as an annual. All zones.
H: 1 ft. S: 3–4 ft.

This is the best geranium for hanging baskets, raised planters, and window boxes. The stems trail like vines. The bright green 5-lobed leaves are thick and glossy. The star-shaped flowers are red, pink, purplish, white, or bicolor, in small clusters on long stalks. Popular everywhere in containers, this is also a fine ground cover for Zone 9 gardens.

How to grow: Like *P.* × *domesticum.*

scented geraniums (p. 287)
Tender perennials grown as annual herbs.
All zones.
H: varies. S: varies.

This group includes dozens of species and hybrids grown for their attractive and strongly scented foliage. Their delicate white, pink, or lavender flowers are pretty, too, blooming in winter or spring. Most grow well year-round in containers, outdoors from spring to fall and moved to a sunny windowsill in winter. Try planting them in the ground, near a path, bench, or patio where you can stroke the foliage to release the lovely fragrances. A plant from a 4-in. pot in spring can make a big mound by fall. The leaves are used in potpourri and perfumery, as garnishes, and to flavor jellies and cakes.

P. crispum, the lemon-scented geranium, has erect stems that reach 3 ft. tall, small round leaves with crinkled margins, and a rich lemony fragrance. There are several cultivars, including some variegated ones. *P. graveolens,* the rose geranium, is a bushy 2–3-ft. plant with branching stems and softly pleated, toothed, deeply lobed leaves. There are several cultivars and hybrids with different flowery and fruity scents. *P. tomentosum,* the peppermint geranium, spreads wider than tall and has large round-lobed leaves covered with soft furry hairs. The fragrance is intensely minty.

How to grow: Like *P.* × *domesticum.*

Pennisetum
Pen-ni-see´tum.
Gramineae. Grass family.
Annual or perennial grasses with flat leaves and dense flower heads. About 70 spp., most native to tropical or warm climates.

alopecuroides (see below for photo)
Fountain grass.
Perennial grass. Zone 5.
H: 3–4 ft. S: 3–4 ft.

Offers 3-season interest and requires very little care. Makes a vibrant flowing fountain of 3-ft. leaves, dark green in summer and warm apricot, almond, or orange in fall. It flowers freely from July to October, with many fluffy spikes 6–8 in. long, shading from reddish purple to coppery tan. An excellent plant to combine with spring bulbs—its fresh spring growth complements the bulb flowers, and it soon grows to cover the yellowing bulb leaves. Also good as a ground cover or transitional plant bridging natural and more formal areas. Lovely beside a pond, where its shape is mirrored in the water. 'Hameln' is more compact, with foliage 18–24 in. tall and flower stalks to 30 in. 'Little Bunny' is extremely dwarf, growing only 8–10 in. high.

P. orientale (p. 213) is a similar plant hardy only to Zone 7. It's more compact, forming upright clumps of gray-green foliage 1–2 ft. tall, topped with long, fluffy, arching spikes of pinkish purple flowers. Grown as an annual in northern climates, it starts flowering 2–4 weeks earlier than *P. alopecuroides,* but the flowers disintegrate by fall.

How to grow: Full sun in the North, part shade in hotter climates. Grows in acidic or alkaline soils. Tolerates dry spells, but the leaves get pale and curl up. Space 2–3 ft. apart. Cut back old foliage in February or March, especially if interplanted with bulbs. Can be (but doesn't need to be) divided every 5–6 years. The center of the clump may die out, but that gap is noticeable only in early spring and doesn't matter later. No insect pests, but voles and mice may feed on the crown in winter.

setaceum (p. 213)
Crimson fountain grass.
Perennial grass, grown as an annual north of Zone 8.
H: 2–3 ft. S: to 2 ft.

Makes an arching or mounded clump of fine-textured rusty green foliage. The fluffy nodding spikes of rose or purple flowers are 6–12 in. long, 2–4 in. wide, held well above the foliage from June through fall. Effective as a specimen or massed. Nice with pink flowering tobacco, which accents the pink tints of the grass flowers. This species self-seeds and has become a weed in warm climates such as California. The following two cultivars are preferable, because they don't set seed. 'Purpureum' (also called 'Atropurpureum') has purple leaves and deep crimson flowers. 'Rubrum' (or 'Cupreum') has bronze-maroon leaves and deep burgundy flowers.

How to grow: Full or part sun. Ordinary or unimproved soil. Somewhat drought-tolerant. Plant 18–24 in. apart. When grown as an annual, it may need staking, especially in windy areas. As a perennial, cut foliage down in fall or spring. Propagate colored forms by division.

villosum (p. 213)
(*P. longistylum*)
Feathertop.
Perennial grass, grown as an annual north of Zone 8.
H: 2–2¹/₂ ft. S: 1¹/₂–2 ft.

Valued for its fluffy white flower plumes, 3–5 in. long and 2 in. wide. It blooms from July through September. Best combined with annuals or perennials that can cover the irregular mound of foliage, which isn't particularly attractive, and

Pennisetum alopecuroides

help support the flower stalks during rains or stormy weather.

How to grow: Full or part sun. Ordinary soil and watering. Propagated by seed. Not seriously weedy, but it has escaped in areas from Michigan to Texas. Doesn't last into winter; cut to the ground in fall.

Penstemon

Pen´ste-mon. Beard-tongue.
Scrophulariaceae. Foxglove family.

A large genus of perennials and some shrubs. All have tubular 2-lipped flowers that attract hummingbirds; some are very showy. There are about 250 spp., almost all native to western North America.

Penstemon barbatus

barbatus (p. 263)
Perennial. Zone 3.
H: to 3 ft. S: 3 ft.

A bushy open plant with sprawling stems, narrow leaves, and loose spikes of bright red flowers, 1 in. long, in early summer. There are several cultivars with different flower colors, including pink, purple, orange, and white. Excellent for dry sites or xeriscape gardens.

How to grow: Full sun. Needs very good drainage and thrives in sandy or gravelly soil where few other perennials would grow. Native to the Rocky Mountain region, it is very cold-hardy and also puts up with hot summers. Deadhead to prolong bloom. Usually dies after a few years but may self-seed. Pest-free.

digitalis (p. 263)
Perennial. Zone 3.
H: 2–4 ft. S: 2 ft.

One of the larger, more robust penstemons, with thick-textured, lance-shaped leaves and large flowers like white foxgloves. Blooms for up to a month in early summer. Even if it didn't bloom, 'Husker's Red' would deserve a space in the border for its dark reddish purple foliage.

How to grow: Full or part sun. Prefers fertile, well-drained, organic soil. Tolerates moisture better than most penstemons do. Cut stalks after flowering, or let seeds mature to self-sow. Foliage is semievergreen in mild winters.

other species (p. 263)
Several other species, including the following, are available as seeds or plants from native-plant nurseries. Almost all need dry, gravelly soil and full sun.

P. heterophyllus is a neat low plant with narrow evergreen leaves and blue or violet flowers from April to July. Subsp. *purdyi* has rich blue flowers and is sold as 'Blue Bedder' penstemon.

P. pinifolius makes a low evergreen cushion of short needlelike leaves topped with spikes of orange-red flowers in May and June. Tolerates clay soil and part shade.

P. smallii has upright stems that branch at the top to bear many clusters of lilac flowers in early summer. The dark green foliage is usually evergreen. Good on dry banks or in dry soils around tree roots.

P. strictus forms a low mat of evergreen foliage but has flower stalks up to 3 ft. tall, with blue-purple flowers in May and June. Fairly tolerant of heavy or wet soils.

Perovskia

Pe-rof´skee-a.
Labiatae. Mint family.

Woody-based perennials with opposite leaves, square stems, and small 2-lipped flowers. Only 7 spp., native from Iran to India.

atriplicifolia (p. 264)
Russian sage.
Shrubby perennial. Zone 5.
H: 3–5 ft. S: 4 ft.

Graceful, aromatic, and easy, this is a wonderful plant for sunny borders. Stems and leaves are silver-gray, topped in late summer with tiered whorls of lavender flowers. Stems are square; leaves are coarsely toothed, 1–3 in. long. Grows erect, sometimes flopping by late summer, and makes a large but airy mass. Combines well with late-flowering pale yellow daylilies, white or pink boltonias, or asters.

How to grow: Full sun. Ordinary soil and watering. Needs good drainage, especially in winter. Remove old stems, leaving short stubs, in late fall or early spring. Use pine boughs as a winter mulch in Zones 6 and 5, and don't remove too early in spring. Established clumps endure for years. Problem-free.

Petroselinum

Pet-ro-se-lee´num. Parsley.
Umbelliferae. Carrot family.

Biennials with thick roots, finely divided leaves, and small flowers in compound umbels. Only 3 spp., native to Europe and the Mediterranean region.

crispum (p. 287)
Parsley.
Biennial herb grown as an annual. All zones.
H: 1 ft. (foliage). S: 1 ft.

A favorite for flavoring soups, salads, and main dishes, parsley is also a fine ornamental. It forms a low rosette of dark green leaves, triangular in outline but divided into many flat or curly leaflets. It's useful for edging beds of annuals or herbs and also grows well in containers.

Penstemon smallii

Curly-leaf types are attractive and widely used for garnishes, but gourmets insist that the Italian flat-leaf type is more flavorful. Started from seed, the plants are attractive until hard frost, or all winter in mild climates. The second year, this biennial sends up 3-ft. stalks topped with umbels of tiny greenish flowers. (May flower the first year if transplanted too early, while the weather is still cold.) Sometimes self-seeds.

How to grow: Full or part sun. Does best in well-drained but constantly moist soil amended with plenty of organic matter. Soak seeds overnight in hot water to speed germination. Sow indoors 8 weeks before last frost. Space 8 in. apart. Harvest leaves from around the edge; new growth comes up in the center. May host green-and-yellow caterpillars of the swallowtail butterfly; grow enough to share with these beautiful creatures.

Petunia
Pe-too'nee-a.
Solanaceae. Nightshade family.

Annuals or perennials with sticky hairy stems and leaves and showy, sometimes fragrant, funnel-shaped flowers. About 35 spp., native to warm and tropical regions in Latin America.

× *hybrida* (p. 302)
Common garden petunia.
Tender perennial grown as an annual.
All zones.
H: 1–3 ft. S: 1–3 ft.

One of the most popular summer bedding plants, easy and colorful. Blooms profusely for months. The round flowers are single or double, in shades of red, rose, pink, purple, violet-blue, pale yellow, white, or striped combinations. Some kinds are very sweetly fragrant, especially at night. All have straggly stems and small oval leaves covered with sticky hairs. Scores of cultivars are available from seed, in solid and mixed colors. Most cultivars fall into 2 groups. The Grandiflora types are larger plants with flowers 4–5 in. wide and are subject to botrytis, which disfigures the leaves and flowers. The Multiflora types are more compact, with flowers 2–3 in. wide, and are resistant to botrytis—a big advantage in humid climates.

How to grow: Full sun. Ordinary or improved soil and regular watering. Start the tiny seeds indoors 8 weeks before last frost. Space seedlings or purchased transplants 1 ft. apart for bedding. Use 1–3 plants in a 12-in. hanging basket. Fertilize monthly. Frequent deadheading prolongs bloom, and frequent pinching makes the plants bushier. Generally problem-free but can be damaged by air pollution or attacked by tobacco budworm, aphids, and leaf viruses.

Phalaris
Fa-lay'ris.
Gramineae. Grass family.

Annual or perennial grasses, most with spreading rhizomes. Seeds of some species are used for bird feed. About 15 spp., from around the north temperate zone.

arundinacea 'Picta' (p. 213)
Ribbon grass.
Perennial grass. Zone 4.
H: 2–4 ft. S: invasive.

One of the first grasses grown as an ornamental, this plant is noted for its variegated foliage and fortitude. The upright stems hold leaves 4–10 in. long, bright green with lengthwise white stripes. One clump can lighten a dark corner or provide a foil for clashing colors in a perennial border. The pinkish white flowers in midsummer are not particularly ornamental. Invasiveness is the main concern. You can control its spread by planting in a bottomless container or in defined areas such as parking lot islands. Can also be grown as an aquatic—it won't spread from a container surrounded by water! Planted in mass, it makes a tough ground cover and the rhizomes are an effective soil stabilizer.

How to grow: Full or part sun. Not fussy about soil; tolerates sand or clay, acidic or alkaline conditions, wet or dry sites, some sea salt, and standing water. In most areas, the foliage is pretty in spring and early summer but turns brown by August. Cut it back to 6 in. and it will sprout fresh new growth. Easily propagated by division.

Phellodendron
Fell-o-den'dron. Cork tree.
Rutaceae. Citrus family.

Deciduous trees with opposite, pinnately compound leaves and small greenish flowers. About 10 spp., native to eastern Asia.

amurense (p. 122)
Amur cork tree.
Deciduous tree. Zone 4.
H: 30–45 ft. S: 30–45 ft.

A medium-size tree with a broad, spreading, rounded crown. Leaves are pinnately compound, 10–15 in. long, with 5–13 leaflets, and cast a light shade. The bark matures into attractive corky ridges. The creamy white flowers in May are not very showy. The black fruits, $1/2$ in. wide, are ornamental in fall and winter but messy if they drop on a sidewalk and produce unwanted volunteer seedlings. No longer recommended as a street tree but is a good tree for large lawns and parks. Can be used to shade perennials and ground covers, but remember to provide enough water and nutrients for both the tree and the perennials.

How to grow: Full sun. Ordinary soil. Needs regular watering and mulch during hot weather. Easily transplanted. Needs little pruning.

Philadelphus

Fill-a-del'phus. Mock orange.
Saxifragaceae. Saxifrage family.

Deciduous shrubs with opposite oval leaves and white flowers, sometimes very fragrant, in spring. About 65 spp., native to the north temperate zone, and many hybrids.

Philadelphus coronarius

coronarius (p. 143)

Common mock orange, sweet mock orange.
Deciduous shrub. Zone 4.
H: 10 ft. S: 10 ft.

An old-fashioned shrub, common around old farmhouses. It's delightful for a week or two in late spring, when each twig is tipped with a small cluster of 4-petaled or double snow-white flowers, 1–1¹/₂ in. wide. The flowers have a penetrating sweet fragrance. Unfortunately, the shrub itself is bulky and graceless, and the leaves are plain green with no fall color. Enjoy it if you already have one, but for a new planting, save space by choosing a dwarf cultivar, such as *P.* × *virginalis* 'Miniature Snowflake'. It's a compact mounded shrub, 3 ft. tall, that covers itself with fragrant double flowers. *P.* × *lemoinei* 'Avalanche' is another good compact form, 4 ft. tall, with fragrant single flowers.

How to grow: Full or part sun. Grows in any soil with regular watering. Prune immediately after flowering to reduce size and to improve shape. Renew old plants by cutting to the ground. Very tough and carefree.

Phlomis

Flo'mis. Jerusalem sage.
Labiatae. Mint family.

Perennials or shrubs with square stems and opposite leaves, often quite woolly, and tubular 2-lipped flowers. About 100 spp., most native to dry stony habitats in Europe and Asia.

fruticosa (p. 264)

Jerusalem sage.
Shrubby perennial. Zone 7.
H: 4 ft. S: 6 ft.

A good plant for dry, sunny gardens. The habit is round and bushy with many stems that are woody at the base and soft on top. The thick wrinkly leaves, 2–4 in. long, are gray-green above, white and woolly below. Stems are topped with a series of ball-shaped whorls of fuzzy buds and tubular 1-in. yellow flowers. Blooms in spring or summer, and repeats several times if you cut it back after each cycle. Combine it with lavender, rosemary, salvias, or other shrubby perennials that take dry heat. *P. russeliana* (also sold as *P. viscosa*) is hardy to Zone 5 or 4 but dies to the ground each winter. It has green leaves on 4–5-ft. stems topped with big round whorls of showy yellow flowers.

How to grow: Full sun. Tolerates poor soil and dryness but grows even better in ordinary garden soil with regular watering. Usually planted as a single specimen. Prune after flowering. Evergreen in mild winters but dies back in severe cold. Cut off dead shoots in spring; it will soon recover.

Phlox

Flox.
Polemoniaceae. Phlox family.

Annuals, perennials, or small shrubs with simple leaves and round 5-petaled flowers. More than 60 spp., all but one native to North America.

divaricata (p. 264)

Wild sweet William, woodland phlox.
Perennial. Zone 3.
H: 8–12 in. S: 2 ft. or more.

An ideal ground cover or filler for shady gardens, where it wanders and spreads but never dominates. Native to eastern woodlands, where it blooms for many weeks in spring, along with foamflowers, bleeding-hearts, and other woodland wildflowers. The starry 5-petaled flowers, about 1 in. wide, form loose clusters at the tops of the stems. Some people notice a slight fragrance. The standard color is blue, but 'Fuller's White' has white flowers and var. *laphamii* has deep blue-purple flowers. *P. pilosa*, or prairie phlox, grows 1–1¹/₂ ft. tall and has pink flowers. It tolerates sun, heat, and dry soil better than *P. divaricata* does and forms a nice clump in a sunny border. *P.* × *chattahoochee* is a hybrid that has lavender flowers with dark purple eyes.

How to grow: Afternoon sun or light shade. Does well under deciduous trees, blooming before their leaves expand fully. Prefers fertile, acidic, organic soil, well drained but moist. Space 1 ft. apart; it spreads by rhizomes and will soon fill in. Propagate by division.

Phlox divaricata

Phlox pilosa

drummondii (p. 302)

Annual. All zones.
H: 6–18 in. S: 8 in.

Native to eastern and central Texas, where it grows wild along the roadsides, this is a fast-growing annual with weak sprawling stems that can hardly support the clusters of red, pink, or white flowers. (New cultivars offer more colors.) Combines well with flossflower and sweet alyssum as a low bedding plant or edger. Blooms all summer if you deadhead it regularly.

How to grow: Full sun. Tolerates poor, dry soil and hot weather. Sow seeds around the last frost date; thin seedlings to 6 in. apart. Usually doesn't self-sow in gardens.

maculata (p. 264)
Spotted phlox, wild sweet William, meadow phlox.
Perennial. Zone 3.
H: 2–4 ft. S: 2 ft.

A handsome healthy plant for sunny borders. Blooms for 2–3 weeks in early summer, with cylindrical clusters of fragrant purplish pink flowers 1/2 in. wide. (There are a few cultivars with other flower colors.) The lance-shaped leaves, 2–4 in. long, are thick, glossy, and dark green. Stems are sometimes spotted with dark red or purple. Carolina phlox, identified as *P. carolina* or *P. suffruticosa,* is very similar but has spotless stems. Both species grow wild in the East in moist meadows and along streams and roads. 'Miss Lingard' belongs to one or the other species, or it may be a hybrid; in any case, it's an excellent plant with large heads of white flowers.

How to grow: Full or part sun. Prefers fertile, organic soil. Needs regular watering and tolerates constant moisture. Space 1 1/2–2 ft. apart. Increase by division in spring or fall. Unlike with most species of phlox, the thick foliage of *P. maculata* and *P. carolina* resists mildew and spider mites and looks good all season.

paniculata (p. 265)
Garden phlox, summer phlox.
Perennial. Zone 4.
H: 2–4 ft. S: 2–3 ft. or more.

Indispensable for late-summer bloom in sunny borders, this phlox makes erect clumps of leafy stems, topped with domed clusters of fragrant flowers 3/4 in. wide. It is tall but doesn't need staking, and it spreads over time to form large patches. There are dozens of cultivars of different heights and flower colors. 'Bright Eyes' (2 ft.) has pale pink flowers with crimson eyes. 'Dodo Hanbury Forbes' (3 ft.) is an extraordinary bright salmon-pink. 'Mt. Fuji' ('Fujiyama'; 3–3 1/2 ft.) has the best white flowers and is notably strong and healthy. 'Starfire' (3 ft.) is a brilliant cherry red. 'The King' (2–2 1/2 ft.) is deep purple.

How to grow: Full sun. Needs well-prepared, fertile soil amended with plenty of compost or aged manure, well drained but moist. Space 2 ft. apart. Divide clumps every 2–3 years in early fall, retaining only strong outer divisions, and enrich the soil before replanting. In spring, thin clumps to 5–6 stems to improve air circulation. Subject to spider mites in hot, dry weather; powdery mildew in hot, humid weather. Regular watering helps prevent these problems. Deadhead after flowering to avoid seedlings that revert to the wild magenta-flowered type.

stolonifera (p. 264)
Creeping phlox.
Perennial. Zone 2.
H: 6–12 in. S: 1–2 ft. or more.

Forms loose mats of medium green foliage, spreading where space allows. Blooms for 2–4 weeks in midspring, with small clusters of mildly fragrant flowers, 1 1/2 in. wide, normally blue with yellow eyes. Both foliage and flowers are soft-textured. 'Blue Ridge' (lilac-blue flowers) and 'Pink Ridge' (pink) grow about 1 ft. tall. 'Bruce's White' (white) and 'Sherwood Purple' (violet) grow about 6 in. tall. All kinds look good under and around spring bulbs or trailing along a woodland path.

How to grow: Like *P. divaricata.*

subulata (p. 265)
Moss phlox.
Perennial. Zone 2.
H: 6–9 in. S: 1 ft. or more.

The most common creeping phlox, it makes wonderful swaths of color in spring and is tough and easy to grow. It forms dense mats of somewhat woody stems with stiff needlelike leaves 1/2 in. long. Foliage is evergreen in mild climates, semievergreen in the North. Covers itself with flat flowers 1/2 in. wide. Combine it with tulips or other spring bulbs, or use it to paint a tapestry on a sunny bank. There are several named cultivars, but it's often sold simply by color: white, pink, blue, lavender, or red.

How to grow: Full sun. Sandy, well-drained soil is best; otherwise plant on slopes or in raised beds. Space 1 ft. or more apart. As a ground cover, it's dense enough to eliminate most weeds, except grass. If grass invades, you must fork up all the phlox and replant clean pieces. Shear back after flowering (use a lawn mower for big areas). Increase by division in early fall.

_____

Phoenix
Fee´nix.
Palmae. Palm family.

Palm trees with long pinnately divided leaves on short or tall trunks. The fruits are used for food, the leaves for thatched roofs and basketry. About 17 spp., native to Africa and Asia.

canariensis (p. 165)
Canary palm.
Feather palm. Zone 9 or 8.
H: 50 ft. S: 50 ft.

A large palm with a thick erect trunk topped with an umbrella of arching fronds 15–20 ft. long. The featherlike fronds have coarse dark green leaflets. Slow-growing when young. Eventually gets too large for most gardens, but is popular along boulevards in California. *P. dactylifera,* the date palm, grows up to 80 ft. tall, with one or several slender trunks, and bears tasty sweet dates in huge drooping clusters. Native to the Middle East, it's the common palm at Palm Springs, California.

How to grow: Full sun. Ordinary or dry soil. Very tolerant of heat and drought. Remove old leaf bases to expose the patterned trunk. Recovers slowly from severe frosts, which kill the leaves.

Phlox carolina

Phormium

For'mee-um.
Agavaceae. Agave family.

Large clumping plants with spearlike leaves. Fibers from the leaves are woven into nets and fabrics. Only 2 spp., native to New Zealand.

tenax (p. 213)

New Zealand flax.
Perennial used like an ornamental grass. Zone 8.
H: 8–9 ft. S: 8–9 ft.

A dramatic plant that adds a tropical look to any garden. The sword-shaped leaves, up to 9 ft. long and 5 in. wide, grow in fans, like irises, and make crowded clumps. New cultivars offer a variety of foliage colors—bronzy, purplish, reddish, and striped with cream or yellow. The dull reddish brown flowers are trumpet-shaped, 2 in. long, and borne in branched clusters atop tall naked stalks in summer. Compact 3–5-ft. cultivars fit into smaller gardens and make bold punctuation marks in a flower border.

How to grow: Full or part sun. Ordinary, well-drained soil and regular watering. Plant from containers and allow plenty of space— these plants get big fast. Needs no care beyond the removal of dead or damaged leaves and old flower stalks. May freeze back in cold winters but recovers in one season. Can be divided, but you'll need several helpers to tackle a large specimen.

Photinia

Fo-tin'ee-a.
Rosaceae. Rose family.

Deciduous or evergreen shrubs or trees with simple leaves, clusters of 5-petaled white flowers, and small red fruits. About 40 spp., native to Southeast Asia.

× *fraseri* (p. 181)

Red-tip photinia.
Evergreen shrub. Zone 7.
H: 10–12 ft. S: 10 ft.

A cliché, but useful. Widely planted in home and commercial landscapes wherever it is hardy. Forms a large oval shrub with many upright stems. Most often used for hedges and foundation plantings but can also be trained as a small specimen tree. New leaves and stems are shiny bright red in spring, later turning dark green. Leaves are smooth and leathery, 2–5 in. long. Annual summer shearing maximizes the display of red tips but reduces or prevents flowering. Unpruned plants bear 3–5-in. clusters of white flowers at the same time as the new leaves develop in spring.

How to grow: Full or part sun. Not fussy about soil pH but needs good drainage. Tolerates heat and drought when established. Space 6–10 ft. apart for a hedge. Prune often when young to establish the desired shape and to increase density (or choose one or more stems to train a specimen tree). No serious pests or diseases.

serrulata (p. 181)

(now *P. serratifolia*)
Chinese photinia.
Evergreen shrub or tree. Zone 8 or 7.
H: to 30 ft. S: 15–20 ft.

Less common but prettier than red-tip photinia. Usually grows as a multitrunked shrub or tree with a dome-shaped crown. The glossy evergreen leaves are coarse and stiff, 4–8 in. long, with fine-toothed edges. New leaves are coppery red, changing to dark green. Slightly fragrant white flowers in dense round clusters, 4–6 in. wide, cover the canopy in spring. Small round fruits are bright red in fall, darkening to black in winter. A fine specimen for patios or courtyards. Can be used for a tall hedge but needs repeated pruning to encourage branching.

How to grow: Like *P. × fraseri*. Susceptible to mildew, especially in shaded sites with poor air circulation.

Phyllostachys

Fil-lo-stak'is.
Gramineae. Grass family.

A large and useful group of hardy bamboos. Some grow quite tall, and all spread to make thickets or groves. The young shoots are eaten as a vegetable, and mature culms are used for fishing rods, plant stakes, fences, and timber. About 60 spp., native to China.

Photinia × fraseri

aureosulcata (p. 214)

Yellow-groove bamboo.
Bamboo. Zone 6.
H: 15–20 ft. S: indefinite.

This is the hardiest of the running (grove-making) bamboos. The woody upright stems, called culms, are rich green with yellow grooves that run vertically from node to node. They grow up to $1^{1}/_{2}$ in. thick and are good for plant stakes or light fencing. The narrow lance-shaped leaves are papery, thin, and light green. Can be used as a screen or hedge if you curb its spread.

P. bambusoides, the giant timber bamboo, makes groves you can walk through, with culms 3–5 in. thick and up to 45 ft. tall. *P. nigra*, the black bamboo, has shiny black culms 15–25 ft. tall and 1 in. thick and narrow dark green leaves 1–4 in. long. A confined grove is lovely in a Japanese-style garden. Both are hardy to Zone 7.

How to grow: Full or part sun. Ordinary soil and watering. Plant divisions in spring, container-grown plants anytime. These bamboos all spread by underground rhizomes and can send up new shoots 20–30 ft. into your neighbor's yard. Mowing the shoots with a lawn mower won't keep the plant from spreading; you need to dig a trench and install a concrete, metal, fiberglass, or heavy plastic curb 18–24 in. deep. Do this when you first plant the bamboo. It's a hard job, but it's easier than trying to eradicate an established grove that's gotten out of bounds.

In the zones listed, these bamboos should overwinter with little damage to the foliage or culms. Zone 5 gardeners can grow these species

Phyllostachys nigra

like herbaceous perennials. The culms may freeze to the ground, but the rhizomes are hardy to -20° F if protected with a layer of snow or mulch.

Maintenance is simple. Remove the oldest, tattered culms at ground level. Thin culms to create a grove. Shear hedges as desired.

Physostegia virginiana

Physostegia
Fy-so-stee´jee-a.
Labiatae. Mint family.

Perennials with opposite leaves and showy 2-lipped flowers. Only 12 spp., native to North America.

virginiana (p. 265)
Obedient plant.
Perennial. Zone 2.
H: 3–4 ft. S: 3 ft. or more.

An eastern wildflower with leafy branching stems topped with dense spikes of pink, lilac, or white flowers like little snapdragons. Blooms for 3–6 weeks in late summer and makes a good cut flower. (It's called obedient plant because the flowers stay put if you adjust their position on the stalk.) The glossy leaves, 3–5 in. long, are slender with toothed edges. Good for natural areas and streamside plantings, where it can spread freely. Pretty but invasive in borders. 'Alba' and 'Summer Snow' have white flowers. 'Vivid' has pink flowers on a more compact plant.

How to grow: Full sun. Prefers fertile, organic, acidic soil and constant moisture. Prune in early summer to reduce height and floppiness. Restrain its spread by limiting water and nutrients and by pulling new shoots that sprout from underground runners. Propagate by division anytime. Pest-free.

Picea
Py-see´a. Spruce.
Pinaceae. Pine family.

Evergreen coniferous trees with drooping cones and stiff needles that make a distinct pattern of bumps where they attach to the twigs. Widely harvested for paper pulp and timber (the resonant wood is used for string instruments); grown for Christmas trees and as ornamentals. About 34 spp., native to cool regions of the Northern Hemisphere. Spruces grow very well in the Northeast and Northwest and are the best conifers for the Upper Midwest. They don't, however, do well in the hot summers of the South and Southwest.

abies (p. 193)
Norway spruce.
Conifer. Zone 3.
H: 100 ft. or more. S: 30–40 ft. or more.

Like a Christmas tree that gets bigger every year. Young trees have stiff angular branches. Old specimens have wide upswept limbs and branchlets that droop like long fringe. Looks most graceful with the lower limbs intact; clear-

ing the trunk up to 8–10 ft. lets you walk under the tree but makes it look funny. The dark green needles are stiff and sharp, up to 1 in. long. Sausage-shaped cones, 6 in. long, hang from the upper limbs all winter; many birds flock to eat the seeds. (Birds also sleep and nest in these trees, attracted by the dense shelter.) Widely planted as windbreaks and dooryard trees throughout the Midwest and East in past decades but less so now that people see how big they can get. There are several dwarf cultivars—conical, mounded, spreading, or weeping. Slow-growing but tough, they're good for rock gardens, mixed borders, foundation plantings, and containers.

How to grow: Full sun. Prefers well-drained, acidic or neutral soil and needs regular watering. Protect the root zone with a layer of mulch; the roots are too shallow for underplanting. Container-grown or balled-and-burlapped plants are easy to transplant. Shapes itself naturally and doesn't need pruning. Subject to various insect pests, sometimes serious, usually minor.

glauca (p. 193)
White spruce.
Conifer. Zone 3.
H: 60–70 ft. S: 25 ft.

Native across Canada, this spruce withstands heat, wind, and dryness but needs cold winters. It's useful as a windbreak or specimen in the Upper Midwest. Makes a dense cone of foliage, with bluish green needles 3/4 in. long and 2-in. cones. More common than the species is 'Conica', a dwarf form with pale green needles, 1/4–1/2 in. long, densely crowded on the twigs. It looks like a cone upholstered with slightly prickly fake fur, and it takes decades to reach 10 ft. tall. 'Densata', often called Black Hills spruce, is a conical form that grows about 6 in. a year, with dense, dark blue-green needles.

How to grow: Like *P. abies*.

omorika (p. 193)
Serbian spruce.
Conifer. Zone 4.
H: to 100 ft. S: to 25 ft.

A narrow and graceful tree, it makes a fine specimen; several planted together form an excellent backdrop or screen. Forms a slender pyramid, growing only one-quarter as wide as it is tall. The stiff branches point up at an angle. Needles are flat, 1/2 in. long, dark green above with 2 white stripes below. 'Pendula' has weeping branches but is an upright tree.

How to grow: Full sun or part shade. Prefers deep, well-drained, moist soil but tolerates both acidic and alkaline conditions. An adaptable tree that does especially well in the East.

orientalis (p. 193)
Oriental spruce.
Conifer. Zone 5.
H: 60 ft. or more. S: 20 ft. or more.

A magnificent evergreen, slower-growing than other spruces. Makes a narrow pyramid with spreading branches and drooping branchlets. Needles are glossy green, less than 1/2 in. long, and densely crowded on the twigs. An excellent specimen, already handsome when young, getting better all the time.

How to grow: Full sun. Needs good drainage; tolerates sandy or gravelly soil but not clay. Dry winter winds turn the needles brown, but fresh new growth soon restores this tree's beauty.

pungens (p. 193)
Blue spruce, Colorado spruce.
Conifer. Zone 3.
H: 80–100 ft. or more. S: 30–40 ft.

A symbol of the Colorado Rockies, where its erect pyramidal shape echoes the mountain peaks. Popular in other regions for its colored foliage and rigid posture. Young trees are especially neat and formal, with tiers of horizontal branches. Older specimens often lose their lower limbs and may get straggly and irregular. The needles are very stiff and sharply pointed, about 1 in. long. "Blueness" varies among seedlings; some trees are pale silvery blue, others a drab gray-green. Grafted cultivars cost more than seedlings but have reliably blue color. 'Hoopsii' is one of the best cultivars, with beautiful bright blue needles and rapid dense growth. 'Fat Albert' grows slowly into a compact chubby cone with good blue color. 'Blue Spreader' is a dwarf form with creeping branches, good for trailing over a stone wall.

How to grow: Like *P. abies.*

Pieris
Pee-air´is.
Ericaceae. Heath family.

Evergreen shrubs or trees with simple leaves and small white flowers. Only 7 spp., native to eastern Asia and the eastern United States.

floribunda (p. 181)
Mountain andromeda.
Evergreen shrub. Zone 4.
H: 4–6 ft. S: 4 ft.

Harder to find than Japanese andromeda but worth looking for. This southeastern native doesn't suffer from as many insect problems; is more tolerant of cold, heat, and alkaline soil; and doesn't outgrow its space in foundation plantings. It's an erect mounded shrub with oval leaves 2–31/2 in. long, pointed at the tips. The leaves are shiny, smooth, and thick, red or bronzy when new, darkening to green. The flower buds form in fall and are attractive all winter, opening in March or April to pitcher-shaped, fragrant white flowers in upright 4-in. clusters at the branch tips.

'Brouwer's Beauty' is a hybrid between *P. floribunda* and *P. japonica.* It grows 3–6 ft. tall, with a dense compact habit and shiny dark green leaves. Horizontal clusters of deep purplish-red flower buds open into small white flowers.

How to grow: Full or part sun. Needs protection from winter sun in cold areas, from summer sun in hot areas. Does best in fertile, organic, acidic soil but tolerates ordinary garden soil. Regular watering. Mulch with pine needles or composted leaves. Develops slowly and doesn't outgrow its space. Needs little care.

japonica (p. 181)
Japanese pieris, Japanese andromeda.
Evergreen shrub. Zone 5.
H: 9–12 ft. S: 6–8 ft.

A popular evergreen shrub with glossy foliage that's buried under masses of white, pink, or rosy flowers in early spring. Flower buds form at the branch tips in fall, in many drooping clusters 3–5 in. long. The oblong leaves, 11/2–3 in. long, are clustered on the stiff erect branches. New leaves expand after flowering and are red, pink, or bronze at first, maturing to dark green. Combines easily with rhododendrons, azaleas, mountain laurels, hollies, and conifers. There are dozens of cultivars, selected mostly for unique foliage and flower colors. 'Mountain Fire' is one of the most popular, with bright gold and red new growth and white flowers.

How to grow: Part sun. Needs well-drained, fertile, organic, acidic soil. Regular watering. Protect from cold winter winds. Fairly slow growing. Prune after flowering, removing fruit clusters. Subject to various fungal diseases, and badly damaged by lace bugs throughout the eastern United States.

Pinus
Py´nus. Pine.
Pinaceae. Pine family.

Evergreen coniferous trees with needlelike leaves, almost always borne in clusters of 2–5. The main trunk is strongly upright. Each year's growth makes a new whorl of branches on the main trunk and the side limbs. The woody cones may be small or large; a few kinds have edible seeds. The timber is very important for carpentry and woodworking, and the trees also provide turpentine, rosin, and fragrant oils. More than 90 spp., native to both temperate and tropical climates in the Old and New World.

Most pines are propagated by seed, and plants within a species may vary in habit, vigor, hardiness, and needle color. There are only a few vegetatively propagated cultivars. Several Old World species are planted throughout the United States, but our various native pines are also very common and are versatile, reliable, popular trees.

How to grow: Most pines do best in full sun; a few can take part shade. Except where noted, they need good drainage, but they do not require rich soil. Some kinds tolerate considerable drought when established. Plant in early spring, before bud break, or in fall. The roots are vulnerable to drying out—even a few minutes' exposure to wind and sun can hinder subsequent growth, so be sure to keep the roots covered or protected while digging the planting hole. Water new trees regularly for the first year.

Summer winds, winter sun, and ocean or road salt can damage the foliage of susceptible species. Various borers, beetles, rusts, and blights can also cause problems, but in general, pines are tough, adaptable trees. Pruning is not required, but if you want to improve the shape or reduce the size of a tree, you can thin or shorten the expanding buds, called candles, in spring. Snapping off the ends of the candles produces more compact growth.

bungeana (p. 194)
Lace-bark pine.
Conifer. Zone 5.
H: 50 ft. S: 25 ft.

Valued for its handsome bark, which flakes off in large patches like a sycamore's. Often grown with multiple trunks and lower branches removed to showcase the bark. Needles are stiff and sharp, dark green, 2–4 in. long, in groups of 3. Cones are 2–3 in. long. Plant it near a path or building where you can enjoy it all year.

How to grow: See main entry. Quite tough; it tolerates winter cold and desert heat. Grows very slowly.

cembra (p. 195)
Swiss stone pine.
Conifer. Zone 4.
H: 35 ft. or more. S: 15 ft. or more.

Uncommon but desirable. Young trees are narrowly erect and fit easily into small gardens. Mature trees have a broad open crown. Foliage is dense and rich. Needles are stiff and fine, 3–5 in. long, glossy dark green, in groups of 5. The closed cones, 3 in. long, hang on for 2 years.

How to grow: See main entry. Native to the Alps, it is cold-hardy but can't take extreme heat. Grows very slowly.

densiflora 'Umbraculifera' (p. 195)
Tanyosho pine, Japanese umbrella pine.
Conifer. Zone 5.
H: 10–25 ft. S: wider than tall.

An unusual pine that makes a distinct umbrella-shaped crown with many close-set branches. Grows slowly and is handsome at all ages. Makes a fine specimen for any garden. The multiple trunks have attractive, flaking, red-orange bark. Needles are soft, twisted, 3–5 in. long, in groups of 2. Cones are 2 in. long, borne even on young trees. This cultivar is more widely grown than the species, which is a round-headed tree, to 60 ft. or more, with interesting irregular branching.

How to grow: See main entry. Can't take hot, dry winds.

halepensis (p. 195)
Aleppo pine.
Conifer. Zone 8.
H: to 60 ft. S: 25 ft.

This Mediterranean species is commonly planted in the arid Southwest. Grows quickly and has interesting irregular branching even when young. Older trees have a rounded crown

Pinus halepensis

of short upturned branches that look windswept. Needles are soft, thin, light green, 3–4 in. long, in groups of 2. Cones are 3 in. long. *P. eldarica* (now *P. brutia* var. *eldarica*), the Afghan pine, is similar and just as tough. It grows faster and has a more regular shape. It is sometimes planted for Christmas trees. Needles are longer and greener than those of Aleppo pine.

How to grow: See main entry. Useful in difficult conditions; it tolerates desert heat, drought, sea spray, and poor soil.

mugo (p. 194)
Mugo pine.
Conifer. Zone 3.
H: 15 ft. or more. S: 15 ft. or more.

More like a shrub than a tree, this pine is broad and bushy. Most of the plants sold are labeled as dwarfs (sometimes listed as *P. mugo* var. *mugo*), but some are more compact than others. True dwarfs are excellent for foundation plantings and small beds or rock gardens. Larger forms make good screens or boundary plantings. All have dense dark green foliage. The stout needles are crowded on the stems, 2 in. long, in groups of 2. The oval cones are 1–2 in. long. Var. *pumilio* is a prostrate form that can spread 8–10 ft. wide.

How to grow: See main entry. Hardy to cold but can't take extreme heat. Good for coastal gardens; not damaged by salt spray.

nigra (p. 194)
Austrian black pine.
Conifer. Zone 4.
H: 40–60 ft. S: 20–30 ft.

Very adaptable and widely planted. Conical when young, broad and flat-topped with age. The trunk is stout; the limbs spread horizontally. The foliage is especially dark green, even in winter, and makes a good background for other plantings. Also used as a screen or windbreak. Needles are 4–6 in. long, in groups of 2. Cones are 3 in. long.

How to grow: See main entry. Tolerates cold, wind, salt, and dry or damp soil. In recent years, trees in the Midwest (but not in other areas) have succumbed to a fatal blight.

strobus (p. 195)
Eastern white pine.
Conifer. Zone 3.
H: 80 ft. or more. S: 20–40 ft.

One of the most ornamental pines. Its soft texture, attractive form, and fast rate of growth make it ideal as a specimen, in groups, or for

Pinus strobus

screening. Can be sheared to form tall hedges. Needles are very soft, bluish green, 2–4 in. long, in groups of 5. The slender cones are 6–8 in. long. The many cultivars include compact, fastigiate, and weeping forms.

How to grow: See main entry. Prefers rich, moist, organic soil. Grows best in its native area—the Northeast, Great Lakes, and Appalachians. Is damaged or killed by salt and by air pollution. Susceptible to blister rust and white pine weevil.

sylvestris (p. 195)
Scotch pine.
Conifer. Zone 3.
H: to 70 ft. or more. S: 30–40 ft.

Young plants quickly develop a conical shape and are widely planted for Christmas trees. Older trees become quite picturesque, with open branching and an irregular rounded crown. Twigs and branches have orange bark that peels off in papery layers. The stiff twisted needles have sharp points and are 1–4 in. long, in groups of 2. The rounded cones, 2–3 in. long, drop in late spring. There are dwarf, fastigiate, and blue-needled cultivars.

How to grow: See main entry. Tolerates poor, dry, sandy, acidic soil. Hardy to cold but suffers in extreme heat and drought.

thunbergiana (p. 195)
(*P. thunbergii*)
Japanese black pine.
Conifer. Zone 6.
H: 20–80 ft., depending on conditions.
S: 20–40 ft.

Planted across the United States because it is fast-growing, adaptable, and picturesque. Needles are stiff, dark green, about 3 in. long, in groups of 2. Cones are 2–3 in. long. Young trees are more or less conical and can be pruned or sheared for dense rounded growth. Older trees develop a crooked trunk and an irregular spreading crown. Indispensable for Japanese-style gardens.

How to grow: See main entry. Highly recommended for seaside plantings because it tolerates coastal salt spray and winds. Sometimes listed for Zone 5 but is subject to freeze damage there. In recent years, many trees in the Northeast have died from blue canker stain disease. No cure is known.

native southern pines
This group includes several native pines that are widespread throughout the South. They sprout quickly in abandoned fields and cut-over forests and are grown on plantations for timber and for Christmas trees. Existing pines are usually preserved when new homes are built in the South, and pines are often planted as shade for azaleas and camellias. These southern species are sometimes called yellow pines because the wood has a yellow color. Most are hardy to Zone 7; a few will grow in Zone 6.

P. echinata, the shortleaf pine, grows fast and gets 50–60 ft. tall. Young trees are cone-shaped. Older trees have a narrow open crown. The soft flexible needles are 3–5 in. long, in groups of 2. The prickly cones hang on the branches for years. Adapts to most soils except wet, heavy clay.

P. elliotii, the slash pine, is notable for its tolerance of poorly drained soil. Grows quickly and reaches 80 ft. or taller, with an upright trunk and spreading limbs. Pairs of yellow-green to green needles, 8–10 in. long, cluster at the ends of the limbs. The prickly cones, 4–6 in. long, drop after 2 years. Not a classy tree, but it provides shade and can be underplanted with flowering shrubs or perennials.

P. glabra, the spruce pine, has character even as a young tree, with irregular branches and a trunk that often twists or curves. It grows at a moderate rate, reaching 60 ft. or more. The slender twisted needles are bright green, 3–4 in. long, in groups of 2. The stout cones, 2–3 in. long, are not prickly.

P. palustris, the longleaf pine, has needles 8–18 in. long in groups of 3. Seedlings look like hummocks of grass for a few years before they form a trunk and start to grow up. Old trees reach 80–100 ft. The high, airy, fragrant canopy of a mature stand makes fine shade; individuals make striking specimens. Tolerates all but swampy conditions. The large cones, 6–10 in. long, have spine-tipped scales.

P. taeda, the loblolly pine, grows quickly on eroded soil and exposed sites, providing shade and screening. Conical when young, its crown gets rounder and lower branches drop off with age. Old trees get straggly, but they still provide shade. Needles are 6–9 in. long, in bundles of 3, light green in summer but often yellowish in winter. Clusters of 3–4-in. cones hang on the branches for years.

P. virginiana, the Virginia pine, is grown on Christmas tree plantations because it quickly develops a neat conical shape. Tolerates infertile soil, clay or sand. Needles are stiff and twisted, 2–3 in. long, in groups of 2. Clusters of small prickly cones hang on 2 years or more.

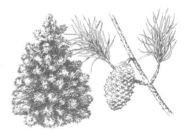

Pinus virginiana

native western pines (p. 195)
Several species of native pines are commonly retained or planted on homesites throughout the Rocky Mountain and western states. They are quite cold-hardy (Zone 5 or 4) and tolerate strong wind, hot sun, and dry gravelly soil.

P. aristata, the bristlecone pine, grows very slowly but lives indefinitely—some old-timers are judged to be more than 4,000 years old. It makes a picturesque specimen, eventually reaching 20–25 ft. tall and 12–15 ft. wide. It has irregular crooked limbs covered with stout needles 1–1¹/₂ in. long, dark green with white specks of resin, in groups of 5.

P. edulis, the pinyon pine, and *P. cembroides,* the Mexican pinyon pine, are bushy rounded trees that grow only 10–20 ft. tall, with stiff limbs and short thick needles. Their small rounded cones contain plump tasty seeds. Both are very drought-tolerant, good for screening or specimens on dry windy sites.

P. flexilis, the limber pine, grows wild on exposed rocky ridges and makes a fine windbreak, screen, or specimen. It can substitute for eastern white pine on difficult sites. Mature trees form a broad open pyramid 25–50 ft. tall and 15–25 ft. wide. The limbs are slender and limber. Needles are stiff, dark green, 2–3 in. long, in groups of 5. Cones are resinous, 3–5 in. long. 'Glauca' has bluish green needles.

P. ponderosa, the ponderosa pine, is a large tree that grows 60 ft. or taller, with an upright trunk and horizontal limbs. Pyramidal when young, it opens with age, revealing rusty orange, deeply furrowed bark. Needles are coarse, yellow-green to dark green, 4–8 in. long. The prickly cones are 4–6 in. long. A grove of ponderosas is a lovely place, and the shade is light enough to allow underplanting. *P. jeffreyi* is similar but has more bluish needles and larger cones without prickles. Its bark smells like vanilla.

Pinus edulis

Pistacia

Pis-tash´ee-a. Pistachio.
Anacardiaceae. Sumac family.

Deciduous or evergreen trees or shrubs with pinnately compound leaves, small flowers, and dry single-seeded fruits. *P. vera* is the source of pistachio nuts. Only 9 spp., from the Old and New World.

chinensis (p. 122)
Chinese pistache.
Deciduous tree. Zone 7 or 6.
H: 40 ft. or more. S: 30 ft. or more.

One of the best trees for fall color in warm climates. The large compound leaves with 10–14 paired leaflets turn bright orange or scarlet. The umbrella-like canopy casts a light shade. Flowers and fruits are inconspicuous. Tough, adaptable, and neat, this is a good tree for urban settings and makes a fine shade tree on small lots. *P. texana,* the Texas pistachio, is native to Texas and Mexico and thrives in hot, dry weather. Usually a large multitrunked shrub, it has glossy semievergreen foliage and long clusters of red berries that attract birds.

How to grow: Full sun. Tolerates poor or alkaline soil. Drought-tolerant when established. Stake and train young trees to develop a strong single trunk and to establish a good branch structure. Older trees need little pruning. No serious pests or diseases.

Pittosporum tobira

Pittosporum
Pit-o-spo´rum.
Pittosporaceae. Pittosporum family.

Evergreen shrubs or trees with shiny leathery leaves and attractive, often fragrant flowers. Some have valuable timber. About 200 spp., native to warm and tropical climates in the Old World.

crassifolium (p. 182)
Evergreen shrub. Zone 8.
H: 10 ft. or more. S: 10 ft. or more.

Used mostly for hedging, kept neat and compact with annual pruning. This can also make a small rounded tree. Its gray-green leaves are thick and leathery, 1–2 in. long, with rounded tips. Foliage is dense and handsome but tough, and holds up well to wind, sun, and salt spray. The clusters of small purple flowers in late spring are less conspicuous than the blue-purple fruits that follow. 'Compactum' is a dwarf form.

How to grow: Full or part sun. Ordinary soil and watering. Tolerates dry spells. Space 2 ft. apart for a pruned hedge, 5 ft. apart for an unpruned screen or windbreak. Can be infested with scale or aphids.

eugenioides (p. 182)
Evergreen shrub or tree. Zone 9.
H: to 40 ft. S: to 20 ft.

Where hardy, its light green, dense, shiny foliage makes it an excellent choice for year-round good looks. Leaves are narrow ovals, 2–4 in. long, with a crisp texture and wavy edges. The clusters of tiny star-shaped yellow flowers are strongly honey-scented and bloom for several weeks in spring. A versatile plant that responds well to pruning, it can make a fine clipped hedge, a tall screen or windbreak, or a specimen tree with a gray trunk and dense canopy. Other tender species are popular in California. *P. tenuifolium* has smaller, darker green leaves and fragrant, dark red (almost black) flowers. It's used as a hedge or screen. *P. undulatum,* or Victorian box, makes a rounded tree 30–40 ft. tall with wavy-edged leaves up to 6 in. long, fragrant white flowers, and orange fruits.

How to grow: Like *P. crassifolium.*

tobira (p. 182)
Evergreen shrub. Zone 8.
H: 10–15 ft. S: 10 ft. or more.

A durable shrub that makes an irregular but dense mound of foliage. Large, thick, glossy dark green leaves with rounded tips are clustered at the tips of the branches. 'Variegata' has gray-green leaves mottled with white and grows about 6 ft. tall. 'Wheeler's Dwarf' has small dark green leaves and grows only 3–4 ft. tall; it does well in planters or containers. All bear clusters of small, creamy white, very fragrant flowers in early summer. Tough and adaptable, they are good for foundation plantings, hedges, or mixed borders.

How to grow: Sun or shade. Tolerates hot, dry sites; unamended soil; and ocean spray. Can be pruned by heading back individual branches, but the leaves are too big for clipping with hedge shears. Subject to scale and aphids.

Platanus

Plat´a-nus. Sycamore, plane tree.
Platanaceae. Plane tree family.

Large deciduous trees with thick trunks, spreading limbs, flaking bark, lobed leaves, and round flower heads and fruits. Only 6 or 7 spp., several native to North America.

occidentalis (p. 123)

American sycamore, buttonwood, buttonball tree.
Deciduous tree. Zone 5.
H: 100 ft. S: 100 ft.

An impressive native tree that makes massive specimens on floodplains and riversides throughout the eastern United States. It has a stout trunk and twisting, wide-reaching limbs. The bark is very distinctive—smooth and white on the new limbs, flaking in irregular patches of cream, gray, olive green, and tan on the trunk and main branches. The large toothed leaves have a soft texture and are medium green in summer, tan in fall. The dry brown seed balls are 1–1¹/₂ in. thick, borne singly. *P. racemosa,* the California sycamore, is a similar tree but has dangling clusters of 3–7 seed balls. If there's a native sycamore on your property, enjoy it, but think twice before planting one. They get big fast, are very susceptible to anthracnose disease, and are attacked by several insect pests.

The hybrid *P.* × *acerifolia,* or London plane tree, has the characteristic sycamore bark, leaves, and seed balls but is tougher and more adaptable than native sycamores. It has been planted by the thousands in towns and cities because it tolerates compacted soil, heat, drought, and air pollution and has fairly good disease resistance. However, it grows too fast and gets too large to plant near utility lines or buildings, and the roots can clog sewers and lift sidewalks. In Europe, London plane trees are pollarded and pruned into dense formal screens along avenues or estate driveways. Severe annual pruning reduces a tree's top growth but doesn't inhibit the roots, and a pollarded trunk is an ugly monster in winter.

How to grow: Full sun. Prefers moist, fertile soil but grows okay with regular soil and watering. All sycamores need plenty of space and grow quickly. Plant them in large, open, parklike settings, where they can spread their limbs and roots.

Platanus racemosa

Platycodon

Plat-i-ko´don. Balloon flower.
Campanulaceae. Bellflower family.

A perennial with unusual balloonlike buds. Only 1 sp., native to eastern Asia.

grandiflorus (p. 265)

Balloon flower.
Perennial. Zone 3.
H: 1¹/₂–3 ft. S: 2 ft.

The unique puffy buds are shaped like hot-air balloons and open from the top into elegant flowers like 5-pointed stars, 2 in. wide, in shades of violet, blue, pink, or white. Forms a small clump of erect stems with many narrow toothed leaves 3 in. long. Continues blooming throughout the summer if spent flowers are removed. Lovely in a border with campanulas, astilbes, and veronicas. 'Mariesii' is a compact form, under 2 ft. tall, with blue, white, or pink flowers. Var. *plenus* is double, with 2 layers of blue petals.

How to grow: Full sun in northern regions; afternoon shade where summers are hot. Ordinary or better soil and regular watering. Set 1¹/₂–2 ft. apart, in spring or fall, and leave undisturbed. Balloon flower is long lived but hates to be moved and is difficult to divide. Easily raised from seed but doesn't bloom for a few years. Very late to emerge in spring; mark the spot to avoid digging and damaging it. Few pests.

Plumbago

Plum-bay´go. Leadwort.
Plumbaginaceae. Plumbago family.

Perennials or shrubs with simple leaves and flowers with long tubes that flare into 5 lobes. About 10 spp., native to tropical climates.

auriculata (p. 182)

(formerly *P. capensis*)
Cape plumbago.
Evergreen shrub. Zone 9.
H: 6 ft. S: 10–12 ft.

A spreading, mounding, or climbing shrub whose cool blue flowers appear throughout the hottest weather, when their color is most appreciated. Although slow to start, it's trouble-free once established. Flowers are pale to sky blue (sometimes white), in rounded terminal clusters. The thin light green leaves are pointed ovals, 1–2 in. long. A good ground cover along driveways or on banks. Can be trained on a fence or trellis or used as a screen or boundary planting.

How to grow: Full sun. Ordinary soil and watering. Tolerates heat and dry soil when established. Buy plants in bloom to choose flower color. Furnish support and tie up stems to train vertically. Remove frost-damaged shoots in spring. Thin out the oldest stems periodically. No serious pests.

Platycodon grandiflorus

Podocarpus
Po-do-kar´pus.
Podocarpaceae. Podocarpus family.
Evergreen coniferous trees or shrubs with flat narrow leaves. Many are harvested for timber. More than 90 spp., most native to the Southern Hemisphere and the tropics.

macrophyllus (p. 196)
Yew pine.
Conifer. Zone 8.
H: to 30 ft. but can be kept much smaller.
S: 10–15 ft.
An upright shrub or tree with glossy, leathery, needlelike leaves 3–4 in. long and 1/4 in. wide. Creamy clusters of male flowers are conspicuous in early summer. Edible reddish purple fruits appear in fall. Responds well to pruning; makes a dense hedge or screen, or can be espaliered or used for topiary. Can also be trained as a columnar or rounded specimen tree. Var. *maki* is a compact form that grows narrowly upright, slowly reaching 10 ft. or more. Popular for foundation plantings, it also does very well in containers.

How to grow: Full sun or part shade. Needs well-drained soil and tolerates drought when established. Easy and adaptable, with no serious pests or diseases. Prune to shape as desired.

Polemonium
Po-lee-mo´nee-um. Jacob's-ladder.
Polemoniaceae. Phlox family.
Perennials with pinnately compound leaves and clusters of 5-petaled flowers. About 25 spp., many native to western North America.

caeruleum (p. 266)
Jacob's-ladder.
Perennial. Zone 2.
H: 2–3 ft. S: 2 ft.
Forms a soft mound of feathery compound leaves and upright stems topped with clusters of nodding bell-shaped flowers, 1 in. wide. Blooms from late spring until midsummer. Foliage is apple green; flowers are indigo blue. Combine it with spring bulbs, hellebores, and hostas in a moist shady bed under deciduous trees or shrubs. *P. reptans,* only 9 in. tall, spreads in damp soil and is covered with blue flowers in spring.

How to grow: Part shade; tolerates sun if the soil is moist. Plant in cool, moist, well-drained, moisture-retentive soil enriched with plenty of organic matter. Divide every 3–4 years in early spring. Trouble-free.

Polygonatum
Po-lig-o-nay´tum. Solomon's-seal.
Liliaceae. Lily family.
Perennials with spreading rhizomes, leafy arching stems, and small starry flowers. About 55 spp., native to the north temperate zone.

Polygonatum odoratum 'Variegatum'

odoratum 'Variegatum' (p. 266)
(*P. odoratum* var. *thunbergii* 'Variegatum')
Variegated Solomon's-seal.
Perennial. Zone 3.
H: 11/2–3 ft. S: 1 ft. or more.
A graceful plant that forms a patch of leafy, unbranched, arching stems. The alternate leaves, 4 in. long, are neatly arranged on the upper half of the stems. The creamy white variegation on the edges of the leaves brings light to shady places. Fragrant white flowers, 1 in. long, dangle singly or in pairs from each leaf axil. Blooms in April or May and attracts hummingbirds. Grows well under trees or shrubs; tolerates dry shade better than most perennials do. *P. biflorum,* the native Solomon's-seal, has solid green leaves and needs moist soil.

How to grow: Part or full shade. Does best in fertile, organic soil. Spreads slowly by thick rhizomes. Divide and replant in early spring or in late fall after the foliage has died back. Space 11/2–2 ft. apart. Top-dress occasionally with compost. Trouble-free.

Polygonum
Po-lig´o-num. Knotweed.
Polygonaceae. Buckwheat family.
Annuals, perennials, or vines, some aquatic. Stems usually have swollen nodes. Leaves are alternate. Flowers are small but sometimes showy. Some species are very weedy, spreading by seed or rhizome. About 150 spp., native worldwide.

aubertii (p. 205)
Silver fleece vine, mile-a-minute vine.
Deciduous vine. Zone 5.
H: 25–35 ft.
Grows fast enough (up to 15 ft. the first year!) to be very helpful in a new garden, and flowers in midsummer when most other vines are finished or haven't started. Has a very soft, relaxed appearance when scrambling over a wall or fence or climbing into shrubs or trees. The soft leaves, up to 4 in. long, are reddish at first, bright green later. Literally covers itself with slender drooping clusters of small, fragrant, white or pinkish flowers.

How to grow: Full or part sun. Ordinary or unimproved soil. Tolerates heat and dry soil. Plant in spring for flowers the first year. Freezes back to the ground each winter in the North. Where winters are mild, cut it back hard in spring to limit its spread. Propagate by division. May be attacked by Japanese beetles.

***bistorta* 'Superbum'** (p. 266)
(*Persicaria bistorta* 'Superbum')
Knotweed, snakeweed.
Perennial. Zone 3.
H: 2–3 ft. S: 2 ft.

Makes clumps of large smooth leaves, 4–6 in. long, with wavy edges and distinct white midribs. Brushy spikes of tiny pink flowers are held above the foliage in late spring and sometimes again in early fall. Makes a good cut flower.

How to grow: Does best with afternoon shade. Ordinary or improved soil. Spreads fast enough to be a ground cover on wet sites but is inhibited by dry soil. Divide in spring or fall. Space 2 ft. apart. May be attacked by Japanese beetles.

Polystichum

Po-lis´ti-kum. Shield fern.
Polypodiaceae. Polypody family.

Evergreen or deciduous ferns with long pinnate fronds. The frond segments, called pinnae, have a round "ear" or "thumb" at the base. Most are native to woodlands. About 135 spp., native worldwide.

acrostichoides (p. 219)
Christmas fern.
Evergreen fern. Zone 3.
H: 2–3 ft. S: 3 ft.

Easy and adaptable, good as a ground cover or combined with spring wildflowers or bulbs. The leathery evergreen fronds are glossy green, up to 5 in. wide and 2–3 ft. long. Sterile fronds spread horizontally; fertile fronds are taller and more erect. *P. braunii*, or Braun's holly fern, has the same erect grace but needs constant moisture and deep shade. *P. tsus-simense*, or rock fern, is similar but smaller. It makes a compact rosette of stiff, leathery, shiny, blackish green fronds, 1–1½ ft. tall and 1 ft. wide. Makes an excellent edging along paths. Needs a cool shady site, rich soil, and constant moisture.

How to grow: Part sun or shade. Grows naturally on shaded slopes in moist woods or along streambanks, throughout the eastern United States. Can't take hot dry summers. Plant 2 ft. apart in acidic or neutral soil amended with plenty of organic matter. Divide in early spring.

munitum (p. 219)
Sword fern, western sword fern.
Evergreen fern. Zone 4.
H: 2–4 ft. S: 1–2 ft.

A West Coast native that's attractive, hardy, and easy to grow. Forms erect clumps of large sword-shaped fronds with a leathery texture and dark green color. Florists use the fronds for greenery. Grow it with other ferns, hostas, begonias, and astilbes in shady beds along north walls or under trees. Ideal for woodland gardens.

How to grow: Part sun or shade. Plant in soil amended with plenty of organic matter. Tolerates some heat or dryness but not both at the same time. Cut off battered fronds in spring, after new growth has begun. Old clumps make offsets that can be removed and replanted. Trouble-free.

polyblepharum (p. 219)
Tassel fern.
Evergreen fern. Zone 4.
H: 2 ft. S: 2–3 ft.

This lovely Japanese fern is very easy to grow if not allowed to dry out. Forms a mounded rosette of stiff, glossy green foliage. The scaly new fiddleheads arch over backwards as they emerge, exposing soft bristles or tassels at the tips of the pinnae. A fine specimen for shady borders, dark corners where flowering plants would be unhappy, or north-facing slopes.

How to grow: Deep shade. Needs rich, acidic soil amended with plenty of organic matter and constant moisture. Mulch well. Protect from sun and dry winds.

setiferum (p. 219)
Soft shield fern.
Semievergreen fern. Zone 5.
H: 3 ft. S: 2 ft.

A popular fern with narrow lance-shaped fronds that spread like a starfish and hug the ground. The fronds have a soft velvety texture, feathery appearance, and dark green color. Plant in a prominent position along a path or near a stepping-stone, and contrast it with grasses, coarser ferns, or hostas. There are many cultivars, each with uniquely lovely foliage. After you've grown one, you'll want to try them all.

How to grow: Part sun or shade. Prefers moist, fertile soil but will grow in poor soil and tolerates drought. Space at least 3 ft. apart. Position the crown right on top of the soil. Fronds produce new plantlets along the center stalk; to propagate, detach a frond and peg it down on moist, gritty, sterile potting soil in a covered container such as a plastic shoebox. When the young plants have rooted and are large enough to handle, plant them in separate pots until they are big enough to put in the ground.

Populus

Pop´you-lus. Cottonwood, poplar, aspen.
Salicaceae. Willow family.

Deciduous trees that are very fast growing but usually short lived. They have soft light wood, simple leaves, and dangling catkins in early spring. Closely related to willows (*Salix* spp.). About 35 spp., native to the north temperate zone, and several hybrids.

deltoides (p. 123)
Eastern cottonwood.
Deciduous tree. Zone 3.
H: 60–100 ft. S: 30–50 ft.

Cottonwoods have many faults—they grow too big for most lots, their wood is brittle and breaks in storms, their roots invade underground pipes, the fluffy seeds from female trees

Populus fremontii

clog window screens and car radiators, and the seedlings are weedy. Despite all that, they're useful as fast-growing shade trees, especially in the Great Plains. The large stiff leaves are triangular or heart-shaped, 3–6 in. long, shiny green in summer and rich gold in fall. They flutter in the slightest breeze and make a rustling sound that's very soothing. Plant selected male forms to avoid the mess of white cottony seeds. Eastern cottonwood grows wild on moist sites or disturbed soil from the Rockies to the Atlantic. Similar trees are *P. fremontii*, or Fremont cottonwood, native to the Southwest and California, and *P. sargentii*, or plains cottonwood, native to the Great Plains. *P.* × *acuminata*, or lanceleaf cottonwood, has slender willowlike leaves and is relatively tidy and well mannered.

How to grow: Full sun. Tolerates infertile soil. Prefers constant moisture but gets by with regular watering. Grows very quickly. Subject to various cankers, galls, and leafspots. Plant at least 50 ft. away from water pipes, sewers, septic fields, sidewalks, or patios.

other poplars and cottonwoods
P. alba, the white poplar, is a European species that's planted throughout the United States. The toothed leaves are dark green on top and white underneath and look very pretty on breezy days. The interesting bark shades from white to green to gray. A very attractive tree that grows fast and tolerates almost any soil and conditions, but it produces many suckers, especially if damaged or stressed, and it has all the other problems associated with cottonwoods.

P. nigra 'Italica', the Lombardy poplar, is a male cultivar shaped like an exclamation point. Often planted along driveways or for quick screening. It grows very quickly until afflicted by fatal cankers, then dies slowly from the top down.

P. tremuloides, the quaking aspen, is a small tree that's very common in cool mountain or northern climates. The glossy leaves are fresh green all summer, warm gold in fall. The smooth gray bark is attractive all year. Needs cool, moist soil and protection from hot sun and dry winds.

"Hybrid poplars" are fast-growing trees bred for the paper-pulp industry but promoted to homeowners for instant shade or screening. They need fertile, moist, well-prepared soil and protection from competing grass or weeds to achieve the advertised rates of growth—5 ft. a year or more.

Populus tremuloides

Portulaca
Por-tew-la′ka. Moss rose, purslane.
Portulaceae. Purslane family.

Low-growing annuals with plump succulent leaves on trailing stems. Some have showy flowers. About 40 spp., nearly all from warm and tropical climates.

grandiflora (p. 302)
Moss rose.
Annual. All zones.
H: under 1 ft. S: 1 ft.

A favorite annual for hot, dry sites. Blooms from early summer until frost. The trailing stems are covered with plump cylindrical leaves and waxy round flowers, 1 in. wide, single or double, in shades of yellow, orange, red, pink, or white. Old-fashioned types closed by late afternoon and didn't open at all on cloudy days, but new strains keep longer hours. Excellent for edging walks, beds, or driveways or in containers.

How to grow: Full sun. Prefers ordinary soil and watering but tolerates infertile soil and long dry spells. Buy bedding plants in spring or direct-sow seeds about the time of last frost. The seeds are tiny, but the seedlings grow fast. It often self-sows. Shear halfway back and fertilize in midsummer to promote fresh growth and to renew flowering.

Potentilla
Po-ten-til′la. Cinquefoil.
Rosaceae. Rose family.

Annuals, perennials, or shrubs with stiff or wiry stems, compound leaves, and 5-petaled flowers. About 500 spp., native to the north temperate zone.

fruticosa (p. 143)
Bush cinquefoil.
Deciduous shrub. Zone 2.
H: 2–3 ft. S: 3–4 ft.

One of the few shrubs that bloom all summer, with 1-in. flowers in shades of yellow or white. Makes a plump round specimen or a low hedge. The palmately compound leaves have 3–7 slender leaflets and are covered with silky hairs. The habit is bushy and dense because the stems branch repeatedly. Hard to beat for ease of care and reliable bloom. 'Abbotswood' has white flowers; 'Goldstar' is deep yellow; 'Katherine Dykes' and 'Primrose Beauty' are pale yellow.

How to grow: Full sun. Prefers ordinary soil and watering but tolerates dry sandy soil or alkaline conditions. Space 24–30 in. apart for hedges or mass plantings. Blooms on first-year wood, so it can be cut to the ground and still flower. This should be done at least every other year in early spring to keep the plant dense and compact. Spider mites can be a problem in hot, dry weather.

Primula
Prim′you-la. Primrose.
Primulaceae. Primrose family.

Low-growing perennials with a rosette of basal leaves and clusters of showy flowers on leafless stalks. About 400 spp., native worldwide, mostly in cool climates.

denticulata (p. 266)
Drumstick primrose.
Perennial. Zone 3.
H: 10–15 in. S: 9–12 in.

One of the easiest primroses to grow. Flower buds emerge in early spring as a small dome centered in the leaf rosette, then the stalk lifts straight up and the buds open into a fluffy 2-in. sphere of lavender, pink, rosy, or white flowers. Leaves are just 3–4 in. long at first but later expand to as long as 12 in. Lovely in a woodland garden or beside a stream.

How to grow: Part sun in spring, shade in summer. Needs fertile soil amended with plenty of organic matter, and a layer of organic mulch. Can survive short dry spells but does better with constant moisture. Often self-sows, or you can gather ripe seed and sow immediately. Divide every 1–2 years in late spring or early summer, after flowering, and reset in freshly enriched soil. Foliage may be attacked by aphids, flea beetles, spider mites, slugs, and snails.

japonica (p. 266)
Japanese primrose, candelabra primrose.
Perennial. Zone 5.
H: 1–2 ft. S: 1–2 ft.

Unusually lovely, with tiers of rosy red, pink, magenta, or white flowers stacked one above another on stalks 1–2 ft. tall. Blooms for 2 weeks or more in May or June. Individual flowers are about 1 in. wide and face out in all directions. The oblong basal leaves form a rosette 1–2 ft. wide.

How to grow: Like *P. denticulata* but needs moist soil all summer long. Where conditions are right—in damp soil near flowing water—these plants self-sow and form vast patches. But if the soil dries out, they die.

× ***polyantha*** (p. 267)
Polyanthus primrose.
Perennial. Zone 3.
H: 8–12 in. S: 8–10 in.

These hybrids are the easiest primroses to obtain and to grow. They're among the earliest plants to bloom in spring—and often the latest in fall, as many strains rebloom after a rainy summer (or if they've been watered regularly). Forms a basal rosette of light green leaves, 3–6 in. long, with crinkled edges. Short stalks carry umbels of upward-facing, almost flat flowers 1–2 in. wide. Fragrant flowers are solid-color or two-tone, usually with a yellow eye, in all colors and combinations. There are several excellent strains, including 'Barnhaven' hybrids, 'Pacific Giants', 'Regal', and 'Cowichan'. 'Hose-in-Hose' types have double flowers, with 2 layers of petals. Plant them among shrubs, in a woodland garden, on the north or east side of a house, or in containers. Where winters are mild and summers are very hot, polyanthus primroses are used as winter annuals that provide color in beds or containers from fall through spring.

How to grow: Like *P. denticulata*.

sieboldii (p. 267)
Japanese star primrose.
Perennial. Zone 4.
H: 9–15 in. S: 8–10 in.

One of the easiest and prettiest primroses for gardeners who must cope with hot summers. It withstands dry conditions by going completely dormant. The basal leaves are pale green hearts with crinkled scalloped edges. Umbels of 6–10 flowers, 1–1 1/2 in. wide, are held well above the foliage. Flowers are white, lilac, pink, or magenta, with deeply notched or frilled petals. There are several cultivars, including some new ones with larger flowers.

How to grow: Like *P. denticulata*.

vulgaris (p. 267)
(*P. acaulis*)
Common primrose, English primrose.
Perennial. Zone 5.
H: 6–9 in. S: 8–10 in.

An English wildflower, beloved by generations of gardeners for its simple charm. The fragrant flowers, 1–1 1/2 in. wide, are pale yellow with a deeper yellow eye, borne singly on thin fuzzy stalks. The basal leaves are scalloped and crinkled, expanding from 2–3 in. to 6–8 in. long as flowering continues in early spring. Excellent for woodland gardens or streamsides, along with dainty wildflowers and early spring bulbs.

How to grow: Like *P. denticulata*.

Primula vulgaris

Prosopis

Pro-soap´is. Mesquite.
Leguminosae. Pea family.

Deciduous or evergreen trees or shrubs with hard wood, spiny limbs, compound leaves, yellow flowers, and beanlike pods with edible seeds. More than 40 spp., most native to hot, arid regions in the New World.

glandulosa (p. 123)
Honey mesquite.
Deciduous tree. Zone 6.
H: to 30 ft. S: to 20 ft.

Despised in some areas—where it forms impenetrable thickets on ranchland—and cherished in others—where it's one of the only trees to cast shade—mesquite grows wild across much of Texas and the Southwest. The single or multiple trunks are twisted and gnarled; the spreading limbs have many thorny twigs. The compound leaves have many tiny leaflets and are bright green. Bees visit the narrow spikes of fragrant yellow flowers in spring and make an excellent honey. Tan pods, 4–10 in. long, ripen in late summer. Mesquite wood burns slow and hot and is prized for barbecues. Other species of mesquite grow wild and are sometimes planted in the Southwest.

How to grow: Full sun. Does well in poor, dry soil. Plant during warm weather. Space 10 ft. apart for a grove or barrier. Thin and shape to create a tree form. Water deeply and infrequently.

Prosopis glandulosa

Prunella

Proo-nel′la.
Labiatae. Mint family.

Low-growing perennials with square stems, opposite leaves, and small flowers arranged in dense heads. Most are spreading and can be weedy. Only 7 spp., native to the Old and New World.

webbiana (p. 267)
(now *P. grandiflora*)
Self-heal, heal-all.
Perennial. Zone 5.
H: 12–18 in. S: 12–18 in.

Forms a compact mat or clump of smooth dark green leaves, attractive at the front of a border or along a pond or stream. Spikes of 2-lipped flowers are held above the foliage and bloom for several weeks in summer. 'Pink Loveliness' has medium-size pink flowers. Other cultivars are white, lilac, or lavender. Doesn't spread like the common weed, *P. vulgaris*.

How to grow: Full or part sun. Prefers fertile, organic soil and constant moisture but tolerates ordinary soil and watering. Can't survive where summers are hot and dry. Space 9–12 in. apart. Divide big clumps in spring or fall.

Prunus

Proo′nus.
Rosaceae. Rose family.

A valuable group of deciduous or evergreen trees or shrubs. All have alternate simple leaves, pink or white flowers, and fleshy fruits with one hard seed or pit. This genus includes cherries, prunes, plums, peaches, and apricots. Many species are grown as ornamentals, and some are used for timber. About 400 spp., most native to the Northern Hemisphere.

Prunus caroliniana

caroliniana (p. 162)
Carolina cherry laurel.
Evergreen tree. Zone 7.
H: 30 ft. S: 20 ft.

A fast-growing tree with an upright oval crown and glossy dark green leaves 2–3 in. long. Crushed leaves and twigs have a strong maraschino cherry odor. Small starry flowers in clusters at each leaf axil release a heavy sweet aroma for a few weeks in early spring. Birds flock to eat the small black cherries when they ripen, and they distribute the seeds throughout the neighborhood. Often used for hedges or screens, but it needs frequent severe pruning to control the size and shape. 'Bright 'N Tight' is a more compact plant with smaller leaves.

How to grow: Full or part sun. Grows fast in any well-drained soil, and grows very fast in fertile soil with regular watering. Can't take extreme heat or dryness. Subject to root rot in wet soil. Sometimes attacked by various insects and foliar diseases, none fatal. Volunteer seedlings are the major problem.

cerasifera cultivars (p. 123)
Purple-leaf plums.
Deciduous trees. Zone 5 or 4.
H: 15–25 ft. S: 10–15 ft.

Purple-leaved trees contrast with common green foliage and make a strong accent in any landscape. These cultivars are fairly small trees with dense rounded crowns. The teardrop-shaped leaves are 1–3 in. long. White or light pink flowers in early spring are a bonus; blossoms are single, $1/2–1$ in. wide, opening just before the leaves expand. The plums are 1 in. long, edible but not tasty. 'Atropurpurea', 'Krauter Vesuvius', 'Newport', and 'Thundercloud' are most commonly offered.

Other common purple-leaf plums include two hybrids derived from *P. cerasifera*. *P. × blireiana* 'Moseri' has fragrant, light pink, double flowers 1 in. wide in early spring and leaves that open bright reddish purple but fade to green in summer. *P. × cistena*, the dwarf purple-leaf plum, is a hardy (Zone 3) medium-size shrub that grows 8–15 ft. tall. Single flowers, white or pale pink, open with the leaves. Foliage is dark reddish purple throughout the season.

How to grow: Full sun produces good foliage color; leaves are green in the shade. Ordinary soil with good drainage and regular watering. Can tolerate heat but not drought. Prune after flowering. Subject to several insect and disease problems that can be serious or fatal if trees are stressed by poor growing conditions. These are generally fast-growing but short-lived trees.

flowering cherries (p. 123)
This group of deciduous trees includes several species and dozens of cultivars grown primarily for their spectacular display of pink or white flowers in early spring. They also provide summer shade and fall color. All are desirable as lawn specimens or accents in formal or Oriental gardens.

P. sargentii, or Sargent cherry, is the largest flowering cherry (40–50 ft. tall) and the best to use as a street tree. The light pink flowers are like single roses, $1 1/2$ in. wide, in clusters of 2–4. Blooms for a long season in midspring. In fall the leaves turn bright orange-red. 'Columnaris' is more upright and narrower, useful near power lines or buildings. Zone 4.

Plants previously described as cultivars of *P. serrulata*, the Japanese flowering cherry, are now classified as the Sato Zakura Group (cultivated cherry group). Many outstanding cultivars have been developed in Japan. Most familiar in the

Prunus serrulata

United States is 'Kwanzan' (also called 'Kanzan' and 'Sekiyama'), an upright flat-topped tree, to 30 ft., with double deep pink flowers and bronzy new leaves. Zone 6.

P. subhirtella var. *autumnalis*, the autumn cherry, is a graceful tree 20–30 ft. tall with double white or pale pink flowers on the bare branches in late fall, during mild spells in winter, and most abundantly in early spring. Plant it near the house so you can enjoy the flowers from indoors. Var. *pendula* is a weeping form with single blossoms on branches that trail to the ground. Zone 6.

P. × yedoensis, or Yoshino cherry, bears clouds of mildly fragrant single blossoms in clusters on the bare branches in early spring. Most of Washington, D.C.'s celebrated cherry trees belong to this species. There are various rounded or weeping forms, 25–45 ft. tall, with single or double, pink or white flowers. Zone 6.

How to grow: Full sun. Ordinary or improved soil and regular watering. Can't take extreme heat. Plant bare-root or container-grown plants in late winter or early spring. Prune to eliminate double leaders and narrow crotches and to establish a crown high enough to walk under. Flowering cherries grow fairly quickly and are lovely for decades under ideal conditions. Borers and cankers can be fatal problems, however, especially if trees are already stressed by soil compaction, root disturbance, or drought.

Prunus laurocerasus

laurocerasus (p. 183)
Cherry laurel, English laurel.
Evergreen shrub or small tree. Zone 7.
H: 10–25 ft. S: varies.

An upright tree with a broad, dense, rounded crown of thick glossy leaves, 4–6 in. long and 2 in. wide. Upright 3–5-in. clusters of very sweet-scented small white flowers stand out like exclamation points against the foliage in midspring. *P. lusitanica,* the Portugal laurel, is a similar tree with slightly smaller leaves and slender flower clusters up to 8 in. long. Both make beautiful specimen trees. They are often misused as hedge plants; shearing chops the big leaves and the result looks quite messy.

Low, spreading cultivars of *P. laurocerasus* include 'Otto Luyken', 'Schipkaensis', and 'Zabeliana'. All stay under 4–6 ft. and spread wider than tall. They flower profusely even in the shade and tolerate the dry shade under tall trees. 'Schipkaensis' and 'Zabeliana' have narrow leaves and are hardy on protected sites in Zone 6.

How to grow: Full sun, part sun, or shade. Grows best with ordinary soil and watering but tolerates dry, infertile soil. Needs little care. Insects occasionally chew the foliage but do no serious damage.

Pterostyrax
Tay-ro-stee´rax.
Styracaceae. Storax family.

Deciduous trees or shrubs with alternate leaves and showy white flowers. Only 4 spp., native to southeastern Asia.

hispidus (p. 124)
Fragrant epaulette tree.
Deciduous tree. Zone 5.
H: 40 ft. S: 20 ft.

An uncommon but desirable shade tree. It blooms in May or June, after the large oblong leaves have fully expanded. The fragrant white flowers are held in drooping clusters 6–10 in. long. Plant it beside a deck, path, or steps where the flowers can be appreciated from below. It grows erect with horizontal branches and develops a round open crown.

How to grow: Full or part sun. Ordinary or improved soil and regular watering. Tolerates heat but not dryness. Prune to shape as desired. No serious pests.

Pulmonaria
Pul-mo-nay´ree-a. Lungwort.
Boraginaceae. Borage family.

Perennials with creeping rhizomes and hairy stems and leaves, sometimes spotted with white. Only 14 spp., native to Europe.

angustifolia (p. 267)
Blue lungwort.
Perennial. Zone 3.
H: 6–9 in. S: 12 in. or more.

Small flowers in a rich shade of pure blue are held above the hairy light green leaves. Blooms for several weeks in early spring. *P. saccharata* 'Mrs. Moon' is similar but has leaves spotted with silver-gray and flowers that open pink and fade to blue. Both spread slowly and make a good edging for woodland trails or a ground cover among early spring bulbs such as small white daffodils, crocuses, or squills.

How to grow: Shade. Ordinary soil and watering. Space 10–12 in. apart for ground cover. Divide in fall. Foliage may disappear in the heat of summer, but new growth will follow the fall rains. Easy and trouble-free.

Pulmonaria saccharata

Punica
Pew´ni-ka. Pomegranate.
Punicaceae. Pomegranate family.

Deciduous shrubs or small trees with showy flowers and large fruits with juicy pulp. Only 2 spp., native to Eurasia.

granatum (p. 143)
Pomegranate.
Deciduous shrub. Zone 8.
H: 15–20 ft. S: 10–15 ft.

An old favorite for hot climates, where it blooms all summer. Flowers are bright orange-red, 1–2 in. wide; double forms such as 'Flore Pleno' resemble carnations. The round fruits, 3–5 in. wide, have a leathery red rind and are stuffed with sweet juicy seeds. The narrow pointed leaves are glossy bright green in summer, yellow in fall. Can be trained as a rounded shrub, as a single-trunked or multitrunked tree with a spreading crown, or espaliered. Grows well in containers, and a patio plant can be over-wintered indoors. 'Wonderful' has the most delicious fruits. 'Nana' is a dwarf form, 1^1/$_2$–3 ft. tall, that can live in a pot for years. It has near-evergreen foliage, single orange-red flowers, and small dry fruits. Other cultivars have pretty salmon-pink, yellow, white, or two-tone flowers.

How to grow: Full sun. Prefers fertile, well-drained soil and regular watering but tolerates ordinary soil and some drought. Train young plants as desired. Prune in spring, removing tangled inner branches and cutting back long shoots. Flowers on new wood. No serious pests or diseases.

Pyracantha

Py-ra-kan´tha. Firethorn.
Rosaceae. Rose family.

Evergreen thorny shrubs with simple leaves, round clusters of white flowers, and red or orange berries. The berries are very showy from fall to spring. Birds don't eat them until other food sources have been depleted. Closely related to *Cotoneaster* and *Crataegus*. Only 6 spp., native to southeastern Europe and Asia.

Pyracantha coccinea

coccinea (p. 183)
Scarlet firethorn.
Semievergreen shrub. Zone 6.
H: 8–10 ft. S: 10–20 ft.

A fast-growing shrub valued for its profuse crops of red berries. The glossy dark green leaves are 1–2 in. long, with shallow teeth along the edge and a narrow rounded or pointed tip. Clusters of small white flowers last for 2–3 weeks in spring; their fragrance pleases some people and offends others. Unpruned, it makes a large upright shrub with stiff thorny branches that project at irregular angles. With persistent training and pruning, it can make a dense barrier hedge, a small multitrunked tree, or a formal espalier on a wall or fence. 'Lalandei' is one of the most common cultivars; it is vigorous and hardy, with orange-red berries.

How to grow: Needs full sun for maximum fruit production but grows fine in part shade. Ordinary soil and watering. Tolerates summer heat and dry soil when established. Prune in early spring, removing frost-damaged shoots and shaping as desired. Subject to fire blight, which makes the shoots die back from the tips; scab,

which makes hard dark spots on the berries and leaves; and various insect pests.

koidzumii (p. 183)
Firethorn.
Semievergreen shrub. Zone 7.
H: 10 ft. S: 5–10 ft.

Just as showy but not as cold-hardy as *P. coccinea*. The flowers and berries are similar to those of *P. coccinea*, but its leaves generally have smooth edges and a slight notch at the tip. It tends to grow as an irregular mounded shrub, with stiff stems that project at odd angles. Doesn't adapt well to espalier and requires diligent pruning as a hedge. Best used as a specimen along property lines or in large shrub borders, where it can develop an interesting shape and reach its full size. The most common cultivars are 'Santa Cruz', a low prostrate grower with bright red berries; and 'Victory', a vigorous upright plant with dark red berries.

How to grow: Like *P. coccinea*.

hybrid cultivars (p. 183)
Many pyracantha cultivars are hybrids of uncertain parentage. All are semievergreen shrubs with glossy foliage, clusters of white flowers in spring, and bright berries. They differ in size, habit, vigor, hardiness, and fruit color.

'Gnome' is compact and dense, usually under 6 ft. tall, with orange berries. Susceptible to scab. Zone 5.

'Mohave' grows narrowly upright to about 10 ft., with huge crops of bright orange berries that color early. Disease-resistant. Zone 7 or 6.

'Navaho' makes a broad mound, 6 ft. tall, with orange-red fruits. Disease-resistant. Zone 7 or 6.

'Red Elf' forms a dwarf compact mound and has bright red fruits. Susceptible to fire blight. Zone 7.

'Teton' grows upright, to 10 ft. or more, with yellow-orange fruits. It is one of the hardiest cultivars. Zone 5.

'Watereri' is a vigorous rounded shrub with dark red berries. Zone 7.

How to grow: Like *P. coccinea*.

Pyrus

Py´rus. Pear.
Rosaceae. Rose family.

Deciduous or evergreen trees with simple leaves, 5-petaled white flowers, and fruits with a gritty texture. Closely related to *Malus*. About 20 spp., native to Eurasia and North Africa.

calleryana (p. 124)
Callery pear.
Deciduous tree. Zone 5.
H: 30–60 ft. S: 25–35 ft.

Widely planted as a street or lawn tree wherever it is hardy, especially in towns and cities where it tolerates compacted soil, drought, heat, wind, and neglect. Neat and shapely, with a round or oval crown. Very showy in early spring, when clusters of round white flowers cover the limbs. The glossy leaves are dark green in summer and usually develop good fall color— red, orange, yellow, or purple, varying from place to place, tree to tree, and year to year. Sometimes makes tiny, hard, inedible pears. 'Aristocrat', 'Bradford', and 'Chanticleer' are the most common cultivars.

How to grow: Full or part sun. Tolerates poor, unamended soil. Drought-tolerant when established. Fairly resistant to fire blight. It was planted by the thousands in recent decades, but some problems are showing up: Older trees have grown too big for their sites, and their weak crotches and brittle limbs are liable to break during storms. Life expectancy may be about 20–30 years.

kawakamii (p. 162)
Evergreen pear.
Evergreen tree. Zone 8.
H: 15–30 ft. S: 15–30 ft.

Among the most graceful of evergreen trees, with a soft weeping habit. Can be trained in different ways—as a standard tree with an upright trunk and a spreading crown, espaliered against a wall or trellis, or as a vinelike "eyebrow" along the top of a fence or balcony. The oval leaves are leathery, glossy, and dark green. Small clusters of scentless white flowers cover the foliage with a sheet of bloom for weeks in late winter. Underplant with primroses, crocuses, and early daffodils to complete the picture.

How to grow: Full or part sun. Ordinary soil and watering. Plant from containers anytime. Stake at once to form a trunk if you want it to grow into a tree, or train the flexible shoots as they grow. Fire blight is a serious threat. Remove blighted stems well below the damaged area, sterilizing clippers with diluted bleach between cuts.

Quercus
Kwer'kus. Oak.
Fagaceae. Beech family.

A great and complex genus of evergreen or deciduous trees, some shrubby and some immense. All have alternate leaves, usually lobed or toothed; dangling catkins of male flowers; and woody acorns. Many are harvested for the hard, durable, attractive timber. There are about 600 spp., nearly all from the Northern Hemisphere. Because oaks hybridize freely, many wild trees are natural hybrids, and even botanists have trouble sorting them out.

Many oaks are evergreen, and several North American species have leaves that turn brown but hang on through the winter. In the listings that follow, only those whose leaves stay green all winter are designated as evergreen. Among the deciduous species, fall color varies from drab tans to vivid crimson, warm gold, and rich purple.

Almost all oaks are propagated by planting acorns. It's very difficult to root cuttings; the few named cultivars are grafted onto seedling rootstocks. Enthusiasts around the country are, however, actively breeding oaks and selecting seedlings with increased beauty, vigor, and hardiness. These new seed strains are starting to show up in specialty nurseries.

Traditionally, gardeners have thought of oaks as trees to appreciate if they already exist on a property, but not as trees to plant. Oaks have the reputation of being hard to transplant and slow to grow. In fact, some oaks transplant readily, especially as young trees, and modern nursery techniques make even the most difficult species much easier to move. (Or you can plant an acorn where you want the tree to grow.) Several oaks grow as much as 2 ft. a year. The key to success is choosing the right oak for any particular site. Given suitable soil, moisture, and climate, oaks grow steadily, require little pruning, and live for hundreds of years.

In general, oaks are trouble-free, but various pests and diseases cause problems in particular regions. In the East, all oaks, even live oaks, are susceptible to defoliation by gypsy moths. In the Upper Midwest, oak wilt disease kills red oaks and can damage white oaks. Oak wilt kills live oaks in Texas. Oak root fungus (*Armillaria*) can weaken and kill oaks (and many other trees) in California and the Southwest. In all areas, "oak decline" is the catchall term for trees that gradually succumb to various combinations of root damage, drought, insect predation, and other stresses.

acutissima (p. 126)
Sawtooth oak.
Deciduous tree. Zone 5.
H: 35–50 ft. S: 35–50 ft.

A trouble-free oak with distinctive chestnutlike foliage. The oblong leaves, 3–7 in. long, are not lobed but have bristles around the edge. Leaves are pale green or yellowish in spring, dark green in summer, and tan or gold in late fall. Male catkins are like golden tinsel in spring. These oaks bear heavy crops of medium-size acorns, starting as young trees. The selection 'Gobbler' is planted for wildlife food. The acorn caps are covered with long curly scales. It is one of the faster-growing oaks, especially in warm climates. *Q. variabilis,* the Chinese cork oak, is similar but has furrowed corky bark. Both are native to eastern Asia.

How to grow: Full sun. Does best in well-drained, acidic soil; does poorly in alkaline conditions. Tolerates dry soil. Can be damaged by late spring or early fall frosts.

agrifolia (p. 162)
Coast live oak.
Evergreen tree. Zone 9.
H: 50 ft. or more. S: 50 ft. or more.

The emblematic tree of coastal southern and central California. The thick gray-green leaves are 1–3 in. long with a few spiny points along the edges. Old trees can reach 100 ft. wide, with a picturesque silhouette and a broad dome-

Quercus agrifolia

shaped crown. Young trees grow quickly, up to 2 ft. a year. They can be planted close together and sheared for a tall hedge. Other West Coast evergreen oaks are also desirable and are increasingly available from native-plant nurseries.

How to grow: Full sun. Needs dry soil and can't take summer irrigation. If you're lucky enough to have an old live oak on your property, be careful not to hurt it with overwatering. Oak root fungus is encouraged by a wet trunk and root crown. Can be underplanted with low-water-use perennials or shrubs, but don't surround it with a lawn. For a lawn specimen, choose the southern live oak, *Q. virginiana.*

Quercus alba

alba (p. 126)
Eastern white oak.
Deciduous tree. Zone 4.
H: 50–100 ft. S: to 100 ft.

A giant tree native to woodlands throughout the East. It has a broad open-domed canopy of spreading limbs. Leaves, 4–8 in. long with deep rounded lobes, are medium green in summer and red or purple in fall. On the limbs of older trees, the bark separates into overlapping vertical plates. A wonderful tree if you already have one but not the best oak to choose for planting. From a gardener's point of view, it is the stereotypical oak, hard to transplant and slow-growing. Another eastern native, *Q. bicolor,* the swamp white oak, is equally hardy and attractive but much easier to transplant, and it tolerates a wider range of soil conditions. It has scalloped rather than deeply lobed leaves.

In California, the native white oak is *Q. lobata* (Zone 7). It grows to 100 ft. or more and develops a massive trunk, a broad crown, and weeping branches. The deeply lobed leaves, 3–4 in. long, are dark green above, pale below. It grows fast and does best in deep soil where its roots can tap groundwater. Transplant when small. Under good conditions, it can grow 2 ft. a year. Tolerates heat and alkaline conditions.

How to grow: Full sun. Eastern white oak prefers rich, deep, well-drained, acidic or neutral soil. Mature trees don't tolerate disturbance or soil compaction. Benefits from a thick layer of organic mulch.

gambelii (p. 126)
Gambel oak, scrub oak, Rocky Mountain white oak.
Deciduous tree or shrub. Zone 5.
H: 15–30 ft. S: 8–15 ft. or more.

Unlike most oaks, this is usually more shrubby than treelike and often spreads by suckers to make a low colony. It can be used for mass plantings or screens. You can make an attractive single-trunked or multitrunked specimen by removing the suckers. The 3–7-in. leaves have deep round lobes, like those of white oak, and turn copper, gold, or red in fall. Native to the dry foothills of the Rocky Mountains in Colorado, New Mexico, Utah, and Arizona. In the Southeast, *Q. marilandica,* the blackjack oak, is similar in most respects.

How to grow: Full sun. Can grow in dry, rocky soil. Needs good drainage and tolerates drought. Sold in containers or balled-and-burlapped. Slow-growing but very tough and hardy.

ilex (p. 162)
Holly oak, holm oak.
Evergreen tree. Zone 8 or 7.
H: 60 ft. S: 60 ft.

A rugged, fairly fast growing, evergreen oak for West Coast gardens. It can grow into a spreading, irregular tree or be sheared or trimmed into a hedge. The leathery leaves are 1–3 in. long and are toothed or smooth-edged. New growth in spring is covered with white down and gives the effect of a flowering tree. Native to the Mediterranean region, it combines well with rock roses, brooms, lavenders, and other Mediterranean plants. Can also be grown in containers.

How to grow: Full sun. Ordinary or unamended soil. Tolerates dry soil, sea salt, and wind. Can be pruned as desired. No serious pests.

laurifolia (p. 162)
Laurel oak.
Semievergreen tree. Zone 8 or 7.
H: 70 ft. or more. S: 40 ft. or more.

A southeastern native that slowly makes a large tree with a wide rounded crown. Can be used as a street tree or shade tree. The smooth-edged leaves are 2–4 in. long, 1–2 in. wide, glossy dark green above and lighter below. Leaves stay green well into winter but drop by spring. Acorns are round, $1/2$ in. wide. *Q. hemisphaerica* is similar but doesn't grow as tall. Some authorities combine the two species.

How to grow: Full sun. Ordinary soil and watering. Tolerates poor drainage. No serious pests.

macrocarpa (p. 127)
Bur oak.
Deciduous tree. Zone 3.
H: 70–80 ft. S: 60 ft. or more.

The prominent oak throughout the Midwest, from the Great Lakes south to Texas, and the best oak for exposed prairie conditions. Similar in form and stature to the eastern white oak, *Q. alba.* Old trees are massive, with an angular profile and spreading limbs. The trunk and branches have thick ridged bark, and the twigs often have corky wings. Even young trees develop furrowed bark and an interesting irregular form. Leaves are 4–10 in. long, round-lobed at the base and broad at the end, dark green above and pale or silvery below. The large acorns are partly enclosed by a cap of curly scales that looks like a tuft of moss.

How to grow: Full sun. Tolerates poor soil, alkaline conditions, and soil compaction, and established plants tolerate drought. Hardy to cold and heat. Sow in place or transplant small container-grown trees. Considered a slow grower, but under good conditions it makes a second spurt of growth in midsummer, which doubles the annual rate.

palustris (see below for photo)
Pin oak.
Deciduous tree. Zone 5.
H: 50–100 ft. S: 25–40 ft.

Pin oaks are sold by the thousands because they are easy to propagate and to transplant and are fast-growing. Given plenty of space and the rich, moist, heavy, acidic soil they prefer, they make beautiful trees with many slender horizontal branches. The lower limbs sweep down and brush against the ground in a very graceful way. The medium to large leaves have deeply cut, pointed lobes and turn bright coppery red in fall. Native to swampy sites in the East. However, many pin oaks are sold in the Midwest and West, where they usually don't grow well; they are weak and chlorotic in alkaline soil. Also, their drooping lower limbs take up too much space on small lots.

Q. coccinea (p. 126), the scarlet oak, is not as common at nurseries but is worth looking for. It has similar leaves and fall color but is more tolerant of dry or alkaline conditions. Its branches spread higher and don't get in the way, and its roots are deeper, so you can underplant with perennials. Native on upland sites in the East, it prefers light, dry soil. Hardy to Zone 5.

How to grow: Full sun. Pin oak does best in moist, fertile, acidic soil. Requires a large space or repeated pruning of the lower limbs. Inexpensive and commonly offered, but not the best oak for many situations.

phellos (p. 127)
Willow oak.
Deciduous tree. Zone 6 or 5.
H: 50–90 ft. S: 30–50 ft.

This oak has long, slender, willowlike leaves, up to 5 in. long and 1 in. wide, glossy dark green in summer and yellow in fall. The foliage looks more delicate than that of other oaks, and the tree is well shaped with a wide round crown. Makes a fine shade tree. Hardy into New York and Ohio but does best in the heat of the Southeast. It prefers damp soil. *Q. imbricaria,* the shingle oak, looks similar but grows faster on drier sites and farther north. It's a medium-size tree with a rounded crown and oblong leaves up to 6 in. long and 3 in. wide. The leaves turn tan or brown in fall but hang on into winter. Although they don't have the typical pointed-lobe leaves, willow oak and shingle oak belong to the red oak group.

How to grow: Full or part sun. Both willow oak and shingle oak are easy to transplant, relatively fast growing, and undemanding. They are highly recommended.

robur 'Fastigiata' (p. 127)
Upright English oak.
Deciduous tree. Zone 6.
H: 50 ft. S: 15 ft.

Useful because of its narrowly upright shape, which fits into tight spaces. Good in cities, where it doesn't interfere with power lines or street traffic. Planted in rows, it makes a magnificent tall screen or colonnade. Young trees are only one-fifth as wide as they are tall, but older trees develop a wider crown. Leaves are 4–6 in. long, broader at the end, with rounded lobes. Acorns are narrow, 1 in. long. There are many other cultivars of English oak. Some of the most promising new oaks are hybrids between English oak and our native white oaks.

How to grow: Full sun. Ordinary soil and watering. Space 5–10 ft. apart for a screen. No serious pests, but leaves get covered with powdery mildew in humid climates.

rubra (p. 127)
Northern red oak.
Deciduous tree. Zone 4.
H: 50–90 ft. S: 40–50 ft.

Faster-growing than most oaks and generally easy to transplant, northern red oaks are widely used as shade and street trees. Tall and conical when young, they develop a round crown at maturity. The trunk has dark bark with vertical ridges and stripes. The large leaves, up to 9 in. long, have distinct pointed lobes that taper to slender bristles. Fall color varies but can be rich bright red. Other members of the red oak group grow in different conditions. *Q. velutina,* the black oak, is a twin for northern red oak but grows on drier sites. *Q. shumardii,* or Shumard red oak, is a southern look-alike that tolerates wetter soils. *Q. falcata,* the southern red oak, has leaves with fewer, narrower lobes and tolerates poor, dry soil.

How to grow: Full sun or part shade. Northern red oak is more shade-tolerant than other native oaks are. Grows wild throughout the Midwest and East. Prefers well-drained, acidic soil but adapts to average soils. Established trees tolerate dry spells. Grows 12–18 in. a year.

suber (p. 162)
Cork oak.
Evergreen tree. Zone 7.
H: 70–90 ft. S: 70–90 ft.

An attractive evergreen oak with glossy dark green foliage and very picturesque bark on the trunk and limbs. The soft pale bark, called cork, is very thick and splits into ridges and grooves. Leaves are narrow ovals, $1^1/2$ in. long, with toothed edges. Can be used to shade a large terrace. Children often carve the bark once they find how soft it is; vandalism disfigures but normally doesn't hurt the tree. (On cork plantations in Spain and Portugal, the outer bark is harvested by cutting it from the trees every 10–15 years.)

How to grow: Full sun. Needs good drainage. Grows in unamended soil but gets chlorotic in alkaline conditions. Tolerates desert heat and drought (when established) but is also surprisingly cold-hardy. Needs little pruning. Pest-free.

Quercus virginiana

Ratibida columnifera

Rhaphiolepis indicia

virginiana (p. 162)
Southern live oak.
Evergreen tree. Zone 7.
H: to 60 ft. or more. S: to 100 ft. or more.

A majestic tree that thrives in hot, humid climates. Old trees have short thick trunks and strong twisted limbs that spread like outstretched arms. Can spread twice as wide as it is tall. Young trees are more erect, with dense rounded crowns. The smooth-edged leaves, 2–5 in. long, are dark green above, fuzzy white below. Old leaves drop in spring, about the time the new ones expand. The bark is dark and breaks into checkered scales. Bears heavy crops of small acorns. Grows wild along the Atlantic and Gulf coasts from Virginia to Texas, where Spanish moss often drapes the limbs. *Q. fusiformis*, native to Texas, looks similar but is more tolerant of alkaline soil, dryness, and winter cold.

How to grow: Full sun. Prefers acidic or neutral soil. Tolerates dry spells but grows better with regular watering. Does well in irrigated lawns. Young container-grown plants transplant readily. Eventually gets huge, but young trees are often planted on 25–30-ft. spacing to achieve the cathedral effect of interlacing branches.

Ratibida

Ra-ti′bi-da. Prairie coneflower.
Compositae. Composite family.

Perennials with rough hairy foliage and daisylike blossoms with drooping rays. Only 6 spp., native to North America.

columnifera (p. 268)
(*R. columnaris*)
Coneflower, Mexican hat.
Perennial. Zone 4.
H: 12–18 in. S: 12–18 in.

A prairie wildflower, good for planting in sunny meadows. The finely dissected leaves blend inconspicuously with neighboring grasses. Blossoms have a few broad rays in shades of yellow, red, or bicolor; the elongated disk is rusty red. Blooms from May to September.

How to grow: Full sun. Needs well-drained soil; roots rot if the soil stays too wet. Tolerates poor or dry soil and heat. Is short lived in gardens but usually self-sows. Needs no special care. Shear or cut back in fall.

Rhaphiolepis

Ra-fee-ol′e-pis, ra-fee-o-leep′is.
Rosaceae. Rose family.

Evergreen shrubs with thick leathery leaves and small but showy flowers. About 14 spp., native to eastern Asia.

indica (p. 183)
Indian hawthorn.
Evergreen shrub. Zone 7.
H: 2–5 ft. S: 4–6 ft.

A mounding shrub with thick, glossy, dark green leaves and abundant clusters of pink or white flowers for several weeks in spring. Individual flowers are only 1/2 in. wide, but clusters can be 4–6 in. wide. Small blue berries ripen in late summer. Oval leaves with pointed tips are clustered at the ends of the branches. Often used in foundation plantings. Also makes a good low hedge or mass planting. *R. umbellata* is a similar species with rounded leaves and fragrant white flowers 3/4 in. wide. Several cultivars that are often listed under *R. indica* may be hybrids between the two species. 'Enchantress' is a compact plant with rose-pink flowers. 'Springtime' is a vigorous upright grower with deep pink flowers. *R.* 'Majestic Beauty' is a hybrid that grows 10 ft. or taller and can be trained into a small standard tree, with larger leaves and 10-in. clusters of fragrant pink flowers.

How to grow: Needs full sun for maximum flowering. Ordinary soil and watering. Tolerates short dry spells but not prolonged drought. Space 3–5 ft. apart for mass plantings. Prune after flowering to shape as desired. Has only minor pest and disease problems.

Rhapis

Ray′pis. Lady palm.
Palmae. Palm family.

Small slow-growing palms with dark green fanlike fronds. Only 9 spp., native to Southeast Asia.

excelsa (p. 165)
Lady palm.
Fan palm. Zone 8.
H: 5 ft. or more. S: to 5 ft.

One of the most elegant plants, especially popular for growing in tubs or containers. Forms a clump of erect stalks wrapped in coarse fibers and topped with tufts of dark green leaves. The fanlike leaves have 3–10 long narrow leaflets. Grows slowly, so it's an expensive plant to buy, but a well-sited specimen can live for decades.

How to grow: Part shade. Needs well-drained, ordinary soil and regular watering. Remove old dead leaves and wash the foliage occasionally to keep it looking fresh. No common problems.

Rhododendron

Roe-doe-den′dron. Rhododendron and azalea.
Ericaceae. Heath family.

This complex and fascinating genus offers gardeners a variety of evergreen or deciduous shrubs with spectacular flowers in spring or summer. There are about 800 spp., most native to the north temperate zone, and thousands of hybrids and cultivars. All have simple alternate leaves, sometimes glossy but often dotted or covered with tiny hairs or scales on the bottom or on both surfaces. The flowers have 5 or more petals or lobes and are borne in round clusters called trusses. The seedpods are small dry capsules. Plant size ranges from tiny shrublets and low creepers to large trees, but most garden specimens are between 3 and 15 ft. tall.

Although gardeners consider azaleas a separate group of plants, botanists include them with rhododendrons. The distinction isn't clearcut. In general, azaleas have smaller leaves, often deciduous, and funnel-shaped flowers with 5 stamens; rhododendrons have larger, evergreen leaves and bell-shaped flowers with 10 stamens. But there are many exceptions, including evergreen azaleas, deciduous rhododendrons, and rhododendrons with small leaves. Plants in this genus often defy categorization; there is considerable variation within some species, and natural or man-made hybrids blur the boundaries between species.

Rhododendrons and azaleas are easy to grow where the soil and climate are suitable, but they're quite challenging in other areas. Generally, rhododendrons do best in the Pacific Northwest, the eastern Great Lakes region, lower New England, and the Mid-Atlantic states. Evergreen azaleas do well along the Pacific Coast and from the Mid-Atlantic states to the Gulf Coast. Deciduous azaleas do well throughout the eastern United States, the Great Lakes area, and the Pacific Northwest. It's difficult to grow any of these plants in the Great Plains, Rocky Mountains, or arid Southwest.

Wherever rhododendrons and/or azaleas are grown, local nurseries stock an assortment of the most popular types, usually in 1–5-gal. containers. For a wider selection, contact mail-order specialists. These plants ship well, so don't hesitate to order from a catalog.

How to grow: Most rhododendrons and azaleas do best when lightly shaded. Too much shade leads to lanky growth and sparse flowering. Some kinds tolerate full summer sun in cool climates, but hot summer sun can bleach or burn leaves. Winter sun and wind desiccate evergreen leaves and cause as much damage as cold temperatures do; avoid this by planting in sheltered locations or by wrapping the plants with burlap for the winter.

Cold-hardiness varies, as noted in the entries below. Winter survival is affected by many factors. Well-established, healthy plants tolerate lower temperatures than do new plantings or plants stressed by drought, poor soil, or pests. As with many woody plants, flower buds can be damaged by temperatures that don't hurt the rest of the plant.

The soil should be well drained but constantly moist, never too wet or too dry. It should be slightly to fairly acidic and rich in organic matter. Alkaline conditions, including lime leaching from concrete building foundations or sidewalks, cause chlorosis (yellowing) of the foliage and can weaken or kill the plant. If your soil is alkaline or poorly drained, plant in raised beds, 1–2 ft. deep. Amend the soil by incorporating several inches of peat moss or composted pine bark. Place the top of the root ball slightly above the soil line when you plant, and cover it with a thick mulch of ground bark, chopped oak leaves, pine needles, compost, or similar material. Renew the mulch annually. Water regularly, especially during the first year or two after planting. Apply diluted acid-type fertilizer, following the manufacturer's directions, in spring or early summer.

Remove faded flowers promptly to prevent seed formation, which wastes the plant's energy. Prune, if necessary, just after flowering.

Various insect and disease problems can damage or kill plants, especially those already stressed by marginal conditions. Ask your Cooperative Extension agent or local nursery to identify which problems might occur in your area.

deciduous hybrid azaleas (p. 146)
These hardy shrubs cover themselves with showy flowers in all shades of red, pink, lavender, orange, yellow, white, and bicolors. Some kinds are very fragrant. Individual shrubs usually bloom for about 2 weeks, most commonly in May, but some kinds start in mid-April and others extend the season through June and July. Plants differ in habit, mature size, and rate of growth. Many form neat compact mounds, often spreading wider than tall, but some are more upright, open, and casual. Most are hardy to Zone 5, and some bloom reliably even in Zone 4 or 3.

After bloom, the fine-textured foliage can make a pleasing background for summer perennials, and the leaves often turn orange, red, or purple for several weeks before dropping in late fall. Some groups, however, are subject to mildew and other fungal diseases, especially where summers are hot and humid. Check locally to see if disease problems are common in your area. If so, consider disease resistance as well as flower color when shopping.

The Ghent hybrids grow upright, 5–8 ft. tall. Their flowers are not large but are usually sweet-scented, in shades of yellow, orange, pink, or red. Zone 5.

The Knap Hill, Exbury, and Ilam hybrids constitute the largest, most popular, and most diverse group of hardy deciduous azaleas. There are hundreds of cultivars. Plants are upright or spreading, 4–8 ft. tall. Flowers are quite large, sometimes fragrant, in shades of white, cream, yellow, orange, red, rose, or pink. Foliage is often disfigured by mildew in summer. Zone 5.

The Mollis hybrids are rounded shrubs, 4–6 ft. tall. Their large flowers open before the leaves, in shades of yellow, orange, or red. They have a scent that some people enjoy, but many consider it skunklike. The Occidentale hybrids are similar but grow up to 8 ft. tall and have fragrant flowers in pastel colors marked with contrasting blotches. Both are hardy to Zone 6 or 5.

The Northern Lights hybrids are particularly hardy, developed at the University of Minnesota. They grow about 6 ft. tall and wide and are covered with fragrant flowers even after severe winters. Colors include white, pink, yellow, orange, and rosy red. Zone 3.

How to grow: See main entry.

deciduous species azaleas (pp. 144, 145)
This diverse group includes many of the parent species used in breeding hybrid azaleas. They are valuable garden shrubs offering hardiness, ease of care, disease-resistant foliage with good fall color, extra-early and extra-late bloom, a wide range of flower colors, and sweet fragrance. Unless otherwise noted, all species listed below are native to the eastern United States.

Several species are notable for their early bloom. *R. vaseyi,* the pink-shell azalea, is a spreading shrub that grows 6–8 ft. tall and is hardy to Zone 6 or 5. Its scentless pink flowers open just before the leaves in late April or early May. *R. periclymenoides* (*R. nudiflorum*), or pinxterbloom azalea, spreads underground to make a colony with many stems, generally 4–6 ft. tall. It tolerates drier sites than many azaleas do. Sweetly fragrant white or pink flowers open with the leaves in April or May. It is hardy to Zone 4. *R. prinophyllum* (*R. roseum*), the rose-shell azalea, is even hardier (Zone 3) but blooms a bit later. Its rosy pink flowers smell like cloves or carnations. *R. canescens,* the Piedmont azalea, is similar to pinxterbloom but grows farther south, where it blooms in March or April. It is hardy to Zone 7. *R. schlippenbachii,* the royal azalea, is an Asian species that grows to about 6 ft. and is hardy to Zone 5. Its large fragrant flowers, clear pink with reddish brown spots inside, open in early spring. The wide rounded leaves are clustered at the ends of the twigs and develop good fall color.

Other species extend the bloom season into summer. *R. atlanticum,* or coast azalea, forms a dense compact mound 3–4 ft. tall with especially nice blue-green leaves and is hardy to Zone 5. It blooms profusely from late May into June, with very sweet-scented white or pale pink flowers. Next to flower is *R. arborescens,* the tree azalea, which is hardy to Zone 5 or 4. It can reach 20 ft. tall after decades but is usually about 6–8 ft. tall in gardens. Its very sweet white or pinkish flowers continue from late June into July. *R. viscosum,* the swamp azalea, also has fragrant white or pink flowers in late June or July. It grows to about 8 ft. tall and, unlike most azaleas, tolerates poorly drained soil. It is hardy to Zone 4. *R. prunifolium,* or plum-leaved azalea, is remarkable for its colorful midsummer blooms. It has large, scentless, orange-red flowers in July or August, blooming for up to a month if shaded from hot afternoon sun. Although the plant grows well in Zone 6 or 5, the flower buds may freeze in severe winters.

This final group also has red, orange, gold, or yellow flowers and offers several alternatives to the more common white and pink azaleas. *R. calendulaceum,* the flame azalea, grows 8–10 ft. tall and is hardy to Zone 5. It has large but scentless yellow, orange, or red flowers in May or June and is the parent of several bright-colored hybrids and cultivars. *R. austrinum,* the yellow wild azalea, grows upright to 12 ft. tall and is hardy to Zone 7. Its fragrant flowers are yellow or gold, sometimes tinged with pink, and open

before or with the leaves in early spring. *R. bakeri,* or Cumberland azalea, spreads horizontally, stays under 4–5 ft. tall, and is hardy to Zone 5. It has scentless orange-red flowers in June or July. It tolerates more shade than most azaleas do and can be used as a ground cover under tall trees.

How to grow: See main entry.

evergreen azaleas (pp. 184, 185)
Evergreen azaleas are very popular for their masses of bright flowers in spring, and their foliage is neat and attractive all year. Most of the cultivars are hybrids developed by individuals or institutions with particular breeding goals, such as increased cold-hardiness or compact habit. Most bloom between mid-April and mid-June, with flowers in shades of pink, rose, red, or white. A few are lavender, salmon, or orange. Many have double flowers with one layer of petals inside the other, called "hose-in-hose." Few of the evergreen azaleas are fragrant, and none offer the intoxicating sweetness found in the deciduous types. Plant habits range from prostrate spreaders that hug the ground and trail over walls, to compact rounded shrubs with branches in layered tiers, to upright growers with erect stems, suitable for background plantings or hedges.

The flowers can be very large, up to 5 in. wide. Some of the largest, loveliest flowers are the Belgian Indicas, often grown in greenhouses and sold by florists. Potted specimens can be maintained for years if overwintered indoors, but they are tender to frost and grow outdoors only in southern California. The Southern Indicas were developed from the Belgian Indicas and have flowers nearly as large, but the plants are hardier, suitable for Zone 9 or 8. Most are vigorous upright shrubs that bloom in April or May. 'Fielder's White' (white), 'Formosa' (rosy purple), 'George Lindley Taber' (light pink), and 'Pride of Mobile' (pink) are popular cultivars.

Gumpo azaleas also have large flowers, on low, spreading plants with small leaves. 'Gumpo Pink', 'Gumpo Rose', and 'Gumpo White' are popular cultivars that flower in June. They are hardy to Zone 7.

Other hybrids have masses of smaller flowers. The Kurume hybrids are compact and bushy, usually 3–4 ft. tall, with small glossy leaves. They are literally covered with bloom in April or May and are hardy to Zone 7. Popular cultivars include 'Coral Bells' (pink), 'Hino Crimson' (bright red), 'Hinodegiri' (cerise), 'Snow' (white), and 'Ward's Ruby' (dark red).

Breeders have been working on hardy evergreen azaleas. The Glen Dale hybrids have flowers like the Southern Indicas but were bred in Maryland for hardiness in Zone 7 or 6. They bloom from May to July. Many have flowers marked with a second-color blotch or stripe, and sometimes whole branches will have flowers that contrast with the rest of the plant. The Girard hybrids, from Ohio, offer a wide range of bright-colored single and double flowers and bloom

Rhododendron austrinum

reliably in Zone 6. Their foliage often turns dark reddish purple in winter.

Compact or spreading azaleas are ideal for small gardens or can be massed as ground covers. The Robin Hill hybrids have exceptionally large flat flowers in soft pastel shades, on compact, low, spreading plants, hardy to Zone 7. The North Tisbury hybrids are prostrate or trailing plants that have large flowers in June and are hardy to Zone 6.

R. kiusianum is an uncommon but desirable Japanese species with a low spreading habit, dense foliage, and very showy masses of flowers in shades of white, pink, orchid, or purple. It is hardy to Zone 6. Although botanists group it with the evergreen azaleas, it loses most of its leaves in winter. *R. yedoense* var. *poukhanense* is another semievergreen plant, with slightly fragrant rose or lilac flowers. One of the tallest of the so-called evergreen azaleas, it can grow 6 ft. tall and is hardy to Zone 6 or 5.

How to grow: See main entry.

rhododendrons (pp. 184, 185)

A rhododendron in full bloom makes a colorful display unequaled by other shrubs. The large flowers come in nearly all colors and last about 2 weeks, longer in cool, cloudy weather. Even if they didn't bloom, many rhododendrons have outstanding foliage that provides year-round interest. Leaves come in several shades of green and can be large or small, thick or thin, glossy or furry, flat or curled. Plant sizes range from compact dwarfs to giants that can hide a two-story house. This group is a collector's dream come true: there are hundreds of species and thousands of cultivars, each with unique flowers and foliage. The following species and the hybrids listed in the box are some of the most popular, widely adapted, and widely available.

Two native species are valued for their hardiness. *R. catawbiense* is native to the southern Appalachians but is hardy to Zone 5 and is a parent of many hardy hybrids. Leaves are large and thick, dark green in summer but olive in cold weather. It grows 6–10 ft. tall and has lilac-purple flowers; related cultivars have purple, lilac, pink, rosy red, or white flowers. *R. carolinianum,* from the same region, is also hardy to Zone 5. It has much smaller leaves and grows only 3–5 ft. tall. Leaves release a pleasant fragrance if crushed, but the white, pale pink, or rosy pink flowers are scentless.

Some Asian species bloom very early, with the forsythias. The flowers last 2 weeks or more. *R. dauricum,* from the mountains of Korea and Japan, is hardy but semievergreen in Zone 6 or 5. It grows slowly to about 5 ft. tall. There are lavender, pink, and white forms. *R. mucronulatum,* from Korea and China, is hardy but deciduous in Zone 5. It grows upright to about 6 ft. The species has scentless rosy purple flowers; 'Cornell Pink' has clear pink flowers. *R. moupinense,* from China, is one of the best species for early bloom. Evergreen and hardy to Zone 7, it's a low spreading plant, under 2 ft.

tall, with small leaves. The fragrant flowers are white or pink with red marks.

R. yakusimanum and its cultivars and related hybrids earn the highest praise from plant connoisseurs. This Japanese species is hardy to Zone 5 and makes a dense, compact, rounded plant about 3 ft. tall. Tender new leaves are covered with soft white fur; mature leaves are shiny dark green on top with golden brown felt below. Pink buds open to snow-white flowers in May, and even young plants bloom heavily. 'Ken Janeck' and 'Mist Maiden' are especially vigorous and attractive cultivars.

How to grow: See main entry.

Rhododendron

Recommended hybrid rhododendrons, by flower color

These are all evergreen shrubs with large or small leaves. Most bloom in April or May. Following the cultivar name are the expected height, the hardiness zone, and additional comments.

Red: 'America', 5 ft., Zone 5; sun-tolerant. 'Elizabeth', 3 ft., Zone 7; low-growing but vigorous. 'Henry's Red', 5 ft., Zone 5 or 4; very dark red—almost black. 'Jean Marie de Montague', 5 ft., Zone 7 or 6; bright green foliage. 'Nova Zembla', 5 ft., Zone 5 or 4; sun-tolerant. 'Scarlet Wonder', 2 ft., Zone 5; low and compact, with excellent foliage.

Pink: 'Anna Rose Whitney', 6 ft., Zone 6; deep rose-pink. 'Bow Bells', 3 ft., Zone 6; a compact mound with excellent foliage. 'Cotton Candy', 6 ft., Zone 7; pastel pink. 'Janet Blair', 6 ft., Zone 6; pale flowers are frilly and fragrant. 'Olga Mezitt', 3 ft., Zone 5 or 4; compact, with small leaves. 'Party Pink', 5 ft., Zone 5; flowers have a yellow splotch. 'Scintillation', 5 ft., Zone 5; a vigorous plant with excellent foliage. 'Waltham', 2 ft., Zone 5 or 4; very compact and hardy.

Lavender/purple: 'Blue Diamond', 3 ft., Zone 6; small flowers on upright stems. 'Blue Peter', 4 ft., Zone 6; lavender-blue with a purple flare. 'Dorothy Amateis', 5 ft., Zone 5; deep purple with a dark eye. 'English Roseum' and 'Roseum Elegans', 6 ft., Zone 5; these are similar plants with lavender-pink flowers. 'P.J.M.', 4 ft., Zone 4; lavender-pink flowers on a very adaptable plant with small leaves. 'Ramapo', 2 ft., Zone 5; violet flowers on a compact plant with lovely foliage.

Yellow/gold: 'Dexter's Champagne', 4 ft., Zone 4; apricot-gold flowers. 'Full Moon', 4 ft., Zone 6; yellow flowers on a compact plant. 'Hong Kong', 5 ft., Zone 5; primrose yellow with a greenish throat. 'Hotei', 3 ft., Zone 7; canary yellow flowers on a compact plant. 'Unique', 4 ft., Zone 6; dark pink buds open to yellow flowers.

White: 'Anna H. Hall', 3 ft., Zone 5; compact, with good foliage. 'Boule de Neige', 5 ft., Zone 5; widely available. 'Dora Amateis', 3 ft., Zone 6; a compact plant with small leaves. 'Gomer Waterer', 5 ft., Zone 6; tolerates full sun. 'Molly Fordham', 4 ft., Zone 5; a compact plant with small leaves.

Rhus

Roos. Sumac.
Anacardiaceae. Sumac family.

Deciduous or evergreen trees, shrubs, or vines with simple or compound leaves, milky or resinous sap, and terminal clusters of small flowers and berries. This genus includes poison ivy, poison oak, and a few other species that cause skin rashes. About 200 spp., native worldwide.

aromatica (p. 147)
Fragrant sumac.
Deciduous shrub. Zone 3.
H: to 6 ft. S: 6–10 ft.

A low shrub that makes a colony of arching or sprawling stems. The compound leaves have 3 toothed leaflets and resemble poison ivy but are harmless. They have a pleasant fragrance when crushed and turn bright red or reddish purple in fall. Small clusters of red berries ripen in late summer. An excellent shrub for difficult sites with poor, dry soil. Spreads faster in better soil but doesn't get out of control. The cultivar 'Gro-Low' stays under 2 ft. tall and spreads up to 8 ft. wide. *R. aromatica* is native to the East; *R. trilobata* is similar but grows in the West. It has smaller leaflets with a more pungent fragrance and smooth upright stems that grow 4–12 ft. tall.

How to grow: Full or part sun. Tolerates infertile and alkaline soil, heat, and drought. Space 6 ft. apart for mass planting or ground cover. Easy to transplant and establish. Pest-free.

Rhus trilobata

copallina (p. 147)
Shining sumac, winged sumac.
Deciduous shrub. Zone 4.
H: 12 ft. or more. S: 10 ft. or more.

This native shrub is tough, trouble-free, and easy to grow, and it has lovely foliage, shiny bright green in summer and crimson in fall. The compound leaves have 9–15 small leaflets connected by thin wings that run along the main stalk. Greenish yellow flower clusters develop in summer and mature into red fruits that last through winter. Given room, it spreads underground to make a dome-shaped colony of upright stems; however, it is easily controlled by mowing or pulling the outer suckers. Makes a good background or screen along property lines, a showy specimen in a sunny corner, or a transition between formal and natural gardens.

How to grow: Like *R. aromatica,* but space plants 10 ft. apart.

Rhus copallina

lancea (p. 163)
African sumac.
Evergreen tree. Zone 9.
H: 25 ft. S: 25 ft.

A tough tree for hot, dry climates, with a graceful, open, soft appearance. The dark green leaves have 3 narrow leaflets, 3–5 in. long, with a smooth leathery texture. The trunk has deeply checkered blackish red bark. The tiny flower clusters are inconspicuous, but female trees make small red or yellow fruits that litter a sidewalk or terrace. A good small tree for lawns or streetside planting. Can also be set close together and pruned for a screen or clipped hedge.

How to grow: Full sun. Ordinary or unimproved soil. Tolerates desert heat; tolerates drought once established. Easily transplanted. Stake and train to establish single or multiple trunks. Pest-free.

typhina (p. 147)
Staghorn sumac.
Deciduous shrub or small tree. Zone 4.
H: 15–25 ft. or more. S: 15–25 ft.

A tough vigorous shrub with excellent red or purplish fall color, crimson fruit clusters that last from fall to spring, and distinctive forked branching that makes an interesting winter silhouette. The compound leaves and thick twigs are covered with downy hairs. 'Dissecta' and 'Laciniata' have large leaves that are divided into many slender segments, like fern fronds. *R. glabra* is a similar plant with smooth twigs and leaves. Both species are native to the Northeast and form large colonies on abandoned farmland. In the garden, mowing or removing suckers controls their spread. To make a dramatic clump with tropical-looking foliage, let a plant grow for a few years to get well established, then start cutting it to the ground each year in early spring. This makes it send up vigorous new shoots with unusually large leaves.

How to grow: Full or part sun. Not fussy about soil. Tolerates heat and drought once established. Pest-free.

Ribes

Ry´beez. Currant, gooseberry.
Saxifragaceae. Saxifrage family.

Bushy shrubs with prickly stems and juicy berries. Gooseberries and currants are especially popular in Europe for juices and preserves. About 150 spp., most native to the north temperate zone.

alpinum (p. 147)
Alpine currant.
Deciduous shrub. Zone 3.
H: 3–6 ft. S: 3–6 ft.

A very hardy shrub, especially useful for mass plantings and hedges in cold climates. It grows naturally into a dense compact mound and responds well to pruning. The small, bright green leaves have 3–5 lobes. Flowers are inconspicuous, and fruits are uncommon, since only male plants are normally sold. 'Green Mound' makes a neat dome 2–3 ft. tall.

How to grow: Grows equally well in sun or shade and adapts to any well-drained soil. Space 3 ft. apart for hedges, and prune as desired or not at all. Trouble-free. Unlike several currants, this species does not host white pine blister rust.

native currants (see below for photo)
Several species of *Ribes* grow wild in the western states. They are desirable ornamentals where

white pine blister rust is not a problem; ask locally before planting. *R. cereum,* or wax currant, grows 3–5 ft. high and wide and has light pink flowers and fuzzy red berries. Drought-tolerant. Zone 4.

R. odoratum, the buffalo or clove currant, has dangling clusters of clove-scented golden flowers in May and edible fruits in July. It grows 3–6 ft. tall in ordinary or dry soil. Zone 4.

R. sanguineum, the flowering currant, has clusters of showy pink or red flowers in very early spring (January to March) and dark blue-black berries in summer. It grows up to 12 ft. tall and prefers moist soil. Zone 6.

R. speciosum (p. 147), or fuchsia-flowered gooseberry, has bristly branches covered with dangling crimson flowers in winter (December to May). It grows to 10 ft. and tolerates dry shade. Zone 7.

Ricinus

Ris´i-nus. Castor bean.
Euphorbiaceae. Spurge family.

A fast-growing tropical shrub, commonly grown as an annual. The seeds are poisonous but produce an oil used in paints and varnishes. Only 1 sp., native to Africa.

communis (p. 303)

Castor bean.
Grown as annual. All zones.
H: 8 ft. or more. S: 4 ft.

Definitely one of a kind, this is a bold dramatic plant with stout stems and giant (up to 3 ft. wide) leaves with pointed lobes. The leaves have a shiny surface and are bright green, bronze, or red. It bears large clusters of bristly pods in fall. Use it for a fast temporary screen or background. The red and bronze forms combine well with red flowers such as cannas, zinnias, and salvias or with the red forms of *Pennisetum setaceum.* 'Zanzibariensis' is especially vigorous and can reach 15 ft. by late summer.

How to grow: Full sun. Ordinary soil and watering. Soak seeds overnight before planting. In cold regions, start indoors 8 weeks before last frost. In mild regions, direct-sow when the soil is warm. Pest-free and alleged to deter moles and gophers. Warn children that the seeds are poisonous. Has spread like a weed in California.

Robinia

Row-bin´-ee-a. Locust.
Leguminosae. Legume family.

Deciduous trees or shrubs with compound leaves, thorny stems, and showy white or pink flowers. A few spp., native to North America.

pseudoacacia (p. 124)

Black locust.
Deciduous tree. Zone 4.
H: 50 ft. or more. S: 30 ft. or more.

Tough and adaptable, this fast-growing native has its pros and cons. A healthy, well-

cared-for specimen is very attractive, with large clusters of very fragrant white flowers in late spring, lacy compound leaves that cast a light filtered shade all summer and turn clear yellow in fall, and rugged bark with deep ridges and furrows. Unfortunately, it can be weedy, spreading by suckers and volunteer seedlings; it also suffers from several insect pests, and the young shoots are studded with pairs of extremely sharp thorns. Wild trees are very common in some parts of the country, and it's often planted in urban sites because it tolerates poor soil and air pollution. 'Frisia' is a unique selection with golden yellow foliage that stays bright all summer.

How to grow: Full sun. Grows best in rich, moist soil but tolerates compacted, infertile, alkaline, sandy, or clay soil. Established trees tolerate drought. Subject to borers, lace bugs, Japanese beetles, leafminers, and other pests. Sometimes forms just a single trunk but often spreads by suckers to make a multitrunked grove.

Romneya

Rom´nee-a. Matilija poppy.
Papaveraceae. Poppy family.

A large perennial with white flowers. Only 1 sp., native to California and Baja California.

coulteri (p. 268)

Matilija poppy.
Perennial. Zone 8.
H: 8 ft. S: to 8 ft.

One of California's most famous wildflowers, blooming from May to July. The giant poppylike flowers have 6 snow-white petals and a tuft of golden stamens. The petals have a crinkled or pleated texture, like crepe paper. The erect branching stems and deeply lobed leaves have a smooth surface and a cool gray-green color. Spreads too fast to combine with other perennials but is ideal for naturalizing on dry sites.

How to grow: Full sun. Tolerates poor soil, heat, and drought. Buy a container-grown plant from a nursery; don't try to transplant wild plants. Plant in fall. In subsequent years, cut back in late summer. New growth comes with the fall rains.

Rosa

Ro´za. Rose.
Rosaceae. Rose family.

Roses are the most popular of all flowers and have been grown in gardens since the days of the ancient Egyptians, Romans, and Chinese. There are about 100 species and literally thousands of cultivars. All are deciduous or evergreen shrubs with thorny stems, compound leaves, and an upright, climbing, or trailing habit. Wild rose flowers have 5 petals and many stamens. Garden roses often have many petals. Rose fruits, called hips, have a fleshy hull with several hairy seeds inside.

Ribes sanguineum

Romneya coulteri

Rose

Everyone loves roses, but some gardeners hesitate to grow them, fearing that the plants will require too much special care. This isn't true. Many roses are as easy, reliable, and trouble-free as lilacs, viburnums, or other common shrubs. Growers today offer both heirloom varieties and new introductions that are hardy, vigorous, and disease-resistant and require no spraying and little pruning.

There isn't room in this book to describe more than a sampling of the many wonderful roses that are currently available, but the listings below should be enough to get you started. Think of roses as shrubs, rather than just flowers, and you'll find many ways to use them in the garden. Of course, roses are excellent specimens for mixed borders, but they can also define a boundary, screen a view, cover a fence, climb a tree, spill over a wall, edge a path, or frame an entryway.

How to grow: Roses require at least half a day of full sun (preferably morning) and bloom best in full sun. Prepare the soil by digging deeply to loosen any compacted zones and working in generous amounts of compost, rotted mature, and/or peat moss. Roses need well-drained soil; in damp areas, plant in beds raised 1–2 ft. higher than the surrounding soil. Wait until the plant is established before applying fertilizer, according to package directions. Water regularly, as needed, to keep the soil moist.

Cold-hardiness is a genetic trait that varies among roses, and they are described in general terms as tender, hardy, or extremely hardy. By convention, roses are not assigned hardiness zone ratings, because minimum temperature is only one of the factors that affect their winter survival. Sudden temperature fluctuations, harsh winter sun, dry winds, dry soil, or waterlogged soil is just as harmful as cold temperature. There are several steps to maximizing hardiness. Choose roses that are known to do well in your area. Provide the best possible conditions throughout the growing season to keep them as healthy as possible. Refrain from pruning, deadheading, or cutting flowers in fall; allow the hips to form. Don't fertilize in fall, but continue watering during dry spells from fall to spring. After hard frost, heap a cone of soil around the base of the plant. When temperatures remain below freezing, apply a thick mulch for additional insulation. Wait until spring is here to stay before removing winter protection.

Roses need careful pruning to establish the shape of the bush, to remove old or damaged shoots, and to promote vigorous growth and abundant flowering. When and how to prune varies among the different groups; for more information, consult *Taylor's Guide to Roses.*

Roses are subject to several pests and diseases, but the occurrence and severity of different problems varies from rose to rose and from place to place. The best policy is to choose disease-resistant varieties, plant them in favorable sites, and provide the best possible care. Healthy plants are less prone to attack. Promptly remove and destroy any damaged or diseased plant parts. Check with local rose growers, nurseries, public gardens, or extension agents for specific advice on growing healthy roses in your area.

climbing roses (pp. 148, 206)

Climbing roses can function like vines in the landscape, covering a wall, fence, or arbor with foliage and flowers. They don't climb on their own, however; they must be tied to a support, and they need regular training and pruning. For maximum bloom, their long canes should be bent over and fastened in a horizontal position. This promotes the development of many short lateral stems that produce flowers. Climbers are vigorous plants that need plenty of space; some can produce canes up to 20 ft. long. Pillars are smaller plants that produce flowers on upright canes and usually stay under 10 ft. tall. Some roses are intermediate and can be grown as climbers or pillars. Ramblers have clusters of small flowers on long pliable canes and bloom later than other climbers.

'Blaze' is an old favorite that blooms over a long season, with semidouble red flowers 2½–3 in. wide on canes up to 12 ft. long. It tolerates cold and heat and can be trained up a post or along a fence. 'Don Juan' has very fragrant, double, dark red flowers 4½–5 in. wide on canes 8–10 ft. tall. It makes a good pillar rose but is not reliably cold-hardy. 'Golden Showers' has fragrant, semidouble, yellow flowers 3½–4 in. wide on upright canes 8–10 ft. tall. It makes a good pillar, blooms abundantly throughout the growing season, and is fairly cold-hardy. 'New Dawn' has fragrant, semidouble, light pink flowers 3–3½ in. wide on canes 12–15 ft. long. It is vigorous and hardy. There are many other fine climbing roses, including some of the species roses listed below.

How to grow: See main entry.

floribundas and polyanthas (p. 149)

Floribundas are bushy plants that are usually hardier and more disease-resistant than most hybrid tea roses. All make good specimens for mixed borders, and the taller types can be used for hedges. Floribundas have well-formed flowers in a wide range of colors, borne in small to large clusters. They bloom prolifically, repeating or continuing throughout the season. 'Angel Face' grows to 3 ft. tall and has small clusters of very fragrant, double, mauve flowers 3½–4 in. wide. 'Betty Prior' grows 5–7 ft. tall with clusters of fragrant, single, pink flowers 3–3½ in. wide that resemble flowering dogwood blossoms. 'Iceberg' grows 4 ft. tall with clusters of fragrant, double, pure white flowers 3 in. wide that resemble hybrid tea roses.

Polyanthas are neat little shrubs that start blooming late in the season but continue until frost. Most are hardy and carefree. Flowers are small but generously produced, in large clusters. 'Cecile Brunner' grows 2½–3 ft. tall and has clusters of double light pink flowers that resemble miniature hybrid tea roses. There's also a fine climbing 'Cecile Brunner', but neither form is reliably cold-hardy. 'The Fairy' is very hardy and healthy and blooms continuously with clusters of very double pink flowers 1–1$1/2$ in. wide. It grows 2 ft. tall and 3 ft. wide and makes a colorful mass planting or low hedge.

How to grow: See main entry.

hybrid teas and grandifloras

Hybrid teas are the most popular roses today, particularly where winters are not too severe. They bloom all season, from spring to fall, and their elegant long-stemmed blossoms are excellent for cutting. The plants, however, require more care than most shrub roses do and often look stiffly formal and out of place in mixed borders. Enthusiasts grow them in special beds. For best results, hybrid teas need careful soil preparation, fertilizing, winter protection, pruning, and a regular spray routine. Some outstanding cultivars are listed in the box, but if you're interested in growing hybrid tea roses, visit a rose display garden to observe plants in bloom and choose your own favorites. Such gardens are sponsored by the American Rose Society and located throughout the United States.

Grandifloras combine the long stems and beautiful blossoms of the hybrid teas with the hardiness and clustered flowers of the floribundas. This group was just introduced in 1954, and so far there are only a few dozen cultivars. They are vigorous tall shrubs that make good hedges or background plantings. The prototype of the grandiflora class is 'Queen Elizabeth', with fragrant, double, medium pink blossoms 3–4 in. wide, borne singly or in small clusters. It grows upright, 5–7 ft. tall. 'Love' has slightly fragrant 3$1/2$-in. flowers, scarlet red with a white reverse, and grows 3–4 ft. tall. 'White Lightnin' has very fragrant, double, white flowers 3–4 in. wide and grows 4–5 ft. tall. These grandifloras all bloom continuously; have glossy, disease-resistant foliage; and are quite cold-hardy.

How to grow: See main entry.

miniature roses

Miniature roses are short plants—usually about 12 in. tall but ranging from 6 to 18 in.—with thin canes, closely spaced small leaves, and perfect little buds and flowers. There are dozens of cultivars in all colors. Miniature roses are most familiar as pot plants for a cool sunny windowsill in winter, but many kinds are fully hardy outdoors. They are excellent for beds, borders, edgings, rock gardens, and patio containers.

How to grow: See main entry.

old garden roses

These are the various roses that were already established in gardens prior to 1867, when one of the first hybrid tea or modern roses was introduced. A diverse group, there are both hardy and tender plants with dwarf, robust, or climbing habits. Some have lovely foliage and good disease resistance. Several have very fragrant flowers. Many of the old garden roses are still

Favorite hybrid tea roses, by color

Multicolor: 'Peace', soft yellow tinged with pink; mild fragrance. 'Chicago Peace', similar to 'Peace', but the colors are deeper pink and canary yellow. 'Sutter's Gold', yellow tinged with orange and red; rich fruity fragrance. 'Voodoo', orange, yellow, and pink; rich fragrance.

Orange: 'Brandy', golden apricot; mild fragrance. 'Cary Grant', orange touched with copper and gold; spicy fragrance. 'Tropicana', fluorescent orange-red; rich fruity fragrance.

Pink: 'Friendship', deep pink; very fragrant. 'Tiffany', medium to deep pink; very fragrant. 'Touch of Class', warm pink shaded with coral and cream; mild fragrance.

Red: 'Chrysler Imperial', deep red; very fragrant. 'Dolly Parton', coppery orange-red; very fragrant. 'Mister Lincoln', rich red; strong fragrance and long-stemmed.

White: 'Garden Party', ivory white tinged with pink; mild fragrance. 'Pascali', pure white; slight fragrance and a profuse bloomer.

Yellow: 'New Day', clear yellow; spicy fragrance. 'Oregold', deep yellow; slight fragrance. 'Summer Sunshine', clear deep yellow; mild fruity fragrance.

considered excellent, and they are available from several specialty growers. Consult *Taylor's Guide to Roses* for more information.

How to grow: See main entry.

shrub roses (pp. 148, 149, 150)

This is a catchall group, including both old favorites and new introductions. The flowers come in many forms, but the plants share several desirable attributes: vigor, adaptability, healthy foliage, good habit, and ease of care. These are the best candidates for gardeners who want to enjoy roses without going to much trouble. Except where noted, all are hardy.

'Bonica' is a dense rounded bush about 4–5 ft. tall and wide. Clusters of small, scentless, double, soft pink flowers bloom nonstop all season. It is carefree, easy, and reliable. The same breeders also introduced 'White Meidiland', 'Pink Meidiland', and 'Red Meidiland'. All are healthy vigorous plants that bloom from spring to fall and make excellent low hedges or tall ground covers for large areas or slopes.

'Carefree Beauty' grows 4 ft. tall and has clusters of fragrant, semidouble, medium pink flowers. It blooms all summer. The orange hips are showy in fall and winter. This is a new rose with good disease resistance and a neat habit.

The English roses have been developed by David Austin, an English rose breeder. They are vigorous shrubs with a compact habit and disease-resistant foliage, and they bear full, rounded, fragrant flowers. One of the most popular cultivars is 'Mary Rose', a 5-ft. shrub with rich pink flowers from spring to fall. 'Constance

Spry' has very fragrant, rounded, pink flowers but doesn't repeat. 'Graham Thomas' has golden yellow flowers all season.

'Harison's Yellow' is an old favorite with double deep yellow blossoms. It blooms once, in early season. The thorny arching canes grow 5–7 ft. tall. The small delicate leaves are light green.

The hybrid musk roses are big bushes with tall arching canes and an open habit. They make good hedges, growing 6–8 ft. tall and wide. Most have generous clusters of fragrant double flowers that open in pastel colors and fade to white. Some are repeat bloomers, and some have colorful hips. 'Buff Beauty' opens apricot-gold and fades to cream. 'Cornelia' opens medium pink and fades to creamy pink. 'Penelope' opens coral-pink and fades to blush.

'Nymphenberg' grows to 8 ft. and can be trained as a pillar or climber. It has salmon-pink flowers with a delicious fragrance, peaking in June but repeating later. Foliage is dark bronzy green. This excellent rose is not reliably hardy.

The rugosa cultivars and hybrids display the hardiness, disease resistance, and adaptability of *R. rugosa* (included with the species roses below). They make fine specimens or hedges and thrive in ordinary soil without special care. The prickly canes are usually 4–6 ft. tall. Leaves are bright green and have a crinkled texture. The single or double flowers are very fragrant and 3–4 in. wide. The colorful hips are large and round. 'Blanc Double de Coubert' has double white flowers. 'Frau Dagmar Hartopp' ('Fru Dagmar Hastrup') has single clear pink flowers. 'Hansa' has thorny upright canes, semidouble purplish red flowers, and large red hips. 'Thérèse Bugnet' is exceptionally hardy and vigorous, with reddish buds that open to fully double lilac-pink flowers. It's usually fruitless, but the almost thornless canes have glossy red bark that looks pretty against the snow.

'Sea Foam' is a low, spreading bush, under 2 ft. tall, that will spread as a ground cover or spill over a wall. It has glossy dark green leaves and clusters of lightly scented, pure white flowers.

How to grow: See main entry.

species roses (pp. 150, 206)

Many kinds of roses grow wild throughout the Northern Hemisphere; some are native to North America, and others have naturalized here. The following are some of the most popular species. Except where noted, all are hardy.

R. banksiae, the Lady Banks rose, is a vigorous plant that can climb, scramble, or spread 20–30 ft. or more. It has small leaves and almost thornless canes. Clusters of 1-in. double flowers open in early spring. The white-flowered form is more vigorous and fragrant but not as common as the yellow-flowered variety. Not cold-hardy.

R. eglanteria (*R. rubiginosa* 'Sweet Briar Rose') has clusters of single pink flowers 1–1¹/₂ in. wide with a sweet rosy fragrance. Wetting or touching the foliage releases a wonderful apple-like aroma. Hips are small red ovals. It grows 8–12 ft. tall but can be kept shorter by pruning.

R. hugonis, or Father Hugo's rose, is one of the best single yellow roses, with slightly fragrant 2-in. flowers early in the season. It has bristly arching canes 6–8 ft. tall and dainty dark green leaves.

R. moyesii has single red flowers about 2 in. wide in early to midseason, followed in fall by a showy display of brilliant red vase-shaped hips. It grows upright to 10 ft., with small leaves.

R. multiflora is a vigorous plant that blooms for weeks in early summer, bearing large clusters of ¹/₂-in. white flowers with a strong honeylike fragrance. It was once promoted as a "living fence," and bird-dispersed plants have naturalized in several parts of the country. It's very tough and very showy but much too big and too invasive for most gardens. This species is the ancestor of many polyantha and floribunda roses.

R. palustris, the swamp rose, is a native wild rose unique for its tolerance of poorly drained soil. It has very sweet-scented, single, pink flowers 2¹/₂ in. wide. The canes are almost thornless and grow upright to 6 ft. or more. *R. arkansana, R. carolina, R. setigera,* and *R. woodsii* are other wild roses with single pink blossoms, available from rose specialists and native-plant nurseries.

R. rubrifolia is grown primarily for its unusual dark reddish purple foliage. Its colorful canes are almost thornless and grow 4–8 ft. tall. The single pink flowers are small and don't last long, but the shiny red hips are showy all fall and winter.

R. rugosa is a very hardy shrub that tolerates cold, wind, dry spells, sandy soil, ocean spray, and road salt. The glossy green, richly textured leaves are relatively immune to blackspot and mildew diseases. Flowers are fragrant, single, about 3 in. wide, and rosy purple or white. The shiny red hips are big and round, like cherries, and very showy from fall into winter. Some people gather them for rose-hip tea or preserves.

R. wichuraiana, the memorial rose, is the parent of many climbing roses. It makes a good ground cover, with trailing stems that root where they touch soil and spread 10–20 ft. wide. Clusters of fragrant white flowers 1¹/₂–2 in. wide are produced in summer. The glossy foliage is semievergreen.

How to grow: See main entry.

Rosa woodsii

Rosa banksiae

Rosmarinus

Ros-ma-ry´nus. Rosemary.
Labiatae. Mint family.

Evergreen shrubs with slender opposite leaves and small 2-lipped flowers. Only 2 spp., native to the Mediterranean region.

officinalis (p. 287)

Rosemary.
Evergreen shrub used as an herb. Zone 8.
H: 4 ft. S: 4 ft.

A favorite culinary herb. The gray-green needlelike leaves, ¹/₂–1¹/₂ in. long, are very aromatic. Small light blue, lilac, or white flowers form on old wood and last for weeks in winter and spring. Makes a bushy, upright, or spreading shrub that can be trained and pruned into formal shapes. Useful as a specimen, hedge, or ground cover. 'Arp' is the cold-hardiest cultivar, surviving on protected sites in Zone 6. 'Blue Spire', 'Collingwood Ingram', and 'Tuscan Blue' are upright growers. 'Huntington Blue', 'Lockwood de Forest', and 'Prostratus' are prostrate forms with sinuous branches.

How to grow: Full sun. Well-drained ordinary or unimproved soil. Tolerates heat and drought. Plant 2 ft. apart for a ground cover (prostrate types) or hedge (upright growers). Pinch growing tips to promote full, bushy growth. Grows well in containers and can be overwintered indoors in a cool, sunny room.

Rudbeckia

Rood-bek´ee-a. Coneflower.
Compositae. Composite family.

Annuals or perennials with showy daisylike blossoms, usually with gold, reddish, or rusty brown rays. About 15 spp., native to North America.

fulgida 'Goldsturm' (p. 268)
Black-eyed Susan.
Perennial. Zone 3.
H: 18–30 in. S: 24 in.

Forms an erect clump of robust branching stems with coarse-textured leaves 3–6 in. long. The composite blossoms have dark gold rays around a dome-shaped, dark brown disk. Makes a big splash of color from summer into fall. Combines well with daylilies, daisies, asters, and grasses. The fresh flowers are good for cutting. Pick off the rays and dry the disks for winter arrangements.

How to grow: Full sun. Ordinary soil. Water it often during hot weather or the leaves will droop. Deadhead to prolong bloom. Easy to grow and trouble-free. Divide older plants in early spring or fall.

hirta (p. 303)
Black-eyed Susan, gloriosa daisy.
Annual or biennial. All zones.
H: 1–3 ft. S: 1 ft.

The species is a common wildflower with rough stems and leaves and gold-and-brown blossoms 2–3 in. wide, blooming from summer to fall. It self-sows freely and continues for years in meadow or prairie plantings, combining well with grasses, asters, and goldenrods. Gloriosa daisies are cultivated forms with yellow, gold, mahogany, red, or bicolored blossoms up to 6 in. wide, sometimes semidouble or double. They make good cut flowers and are very easy to grow.

How to grow: Full sun. Ordinary soil and watering. Tolerates heat and drought. Sow seeds indoors 8–10 weeks before last frost, or direct-sow when the soil is warm. Space 18 in. apart to allow air circulation between plants. Foliage is subject to mildew in damp, crowded beds.

laciniata 'Golden Glow' (p. 268)
Perennial. Zone 3.
H: 6–8 ft. S: 3–4 ft.

An old-fashioned perennial, famous for surviving even when neglected. Its cheerful fluffy yellow blossoms open from summer to fall if it has decent soil and plenty of moisture. It blooms less but keeps going even during droughts. Forms an erect clump of branching stems and dark green foliage. The double flowers are 2–3½ in. wide. Best for informal country gardens or meadow gardens.

How to grow: Full sun. Ordinary or improved soil with constant moisture. Space 3 ft. apart. It spreads underground and can be invasive. May need staking. Propagate from seed, or divide older plants at any time. Doesn't like hot summers.

nitida 'Herbsonne' ('Autumn Sun') (p. 268)
Perennial. Zone 4.
H: 4–6 ft. S: 2 ft.

One of the best in the genus, this plant is easy to care for, long-blooming, and not too tall. It forms erect clumps of branched stems with dark green foliage. The composite blossoms, 3–4 in. wide, have drooping pale yellow rays around a bright green cylindrical disk. Combine it with red dahlias, purple asters, and white boltonia for a dazzling late summer/autumn display. 'Goldquelle' ('Gold Drop') has double yellow flowers in midsummer and grows only 3 ft. tall.

How to grow: Full sun. Ordinary soil and watering. May need staking. Divide established plants in early spring or after flowering in fall. Trouble-free.

Rumohra

Roo-mow´ra.
Polypodiaceae. Polypody family.

An evergreen fern with large leathery leaves. Only 1 sp., native to the Southern Hemisphere.

adiantiformis (p. 219)
(*Aspidium capense*)
Leatherleaf fern.
Evergreen fern. Zone 9.
H: to 3 ft. S: to 3 ft.

A tough fern for warm-winter climates. It makes clumps of firm, leathery, finely divided, dark green fronds up to 3 ft. long. Cut fronds provide excellent greenery for bouquets and arrangements. A good foliage plant for shady beds or foundation planting, it combines well with calla lilies, tuberous begonias, and caladiums.

How to grow: Tolerates part sun where summers are cool but needs shade from hot sun. Prefers fertile, organic soil and constant moisture but tolerates ordinary soil and watering. Needs little care; just remove dead or tattered fronds. Old clumps can be divided.

Rudbeckia fulgida
'Goldsturm'

Ruta

Roo´ta. Rue.

Rutaceae. Rue family.

Shrubby perennials with strong-scented compound leaves. Only 7 spp., most native to Europe and the Middle East.

graveolens (p. 288)

Rue, herb-of-grace.

Shrubby perennial herb. Zone 5.

H: 2–3 ft. S: 2 ft.

This herb has many historic uses but is now grown chiefly as an ornamental. Its smooth blue-gray leaves are divided, fernlike, into many small segments. Clusters of small yellow flowers are held above the foliage for 2–3 weeks in summer. 'Jackman's Blue' has waxy blue foliage and doesn't flower, so it remains compact and bushy, 1¹/₂–2 ft. tall. It combines well with the flowers and foliage of other perennials. 'Variegata' has leaves dappled with cream or white when young; prune often to force new growth.

How to grow: Full or part sun. Well-drained, ordinary soil. Tolerates hot, dry weather. Use conifer boughs or other mulch as winter protection in cold zones, and do not uncover too soon in spring. Prune annually in early spring, cutting back to old wood. Wear long sleeves and gloves when handling this plant—touching the foliage, especially in hot weather, gives some people a terrible rash.

Sabal

Say´bal. Palmetto.

Palmae. Palm family.

Palms with fanlike fronds, often used in basketry or for thatched roofs. About 14 spp., native from the southeastern United States to South America.

Sabal minor

palmetto (p. 165)

Cabbage palm.

Fan palm. Zone 8.

H: 20–40 ft. S: 10–15 ft.

A native palm that slowly grows a tall trunk topped with a crown of coarse, dark green, palmate fronds, 5 ft. or more in diameter. The state tree of South Carolina and Florida, it gives a tropical look to southern gardens. *S. minor*, or palmetto, has a similar crown of fronds, but the trunk is very short, sometimes underground. Both have clusters of small creamy white flowers in May or June, followed by dark berries.

How to grow: Full sun, part sun, or full shade. Tolerates poor, unamended soil. A tough, adaptable plant. Native to river bottoms and swamps, it tolerates both standing water and seasonal drought. Grows slowly but is pest-free. The only care required is the removal of old foliage and bloom stalks.

Salix

Say´licks. Willow.

Salicaceae. Willow family.

Deciduous trees or shrubs with simple leaves and catkins of small male and female flowers, borne separately. Most willows are fast-growing but relatively short-lived. The twigs are used in basketry; the bark was an early source of aspirin. About 300 spp., nearly all native to cold or temperate climates in the Northern Hemisphere.

alba 'Tristis' (p. 125)

(sometimes listed under several other names)

Golden weeping willow.

Deciduous tree. Zone 2.

H: 50 ft. or more. S: 50 ft. or more.

A popular tree with a distinctly graceful shape. The drooping branchlets have bright yellow bark. The slender leaves, 2–4 in. long, are light green on top and silky white below. They unfold in very early spring, along with the yellow catkins, and turn clear yellow before dropping in late fall. It makes a lovely specimen near a large pond or in a well-watered lawn, but it has drawbacks: the roots invade underground water and sewer pipes, the brittle twigs drop with every storm, and there are several insect and disease problems. The species *S. alba* grows upright 75–100 ft. tall and has a broad rounded crown. 'Chermesena' has twigs that turn bright scarlet-orange in winter. 'Vitellina' twigs turn egg-yolk yellow. Grow these two cultivars as shrubs or pollards, and cut them back hard each spring; only the first-year shoots develop bright-colored bark.

How to grow: Full sun. Grows in almost any soil if supplied with plenty of water. Tolerates wet, poorly drained sites. Very easy to propagate—just stick cuttings into moist soil in spring or fall—and easy to transplant. Young trees must be staked to develop a strong trunk high enough to support the weeping branches.

caprea (p. 151)

Goat willow, French pussy willow.

Deciduous shrub or small tree. Zone 4.

H: to 25 ft. S: to 15 ft.

Valued for its soft, silky, pinkish gray catkins, 1–2 in. long, which open in early spring or can be brought indoors and forced in late winter. Male and female flowers are borne on separate plants; the males have prominent yellow stamens. Leaves are dark green above, gray below, 2–4 in. long. Will make a tree or can be cut back regularly to keep it smaller. 'Pendula' is a weeping form that can make a low mound or ground cover or be trained as a standard with a short trunk. *S. discolor*, a native pussy willow, is similar but has silvery gray catkins and leaves that are bluish white below. *S. gracilistyla*, the rose-gold pussy willow, grows only 6–10 ft. tall and has large gray-pink catkins and gray-green or blue-green foliage.

How to grow: Full sun. Ordinary soil and watering. Tolerates constant moisture. Cuttings root easily in water or moist soil. Easy to transplant. Prune after flowering. Cut back to the ground every few years to force vigorous new growth. Grows best where winters are cold.

elaeagnos (p. 151)
Rosemary willow.
Deciduous shrub or small tree. Zone 5.
H: 8–12 ft. or more. S: 8–12 ft. or more.

A fine-textured dense shrub that makes a graceful specimen or hedge. The long narrow leaves are dark green above and covered with woolly white hairs below, giving a wonderful two-tone effect when rippled by the breeze. The slender twigs are reddish brown in winter. Can make a tree 45 ft. tall if unpruned but is usually pruned to make a dense upright clump.

How to grow: Full sun. Not fussy about soil. Tolerates moist or dry conditions. Prune back to the ground every few years to keep it compact and vigorous. Subject to leaf-eating insects but generally trouble-free.

matsudana 'Tortuosa' (p. 125)
Twisted Hankow willow.
Deciduous tree. Zone 5.
H: 30 ft. S: 20 ft.

An upright tree with remarkable gray-brown twigs and stems that twist and spiral like a corkscrew. Position it against a dark evergreen background to enjoy the silhouette in winter. The slender 3-in. leaves are dark green in summer, yellow in fall. Grows quickly into a tree or can be pruned repeatedly to keep it shrub-sized. 'Golden Curls' and 'Scarlet Curls' are hybrids with bright-colored bark on the youngest twigs.

How to grow: Like *S. elaeagnos.*

purpurea 'Nana' (p. 151)
Purple osier willow.
Deciduous shrub. Zone 4.
H: to 5 ft. S: to 5 ft.

A compact shrub with very slender twigs and thin blue-gray leaves 1–2 in. long. Good for planting along streams or ponds, where the fibrous roots help stabilize the soil. Can be used for a low hedge and responds well to annual pruning. Sometimes used as a specimen in mixed borders, for a mound of fine-textured foliage.

How to grow: Like *S. elaeagnos.*

Salvia
Sal′vee-a. Sage.
Labiatae. Mint family.

Annuals, perennials, or shrubs with square stems, opposite simple leaves, and 2-lipped flowers. About 900 spp., native worldwide. A few species have aromatic foliage that is used for seasoning, potpourri, or home remedies. Several species are grown for their bright-colored flowers.

azurea (p. 269)
Azure sage, wild blue sage.
Perennial. Zone 5.
H: 3–5 ft. S: 1–3 ft.

Produces wonderful arching fountains of clear blue flowers, 1/2 in. long, from summer to frost. Bees and butterflies love it. Native to open grasslands and woodlands across the southern United States. It's showy in borders and also good for meadows, as it competes well with grasses and tolerates periodic mowing. The lance-shaped leaves are small, hairy, and dark green. Var. *grandiflora* (*S. pitcheri*) has larger, light blue flowers. *S. patens,* or gentian sage, has beautiful dark blue flowers, 2 in. long, but they are too widely spaced to make a showy display. It grows 2 1/2 ft. tall and is usually grown as an annual.

How to grow: Full or part sun. Prefers poor, dry soil but tolerates heavy, moist soil better than most salvias do. Tolerates heat and humidity. Pinch growing tips a few times in spring and early summer to promote bushiness. Often self-seeds.

clevelandii (p. 269)
Cleveland sage.
Tender shrubby perennial. Zone 9 or 8.
H: 4 ft. S: 6 ft.

A rounded shrubby plant with very aromatic evergreen foliage. The slender gray-green leaves can be used in cooking or dried for potpourri. Whorls of small, sweet-scented, lilac-blue flowers open from spring to summer. Native to dry slopes in southern California, it combines well with rosemary, lavender, and other Mediterranean herbs.

How to grow: Full sun. Tolerates poor, dry soil and heat. Needs no irrigation after the first year. Prune in early spring to keep it compact, and remove old flower stalks to prolong bloom.

elegans (p. 288)
(*S. rutilans*)
Pineapple sage.
Tender perennial herb. Zone 9.
H: 4–5 ft. S: 3–4 ft.

Grows bushy and upright, making a shrub-sized plant in a single season. The rich green leaves have a strong pineapple fragrance and flavor. Use them in fruit salad or for iced or hot tea. Bears 8-in. spikes of slender red flowers from late summer until frost. Hummingbirds love it. Grows well in a container on a sunny windowsill indoors. Herb specialists have other salvias with fruit-scented leaves.

How to grow: Full sun. Ordinary soil and watering. Plant outdoors after danger of frost is past. Pinch once or twice to promote bushiness. Rarely grown from seed. Root a cutting in fall to overwinter indoors, or buy a new plant each spring.

Salvia clevelandii

Salvia farinacea

farinacea (p. 269)
Mealy blue sage.
Perennial. Zone 8 or 7.
H: to 2–3 ft. S: 1 ft.

Blooms and blooms from late spring to hard frost. Branches near the base and makes many upright stalks with small gray-green leaves on the bottom and crowded spikes of violet-blue flowers on top. The long-stalked flower spikes are good for fresh or dried arrangements. Cultivars with dark blue, light blue, or white flowers are available from seed catalogs or as bedding plants in spring. *S. guaranitica,* or blue sage, grows 3–5 ft. tall and wide and has fragrant dark green leaves and dark violet-blue flowers 1–2 in. long. Both are native to Texas and the Southwest. 'Indigo Spires' is a hybrid between these two species, with smooth gray-green leaves and very dark violet-blue flowers on dozens of crowded spikes that extend 2 ft. above the foliage. It blooms from midsummer until hard frost. Hardy to Zone 8, it is sterile and must be propagated by cuttings or by division.

How to grow: Full sun. Tolerates hot weather and poor, dry, alkaline soil. Gets lush with ordinary soil and watering. Plant outdoors about the time of last frost. Keeps blooming even if you don't remove old flower stalks. Perennial in mild climates. May self-sow where winters are cold, or start seeds indoors 8 weeks before last frost.

greggii (p. 269)
Cherry sage, autumn sage.
Tender shrubby perennial. Zone 9 or 8.
H: 3 ft. S: 3 ft.

A low bushy plant with colorful flowers from spring to fall. The small crisp leaves are fragrant and semievergreen. The scented flowers are rosy pink, red, salmon, purple, or white, 1 in. long, arranged in loose clusters. Makes a good low hedge, natural or clipped, or a mounded specimen. Native from Central America into Texas and the Southwest.

How to grow: Full or part sun. Needs good drainage and grows well in poor, dry soil. Trim off spent flowers to stimulate further bloom. Cut back in early spring to keep it bushy. Increase by transplanting self-sown seedlings in spring.

leucantha (p. 270)
Mexican bush sage.
Perennial. Zone 8 or 7.
H: 3–4 ft. S: 2–3 ft.

Forms a large clump of graceful arching stems tipped with long spikes of rosy purple bracts and small white flowers. The gray-green leaves are 1–3 in. long. Neither foliage nor flowers have much fragrance. Thrives in hot, dry weather and blooms nonstop from midsummer to late fall.

How to grow: Full or part sun. Tolerates poor, dry soil. Cut back older stems to promote new growth. Rarely sets seed; propagate by dividing old clumps in spring or fall.

officinalis (p. 288)
Garden sage.
Perennial herb. Zone 5.
H: 2 ft. S: 2 ft.

The fragrant gray-green leaves of this favorite herb are used for seasoning and to make a therapeutic tea. Woody at the base, it is evergreen in mild climates but freezes back where winters are cold. Tall spikes of blue-purple flowers are colorful for weeks in early summer. Variegated cultivars such as 'Tricolor' (white, purple, and green leaves) and 'Icterina' (green and yellow leaves) are hardy only to Zone 8 or 7.

How to grow: Full sun. Needs well-drained soil. Cut back frozen shoots in late spring, before new growth starts, and remove faded blooms in summer. Divide every few years. Root cuttings to overwinter tender cultivars, or buy new plants in spring.

pratensis (p. 270)
Meadow sage, meadow clary.
Perennial. Zone 3.
H: to 3 ft. S: 2–3 ft.

Forms a rosette of large, hairy, fragrant, dark green leaves with toothed edges. Very showy for a month or so when it blooms in summer. The upright branched stalks are crowded with lavender-blue, violet, rosy, or white flowers. Easy to grow in a flower bed or border. Self-sows and naturalizes in a grassy meadow. Native to Europe.

How to grow: Full or part sun. Ordinary soil and watering. Plant size, leaf fragrance, and flower color vary among seedlings. The best forms are propagated by division.

sclarea (p. 288)
Clary sage.
Biennial herb. Zone 4.
H: 3–4 ft. S: 2 ft.

Grows a broad rosette of large, crinkly-textured, gray-green leaves the first year. Sends up several branching flower stalks in early summer the second year, crowded with papery white, pink, or purplish bracts and small white flowers. Bracts remain colorful and showy for many weeks. Bract color and leaf fragrance vary among seedlings. Some plants release a very rich aroma, particularly after a rain. Used for flavoring, fragrance, and medicinally. Var. *turkestana* has larger leaves and flowers. *S. argentea,* or silver sage, is a similar biennial, grown for its large leaves that are densely covered with silvery hairs. The first-year rosette is a striking accent for the front of a border, but the second-year flower stalk is a disappointment compared with that of clary sage.

How to grow: Full sun. Ordinary soil and watering. Tolerates heavy soils. Usually self-seeds. Transplant volunteer seedlings to their permanent location by midsummer.

splendens (p. 303)
Salvia.
Annual. All zones.
H: 1–3 ft. S: 1 ft.

One of the most popular and widely grown bedding plants, with stiff erect spikes of bright flowers all summer. Blooms nonstop even without deadheading. Makes a bushy plant with dark green foliage. There are dwarf, medium, and tall strains. Scarlet flowers are by far the most common, but there are also pink, salmon, lavender, purple, and white forms. All attract hummingbirds and combine well with silver-leaved dusty-millers.

Two Texas species have equally bright red flowers but are looser, more casual-looking plants. *S. coccinea*, or scarlet sage, grows fast from seed and flowers nonstop from early summer to fall. It grows 2–3 ft. tall. 'Lady in Red' is a popular cultivar, grown from seed as an annual. There are also pink and white forms. *S. roemeriana*, or cedar sage, forms a rosette of fuzzy rounded leaves and has flowers on spikes 12–18 in. tall in summer. It thrives in the dry shade between scattered trees. Both species are perennial in Zone 8 or 7.

How to grow: Full or part sun. Ordinary soil. Needs regular watering; wilts in dry soil. Space 12–18 in. apart. Start seeds indoors 10 weeks before last frost; do not cover, as seeds need light to germinate. Transplant after danger of frost is past.

× ***superba*** (p. 270)
(*S. nemorosa*)
Perennial. Zone 4.
H: 1¹/₂–3 ft. S: 2 ft.

One of the most dependable perennials, with no quirks, no enemies, no demands. Blooms from early summer into fall if you remove spent flower spikes. Makes a mass of color in the garden and a good cut flower, too. The basal leaves are thick, wrinkled, pungent, and 1–3 in. long. The branched stems carry dense spikes crowded with rich-colored bracts and flowers. Seedling plants are quite variable. It's best to buy cultivars from a nursery and divide them later. 'Mainacht' ('May Night') is a compact plant with very dark violet-blue flowers on spikes 18 in. tall. It can bloom from May to frost. 'East Friesland' has red-violet flowers on spikes 18–24 in. tall. 'Blue Queen' is deep blue-purple on spikes 24 in. tall.

How to grow: Full or part sun. Ordinary soil and watering. Tolerates dry soil and dry heat but gets floppy in hot, humid conditions. Space 15–18 in. apart. Deadhead to prolong bloom. Divide in fall or early spring.

viridis (p. 303)
(*S. horminum*)
Tricolor sage.
Annual. All zones.
H: 18 in. S: 6 in.

Unusual and easy to grow, this is a slender erect plant that blooms for several weeks or more in midsummer. The unbranched spikes have small inconspicuous flowers, but the leaflike bracts are long-lasting and colorful in the garden or for fresh or dried arrangements. Comes in shades of white, rose, lavender, or blue-purple.

How to grow: Full sun. Ordinary soil and watering. Direct-sow in midspring, or start indoors several weeks before last frost. Often self-sows. May rebloom if you remove spent flowers.

Sanguinaria

Sang-gwi-nay′ree-a. Bloodroot.
Papaveraceae. Poppy family.

A perennial wildflower. The rhizome has bright red sap. Only 1 sp., native to eastern North America.

Sanguinaria canadensis

canadensis (p. 270)
Bloodroot.
Perennial. Zone 4.
H: to 8 in. S: to 18 in.

An early spring wildflower, native to deciduous woodlands. The large, thick, smooth, blue-green leaves are basically round, with irregular lobes around the edge. The round white flowers are about 1 in. wide. Both leaves and flowers grow directly from the spreading rhizome. Gradually forms a patch, and self-sows on suitable sites. Goes dormant by midsummer. 'Multiplex', or 'Flore Pleno', has large double flowers but can be propagated only by division; it doesn't set seed.

How to grow: Part sun in spring, shade in summer. Ordinary soil and watering. Divide every few years in early spring. Trouble-free.

Sanguisorba

Sang-gwi-sor′ba. Burnet.
Rosaceae. Rose family.

Perennials with compound leaves and dense flower heads. Some species are used medicinally. About 18 spp., native to the north temperate zone.

canadensis (p. 271)
(*Poterium canadense*)
Canadian burnet.
Perennial. Zone 3.
H: 3–6 ft. S: 1–2 ft.

A native wildflower with creamy white flowers in showy bottlebrush-like clusters, 6–8 in. long and 1¹/₂ in. thick, held above the foliage for 3–4 weeks in late August or September. Forms an upright clump of many leafy stems. The pinnately compound leaves have oblong leaflets with neatly scalloped edges. Excellent for native gardens, perennial beds, or waterside plantings. The dried rhizomes have been used medicinally.

How to grow: Full sun. Ordinary or poor soil. Prefers constant moisture. Needs staking in all but the leanest soils. Can go years without division.

Santolina
San-to-ly´na.
Compositae. Daisy family.

Perennials or shrubs with pungent foliage and round flower heads. About 18 spp., native to the Mediterranean region.

chamaecyparissus (p. 271)
Lavender cotton, gray santolina.
Shrubby perennial. Zone 7 or 6.
H: 2 ft. S: 3 ft.

A favorite plant for low clipped edgings or miniature hedges around rose beds or herb gardens. Grows naturally into a low, spreading mound that combines well with rosemary, lavender, sages, rock roses, and wild buckwheats. The aromatic silvery gray foliage has a rough curly texture, like terrycloth. Buttonlike yellow flower heads, 3/4 in. wide, perch on 6-in. stalks in summer.

How to grow: Full sun. Needs good drainage and air circulation; subject to root and foliar fungal diseases in wet or humid conditions. Tolerates poor, dry soil and heat. Space 18–24 in. apart for a clipped edging, 30–36 in. apart for mass plantings. Older plants get woody at the base and split open in the middle. Cut back hard in spring to renew, or, better yet, replace them with fresh plants.

virens (p. 271)
(now *S. rosmarinifolia*)
Green santolina.
Shrubby perennial. Zone 6.
H: 2 ft. S: 3 ft.

Forms a low mound of dark green foliage. The slender 1–2-in. leaves look like twisted pine needles. Blooms in summer, with pale yellow, round flower heads, 1/2 in. wide, on stalks 6 in. tall. Often combined with gray santolina and other gray-leaved plants and used as a clipped edging or a mass planting on dry banks. The form most often sold has been labeled 'Primrose Gem'.

How to grow: Like *S. chamaecyparissus* but is slightly hardier and more tolerant of moist soil and humid air.

Sapindus
Sa-pin´dus. Soapberry.
Sapindaceae. Soapberry family.

Deciduous or evergreen shrubs or trees with compound leaves and fleshy or leathery fruits. About 13 spp., all native to warm and tropical climates.

drumondii (p. 125)
Soapberry.
Deciduous tree. Zone 6.
H: 40–50 ft. S: 20–30 ft.

A good medium-size shade tree for difficult sites with very poor, dry soil. Forms an oval crown of pinnately compound leaves that turn a bright clear yellow in fall. Small dense clusters of greenish white flowers in early summer are fol-

lowed by grape-sized yellow fruits that hang on through fall and winter. Crushed fruits yield a soapy lather. Native to Texas and the Southwest.

How to grow: Full sun. Tolerates poor, dry soil and heat. Easy to grow, with no serious pests.

Sapium
Say´pi-um.
Euphorbiaceae. Spurge family.

Deciduous or evergreen trees with simple alternate leaves and milky sap. About 100 spp., all native to warm and tropical climates.

sebiferum (p. 124)
Chinese tallow tree.
Deciduous tree. Zone 7.
H: 25–50 ft. S: 15–30 ft.

This medium-sized, fast-growing tree is praised for its fall color and cursed for its weediness. It has invaded pastures and forests along the humid, hot Gulf Coast, but it is less aggressive in dry California or in cooler Zone 7. It forms a rounded crown and casts medium shade. The aspenlike leaves are dark green in summer, fire-engine red in fall. The flowers are not showy, but the fruits are conspicuous in fall. Small dry pods release white seeds with a waxy covering that has been used to make soaps and candles.

How to grow: Sun or shade. Tolerates poor, dry soil. Grows fast from seed. Needs no care. Pest-free.

Saponaria
Sap-o-nay´ree-a. Soapwort.
Caryophyllaceae. Pink family.

Annual, biennial, or perennial herbs with opposite leaves and 5-petaled pink or white flowers. Crushed leaves make a suds in water. About 30 spp., most native to the Mediterranean region.

ocymoides (p. 271)
Rock soapwort.
Perennial. Zone 4.
H: 4–8 in. S: 12 in.

A trailing plant that makes a low mat of tangled stems and small slender leaves. It's covered with loose clusters of bright pink flowers, 1/2 in. wide, in early summer. A single clump is very showy along a path or at the front of a raised bed or terrace. Sometimes self-seeds but doesn't spread underground and isn't dense enough to inhibit weeds as a ground cover. *S. officinalis,* bouncing Bet or soapwort, grows 1–3 ft. tall and has dense clusters of white or pink flowers with a heavy, sweet, clove fragrance at night. It blooms all summer but spreads fast and is quite invasive.

How to grow: Full sun. Ordinary, well-drained soil. Grows easily from seed. Shear back after flowering to force new growth, which stays fresh and dark green until early winter. Pest-free.

Sapium sebiferum

Sarcococca
Sar-ko-kok´a. Sweet box.
Buxaceae. Box family.

Evergreen shrubs, similar to boxwood. About 14 spp., native from western China to southeastern Asia.

hookerana var. humilis (p. 186)
Sweet box.
Evergreen shrub. Zone 6.
H: 18 in. S: to 8 ft. or more.

A splendid evergreen ground cover for deep shade under trees or wide overhangs. The shiny dark green foliage looks fresh and healthy all year. The oval leaves are about 2 in. long. Clusters of tiny white flowers with a powerful honey scent open from midwinter to early spring, followed by small black berries. *S. confusa* and *S. ruscifolia* have similar foliage and flowers but grow slowly to 5–6 ft. They are good shrubs for shady foundation plantings.

How to grow: Part or full shade; tolerates full sun only where summers are cool. Prefers rich, fertile soil. To help it spread as a ground cover, loosen heavy soil with plenty of organic matter. Ordinary watering okay. Rarely needs pruning or other care. Pest-free.

Sasa
Sa´sa.
Gramineae. Grass family.

Low-growing spreading bamboos. They rarely flower. About 25 spp., native to eastern Asia.

palmata (p. 214)
Running bamboo. Zone 7.
H: 6 ft. or more. S: indefinite.

A vigorous bamboo with slender erect stems. Papery thin, bright green leaves, 12–16 in. long and 2–4 in. wide, are clustered at the tips of the stems and branches. Underground runners spread fast. Use it to control erosion on hillsides or streambanks, or install 18-in.-deep barriers at planting time and use it for a quick tropical or Oriental effect.

How to grow: Sun or shade. Spreads fast in rich, moist soil; not so fast in ordinary conditions. Should be curbed with a deep metal, fiberglass, or concrete barrier. Propagate by division. Dig up sections of 5–6 stems in early spring. Try to keep soil around the roots, and replant quickly. Needs little care—just cut old or shabby stems to the ground in spring. Doesn't tolerate desert heat or drought. Worth a try in Zone 6. It may freeze to the ground but will recover.

veitchii (p. 214)
Running bamboo. Zone 7.
H: 2–3 ft. S: indefinite.

A striking ground cover for shade, with broad, papery, bright green leaves that turn creamy white around the edges in fall. The variegated effect lasts all winter. Leaves are 6–8 in. long, 2 in. wide, clustered at the ends of the slender canes. Indispensable for Japanese gardens with mondo grass, azaleas, water-smoothed stones, and bamboo fences.

How to grow: Like *S. palmata.*

Sassafras
Sas´a-fras.
Lauraceae. Laurel family.

Deciduous trees with aromatic leaves, flowers, bark, and wood. Only 3 spp., one from North America, two from eastern Asia.

albidum (p. 125)
Sassafras.
Deciduous tree. Zone 5.
H: 40–60 ft. S: 25–50 ft.

A beautiful and popular native. All parts have a spicy fragrance. Young plants often form dome-shaped suckering colonies with bright yellow-green bark, antlerlike branch forks, and mitten-shaped leaves with 1 or 2 "thumbs." Can mature into a grove or, if suckers are removed, a single-trunked specimen shade tree. Older trees have thick furrowed bark and simple oval leaves. Fall color is rich red, purple-red, orange, or gold. Small yellow flowers open with the leaves in spring, and blue berries attract birds in fall. The flowers and root bark are used for tea, and the dried leaves are used in gumbo.

How to grow: Full or part sun. Grows best in fertile, moist soil but tolerates poor, dry soil. Difficult to transplant; must be started from seed or grown in containers. Plants dug from the wild rarely survive. Grows fast and needs little care once established. Leaf-eating insects may cause cosmetic but not serious damage. Remove suckers to limit spread or to encourage one or a few trunks to dominate the stand.

Satureja
Sat-you-ree´ya. Savory.
Labiatae. Mint family.

Annuals or perennials with square stems and opposite leaves, used medicinally and for flavoring. About 30 spp., native to the Old and New World.

montana (p. 289)
Winter savory.
Shrubby perennial herb. Zone 6.
H: to 1 ft. S: to 2 ft.

Makes a low compact mound with many small, glossy, pointed, evergreen leaves. The leaves have a strong flavor and are used to season meats and beans. Bees love the small white, lavender, or pink flowers in late summer. *S. hortensis,* or summer savory, is a slender annual with narrow leaves and small pink or white flowers. It has a milder, more versatile flavor and is used in cooking and to make a therapeutic tea. *S. douglasii,* or yerba buena, is native along the Pacific Coast and valued there for the rich minty fragrance of its rounded leaves. It's a creeping perennial, hardy to Zone 8 or 7.

Sasa veitchii

How to grow: Full sun. Needs good drainage. Tolerates dry, sandy soil with occasional watering. Harvest by trimming back in early summer; stop trimming before it blooms. New growth needs time to mature and harden before cold weather. Pest-free. Propagate by seed or by division.

Saxifraga

Sax-i-fra´ga, sax-if´fra-ga.
Saxifragaceae. Saxifrage family.

Perennials and a few annuals, usually forming a compact rosette of basal leaves. About 300 spp., most native to montane or alpine sites.

stolonifera (p. 271)

(*S. sarmentosa*)
Strawberry geranium, strawberry begonia.
Perennial. Zone 7.
H: 6 in. S: 2 ft. or more.

An easy ground cover for mild, shady spots. Forms rosettes of hairy, rounded or heart-shaped leaves, dark green with white veins on top and reddish underneath. The reddish underside shows enough to echo the color of pink azaleas or saucer magnolias growing overhead. Makes graceful loose clusters of small white flowers in early summer. Spreads like a strawberry, making baby plants at the ends of slender runners. Also grows well in hanging baskets and is a popular houseplant in cold regions.

How to grow: Part or full shade. Prefers moist, fertile soil. Tolerates heat if it has shade and water. Spreads quickly and can be invasive. Multiply by transplanting rooted offsets. Subject to mealybugs.

Scabiosa

Ska-bee-oh´sa. Pincushion flower.
Dipsacaceae. Teasel family.

Annuals or perennials with opposite leaves and rounded flower heads on long stalks. About 80 spp., native to the Old World.

caucasica (p. 271)

Pincushion flower.
Perennial. Zone 3.
H: 18–24 in. S: 12–18 in.

A desirable and long-lasting cut flower, also showy in a summer border. Forms a basal clump of gray-green foliage. The round, flattened flower heads, 2–3 in. wide, are held on long slender stalks. The stamens stick out like pins on a cushion. There are several cultivars; colors include pale and deep blue, lilac, lavender pinkish purple, and white. *S. atropurpurea* is an annual with similar flowers.

How to grow: Full sun. Needs well-drained, fertile, neutral or alkaline soil. If your soil is acidic, add lime. Water regularly. Space 12 in. apart and plant in small groups to make a show. Divide every other year. Foliage may be attacked by various insects.

Schinus

Sky´nus.
Anacardiaceae. Sumac family.

Evergreen trees with simple or compound leaves and showy clusters of small flowers and round fruits. About 27 spp., native to tropical America. Fruits of the species below are sold for seasoning as "pink peppercorns"; some people are allergic to them, so use with caution.

molle (p. 163)

California pepper tree, Peruvian pepper tree.
Evergreen tree. Zone 9.
H: to 40 ft. S: to 40 ft.

A study in contrasts—the trunk and branches are sturdy, heavy, and gnarled; the graceful weeping branchlets hold delicate glossy foliage all year and drooping clusters of small rose-pink berries in fall and winter. Old specimens have a lot of character. Can be trained to a single or multiple trunk. Useful along rural roads or suburban streets where the surface roots won't interfere with sidewalks. Can also be planted 2–3 ft. apart and pruned as a hedge.

How to grow: Full sun. Tolerates desert heat. Ordinary or unamended soil with regular watering at first; tolerates drought once established. Train to establish one or more trunks. Remove suckers and low branches that get in the way. Subject to aphids, scale, and psyllids. Roots are aggressive and can invade water pipes or sewers.

terebinthifolius (p. 163)

Brazilian pepper tree, Florida holly.
Evergreen tree. Zone 9.
H: 30 ft. S: 30 ft.

Usually grown with a single trunk and rounded crown, this can be an attractive shade tree with a dense, dark green umbrella of foliage. The compound leaves have a thick leathery texture. Big clusters of small red berries are very showy in fall and winter. It's a showy tree, but it shouldn't be planted in Florida, where bird-sown seedlings have become a major weed problem. So far, it hasn't spread invasively in California.

How to grow: Full sun. Ordinary or unamended soil. Needs regular watering. Thin the crown to reduce wind resistance and subsequent breakage. No major insect pests.

Schizachyrium

Sky-zack´ree-um.
Gramineae. Grass family.

Mostly perennial grasses with a bunching habit. Closely related to *Andropogon*. About 60 spp., mostly tropical.

scoparium (p. 214)

(*Andropogon scoparius*)
Little bluestem.
Clumping grass. Zone 3.
H: 2–3 ft. S: 12–18 in.

A small native grass that forms erect clumps. Leaves are slender, 12–18 in. long, and develop good fall color, ranging from bronze to intense

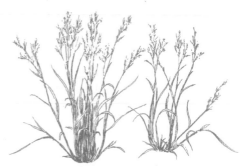

Schizachyrium scoparium

orange. The stout stems stand up to snow and provide winter interest. Summer flowers mature into fluffy seed heads that sparkle when backlit. Can be used as a large-scale ground cover on dry sites, for erosion control, as a transition between tended and natural areas, or as a specimen in borders or foundation plantings. 'Blaze' was selected for outstanding fall and winter color, ranging from purplish orange to russet or reddish purple.

How to grow: Full or part sun. Ordinary or unimproved soil with regular watering. Tolerates hot weather and dry soil. Can self-seed but usually doesn't. Propagate by dividing older clumps. Cut back once a year, in early spring. Pest-free.

Scilla
Sil′la. Squill.
Liliaceae. Lily family.

Low-growing perennials with bulbs, slender leaves, and blue or white flowers. About 40 spp., native to the Old World.

sibirica (p. 272)
Squill, Siberian squill.
Perennial. Zone 3.
H: 4–8 in. S: 3–4 in.

The small starry flowers are the most gorgeous blue on Earth. Just the hope of seeing them again can keep you going through a bad winter. Blooms in early spring, right after the snowdrops (*Galanthus* spp.). Each small bulb sends up 1–4 stalks, each with about 3 flowers, and a few grassy leaves. Buy dozens of bulbs and plant big pools of blue in woods or under trees or shrubs where they can spread undisturbed by hoe or trowel and their foliage can mature unobtrusively. 'Spring Beauty' has larger flowers than the species, with bright blue anthers.

S. tubergeniana blooms a little earlier and has larger, pale blue flowers on stalks 4–6 in. tall. *S. peruviana,* the Cuban lily, has clusters of 50 or more starry blue-purple flowers on 18-in. stalks in early spring. It is hardy only to Zone 9 but grows well in containers in cold climates.

How to grow: Sun in spring and shade in summer, as provided by deciduous trees. Ordinary soil and watering. Plant bulbs in fall, 3 in. deep and 3 in. apart. They will multiply but don't need to be divided for years. Top-dress with compost in fall.

Sedum
See′dum. Stonecrop.
Crassulaceae. Orpine family.

Small perennials, sometimes shrubby, with succulent leaves and stems. There are 300 or more spp., most from the north temperate zone, and several hybrids and cultivars. Authorities disagree on the taxonomy of this group, so some plants are listed under various Latin names, but the cultivar names go along unchanged.

'Autumn Joy' (p. 272)
(a hybrid of *S. spectabile* and *S. telephium*)
Perennial. Zone 3.
H: 2–3 ft. S: 1½–3 ft.

An attractive and easy-to-grow perennial that flowers for many weeks in late summer and fall. Forms a spreading clump of thick unbranched stems surrounded with plump, succulent, blunt-toothed leaves. The tiny starry flowers form clusters like broccoli, 4–6 in. wide, starting out pink, then deepening to dark salmon and finally rusty red. Combines well with white or pink lespedezas, asters, and other autumn flowers. It is commonly used with grasses and rudbeckia 'Goldsturm' in parks and municipal plantings. *S.* 'Indian Chief' may be the same plant as 'Autumn Joy'.

S. spectabile, one of the parent species, grows about 18 in. tall and prefers dry soil. It has thick stems; opposite, egg-shaped, pale green leaves; and flat clusters of star-shaped flowers ½ in. wide. 'Brilliant' has deep pink flowers, 'Meteor' is reddish pink, and 'Stardust' is very pale pink or off-white.

How to grow: An adaptable plant; prefers full sun and well-drained, gritty soil but does well even in somewhat soggy soil and part shade. Space at least 2 ft. apart. Cut back in late fall, or leave the dry stems and seed heads to look at in winter. 'Autumn Joy' often self-seeds. Watch for small plants, which will be true to their parent. Otherwise, propagate by division. Lift and divide the clumps every third year to keep them from flopping open when they flower. No major pests.

kamtschaticum 'Weihenstephaner Gold'
(p. 272)
(*S. floriferum* 'Weihenstephaner Gold')
Perennial. Zone 3.
H: 4–8 in. S: 12 in.

An excellent noninvasive ground cover. Leaves, flowers, and seed heads are all handsome, so it gives good value for a long period in summer. The sprawling stems have dark green, toothed leaves 1½ in. long. Copper-red buds open into yellow blossoms, followed by red seed heads. The flowers form all along the stems, rather than in terminal clusters.

How to grow: Full sun. Quite adaptable; tolerates both dry and heavy soil. Space 6–8 in. apart. Divide when it gets crowded. Requires little attention.

Sedum 'Autumn Joy'

'Ruby Glow' (p. 272)
(a hybrid of *S. cauticola* and *S.* 'Autumn Joy')
Perennial. Zone 3.
H: 12 in. S: 12–18 in.

An easy plant for dry walls, rock gardens, or the front of the border. Forms a lax mound of flexible stems. The fleshy egg-shaped leaves, to 2 in. long, are blue-gray tinged with maroon. Flat 2-in. clusters of brilliant ruby red flowers appear for several weeks in fall. Butterflies love it. Also sold as 'Rosy Glow'. 'Vera Jameson', a related hybrid, has smoky gray-purple leaves and pink flowers in 2–4-in. heads. It spreads about 12 in. wide.

How to grow: Full sun. Needs good drainage and prefers lean, gritty soil. Space 1 ft. apart. Divide every few years to keep stems from falling apart into a flat open ring. Trouble-free.

spurium (p. 272)
Perennial. Zone 3.
H: to 6 in. S: 12–18 in. or more.

An easy, low-maintenance ground cover or edging for sunny spots. Good on walls, in large rock gardens, or along walkways. The creeping stems root at the nodes. The semievergreen leaves are opposite, oval, and about 1 in. long. 'Dragon's Blood', a very popular cultivar, has purple-bronze leaves on reddish stems and rosy red (not blood red) star-shaped flowers for several weeks in summer. 'Tricolor' seldom if ever flowers but has lovely toothed leaves marked with green, cream, and pink. The leaf surface looks sparkly, as if coated with sugar. This cultivar grows steadily but is less invasive than 'Dragon's Blood'.

How to grow: Full or part sun. Needs well-drained soil. Tolerates heat but not humidity. Space about 10 in. apart. Trim back when it gets straggly or crawls into the territory of other plants. Spreads too fast to combine with fragile little alpines in small rock gardens. Trouble-free.

Semiarundinaria

Se-my-uh-run-di-nay´ree-a.
Gramineae. Grass family.

Running bamboos with woody culms. They rarely flower. About 20 spp., native to eastern Asia.

fastuosa (see below for photo)
Narihira bamboo.
Clumping bamboo. Zone 8.
H: 15–25 ft. S: 2–5 ft., eventually more.

An exceptionally erect, narrow, clumping bamboo that spreads at a very moderate rate. The lush foliage is ideal for screening an unpleasant view, such as a telephone pole. Planted in a row, it makes a tall dense screen or windbreak. The jointed culms grow up to 1 1/2 in. thick. The thin, papery, bright green leaves are 4–8 in. long and 1 in. wide. *S. murielae* (p. 214) is similar but smaller—it stays under 15 ft. tall and has 1/2-in. culms—and is hardy to Zone 7.

How to grow: Full or part sun. Grows and spreads very slowly in unimproved soil. Gets taller and lusher in fertile soil amended with organic matter. Ordinary watering. Divide in very early spring, taking clumps of 3–5 stems with a good root ball, and replant promptly. Remove old or damaged stems as necessary. Trouble-free.

Sempervivum

Sem-per-vy´vum.
Crassulaceae. Orpine family.

Low-growing perennials that make a dense rosette of succulent leaves and multiply by offsets. About 40 spp., native mostly to Europe.

tectorum (p. 273)
Hen-and-chickens, hens-and-chicks.
Perennial. Zone 4.
H: 4 in. (foliage); 12 in. (flower stalks).
S: 1 ft. or more.

These little succulents make friends easily. Even the smallest garden has room for several clumps. Put them against a stone, in the crevices of a wall or steps, along a path, or in a shallow container. Each "hen" rosette spreads 4–6 in. wide and is closely surrounded by many smaller "chicks." In midsummer, flat clusters of starry reddish flowers top thick stems that stick up like chimneys. *S. arachnoideum* is a miniature version with marble-sized rosettes of leaves joined by a cobweb of fine hairs. There are dozens of selections in different sizes and colors.

How to grow: Full or part sun. Needs well-drained soil and regular watering. Very easy and trouble-free. Let the colony spread, or detach chicks to plant elsewhere or to give away.

Senecio

Se-nee´see-oh.
Compositae. Composite family.

A huge and diverse group of annuals, perennials, vines, and shrubs, including some succulents. Although many species have been reassigned to other groups in recent years, this is still one of the largest plant genera, with more than 1,500 spp. worldwide.

cineraria (p. 303)
(formerly *Centaurea cineraria*)
Dusty-miller.
Perennial usually grown as an annual. All zones.
H: to 12 in. S: 12 in. or more.

Easy and popular, valued for its beautiful silvery gray or white leaves. It combines well with almost any plant and makes a good foil for bright-colored flowers. Useful for bedding, for edgings, and in containers. It forms a woody crown and a spreading rosette of lobed leaves. Leaf size and shape vary among cultivars—some are very deeply cut and lacy, but others are broad and bold. The leaves are evergreen in mild climates. Overwintered plants have small yellow flowers on 2-ft. stalks the second and following years, but they are insignificant compared with the foliage.

How to grow: Full sun. Ordinary or unimproved soil. Does best with regular watering but tolerates dry spells. Easily propagated by seed or by cuttings. Subject to fungal infections in wet soil or humid weather but otherwise trouble-free.

Sequoiadendron

See-kwoy-a-den′dron. Giant sequoia.
Taxodiaceae. Bald cypress family.

A giant conifer with a massive trunk. Only 1 sp., native to the Sierra Nevada in California.

giganteum (p. 196)
Big tree, giant sequoia.
Conifer. Zone 7.
H: 80 ft. S: 25 ft.

Given thousands of years, these famous trees reach massive proportions—more than 300 ft. tall, with trunks 30 ft. in diameter. A young tree in a garden, however, forms a dense erect pyramid, narrow in proportion to its height, with branches all the way to the ground. The gray-green needles are sharply pointed and less than $1/4$ in. long. The thick furrowed bark is dark reddish brown. A good specimen for large lawns or along rural roads. *Sequoia sempervirens,* redwood or coast redwood, is less hardy (Zone 8) but grows faster (3–5 ft. a year). It has flat sprays of dark green foliage and makes a good clipped hedge (plant 3–4 ft. apart).

How to grow: Full sun. Ordinary soil and watering. Tolerates heat and dry soil once established. Allow plenty of room for eventual growth. Needs no maintenance. Trouble-free.

Sidalcea

Si-dal′she-a.
Malvaceae. Mallow family.

Annuals or perennials with clusters of mallowlike 5-petaled flowers. About 20 spp., native to western North America.

malviflora (p. 273)
Prairie mallow, checkerbloom.
Perennial. Zone 5.
H: $2^1/_2$–4 ft. S: $1^1/_2$ ft.

A graceful wildflower with flowers like small hollyhocks, in shades of rose, pink, or lavender. Flowers are 1 in. wide, with 5 silky petals. Blooms for about 2 weeks in June or July. Forms an erect clump of branching stems with deeply lobed leaves. Combines well with salvias, campanulas, and artemisias. There are several cultivars of different heights and flower colors.

How to grow: Full or part sun. Prefers fertile, organic soil. Ordinary watering okay. Likes dry air but doesn't tolerate heat. May need staking. Cut back after bloom. Some strains can be raised from seed. To propagate purchased cultivars, lift in early fall, separate, discard the center, and replant strong divisions from the outside.

Sisyrinchium

Sis-i-ring′kee-um.
Iridaceae. Iris family.

Low-growing perennials with clumps of grassy foliage and small 6-petaled blue, yellow, or white flowers. About 100 spp., nearly all from the New World.

angustifolium
Blue-eyed grass.
Perennial. Zone 5.
H: 12–18 in. S: 6–8 in.

A good wildflower for damp meadows or around ponds or streams. Many star-shaped light blue flowers top the flattened leaflike stems for several weeks between May and July. The grassy foliage is dark green. Individual plants are small, but it self-sows readily and dots a meadow like stars in the sky.

How to grow: Full or part sun. Native to wet sites across the United States, it prefers constantly moist soil. Sow seeds outdoors in fall. Divide big clumps in spring.

bellum (p. 273)
Blue-eyed grass.
Perennial. Zone 8.
H: 6–18 in. S: 6 in.

A California wildflower, native to open grassy sites. The starry flowers, $1/_2$ in. wide, are blue-violet with a yellow throat, borne in clusters on flat winged stalks. Blooms for several weeks in late spring and early summer. The blue-green grassy leaves are semievergreen. Individual plants are small. Mass several to make a showy display in a border.

How to grow: Full or part sun. Tolerates poor or dry soil and hot weather. Easily grown from seed sown outdoors in fall.

striatum (p. 273)
Perennial. Zone 7.
H: $1^1/_2$–$2^1/_2$ ft. S: 1 ft.

The largest and showiest species in the genus, with irislike fans of gray-green leaves up to 1 in. wide and 12 in. long. Blooms in spring, with crowded clusters on tall stalks. Flowers are creamy yellow with purple stripes on the backs of the petals. The foliage and flowers make an unusual and subtle color combination. 'Variegatum' has gray-green leaves striped with cream.

How to grow: Full or part sun. Prefers well-drained but constantly moist soil; tolerates ordinary soil and watering. Looks messy after flowering and can self-sow to excess. Remove the flower stalks and cut the leaves back to 6 in. Fertilize and water to encourage new growth. Divide every 2–3 years in spring.

Skimmia

Skim′ee-a.
Rutaceae. Citrus family.

Evergreen shrubs with fragrant flowers and red berries. Only 5 or 6 spp., native to eastern Asia.

Sisyrinchium angustifolium

japonica (p. 186)
Evergreen shrub. Zone 7.
H: 3–5 ft. S: 3–5 ft.

A neat, low-growing, naturally rounded shrub for shady sites in mild-winter climates. Grows full and compact without pruning. The oblong leaves, 3–5 in. long, are glossy dark green. The clustered white flowers are conspicuously fragrant in spring. Female plants have shiny red berries in winter. Useful in foundation plantings—put it under a window or near the door. *S. reevesiana* stays under 2 ft. tall, with smaller and narrower leaves, and is self-fertile, bearing dark red fruits.

How to grow: Part or full shade. Ordinary soil and watering. Can freeze back in severe Zone 7 winters. Needs no maintenance. No serious pests.

Smilacina

Smy-la-see´na. False Solomon's-seal.
Liliaceae. Lily family.

Perennials with creeping rhizomes, leafy arching stems, and terminal clusters of small flowers. About 30 spp., native to North America and eastern Asia.

Smilacina racemosa

Recommended goldenrods

S. bicolor, or silverrod, has slender clusters of cream or ivory flowers. 18–24 in. tall. Thrives in poor soil.

S. canadensis 'Golden Baby' has canary yellow flowers. Compact, only 24 in. tall, and noninvasive. Blooms early.

S. odora, or sweet goldenrod, has smooth leaves with a strong anise fragrance, sometimes used to make an herbal tea. Bright yellow flowers are showy for a very long season. 2–4 ft. tall. Not reliably hardy above Zone 6.

S. rugosa, or rough-leaved goldenrod, has sturdy stems that branch near the top into many flowering side shoots, making a fountain of gold in fall. 4–5 ft. tall. Doesn't spread as fast as most large goldenrods.

S. sempervirens, or seaside goldenrod, has large clusters of bright yellow flowers. 4–6 ft. tall. Basal leaves are evergreen. Tolerates ocean spray and road salt. Will grow in sandy or marshy soil.

S. sphacelata 'Golden Fleece' has narrow arching clusters of yellow flowers. Heart-shaped basal leaves are semievergreen. 12–18 in. tall. Can be used as a ground cover.

S. vigaurea is a European species sometimes grown in this country. The following cultivars may be hybrids. 'Cloth of Gold' has primrose yellow flowers for months, starting in July, and grows to 18 in. 'Goldenmosa' has fluffy yellow flowers and unusual light green foliage and grows to 30 in. 'Peter Pan' has canary yellow flowers in fall and grows 2–3 ft. tall.

---

racemosa (p. 273)
False Solomon's-seal.
Perennial. Zone 3.
H: 2–3 ft. S: 6–12 in. per year.

A woodland wildflower that spreads slowly to form wide colonies. The pointed leaves, about 6 in. long, are arranged alternately on slender arching stems. Fluffy-looking clusters of tiny white flowers in spring are followed by small berries that slowly ripen from green to red.

How to grow: Shade. Best in deep, loose, acidic, organic soil, moist but well drained. Sow seeds outdoors in fall, or space plants 6–12 in. apart. Increase by dividing older plants into clumps with at least one bud each. Trouble-free.

Solanum

So-lay´num.
Solanaceae. Nightshade family.

A very large and diverse group of herbaceous and woody plants, including potatoes, eggplants, and many poisonous or medicinal species. All have 5-petaled flowers and seedy fruits. About 1,400 spp., native worldwide.

jasminoides (p. 206)
Potato vine.
Semievergreen vine. Zone 10 or 9.
H: 15 ft. or more.

Quickly covers a trellis or wall with a mass of smooth, medium green to purplish leaves. Can also spread on the ground. Blooms prolifically in spring, continuing all year in very mild areas. The blue-white flowers are star-shaped, 1 in. wide, in clusters of 8–12. Though a vigorous grower, potato vine is much easier to control than bougainvillea or other heavy climbers. It is unarmed and easy to renew by hand pruning. *S. rantonnetii* 'Grandiflorum', the blue potato bush, has larger flowers in a dark blue-violet color and can be grown as a climbing vine, spreading ground cover, scrambling shrub, or standard.

How to grow: Full or part sun. Ordinary soil and watering. One plant is enough. Cut back as needed to control size or to remove unattractive tangled growth.

Solidago

Sol-i-day´go. Goldenrod.
Compositae. Composite family.

Perennials with leafy erect stalks and clusters of gold flowers in late summer or fall. About 100 spp., most native to North America.

species and cultivars (p. 274)
Goldenrods.
Perennials. Most are hardy to Zone 4.
H: 1–5 ft. S: at least 2 ft. or more.

Wild goldenrods are so abundant in some parts of the United States that they illuminate whole landscapes in late summer and fall. In the garden, they provide a welcome splash of color when many other plants are finished, and they combine well with heleniums, Joe-Pye weed,

Solidago canadensis

perennial sunflowers, asters, and grasses. They make good fresh cut flowers. Gather just before the flowers open to use for dried arrangements. If not picked or cut back, the dried stalks turn a warm brown and stand up through winter rains and snows.

Goldenrods have spreading rhizomes, dark green foliage, and unbranched stalks topped with fluffy clusters of small flowers. There are dozens of species, available as seeds or plants from native-plant specialists. Selected cultivars and hybrids tend to be more compact and less invasive than the species.

How to grow: Full sun. Most thrive with ordinary soil and watering, but they may spread too fast in rich soil. Many tolerate poor, dry soil. Plants bloom the second year when grown from seed. Easily propagated by dividing the rhizomes in spring. Subject to some insect pests and foliar diseases, none serious. Generally long lived and trouble-free.

Sophora
So-for´ra.
Leguminosae. Pea family.

Deciduous or evergreen trees with alternate compound leaves and showy pealike flowers. Woody pods are constricted between the beanlike seeds. More than 50 spp., native to the Old and New World.

japonica (p. 128)
Pagoda tree, scholar tree.
Deciduous tree. Zone 4.
H: 50–75 ft. S: to 50 ft.

One of the last trees to bloom, it has very showy 6–12-in. clusters of creamy white, mildly fragrant flowers for a few weeks in midsummer. The woody pods, like dry bean pods, are 2–4 in. long. The compound leaves with many oval leaflets are glossy, medium-green above and gray-green below. The flowers and fruits are messy on pavement, but it makes a wonderful lawn specimen. 'Regent' grows faster, has better foliage, and blooms at an early age.

How to grow: Full sun. Ordinary soil and watering. Tolerates heat, dry soil (once established), and urban pollution. Young trees are sensitive to cold. Wrap with burlap for the first year or two and hope for mild winters. Subject to powdery mildew and leafhoppers but generally trouble-free.

secundiflora (p. 186)
Texas mountain laurel, mescal bean.
Evergreen shrub. Zone 7.
H: 10–30 ft. S: 10 ft. or more.

A showy flowering shrub for well-drained sites. Native to Texas. Makes an upright rounded specimen, often with multiple trunks. The compound leaves have thick, glossy, rounded, dark green leaflets. Large purple wisteria-like flowers form clusters 3–9 in. long and have a sweet fruity fragrance like grape Koolaid. The gray pods contain large scarlet seeds, sometimes strung in bead necklaces. The seeds contain poisonous compounds but are too hard to chew and if swallowed accidentally would probably pass undigested. Warn children about them, but don't let them scare you away from planting the tree. *S. affinis,* or Eve's necklace, is another Texas native with smaller, deciduous leaves; long clusters of pink flowers; and long pods that look like a string of black pearls.

How to grow: Full sun. Tolerates poor, unamended soil, including limestone outcrops. Needs good drainage; gets root rot in wet soil. Grows slowly but needs no care. No serious pests.

Sorbus
Sor´bus. Mountain ash.
Rosaceae. Rose family.

Deciduous trees or shrubs with clusters of white flowers in spring and bright berries in fall. About 85 spp., native to the Northern Hemisphere.

alnifolia (p. 128)
Korean mountain ash.
Deciduous tree. Zone 5 or 4.
H: 40–50 ft. S: 20–30 ft.

A small tree with 4-season interest. Flat clusters of white flowers bloom in spring. The oval leaves, 2–4 in. long, are glossy green in summer, bright orange-red in fall. (Leaves are simple, not compound like those of most mountain ashes.) Round red-orange berries, about 1/2 in. in diameter, ripen in fall and hang on into early winter. The smooth gray bark, like that of a beech, is attractive in winter. Makes a fine lawn specimen.

How to grow: Full sun. Ordinary soil and watering. Doesn't tolerate pollution or salt, so avoid urban or roadside sites. Subject to the same diseases and pests as apple trees but is much healthier than the following species.

Sophora japonica

aucuparia (p. 128)
European mountain ash, Rowan tree.
Deciduous tree. Zone 3.
H: 20–40 ft. S: 15–25 ft.

A small tree with very showy clusters of bright red, orange, pink, or yellow fruits in fall. It is familiar and popular in cold-winter regions and can make a handsome lawn specimen, but it is subject to several pests and diseases and can be short lived. The compound leaves have 9–15 small oblong leaflets and are medium green in summer, often turning yellow or red in fall. Flat clusters of malodorous white flowers bloom in May. Birds like the fruits and have spread the tree from gardens to roadsides and fields across Canada and the northern United States.

How to grow: Full sun. Prefers acidic soil. Needs regular watering. Doesn't tolerate heat well. Subject to fire blight, canker, rust, scab, aphids, mites, leafhoppers, borers, scale, and more. Look for existing trees in your area and see if they are healthy before deciding to plant one in your own yard.

Sorghastrum
Sor-gas´trum.
Gramineae. Grass family.

Perennial grasses with narrow leaves, important chiefly as fodder. About 13 spp., mostly from tropical regions.

nutans (p. 215)
(*S. avenaceum*)
Indian grass.
Clumping grass. Zone 4.
H: 3–5 ft. S: 2 ft.

Native to the tall-grass prairie, this grass forms tall narrow clumps that make a good vertical accent or can be massed as a background or screen. The slender leaves are light green or blue in summer, bronze or burnt orange in fall. The thin flower heads open yellow-tan and darken to bronze. They're conspicuous for several weeks in late summer and fall and look graceful in fresh or dried arrangements.

How to grow: Full or part sun. Can get floppy if the soil is too rich and moist but stands up well if grown in lean, dry soil. Tolerates heat but appreciates an occasional watering during long dry spells. Can be propagated by seed or by division. Set out plants in spring or early summer. Cut back once a year, in spring. Pest-free.

Sorghastrum nutans

Spiraea
Spy-ree´a. Spirea.
Rosaceae. Rose family.

Deciduous shrubs with simple alternate leaves and clusters of small white or pink flowers. About 70 spp., native to the north temperate zone.

× *bumalda* cultivars (p. 151)
(now grouped with *S. japonica*)
Deciduous shrubs. Zone 3.
H: to 3 ft. S: 2–4 ft.

These adaptable shrubs grow well in gardens from coast to coast. They form low, twiggy, fine-textured mounds that need little pruning. Leaves are small, usually under 1 in. long. The round flat clusters of dainty little flowers last for several weeks in summer. The following cultivars are the most popular. 'Anthony Waterer' has rosy pink flowers and green foliage. 'Coccinea' is similar but has deeper reddish pink flowers. 'Crispa' has light pink flowers and crinkled toothed leaves

Spiraea japonica

that darken from pinkish to red to green as they mature. 'Goldflame' has crimson flowers and leaves that are pure gold in summer, touched with red and copper in both spring and fall. 'Lime Mound' has light pink flowers and leaves that change from yellow to lime green to orange-red as the season progresses.

How to grow: Full or part sun. Ordinary soil with good drainage and regular watering. Tolerate heat and dry soil but not prolonged drought. Plant from containers in spring or fall, 2 ft. apart. Remove spent blooms to prolong flowering. Prune to shape in early spring. Easy to grow. No serious pests or diseases.

× *cinerea* 'Grefsheim' (p. 151)
Deciduous shrub. Zone 4.
H: 5–6 ft. S: 4–5 ft.

An excellent intermediate-size shrub that makes a fine informal hedge or a graceful specimen. It has an upright arching habit that looks like a surging fountain; in bloom, it's like a fireworks display. Clusters of fragrant small white flowers line the stems before the leaves open in April or May. Foliage is pale green in summer, warm golden yellow in fall. Very useful in a mixed border, where it adds interest in spring, fall, and winter and makes a good background for flowering perennials all summer.

How to grow: Full or part sun. Ordinary soil and watering. Tolerates poor, dry soil. Space 4–5 ft. apart for a hedge. Renew every 3–5 years by cutting the oldest stems to the ground. Doesn't need annual pruning. Pest-free.

japonica (p. 152)
Japanese spirea.
Deciduous shrub. Zone 3.
H: 2–3 ft. S: 2–3 ft. or more.

A compact shrub that blooms in summer, after the other spireas. Stays low and spreads wider than tall; good for foundation planting, edging beds or borders, or containers. It is twiggy and fine-textured, with small dark green leaves. 'Albiflora' has white flowers. 'Little Princess' and 'Nana' (also called 'Alpina') have pink flowers and are very compact, about 1 1/2 ft. tall by 2 ft. wide. 'Shirobana' has a mixture of dark rosy pink, pale pink, and white flowers, all at the same time, and grows 2–3 ft. tall.

How to grow: Like *S. × bumalda.*

nipponica 'Snowmound' (p. 152)
Deciduous shrub. Zone 4.
H: 4 ft. S: 4 ft.

This is a compact bush with arching branches that make a spreading rounded profile. The small thin leaves are blue-green and make a fine-textured background for other plants, but they don't show much fall color. Round clusters of pure white flowers cover the stems in May or June. *S. trilobata* 'Swan Lake' and 'Fairy Queen' are also compact (to 3 ft.), with green foliage and profuse white flowers in May or June.

How to grow: Like *S. × cinerea* 'Grefsheim'. Space 3 ft. apart for mass plantings.

× *vanhouttei* (p. 152)
Deciduous shrub. Zone 4.
H: 6–8 ft. S: 8 ft.

The most commonly planted spirea, very tough and easy to grow. Needs plenty of space for the arching branches to spread into a graceful fountain shape. Makes a big lawn specimen or a wide boundary hedge. (If space is limited, plant a smaller spirea instead of chopping at this one.) Leaves are blue-green with no fall color. Foliage is semievergreen in mild climates. White flowers form rounded clusters that line the branches in May or June.

S. cantoniensis 'Lanceata' (*S. reevesiana*), or bridal-wreath, is a closely related, similar plant but has double flowers like tiny white camellias and is hardy to Zone 5. *S. prunifolia* 'Plena', also called bridal-wreath, is an old favorite, hardy to Zone 4, with small double white flowers in April and dark green leaves that turn orange-red in fall. It grows to 6 ft. but tends to get sparse and leggy; prune every year, right after it blooms, to make it denser and more compact. Both kinds of bridal-wreath make good cut flowers. Gather whole branches just as the flowers open.

How to grow: Like *S.* × *cinerea* 'Grefsheim'.

Sporobolus
Spo-ro′bo-lus. Dropseed.
Gramineae. Grass family.

Annual or perennial grasses, usually clump-forming. Ripe seeds drop out of their hulls. About 100 spp., native to the Old and New World.

heterolopis (p. 215)
Prairie dropseed, northern dropseed.
Clumping grass. Zone 3.
H: 18–24 in. S: 18–24 in.

An excellent plant to start with if you are new to ornamental grasses. It forms an upright arching mound of delicate fine leaves, 2–3 ft. long, emerald green in summer, turning gold with orange tints in fall. The color is stunning in winter. The small delicate flowers are held 2–3 ft. above the foliage in late summer and have a unique fragrance—some compare it to buttered popcorn, others to melted wax! Can be grown as an accent plant, included in foundation plantings or mixed borders, or massed as a ground cover. Makes a good transition between manicured gardens and natural areas. Native to moist prairies.

How to grow: Prefers full sun but tolerates part shade. Thrives with ordinary soil and watering but tolerates dry, rocky soil. Space 18 in. apart for mass planting. Cut back or mow in spring. Sow seeds in fall, or propagate by dividing older plants. Trouble-free.

Stachys
Stay′kis.
Labiatae. Mint family.

Perennials or shrubs with square stems and opposite leaves. Some kinds are used in medicine or cooking. About 300 spp., native to temperate climates.

byzantina (p. 274)
(*S. lanata, S. olympica*)
Lamb's-ears.
Perennial. Zone 5.
H: 8 in. (foliage); to 18 in. (flowers). S: 18 in.

A classic edging plant that forms low mats of woolly white foliage. Helps blend and unify flowers of mixed colors. The ear-shaped leaves, 3–6 in. long, are very soft and thick and semievergreen. Fat stalks of scattered pink or purple flowers develop in late spring or early summer but aren't particularly attractive. Many gardeners remove them or choose 'Silver Carpet', a nonflowering cultivar.

How to grow: Full or part sun in most regions. Tolerates heat but not high humidity. Leaves and stems rot in hot wet weather. Needs well-drained average soil. Water during long dry spells. Space 12–18 in. apart for edging or a small-scale ground cover. Trim back in spring and groom frequently to remove old leaves. Divide in early spring or fall. Subject to a few pests, none too serious.

Stewartia
Stew-art′ee-a.
Theaceae. Tea family.

Deciduous shrubs or small trees with simple alternate leaves and showy white flowers. Only 6 spp., native to eastern North America and eastern Asia.

pseudocamellia var. *koreana* (p. 128)
(*S. koreana, S. pseudocamellia*)
Deciduous tree. Zone 5.
H: 30–40 ft. S: 20 ft.

A perfect small tree for courtyards or patios, with no down time—it is lovely during every season. New spring growth is tinted with purple and maroon; the summer flowers are large and unexpected; fall color is a soft blend of yellow, orange, scarlet, and plum; and the smooth multicolored bark—with blotches of buff, tan, cinnamon, and plum—is without peer. Grows erect with a vase-shaped or spreading crown. The oval leaves are 2–4 in. long, somewhat thick, with slightly quilted venation. Round flowers, 2^1/$_2$ in. wide, have 5 white petals with ruffled edges and a tuft of gold stamens. Position it where every feature can be admired at close range.

S. monadelpha can tolerate more sun and heat. It has similar habit and foliage, with smaller flowers, soft maroon fall color, and flaky cinnamon-colored bark, and is hardy to Zone 6.

S. ovata var. *grandiflora*, or mountain stewartia, is native to the Southeast. It's a wonderful plant, hardy to Zone 6, but not widely available.

Stachys byzantina

**Stewartia pseudocamellia
var. koreana**

It makes a large 15-ft. shrub or can be trained as a small tree. The large (to 4 in. wide) flowers are very showy for about 3 weeks in July or August. They resemble white camellias, with 5 or more crinkled white petals and a prominent tuft of violet-purple stamens. Use it to anchor a perennial border, and choose blue or purple flowers to echo the color of the stamens.

How to grow: Dappled light or part-day shade. Prefers fertile soil amended with plenty of organic matter. Apply a thick layer of organic mulch to keep the roots cool and moist. Water during dry spells. Can't take extremely hot, dry weather. No serious insect or disease problems.

Stokesia

Sto-kee′zhi-a. Stoke's aster.
Compositae. Composite family.

A perennial with blue flowers. Only 1 sp., native to the Southeast.

Stokesia laevis

laevis (p. 274)
Stoke's aster.
Perennial. Zone 5.
H: to 2 ft. S: 1¹/₂ ft.

An old favorite for perennial borders. The asterlike flowers, up to 3 in. wide, are surrounded by a ring of spiny bracts. Cultivars offer different flower colors, including pale and rich blue, lavender-blue, pink, white, and pale yellow. Blooms for 3–5 weeks in summer, and the bracts dry and remain attractive afterward. The long, lance-shaped basal leaves are evergreen. One of the few composites for light shade, where it is striking among ferns or along a path.

How to grow: Sun or part shade. Tolerates poor or dry soil and heat. Avoid wet spots. Increase by division in spring or fall. Carefree and easy to grow.

Strelitzia

Streh-lit′see-a. Bird-of-paradise.
Zingiberaceae. Ginger family.

Tropical plants with giant leaves and showy flowers displayed in a colorful spathe. Only 5 spp., native to South Africa.

reginae (p. 274)
Bird-of-paradise.
Tender perennial. Zone 9.
H: to 5 ft. S: 3–5 ft.

The official flower of Los Angeles, with exotic flowers and tropical-looking foliage. Forms an erect clump of sturdy leaves shaped like large canoe paddles. Leaves overlap at the base, like iris foliage. Very long-lasting orange and blue flowers perch on a leaflike spathe, supported by a long bare stalk. Makes an excellent cut flower. It grows well in large containers, makes a dramatic accent for an entryway, or combines with other tropicals around a pool. *S. nicolai,* the giant bird-of-paradise, forms a clump of leaning or twisting trunks topped with fans of

5–6-ft. leaves and reaches 25–30 ft. Use it for big tropical effects. The blue-and-white flowers aren't as showy.

How to grow: Full or part sun. Needs rich, organic soil. Water and feed heavily until the plant reaches the desired size, then ease off. Remove faded bloom stalks and dead leaves. Large plants can be divided, but the divisions take some time to get established. Recovers slowly from even slight frost damage.

Styrax

Sty′racks. Snowbell.
Styracaceae. Storax family.

Deciduous or evergreen shrubs or trees with simple alternate leaves and white flowers. Resins of some species are used in medicines and flavorings. About 120 spp., native to the Northern Hemisphere. Similar to silverbell (*Halesia* spp.), but silverbells have 5-petaled flowers and winged fruits, whereas snowbells have 4-petaled flowers and round fruits.

japonica (p. 128)
Japanese snowbell.
Deciduous small tree or large shrub. Zone 5.
H: 15–30 ft. S: 10–25 ft.

A pleasant little tree, beautiful in bloom. Dangling clusters of fragrant, bell-shaped, white flowers swing under the branches in May or June. Plant one beside a path or on a hill, where you can look up at the flowers. Forms a rounded crown with horizontal branching. The oval leaves are dark green, up to 3 in. long. The small round fruits aren't very showy and birds ignore them. 'Pink Chimes' has pink flowers. 'Pendula' is a weeping form. *S. obassia,* or fragrant snowbell, grows more upright and has larger leaves (to 8 in.) that are glossy on top and furry underneath. Flowers are larger and open a bit earlier. *S. americanus* and *S. grandifolius* are desirable native species, hardy to Zone 6, but not commonly available.

How to grow: Full sun or part shade. Prefers moist, acidic soil rich in organic matter but tolerates average well-drained soil. Needs regular watering. Needs some pruning and training when young to shape it as a tree rather than as a shrub. Susceptible to stem borers and some leaf-eating insects but generally trouble-free.

Symphoricarpos

Sim-for-i-kar′pos.
Caprifoliaceae. Honeysuckle family.

Hardy deciduous shrubs with thin stems, opposite leaves, small flowers, and showy fruits borne in pairs or small clusters. About 17 spp., all native to the United States except for one Chinese species.

albus (p. 152)
Snowberry.
Deciduous shrub. Zone 3.
H: 3–6 ft. S: 3–6 ft.

Not a sophisticated plant, but a useful one: it thrives where little else will. Grows in almost any soil and tolerates the dry shade under trees. Spreads by suckers and can stabilize a steep bank. Has an upright open habit. The small blue-green leaves are usually oval, sometimes slightly lobed. Clusters of small pinkish flowers appear at the tips of the branches in late spring, and juicy white berries, the size of marbles, are produced in fall. The berries look especially bright against a background of dark evergreens, and they last a few months before birds take them. *S. orbiculatus*, the coralberry or Indian currant, has profuse clusters of small reddish purple berries on arching stems.

How to grow: Sun or shade. Tolerates limestone and dry gravelly soil but not swampy sites. Very easy to move. Prune in early spring so that flowers and subsequent fruits aren't cut off. Remove old stems and unwanted suckers to the ground, and cut the most vigorous shoots back partway to induce branching. Subject to aphids and powdery mildew.

***

Syringa
Sir-ring´a. Lilac.
Oleaceae. Olive family.

Deciduous shrubs or small trees with opposite leaves and clusters of small flowers, often very fragrant. About 25 spp., most native to Asia.

laciniata (p. 152)
Cut-leaf lilac.
Deciduous shrub. Zone 4.
H: 4–6 ft. S: 4–6 ft.

Unusual for its foliage—the leaves are very deeply lobed and finely divided and give an overall lacy effect. Has small clusters of fragrant lilac flowers all along the branches in spring. Makes a graceful small shrub with a rounded bushy shape. Foliage is fairly mildew-resistant. Tolerates hot weather.

How to grow: Full or part sun. Ordinary soil and watering. Add lime to acidic soil. Prune after flowering, removing spent blooms. Can be rejuvenated by cutting to the ground in early spring.

meyeri 'Palibin' (p. 152)
Dwarf lilac, dwarf Meyer lilac.
Deciduous shrub. Zone 4.
H: 6–8 ft. S: 6–8 ft.

A compact lilac with many advantages. It starts blooming when very young, making 4-in. clusters of lilac to lavender flowers with excellent fragrance. It blooms profusely for 2 weeks in midspring and often repeats in September. The neat small leaves resist mildew and sometimes develop fall color.

How to grow: Like *S. laciniata*.

patula 'Miss Kim' (p. 152)
(*S. palibiniana, S. velutina*)
Miss Kim lilac.
Deciduous shrub. Zone 4.
H: 4–8 ft. S: 3–5 ft.

Another compact lilac that won't outgrow its space. Plant it near a window or porch so you can smell it often when it flowers. Blooms reliably each year in early summer, with pale lavender-blue flowers in 3-in. clusters. The mildew-resistant leaves are dark green in summer and turn purple in fall.

How to grow: Like *S. laciniata*.

reticulata (p. 129)
Japanese tree lilac.
Deciduous tree or large shrub. Zone 3.
H: to 30 ft. S: 15–25 ft.

A showy tree for northern gardens. Can be single-trunked or multitrunked, with an upright oval crown. Has large fluffy clusters of creamy white flowers for about 2 weeks in June. The flowers are quite fragrant, but they smell like privet, not like common lilacs. The 5-in. oval leaves are fairly disease-resistant but have no fall color. The cherrylike bark adds winter interest; it is smooth, glossy, and reddish brown, with small white horizontal marks. *S. pekinensis* has similar flowers, foliage, and bark but usually grows only 15–20 ft. tall.

How to grow: Full sun. Average well-drained soil and regular watering. Grows well in the Midwest but can't take hot summers in the South or Southwest. Remove spent blooms and prune to shape after flowering. Rejuvenate by cutting old stems to the ground in late winter or early spring. Generally vigorous and trouble-free.

vulgaris (p. 153)
Common lilac.
Deciduous shrub. Zone 4.
H: to 20 ft. S: to 15 ft.

Sentimental favorites for their sweet fragrance, lilacs have big clusters of single or double flowers in mid- to late spring. An individual plant's buds and flowers are colorful for several weeks, and some cultivars open earlier or later than others. Colors include lilac, violet, blue, purple, magenta, pink, and white. Most grow quickly, with many upright stems and ascending branches. The dark green leaves are oval or heart-shaped, 3–5 in. long, with no fall color.

There are hundreds of cultivars of *S. vulgaris* and some hybrids between this and other species. Favorites include 'Alphonse Lavalle' (double lilac), 'Charles Joly' (double magenta), 'Ellen Willmott' (double white), 'Lucie Baltet' (single rose-pink), 'Monge' (single deep purple), 'President Lincoln' (single blue), 'Primrose' (single creamy yellow), and 'Sensation' (single purple with white picotee edge).

The cultivars listed above, like most common lilacs, have a "chilling" requirement—they need several weeks of cold weather to induce flowering. This limits their use in mild-winter climates. The Descanso hybrids, developed in

Symphoricarpos albus

Syringa vulgaris

southern California, bloom reliably even where winters are warm. 'Lavender Lady', with fragrant lavender flowers, is the most popular and widely available. 'Blue Skies' is a rapid grower with light lavender-blue flowers. 'Angel White' has fragrant white flowers. Although developed for warm climates, these are hardy to Zone 4.

Common lilacs are widely planted but sometimes difficult specimens. They may seem carefree, because old plants persist for decades with absolutely no care around farmhouses in the Northeast and Upper Midwest. Planted in a garden, however, where you see them every day, you'll note that they are easily stressed by heat or drought and prone to mildew, borers, and other plagues. They get leggy at the base and offer little interest when not in bloom. Before planting a common lilac, consider the less common species described above.

How to grow: Like *S. laciniata*.

Tabebuia

Ta-be-bew´ee-a.
Bignoniaceae. Trumpet creeper family.

Chiefly tropical trees and shrubs, some harvested for valuable timber. Most have palmately compound leaves and large clusters of showy trumpet-shaped flowers. About 100 spp., native from Mexico to South America.

chrysotricha (p. 129)
Golden trumpet tree.
Semievergreen tree. Zone 9.
H: to 25 ft. S: to 25 ft.

A very showy small tree for warm climates. The bright green compound leaves have 5 leaflets 2–4 in. long. The leaves drop briefly in spring, when masses of scentless, bright yellow flowers make a dazzling display. Flowers reappear, a few at a time, through summer or fall.

How to grow: Full sun. Ordinary soil and watering. Tolerates dry soil once well established. Needs only routine training and pruning. Trouble-free.

Tagetes

Tay-gee´teez, taj´eh-tees. Marigold.
Compositae. Composite family.

Annuals or perennials with strong-scented leaves, mostly opposite and usually finely dissected. The composite flowers are most often yellow. About 50 spp., one from Africa, the rest from Central and South America.

erecta (p. 304)
African marigold.
Annual. All zones.
H: to 3 ft. S: to 2 ft.

Provides easy summer color for bedding, edging, and planters. The big bushy plants have many erect branched stems covered with smooth, green, pinnately divided leaves. The rounded, double flower heads are 2–5 in. wide, in shades of yellow, orange, or creamy white. Blooms nonstop from early summer to frost. Many strains are available as seeds or bedding plants.

How to grow: Full sun. Ordinary soil and watering. Direct-sow seeds, or start indoors 6–8 weeks before last frost. Plant outdoors after the soil has started to warm. Pinch off the tips and the first few flowers to promote bushiness. Leggy or top-heavy plants are liable to tip over in summer storms. Deadheading helps improve the appearance and prolong bloom. Marigolds are generally pest-free, but Japanese beetles will eat the flowers. Wet soil, humid air, and excess rain can rot the roots, foliage, and flowers.

lemmonii (p. 274)
Mexican bush marigold.
Tender perennial. Zone 9.
H: 3–6 ft. S: 3–6 ft.

A bushy plant with many erect and/or sprawling stems. The evergreen foliage has a strong marigold odor. The dark green leaves are pinnately divided into many narrow leaflets. Bright orange-yellow daisylike blossoms, 1 in. wide, are borne in clusters at the branch ends. Bloom continues all year but is heaviest in winter and spring. Popular in southwestern gardens, combined with rosemaries, lavenders, artemisias, and other Mediterranean and native plants.

How to grow: Full or part sun. Ordinary soil and watering. Tolerates dry soil once established. Prune to improve shape and to prevent sprawl. Hard frost will kill it, but it survives mild winters. Trouble-free.

lucida (p. 289)
Mexican mint marigold.
Perennial herb. Zone 8 or 7.
H: to 3 ft. S: to 3 ft.

A good substitute for French tarragon in hot climates. The foliage, stems, and flowers have a rich anise fragrance and flavor and can be used for tea or seasoning. Makes a bushy clump of erect stems covered with narrow leaves about 1 in. long. May be evergreen in mild winters. Has small, single, yellow blossoms in summer and fall.

How to grow: Full or part sun. Average well-drained soil. Harvest leaves whenever you choose. Cut back to the ground in early spring. Grows well as an annual and produces plenty of fragrant foliage but few flowers in northern gardens. Doesn't overwinter well indoors, so start from seed or buy a new plant each year.

patula (p. 304)
French marigold.
Annual. All zones.
H: 6–18 in. S: 6–18 in.

More compact than African marigold, with several dwarf cultivars, this is a favorite edging or bedding plant. The smooth, aromatic, dark green leaves have many toothed segments. The single or double flower heads, 1–3 in. wide, come in shades of yellow, orange, red, mahogany, or bicolor. Flowers from early summer until frost whether you deadhead it or not.

How to grow: Like *T. erecta*.

***tenuifolia* 'Lemon Gem'** (p. 304)
(*T. pumila*)
Lemon gem marigold.
Annual. All zones.
H: to 8 in. S: to 8 in.

Less familiar than African or French marigolds but just as easy to grow. This makes a bushy ball of delicate lacy foliage with a lemony fragrance. Blooms profusely until frost. The single blossoms have the charm of wildflowers, in a shade of clear yellow that combines with other colors more easily than the typical gold of most marigolds does. Use it to fill the gaps in a border, for edging, or in containers.

How to grow: Like *T. erecta.*

Tanacetum
Tan-a-see´tum.
Compositae. Composite family.

Annuals or perennials with strong-scented foliage and composite flowers. Closely related to *Chrysanthemum*, and some species keep getting shifted back and forth. 50–70 spp., most native to the Old World.

vulgare (p. 289)
Tansy.
Perennial herb. Zone 4.
H: to 3 ft. S: 3 ft. or more.

A strong-scented plant with pungent dark green foliage, formerly used medicinally. Now organic gardeners brew a tea from the leaves and spray it on other plants to repel insect pests. Forms a clump of basal leaves and several tall stems topped with flat clusters of many buttonlike flower heads, about 1/2 in. wide. Flowers are bright golden yellow. Var. *crispum* is prettier than average, with crisp-textured, finely divided leaves.

How to grow: Full or part sun. Grows in any well-drained soil. Tolerates poor, dry soil. Spreads fast by underground runners and is invasive in most garden beds. Easily propagated by division in spring or fall. Trouble-free.

Taxodium
Tax-oh´dee-um. Bald cypress.
Taxodiaceae. Bald cypress family.

Only 3 spp. of deciduous or semievergreen conifers, native to the southeastern United States and Mexico.

distichum (p. 196)
Bald cypress.
Deciduous conifer. Zone 5.
H: to 100 ft. S: to 30 ft.

An adaptable tree, native to swampy sites in the Southeast but well suited to other soils and regions. Grows quickly, making a narrow upright cone when young, spreading wider with old age. The flat needlelike leaves, about 1/2 in. long, are soft yellow-green in spring, dark green in summer, and turn rusty red before dropping in late fall. Small round cones and fibrous

reddish brown bark are conspicuous in winter. In waterlogged soil, the roots make woody "knees" that stick up like fire hydrants. Even in average soil, surface roots can interfere with lawn mowing. *T. ascendens,* the pond cypress, is very similar but grows more narrowly upright. *T. mucronatum,* or Montezuma cypress, has spreading limbs and makes a broader crown. It grows very quickly and has semievergreen foliage. Native to Mexico, it is under trial for hardiness and adaptability.

How to grow: Full sun. Prefers fertile, moist, well-drained soil but grows well in average garden soil. Tolerates standing water, but established trees can also survive dry conditions. Use only container-grown plants; volunteer seedlings don't transplant well. Needs little pruning. No common pests or diseases.

Taxodium distichum

Taxus
Tax´us. Yew.
Taxaceae. Yew family.

Conifers with dense fine-grained timber, flat needlelike leaves, and fleshy red or brown fruits with one hard seed inside. The foliage and seeds contain poisonous compounds. Only 7 spp., native to the Old and New World.

cultivars (pp. 196, 197)
Conifers. Hardiness varies.
H: varies. S: varies.

Yews are among the most popular and versatile evergreens for hedges, backgrounds, and foundation plantings. Most are slow-growing, with dense, dark green foliage. They tolerate repeated pruning and are often sheared into formal shapes. Needles are flat and narrow, under 1 in. long, with pointed tips. Male plants produce a cloud of pollen in spring. Females bear fruits in fall. The foliage and seeds of all yews contain dangerously poisonous compounds, but birds eat the fruits safely because the seeds are so hard that they pass undigested.

Nearly all the yews grown in this country are cultivars of *T. baccata*, the English yew, or *T. cuspidata,* the Japanese yew, or are hybrids between those species, classified as *T. × media,* the hybrid yew or AngloJap yew. The cultivars differ in cold-hardiness, ultimate size, habit, rate of growth, foliage color, ability to retain good foliage color during cold weather, and berry production (only female clones set fruit). Yews are a long-term landscape investment, so consider all of these attributes when choosing which cultivar to plant.

How to grow: Full sun, part sun, or shade. Yews tolerate more shade than other conifers do and grow well on the north or east side of a building. They need good drainage and tolerate dry sites, such as that difficult area next to a house foundation and under a roof overhang. Soil can be neutral or moderately acidic or alkaline. Plant container-grown or balled-and-burlapped plants in spring or fall. Water regularly for the first year or two, until plants are

Taxus baccata 'Repandens'

Recommended yew cultivars

Cultivars of *T. baccata* have the darkest green—sometimes almost black—foliage but are reliably hardy only to Zone 6. 'Adpressa' has short dark green needles, red fruits, and spreading branches and grows wider than tall. 'Repandens' is another spreading form, growing 2–3 ft. tall and several feet wide, with dark green needles that are larger than those of most yews. 'Fastigiata', or 'Stricta', often called Irish yew, grows narrowly upright into a dense column of foliage, about one-fourth as wide as it is tall, and reaches 20 ft. or taller.

Most cultivars of *T. cuspidata* are hardy to Zone 4. Needles are medium or dark green in summer but may discolor to a dirty tan or brown on exposed sites in winter. 'Capitata' is commonly sold, but it has drawbacks: its foliage turns bronze in winter, and it gets too big, too fast, for foundation plantings—it can reach 25 ft. or more. Use it for tall screens or hedges. 'Columnaris' is even better for hedges, because it grows more narrowly upright, stays green in winter, and sets red berries. There are several slow-growing, spreading forms, good for foundation plantings. 'Greenwave' forms a low mound with arching branches. 'Nana' is very dense and spreads about twice as wide as it is tall. Both have good green winter color.

The most common and popular yews are cultivars of *T. × media*. Most are hardy to Zone 5 or 4. 'Brownii' is a dense, rounded, spreading form that can reach 8 ft. tall but is easily kept shorter by pruning. 'Densiformis' grows fast into a spreading mound, twice as wide as it is tall but low enough to fit under windows. Its new growth turns bronze in winter. 'Hatfield' ('Hatfieldii') is good for hedging. It grows slowly, makes a broad dense pyramid up to 12 ft. tall, and stays bright green all year. 'Hicksii' is similar to *T. baccata* 'Fastigiata' but hardier. It's narrowly upright and fast-growing, with dark green needles and red fruits.

well established. Yews are affected by a few pests and diseases, but they are generally trouble-free.

Yews tolerate and respond well to repeated pruning, but you can minimize the need for pruning by choosing cultivars of appropriate size, habit, and rate of growth. If you do want a formal, neatly sheared effect, clip new growth after it has lengthened but before it has hardened. Otherwise, an occasional trimming to remove stray or damaged shoots will suffice.

Old overgrown plants will recover if you cut them back to 1–2-ft. stumps, but they'll look as ugly as a bad haircut in the meantime. Rather than trying to salvage an outdated foundation planting, consider digging it out and replacing the overgrown plants with compact new ones.

Tecoma

Te-ko´ma.
Bignoniaceae. Trumpet creeper family.
Shrubs or small trees with compound leaves and bright yellow flowers. Only 12 spp., native from the southwestern United States through South America.

stans (p. 186)

Yellowbells.
Semievergreen shrub. Zone 8 or 7.
H: to 20 ft. S: to 10 ft.
A fast-growing, long-flowering shrub for California and the Southwest. The compound leaves with many toothed leaflets look crisp and fresh all season. Clusters of large, bell-shaped, yellow flowers are borne at the branch ends from spring to late fall. Makes a very showy specimen and requires little care.

How to grow: Full or part sun. Prefers dry, well-drained soil. Water deeply every few weeks in warm weather. In colder areas, withhold water in late summer and fall to suspend new growth, which is frost-tender. May freeze to the ground in cold winters but regrows fast enough to use as a seasonal hedge. Even if it doesn't freeze back, it's a good idea to prune it to the ground in early spring: the new growth is most attractive and bears the flowers. Trouble-free.

Ternstroemia

Tern-stro´mee-a.
Theaceae. Tea family.
Evergreen shrubs or trees with leathery leaves and 5-petaled flowers. About 85 spp., native to tropical regions in the Old and New World.

gymnanthera (p. 187)

(often sold as *Cleyera japonica*)
Evergreen shrub. Zone 7.
H: 4 ft. or more. S: 4 ft. or more.
A low rounded shrub, very useful for foundation planting. The glossy foliage is deep green in shade, turning reddish purple in full sun, especially during cold weather. The oval leaves, 3 in. long, are arranged in rosettelike tufts at the ends of the twigs. It has yellow flowers, small but fragrant, in summer. Red-orange berries ripen in fall.

How to grow: Full sun, part sun, or shade; if planted in full sun, give it plenty of water. The soil should be acidic, fertile, well drained, and moist, as for camellias and azaleas. Grows slowly and develops a nice shape with little pruning. Generally pest-free.

Teucrium

Too´kri-um. Germander.
Labiatae. Mint family.
Perennials or small shrubs with square stems, opposite leaves, and clusters of small 2-lipped flowers. Several species have aromatic foliage with various medicinal uses. About 100 spp., native worldwide.

chamaedrys (p. 289)

Germander.
Shrubby perennial herb. Zone 5.
H: 1 ft. S: 1 ft.
A bushy little plant with lots of shiny scalloped leaves. The pungent semievergreen foliage

was formerly used medicinally. It responds well to pruning and makes a neat edging or mini-hedge around rose beds or herb gardens. Unpruned, it makes a low mound that combines well with other Mediterranean herbs, heaths and heathers, or dwarf conifers. The clusters of small purple flowers are showy and attract bees for a few weeks in midsummer. Herb nurseries offer a few other species of germanders, some low and spreading, some larger and erect. Most are aromatic, attractive, and trouble-free.

How to grow: Full or part sun. Needs good drainage. Tolerates poor, dry soil and hot weather. Shear after flowering to keep it compact, and shear or trim to renew plants in early spring. Propagate by seed or by division in spring. Pest-free.

Thalictrum

Tha-lick´trum. Meadow rue.
Ranunculaceae. Buttercup family.

Perennials with delicate-textured compound leaves and big clusters of tiny flowers. About 85 spp., native worldwide.

aquilegifolium (p. 275)
Columbine meadow rue.
Perennial. Zone 4.
H: 2–3 ft. S: 2 ft.

A graceful plant for wood's edge or mixed border. Makes a lacy mound of basal foliage with many small, scalloped, blue-green leaflets. The foliage is attractive all season and provides a soft background for spring-flowering bulbs or summer lilies. The tall hollow stalks branch near the top to bear countless fluffy round clusters of tiny flowers with no petals but with many purple, pink, or white stamens. They are showy for about 2 weeks in late spring or early summer. 'Purpureum' has dark purple stems and flowers; 'White Cloud' has white flowers; 'Roseum' has rosy pink flowers.

Perennial nurseries sometimes offer several other species of *Thalictrum*. *T. delavayi* (*T. dipterocarpum*), or Yunan meadow rue, has tiny mauve flowers with pale yellow stamens and grows to 5 ft. *T. rochebrunianum* 'Lavender Mist' has rosy purple flowers with yellow stamens and grows 4–6 ft. tall. *T. speciosissimum* (also sold as *T. flavum* or *T. glaucum*) has especially attractive blue-green foliage and large fluffy heads of sulphur yellow flowers on stalks 3–5 ft. tall. It tolerates hot, dry weather better than other meadow rues do.

Thalictrum rochebrunianum

How to grow: Morning sun is best. Prefers fertile soil amended with organic matter, well drained and moisture-retentive. Space plants 18 in. apart and mulch well. Flower stalks may need staking. Cut them back after bloom. May self-sow, or can be divided in early spring. Unless you want more plants, established clumps can go 4–5 years without being divided. No serious pests.

Thelypteris

Thel-ip´ter-is.
Polypodiaceae. Polypody family.

Clumping ferns with finely divided fronds. Formerly grouped with *Dryopteris*. Only 2 spp., native to tropical regions.

kunthii (p. 219)
(*Dryopteris normalis*)
Wood fern.
Deciduous fern. Zone 8 or 7.
H: to 3 ft. S: 3 ft. or more.

One of the best ferns for southern gardens. The fine-textured fronds are divided into many long, slender segments. Green all summer, they turn brown after hard frost but stand up until spring. Spreads steadily by rhizomes but isn't invasive. Makes a good ground cover for shady corners, along the north or east side of a building, or under evergreen trees such as live oaks or southern magnolias.

How to grow: Part or full shade. Ordinary soil and watering. Shaded plants are quite drought-tolerant; the more sun they get, the more water they need. Propagate by division in spring or fall. Trim fronds to the ground in early spring.

Thermopsis montana

Thermopsis

Ther-mop´sis.
Leguminosae. Pea family.

Upright perennials with trifoliate leaves and tall spikes of showy flowers in spring. More than 20 spp., native to North America and Asia.

caroliniana (p. 275)
(*T. villosa*)
Carolina lupine.
Perennial. Zone 4.
H: 3–6 ft. S: 3 ft.

A carefree, long-lived wildflower for sunny sites. The erect stalks are topped with 8–12-in. spikes of bright yellow pealike flowers for 1–2 weeks in late spring. The show of color is brief but intense. The flat fuzzy pods and smooth gray-green leaflets are handsome for the rest of the season. Combines well with other native wildflowers and grasses, or makes a specimen for the back of the border. *T. montana*, or golden banner, is a western species that looks similar but grows only 3 ft. tall.

How to grow: Full sun. Grows best in well-drained, fertile, organic soil but does very well in poor, dry soil. May need staking in rich, moist soil or if partly shaded. Difficult to divide and does not transplant well. Choose where to put it, then plant it and leave it alone. A clump can go for years with minimal care, slowly spreading wider. Trouble-free.

Thuja

Thew´ya. Arborvitae.
Cupressaceae. Cypress family.

Tall evergreen conifers, usually with scalelike foliage arranged in flat fans or sprays. Only 5 spp., native to eastern Asia and North America, and hundreds of selected cultivars.

occidentalis (pp. 196, 197)
American arborvitae, eastern white cedar.
Conifer. Zone 3.
H: 40–60 ft. S: 10–15 ft.

A useful evergreen for the Northeast and Upper Midwest, with fewer pest and disease problems than pines, spruces, or firs. Selected cultivars are popular for hedges and screens, shelter belts, and foundation planting. The rich green foliage is quite fragrant when crushed. The tiny scalelike leaves are arranged in flat sprays that tilt in all directions. Seedling trees and some cultivars are prone to winterburn and turn dingy tan or brown if damaged by cold dry winds or bright winter sun. Except where noted, the cultivars described in the box stay rich green all winter. The small woody cones have overlapping scales that open in midwinter. Chickadees, nuthatches, and other birds eat the seeds.

How to grow: Needs sun; gets loose and leggy if grown in shade. Ordinary soil and watering. Tolerates moist, heavy, or clay soil but not dry or sandy soil. Easy to transplant in spring or fall. Responds well to pruning, but dwarf cultivars don't need it. The most common problem is winter storm damage. Heavy wet snows can open up the center and spread the leaders apart or leave them sprawling on the ground. Prevent this by using wire or rot-resistant twine to tie the leaders together in several places. Susceptible to bagworms and spider mites but generally trouble-free. Suffers in hot summers and doesn't do well across the southern United States.

orientalis **cultivars** (p. 196)
(called *Platycladus orientalis* by some botanists but few gardeners)
Oriental arborvitae.
Conifer. Zone 6.
H: varies. S: varies.

The best arborvitae for gardens across the southern United States. They're not as cold-hardy, but they tolerate hot dry weather and alkaline soil better than *T. occidentalis* does. Form a core of upright stems with many horizontal limbs that branch into flat vertical sprays of tiny twigs, densely covered with scaly or prickly foliage. The foliage has only a slight fragrance. Odd fleshy cones have a bumpy surface and might be confused with insect galls. They are blue-green for several months, turning brown when they mature.

The following cultivars are popular for hedges, specimens, and foundation plantings. 'Aurea Nana' ('Golden Ball') is a compact dwarf that makes a rounded cone about 3 ft. tall. The golden foliage turns bronze in winter. 'Beverlyensis' makes an upright rounded cone, up to 10 ft. tall. Foliage is lime green tipped with yellow, turning bronze in winter. 'Fruitlandii' is conical, 4–6 ft. tall, with rich green foliage. 'Juniperoides' is conical, 4–6 ft. tall, with feathery gray-green foliage that turns plum-purple in winter. 'Westmont' makes a small dense cone, slowly growing to 2–3 ft. Foliage is deep green tipped with yellow, turning bronze in winter.

How to grow: Full sun or afternoon shade. Not fussy about soil. Prefer regular watering but tolerate dry soil once established. Easy to transplant in spring or fall. Respond well to pruning, but dwarf cultivars don't need it. Trees split apart in heavy snow or ice storms. Susceptible to bagworms and spider mites. Hose the foliage to remove dust and dirt that collects during dry weather or in urban conditions.

plicata (p. 197)
Western arborvitae, giant arborvitae.
Conifer. Zone 5.
H: 50–70 ft. S: 15–25 ft.

A magnificent evergreen, native to the Pacific Northwest, where it can reach 200 ft. tall.

Cultivars of American arborvitae

'Aurea' ('Golden') is bright yellow in summer, bronzy in winter, and grows to about 3 ft. tall and wide.

'Emerald' ('Smaragd') makes a narrow cone up to 15 ft. tall, with vertical sprays of emerald green foliage.

'Hetz Midget' starts out like a basketball, grows only 1–2 in. per year, and eventually matures at 3 ft. tall and wide.

'Nigra' has dark green foliage and makes a conical tree up to 25 ft. or taller but is easily maintained as a tall hedge.

'Rheingold' makes a small cone of foliage in metallic shades of gold, copper, and bronze. Sometimes seen with prickly (juvenile) rather than scaly (adult) foliage. Usually under 5 ft.

'Techny' ('Mission') has excellent green color in winter and makes a broad-based pyramid 10–15 ft. tall.

'Wintergreen' is not as fine-textured as other cultivars, but it makes a narrow column with a single leader, which minimizes snow damage. Reaches 15 ft. or more.

'Woodwardii' is a naturally rounded form that grows to 8 ft. or more. Common and popular for specimens and hedges but subject to winterburn.

Does well in gardens throughout the Upper Midwest, Great Lakes, and Northeast. Young trees grow fast and make a narrow cone or pyramid. Older trees slow down and spread wider. Flat fans of fragrant, ferny-looking foliage spread from the graceful drooping branches. Foliage is glossy bright green in summer, turning golden brown in cold winters. Holds its branches and foliage all the way to the ground unless you remove them. Makes a lovely specimen or tall hedge and has three important virtues: it is deer-resistant, perhaps even deer-proof; it has a single leader, so it doesn't fall apart in the snow; and it is more shade-tolerant than other arborvitae. There are dwarf, columnar, golden, and variegated cultivars, but the species is most commonly available.

How to grow: Full sun or part shade. Ordinary soil and watering. Tolerates heavy clay soil and alkaline conditions. Can't take extreme heat or dryness. Easy to transplant but may pause a year or two before it regains speed. Needs no pruning. Subject to bagworms but generally trouble-free.

Thymus

Thy′mus. Thyme.
Labiatae. Mint family.

Perennials or small shrubs with very small opposite leaves and clusters of small white, pink, rosy red, or purple flowers. Most are aromatic and can be used as seasoning. About 350 spp., native to Europe and Asia.

vulgaris

Common thyme.
Perennial herb. Zone 4.
H: to 12 in. S: to 8 in.

A bushy little plant, woody at the base, with many erect wiry stems covered with fragrant semievergreen foliage. The small rounded leaves are gray or gray-green. Masses of tiny lilac flowers attract bees in summer. Fresh or dried thyme leaves are indispensable for cooking, but fragrance and flavor vary widely among seedlings and cultivars. Raise your own seedlings if you want several plants to make a low edging or mini-hedge, but go to the nursery and sniff the leaves to choose a good specimen for a kitchen herb garden.

How to grow: Full sun. Well-drained average soil. Established plants can tolerate considerable dryness but can't take soggy soil, especially in winter. A raised bed or south-facing slope is ideal. Use sand or gravel, rather than organic material, as a mulch. Where winters are cold and windy but snow is unreliable, cover plants with pine boughs in early winter to limit dieback (unprotected plants survive but recover slowly). Cut back in early spring, removing frost damage and old woody stems. Shear after flowering to reduce self-seeding and to promote new growth. No common insect pests, but leaves and roots may rot in wet soil, in humid weather, or if shaded by neighboring plants.

other thymes (p. 289)

There are dozens of species and hundreds of cultivars of thyme. Some are used for flavoring or fragrance. Others are valued for their handsome foliage and masses of tiny but colorful flowers. *T. × citriodorus,* or lemon thyme, makes a low spreading mound of glossy dark green leaves with a distinct lemony fragrance; the cultivar 'Aureus' has leaves with yellow edges. *T. herba-barona,* or caraway thyme, has caraway-flavored dark green leaves, and spreads to make a good ground cover. *T. pseudolanuginosus,* or woolly thyme, makes a very flat mat of fuzzy silver-gray foliage; fragrance and flowers are secondary to its woolliness. Various forms of *T. pulegioides,* or mother-of-thyme, are often sold as *T. serpyllum;* most are vigorous spreaders, showy in bloom, with fragrant foliage. This species has naturalized in parts of New England and grows well in meadows and lawns.

How to grow: Like *T. vulgaris.*

Tiarella

Tee-a-rel′a.
Saxifragaceae. Saxifrage family.

Low-growing perennials with clusters of small white or pinkish flowers in spring. Only a few spp., all but one native to North America.

cordifolia (p. 275)

Foamflower.
Perennial. Zone 3.
H: 6–12 in. S: 12–18 in.

An excellent ground cover or edging for a woodland garden or shady border. Spreads by underground runners that send up little clumps of semievergreen foliage. The lobed leaves are 4 in. wide, hairy on top and downy underneath. Plump spikes of white or pinkish flowers are held above the foliage for several weeks in late spring. Combines well with spring-flowering bulbs, trilliums, columbines, anemones, and ferns. A woodland wildflower, native to the eastern United States. *T. wherryi* makes clumps and doesn't spread. Its leaves are more deeply indented, and the flowers are usually pink and bloom later in the season.

How to grow: Part sun or shade (where grown in part sun, the leaves turn red or reddish purple in fall). Not for hot, dry climates. Plant 12 in. apart in cool, moist, acidic, humus-rich soil and mulch lightly. Increase by division; separate and replant rooted runners in spring or fall. Trouble-free.

Tilia

Till′ee-a. Linden, basswood.
Tiliaceae. Linden family.

Deciduous trees with large alternate leaves, fibrous inner bark, versatile white timber, and fragrant flowers that dangle from the middle of a leafy bract. About 45 spp., native to the north temperate zone.

Tiarella cordifolia

cordata (p. 129)
Littleleaf linden.
Deciduous tree. Zone 3.
H: to 50 ft. S: to 30 ft.

An adaptable and attractive tree that forms a dense fine-textured crown and casts plenty of shade. In Europe, this tree is used successfully for tall formal hedges that are pruned into outdoor "walls." Here, it is grown mostly as a lawn specimen or street tree. Leaves are nearly round with a pointed tip, 1 1/2–3 in. long, dark green above and silvery below, turning yellow in fall. Very fragrant flowers dangle in small clusters from the center of a leaflike stalk. Europeans dry the flowers to make a fragrant tea. Bees visit the flowers and make a tasty honey. Mature trees can spread to shade a large area, but the shade is so dense that it's hard to grow grass underneath. Cultivars such as 'Greenspire' and 'Chancellor' develop narrower, more upright crowns.

How to grow: Full sun. Ordinary soil and watering. Tolerates heat (if the soil is moist), alkaline soil, and air pollution. Specimen trees need only routine pruning. Subject to aphids, which produce messy, sticky honeydew. Japanese beetles may attack the foliage and flowers.

other lindens (p. 129)
T. × *euchlora,* or Crimean linden, resembles European linden but has graceful, somewhat drooping branches, a more open crown, and larger leaves. It is less susceptible to aphid infestations. Hardy to Zone 3.

T. americana, the American linden or basswood, is fairly common throughout the central and eastern United States. It can reach 80 ft. tall and 50 ft. wide. The heart-shaped leaves, with toothed edges, are about 6 in. long. It's good for large open sites but grows too big, too fast for most suburban lots. Hardy to Zone 3. *T. tomentosa,* or silver linden, has rounded leaves 3–5 in. long, dark green above and silvery white below. The shimmering foliage is gorgeous on a breezy day. Tolerates heat and drought better than other lindens do but is hardy only to Zone 6.

How to grow: Like *T. cordata.*

Tithonia
Ti-tho′nee-a. Mexican sunflower.
Compositae. Composite family.

Fast-growing annuals, perennials, or shrubs with large coarse leaves and bright orange or gold blossoms. About 10 spp., native to Latin America.

rotundifolia (p. 304)
Mexican sunflower.
Tender perennial grown as an annual. All zones.
H: 6 ft. S: 3–4 ft.

Use this for a quick specimen or temporary hedge or screen. Seedlings quickly develop into leafy bush-sized plants with many branching stems. The large green leaves are covered with soft hairs. The dark orange blossoms, about 3 in. wide, resemble single zinnias or small sunflowers. Hummingbirds come for the nectar, and finches eat the seeds. There's no way to tone down the color, so go ahead and combine it with other orange, red, and gold flowers and call it a fiesta garden.

How to grow: Full sun. Ordinary soil and watering. Thrives in hot, dry weather. Plants growing in rich, moist soil get soft and may flop over in summer storms. Direct-sow when the soil is warm, or start indoors 4–6 weeks before last frost. Blooms all summer without deadheading. Trouble-free.

Trachelospermum
Tra-kel-o-sper′mum.
Apocynaceae. Dogbane family.

Woody vines with twining stems, evergreen leaves, milky sap, and fragrant 5-petaled flowers. About 20 spp., all but one native to southeastern Asia.

asiaticum (p. 207)
Asian jasmine.
Evergreen vine. Zone 8.
H: 12 in. (as a ground cover).

This tough evergreen vine doesn't climb well, but it spreads to make an impermeable ground cover. The woody stems tangle into a dense mat covered with glossy dark green foliage. The small rounded or oval leaves are stiff and waxy. Usually doesn't produce flowers. Useful on slopes or trailing over the edge of raised beds. Can be interplanted with daffodils, tulips, or other spring bulbs. Grows well around the base of trees and shrubs.

How to grow: Sun or shade. Not fussy about soil. Tolerates heat and drought. Space small plants 6 in. apart; put 1-gal. plants 2 ft. apart. Regular mowing will keep it from spreading into an adjacent lawn. Mow or shear in late winter to renew established plantings and to keep them from getting too leggy and woody. Although sometimes sold and planted in Zone 7, it is badly damaged by severe winters there. No serious insect or disease problems.

jasminoides (p. 207)
Confederate jasmine, star jasmine.
Evergreen vine. Zone 8.
H: to 20 ft.

Very popular in California and the Southwest, this versatile vine is usually used as a ground cover, but it can be trained up a tree trunk or trellis, and its stems are stiff and woody enough to stand unsupported as a small shrub. The shiny dark green leaves are stiff ovals. Blooms heavily for several weeks in late spring and early summer, with clusters of pinwheel-shaped flowers 1/2 in. wide, opening white and fading to creamy yellow. They are very fragrant, especially in the evening.

How to grow: Sun or shade. Not fussy about soil. Tolerates some dryness, but needs watering during droughts. For a ground cover, space 1-gal. plants 2 ft. apart. Use one plant against a

Trachelospermum
jasminoides

tree or trellis, and start training it right away. Fasten the stems to the support until they catch on. Prune out old woody stems as needed to renew growth. Trouble-free.

Trachycarpus

Tra-kee-kar'pus.
Palmae. Palm family.

Small to medium-size fan palms that provide fibers and fronds for cordage and basketry. Only 4 spp., native to the Himalaya region.

fortunei (p. 165)
Windmill palm.
Fan palm. Zone 8.
H: 20 ft. S: 8 ft.

A rather small palm that's quite hardy and easy to grow. Forms a single trunk covered with coarse black fibers, topped with an umbrella-shaped or rounded crown. The long-stalked fronds, about 3 ft. in diameter, are palmately divided into dozens of long slender segments that droop at the tips. Flowers and fruits are not showy. Use as a specimen, in the ground or a container.

How to grow: Full or part sun. Grows best in well-drained soil with regular watering. Tolerates salt spray and some dryness but not constantly wet soil. Needs only occasional grooming. Trouble-free.

Tristania

Tris-tay'nee-a.
Myrtaceae. Myrtle family.

Evergreen trees or shrubs with simple alternate leaves and small white or yellow flowers. About 20 spp., most native to Australia.

conferta (p. 163)
(now *Lophostemon confertus*)
Brisbane box.
Evergreen tree. Zone 9.
H: 40–60 ft. S: 20–30 ft.

A neat tree with leathery, bright green, 4–6-in. leaves and small white flowers that look like snowflakes in summer. The dark red-brown outer bark peels off to expose smooth tan inner bark. *T. laurina* (now *Tristaniopsis laurina*) is smaller and slower-growing, with smooth dark green leaves, bright yellow flowers, purple-red outer bark, and clean white inner bark. A large shrub or small tree, it can be used for tall screens or as a patio or courtyard specimen.

How to grow: Full or part sun. Ordinary soil and watering. Tolerates dry soil once established. Needs only routine training and pruning. Easy and trouble-free.

Tropaeolum

Tro-pee'oh-lum. Nasturtium.
Tropaeolaceae. Nasturtium family.

Annuals or perennials with showy red, orange, or yellow flowers. More than 80 spp., native to the mountains of Central and South America.

majus (p. 304)
Nasturtium.
Annual. All zones.
H: 1 ft. S: 2 ft.

Easy, adaptable, and colorful. The fleshy stems can climb or sprawl to 2 ft. or more (dwarf kinds remain compact). Leaves are like parasols, with a long stalk attached in the center and a rounded blade up to 6 in. wide. The surface is smooth, almost waxy. The large long-stalked flowers have a spicy fragrance and come in bright shades of yellow, orange, red, mahogany, cream, or bicolor. The flowers are edible and make a colorful garnish or salad item. Looks cheerful in containers, trailing over walls, or edging annual flower beds or vegetable gardens. Self-sows readily but isn't an aggressive weed. Seed catalogs list several strains, including one with white-variegated leaves.

How to grow: Full or part sun. Ordinary soil and watering. The seeds are large enough that children can handle them easily. Direct-sow in early spring, covering $1/2$ in. deep. Thin to 6–12 in. apart. Subject to aphids but generally carefree.

Tsuga

Soo'ga. Hemlock.
Pinaceae. Pine family.

Evergreen conifers with flat needles and small woody cones. Only 10 spp., native to North America and eastern Asia.

canadensis (p. 197)
Canada hemlock.
Conifer. Zone 4.
H: 50–100 ft. S: 25–35 ft.

One of the most graceful conifers, native to cool moist sites in the Great Lakes, Northeast, and Appalachians. Makes a tall pyramid with relaxed spreading branches that are soft enough to sway in the breeze. Short flat needles are crowded on two sides of the twigs, forming feathery sprays of foliage that stays rich green all year. The small cones are like miniature pinecones. Responds well to pruning and can be shaped into a dense fine-textured hedge. Var. *sargentii* is a weeping form that spreads wider than tall. There are a few dwarf forms.

T. caroliniana, the Carolina hemlock, has slightly larger needles on all sides of the twigs and stiffer branches. It makes a good hedge, is more tolerant of dry air and wind, and is hardy to Zone 5. *T. heterophylla*, the western hemlock, makes a beautiful specimen in the Pacific Northwest but is hardy only to Zone 7.

How to grow: Part shade. Prefers a north or east exposure that provides some sun in summer and shade in winter. Needs cool, rich, moist, well-drained, acidic soil with a thick layer of organic mulch. Water regularly during dry spells. Can't take heat or drought. Space 6 ft. apart for

Tsuga canadensis

a hedge, and prune to encourage dense growth. Subject to a few insect and disease problems, some locally serious. Check with a local nursery or extension agent before planting.

Tulbaghia

Tul-baj´ee-a.
Amaryllidaceae. Amaryllis family.

Small perennials that smell like onions or garlic, with small bulbs, grassy foliage, and umbels of 6-petaled flowers. More than 20 spp., native to Africa.

violacea (p. 275)
Society garlic.
Tender perennial. Zone 9.
H: 1–2 ft. S: 6–12 in.

A pretty little plant for mild climates or containers. Blooms most in summer but repeats throughout the year. Clusters of starry white or lilac flowers are held on 1–2-ft. stalks and make good cut flowers. The garlic-scented foliage is evergreen. Leaves are flat and slender, up to 12 in. long. There are variegated forms with white-striped leaves.

How to grow: Full or part sun. Ordinary soil and watering. Put one plant in a 6-in. or 8-in. pot. Propagate by division. Easy and trouble-free.

Tulipa

Too´li-pa. Tulip.
Liliaceae. Lily family.

Spring-blooming perennials with edible bulbs, broad flat leaves, and showy flowers. About 100 spp., most native to Central Asia, and countless hybrids and cultivars.

garden tulips (p. 276)
Perennials, often short lived. Zone 4.
H: 1–3 ft. S: 6 in.

Modern garden tulips are complex hybrids, the result of centuries of deliberate breeding. There are thousands of named forms, divided into several classes based on time of bloom, flower form, and genetic background. As a group, tulips flower over a season of many weeks from early to late spring. Individual flowers last just a week or two. The flowers are held singly on long stiff stalks (good for cutting) and come in all shades of red, orange, yellow, pink, purple, white, bicolor, or multicolor. Some kinds have a pleasant fragrance. The flowers can be single or double, 2–6 in. wide, in various rounded shapes. The petals usually spread wide open on sunny days, closing again at night or during cloudy weather. Each bulb usually makes one flower and a few broad basal leaves. The gray-green leaves make a pleasant backdrop for the flowers, but they aren't very attractive in subsequent weeks as they mature and finally wither.

Some of the most popular classes are the Cottage tulips, Darwin tulips, and Darwin hybrids; all have large egg-shaped or cup-shaped flowers on tall stems in late spring. There are early and late classes of double tulips, with peony-like flowers on short stems. The Greigii tulips have leaves striped or mottled with dark reddish purple and large flowers on short stems. Lily-flowered tulips have long slender flowers, narrow in the middle, with pointed petals that flare out at the top. Rembrandt tulips are like Darwins with striped or streaky petals, and Parrot tulips have fringed petals with bright multicolored streaks and splotches. Plant these in containers, not in mixed borders; their markings are caused by a virus that can infect other tulips and lilies.

How to grow: Most garden centers have an assortment of tulip bulbs in the fall. For a wider selection, refer to mail-order bulb catalogs. Order in spring for fall delivery. Store bulbs in a cool place prior to planting.

Tulips need full sun until flowering is completed, but it's okay if they're shaded by deciduous trees later in the season. Any well-drained soil will do. Plant bulbs 4–8 in. deep and 4–6 in. apart, depending on size. Use wire mesh cages or a handful of gravel in the planting hole to protect them from chipmunks, gophers, mice, and voles, if those critters are common in your area. Water regularly if the weather is dry in spring. After flowering, continue watering and let the foliage develop; it requires several weeks to mature. In cold climates, deep-planted tulips will rebloom for a few years before declining. The bulbs split apart and make smaller flowers each year, or they may disappear altogether. You can separate and replant the smaller bulbs; sometimes they perform quite well, but usually it's better to buy new bulbs.

Gardeners in warm climates treat tulips as annuals, discarding them after bloom and buying new bulbs each fall. In very mild regions, bulbs must be refrigerated for 6–8 weeks to give them an artificial "winter" before planting, or else they will not bloom. A similar treatment is used to force potted bulbs for indoor bloom.

Aphids may infest the leaves and buds; wash them off with soapy water. Fungal infections sometimes disfigure the leaves and flowers; pull and destroy infected plants.

species tulips (p. 276)
Most species or wild tulips are small plants that bloom earlier than garden tulips. They have the charm of wildflowers and are lovely in rock gardens or informal naturalized plantings. The bulbs are uncommon at local garden centers but listed in several catalogs.

T. clusiana, the lady tulip or candy tulip, has slender red-and-white flowers that open wide on sunny days. The slender leaves and flower stalks both grow about 12 in. tall. Var. *chrysantha* has pink-and-yellow flowers on stalks 6–8 in. tall. Both persist in mild areas where hybrid tulips rarely come back the second year, and they are hardy to Zone 5. They spread by forming new bulbs at the ends of underground runners.

T. saxatilis is another good perennial tulip

that multiplies readily. It has wide glossy leaves and clusters of 1–4 flowers on 12-in. stalks. The fragrant flowers are pale lilac with yellow in the center. Good for mild climates and hardy to Zone 6.

T. tarda forms a flat rosette of bright green leaves and bears groups of 3–6 flowers on short stalks. The star-shaped flowers open 2 in. wide and are bright yellow with white tips. Blooms for about 2 weeks in early spring. Will spread by seed on a well-drained, sunny site. Zone 4.

How to grow: Like garden tulips.

Ulmus

Ul′mus. Elm.
Ulmaceae. Elm family.

Deciduous or semievergreen trees with tough wood, simple alternate leaves, and flat round fruits. About 18 spp., native to the north temperate zone.

Ulmus parvifolia

parvifolia (p. 129)
Lacebark elm, Chinese elm.
Deciduous tree. Hardiness varies among cultivars.
H: 40–50 ft. S: 30–40 ft.

A tough, adaptable, fast-growing tree with mottled multicolored bark, clean foliage, and good resistance to Dutch elm disease. The bark flakes off the trunk and limbs, making a lacy pattern in shades of gray, brown, green, and orange. The small oval leaves, 1–1½ in. long, are set close together on very slender, drooping twigs. The dark green foliage doesn't turn yellow and drop until late fall. Some cultivars are semievergreen where winters are mild. Small flowers and fruits develop in fall but are often overlooked. The species and most deciduous cultivars are hardy to Zone 5 or 4. 'Drake', 'Sempervirens', and 'True Green' are semievergreen cultivars, hardy only in Zone 7 or warmer.

U. pumila, the Siberian elm, is also called Chinese elm. Although very hardy, it is an inferior tree with weak wood, shallow roots, and weedy seedlings.

How to grow: Full or part sun. Grows best in well-drained, moist, fertile soil but tolerates infertile, dry, compacted soil and restricted root runs in urban sites. Stake and train to develop a crown high enough to walk under, and remove suckers as soon as they form. No serious insect or disease problems.

other elms
U. americana, the American elm, is a sentimental favorite because it once lined the streets of many American towns and cities, forming tunnels of shade in summer. It is uncommon now, virtually eliminated in recent decades by Dutch elm disease. Treatment for infected trees is expensive and only delays inevitable death. Even without the disease, the tree has drawbacks. It gets too big, has shallow roots, suffers from various insects, and makes too many seedlings.

U. crassifolia, the cedar elm, is a tough native elm that tolerates alkaline soil, drought, and urban conditions. The small, oval, dark green leaves are stiff and glossy. Hardy to Zone 7, it is planted mostly in Texas and the Southwest.

U. glabra 'Camperdownii', or Camperdown elm, is sold as a standard with a short erect trunk and many weeping branches that soon reach down to the ground. The dense leafy canopy makes a shady playhouse for small children. Zone 4.

U. 'Regal' and other hybrid elms with Dutch elm resistance have been introduced by plant breeders. They show promise as shade trees but are not yet widely available.

Vaccinium

Vak-sin′i-um. Blueberry, cranberry.
Ericaceae. Heath family.

Deciduous or evergreen shrubs and a few small trees or vines. Many have edible fruits. About 450 spp., native worldwide.

Vaccinium corymbosum

corymbosum (p. 153)
(now includes many plants previously assigned to *V. ashei* and various other species)
Highbush blueberry.
Deciduous shrub. Zone 4.
H: 6–15 ft. S: to 8 ft.

An excellent shrub, both attractive and productive. It has small pinkish white flowers for weeks in spring, fine-textured foliage with good fall color, and bright twiggy stems in winter. Birds flock to eat the tasty dark blue berries, and pie makers may have to protect the crop with netting. Numerous cultivars have been selected for fruit production and fall color. Makes a nice informal, rounded hedge with no pruning if planted 6 ft. apart.

How to grow: Full sun or part shade (the more shade, the fewer berries). Needs fertile, moist, acidic soil. If your native soil is not suitable, plant in raised beds filled with a mixture of soil and peat moss or composted pine bark. Use a thick layer of mulch to protect the shallow roots and keep them cool and damp. Prune after harvest to remove old or weak stems.

other species
V. angustifolium, or lowbush blueberry, grows in New England. It's a twiggy little deciduous shrub, 1–2 ft. tall, that makes a good ground cover for sunny sites with well-drained, acidic

soil. It has very tasty berries and good fall color. Needs a good shearing every few years to keep it low and dense. Zone 3.

V. arboreum, sparkleberry or tree huckleberry, grows in the Southeast. It makes a multi-trunked shrub or small tree up to 25 ft. tall and 5 ft. wide, with glossy, fine-textured, semievergreen foliage, and produces small white flowers and shiny black berries. It tolerates heat and grows well in dry, acidic soil in part shade or sun. Zone 7.

V. ovatum, or evergreen huckleberry, grows in the Northwest. Its glossy dark green foliage lasts well in water and is a favorite florist's filler. It has pinkish white flowers in spring and small tasty berries in summer and fall. Grows 8–10 ft. tall and 4–5 ft. wide in part shade; stays smaller and more compact in sun. Zone 7.

Verbascum

Ver-bas′kum. Mullein.
Scrophulariaceae. Foxglove family.

Mostly biennials with basal rosettes of simple leaves and 5-petaled flowers on erect stalks. About 350 spp., native to Eurasia; a few species have naturalized in North America.

chaixii (p. 277)

Short-lived perennial. Zone 5.
H: 3 ft. S: 2 ft.

A showy plant for borders or naturalizing. Makes a rosette of gray-green leaves 3–6 in. long. The basal foliage is semievergreen; even in the North, it looks fresh until early winter. Thick flower stalks hold dense spikes of yellow or white flowers in summer. Remove the first spent flower stalks to prolong bloom, but let the later ones go to seed. The dry stalks hold up well if you want to leave them for winter interest. Several other species are sometimes listed in seed or plant catalogs. *V. bombyciferum* and *V. olympicum* are exciting as foliage plants. They make wonderful wide rosettes of large woolly white leaves. Both have yellow flowers on tall stalks.

How to grow: Full sun. Needs well-drained average soil; does well in dry sites. Raise from seed, or purchase small plants to set out in spring or summer. Space 2–3 ft. apart. Flowers in the second year. Stalks may need staking. May die that year or continue for a few more, but often replaces itself with volunteer seedlings. Spider mites are a common problem in hot, dry weather. Fungus can rot the leaves in extremely rainy or humid conditions.

Verbena

Ver-bee′na.
Verbenaceae. Verbena family.

Annuals, perennials, or shrubs with toothed or dissected foliage and spikes or clusters of small flowers. About 250 spp., nearly all native to the New World.

bonariensis (p. 277)

Perennial often grown as an annual. Zone 7.
H: 3–4 ft. S: 3 ft.

An airy filler for annual or perennial beds. Doesn't take much space at ground level, but fills a large air space with dots of color. Clusters of small violet flowers open continually from early summer until frost and attract many butterflies. The thin branching stems are stiff and wiry with little foliage, so you can see the plants below and behind. Plant in masses, or weave a strand of individual plants throughout a bed. *V. rigida* is similar but grows only 1–2 ft. tall.

How to grow: Full sun. Ordinary soil and watering. Tolerates poor, dry soil. Pinch first shoots to encourage branching. Subject to powdery mildew but generally trouble-free. Perennial only in mild climates, it makes a good annual in the North. It grows quickly from seed and starts blooming early the first year. Often self-sows.

Verbena canadensis

canadensis (p. 277)

Rose verbena.
Perennial. Zone 6.
H: 1 ft. S: 3 ft.

A tough wildflower, good for mass plantings on dry, sunny slopes. Bears many round clusters of rosy pink flowers over a long season. (A few cultivars have been selected for rose, lavender, or pink flowers.) Floppy stems root where they touch the ground. The deeply lobed leaves have a sticky surface and sometimes look dirty because they catch dust, pollen, and bits of debris. *V. bipinnatifida,* or prairie verbena, is very similar, with clusters of lavender or purple flowers. *V. peruviana* spreads flatter and has scarlet red flowers. Its cultivars have pink, white, or purple flowers.

How to grow: Full sun. Thrives in dry, sandy soil. Space 1 ft. apart for mass planting. Trouble-free and very easy to grow. Usually short lived but self-sows.

× hybrida (p. 305)

Garden verbena.
Annual. All zones.
H: 6–12 in. S: 12 in.

A colorful annual for bedding, edging, or containers. Thrives in hot sunny weather and blooms nonstop all summer. The starry flowers form dense round clusters, 2–3 in. wide, in bright shades of red, pink, purple, or white. Usually forms a sprawling mat of stems, although some kinds are supposed to grow upright.

How to grow: Full sun or afternoon shade. Well-drained average soil. Seeds are difficult to germinate; it's easier to buy transplants, and garden centers have mixed or solid-color packs. Space 8 in. apart. Deadhead to prolong bloom.

Veronica

Ver-on´i-ka.
Scrophulariaceae. Foxglove family.

Mostly perennials with opposite or whorled leaves and spikes of small flowers. About 250 spp., native to the north temperate zone.

cultivars (p. 278)
Perennials. Most are hardy to Zone 3.
H: usually 1–2 ft. S: 1–2 ft.

Veronicas are wonderful garden plants, but their taxonomy is a riddle. Some species are quite variable; others are distinguished only by minute details. Many of the cultivars are hybrids of unknown parentage, and they are often listed under different species in different catalogs. Don't worry; just look for the cultivar name, and you can trust that it will be the right plant.

The most popular cultivars differ in flower color, height, and growth habit. The mat-forming types will spread along the front of a border, terrace, or raised bed. The clumping types hold their flowers higher and combine easily with other sun-loving perennials. Any of the blue veronicas, in particular, look especially lovely with clear lemon yellow flowers—irises, lemon lilies, daylilies, anthemis, feverfew, or daisies.

How to grow: Full sun or part shade. Well-drained average soil. Water during long dry spells. Need afternoon shade and regular watering to survive in hot climates. Some kinds get floppy and need staking in too-rich soil. Space about 1 ft. apart. Divide clumps every 2–3 years in spring, as soon as growth has started. Cut back spent flower stalks to prolong bloom. No serious pests or diseases.

incana (p. 278)
Woolly speedwell.
Perennial. Zone 3.
H: 1–2 ft. S: 1–2 ft.

Valued for its foliage, which is covered with silver-gray hairs. It makes low, dense, spreading clumps that brighten the front of a terrace, border, or rock garden. It has pale lilac-blue flowers on slender stalks that may lean over, but they're too delicate to stake unobtrusively. Blooms for several weeks in summer; combines well with dianthus, sedums, thymes, and blue fescue grass.

How to grow: Full sun. Needs very good drainage and thrives in dry sandy or gravelly soil. Don't apply a thick mulch or crowd it with other plants. Allow space for air to circulate around the foliage, so that rain or dew dries quickly. If the leaves stay wet, they are liable to mildew or rot. Cut off stalks after the flowers fade. Divide clumps every 2–3 years in early spring.

Popular veronica cultivars

'Crater Lake Blue' (often assigned to *V. teucrium* or *V. latifolia*) grows about 1 ft. tall and wide. Has dense spikes of true blue flowers for about 2 weeks in spring; unfortunately, the lax stalks tend to flop over. 'Royal Blue' is similar, with deep sky blue flowers on sturdier stalks. Out of bloom, both form low clumps of green foliage.

'Goodness Grows' has long slender wands of bright blue flowers from early summer to fall. Grows about 1 ft. tall. Makes a low, spreading mat of shiny green foliage.

'Icicle' (often listed under *V. spicata*) is the best tall white veronica, with pure white flowers from June to September. Forms a vase-shaped clump that reaches 18–24 in. tall. Foliage is gray-green.

'Minuet' has lots of clear soft pink flowers in early summer. Grows 1 ft. tall. Forms a mat of silvery foliage.

'Red Fox' (often listed under *V. spicata*) has deep rosy pink (not true red) flowers. Blooms for 4–6 weeks in June and July. Grows 15 in. tall. Forms a mat of glossy green leaves.

'Sarabande' has lavender-blue flowers on upright stalks that don't flop. Grows 15–18 in. tall. Forms a dense compact mat of gray leaves.

'Sunny Border Blue' (sometimes listed under *V. longifolia*) has dense racemes of deep blue-violet flowers. Blooms all summer. Forms a bushy upright clump that reaches 24 in. tall. Shiny dark green leaves are thick and crinkled.

Viburnum

Vy-bur´num.
Caprifoliaceae. Honeysuckle family.

Deciduous or evergreen shrubs or small trees with simple opposite leaves and showy clusters of 5-petaled flowers, usually white or pink and sometimes very fragrant. About 150 spp., native to the Old and New World, and several hybrids. Many excellent hybrids were developed by Dr. Donald Egolf at the National Arboretum; they have Native American names such as 'Mohawk', 'Seneca', 'Iroquois', and 'Chesapeake'.

Dozens of viburnums are cultivated for their many attractive features; several favorites are described below. The evergreen species have handsome foliage year-round, and the deciduous species offer rich fall color. Several are very showy in bloom, and some have an unforgettable spicy fragrance. Many produce colorful berries that attract birds in fall and winter. Nearly all are upright growers with multiple stems. Some are (or can be kept) bushy and compact; others tend to get leggy. A few spread by suckers and form thickets, and a few mature into small trees.

How to grow: Full or part sun. Average well-drained garden soil and regular watering. Apply a thick organic mulch to keep the roots cool and moist. Transplant from containers in spring or early fall. You can prune after flowering to improve shape and make plants denser and more compact, but pruning removes the fruits. Renew established plants by cutting old and weak stems to the ground in early spring. Viburnums are generally trouble-free but can be infested with aphids and other pests, or powdery mildew and other foliar diseases.

carlesii and its hybrids (pp. 154, 155)
Korean spice viburnums.
Deciduous shrubs. Zone 4.
H: 4–5 ft. or more. S: equal to height.

A species valued for its extremely fragrant flowers, which form dome-shaped clusters 2–3 in. wide. Pink buds open into white flowers. Blooms in April, as the leaves expand. Fruits are not showy. The broad oval leaves are covered with soft hairs and are dull green in summer, sometimes turning reddish in fall. 'Compactum' has similar flowers and foliage but makes a neat sphere only 3 ft. tall and wide. 'Cayuga' is a hybrid with especially healthy and attractive foliage and generous clusters of pink buds and white flowers. It grows about 5 ft. tall and wide.

V. × burkwoodii is an old hybrid of *V. carlesii* with equally fragrant flowers. It grows 8–10 ft. tall and 6–8 ft. wide but tends to get loose and leggy. It is hardy to Zone 4. 'Mohawk' is a more recent hybrid that improves on *V. × burkwoodii*. Dense and bushy, it grows 7–8 ft. tall and 8–9 ft. wide. The shiny, deep green, oval leaves hang on late into fall, turning orange-red as the weather cools. Dark red buds are colorful for weeks before opening into very fragrant white flowers in May. The rounded flower clusters are about 3 in. wide. Fruits are not showy. It is hardy to Zone 5.

V. × juddii is another hybrid of *V. carlesii* with domed clusters of very fragrant white flowers in April or May. It can reach 6–8 ft. tall and wide but looks better if sheared or pruned after flowering to keep it dense and compact. The medium green leaves, 2–4 in. long, turn dark purple in fall.

How to grow: See main entry. Think twice when choosing a site for one of these fragrant early viburnums. They bloom when it's still too cool to sit outdoors or open a window, so don't plant one next to a patio or by the house. Put it next to the mailbox, driveway, or sideway, where you'll pass it daily during bloom.

davidii (p. 187)
Evergreen shrub. Zone 7.
H: 3 ft. S: 3–4 ft.

A compact evergreen, good for foundation plantings. The dark green leaves are smooth ellipses, up to 6 in. long, with 3 deep parallel veins. Flat 3-in. clusters of scentless, dull white flowers are followed by extremely pretty blue berries. Plant 2 or more shrubs to increase berry set. Popular in California and the Northwest but usually not grown in the East.

How to grow: See main entry. Prefers acidic soil.

dentatum (p. 154)
Arrowwood.
Deciduous shrub. Zone 3.
H: to 15 ft. S: to 15 ft.

A native shrub with many upright stems, straight enough to use for arrow shafts. It spreads underground to form a patch or thicket and makes a good hedge, screen, or background for informal or country gardens. The rounded leaves have coarse teeth and deep veins and are glossy dark green in summer, turning rich red, purple, or orange in fall. Blooms for 1–2 weeks in early summer, with flat 4-in. clusters of small creamy flowers. Birds eat the pretty blue berries as soon as they ripen in late summer or fall. Several other native viburnums are also interesting, adaptable plants. Many have good fall color and berries.

How to grow: See main entry. Tolerates sun or shade and grows in any well-drained soil. Suckers are easily controlled by pruning or mowing them off.

dilatatum 'Erie' (p. 154)
Deciduous shrub. Zone 5.
H: 6 ft. or more. S: 10 ft.

A good choice for fall and winter interest. The dark green leaves turn yellow, orange, and red in fall. Flat clusters of small berries ripen red in fall and hang on well into winter, gradually fading to a coral or salmon color. Blooms abundantly in May or June, when clusters of small white flowers cover the foliage for 7–10 days. A rounded shrub that makes a good lawn specimen. Other cultivars differ in size, habit, and fruit color.

How to grow: See main entry.

lantana 'Mohican' (p. 155)
Wayfaring tree.
Deciduous shrub. Zone 4.
H: 10 ft. S: 10 ft.

A compact mounded shrub with many strong stems and branches, this makes a good hedge, screen, or background for perennial borders. Foliage is thick-textured and healthy, dull dark green in summer, sometimes turning red or purple in fall. The flat clusters of scentless white flowers last about 2 weeks in May. Berries change color as they ripen, darkening from orange to red to black.

How to grow: See main entry. Tolerates dry and alkaline soil conditions. Widely adapted and trouble-free.

opulus (see below for photo)
European cranberry bush.
Deciduous shrub. Zone 3.
H: 8–12 ft. or more. S: 10–15 ft.

An attractive upright shrub with showy flowers in May, shiny red fruits in fall and winter, and fall color ranging from yellow-red to reddish purple. The dark green leaves have 3 lobes with toothed edges and resemble maple leaves. Like lacecap hydrangeas, the flower clusters contain an inner group of small fertile flowers surrounded by a lacy ring of sterile flowers with round white petals. 'Compactum' grows only half as big—a better size for today's smaller gardens—and has excellent flowers and fruits. 'Nanum' is a true dwarf, maturing at 18–24 in., with pretty little leaves. It doesn't often flower or fruit. 'Notcutt' is a vigorous grower with flowers and fruits larger than the species. 'Xanthocarpum' is hard to find, but it has glowing yellow-gold fruits that show up well in winter.

'Roseum', also sold as 'Sterile', is an old-fashioned favorite called the snowball bush. It makes fluffy white 3-in. balls of flowers in early May. Because it has only sterile flowers, it doesn't make fruits, but the fall color is a good reddish purple. This cultivar is particularly subject to aphids.

V. trilobum (p. 155), the American cranberry bush, is very similar to European cranberry bush but even hardier, surviving in Zone 2. 'Compactum' and other dwarf forms reach about 6 ft. tall and wide and make good hedges. 'Wentworth' and 'Hahs' grow about 8–10 ft. tall and wide and have beautiful large fruits that ripen from gold to red and hang on all winter. They are edible but taste more sour than sour cherries.

How to grow: See main entry. Both *V. opulus* and *V. trilobum* are stressed by hot, dry weather; water before the leaves start to wilt. Stressed plants are more subject to aphids, borers, and diseases.

Viburnum plicatum
var. *tomentosum*

plicatum var. *tomentosum* (p. 155)
Double file viburnum.
Deciduous shrub. Zone 6.
H: 8–10 ft. S: 10–12 ft.

One of the most beautiful ornamental shrubs, with true 4-season appeal. Spreads wider than tall, with layer upon layer of horizontal tiered branches. Paired leaves with neat distinct veins hang below the twigs like a line of fresh laundry. Foliage is rich green in summer, turning deep red-purple in fall. Best of all are the flowers. They form flat clusters like 2–4-in. snowflakes, held well above the foliage for about 2 weeks in April or May. The fruit clusters are bright red in July, turning black later if the birds don't eat them first. 'Mariesii' is the most common cultivar and sets a heavy crop of berries. 'Shasta' has flowers twice as large as normal and

grows about 6 ft. tall and 12 ft. wide. 'Summer Snowflake' and 'Watanabei' (they may be the same plant) have smaller flowers but continue blooming on new growth all summer. More compact and rounded than other cultivars, they grow about 6 ft. tall and wide.

How to grow: See main entry. Prefers moist soil and can't take hot, dry weather.

rhytidophyllum (see below for photo)
Leatherleaf viburnum.
Semievergreen shrub. Zone 6.
H: 10–15 ft. S: 10–15 ft.

An upright rounded shrub that holds its foliage until midwinter in the North and can be evergreen in the South. The long narrow leaves are shiny dark green on top with fuzzy tan hairs below. Has large flat clusters, 4–8 in. wide, of creamy white flowers in April or May. Berries darken from red to black and hang on for 2–3 months in fall. Considered hardy to Zone 5, but it freezes back hard in severe winters there.

V. 'Pragense' (p. 187) is a hardy (Zone 5), semievergreen hybrid of *V. rhytidophyllum* and *V. utile*. The small leaves are shiny dark green and remain attractive well into winter, even in the North. Farther south, it is reliably evergreen. Flat 3–6-in. clusters of slightly fragrant, creamy white flowers open in spring. Red berries turn black as they age. Vigorous and fast-growing, it can reach 10 ft. tall and wide with arching stems, or you can prune it into a smaller, more compact shape.

V. × *rhytidophylloides*, a hybrid between *V. rhytidophyllum* and *V. lantana*, is a large upright shrub, reaching up to 10 ft. tall and wide. It is hardy to Zone 5. The leathery dark green leaves are semievergreen. Creamy white flowers are showy for 1–2 weeks in April or May. Clusters of berries change from yellow to red to black and last from late summer until December. 'Allegheny' is an excellent cultivar, hardy as far north as Minneapolis. 'Willowwood' has coarse-textured, gray-green foliage and a tendency to rebloom in fall—sometimes displaying flowers and fruits at the same time.

How to grow: See main entry.

suspensum (p. 187)
Sandankwa viburnum.
Evergreen shrub. Zone 8.
H: 10 ft. S: 10 ft.

A large round shrub with dense evergreen foliage. The oval leaves are 2–4 in. long, with a shiny surface and a thick texture. Loose clusters of star-shaped flowers form at the branch tips in spring. The flowers are fragrant or smelly, depending on your point of view. Birds eat the berries soon after they ripen. Makes a good screen or hedge for large properties.

How to grow: See main entry. Does best in part shade; hot summer sun can scorch the foliage.

Viburnum tinus

tinus (p. 187)
Laurustinus.
Evergreen shrub. Zone 7.
H: 6–12 ft. S: 3–8 ft.

An erect narrow shrub that responds well to pruning and makes a good hedge for smaller gardens. The dark green leaves are smooth, shiny, 2–3-in. ovals. Dense clusters of pink buds and white flowers, slightly fragrant, last for weeks in late winter and early spring. Pretty blue berries ripen in summer. There are a few cultivars with larger, smaller, or variegated leaves.

How to grow: See main entry. Needs good drainage and air circulation; subject to root rot and mildew in wet or humid sites.

Vinca
Ving′ka. Periwinkle.
Apocynaceae. Dogbane family.

Trailing vinelike perennials with opposite leaves and 5-petaled flowers. Only 7 spp., native to the Old World. Closely related to *Catharanthus*.

major (p. 278)
Large periwinkle.
Perennial. Zone 7.
H: 1 ft. S: 3 ft. or more.

An evergreen ground cover for mild climates. Trailing stems root where they touch the ground. The paired oval leaves are smooth and glossy, 1–3 in. long. The short upright stems bear violet-blue flowers with 5 wide petals. Blooms mostly in early spring, but a few flowers may appear in summer or fall. A variegated form with white blotches on the leaves is often used in window boxes or other containers. It spills over the edge and combines well with upright growers such as geraniums or coleus.

How to grow: Sun or shade. Needs moist soil and regular watering in full sun. Shaded plants can tolerate short dry spells but will grow slowly. Easy to propagate by division; dig up rooted runners and space them 6 in. apart for a ground cover. Shear or prune long runners to encourage branching and make a denser cover. Established plantings need minimal care. Pest-free.

Vinca minor

minor (p. 278)
Common periwinkle.
Perennial. Zone 4.
H: 6–12 in. S: 3 ft. or more.

One of the most versatile evergreen ground covers, good for both cold and warm climates. Grows well in sun or shade. It makes a dense weed-proof mat of wiry stems, and its tenacious roots can secure steep banks against erosion. The paired leaves are small ovals, about 1 in. long. Soft-textured and light green when they unfold in early spring, they turn thick, leathery, and dark green by summer. Winter sun and cold can color the foliage a dull purplish bronze. Short upright stems hold flat round flowers, about 1 in. wide, for several weeks in spring. The more

sun, the more flowers; plants in deep shade may not bloom at all. The flowers are usually lavender-blue, but pale blue, darker purple, and white forms are also available.

How to grow: Like *V. major*, but it's more adaptable. Tolerates cold, heat, deep shade, and dry soil. Very long lived and trouble-free. Established plantings survive for decades with no care. Has naturalized in the Northeast.

Viola
Vy-oh′la. Violet, pansy.
Violaceae. Violet family.

A diverse group of annuals, perennials, and a few small shrubs. Most have characteristic violet-type flowers, but the leaves and habit are variable. About 500 spp., native to the Old and New World. Many of the species are distinguished by minor differences, and they hybridize readily. The identity of some cultivars is uncertain.

labradorica (p. 278)
Labrador violet.
Perennial. Zone 3.
H: 4 in. S: 12 in.

A low-growing violet, with medium green leaves about 1 in. wide on short stalks. It has small violet-blue flowers in spring and occasionally in summer. Looks pretty and dainty but is actually quite tough. Use it to edge beds or paths or as a shallow-rooted ground cover over little bulbs. Var. *purpurea* is a form with shiny dark leaves that unfold purple and gradually turn purple-green. It comes true from seed.

How to grow: Sun (where summers are cool), part shade, or shade (in hot climates). Prefers moist, humusy, well-drained soil but grows fine in ordinary garden soil with regular watering. Space 10–15 in. apart. It spreads quickly. Lift every year or two and reset the pieces in renewed soil. Also spreads by self-seeding.

odorata (p. 278)
Sweet violet.
Perennial. Zone 4.
H: 4–6 in. S: 12 in.

Treasured for centuries for their sweet fragrance, these violets are vigorous and easy to grow. The lavender, white, or dark blue flowers open for many weeks in late winter and early spring, often repeating in fall. The dark green

Viola odorata

leaves are heart-shaped or kidney-shaped, about 2 in. wide, arranged in tufts or clumps. Spreads fast by runners to fill in an area. Competes well with grass and will spread into a lawn. 'Czar' (dark violet) and 'Rosina' (dusty pink) are hardy plants with single flowers. The cultivars called Parma violets have double flowers that are especially fragrant, but the plants are hard to obtain and hardy only to Zone 6.

'Royal Robe' (deep blue) and 'White Czar' (white) are sometimes listed under this species and sometimes under *V. cucullata*. Either way, they are hardy, vigorous plants with fragrant single flowers on long stalks. *V. cucullata* 'Freckles' is another favorite violet with pale blue flowers dotted with deep blue-purple specks.

How to grow: Like *V. labradorica*.

tricolor (p. 304)
Johnny-jump-up.
Self-seeding annual or short-lived perennial.
Zone 4.
H: to 12 in. S: to 12 in.

Charming, cheerful, and easy to grow. Once started, you'll always have it. Although the flowers are much smaller than pansies, they're produced abundantly. The most common form is blue-purple, yellow, and white (hence the name "tricolor"), but other colors and combinations are available. Blooms in spring and early summer, continuing until the weather gets hot. Forms a tuft or clump of leafy branching stems. Plants often overwinter and can continue for a few years. Seedlings will surprise you, showing up here and there in a mixed border or along a path.

How to grow: Full or part sun. Ordinary soil and watering. Grows easily from seed, and several strains are listed in catalogs. Self-sows freely. Carefree.

× wittrockiana (p. 304)
Pansy.
Annual or short-lived perennial. All zones.
H: to 12 in. S: to 12 in.

Pansies are popular bedding plants, blooming from fall to spring where winters are mild and from spring to fall where summers are cool. They have shiny evergreen leaves. Young plants form compact clumps; later the stems stretch and sprawl. The wide (1–4 in.), flat, facelike flowers are loaded with personality and come in a very wide range of colors—red, pink, yellow, white, blue, and mahogany, usually marked with dark blotches. There are dozens of seed strains, selected for flower color and size. The flowers have a pleasant fragrance. Long-stemmed types are good for cutting and last several days in water. Pansies grow quickly from seed and are usually raised as annuals and discarded when the plants get straggly. Across the South and Southwest, they die out in the heat of summer. In the North, they may overwinter and go on for a few years.

Violas, *V. cornuta,* have solid-colored pansy-like flowers, 1–2 in. wide, in shades of white,

Viola canadensis

Viola pedata

Native violets

Violets are common wildflowers in many parts of the United States, and several species are available from native-plant specialists or perennial nurseries.

V. canadensis, or Canada violet, grows in eastern woodlands and needs shade and rich, moist soil. It makes a loose clump of large leaves. White flowers with purple backs bloom in spring. Zone 3.

V. nuttallii, or Nuttall's violet, grows in western meadows and needs well-drained sandy or gravelly soil and part or full sun. It has yellow flowers with brownish purple veins in early summer. Zone 4.

V. pedata, the bird's-foot violet, has palmately lobed leaves divided into 3–5 segments, like a bird's foot. Flowers are large (3/4–1 1/2 in. wide), in shades of blue or violet with a white throat and golden yellow stamens. It needs well-drained sandy or gravelly soil and part or full sun. Zone 4.

V. pubescens (*V. pensylvanica*), the downy yellow violet, has heart-shaped leaves, 2–3 in. wide, covered with soft down hairs. Small clear yellow flowers open in early spring. Spreads to make an excellent ground cover in moist, fertile soil. Needs a shady, sheltered site. Zone 3.

V. sororia, the blue woods violet or confederate violet, is a catchall species that includes many varieties. All have lovely small flowers in shades of pale to deep blue or white. Blooms in early spring. Grows 6–8 in. tall and spreads fast to make a good ground cover for average soil and part shade. Zone 3.

yellow, apricot, pink, ruby, blue, purple, or near-black. A few cultivars are grown as perennials and propagated by division, but most seed strains are grown and used as annuals, like pansies. Both pansies and violas do very well in window boxes or containers.

How to grow: Full sun or afternoon shade. Grows best in moist, fertile, organic soil but does okay in average garden soil. Space seedlings 6–12 in. apart. In mild climates, plant when the weather starts to cool in fall. Otherwise, plant in fall or spring. Fall-planted seedlings overwinter with no protection even in Zone 6 and start blooming earlier than spring transplants. Deadhead to prolong bloom and to reduce self-seeding. Occasionally infested with aphids or spider mites.

Vitex

Vy′tex.
Verbenaceae. Verbena family.

Deciduous or evergreen shrubs or trees with opposite compound leaves and clusters of small flowers. Both foliage and flowers can be aromatic. About 250 spp., mostly tropical, native to the Old and New World.

agnus-castus (p. 153)
Chaste tree, pepperbush.
Deciduous shrub or small tree. Zone 7.
H: 10–20 ft. S: 10–15 ft.

A multitrunked shrub or small tree with a loose, open, umbrella-shaped crown. Leaves are palmately compound with 3–9 toothed leaflets. Dark green above and gray-green or silvery below, they release a spicy or peppery fragrance when crushed. Clustered 4–10-in. spikes of small lilac or lavender flowers bloom on the new growth from midsummer through fall. Adaptable and easy to grow, it makes a fine lawn or border specimen. Selections with white or pink flowers are also available. *V. negundo* var. *heterophylla,* the cut-leaved chaste tree, has similar flowers and finely divided, feathery, gray-green foliage that turns bronze or purplish in fall. The top dies back, but the roots are hardy to Zone 5. Grow it like a buddleia, cutting the stems to the ground each spring. It recovers fast and starts blooming by midsummer.

How to grow: Full sun. Thrives in hot weather. Tolerates poor, dry soil but grows faster with ordinary garden soil and regular watering. May freeze back in cold winters. Remove damaged shoots in spring. Trouble-free.

Vitis rotundifolia

Vitis

Vy′tis. Grape.
Vitaceae. Grape family.

Deciduous woody vines that climb by tendrils, with lobed leaves and clusters of round fruits. About 65 spp., native to the Northern Hemisphere.

grapes (p. 207)
Deciduous vines. Hardiness varies.
H: 20 ft. or more.

Grapes are very popular for shading patios and arbors or covering trellises and fences. They're fast-growing, vigorous, long-lived vines. The main trunk develops an interesting gnarled character and decorative shredding bark. The large handsome leaves have distinct veins and lobed or scalloped edges. Many develop rich gold, red, or purple fall color.

Different varieties of wine and table grapes are adapted to different climates; ask locally to determine which will do well in your area. In general, the *V. vinifera* grapes are limited to the mild climates of California and the West Coast, where summers are warm and dry. Selections of *V. rotundifolia,* the muscadine grapes, thrive in the heat and humidity of the South; 'Carlos' and 'Noble' are highly recommended. Where winters are cold and summers are short and cool, choose 'Concord', 'Niagara', or other types of *V. labrusca,* the fox grape.

How to grow: Full sun. Deep, well-drained, fertile soil. Prepare the soil well and install a trellis or other support before you plant. Careful training and pruning are required for maximum fruit production. If you just want to shade an arbor, simply cut the canes back in late winter. Grapes are subject to various diseases and pests. Ask locally to see if any problems are common in your area.

Waldsteinia

Wald-sty′nee-a. Barren strawberry.
Rosaceae. Rose family.

Low-growing perennials, like strawberries, with creeping stems and yellow flowers. Only 6 spp., native to the Northern Hemisphere.

ternata (p. 279)
Barren strawberry.
Perennial. Zone 4.
H: 4–6 in. S: 12 in.

Grown principally for its foliage, but the flowers are a nice bonus. The shiny 3-parted leaves are semievergreen (often turning reddish purple in cold weather). Yellow saucer-shaped flowers, 3/4 in. wide, are held well above the foliage in late spring and early summer. Forms compact mats and makes an excellent ground cover. Try using it on the sunny side of shrubs or small trees.

How to grow: Full or part sun. Needs well-drained soil and regular watering. Can't take extreme heat or humidity. Space 10–12 in. apart; divide in spring or fall. Needs very little care. Pest-free.

Washingtonia

Wash-ing-toe′nee-a.
Palmae. Palm family.

Large palms with tall trunks and palmately divided leaves. Only 2 spp., native to the arid Southwest.

filifera (p. 165)
Washington palm.
Fan palm. Zone 8.
H: 30–50 ft. S: 15–20 ft.

A tall, large palm that adapts to various growing conditions. Fronds are 6–9 ft. long, clustered in a round crown atop an erect trunk. Loose fibers dangle like fringe from the ends and edges of the leaflets. Large clusters of small white flowers hang below the fronds in spring, followed by black fruits in fall. Often used as a street tree, sometimes lined out for many blocks to create the effect of a tropical promenade. Individual specimens are good for poolside or xeriscape plantings. *W. robusta* looks similar but can grow to 100 ft. tall.

How to grow: Full or part sun. Tolerates heat and drought. Grows in any well-drained soil. Pest-free.

Weigela
Wy-gee′la.
Caprifoliaceae. Honeysuckle family.

Deciduous shrubs with opposite leaves and showy clusters of pink, purplish, or white flowers. About 10 spp., native to eastern Asia.

florida (p. 153)
Weigela.
Deciduous shrub. Zone 5.
H: to 10 ft. S: to 8 ft.

An old-fashioned favorite, easy to grow and very showy when blooming. Loose clusters of funnel-shaped flowers, 1 1/2 in. long, cover the stems for about 2 weeks in late spring. Rose-pink is the most common color, but dark pink and white forms are available. After bloom, the standard full-size shrub is a waste of space—its foliage is drab, and the profile is angular and lumpy. If your garden is small, consider using a compact cultivar with interesting foliage. 'Variegata' grows 4–6 ft. tall, with pink flowers and creamy-edged leaves. 'Minuet' is very compact, only 30 in. tall, with dark red flowers and purple-green leaves. 'Foliis Purpureis', about 4 ft. tall, has pink flowers and purple-green leaves.

How to grow: Full or part sun. Grows best with ordinary soil and watering but tolerates poor, dry soil. Tolerates hot summers. Prune to shape after flowering. Renew by cutting old shoots to the ground. Tough and trouble-free.

Wisteria
Wis-tee′ree-a, wis-tair′ee-a.
Leguminosae. Pea family.

Woody vines with twining stems; pinnately compound leaves; clusters of pealike blossoms, often very fragrant; and thick pods. All parts are poisonous. Only 6 spp., native to North America and eastern Asia.

floribunda (p. 207)
Japanese wisteria.
Deciduous woody vine. Zone 5.
H: 30 ft. or more.

A tough vigorous vine that spreads a curtain of bloom over a trellis, fence, arbor, or tree. Violet, blue, or white flowers hang in slender clusters 1–3 ft. long. Blooms in spring, as the new leaves expand. Large velvety pods ripen from green to brown and persist into winter. The compound leaves have 13–19 leaflets; stems twine in a clockwise motion. *W. sinensis,* or Chinese wisteria, has shorter clusters of more fragrant flowers, leaves with 7–13 leaflets, and stems that twine counterclockwise. Both form thick woody trunks and need a strong support, or they can be trained into a small weeping standard. There are many cultivars, selected for flower color and length of the flower clusters.

Grafted plants of named cultivars tend to flower earlier and more freely than unnamed seedling plants.

How to grow: Tolerates part shade but needs full sun for maximum flowering. Ordinary soil and watering. Requires several years to reach flowering size and may be balky. Administer treatment in early summer to promote flowering the following spring. Cut back vigorous shoots, prune the roots by cutting vertically with a sharp shovel, then fertilize with superphosphate. Established plants can be very aggressive and cover whole trees. Don't hesitate to prune back severely. No serious pests.

Xylosma
Zy-loz′ma.
Flacourtiaceae. Flacourtia family.

Evergreen trees or shrubs with simple alternate leaves, small flowers, and small berries. About 85 spp., all tropical.

congestum (p. 187)
Xylosma.
Evergreen shrub. Zone 8.
H: 8–10 ft. S: 10–12 ft.

A versatile shrub for hot, dry climates. It's most commonly grown as a clipped 3–5-ft. hedge; unpruned, it makes a graceful, spreading, 6–10-ft. screen. It can also be trained as an espalier to cover a hot, bright wall. The glossy leaves are 3–4 in. long, bronzy red when new, yellow-green when mature. Flowers are inconspicuous.

How to grow: Full or part sun. Ordinary or unimproved soil. Tolerates drought once well established. Plant anytime, and train and prune as desired. May need supplemental iron in alkaline soils. Generally problem-free.

Yucca
Yuk′a.
Agavaceae. Agave family.

Woody perennials with short or medium-height trunks; stiff, swordlike, fibrous leaves; erect branched stalks of large flowers, usually white; and large woody or fleshy fruits. About 40 spp., native to North America.

filamentosa (p. 215)
Bear grass, Adam's-needle.
Grasslike perennial. Zone 5.
H: 2–3 ft. (foliage); 5–6 ft. (flowers). S: 5–6 ft.

This southeastern native is the most commonly offered yucca. It spreads slowly to make a wide patch with many rosettes of sword-shaped leaves 2–3 ft. long. The evergreen leaves have sharp tips and curly fibers along the edges. The tall branched stalks of large white flowers are very showy in June. Gather the woody pods in fall for dried arrangements. 'Golden Sword' and other variegated forms have pretty gold or cream

Wisteria sinensis

Yucca filamentosa

stripes on the leaves. Plants sold as *Y. filamentosa* may actually be *Y. flaccida* or *Y. smalliana;* it's hard to distinguish these similar-looking plants.

Yuccas aren't restricted to dry climates or xeriscape gardens. They combine well with perennials or grasses in any well-drained, sunny bed or border. Individual clumps make a dramatic accent or focal point.

How to grow: Full sun. Needs well-drained soil; tolerates poor, dry soil. Tolerates winter cold, summer heat, and wind. Transplant container-grown plants in spring. Established plants form offsets at the base that can be removed and transplanted. Only care required is the removal of old flower stalks and dead leaves.

other yuccas

Y. elata, or soaptree, is a southwestern species with stiff, narrow, gray to blue-green leaves. Older plants develop several heads on erect trunks 10–20 ft. tall. The branching flower stalks, 3–7 ft. tall, are covered with creamy white flowers in May and June. Other southwestern species include *Y. angustifolia,* or Spanish dagger, which has slender leaves on stems to 6 ft. tall; and *Y. baccata,* or datil, which makes broad patches of thick-leaved rosettes and has short flower stalks. All are hardy to Zone 7 or 6 and require well-drained soil.

Y. glauca, or bear grass, is common on the western Great Plains. It forms pincushion-like rosettes of narrow spiky leaves, gray-green with pale edges. White flowers line a slender 3–6-ft. stalk in June. Zone 3.

Y. whipplei, or Whipple's yucca, is native to southern California. It makes a 2-ft. rosette of gray-green leaves tipped with very sharp spines and bears pale yellow or creamy flowers on a thick stalk up to 12 ft. tall in May or June. The parent rosette dies after flowering but produces offsets at the base. Zone 7.

Yucca whipplei

Zantedeschia

Zan-tee-des´kee-a. Calla.
Araceae. Arum family.

Perennials with rounded storage rhizomes, large long-stalked leaves, and white or colored spathes that curl around the thumblike cluster of tiny flowers. Only 6 spp., native to Africa.

albomaculata (p. 305)

Calla lily.
Tender perennial often grown as an annual.
Zone 8.
H: 24 in. S: 12 in.

Like gladioli, callas provide excellent cut flowers and are easy to grow if you don't mind digging the rhizomes each fall and storing them over winter. They start blooming in 6–8 weeks after the rhizomes are planted in late spring and continue flowering until midsummer. The white spathes are about 4 in. long. The white-spotted leaves have long stalks and arrowhead-shaped blades. Combines well with cannas, gingers, and other tropical-looking plants. *Z. aethiopica,* the white calla, is a larger plant with white spathes up to 8 in. long. It is evergreen and doesn't go dormant, so it must be overwintered in a pot. There are several new hybrid callas with pastel pink or yellow flowers; most are small plants with spathes less than 3 in. long.

How to grow: Part shade or sun. Ordinary soil and watering. Also tolerates constantly wet soil and can be grown along the edge of a stream or pond. Plant rhizomes 2–3 in. deep, about the time of last frost. Dig when the leaves turn yellow or after frost in fall. Shake off the soil and let the rhizomes dry for a few days, then remove leaf bases and roots before packing the rhizomes in dry peat, sawdust, or crumpled newspaper. Store in a dark place at 50°–60° F for the winter. Usually overwinters outdoors with no problems in Zone 8 and sometimes survives in Zone 7 or 6. Japanese beetles and spider mites attack the leaves.

Zauschneria

Zowch-nay´ree-a.
Onagraceae. Evening primrose family.

Perennials, often woody at the base, with leafy stems and spikes of bright red flowers. Only 4 spp., native to California. Many botanists now combine this genus with *Epilobium.*

californica (p. 279)

(now *Epilobium canum*)
California fuchsia.
Perennial. Zone 8.
H: 1–2 ft. S: 1–2 ft.

A rangy plant that spreads widely and quickly, it's a good candidate for casual gardens. Grows well with other California wildflowers among scattered shrubs. The bright scarlet trumpet-shaped flowers, 1½–2 in. long, attract hummingbirds from July to October. Flower spikes extend up to 2 ft. above the gray-green foliage. There are also pink and white forms.

How to grow: Sun or part shade. Does best with ordinary soil and watering but tolerates poor soil and dry spells. Cut to the ground after bloom; in mild areas, it will begin to regrow immediately. Propagate by seed, or divide in fall or spring.

Zelkova

Zel-ko´va.
Ulmaceae. Elm family.

Deciduous trees or shrubs with alternate toothed leaves, like elm leaves. Only 5 spp., native to Asia.

serrata (p. 129)

Japanese elm.
Deciduous tree. Zone 4.
H: 40–80 ft. S: 40–60 ft.

A tough fast-growing tree that is recommended as a substitute for the now-lamented

American elm. Makes a good shade tree for lawns or streets. The oval leaves, 3–5 in. long, have toothed margins and are dark green in summer; fall color is variable. The attractive bark is smooth on young trees and shoots and flaky on mature trunks. Notable cultivars include 'Village Green', a fast grower with reddish fall color; and 'Green Vase', which grows even faster and makes a graceful, arching, vase-shaped canopy.

How to grow: Full sun. Does best in rich, moist soil but tolerates poor soil and adapts to acidic or alkaline conditions. Established trees tolerate some drought. Has some pest and disease problems but is immune to Dutch elm disease.

Zelkova serrata

Zephyranthes

Zef-i-ran´theez.
Amaryllidaceae. Amaryllis family.

Small annuals or perennials with bulbs, a basal tuft of grassy leaves, and 6-petaled flowers on short stalks. About 70 spp., native to warm and tropical regions in the New World.

atamasco (see below for photo)
Fairy lily, zephyr lily, Atamasco lily.
Perennial. Zone 7.
H: 1–2 ft. S: 1–2 ft.

A cheerful plant with fragrant white or pinkish white flowers, about 3 in. wide, that open between April and June. Forms a basal clump of slender dark green leaves. Native to the Southeast, where it used to form large colonies in damp woods and meadows (it's uncommon now because of over-collection). Can be naturalized in a lawn if you delay mowing until after it blooms. Other species are hardy only to Zone 10 or 9 but make good container plants elsewhere. *Z. candida* (p. 279) has clear white flowers 2 in. wide. *Z. grandiflora* has red or pink flowers 3 in. wide. *Z. rosea* has pink flowers 1 in. wide.

How to grow: Full or part sun. Ordinary soil and watering in summer; subject to root rot if the soil stays too wet in winter. Plant bulbs 6–12 in. apart; divide every few years in fall. Plant several bulbs in a 6- or 8-in. pot for the patio. Overwinter potted bulbs in a cool dark spot, and don't let the soil dry out completely. No serious pests.

Zinnia

Zin´ee-a.
Compositae. Composite family.

Annuals, perennials, and a few small shrubs with simple opposite leaves and showy composite flowers, often with bright-colored rays. About 20 spp., mostly from Mexico.

angustifolia (p. 305)
(*Z. linearis*)
Annual. All zones.
H: 12 in. S: 12 in.

Quite different from common zinnias, this looks more like a wildflower than a bedding plant. It makes a loose mound of thin stems with sparse narrow leaves but blooms throughout the hottest weather and bears scores of blossoms 1–1½ in. wide. The species has orange rays, but new cultivars with white rays are more versatile. Combines well with grasses and prairie plants.

Z. haageana, or Mexican zinnia, is a similar species that also thrives in hot, dry conditions. It has bicolored flowers in shades of yellow, gold, red, mahogany, or maroon. 'Old Mexico' and 'Persian Carpet' are old but still-popular strains.

How to grow: Full sun. Ordinary soil and watering. Tolerates dry soil and hot weather. Start seeds indoors 6 weeks before last frost, or direct-sow after the soil has warmed. Doesn't grow well until the weather is warm. Japanese beetles eat the flowers.

elegans cultivars (p. 305)
Common zinnias.
Annuals. All zones.
H: 1–3 ft. S: 1 ft.

Zinnias are among the easiest annuals to grow, and there are dozens of strains to choose from. Most have double flowers, ranging from 1 to 6 in. wide, available in all colors but blue. Plants range from 1-ft. dwarfs, good for edging and bedding, to cut-flower types that reach 3 ft. tall. Arrangers grow a row of zinnias in a cutting garden, but you can also tuck a few plants here and there to fill gaps in a mixed border. Local nurseries usually grow mixed colors of different strains for spring planting. If you want one particular color, order seeds and grow your own plants.

How to grow: Like *Z. angustifolia*, but they do best in good garden soil with regular watering. Tolerate heat but not dryness. Foliage is subject to mildew, which disfigures and weakens the plants. Allow plenty of space between plants for good air circulation, and don't wet the foliage when watering. Cut flowers for arrangements when they just open, and strip all the leaves off the lower part of the stems.

grandiflora (p. 279)
Desert zinnia, Rocky Mountain zinnia.
Perennial. Zone 5.
H: 6–8 in. S: 12 in. or more.

Possibly the toughest low ground cover in the West, it provides color for a long season even on hot, exposed sites. The daisylike blossoms, 1 in. wide, open bright yellow, fading to straw color as they mature. The wiry grasslike leaves are pale green, curing to tan in winter. Spreads slowly by root sprouts, eventually forming a long-lived, dense, indestructible ground cover. Add verbena to young plantings for a colorful display while the zinnia fills in.

How to grow: Full sun. Needs dry soil. Tolerates poor soil and heat. Sold as plants; seeds are rarely offered. When the soil has warmed, space plants 6–8 in. apart (12 in. if combined with verbena or other plants). Increase by division in spring. Mow 4 in. high in early spring. Trouble-free.

Zinnia grandiflora

Growing Healthy Plants

Garden know-how

Deciding what to grow and where to grow it is an exciting part of gardening. But it is only a beginning. The garden of your dreams is brought to life by a lot of dirt-under-the-fingernails effort. These day-to-day gardening activities—preparing soil; planting trees, shrubs, and flower beds; watering; fertilizing; pruning; and maintaining your plants—may be harder work than poring over gardening catalogs, but they can be no less enjoyable. The chapters in this section of the book seek to help you accomplish these and other gardening tasks.

Understanding how plants grow and respond to different conditions and care is the key to successfully employing all the techniques discussed in the chapters that follow. Although this knowledge can be gleaned from books, it is careful personal observation that makes it meaningful to you and your garden.

Observe the plants in your community

Taking a close look at the plants in your area can tell you a lot about the possibilities and problems of creating and maintaining a garden on your property. Undeveloped or neglected lots show what nature accomplishes without a gardener's assistance. Is the untended vegetation sparse or dense? Can you see bare soil between the plants, or do they crowd together and cover the soil? How fast do the shrubs and trees grow?

Naturally dense growth indicates plenty of precipitation and normal or good soil. Sparse growth usually is a sign of low moisture, but it may also imply extremely poor soil. If the untended environment is sparse, you'll probably have to irrigate and may have to work at improving the soil if you want to create a lush garden on your property. And where woody plants grow quickly, pruning hedges, foundation shrubs, and shade trees will be a constant chore unless you choose compact or slow-growing varieties.

Once you start, more questions will come to mind. Be inquisitive when you visit a friend's garden, and as you walk around your own property. It's important, for example, to recognize that conditions may vary quite a bit from one spot to another on your site. By observing the patterns of sun, shade, water runoff and accumulation, and air movement, and by digging test holes to determine the depth and characteristics of the soil, you can identify areas with different growing conditions.

As you learn more about local conditions and their effect on plants, you'll realize that some conditions are more amenable to change than others. There's nothing you can do to raise winter temperatures in Minnesota or to brighten cloudy days in Seattle. And providing an inch of water a week to a lawn in the Sonoran Desert may be far too costly in time, energy, or money. Selecting plants that tolerate the given conditions is the easiest way to make and maintain a garden.

Part of the challenge of gardening, however, is growing a wide variety of plants. By watering, improving the soil, providing shelter from wind and cold, and creating or removing shade, you can introduce many kinds of plants that wouldn't occur naturally in your area. How many of these "exotic" plants you choose to grow depends on how maleable your gardening conditions prove to be and how much work you're willing to expend altering them to suit your plants.

Figuring out what each plant needs comes with experience, but it helps to have a basic understanding of how plant growth is affected by the environment—temperature, light, water, and nutrients.

Temperature

Air and soil temperatures affect root growth, leaf development, foliage color, stem elongation, flowering, fruit set, and other aspects of plant growth and development. Often a plant's response is keyed to a particular minimum or maximum temperature. For example, daffodil roots begin to develop when soil temperatures drop below 60° F in the fall. Gardenias don't bloom unless the air temperature is above 60° F at night. Other plants respond to warmth over time. Most spring-flowering shrubs don't bloom until there have been a certain number of days above a certain minimum temperature. And some responses depend on the contrast between day and night temperatures. Fall foliage colors are most intense if the days are warm and the nights are frosty.

In general, the plants you'll find in the Gallery of Plants and the Encyclopedia of Plants in this book can actively grow at temperatures ranging between freezing and 90° F or hotter. They may sulk in cool weather or wilt on hot days, but they will survive and recover. When temperatures get too cold or too hot, plants stop growing. They may even drop their leaves and go dormant. Daffodils, tulips, other spring-flowering bulbs, many woodland wildflowers, and some lawn grasses go dormant through the heat of summer. Many herbaceous and woody perennials go dormant through the cold of winter; some actually require several weeks of cold to trigger renewed growth the following year.

Temperature can be a matter of life or death. Heat alone rarely kills plants, but the combination of heat and dryness (dry soil and/or dry air) can be fatal. Cold does kill plants, but sensitivity to cold varies widely among plants and between different parts of the same plant. Some plants are killed outright at 32° F, but others can tolerate 0° F or even -30° F. The tops of herbaceous perennials and many shrubs die back at temperatures below freezing, but the roots and ground-level buds survive. Cold often kills the leaves of broad-leaved evergreen trees and shrubs, but if buds remain, the plants recover. If you're not familiar with a plant's cold tolerance, its hardiness-zone rating is a good guide. (These ratings are given in the Encyclopedia entries, and the USDA Hardiness Zone map is reprinted on pages 576–577.)

You can't do much to change the temperatures in your garden, but it's important to keep temperature in mind as you choose and locate plants. Some people go to great lengths to grow plants in conditions more extreme than the plants are adapted to, but almost everyone can accommodate some plants that are heat or cold sensitive in their region just by careful placement. Put plants that are less tolerant of heat in a shaded area where you can water them regularly. Put plants of questionable cold hardiness against a brick or stone wall that retains heat, sheltered from prevailing winter winds, and be sure that the soil drains freely and doesn't stay wet.

Light

Two aspects of sunlight—its intensity or brightness, and the daylength or photoperiod—greatly affect plants in a garden. Both influence the daily photosynthetic output, which is the basis for plant growth. In that regard, fewer hours of bright light

are equivalent to more hours of weak light. A rosebush can grow equally well in Phoenix, with 15 hours of glaring sun on a summer day, or in Seattle, with 18 hours of gentler light. At any latitude, growth slows in the fall and winter as both brightness and daylength decrease.

All plants can tolerate a range of light intensities; they must, since all climates have sunny and cloudy days. On a long-term basis, however, some plants do best in full sun, generally defined as unblocked sun for at least six hours a day during the growing season. Others prefer partial sun, which is full sun for fewer than six hours a day, preferably in the morning, or light shade, such as that cast by a sparse foliage or tree limbs high overhead. Fewer garden plants perform well in the deep shade of a building or a densely leaved tree. These categories aren't absolute, and, of course, the amount and intensity of sunlight vary considerably across the country.

Light intensity influences a plant's size, shape, foliage, and flowering. Light that's too intense can stunt a plant and usually bleaches or discolors the foliage. Moving a plant suddenly from shaded to sunny conditions often causes white or brown splotches on the leaves, and the leaves may soon drop off. The plant may recover and adapt to the brighter light, producing a new set of leaves within a few weeks, or it may die. Plants permanently exposed to light that's too bright may have leaves that are smaller, more leathery, and yellower than normal. The plants may flower profusely, but the petals are likely to be faded in color.

Light that's too weak can also stunt a plant, producing long, weak stems with a few widely spaced, dark green leaves that are larger and thinner than normal. Young seedlings—especially plants started indoors—are so weakened by low light intensity that they usually flop over and die. An older plant, such as a shrub growing under a tree, may survive with inadequate light, but it will grow slowly, if at all, and won't flower or fruit.

Some plants are sensitive to daylength (actually, they measure hours of darkness) and respond by forming flower buds when the photoperiod is either less or more than that plant's critical limit. Chrysanthemums form buds when daylength is shorter than 15 hours, and violets need less than 11 hours; both are categorized as short-day plants. Long-day plants include dill, which flowers only when the photoperiod exceeds 11 hours, and baby's-breath, which needs more than 16 hours. Many plants are insensitive to daylength; called day-neutral plants, they flower whenever they're ready.

Water

Constituting 90 percent or more of a plant's weight, water is essential for photosynthesis. But for every cup of water that a plant uses or stores, many gallons merely pass through in the process of transpiration—the continuous movement of water into the roots, up through the stems, and evaporating out tiny holes called stomata on the bottom of the leaves. Transpiration is essential for bringing water and dissolved nutrients up from the soil, and evaporation cools the leaves on hot days.

Plants differ greatly in their ability to absorb water from the soil, store it in their tissues, and reduce water loss through the leaves. Gardeners in rainy climates have the widest choice of plants, but gardeners in dry regions or where irrigation water is limited have identified hundreds of herbaceous and woody plants that use water efficiently.

Sooner or later, plants die if they don't get enough water. First their leaves and flowers wilt, turn brown, and fall off, and then their stems and roots wither and shrink. Plants also die from too much water, especially if it accumulates in the soil around their roots. In that case, the leaves and flowers turn black and fall off, and the roots and stems rot and get mushy. In between these extremes, the right amount of water is that which produces vigorous but sturdy growth and firm, healthy foliage and flowers.

Nutrients

Compared with their water needs, plants use a tiny volume of nutrients. These essential elements—nitrogen, potassium, phosphorus, calcium, magnesium, iron, sulfur, and others—are absorbed from the soil by the roots, dissolved in the sap, and transported throughout the plant, where they are incorporated into proteins, enzymes, vitamins, pigments, and other molecules.

Plants need different amounts and proportions of nutrients and have different abilities to extract these nutrients from the soil. Gardeners respond in two ways. One approach is to supply custom fertilizers for each kind of plant—one preparation for azaleas, another for roses, something else for spring bulbs. The other way is to amend the soil with plenty of organic matter, apply an all-purpose natural or synthetic fertilizer, and let different plants pick and choose what they need. Either method works, but combining general all-purpose fertilization with supplements for particular plants works especially well.

It's uncommon to see garden plants damaged by overfertilization. (It's easier to overfertilize and damage plants grown in containers.) As long as plenty of water is available, more nutrients means more growth.

Nutrient deficiencies are common, but the symptoms vary from plant to plant and nutrient to nutrient. They include slow or no growth, failure to bloom, and pale or discolored leaves. It's often difficult to distinguish such symptoms from the effects of cold temperatures, of too little or too much light, or of drought—and, of course, all these factors interact. If conditions seem favorable but a plant just isn't growing, adding fertilizer usually gives it the necessary boost.

What is soil?

Soil is the layer of transition between the rock core of the Earth and the web of life on its surface. It is a very thin layer, measured in inches or feet, but it is the basis for all that stands between life and lifelessness.

Soil is a complex and dynamic mixture of several components: rock and mineral particles, water and dissolved substances, air, living organisms, and more or less decomposed organic matter. An "ideal" soil is said to contain a little less than 50 percent solid particles, about 25 percent liquid, 25 percent air, and less than 5 percent living organisms and organic matter. In actual soils, of course, the relative proportions of these components vary from region to region, and the makeup of any given soil changes with the weather and the seasons.

Soil texture

Soil is composed primarily of broken-down rocks; mineral particles constitute more than 95 percent of the bulk of most soils. The size of these particles determines the texture of any particular soil. All soil particles are relatively small, but soil scientists divide them into small (sand), smaller (silt), and smallest (clay).

Sandy soil has a coarse, grainy, gritty texture. If you squeeze a handful and release it, sandy soil falls apart and runs between your fingers. Wet or dry, sandy soil is easy to dig and till and easy for plant roots to penetrate. Water and air pass freely through the large pores between sand particles, and sandy soil dries out quickly after a rain and doesn't hold a large reservoir of water.

Silty soil has a slippery texture, like talcum powder. If you squeeze a handful and release it, it slides apart. When silty soil is very dry, water beads and runs off the surface rather than penetrating. Once it's moistened, however, silty soil absorbs and retains more water than does sandy soil.

Clay particles are microscopic. Clay soil feels sticky when wet, and it holds its shape when you mold or model it. When dry, clay hardens into dense, bricklike clods. Clay tends to swell when wet, but it shrinks and cracks apart when dry.

In practice, any soil is a mixture of particles of different sizes. Soils with moderate amounts of sand, silt, and clay are known as loam. Loamy soils are considered ideal for gardening because they combine the advantages of easy tillage and good water and nutrient retention.

Water and air in the soil

The spaces or pores between soil particles can be filled with water or with air. Gravity pulls water down, whereas adhesion (the tendency of water to stick to surfaces) slows its movement. Water doesn't spread far laterally through soil, except when it's running down a slope. Draining water slows down when it reaches a transition between finer and coarser soils—no matter which lies above the other—and "perches" in the soil immediately above the transition zone.

Plant roots need water, but they also need oxygen, which they get from air. If soil is waterlogged and the pores are filled with water, plants suffer. Deprived of oxygen, roots—and thereby whole plants—can drown in a matter of days. Worse, bacteria in waterlogged soil give off a gas that's poisonous to roots. And dead roots are vulnerable to fungal infection, which can proceed into living tissue and kill off an already weakened plant.

Organic matter and humus

Organic matter is a catchall term for living organisms and plant and animal residues in various stages of decomposition. As the tiny animals and microorganisms that live in the soil gradually bite, chew, and digest dead leaves, stems, and roots as well as other debris, they break this material down into unidentifiable crumbs. In the process, elements such as nitrogen, phosphorus, and sulfur are converted into forms that can be absorbed as nutrients by plants. Also produced are acids that help dissolve rocks and release minerals needed for plant growth.

The volume of residues is greatly reduced, until all that's left is humus, a complex and concentrated molecular stew with a characteristic dark brown or black color. (Humus clinging to the surface of mineral particles is what makes soil look dark.) Humus itself continues to decompose at a rate that depends on temperature—as slowly as 1 percent a year in very cool climates or as fast as 25 percent a year in the tropics. Decomposing humus provides a steady supply of nutrients for plant growth.

In addition to furnishing nutrients, organic matter changes the physical condition or structure of the soil. Increasing the organic content of a given soil makes it easier to till and easier for roots to penetrate. Water soaks in faster and more deeply.

Soil structure

The way in which individual soil particles cluster, or aggregate, is called soil structure. Soils range in structure from single-grain soil, such as beach sand, to massive soil, where the entire soil mass clings together like modeling clay.

A granular, crumblike soil structure is most desirable. Soil that's well aggregated—that crushes easily but will hold together if pressed—is said to be friable, or to have good tilth. Either term means that the soil is easy to till and ideal for plant root growth. Adding plenty of organic matter is a good way to improve your soil's structure.

If the soil is disturbed when it's wet, aggregates can melt, collapse, or break apart, compacting the soil and making it harder for water and air to penetrate. Aggregates of clay soil are particularly vulnerable to disturbance, so be especially careful not to till or cultivate clay soil when it is wet.

Soil chemistry

Soil is a reservoir for the water and nutrients that plants need. The water comes from natural precipitation and irrigation. The nutrients come from mineral particles, organic matter, and fertilizers. Only nutrients that are dissolved in the soil water are available for plants to absorb. The water and dissolved nutrients form a thin film that coats the surface of the soil particles and clings to the tiny pore spaces between particles.

Soils differ greatly in their capacity for storing and providing water and nutrients. In general, clay soils and soils high in organic matter can retain more water and nutrients than can sandy soils or pure mineral soils. This is because clay particles and organic matter have greater total surface area and more small pore spaces than do sandy soils.

Soil pH. A soil's pH is the measure of its acidity or alkalinity. The pH scale ranges from 0 to 14. At pH 7, the midpoint, the soil solution (the soil water and everything that is dissolved in it) is neutral, neither acidic nor alkaline. As pH numbers go down from 7, the soil solution becomes increasingly acidic. As the numbers increase from pH 7, it becomes more alkaline. Each number on the scale differs from the preceding one by a factor of 10. That is, pH 5 is 10 times as acidic as pH 6, and pH 4 is 100 times as acidic as pH 6.

Soil pH typically varies from about pH 4 to pH 8, although it may range lower or higher. Regions of high rainfall tend to have soil that is more acidic. Regions with dry climates tend to have alkaline soils. This is because alkaline substances dissolve and leach, or drain, out of the soil faster than do acidic substances.

The importance of a soil's pH to plants (and therefore to gardeners) is its influence on nutrient availability. The nutrients needed for plant growth are most readily available at slightly acid to neutral pH, which is why that range is recommended. Many plants are adapted to grow best at a certain soil pH level, but they may tolerate conditions that are two to three points on either side of their preferred level.

"Sour" and "sweet" are old-fashioned terms for acidic and alkaline soils, respectively, and old-time gardeners claimed to be able to determine a soil's pH by tasting it. Acidic substances do taste sour, but you'd be unlikely to detect this in soil. Alkaline substances actually taste bitter, not sweet. A chemical soil test is the only sure way to measure soil pH.

Soil fertility. At least 16 elements are considered necessary for the growth of green plants: carbon, hydrogen, oxygen, nitrogen, phosphorus, sulfur, potassium, calcium, magnesium, iron, manganese, zinc, copper, molybdenum, boron, and chlorine. Plants obtain the first three—carbon, hydrogen, and oxygen—from water and air. All the rest are absorbed from the soil. These elements are called nutrients, and soil rich in nutrients is called fertile soil.

Soil fertility is a complex subject. Many soils have adequate supplies of some nutrients but insufficient amounts of others. For example, many soils have adequate phosphorus to support healthy plants but are deficient in nitrogen. In cases such as this, fertilizing with the missing element can greatly enhance plant performance. But even though a nutrient is present in the soil, it may not be in a form that is available to plants. Plants need iron, for instance, but roots can't absorb iron oxide (rust), which is one of the most common forms of iron in the soil. Interactions between the different nutrients can also limit availability. For example, if a soil is high in calcium, plants may have difficulty absorbing magnesium and potassium. Finally, nutrient availability changes at different pH levels.

Fortunately, plants have a remarkable ability to extract nutrients from the soil. They actively pump in nutrients and concentrate them at levels as much as 30,000 times greater inside the root than in the soil immediately outside. Different plants require different amounts and proportions of the essential nutrients, but many garden plants do fine in soil of average fertility.

As a final note on the topic of soil fertility, it's worth mentioning soil color. Soil comes in many colors—brown, black, red, yellow, and white are common—depending on its origins and history. Most gardeners think that the blacker the soil, the more fertile it is. This is not necessarily so. Black soils aren't always fertile, and soils of other colors are sometimes quite fertile. If you're new to a region and the soil color is unusual to you, ask a local gardener, farmer, or extension agent about the soil's fertility.

Life in the soil

Soil not only supports life, it contains life. A huge and diverse population of organisms, ranging from microscopic bacteria to wriggling worms, is at home in the soil. Their presence is beneficial in many ways, and they should be encouraged in the garden. They recycle nutrients, mix and churn soil particles, and improve soil structure.

Soil microorganisms. Healthy soil teems with microorganisms—a teaspoon of it may contain billions of bacteria, an ounce may have thousands of yards of fungal mycelia. These organisms may be useful to plants. Some bacteria, for example, transform atmospheric nitrogen, a gas that plants cannot use, into nitrates, nutrient compounds that plants readily absorb and need. Other soil organisms give off compounds that can stimulate or inhibit root growth. Some "good guys" act as a shield that defends plants from harmful organisms. Others extend the surface area of plant roots, collecting nutrients that are shared with the plant.

Some soil microbes are harmful to plants. Soil-borne diseases cause root rots and also rots and blights that penetrate stems and affect aboveground plant parts, usually causing wilting or even death. Anthracnose, fusarium, and verticillium are common soil-borne diseases that afflict a wide variety of plants. Some plant species and varieties show resistance to these diseases, but there are few treatments to protect or to cure susceptible plants, and it's almost impossible to eradicate these diseases from infected soil.

Earthworms and other soil animals. Earthworms are good for soil. Their vertical burrowing carries and mixes material up and down through the soil, improving its aeration and tilth. (Contrary to folklore, earthworms don't by themselves make soil more fertile.) As long as there is moisture and enough organic matter for them to feed on, earthworms can be found in all types of soils. The more organic matter, the more earthworms. Their populations can reach several hundred thousand per acre. They are most active near the surface, but they can burrow 6 feet deep.

Other small soil animals and insects greatly affect the makeup of the soil, feeding on living and dead plant parts, on litter, on bacteria and other soil microorganisms, and on each other. They mix the soil and transport material up and down and sideways. Their tunneling opens passageways that enhance air and water infiltration. A few soil-dwellers, such as nematodes and grubs that damage plant roots, are pests. But the vast majority of soil animals are beneficial to the garden.

Evaluating your soil

Before beginning a garden, you should spend some time observing and assessing your soil. You can evaluate the soil's texture, depth, profile, drainage, and exposure; check for compaction and contamination; and test its pH and nutrient levels.

Soil conditions vary across even a small garden, due to natural factors or to human activity. Watch for differences in the soil itself and in how plants grow in different parts of the garden.

Testing soil texture

The simplest way to assess your soil's texture is to take a handful and feel how it responds when you rub and squeeze it. Soil that feels gritty is high in sand. Sticky soil is high in clay. For a more precise evaluation, take spoonfuls of soil from a few inches below the surface at several spots in your garden. Remove any pebbles, debris, leaves, or roots, and break up any lumps. Mix the samples together, then put a cup of the soil and a cup or two of water into a clear glass jar. Secure the jar lid and shake the jar vigorously until all the soil is suspended in the water.

Set the jar on a table and get a ruler. After about a minute, the largest particles will have settled to the bottom. Measure and record the depth of that layer, which is the sand. (See the drawing at right.) After about an hour, the intermediate-size particles—the silt—will have settled out. Measure the depth again, then subtract the amount that was sand in order to obtain the depth of the silt layer. After about 24 hours, measure and subtract the amounts of sand and silt in order to obtain the depth of the clay particles.

To calculate the percentages of sand, silt, and clay, divide the depth of each layer by the total depth of soil, then multiply by 100. For example, if the sand layer is 1/2 inch deep and the soil totals 3 inches deep, the percent of sand is 1/2 divided by 3, or 0.17; multiplying by 100 gives 17 percent sand.

Loam, that ideal garden soil, can vary considerably in its makeup. Loam soils contain less than 52 percent sand, between 28 and 50 percent silt, and 7 to 27 percent clay. If the makeup of your soil falls very far outside these ranges, you may wish to amend it.

Looking at your soil profile

It's easy to examine the profile of your soil. Just dig a straight-sided hole from one to several feet deep (depending on local conditions) and look at the soil that's exposed. Are there differences in color and texture? How deep are the different layers? What

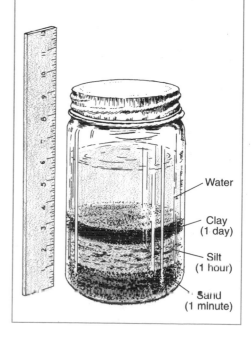

Evaluating soil texture

Mix several small samples of soil with about twice as much water (by volume). Shake vigorously and allow to settle. Measure the layers within the times indicated. To find the percentage of sand, silt, or clay in the soil, divide the depth of each layer by the total depth of all the settled soil and multiply by 100.

Water

Clay
(1 day)

Silt
(1 hour)

Sand
(1 minute)

you observe will inform you about the soil's history, the conditions that plant roots will encounter, and the soil's potential to supply the support, water, and nutrients that all plants need.

Watch for hardpans—dense layers that are particularly hard to penetrate with a spade or a shovel. These compacted layers form barriers to water movement and root growth. If there is a compacted layer, note how deep it is and how thick it is. Check to see if it underlies the entire garden, or if it is limited to certain areas.

Testing drainage

You can test drainage by digging one or more holes about 2 feet deep. Fill the hole(s) with water, and check to see if any water remains in the bottom of the hole after 24 hours. If all the water is gone, the drainage is fine. If just a little water remains, the drainage will be adequate for some plants but not for all. If most of the water remains, drainage is so poor that many plants will suffer.

Also, watch the flow of water on your property during and after a heavy rain. Note the areas where water runs off quickly and the low spots where water collects, and select plants for those spots accordingly.

Checking for contamination

Soil around houses and other buildings or near roads or driveways is sometimes contaminated with trash and debris, concrete, oil, or lead. Check for buried trash from construction or renovation projects. Remove any chunks of concrete or plaster, which release alkaline lime into the adjacent soil. Look near driveways or parking areas for oil-stained soil, which must be dug up and removed. In cold-winter areas, road salt may also cause trouble.

Lead contamination can be a problem in soil that is adjacent to busy streets and freeways and in soil near the foundations of older houses and buildings that have been painted repeatedly with lead-based paints. Lead in the soil usually doesn't damage plants, but it can accumulate in their roots and leaves, and if these are eaten, the lead can harm humans. If you suspect lead contamination on parts of your property, have the soil tested for lead; where results indicate danger, grow ornamental plants, not vegetables.

Testing soil pH and nutrient levels

Experienced gardeners can often judge soil pH and soil fertility by looking at the plants growing in that soil. A much more reliable method is to test the soil at home or send a sample of the soil to a state or private laboratory.

Home soil-test kits are generally inexpensive and easy to use, but they are much less accurate than are laboratory tests. Soil-test labs report pH and availability of major nutrients, and they recommend how much lime, sulfur, or fertilizer to add to improve the soil for growing whatever plants you specify. A single test can serve as a baseline appraisal of your soil. A series of tests repeated over time will monitor the effect of the treatments you apply to the soil.

Whether you test at home or at a lab, collecting a representative sample is essential for meaningful results. Dig a few inches deep (but avoid sampling from the subsoil) and gather small amounts of soil from 10 or more places around the garden. Then mix these to make a composite sample. If you want to compare different parts of the garden—for example, an area that has been limed and fertilized with one that hasn't—prepare samples for each area and keep them separate. (Be sure to label which sample is which.)

Improving your soil

Many people move into new homes and discover that their soil is too sandy, too clayey, too shallow, too infertile, too wet, or too compacted for plants to grow easily and well. This is discouraging at first, but with a little work, nearly all soils can be improved.

There are several approaches to soil improvement. One is to buy organic, inorganic, and chemical materials to mix with your existing soil. Slower but less expensive approaches are to grow green manures and to make compost. Adding chemical and organic amendments can help neutralize overly acidic or alkaline soils. Rototilling, hand digging, and well-timed cultivation can all help loosen and aerate soil. Installing drainage systems or planting in raised beds improves the movement of water and air through the soil.

Deciding which areas to improve

Focus your soil-improvement efforts on those areas where they will have the most effect. Annual flowers and vegetables have fine roots that are too weak to penetrate hard soil, and they look best and produce most if pampered with optimum conditions.

It's also worth spending extra time and effort on the soil when planting perennial beds, lawns, and ground covers. Once established, these plantings last for years. Given deep, loose, well-drained, and fertile soil, perennial plants of all kinds survive much better through winter cold, summer heat, and droughts.

The majority of trees and shrubs do better if planted into native, unamended soil. The nursery trade used to recommend that the gardener add quantities of peat moss or compost to the soil when refilling the hole around the root ball. In recent years, however, researchers have observed that trees planted in holes filled with fluffed-up soil never root out into the surrounding territory. Such trees are limited to the supply of water and nutrients in the volume of the hole, as if they were growing in containers.

Materials to improve your soil

The easiest and fastest way to start a garden on a site with poor soil is to fill beds and prepare planting areas with large quantities of topsoil or soil blends. Buying topsoil can be an uncertain business. You may get an unwelcome crop of weeds as well as stones and debris, and the soil itself may be less than "top" quality. Before buying a truckload, ask where the soil is coming from.

Soil blends (frequently called improved soil) consist of topsoil amended with composted tree leaves, sawdust or bark chips, manure, and other organic materials. Blends are more expensive than plain topsoil, but they're a worthwhile investment for small areas such as flower beds.

Organic materials. Adding organic material—peat moss, reed-sedge peat, composted bark, or other composted materials—helps soil in many ways. It increases the microbial activity, which in turn improves the soil structure and makes it easier for water, air, and roots to penetrate. It increases the soil's capacity to hold water and nutrients. And it provides a small supply of nutrients, particularly micronutrients. The different forms of organic material all have desirable effects, so choosing among them is mostly a matter of price, availability, and convenience.

Peat is a general category of compost that forms naturally in wet areas. Old, dark, dead, compressed sphagnum moss is the most common form of this amendment. Called peat moss, sphagnum peat, or simply peat, it is sold under several brand names in bags, bales, and bulk. Reed-sedge peat, collected from natural deposits of decomposed reeds, sedges, cattails, and similar marsh plants, is typically much less expensive than sphagnum peat. All forms of sphagnum moss and peat are acidic and may have an effect on soil pH. Although water tends to bead up on the surface of dry peat, once peat is wet, it retains moisture well.

Locally produced compost is an inexpensive alternative to peat moss. Many municipalities now make and sell compost from lawn clippings, tree leaves, and chipped brush. Some sell composted sewage sludge, usually as a dark granular substance that bears little trace of its origins. (See "Making compost" later in this section for information on how to make your own.)

Consider agricultural waste, such as bedding and manures from cattle, poultry, or horse farms; processing wastes from canneries; spent mushroom compost; and hulls and stalks from cotton gins and grain mills. You might need to drive a pickup truck to the source, but chances are the price will be low. Aged material—the older, darker stuff—will benefit the soil structure immediately. Use fresh material as a mulch, or layer it in a compost pile for a season before adding it to the soil.

Sawdust and bark chips are cheap and abundant in some parts of the country. Give fresh or coarse wood chips time to decompose before adding them to the soil, since the microorganisms that decompose wood need nitrogen to do the job and can "steal" nitrogen that would otherwise be available to plants. Adding 1 pound of ammonium sulfate for each 1-inch-deep layer of wood chips spread over 100 square feet will speed decomposition. When they've turned dark, soft, and crumbly, mix the chips into the soil. Composted sawdust or bark chips increase soil aeration and improve soil structure, but they don't absorb or retain water or nutrients as well as sphagnum moss or peat products do.

Improving clay soil. Gardeners are often tempted to try to improve clay soil by adding sand. Unfortunately, adding a small percent of sand to clay soil produces a cementlike mixture. Don't add any sand to clay unless you can add at least one-quarter by volume. Look for coarse, clean, washed sand—the washing removes salt and fine particles.

Both calcium carbonate (lime) and calcium sulfate (gypsum) can be used to improve a clay soil's water and air penetration and make the soil easier for roots to penetrate. Adding lime raises the pH of acidic soil, which may be an additional useful correction. Gypsum has no effect on pH, so it is recommended for neutral or alkaline soils.

Green manures

One way to improve poor soil before starting a garden is to devote a season or two to growing green manures (sometimes called cover crops). While growing, these plants cover the soil, protecting it from wind and water erosion. When cut down and mixed into the soil, they decompose and provide energy to soil microorganisms, produce acids that dissolve mineral nutrients from the soil, and increase the amount of humus in the soil.

Sow cover-crop seeds evenly onto a smooth bed, press the seeds into the soil, and water regularly to ensure good germination. It's usually best to turn under a crop just before it begins to bloom. Mow dense, tall stands, then dig or till to mix the plants—tops and roots—with the soil. Allow one or more weeks for the turned-under plants to wilt and begin to decompose before planting in the bed.

Rye, wheat, and barley are often sown in the fall and turned under in the spring. Oats are sown in the spring and turned under in summer. These crops all make a dense stand of grassy foliage aboveground and a soil-binding mass of fine roots underground. Buckwheat, a broad-leaved grain, is one of the fastest-growing green manures; sown in early summer, it can be ready to turn under within 10 weeks. Several legumes, including different kinds of clover, alfalfa, sweet clover, cowpeas, and vetch, are useful as green manures. Legumes convert nitrogen from the air into a form that can be used by plants.

Changing soil pH

Chances are good that the common plants that are doing well in other gardens in your neighborhood are fairly tolerant of the existing soil pH, so choosing these plants is an easy way to begin a garden. It is possible, however, to change the soil pH in order to grow less-common plants.

A soil test will indicate the pH of your garden soil. Lime is used to treat acidic soil, and sulfur to treat alkaline soil. Both are inexpensive chemicals that can be purchased at a local garden center. The finer the soil texture or the greater the amount of organic material, the more lime or sulfur will be needed to raise or lower pH by one point. Also, because a change of one point in pH (from pH 4 to pH 5, for example) represents a tenfold change in acidity or alkalinity, it takes a lot more lime or sulfur to change pH by two points than by one point. These variables lead to one important conclusion: Test your soil at regular intervals to monitor the effects of the treatments you apply.

Improving acidic soil—raising soil pH. There are several forms of lime appropriate for use in the garden. Fine-ground limestone (calcium carbonate) and dolomitic limestone (which contains both calcium carbonate and magnesium carbonate) are the cheapest, easiest, safest to use, and most readily available. Dolomitic limestone supplies magnesium, an essential plant nutrient, as well as reducing soil acidity. Both of these materials are ground-up rocks; the more finely ground, the better, as smaller particles react more quickly to neutralize soil acids. (Quick lime and hydrated lime are caustic powders that can damage your skin and your plants.)

Lime can be applied to the surface of the soil and watered in, but it's more effective if you mix it thoroughly with the soil. You can apply lime at any season, but don't apply it at the same time as chemical fertilizer. If you want to raise the pH of acidic soil by more than one point, it's a good idea to apply small doses of lime once or twice a year, retesting the soil pH from time to time to monitor its changes. Lime has a slow and gradual effect on soil pH, but it eventually does its job.

Wood ashes can neutralize acidic soil. Hardwood ashes (from broad-leaved trees) generally are more effective than are softwood ashes (from conifers). Wood ash supplies some potassium, an essential plant nutrient, as well as reducing acidity.

Improving alkaline soil—lowering soil pH. Applying sulfur is the fastest way to lower soil pH. Elemental sulfur, often called flowers of sulfur, can lower soil pH in as little as six to eight weeks, but the treatment isn't long-lasting and must be repeated after six months to a year. Sulfur-containing compounds, such as ammonium sulfate, aluminum sulfate, and iron sulfate, have a rapid but short-term effect, lasting as little as three to four weeks in very alkaline soils.

As an amendment or mulch, peat moss, composted sawdust or bark, and composted leaves and pine needles all have a slow but long-term effect on reducing soil pH. Cottonseed meal—a by-product of pressing oil from cotton seeds—is another organic product that lowers soil pH.

Loosening compacted soil

It's easier to prevent soil compaction than to cure it. Construction equipment, vehicle traffic, and foot traffic all compact soil enough to cause problems for your plants—the flow of water and air and the movement of plant roots are all hindered by compacted soil. If possible, prevent such damage by restricting vehicle movement to driveways and designated parking spots and by restricting foot traffic to clearly marked paths.

The fastest way to treat large areas of compacted soil is to hire tractor-drawn equipment that can break through the compacted zone. If you have more time and patience, plant a crop of a deep-rooted legume such as sweet clover or alfalfa. After a year or two of vigorous growth, the roots of these plants will have penetrated several feet down into the soil. Then till the roots and tops into the soil before planting a lawn or making beds or borders. For smaller areas, hand digging or rototilling is a good way to loosen compacted soil. However you loosen the soil initially, add plenty of organic matter to help it stay loose and porous.

Improving water penetration and drainage

In addition to improving soil structure and loosening compacted soil, keep the soil covered with growing plants or mulch to help retain water that would otherwise run off. If the site slopes, consider making terraces.

In arid climates, try digging sunken beds 24 to 30 inches deep and filling the beds with a mixture of soil and compost. Make the top of the bed a few inches lower than the original grade. Border the beds with paths, so rainwater will run off these compacted surfaces into the beds.

Water accumulates in low spots, flat places, and where the soil is compacted, shallow, or underlain by an impermeable layer. Most plants die if their roots are under water for an extended period of time. Major problems with standing water may require the services of a landscape architect, who can advise you on how to change the grade and drainage patterns of your property. Minor problems can be solved by digging drainage ditches, installing drains, or planting in raised beds or on mounds.

Open drainage ditches can be wide, shallow swales leading to an outlet, stream, or reservoir of some kind. Ditches can be lined with gravel or stones, or they can be planted with turf or low-growing ground covers.

Where runoff is frequent, open ditches may be muddy and undesirable, making buried clay or plastic drain tiles preferable.

If there's no place to direct water away from your garden site, you can lead the drain tiles into a "dry well," a large hole filled with rocks, gravel, or rubble and covered with topsoil. A dry well holds runoff until it can gradually seep down into the water table. Check with a local nursery or landscape contractor about the type, size, and layout of the drain tiles and, if necessary, the dry well best for your site.

Planting in beds where the soil level is higher than the surrounding grade solves the problem of wet surface soil. Depending on the severity of the drainage problem, you can raise the beds anywhere from 3 to 12 inches or more. Individual shrubs and trees can also be planted on shallow mounds of soil to protect their crowns—the junction between roots and stems—from excess moisture and guarantee that the fine roots near the surface will be in well-drained soil. Deeper roots can reach down for water in the underlying soil.

Soil for container plants

If you want to grow plants in flowerpots, hanging baskets, window boxes, or half-barrels, you need potting soil. Ordinary garden soil doesn't work well in containers because it packs into a dense mass that limits water and air penetration. By contrast, potting soil is crumbly and porous enough for rapid drainage and generous aeration.

You can make your own potting soil or buy it in bags at a local garden center. Either way, there are advantages to using the same mix for as many of your plants as possible. It isn't necessary to have special mixes for different kinds of plants, and standardizing the soil simplifies your watering, fertilizing, and repotting routines. Potting soil is cheap compared with the plants you buy and the time you spend growing and tending them. It's false economy to let valuable plants languish in inferior soil. Mix or buy the best soil you can find, and your plants will respond with superior growth and appearance.

Making your own potting soil

To mix your own potting soil, simply combine equal parts of loamy garden soil, compost or peat moss, and coarse sand. The soil provides nutrients, the compost aids in water retention, and the sand helps the mixture drain well.

Start with some of the best soil from your garden, and sift it through a 1/4-inch mesh screen to separate out any sticks and stones. Some gardeners take the extra precaution of pasteurizing the soil to kill any insects, weed seeds, or organisms that might cause disease. Heating damp soil to a temperature of 180° F for 30 minutes will do the job. You can heat it in an oven or a microwave, or over the barbecue grill outdoors—hot soil gives off some odors that you might not want in the house. It's a good idea to sift any chunks from the compost or peat moss, but it isn't necessary to pasteurize these ingredients.

For sand, choose the coarsest grit you can get. Anything that passes through the mesh of a window-screen sieve is too fine. Using sand adds considerable weight to a potting-soil mix. The added weight is an advantage for tall, top-heavy plants that might otherwise blow or tip over, but it's a disadvantage when you have to carry or move the potted plants. Instead of using sand in container mixes, you might buy a bag of perlite, a kind of crushed volcanic rock that's very lightweight.

Buying potting soil

Most bags of ready-mixed potting soil don't contain any real soil at all. These "soilless" mixes are generally composed of peat moss, ground pine bark, and vermiculite and/or perlite, with lime and nutrients added. They vary in texture; in general, coarser mixes don't mat down the way fine-textured mixes do. Nearly all modern nurseries use soilless mixes because these blends are of consistent quality, lightweight, and sterile. Several brands give good results, but it takes practice to learn the best way to water and to fertilize plants growing in soilless mixes.

One approach is to visit your favorite local nursery, ask what kind of potting soil they use, and ask if they'll sell you some. The nursery staff can answer your questions on the best way to water and to fertilize plants in that soil mix. Also, plants you buy from that nursery will have an easy adjustment when it comes time for repotting if you use the same type of soil that they've been growing in.

Whether or not you buy through a nursery, when you find a mix you like, buy it in quantity to get the best price. A 40-pound bale may cost only three to four times as much as a 4-pound bag. You can share the savings by shopping with a gardening friend, or stockpile the surplus for future use. Kept dry, most soil mixes can be stored indefinitely.

Making compost

Every gardener should consider making compost. This highly decomposed organic matter has the crumble and feel of fertile garden soil, and plants grow exceptionally well where it is used as a soil amendment or as mulch.

There are two basic approaches to composting: hot and cold. At their simplest, both involve making large piles of organic matter. Grass clippings, crop residues, hay, manure, and leaves are just some of the many materials that can be composted. Hot composting, in which high temperatures hasten decomposition and kill weed seeds and pathogens, requires a lot of planning, attention, and work, so we'll concentrate on the much simpler method of cold composting.

Cold composting involves little more than making piles of suitable material (discussed below) and letting them sit until they decompose, aided by an occasional turning to aerate the pile and to put material on the outside of the pile inside. About the only other care you need to provide is to keep the pile moist, but not soggy. Given enough oxygen, microbes will break down the material and create compost in a few months to a year or so.

Simply piling material on the ground is sufficient for cold composting. But bins make it easier to turn the piles and to compost material that might get blown away or that might attract animals. Homemade bins can be simple wire cages or elaborate wooden constructions, as shown in the drawing. You will need at least two bins, one to start the compost, another to turn it into. A third or fourth bin can be used for storing raw material or finished compost. (If you need to compost only small amounts of material, consider one of the small, commercially made bins available at garden centers or from mail-order suppliers.)

Select a level site for the bins or piles, avoiding low spots where water can collect. If your pile is near trees or shrubs, you might lay down a sheet of plastic to keep roots from growing up into the pile. Place closely spaced rows of bricks on top of the plastic to let oxygen into the pile from below.

Materials for composting

Prunings, leaves, stalks, and similar garden detritus all make good compost. Fresh, green plant residues are a good source of nitrogen. Don't compost diseased plants,

though; burn them instead. Lawn clippings are wet and dense, so mix them with hay or straw before adding them to the pile so that they don't compact. (If you can't get hay or straw, mix the clippings with soil or sun-dry them on the driveway before adding them to the pile.) Fresh, green, and undried hay makes excellent compost by itself. Deciduous leaves compost well when shredded; left whole, they can form a dense, impermeable mat and hinder biological activity. Evergreen needles decompose very slowly and are better used as a mulch.

Kitchen wastes such as vegetable trimmings, fruit peels, and coffee grounds are fine, but don't compost meat products—they attract animals, and the fats in them hinder the composting process. Cover kitchen wastes with a layer of soil to absorb odors.

The best way to break down sod removed from a new garden is to cold-compost it with only the soil attached to its roots. The sod will break down within a few months.

Wood wastes, such as sawdust and shavings, are reasonably good compost materials, but they're especially low in nitrogen. Softwoods are less desirable, as

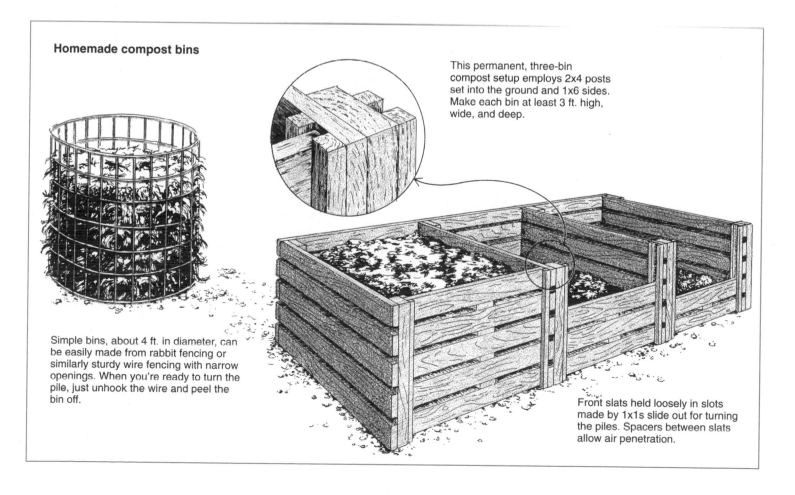

Homemade compost bins

This permanent, three-bin compost setup employs 2x4 posts set into the ground and 1x6 sides. Make each bin at least 3 ft. high, wide, and deep.

Simple bins, about 4 ft. in diameter, can be easily made from rabbit fencing or similarly sturdy wire fencing with narrow openings. When you're ready to turn the pile, just unhook the wire and peel the bin off.

Front slats held loosely in slots made by 1x1s slide out for turning the piles. Spacers between slats allow air penetration.

they are much more resistant to attack by microorganisms than are hardwoods. Wood shavings break down more slowly than does sawdust.

Animal manure is the most common source of nitrogen for composting. Cow, horse, and poultry manures are most readily available from local farms, or you can add bagged, dry manures. Dog and cat droppings may contain disease organisms that affect humans and should not be in compost used for food crops, although they may be satisfactory for ornamentals.

Preparing and tending a compost pile

Plant stalks, leaves, straw, and other large materials compost best when broken into small pieces. Gas- or electric-powered shredding machines are helpful, but they're probably not worth the expense unless you regularly compost a lot of bulky material. You can shred leaves and smaller stalks with a lawn mower, or bruise bulky material with a sharpened garden spade. It also helps to break up bulky material that is already in a pile with a mattock before you turn the pile.

Adequate aeration is essential for providing oxygen to the microbes that digest the raw materials. Adding soil liberally to a pile usually ensures an adequate supply of oxygen, especially with wet or compactible materials. You can also build a pile around a number of loose poles, then withdraw the poles to create air holes; this works well for larger piles. Alternatively, after you've built a pile, you can punch air holes with a crowbar. The most effective aeration technique is to turn the pile frequently, but it's also the most labor intensive.

Preparing a planting bed

Whether you plant a small plot of annual flowers or several large perennial borders, you'll need to know how to prepare a bed for planting. There are three basic steps in making a garden bed. Site selection comes first, design and choice of plants is next, and last comes the plain old hard work of making the bed. Skimp on any of these, and you'll probably be disappointed with the results. The first two steps are discussed in the first section of this book, Creating a Garden. Here we'll concentrate on the third, dirt-under-the-fingernails step.

Laying out the bed

Before you dig, you need to lay out the shape of the bed. If you're working from a plan, measure from existing points of reference (trees, structures, or the stakes you set when measuring to make the plan) and pound in as many stakes as you need to establish the basic position and outline. To lay out a circle, drive a stake at the center point and attach to it a string cut to the radius. Use the string to set stakes at various points on the circumference. If the sides of the bed are straight, connect the stakes with string to establish the outline. If the bed curves, use a garden hose, some powdered limestone, or a can of spray paint to mark smooth curves connecting the stakes. Don't be afraid to change the shape if you're not satisfied—better now than after you've done a lot of digging.

Eliminating existing vegetation

Most new garden sites are already covered with plants, and you've got to get rid of them. If you're in luck, there'll be only a few shrubs to dig up. A pick, ax, or mattock can help get the more stubborn denizens out. Removing trees that are larger than saplings can be dangerous. If you're inexperienced, call a professional, who may also have equipment for removing tree stumps.

More than likely, your site will be populated by a ground cover of tenacious perennial weeds, tenacious perennial garden plants, or lawn grass (a very tenacious weed when not wanted). No matter which confronts you, do a thorough job of removing it, or it will come back to plague you. Complete eradication is particularly impor-

tant for plants with underground runners, such as Bermudagrass or bindweed. If you merely chop the running root system to bits, then turn and aerate the soil, the little bits of root will soon send out a host of new shoots—in, among, and over your new plants. To eliminate such plants, you must smother them.

Smothering unwanted plants. Smothering plants is cheaper and environmentally safer than killing them with an herbicide, but it is slower, taking months rather than days. First mow or cut the plants as close to the ground as possible. Then spread black plastic or thick, overlapping layers of newspaper. Overlap the newspaper generously so that there are no places where light can penetrate—the plants will find these gaps in a hurry and grow through them. Wetting the paper helps the layers stick together.

Both plastic and newspaper must be anchored to keep them in place. Use stones, bricks, or other heavy objects, or dig and bury the edges. All this can create an eyesore. A thick layer of wood chips or other organic matter will mask it, and you can reuse the mulch when you remove the plastic, or dig it in with the decomposed newspaper. To be effective, you have to smother plants while they're actively growing. A few fiercely competitive weeds, such as Russian thistle, may take 15 months or so to smother, from early one spring to early summer the following year.

Digging and pulling unwanted plants. The fastest and simplest method of removing many undesirable plants is to dig or pull them out. Make sure that you get all the root of taprooted offenders, such as dandelions, which can resprout from small pieces of root.

Most annual weeds can be easily pulled or hoed off when young. Remember that weeds live on in their seeds. Some buried seeds can remain viable for years, then germinate quickly after cultivation disturbs the soil. It's a good idea to dig the bed and then keep it moist for a couple of weeks. (Do this during warm weather; most seeds won't germinate in cold soil.) Many of the weed seeds will germinate, and you can then hoe them off while they're small.

Removing lawn grass. A lawn can produce better-than-average soil due to the breakdown of grass clippings and dead roots over the years and to the many insects, worms, and other creatures that the grass supports. The challenge is getting rid of the turf. If it's not too dense, you can lift it with a digging fork or a spade, or chop through it with a rototiller.

If the turf is dense, you can smother it, or you can strip it with a spade or with a gasoline-powered machine that cuts the sod like a carpet. You can rent these machines, which are heavy but simple to run. Sod stripping is a quick, neat method, but a good deal of topsoil comes off with the sod, so be sure to compost the sod rolls, or use them to patch areas of thin lawn.

Plan to spend half a day or more stripping sod by machine from areas larger than 20 feet square. The soil should be moist, but not wet. A helper to remove and shake out the heavy rolls of sod and soil as you move along makes the whole process a lot faster and easier. Be sure to cut deeply—4 inches is generally advised for deep-rooted varieties such as Kentucky bluegrass.

Digging a new bed

If the ground isn't frozen, you can dig a new garden bed at any time of year. But if you're adding a lot of organic matter or other amendments, do so at least a few months before you plant. This gives the microbes and bacteria in the soil time to break down the amendments.

Before you start digging, squeeze a handful of soil to see how moist it is. If it makes a tight ball that holds together after you open your hand, it's too wet. Wait a couple of hours or a day and check again. If the soil is dust-dry, give the site a good soaking, then test again. Digging dry soil can be backbreaking. Digging wet soil can be backbreaking, too, and if the soil contains a lot of clay, digging can compact it and produce concrete-hard clods.

If you've never dug a garden bed before, it might seem that nothing could be simpler. Hard work, to be sure, but simple. There are, however, several different methods of digging a bed to choose from. Your choice should be determined by the condition of your soil, the condition of your body, and careful consideration of the benefits and drawbacks of each method.

The two most basic methods are single and double digging. As the names suggest, the latter method goes twice as deep, and requires double the effort. Both aerate the soil; enable you to remove rocks, roots, and debris; and give you a much-needed chance to incorporate amendments and organic matter deeply.

For most soils and for most perennials, annuals, ground covers, and small shrubs, the foot-deep preparation of single digging is ample. (If conditions permit, you may be able to avoid digging and prepare the bed with a rototiller.) If your soil is very poor, or if you discover a nasty layer of subsoil near the surface, or if you're planting many deeper-rooted shrubs in the bed, you should consider double digging. Whichever method you choose, when you're finished, rake the surface of the bed smooth.

Single digging. Turning the soil to the depth of a spade or a shovel is called single digging. Starting at one end of the bed, dig out a trench as deep as your spade and about 2 feet wide, as shown below. Pile the soil in a wheelbarrow or a cart and haul it to the far end of the bed, onto a tarp. This load will fill your last trench. Add whatever amendments and organic matter you have in mind, and mix them with the soil at the bottom of your trench. Then dig another trench adjacent to the first, throwing the soil into the first trench, and add amendments. Continue this way across the bed. Fill the final trench with the first load of soil. Because you've loosened the soil and added amendments, the bed will be higher than the surrounding ground, but it will settle back.

Double digging. Double digging starts off the same way as single digging. Dig a spade-deep trench about 2 feet wide and cart the soil to the far end of the bed. Now dig the trench down another shovel's depth.

If the soil at the bottom of the trench is reasonably good, loosen or turn it with a spade or a garden fork to the full depth of the blade or tines, then mix in the amendments thoroughly. If the soil at the bottom is compacted, rocky, or very poor, you can remove it from the trench, pick out the rocks or roots, mix in amendments, then return it to the trench.

To continue, dig the next one-spade-deep, 2-foot-wide trench and turn this soil into the previous trench. This keeps the topsoil on top—inverting the layers would bring poorer subsoil to the surface. You can

---

Digging a garden bed

Whether you single-dig or double-dig, the first step is to dig a trench across one end of the bed, one spade deep and about 2 ft. wide. Haul the soil to the other end of the bed. Single-diggers spread amendments on the bottom of the trench.

If you're double-digging, loosen or dig out the soil in the bottom of the trench to another spade depth, mixing in amendments thoroughly and removing stones and roots.

Now dig a second, adjacent trench, one spade deep, throwing the soil into the first. Add amendments to the bottom of the new trench, or double-dig the bottom and amend it. Continue across the bed in this manner, filling the last trench with the soil from the first.

also combine sod removal with double digging. Just place the pieces of stripped sod at the bottom of the previous deep trench.

Double digging is a lot of work, but it alleviates potential subsoil problems and gives plant roots a much deeper, healthier area to push into. It prepares a bed for years of healthy growth and is particularly valuable for perennial beds, where it's difficult to correct major soil problems after planting.

Rototilling. Gas- or electric-powered machines that churn the soil with rotary tines have long been employed by vegetable gardeners to prepare beds each year. Rototilling is a fast way to loosen compacted soil and to mix in amendments.

Rototilling works best if your soil is reasonably fertile and friable, free of rocks, tree roots, and subsoil problems. In these conditions, 6 to 8 inches of rototilled soil (amended if you wish) will give your plants a good start. In heavy clay soils, rototilling can create a compacted layer of soil at the depth of tine penetration. Dig down and check; loosen compacted soil with a garden fork. If you rototill, protect your eyes from flying bits of soil and stone and your ears from the roar of the motor. Heavy shoes will protect your feet from errant tines.

Raised beds

A raised bed—created by mounding soil above ground level—can solve a number of gardening problems. With a raised bed you can make a deeper zone of good soil without deep digging, or solve a minor drainage problem without putting in drain tiles. If your entire property is laced with greedy, shallow tree roots, or your prime garden site possesses a drainage problem too difficult or too expensive to fix, building a garden on top of these problems may be the only reasonable solution. Raised beds also allow you to extend your gardening horizons and pleasure. You can create a special soil for particular plants, such as a peat bed for acid-lovers or a rocky bed for alpine plants.

You can raise a bed 6 to 8 inches above ground level without building a wall to hold the soil in place. Just keep the bed tidy with a rake or a hoe. Contained beds require more initial work, but if they're well built, they'll last. Low walls can be made by simply stacking stones or by anchoring treated planks (2x6s or wider) with stakes. But a casually built wall won't last as well as one built on a proper base and assembled with some care. The higher the wall, the stronger it must be to withstand the pressure of the soil it contains—and wet soil can exert a great deal of pressure. If you wish to make a deep, long-lasting raised bed, see the guidelines for building retaining walls in the next chapter.

Inside the enclosure, prepare the bed as the soil and your plans require. The existing soil may be good, and you'll just need to add amendments and, possibly, soil brought from elsewhere to raise the level of the bed. Or the underlying soil may be so problematic that you'll need to treat the bed as a huge container and bring everything in. If you're building a raised bed on top of a tree-root-infested site, lay weed-suppressing cloth, available at garden-supply stores, under the new soil to discourage roots from invading.

Making a no-dig bed

If your native soil is in good enough condition, you might want to consider making a garden bed without digging or rototilling at all. Although digging allows you to improve the soil in many ways, it has some drawbacks. New beds are often thick with young weeds because long-dormant seeds germinated when the soil was disturbed. Newly turned soil is an inviting site for migrating weed seeds, too. Digging and, in particular, rototilling can also damage the structure of certain soils. And fluffed-up bare earth loses more moisture to the air than does undisturbed soil.

No-dig gardening (also called no-till gardening) leaves the soil largely undisturbed and avoids these problems. A mulch of black plastic, weed cloth, newspapers, or organic matter is spread to smother existing vegetation, then left in place and the garden planted through it. Acted on by organisms already in the soil, the smothered vegetation (along with organic mulches) decomposes, enriching the soil. As the garden matures, additional amendments can be added as topdressing. (Plastic or weed cloth can be pulled away eventually to allow topdressing.) In its simplest form, no-dig gardening relies on the creatures in the soil to do the work rather than on the gardener.

There are significant drawbacks and limitations to no-dig gardening. Many soils are too poor to support enough organisms to get the process going in the first place. Such soils also need a larger infusion of organic matter than that provided by the smothered vegetation. And the benefits of organic matter piled on top of the soil are not as great as or seen as quickly as when it is incorporated more deeply.

If you're making a garden in an old established lawn, meadow, or pasture, and the site is already supporting a variety of healthy plants, consider a no-dig bed. It's fast and easy; from mulching to planting takes only a few months. It's great for large areas that you want to plant quickly. But if you're starting out around a newly built house or a lot infested with a few scraggly weeds, digging and amending is probably the best route to a garden.

Tools for making a bed

You don't need a lot of tools to make a garden bed. A good sharp spade, a digging fork, a flat metal rake, and something for hauling material are ample. If you have to remove large rocks, a large crowbar, a mattock, and a pick will be a big help. A claw-like tool with four tines, sometimes called a potato hook, works wonders removing small rocks. To sever big roots, you'll need an ax or a coarse saw.

Buy good-quality tools and take care of them and they'll last a long time. To prevent rust during the gardening season, clean excess soil off metal parts and wipe them with an oily rag. You can stick blades and tines in a bucket of coarse sand to which a little motor oil has been added. When you store tools for any length of time, give the metal parts a good coating of oil. Stainless-steel tools won't rust, but they are harder to keep sharp and very expensive.

The terms *spade* and *shovel* are often used interchangeably to describe a variety of digging tools. Spades and shovels may be flat or convex, round-bottom or square-bottom, with short or long handles. For single and double digging, a flat blade cuts straighter and deeper and will make your work a lot easier. A convex blade, however, is better for sandy soil, which just crumbles off the side of a flat tool.

A sharp spade or shovel is to a gardener what a finely honed knife is to a cook: indispensable. File a shallow, even bevel on the front side of the blade. You'll create a burr of steel on the back of the blade as you file; when you're finished with the bevel, run the file flat on the back to remove the burr.

Garden forks with three or four strong, thick tines are ideal for breaking through compacted layers of soil, for the initial groundbreaking of a new bed, and for mixing coarse-textured organic matter into the soil. If your soil is rocky, invest in a fork with thick tines that are square in cross section rather than flat. Thin tines quickly bend out of shape.

When buying a shovel, a spade, or a fork, look for smooth wooden handles with straight grain—these are less prone to splintering and breakage. The tapered wooden handle should fit tightly into a closed socket or be held by straps that extend up the front and back of the handle. The socket or straps should be formed from the same piece of metal as the blade or tines. Cheaper tools are attached by separate pieces of metal, often a tang-and-ferrule arrangement, which are weaker. Avoid open-ended sockets that let moisture in, which rots the end of the handle.

Gasoline-powered rototillers are strong tools that make quick work of tearing apart sod, breaking new ground, turning under cover crops, mixing organic material with soil, and loosening and homogenizing the soil in a bed. Most of these jobs are done infrequently enough in an ornamental garden that it may make sense to rent or bor-

Edgings

EDGINGS HELP KEEP PLANTS in your bed from creeping out and plants outside the bed from creeping in. In addition, they improve the looks of a bed or make mowing adjacent lawn much easier. There are many methods of edging a bed. The three shown here will serve many needs.

Cut edges

The cheapest and simplest edging is a cut edge. Plants tend not to cross the small ditch formed by a cut edge. Cut edges erode quickly and lose their definition, so you'll need to recut them every year or two.

Strip edgings

Prefabricated barrier strips of steel, aluminum, or plastic require more initial work and expense but less maintenance. Plastic is easy to handle and to cut, and it readily bends around curves. Steel is heavy and hard to cut, and it rusts, but it has a distinctive look many people find appealing. Aluminum is expensive, but it's relatively easy to cut and it won't rust. None of these materials bends particularly well over a slope. All strip edgings are installed more or less as shown here.

Mowing strips

Wide edgings of stone, brick, or wood make mowing easy (hence the name) and give strong visual definition to a bed. If you choose brick, use brick specifically made for use in walkways. Secondhand bricks are charming, but most were not made to withstand this type of use and will break apart as a result.

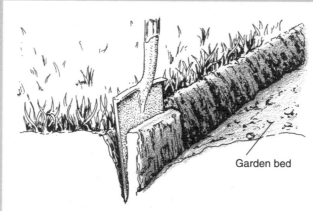

Cut edge

Cut around the bed perimeter with a flat-bladed spade or a semicircular-bladed edging tool. Slope the soil in the bed away from the cut with a rake.

Garden bed

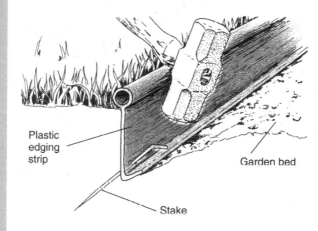

Strip edging

Dig a trench 4–5 in. deep. Position the top of the plastic, steel, or metal strip just above the sod root zone and drive in the fixing stakes. Backfill soil in the bed 1–2 in. below the top of the strip.

Plastic edging strip

Garden bed

Stake

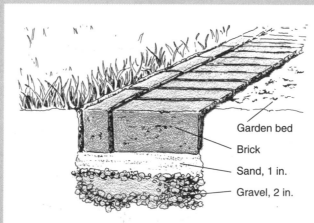

Mowing strip

All mowing strips are laid flush to the soil level. Lay brick, landscape timber, or flagstone on a bed of sand and gravel. Level and tamp the sand and gravel, then water it in. Lay the brick, stone, or timber and tamp it in place. After you've laid an area, fill the gaps between pieces with sand.

Garden bed

Brick

Sand, 1 in.

Gravel, 2 in.

row a tiller rather than to buy one. A day or two with a tiller is enough to prepare a bed for planting perennials, for example, and that bed won't need reworking for years.

Small, lightweight, gasoline- or electric-powered tillers can be used for some of the same jobs performed by bigger tillers, although they take longer to work the same area to the same depth. But small tillers have advantages that the big ones don't.

They fit into narrow or tight spaces, between existing plants or next to paths or walls, and they can till a strip as narrow as a spade's blade.

Even if you're making a small bed, you'll need to move a lot of stuff around—soil, rocks, plants, manure, compost, and so on. There are numerous types and styles of garden carts and wheelbarrows on the market. Carts, which have two or more wheels supporting a bin of some sort, can

handle large loads. They're more stable but less maneuverable than wheelbarrows. (Be careful, though—a heavily loaded cart can gather enough momentum going downhill to escape your control.) Wheelbarrows can weave gracefully in and out of narrow spaces on their single wheel, and they're a breeze to dump. Carts, unless they have a removable front panel, have to be shoveled out, and who wants to shovel out what they just shoveled in?

Terracing

Terraces can enhance gardens on both sloped and flat sites. Slopes present many garden-design opportunities, but steep slopes pose problems of erosion and access. Terraces allow you to combine the practical advantages of working on flat or slightly sloped surfaces with the design advantages of a sloping site. On a flat site, constructing terraces of varying heights adds interest, although it requires moving large quantities of earth.

The soil in a garden terrace is usually held in place by a retaining wall. The higher the wall, the more critical its engineering and construction. If you want to retain more than a gentle slope, consult a professional for advice.

Building a dry-stone retaining wall

Dry-stone walls (assembled without mortar) are ideal for gardens because they give when the ground moves (frost heaving, for example) and they drain well. As the drawing at top right shows, a dry-stone wall is basically a well-organized pile of stones. It should be at least as wide at its base as it is high, and it should rest on a firm foundation. For obvious reasons, flat stones are much easier to build with than are round, although with enough patience you can build a serviceable wall with round stones.

Several inches of gravel is sufficient base for most dry-stone walls. The gravel aids drainage and lessens the effects of frost heaving in northern climates. Make the trench for the gravel level from front to back. A stone wall can rise and fall along its length with gentle undulations in the grade. If the grade rises too rapidly, however, you'll want to stairstep the wall, digging into the slope to make sections of the foundation trench level along their length as well as their width.

Tamp loose soil in the trench, rake the gravel, then set the first course of stones. Put the largest stones at the bottom of the wall, flattest side up. Position subsequent courses so that the face of the wall "leans" back slightly into the soil it retains.

The secret to dry-stone walling is to overlap stones at every opportunity through the thickness and along the length of the wall. Tying the wall together in this fashion gives it strength beyond its simple weight and mass. Shovel in small gravel every course or so to fill in among the backing stones. If you want to grow plants on the face of the wall, fill in between and behind the face stones with soil. If the wall

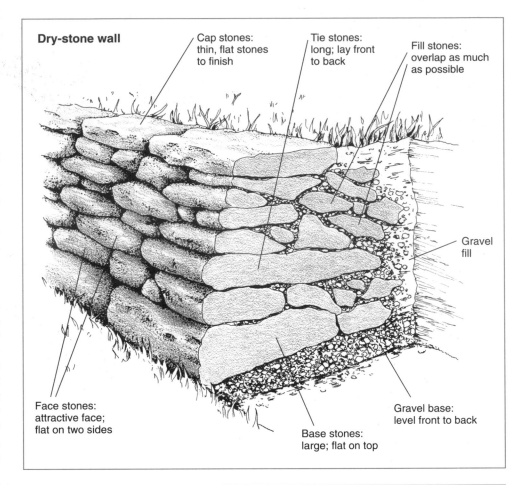

Dry-stone wall

Cap stones: thin, flat stones to finish

Tie stones: long; lay front to back

Fill stones: overlap as much as possible

Gravel fill

Face stones: attractive face; flat on two sides

Base stones: large; flat on top

Gravel base: level front to back

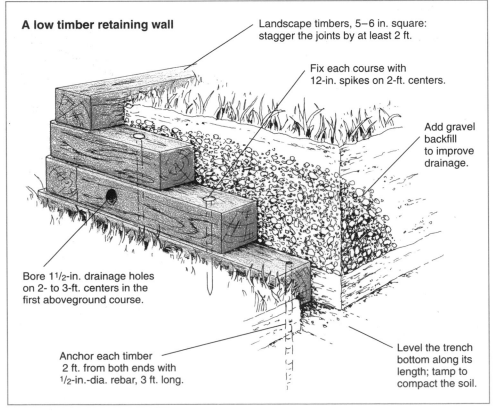

A low timber retaining wall

Landscape timbers, 5–6 in. square: stagger the joints by at least 2 ft.

Fix each course with 12-in. spikes on 2-ft. centers.

Add gravel backfill to improve drainage.

Bore 1½-in. drainage holes on 2- to 3-ft. centers in the first aboveground course.

Anchor each timber 2 ft. from both ends with ½-in.-dia. rebar, 3 ft. long.

Level the trench bottom along its length; tamp to compact the soil.

is cut into an existing slope, a layer of gravel between the stone and the soil will aid drainage.

Building a timber retaining wall

A timber retaining wall must make up for with engineering what it lacks in sheer weight and mass. The method described here is adequate for retaining walls and raised beds up to 18 inches high; taller timber walls need additional reinforcing to counter the weight of the contained soil.

Timber walls require 5- to 6-inch-square timbers, usually available as landscaping timbers or railroad ties. Avoid ties or timbers treated with creosote, which is toxic to plants. Pressure-treated wood will last longer than naturally rot-resistant wood, such as cedar, or wood treated by painting or by soaking or dipping in preservatives. The two most common preservatives, pentachlorophenol and CCA (a mixture of chromium, copper, and arsenic compounds), can be hazardous to you and to your plants. Be particularly careful when working with penta-treated wood. If the wood is still wet, let it dry thoroughly—penta vapors stunt and kill plants. It's also a good idea to wear gloves and safety goggles and to avoid inhaling sawdust while working with penta- or CCA-treated wood.

Timber walls can't rise and fall with the grade, so the base must be level along the wall's length as well as across its width. For anchorage, the first course of a retaining wall is almost buried in a trench about 1 inch shallower than the timber's thickness. Lay the first course directly on firm, compacted soil at the bottom of the trench or, for loose, sandy soils, on a bed of gravel 2 to 3 inches deep. It's important that the first course be dead level; any error will be compounded as subsequent courses are added, and you'll soon have a leaning wall.

Fill the trench on either side of the leveled timbers with soil and tamp it in place. Bore $1/2$-inch holes in each timber, 2 feet from each end, and drive 3-foot-long lengths of $1/2$-inch rebar through the holes to anchor the wall securely. Check to see that the pounding hasn't shifted the timber out of level. Now stack and spike the remaining two or three courses in place, as shown in the drawing on the facing page. Stagger the joints and overlap at the corners. Set the face of each course slightly back from the course below if you wish. If you find driving 12-inch spikes hard going, drill pilot holes to ease their passage.

For drainage, drill $1^{1}/_2$-inch-diameter holes every 2 to 3 feet in the first above-grade timber course. Cover these holes with several shovelfuls of rock as you backfill behind the wall—this will keep the soil from clogging them.

Buying plants

Planting a garden is a little like furnishing a house. There are plants to fill practical needs, plants that are combined with care to create a particular effect in a garden "room," plants that accumulate over the years in a pleasant, colorful jumble. As the garden matures, age or changing taste banishes some plants, while newcomers compete for attention with old favorites.

Where do all these plants come from? As with the furnishings of a house, their sources are varied. Some arrive as gifts, passed on in a family like heirlooms or given as thanks for a favor or for hospitality. Gardeners are a generous lot and are constantly distributing divisions and cuttings among friends.

Plants from these personal sources can sometimes give a new gardener a very good start, as well as add a sentimental dimension to a garden. But many of your plants will come from commercial suppliers: local garden centers and nurseries, mail-order suppliers, and sales at garden clubs and botanical gardens.

Local nurseries

For beginning gardeners, a local nursery, stocked with a range of plants that do well in your area and staffed with knowledgeable, helpful people, is an invaluable resource. From the staff you can learn how this or that plant performs in local conditions and how best to care for it. You can personally inspect the plants to be sure that they're healthy before spending your money. And if you have problems, you can go back for help.

Nurseries sell most of their plants in plastic containers. Annuals usually come in small plastic pots or in packs of two, four, six, or more cells, linked like an egg carton. Perennials often require larger, individual containers that typically hold a quart or a gallon of soil. Most trees and shrubs are sold in containers or are balled and burlapped (the excavated root ball and soil held together with a wrapping of burlap or plastic tied with twine); in early spring, some are sold without soil, their bare roots wrapped in plastic.

Buying plants

Seedlings of annuals and some perennials are often sold in packs of four to six linked cells.

Larger plants, including annuals, perennials, shrubs, and trees, may be sold in individual containers.

Dormant shrubs, trees, and some perennials are sold bare-root.

Trees and sometimes shrubs may be sold with an intact ball of soil wrapped in burlap or other material.

Some small nurseries propagate and grow all the plants they sell. Many others buy most of their stock from large wholesale suppliers. Supermarket garden centers and discount nurseries buy all their plants. (As you gain experience in judging quality, don't be afraid to buy from a discount nursery—they may have bought their stock from the same wholesale nursery supplying the high-priced nursery down the road.) In general, plants propagated and raised by a reputable local nursery are likely to be excellent value—species or cultivars proven to do well in your area, they'll be well cared for and won't have suffered the stress of a relocation from a wholesale supplier.

Selecting annuals

Years ago, nurseries sold annuals before the plants developed flower buds or blossoms—very young plants suffer less transplanting shock and resume growth more quickly, so they soon catch up with older transplanted flowers. Then, to satisfy a new generation of buyers who wanted instant color, growers began delivering older plants that were already in bloom. Soon any variety that was slow to bloom in containers disappeared from garden-center shelves. Today it's difficult to find garden-center annuals that aren't in early or full bloom.

Some plants, such as petunias, dwarf marigolds, and impatiens, are so vigorous that they hardly slow down when transplanted in full bloom. But others, such as celosia, put so much of their strength into forming large flower heads that if transplanted when in bloom they may barely survive the ordeal.

For best results, then, choose the youngest annuals available. Look for plants with healthy green leaves all the way down to soil level. If the seedlings have begun to branch, all the better. Tall, wiry plants that are shedding their bottom leaves are probably suffering from lack of water and will take longer to establish in your garden. Yellowed or discolored plants haven't been fertilized enough and may be permanently stunted. Look for signs of insects and disease, misshapen flowers, distorted growth, and other damage.

If you can, carefully pop a small seedling out of its plastic cell or tap a larger plant out of its pot and look at the root ball. A mass of roots spiraling around the container indicates a root-bound plant that will adjust slowly when you transplant it, no matter how carefully you untangle and spread out the roots.

Selecting perennials

Perennials are most often older than seedlings when sold. Grown in containers for up to a year (occasionally longer for some species), these larger, more mature plants can make a splash in your garden more quickly than can plants grown from

Obtaining native plants

WILDFLOWER GARDENING has become increasingly popular, and it's tempting to stop and dig an admired wildflower on the side of a road or in a meadow. After all, there seem to be lots more out there. But the increasing encroachment of commercial, industrial, agricultural, and residential development on natural habitats is eliminating whole populations of native plants. These plants may grow elsewhere, even in large numbers, but their disappearance from a particular location impoverishes that landscape and ecosystem.

So, admire wildflowers in the wild, but for your garden, buy nursery-propagated plants or grow plants from seed. Many nurseries sell wildflowers and native plants. Be careful, however, of those that offer "nursery-grown" plants. Too often these plants have been dug in the wild and transplanted to a nursery bed or pot before sale. Buying collected plants contributes to habitat destruction—and they're a poor investment, less likely to survive in cultivation than plants propagated in a nursery from seeds or by vegetative means (division, cuttings, and so on). Don't be afraid to ask how the plant was propagated. If the nursery can't or won't tell you, look elsewhere. Many botanical gardens, arboretums, or native-plant societies sell native plants or can supply you with a list of mail-order nurseries that grow nursery-propagated plants.

seeds or seedlings, but they're likely to be more expensive.

The size of the plants and containers varies considerably; pots range from 4 inches across to those containing 2 gallons of soil. Pot size doesn't necessarily correlate with performance. For a fast-growing species, a plant purchased in a quart pot may have attained the same size at the end of a season in the garden as one purchased in a gallon pot.

As with annuals, look for bare stems, discolored leaves, insects, and disease in container-grown perennials. A big plant in a small pot is likely to be root-bound. Look for exposed roots on the soil surface or roots protruding from the container's drainage holes.

Buy perennials early in the season to give them as much time as possible to become established in the garden. (Nurseries in warm-winter areas target fall, as well as spring, as a prime planting time.) Get the plants into the ground as soon as you can. If you have to leave them in their pots for a while, be sure to water them as often as the soil dries out, which may be daily.

As the growing season progresses, you'll probably think of more plants you'd like, or discover something irresistible at a nursery. You can often find bargain perennials during the summer, plants that were passed over earlier and that now look a bit overgrown and ratty. With some judicious pruning of top growth when you plant them, and regular attention to watering, these plants can be brought to full health again. They may not look their best for a year or so, but the pleasure of the rescue makes the wait worthwhile.

Buying trees and shrubs

Large, long-lived, and often expensive, trees and shrubs are a daunting purchase for a novice gardener. If possible, take a knowledgeable friend with you to the nursery or even hire a professional landscaper or arborist to help you choose.

Shrubs are frequently sold in 1- or 5-gallon containers. As with perennials, make sure that their foliage isn't discolored, damaged, or diseased and that no roots are poking out of the drainage holes. Check that branches and stems are undamaged and healthy and that the plant's overall form is pleasing.

Most trees are sold balled-and-burlapped or in containers. Check to see if the root ball is firm or if the tree is settled snugly in the can. Reject trees with dry or cracked root balls or wobbly trunks.

Look for sturdiness rather than height in a tree. Check branching. Buggy whips and fishing poles make poor trees. Branches should be well spaced, not sparse and not crowded. Unless you're buying a narrowly upright cultivar, branches should join the trunk at a generous angle (45° or so); tighter junctures split more easily as the tree grows older.

Inspect the trunk. Reject trees with scars from careless handling and ragged pruning. Pass by those with cankers, holes, or splits in the bark. Inspect the foliage and rule out plants with spotted or holed leaves and those with undersized or poorly colored leaves. Insufficient water is the greatest enemy of nursery stock; do not accept plants with severely wilted or dry foliage.

Bare-root trees and shrubs, dug during their dormant season and sold before new growth resumes, are usually much less expensive than container-grown or balled-and-burlapped plants because they are cheaper for growers to process and ship. This doesn't mean that they are inferior plants, or that they will grow less rapidly than container-grown types (unless they are species of trees or shrubs that resent the disturbance of their roots). The major differences are that you will need to give them more care after transplanting and that it may take a year or two for them to catch up in size to their container-grown counterparts. In addition to inspecting the trunk, branches, and leaves as described previously, look for a full, fibrous, and symmetrical root system that is moist and flexible.

Container-grown and balled-and-burlapped trees and shrubs may be encircled by major roots, which can effectively strangle the plant. Sometimes pruning the girdling roots can save the plant, but it's best to avoid purchasing such plants. Look for thick, encircling roots on the surface of the root ball or under the surface, where they may be betrayed by bulges you can see or feel.

Use good sense when bringing a tree home. Fresh, unprotected foliage can be desiccated and injured on the ride home. Ask the seller to wet the foliage and to wrap the branches in damp burlap for a long trip. Wrap and secure the trunk to prevent injury from jostling, and wrap the roots of bare-root plants in plastic or damp cloth.

Mail-order plants

Even the best local nurseries can stock only a small portion of the many desirable garden plants. As your gardening horizons expand, you'll want to explore the vast and tantalizing offerings of mail-order suppliers. Many specialize in particular groups of plants or in plants that do well in particular conditions. Ranging from tiny mom-and-pop nurseries to large, well-oiled corporations, mail-order suppliers put the world of horticulture at your fingertips.

As with so much in gardening, the best place to start when looking for mail-order companies is with gardening friends—find out where they order their daylilies, bulbs, rock-garden plants, and so on. Check the advertisements in gardening magazines; several valuable books listing mail-order gardening suppliers are noted in the bibliography of this book.

Many of the smaller mail-order suppliers propagate and grow their own plants, but larger firms purchase some of their plants from wholesale suppliers. Container-grown plants are available from early spring through late autumn. Bare-root plants are dug in autumn, then stored in refrigerators for early spring delivery. Plants for fall delivery are freshly dug and shipped just as they begin to go dormant.

Study the suppliers' terms of sale, shipping dates, and plant guarantees. Don't be overly swayed in your choice of supplier by low prices. Inexpensive plants may be small and take additional time to become established in your garden.

If you've never bought a mail-order plant, don't be alarmed by what you receive. Dormant plants are little more than rootstocks; don't worry if you don't see any green top growth or buds. Planted and cared for, they'll soon fill out. Growing plants shipped in pots may have some bent stems or bruised leaves, but they'll usually shape up again.

When you receive a shipment, unpack the plants immediately and inspect them for damage. If they're acceptable, plant them as soon as possible. (See the chapters on planting later in this section.) If the plant arrives broken, rotted, dried out, diseased, or in some other unacceptable condition (including too small), notify the supplier immediately. Perennials that look bad at first may surprise you and grow magnificently. You might put them in a nursery bed to see how they do.

Other sources

Gardeners are generous people, and plants, which grow and multiply, help foster these unselfish instincts. In addition to swapping plants and giving them as gifts, gardeners often donate plants to fund-raising sales. These plants, which have done well enough to multiply in your neighbors' gardens, are likely to grow well in yours.

There are, however, some drawbacks to gift and plant-sale plants. Soil-borne diseases are easily transferred, which is why some states prohibit or restrict plant importation. There is little chance that your friends will know if their gift carries an unwelcome microbe. But take a good look at the plant prior to transplanting—if it shows any signs of disease, think twice about adding it to your garden. Also, before transplanting, do some research to determine if the plant is invasive—you want a gift to join in, not take over.

Plants from seeds

Growing plants from seed is probably the first gardening experience most of us have—what child doesn't plant a bean or radish seed and marvel at the magic of its emergence from the soil? For adults, planting seeds is a simple, easy, and inexpensive way to acquire garden plants. Not all the plants you'll want can be grown from seed; many ornamental hybrids and cultivars retain desired characteristics only when propagated vegetatively. (See "Multiplying by division" later in this section.) But the variety and merit of plants commonly grown from seed is enough to keep even the most ardent seed starter busy for years.

The simplest way to start plants from seeds is to sow the seeds in the garden where the plants are to grow. Called direct seeding, this process is particularly effective where a large swath of a certain plant is desired or for plants whose roots don't tolerate disturbance. For many plants, though, it's better to sow seeds in containers and nurse them through germination and early growth indoors or in a greenhouse or a cold frame, where light, moisture, and temperature can be monitored and controlled. In cold-winter climates, this method also allows the gardener to get a jump on the growing season; you can be transplanting sturdy seedlings when seeds sown outdoors would just be germinating.

Starting seeds in containers

Like school children, gardeners can start seeds indoors with no more than a cut-down milk carton, some soil, and a sunny window. A slightly more sophisticated approach, using plastic containers, commercial soil mix, and fluorescent lights, will greatly increase your capacity and improve your results.

Soil. Garden soil, even the best, is usually unsuitable for starting seeds in containers. Watered and allowed to settle in the container, it often resembles concrete. And it may be contaminated with weed seeds and disease organisms, which can devastate seedlings. Gardeners have long made their own mixes from equal amounts of sand, soil, and peat moss, but these homemade blends have been largely supplanted by commercially made mixes.

Relatively cheap and readily available, commercial mixes frequently contain no soil at all, instead combining two or more of the following non-soil ingredients: peat moss, perlite, ground bark, sawdust, and vermiculite. (Despite the absence of true soil, these mixes are commonly referred to as soil mixes.) In addition to appropriate moisture retention, aeration, drainage, and pH, most mixes provide at least a modicum of nutrients. Commercial mixes are highly uniform, lightweight, and easy to store. And they contain few, if any, insects, disease organisms, or weed seeds.

Almost any reputable seed-starting mix will do the job. But mixes do differ. Particle sizes vary, some take up water or drain more readily than others, some form a firmer root ball than others, and so on. Some differences are more subjective—one mix will "feel" better in your hands than another, for example. So if you're just starting out, experiment with different mixes to find the one that suits you, as well as your seeds, best.

Containers. Almost any container that can hold soil and drain excess water from its base can be used to germinate seeds. Garden centers usually carry plastic containers: large, rectangular flats; individual pots in a variety of sizes; or cell packs. The width of the container is not important; you can use a small pot to sow a few seeds or large flats to sow hundreds. The container's depth, however, does matter. Soil at the bottom of a container will hold more water and less air than will the soil above it, and roots don't grow well in poorly aerated soil. Most commercial seed-starting mixes have been formulated for use in containers only $1^1/_2$ to 2 inches deep, but 3 inches of soil shouldn't cause problems.

Containers can be reused, but they must be cleaned and sterilized to control diseases. Scrub them with a soapy solution and a stiff brush to loosen and remove larger soil particles. Then soak them for 30 minutes in a solution of nine parts water to one part laundry bleach to sterilize them.

Containers should be filled with already moistened soil. Pour some mix in a bucket or a pan (cleaned and sterilized if it has previously contained soil) and mix with water. To check the moisture content, firmly squeeze a handful. The soil shouldn't fall apart when you release your fingers, but it should fall apart when you shake your hand.

Fill each container to overflowing, working the soil into the corners. Then draw a straightedge across the top of the container to remove the excess. Lightly tamp to firm the seedbed to within $1/_4$ to $1/_2$ inch of the container's rim.

Don't put a layer of gravel or other "drainage" material in the bottom of the container—it will just lessen drainage, moisture retention, and aeration. Place a few small pebbles or similar objects over the drainage holes if you're worried about mix washing through them.

Sowing the seeds. You can sprinkle, or "broadcast," seeds evenly across the surface of the mix. For flats or other larger contain-

Starting seeds in containers

Carefully sprinkle seeds onto moistened soil mix in the container.

A fluorescent lamp allows you to control the light to your seedlings. Keep the tubes positioned about 2 in. above the top leaves.

After the first true leaves appear, transplant the seedlings to larger containers. Prick clumps out with your finger or a pencil and gently tease them apart.

Holding the seedling by a leaf, coax it into a hole poked in the mix in a new container. Put the new transplants under lights again and keep them well watered until they're ready to begin hardening off outside.

ers, sow seeds in rows about 1 inch apart. Seedling diseases, which can spread quickly through a container of broadcast seeds, are often contained in a row, sparing seedlings in other rows. Row-sown seedlings are also easier to transplant.

After sowing, cover most seeds with soil mix to a depth two to three times the thickness of the seeds. Some seeds require light to germinate, however, and should not be covered. (See the discussion of light on the facing page.)

The number of seeds you sow depends on how many plants you want, the germination rates, and the anticipated mortality rate of the seedlings. Many suppliers indicate germination rates on the seed packets. Seeds are generally inexpensive, so you can sow more than you need and choose the healthiest seedlings for growing on. As a rule, give seeds more rather than less room in a container. Crowded seedlings are weaker, not uniform in size, more susceptible to disease, and more difficult to separate and transplant. It's usually a good idea to

sow only one species or cultivar to a container unless you're combining seeds that will germinate and grow at the same rate.

Watering. Sown in properly moistened mix, many seeds will germinate before additional water is required. You can cut down on evaporation by covering the container with a sheet of plastic or glass or by placing it inside a plastic bag. Don't put covered containers in direct sunlight; temperatures inside the covering can quickly reach levels lethal to seeds or emerging seedlings. Remove the coverings once seedlings have emerged.

Check the mix in uncovered containers several times a day. Never let it dry out. When you need to water, immerse the container in a pan containing an inch or so of water; capillary action will draw the water up through the soil. Or, gently wet the surface with a fine overhead spray. Immersion is best for watering very fine seeds, which are easily washed away by even the finest spray. Use water that is room temperature or warmer. Cold water applied to seeds or seedlings can retard germination and growth. After watering, let the container drain completely.

After germination, water so that the seedlings, but not the soil, are dry by nightfall. Nighttime temperatures are usually lower and air movement is stilled, conditions that are conducive to the start and spread of disease. You can judge the soil's moisture content by its color (wetter is darker) and by the weight of the container (wetter is heavier). Immersion and spray will both work for seedlings, but if you spray, be careful not to wash the seedlings out. Allow all excess water to drain completely away rather than catching it in a saucer or pan beneath the container. As seedlings grow, water them less frequently, allowing the soil surface to dry slightly between waterings. This will aid in the control of water-borne diseases.

Temperature. Different plants respond to different soil temperatures, but in general plants fall into one of two groups. Those whose seeds and seedlings require warm soil (above 70° F) include tropical and subtropical plants, summer vegetables, plants of the bean and nightshade families, gaillardia, and lobelia. Those requiring cool soil (below 70° F) include cosmos, delphinium, penstemon, perennial baby's-breath, freesia, and cyclamen. Seed packets may specify optimum temperatures; if not, you'll have to rely on experience. Many seeds will germinate at other than optimum temperatures; they'll just take longer to do so.

An easy way to keep soil warm is to place the containers on heating elements. A number of heating strips and blankets designed for this purpose are available from garden centers or mail-order suppliers.

After germination, most seedlings grow best in daytime air temperatures between 60° and 80° F, depending on the species, and in nighttime temperatures about 10° F cooler. Normal room temperatures are usually acceptable.

Light. Seeds and seedlings also vary in their reaction to light. Most species with small seeds germinate best in the presence of light. The germination of other species, including delphinium, phlox, allium, and amaranthus, is inhibited by light. The length of the exposure to light each day may also affect germination. The seed packet will often tell you whether light is needed for germination.

Light falling naturally on a windowsill should be sufficient to germinate seeds that need light. You can also place sown containers approximately 6 inches beneath 40-watt fluorescent lamps that are on about 16 hours a day. (Although special lamps are available for this purpose, ordinary fluorescent tubes work just fine.)

The intensity and duration of light needed by seedlings also varies. Some thrive when subjected to continuous light, while others benefit from a daily period of darkness. If you're not sure of a species' light needs, place the seedlings several inches beneath fluorescent lamps for 16 hours or more per day and watch them closely. Spindly, weak seedlings are probably suffering from too little light. Those with "burned" or discolored leaves may be receiving too much light.

Seedling nutrition. Seeds need no additional nutrients before germination (don't add it to soil mixes). Young seedlings soon use up the small amount of nutrients in soil mixes, or the nutrients will be washed out by watering. (Not all mixes contain nutrients, and those that do may not say so on the label, due to curious labeling regulations.) You can use almost any general soluble fertilizer containing approximately equal amounts of nitrogen, phosphorous, and potassium on seedlings. Some gardeners fertilize once a week, others do so each time they water. Either way, observe your plants. Weak, spindly growth often accompanied by yellowing of the leaves and increased susceptibility to disease can indicate nutrient deficiency. Too much fertilizer causes the leaf edges to "burn" and the stems to collapse. Too much fertilizer can also cause a white, salty substance to form on the surface of the soil or container. You can wash this out of the mix by watering several times in quick succession with clear water and allowing the excess to drain completely away from the bottom of the container.

If the label does not provide recommendations for diluting the fertilizer for seedlings, halve or quarter the ordinary rate for once-a-week fertilizing. If you fertilize with each watering, you'll need to dilute even more, perhaps as much as one-tenth of the recommended rate.

Transplanting. Seedlings are usually transplanted after they've grown a set of "true" leaves. These leaves, which resemble those of a mature plant, follow the expanded cotyledons, often called "seed" leaves, that normally appear first.

Although a coarser soil mix can be used for transplanting than for germinating, most gardeners prefer the same kind of mix for both. Again, almost any container that will drain is fine. (To guard against disease, wash and sterilize containers, and don't reuse mix.) Choose a container size adequate for the plant's habit and rate of growth. You can transplant bedding plants into cell packs (usually containing four or six cells) or into flats, spacing the plants to avoid crowding as they grow. Plants that will grow larger before transplanting into the garden can be put in individual pots, 2 to 4 inches wide.

The day before transplanting, water

Germination problems

A POT FULL OF SPROUTING seedlings can provide satisfaction out of all proportion to their tiny size. But sometimes things don't work out. One week, then two and more go by with no hint of green above the soil. It's often difficult to determine what went wrong. Given the importance of water, light, temperature, and heat to germination, it's likely that one or more of these factors was to blame. But before you fill another container with soil mix and try again, check two other possibilities.

First, how old are the seeds? It's tempting to finish off a pack of seeds purchased last year, but their viability may be reduced. Although seeds with hard seed coats can be stored for long periods without special care, most seeds rapidly lose viability in the hot or humid conditions found in kitchens, attics, damp cellars, or greenhouses. Storage requirements vary among species, but in general you need to keep seeds dry and cool. Seal them inside a closed, airtight, and moisture-proof jar, plastic tub, or other container and store in the refrigerator at 35° to 40° F until you're ready to sow them.

The second problem to consider is the nature of the seeds themselves. Some seeds need more than just warmth and moisture to germinate. Many of the native woody plant species and species from alpine or desert climates have evolved seeds that will germinate only after passing through a particular sequence of conditions or treatments.

Some seeds require abrading, puncturing, or softening to allow water and air to penetrate the seed coat. Others need a certain amount of time in moist, cool conditions before they'll germinate. If you suspect that your troublesome seeds might have these or other natural impediments to germination, consult one of the books on seed starting listed in the bibliography for the remedy. Growing these plants from seed can be challenging, but rewarding.

the seedlings well. This helps limit the shock of transplanting and ensures that the seedlings are turgid. Moist, well-drained mix also separates more easily than dry or overly moist mix.

Fill the new containers with moistened soil and tamp just as you did when preparing seedbeds. Then, with your finger or a pencil, gently remove seedlings from their original containers, individually or in clumps, lifting as much of the root system and its attached soil as possible. Place the plant or clump in the palm of your hand or on a flat surface. Holding only the leaves (not the stems or the roots), carefully tease individual seedlings free of a clump. Disturb the soil adhering to the roots as little as possible.

Poke a hole in the soil in the new container. Then, aided by your finger or a pencil, guide the roots into the hole so that all are buried. If the roots are too big for a narrow hole, hold the plant by a leaf in an empty cell and spoon soil around the roots. You can't go wrong positioning the seedling at the same depth it was growing, but many seedlings can be buried up to the cotyledons, which gives little stems more support. Water the seedlings by immersion or with a light spray soon after transplanting (this will settle the soil, too), and put them back under the lights.

Continuing care. Most seedlings are transplanted only once before they reach their final destination in the garden. As they approach a size suitable for the garden, you'll need to harden them off, gradually subjecting them to conditions similar to those in the garden. Place seedlings that were grown indoors or in a cold frame in increasingly more exposed conditions outdoors. Start by setting them in a shady place out of the wind during the daytime. Then gradually expose them to sun and open air, finally leaving them out overnight. (For information on transplanting into the garden, see the next chapter.)

Seedling diseases

The warm, humid conditions that promote germination and seedling growth are also ideal for the growth of fungal disease, called "damping-off." Found in soil and infected plant tissues and on seeds, containers, and tools, these fungi can prevent seeds from germinating or can wipe out a batch of new seedlings in a matter of hours. Infected seedlings collapse suddenly due to restricted movement of water and nutrients through either the roots or the stems. If you inspect the seedlings closely, you'll find dark, rotted roots or dark, shrunken stems that appear to be girdled, usually at the soil surface.

Damping-off can occur when seedlings are overwatered, crowded, or poorly ventilated; when the soil mix drains or aerates poorly; when temperatures are cold; or

Cold frames

GARDENERS IN COLD-WINTER areas who are short of indoor space for seedlings should consider building a cold frame. Nestled in the frame, seedlings are protected from cold and wind, while receiving ample sunlight. To accustom seedlings to outdoor conditions prior to transplanting them in the garden (a process called hardening off), just lift the top of the frame for increasingly long periods each day.

A cold frame is simply a bottomless box with a movable top. Commercially made frames are available, but it's easy to make one yourself. Just nail the sides together and salvage old storm windows or a piece of clear fiberglass for the top. (Size the frame to suit the material you find for the top.) Slant the top so that water and melting snow will run off. Rest the frame on the ground and bank soil around the bottom to seal gaps.

Sunlight provides the only heat, so you need to keep an eye on the temperatures inside. During the winter, you can bank bales of hay or straw, compost, or leaves against the outside of the frame for insulation, and you can cover the top with an old quilt or blanket on cold nights.

Overheating is a more common and serious problem. A little sunlight can heat a frame to plant-killing temperatures very quickly. Garden centers and mail-order suppliers sell hydraulic gadgets filled with temperature-sensitive fluids that automatically open and close the top for ventilation. If you're home during the daytime and can monitor the cold frame, you can hinge the top and use sticks to prop it open for ventilation, or just rest the top on the frame and slide it partially or completely off to ventilate.

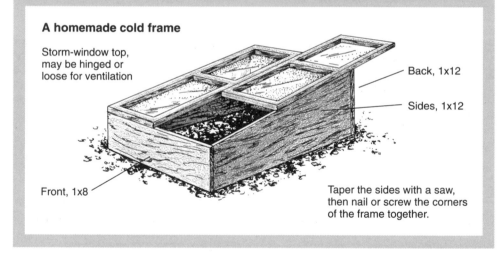

A homemade cold frame

Storm-window top, may be hinged or loose for ventilation

Back, 1x12

Sides, 1x12

Front, 1x8

Taper the sides with a saw, then nail or screw the corners of the frame together.

when equipment, soil, hands, or seeds are contaminated with fungal spores or vegetative matter.

Since there is no cure for affected seedlings, prevention is essential. Use only clean soil mix, containers, and tools. Never combine clean mix with previously used mix. Avoid crowding seedlings or watering with cold or dirty water, and ensure that seedlings have good air circulation.

Direct seeding

Gardeners can grow a great many plants, particularly annuals, by seeding them directly into the garden. Some species require you to do little more than toss the seeds on the ground. Most others are fussier. It is sobering to remember that plants in the wild may expend thousands of seeds to produce a single mature plant, the rest succumbing to drought, drowning, disturbance, disease, or herbivores.

Prepare the bed carefully, raking the surface smooth. If you want to establish just a few plants, sprinkle several seeds where you want a single plant to grow and thin down to one seedling later. (Don't be stingy with seeds.) You can broadcast seeds over a large area and thin them as necessary. Mixing small seeds with fine sand makes broadcasting them easier.

Of the factors affecting germination, the most critical for success in direct seeding is moisture. Keep your seeds moist and you'll have a good chance of success. A light cover of straw or a layer of row-cover fabric helps retain moisture. If the seeds don't require light for germination, you can cover them with a board or a piece of cardboard until they germinate. Seedlings, too, need moisture to become well established. As they extend their root systems, water less frequently but more deeply to encourage deep rooting.

Planting annuals and perennials

Setting plants out in a freshly prepared garden bed is a time of pleasant anticipation. As you firm the soil around young roots, in your mind's eye you can conjure a picture of the display of brilliant flowers or striking foliage that will be the reward of your careful husbandry in the months and years ahead.

Whether you've grown them yourself from seed or purchased them from a plant sale, nursery, or mail-order supplier, you'll want to give your new plants the best start possible. Elsewhere in this section we discuss how to prepare the soil and make a planting bed. Here we'll outline how best to settle annual and perennial plants in their new homes.

Planting seedlings

Annuals are most often transplanted into the garden as seedlings only 8 to 12 weeks old. Some perennials are sold as seedlings, and you can grow many perennials yourself from seed and set them out as seedlings.

Ask at the nursery whether the seedlings have been acclimatized to outdoor conditions, a process called hardening off. If not, don't plant them right away, but introduce them to full sun and cool night temperatures gradually. If you're buying frost-tender plants, remember not to transplant them before the last frost is expected.

Seedlings in moist (but not wet) soil are easy to handle and resilient when transplanted. Water the containers several hours before transplanting if the soil is dry. If you can pick your planting time, transplant on a cool, overcast day, which will stress the seedlings less than will hot, sunny conditions.

Seedlings are sometimes sold in groups of four to six plants in a single small container. To plant them, gently tap out the entire mass of earth and roots. If the roots haven't grown together much, you can break off each plant and its clump of soil. Intertwined roots are more problematic. Plants with larger, tougher roots can be teased apart by hand, disturbing the soil as little as possible. For those with delicate roots, it's probably wiser to cut the soil into sections with a knife, centering a seedling in each section. Seedlings grown in packs of four to six individual cells or in small, individual pots should be gently tapped out, with the root ball intact. The less the roots are disturbed, the faster the plant will become established.

To plant a seedling, dig a hole large enough for the root ball. If the soil is dry, you might want to fill the planting hole with water and let it drain before setting the plant. Hold the seedling in the hole at the same level at which it grew in the pack, or a little deeper (up to the first leaves), then add and firm the soil around the plant. If the plants are leggy, you may want to pinch off the tops to encourage new shoots and a bushier form. Simply take off a section at the top just above a leaf or a pair of leaves.

Water is essential to the health of seedlings, even those of drought-tolerant species. After planting, water the seedlings well with a fine spray, and keep watering once or twice a day until the plants no longer wilt and they begin to send out new shoots.

Planting perennials from containers

Most of the perennials you buy at a local nursery and some from mail-order suppliers are likely to be sold in containers. Water the soil in the container as suggested above for seedlings, and plant on the same kind of cool, overcast day if possible.

Dig a planting hole slightly larger than the container, loosening the soil in an even larger area to encourage root penetration. If you're planting into an established bed, you might add soil amendments—compost, rotted manure, and so on—to the hole at this time.

To remove the plant, slide your hand over the top of the soil, placing the plant's stem between your fingers. Turn the container upside down and tap or press on the pot as needed until it slides off the root ball. If the plant and container are large, place the container on its side and slide it off. If the plant is stuck, dislodge it by hitting the rim of the overturned pot sharply against a solid object (such as the edge of a picnic table), or slide a long knife around the inside of the pot (as you'd do to remove a cake from a baking pan). Avoid picking up the plant by its stem, which can put considerable strain on it.

Some gardeners advise pruning off broken roots, or even the bottom inch of the

Planting seedlings and container-grown plants

Carefully remove the seedling or young container plant.

Set the plant in the soil at the same height at which it grew in the container. Firm the soil around it and water well.

root ball of container-grown plants, before planting. But these plants rarely need either root pruning or the pruning of the above-ground growth that is sometimes recommended to compensate for lost roots.

Once the plant is out of its pot, gently loosen some of the side and bottom roots to encourage them to grow out into the new soil. Set the plant in the hole at the same depth at which the soil ball sat in the container. Add enough soil around the plant to fill the hole halfway, then fill the hole to the brim with water. After the soil has settled and the water drained, fill the hole completely with soil, then tamp it down gently with your hands.

As with seedlings, water is critical for establishing container-grown plants. If nature doesn't provide it, make sure that new plants have about an inch of water each week throughout the growing season. If you're planting during a dry season, or if your climate is particularly dry, build a low wall of soil around the plant, just outside the original hole. This dike will help hold water, as will a layer of mulch.

New transplants often benefit from temporary shade for a few days. If you notice wilting leaves, cover the plant with a lightweight fabric, an inverted basket, or a lath-covered frame. Container-grown plants can be planted throughout the summer and early fall in cold-winter climates, but cover them with a generous mulch of leaves or evergreen boughs before winter sets in to prevent frost heaving, which can lift unprotected plants completely out of the ground. In climates with mild winters, fall planting works well with no special care other than regular watering.

Root-bound plants

If seedlings or container-grown plants are left too long in a container, they can develop too many roots for the available space and become root-bound. If you pop a root-bound plant out of its pot, you'll see more root than soil on the surface of the root ball, sometimes with large roots wound tightly around the perimeter. No matter how much room you create in the new planting hole, the roots will continue to grow around the ball. Although most annuals and perennials will grow out of this condition, you may be able to help them on their way. (Some perennials may be sensitive to root disturbance, but your efforts are unlikely to hurt them any more than their root-bound condition would.)

To rescue a root-bound plant, you must gently tease out the largest of the encircling roots and spread them out into the prepared soil. For larger plants with very tightly meshed roots, you may need to spray the soil away with a garden hose set at full force and then separate the major roots. If that doesn't work, you can cut off some of the roots so that you can untangle

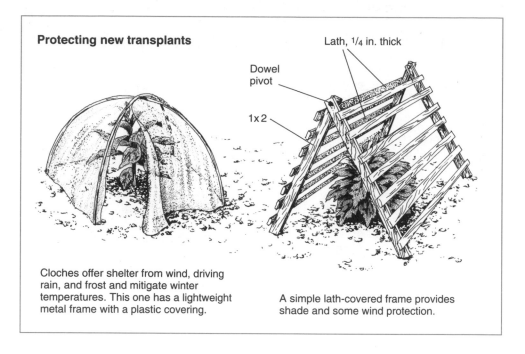

Protecting new transplants

Dowel pivot

Lath, 1/4 in. thick

1 x 2

Cloches offer shelter from wind, driving rain, and frost and mitigate winter temperatures. This one has a lightweight metal frame with a plastic covering.

A simple lath-covered frame provides shade and some wind protection.

the rest. Slicing longitudinally through the root ball in several places with a knife can also stimulate new root growth. Perform this rather drastic surgery only if you can water the plant regularly for the remainder of the season.

Bare-root plants

Some perennials are sold, usually through the mail, with little or no soil surrounding their roots. Such bare-root plants are sold when they're dormant, in very early spring or in the fall.

Plant bare-root plants as soon as possible. Many suppliers include instructions for planting and care. In general, clip off any broken stems or roots. If a plant appears dry, soak its roots for 12 to 24 hours in water or in a quarter-strength solution of soluble fertilizer before planting. If you can't plant in the garden right away, plant temporarily in a nursery bed or a cold frame, mulching and watering well. Or, pot the plant in a suitable container and store it in a cool, sheltered place.

Dig a planting hole wide and deep enough to allow you to spread the roots out. Add soil amendments if needed. As a rule, plant bare-root plants at the same depth at which they grew in the nursery. Look closely at the base of the stem, where the roots begin, and you may see a slight change in color, indicating the previous soil line. If you can't see a line, position the stem to ensure that the roots will be covered with soil.

Suspend the plant in the hole at the correct depth and add soil, working it in among the roots with your fingers. When the hole is half full of soil, fill it with water, wait for it to drain, then add the remainder of the soil. Make a dike of soil around the outermost limits of the planting hole (to hold water) and mulch generously. As with

other transplants, bare-root perennials need regular watering during their first season.

Planting herbaceous ground covers

Low-growing perennial ground covers can save you a great deal of weeding and mowing, while creating an attractive carpet of color in the landscape.

The closer you space ground-cover plants, the quicker they will fill in. But the mature plants may be crowded and need thinning. If you're placing ground-cover plants among other, larger plants, mulch before planting; the mulch will keep the weeds down until the ground cover is established. Just dig down through the mulch layer to plant each ground-cover plant. Plastic mulch controls weeds effectively, but it is unattractive, inhibits moisture penetration, does not decompose, and must eventually be removed. Small pebbles and gravel look better, but they don't add anything to the soil. Bark chips, shredded leaves, straw, or grass clippings are often used.

Ground covers are very useful on steep slopes, where they help hold the soil and preclude struggling up and down with a lawn mower. But slopes present special problems for planting. They are difficult to work on and don't hold water well. Heavy rains or winds can wash away newly placed plants and much soil. To counter these problems, build small "terraces" for single plants or groups of plants. You can dig into the slope, mounding soil on the downhill side of the planting hole. If needed, add one or more bricks or stones to shore up the soil. Wooden shingles work very well; just push them into the soil to form a small retaining wall for each plant. Work from the top of the slope down, mulching heavily as you go to help hold water and the bare soil. Water regularly until the plants become established.

Planting trees and shrubs

Whereas most gardeners look forward to planting annuals and perennials, beginners are likely to be less eager to set a tree or a shrub in its permanent home. Lugging large, heavy plants around and digging good-size holes in often recalcitrant soil isn't everybody's idea of fun. Even if the plants are small and easily maneuvered, they are often expensive, and the cost of failure is daunting.

One solution to this dilemma is easy. Hire a trained arborist or experienced landscaper to plant large trees and shrubs. The nursery where you bought the plant will usually offer this service as well as a guarantee, saving you the work and making replacement less of an issue if something goes wrong.

Small trees and shrubs, however, aren't much more difficult to plant than large perennials. And, if you find that you enjoy the process with these plants, you'll feel more confident tackling larger specimens.

Trees and shrubs are most commonly sold in containers, bare-root, or balled-and-burlapped. You can plant a small container-grown or bare-root tree or shrub in the same way as described for perennials. The drawing below shows how to plant a bare-root shrub. Planting balled-and-burlapped plants, which requires slightly more work, is discussed in this chapter.

As mentioned in the chapter on soil improvement, it's best to plant most trees and shrubs into unamended soil. Research has shown that roots don't seem inclined to venture beyond the cozy confines of fluffed-up, amended soil.

Balled-and-burlapped plants

With its root ball wrapped in burlap or a similar material, tied securely for transport, a balled-and-burlapped tree or shrub might be said merely to have a fabric container. But because these plants dry out more rapidly than do container-grown plants, make sure to keep the roots moist if there's any delay between purchase and planting.

It used to be possible to plant the root ball with the burlap and twine in place. The roots would push through the loosely woven fabric, and the fabric eventually rotted away. Today the "burlap" and "twine" are often nonbiodegradable materials. If you don't recognize this, your plant will slowly strangle to death as its roots circle around inside the impenetrable fabric. To be safe, take the extra time to unwrap the fabric as you plant.

First, dig a hole that will easily accommodate the root ball. It should be deep enough to allow you to position the trunk or stems at the same height at which they grew in the field—look for a change of

Planting a balled-and-burlapped plant

Dig a hole wider than the root ball and as deep. (The plant should be at the same depth at which it grew previously—check for a soil line on the stem.) Rough up the sides of the hole if they're smooth, and add stakes for support if necessary. If the root ball isn't intact enough to permit unwrapping the ball outside the hole, lower the wrapped ball into the hole, as shown.

Cut the twine and carefully work the wrapping down the sides, then slide it out from under the ball.

Backfill with native, unamended soil, working the soil around the ball. Water when the hole is half full of soil. Then fill to the soil line, build a soil dike to retain water, and add mulch. Water regularly.

Planting a bare-root shrub

Spread and support the roots on a mound of earth in the planting hole, positioning the stem at the same depth at which it was growing previously. (Place a long stick across the hole as a gauge.) Work backfill soil among the roots with your free hand until the hole is more than half full, then soak the plant and soil.

Allow the water to drain, adjust the depth of the stem if necessary, and work in more soil to fill the hole. Make a dike of soil around the perimeter of the root zone, mulch, and keep the plant well watered during its first growing season.

color near the base indicating the old soil line. Drive in any stakes you need to support the plant as described in the next chapter. Rest the tree or shrub on a ground sheet or tarp beside the hole. You won't be able to turn the plant easily in the hole, so orient its limbs in the directions you prefer while it's on the tarp.

Begin to unwrap the root ball. If the soil and roots appear to cohere, completely unwrap the root ball and gently lower it into the hole. Support the base of the ball—don't dangle the plant by its trunk or stem. Enlist a friend to help you if necessary. If the partially unwrapped root ball appears to be too crumbly to hold together on its own, lower the plant into the hole with the fabric in place. Finish unwrapping the plant there and carefully slide the fabric out from under the ball.

As you refill the hole with soil, take time to stand back and make sure that the trunk and stems are vertical. Work the soil around the root ball. When the hole is half full of soil, fill it with water, let it drain, then add the remaining soil. Encircle the planting hole with a low mound of soil to hold water, then spread mulch. As with any transplant, monitor the tree or shrub's water carefully during its first season.

Pruning and wrapping

Arborists used to recommend pruning the top growth of newly transplanted trees to compensate for the corresponding loss of or damage to the roots. Current research, however, seems to indicate that the practice may actually retard root growth. You may not need to do any pruning when you plant other than removing branches damaged in transport. (Unless you're an experienced pruner, when you buy the tree or shrub, ask the nursery to do whatever pruning is necessary to enhance its form. If you don't trust the nursery, hire an arborist.)

Another traditional practice—wrapping the trunk of a young tree—seems also to miss its intended mark. Although wrapping may reduce insect damage, it doesn't seem to prevent sunscald or other winter injury. A coat of white latex paint or other reflective material reduces sunscald, but it may be an eyesore. Rabbits often eat the bark at the base of trees, girdling the trunks so badly that young trees may die. A cylinder of 1-inch mesh chicken wire, positioned high enough to remain above expected snow cover, will protect the bark from small, sharp incisors.

Supporting plants

Many large annuals, perennials, shrubs, and trees sometimes need support. Newly transplanted, they may need help to resist strong winds or to encourage young trunks or stems to grow straight. Large mature annuals or perennials may flop and sprawl unless given some discreet support.

Several simple methods of providing support are shown in the drawings below. All are best installed when you plant or in the spring when perennials are small. A thicket of twigs or brush, frequently used to support beans in the vegetable garden, will do the same for floppy ornamentals. Wire supports, homemade or purchased at a nursery, also do the job.

Stakes of various sizes can be used singly or in groups. Bamboo and metal stakes are stronger than wooden stakes of comparable size and don't rot as easily as untreated wood. If you can, place the stakes when you plant, so that you won't risk pounding them through major roots later on. Ties should be strong, should not cut into the stems, and should allow for growth.

In areas exposed to steady or gusting winds, newly planted trees 5 feet tall or more will need the support of stout posts until their root systems become established. Pound two or three posts into the soil outside of the planting area prior to planting and tie the tree to them. If you use wire, cover it with a section of an old garden hose where it comes in contact with the tree. The fastenings should be loose enough to allow some movement of the trunk in the wind—like an arm in a sling, a rigidly tied trunk will become weak.

Check periodically to see that the ties are not cutting into the bark. After a season, remove all supports and try to wobble the trunk. The base of the tree shouldn't move any more than that of an established tree of similar size. If it does, the root base may have problems; consult an arborist to find out.

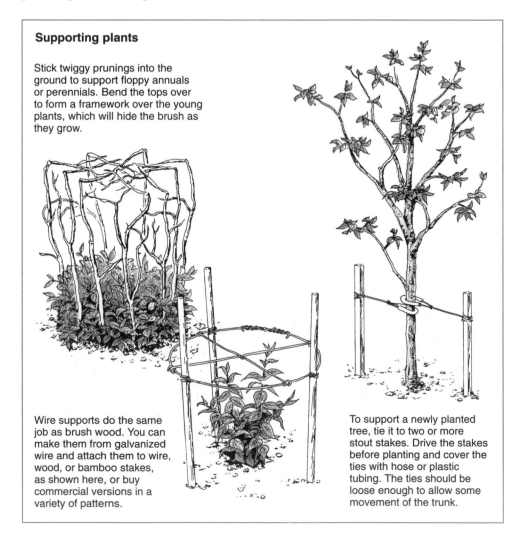

Supporting plants

Stick twiggy prunings into the ground to support floppy annuals or perennials. Bend the tops over to form a framework over the young plants, which will hide the brush as they grow.

Wire supports do the same job as brush wood. You can make them from galvanized wire and attach them to wire, wood, or bamboo stakes, as shown here, or buy commercial versions in a variety of patterns.

To support a newly planted tree, tie it to two or more stout stakes. Drive the stakes before planting and cover the ties with hose or plastic tubing. The ties should be loose enough to allow some movement of the trunk.

Growing hardy bulbs

When many of us think of spring, we think of bulbs—crocuses, daffodils, and tulips. But bulbs are with us throughout the year: showy summer-flowering lilies and gladioli, autumn-flowering colchicums, and snowdrops, which peek through the late-winter snow cover.

Bulb is the common designation for plants that store food in swollen underground stems. We use the term here to include plants such as daffodils, tulips, and lilies, which form true bulbs; and other plants such as crocuses and colchicums, which form bulblike structures called corms.

Bulbs, like other plants, are classified as tender or hardy. Tender bulbs can't withstand cold temperatures and must be dug up and stored over cold winters. Hardy bulbs can survive freezing temperatures in the ground; in fact, most need a period of cold during dormancy in order to grow and flower later.

Planting

In cold-winter areas, spring-blooming bulbs are best planted in early fall so that they have time to set roots to help them through the winter. In warmer climates, however, you may be able to plant them well into December or even later, as long as the ground can still be worked. Summer- and autumn-flowering bulbs are best planted in the spring.

In general, bulbs should be planted two to three times as deep as the bulb is tall. Place the flat side, where the roots will grow, pointing down; if both ends look the same to you, don't worry too much—a bulb planted upside down will right itself within a season. Some smaller bulbs will work their way to the surface within a year and flourish right under the mulch without any soil covering. Indeed, all bulbs somehow reach their optimum depth within a few years. Bulbs planted in good garden soil need no special amendments. (For a more intensive fertilizing program, see "Applying fertilizers" later in this section.)

Space bulbs according to the effect you desire. If you want a daffodil bed to look ancestral immediately, lift whole shovelfuls of soil and plant half a dozen or more bulbs in each large hole. If you can wait a few years for a mature look, plant one bulb per hole and space the holes 6 inches to a foot or two apart, depending on the size of the plant. The planting will look sparse that first season, but it will fill in later. In some

areas, burrowing varmints consider bulbs, particularly those of tulips and lilies, a great delicacy. Planting groups of bulbs underground in little wire or plastic baskets will help deter these critters.

If you plant spring bulbs early in the fall, rainfall will provide enough moisture to prepare them for winter. If you're late, soak the area well after planting to settle the soil before a hard freeze sets it.

After the plants bloom in the spring, the foliage replenishes each bulb's food supplies, then turns brown and withers as the bulb goes dormant. Some gardeners apply special bulb fertilizers to the soil around the bulbs while they are actively growing. They also deadhead, or remove the flowers and small seedpods so that all the plant's resources help replenish the bulb. But other gardeners do neither and their bulbs continue to flourish.

If you plant spring bulbs in beds with other annuals and perennials, you may not appreciate the unsightly foliage of dormant plants. You can dig the plants immediately after blooming and transplant them to an inconspicuous area of the garden until their foliage has withered, but that's a lot of work. It's better to plant bulbs among other plants that will screen the dying bulb foliage from view.

Naturalizing spring bulbs

Bulbs spread throughout a lawn or meadow are a lovely sight in spring. Some people plant one or a few bulbs in the bottom of small holes made with a special bulb-planting tool that cuts a plug of soil several inches in diameter and up to 5 to 6 inches deep. Others skim off large areas of sod, dig to the required depth and scatter the bulbs, then replace soil and sod. Whether you plant in small or large holes, if the soil is poor, work in bone meal or bulb fertilizer, covering the fertilizer with a sprinkling of soil or sand before planting to protect the bulb from burning.

Naturalized bulbs pose a dilemma for lawn care. Mowing the lawn, and therefore the bulb foliage shortly after bloom, prevents the plant from replenishing its food supplies. In areas of naturalized bulbs, you must be willing to let the grass grow until the bulb foliage has yellowed (anytime from June to August, depending on climate). You could naturalize only small bulbs, such as crocuses, and mow high, over their foliage. Or you could naturalize bulbs in an area where regular mowing isn't needed, such as along the edge of a woods or in a meadow.

Making a meadow garden

It's easy to understand the popularity of meadow gardening—a field of colorful flowers dancing in the breeze is a happy sight to anyone. For the gardener, the thought of growing such a thing is seductive indeed, particularly when it is advertised as easy to start and maintain. Unfortunately, the enticing pictures and promises offered by various brands of "canned" meadows are, at best, simplistic.

True meadows are not a broad sweep of cheerful flowers but a mixture of plants—herbaceous annuals and perennials and grasses. In addition, meadows are home to a wide variety of wildlife. The result is a

diverse, constantly changing community.

In North America, the prairies of the Great Plains and the meadows of the western mountains are the only long-lived meadows. When meadows are found elsewhere, they're usually transitory, the first of a succession of stages of regrowth in a disturbed or cleared area. In the eastern woodlands, for example, a meadowlike mix of native grasses and herbaceous plants may quickly colonize a cleared area, but after a few years it will have given way to brambles and fast-growing trees such as red cedar.

Maintaining a meadow garden in such an area requires regular intervention to forestall the natural course of events. You'll need to mow, burn, or pull out undesirable plants by hand. In addition, the balance of plants in the meadow will change if the field is left to its own devices. Certain grasses and herbaceous plants may crowd out other plants, and these too may need to be controlled. Clearly, meadows in these areas are not low maintenance.

Few gardeners have the space, conditions, or energy to establish a true meadow. But many, regardless of where they live, can establish and enjoy a meadowlike mixture of wildflowers and grasses. A few general tips: If this is your first attempt, start small; you can create a little "meadow" in an area no bigger than one of your flower beds. Mow a strip around the area—meadow gardening requires acceptance and appreciation of "weedy" appearances in between colorful flowering periods, and when the meadow is looking unkempt, a mown border will remind you and your neighbors that this is not merely a neglected spot in the landscape.

Serendipity or control?

The simplest approach to making a meadow is to just stop mowing a sunny area on your property. You'll be surprised at the variety of plants that appear. You might plant a few additional wildflowers to achieve more diversity.

If you want to control the composition of your meadow, you'll need to remove the existing vegetation. You can deep-till the area, as for a flower bed, or shallow-till it, removing the surface vegetation and disturbing the underlying soil as little as possible. Any soil disturbance will bring weed seeds to the surface, requiring one or more subsequent tillings to eradicate the seedlings. If you're not in a hurry, you can till as needed over an entire season, then plant the meadow in the fall or the following spring.

You can also destroy existing vegetation by smothering it under black plastic or layers of newspaper. Both of these methods also work best if extended over the course of a year. After the existing vegetation has

been killed, you can either till the area (which risks bringing up more weed seeds) or rake away the debris and sow or plant into untilled soil.

A meadow does not require heavy fertilization. It is helpful to test the soil, but adding copious amounts of manure or inorganic fertilizers is generally not necessary. If the land is exhausted from extensive farming, or if the topsoil was removed during land development, you can incorporate organic matter (mulch or compost) to slowly restore the soil.

Seeding a meadow

Sowing seeds on the plot is the simplest and, for large areas, the least costly method of starting a meadow. You can sow seeds in the spring or the fall. Fall seeding takes advantage of fall and winter rains and provides the cool, moist period that many native plants need in order to germinate. The seeds will germinate early in the spring when the soil begins to warm up, and the seedlings will be well established before the arrival of the hot, dry days of summer.

For large areas, sow at a rate of roughly 10 pounds of seed per acre. Sow smaller areas at 4 to 5 ounces per 1,000 square feet. For very small areas, you can double the rate for more intense color. Mix tiny seeds, such as those of bee balm, with fine sand for more even dispersal.

After broadcasting the seeds, tamp them in with a roller or the back of a rake. Irrigate regularly—don't let the seeds dry out before germination, and keep seedlings well watered until they've become established. During the first year, water during dry periods.

"Plugging" a meadow

A meadow, like a garden bed or border, can be planted with seedlings grown in trays or containers; you can start the seedlings yourself or purchase them from a nursery. This method of "plugging" seedlings into a meadow can be time-consuming or expensive, but it allows you to get the jump on weeds by mulching around the seedlings. A middle course is to sow native grass seed

and plant "plugs" of wildflower seedlings. Depending on the species and on the look you want, plugs can be spaced as close as 1 foot on center; larger plants need more space—unless you want to mimic the effects of competition in the wild.

Choosing plants

Be wary of the "canned" meadow approach. Many of these mixes are predominantly annuals; some may reseed, but after the first year, such meadows usually decline. Take a little more time and effort to compile your own plant list. If you live in a region with natural meadows, study them; if not, note the plants that colonize roadsides and open spaces.

Remember that some perennial wildflowers (for example, coneflowers, butterfly weed, and blazing-star) may not flower for three to five years when grown from seed. Consider buying some container-grown perennials and include some native annuals to provide color in the meadow's first years. If you select species that self-seed aggressively and crowd out others, plant them sparingly and be prepared to pull out some of the seedlings to maintain diversity in the planting.

Designing a meadow

It may sound odd to "design" a meadow. If you're seeding, it is certainly possible to mix all the seeds together and see what effect broadcasting them creates. But meadows in the wild are seldom, if ever, collections of single plants randomly dotted about the landscape. Competition among plants, grazing, pockets of moisture, soil fertility, and other small-scale differences "organize" the landscape. Some plants grow as individuals; others form drifts, the boundaries of which are indistinct. It takes some effort to capture the essence of a wild meadow in a garden. In general, plant smaller plants in large drifts. Larger plants read well in a meadow when planted in smaller numbers.

Maintenance

As we've noted, in many parts of the country, meadows are transitory. The meadow gardener seeks to freeze the natural succession as well as to maintain some control over the mix of plants. Annual mowing can accomplish a great deal; old-fashioned weeding does the rest.

If you mow, start at the end of the second year, sometime after most of the seeds have ripened. (A meadow is a miniature nursery, providing seeds and seedlings that can be collected and used to fill in bare spots.) Set the mower blades as high as possible to avoid damaging the crowns of plants. Mowing during the growing season can yield interesting results, delaying bloom on some species, providing plants you didn't know were there the opportunity to grow—you might want to experiment.

Multiplying by division

Unlike animals, plants have the wondrous ability to produce a new individual from a part of an old one. Under certain conditions, a portion of a leaf, stem, shoot, or root can generate a completely new plant, genetically identical to its parent. Over centuries, gardeners and horticulturists have developed techniques to initiate or to enhance this natural phenomenon in order to increase their stock of plants.

Almost all the vegetative parts of a plant (virtually everything but the seeds and associated sexual parts) are candidates for this asexual type of propagation. Although some of these propagation techniques are difficult or fussy, several are not. In the next chapter we'll discuss propagation from cuttings. Here we'll examine the easiest vegetative propagation technique: division.

In nature, plants often grow and divide themselves over the years into two or more independent plants. Gardeners can duplicate this process by lifting an entire plant and dividing it into pieces, each piece a small plant complete with leaves or buds, stems, and roots. Crowns can be divided, as can roots and rhizomes and the plants arising from them. Specialized plant structures, such as bulbs and corms, can be divided or forced into growth that can later be divided and multiplied.

Plants are usually divided in the early spring or in the fall. Spring weather promotes good shoot and root growth in the newly separated plants, which have a full growing season to become established. In northern regions, plants divided in the fall, after deciduous plants have lost their leaves but before the ground freezes, have some opportunity to continue growing roots before very cold weather prevails. In southern regions, where excellent root-growing temperatures occur throughout the winter, gardeners may prefer to divide in the fall rather than the spring.

Dividing plants that form crowns

Many herbaceous perennials and woody plants form crowns and can be easily divided. A close-knit collection of stems at the base of a plant, a crown forms over a period of years and increases the diameter of the plant. Dividing plants with crowded crowns or those that are flowering less abundantly can restore their vigor. You can also divide healthy, flourishing plants to increase your stock.

As a rule, most species are best divided

Dividing crown-forming plants

Dig a generous root ball.

Smaller plants can be teased apart with your fingers or cut apart with a knife. Large, tangled root masses can be forced apart with two garden forks.

Replant the divisions quickly, setting them in place as you would any new plant.

in early spring before growth begins. Some plants, however, will do best if divided at specific times of year according to their growth cycle. Plants that normally bloom in the spring can be divided in late spring and early summer, or even in fall. Plants that bloom in late spring and become dormant shortly thereafter, such as Oriental poppies, can be divided in the summer; wait until they have bloomed and the foliage has begun to discolor before dividing. Many herbaceous species can be divided at any time of year, so successful are they at reestablishing themselves.

Before you lift and divide a plant, thoroughly water the surrounding ground and allow it to drain, and prepare the soil in which you will plant the divisions. If possible, divide plants on cloudy days; the lower temperature and higher humidity will reduce moisture stress. Dig around and under the plant with a shovel or a garden fork to create a generous root ball. Then lift the plant and as many roots as possible and place it on a firm surface.

Although it is best to leave as much soil as possible on the roots, you may have to shake off or wash away some soil so that you can locate the growing points— each division must contain structures capable of producing new roots and shoots. (Some plants, as noted in the Encyclopedia entries, do not reestablish quickly from divisions, even if you disturb their roots as little as possible.)

Some plants can be separated easily with your fingers or a hand fork. Others may need to be cut apart with a sharp shovel or a sturdy knife. Large plants with tough, compact, or tangled roots, such as daylilies, can be forced apart by thrusting two garden forks back to back into the center of the crown and levering one against the other. Some plants may be too large to comfortably lift. If so, you can divide them in the ground by slicing off portions from the edges of the crown.

After it has been separated from its parent, a new division should be treated like any other new plant. Don't let the roots dry out, and replant it as soon as possible. Water it immediately and thoroughly. Keep it watered and protected from intense sunlight, heat, and wind until it's well established. If you have the space, you can plant small divisions in a nursery bed where they can grow to a decent size before transplanting them in their final location. If you plant small divisions in the fall, mulch the soil around them to prevent subsequent freez-

Propagating by runners and stolons

Pin the runner or stolon to the ground at a node and keep the surrounding soil moist. When the new plant offers resistance to a tug, dig and transplant it.

Pin

Dividing rhizomes

Carefully dig up the clump.

Break or cut young branching rhizomes from the older parent. (Iris rhizomes, illustrated here, will contain a leaf fan.)

Trim dead growth and plant the divisions at their previous depth.

ing and thawing from pushing them out of the ground.

As with newly transplanted trees and shrubs, you need not prune back the tops of woody plants before division. Leaving the top intact allows the plant to develop as many leaves as possible, each of which manufactures foods that aid the plant's recovery. Large, unwieldy plants may need to be pruned so that they can be maneuvered during division and replanting.

Herbaceous crown-forming plants include coreopsis, bleeding-heart, foxgloves, asters, campanulas, anemones, columbines, daisies, primroses, herbaceous peonies, sedum, dianthus, veronica, viola, and rudbeckia. Woody plants that form crowns include barberries, heaths, spireas, and potentilla.

Dividing plants with runners, stolons, or offsets

Runners and stolons are specialized stems that run along the surface of the ground. Where conditions permit, the nodes on these stems can develop roots and shoots and become independent of the parent plant. Plants producing runners often grow as a rosette or a crown; they include a large number of ground covers. Among the plants that produce stolons are Bermudagrass, ajuga, mint, and lamb's-ears.

Gardeners can propagate plants with runners or stolens merely by enhancing the plant's natural tendencies. Pin or peg a runner or stolon to the ground at one or more nodes. Keep the soil around the pinned nodes moist to allow any roots that are formed to become established. When you tug gently on the new plant and feel some resistance, cut the plant free of its parent, then dig and transplant it. Some plants, such as strawberries, are ready to separate in a few weeks; others, such as red-twig dogwood, can take as long as a year.

Offsets are little plants that develop from the base of the main stem of plants such as aloes, yuccas, date palms, and cen-

tury plants. In nature, offsets often become independent of the parent plant by establishing their own root systems. This is most apparent in agaves, where, in most species, the parent plant dies after blooming. You can take advantage of this natural means of reproduction by separating and transplanting offsets that have formed their own roots.

Dividing suckering plants

A sucker is a shoot that arises from root tissues below ground, but the term is also commonly used for shoots arising from stem tissue near the crown of the plant. Suckers may appear at any distance from the parent plant. Many woody plants form suckers, including lilacs, sumacs, serviceberries, poplars, jasmines, mock oranges, nandina, flowering quince, and rugosa roses.

You should divide and transplant suckers during the dormant season, in the spring or, second best, in the fall. Dig down carefully and examine the sucker's roots; if they appear healthy and prolific, cut the root connecting the sucker to the parent plant with pruners. Lift the sucker with as many remaining roots and as much soil as possible, and transplant it. As for other woody divisions, don't prune healthy roots or top growth if you can help it.

Dividing plants with rhizomes

Rhizomes are storage structures that grow horizontally at or just beneath the surface of the soil. These specialized segmented stems have nodes and internodes from which roots and lateral branches grow. Leaves, flowering stems called culms, and upright, aboveground shoots also develop from the rhizome or its lateral branches. Rhizome-bearing plants include lily-of-the-valley, pachysandra, rhizomatous irises, many grasses (including bamboo), and some ferns.

Rhizomes may be skinny or fat and may form dense mats or wide-spreading networks. Bearded irises, for example, form

clumps of large rhizomes, which should be divided every few years before they become overcrowded, a condition that results in weakened plants and declining flower production. Lily-of-the-valley, on the other hand, has thinner rhizomes that spread widely and can grow for decades without division.

Rhizomes are best divided when growth begins in early spring or when it ends in late summer to early fall. Dig up the rhizomes; cut or break them into smaller segments, each with roots and buds or shoots; and replant them at the same depth, as shown above. It's easy to see where to make the cuts for some rhizomes, such as bearded irises, because each branch will contain one or two leaf fans. Sometimes it's less obvious because dormant buds may be quite small.

Dividing tubers

We're all familiar with that most common tuber, the potato, but ornamental plants such as caladiums, calla lilies, dahlias, and tuberous begonias also form tubers. Like a rhizome, a tuber is a swollen, specialized, underground stem that stores food.

Technically speaking, there are several types of tubers. Some, such as potatoes, are connected to the parent by stolons and are dotted with eyes, which consist of one or more buds. Other plants, including dahlias and tuberous begonias, form tuberous roots or stems that have no eyes. Instead, buds are found only on the crown of the swollen structure, and the fibrous roots are only at the opposite end.

All of these types of tubers are simple to propagate. Most are partly tender and in cold-winter areas will need to be dug in the fall and stored for planting in the spring. Dig them when the tops have fallen over or break off easily, then spread them out in the air for several days until their surfaces have become leathery. Pack them in wadded newspaper, dried peat moss, or sawdust and store in a cool, dry place.

Divide and plant the tubers in the spring. You can divide some tubers merely by snapping off branches containing at least one bud. Try not to damage any roots that have already developed. Tubers with several buds or eyes on the surface can be cut apart, one eye or bud and enough tuber to sustain initial growth per division. Dust the pieces immediately with a protective fungicide and leave them for several days where it is warm (70° F) and humid to form a protective layer of cells over the cut surfaces. This process, called suberization, helps prevent the tuber from further drying and decay.

Finally, plant the cured pieces. Cover eyed tubers with a layer of soil equal to their size (a tuber 2 inches in diameter goes 2 inches deep). Plant dahlias, tuberous begonias, and other root or stem tubers so that the crown bud is just at the soil surface. Small tubers may produce only foliage the first year but will flower if replanted the following year.

Dividing bulbs

Bulbs have a short, compact stem and embryonic leaf and flower buds enclosed in specialized leaves or leaf bases called bulb scales. The outer layers of bulb scales usually appear fleshy, whereas the interior layers appear more leaflike.

There are two general types of bulbs. Onions, daffodils, and tulips are examples of bulbs whose outer scales are dry and papery and provide protection against

Dividing bulbs

Divide bulbs after the foliage has yellowed. Replant them twice as deep as their height.

moisture loss. These outer, protective scales resemble tunics, so these bulbs are referred to as tunicate bulbs. Inside these protective layers, the bulb scales are tightly held together.

Bulbs such as lilies and fritillarias lack protective coverings and are called nontunicate or naked bulbs. Their bulb scales are held together only loosely and can easily come apart, so they're easy to divide, but they must be handled carefully and protected from moisture loss.

Small bulbs, called bulblets, often form at the base of tunicate and nontunicate bulbs, as shown at left. After the aboveground foliage has yellowed or died down, you can dig the parents up and easily pull off these bulblets, sometimes called offsets. You can replant them immediately, or you can store them in a cool, dry spot and replant them when you'd normally plant bulbs of that type. Plant them just as you would a full-size bulb but at a depth only twice their own height. Small bulblets may take several years to grow to flowering size.

Dividing corms

Corms, like bulbs, are swollen underground stems that store food for the new plant, and they're frequently confused with bulbs. Gladioli, crocuses, colchicums, and freesias form corms. If you dig corms during their dormant period, you'll typically find a new corm growing on top of the previous season's shriveled and depleted corm. Enclosed by dry, leaflike scales, the new corm will have a growing point at the top, lateral buds, and offspring called cormels attached to its base.

Hardy corms such as crocuses can be divided after their foliage has died back and replanted immediately or in the fall. Just remove the cormels and plant them, large ones at a depth of about twice their height, smaller ones about 2 inches deep. In cold climates, tender corms such as gladioli are lifted each fall. The new corms are separated from the old; stored in a cool, dry place; and replanted in the spring. Cormels will form only grasslike leaves during their first growing season, and small ones may take two seasons to reach blooming size.

Increasing by cuttings

Whereas division is widely practiced by gardeners—there always seems to be a clump of asters or daffodils to split up—many people garden for years without attempting to propagate plants by cuttings. Although the basic techniques are fairly simple, a lot more can go wrong with cuttings than with divisions. Nevertheless, cuttings are a useful way to propagate many woody and some herbaceous plants that are difficult or impossible to divide. In addition, a parent plant that yields a few divisions might supply dozens of cuttings.

Unlike divisions, which contain the necessary growing points for both shoots and roots, cuttings have to regenerate either the shoots or the roots, or both. The propagator's task is to take cuttings from those parts of the plant in which cells will most readily regenerate and to provide the levels of moisture, temperature, and light conducive to their doing so.

Professional propagators produce most ornamental shrubs and many greenhouse plants by cuttings, and they leave little to chance in their procedures. Drawing on long experience and research, they know just when and where to make the cuts. Then they tend the cuttings in closely monitored greenhouse conditions.

Few gardeners have the resources or

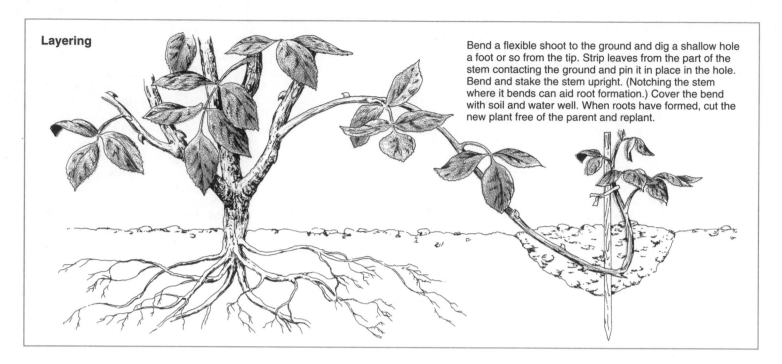

Layering

Bend a flexible shoot to the ground and dig a shallow hole a foot or so from the tip. Strip leaves from the part of the stem contacting the ground and pin it in place in the hole. Bend and stake the stem upright. (Notching the stem where it bends can aid root formation.) Cover the bend with soil and water well. When roots have formed, cut the new plant free of the parent and replant.

the inclination to duplicate a professional propagating setup. But if you're willing to experiment—and to fail—you can have fun with a simpler, hit-or-miss approach. First, however, we'll discuss a propagation technique that, technically, doesn't involve cuttings at all.

Layering

Occasionally when a branch or stem of a plant rests on the ground or becomes buried underground, it forms roots and, with time, becomes a separate plant. You can mimic this natural process, called layering, to propagate new plants. As with a cutting, you're trying to induce a stem to produce roots, but by leaving the stem attached to the parent plant you mitigate problems that might arise if you severed it to make a cutting.

Many plants (for example, magnolias, rhododendrons, lilacs, and dogwoods) naturally layer, but you can try the technique with almost any plant whose stems can be bent to the ground. The long, flexible stems of vines and ground covers such as wisteria, clematis, and rambling roses can be layered at several points at once along their length.

In early spring, before growth starts, select a plant with low, flexible, one-year-old shoots. A short distance from the tip of a shoot, strip the leaves off a portion of the stem. Then bend and bury it 3 to 5 inches deep in soil that you've loosened and amended. Depending on its stiffness, you may have to pin the stem in place with sticks, wires, or a rock.

Rooting can be enhanced on many species by wounding the stem before burying it. With a sharp knife, girdle, notch, or slice the stem halfway through. If necessary, keep the wound open by inserting a small stem or a toothpick. Dust the wound with

rooting hormone, then bury it and water thoroughly.

Keep layered stems well watered while roots form; this may take up to two full growing seasons. If the stem resists gentle tugging, it has developed roots, and you can sever it from the parent and transplant it. Care for it as you would any new plant.

Cuttings

Propagating a cutting can be almost as easy as layering. Just snip off a stem, strip the bottom leaves, stick the stem in the ground beneath the parent plant, and keep it well watered. Although the failure rate is very high, gardeners have been propagating plants this way for centuries.

Even the most sophisticated methods differ from this basic one mostly in the measures taken to control the conditions in which the cutting roots—soil, moisture, temperature, and light. Here are some tips to increase your chances of success.

When to take cuttings varies from species to species. For some, the soft succulent spring growth roots best; others should be cut after the first flush of growth is past; still others are made from mature, dormant stems. If you can't find out the timing for a particular plant (check the references in the bibliography), try taking cuttings at each stage.

In general, take cuttings early in the morning from well-watered plants. Cut back from the tip of a healthy stem at least two nodes (the slight swellings where leaves attach). Cut with a very sharp, disinfected knife or pruners slightly below the node.

It's best to prepare and "stick" (plant) cuttings immediately. But you can refrigerate them in a plastic bag for several hours or, occasionally, for several days. Chrysanthemum cuttings, for example, are shipped worldwide and retain the ability to root.

Before sticking, strip the bottom leaves with a sharp knife. Make a fresh cut at the base of the cutting, then dip the base into rooting hormone, sold at garden centers as a powder. Tap the cutting to remove excess powder, which could harm the cutting.

Propagators root cuttings in various mixtures of sand, peat moss, vermiculite, pumice, and perlite. Perlite is a good, all-purpose material, but commercial potting soil may work fine. Put 2 to 3 inches of moist planting medium in a container, make a hole slightly larger than the diameter of the cutting and 1 to 2 inches deep, then insert the cutting. Gently push the surrounding medium into the hole and water thoroughly.

Ideal rooting temperatures are 70° to 80° F during the day and 60° F at night, but many cuttings tolerate a wider range. Unfortunately, there are no clear-cut ways of determining the best light level for cuttings. You'll have to rely on your own experiences and those of others, which are sometimes given in books.

Moisture is critical. Too much can rot stems or leaves. Too little can kill a cutting quickly, sometimes within minutes. You can cover a cutting stuck in the ground outdoors with the top half of a cut-off plastic milk container to conserve moisture. Prop a corner of the container up on a stone or a twig and leave its mouth open for ventilation. Cold frames, terrariums, or a clear plastic bag will retain moisture for cuttings in containers. But they all must be checked periodically. Remember that any transparent propagating tent quickly overheats in direct sunlight.

Cuttings may take weeks or months to root. When the stem resists gentle tugging, transplant the cutting as you would a seedling into a larger pot, or harden it off and plant outside.

Feeding your plants

Plants draw the nutrients they need to live and to grow from air, water, and soil. Although gardeners may be concerned about the effects of air pollution on their plants, we need not worry yet about the air's ability to deliver sufficient quantities of oxygen to plants. The supply of nutrients in the soil, however, is a constant concern. Fortunately, there is much that we can do about soil. We can improve its structure, texture, aeration, and drainage, as outlined in the chapters on soil earlier in this section. And we can fertilize.

Some soils have inherently low fertility. Sandy soils and certain clay soils, for example, are incapable of holding sufficient nutrients and releasing them gradually to plants. Some soils contain all the nutrients plants need but in forms they cannot use. More common are soils whose nutrients have been depleted by plants, by leaching, or by erosion. Natural processes in soils act to replenish the supply of nutrients. In nature, nutrients are returned to the soil as leaves, stems, and branches decompose. In the garden, regular applications of compost and other organic matter can accomplish the same thing. These processes are relatively slow, however, and may not be able to keep up with plant needs.

Fertilizer provides nutrients that are unavailable in the soil and replaces nutrients that plants have used. With fertilizer, you can speed the growth and increase the size of young plants, and you can maintain the quality and healthy growth of older ones. But you shouldn't look to fertilizers to provide all your plants' needs or to solve all their problems. Remember that temperature, moisture, wind, sunlight, insects, disease, and soil pH all affect plants, too. Indeed, fertilizer can sometimes compound a problem. So, to use fertilizer effectively, you should know your plants, your soil, and your climate, and you should know some background about plant nutrients and how fertilizers provide them.

Plant nutrients

Fertilizers come from many different sources. They may be organic or inorganic, natural or manufactured compounds. Whatever their origin, we use them because they contain one or more of the 16 chemical elements that scientists currently identify as essential for plant growth.

Although gardeners may speak of "plant food" or "feeding plants," those terms are a little misleading. Foods are ready-made sources of energy and chemical

compounds. Both plants and animals need food, but green plants are unique in their ability to manufacture their own food. The raw materials from which plants make food are light and nutrients—the 16 essential elements. (The terms *nutrient* and *element* are interchangeable in this context.)

The role that essential elements play in plant growth is complex. Some are incorporated into plant tissues; others are involved in processes inside the cells without becoming part of the cells. For our purposes, it's enough to know that if any one of the essential elements is missing or deficient, plants grow, reproduce, and develop abnormally.

The essential elements are classified in two groups. The major elements, or macronutrients, are carbon, oxygen, hydrogen, nitrogen, phosphorus, potassium, sulfur, calcium, and magnesium. The second group, called trace elements or micronutrients, contains iron, manganese, boron, copper, zinc, molybdenum, and chlorine. Although carbon, oxygen, and hydrogen make up more than 90 percent of the dry weight of plant tissues and play many important roles in plant growth, plants obtain them from air and from water, rather than from the soil. Therefore we normally don't take these elements into account when considering fertilizers.

The macronutrients are further divided into primary and secondary nutrients. Nitrogen (N), phosphorus (P), and potassium (K) are called primary nutrients because they are required in the largest amounts. (Scientists abbreviate the elements using the chemical symbols given in parentheses; you'll also see these letters on fertilizer labels.) Anyone who has bought a bag, box, or bottle of fertilizer will have encountered the primary nutrients, the relative amounts of which are prominently listed on labels as a ratio of nitrogen to phosphorus to potassium (always in that order)—10:10:10, for example.

Sulfur (S), calcium (Ca), and magnesium (Mg) are known as secondary nutrients since they are usually required in smaller amounts. These categories indicate only the relative quantities needed by plants. All of the essential elements are equally important for normal plant growth.

Iron (Fe), manganese (Mn), boron (B), copper (Cu), zinc (Zn), molybdenum (Mo), and chlorine (Cl)—the trace elements, or micronutrients—are required in very small quantities in comparison to the macronutrients, but a deficiency of any of

them affects plant growth and development just as severely as does a macroelement deficiency. Too much of a trace element can also prove toxic to plants. The margin between too little and too much is relatively narrow for trace elements, so you must take great care when fertilizing plants with them.

It's best to apply a trace element only if you're sure that a symptom is due to a deficiency of that element (laboratory plant analysis can confirm this), or if the soil in a particular area of your garden is chronically deficient. Apply only the deficient element; blanket applications of trace elements may result in toxic levels of one or more of them. Nevertheless, many fertilizers formulated for ornamentals include small amounts of trace elements as insurance against deficiencies. These are reasonably safe to use unless you frequently apply large amounts of them.

Fertilizer choices

You have only to visit your local garden center to discover how many different products you can use to provide your plants with essential nutrients. An understanding of the basic fertilizer types will help you make choices between all these alternatives. Fertilizers can be characterized by the selection of nutrients they contain, by the compounds or forms in which the nutrients are provided, by the origin of the materials used (organic or inorganic, natural or manufactured compounds), and by the form of the fertilizer (liquid, powder, granules, and so on).

Nutrient selection. A complete fertilizer contains all three of the primary nutrients. A fertilizer with a 5-10-5 rating, for example, contains 5 percent by weight of nitrogen, 10 percent phosphate, and 5 percent potash.

Some fertilizers contain only one or two of the primary elements. Superphosphate (0-20-0) is 20 percent phosphate; the balance is primarily gypsum. Diammonium phosphate (21-53-0) contains 21 percent nitrogen, 53 percent phosphate, and no potassium. A number of fertilizers also contain secondary nutrients and trace elements.

Organic versus inorganic. Fertilizers are formulated from organic materials and from natural or manufactured inorganic compounds, but plants absorb *all* of their nutrients in the form of inorganic ions. Whether these ions originate from an organic source, such as cow manure or fish meal, or from an inorganic one, such as rock phosphate or lime, makes no difference to their effect on the plant. Likewise, nutrients in fertilizers formulated from natural sources and those in fertilizers synthesized in a chemical factory are used by the plant in exactly the same way.

Organic fertilizers

Fertilizer	Nitrogen	Phosphorus	Potassium	Application rate (per 100 sq. ft.)
Activated sewage sludge "milorganite"	4–6%	2–4%	trace	4–6 lb.
Alfalfa pellets	2.7%	0.5%	2.8%	5 lb.
Blood meal	9–14%	1.6%	0.84%	2 lb.
Bone meal	2%	25–30%	0%	4 lb.
Cottonseed meal	6–7%	2–3%	1–2%	5 lb.
Cow manure, dried	2%	1.8%	2.2%	6–8 lb.
Fish emulsion	12%	0%	1%	25 gal. (1 tbsp./gal.)
Fish meal	4–9%	7%	trace	2–4 lb.
Horse manure, dried	0.7%	0.3%	0.6%	6–8 lb.
Poultry manure, dried	6%	4%	3%	2 lb.
Seaweed extract (kelp)	2%	1%	4–13%	2–3 lb.
Soybean meal	6%	1%	2%	4–5 lb.
Wood ash	0%	trace	5–10%	5 lb.

You may have concerns about the energy consumed and the pollution entailed in the creation of synthetic fertilizers, but remember that plants, and the environment in general, cannot distinguish between a synthetic fertilizer and a natural one—too much manure can pollute a stream just as too much granular fertilizer can.

That said, there are ways in which organic and inorganic fertilizers perform differently in the garden. In certain circumstances these differences may be important enough to influence your choice of which fertilizer to use.

Organic fertilizers. Manures, composts, and other plant and animal residues contain varying amounts of plant nutrients, as shown in the chart above. Most gardeners, however, use them primarily to improve the physical structure of the soil, valuing their organic matter more than their nutrient content. Manures and composts are quite coarse and bulky and are difficult to spread uniformly. As with other organic fertilizers, the nutrients in manures are not available until soil microorganisms break them down. To reduce nitrogen loss during this process, turn the manure into the soil or, in established plantings, work as much as possible into the top layer of soil.

Other organic materials, including bone meal, blood meal, dried sewage sludge, cottonseed meal, and fish emulsion, are dried, pulverized, or processed before they are packaged as fertilizers. (Some animal manures are treated this way as well.) These materials do not condition the soil; their purpose is to supply nutrients.

Organic fertilizers have several advantages over inorganic compounds. Because they must first be processed by microorganisms, they are available to plants over a longer period of time. They are safer to use because they do not burn plants as readily. And they are less likely to leach from the soil. They also have disadvantages. They cost more per unit of nutrient, and many of them are not a balanced source of nutrients. The release of nutrients by the microorganisms is also unpredictable, due to the influence of soil temperature, moisture level, and pH on the organisms' activity.

Inorganic fertilizers. In contrast to organic fertilizers, inorganic fertilizers provide maximum control over nutrient levels. The nutrients are in a soluble form, and they dissolve into ions that are immediately available to plants. They also readily leach from the soil. Since they are usually more concentrated, inorganic fertilizers are more economical per unit of nutrient. But because it takes a smaller amount of inorganic fertilizer to supply a specific quantity of nutrients, you must be careful not to apply too much and burn your plants.

Inorganic fertilizers are also available in several specialized forms, such as starter solutions and slow-release compounds. Starter solutions are fertilizers high in phosphorus and readily available nitrates. They help plants recover more rapidly from the shock of transplanting, when damage to the root system limits its capacity to absorb water and nutrients.

Slow-release fertilizers release nutrients at a relatively slow rate. Some slow-release lawn fertilizers, for example, are formulated to make it possible to apply relatively large amounts of nitrogen without burning the grass. Some of the nitrogen is water soluble and immediately available, but the release of most of the nitrogen depends on temper-ature, moisture, and the activity of soil microorganisms.

Another type of slow-release inorganic fertilizer consists of individual granules coated with a plastic membrane. Water passes through the membrane and dissolves the fertilizer, which then diffuses out through the membrane. The process is not affected by soil pH or soluble-salt levels, and the activity of soil microorganisms is not required. The release rate varies with temperature—almost none is released in cool weather, but release is rapid in hot weather.

Ground limestone, dolomite, and superphosphates are also, in effect, slow-release fertilizers. A single application can supply all of the calcium, magnesium, phosphorus, and sulfur that most ornamentals will need for a growing season and may be adequate for several seasons, depending on soils and growing conditions.

Reading a fertilizer label

The label on a fertilizer container provides important information and can help you choose the fertilizer appropriate to your needs.

Prominently displayed are the percentages by weight of the primary nutrients: nitrogen, phosphorus, and potassium, always in that order. The nitrogen is measured in its elemental form, whereas phosphorus is measured as phosphoric acid and potassium as potash. The balance of the material in the bag consists of fillers (gypsum and ground limestone are the most common) or other elements in compounds with nitrogen, phosphorus, or potassium.

The concentrations of primary and secondary nutrients and trace elements listed on the label are guaranteed by law. The percentages represent the minimum concentration of an element; the fertilizer typically contains a small amount more. (Fillers do not change the guaranteed N-P-K analysis.) The label also provides information about the compounds used to supply the essential elements that are guaranteed to be in the fertilizer.

Inorganic fertilizers can acidify soil, and most labels indicate the fertilizer's potential effect on acidity. This is usually expressed as the amount of calcium carbonate (ground limestone) that would be necessary to neutralize the change in pH that a ton of the fertilizer could cause. The higher the amount, the more acidic the soil will become.

In many soils, the changes in pH induced by fertilizer will not cause problems. But when fertilizer is applied to soils with an already low pH, the increased acidity can affect the availability of nutrients. Most gardeners save highly acidic fertilizers for acid-loving plants such as azaleas and rhododendrons, especially if they are growing in alkaline soil.

Applying fertilizers

Fertilizers come in a variety of physical forms. Inorganic fertilizers may be loose, dry granules; solid tablets or spikes; soluble powders or liquids; or slow-release compounds. Organic fertilizers may be bulky raw materials or may be processed into concentrated powders, granules, or liquids. Some forms are better suited to certain plants or garden conditions than are other forms.

Granular fertilizer

Loose, dry, granular fertilizer can be spread over small areas by hand or over large ones, such as a lawn, with a mechanical spreader. Distribute the fertilizer on the surface as uniformly as you can, then mix it into the soil. This is the most effective way to apply lime and superphosphate, and to get the nutrients in a complete fertilizer (especially phosphorus) down near plant roots.

In a bed of established plants, you can use a technique called side-dressing. Sprinkle the granules on the soil surface in narrow bands along one or both sides of a row of plants or in a circle around individual plants. Leave the fertilizer on the surface or scratch it into the soil (but not too deeply, to avoid damaging roots). Be careful not to leave granules of fertilizer on plant leaves; it can burn them.

Solid tablets

Fertilizer tablets, which are buried in the soil, are most often used for container plants. Long-lasting types are available for treating clumps of perennials and small shrubs. Solid spikes, which are driven into the soil, are made for large shrubs and trees.

Space the tablets or spikes carefully to avoid concentrating the fertilizer in a few spots, and use enough of them to distribute nutrients uniformly. Follow the manufacturer's recommendations for depth. Fertilizers in this form are expensive in relation to the nutrients they supply.

Soluble powders and liquids

Effective and easy to use, these fertilizers provide immediately available nutrients to plants. Both types are used in the same way, although liquids are usually more expensive per unit of nutrient. Dissolve the specified amount of powder or liquid in a container of water and drench the soil. Apply just enough solution to wet the soil down to root depth; more just wastes fertilizer.

If you have a very large garden, you can apply the fertilizer with a garden hose. A hose-end sprayer, which mixes concentrated fertilizer with the spray of water, is simplest. Attaching a metered siphoning device between the faucet and hose gives more control over the concentration of fertilizer delivered. (You can use a similar device with more extensive irrigation systems.) Go over the same plants several times, and direct the spray carefully to ensure even distribution. The nutrients that land on the leaves will be absorbed quickly, but water after you've finished spraying to push the fertilizer on the soil down to the roots. Plan to make several applications during the growing season, rather than supplying all nutrients at one time. Too high a concentration will damage leaves and stems.

Foliar fertilization

Spraying plants with a fertilizer solution as described above is a form of foliar fertilization, but it is inefficient. The water droplets are large, and much of the fertilizer solution ends up on the soil surface. It's much better to apply the nutrients with a fine-mist sprayer and just enough water to wet the leaves.

Foliar fertilizers can't provide enough of the primary elements at one time to meet plant requirements without burning the leaves. So this method is used most often to supply trace elements. Absorption through the leaves is normally very rapid, and symptoms of deficiency frequently can be alleviated in a few days.

Fertilizing a new bed

When you make a new bed or replant an old one, you may wish to incorporate fertilizer. If you plan to grow perennials in the bed, this may be your only opportunity for quite a while to add large quantities of bulky organic matter, such as manure or compost. Once the plants are in place, it's not easy to incorporate these amendments deeply into the soil.

Before fertilizing, it's advisable to have your soil tested. A good soil test will indicate what, if anything, you need to do about the soil's pH and nutrient levels. If the test indicates a lack of calcium or phosphorus, add those elements as you prepare the bed. Since neither of these elements moves through the soil, work in lime or a high-phosphorus fertilizer, such as superphosphate, as thoroughly and as deeply as you can with a spading fork or a small garden tiller. (Dig it in at least 6 to 9 inches and up to 15 inches deep if you can.)

Because other macronutrients are more transient, wait until you plant to incorporate them. Remember that the organic matter you added will provide a steady source of nutrients, including trace elements, as it breaks down. If the soil test indicated a need for nitrogen and potassium, and the organic matter you added will not supply enough, mix in some organic nitrogen or a slow-release fertilizer containing nitrogen and potassium. At most, apply 2 to 3 pounds of inorganic complete fertilizer per 100 square feet, and mix it into the soil well. Once the plants are in the ground (given a boost by a shot of a water-soluble fertilizer when transplanted), you can fertilize them on a regular basis.

Fertilizing programs for specific plants

Most ornamental plants benefit from a basic program of fertilizer application to maintain their health and to promote vigorous growth. As a general rule of thumb, use a fertilizer relatively low in nitrogen and high in phosphorus (such as a 5-10-10 or 5-10-5) for fruiting and flowering plants and one relatively high in nitrogen (a 20-10-10 or a 20-10-20, for instance) for foliage plants. An excess of nitrogen can encourage lush vegetative growth but few flowers and fruits.

Flowering annuals. Whether you purchase them from a garden center or grow them from seed in flats, give flowering annuals some water-soluble fertilizer when you transplant them to the garden. As soon as they show signs of new growth, begin fertilizing regularly, once a week in sandy soils and every ten days to two weeks in heavier soils.

Use a soluble powder, such as a 20-20-20 or a 15-30-15, at the rate of 1 tablespoon per gallon of water. Apply about a quart of solution per square foot to wet the soil thoroughly. Water dry soil before you apply the fertilizer solution.

Spring bulbs. Most spring-flowering bulbs need more fertilizer than gardeners usually provide. Research indicates that the reason tulips, for example, fade out after a few years is lack of nutrients. At the time of planting, apply 4 to 5 pounds of bone meal or superphosphate per 100 square feet, and mix it in as deep as you expect to plant the bulbs. In early spring as soon as leaves begin to emerge, apply about 1 pound of a 5-10-10 per 100 square feet. Try to keep the granules from touching the leaves.

Calculating how much fertilizer to apply

ONCE YOU'VE HAD YOUR SOIL TESTED, you'll need to figure out how much packaged fertilizer it will take to meet the lab's recommendations. This is relatively simple and requires only basic arithmetic. The easiest way to explain the calculations is by example:

The soil-test report recommends 2 pounds of actual nitrogen per 1,000 square feet. You are fertilizing 100 square feet with a 5-10-10 fertilizer. How much should you apply?

Start by asking how much 5 percent fertilizer it takes to supply 2 pounds of nitrogen. Set up a simple equation, using $\times$ as the unknown amount of fertilizer:

$$.05\times = 2 \text{ lb.}$$

$$\times = 2 \div .05$$

$$\times = 40 \text{ lb.}$$

It will take 40 pounds of a 5-10-10 fertilizer per 1,000 square feet to supply 2 pounds of nitrogen. Since you are fertilizing one tenth as much area, you need to spread only 4 pounds of a 5-10-10 fertilizer to meet the lab's nitrogen recommendation. Calculations for the other elements are, of course, done in the same manner.

When flowers begin to fade, repeat the application of bone meal or superphosphate and apply an organic source of nitrogen, or make a second application of the 5-10-10 to keep the leaves green longer. This allows the bulbs to store more food, which is so important for the formation of flowers the following year. An alternative program is to apply a four-month-duration slow-release fertilizer in place of the 5-10-10 early in the spring. Use the equivalent of 2 pounds of 5-10-10, but apply the coated fertilizer only once.

Herbaceous perennials. For new perennials, follow the fertilizing schedule for flowering annuals. Stop applying fertilizer toward the end of July in cool regions, in mid-August in moderate areas, and later in warmer sections to allow plants to slow down soft vegetative growth and to harden off tissues in preparation for winter dormancy. If you use organic or slow-release fertilizers, time the application and use amounts that will be depleted before the end of the summer. Plants that are fertilized too late in the season can be damaged, even killed, by cold weather.

Roses. Prepare the soil well for new roses. Add large amounts of organic matter, adjust the pH to 6.5 to 6.8, and mix in 3 to 4 pounds of superphosphate or 3 to 6 pounds of bone meal per 100 square feet.

After planting, do not fertilize new plants until they have become established, usually in three to four weeks. Then begin a program of regular fertilizing, using soil tests as a guide.

For mature plants, make the first application of fertilizer just as growth starts in the spring, using 1/4 pound of a 5-10-10 or its equivalent per plant. After the first flush of flowers, repeat about once a month until midsummer to late summer, no later than mid-August in the North, into the fall in the South. Stop in time to give stems and buds time to harden off sufficiently for winter dormancy.

Shrubs and trees. For young shrubs and trees, follow the fertilizing program for roses. (Add the superphosphate or bone meal to unamended native soil when you plant lawn trees or shrubs.) As shrubs and trees approach full size, you can cut back on fertilizing. In general, trees in good health need little fertilizer, and then only nitrogen. A soil test will indicate what your trees need; if you haven't tested, apply only nitrogen at a rate of 3 to 4 pounds of actual nitrogen for each 1,000 square feet every two years. (Your lawn fertilizer may supply more than enough.) Flowering shrubs benefit from an annual application of a balanced fertilizer, and broad-leaved evergreens may need iron to stay green.

Ornamentals in containers. The small volume of soil in containers holds a limited supply of water and nutrients, and both must be replenished at frequent intervals. Watering daily or more often can leach nutrients from the soil.

Before you plant, mix lime and superphosphate into the soil, adding about 4 ounces of dolomitic limestone and 2 ounces of superphosphate per bushel of loose, well-drained soil mixture. Then each time you water, apply a fertilizer solution containing about 1/4 teaspoon of a 20-20-20 or its equivalent per gallon of water. (If you apply fertilizer only once a week, use roughly 1 teaspoon per gallon.) Instead of applying fertilizer solutions all summer, you can mix a slow-release fertilizer into the soil before you plant or sprinkle some on the surface of the soil in the pot, at rates specified on the package.

Recognizing nutrient problems

Well-prepared soil and a regular program of fertilizing go a long way toward keeping your plants healthy. But at times plants develop problems due to a deficiency or excess of nutrients. These problems include slow or abnormal growth, discolored foliage, or failure to flower or to fruit. You can diagnose nutrient problems by noting visual symptoms, by soil testing, and by leaf analysis. Keep in mind that nutrients are only one of many possible causes of plant problems. As you search for the answer, remember to consider temperature, moisture, insects, disease, and so on.

You should look at your plants regularly with a critical eye. In doing so, you'll gain a sense of how plants grow when they're healthy and when they're not. With experience, you'll be able to spot problems before they get out of hand. Be vigilant. By the time deficiency symptoms become very distinct, plant growth probably has been drastically reduced. Even with treatment, the plant may not be able to gain back all the growth and quality that it has lost.

Unfortunately, spotting a problem is much easier than identifying its cause. Certain symptoms can have any of several causes. Brittle, brown leaf edges or other leaf damage, for example, might be caused by extremely dry soil or by a deficiency or an excess of different nutrients. Many gardeners, regardless of experience, will probably need to turn to soil or leaf analysis or some expert assistance to pin down the exact cause of a problem. Even specialists often rely on tests to confirm a diagnosis. (Your county extension agent can usually recommend a reliable state or private lab for tests.)

Watering your plants

Water is essential for seeds to germinate and for plants to grow, flower, and produce fruit. How well seeds and plants do these things depends on when and how much water is available. Yet of all the gardening techniques, watering is the most elusive. To understand how to water your plants, it's useful first to learn about how plants use water and how water behaves in the soil.

How plants use water

Water plays a role in every plant process from germination to seed production. It is a critical raw material for photosynthesis and for the formation of chlorophyll. Dissolved in water, the sugars formed by photosynthesis and the minerals taken up through the roots are moved through the plant's circulation system.

Cells, the basic building blocks of plant life, are inflated by water. If cells lose water and deflate, the plant wilts and cell processes suffer. Desiccated plants may be dwarfed; have shortened stems, small leaves, and weak foliage and flower color; and produce small flowers and fruits, or none at all.

As important as water is to plants, only 1 to 5 percent of the water absorbed by the roots is actually used by the plant. The rest is transpired, passing through leaf pores back to the atmosphere as water vapor. Transpiration cools plants in much the same way that perspiration cools humans. Most transpiration occurs during daylight hours, responding to the heat of the sun or even the slightest drying breeze. Wind and high temperatures can quickly desiccate plants, especially young transplants or seedlings.

Plants have adapted to different environments by taking on various forms and structures. Because the water needs of different plants vary, you should grow plants of the same group together, rather than trying to mix them.

Plants classed as hydrophytes are adapted to growing in water; some float, some are rooted in the mud. Most traditional garden plants are mesophytes. They generally have broad, thin leaves of varying textures and color and prefer moist soil and high relative humidity. Xerophytes are increasingly grown by gardeners as water conservation becomes more important. Native to semiarid to arid climates where the relative humidity is often as low as 5 to 35 percent and the evaporation rate is high, xerophytes have evolved many features (such as small, hairy, or waxy leaves or extensive root systems) that allow them to survive on limited amounts of water.

Water and soil

Most plants in the garden extract their moisture from the soil. The ease or difficulty with which they do so depends on the soil's texture and structure. As we discussed in the chapters on soil, most soils are mixtures of sand, silt, and clay, which clump together to form aggregates. Air and water reside and move in the spaces between the particles and between aggregates. Water moves rapidly and drains freely through the large pore spaces of sandy soils; its movement is more restricted in the smaller pore spaces of clay soils.

Air and water can displace each other in the pore spaces. If the soil is overwatered and kept too wet, water displaces too much air, and the plant roots, starved of oxygen, "drown." Waterlogged soil also supports certain disease organisms that survive without oxygen, which can affect the health and vigor of the plant.

When and how much to water?

Plant roots absorb water most readily when the surrounding soil is moist but drains freely. One approach to watering is to strive to keep the soil in this optimum condition, continually replacing the water that the plants absorb and that evaporates from the soil. Another approach is to water thoroughly and deeply, then allow the soil to dry out until the plants begin to show signs of mild water stress (some wilting, dull, or drooping foliage), and then water deeply again. The first approach undoubtedly produces healthy plants, but it may require a lot of water and, unless you spend hours each day in the garden, an expensive automatic delivery system. The second system is a little harder on the plants, but it may use less water and requires less vigilance.

Regardless of which watering method you choose, it's helpful to learn how to gauge the amount of water in your soil. You can conduct a "feel test" by taking a handful of soil and squeezing it firmly. In general, when good garden loam is optimally moist, it will form a ball, and if you roll the ball between your fingers, a little damp soil will stick to your fingers and leave an outline of the ball. Different soils, however, have different "feels," and it may take a while before you're able to recognize the moisture content of your soil by feel.

When you water, it's important to moisten the root zone to its full depth. This encourages deep rooting, and the deeper the roots, the longer plants can go between irrigations. Some books give rooting depths for specific plants—shallow, deep, taprooted, for example. You can also learn a lot by taking note of the roots when you divide or transplant. In general, with the exception of shallow-rooted plants, most plants grow roots 6 to 18 inches deep.

To estimate how much water is needed to reach roots at different depths, you can use the following rule of thumb: On the average, 1 inch of water will penetrate about 12 inches deep in a sandy soil, 7 inches in a loam soil, and 4 to 5 inches in a clay soil. Use the rule to get you started, then check to see how water actually behaves in your soil. About 24 hours after watering, dig into the soil with a trowel or a shovel to see how far the water has penetrated. To keep from wasting water through runoff, water less-absorbent soils with small amounts of water applied over longer periods of time.

Different soil types also lose moisture at differing rates. Coarse, porous soils dry out rapidly. Plants growing in them can appear healthy, then suddenly wilt overnight. And the time between wilt and permanent damage can be very short, especially in very hot weather. Clay soils, on the other hand, dry out more slowly, and plants grown in them will have a gradual curve of drought stress. Some soil types have peculiarities that affect watering. Clay, for example, shrinks and cracks when dry and expands when wet. Water runs through the cracks without wetting the plants. If your soil is cracked, try watering twice, first to seal the cracks and again to provide moisture for the plants. Learn about your soil's idiosyncrasies by paying attention to how it behaves in different conditions.

Applying water

Years ago, most gardeners simply hauled water to their plants in a sprinkling can or a bucket. Hand watering is still one of the most therapeutic and valuable gardening activities. As you stand with the hose or watering can in hand, you can really observe the individual plants. Unfortunately, hand watering can be very time consuming, prohibitively so if you're deep watering. It's also haphazard—it's difficult to gauge the amount of water you've applied, and the amounts vary from one watering to the next.

Despite the pleasures of hand watering, most gardeners soon find themselves employing one or more of the many mechanical watering devices available today. These can be as simple as a portable sprin-kler or soaker hose connected to a hose bibb (an outside faucet)—you put it where it's needed, turn it on, and go do something else. Or they can involve a complex system of in-ground pipes that feed permanently located sprinklers, soaker hoses, drip tapes, or subsurface irrigation lines. Fitted with a programmable timer and automatic valves, such a system can keep your plants happy for days or weeks while you're away.

Given the variety of watering devices and systems available, it can be difficult to choose which best suits you. Ask yourself some basic questions: During how much of the growing season will you have a need for supplemental water? How large is your garden or landscape? What kinds of plants will you be growing? What is your source of water? How much money can you afford to spend?

Simpler alternatives are easy enough to evaluate by trial and error. If one doesn't work out, you haven't lost a lot of money or time. But the more complex systems call for thought and planning. If you're planning a new landscape or garden, don't do so without considering irrigation. Difficult landscape designs incorporating tapering and odd-shaped beds, slopes, or combinations of plants that require different amounts of water can make water-system plans more complicated. Design the system for the maximum demand, so you don't come up dry at a critical moment. If you're short on experience or confidence, consult a landscape architect or contractor. A modest amount of money spent on professional help at the beginning may save you a lot of money later on.

Flood irrigation

Used for centuries in agriculture, this simple irrigation technique can work well in some ornamental gardens. If the site is fairly level and a large enough volume of water is available, you can flood the entire garden with enough water to wet the root zone.

On a smaller scale, many people employ another type of flooding, called basin irrigation, for watering large and deeply rooted trees and shrubs. Around each plant, build a soil dike up to 6 inches high, extending a short distance beyond the spread of the plant's branches. Slowly fill the basin with water, which will then percolate through the soil profile to the root zone.

Basin irrigation can also be used for small beds (about 4 feet by 5 feet) of annuals or perennials. Surround each bed with a dike (which can also serve as a walkway) and inside make the surface of the bed slightly below ground level. Good drainage is critical, so amend the soil in the bed to a depth of 18 to 24 inches if necessary. Basin irrigation is useful in arid climates, where it offers protection from drying winds that increase evaporation rates. In areas of abundant rainfall, however, basin irrigation can lead to overwatering.

Sprinklers

These familiar devices emit fine sheets, fans, or pulsating streams of water. They vary greatly in size and coverage, from tiny microsprinklers that emit a cone of spray several feet in diameter to large rotary

In-ground irrigation systems

If you're watering your garden by hand, or hauling portable sprinklers or drip hoses from one bed to another, you may soon find that watering has become your main gardening activity. If your garden is large and your climate dry, you may also discover that you can't keep up and you begin to lose some of your favorite plants. An in-ground irrigation system may be what you need to save your plants, save water, and save time.

In an in-ground system, buried pipe replaces aboveground hoses. The pipe connects the water supply to one or more valves that control the flow of water through additional buried pipes to sprinklers, drip or subsurface irrigation lines, or hose bibbs. A simple system can be run from a single, existing hose bibb. Larger systems connect the water main or well directly to a number of valves, each valve controlling one or more lines that serve a portion of the landscape. The valves can be distributed individually throughout the garden, or they can be ganged together in one or more manifolds. You can open and close the valves manually, or install automatic controls and a timer.

An irrigation system must deliver water to the sprinklers or irrigation lines at an adequate flow and pressure. Pipe, pipe fittings, valves, and other components of the system all reduce water pressure and flow. The more extensive the system, the greater these reductions can be. The smaller the pipe, the larger the loss of pressure, so, in general, use the largest-diameter pipe and fittings you can work with and afford. Charts to help you determine the size of pipe, fittings, and valves best for your system (based on simple calculations you make about water flow and pressure) are available from suppliers and manufacturers of irrigation equipment.

All in-ground systems, whether simple or elaborate, require pipe and a range of pipe fittings and valves. Most city and town codes call for some form of backflow prevention, to keep water in the irrigation lines from being sucked back into the municipal water system. Drip lines will usually need a filter and a pressure regulator.

You should have little trouble installing a simple system guided by the brochures available from suppliers and manufacturers of irrigation equipment. But even if you're a confident do-it-yourselfer, it's prudent to consult with a knowledgeable landscape architect or contractor before installing an extensive irrigation system.

sprinklers that can cover an area 200 feet in diameter. Depending on size and coverage, sprinklers can deliver between 1/4 inch and 2 inches of water per hour. Small fixed-head sprinklers are good for low-growing, closely spaced plants. Those attached permanently to in-ground systems are usually mounted on lengths of pipe above interfering foliage to provide best coverage. Rotary sprinklers are best for lawns and large areas of ground cover, especially where there is foot traffic.

Sprinklers offer fairly uniform coverage and allow you to control how much water is applied. But one disadvantage to sprinklers is that only 65 to 75 percent of the water they emit ends up in the soil, where you want it; the rest evaporates, is intercepted by foliage, or is blown away by the wind. And they're not selective—everything in their path gets watered, whether it needs it or not.

To find out how long it takes a sprinkler to apply an inch of water in a specific area, distribute flat-bottomed cans at a regular spacing over the area covered by the sprinkler. Turn on the water and record the time it takes for 1 inch to accumulate in each can. Some cans will fill faster than others. You can average the time between the first to fill and last to fill if you want to be precise.

Drip irrigation
Drip systems apply water slowly and evenly close to the soil. Water flows through flexible plastic tubing and drips out emitters, tiny water meters rated by gallons of water delivered per hour. Drip tape is tubing with regularly spaced emitters installed at the factory. Drip tubing with plug-in emitters allows you to tailor the spacing to suit different situations.

Because drip systems apply water only where the plant needs it and not on walks, streets, or weeds, they can save a lot of water. They wet the ground, not the foliage, so they can reduce the incidence of foliar diseases. They're unlikely to cause erosion on even steep slopes. If you wish to keep the soil at its optimum moisture level, a drip system or a subsurface system (discussed next) is the most effective way to do so. There are disadvantages to drip. Although a simple drip system can be run off a hose bibb, an extensive system can be expensive. Beyond a certain length, drip tubing can lose pressure and flow. And emitters can clog.

All drip systems, however simple or complex, require water pressure of 8 to 15 pounds per square inch (psi) rather than the 40 to 60 psi most community water systems provide. Some drip emitters are designed to step the pressure down themselves. For those that aren't, you'll need a pressure regulator. Every system should have a filter to help keep debris from clogging the system. Where you place emitters depends on your soil and the root structures of your plants. Emitters are usually spaced wider for clay soils than for sandy soils and closer for shallow-rooted plants than for deep-rooted ones.

Subsurface irrigation
These are essentially drip-irrigation systems buried 4 to 6 inches underground. Water seeps through porous plastic tubing or special emitters fitted in plastic tubing. Like drip systems, they supply water directly to the root zone, with no waste from overspray or evaporation. You also don't need to worry about trimming around sprinkler heads.

Because subsurface systems are invisible and silent, however, you don't know if they're working properly until your plants show signs of stress. The initial cost is up to 20 percent higher than for standard aboveground systems. Also, subsurface systems aren't suitable on rocky or extremely porous soils. (Effective positioning in other soils depends on a knowledge of the soil type and profile.) And once installed, they're difficult to modify.

Pruning

Pruning is one of the most important, most commonly practiced, and yet most universally misunderstood gardening techniques. When most people think of pruning, they think of removing a limb from a tree or a branch from a shrub. But pruning is also the plucking of spent flowers to conserve plant energy or to induce reblooming, or the pinching of selected buds or growing tips to direct new growth in a specified pattern. In fact, the term *pruning* is applied to the intentional removal of any plant part, except perhaps harvesting cut flowers or ripe fruit and vegetables.

If you've chosen your plants wisely, selecting those that thrive in the conditions and space constraints of your site, you won't need to do a lot of pruning. You'll trim away dead, diseased, or weak portions of plants or repair damage from ice, wind, or exuberant children. Occasionally you'll thin dense stems or branches to allow more light or air to reach a plant's interior.

Despite your best attempts to pick appropriate plants, you'll probably have to do some pruning to reduce the size of overgrown plants. And some plants may need to be rejuvenated from time to time, cut back at or near the ground to promote vigorous new growth.

You may choose to be more active, even creative, with your pruning. You may decide to remove selected branches or stems to make the most of a plant's "natural" form, or prune to encourage bushy or compact growth or to direct a branch into a certain area. You may tackle the task of training and shearing a formal hedge. Or, if you really get hooked, you'll explore the specialized techniques of espalier, topiary, or bonsai, and shape plants to your own designs, rather than nature's.

In subsequent chapters we'll discuss the pruning techniques gardeners typically use for herbaceous plants, shrubs, vines, and trees. First, however, we'll introduce a little basic plant physiology. Almost every pruning cut you make will induce or suppress growth, for better or worse, in the plant you are treating. Understanding what causes this growth will make pruning easier, more efficient, and more effective.

How plants respond to pruning
A great many factors affect a plant's growth—sunlight, nutrients, water, temperature, pathogens, plant hormones, and genes. Of principal interest for understanding pruning is the way in which hormones called auxins control growth. Produced continuously in the growing tips of shoots, auxins promote growth at the tip while inhibiting the growth of buds along the sides of the shoot (lateral buds).

This process of growth regulation by a shoot tip is called apical dominance. If you cut off a growing tip (thereby cutting off its production of auxins), some of the previously dormant lateral buds behind it will develop into side shoots, making a shorter and bushier plant. Thus you can change the entire shape of a plant with a simple pruning cut.

Whether you're pinching the leading shoots of snapdragon seedlings, shearing a privet hedge, or heading back canes of a rosebush, you're seeking to direct growth by manipulating apical dominance. Remember that cutting the growing point of a stem will stimulate growth even if that isn't your intention. When you cut back a shrub to reduce its size, you may inadvertently produce a thicket of unwanted growth. Apical dominance is much stronger in some plants than in others. Some, such as bushes that branch a lot naturally, barely show it. Others, such as chrysanthemums, exhibit strong

Pruning and apical dominance

Left unpruned, the tip of a shoot, stem, or branch will grow longer than the buds behind it. Removing the tip induces more growth in the shoot's lateral buds.

Basic pruning tools

Bypass shears

Blade

Hook

Anvil shears

Blade

Anvil

Loppers (may be bypass or anvil)

apical dominance, and pruning makes a big difference in their growth and form.

However beneficial our intentions, a pruning cut is still a wound, a potential site for fungal spores, insects, or a variety of disease vectors. Plants, like animals, have developed mechanisms to protect themselves from disease and decay when wounded. Woody plants, for example, cover the cut with a layer of new cells to seal it from infection. In general, plants in good health and well supplied with nutrients and water suffer few problems from pruning that is undertaken with good judgment and care.

Pruning tools

Pruning can be done with fingernails, or a chain saw, or anything in between. Most gardeners rely primarily on pruning shears (also called pruning clippers or secateurs). Loppers and a brush saw or pruning saw come in handy for branches that are too big for pruning shears. Maintaining hedges or other sheared shrubs and trees requires hedge clippers.

Pruning shears. Pruning shears come in two basic designs, bypass and anvil. Bypass shears cut like scissors—a sharp convex cutting blade slides past a blunt concave hooked blade that supports the stem being cut. Anvil shears cut like a knife on a cutting board—a straight blade cuts against a soft metal surface, the anvil, which also supports the stem. Bypass shears tend to damage a stem less than anvil shears; they're also better able to reach into tight spots. Anvil shears, however, are the more powerful of the two tools.

Hand shears come in a huge range of models and prices, including designs for large and small hands and left-handers. If

you have weak hands, consider shears with ratchet mechanisms. Inexpensive shears are very serviceable for weekend gardeners if the blades are kept sharp and properly adjusted. Examine the blades closely when purchasing shears. As you slowly close bypass shears, make sure that the cutting blade is in constant contact with the hook as it slides past. Likewise, the blade and anvil should be in contact along their full length when closed. If you regularly work with gloves on, remember to wear them when you try out new hand shears.

Loppers. These are essentially heavy-duty bypass or anvil shears attached to long handles. Requiring two hands to use, they provide considerable leverage and cutting power—some can handle branches up to 2 inches in diameter. Gardeners with small or weak hands or stiff joints may find loppers easier to use than shears; there are ratchet models, too. Loppers can be expensive, and there is nothing they do that can't be done with either hand shears or a saw. But if you maintain a lot of trees and shrubs, a good pair of loppers will save you time and work.

Pruning herbaceous plants

Although we may not think of it as such, much of the pruning gardeners do involves nonwoody annuals and perennials. With the aim of producing more flowers or fruit, we pinch, thin, and deadhead these plants. During the course of the growing season, we also prune them to keep them tidy, cutting back dead, dormant, damaged, or merely unsightly stems and foliage.

Pinching and heading back

By pinching or snipping off growing tips, you can induce branching and make plants

more compact. More branches also means more flowers or foliage. Pinching or cutting stems along their length, called heading back, has the same effect. It also helps reduce the size of—and therefore the need to stake—tall, floppy plants. You can head back plants that develop leafy stems with terminal flower clusters, such as heliopsis and asters.

To encourage bushiness in flowering plants, pinch them back before they set flower buds. Pinch the stems or shoots just above a leaf or a pair of leaves. You can pinch off the central stems of annual or perennial seedlings with your fingers when you transplant the seedlings into the garden. For most plants, pinching back once is enough, although chrysanthemums can be pinched as frequently as once a week.

With foliage plants, such as coleus and basil, the purpose of pinching is to prevent blooming and encourage the growth of shoots and leaves. On these plants, pinch off new terminal flower buds whenever they form.

Annuals and perennials can be headed back by one third when they reach half their mature height. For example, when a plant that is ordinarily 4 feet tall at maturity reaches 2 feet, cut it back to about 16 inches high. Cut just above a healthy leaf or pair of leaves. You may want to thin out some stems of plants with dense habits, to give the remaining, headed-back stems room to fill out.

If your objective is to produce a few prizewinning specimen flowers, you can concentrate your plant's energy wonderfully by pinching off secondary flower buds and by removing surplus shoots. Many gardeners do so with phlox (by thinning shoots) and peonies (by disbudding). Unfortunately, this technique may result in a few very large flowers on an unattractive plant. Aficionados often maintain their special cut-flower plantations behind the garage or in the vegetable garden.

Deadheading

Spent flowers that remain on a plant will begin to form seeds, a process that claims energy that the plant could otherwise use to produce more flowers, foliage, or roots. By removing spent flowers (a practice called deadheading), you can get more flowers or more robust plants.

Most annuals will produce additional flowers if deadheaded; just cut the flowering stem back to a healthy leaf. Deadheading will also increase flowering in some perennials. Plants that bloom on leaf-bearing stems, such as phlox, are good candidates. Plants with leafless flower stalks rising above clumps of basal leaves, such as hostas and daylilies, are less likely to rebloom, but deadheading will direct their energy to forming more roots and healthy foliage, as well as tidy up appearances. When a stalk has finished blooming, cut it off at the base. (Some daylilies, such as 'Stella d'Oro', will often send up a second growth of flowering stalks.) Don't deadhead baptisia, lunaria, blackberry lily, or any other plant that has decorative seed heads or pods later in the season.

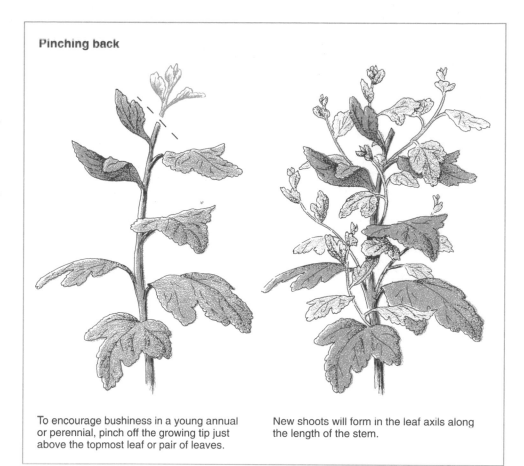

Pinching back

To encourage bushiness in a young annual or perennial, pinch off the growing tip just above the topmost leaf or pair of leaves.

New shoots will form in the leaf axils along the length of the stem.

Heading back

To limit the size of tall, floppy perennials, head them back by one third when they reach half their usual mature size. Cut stems just above a leaf or a pair of leaves.

That season's mature growth will be shorter and bushier, less likely to require staking.

Pruning shrubs and woody vines

When faced with pruning a shrub or a vine, many gardeners, particularly beginners, grow nervous. Unlike herbaceous annuals and perennials, which live only one year or die back to the ground in winter, these woody plants are permanent presences, visible throughout the year. If you mess up pruning a perennial, you can wait a year and try again on a completely new set of stems and shoots. But if you mess up a woody plant, you may have to live with your mistake for a long time. Or, worse, you may entirely lose an expensive or important element in your landscape.

Take heart. When carefully chosen to match the conditions and size of their site, many shrubs will thrive for years with no more than timely thinning of worn-out, dead, or overcrowded stems. (Plants that require constant pruning to reduce their size are in the wrong place.) With some background knowledge and the courage to make that first cut, even beginning gardeners can learn to enhance the shape of a shrub, maintain many common shrubs and vines, or train a hedge.

The basic pruning procedures outlined below will get you started. Remember, however, that real plants are tremendously varied, even within a species or a cultivar. Your plant may well have much longer stems or four times as many of them as specified in a reference book's example or shown in its schematic drawing. So how do you figure out which stem to cut and where?

You can reason your way to a solution. Think about the purpose of your pruning—to thin out dense, tangled stems, for example—and recall the ways in which pruning affects a plant's growth. Put the two together, take a deep breath, and begin to cut. Even better, before you prune, study well-maintained examples of the plant in your neighborhood or at a local arboretum. Ask experienced pruners for advice. Observe how your plants grow before and after pruning.

If you're really baffled, or worried about damaging a plant, ask a knowledgeable friend or hire a reputable arborist to prune it for you. Watch him or her carefully and ask questions. A short "apprenticeship" like this can be worth thousands of words and dozens of pictures in books.

When to prune

Dead, damaged or diseased wood should be removed as soon as possible in order to prevent infection or the spread of disease. The best time to prune healthy wood on flowering shrubs depends mainly on whether they bloom on new wood—that is, the current season's growth—or on old wood, formed the previous year.

In general, spring-flowering plants, such as azalea, lilac, viburnum, flowering quince, and forsythia, bloom on old wood. Prune them after they've flowered, so they can form new growth for next year's display. Plants that bloom later, such as potentilla, oakleaf hydrangea, clethra, caryopteris, and hypericum, usually do so on new wood. Prune them in fall, winter, or early spring. Some plants bloom twice or throughout the growing season; prune them when they are dormant. There are some exceptions to these rules, so it's best to ask about the correct pruning time when you buy a shrub.

If bloom is not a consideration, other factors influence when you prune. The branch structure of all deciduous shrubs is easiest to see before the plant is in full leaf, making winter or early spring a good time to prune. If you're pruning to encourage growth, doing so early in the growing season (or before) will give the new growth a full season to develop. If you prune in the fall, before the onset of dormancy, remember that tender new growth induced by pruning may be damaged by winter cold, wind, or snow.

Pinching, heading back, and deadheading

Pinching or cutting off growing tips induces branching and compact growth in shrubs just as it does in herbaceous plants. Some shrubs, such as rhododendrons and azaleas, are pinched to increase the number of buds the plant sets.

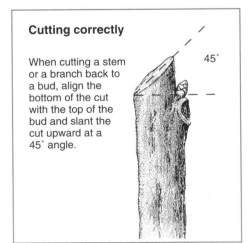

Cutting correctly

When cutting a stem or a branch back to a bud, align the bottom of the cut with the top of the bud and slant the cut upward at a 45° angle.

45°

Woody plants are headed back (the process of cutting branches or stems somewhere along their length) for a variety of reasons: to remove dead, damaged, or diseased wood; to control size or to direct growth; to eliminate crossed or crowded branches; to admit more light; to promote flowering; and to reduce structural stress from weight or wind. Head back to a bud facing in a direction you wish growth to develop (usually out from the center of the shrub).

New growth of conifers, like that of deciduous plants, can be pinched or headed back to induce more branching. Removing half or all of the tender new growth "candles" of spruces, firs, and most pines will force buds along the length or at the base of the candles into growth. (New growth is often a lighter green than the old.) Likewise, new growth of junipers, arborvitae, hemlocks, and certain other evergreens can be pinched, sheared, or headed back.

But be careful when heading back conifers into old wood. Some species will initiate new growth from old wood readily, others won't. If you head back into the old wood of spruces and firs, for example, make sure that you cut back to a branching, where latent buds can sprout, rather than to bare wood. The old wood of yews contains no latent buds, but it will form adventitious buds (new buds where none existed before). Junipers, arborvitae, hemlocks, and most pines, however, won't sprout at all from old wood, so don't cut beyond the green zone of live foliage.

As with herbaceous plants, deadheading can improve the appearance of flowering shrubs and make available to roots and shoots energy that would otherwise be spent setting seed or fruit. (Thus it improves the next year's bloom on plants such as lilacs and mountain laurels.) Remove only the spent flowers, taking care not to cut any buds at the base. For most shrubs, deadheading will not stimulate reblooming, and it isn't practical unless, like rhododendrons and azaleas, the shrub bears flowers in large clusters.

Thinning

Thinning removes entire stems or branches and is done for the same reasons as heading back. Canes or stems that arise from a crown can be cut back to the ground. Thin treelike woody shrubs by removing the unwanted branches back to a crotch. Don't leave a stub, which invites disease—if you can hang your hat on it, it's too long.

Thinning

Removing entire stems and branches can improve the looks and health of a shrub.

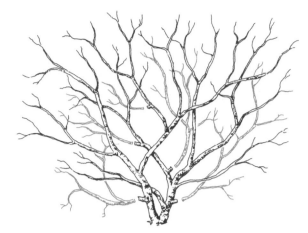

Where numerous stems sprout from a crown, you can cut stems back to the ground.

You can also thin by cutting branches back to a crotch. This is useful for shrubs with just a few main stems or trunks.

Pruning or natural causes can induce unwanted sprouts from latent or adventitious buds. Prune off these shoots, called water sprouts or feather growths, at their point of origin. A number of shrubs, such as lilacs, also produce suckers, vigorous vertical shoots generated from the base of a trunk or buds on roots. Removing these helps keep your garden tidy and directs a plant's energy into the remaining growth. Suckers are less liable to grow back if you pull them rather than cut them, preferably during their first growing season.

Rejuvenation

This is radical pruning, intended to promote new growth and to restore vigor. Paring away all but a base or skeleton forces dormant buds into growth or new buds to form and sprout where none previously existed. A healthy shrub with adequate energy reserves will respond with vigorous growth that can, over time, be pruned and trained into a shapely specimen.

Some gardeners rejuvenate certain shrubs every year, cutting back into old wood, leaving a few buds in new wood, or cutting all stems down to the ground, depending on the nature of the specific plant. Caryopteris, ceanothus, hardy fuchsias, plumbago, and roses are often pruned this way. When you buy a shrub, ask whether it needs yearly rejuvenation. Many gardeners successfully treat plants such as these with subtler combinations of thinning and heading back. Benign neglect has its advocates, too.

Many shrubs that are hardy in the South die back to the ground each winter in the North. These "die-back" shrubs, including caryopteris, vitex, buddleia, perovskia, plumbago, and hardy hibiscus, should be trimmed to the ground, like herbaceous perennials.

Old, neglected, or overgrown shrubs can often be renewed by a single radical

Rejuvenating shrubs

Some shrubs look their best when cut back hard each year. Some, such as the spirea shown here, can be cut within a few inches of the ground.

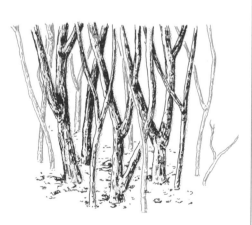

Severe pruning can give old or overgrown shrubs a new life. Some plants, such as the lilac shown here, do best when some old wood is retained. The stems shown in green are cut at ground level; the retained stems (black) include old growth cut between 2 and 6 ft. high, and a few suckers kept to form new stems.

pruning. Not all shrubs are good candidates. If you aren't sure about a plant, it's best to ask at a nursery. You can also look among the older stems for suckers. A cloud of suckers surrounding the old diseased and dead stems of a neglected shrub—a lilac, for example—indicates an excellent candidate for rejuvenation.

Rejuvenate old or overgrown plants in late winter or early spring. When overgrown, some shrubs, such as pussy willow and mahonia, can be cut to within a few inches of the ground. Some aged or crowded shrubs may not require or respond well to such drastic treatment, and can be cut to 2 feet or more above the ground. Cotoneaster, privet, and lilac can be rejuvenated in this way. Suckering plants can be rejuvenated by removing the old growth and encouraging selected suckers.

If radical pruning of the entire plant will be too much of a shock (for the plant or for you), you can rejuvenate it in stages, removing a portion of the oldest stems each year for two or three years. Remember to burn or send pruned wood to the landfill to control disease and insect infestation. Once a rejuvenated shrub has begun to thrive again, thin it out annually to keep it growing and looking its best.

Shearing

Formal hedges, some specimen shrubs (often those in foundation plantings), and topiary are pruned and trained to a specific outline or shape, then maintained by shearing. When you shear, you make no attempt to cut each shoot or branch near a bud, as you do for other forms of pruning. Instead, you cut wherever necessary to create the desired flat or contoured surface. Properly tended, a sheared plant can remain vigorous through periods of controlled, almost unnoticeable growth.

Shearing is a relatively drastic form of pruning and can prove disastrous if performed on the wrong plants. Some plants, such as privet and boxwood, can recover from even the most radical shearing and form a respectable hedge. Other, more open shrubs, such as forsythia, may survive the ordeal but will look terrible. They're best used in a natural hedge or shrub border. If you're planning a formal hedge, make sure to select a species that not only tolerates shearing but that looks good when sheared.

Pruning of a formal hedge begins a few weeks after planting when you head back the new plants by one third to one half to encourage dense, bushy growth. (Don't head back most conifers.) You can do the same to rejuvenate existing overgrown hedge plants.

In subsequent years, beginning in spring and continuing to midsummer, shear the new growth to the desired shape. Make sure that the base is broader than the top, to allow light to reach the bottom leaves. Initially, the hedge will look like a small version of what you desire. Increase its size slightly each year for several years, until a dense peripheral branch structure develops.

Mature formal hedges many need to be pruned two or three times a year to look their best. To minimize sunscald on leaves and twigs, avoid heavy shearing during extremely hot, sunny periods. In cold climates, stop shearing early enough to give subsequent new growth time to harden off before winter.

Pruning vines

Many vines are pruned primarily to keep them from taking over. Cut these rampant growers whenever and wherever they extend beyond their intended bounds. Vines, like other plants, are pruned to remove dead stems, to regulate flowering, and to keep the flowers where you'll see them—most vines flower on new wood, and you won't want that 60 feet up in the air.

Some vines grown for their attractive flowers, such as wisteria, can be pinched or headed back to encourage more flowers. During the winter, you can cut wisteria shoots back to within two or three buds from their base. Clematis doesn't need pruning to increase flowers, but you may want to thin out the shoots to make the plant look better.

Wisteria, Boston ivy, or grape vines can be very picturesque trained on an arbor or a large tree. Over the years, the effect is enhanced by development of a massive stem. Begin training and anchoring the woody shoots of these plants when the plants are young, pruning them as necessary to fit the supporting structure.

Pruning roses

Roses are a specialty, and beginners will save themselves a lot of confusion and frustration by consulting an experienced rose grower about pruning. A few general guidelines, however, may be helpful.

Other than removing dead or damaged canes, don't prune newly planted bushes. If you want to increase the number of canes and their vigor, rub off the first set of buds that appear.

When you begin to prune, use bypass rather than anvil clippers, which can crush the cane. Roses can be thinned and headed back in much the same way and for the same reasons as other shrubs. In the spring, cut away winter-killed portions of canes, and thin to eliminate canes that cross or form a tangle in the center of the bush. Cut to an outward-facing bud eye, to promote growth away from the plant's center. (When a leaf drops off or is removed from a cane, it leaves a crescent-shaped scar. The area above the scar will produce a swelling, from which a new cane will form; such a swelling is known as a "bud eye.")

When you cut a cane, examine the color of the center, or pith. A healthy pith is white; if the pith is brown, keep cutting down the cane until you reach a white center, then cut above the nearest outward-facing bud eye. (After a particularly severe winter, you can accept pith that is slightly colored.)

Pruning trees

In many ways, pruning trees is not much different from pruning shrubs. The stems, branches, and buds of both respond to pruning in exactly the same ways; therefore they share many pruning techniques. Trees, like shrubs, can be maintained largely by prompt removal of dead, damaged, or diseased wood. If you choose to go further and enhance or alter what nature produces, you'll find that most of the techniques used to remove, induce, or direct the growth of shrubs are employed for trees, too.

For the gardener pruning his or her own plants, there is one very important difference between trees and shrubs—size. You can do everything you need to do to most shrubs while standing firmly on the ground. Cuts seldom require more than pruning clippers, loppers, or a small pruning saw. And the severed stems and branches are almost never heavy enough to knock you off balance when they fall or to strain your back when you drag them away.

Pruning all but young or small trees can be a dangerous business. It's easy to see that training and experience are essential when the task is to remove a 300-pound, 10-inch-diameter branch growing 30 feet off the ground. But simpler jobs can be dangerous, too. It's surprisingly easy to tumble off the top of a stepladder, jarred by the sudden release of the 3-inch-thick branch you were sawing off. Broken bones are bad enough; imagine the outcome if you were perched on a ladder wielding a chain saw.

So, for safety reasons alone, we strongly recommend that you hire a professional arborist to do any tree pruning you can't accomplish while standing on the ground (or perhaps a low stool) using pruners or a small handsaw.

Given this restriction, there is still a fair amount of pruning you can do on smallish, mature trees. And with just a few simple techniques, you can help give young trees a good start.

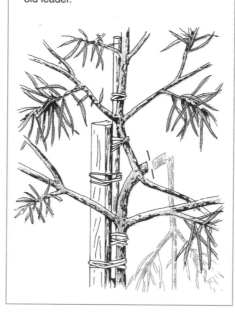
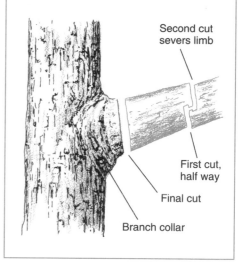
Training young trees

Governed by genetic and environmental forces, trees develop characteristic shapes. Some trees are purchased because of their distinctive branching pattern and silhouette. For others, desirable height, spread, or fall color may outweigh undistinguished or even problematic branching patterns.

If attended to early enough, it is possible to alter potentially troublesome or unattractive growth patterns. It's relatively easy, for example, to widen a narrow crotch or to remove a crossing branch on a young tree. You can also prune young trees for aesthetic reasons; by selective thinning, pinching, and heading back, for instance, you can create an open tree that will display attractive bark, flowers, or fruit to best advantage.

Thoughtful pinching and heading back can accomplish much. Cut just above buds and young shoots that are well spaced and oriented in the pattern that you want the tree to follow. Keep your eye out for the development of branches that, if left to mature, will alter the shape that you're trying to encourage.

Branches that join the trunk at a narrow angle frequently cause problems as the tree ages—bark becomes trapped in the crotch, which weakens and sometimes splits as a result or provides an entry point for disease or insects. With a simple brace, you can widen a narrow crotch on a young tree. Cut a light stick or wooden lath to size, notch each end, and insert the brace between the branch and the trunk or the collar of a higher branch. (A branch collar is a swelling where branch and trunk join.) Be careful not to force a branch too far all

at once and split the crotch. Leave the brace in place only during the growing season to minimize abrasions to the bark. You can also widen the angle of a crotch or otherwise direct a branch's growth by attaching ties to the stakes supporting young trees.

Many of our most prized trees—ash, oak, pine, and spruce—have a characteristic columnar or pyramidal shape. The backbone of this shape is usually a single, strong trunk. The leading shoot of young trees sometimes forks, creating two competing leaders. If these both mature, the tree won't have its distinctive shape. For some trees, such as conifers, trim the second leader off at its base. On other trees you may wish to cut the second leader back to a bud about halfway down its length and force it to send out side shoots.

Occasionally, the weather, animals, or humans damage or destroy a young tree's leader. Fortunately, you can establish another leader simply by tying a healthy branch from below the point of damage to a vertical splint made of wood or bamboo. Attach the splint to the trunk and new leader with twine. (If the trunk alone won't support it easily, tie the splint to a stout stake driven into the ground.) Trim off the old leader just above the new one. Leave the splint in place until the new leader can support itself, which may take a year or two.

Pruning mature trees

If you've purchased a well-formed young tree and pruned it judiciously, there's little pruning you'll need to do when it's mature. (This is particularly true of conifers.) Rejuvenation of neglected mature trees, treat-

ment of disease, and any other pruning required above a height you can comfortably reach from the ground are best left to professionals. Still, there are some things you can do for mature trees with easily reached branches.

From time to time, you may need to trim off water sprouts, straight, thin shoots arising on mature branches. Snip them off at their base with pruning clippers or loppers. Older limbs sometimes die, get damaged or contract diseases, or begin to interfere with a view or some activity in the garden. Because their weight may tear them loose from the tree before you've completed the cut, remove these larger branches in two stages as shown above. Take some care to position the final cut so that you don't injure the branch collar. (See "Healing wounds" below.)

Sometimes a branch grows too long, giving the tree an unbalanced look. Figure out how much of the limb to remove to restore the tree's visual equilibrium, then make the cut just above the nearest side shoot that grows in a direction you prefer. If the portion you're removing is large or heavy, you may want to cut it back in several stages. (Remember that most pines and some other conifers won't sprout new growth from old wood.)

Shearing individual conifers to geometric shapes isn't quite as popular as it once was, due in part to a desire to minimize maintenance and in part to an increased interest in using plants in their natural forms. If you decide to shear a conifer, start pruning and shearing when the tree is young to build up a dense branching structure, as described for a hedge in the previous chapter. When you buy the tree, ask for information about specific pruning techniques and timing. Remember that once you begin to shear a conifer, you will have to continue the treatment every season, or else contend with a corona of loose growth around a dense core, which is not a pretty sight.

When to prune trees

Many experts say that the correct time to prune a tree is whenever you have the saw in your hand. Timing does, however, pose some problems. Maples, elms, walnuts, birches, and some other trees will "bleed" if cut when the sap is rising in late winter and early spring, inviting unsightly bacterial infections and sooty molds. Oaks are more liable to become infected with the fatal oak wilt disease if pruned in May or June. Pruning wounds made in late summer or fall won't close until the following year, exposing the tree to winter damage. Trees become increasingly brittle and more easily damaged if they are pruned during extremely cold weather. Succulent new growth resulting from heavy late-summer pruning may not harden sufficiently before cold weather sets in.

With all these possible pitfalls, it almost seems as if there is no good time to prune. In general, however, most trees respond well to late-winter pruning. On species that bleed readily, you might defer heavy pruning until midsummer, when new growth is hardened, or even until early winter, after the leaves have fallen. You should remove dead or diseased branches as soon as you notice them; prune water sprouts and suckers at any time.

Healing wounds

Untended trees naturally shed their lower limbs as they grow. The limbs detach at the swellings, or branch collars, at their bases, then a callus forms over the wound. The damaged wood does not regenerate; the tree simply concentrates preservatives around the wound to isolate it. Even if the wound becomes infected before it closes, a healthy tree's chemical defenses will usually contain the infection. Cutting off a branch at the outer edge of its collar allows the tree to use its inherent closure and decay-resistance mechanisms most effectively.

The effectiveness of tree-wound dressings has been debated for decades. Many of the substances used to coat tree wounds do more harm than good, and they are seldom necessary. Some of the newer dressings suppress the growth of water sprouts and suckers and may be helpful where such problems are likely. In general, however, it's best to leave the tree to its own devices.

Controlling pests and diseases

Gardeners have been battling plant pests and diseases since they first scratched up the soil to plant a seed. For centuries these wars were largely hand-to-hand combat. What gardeners couldn't pluck, stomp, or trap, they fought with concoctions derived from minerals or plants. With limited technological resources, gardeners had to be keenly aware of the connection between their garden and the surrounding environment. They looked closely to nature's ways for guidance.

When synthetic chemical pesticides, such as DDT, first came on the scene in the 1940s, they promised speedy and long-term relief from many plant pests and diseases. What could be more appealing to a gardener who has watched helplessly as a majestic old tree succumbed to fire blight disease or young seedlings fell prey to a plague of slugs? Gardeners switched to synthetic pesticides in droves.

Over the years, however, it has become evident that these compounds too often create as many problems as they solve. As awareness of the environmental liabilities of many synthetic pesticides has increased, gardeners have become uneasy about their use. Once again, gardeners are turning to a natural, or organic, approach.

The appeal of organic practices is broad and varied. Some gardeners are concerned primarily about the risks of exposing themselves, their families, friends, and pets to toxic compounds. Others want to steer clear of materials that pollute the environment and kill beneficial insects, fish, and wildlife. Some regard organic gardening as a viable way to sustain our natural resources for future generations. Still others embrace organic gardening as part of living in harmony with nature. Whatever their motivation, today's organic gardeners can draw upon the best of old practices as well as the newest information and techniques.

Pest-control choices

To better understand the organic approach to pest and disease control, it will help to take a closer look at the other major methods practiced today: the conventional (or "chemical") approach and integrated pest management (called IPM).

Chemical controls. This approach relies heavily on synthesized compounds derived from petrochemicals. These chemicals range from highly toxic to less toxic in their effect on pests, other living organisms, and the environment. Chemical controls offer quick knockdown of pests; usually require less time, effort, and thought on the part of the gardener; and often give an initial appearance of complete control.

On the down side, chemical controls can leave toxic residues in the soil, water, and plants. Many are quite toxic to mammals, birds, honeybees, and other organisms, and the long-term effects of exposure are still not clear. Chemical controls also have unintended effects. Once the primary pest is killed, secondary pests that were kept in check by the primary pest increase, creating a new problem that requires another chemical control. Some of the treated pests develop resistance to chemical sprays and then require stronger control measures. Beneficial insects and other natural controls are frequently wiped out by broad-spectrum chemicals, and pest populations soar.

Integrated pest management. IPM is a systematic approach that relies on regular monitoring of pest populations to determine if and when to take action. When control is warranted, you employ nontoxic strategies first—traps, mulch, beneficial insects—then, if necessary, natural or synthetic pesticides.

By focusing on a pest in the context of the garden ecosystem rather than as an isolated nuisance to be eliminated, IPM provides the means to carefully target your control efforts. The infrequent use of synthetic pesticides reduces the potential for harming people and the environment but still offers the advantages of these products. IPM does not provide quick fixes. It requires more careful planning and observation, and often more time and effort up front, than methods employing synthetic chemicals require, but IPM can be less work over the long haul.

Organic gardening: basic principles

An organic approach emphasizes prevention of problems through careful garden design, sound horticultural practices, and an understanding of pest and disease life cycles. In addition to cultural measures, organic gardeners control pests by physical and mechanical means and with naturally occurring or naturally derived materials or organisms, such as insecticidal soaps, sulfur dust, beneficial insects, or pesticidal compounds derived from plants (called "botanicals").

Compared with synthetic chemicals, many organic controls pose little or no risk to you, other creatures, or the environment. This makes it easier for existing predators and parasites to come to your aid. Some pesticides that are derived from plants are highly toxic to mammals or to some beneficial organisms, but they all tend to break down quickly into harmless compounds. Naturally derived pesticides sometimes act slowly, and those that break down rapidly may need frequent application.

Like IPM, the organic approach requires careful planning and observation. But your extra work is likely to be rewarded.

Learning from nature

Organic pest control involves much more than a bagful of environmentally safe remedies. Practitioners view the garden as a complete system whose sum is greater than its parts. They model the garden's design and care on natural processes, and they take action only if it's needed.

This approach, often called "holistic," is more than a philosophical preference—it's based on a biological reality. Everything in your garden, living and nonliving, is interrelated in one way or another—bugs and blight, roots and shoots, sun and soil, water and wind make up an ecosystem, which is part of still larger ecosystems around it.

Almost anything you do with one part of your garden will eventually cause something to happen in another part of it, for better or worse. Sometimes the connection is simple—in some regions, if you mulch deeply with leaves during the rainy season, you're likely to create a snail haven. Other times, cause and effect may be nearly impossible to pinpoint. The more you try to understand how each aspect of your garden fits into the big picture, the better able you'll be to know when to take action and when to sit back and let nature take its course.

With nature as a model, you can design many potential pest and disease problems out of your landscape and design in buffers against future problems, all before you ever put spade to soil. Common sense indicates a number of important things you can do:

Choose plants that are well adapted to your soil, climate, and any special characteristics of your site—a steep hillside or high winds, for instance. Consider plants native to your area as well as those from other regions with similar conditions. Whether you grow native or exotic plants, learn about their soil, nutritional, and water needs, and do your best to meet them.

Don't overcrowd plants, and group together those that prefer similar conditions. Healthy plants aren't necessarily less appealing to pests and pathogens, but they are usually better able to tolerate the damage.

Encourage diversity. By including many different species, and avoiding planting all of one kind together, you're more likely to create a stable ecosystem with an abundance of beneficial organisms that will help keep problems in check. Plant plenty of flowering plants to provide food for beneficial insects. Create habitats for other natural predators, such as toads, frogs, and birds.

Diagnosing pest and disease problems

No matter how carefully thought out and tended, no garden escapes pest problems. To prepare yourself, find out as much as you can about the pests and diseases that are most common in your area on the plants you're growing. Learn their symptoms and when they're likely to appear. Experienced gardeners and staff at local nurseries or botanical gardens are excellent resources.

Once you see damage to a plant, the first task is to identify the culprit. This is easier said than done, but essential. Not every problem is caused by an insect or other pest organism—damage can also be caused by cold, heat, wind, air pollution, too much or too little water or fertilizer, or other environmental and cultural factors. To make matters more confusing, sometimes this damage looks similar to that caused by pests.

When pests or diseases are the problem, they often are misidentified. Many insects look similar to the untrained eye. Sometimes the perpetrator has left the scene before you arrive, and whatever insect is present at that time is blamed. Pests also sometimes hide within the plant or operate underground. Applying controls for the wrong pest frequently fails to solve the problem or, even worse, aggravates it. Here are some activities to help you figure out who done it.

Be vigilant. Check your garden regularly for damaged plants, insects, and other organisms. Over time, careful observation will help you recognize when something's gone awry and will give you a better sense of local pest and disease cycles. Take an upclose look: check the top and underside of the leaves, along the stems, where the branches meet the stem, buds and flowers, the base of the plant, and the surrounding soil surface. Note leaves that are munched, covered with webbing, or abnormal in shape or color. Pay attention to whether the damage occurs along the leaf margin, along the veins, or throughout the leaf; whether holes or discolored areas are regular or irregular in shape. Look for wilted, blackened, or chewed stems; sticky exudate on branches; withered or browned flower buds; or loose mounds of soil near the plant.

Look for insects—a 10X hand lens will expose tiny ones. Check for egg masses on or near the plants. Also take a look at plants in wild areas adjacent to your property, where pest species may find a habitat to their liking. Occasional nighttime forays into the garden with a flashlight might reveal critters that are hidden from view in the day. Collect samples of any insects or damage that you want to identify.

Although it may initially seem like a lot of trouble, record your observations in a notebook. Note the date you first notice the problem and how it changes over time. Your jottings may help you discover correlations between pest or disease problems and gardening practices or environmental conditions.

Identification. One of the best clues to the identity of a pest is the damage it causes. Chewing insects, such as beetles, caterpillars, and grasshoppers, eat holes in leaves or munch away surface leaf tissue, leaving a sort of leaf "skeleton." Cutworms often nip off seedlings at ground level. White, irregularly shaped pathways on the surface of a leaf mark the trails of leafminers, which tunnel their way between the layers of leaf tissue. Borers burrow into stems and branches, sometimes leaving oozing, sticky sap or sticky sawdust in their wake. Slugs and snails also chomp leaves.

Insects such as aphids, mealybugs, scale, and whiteflies, as well as mites (which are more closely related to spiders than to insects), all suck the sap from plants. This causes a variety of symptoms, ranging from wilted, twisted, yellowed, spotted, or curled leaves to stunted or dead plant parts. If aphids or scale is causing the damage, there will often be an accumulation of honeydew, a sticky, shiny substance, on leaf surfaces as well.

Plant diseases are caused by fungi, bacteria, or viruses. But pathogens are more elusive than are insect pests—most are microscopic—so your best bet is to try to identify them by their typical symptoms or signs. Mildews are recognized by a gray-white powdery coating on leaf surfaces, stems, or fruit, sometimes with yellowed or dead areas beneath. Leaf spots, which can result from fungi or bacteria, appear as discolored lesions on the leaves—yellow, red, brown, tan, gray, or black spots. Sometimes the infected leaves wilt and rot. Blights cause leaves, branches, twigs, or flowers to suddenly wilt or become brown and die. Frequently the stem appears water-soaked and blackens at the soil line. Rots, caused by fungi or bacteria, can cause similar decay of roots, of the lower part of the stem, or of other succulent plant tissue. Viruses can produce white, yellow, or pale-green discolored, patterned, or spotted areas on leaves and less commonly on stems, fruit, or roots. Virus-infected plants often become stunted. While these symptoms are generalizations at best, they should point you in the right direction.

For help in identifying the insects, other organisms, or symptoms, you can refer to books or a local expert. Books with good color photos and/or diagnostic keys are likely to be the most helpful for beginners (several are listed in the bibliography). Reliable diagnosis of plant problems is usually tricky business, so you shouldn't feel reluctant to turn to an expert for assistance. Your Cooperative Extension Service (listed under government offices in the phone book) or a local nursery or garden center may be able to help or to refer you to someone who can.

Before you take action. Learn as much as you can about the pest's life cycle and preferred environment before you take action. Find out at which stage in its life cycle the damage occurred—if a caterpillar is chomping your leaves, you'll need to control it, not the butterfly or moth it will become. Monitor pest populations to see if their numbers are increasing, decreasing, or holding steady. Check for insects or other organisms that prey on the pest; given time, they may provide adequate control. Remember that populations of beneficial organisms are often slower to build up than populations of the pests—taking action too soon could wipe them out. Even an ill-timed spray of an apparently harmless substance such as water can wash off beneficial predators.

Decide if you and your plants can live with the damage. Keep in mind that beneficial insects need a supply of pests to maintain their populations. If a pest-covered plant is seriously damaged and going downhill fast, and there are no natural enemies in sight, you need to think seriously about taking action. On the other hand, if you spot a few pests here and there, but they aren't causing much harm, and they aren't on the increase, then you might take a "wait and see" attitude. You'll also need to think about your aesthetic standards and decide just how much damage is acceptable to your eye.

Controls

It is impossible here to address individually the many pests and the controls for each one. Instead, we offer an overview of a range of controls. Each particular problem will require some research on your part—consulting an experienced gardener, a local professional, or detailed reference books. This research can be interesting, and with experience you'll become an expert yourself.

To choose the most appropriate, safest

control, ask yourself the following questions. Do you need a control with immediate impact, or can you wait for a long-term control to take effect? Is this the most specific control for the problem? Is this the right time to take this action? Is this control the least disruptive of beneficial insects and the safest for humans, other animals, and the environment? If the control requires repeated action, such as handpicking insects off plants, do you have the time and patience to follow through?

Once you decide to take action, start with the most benign controls, ones that you can accomplish with just your own hands (or feet), and move on to other tactics as needed. In the end, a combination of strategies often proves most successful.

Cultural and mechanical controls. First, change any cultural practices that might make your plants more susceptible to a particular pest. For example, planting earlier might give your plants a chance to establish themselves before the pests that attack them are up and running. Another strategy is to modify the pest's habitat in a way that discourages its survival. You might remove a thick mulch or clear out adjacent weedy areas where the pests hide when they're not feeding in your garden.

Traps, barriers, cages, row covers, and other mechanical devices can capture or exclude pests. Handpicking pests or crushing them underfoot is particularly successful for larger critters such as beetles, snails, and slugs. Strong water sprays can physically dislodge certain insects.

Biological controls. Increasingly, gardeners are making use of their pests' naturally occurring enemies: predators, which are free-living organisms that feed on other organisms; parasitoids, which kill the hosts they live on; and pathogens, which are microorganisms that release toxins into the insects that ingest them. These beneficial insects, mites, nematodes, and microorganisms are probably already at work naturally in your garden. Under the best of circumstances, you can just sit back and enjoy the fruits of their labor.

If, however, these beneficial organisms haven't appeared yet or are in short supply, you can purchase laboratory-reared populations to release in your garden. There are commercially available beneficials that control pest insects, mites, or snails. Some, such as the larvae of the green lacewing, can be quite effective, while others, such as the

convergent lady beetle, often fly away before they've adequately controlled their prey. Sometimes the introduced beneficials will establish large enough populations in your garden to provide ongoing control; other times you'll need to replenish the supply periodically.

Microbial insecticides are commercially available as well. These pathogens include bacteria, fungi, and viruses that are effective against insects and in some cases against other plant diseases. One of the most common microbial pesticides, *Bacillus thuringiensis* (commonly called Bt), is a toxin-producing bacteria that kills caterpillars and insect larvae after these pests have eaten leaves or stems sprayed with it.

Naturally derived pesticides. A wide range of compounds derived from natural sources are sprayed or dusted on plants to control pests and diseases. Most common are insecticidal soaps, horticultural oils, botanical pesticides, and minerals.

Insecticidal soaps penetrate the coating of susceptible insects and dissolve their cell membranes, causing death. They are most effective against soft-bodied insects with sucking mouthparts, such as aphids, mites, whiteflies, and thrips. Fungicidal soaps are sprayed on plants to control diseases such as mildews, rots, leafspots, and rust. They are very safe to use and break down rapidly in the soil, but they can be poisonous to plants (phytotoxic). Test them on a small portion of the plant first. Thorough coverage and periodic reapplication are needed for good control.

Horticultural oils smother the adults and eggs of a variety of pests, including certain aphids, scale, caterpillars, and mites. Although traditionally these are sprayed when the plant is dormant, newer formulations are safe for spraying on leafed-out plants as well. Follow label precautions to avoid potential phytotoxicity, and wear protective clothing to prevent eye and skin irritation during application. The oils have a low toxicity to humans and wildlife and biodegrade rapidly.

Botanical pesticides are derived from plants that contain substances toxic to insects. Some botanicals, such as pyrethrin, are effective against a wide variety of pests (they're called broad-spectrum pesticides), while others, such as sabadilla, kill a more limited range of pests. Botanicals also vary widely in their toxicity to humans, other mammals, and insects—pyrethrins and sabadilla have low mammalian toxicity, while nicotine and rotenone are highly toxic to mammals. On the other hand, rotenone is not toxic to honeybees, but sabadilla is. Regardless of their toxicity, botanicals quickly break down into nontoxic compounds in the presence of sunlight or in the soil. They may require frequent reapplication, but their short period of toxicity minimizes potential harm to organisms other than the targeted pests.

The minerals sulfur, copper, and lime are used primarily to control fungal and bacterial diseases, including mildews, rots, leafspots, and blights. Sometimes these minerals are sold in combined formulations, such as copper sulfate. Sulfur dust, lime, and lime sulfur control some plant-sucking pests as well. Sulfur is relatively nontoxic to humans; the toxicity of copper varies depending on the formulation. Whether you apply minerals as a dust or a spray, protect your eyes, lungs, and skin to avoid irritation.

Safety

Pesticides derived from natural substances should not be treated casually. Labels are quite specific about the dangers posed by the product and about how to use it and on what. (It is, in fact, illegal to apply a pesticide to plants other than those specified on the label.) Do just what the label says.

It's wise to wear protective clothing when you apply any pesticide. This includes a long-sleeved shirt and long pants, rubber gloves, boots, goggles, and a respiratory mask. Don't spray on windy days. Mix only in the specified proportions—a higher concentration or bigger dose doesn't make an insect any deader and can be very dangerous.

Preventing diseases

Diseases can be transmitted to your plants quite rapidly by a variety of means—air, soil, water, insects, humans, and propagation tools. They can be carried in seeds, cuttings, and divisions. Since pathogens are rarely visible, it's hard to control them by mechanical or physical means.

Prevention plays a more important role in controlling disease pathogens than in controlling insect or animal pests. It's much easier to protect a plant from disease than to cure it. To minimize disease problems in your garden, buy healthy plants, choosing disease-resistant varieties if available. In addition, certain cultural practices can create unfavorable conditions for many pathogens and minimize the spread of existing ones. Space plants far enough apart to allow good air circulation. Don't overwater. Provide adequate drainage. Don't over-fertilize, especially with nitrogen. Avoid mechanical damage to your plants—lawn mowers are so frequently rammed into trees that the aftermath has been dubbed "lawn-mower blight." Prune out diseased or dead plant parts. Don't leave long stubs of pruned branches or stems, which can serve as a conduit for disease organisms. Remove healthy plant debris from the garden and compost it. To avoid transmitting disease, discard diseased material rather than composting it.

Starting a new lawn

Fashions in lawns are changing. The broad sward of crew-cut, weedless turf, intensely maintained with chemical additives and generous doses of water and hard labor, is giving way to smaller, less demanding lawns, often bordered by large areas of easily maintained ground covers. In drought-prone areas, legal restrictions on watering combine with personal factors (changing tastes, less free time and money) to make low-maintenance, low-input lawns a necessity.

Keeping up a putting-green-quality lawn is a science in itself. Every effort to achieve perfection begets yet more effort. Heavily fertilized lawns need more frequent mowing. Closely mowed lawns need more irrigation. Well-irrigated lawns are more prone to diseases and weed infestation. What's more, chemicals used to cure diseases or to kill weeds often give rise to new diseases.

Fortunately, you can have a good-looking lawn without devoting your life or your pocketbook to it. If you prepare the soil well, select an appropriate turfgrass, and provide moderate amounts of thoughtful, timely care, you can have an attractive, durable lawn.

In this chapter we'll discuss the basics of making a new lawn—whether you're starting from scratch on the site of a newly built house or replacing an existing lawn.

Choosing the best grass

The best way to reduce the maintenance requirements of your lawn is to grow a species of grass suited to your climate and to your tolerance for maintenance. There are varieties that resist drought, insects, and diseases; varieties that stand up to heavy foot traffic; and varieties that need less frequent mowing.

This range of choices may overwhelm many gardeners, and we can't provide more than an overview here. (A selection of the most popular varieties is given in the charts on the following pages.) If you don't have the time or inclination to become a turfgrass expert, consult with a local landscape architect or contractor or a knowledgeable person at a nursery to find out which varieties do best in your area.

Lawn grasses may be sold in one or more forms (seed, sod, sprigs, and plugs). Seed is sometimes sold as blends, which contain a mix of different varieties, each contributing one or more important qualities. The grasses that are most often used in American lawns are categorized in several ways: fine-bladed or coarse-bladed; sod-forming or bunching; annual or perennial; warm-season or cool-season.

Fine-bladed grasses include any variety with blades less than $1/4$ inch wide; they're used to create carpetlike lawns. Bentgrass, Kentucky bluegrass, and zoysiagrass are the most common fine-textured grasses. Wider, coarse-bladed grasses (annual ryegrass, tall fescue, and St. Augustine grass) can look weedy, but they offer other redeeming qualities, such as durability and shade or drought tolerance.

Grasses are also classified by the way they grow. Sod-forming grasses spread by stolons (horizontal stems that creep above ground) or rhizomes (underground stems), filling in bare patches, forcing out weeds, and creating a thick lawn. Sod-forming grasses include bentgrass, Bermudagrass, and zoysiagrass. Bunchgrasses, by contrast, grow in clumps and spread only by expanding their basal growth. They are often fast growers that stand up well to traffic. Bunch grasses, such as perennial ryegrass, tall fescue, and blue grama grass, are sometimes mixed with sod-forming grasses.

Perennial grasses are usually the only types you should consider for a permanent lawn. You might want to plant annual types to provide cover while a perennial grass becomes established or, in southern areas, for winter color.

The most basic division among lawn grasses describes their growth habits. Warm-season grasses, such as Bermudagrass and St. Augustine grass, grow rapidly in hot weather and go dormant (turning brown) when it's cool. Cool-season grasses (Kentucky bluegrass, bentgrass, perennial ryegrass, and the fescues) do the opposite. Warm-season grasses are normally planted south of the so-called bluegrass line, which runs approximately along the northern borders of North Carolina, Tennessee, Arkansas, Oklahoma, and Texas and through New Mexico and Arizona to the Pacific, passing through southern California. Cool-season grasses perform best north of the bluegrass line. Some gardeners south of the line also plant cool-season grasses in the fall to provide winter color.

In many areas, traditional turfgrasses are ideal ground covers. But they can't survive in the driest areas of the country without heavy irrigation. If you live in a dry area and don't want to make heroic efforts to grow turfgrass, you should consider making a lawn of more drought-tolerant native grasses, such as buffalograss and blue grama grass. You can also cut down the size of your lawn, installing imaginative combinations of drought-tolerant ornamental grasses and other ground covers. Or, you might do away with grass entirely. Some gardeners in the Southwest have created spectacular home landscapes with just native plants, stone mulch, paths, and bare soil.

Preparing the soil

The most carefully chosen and tended grass will not grow well unless the soil beneath it is reasonably healthy. Once a lawn is started, it's much more difficult, though not impossible, to loosen compacted soil and to improve drainage. Time spent at the beginning testing the soil, correcting deficiencies, and improving drainage and grading will pay off for years to come. Remember that the preparation outlined below is important whether you sow seed, lay sod, or plant sprigs or plugs.

Grading. Let's start with the largest consideration first, the grading on the site. Ideally, the surface should drop away from the house in all directions, about 1 foot for every 100 feet of distance. Water may stand on flatter grades or run off steeper ones.

Few of us will be blessed with an ideal site, and changing grades requires heavy equipment, which can be expensive and disruptive. If you're building a new house or overhauling the entire landscape of an older site, talk with the builder or a landscape contractor about making major changes to improve conditions. Soil around new houses usually has been compacted by heavy construction equipment. Make sure that the builder remedies this by loosening the soil as deeply as possible, with tractor-drawn equipment if necessary, not just by spreading a few inches of topsoil over a rock-hard surface.

If regrading isn't practical, consider other solutions. Terraces or berms can create flat or gently sloping areas on a steep site. If the property is relatively flat but too damp, or if there are swales or depressions where water collects, consider installing drain lines. For all large-scale grading and drainage projects, it's prudent to seek the advice of a landscape architect or contractor. Smaller problems, such as bumps, potholes, or low spots, can often be corrected with a shovel, rake, wheelbarrow, and some elbow grease.

If your site has problems that seem likely to exhaust your pocketbook or your energy, don't give up hope. Satisfactory lawns do grow on less than ideal sites. Where moisture and sunlight are ample and foot traffic light, grass can do quite nicely on slopes much steeper than the ideal. Look around town for properties with conditions similar to yours and see how they fare; talk with the owners to see what effort is required to produce good results. Finally, consider planting alternative grasses or ground covers where the conditions or the cost of maintenance rules out turfgrass.

Improving the soil. There is nothing mysterious about a lawn's fertility needs. Like other plants, grasses need soil rich in nitrogen, phosphorus, and potassium. Take the time to test your soil, sending the samples to your state's Extension Service lab or to a reputable private lab. Be sure to specify that the test is for a lawn. If the test indicates nutrient deficiencies, amend the soil accordingly. If the test is in the normal range, broadcast a starter fertilizer over the area; use about 50 pounds of a 5-10-5 fertilizer per 1,000 square feet or 25 pounds each of blood meal, bone meal, and greensand per 1,000 square feet.

Most grasses prefer a neutral pH, in the range of 6.5 to 7.5. Your soil test should indicate how much (if any) limestone or sulfur you need to add to raise or lower the pH of your soil.

Before adding any amendments, take a close look at your soil's structure. Knowing whether you are working with sand, clay, loam, or something in between will aid you in choosing grass types and in setting your irrigation schedule. (See "Evaluating your soil" for a simple method of testing soil texture and composition.) If your soil is more than 60 percent clay or 70 percent sand, work at least a 2-inch layer of organic matter (compost, peat moss, or dried manure, for instance) or a 3-inch layer of rich topsoil into it.

When you've determined the additives necessary for improving structure and fertility, spread them on the soil along with the lime or sulfur required to adjust the pH. Till to a depth of 6 inches, or make one or two passes with a tractor-mounted disk. Then broadcast the starter fertilizer and rake the surface smooth.

A selection of warm-season grasses

Grass	Texture	Water needs	Wear resistance	Shade tolerance	Fertilizer needs	How to establish	Mowing height (in.)	Comments
Common Bermudagrass (*Cynodon dactylon*)	medium to fine	low	high	poor	heavy	seed	$1/2$–1	Toughest of the tough in hot climates.
Hybrid Bermudagrasses	fine	low	high	poor	heavy	sod, plugs	$1/2$–1	'Tifway', 'Santa Ana' are good strains. 'Tifdwarf' is low, slow growing.
St. Augustine grass (*Stenotaphrum secundatum*)	coarse	heavy	high	good	heavy	sod, plugs	$1^1/2$–2	Great heat resistance; tolerates saline conditions near beach.
Seashore paspalum (*Paspalum vaginatum*)	fine	moderate	good	some	moderate	sod, plugs	$3/4$–1	Salt- and heat-resistant.
Zoysiagrasses (*Zoysia japonica, Z. matrella*)	fine	moderate	high	some	low	sod, plugs	1–2	Long dormancy, slow growth. Good choice for South.
Zoysia tenuifolia	fine	moderate	high	some	low	sod, plugs	NA	Low-growing bank or ground cover; never needs mowing.
Dichondra (*Dichondra micrantha*)	coarse	moderate to heavy	moderate	some	heavy	seed, plugs, sod	1–2 (in shade)	Tolerates heat but not hard freezing. Rarely needs mowing in full sun and moderate foot traffic.

A selection of cool-season grasses

Grass	Texture	Water needs	Wear resistance	Shade tolerance	Fertilizer needs	How to establish	Mowing height (in.)	Comments
Colonial bentgrass (*Agrostis tenuis*)	fine	average to light	moderate	some	low	seed	1/2–1	Beautiful, but fussy.
Creeping bentgrass (*Agrostis stolonifera*)	fine	high	high	some	moderate	seed	1/2 or less	Beautiful, but even fussier.
Kentucky bluegrass (*Poa pratensis*)	medium to fine	high	high	poor	heavy	sod, seed	11/2–2	The classic cool-season grass, but needs care.
Rough-stalked bluegrass (*Poa trivialis*)	fine	high	poor	good	low to moderate	seed	11/2–2	Grown for finer texture, greater tolerance of shade.
Creeping red fescue (*Festuca rubra*)	fine	low to moderate	poor	good	low to moderate	seed	11/2–2	Widely used in southern California as a ground cover; mow once a year.
Hard or sheep fescue (*Festuca ovina*)	bunchy	low	moderate	moderate	low	seed	11/2–2	Tolerant of extreme heat, cold, drought.
Tall fescue (*Festuca arundinacea*)	coarse to fine	moderate	good	moderate	low to moderate	sod, seed	2–3	Withstands drought.
Annual ryegrass (*Lolium multiflorum*)	coarse	moderate to high	moderate	poor	low to moderate	seed	11/2–2	Quick sprouting; short-lived in hot weather.
Perennial ryegrass (*Lolium perenne*)	medium to fine	high	high	some	moderate	seed	11/2–2	Dislikes extreme heat or cold.

At this point, the soil will be rather soft and in need of settling. To speed the process, rent a roller (basically a big barrel with handles attached). Fill the barrel one-third to one-half full with water and roll it over the soil to smooth and firm it. Don't wait too long to plant after rolling—a heavy downpour can wash bare soil away in the wink of an eye.

Eliminating weeds. The more weeds you can eradicate before installing a lawn, the fewer you'll have to deal with later. You can kill weed seeds and seedlings at the same time as you prepare your soil. Stretch a sheet of clear plastic tightly over tilled and thoroughly watered soil and leave the plastic in place for about four weeks. This process, called solarization, will kill weeds and weed seeds in the top layer of soil.

You can also eliminate weeds by successive tillings. Your first tilling will destroy established weeds while bringing new weed seeds to the surface to germinate. Wait at least two weeks until a solid crop of new weeds sprouts, then do them in with another tilling. Two or three tillings will eliminate many of the resident weeds.

Removing an old lawn. If your lawn is an unsightly, unhealthy quilt of bare patches, weeds, and anemic grass, you may want to tear it out and start over. In exchange for some hard work, you will get the opportunity to evaluate and amend the soil, fix drainage problems, and wipe out weeds. Correcting underlying problems will give the new lawn excellent chances of long-term health.

First you need to remove the existing vegetation, consisting of old sod, weeds, and thatch (an accumulated residue of dead plant parts). Then you prepare the site as outlined above. There are several ways to remove an old lawn. You can rent a sod stripper (a machine about the size of a lawn mower that slices off the top layer of sod), or you can hire someone to do the job for you. Be prepared to lose some of your topsoil along with the sod.

Alternatively, you can hire someone with a plow to turn the whole lawn over. (Doing this with a rotary tiller is far too time-consuming and arduous a process for all but postage-stamp lawns.) If your lawn is not too large and time is not of the essence, you can also mulch the vegetation to death. Cover the lawn with sheets of black plastic, firmly anchored, and wait for the grass to shrivel. Depending on the type

A selection of native lawn grasses

Grass	Texture	Water needs	Wear resistance	Shade tolerance	Fertilizer needs	How to establish	Mowing height (in.)	Comments
Wheatgrass (*Agropyron cristatum*)	medium	low	moderate	low	low	seed	2	'Fairway' is improved strain. *A. smithii* sometimes used.
Blue grama grass (*Bouteloua gracilis*)	medium	low	moderate	low	low	seed	11/2	Bunch grass.
Buffalograss (*Buchloe dactyloides*)	fine	low	good	low	low	seed, plugs	NA	Maximum height of 4 in. without irrigation.

of grass and the temperature, this can take from three to six weeks.

Planting

You can start a new lawn from seed, sod, sprigs, or plugs. Seeding is the cheapest, easiest, and most common method, and it offers the greatest choice of turfgrass varieties. If you need a lawn in a hurry, sod is best, but it is much more expensive and takes more work. Sprigs and plugs (individual grass plants or parts of plants) are less expensive than sod, because you do not plant them in a solid blanket. But they demand patience. It may take several years for plugs to fill in and cover an area. In the meantime, you have to keep the remaining bare soil free of weeds.

Seeding a lawn. In theory, you want to sow a lawn at a time when the young grass plants will have an advantage over weeds. In the North, the best time is autumn, at least six weeks before the first frost. The cool-season grasses are ready to take off once the heat breaks, but most annual weeds are not programmed to germinate in the fall. Northerners can also sow in early spring, as soon as the ground can be worked, which will give the grass plenty of time to establish itself before the summer heat sets in. In the South, sow warm-season grasses in late spring or early summer and cool-season grasses in late summer or early fall.

When you've decided what variety or blend of seed to buy, take a close look at the labels of the various brands. They should list the species and varieties included, the percentage of each, and whether they are fine- or coarse-textured. Look for named varieties of seed whenever possible; 'Merion' Kentucky bluegrass, for example, rather than just a generic Kentucky bluegrass. The label will also tell you how much weed seed, crop seed, and inert matter are present. Good-quality grass seed contains less than 1 percent of weed or crop seed and less than 3 percent inert matter.

The label will list a germination-rate number for each type of seed in the package and a date the seed was tested. Don't buy seed with a germination rate less than 80 percent or a test date over one year old.

The easiest and most accurate way to sow grass seed is with a broadcast or drop spreader, but you can also do a perfectly acceptable job by hand. When you're ready to sow, divide the seed into two equal portions. Put half in the spreader or, if you're sowing by hand, in a bucket. Make one pass over the area with the first batch of seed. Then with the rest of the seed, make a second pass at right angles to the first. This will give you good coverage.

After sowing all the seed, rake a thin layer of soil over it. Firm down the seedbed with a lawn roller or tamp it with the back

---

Growing a lawn in shade

SHADE, ESPECIALLY HEAVY shade, poses problems for many plants, and grass is no exception. Grasses need sunlight, and grown in too much shade, they may be anemic and prone to disease. Competition from shallow-rooted trees or shrubs can make the problem worse. It is possible to grow a healthy lawn in moderate shade if you do it correctly right from the start.

First, make sure that the soil is fertile and well drained, and remove all perennial weed roots from the top 6 inches of the soil. Then plant a suitable type of grass. Check at your nursery to find out what shade-tolerant varieties do best in your area. In general, fescues handle the shade well; Kentucky bluegrass does not.

Once the grass is up, you must care for it differently than if it were growing in full sun. Since low light levels cut down on how much food the plants can manufacture, increase the leaf surface by mowing 1 inch higher than the variety's recommended height for full sun. Provide a little extra fertilizer and water. If necessary, prune nearby trees and shrubs to increase air circulation.

---

of a rake. To keep the soil moist, which is critical for germination, cover it thinly with weed-free straw. (Hay contains weed seed; peat moss and sawdust crust over into an impenetrable layer.)

Don't allow the soil surface to dry out until the grass is 2 inches tall, even if you must water it lightly several times a day. But be careful not to saturate the soil. When the grass emerges, stay off it, and do not mow until it is 2 to 3 inches high. (Leave the straw to rot.) Then treat it as you would an established lawn.

Laying sod. The best time for laying sod is the same as for seeding: fall or early spring in the North, spring in the South. Never plant during hot, dry weather—you can't afford to let the sod dry out before its roots have knitted into the soil.

It's just as important to start with good sod as with good seed. Buy sod guaranteed to be free of insects, diseases, and weeds. Inspect it carefully, if possible before it is delivered to your home. Pieces should be green, moist, and firm, with a thick set of roots. Reject any sod that is sparse, brown, yellow, or flimsy.

Prepare the soil exactly as you would for seed, including rolling it. Water the area thoroughly the night before laying the sod (ideally to a depth of 8 inches). Water uniformly and gently so that no puddles or mud forms.

Lay sod as quickly as possible; if it sits in a pile and heats up, the roots may be permanently damaged. If you can't finish on the day of delivery, store the remainder in a cool, shaded place and lay it first thing the next day.

Laying sod is a bit like building a brick wall, and it requires some precision. Lay the first course in a straight line—against the edge of a walk or a driveway, or a string stretched between two stakes. Butt the ends and edges of the strips tightly together without overlap. Stagger the joints of adjacent courses. If you need to work on top of laid sod, place a piece of plywood on it to distribute your weight and prevent damage.

Once the sod is in place, go over it once or twice with a light lawn roller. Then spread a thin layer of topsoil over the sod, working the soil into the cracks with a broom or the back of a wooden rake. Keep the sod moist by watering during the warmest part of each day until the roots have knitted into the soil; you can pull up a corner to check.

If you lay sod on a slope, orient the long edges of the sod across rather than up and down the slope. If pieces slip, peg them in place with wooden stakes or large staples made from coat hangers. (Pull the pegs or staples out before you use the roller.)

Plugs and sprigs. Some grasses, such as zoysias and improved varieties of Bermudagrass, aren't readily available from seed and have to be planted as sod, plugs, or sprigs. To plug a lawn, you set 2- to 3-inch cubes of turf (the plugs) into the lawn in a checkerboard pattern. You can buy plugs in trays or make them yourself from sod (these will be thinner). The plugs may take anywhere from a few weeks to a year or two to fill in completely. Plugs of most warm-season grasses are spaced about 18 inches apart; zoysiagrass takes longer to spread and should be spaced about 12 inches apart.

Prepare the soil as for seeding. Excavating for each plug is quickly done with a special plugging tool, a sort of miniature posthole digger, which you may be able to rent. You can plant plugs anytime during the growing season.

Sprigs are small sections of stems with roots attached. You can buy them by the bushel or make your own by shredding pieces of sod. Plant them in regularly spaced furrows or spread them evenly across the prepared soil, then cover them with 1/4 inch of topsoil. After planting, roll the lawn and water thoroughly.

Lawn care

Maintaining a lawn is like caring for a house or an automobile—a little regular attention can prevent major headaches later on. By promptly and properly mowing, watering, fertilizing, and attending to weeds, insects, or diseases, you can keep your lawn healthy without spending a great deal of time or money.

Think before you mow

Most people cut their grass purely for appearance' sake. But there's much more at stake here than keeping your lawn tidy and attractive. How and when you cut your grass can make the difference between a healthy lawn and an ailing one.

A grass plant, of course, works like other plants. The larger its aboveground parts, the more food it produces and the longer its roots grow. Mowing shocks grass, no matter how high or low the cut. But when grass blades are cut too short, food production drops and roots may stop growing altogether. The weakened plants are more susceptible to disease and the stress of heat or drought.

Ideal mowing height varies by species and variety. Some grasses are naturally low-growing and do best when kept short. Let them grow long, and you'll get thatch buildup, seed-head formation, and a poor appearance. Others do better when cut high. (The charts in the previous chapter indicates recommended mowing heights.)

Because vigorously growing grass can bounce back from stress, you can mow lower than the ideal in the spring and fall in the North, when cool-season grasses are most active, and during the summer in the South, when warm-season grasses are most vigorous. During other seasons, when the grass naturally slows down, or when times are tough, as during heat and drought, mow higher.

When in doubt, follow these two mowing rules and you won't go far wrong. First, never remove more than one third of the top growth at any one time. For example, trim only 1 inch off 3-inch-tall grass; any more will weaken the grass. Second, mow high and mow often. Studies have shown that high and frequent mowing imparts the greatest vigor, making a healthier lawn with fewer weeds.

Clippings. Most people bag and discard grass clippings as a matter of course. In most cases, however, it would benefit the lawn to leave them right where they are. Clippings contain a significant amount of nutrients, which return to the lawn when the clippings decompose. By some estimates, you can reduce your lawn's fertilizer requirements by 25 percent if you leave clippings where they fall.

Interestingly, clippings from properly managed lawns do not contribute to thatch, which consists primarily of the tougher parts of the grass plants—the stems, stolons, rhizomes, and roots. To prevent unsightly mats of fresh clippings from accumulating and smothering grass beneath them, cut the lawn when the grass is dry, and cut it before it grows more than 1 inch taller than its recommended mowing height.

Watering

When it comes to watering, many people are guilty of killing their lawns with kindness. Provided frequently with small amounts of water, grass plants won't put down deep roots. If the water supply is cut off, the shallow roots will dry out quickly and the grass wilts, and perhaps dies. Also, a great deal of water is wasted on lawns. Sprinklers are too often whirling during the hottest part of the day, when much water is lost to evaporation, or they're left on after the soil is saturated, and water runs off down the storm sewers.

Grass needs as much as 1 to 2 inches of water per week to grow, but in many parts of the country nature provides much of that. When you need to supplement rainfall, water deeply. A good rule of thumb is to provide an inch of water in a single soaking per week. With increased concern about water conservation, many gardeners are deciding to water only when the grass absolutely needs it. The lawn will tell you when it's time: blades will begin to wilt and their color dull, the turf won't spring back

when you walk on it. Remember that clay soils store more water than do sandy soils and will need watering less frequently.

Early morning watering minimizes evaporation (the air is cool) and gives the blades time to dry off during the day, reducing the chance of fungal infections. A sprinkler with a low flow rate (less than 1/4 inch per hour) will minimize runoff. To determine how long a sprinkler takes to deliver an inch of water, spread some empty 1-inch-deep tuna cans under the sprinkler and see how long it takes them to fill.

Inevitably, there will be times when you forget to water and the lawn turns brown. Does this mean that the grass is dead? Not usually. Many grasses will survive a summer drought by going dormant. They may stop growing, and even turn brown, but once the weather cools and the rain returns in the fall, they will come back to life.

Fertilizing

After years of recommending that home-owners pour on fertilizer spring, summer, and fall, experts are now concluding that we feed our lawns too much. True, grass that doesn't get enough fertilizer grows slowly and sparsely; it loses the battle against certain weeds and is more vulnerable to damage from insects, disease, and drought. But overfertilized grass has problems as well, some of them the same as those caused by too little fertilizer—reduced root growth and drought resistance, increased susceptibility to pests and disease, and thatch formation.

Grass grows best when it receives a slow, steady supply of fertilizer. How much and when depends on the type of grass and the climate. In the North, most turfgrasses can get by with one or two applications of a slow-acting fertilizer annually. In the South, grass grows best with two or three small doses during the growing season.

In the North, the best time to fertilize is September or October. This will help the plant roots create and store enough food to get the plant off to a good start in the spring. If you don't have to feed grass in the spring, you'll deny hungry young weeds free food. Alternatively, you can give northern grass a half-dose in the spring (May or June) and another in the fall.

Warm-season grasses, on the other hand, are natural summer feeders. Their requirements vary more than do those of northern grasses. Some varieties can do quite well with two feedings, one in early summer, perhaps June, and one in late summer, around August. Others need feeding every month. But again, the more frequent the feedings, the smaller the dose of fertilizer required.

Different types of grass need different amounts of fertilizer. Some, such as bent-grass, are heavy feeders, requiring 2 to 4 pounds of actual nitrogen for each 1,000 square feet per year. Others, such as buffalograss and fine fescue, require only half as much, while Bermudagrass and Kentucky bluegrass fall between the two extremes. Get advice on amounts from your nursery or extension agent, or follow the recommendations on the fertilizer bag. Be aware, however, that these rates are usually based on a high-fertility regime.

Turf fertilizers come in several different forms. They may be liquid or granular, fast-acting or slow-release. Liquid fertilizers are fast-acting, and go right to work greening up your lawn. But they run out of steam quickly, and many of the nutrients may leach out of the soil before the roots can make use of them. A lawn fed with liquid fertilizers will become hooked on that quick fix and will require repeated applications throughout the year.

It's better to follow the old gardening principle of feeding the soil instead of the plant. For that, you'll want to use dry fertilizers. There are many brands on the market, but some are nearly as quick to disappear as are liquid fertilizers. Check the analysis on the back of the bag, which will tell you what percentage of nitrogen is water-soluble and what percentage is insoluble. The higher the percentage of insoluble nitrogen (which isn't actually insoluable

at all), the greater the staying power of the fertilizer. Those with at least 25 to 33 percent of the nitrogen in an insoluble form are sometimes labeled "slow-release" or "controlled-release."

To distribute fertilizer across the lawn, you'll need a spreader. The two types commonly used are the drop spreader and the rotary spreader. A drop spreader drops a trail of fertilizer behind it as wide as its hopper. A rotary spreader uses a propeller-like device to sling fertilizer out. It takes a lot longer to cover the lawn using a drop spreader. But it's much more precise than a rotary spreader, which often scatters fertilizer on walks, driveways, ground covers, and flowers.

Weeds, diseases, and pests

The best way to control weeds, diseases, and insects in the lawn is to keep them from getting started in the first place. If you follow proper procedures for mowing, watering, and fertilizing, serious lawn problems will seldom arise.

When it comes to weeds, many gardeners automatically reach for the herbicide. People who spend hours weeding or hoeing their vegetable gardens and flower borders never think of hand-weeding their lawns too. But it can be done. Just take care to remove as much of the weed and its root as possible, while disturbing as little of the lawn as you can. With a long-handled lawn weeding tool, you can even avoid crawling around on your hands and knees.

Remember that weeds are vigorous invaders that will quickly colonize a bare spot on the lawn. So it's a good idea to carry around a bag of topsoil and some grass seed as you weed. When a weed comes out, fill in the divot with soil and sprinkle some seeds.

Most homeowners find lawn diseases and insect problems difficult if not impossible to diagnose. The truth is that a brown spot on the lawn may be caused by one of several different things. If you discover a problem area, watch it carefully. If it begins to spread, consider asking a lawn-care professional to come out and identify the cause. Many lawn-care companies offer diagnostic services to their customers. Your county agricultural extension agent may also be able to help.

Rejuvenating an old lawn

Your new lawn may start out nearly perfect, but chances are it won't stay that way. Or you may have purchased an existing lawn that doesn't look its best. Cold, heat, drought, insects, and disease all take their toll, as do hordes of football-playing children. Regular maintenance may whip a neglected lawn into shape, but sometimes more is needed. You may need to renovate or reseed.

Renovation

A shabby lawn may be choking on its own debris or suffering from soil compacted by too much traffic. Fixing these problems can invigorate a lawn.

Thatch, the layer of dead plant debris on the soil surface, can cause problems. A thin layer of thatch can help retain soil moisture and shield roots from extreme heat. But a thick layer prevents water from reaching the grass roots, and it harbors insects and diseases. By blocking light, it can weaken grass plants and prevent turf from spreading as it should. A layer of thatch more than 1/2 inch thick should be removed.

You can remove thatch by hand with a special rake whose heavy, double-edged, crescent-shaped blades slice through and pull up thatch. But raking thatch is hard work. If your lawn is large, you'll want to rent a gasoline-powered dethatcher, sometimes called a verticutter or vertimower. These machines operate like lawn mowers with short, vertical blades that slice through the thatch and lift it to the surface, where you can rake it away.

Compacted soil starves plant roots of water and oxygen, in the process causing thatch to build up. You can relieve compaction with another readily rented machine, a core cultivator, which pounds the lawn with hollow tubes that extract thin cores of soil a few inches long. (A foot-operated tool that looks something like a garden fork can aerate small plots.) Rake the soil cores up and compost them, or leave them in place and pulverize them with a rake.

After aerating the soil, you can further improve it by spreading a layer of topsoil, sand, or compost. This material seeps into the holes, where it improves the tilth, aeration, and drainage of the soil. Top-dressing with organic matter will increase soil microorganisms and earthworms, both of which help reduce thatch. Spread about 3/4 cubic yard of topsoil for every 1,000 square feet of lawn. The best time to top-dress is in the fall.

Reseeding

If thatch or compaction isn't a problem, a neglected, thin, weedy, disease-prone lawn or part of a lawn can sometimes be restored with regular maintenance and reseeding. If the area drains well and less than 25 percent of it is weeds, try reseeding. Most new grasses are so vigorous that they will eventually crowd out old, weaker grass. But the new seed must get off to a good start, so sow in the fall or early spring in the North and spring or early summer in the South.

Before you sow, mow the grass closely, at half the normal mowing height—as low as 1/2 inch, depending on the species of grass. Next, rake thoroughly and vigorously. Remove all the clippings and as much thatch as you can. Expose and rough up as much soil as possible, and pull up or hoe out all the weeds you find. (You may find it easier to rent a verticutter for large lawns.)

Because you are not sowing the seed into bare soil, spread it more thickly, one and a half times the amount recommended on the package. Then rake the entire area lightly and top-dress the lawn with a thin layer of sand or topsoil. About 1/2 cubic yard of soil should cover 1,000 square feet. Finally, water the area thoroughly, putting down at least an inch of water. Keep the reseeded area well watered, and stay off it until the grass has come up. Then don't mow until it has reached its maximum mowing height (2 to 4 inches, depending on variety).

Hardiness Zone map

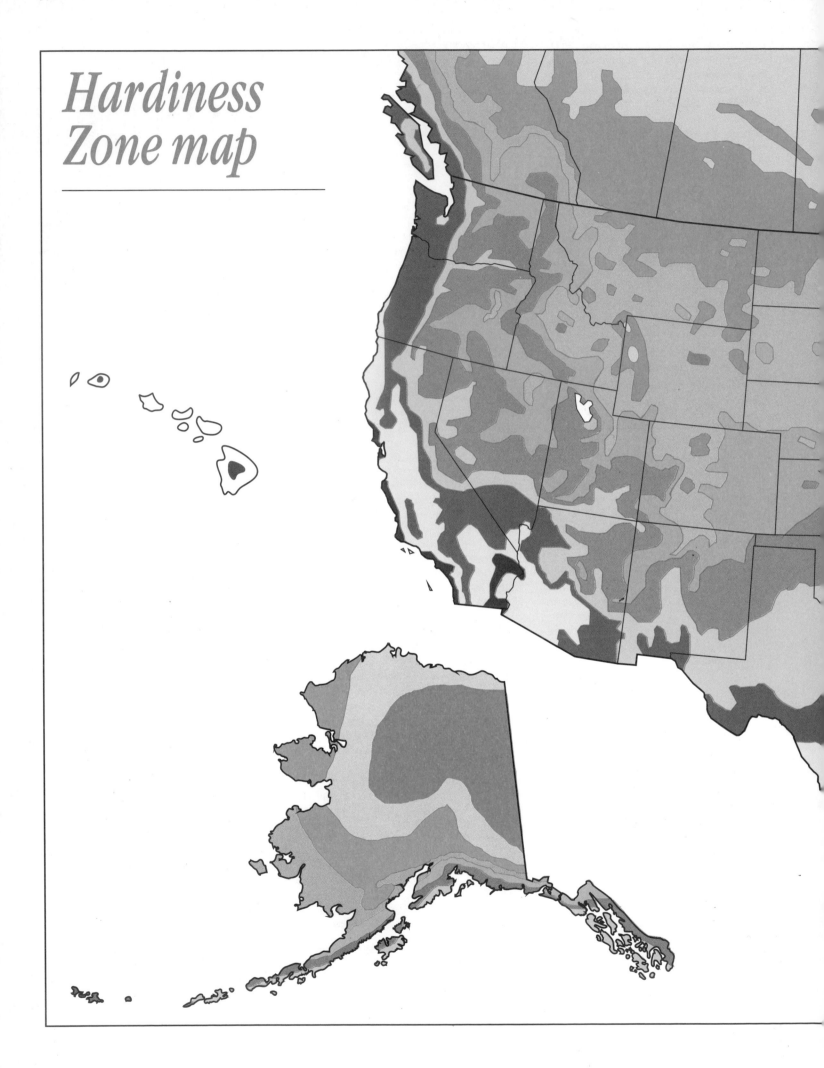

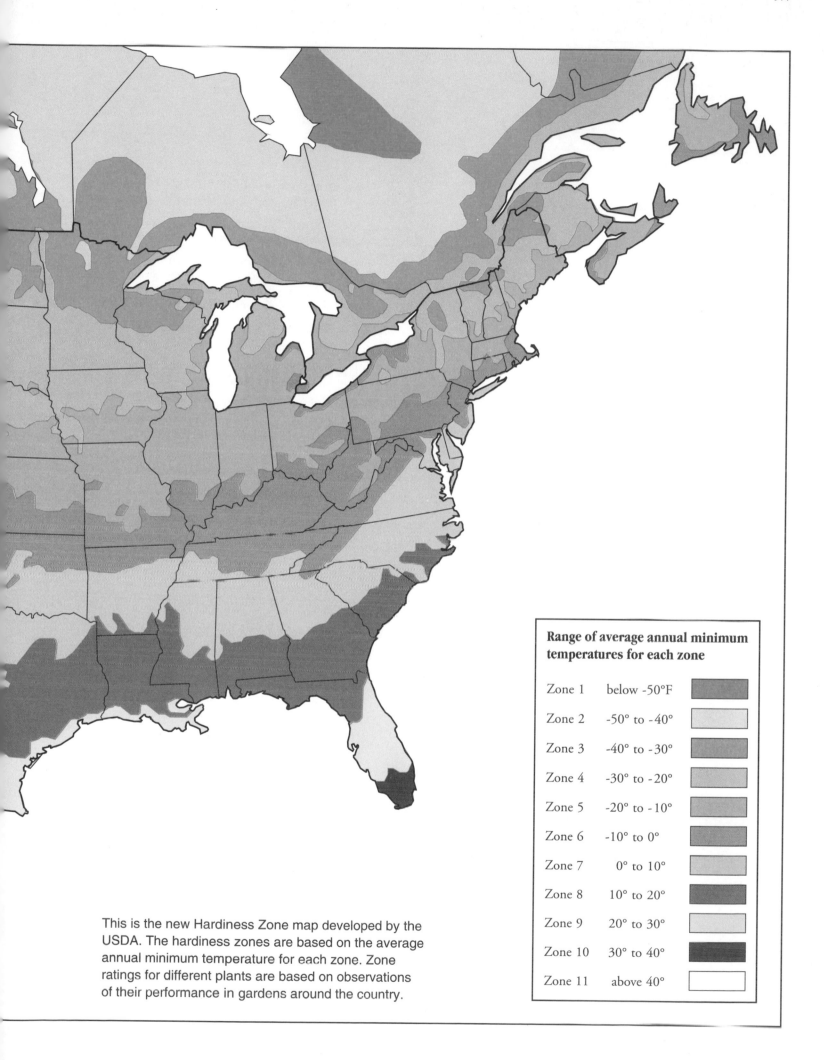

Range of average annual minimum temperatures for each zone

Zone 1   below -50°F

Zone 2   -50° to -40°

Zone 3   -40° to -30°

Zone 4   -30° to -20°

Zone 5   -20° to -10°

Zone 6   -10° to 0°

Zone 7   0° to 10°

Zone 8   10° to 20°

Zone 9   20° to 30°

Zone 10   30° to 40°

Zone 11   above 40°

This is the new Hardiness Zone map developed by the USDA. The hardiness zones are based on the average annual minimum temperature for each zone. Zone ratings for different plants are based on observations of their performance in gardens around the country.

Glossary

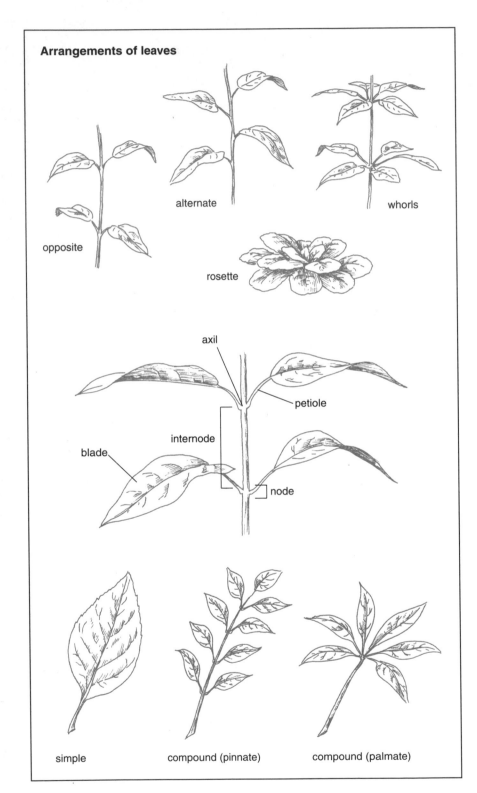

Arrangements of leaves

opposite

alternate

whorls

rosette

axil

petiole

internode

blade

node

simple

compound (pinnate)

compound (palmate)

Accent plant An individual plant that contrasts with its surroundings and catches your attention.

Acid soil Soil with a pH lower than 7. Common in high-rainfall regions.

Adventitious Growing in an unexpected or unusual position, such as new shoots growing out of the trunks of trees or roots growing from the climbing stems of vines.

Aerial root A root that emerges from a stem above ground.

Alkaline soil Soil with a pH higher than 7. Common in low-rainfall regions.

Alpine A small plant suitable for growing in a rock garden. Most (but not all) alpines are native to mountain habitats.

Alternate Occurring singly on alternate sides of a stem, not in pairs or whorls.

Amendment An organic or mineral material such as peat moss or perlite that is used to improve the soil.

Annual A plant that germinates, grows, flowers, produces seeds, and dies in the course of a single growing season.

Anther The part of a flower where pollen is produced.

Anti-transpirant A substance that is sprayed on the stems and leaves of plants to reduce the rate of transpiration, or water loss. Often used to protect evergreens from dry winter winds.

Apical dominance The tendency of the central or terminal shoot that grows upward to inhibit the development of branching side shoots.

Auxin A plant hormone that affects the growth of shoots and roots.

Axil The angle between a stem and a leaf. Each axil contains an axillary bud, which may develop into a new shoot.

Backfill Soil returned to a planting hole after the plant's roots have been positioned. This can be original soil or soil with added amendments.

Balled-and-burlapped Dug out of the ground with a ball of soil around the roots, which is wrapped in burlap and tied for transport.

Bare-root Dug out of the ground when dormant, then shaken or washed to remove the soil from the roots before storage or shipment.

Basal leaf A leaf that grows at the base of a plant, often different in size and shape from leaves that grow on the upright flowering stems.

Bedding plant A fast-growing plant used to create a mass display of colorful flowers or foliage. These are short-term plantings that must be replaced each season.

Biennial A plant that germinates and grows leaves for one growing season, lives through the winter, and then flowers, produces seeds, and dies the second year.

Blade The broad flat part of a leaf.

Bolting The rapid growth of a stem prior to flowering. Usually refers to annuals or biennials that have been stressed by heat, cold, drought, crowding, or transplanting.

Bracts Special leaves located at the base of a flower or inflorescence. May be small or large, green or colored.

Broadcast To distribute seeds, fertilizer, and the like evenly over an area.

Broad-leaved evergreen An evergreen tree or shrub that is not a conifer.

Bulb A storage organ, usually formed underground, made of overlapping scales or swollen leaf bases attached to a short flat stem.

Caliche A hard deposit of white limestone that sometimes underlies alkaline soils in arid climates.

Calyx Collectively, the sepals of a flower.

Catkin A dense spike of small, petalless, often unisexual flowers, most often found on wind-pollinated trees or shrubs.

Chlorosis Yellowing of the leaves, often caused by a shortage of iron.

Clone A group of genetically identical plants all produced by vegetative propagation from a single parent.

Cold frame A low boxlike structure like a miniature greenhouse used to shelter small plants.

Complete fertilizer A fertilizer that supplies nitrogen, phosphorus, and potassium, the three elements required in greatest quantities by plants. Note that a "complete" fertilizer does not necessarily supply the trace elements that are also required for healthy plant growth.

Composite A plant in the composite or daisy family, whose members have many small flowers packed tightly together into inflorescences that resemble single blossoms.

Compound leaf A leaf with two or more leaflets branching off a single stalk. Cf. simple leaf.

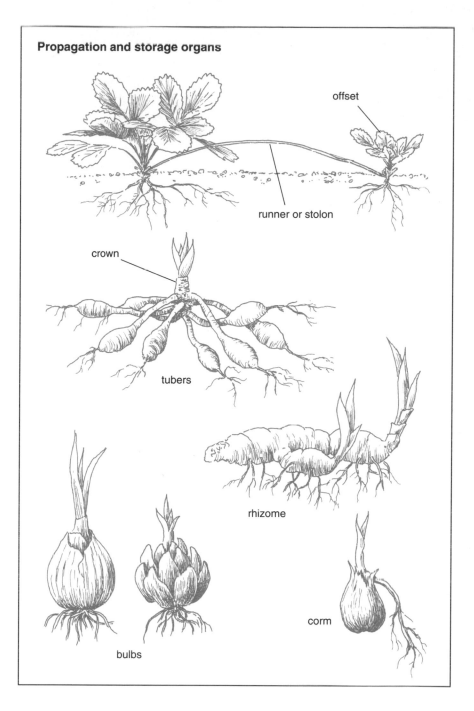

Propagation and storage organs

offset

runner or stolon

crown

tubers

rhizome

corm

bulbs

Conifer A cone-bearing tree or shrub, often evergreen, usually with needlelike leaves.

Container-grown Raised in a pot that is removed before planting.

Corm A short swollen underground stem that serves as a storage organ.

Corolla Collectively, the petals of a flower.

Corymb A flat-topped cluster of flowers, which begin blooming at the edge and proceed toward the center.

Cotyledon A food-storage organ in seeds. Cotyledons often develop into a seedling's first leaves.

Crown That part of a plant where the roots and stem meet, usually at soil level.

Crucifer A plant in the crucifer or mustard family, whose members have flowers with four petals arranged like a cross.

Cultivar A plant variety maintained in cultivation by vegetative propagation or inbred seed.

Cutting A part of a plant removed from its parent and treated so that it produces roots and becomes a new plant. Most cuttings are taken from stems or shoots, but sometimes leaf or root cuttings are used.

Cyme A branching flower cluster that blooms from the center toward the edges.

Damping-off A common fungal disease that attacks seedlings, weakening the stems right at the soil level. Infected seedlings usually die.

Deadheading Removing old flowers during the growing season to encourage the development of new flowers and to prevent seed formation.

Deciduous Dropping all its leaves in one season.

Dicot A plant having two cotyledons, usually with a netlike pattern of veins in the leaf blades and flower parts in groups of four or five. This group includes all the broad-leaved trees and shrubs and many common flowers such as daisies, phlox, carnations, and peonies. Cf. monocot.

Dieback shrub A tender shrub that can be grown in cold climates; it freezes to the ground in winter but sends up new shoots in spring.

Dioecious Having male and female flowers on separate plants. Cf. monoecious.

Direct seeding Sowing seeds directly in the soil where they are to grow; not transplanting.

Disbudding Removing most of the immature buds from a plant to boost the size of the few selected to remain.

Disk flower A small tubular flower in the center of a composite blossom. These make up the "eye" of a black-eyed Susan or daisy, for example.

Division Propagation of a plant by separating it into two or more pieces, each of which has at least one bud and some roots.

Dormancy A state of reduced activity that enables plants to survive conditions of cold, drought, or other stress. Most plants drop their leaves before going dormant.

Double flower A flower with more than the usual number of petals, usually arranged in extra rows.

Drainage Movement of water down through the soil. Good drainage means water disappears from a planting hole in less than an hour. If water remains standing overnight or longer, the drainage is poor.

Drift A group of plants arranged in a graceful curved shape, spaced closer together in the center or at one end, then gradually farther apart at the edges or other end.

Drip line An imaginary line on the soil around a tree that mirrors the circumference of the branches above.

Edging A shallow trench or physical barrier of steel, plastic, brick, or boards used to define the border between a flower bed and adjacent turf.

Entire A term used to describe leaves having a smooth edge with no teeth or lobes.

Ericaceous Belonging to the heath family, most of whose members prefer acidic soil. Examples are azaleas, rhododendrons, blueberries, and heathers.

Escape An exotic plant that has spread from cultivation and grows successfully in the wild.

Espalier A plant that has been trained to grow flat against a wall or framework.

Exfoliating A term used to describe bark that peels off in thin layers and has a patchy or shredded appearance.

Exotic A garden plant that is native to another part of the world.

Exposure The intensity, duration, and variation in sun, wind, and temperature that characterize any particular site.

Family A group of plant genera with similarities in flower and fruit form. Important examples are the grass, lily, mint, and daisy families.

Feeder roots Slender branching roots that spread close to the surface of the soil and absorb most of the nutrients for a tree or shrub.

Fertile
1. Fertile soil has a ready supply of nitrogen, phosphorus, potassium, and the other nutrients needed by plants. To fertilize plants is to supply these nutrients.
2. A fertile seed has an embryo capable of developing into a new plant. To fertilize flowers is to transfer pollen from the anther of one flower to the stigma of the same or a different flower.

Filament The slender stalk that supports the pollen-bearing anther.

Flora All the kinds of plants that grow wild in an area.

Formal garden A garden laid out in regular geometric patterns with defined paths and pruned hedges.

Foundation planting A narrow border of evergreen shrubs planted around the foundation of a house.

Friable Soil texture that is loose and crumbly, easily penetrated by roots and water.

Fruit The mature or ripened ovary of a flower, containing one or more seeds.

Full sun Receiving a minimum of six hours of direct sun each day during the growing season.

Fungicide A compound that kills fungal organisms.

Genus (plural: **genera**) A group of plant species with similarities in flower form and often in general appearance, growth habit, and cultural requirements. A genus may include from one to a thousand or more species. The genus is the first word in a two-part Latin name. The common names for many groups of plants, such as aster, cosmos, magnolia, and rhododendron, are also the Latin names for those genera.

Germination The initial sprouting of a seed.

Grade The degree and direction of slope on a piece of ground.

Grafting Joining a bud or shoot from one plant onto the roots or trunk of another plant so that the two parts will unite and grow together.

Ground cover Plants such as ivy, liriope, or juniper used to cover the soil and form a continuous low mass of foliage. Often used as durable, undemanding substitutes for turfgrass.

Habit The characteristic shape or form of a plant, such as upright, spreading, or rounded.

Half-hardy Able to withstand a few degrees of frost but not extreme cold.

Hardening off Gradually exposing a plant that had been growing under sheltered conditions to cold, heat, sun, and wind.

Hardiness A term that usually refers to a plant's ability to survive the winter without protection from the cold. Can also refer to a plant's ability to survive summer heat and drought.

Heeling-in Temporarily storing a plant by covering its roots with soil.

Herbaceous perennial A nonwoody plant that produces new shoots each year. Some herbaceous perennials are evergreen, but most go dormant and die down to the ground for part of the year.

Herbicide A chemical used to kill plants. Selective herbicides kill only particular kinds of plants. Nonselective herbicides kill or damage a wide range of plants.

Horticultural oil A light, highly refined mineral oil, mixed with water and used as an insecticidal spray.

Humus Organic matter in the soil derived from decomposed plant and animal remains.

Hybrid A plant resulting from a cross between two parents that belong to different varieties, species, or genera. A hybrid may show some of the characteristics of each parent.

Hybrid vigor The tendency of many hybrids to grow faster, get larger, bear more flowers and fruit, or be hardier than their parents.

Inflorescence A cluster of flowers arranged in a particular way on a stem. Spikes, racemes, umbels, whorls, panicles, cymes, corymbs, and composites are common types of inflorescences.

Insecticidal soap A particular kind of soap that is mixed with water and used as an insecticidal spray.

Interplant To combine plants with different bloom times or growth habits. This makes it possible to fit more plants in a single bed and prolongs the season of interest.

Juvenile foliage Distinct forms of leaves present only on young plants or new growth. In many junipers, for example, the juvenile foliage is needlelike, while the adult leaves are flattened like scales.

Layering Starting a new plant by fastening a stem down to the ground and partially covering it with soil to induce roots to develop. The rooted stem can later be removed and planted separately.

Leaching Loss of nutrients when rain or irrigation carries them down through the soil and out of the root zone.

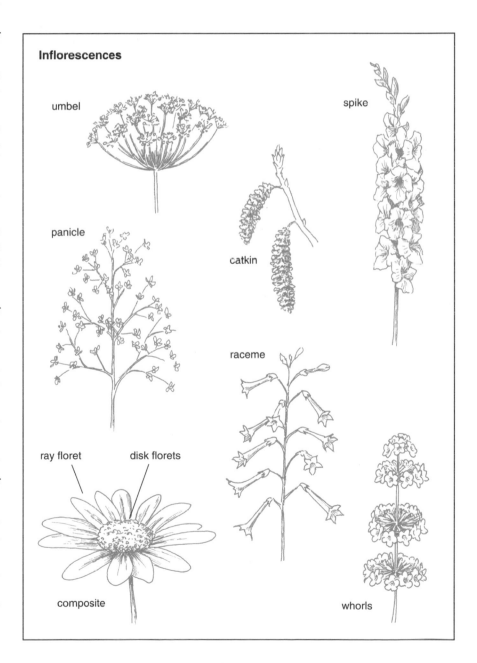

Inflorescences

umbel

spike

panicle

catkin

raceme

ray floret   disk florets

composite

whorls

Leader The central upward-growing stem in a single-trunked tree.

Legume A member of the legume or pea family, a group that includes annuals, perennials, shrubs, vines, and trees.

Limbing up Removing the lower limbs of large trees to open space and allow light and air to reach lower plants.

Lime, limestone White mineral compounds used to combat soil acidity and to supply calcium for plant growth. Quicklime is calcium oxide; slaked lime is calcium hydroxide; limestone is calcium carbonate.

Loam An ideal soil for gardening, containing plenty of organic matter and a balanced range of smaller to larger mineral particles.

Mass planting Filling an area with just one or a few kinds of plants spaced close together. Often done to create a bold dramatic effect or to reduce maintenance.

Meadow A mixed planting of herbaceous perennial plants, usually including grasses and native or naturalized wildflowers, maintained (once established) by annual mowing.

Microclimate Local conditions of shade, exposure, wind, drainage, and other factors that affect plant growth at any particular site.

Micronutrients Elements that are essential for plant growth but that are needed in very small quantities. Also called trace elements.

Monocot A plant having only one cotyledon or seed leaf and usually having parallel-veined leaves and flower parts arranged in groups of three. Common examples are grasses, bamboos, palms, lilies, daffodils, irises, and orchids. Cf. dicot.

Monoecious Having separate male and female flowers but on the same plant. Cf. dioecious.

Mulch A layer of bark, peat moss, compost, shredded leaves, hay or straw, lawn clippings, gravel, paper, plastic, or other material spread over the soil around the base of plants. During the growing season, a mulch can help retard evaporation, inhibit weeds, and regulate soil temperature. In the winter, a mulch of evergreen boughs, coarse hay, or noncompacting leaves is used to protect plants from freezing.

Native A plant that grows naturally in a particular region and was not introduced from some other area.

Naturalized A plant that grows without assistance and reproduces in an area other than its native region (cf. exotic). Many roadside wildflowers are European natives that have naturalized in the United States. Garden plants such as daffodils are naturalized when they spread by themselves and persist for years with no human care or intervention.

Nematode A microscopic round worm that lives in the soil. Some kinds of nematodes are beneficial and prey on harmful insect larvae, but many nematodes are serious pests that weaken plants by damaging their roots.

Node A place on a stem where leaves or branches are attached. An internode is a section of stem between two nodes.

Nutrients Nitrogen, phosphorus, potassium, calcium, magnesium, sulfur, iron, and other elements needed by growing plants. Nutrients are supplied by the minerals and organic matter in the soil and by fertilizers.

Offset A short lateral shoot arising near the base of a plant and readily producing new roots. Offsets can be detached and replanted away from the parent plant.

Opposite A term used to describe parts such as leaves that are arranged in pairs along a stem or shoot.

Organic matter Plant and animal residues such as leaves, trimmings, and manure in various stages of decomposition.

Orientation The location or arrangement of a garden relative to the points of the compass.

Ovary, ovules The ovary is the part of a flower that develops into a fruit; the ovules develop into seeds.

Palmate Having veins or leaflets arranged like the fingers on a hand, radiating out from a center point.

Panicle A loose, open, branching cluster of flowers that bloom from the center or bottom toward the edges or top. Examples of plants that produce panicles are yucca, catalpa, and baby's-breath.

Peat moss Partially decomposed mosses and sedges, mined from boggy areas and used to improve garden soil or to prepare potting soil.

Pedicel The stalk of an individual flower.

Peduncle The stalk of an inflorescence.

Perennial A plant that lives for a number of years, generally flowering each year. Gardeners often use the term *perennial* to mean herbaceous perennial, but woody plants such as shrubs and trees are also perennial.

Perfect A flower that has both male and female parts, as opposed to one that is unisexual or sterile.

Perianth All the sepals and petals of a flower, which may be green or colored.

Pesticide A general term for compounds used to kill insects, mites, weeds, fungi, bacteria, or other pests.

Petal One of a series of flower parts, often bright-colored and sometimes patterned.

Petiole The stalk of a leaf.

pH scale A system of describing acidity or alkalinity, ranging from pH 0 to 14. pH 7 is neutral. Values lower than 7 indicate acidity; those higher than 7 indicate alkalinity.

Pinching Removing the top or central growing point of a plant to promote the development of side shoots.

Pinnate Having leaflets arranged in two rows on either side of a central axis.

Pistil The female parts of a flower, consisting of ovary, style, and stigma.

Pollination The transfer of pollen from stamens to pistils, usually between two flowers on the same or different plants.

Propagate To produce new plants by sowing seeds, rooting cuttings, making divisions, layering, grafting, or other means.

Raceme A long inflorescence with individual flowers borne on short side stalks off a larger central stalk.

Ray flower A small flower with a single straplike petal, borne at the edge of daisy, sunflower, cosmos, or other composite inflorescences.

Rhizome A horizontal underground stem, often swollen into a storage organ. Both roots and shoots emerge from rhizomes. Rhizomes generally branch as they creep along and can be divided to make new plants.

Root-bound A term used to describe a condition that results from leaving a plant too long in a too-small container. The restricted roots grow around in a tangled mat; once set in this circular pattern, they may never recover and grow outward.

Rooting hormones Powder or liquid preparations of plant hormones that stimulate a cutting to form roots.

Rosette A low flat cluster of leaves arranged like the petals of a rose.

Runner A slender shoot that grows along the ground, forming roots and a new plant at its tip end.

Scape A flower stalk that grows directly from the base of a plant, as in daffodils and daylilies. It is often leafless.

Scarify To penetrate hard seed coats by scratching or nicking the seeds or immersing them briefly in hot water, acid, or bleach.

Self-sow To produce seeds that germinate and grow with no care from the gardener.

Sepal One of the outermost series of flower parts, arranged in a ring outside the petals and usually small, green, and leaflike.

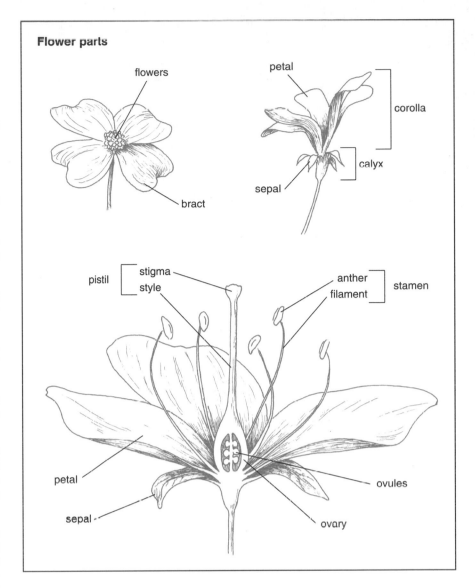

Flower parts

Simple leaf A leaf with only one blade. It may be toothed, scalloped, or lobed but is never divided all the way to the leafstalk. Cf. compound leaf.

Species A group of individual plants that share many characteristics and interbreed freely.

Specimen plant A plant placed conspicuously alone, usually in a prominent place, to show off its ornamental qualities.

Spike An elongated flower cluster, with individual flowers borne on very short stalks or attached directly to the main stem.

Stamen A male reproductive organ of a flower.

Standard A plant trained to grow a round bushy head of branches atop a single upright stem.

Sterile A term used to describe a plant that is unable to produce seeds.

Stigma The part of a flower that receives pollen.

Stolon A stem that runs along the ground, forming roots and new plants at intervals along its length.

Stratify To keep seeds under cool, dark, moist conditions for a period of weeks or months so that they will subsequently germinate.

Subshrub A perennial plant with woody stems at the base and tender new growth that dies back more or less each winter.

Succulent A plant with thick fleshy leaves or stems that can store water. Cacti and sedums are examples.

Suckers Shoots arising from underground buds on the roots of a plant. They can be removed and replanted as new plants.

Tender Damaged by freezing temperatures.

Tepal A term used to describe sepals and petals that are similar in size, shape, and color, as in the flowers of tulips, alliums, and many lilies.

Terminal Borne at the tip of a stem or shoot.

Tetraploid Having twice the normal number of chromosomes and characteristically larger and more vigorous than normal plants.

Tissue culture A laboratory technique of propagating new plants from tiny portions of the mother plant.

Top-dress To apply fertilizer, compost, or manure to the soil around the base of a growing plant.

Trace elements Elements that are essential for plant growth but that are needed in very small quantities. Also called micronutrients.

Tuber A swollen underground stem that serves as a storage organ and has buds where new shoots and roots develop after a dormant period.

Umbel A flower cluster in which the individual flower stalks emerge from the same point on the stem, like the ribs of an umbrella.

Variegated Marked, striped, or blotched with some color other than green.

Variety A population of plants that differ consistently from the typical form of the species, occurring naturally in a geographical area. Also applied, incorrectly but popularly, to forms produced in cultivation. The latter are properly called cultivars.

Vegetative propagation The production of new plants by means other than seeds.

Vigor Strong healthy growth and the ability to withstand stress.

Virus A disease organism that often causes a streaky discoloration of leaves or petals, distorts buds and new growth, and weakens plants.

Volunteer A plant that grows from self-sown seed.

Whorl A group of three or more leaves or shoots that emerge from a single node.

Wildflower A native or exotic plant that grows wild in a region and has conspicuous flowers.

Xeriscape A landscape designed to conserve water.

Further Reading

The only thing gardeners seem to want more of than plants is information and inspiration. We hope this book has given you a good start; the following titles have been selected to help you expand your horizons. They are grouped by topic, but many will be of use outside the confines of our categories. Found in bookstores, mail-order catalogs, or at the library, they will make a valuable addition to your gardening library. In addition, contact local botanical gardens and arboretums and your state extension service for lists of the many informative books, pamphlets, and information sheets they offer.

GARDEN PLANNING AND DESIGN

General

Brookes, John. *The Book of Garden Design*. New York: Macmillan, 1991.

Carpenter, Philip L., and Theodore D. Walker. *Plants in the Landscape,* 2d ed. New York: W. H. Freeman, 1989.

Church, Thomas. *Gardens Are for People,* 2d ed. New York: McGraw-Hill, 1983.

Eckbo, Garrett. *Home Landscape: The Art of Home Landscaping,* rev. ed. New York: McGraw-Hill, 1978.

Johnson, Hugh. *The Principles of Gardening*. New York: Simon & Schuster, 1984.

Leighton, Phebe, Calvin Simonds, and Penny Thompson. *The New American Landscape Gardener*. Emmaus, PA: Rodale Press, 1987.

Taylor's Guide to Garden Design. Boston: Houghton Mifflin, 1988.

Verey, Rosemary. *The Art of Planting*. Boston: Little, Brown & Co., 1990.

Beds and borders

Brown, Emily. *Landscaping with Perennials*. Portland, OR: Timber Press, 1986.

Cox, Jeff, and Marilyn Cox. *The Perennial Garden: Color Harmonies Through the Seasons*. Emmaus, PA: Rodale Press, 1992.

Harper, Pamela J. *Designing with Perennials*. New York: Macmillan, 1991.

Lovejoy, Ann. *The American Mixed Border: Gardens for All Seasons*. New York: Macmillan, 1993.

Murphy, Wendy. *Beds and Borders: Traditional and Original Garden Designs*. Boston: Houghton Mifflin, 1993.

Bird and butterfly gardens

Dennis, John, and Mathew Tekulsky. *How to Attract Hummingbirds and Butterflies*. San Ramon, CA: Ortho Information Services, 1991.

Kress, Stephen. *The Audubon Society Guide to Attracting Birds*. New York: Macmillan, 1985.

Xerces Society Staff. *Butterfly Gardening: Creating Summer Magic in Your Garden*. San Francisco: Sierra Club Books and National Wildlife Federation Books, 1990.

Color

Hobhouse, Penelope. *Color in Your Garden*. Boston: Little, Brown & Co., 1985.

Jekyll, Gertrude. *Color Schemes for the Flower Garden,* rev. ed. Salem, NH: Ayer Company Publishers, 1984.

Keen, Mary. *Gardening with Color*. New York: Random House, 1991.

Wilder, Louise Beebe. *Color in My Garden*. New York: Atlantic Monthly Press, 1990.

Natural landscaping

Austin, Richard L. *Designing the Natural Landscape*. New York: Van Nostrand Reinhold, 1984.

Cox, Jeff. *Landscaping with Nature: Using Nature's Designs to Plan Your Yard*. Emmaus, PA: Rodale Press, 1990.

Taylor's Guide to Natural Gardening. Boston: Houghton Mifflin, 1993.

Wilson, William H. W. *Landscaping with Wildflowers and Native Plants*. San Ramon, CA: Ortho Information Services, 1985.

Rock gardens

Foster, H. Lincoln. *Rock Gardening*. Portland, OR: Timber Press, 1982 (reprint of 1968 ed.).

Lawrence, Elizabeth. *A Rock Garden in the South*. Durham, NC: Duke University Press, 1990.

Seasonal interest

Lacy, Allen. *The Garden in Autumn*. New York: Grove/Atlantic Inc., 1990.

Shade gardens

Druse, Ken. *The Natural Shade Garden*. New York: Crown Publishing, 1992.

Morse, Harriet K. *Gardening in the Shade*. Portland, OR: Timber Press, 1982.

Schenk, George. *The Complete Shade Gardener*. Boston: Houghton Mifflin, 1991.

Water gardens

Hériteau, Jacquiline. *Water Gardens.* Boston: Houghton Mifflin, 1994.

Paul, Anthony. *The Water Garden.* New York: Viking Penguin, 1986.

Water-saving gardens

Ellefson, Connie, Thomas Stephens, and Douglas Welsh. *Xeriscape Gardening: Water Conservation for the American Landscape.* New York: Macmillan, 1992.

Johnson, Eric A., and Scott Millard. *Low-Water Flower Gardener.* Tucson, AZ: Ironwood Press, 1993.

Sunset Magazine and Book Editors. *Waterwise Gardening: Beautiful Gardens with Less Water.* Menlo Park, CA: Sunset Publishing Co., 1989.

Taylor's Guide to Water-Saving Gardening. Boston: Houghton Mifflin, 1990.

Other topics

Brookes, John. *The Small Garden Book.* New York: Random House, 1991.

Creasy, Rosalind. *The Complete Book of Edible Landscaping.* San Francisco: Sierra Club Books, 1982.

Evans, Hazel. *The Patio Garden.* New York: Viking Penguin, 1986.

Smith, Mary R. *Front Garden: New Approaches to Landscape Design.* Boston: Houghton Mifflin, 1992.

Sunset Magazine and Book Editors. *Landscaping for Privacy.* Menlo Park, CA: Sunset Publishing Co., 1985.

Verey, Rosemary. *The Flower Arranger's Garden.* New York: Little, Brown & Co., 1989.

Verey, Rosemary. *The Scented Garden.* New York: Random House, 1989.

PLANTS

General and reference

Bailey, Liberty H. *Hortus Third: A Concise Dictionary of Plants Cultivated in the United States and Canada.* New York: Macmillan, 1976.

Ferguson, Nicola. *Right Plant, Right Place.* New York: Summit Books, 1984.

Griffiths, Mark, ed. *Index of Garden Plants: Based on the New Royal Horticultural Society Dictionary of Gardening.* Portland, OR: Timber Press, 1993.

Mabberly, D. J. *The Plant-Book: A Portable Dictionary of the Higher Plants.* New York: Cambridge University Press, 1987.

Stearn, William T. *Stearn's Dictionary of Plant Names for Gardeners.* New York: Sterling, 1992.

Wright, Michael. *The Complete Handbook of Garden Plants.* New York: Facts on File, 1984.

Annuals

Bennett, Jennifer, and Turid Forsyth. *The Harrowsmith Annual Garden.* Buffalo, NY and Willowdale, Ontario: Firefly Books, 1990.

Fell, Derek. *Annuals: How to Select, Grow and Enjoy.* Los Angeles: Price Stern Sloan, 1983.

Proctor, Rob. *Annuals.* New York: Harper-Collins, 1991.

Sunset Staff, eds. *Annuals.* Menlo Park, CA: Sunset Publishing Co., 1992.

Taylor's Guide to Annuals. Boston: Houghton Mifflin, 1986.

Winterrowd, Wayne. *Annuals for Connoisseurs.* New York: Prentice-Hall, 1992.

Bulbs

Bryan, John E. *Bulbs,* 2 vols. Portland, OR: Timber Press, 1989.

Horton, Al. *All About Bulbs,* rev. ed. San Ramon, CA: Ortho Information Services, 1986.

Mathew, Brian, and Phillip Swindells. *The Complete Book of Bulbs.* New York: The Reader's Digest Association, 1994.

Proctor, Rob. *The Outdoor Potted Bulb.* New York: Simon & Schuster, 1993.

Scott, George H. *Bulbs: How to Select, Grow and Enjoy.* Los Angeles: Price Stern Sloan, 1982.

Taylor's Guide to Bulbs. Boston: Houghton Mifflin, 1986.

Ground covers

Lacy, Allen. *Gardening with Groundcovers and Vines.* New York: HarperCollins, 1993.

McCaskey, Michael. *Lawns and Ground Covers: How to Select, Grow and Enjoy.* Los Angeles: Price Stern Sloan, 1982.

MacKenzie, David S. *Complete Manual for Perennial Ground Covers.* Englewood Cliffs, NJ: Prentice-Hall, 1989.

Ortho Books Editorial Staff. *All About Groundcovers.* San Ramon, CA: Ortho Information Services, 1982.

Sunset Magazine and Book Editors. *Lawns and Ground Covers.* Menlo Park, CA: Sunset Publishing Co., 1989.

Taylor's Guide to Ground Covers, Vines and Grasses. Boston: Houghton Mifflin, 1987.

Thomas, Graham S. *Plants for Ground Cover,* rev. ed. Portland, OR: Timber Press, 1990.

Herbs

Kowalchik, Claire, and William Hylton, eds. *Rodale's Illustrated Encyclopedia of Herbs.* Emmaus, PA: Rodale Press, 1987.

Lathrop, Norma Jean. *Herbs: How to Select, Grow and Enjoy.* Los Angeles: Price Stern Sloan, 1981.

Lima, Patrick, and Turid Forsyth. *The Harrowsmith Illustrated Book of Herbs.* Camden East, Ontario: Camden House, 1986.

Wilson, Jim. *All About Herbs.* San Ramon, CA: Ortho Information Services, 1990.

Perennials

Armitage, Allan M. *Herbaceous Perennial Plants: A Treatise on Their Identification, Culture and Garden Attributes.* Athens, GA: Varsity Press, Inc., 1989.

Clausen, Ruth R., and Nicolas H. Ekstrom. *Perennials for American Gardens.* New York: Random House, 1989.

Hudak, Joseph. *Gardening with Perennials Month by Month,* 2d rev. ed. Portland, OR: Timber Press, 1993.

McGourty, Fred, and Pam Harper. *Perennials: How to Select, Grow and Enjoy.* Los Angeles: Price Stern Sloan, 1985.

Phillips, Ellen, and C. Colston Burrell. *Rodale's Illustrated Encyclopedia of Perennials.* Emmaus, PA: Rodale Press, 1993.

Still, Steven. *Manual of Herbaceous Ornamental Plants,* 4th ed. Champaign, IL: Stipes Publishing Co., 1993.

Taylor's Guide to Perennials. Boston: Houghton Mifflin, 1986.

Woods, Christopher. *Encyclopedia of Perennials: A Gardener's Guide.* New York: Facts on File, 1992.

Regional gardening

Dry Climate Gardening. San Ramon, CA: Ortho Information Services, 1989.

Duffield, Mary R. *Plants for Dry Climates: How to Select, Grow and Enjoy.* Los Angeles: Price Stern Sloan, 1992.

Flint, Harrison L. *Landscape Plants for Eastern North America.* New York: John Wiley & Sons, 1983.

Grant, John A., and Carol L. Grant. *Trees and Shrubs for Pacific Northwest Gardens,* 2d ed. Portland, OR: Timber Press, 1990.

Halfacre, R. G., and A. R. Shawcroft. *Landscape Plants of the Southeast,* 5th ed. Raleigh, NC: Sparks Press, 1989.

Hunt, William L. *Southern Gardens, Southern Gardening.* Durham, NC: Duke University Press, 1982.

Phillips, Judith. *Southwestern Landscaping with Native Plants.* Santa Fe, NM: Museum of New Mexico Press, 1987.

Sabuco, John J. *The Best of the Hardiest,* 2d ed. Flossmoor, IL: Good Earth Publishing, 1987.

Snyder, Leon C. *Gardening in the Upper Midwest,* 2d ed. Minneapolis, MN: University of Minnesota Press, 1985.

Snyder, Rachel. *Gardening in the Heartland.* Lawrence, KS: University Press of Kansas, 1991.

Sunset Magazine and Book Editors. *Western Garden Book,* 5th ed. Menlo Park, CA: Sunset Publishing Co., 1988.

Taylor's Guide to Gardening in the South. Boston: Houghton Mifflin, 1992.

Taylor's Guide to Gardening in the Southwest. Boston: Houghton Mifflin, 1992.

Vick, Roger. *Gardening: Plains and Upper Midwest.* Golden, CO: Fulcrum Press, 1990.

Welch, William C. *Perennial Garden Color for Texas and the South.* Dallas: Taylor Publishing, 1989.

Trees and shrubs

Clarke, J. Harold. *Getting Started with Rhododendrons and Azaleas.* Portland, OR: Timber Press, 1982 (reprint of 1960 ed.).

Dirr, Michael. *Manual of Woody Landscape Plants: Their Identification, Ornamental Characteristics, Culture, Propagation and Uses,* 4th ed. Champaign, IL: Stipes Publishing Co., 1990.

Hightshoe, Gary. *Native Trees, Shrubs, and Vines for Urban and Rural America: A Planting Design Manual for Environmental Designers.* New York: Van Nostrand Reinhold, 1987.

Moody, Mary, and Peter Harkness, eds. *The Illustrated Encyclopedia of Roses.* Portland, OR: Timber Press, 1992.

Reddell, Rayford C. *Growing Good Roses.* New York: HarperCollins, 1987.

Taylor's Guide to Roses, rev. ed. Boston: Houghton Mifflin, 1994.

Taylor's Guide to Shrubs. Boston: Houghton Mifflin, 1987.

Taylor's Guide to Trees. Boston: Houghton Mifflin, 1988.

Wildflowers and native plants

Art, Henry. *A Garden of Wildflowers: 101 Native Species and How to Grow Them.* Pownal, VT: Storey Communications, 1986.

Ferreniea, Viki. *Wildflowers in Your Garden.* New York: Random House, 1993.

Martin, Laura C. *The Wildflower Meadow Book: A Gardener's Guide,* 2d ed. Chester, CT: Globe Pequot, 1990.

Phillips, Harry R. *Growing and Propagating Wildflowers.* Chapel Hill, NC: University of North Carolina Press, 1985.

Sperka, Marie. *Growing Wildflowers: A Cultivator's Guide.* New York: Macmillan, 1984.

Wilson, Jim. *Landscaping with Wildflowers.* Boston: Houghton Mifflin, 1993.

Miscellaneous

Foster, Gordon. *Ferns to Know and Grow.* Portland, OR: Timber Press, 1993.

Gardner, JoAnn. *The Heirloom Garden.* Pownal, VT: Storey Communications, 1991.

Greenlee, John. *The Encyclopedia of Ornamental Grasses.* Emmaus, PA: Rodale Press, 1992.

Jefferson-Brown, Michael. *Hardy Ferns.* New York: Sterling, 1992.

Overy, Angela. *The Foliage Garden.* New York: Crown Publishing, 1993.

Reinhardt, Thomas A., Martina R. Reinhardt, and Mark Moskowitz. *Ornamental Grass Gardening.* Los Angeles: Price Stern Sloan, 1989.

GARDENING TECHNIQUES

General

Damrosch, Barbara. *The Garden Primer.* New York: Workman Publishing, 1988.

Taylor's Guide to Gardening Techniques. Boston: Houghton Mifflin, 1991.

Construction

Burch, Monte. *Brick, Concrete, Stonework.* Upper Saddle River, NJ: Creative Homeowner Press, 1980.

Hayward, Gordon. *Garden Paths: Inspiring Designs and Practical Projects.* Charlotte, VT: Camden House Publishing, 1993.

Meyers, L. Donald. *The Complete Outdoor Building Book: Patios, Decks, Fencing, Landscaping, etc.* New York: Prentice-Hall, 1991.

Vivian, John. *Building Fences of Wood, Metal, Stone, and Plants.* Charlotte, VT: Williamson Publishing, 1987.

Williams, T. Jeff. *Garden Construction,* ed. by Jim Beley. San Ramon, CA: Ortho Information Services, 1985.

Pests and diseases

Bradley, Fern M. *Rodale's Chemical-Free Yard and Garden.* Emmaus, PA: Rodale Press, 1991.

Olkowski, William, Sheila Daar, and Helga Olkowski. *Common-Sense Pest Control.* Newtown, CT: The Taunton Press, 1991.

Pirone, Pascal. *Diseases and Pests of Ornamental Plants,* 5th ed. New York: John Wiley & Sons, 1978.

Schultz, Warren. *The Chemical-Free Lawn.* Emmaus, PA: Rodale Press, 1989.

Smith, Miranda, and Ana Carr. *Rodale's Garden Insect, Disease and Weed Identification Guide.* Emmaus, PA: Rodale Press, 1988.

Propagation

Hartmann, Hudson T., Dale E. Kester, and Fred Davies, Jr. *Plant Propagation: Principles and Practice,* 5th ed. Englewood Cliffs, NJ: Prentice-Hall, 1990.

Hill, Lewis. *Secrets of Plant Propagation.* Pownal, VT: Storey Communications, 1985.

Pruning

Coombs, Duncan, et al. *The Complete Book of Pruning.* New York: Sterling, 1992.

Hill, Lewis. *Pruning Simplified.* Pownal, VT: Storey Communications, 1986.

Sunset Magazine and Book Editors. *Sunset Pruning Handbook.* Menlo Park, CA: Sunset Publishing Co., 1983.

Soil and fertilizers

Campbell, Stu. *The Mulch Book: A Complete Guide for Gardeners,* rev. ed. Pownal, VT: Storey Communications, 1991.

Gershuny, Grace, and Deborah L. Martin, eds. *The Rodale Book of Composting: Easy Methods for Every Gardener.* Emmaus, PA: Rodale Press, 1992.

Parnes, Robert. *Fertile Soil: A Grower's Guide to Organic and Inorganic Fertilizers.* Davis, CA: Ag Access, 1990.

GENERAL GARDENING

Bagust, Harold. *The Gardener's Dictionary of Horticultural Terms.* New York: Sterling, 1993.

Bradley, Fern, and Barbara Ellis. *Rodale's All New Encyclopedia of Organic Gardening.* Emmaus, PA: Rodale Press, 1993.

Brooklyn Botanic Garden Handbooks. A series of booklets, frequently added to and revised, covering a wide range of gardening subjects, including titles such as *Annuals, Water Gardening,* and *Gardening with Wildflowers and Native Plants.* For a list of current publications, write to Brooklyn Botanic Garden, 1000 Washington Ave., Brooklyn, NY 11225-1099.

Bush-Brown, James, and Louise Bush-Brown. *America's Garden Book,* rev. ed. New York: Macmillan, 1980.

Wyman, Donald. *Wyman's Gardening Encyclopedia,* updated ed. New York: Macmillan, 1987.

SOURCES OF PLANTS AND GARDENING SUPPLIES

Barton, Barbara. *Gardening by Mail,* 4th ed. Boston: Houghton Mifflin, 1994.

Barton, Barbara. *Taylor's Guide to Specialty Nurseries.* Boston: Houghton Mifflin, 1993.

Dean, Jan. *The Gardener's Reading Guide: The Best Books for Gardeners.* New York: Facts on File, 1993.

Dobson, Beverly. *The Combined Rose List.* Annually compiled. From the author: 215 Harriman Rd., Irvington, NY 10533.

Ettlinger, Stephan R. *The Complete Illustrated Guide to Everything Sold in Garden Centers (Except the Plants).* New York: Macmillan, 1990.

Index

Numbers in italic refer to pages on which photographs or drawings appear.